A Commentary
on
Cicero, *De Legibus*

A Commentary
on
Cicero, *De Legibus*

ANDREW R. DYCK

THE UNIVERSITY OF MICHIGAN PRESS
Ann Arbor

Copyright © by the University of Michigan 2004
All rights reserved
Published in the United States of America by
The University of Michigan Press
Manufactured in the United States of America
ⓢ Printed on acid-free paper

2007   2006   2005   2004   4   3   2   1

A CIP catalog record for this book is available from the British Library.

Library of Congress Cataloging-in-Publication Data

Dyck, Andrew R. (Andrew Roy), 1947–
    A commentary on Cicero, De legibus / Andrew R. Dyck.
       p.   cm.
    Includes bibliographical references and indexes.
    ISBN 0-472-11324-0 (alk. paper)
    1. Cicero, Marcus Tullius. De legibus.   2. Dialogues, Latin—History and criticism.
3. Atticus, Titus Pomponius—In literature.   4. Cicero, Quintus Tullius—In literature.
5. Law and literature—History—To 500.   6. Roman law.   I. Cicero, Marcus Tullius. De
legibus.   II. Title.

PA6296.D323D93   2003
340.5′01—dc21   2003053335

For J.G.F.P.

Preface

The neglect of Cicero, *de Legibus,* is striking. The edition in general use, intended merely as a stopgap, is not based upon rigorous application of the stemmatic method (see § 10 of the Introduction), and the last commentary on the whole work, dating from 1881, was conceived for the needs and interests of a very different generation of readers, not to mention being written too early to take advantage of standard works on lexicography, prosopography, etc., that began appearing at the end of the nineteenth century. The diversity of content—natural law theory, religious law, constitutional law—have made the work difficult to grasp and interpret as a unity, so that the parts have come in for more attention than the whole. Not surprising that Rawson, 1991, 125, remarks "it is depressing to see how little solid advance has been made in the last hundred years." The neglect by specialists has led in turn to neglect by students of related subjects that might have benefited. Thus, in spite of the rise in interest in natural law theory among students of ancient philosophy, the lack of recent literature on *Leg.* from a philosophical angle is conspicuous.[1] Again, *Leg.* receives only cursory and unsympathetic treatment in a recent paper on Roman priesthoods by Mary Beard, who contrasts the treatment of the topic in Plato's *Laws* and concludes that "the multifarious variety of the Roman priestly groups . . . presented Cicero with serious difficulties in generalizing in Hellenizing terms, which he did not fully overcome";[2] but is "generalizing in Hellenizing terms" really what Cicero was seeking to do?[3] Assessments of Cicero's political philosophy can profit from attention to our work; yet in his influential *RE*-article "Cicero als Politiker" M. Gelzer devotes almost four columns to analysis of *de Republica* but no connected treatment to *Leg.*[4]

Incomplete, bristling with lacunae and other textual problems as well as archaic or pseudo-archaic language, with a problematic relation to Plato's *Laws* on the one side and Cicero's own *de Republica* on the other, more than most ancient works, *Leg.* needs to be read in a high quality critical edition with the aid of a detailed modern commentary. The need for a new

---

1. See below p. 1 and n. 1.

2. Mary Beard, "Priesthood in the Roman Republic," in Beard-North, 45.

3. Contrast Mehl, 167, who emphasizes that "the religious laws of *De Legibus* can only be comprehended in the context of the work in which they appear."

4. Gelzer, *RE* 7A (1948), 972.37–976.20 (on *Rep.*).

text has been catered for by J.G.F. Powell, whose new OCT should appear next year. In presenting a commentary, I am keenly aware that the task requires a formidable array of specialized knowledge—in philology, history of philosophy and religion and constitutional history, in each of which I can hope, at best, to approximate a beta.[5] The method and goals outlined in the Preface to my commentary on *de Officiis* apply here as well; here I can focus on the needs of scholarly readers in the knowledge that the general reader has been catered for in the recent annotated translations by Rudd-Powell and Zetzel.

I owe thanks to many persons and institutions who made my work easier: to J.N. Adams, Clifford Ando, Catherine Atherton, Andreas Bendlin, David Blank, Mortimer Chambers, Peter Cohee, Thomas Frazel, Sander Goldberg, Brad Inwood, Christina S. Kraus, Andrew Lintott, Angelo Mercado, Sarah Morris, Paul Naiditch, David Phillips, Amy Richlin, P.L. Schmidt, Christine Schmitz, R.R.R. Smith, and Brent Vine for advice on various problems, passages, or parts of my commentary, and to Barbara Landis and M.D. Pike for help in preparing and correcting the indices; to All Souls College, Oxford, and Clare Hall, Cambridge, for providing me visiting fellowships during the academic year 1998–99, when the bulk of the commentary was completed; to Gisela Striker for kindly inviting me to participate in the 1999 Cambridge Mayweek seminar devoted to *Leg.* 1.1–2.14 and to all the other participants for sharing their views, which I have gratefully used and/or reacted to in the following pages; I regret that my notes enable me to attribute some, but not all, to their authors; to the Academic Senate of the University of California, Los Angeles, for providing research assistance and supplies to support work on this project; to the chancellor of the University, provost of the college, and dean of humanities for providing me with sabbatical leave during said academic year; to D.R. Shackleton Bailey, who read the whole commentary for the Press and provided a series of characteristically learned and acute comments from which I have benefited enormously; to W. Jeffrey Tatum for his valuable and detailed comments as Press reader; to the University of Michigan Press, in particular to Collin Ganio and Christina L. Milton for their enormous patience and help in seeing the manuscript through to publication; to J.G.F. Powell for giving me access to his texts of *Leg.* and *Rep.* in advance of publication and for patient, acute, and very fruitful dialogue extending over many months about textual problems; and, last but not least, to my wife, Janis, for considerable understanding and support during the gestation of the project.

---

5. Cf. Su. ε 2898 (of Eratosthenes): διὰ δὲ τὸ δευτερεύειν ἐν παντὶ εἴδει παιδείας τοῖς ἄκροις ἐγγίσαντα (Meursius : ἐγγίσαι) τὸ βῆτα (Ps.-Hesych. : τὰ βήματα) ἐπεκλήθη.

Contents

Works Cited by Author

Early Imprints

Sweynheym-Pannartz, Rome, 1471
Minutianus, Milan, 1499
Ascensius, Paris, 1521
Aldus, Venice, 1523
Cratander, Basel, 1528
P. Manutius, Venice, 1546
R. Stephanus, Paris, 1546–47
Lambinus, Paris, 1565–66
"Lambinus," Paris, 1572–73
Aldus (nepos), Venice, 1578–83
Graevius, Amsterdam, 1677–1761
Davies, Cambridge, 1727, 2d ed. 1745

Other Editions, Translations, and Commentaries

Bake	Bake, Iohannes, ed. and comm. M. Tulli Ciceronis *De Legibus libri tres*. Leyden, 1842.
Büchner, ed.	Büchner, Carolus, ed. M. Tulli Ciceronis *De Legibus libri tres*. Turin, 1973.
Büchner, tr.	Büchner, Karl, tr. Cicero. *Über die Rechtlichkeit (De Legibus)*. Stuttgart, 1969.
Busuttil	Busuttil, J. *Cicero: De Legibus Book 1: An Introduction, a Translation and a Commentary*. Diss. London, 1964.
Costa	Costa, Carlo Alberto, ed. M. Tullii Ciceronis *De Legibus liber secundus*. Turin, 1937.
Feldhügel	Feldhuegelius, C.F., ed. and comm. M. Tullii Ciceronis *De Legibus libri tres*. 2 vols. Zeitz, 1852–53.
Görler	Görler, Woldemar. M. Tullius Cicero. *De Legibus*. Ed. Konrat Ziegler. 3d ed. rev. W.G. Freiburg-Würzburg, 1979.

Huschke	Huschke, P. Eduardus, ed. *Iurisprudentiae anteiustinianae quae supersunt*. 4th ed. Leipzig, 1879. Pp. 19–84.
Kenter	Kenter, L.P. M. Tullius Cicero. *De Legibus. A Commentary on Book 1*. Amsterdam, 1972.
Keyes	Keyes, Clinton Walker, ed. and tr. Cicero. *De Re Publica, De Legibus*. Cambridge, Mass.–London, 1928.
du Mesnil	du Mesnil, Adolf, ed. and comm. M. Tullii Ciceronis *De Legibus libri tres*. Leipzig, 1879.
Moser-Creuzer	Moser, Georgius Henricus, and Fridericus Creuzer, eds. M. Tullii Ciceronis *De Legibus*. Frankfurt am Main, 1824.
Müller	Müller, C.F.W., ed. M. Tulli Ciceronis *Scripta quae manserunt omnia*. 4 pts. in 10 vols. Leipzig, 1878–98 (*Leg.* in pt. 4, vol. 2, 1878).
Nickel	Nickel, Rainer, ed. and tr. M. Tullius Cicero. *De Legibus, Paradoxa Stoicorum*. Zurich, 1994.
Ottolini	Ottolini, Angelo, ed. and comm. M. Tullio Cicerone. *De Legibus Liber Secundus*. Milan, 1935.
Pearman	Pearman, W.D., ed. and comm. M.T. Ciceronis *De Legibus libri III*. Cambridge, 1881.
de Plinval	Plinval, Georges de, ed. and trans. Cicéron. *Traité des lois*. Paris, 1959.
Powell	Powell, J.G.F., ed. M. Tulli Ciceronis *De Republica, De Legibus, Cato Maior, Laelius*. Oxford, in press.
Rudd-Powell	Rudd, Niall, and Jonathan Powell. Cicero. *The Republic and The Laws*. Tr. N.R. with Introduction and Notes by J.P. and N.R. Oxford, 1998.
Rudd-Wiedemann	Rudd, Niall, and Thomas Wiedemann. Cicero. *De Legibus I*. Ed. with Introduction and Commentary. Bristol, 1987.
Schiche	Schiche, Theodorus, ed. M. Tullius Cicero. *Paradoxa Stoicorum, De Legibus libri*. Leipzig, 1913.
Sichirollo	Sichirollo, D. Giacomo. *I tre libri di M.T. Cicerone intorno alle leggi. Testo colla versione e commento*. Padua, 1878.
Turnebus	Turnebus, Adrianus. Notes on *Leg.* printed as an

appendix to Davies. See also Secondary Literature s.v.

Vahlen[1], Vahlen

Vahlen, Iohannes. M. Tullii Ciceronis *De Legibus libri*. Berlin, 1871, 1883.

Zetzel

Zetzel, James E.G., tr. Cicero. *On the Commonwealth and On the Laws*. Cambridge, 1999.

Ziegler

Ziegler, Konrat, ed. M. Tullius Cicero. *De Legibus*. 2d ed. Heidelberg, 1963.

Ziegler, 1974

Ziegler, Konrat, ed. and tr. Cicero. *Staatstheoretische Schriften*. Berlin, 1974.

Zumpt

Zumpt, A.W., trans. Von den Gesetzen. In *Cicero's philosophische Schriften in deutscher Übertragung*. Ed. Reinhold Klotz. 2. Theil. Leipzig, 1841.

Other Works of Cicero

Att.

Shackleton Bailey, D.R., ed. M.T. Cicero. *Epistulae ad Atticum*. 2 vols. Stuttgart, 1987 (for Latin text). Or Shackleton Bailey, D.R., ed. Cicero's *Letters to Atticus*. 7 vols. Cambridge, 1965–70 (for commentary). His four-volume Loeb ed. (Cambridge, Mass., 1999) is sometimes also cited.

Cons.

Vitelli, Claudius, ed. M. Tulli Ciceronis *Consolationis fragmenta*. Turin, 1979.

Fam.

Shackleton Bailey, D.R., ed. M. Tulli Ciceronis *Epistulae ad Familiares*. Stuttgart, 1988 (for Latin Text). Or Shackleton Bailey, D.R., ed. Cicero. *Epistulae ad Familiares*. 2 vols. Cambridge, 1977 (for commentary). His three-volume Loeb ed. (Cambridge, Mass., 2001) is sometimes also cited.

fr. ep.

Shackleton Bailey, D.R., ed. Fragmenta epistularum in M. Tulli Ciceronis *Epistulae ad Quintum fratrem, Epistulae ad M. Brutum,* etc. Leipzig, 1988.

fr. orat.

Crawford, Jane W., ed. Cicero. *The Fragmentary Speeches*. 2d ed. Atlanta, 1994.

fr. phil.

Garbarino, I., ed. M.T. Cicero. *Fragmenta ex libris philosophicis, ex aliis libris deperditis, ex scriptis incertis*. Turin, 1984.

| *Hort.* | Grilli, A., ed. M. Tulli Ciceronis *Hortensius*. Milan, 1962. |

Other Sources

Aristippus	Mannebach, Erich, ed. *Aristippi et Cyrenaicorum Fragmenta*. Leiden-Cologne, 1961.
auct. inc. *de verbo*	Passalacqua, Marina, ed. Auctoris incerti *de verbo tractatus*. In M.P., ed. *Tre testi grammaticali Bobbiesi (GL V 555–566; 634–654; IV 207–216 Keil)*. Sussidi Eruditi, 38. Rome, 1984. Pp. 21–60.
Carneades . . . M.	Mette, Hans-Joachim. Weitere Akademiker heute: Von Lakydes bis zu Kleitomachos. *Lustrum* 27, 39–148 at 53–141, 1985.
Carneades . . . W.	Wisniewski, Bohdan, ed. Karneades. *Fragmente*. With commentary. Wroclaw-Warsaw-Cracow, 1970.
Cirenaici	Giannantoni, Gabriele, ed. *I Cirenaici*. Florence, 1958.
Courtney	Courtney, Edward. *The Fragmentary Latin Poets*. Oxford, 1993.
Demetrius of Phalerum . . . S.O.D.	Stork, Peter, Jan Max van Ophuijsen, Tiziano Dorandi, eds. *Demetrius of Phalerum: The Sources, Text and Translation*. In Fortenbaugh-Schütrumpf. Pp. 1–310.
Demetrius of Phalerum . . . Wehrli	Wehrli, Fritz, ed. *Demetrios von Phaleron*. 2d ed. Die Schule des Aristoteles 4. Basel-Stuttgart, 1968.
Demetrius of Scepsis . . . Gaede	Gaede, Ricardus, ed. Demetrii Scepsii *Quae supersunt*. Diss. Greifswald, 1880.
Epicurea	Usener, Hermannus, ed. *Epicurea*. Leipzig, 1887.
FLP	Preibisch, Paul, ed. *Fragmenta librorum pontificiorum*. Tilsit, 1878.
Font. iur.	Bruns, Carolus Georgius, ed. *Fontes iuris Romani antiqui*. Vol. 1: *Leges et negotia*. Post curas Theodori Mommseni . . . septimum ed. Otto Gradenwitz. Tübingen, 1909.
gram.	Funaioli, Hyginus, ed. *Grammaticae Romanae fragmenta*. Vol. 1. Leipzig, 1907.

hist.	Peter, Hermann, ed. *Historicorum Romanorum Relliquiae.* 2d ed. Bibliographical suppl. by W. Schaub and J. Kroymann. 2 vols. Stuttgart, 1993.
iur.	Seckel, E., and B. Kuebler, post P.E. Huschke, eds. *Iurisprudentia anteiustiniana.* Vol. 1. 6th ed. Leipzig, 1908.
iur. anteh.	Bremer, F.P., ed. *Iurisprudentia antehadriana.* Vol. 1: *Liberae rei publicae iuris consulti.* Leipzig, 1896.
Leg. Gr. sac.	Prott, Ioannes de, and Ludovicus Ziehen, eds. *Leges Graecorum sacrae e titulis collectae.* 2 vols. Leipzig, 1896–1906.
Leg. sac.	Krueger, Ericus. *De Romanorum legibus sacris commentationes selectae.* Diss. Königsberg, 1912.
Lex XII	Crawford, M.H., ed. XII Tabulae. In *RS*. Vol. 2. Pp. 555–721.
Long-Sedley	Long, A.A., and D.N. Sedley. *The Hellenistic Philosophers.* 2 vols. Cambridge, 1987–88.
Macr. *diff.*	Ianus, Ludovicus, ed. *E Macrobii . . . libro De differentiis et societatibus Graeci Latinique verbi excerpta.* In L.I., ed., Macrobii Ambrosii Theodosii *Opera quae supersunt.* 2 vols. Quedlinburg-Leipzig, 1848–52. Vol. 1, pp. 227–77.
Panaetius fr. . . . A.	Alessa, Francesca, ed. Panezio di Rodi. *Testimonianze.* Naples, 1997.
Panaetius fr. . . . S.	van Straaten, Modestus, ed. Panaetii Rhodii *Fragmenta.* 3d ed. Leiden, 1962.
Petr. *Fam.*	Rossi, Vittorio, ed. Petrarca, Francesco. *Le familiari.* 4 vols. Florence, 1933–42.
Polemo . . . G.	Gigante, M., ed. I frammenti di Polemone academico. *Rendiconti della Accademia di Archeologia, Lettere e Belle Arti* n.s. 51. Naples, 1976. Pp. 91–144.
Polystratus . . . Indelli	Indelli, Giovanni, ed. Polistrato. *Sul disprezzo irrazionale delle opinioni popolari.* Naples, 1978.
PT	Thesleff, Holger, ed. *The Pythagorean Texts of the Hellenistic Period.* Acta Academiae Aboensis, ser. A. Humanistiska Vetenskaper. 30.1. Abo, 1965.

RRC	Crawford, Michael H. *Roman Republican Coinage.* 2 vols. Cambridge, 1974.
RS	Crawford, M.H., ed. *Roman Statutes.* Bulletin of the Institute of Classical Studies Suppl. 64. 2 vols. London, 1996.
Sen. . . . Vottero	Vottero, Dionigi, ed. Lucio Anneo Seneca. *I frammenti.* Bologna, 1998.
Socr.	Giannantoni, Gabriele, ed. *Socratis et Socraticorum reliquiae.* 4 vols. Naples, 1990.
Solon . . . M.	Martina, Antonius, ed. Solon. *Testimonia veterum.* Rome, 1968.
Solon . . . R.	Ruschenbusch, Eberhard. ΣΟΛΩΝΟΣ ΝΟΜΟΙ. *Die Fragmente des Solonischen Gesetzeswerkes, mit einer Text- und Überlieferungsgeschichte.* Historia Einzelschriften 9. Wiesbaden, 1966.
Speusippus . . . I.P.	Isnardi Parente, Margherita, ed. Speusippo. *Frammenti.* Naples, 1980.
Speusippus . . . L.	Lang, Paul, ed. *De Speusippi Academici scriptis. Accedunt fragmenta.* Hildesheim, 1965.
Speusippus . . . T.	Tarán, Leonardo. *Speusippus of Athens: A Critical Study with a Collection of the Related Texts and Commentary.* Leiden, 1981.
Theophr. . . . F.	Fortenbaugh, W.W., et al., eds. Theophrastus of Eresus. *Sources for His Life, Writings, Thought and Influence.* 2 vols. Leiden, 1992.
Var. *ARD*	Cardauns, Burkhart, ed. M. Terentius Varro. *Antiquitates rerum divinarum.* Akademie der Wissenschaften und der Literatur, Mainz. Abhandlungen der Geistes- und Sozialwissenschaftlichen Klasse. Einzelveröffentlichung. 2 vols. Wiesbaden, 1976.
Var. *Cur.*	Cardauns, Burkhart, ed. *Varros Logistoricus über die Götterverehrung (Curio de cultu deorum).* Würzburg, 1960.
Var. *VPR*	Riposati, Benedetto, ed. M. Terenti Varronis *De vita populi Romani.* Pubblicazioni dell' Università Cattolica del S. Cuore 4, 33. Milan, 1939.
Vetter	Vetter, Emil. *Handbuch der italischen Dialekte.* Vol. 1. Heidelberg, 1953.
Xenocrates . . . H.	Heinze, Richard. *Xenokrates. Darstellung der*

	Lehre und Sammlung der Fragmente. Leipzig, 1892.
Xenocrates . . . I.P.	Isnardi Parente, Margherita, ed. Senocrate, Ermodoro. *Frammenti*. Naples, 1982.
Zeno of Sidon . . . Angeli-Colaizzo	Angeli, Anna, and Maria Colaizzo. I frammenti di Zenone Sidonio. *CErc* 9, 47–133, 1979.

Secondary Literature, Works of Reference, Databases

Achard	Achard, Guy. *Pratique rhétorique et idéologie politique dans les discours "optimates" de Cicéron*. Mnemosyne Suppl. 68. Leiden, 1981.
Adams, 1972	Adams, J.N. The Language of the Later Books of Tacitus' *Annals*. *CQ* n.s. 22, 350–73, 1972.
Adams, 1978	Adams, J.N. Conventions of Naming in Cicero. *CQ* 72, 145–66, 1978.
Adams, 1994	Adams, J.N. *Wackernagel's Law and the Placement of the Copula <u>esse</u> in Classical Latin*. Cambridge, 1994.
Agahd	Agahd, R., ed. M. Terenti Varronis *Antiquitatum rerum divinarum libri I, XIV, XV, XVI. Praemissae sunt quaestiones Varronianae*. Leipzig, 1898.
von Albrecht, 1973	von Albrecht, Michael. M.T. Cicero, Sprache und Stil. *RE* Suppl. 13 (1973). Col. 1104–92.47.
von Albrecht, 1983	von Albrecht, Michael. *Meister römischer Prosa von Cato bis Apuleius*. 2d ed. Heidelberg, 1983 = *Masters of Roman Prose from Cato to Apuleius*. Tr. Neil Adkin. Leeds, 1989.
Alexander	Alexander, Michael C. *Trials in the Late Roman Republic, 149 BC to 50 BC*. Phoenix Suppl. 26. Toronto, 1990.
Algra	Algra, K.A. Chrysippus, Carneades, Cicero: The Ethical *Divisiones* in Cicero's *Lucullus*. In Inwood-Mansfeld. Pp. 107–39.
W. Allen	Allen, Walter, Jr. Cicero's House and *Libertas*. *TAPhA* 75, 1–9, 1944.
W.S. Allen	Allen, W. Sidney. *Vox Latina: A Guide to the Pronunciation of Classical Latin*. 2d ed. Cambridge, 1978.

Anselmo   Anselmo, Giuseppina Arico. *Ius publicum—Ius*
                         privatum in Ulpiano, Gaio e Cicerone. *Annali del*
                         seminario giuridico della Università di Palermo
                         37, 445–787, 1983.
Astin, 1964   Astin, A.E. Leges Aelia et Fufia. *Latomus* 23,
                         421–45, 1964.
Astin, 1988   Astin, Alan E. *Regimen morum. JRS* 78, 14–34,
                         1988.
Austin *ad Cael.*   Austin, R.G., ed. M.T. Ciceronis Pro M. *Caelio*
                         oratio. 3d ed. Oxford, 1960.
Badian, 1966   Badian, E. The Early Historians. In T.A. Dorey,
                         ed. *Latin Historians.* New York, 1966. Pp. 1–38.
Badian, 1996   Badian, Ernst. *Tribuni plebis* and *res publica.* In
                         J. Linderski, ed. *Imperium sine fine: T. Robert S.*
                         Broughton and the Roman Republic. Historia Ein-
                         zelschriften 105. Stuttgart, 1996. Pp. 187–213.
Bailey *ad* Lucr.   Bailey, Cyril, ed. and comm. T. Lucreti Cari *De*
                         Rerum Natura libri sex. 3 vols. Oxford, 1947.
Baltrusch   Baltrusch, Ernst. *Regimen morum. Die*
                         Reglementierung des Privatlebens der Senatoren
                         und Ritter in der römischen Republik und frühen
                         Kaiserzeit. Munich, 1989.
Barnes, 1989   Barnes, Jonathan. Antiochus of Ascalon. In
                         Philosophia Togata. Ed. Miriam Griffin and Jona-
                         than Barnes. Oxford, 1989. Pp. 51–96.
Barnes, 1997   Barnes, Jonathan. Logic in *Academica* I and the
                         Lucullus. In Inwood-Mansfeld. Pp. 140–60.
Bauman   Bauman, Richard A. *Lawyers in Roman Republi-*
                         can Politics: A Study of the Roman Jurists in
                         Their Political Setting, 316–82 BC. Munich,
                         1983.
Beard, 1980   Beard, Mary. The Sexual Status of the Vestal Vir-
                         gins. *JRS* 70, 12–27, 1980.
Beard, 1986   Beard, Mary. Cicero and Divination: The Forma-
                         tion of a Latin Discourse. *JRS* 76, 33–46, 1986.
Beard, 1998   Beard, Mary, John North, and Simon Price. *Reli-*
                         gions of Rome. 2 vols. Cambridge, 1998.
Beard-North   Beard, Mary, and John North. *Pagan Priests: Reli-*
                         gion and Power in the Ancient World. Ithaca,
                         1990.

Becker	Becker, Ernst. *Technik und Szenerie des ciceronischen Dialogs.* Diss. Münster, 1938.
Behrends, 1970	Behrends, Okko. Ius und Ius Civile. Untersuchungen zur Herkunft des *ius*-Begriffs im römischen Zivilrecht. In *Sympotica Franz Wieacker sexagenario Sasbachwaldeni a suis libata.* Ed. Detlef Liebs. Göttingen, 1970. Pp. 11–58.
Behrends, 1978	Behrends, Okko. Grabraub und Grabfrevel im römischen Recht. *Abhandlungen der Akademie der Wissenschaften,* philol.-hist. Kl. 3.113. Göttingen, 1978. Pp. 85–106.
Benardete	Benardete, Seth. Cicero's *De Legibus* I: Its Plan and Intention. *AJPh* 108, 295–309, 1987.
Bendlin, 1998	Bendlin, Andreas E. *Social Complexity and Religion at Rome in the Second and First Centuries BCE.* Diss. Oxford, 1998.
Bendlin	Bendlin, Andreas E. Ms. notes placed at my disposal by Andreas E. Bendlin.
H. Benner	Benner, Herbert. *Die Politik des P. Clodius Pulcher. Untersuchungen zur Denaturierung des Clientelwesens in der ausgehenden römischen Republik.* Historia Einzelschriften 50. Stuttgart, 1987.
M. Benner	Benner, Margareta. *The Emperor Says: Studies in the Rhetorical Style in Edicts of the Early Empire.* Göteborg, 1975.
Beretta	Beretta, Dante G. *Promoting the Public Image: Cicero and His Consulship.* Diss. Johns Hopkins, 1996.
Berger	Berger, Adolf. *Encyclopedic Dictionary of Roman Law.* Transactions of the American Philosophical Society. N.s. 43.2. Philadelphia, 1953.
Bernstein	Bernstein, Frank. *Ludi Publici. Untersuchungen zur Entstehung und Entwicklung der öffentlichen Spiele im republikanischen Rom.* Historia Einzelschriften 119. Stuttgart, 1998.
Berry *ad Sul.*	Berry, D.H., ed. and comm. Cicero. *Pro P. Sulla oratio.* Cambridge, 1996.
Bleicken, 1955	Bleicken, Jochen. *Das Volkstribunat der*

	klassischen Republik. Studien zu seiner Entwicklung zwischen 287 und 133 v.Chr. Zetemata 13. Munich, 1955.
Bleicken, 1972	Bleicken, Jochen. *Staatliche Ordnung und Freiheit in der römischen Republik.* Frankfurter Althistorische Schriften 6. Kallmünz, 1972.
Bleicken, 1981a	Bleicken, Jochen. Das römische Volkstribunat. Versuch einer Analyse seiner politischen Funktion in republikanischer Zeit. *Chiron* 11, 87–108, 1981.
Bleicken, 1981b	Bleicken, Jochen. *Zum Begriff der römischen Amtsgewalt.* Nachrichten der Akademie der Wissenschaften, philol.-hist. Kl., 1981, 9. Göttingen, 1981.
Blümner	Blümner, Hugo. *Die römischen Privataltertümer.* Munich, 1911.
Bögel, 1907	Bögel, Theodor. *Inhalt und Zerlegung des zweiten Buches von Cicero de legibus.* Kreuzburg, O.-S., 1907.
Bögel, 1911	Bögel, Theodor. Zum zweiten und dritten Buch von Ciceros Schrift De Legibus. In ΧΑΡΙΤΕΣ *Friedrich Leo zum 60. Geburtstag dargebracht.* Berlin, 1911. Pp. 297–321.
Boesch	Boesch, Fridericus. *De XII tabularum lege a Graecis petita quaestiones philologicae.* Diss. Göttingen, 1893.
Bonjour	Bonjour, Madeleine. *Terre natale. Études sur une composante affective du patriotisme romain.* Paris, 1975.
Boyancé, 1963.	Boyancé, Pierre. Études philoniennes. *REG* 76, 64–110, 1963.
Boyancé, 1970	Boyancé, Pierre. *Études sur l'humanisme cicéronien.* Collection Latomus 121. Brussels, 1970.
Boyancé, 1971	Boyancé, Pierre. Cicéron et les parties de la philosophie. *REL* 49, 127–54, 1971.
Boyancé, 1975	Boyancé, Pierre. L'éloge de la philosophie dans le *De legibus* I, 58–62. *Ciceroniana* n.s. 2, 21–40, 1975.
Brecht	Brecht, Christoph Heinrich. *Perduellio. Eine Studie zu ihrer begrifflichen Abgrenzung im*

römischen Strafrecht bis zum Ausgang der Republik. Munich, 1938.

Bruck   Bruck, Eberhard F. Cicero vs. the Scaevolas: RE: Law of Inheritance and Decay of Roman Religion (*De Legibus* II, 19–21). In *Seminar: An Annual Extraordinary Number of The Jurist* 3, 1–20, 1945.

Brunt, 1979   Brunt, P.A. Cicero and Historiography. In φιλίας χάριν. *Miscellanea di studi classici in onore di Eugenio Manni.* Vol. 1. Rome, 1979. Pp. 311–40.

Brunt, 1990   Brunt, P.A. *Roman Imperial Themes.* Oxford, 1990.

Büchner   See under "*De Legibus:* Editions, Translations, and Commentaries."

Büchner, 1961   Büchner, Karl. Sinn und Entstehung von "De Legibus." *Atti del I Congresso Internazionale di Studi Ciceroniani.* Vol. 2. Rome, 1961. Pp. 81–90.

Büchner, 1970   Büchner, Karl. Römische Konstanten und De Legibus. In K.B. *Studien zur römischen Literatur.* Vol. 8: *Werkanalysen.* Wiesbaden, 1970. Pp. 21–39.

Büchner *ad Rep.*   Büchner, Karl. M. Tullius Cicero. *De re publica.* Kommentar von K.B. Heidelberg, 1984.

Bunbury   Bunbury, E.H. Art. Fibrenus *apud* Smith.

Burckhardt   Burckhardt, Leonhard A. *Politische Strategien der Optimaten in der späten römischen Republik.* Historia Einzelschriften 57. Stuttgart, 1988.

Burkert, 1965   Burkert, Walter. Cicero als Platoniker und Skeptiker. *Gymnasium* 72, 175–200, 1965.

Burkert, 1985   Burkert, Walter. *Greek Religion.* Tr. John Raffan. Cambridge, Mass., 1985.

Burkert, 1987   Burkert, Walter. *Ancient Mystery Cults.* Cambridge, Mass.–London, 1987.

Burkert, 1996   Burkert, Walter. *Creation of the Sacred: Tracks of Biology in Early Religions.* Cambridge, Mass.–London, 1996.

Busolt   Busolt, Georg. *Griechische Geschichte bis zur Schlacht bei Chaeroneia.* 4 vols. in 3. Gotha, 1893–1904.

Busolt-Swoboda   Busolt, Georg, and Heinrich Swoboda.
                      Griechische Staatskunde. 3d ed. 2 vols. Munich,
                      1920–26.
Byrne-Cueva   Byrne, Shannon N., and Edmund P. Cueva, eds.
                      *Veritatis Amicitiaeque Causa: Essays in Honor of
                      Anna Lydia Motto and John R. Clark.*
                      Wauconda, Ill., 1999.
CAH   *The Cambridge Ancient History.* 2d ed. Cam-
                      bridge, 1984–.
Cambeis   Cambeis, Herbert. Das monarchische Element
                      und die Funktion der Magistrate in Ciceros
                      Verfassungsentwurf. *Gymnasium* 91, 237–60,
                      1984.
Cancelli   Cancelli, Filippo. Per l'interpretazione del De
                      legibus di Cicerone. *RCCM* 15, 185–245, 1973.
Cancik, 1994   Cancik, Hubert, and Hildegard Cancik-
                      Lindemaier. *patria—peregrina—universa.*
                      Versuch einer Typologie der universalistischen
                      Tendenzen in der Geschichte der römischen Reli-
                      gion. *Tradition und Translation. Zum Problem
                      der interkulturellen Übersetzbarkeit religiöser
                      Phänomene. Festschrift für Carsten Colpe zum
                      65. Geburtstag.* Ed. Christoph Elsas et al. Berlin–
                      New York, 1994. Pp. 64–74.
Cancik, 1995   Cancik, Hubert. M. Tullius Cicero als
                      Kommentator. In *Text und Kommentar.
                      Archäologie der literarischen Kommunikation IV.*
                      Ed. Jan Assmann and Burkhard Gladigow. Mu-
                      nich, 1995. Pp. 293–310.
Canetti   Canetti, Elias. *Masse und Macht.* Hamburg, 1960
                      = *Crowds and Power.* Tr. Carol Stewart. New
                      York, 1962.
Classen   Classen, C. Joachim. Romulus in der römischen
                      Republik. *Philologus* 106, 174–204, 1962.
Constans   Constans, Léopold Albert. *Un correspondant de
                      Cicéron: Ap. Claudius Pulcher.* Thèse. Paris,
                      1921.
Coarelli   Coarelli, Filippo. *Il foro Romano.* 2 vols. Rome,
                      1983–85.

Corbeill	Corbeill, Anthony. *Controlling Laughter: Political Humor in the Late Roman Republic*. Princeton, 1996.
Cornell	Cornell, Tim. Some Observations on the "crimen incesti." In *Le délit religieux dans la cité antique*. Collection de l'École française de Rome 48. Rome, 1981.
Courtney	See under "Other Sources."
Courtney, 1999	Courtney, Edward. *Archaic Latin Prose*. Atlanta, 1999.
Courcelle	Courcelle, Pierre. Cicéron et le précept delphique. *Giornale italiano di filologia* 21, 109–20, 1969.
J. Crawford	Crawford, Jane W. *M. Tullius Cicero: The Lost and Unpublished Orations*. Hypomnemata 80. Göttingen, 1984.
Cumont	Cumont, Franz. *After Life in Roman Paganism*. New Haven, 1922.
Daube	Daube, David. *Forms of Roman Legislation*. Oxford, 1956.
Delatte	Delatte, A. *Essai sur la politique Pythagoricienne*. Liège-Paris, 1922.
Delz	Delz, Josef. Der griechische Einfluß auf die Zwölftafelgesetzgebung. *MH* 23, 69–83, 1966.
Denniston	Denniston, J.D. *The Greek Particles*. 2d ed. Oxford, 1954.
Denniston *ad Phil.*	Denniston, J.D., ed. and comm. M.T. Ciceronis *In M. Antonium orationes Philippicae prima et secunda*. Oxford, 1926.
Dickey, 1997	Dickey, Eleanor. *Me autem nomine appellabat*: Avoidance of Cicero's Name in His Dialogues. *CQ* 47, 584–88, 1997.
Dickey, 2002	Dickey, Eleanor. *Latin Forms of Address from Plautus to Apuleius*. Oxford, 2002.
Diehl	Diehl, Hermann. *Sulla und seine Zeit im Urteil Ciceros*. Hildesheim–Zurich–New York, 1988.
Dodds	Dodds, E.R. *The Greeks and the Irrational*. Berkeley–Los Angeles, 1951.
Dörrie, 1973	Dörrie, Heinrich. Ciceros Entwurf zu einer Neuordnung des römischen Sakralwesens. Zu den

geistigen Grundlagen von de legibus, Buch 2. *Classica et Mediaevalia Francisco Blatt septuagenario dedicata.* Classica et mediaevalia Dissertationes 9. Copenhagen, 1973. Pp. 224–40.

Dörrie, 1978   Dörrie, Heinrich. Summorum virorum vestigia. Das Erlebnis der Vergangenheit bei Cicero leg. 2, 4 und fin. 5, 1–8. *GB* 7, 207–20, 1978.

Douglas *ad Brut.*   Douglas, A.E., ed. and comm. M. Tulli Ciceronis *Brutus.* Oxford, 1966.

Dyck *ad N.D.* 1   Dyck, Andrew R., ed. and comm. Cicero. *De Natura Deorum liber I.* Cambridge, 2003.

Dyck *ad Off.*   Dyck, Andrew R. *A Commentary on Cicero, De Officiis.* Ann Arbor, 1996.

Dyck, 1998   Dyck, A.R. Narrative Obfuscation, Philosophical *Topoi,* and Tragic Patterning in Cicero's *Pro Milone. HSPh* 98, 219–41, 1998.

Engels   Engels, Johannes. *Funerum Sepulcrorumque Magnificentia. Begräbnis- und Grabluxusgesetze in der griechisch-römischen Welt mit einigen Ausblicken auf Einschränkungen des funeralen und sepulkralen Luxus im Mittelalter und in der Neuzeit.* Hermes Einzelschriften 78. Stuttgart, 1998.

England *ad* Pl. *Lg.* England, E.B., ed. and comm. *The Laws of Plato.* 2 vols. London–New York, 1921.

Ernesti   Ernesti, Johann Christian Gottlieb. *Lexicon technologiae Latinorum rhetoricae.* Leipzig, 1797.

Fantham   Fantham, E. *Stuprum:* Public Attitudes and Penalties for Sexual Offences in Republican Rome. *EMC* n.s. 10, 267–91, 1991.

Fantham *ad Fast.*   Fantham, Elaine, ed. and comm. Ovid. *Fasti. Book 4.* Cambridge, 1998.

Farrell   Farrell, Joseph. *Latin Language and Latin Culture from Ancient to Modern Times.* Cambridge, 2001.

Ferrary, 1974   Ferrary, Jean-Louis. Le discours de Laelius dans le troisième livre du *De re publica* de Cicéron. *MEFRA* 86, 745–71, 1974.

Ferrary, 1995   Ferrary, Jean-Louis. The Statesman and the Law in the Political Philosophy of Cicero. In Laks-Schofield. Pp. 48–73.

Festugière	Festugière, A.J. *La révélation d'Hermès Trismégiste*, 2: *Le Dieu cosmique*. Paris, 1949.
Finger	Finger, Philipp. Die drei Grundlegungen des Rechts im 1. Buche von Ciceros Schrift De Legibus. *RhM* N.F. 81, 155–77, 243–62, 1932.
Fladerer	Fladerer, Ludwig. *Antiochos von Askalon. Hellenist und Humanist*. Grazer Beiträge Suppl. 7. Graz-Horn, 1996.
Fleck	Fleck, Martin. *Cicero als Historiker*. Beiträge zur Altertumskunde 39. Stuttgart, 1993.
Flobert	Flobert, Pierre. *Les verbes déponents latins des origines à Charlemagne*. Paris, 1975.
Flower	Flower, Harriet. *Ancestor Masks and Aristocratic Power in Roman Culture*. Oxford, 1996.
Fontanella, 1997	Fontanella, Francesca. Introduzione al *De Legibus* di Cicerone. I. *Athenaeum* 85, 487–530, 1997.
Fontanella, 1998	Fontanella, Francesca. Introduzione al *De Legibus* di Cicerone. II. *Athenaeum* 86, 179–208, 1998.
Forcellini	Forcellini, Aegidius, et al., eds. *Lexicon totius Latinitatis*. 4th ed. Padua, 1864–1926; rp. Bologna, 1965.
Fordyce *ad* Cat.	Fordyce, C.J. *Catullus: A Commentary*. Oxford, 1961.
Forschner	Forschner, Maximilian. *Über das Handeln im Einklang mit der Natur. Grundlagen ethischer Verständigung*. Darmstadt, 1998.
Fortenbaugh-Schütrumpf	Fortenbaugh, William W., and Eckart Schütrumpf, eds. *Demetrius of Phalerum: Text, Translation and Discussion*. Rutgers University Studies in Classical Humanities 9. New Brunswick–London, 2000.
Fortenbaugh-Steinmetz	Fortenbaugh, William W., and Peter Steinmetz, eds. *Cicero's Knowledge of the Peripatos*. Rutgers University Studies in Classical Humanities 4. New Brunswick–London, 1989.
Fowler	Fowler, W. Warde. *The Religious Experience of the Roman People from the Earliest Times to the Age of Augustus*. London, 1911.

Frank   Frank, Hansgerd. *Ratio bei Cicero*. Frankfurt am
                     Main, 1992.
Frede   Frede, Dorothea. Peripatetic Influence on Cicero's
                     Political Conceptions in *De Re Publica*. In
                     Fortenbaugh-Steinmetz. Pp. 77–100.
Freyburger   Freyburger, Gérard. *Fides. Étude sémantique et
                     religieuse depuis les origines jusqu' à l'époque au-
                     gustéenne*. Paris, 1986.
Frier   Frier, Bruce W. *The Rise of the Roman Jurists:
                     Studies in Cicero's pro Caecina*. Princeton,
                     1985.
Frisk   Frisk, Hjalmar. *Griechisches Etymologisches
                     Wörterbuch*. 3 vols. Heidelberg, 1973–79.
Fuchs   Fuchs, Harald. Ciceros Hingabe an die Philo-
                     sophie. *MH* 16, 1–28, 1959.
Fugier   Fugier, Huguette. *Recherches sur l'expression du
                     sacré dans la langue Latine*. Publications de la
                     Faculté des Lettres de l'Université de Strasbourg
                     146. Paris, 1963.
Gagarin, 1986   Gagarin, Michael. *Early Greek Law*. Berkeley,
                     1986.
Gagarin, 2000   Gagarin, Michael. The Legislation of Demetrius
                     of Phalerum and the Transformation of Athenian
                     Law. In Fortenbaugh-Schütrumpf. Pp. 347–65.
Garnsey   Garnsey, Peter. *Social Status and Legal Privilege
                     in the Roman Empire*. Oxford, 1970.
Gasser   Gasser, Franziska. *Germana Patria. Die
                     Geburtsheimat in den Werken römischer Autoren
                     der späten Republik und der frühen Kaiserzeit*.
                     Beiträge zur Altertumskunde 118. Stuttgart-
                     Leipzig, 1999.
Gawlick-Görler   Gawlick, Günter, and Woldemar Görler. Cicero.
                     In Überweg. Pp. 991–1168.
Gehrke   Gehrke, Hans-Joachim. Das Verhältnis von
                     Politik und Philosophie im Wirken des Demetrios
                     von Phaleron. *Chiron* 8, 149–93, 1978.
Gelzer   Gelzer, Matthias. *Cicero. Ein biographischer
                     Versuch*. Wiesbaden, 1969.
Gelzer, *Caesar*   Gelzer, Matthias. *Caesar. Der Politiker und*

	Staatsmann. 6th ed. Wiesbaden, 1960 = *Caesar: Politician and Statesman.* Tr. P. Needham. Cambridge, Mass., 1968.
Gelzer, *Pompeius*	Gelzer, Matthias. *Pompeius. Lebensbild eines Römers.* 2d ed. rev. Elisabeth Herrmann-Otto. Stuttgart, 1984.
Gentili and Cerri	Gentili, Bruno, and Giovanni Cerri. *History and Biography in Ancient Thought.* Studies in Classical Philology 20. Amsterdam, 1988.
Girardet, 1977	Girardet, Klaus M. Ciceros Urteil über die Entstehung des Tribunates als Institution der römischen Verfassung (rep. 2,57–59). In *Bonner Festgabe für Johannes Straub.* Ed. Adolf Lippold, Nikolaus Himmelmann. Bonn, 1977. Pp. 179–200.
Girardet, 1983	Girardet, Klaus M. *Die Ordnung der Welt. Ein Beitrag zur philosophischen und politischen Interpretation von Ciceros Schrift De Legibus.* Historia Einzelschriften 42. Wiesbaden, 1983.
Glucker	Glucker, John. Cicero's Philosophical Affiliations. In J.M. Dillon and A.A. Long, eds. *The Question of "Eclecticism": Studies in Later Greek Philosophy.* Berkeley–Los Angeles–London, 1988. Pp. 34–69.
Gnauk	Gnauk, Rudolf. *Die Bedeutung des Marius und Cato maior für Cicero.* Diss. Leipzig. Berlin, 1935.
Goar	Goar, R.J. *Cicero and the State Religion.* Amsterdam, 1972.
Goldberg	Ms. notes placed at my disposal by Sander M. Goldberg.
Görler, 1974	Görler, Woldemar. *Untersuchungen zu Ciceros Philosophie.* Heidelberg, 1974.
Görler, 1989	Görler, Woldemar. Cicero und die "Schule des Aristoteles." In Fortenbaugh-Steinmetz. Pp. 246–63.
Görler, 1994	Görler, Woldemar. Älterer Pyrrhonismus, Jüngerer Akademie, Antiochus von Askalon. In Überweg. Pp. 732–989.

Görler, 1995   Görler, Woldemar. Silencing the Troublemaker:
                      De Legibus 1.39 and the Continuity of Cicero's
                      Scepticism. In Powell, 1995. Pp. 85–113.

Görler, 1997   Görler, Woldemar. Cicero's Philosophical Stance
                      in the *Lucullus*. In Inwood-Mansfeld. Pp. 36–57.

Gomme *ad* Thuc.   Gomme, A.W. *A Historical Commentary on Thu-
                      cydides.* 5 vols. (the last in collaboration with A.
                      Andrewes and K.J. Dover). Oxford, 1956–81.

Gonda   Gonda, J. The History and Original Function of
                      the Indo-European Particle K^uE, especially in
                      Greek and Latin. *Mnemosyne* ser. 4, 7, 177–214
                      and 265–96, 1954.

Graff   Graff, Jürgen. *Ciceros Selbstauffassung.* Heidel-
                      berg, 1963.

Greenidge   Greenidge, A.H.J. *The Legal Procedure of Cic-
                      ero's Time.* Oxford, 1901.

Gruen, 1974   Gruen, Erich S. *The Last Generation of the Ro-
                      man Republic.* Berkeley, 1974.

Gruen, 1991   Gruen, Erich S. The Exercise of Power in the Ro-
                      man Republic. In *City-States in Classical Antiq-
                      uity and Medieval Italy.* Ed. Anthony Molho,
                      Kurt Raaflaub, and Julia Emlen. Stuttgart, 1991.
                      Pp. 251–67.

Häfner   Häfner, Siegfried. *Die literarischen Pläne Ciceros.*
                      Diss. Munich. Coburg, 1928.

Häussler   Häussler, Reinhard, ed. *Nachträge zu A. Otto,
                      Sprichwörter und sprichwörtliche Redensarten
                      der Römer.* Darmstadt, 1968.

Hainsworth *ad* Od.   Heubeck, Alfred, Stephanie West, and J.B.
                      Hainsworth. *A Commentary on Homer's Odys-
                      sey.* Vol. 1. Oxford, 1988.

Hall, 1990   Hall, Ursula. Greeks and Romans and the Secret
                      Ballot. In *"Owls to Athens": Essays on Classical
                      Subjects Presented to Sir Kenneth Dover.* Ed.
                      E.M. Craik. Oxford, 1990. Pp. 191–99.

Hall, 1998   Hall, Ursula. "Species Libertatis": Voting Proce-
                      dures in the Late Roman Republic. In *Modus Ope-
                      randi: Essays in Honour of Geoffrey Rickman.*
                      Ed. M. Austin, J. Harries, and C. Smith. London,
                      1998. Pp. 15–30.

Hanssen	Hanssen, Jens S.T. *Latin Diminutives: A Semantic Study.* Bergen, 1952.
Haury	Haury, Auguste. *L'ironie et l'humour chez Cicéron.* Leiden, 1955.
Hand	Hand, Ferdinand. *Tursellinus seu De particulis Latinis commentarii.* 4 vols. Leipzig, 1829–45.
Hartung	Hartung, Hans-Joachim. *Ciceros Methode bei der Übersetzung griechischer philosophischer Termini.* Diss. Hamburg, 1970.
Heck	Heck, Eberhard. *Zur Textgestaltung von Cicero, De legibus.* Unpublished ms. used with permission of the author.
Heck, 1966	Heck, Eberhard. *Die Bezeugung von Ciceros Schrift De re publica.* Spudasmata 4. Hildesheim, 1966.
Heikkilä	Heikkilä, Kai. *Lex non iure rogata:* The Senate and the Annulment of Laws in the Late Republic. In U. Paananen et al. *Senatus Populusque Romanus: Studies in Roman Republican Legislation.* Acta Instituti Romani Finlandiae 13. Helsinki, 1993. Pp. 117–42.
Heinemann	Heinemann, Isaak. *Poseidonios' metaphysische Schriften.* 2 vols. Breslau, 1921–28.
Hellegouarc'h	Hellegouarc'h, Joseph. *Le vocabulaire latin des relations et des partis politiques sous la république.* Paris, 1963.
Heuss	Heuss, Alfred. *Ciceros Theorie vom römischen Staat.* Nachrichten der Akademie der Wissenschaften in Göttingen. Philologisch-Historische Klasse, 1975, 8. Göttingen, 1976. Pp. 195–272.
Hirzel, 1877–83	Hirzel, Rudolf. *Untersuchungen zu Cicero's philosophischen Schriften.* 3 vols. Leipzig, 1877–83.
Hirzel, 1895	Hirzel, Rudolf. *Der Dialog. Ein literarhistorischer Versuch.* Vol. 1. Leipzig, 1895.
Hofmann	Hofmann, J.B. *La lingua d'uso latina.* Rev. L. Ricottilli. Bologna, 1985.
Hofmann-Szantyr	Hofmann, J. B., and Anton Szantyr. *Lateinische Syntax und Stilistik.* Munich, 1965.

Holst — Holst, Hans. *Die Wortspiele in Ciceros Reden.* Symbolae Osloenses Suppl. 1. Oslo, 1925.

Homeyer — Homeyer, Helene. Zur Bedeutungsgeschichte von "sapientia." *AC* 25, 301–18, 1956.

Hopkins — Hopkins, Keith. *Sociological Studies in Roman History.* Vol. 2: *Death and Renewal.* Cambridge, 1983.

Horsfall *ad* Nep. — Horsfall, Nicholas, tr. and comm. Cornelius Nepos. *A Selection, Including the Lives of Cato and Atticus.* Oxford, 1989.

Hoyer — Hoyer, R. *De Antiocho Ascalonita.* Diss. Bonn, 1883.

Humbert — Humbert, Michel. Le tribunal de la plèbe et le tribunal du peuple. Remarques sur l'histoire de la provocatio ad populum. *MEFRA* 100, 431–503, 1988.

Hutchinson, 1995 — Hutchinson, G.O. Rhythm, Style, and Meaning in Cicero's Prose. *CQ* 45, 485–99, 1995.

Hutchinson, 1998 — Hutchinson, G.O. *Cicero's Correspondence: A Literary Study.* Oxford, 1998.

Ierodiakonou — Ierodiakonou, Katerina. The Stoic Division of Philosophy. *Phronesis* 38, 57–74, 1993.

Inwood — Ms. notes placed at my disposal by Brad Inwood.

Inwood, 1985 — Inwood, Brad. *Ethics and Human Action in Early Stoicism.* Oxford, 1985.

Inwood, 1987 — Inwood, Brad. Commentary on Striker. *Proceedings of the Boston Area Colloquium in Ancient Philosophy* 2, 95–101, 1987.

Inwood-Mansfeld — Inwood, Brad, and Jaap Mansfeld, eds. *Assent and Argument: Studies in Cicero's Academic Books.* Proceedings of the 7th Symposium Hellenisticum. Leiden, 1997.

Jahn — Jahn, Joachim. *Interregnum und Wahldiktatur.* Frankfurter Althistorische Studien 3. Kallmünz, 1970.

Johannemann — Johannemann, Richard. *Cicero und Pompeius in ihren wechselseitigen Beziehungen bis zum Jahre 51 v. Chr. Geb.* Emsdetten, 1935.

Jones — Jones, A.H.M. *The Criminal Courts of the Roman Republic and Principate.* Oxford, 1972.

Jordan	Jordan, H. Zur Beurtheilung des archaistischen Lateins: 1. Cicero's Archaismen in den Gesetzen. *Kritische Beiträge zur Geschichte der lateinischen Sprache.* Berlin, 1879. Pp. 225–50.
Kallet-Marx	Kallet-Marx, Robert M. *Hegemony to Empire: The Development of the Roman Imperium in the East from 148 to 62 BC.* Berkeley, 1995.
Kaser, 1949	Kaser, Max. *Das altrömische Ius. Studien zur Rechtsvorstellung und Rechtsgeschichte der Römer.* Göttingen, 1949.
Kaser, 1971	Kaser, Max. *Das römische Privatrecht.* Vol. 1. 2d ed. Munich, 1971.
Kaser, 1978	Kaser, Max. Zum römischen Grabrecht. *ZSS* 95, 15–92, 1978.
Kaser, 1986	Kaser, Max. "Ius publicum" und "ius privatum." *ZSS* 103, 1–101, 1986.
Kaser-Hackl	Kaser, Max, and Karl Hackl. *Das römische Zivilprozeßrecht.* 2d ed. Munich, 1996.
Kaster *ad* Suet. *Gram.*	Kaster, Robert A., ed. and comm. C. Suetonius Tranquillus. *De Grammaticis et Rhetoribus.* Oxford, 1995.
Keaveney	Keaveney, Arthur. *Sulla: The Last Republican.* London and Canberra, 1982.
Keyes	See under "*De Legibus:* Editions, Translations, and Commentaries."
Keyes, 1921	Keyes, Clinton Walker. Original Elements in Cicero's Ideal Constitution. *AJPh* 42, 309–23, 1921.
Kiessling-Heinze	Kiessling, A., and R. Heinze, eds. *Q. Horatius Flaccus.* 3 vols. Berlin, 1914–30.
Klose	Klose, Friedrich. *Die Bedeutung von honos und honestus.* Diss. Breslau, 1933.
C. Koch	Koch, Carl. *Religio. Studien zu Kult und Glauben der Römer.* Nuremberg, 1960.
E. Koch	Koch, Ernestus. *Ciceronis carmina historica restituta atque enarrata.* Diss. Zurich, 1922.
H.A. Koch	Koch, H.A. Review of Vahlen[1]. In *Philologischer Anzeiger* 5, 104–7, 1873.
Kraus	Kraus, Walther. Lateinische Lesungen I. *WS* 69, 303–7, 1956.

Kretschmar — Kretschmar, Marianne. *Otium, studia litterarum, Philosophie und* βίος θεωρητικός *im Leben und Denken Ciceros.* Diss. Leipzig. Würzburg-Aumühle, 1938.

Kroon — Kroon, Caroline. *Discourse Particles in Latin: A Study of nam, enim, autem, vero, and at.* Amsterdam, 1995.

Krostenko — Krostenko, Brian A. *Cicero, Catullus, and the Language of Social Performance,* Chicago, 2001.

Kühner *ad Tusc.* — Kühner, Raphael, ed. and comm. M.T. Ciceronis *Tusculanarum Disputationum libri V.* 4th ed. Jena, 1853.

Kühner-Holzweissig — Kühner, Raphael, and Friedrich Holzweissig. *Ausführliche Grammatik der lateinischen Sprache,* 1: *Morphologie.* 2d ed. Hannover, 1912.

Kühner-Stegmann — Kühner, Raphael, and Carl Stegmann. *Ausführliche Grammatik der lateinischen Sprache,* 2: *Satzlehre.* 2 vols. With corrections to the 4th ed. by A. Thierfelder. Darmstadt, 1966.

Kunkel — Kunkel, Wolfgang. *Untersuchungen zur Entwicklung des römischen Kriminalverfahrens in vorsullanischer Zeit.* ABAW. Phil.-hist. Kl., N.F. 56. Munich, 1962.

Kunkel-Wittmann — Kunkel, Wolfgang, and Roland Wittmann. *Staatsordnung und Staatspraxis der römischen Republik.* Vol. 2: *Die Magistratur.* Munich, 1995.

Kurtz-Boardman — Kurtz, Donna C., and John Boardman. *Greek Burial Customs.* London, 1971.

Laks-Schofield — Laks, André, and Malcolm Schofield, eds. *Justice and Generosity: Studies in Hellenistic Social and Political Philosophy.* Proceedings of the Sixth Symposium Hellenisticum. Cambridge, 1995.

Landgraf — Landgraf, Gustav, ed. *Historische Grammatik der lateinischen Sprache.* 3.1: *Syntax.* Leipzig, 1903.

Landgraf *ad Sex. Rosc.* — Landgraf, Gustav. *Kommentar zu Ciceros Rede Pro Sex. Roscio Amerino.* 2d ed. Leipzig-Berlin, 1914.

Laser — Laser, Günter. *Populo et scaenae serviendum est.*

	Die Bedeutung der städtischen Masse in der Späten Römischen Republik. Trier, 1997.
Latte, 1960	Latte, Kurt. *Römische Religionsgeschichte.* Munich, 1960.
Latte, 1968	Latte, Kurt. *Kleine Schriften zu Religion, Recht, Literatur und Sprache der Griechen und Römer.* Ed. Olof Gigon, Wolfgang Buchwald, and Wolfgang Kunkel. Munich, 1968.
Laughton	Laughton, Eric. *The Participle in Cicero.* London, 1964.
Lausberg	Lausberg, Heinrich. *Handbuch der literarischen Rhetorik.* 3d ed. Stuttgart, 1990. Or *Handbook of Literary Rhetoric: A Foundation for Literary Study.* Tr. M.T. Bliss, A. Jansen, and D.E. Orton. Ed. D.E. Orton and R.D. Anderson. Leiden, 1998.
Lazič	Lazič, Gregor. *Über die Entstehung von Ciceros Schrift "De Legibus."* Vienna, 1912.
Lebek	Lebek, Wolfgang Dieter. *Verba prisca. Die Anfänge des Archaisierens in der lateinischen Beredsamkeit und Geschichtsschreibung.* Hypomnemata 25. Göttingen, 1970.
Le Bonniec	Le Bonniec, Henri. *Le culte de Cérès à Rome.* Paris, 1958.
Lebreton	Lebreton, Jules. *Études sur la langue et la grammaire de Cicéron.* Paris, 1901.
Leeman	Leeman, A.D. Le genre et le style historique à Rome: théorie et pratique. *REL* 33, 183–208, 1955.
Leeman et al. on *de Orat.*	Leeman, A.D., et al. M.T. Cicero. *De Oratore libri III. Kommentar.* Heidelberg, 1981–.
Lefkowitz-Fant	Lefkowitz, Mary R., and Maureen B. Fant. *Women's Life in Greece and Rome.* Rev. ed. Baltimore, 1982.
Lehmann	Lehmann, Gustav Adolf. *Politische Reformvorschläge in der Krise der späten römischen Republik. Cicero De legibus III und Sallusts Sendschreiben an Caesar.* Beiträge zur klassischen Philologie 117. Meisenheim am Glan, 1980.

Lenel
Lenel, Otto. *Das Edictum perpetuum. Ein Versuch zu seiner Wiederherstellung.* 3d ed. Leipzig, 1927.

Leumann
Leumann, Manu. *Lateinische Laut- und Formenlehre.* New ed. Munich, 1977.

Leutsch-Schneidewin ad Zenob.
Leutsch, E. von, and F.G. Schneidewin, eds. *Corpus paroemiographorum Graecorum.* 2 vols. Göttingen, 1839–51 (Zenobius = 1, 1–175).

Lévy
Lévy, Carlos. *Cicero Academicus. Recherches sur les Académiques et sur la philosophie cicéronienne.* Rome, 1992.

de Libero
de Libero, Loretana. *Obstruktion. Politische Praktiken im Senat und in der Volksversammlung der ausgehenden römischen Republik (70–49 v.Chr.).* Hermes Einzelschriften 59. Stuttgart, 1992.

Liebeschuetz
Liebeschuetz, J.H.W.G. *Continuity and Change in Roman Religion.* Oxford, 1979.

Linderski, 1986
Linderski, Jerzy. The Augural Law. *ANRW* 2.16.3, 2146–2312, 1986.

Linderski, 1995
Linderski, Jerzy. *Roman Questions: Selected Papers.* Heidelberger Althistorische Beiträge und Epigraphische Studien 20. Stuttgart, 1995.

Lintott
Ms. notes placed at my disposal by Andrew Lintott.

Lintott, 1968
Lintott, A.W. *Violence in Republican Rome.* Oxford, 1968.

Lintott, 1972
Lintott, Andrew W. Provocatio. From the Struggle of the Orders to the Principate. *ANRW* 1.2, 226–67, 1972.

Lintott, 1992
Lintott, Andrew. *Judicial Reform and Land Reform in the Roman Republic: A New Edition, with Translation and Commentary, of the Laws from Urbino.* Cambridge, 1992.

Lintott, 1999
Lintott, Andrew. *The Constitution of the Roman Republic.* Oxford, 1999.

Leonhardt
Leonhardt, Jürgen. *Ciceros Kritik der Philosophenschulen.* Zetemata 103. Munich, 1999.

Löfstedt
Löfstedt, Einar. *Syntactica. Studien und Beiträge*

	zur historischen Syntax des Lateins. 2 vols. Lund, 1956.
Long, 1995a	Long, A.A. Cicero's Politics in *De officiis.* In Laks-Schofield. Pp. 213–40.
Long, 1995b	Long, A.A. Cicero's Plato and Aristotle. In Powell, 1995. Pp. 37–61.
LSJ	Liddell, Henry George, and Robert Scott. *A Greek-English Lexicon.* 9th ed. rev. H.S. Jones. Oxford, 1940.
LTUR	Steinby, Eva Margareta, ed. *Lexicon topographicum urbis Romae.* 6 vols. Rome, 1993–2000.
Luck	Luck, Georg. *Der Akademiker Antiochos.* Noctes Romanae 7. Bern-Stuttgart, 1953.
Madvig, 1826	Madvig, Joh. Nic. *Emendationes in Ciceronis libros philosophicos.* Pt. 1. Copenhagen, 1826.
Madvig, 1871–84	Madvig, Joh. Nic. *Adversaria critica ad scriptores Graecos et Latinos.* 3 vols. Copenhagen, 1871–84.
Madvig, 1887	Madvig, Io. Nicolai. *Opuscula academica.* Copenhagen, 1887.
Madvig *ad Fin.*	Madvig, I. N., ed. M.T. Ciceronis *De Finibus Bonorum et Malorum libri quinque.* 3d ed. Copenhagen, 1876.
Magdelain	Magdelain, André. *Jus imperium auctoritas. Études de droit romain.* Rome, 1990.
Maltby	Maltby, Robert. *A Lexicon of Ancient Etymologies.* Leeds, 1991.
Marincola	Marincola, John. *Authority and Tradition in Ancient Historiography.* Cambridge, 1997.
Marinone	Marinone, Nino. *Cronologia ciceroniana.* Rome, 1997.
Marx *ad* Pl. *Rud.*	Marx, Friedrich, ed. and comm. Plautus, *Rudens.* Abhandlungen der sächsischen Akademie der Wissenschaften. Philol.-hist. Kl., 38.5. Leipzig, 1928.
McDermott	McDermott, William C. Q. Cicero. *Historia* 20, 702–17, 1971.
Mehl	Mehl, David Duane. *Comprehending Cicero's De Legibus.* Diss. University of Virginia, 1999.
Meiser	Meiser, Gerhard. *Historische Laut- und*

	Formenlehre der lateinischen Sprache. Darmstadt, 1998.
de Meo	de Meo, Cesidio. *Lingue technice del Latino.* Bologna, 1983.
Merguet, *Phil.*	Merguet, H. *Lexikon zu den philosophischen Schriften Cicero's.* 3 vols. Jena, 1887–94.
Merguet, *Reden*	Merguet, H. *Lexikon zu den Reden des Cicero.* 4 vols. Jena, 1877–84.
Meyer	Meyer, Hans Dieter. *Cicero und das Reich.* Diss. Cologne, 1957.
Michels	Michels, Agnes Kirsopp. *The Calendar of the Roman Republic.* Princeton, 1967.
Mitchell, 1979	Mitchell, Thomas N. *Cicero: The Ascending Years.* New Haven–London, 1979.
Mitchell, 1991	Mitchell, Thomas N. *Cicero, the Senior Statesman.* New Haven–London, 1991.
Mitsis, 1988	Mitsis, Phillip. *Epicurus' Ethical Theory.* Ithaca-London, 1988.
Mitsis, 1994	Mitsis, Phillip. Natural Law and Natural Right in Post-Aristotelian Philosophy: The Stoics and Their Critics. *ANRW* 2.36.7, 4812–50, 1994.
Moatti	Moatti, Claudia. *La raison de Rome. Naissance de l'esprit critique à la fin de la République.* Paris, 1997.
Mommsen, *RG*	Mommsen, Theodor. *Römische Geschichte.* 8 vols. Munich, 1976 (rp. of 5 vol. ed. Berlin, 1874, and later, which is the pagination cited here).
Mommsen, *Staatsr.*	Mommsen, Theodor. *Römisches Staatsrecht.* 3 vols. in 5. Leipzig, 1887–88.
Mommsen, *Strafr.*	Mommsen, Theodor. *Römisches Strafrecht.* Leipzig, 1899.
Morrow	Morrow, Glen R. *Plato's Cretan City: A Historical Interpretation of the Laws.* Princeton, 1960.
Morstein-Marx	Morstein-Marx, Robert M. *Rhetoric and Politics: Mass Oratory and Political Power in the Late Roman Republic.* Cambridge, in press.
MRR	Broughton, T. Robert S. *The Magistrates of the Roman Republic.* 3 vols. American Philological Association. Philological Monographs 15. New York, 1951–Atlanta, 1986.

Mueller	Mueller, Hans-Friedrich. *Vita, Pudicitia, Libertas:* Juno, Gender, and Religious Politics in Valerius Maximus. *TAPhA* 128, 221–63, 1998.
H. Müller	Müller, Helmut. *Ciceros Prosaübersetzungen. Beiträge zur Kenntnis der ciceronischen Sprache.* Diss. Marburg, 1964.
R. Müller	Müller, R. Βίος θεωρητικός bei Antiochos von Askalon und Cicero. *Helikon* 8, 221–37, 1968.
Münzer, 1905	Münzer, F. Atticus als Geschichtsschreiber. *Hermes* 40, 50–100, 1905.
Murphy	Murphy, Trevor. Cicero's First Readers: Epistolary Evidence for the Dissemination of His Works. *CQ* 48, 492–505, 1998.
Neue-Wagener	Neue, Friedrich, and C. Wagener. *Formenlehre der lateinischen Sprache.* 3d ed. 4 vols. Berlin, 1892.
Nicholson	Nicholson, John. *Cicero's Return from Exile: The Orations Post reditum.* New York, 1992.
Nicolet, 1966–74	Nicolet, Claude. *L'ordre équestre à l'époque républicaine (312–43 av. J.-C.).* 2 vols. Paris, 1966–74.
Nicolet, 1967	Nicolet, Claude. Arpinum, Aemilius Scaurus et les Tullii Cicerones. *REL* 45, 276–304, 1967.
Nicolet, 1980	Nicolet, Claude. *The World of the Citizen in Republican Rome.* Tr. P.S. Falla. London, 1980.
Nippel, 1980	Nippel, Wilfried. *Mischverfassungstheorie und Verfassungsrealität in Antike und früher Neuzeit.* Stuttgart, 1980.
Nippel, 1995	Nippel, Wilfried. *Public Order in Ancient Rome.* Cambridge, 1995.
Nisbet-Hubbard	Nisbet, R.G.M., and Margaret Hubbard. *A Commentary on Horace: Odes 1–2.* 2 vols. Oxford, 1970–78.
Nizolius	Nizolius, Marius. *Lexicon Ciceronianum* ex rec. A. Scoti. 3 vols. London, 1820.
Norden, 1913	Norden, Eduard. *Agnostos Theos. Untersuchungen zur Formengeschichte religiöser Rede.* Leipzig-Berlin, 1913.
Norden, 1939	Norden, Eduard. *Aus altrömischen*

	Priesterbüchern. Acta regia Societatis Humaniorum Litterarum Lundensis 29. Lund, 1939.
Norden *ad Aen.* 6	Norden, Eduard, ed. and comm. P. Vergilius Maro. *Aeneis Buch VI.* 2d ed. Leipzig-Berlin, 1916.
NP	Cancik, Hubert, and Helmuth Schneider, eds. *Der neue Pauly. Enzyklopädie der Antike.* 15 vols. Stuttgart-Weimar, 1996–2002.
Oakley *ad* Liv.	Oakley, S.P. *A Commentary on Livy, Books VI–X.* 2 vols. to date. Oxford, 1997–.
Obbink, 1992	Obbink, Dirk. "What All Men Believe—Must Be True": Common Conceptions and *Consensus Omnium* in Aristotle and Hellenistic Philosophy. *OSAP* 10, 193–231, 1992.
Obbink, 1999	Obbink, Dirk. The Stoic Sage in the Cosmic City. In Katerina Ierodiakonou, ed. *Topics in Stoic Philosophy.* Oxford, 1999. Pp. 178–95.
OCD³	Hornblower, Simon, and Antony Spawforth, eds. *The Oxford Classical Dictionary.* 3d ed. Oxford–New York, 1996.
Ogilvie *ad* Liv.	Ogilvie, R.M. *A Commentary on Livy Books 1–5.* Oxford, 1965.
OLD	Glare, P.G.W., ed. *Oxford Latin Dictionary.* Oxford, 1982.
Oliver	Oliver, James H. *The Athenian Expounders of the Sacred and Ancestral Law.* Baltimore, 1950.
Oppermann	Oppermann, Irene. *Zur Funktion historischer Beispiele in Ciceros Briefen.* Beiträge zur Altertumswissenschaft 138. Munich-Leipzig, 2000.
Orlin	Orlin, Eric M. *Temples, Religion and Politics in the Roman Republic.* Mnemosyne Suppl. 164. Leiden, 1997.
A. Otto	Otto, A. *Die Sprichwörter und sprichwörtlichen Redensarten der Römer.* Leipzig, 1890.
W.F. Otto	Otto, Walter F. *Die Manen oder von den Urformen des Totenglaubens.* 3d ed. Darmstadt, 1962 (orig. Berlin, 1923).
Page *ad* Verg. *Ecl.*	Page, T.E., ed. and comm. P. Vergili Maronis *Bucolica et Georgica.* London, 1898.

Parker	Parker, Robert. *Miasma: Pollution and Purification in Early Greek Religion.* Oxford, 1983.
Parzinger	Parzinger, Peter. *Beiträge zur Kenntnis der Entwicklung des Ciceronischen Stils.* Diss. Erlangen. Landshut, 1910.
Pascucci, 1968	Pascucci, Giovanni. Aspetti del latino giuridico. *SIFC* 40, 3–43, 1968.
Pascucci, 1970	Pascucci, Giovanni. L'arcaismo nel *De Legibus* di Cicerone. *Studia Florentina Alexandro Ronconi sexagenario oblata.* Rome, 1970. Pp. 311–24.
Pascucci, 1981	Pascucci, Giovanni. Parafrasi e traduzioni da autori greci nel *De legibus* di Cicerone. *Letterature comparate. Problemi e metodo. Studi in onore di Ettore Paratore.* Vol. 1. Bologna, 1981. Pp. 413–27.
Pease *ad Div.*	Pease, Arthur Stanley, ed. and comm. M.T. Ciceronis *De Divinatione libri duo.* University of Illinois Studies in Language and Literature 6 and 8. Urbana, 1920–23 (rp. Darmstadt, 1963).
Pease *ad N.D.*	Pease, Arthur Stanley, ed. and comm. M. Tulli Ciceronis *De Natura Deorum.* 2 vols. Cambridge, Mass., 1955–58.
Perelli	Perelli, Luciano. *Il pensiero politico di Cicerone. Tra filosofia greca e ideologia aristocratica romana.* Florence, 1990.
Perlwitz	Perlwitz, Olaf. *Titus Pomponius Atticus. Untersuchungen zur Person eines einflussreichen Ritters in der ausgehenden römischen Republik.* Hermes Einzelschriften 58. Stuttgart, 1992.
Petzold	Petzold, Karl-Ernst. Cicero und Historie. *Chiron* 2, 253–76, 1972.
PHI 5.3	Database of Latin authors to AD 200: cd rom 5.3 produced by Packard Humanities Institute. Palo Alto, Calif.
Philippson, 1929	Philippson, R. Review *inter alia* of Keyes' ed. *Philologische Wochenschrift* 49, 965–79, 1929.
Philippson, 1939	Philippson, R. M. Tullius Cicero (Philosophische Schriften). *RE* 7A1 (1939). Col. 1104–92.47.

de Plinval   See under "Other Editions, Translations, and
                      Commentaries."
de Plinval, 1969   Plinval, Georges de. Autour du *De Legibus*. *REL*
                      47, 294–309, 1969.
Pohlenz, 1938   Pohlenz, Max. Der Eingang von Ciceros
                      Gesetzen. *Philologus* 93, 102–27, 1938 = *Kleine
                      Schriften*. Ed. Heinrich Dörrie. Hildesheim, 1965.
                      Vol. 2. Pp. 410–35.
Pohlenz, 1940   Pohlenz, Max. *Grundfragen der stoischen
                      Philosophie*. Abhandlungen der Gesellschaft der
                      Wissenschaften zu Göttingen. Philolog.-hist.
                      Klasse 3:26. Göttingen, 1940.
Pohlenz, *Stoa*   Pohlenz, Max. *Die Stoa*. 2d/3d ed. 2 vols. Göt-
                      tingen, 1959–64.
Powell *ad Sen.*   Powell, J.G.F., ed. and comm. Cicero. *Cato maior
                      de Senectute,* Cambridge, 1988.
Powell, 1995   Powell, J.G.F., ed. *Cicero the Philosopher:
                      Twelve Papers*. Oxford, 1995.
Powell-North   Powell, J.G.F., and J.A. North, eds. *Cicero's Re-
                      public*. BICS Suppl. 76. London, 2001.
Rambaud   Rambaud, Michel. *Cicéron et l'histoire romaine.*
                      Paris, 1953.
Rawson, 1982   Rawson, Elizabeth. Review of Lehmann. *Gno-
                      mon* 54, 705–7, 1982.
Rawson, 1991   Rawson, Elizabeth. *Roman Culture and Society:
                      Collected Papers*. Oxford, 1991.
Reesor   Reesor, Margaret E. *The Political Theory of the
                      Old and Middle Stoa*. New York, 1951.
Reid   Reid, J.S. Ms. notes in Vahlen[1]. Cambridge Uni-
                      versity Library: Adv.c.93.7.
Reid *ad Ac.*   Reid, J.S., ed. and comm. M. Tulli Ciceronis *Aca-
                      demica*. London, 1885.
Reid *ad Luc.*   See "Reid *ad Ac.*"
Reifferscheid   Reifferscheid, A. Kritische Beiträge zu Cicero De
                      Legibus. *RhM* 17, 269–96, 1862.
Reijnders   Reijnders, Hendricus Franciscus. *Societas generis
                      humani bij Cicero*. Diss. Utrecht. Groningen-
                      Jakarta, 1954.
Reitzenstein   Reitzenstein, Richard. *Drei Vermutungen zur*

	Geschichte der römischen Litteratur. Marburg, 1894.
Richardson	Richardson, L., Jr. *A New Topographical Dictionary of Rome.* Baltimore-London, 1992.
Riemer	Riemer, Ulrike. *Das Caesarbild Ciceros.* Hamburg, 2001.
Riggsby	Riggsby, Andrew M. *Crime and Community in Ciceronian Rome.* Austin, 1999.
Rilinger	Rilinger, Rolf. "Loca intercessionis" und Legalismus in der späten Republik. *Chiron* 19, 481–98, 1989.
Risselada	Risselada, Rodie. And Now for Something Completely Different? Temporal Discourse Markers: Latin *nunc* and English *now.* In *On Latin: Linguistic and Literary Studies in Honour of Harm Pinkster.* Ed. R. Risselada et al. Amsterdam, 1996. Pp. 105–25.
E.A. Robinson	Robinson, Edward Anthony. *The Date of Cicero's De Legibus.* Diss. Harvard, 1950.
O.F. Robinson	Robinson, O.F. *The Criminal Law of Ancient Rome.* London, 1995.
Roloff	Roloff, Heinrich. *Maiores bei Cicero.* Diss. Göttingen, 1938.
Rosenberger	Rosenberger, Veit. *Gezähmte Götter. Das Prodigienwesen der römischen Republik.* Stuttgart, 1998.
Rosenstein	Rosenstein, Nathan. *Imperatores Victi: Military Defeat and Aristocratic Competition in the Middle and Late Republic.* Berkeley–Los Angeles–Oxford, 1990.
Rotondi	Rotondi, Giovanni. *Leges publicae populi Romani.* Milan, 1912.
Rowe-Schofield	Rowe, Christopher, and Malcolm Schofield, eds. *The Cambridge History of Greek and Roman Political Thought.* Cambridge, 2000.
Ruch	Ruch, Michel. *Le préambule dans les oeuvres philosophiques de Cicéron. Essai sur la genèse et l'art du dialogue.* Paris, 1958.
Rüpke, 1990	Rüpke, Jörg. *Domi Militiae. Die religiöse*

Konstruktion des Krieges in Rom. Stuttgart, 1990.

Rüpke, 1995   Rüpke, Jörg. *Kalender und Öffentlichkeit. Die Geschichte der Repräsentation und religiösen Qualifikation von Zeit in Rom.* Religionsgeschichtliche Versuche und Vorarbeiten 40. Berlin–New York, 1995.

Ryan   Ryan, Frances X. *Rank and Participation in the Republican Senate.* Stuttgart, 1998.

Sabine-Smith   Sabine, George H., and Stanley B. Smith, trs. Cicero. *On the Commonwealth.* Columbus, 1929 (rp. 1976).

Saller   Saller, Richard P. *Patriarchy, Property and Death in the Roman Family.* Cambridge, 1994.

Sandbach   Sandbach, F.H. Ennoia and Prolepsis. In *Problems in Stoicism.* Ed. A.A. Long. London, 1971. Pp. 22–37.

Sandys   Sandys, John Edwin. *A History of Classical Scholarship.* 3 vols. Cambridge, 1903–8.

Santalucia   Santalucia, Bernardo. *Diritto e processo penale nell' antica Roma.* 2d ed. Milan, 1998.

Saunders   Saunders, Trevor J. *Plato's Penal Code: Tradition, Controversy, and Reform in Greek Penology.* Oxford, 1991.

Scanlon   Scanlon, Thomas F. Reflexivity and Irony in the Proem of Sallust's *Historiae.* In *Studies in Latin Literature and Roman History.* Ed. Carl Deroux. Vol. 9. Brussels, 1998. Pp. 186–224.

Scheid   Scheid, John. Le délit religieux dans la Rome tardo-républicaine. In *Le délit religieux dans la cité antique.* Collection de l'École française de Rome 48. Rome, 1981. Pp. 117–71.

Schmekel   Schmekel, August. *Die Philosophie der mittleren Stoa.* Berlin, 1892.

O.E. Schmidt   Schmidt, Otto Eduard. *Ciceros Villen.* Leipzig, 1899.

Schmidt, 1959   Schmidt, Peter Lebrecht. *Interpretatorische und chronologische Grundfragen zu Ciceros Werk De Legibus.* Diss. Freiburg, 1959.

Schmidt, 1965   Schmidt, Peter Lebrecht. Zeugnisse antiker

	Autoren zu Ciceros Werk De Legibus. In *Miscellanea Critica*. Vol. 2. Leipzig, 1965. Pp. 301–33.
Schmidt, 1969	Schmidt, Peter Lebrecht. *Die Abfassungszeit von Ciceros Schrift über die Gesetze.* Collana di Studi Ciceroniani 4. Rome, 1969.
Schmidt, 1973	Schmidt, Peter Lebrecht. Die handschriftliche Überlieferung von "De Legibus." Resultate und Perspektiven. *Ciceroniana* n.s. 1, 83–89, 1973.
Schmidt, 1974	Schmidt, Peter Lebrecht. *Die Überlieferung von Ciceros Schrift "De Legibus" in Mittelalter und Renaissance.* Studia et Testimonia Antiqua 10. Munich, 1974.
Schmidt, 2000	Schmidt, Peter Lebrecht. *Traditio Latinitatis. Studien zur Rezeption und Überlieferung der lateinischen Literatur.* Ed. J. Fugmann, M. Hose, and B. Zimmermann. Stuttgart, 2000.
Schmidt, 2001	Schmidt, Peter Lebrecht. The Original Version of *De Re Publica* and *De Legibus*. In Powell-North. Pp. 7–16.
Schofield, 1991	Schofield, Malcolm. *The Stoic Idea of the City.* Cambridge, 1991.
Schofield, 1995	Schofield, Malcolm. Cicero's Definition of *Res Publica*. In Powell, 1995, 63–83.
Scott	Scott, Dominic. *Recollection and Experience: Plato's Theory of Learning and Its Successors.* Cambridge, 1995.
Scullard	Scullard, H.H. *Festivals and Ceremonies of the Roman Republic.* London, 1981.
Seyffert-Müller *ad Amic.*	Seyffert, Moritz, and C.F.W. Müller, eds. M. Tullii Ciceronis *Laelius de Amicitia Dialogus. Mit einem Kommentar.* 2d ed. Leipzig, 1876 (rp. Hildesheim, 1965).
Shackleton Bailey, 1991	Shackleton Bailey, D.R. *Two Studies in Roman Nomenclature.* 2d ed. Atlanta, 1991.
Shackleton Bailey, 1992	Shackleton Bailey, D.R. *Onomasticon to Cicero's Speeches.* 2d rev. ed. Stuttgart-Leipzig, 1992.
Shackleton Bailey, 1995	Shackleton Bailey, D.R. *Onomasticon to Cicero's Letters.* Stuttgart-Leipzig, 1995.
Shackleton Bailey, 1996	Shackleton Bailey, D.R. *Onomasticon to Cicero's Treatises.* Stuttgart-Leipzig, 1996.

Shackleton Bailey, 1997	Shackleton Bailey, D.R. *Selected Classical Papers.* Ann Arbor, 1997.
Shatzman	Shatzman, Israel. *Senatorial Wealth and Roman Politics.* Collection Latomus 142. Brussels, 1975.
Shaw	Shaw, Brent. Bandits in the Roman Empire. *Past and Present* 105, 3–52, 1984.
Shewring	Shewring, W.H. Prose Rhythm and the Comparative Method. II. *CQ* 25, 12–22, 1931.
Siewert	Siewert, Peter. Die angebliche Übernahme solonischer Gesetze in die Zwölftafeln. Ursprung und Ausgestaltung einer Legende. *Chiron* 8, 331–44, 1978.
Sihler	Sihler, Andrew L. *New Comparative Grammar of Greek and Latin.* New York–Oxford, 1995.
Skutsch *ad* Enn. *Ann.*	Skutsch, Otto, ed. and comm. *The Annals of Q. Ennius.* Oxford, 1985.
Smethurst	Smethurst, S.E. Cicero and Dicaearchus. *TAPhA* 83, 224–32, 1952.
Smith	Smith, William, ed. *Dictionary of Greek and Roman Geography.* 2 vols. Boston, 1865.
Solmsen	Solmsen, Friedrich. *Kleine Schriften.* 3 vols. Hildesheim, 1968–82.
Solodow	Solodow, Joseph B. *The Latin Particle Quidem.* American Classical Studies 4. Boulder, 1978.
F. Sommer	Sommer, F. *Studien zur Geschichte der Rechtswissenschaft im Lichte der Philosophiegeschichte.* Görresgesellschaft: Sektion Rechts- und Staatswissenschaft 65. Paderborn, 1934.
R. Sommer	Sommer, Richard. T. Pomponius Atticus und Ciceros Werke. *Hermes* 61, 389–422, 1926.
Sorabji	Sorabji, Richard. *Animal Minds and Human Morals: The Origins of the Western Debate.* London, 1993.
Spaeth	Spaeth, Babette Stanley. *The Roman Goddess Ceres.* Austin, 1996.
Sprey	Sprey, Karel. *De M. Tullii Ciceronis politica doctrina.* Diss. Zutphen, 1928.
Sprute	Sprute, Jürgen. Rechts- und Staatsphilosophie bei Cicero. *Phronesis* 28, 150–76, 1983.

Stalley	Stalley, R.F. *An Introduction to Plato's Laws*. Oxford, 1983.
Stambaugh	Stambaugh, John E. The Functions of Roman Temples. *ANRW* 2.16.1, 554–92, 1978.
Stockton, 1971	Stockton, David. *Cicero: A Political Biography*. Oxford, 1971.
Stockton, 1979	Stockton, David. *The Gracchi*. Oxford, 1979.
Strachan-Davidson	Strachan-Davidson, James L. *Problems of the Roman Criminal Law*. 2 vols. Oxford, 1912.
Strasburger	Strasburger, Hermann. *Ciceros philosophisches Spätwerk als Aufruf gegen die Herrschaft Caesars*. Ed. G. Strasburger. Hildesheim, 1990.
Striker	Striker, Gisela. Origins of the Concept of Natural Law. *Proceedings of the Boston Area Colloquium in Ancient Philosophy* 2, 79–94, 1987.
Suolahti	Suolahti, Jaakko. *The Roman Censors: A Study on Social Structure*. Annales Academiae Scientiarum Fennicae. Ser. B, 117. Helsinki, 1963.
Szegedy-Maszak, 1978	Szegedy-Maszak, Andrew. Legends of the Greek Lawgivers. *GRBS* 19, 199–209, 1978.
Szegedy-Maszak, 1981	Szegedy-Maszak, Andrew. *The Nomoi of Theophrastus*. New York, 1981.
Szemler	Szemler, G.J. *The Priests of the Roman Republic*. Collection Latomus 127. Brussels, 1972.
Szlezák	Szlezák, Thomas A. *Platon und die Schriftlichkeit der Philosophie. Interpretationen zu frühen und mittleren Dialogen*. Berlin–New York, 1985.
Tarrant *ad* Sen. *Thy.*	Tarrant, R.J., ed. and comm. *Seneca's Thyestes*. Atlanta, 1985.
Tatum, 1990	Tatum, W. Jeffrey. The *Lex Clodia de Censoria Notione*. *CPh* 85, 34–43, 1990.
Tatum, 1999	Tatum, W. Jeffrey. *The Patrician Tribune: Publius Clodius Pulcher*. Chapel Hill–London, 1999.
Taylor, 1949	Taylor, Lily Ross. *Party Politics in the Age of Caesar*. Berkeley, 1949.
Taylor, 1966	Taylor, Lily Ross. *Roman Voting Assemblies from the Hannibalic War to the Dictatorship of Caesar*. Ann Arbor, 1966.
Theiler	Theiler, Willy. *Die Vorbereitung des Neuplatonismus*. Problemata 1. Berlin, 1930.

Thiaucourt	Thiaucourt, C. *Essai sur les traités philosophiques de Cicéron et leurs sources grecques*. Paris, 1885.
Thomas	Thomas, Yan. Cicéron, le Sénat et les tribuns de la plèbe. *Revue historique de droit français et étranger* 55, 189–210, 1977.
Thommen, 1988	Thommen, Lukas. Das Bild vom Volkstribunat in Ciceros Schrift über die Gesetze. *Chiron* 18, 358–75, 1988.
Thommen, 1989	Thommen, Lukas. *Das Volkstribunat der späten römischen Republik*. Historia Einzelschriften 59. Stuttgart, 1989.
TLL	*Thesaurus Linguae Latinae*. Leipzig, 1900–.
Toynbee	Toynbee, J.M.C. *Death and Burial in the Roman World*. London, 1971.
Treggiari	Treggiari, Susan. *Roman Marriage. Iusti Coniuges from the Time of Cicero to the Time of Ulpian*. Oxford, 1991.
Turnebus	Turnebus, Adrianus. *Apologia adversus quorundam calumnias ad librum primum Ciceronis De Legibus*. 1596. Rp. *apud* Moser-Creuzer. Pp. 745–80.
Turpin	Turpin, José. Cicéron, De legibus I–II et la religion romaine: une interpretation philosophique à veille du principat. *ANRW* 2.16.3, 1877–1908, 1986.
Twele	Twele, Jochen R.A. "Columellam . . . aut Mensam . . . aut Labellum": Archaeological Remarks on Cicero's De Legibus II 66. *The J. Paul Getty Museum Journal* 2, 93–98, 1975.
Überweg	Überweg, Friedrich, founding ed. *Grundriss der Geschichte der Philosophie: Philosophie der Antike*. New ed. Vol. 4. Basel, 1994.
Urlichs	Urlichs, L. Zur Kritik Ciceros. *RhM* N.F. 33, 150–56, 1878.
Vairel-Carron	Vairel-Carron, Hélène. *Exclamation, ordre et défense. Analyse de deux systèmes syntaxiques en latin*. Paris, 1975.
Vanderbroeck	Vanderbroeck, Paul J.J. *Popular Leadership and Collective Behavior in the Late Roman Republic (ca. 80–50 BC)*. Amsterdam, 1987.

Vander Waerdt, 1994a	Vander Waerdt, Paul A. Zeno's *Republic* and the Origins of Natural Law. In *The Socratic Movement*. Ed. P.A.V.W. Ithaca, 1994. Pp. 272–308.
Vander Waerdt, 1994b	Vander Waerdt, Paul A. Philosophical Influence on Roman Jurisprudence? *ANRW* 2.36.7, 4851–4900, 1994.
Vasaly	Vasaly, Ann. *Representations: Images of the World in Ciceronian Oratory*. Berkeley, 1993.
Versnel	Versnel, H.S. *Transition and Reversal in Myth and Ritual* (= *Inconsistencies in Greek and Roman Religion*, 2). Leiden, 1993.
Vicaire *ad* Pl. *La.*	Vicaire, Paul, ed. and comm. Platon. *Lachès et Lysis*. Paris, 1963.
Ville	Ville, Georges. *Gladiature en occident des origines à la morte de Domitien*. Rome, 1981.
Vine	Ms. notes placed at my disposal by Brent Vine.
de Visscher	de Visscher, Fernand. *Le droit des tombeaux romains*. Milan, 1963.
Wachter	Wachter, Rudolf. *Altlateinische Inschriften. Sprachliche und epigraphische Untersuchungen zu den Dokumenten bis etwa 150 v.Chr.* Europäische Hochschulschriften 15.38. Bern, 1987.
Wackernagel	Wackernagel, Jacob. *Vorlesungen über Syntax*. 2d ed. 2 vols. Basel, 1926–28.
Walt	Walt, Siri. *Der Historiker C. Licinius Macer. Einleitung, Fragmente, Kommentar*. Stuttgart-Leipzig, 1997.
Wankel *ad* Dem. 18	Wankel, Hermann, comm. Demosthenes. *Rede für Ktesiphon über den Kranz*. 2 vols. Heidelberg, 1976.
Watkins	Watkins, Calvert. *How to Kill a Dragon: Aspects of Indo-European Poetics*. New York, 1995.
Watson, *Property*	Watson, Alan. *The Law of Property in the Later Roman Republic*. Oxford, 1968.
Watson, *Law Making*	Watson, Alan. *Law Making in the Later Roman Republic*. Oxford, 1974.
Watt, 1986	Watt, W.S. Notes on Cicero, *De Legibus*. In Carl Deroux, ed. *Studies in Latin Literature and Roman History*. Vol. 4. Collection Latomus 196. Brussels, 1986. Pp. 265–68.

Watt, 1997   Watt, W.S. Tulliana. *Hermes* 125, 241–43, 1997.
Wegner   Wegner, Michael. *Untersuchungen zu den lateinischen Begriffen socius und societas.* Hypomnemata 21. Göttingen, 1969.
Weinstock   Weinstock, Stefan. *Divus Julius.* Oxford, 1971.
Wieacker, 1967   Wieacker, Franz. Die XII Tafeln in ihrem Jahrhundert. In *Les origines de la république romaine.* Entretiens sur l'antiquité classique 13. Geneva, 1967. Pp. 293–356.
Wieacker, 1988   Wieacker, Franz. *Römische Rechtsgeschichte. Quellenkunde, Rechtsbildung, Jurisprudenz und Rechtsliteratur.* Vol. 1. Munich, 1988.
Wilamowitz   Wilamowitz-Moellendorff, Ulrich von. Erkenne dich selbst. In *Reden und Vorträge.* Vol. 2. 4. Aufl. Berlin, 1926. Pp. 171–89.
Wilhelms   Wilhelms, John William. *The Language of Cicero's De Legibus.* Diss. University of Minnesota, 1942.
Wilkins on *de Orat.*   Wilkins, A.S., ed. and comm. M.T. Ciceronis *De Oratore libri tres.* Oxford, 1892.
Wille   Wille, Günther. *Musica Romana. Die Bedeutung der Musik im Leben der Römer.* Amsterdam, 1967.
Wills   Wills, Jeffrey. *Repetition in Latin Poetry: Figures of Allusion.* Oxford, 1996.
Wiseman, 1971   Wiseman, T.P. *New Men in the Roman Senate 139 BC–AD 14.* Oxford, 1971.
Wiseman, 1974   Wiseman, T.P. *Cinna the Poet and Other Roman Essays.* Leicester, 1974.
Wiseman, 1979   Wiseman, T.P. *Clio's Cosmetics: Three Studies in Greco-Roman Literature.* Totowa, N.J., 1979.
Wiseman, 1987   Wiseman, T.P. *Roman Studies: Literary and Historical.* Liverpool, 1987.
Wiseman, 1994   Wiseman, T.P. Lucretius, Catiline, and the Survival of Prophecy. In *Historiography and Imagination: Eight Essays on Roman Culture.* Exeter Studies in History, 33. Exeter, 1994. Pp. 49–67.
Wissowa   Wissowa, Georg. *Religion und Kultus der Römer.* 2d ed. Munich, 1912.

Wood	Wood, Neal. *Cicero's Social and Political Thought*. Berkeley, 1988.
Woodman and Martin *ad* Tac. *An.* 3	Woodman, A.J., and R.H. Martin, ed. and comm. *The Annals of Tacitus: Book 3*. Cambridge, 1996.
Wülker	Wülker, Ludwig. *Die geschichtliche Entwicklung des Prodigienwesens bei den Römern. Studien zur Geschichte und Überlieferung der Staatsprodigien*. Diss. Leipzig, 1903.
Yakobson, 1995	Yakobson, Alexander. Secret Ballot and Its Effects in the Late Roman Republic. *Hermes* 123, 426–42, 1995.
Yakobson, 1999	Yakobson, Alexander. *Elections and Electioneering in Rome: A Study in the Political System of the Late Republic*. Historia Einzelschriften 128. Stuttgart, 1999.
Zellmer	Zellmer, Ernst. *Die lateinischen Wörter auf -ura*. 2d ed. Frankfurt am Main, 1976.
Zelzer, 1981	Zelzer, Michaela. Die Umschrift lateinischer Texte am Ende der Antike und ihre Bedeutung für die Textkritik. Bemerkungen zur Entstehung des Minuskel-B und zu frühen Verderbnissen in Cicero, De legibus. *WS* N.F. 15, 211–31, 1981.
Zelzer, 2001	Zelzer, Michaela and Klaus. Zur Überlieferung des Leidener Corpus philosophischer Schriften des Cicero. *WS* 114, 183–214, 2001.
Zetzel	See under "*De Legibus*: Editions, Translations, and Commentaries."
Zetzel *ad Rep.*	Zetzel, James E.G., ed. Cicero. *De Re Publica: Selections*. Cambridge, 1995.
Ziegler	See under "*De Legibus*: Editions, Translations, and Commentaries."
Ziegler, 1953	Ziegler, Konrat. Zur Textgestaltung von Cicero De Legibus. *Hermes* 81, 303–17, 1953.
Zielinski, 1904	Zielinski, Thaddäus. *Das Clauselgesetz in Ciceros Reden. Grundzüge einer oratorischen Rhythmik*. Philologus Suppl. 9.4. Leipzig, 1904.
Zielinski, 1929	Zielinski, Thaddäus. *Cicero im Wandel der Jahrhunderte*. 4th ed. Leipzig, 1929.
Zwierlein	Zwierlein, Otto. Cic. Leg. I, 26. *Hermes* 104, 120–23, 1976.

Introduction

"There has been surprisingly little recent work on *De Legibus*, despite the renaissance of interest in Hellenistic philosophy." That is the recent assessment by Paul Vander Waerdt.[1] Indeed there have been grounds of convenience for ignoring *Leg*. But though it is bristling with lacunae, patches of pseudoarchaic Latinity, technical terms, and textual problems, one will also find here passages of rare charm, intimacy, and eloquence: the description of the *locus amoenus* where the Fibrenus flows into the Liris (2.6); the account of the ancestral house of the Tullii Cicerones, where both Cicero and his brother Quintus were born (2.3); the definition of law and the account of the community of gods and men based upon it (1.18–19 and 22–23); or the grand encomium of philosophy (1.58–62). But the work is not merely worth reading for the sake of a handful of purple passages that could be extracted and anthologized. The concept of natural law, so influential in modern times, is known from other sources for Stoicism, but there we have individual points separated from context; here we have them, uniquely, arranged in a continuous argument. We also find here the maturest reflections of a very intelligent observer on needed reforms of Roman religion and government in light of the experience of the 50s. The following will introduce this text and set it into context.

1. The Literature on Law prior to *De Legibus*

If the law codes of the Near East stood under the sign of the ruler's self-advertisement,[2] those of Greece were created in the course of the struggle of the archaic city-state to assert its authority and impose order on the lives of citizens so as to obviate the need for self-help and vendetta. The drafting was often placed in the hands of someone clearly above political faction—a political outsider or even a foreigner.[3] The older law at Athens, for instance, was never invalidated as a whole but superseded piecemeal by newer laws.

---

1. Vander Waerdt, 1994b, 4867, n. 60; cf. Perelli, 1990, 113 (". . . negli ultimi anni la tendenza si è invertita, e gli studi generali sul *De legibus* sono più numerosi di quelli sul *De republica*"); but that conclusion will not survive a look at Gawlick-Görler, 1060 ff.

2. Cf. *ad* 2.14b.

3. Cf. in general Gagarin, 1986, 121–41.

Hence the need for the appointment by the Athenian assembly of a board of expounders (ἐξηγηταί) of the sacred and ancestral law from among the old aristocratic families (the εὐπάτριδαι), whose exclusive preserve it had been prior to Draco's homicide law.[4] But there was not, to our knowledge, a body of exegetical literature.

A literature on law in Greek, as opposed to the texts of the laws themselves, begins with Plato. The work of his middle period shows some distrust of legislation, as of writing in general.[5] Thus at *Rp.* 425d–e Socrates and Adimantus agree that it is unfitting to legislate in detail for the καλοὶ κἀγαθοί: they would take up their entire life in passing and emending laws. The "philosopher-king" is among other things meant to do away with any such necessity, as is clear from *Plt.* 294a7–8: τὸ δ' ἄριστον οὐ τοὺς νόμους ἐστὶν ἰσχύειν, ἀλλὰ ἄνδρα τὸν μετὰ φρονήσεως βασιλικόν. The *Politicus* adumbrates the *Laws,* however, in its doctrine that, in default of any such king, those pursuing the truest polity must draft legislation (301d–e).[6]

Plato's *Laws* is based on a critical evaluation of the laws of several Greek communities.[7] The choice of interlocutors enables him to confront different approaches to law. Clinias the Cretan and Megillus the Spartan hail from communities governed according to traditional Doric law,[8] the limitations of which are highlighted by the Athenian Stranger, who points out that such systems provide for courage but not for the other virtues.[9] The resulting legislation is in recognizable contact with Athenian law, but an Athenian law tested against its own ideals and purified of excesses.[10]

This empirical interest of the late Plato was continued on a more systematic basis by Aristotle,[11] who gathered and published the constitutions of 158 Greek communities, of which only that of Athens survives *in extenso*,[12]

---

4. Cf. Oliver, 48 ff.; for examples of their work cf. Pl. *Euthphr.* 4c; [Dem.] 47.68–71 with Oliver, 29.

5. On the latter cf. Szlezák.

6. Cf. Szegedy-Maszak, 1981, 2–5.

7. Cf. his adoption of a law of Charondas in effect prohibiting purchase by credit cited at Theophr. F 650.56 ff. F. (*Lg.* 849e, 915d).

8. Cf. Morrow, 32–35.

9. Cf. Stalley, 35–40.

10. Cf. (à propos procedure) Morrow, 295–96, and his General Index s.v. "Athenian institutions, influence of on the *Laws.*"

11. The importance he attached to Plato's *Laws* is indicated by the three books of extracts he prepared from it, apparently for the use of his pupils (D.L. 5.22).

12. The fragments of the πολιτεῖαι are gathered at pp. 258–367 Rose. Νόμοι in four books attributed to Aristotle at D.L. 5.26 is probably corrupted from νόμιμα, attested in another list of Aristotle's works; cf. Paul Moraux, *Les listes anciennes des ouvrages d' Aristote* (Louvain, 1951), 130–31.

and exploited this rich material in Books 4 through 6 of his *Politics*. The twenty-four books of νόμοι of his collaborator and successor Theophrastus also grew out of this research.[13] How widely the Peripatetics cast their net is seen in the longest fragment of Theophrastus' work, in which he cites laws of Athens, Mytilene, Cyzicus, Locris, and Thurii as well as Plato's *Laws*.[14] Of other Peripatetics, Demetrius of Phalerum and Heraclides Ponticus are known to have written περὶ νόμων,[15] Aristoxenus has works on παι-δευτικοὶ νόμοι and πολιτικοὶ νόμοι,[16] and a fragment disputed between Aristo of Ceus and the Stoic Aristo of Chios deals with the Spartan laws on marriage.[17]

For Rome, as for the Greek city-states, the writing down of law was an important step toward establishing state authority over the lives of citizens. The historical tradition offers a detailed account, which can be accepted in outline, of how the Twelve Tables were drafted by a special commission (the Decemviri) in the middle of the fifth century in response to demands of the plebs and with some influence from Greek (probably south Italian) law.[18] As in Athens, the preexisting traditional law was not superseded *en bloc*, with resulting conflicts between new *lex* and old *ius*.[19] The publication in 304 by the aedile Cn. Flavius of the *dies fasti* and the *actiones* completed the process of making the law explicit and public.[20]

In Rome, apparently unlike Greece, a substantial body of interpretative literature on the positive law soon grew up, evidently beginning with the *Tripertita* of Sex. Aelius Paetus (cos. 198), the three sections consisting of

---

13. Theophrastus' collaboration is inferred from Phld. *Rhet.* col. LIII.41; cf. Szegedy-Maszak, 1981, 79.—There was also an epitome in ten books as well as a work on legislators (νομοθέται) in three; parts of the large work were also cited separately; cf. evidence for titles gathered at Theophr. F 589.17–22 F.

14. F 650 F. = 21 Sz.-M.; cf. Szegedy-Maszak, 1981, 85.

15. On Demetrius cf. *ad* 3.14; this is in addition to the work on his own legislation (περὶ τῆς Ἀθήνησι νομοθεσίας, combined with περὶ τῶν Ἀθήνησι πολιτειῶν at frr. 139–47 Wehrli; cf. F 80 S.-O.-D.); for possible influences of Theophrastus on Demetrius' legislation cf. Szegedy-Maszak, 1981, 141–42 n. 150, with literature. The remains of Heraclides' work (frr. 146–50 Wehrli), dealing with Solon, Pisistratus, and Protagoras as lawgivers, make one wonder if the transmitted title is not a slip for περὶ νομοθετῶν.

16. Frr. 42–46 Wehrli; for possible influence on Cicero see *ad* 3.5.

17. Fr. 26 Wehrli = *SVF* 1, 89.35–37.

18. Cf. *ad* 2.59; Wieacker, 1988, 287–89.

19. See further *ad* 1.23.

20. Cf. *iur. anteh.* 6; Wieacker, 1988, 524–25; Rüpke, 1995, 245–74 (esp. 272–73 on "das Ziel der Fasten"); on the *ius civile Flavianum* and the possible involvement of App. Claudius Caecus cf. Endre Ferenczy, *From the Patrician State to the Patricio-plebeian State* (Amsterdam, 1976), 189–90.

4 A Commentary on Cicero, *De Legibus*

the Twelve Tables, interpretation thereof, and a treatment of *legis actio*.[21] Works on the civil law in general dominate roughly the next hundred years of legal literature, including contributions by M. Porcius Cato,[22] M. Junius Brutus (praet., date unknown; *RE* s.v. Iunius no. 49),[23] possibly P. Mucius Scaevola (cos. 133),[24] and Q. Mucius Scaevola ("the Pontifex"; cos. 95);[25] such a work is also attributed to Varro.[26] The public law is also represented, however, from fairly early times, both sacred law[27] and the law of magistrates,[28] as well as procedural law.[29]

In this context a work *de Legibus* from Cicero's pen might well have roused the expectation that he, too, is writing in such a vein. Hence he is careful to distance himself from that notion at the very beginning of *Leg.*: *quamobrem quo me vocas, aut quid hortaris? ut libellos conficiam de stillicidiorum ac de parietum iure, an ut stipulationum et iudiciorum formulas componam? quae et scripta a multis sunt diligenter, et sunt humiliora quam illa quae a nobis exspectari puto* (1.14). No jurist having held the consulship since Q. Mucius Scaevola (cos. 95), Cicero apparently regards such work as beneath a man of his rank.[30] He goes on to clarify that in his present project the *iuris disciplina* is to be drawn, as Atticus observes, *ex intima philosophia* (1.17). The separation is not total, however, as Marcus goes on to explain in

21. *Iur.* 1; *iur. anteh.* 15–16; see *ad* 2.59; for a skeptical assessment of Pomponius' reports (*Dig.* 1.2.2.35 ff.) of juristic writing prior to Paetus cf. Wieacker, 1988, 533–35.

22. Surely the Censor, not his son; cf. *iur.* 2 against *iur. anteh.* 20–21.

23. *Iur.* 7; *iur. anteh.* 24–25.

24. *Iur.* 7–9; *iur. anteh.* 34 (with query).

25. *Iur.* 17–19; other fragments 19–22; *iur. anteh.* 58–104.

26. *Iur. anteh.* 126–27; cf. Dahlmann, *RE* Suppl. 6 (1935), 1254.33 ff.

27. Note the works on pontifical law of Fabius Pictor (*iur.* 2–5; *iur. anteh.* 9–12) and Q. Fabius Maximus Servilianus (cos. 142; *iur anteh.* 28), as well as the work on augurs or auspices of L. Julius Caesar (cos. 90; *iur.* 46–47, 1 = *iur. anteh.* 106, 1); possibly to this period belongs a work *de Iure Sacro* attributed to a certain Manilius (title with a query at *iur. anteh.* 107); Cicero's young friend C. Trebatius Testa would make an important contribution to the genre with his nine or ten books *de Religionibus* (*iur.* 43–45; *iur. anteh.* 404–6).

28. C. Sempronius Tuditanus (cos. 129) wrote at least thirteen *magistratuum libri* (*iur.* 9–10; *iur. anteh.* 35–36); attribution of *de Censoribus libri* to L. Cassius Hemina (*iur. anteh.* 28) is doubtful: cf. Cichorius, *RE* 3.2 (1899), 1724.6 ff.; on the *de Potestatibus* of M. Junius Congus Gracchanus cf. *ad* 3.49; Nicostratus *de Senatu Habendo* (*iur. anteh.* 110) handled senatorial procedure, as did Varro's εἰσαγωγικὸς *ad Pompeium*, on which cf. Dahlmann, *RE* Suppl. 6 (1935), 1249.15 ff. This literature was augmented by Cicero's (older?) contemporary L. Cincius, who wrote *de Consulum Potestate* as well as *de Comitiis* and *de Fastis: iur.* 24–26; *iur. anteh.* 252–54; cf. Wissowa, *RE* 3.2 (1899), 2555.24 ff.

29. Besides the third section of the *Tripertita* works on *actiones* are attributed to M'. Manilius (cos. 149; *iur.* 5–6; *iur. anteh.* 26–27) and Hostilius (ibid. 40–41).

30. See further *ad* 1.14.

response to Atticus' remark just quoted: after presenting and offering commentary on each set of laws, there will be opportunity for remarks on the *iura et iussa populorum,* including those of Rome (ibid.).[31] *Leg.* is, in fact, in contact with views Cicero expresses elsewhere on the civil law. He thus complains that the jurisconsults have spread out into countless ramifications points that belong to a single idea (2.47); this is in line with his call for an *ars* reducing the bewildering variety of the *ius civile* to *genera* so as to facilitate learning (*de Orat.* 1.185–90), a project handled in the *de Iure Civili ad Artem Redigendo.*[32]

2. The Composition

a. Date

Turnebus, 250, already saw that *Leg.* must have been written after the death of P. Clodius, alluded to clearly at 2.42; he also placed the work before the civil war, perhaps because of the references to Pompey as living (1.8, 2.6, 3.22 and 26), though these might bear on the fictive date rather than that of composition. In any case, Turnebus' was the view that long prevailed.[33] While agreeing that the main part of *Leg.* was written after or in tandem with *Rep.,* Reitzenstein, esp. 31, called attention to differences in treatment between Books 1 and 2 (see the introduction to Book 2) and suggested that Book 1 was composed later, after the spring of 45, so as to be close to Cicero's writing about the *finis bonorum* in *Fin.* But Cicero was, of course, familiar with Antiochus' views on the *finis bonorum* much earlier, as is shown by *Fin.* 5.1 ff., harking back to his student days in Athens, ca. 78. E.A. Robinson, however, went further than Reitzenstein and sought to date the whole of *Leg.* to the first three months of 43. One consideration emphasized by Robinson is the division in Cicero's corpus between "Heraclidean"

31. Cf. 2.46 ff., combining the execution of this plan for sacred law with a commentary on the last *leges sacrae;* the discussion of existing or past laws for magistrates has evidently been lost through the mutilation of the archetype of the Leiden corpus; cf. *ad* 3.49.

32. In view of Quint. *Inst.* 12.3.10 (*M. Tullius . . . componere aliqua de eo* [sc. *iure*] *coeperat . . .*) it seems likely that the work never reached completion; see further *ad* 1.13.

33. Cf., e.g., Conyers Middleton, *The History of the Life of M. Tullius Cicero,* 1 (London, 1741), 548: "Soon after the death of Clodius, Cicero seems to have written his *Treatise on laws*" with attached reference to *Leg.* 2.17 (= 42–44); John Chapman, whose *Dissertatio de aetate Ciceronis librorum De Legibus* was printed as an appendix to J. Tunstall, *Epistola ad C. Middleton* (Cambridge, 1741), was a notable dissentient, on grounds of *Div.* 2.76 (but see p. 10 n. 45 *infra*) and the distinction between "Heraclidean" and "Aristotelian" types of dialogue; see below.

and "Aristotelian" dialogues; though Cicero states *quae . . . his temporibus scripsi* 'Αριστοτέλειον *morem habent* (*Att.* 13.19.4; 29 May 45; for fuller context see *infra,* n. 91), i.e., that he himself was the main speaker, it does not follow that this was an absolute chronological division of styles, for he returned to the "Heraclidean" form in *Sen.* and *Amic.;* and his statement does not exclude that he began his experiments with the form prior to *Brut.* (46). Moreover, during the first three months of 43 Cicero was busy writing most of the *Philippic* speeches and active in the senate in opposition to the designs of Antony; he surely would not have found the time for writing at least five books *de legibus;* and points of contact between *Leg.* and the *Philippics* can be more plausibly explained as reminiscences in the latter of the former (cf. *ad* 1.23). The arguments of Reitzenstein and Robinson have been refuted in detail by Schmidt, to whose definitive treatment of the dating problem of *Leg.* (1959; 1969, esp. 259 ff.) the interested reader should refer.[34] In the preface of his second edition of the text Ziegler, 5, though familiar with Schmidt, 1959, tries to save the hypothesis of a later dating of parts of *Leg.* by reference to the plan announced by Cicero at *Fam.* 9.2.5 (22 April 46) to read and write about πολιτεῖαι and investigate *de moribus ac legibus;* but it has not been shown that any contemplated revision to *Leg.* in 46 has left traces in the text;[35] and the obscure allusion at *Brut.* 16 surely has no connection to *Leg.*[36]

Cicero did not seal off his theoretical writing from his other, mostly political, concerns, and some of these spill over into *Leg.* or are telling indicators by their absence. For instance, on commands in the provinces "Marcus" seems to take a line similar to the lex Pompeia of 52 (Rotondi,

---

34. Schmidt, 1969, 229 ff., argues that one must, contrary to the theory of Reitzenstein and Büchner, assume continuous composition of *Leg.,* rather than composition of Book 2 before Book 1, since the subsequent books follow the plan formulated at 1.17; on the theory of the priority of Book 2 cf. also the introduction to that Book; on one of Reitzenstein's indices for the late composition of Book 1 see *infra* p. 370 n. 111.

35. Häfner, 97, already connected this passage with *Leg.;* sim. Erich Kalbe, *Quibus temporibus M. Tullius Cicero libros De Legibus III scripserit* (Leipzig diss.; Dresden, 1934), 5; Keyes, 289 of his edition; see further p. 64 n. 31 *infra;* Schmidt, 1969, 269–72.

36. *Seremus igitur aliquid tamquam in inculto et derelicto solo* etc., where the future tense seems to point to a future project; so Schmidt, 1969, 274–75, followed by Rawson, 1991, 128–29. Alberto Grilli, "Data e senso del De Legibus di Cicerone," *P.P.* 45 (1990), 175–87, esp. 180–81, writing evidently without knowing Schmidt's work, uses the *Brutus* passage to argue—most implausibly—that *Leg.* as a whole was composed between *Brut.* and *Tusc.* 1; a similar premise on the date informs the same author's paper "L'idea di stato dal De re publica al De legibus," *Ciceroniana* n.s. 7 (1990), 249–62. On *Brut.* 16 and *Leg.* see also p. 11 n. 46 *infra;* on the form of address used for Attticus as a possible dating criterion see below.

411–12; *MRR* 2, 234; cf. the introduction to Book 3).[37] Now *Leg.* presupposes *Rep.* (1.15, 2.14), which was published just before Cicero's departure to take up post as governor of Cilicia, with the public reaction reported to the author thereafter (*Fam.* 8.1.4; 24 May 51). If *Leg.* had been written or revised after his term as governor, one would have expected at 2.33 a reference such as that at *Div.* 1.2 to *Cilicum . . . et Pisidarum gens et his finitima Pamphylia, quibus nationibus praefuimus ipsi . . .* There is, however, a discussion of the views on augury of App. Claudius, Cicero's predecessor in the governorship, with whom he conducted a detailed and in part acrimonious correspondence in connection with the supersession, including reference to the book on augury Appius dedicated to Cicero (*Fam.* 3; see further *ad* 2.32); Appius and his book were clearly much on Cicero's mind around the time of the posting. Likewise at *Att.* 6.1.18 (20 February 50, from Cilicia) there is reference to the disagreement of Theophrastus and Timaeus about the existence of Zaleucus, also mentioned at *Leg.* 2.15.[38] Finally "Atticus," used in *Leg.* to designate his friend T. Pomponius, seems to have become regular in or just before 51; cf. Shackleton Bailey, 1995, 26–27. All things considered, *Leg.* seems likely to have been written mostly in tandem with *Rep.*; in Cilicia he may conceivably, to the degree possible, have continued the writing; at the very least, as the letter to Atticus shows, he went on thinking about the problems raised in the work.

b. Motives; Consequences

A consequence of the dating of work on *Leg.* to the late 50s is that, though we are fortunate in being able to trace the genesis of many of Cicero's works through references in his correspondence with Atticus, work on *Leg.* falls within the gap in that correspondence between November 54 and the departure for Cilicia in May 51. Nonetheless we can point to the moment when Cicero began to visualize a work embodying some of the components of *Leg.* The evidence comes from a letter to his brother Quintus dated to the end of October or beginning of November 54 (the major points are underlined):

Q.fr. 3.5.1–2: *Quod quaeris quid de illis libris egerim quos cum essem in Cumano scribere institui, non cessavi neque cesso, sed saepe iam scribendi*

---

37. On the other hand, any possible connection between *Leg.* and the plan that Pompey as consul formed but later abandoned to codify Roman law (Isid. *Orig.* 5.1.5; cf. Frier, 265) must remain moot; E. Pólay, "Der Kodifikationsplan des Pompeius," *Acta Antiqua* 13 (1965), 85–95, seeks to set that project into a political context.

38. Cf. Reitzenstein, 2.

*totum consilium rationemque mutavi. nam iam duobus factis libris, in
quibus novendialibus feriis quae fuerunt Tuditano et Aquilio consulibus
sermo est a me institutus Africani paulo ante mortem et Laeli, Phili, Ma-
n⟨i⟩li, ⟨P. Rutili,⟩ Q. Tuberonis, et Laeli generorum, Fanni et Scaevolae,
sermo autem in novem et dies et libros distributus de optimo statu civitatis et de optimo cive (sane texebatur opus luculente hominumque dignitas
aliquantum orationi ponderis adferebat), ii libri cum in Tusculano mihi
legerentur audiente Sallustio, admonitus sum ab illo multo maiore auctoritate illis de rebus dici posse si ipse loquerer de republica, praesertim
cum essem non Heraclides Ponticus sed consularis et is qui in maximis
versatus in republica rebus essem; quae tam antiquis hominibus attri-
buerem, ea visum iri ficta esse; oratorum sermonem in illis nostris libris,
quod esset de ratione dicendi, belle a me removisse, ad eos tamen rettu-
lisse quos ipse vidissem; Aristotelem denique quae de republica et prae-
stanti viro scribat ipsum loqui.*

*Commovi⟨t⟩ me, et eo magis quod maximos motus nostrae civitatis
attingere non poteram, quod erant inferiores quam illorum aetas qui
loquebantur. ego autem id ipsum tum eram secutus, ne in nostra tempora
incurrens offenderem quempiam. nunc et id vitabo et loquar ipse tecum et
tamen illa quae institueram ad te, si Romam venero, mittam. puto enim te
existimaturum a me illos libros non sine aliquo meo stomacho esse
relictos.*

Here Cicero reports reading for an audience on his Tusculan estate two
books of a work *de optimo statu civitatis et de optimo cive*, set shortly
before the death of the younger Africanus and involving a cast of speakers
familiar to us from *de Republica* as his friends. The differences from *Rep.* as
we know it are that this version is divided not into six but into nine books,
spread over nine days, has a preface for each book instead of alternate
books, and makes no mention of Sp. Mummius as a speaker (though this
may be due to an oversight by Cicero or fault of transmission). But this
Urversion of *Rep.* has been criticized by Cicero's friend Sallustius (not the
historian)[39] on grounds that Cicero as a consular and one who has been
engaged in matters of supreme state importance should be speaking in his
own person, not through a mouthpiece (for the *auctoritas* enjoyed by a
writer who has occupied such a position cf. *Fam.* 5.12.7). Cicero adds his

---

39. Perhaps rather the author of *Empedoclea* alluded to by Cicero at *Q.fr.* 2.10.3 as a point
of comparison to Lucretius' *poemata;* cf. Shackleton Bailey *ad Q.fr.* 14.3 in his edition. It is
interesting that Cicero shared the work at this stage with this man; for his practices in such
matters cf. Murphy.

own observation that a second-century setting would debar him from dealing with events of his own time. He did this deliberately, he says, to avoid giving offense, but has now changed his mind. He will incorporate Quintus and himself (*loquar ipse tecum*) but send his earlier draft, which he is reluctant to abandon.

This letter has given rise to several competing interpretations. The issues are: (1) what is the nature of the *offensio* Cicero sought to avoid? and (2) what is the precise nature of the innovation of the new version he now plans (*loquar ipse tecum*)? The *offensio* is not explained in this context. It is evidently something that Quintus will grasp automatically. Several different types of offense are conceivable, political and personal. Dealing with the events of his consulate and his exile with any candor would inevitably have given offense to one or more of the coalition of Caesar, Pompey, and Crassus, who had so recently curtailed Cicero's political independence and imposed upon him such odious tasks as the defense of Gabinius and Vatinius. Even in the 40s, when he did begin work in earnest on a history of his times, he called it an ἀνέκδοτον and meant it originally for the eyes of Atticus alone. Personal offense would also be conceivable since Cicero would have to choose among living speakers, and some might be annoyed at being left out.[40] The innovation, on the other hand, is likely to be a dialogue between Marcus and Quintus Cicero only (*loquar ipse tecum*). Zetzel thinks that these words refer to the prefaces addressed to Quintus that Cicero added at the beginning of alternate books of the later version of *Rep.*[41] But the following words are telling: . . . *et tamen illa quae institueram ad te* . . . *mittam. puto enim te existimaturum a me illos libros non sine aliquo meo stomacho esse relictos.* If what Cicero had in mind at this stage was merely the addition of prefaces addressed to Quintus, his annoyance (*stomachus*) at the prospect of abandoning the earlier version seems unreasonable. It must have been a thoroughgoing rewriting as a two-person dialogue that he was contemplating at this point.[42] This would enable him to avoid offense in that a frank assessment of his achievements, of his exile and recall, would be

---

40. For the political interpretation of the *offensio* cf. Häfner, 53, n. 1; Ruch, 130; Zetzel *ad Rep.* p. 4; *contra* Schmidt, 1969, 33–41, who thinks, rather, that Cicero's friends were competing for a place in his dialogues and would be offended if omitted and that by making his brother the sole interlocutor Cicero could avoid this type of offense. He cites *Att.* 12.12.2 (with reference to *Fin.* 1–2), 13.19.3, and other letters describing Varro's eagerness to be included in a dialogue.—On the ἀνέκδοτον or *Expositio consiliorum suorum* cf. *ad* 1.8.

41. Zetzel *ad Rep.*, p. 4 n. 11.

42. Even though, as Zetzel, *loc. cit.*, observed, such a dialogue would be less compelling than *Rep.*

acceptable if the interlocutor were a family member (cf. *Off.* 1.78: *licet enim mihi, Marce fili, apud te gloriari* . . . ; Leg. 2.41–42, where Atticus is also present but counts as family in view of the tie by marriage).[43]

The plan to rewrite *Rep.* as a two-person dialogue was quickly abandoned but yields insight into Cicero's thinking at a critical point in the creative process. It suggests that he saw a need to go beyond the constitutional theory and general principles of *Rep.* and create a framework for commentary on problems of the present and recent past. In the end he followed neither of the alternatives he was then contemplating, namely keeping the original plan of *Rep.* or transferring the parts to himself and Quintus. He contrived, however, to eat his cake and have it, too. Dividing *Rep.* into six books rather than nine, he added, in *Leg.*, a contemporary pendant. The altered format of *Rep.* suggests a shortening; such a move could have followed from a decision that some of the planned topics could be better illustrated with reference to recent events in *Leg.*[44]

Given the lack of reference to *Leg.* in the catalogue of his philosophical works he prefaced to *Div.* 2, it is likely that Cicero never published the essay.[45] The reason surely has to do with the timing of work on the dialogue. Cicero explains à propos the suggestion that he write history the difficulty he has in finding sufficient leisure for systematic writing; he can merely use "left-over time" (*subsiciva quaedam tempora:* 1.9). The unexpected and unwelcome posting to Cilicia probably hindered Cicero from putting *Leg.* into final form, just as the pressure of events in late 44 would hinder the addition of the *summa manus* to *Off.* (cf. Dyck *ad Off.*, pp. 8–10). On the other hand, at the end of his governorship, the Roman world was thrust into crisis over Caesar's

---

43. This possibility is not considered by Schmidt, *loc. cit.*, n. 40 *supra*, who only thinks of Quintus as the interlocutor obviating offense to other possible living participants in the dialogue.

44. Cf. Otto Plasberg, *Cicero in seinen Werken und Briefen*, ed. Wilhelm Ax (Leipzig, 1926), 114–15: "Ob es sich bei dieser Differenz [sc. of 6 vs. 9 Books of *Rep.*] nur um eine andere Abgrenzung der Bücher handelt, oder ob von dem ursprünglichen Umfang ein Stück weggeschnitten ist, können wir nicht sagen. Ist aber dies letztere der Fall, so darf man vermuten, daß der Inhalt des weggeschnittenen Stückes in die Schrift Von den Gesetzen (*De legibus*) übergegangen ist . . . so darf man vermuten, daß Cicero sie [sc. *Leg.*] im Anschluß an jenen zweiten Entwurf von *De re publica* oder vielleicht eher als eine Art Ersatz für ihn zu schreiben begonnen hat, als er zum ersten ⟨mit der erwähnten Modifikation⟩ zurückgekehrt war." Schmidt, 2001, 13–14, offers a reconstruction of the stages of composition; see p. 29 n. 98 *infra*.

45. Lazič, 18, suspected that *sed hoc loco plura in aliis* (*Div.* 2.76) was a reference to *Leg.* 2.32–33, which would, if true, suggest at the very least that Cicero was planning to publish *Leg.* at the time of his work on *Div.* (spring, 44); however, Pease *ad loc.* more plausibly suspects a reference to the lost treatise *de Auguriis*, the composition of which he may have had in view (cf. Garbarino, fr. phil., 29); see also p. 30 n. 101 *infra*.

supersession in Gaul, with Cicero trying at first to mediate and then, when that proved futile, deciding with difficulty which side to choose. After the hiatus of the civil war and the establishment of Caesar's dictatorship, the political situation was so changed that *Leg.*, taking the traditional *respublica* as its premise, must have seemed impossible to update in any meaningful fashion, quite apart from the fact that his relation to Quintus dissolved in quarrels for some while in the aftermath of Pharsalia.[46]

Various bits of internal evidence also point to the incompleteness of *Leg.*, quite apart from the obvious damage it has suffered in transmission. The most evident case is 3.40, possibly still at the rough draft stage, since it reads more like a series of individual observations than a connected argument. There is likewise an incoherence of argument at 2.8–13, where Cicero at first launches in on a discussion of the *vis naturaque legis* along similar lines to Book 1 but then at 2.9b shifts to the more inductive approach that will, in fact, form the basis of Books 2 ff.; see further *ad* 2.8–9a. It looks, then, as though Cicero is shifting his dialectical approach in the course of writing. Similarly at 2.39 and 45 he begins as if in full agreement with Plato but then unexpectedly modifies this stance; see *ad locos*. It is odd, too, that the long discussion of voting laws at 3.33–39 is based upon Quintus' assumption that Marcus wants to retain the secret ballot, when, in fact, he means to modify it, the true position only emerging in the course of discussion. In addition, there are the unclear references at 2.17 (*istas leges de religione*) and 2.68 (*deinceps dicit eadem illa de immortalitate animorum*): do these refer to matter lost in preceding lacunae (1.57 and 2.53, respectively), or did Cicero mean to clarify in revision? In revising Cicero would presumably have added cross-references, the lack of which is sometimes felt (cf. *ad* 2.26, 31, 44, and 3.16). Finally, there is the basic problem of the coherence of Books 2 ff. with the plan of Book 1, which suggests that "nature" will be the criterion used to establish laws, whereas in practice Roman (and to a limited degree Greek) tradition mostly assumes that rôle; but one wonders whether Cicero himself would have perceived this as a problem to be addressed in revision.

---

46. It is therefore difficult to credit that Cicero went back to work on *Leg.* in 46, as proposed by Ziegler, 9. M. Brutus substitutes for Quintus as the third speaker in *Brut.* (46). Cf. also Marcus' point about his writing habits at 1.9: . . . *neque tam facile interrupta contexo quam absolvo instituta*; Boyancé, 1975, 38; Lehmann, 6. At *Brut.* 16 Cicero rejects the possibility of making return to Atticus for the dedication of the *Liber annalis . . . ex conditis, qui iacent in tenebris et ad quos omnis nobis aditus, qui paene solis patuit, obstructus est*; this is often taken to be an oblique reference to *Leg.*; cf. Douglas *ad loc.*; Lehmann, 7–8 n. 13 with literature.

Leg., then, was clearly conceived and executed—insofar as it was executed—at a specific historical moment with the aim of supplementing *Rep.* in various ways (for one example cf. *ad* 2.25) and in particular adding some conclusions drawn from recent events. Its premise is the Roman Republic in its traditional form, and once that form of government seemed to have become obsolete, the project was abandoned to be exhumed from the author's papers (by Atticus?[47]) only after his death.

3. Sources and Originality

Contrary to what Cicero's words at 1.14 might seem to imply, he did receive stimulus from earlier literature on law, but not so much the Roman literature—as his countrymen would have expected—as the Greek. The idea of affixing a preamble to his laws, as he does at 2.15b–16, is one that he owes to the Greek lawgivers Zaleucus and Charondas, as well as Plato's *Laws* (2.14b).[48] From Plato he also took the idea that a work on laws could complement a work on the state in such a way that the statement and explanation of the laws themselves serve to educate citizens in proper behavior. But, in spite of the Platonic inspiration of the design, the Platonic echoes in the literary frame,[49] the translation and paraphrase from Plato's *Laws* at 2.45 and 67–68, and the occasional praise of Plato interspersed,[50] the content of *Leg.* is in general, as Marcus insists (2.17), rather different from that of Plato's *Laws*. The philosophical doctrines of Book 1 are Stoic or Stoicizing;[51] in the other books purified Roman institutions substitute for the purified Athenian institutions of Plato's *Laws*.

Cicero is also well aware of several other Greek authors on law. Theophrastus, for one, had devoted considerable work to the subject,[52] and Cicero cites him on the historicity of Zaleucus (2.15; F 598C F.); Cicero probably owes to him his knowledge of the shrines of Ὕβρις and Ἀναίδεια at Athens (cf. *ad* 2.28), and the report of Pittacus' legislation (2.66) will go back to him directly or via Demetrius of Phalerum.[53] If Szegedy-Maszak is right in supposing that Theophrastus divided his *Laws* in half with the first

47. Cf. § 8 *infra.*
48. See *ad loc.*; M. Benner, 180–81; Herbert Hunger, *Prooimion. Elemente der byzantinischen Kaiseridee in den Arengen der Urkunden,* Wiener Byzantinistische Studien, 1 (Vienna, 1964), 29 ff.
49. Cf. § 5 *infra.*
50. Cf. 1.15, 2.14, 3.1.
51. Cf. the introduction to Book 1.
52. Cf. 3.14: *Theophrastus . . . habitavit . . . in eo genere rerum . . .*
53. See below and *ad loc.*

half covering the fundamental elements of the constitution, the second half civil, criminal, and commercial law,[54] Cicero may have been influenced by this way of organizing the material insofar as he gives priority to the elements that hold the state together (2.69), namely religion and the law of magistrates, dealt with in Books 2 and 3, then perhaps went on to topics of the courts and the criminal and civil law.[55] Cicero also knew the work of Demetrius of Phalerum on his own legislation; probably his knowledge of earlier Athenian funerary practices, including Solon's law, derives from it as well.[56]

Demetrius seems likely to have cited Solon's sumptuary legislation and presented his own as a revival and updating of it (cf. *ad* 2.64); but Cicero goes much further in the weight he gives to tradition (*privatim colunto quos rite a patribus ⟨cultos* [sc. *deos] acceperint⟩*: 2.19.4; *ex patriis ritibus optima colunto*: 2.22.3, with commentary at 40). This gives the latter part of Book 2 (54 ff.), where Cicero seeks to formulate appropriate legislation for funerals and grave monuments, an antiquarian cast that might not have been expected per se. Thus the Twelve Tables—learned by heart by Marcus, Quintus, and Atticus as boys (2.59)—and their exegetes play a leading rôle here, even though there was subsequent legislation on the subject (cf. *ad* 2.54–68). The focus on the Twelve Tables and their exegesis suggests that Cicero is following the leading interpreter of early Latinity, L. Aelius Stilo Praeconinus, for §§ 58–62a directly and/or via Varro (the question must remain open, given the uncertainties over the date of publication of relevant works of Varro[57]).

Briefly stated, the originality of Cicero's dialogues of the 50s consists in his taking over a Greek form—the philosophical dialogue—and filling it with a content that is a subtle mixture of Greek and Roman. Thus in *de Orat.* the initial placement of the speakers beneath a plane-tree is a nod to the setting of Plato's *Phaedrus* (see p. 20 and n. 77 *infra*), and the basic skeleton of the rhetorical system is Greek, but the dialogue is animated by the ethos of the Roman aristocracy, which not only provides the setting and examples but also informs and conditions the entire discussion.[58] Similarly in *Rep.* the constitutional theory is a version of that of Polybius (modified by subtracting the inevitability of change: cf. Zetzel *ad Rep.*, pp. 18–19), but,

---

54. Szegedy-Maszak, 1981, 82–83.

55. Cf. § 7 *infra*. Rawson, 1991, 135 n. 28, already suggested that "Cicero's careful division of subject matter between Books (unlike Plato's chaotic *Nomoi*) might echo Theophrastus' organization . . ."

56. Cf. *ad* 2.66.

57. Cf. the introduction to Book 2; on Varro's *de Iure Civili* cf. n. 26 *supra*.

58. Cf. Wolf Steidle, "Einflüsse römischen Lebens und Denkens auf Ciceros Schrift De oratore," *MH* 9 (1952), 10–41; Jon Hall, "Social Evasion and Aristocratic Manners in Cicero's *De Oratore*," *AJPh* 117 (1996), 95–120.

when it is presented in a circle of eminent Romans, the upshot is an appreciation of the historical development of the Roman state that goes well beyond Polybius; and the concern for real-life maintenance of the social order goes beyond Plato. *Leg.* is like *de Orat.* and *Rep.* in that the literary and theoretical framework is Greek (for the former see § 5 below; for the Stoic or Stoicizing theory of *ius* and *lex,* the introduction to Book 1), but the specific laws proposed in Books 2 and 3 are mostly based upon Roman practice, present or past. This evaluation, selection, and modification of Roman public law in Books 2 and 3 in light of Greek theory is Cicero's major original contribution in *Leg.*[59]

As soon as the laws have been pronounced in Books 2 and 3, Quintus notes their similarity to Roman tradition (2.23, 3.12; cf. also Atticus' remark at 2.62). This comment, however, is not to be taken at face value but needs to be seen in the context of the general rhetoric of optimate political culture,[60] deferential to the *mos maiorum;* and it was primarily for the optimates that Cicero was writing, as several indicators show.[61]

Under religion the main innovations are the legislation (1) providing for capital punishment for disobeying an augur's finding (2.21.6); against (2) unseemly types of music (2.22.2, 38–39), (3) participation of an *impius* in cult (2.22.8, 41), or (4) consecration of arable land (2.22.11, 45); (5) placing limits on (a) alms (2.22.4 and 40) and (b) expenditure for funerals and tombs (2.22.16 and 62 ff.). Of these, (2) and (4) are clearly inspired by Plato (see *ad locos*); (5a) is in accord with the principle *opes amovento* (2.19.1), inferred

---

59. And not "the idea of drafting a document containing a complete constitution and excluding all other kinds of law," which Keyes, 1921, 312, thought was the "most striking element of originality in the De Legibus." A constitution in the sense of a written document setting out the basic structure of the state was a concept that Cicero did not have (and Keyes' notion, ibid., 311, that "the idea of his 'laws' being made superior to other laws might easily have existed in Cicero's mind" is speculation without support in the text). In laying out in writing basic law for the state, Cicero was explicitly following the example of Plato (1.15; 2.14); his originality is to be sought elsewhere.—What strikes one at first glance as an original touch is the inclusion in these laws of a certain number of informing ideals, presumably so that one can extrapolate from them to specific situations; but cf. *ad* 3.6.1.—I am grateful to Clifford Ando for help in formulating some of the arguments in this paragraph.

60. The terms *optimates* and *boni* in our sources vary notoriously depending on the position and aims of the writer; cf. Erich S. Gruen, review of Burckhardt, *Gnomon* 62 (1990), 179–81; for *optimates* cf. Wood, 195–97, and, with reference to *Sest.* 97, Riggsby, 93; for Cicero's use of *bonus* Achard, 365–66. I designate as "optimates" those whose policies are oriented toward protecting the status quo and the leading rôle of the senate and as "extreme optimates" those who aim to turn the clock back to an earlier stage of the constitution; "conservative" and "archconservative" would be acceptable English equivalents.

61. Cf. *ad* 3.33–39.

from early Roman practice (cf. *ad loc.*), but (5b) is also supported by parallel Greek legislation (2.64–66). On the other hand, (1) and (3) provide sanctions to counter abuses that have grown up in recent times, the Aelian and Fufian laws on respecting auspices having been, on Cicero's view, too often flouted, and the lack of effective sanctions against violation of sacred rites having been underlined by Clodius' acquittal in the Bona Dea affair.

The legislation on magistrates can be summarized as "strengthened control from the top," insofar as Cicero proposes to reinforce the rôle of the senate and the censors, ban violence in assemblies, and pin responsibility, if it should occur, on the presiding magistrate; at the same time the coercive power of magistrates is strengthened by the repeal of the lex Porcia against flogging and by the denial of *provocatio* to soldiers (3.6.2 and 4); he will also change the voting laws so that the contents of ballots are "known to the optimates" (3.10.6). The senate, a more elite body with the quaestors excluded, is to be an independent legislative organ again with no need for its decrees to be ratified by popular assembly (*eius decreta rata sunto:* 3.10.3); it, not the consuls, may appoint a dictator to deal with military crises or internal strife (but the dictator's term is limited to six months), thus obviating the need for consular action under the problematic *senatusconsultum ultimum* (3.9.2). Roman tradition is the source of these reforms. The exclusion of the quaestors and limitation of the dictator's term restore the pre-Sullan position; the increased legislative competence of the senate turns the clock back still further—to the lex Publilia *de patrum auctoritate* of 339. The appointment of a dictator to handle not only military but also civil crises is the explanation offered by some sources for the appointment of the first dictator T. Larcius Flavus (cf. *ad* 3.9.2). Cicero was inclined to identify "oldest" and "best" (2.40), and his reforms in general seek to restore and, through sanctions not provided for in the past,[62] stabilize an earlier state of Roman public life, though on rare occasions he seeks aid from Greek laws to fill what he regards as gaps (the augmentation of censorial power after the analogy of the νομοφύλακες [3.46–47]; the ban on costly tombs [2.62 ff.]). The product can claim originality as a kind of tradition that has been purified and provided with sharper weapons with which to defend itself.

4. *De Legibus* and Politics

Scholars have had difficulty finding the right context into which to set the political views of *Leg.* Thus Keyes, 1921, treats the innovations of Book 3 as

---

62. The death-penalty for disobeying an augur's finding (2.21.6); the presiding magistrate's responsibility for *vis* (3.11.3–5).

a purely theoretical exercise in increasing the powers of certain organs of government without reference to any formative experiences behind Cicero's views. On the other hand, in his 1969 biography, written without knowledge of Schmidt's work on the dating (cf. § 2a above), Gelzer, 273, inserts *Leg.* in the wrong place, in 46, just after Thapsus. Again, Mitchell, 1991, discusses *Leg.* along with *de Orat.* and *Rep.* in a chapter entitled "The Political Ideas behind the Policies of 63" and structures the argument so as to arrive at the conclusion (62): "Nothing had changed from the goals and outlook of 63"—a strangely anti-historical approach. In fact, in light of Schmidt's work on the dating, *Leg.* can be seen as embodying the conclusions Cicero drew for Rome from the experience of the 50s.[63]

If the 50s were a turbulent decade in Roman politics generally, for Cicero they were a time of the bitter disappointment and humiliation of exile, redeemed somewhat by his triumphant recall but without his ever regaining the influential position he had enjoyed in the immediate aftermath of the Catilinarian conspiracy. Looming over most of that decade was the figure of his bitter enemy P. Clodius, resolved to wreak vengeance on the orator for destroying his alibi during his trial in 61 for profaning the rites of the Bona Dea.[64] Having escaped conviction through lavish use of bribery, Clodius transferred to the plebs and went on to make violence a "standard weapon in the political armoury."[65] Besides Cicero's own exile, Clodius effected other measures, including a limitation on the Aelian and Fufian laws on honoring adverse omens reported at public assemblies[66]—a time-honored

---

63. This approach also informs the dissertation of Mehl, which came into my hands shortly before this work went to press; there the reader will find a good review of scholarship on Cicero's political views in the 50s (ch. 1) and a number of other good points. Though one might have expected Cicero to want to reduce consular power in light of events of the 50s, Mehl exaggerates (225 ff.) the degree to which Cicero does, in fact, so do: he removes from the consuls the power of creating a dictator, but this had not been used since the Hannibalic War, and he increases the power of *coercitio* of magistrates in general, repealing the leges Porciae; cf. *ad* 3.6.2 and 9.2. Moreover, Mehl's (false) assumption that, in spite of 1.37 (*ad respublicas firmandas . . . omnis nostra pergit oratio;* cf. also 2.35), "Cicero in fact had in mind only the Republic of Rome" (10) vitiates his analysis insofar as it is founded on Cicero's own self-identification with the Roman state.

64. H. Benner, 39, raises the question whether Clodius may have deliberately involved Cicero in his alibi in order to obtain an excuse to destroy him; but cf. *ad* 3.21.

65. Lintott, 1968, 193; cf. Nippel, 1995, 47 ff.

66. Cf. H. Benner, 51; Tatum, 1999, 125 ff., argues (132) that "Clodius's law only codified into public law what was in fact sound augural doctrine," i.e., that the adverse auspices must be announced in person and the mere announcement *de caelo servasse* does not suffice to break up a public assembly; sim. T.N. Mitchell, "The *Leges Clodiae* and *Obnuntiatio*," *CQ* 36 (1986), 172–76; see further *ad* 2.14a.

method of aristocratic control—and a weakening of the power of the censors such that both censors had to be present at public hearings and give explicit approval regarding any person whose civil status was changed.[67] Some of the major innovations Cicero proposes can be seen as a direct response to Clodius' program.[68]

Now precisely because *Leg.* is not set in the remote past but in the present, or rather the future (the publication of *Rep.* is presupposed; cf. § 5 *infra*), there are thematic overlappings with his other public attempts to come to terms with the events of the 50s, the *post reditum* speeches, with the term taken here in a broad sense to cover the speeches beginning with *Red. Sen.* down through *Mil.*[69] Cicero's complaints in the speeches about Clodius' violation of the Aelian and Fufian Laws (providing for suspension of public meetings in the event of adverse omens) and his limitations on censorial power[70] find their counterpart in legislation designed to strengthen the augurate (2.21.1–6 and 31–33) and the censorship (3.7.3 and 11.13–14, 46–47). Another theme, sounded already in *Red. Sen.* 29 and repeated with great vehemence at *Dom.* 43, is the interpretation of Clodius' law against Cicero as a *privilegium*. The point of law is controversial, and Cicero's interpretation is not inevitable.[71] But in any case Cicero clung to his interpretation and to the assertion, unsubstantiated by other evidence and widely doubted by modern scholars, that *privilegia* were outlawed by the Twelve Tables, and he enshrined in his own legislation in *Leg.* a law against *privilegia* (3.11.9 and 44; see *ad locos*). Above all Cicero makes in *Leg.* of Clodius' life and death and of his own exile and return a moral tale of crime punished and virtue rewarded, just as he does in the *post reditum* speeches (2.41–42; cf. *Red. Sen.* 23; *Mil.* 83–91). Thus, though one might have expected *Leg.* to show greater philosophical

---

67. Astin, 1988, 20 n. 25; A.E. Astin, "Censorships in the Late Republic," *Historia* 34 (1985), 187–88; Tatum, 1999, 133–35, and id., 1990.

68. See below.

69. Cf. Dyck, 1998, 240 and n. 87.

70. *Red. Sen.* 11; *Har.* 58; *Pis.* 9–10.

71. It should be clarified that Cicero is referring to Clodius' second law against him, the *lex Clodia de exilio Ciceronis*, which was passed after Cicero had fled in light of the *lex Clodia de capite civis Romani*; cf. *Att.* 3.15.5; Wilhelm Sternkopf, "Über die 'Verbesserung' des Clodianischen Gesetzentwurfes de exilio Ciceronis," *Philologus* 59 (1900), 273–74; Tatum, 1999, 156–57. Greenidge, 363, explains the legal problem: "the question . . . is the technical one whether—supposing a man had gone into exile to escape prosecution, but had never been formally prosecuted—the bill of outlawry might be passed against him. It is one we have no means of deciding; but it is at least possible that the annual bill passed by the tribunes covered the cases of men who had obviously sought exile for the purpose of avoiding prosecution"; cf. also Nicholson, 30–31.

detachment, in fact, the political commentary of *Leg.* is surprisingly similar in tone and content to that of the *post reditum* speeches.[72]

In his political commentary Cicero is careful to position himself as a moderate. At the end of his presentation of the constitutional laws he comments that such measures are needed to insure *temperatio;* the term is reminiscent of the *genus temperatum,* the mixed constitution recommended by Scipio in *Rep.* (3.12; cf. ibid. 1.69 and 2.65). Thus, on the basis of his reading of Greek and Roman constitutional history, Cicero does not advocate turning back the clock to a time before the tribunes existed. Though he begins his argument as if a total opponent of the tribunate, Quintus in the end advocates the weaker Sullan version of the office, not the one used since the restoration of its powers by Pompey in 70.[73] Marcus, however, rejects this view as too extreme, regarding the otherwise unchecked power of the consuls as an invitation to tyranny. Cicero is at pains, in other words, to avoid upsetting the *concordia ordinum,* which has been his catchphrase from the time of his consulate.[74] He sees the problem not in the tribunate as such (cf. *ad* 3.25)—after all, the friendly tribunes of 57 spearheaded the drive for his own recall from exile—but in violence (*vis*) in public assemblies, which one of his proposed laws would ban (3.11.3).

If "Quintus" represents in this dialogue the extreme optimates, whose position is given a respectful hearing, albeit not endorsed, and Clodius, repeatedly excoriated *tacito nomine,* is portrayed as the disapproved extreme on the other side of the political spectrum, the representative of the middle ground sought in *Leg.* is, besides "Marcus," Demetrius of Phalerum, who is described in glowing terms: *fuit enim hic vir, ut scitis, non solum eruditissimus, sed etiam civis e republica maxime tuendaeque civitatis peritissimus* (2.66). In another passage Cicero describes Demetrius as one who brought his learning out of shade and leisure into the very crisis and line of battle (*in ipsum discrimen aciemque:* 3.14). He goes on to portray him as outstanding in both statesmanship and learning and poses the pregnant question whether anyone else could combine these abilities, to which Atticus replies as if on cue that he thinks one of the three interlocutors could do, in fact. Cicero's strategy here is transparent: the ancients recognized, as Plu-

---

72. For continuity from the speeches to *Leg.* cf. also Mehl, 200 ff.; on similar themes in the letters of the 50s, ibid. 11 ff.

73. Cf. *ad* 3.19b–22. A similar conclusion to that of "Quintus" was reached by Josef Lengle, *Römisches Strafrecht bei Cicero und den Historikern* (Leipzig-Berlin, 1934), 25.

74. Cf. *TLL* s.v. *concordia* 84.20 ff.; s.v. *ordo* 962.48 ff.; Achard, 73, and in general Hermann Strasburger, *Concordia Ordinum. Eine Untersuchung zur Politik Ciceros* (Amsterdam, 1956).

tarch remarks, that the odium of self-praise can be mitigated if one praises not oneself but another sharing the same qualities (*de Laude ipsius* 542c). This consideration clearly underlies Cicero's allusions to Demetrius here and elsewhere (see further *ad* 3.14). In any case, what Cicero is looking for in a statesman is made clear here no less than in *de Orat.* and *Rep.*: *eruditio* engaged in managing public affairs. As Pohlenz already hinted, these three works need to be read together as a corpus.[75]

A terse and powerful formulation of the political message of *Leg.* appears in the law *Intercessor rei malae salutaris civis esto* (3.11.6). In context this refers to intercession by a magistrate of equal or greater authority than the presiding magistrate in an assembly. But in a larger, metaphorical sense, Cicero's work in *Leg.* can be seen as that of an *intercessor rei malae,* aiming to prevent the tactics of a Clodius from gaining ground, just as later, in *Off.,* he would rail against Caesar's tyranny and try to cut out the ground from under any would-be imitators. He hopes, for his efforts, to be recognized as a *salutaris civis,* that is, a citizen who protects the well-being, the *salus,* of the state, just as he had in the struggle against Catiline, or, similarly, as a citizen who is, as he said of Demetrius, patriotic (*e republica* [2.66]); see further *ad* 3.8.2.

The final question to be addressed about the relation of *Leg.* to politics is that of the intended use of its proposals: were they put forward with a view toward adoption in Rome in the foreseeable future or with a more vague hope of doing political good? Both of these views have been held by recent students of the treatise (cf. *ad* 2.14b).

Those who, like Girardet, 1983, 9–11 and 164 ff., believe that Cicero was aiming for a fairly immediate political effect emphasize particularly the statement at 1.37: *ad respublicas firmandas . . . omnis nostra pergit oratio.* But within its context this is given as a reason for pursuing a discussion of *ius* being by nature on a point by point basis (*articulatim distincte⟨que⟩*: 1.36). The implication is that a proper understanding of *ius* will have the effect described, and indeed Cicero goes on to argue that *ius* must be conceived as something independent of personal advantage. His account, then, should instill respect for *ius* and in this sense contribute to strengthening and stabilizing political entities. Cicero need not be thinking of the enactment of the specific laws proposed in Books 2 and 3.

Indeed 2.14 contrasts two types of lawgivers, Zaleucus and Charondas

75. Cf. Pohlenz, 1938, 126 = 434; the idea is elaborated by Friedrich Klingner, *Römische Geisteswelt,* 5th ed. (Munich, 1965), 133–40; Mehl, esp. 274–78, draws some connecting lines, albeit he reads too much of the "wise man" into the augur of *Leg.* 2 and too much of Plato into the censor of *Leg.* 3.

on the one side, Plato on the other. The former gave laws *reipublicae causa,* the latter, implicitly, *studi et delectationis . . . causa.* Cicero clearly does not take seriously Socrates' ironic claim that his constitution might be adopted at some remote time or place (*Rp.* 499c–d). Now Plato is, of course, Cicero's model in *Leg.* (1.15, 2.14); hence it seems clear that Cicero's own laws are offered, like Plato's, *studi et delectationis . . . causa.* The thought that Cicero had the immediate adoption of his proposals in mind is likewise discouraged by Marcus' comment at 3.29: *non enim de hoc senatu nec his de hominibus qui nunc sunt, sed de futuris, si qui forte his legibus parere voluerint, haec habetur oratio.* The adoption of the laws is thus placed in a vague future when there will be a better sort of men; in this way he seeks to avoid a too close comparison of his laws with present realities, though the premise is not maintained consistently; see further *ad loc.*

In accord with Quintus' request for *leges vivendi et disciplina* (1.57), Cicero provides a text that educates in the first principles, through the proem to his laws (2.15b–16), the inclusion within the laws of general principles of conduct (e.g., *duella iusta iuste gerunto* [3.9.4]), and the case he makes for the individual laws in his commentary. These features suggest that Cicero's concern is less with the enactment of specific points than with inculcating attitudes toward law (see above à propos 1.37), toward the gods, and toward magistrates and of magistrates toward citizens.[76] In this broad, educative sense *Leg.* could be said to embody a political program, but not in the narrower, ordinary sense.

5. The Scene and Fictive Date

If Cicero owed to Plato the idea of writing separate works *de republica* and *de legibus* (1.15, 2.14), he also owed to him a good deal of inspiration for the enclosing frame, perhaps the most attractive of any Ciceronian dialogue. But the motifs derive less from Plato's *Laws* than from his *Phaedrus.* To be sure, the scene is transferred from outside the walls of Athens to the Italian soil in and near Cicero's native Arpinum. This is the first step in Cicero's "personalization" of the scene. As there Socrates proposes that he and Phaedrus should make their way along the Ilissus river (229a), so here Atticus suggests they walk along the Fibrenus (1.14: the river is named at 2.1). As Phaedrus points to a plane-tree as the place for him and Socrates to take their ease (229a),[77] so Atticus suggests the island in the Fibrenus as a

---

76. Cf. for these last two points 3.5.

77. There is a reminiscence of the conversation beneath the plane-tree at *de Orat.* 1.28–29 with the upper-class Roman refinement of cushions added.

suitable place for continuing the discussion sitting down (2.1), and the space they will occupy is compared to a *palaestra,* a typical setting for a Socratic dialogue (cf. *ad* 2.6). There is even a reference to Socrates' testing of the water with his foot, something Atticus is reluctant to do in the case of the Liris (2.6; cf. 230b).

But, besides these scenic details, the early course of the conversation of Book 1 takes its cue from the *Phaedrus* in other ways. Here Cicero found a model for the natural environment giving rise to intellectual questions. Phaedrus asks Socrates whether the place they are now passing is where Orithyia was abducted by Boreas; he explains that he infers this from the charming and limpid water, suitable for girls to play in (229b). Similar is Atticus' opening query as to whether a certain oak is the one he has read about in Cicero's poem *Marius,* which is thus given the status of a famous cultural artifact; Atticus draws his inference from its age (*etenim est sane vetus:* 1.1). Socrates has a ready answer: no, the spot is commemorated by an altar of Boreas two or three stades further down; Phaedrus then follows up by asking whether he believes in the historicity of the tale (229c); Socrates offers a rationalizing explanation such as the σοφοί would give but does not commit himself to a definite answer; he would need more leisure (σχολή) in order to look into the matter properly; he has no time to handle ἀλλότρια since he still has not come to know himself (229c–230a). In Cicero, Phaedrus' two questions are fused into one, the identifiability of the oak implying the historicity of the tale, and never receive, in spite of Atticus' persistent efforts, any clear-cut answer. Especially in view of Marcus' authorship of the *Marius,* this would more naturally be a two-person dialogue, as in Plato, and the fact that Quintus, rather than Marcus, gives the first responses to Atticus is a bit awkward. Now Marcus can hardly say that he has not had time to look into the historicity of the "Marian oak," as Socrates says of the story of Orithyia's abduction. When Quintus abstracts from Marcus' examples the principle that he holds the "laws" of history and poetry to be distinct, Atticus turns the discussion to Marcus' possible writing of history (1.5–7), and it is Marcus' reply to this proposition that echoes Socrates' complaint of lack of leisure, though what fills up Marcus' time is not trying to know himself, but "work" (*viz.,* in the courts).

Thus Cicero has taken a recognizably Platonic structure but by changing the scene and making corresponding adjustments of topic has created something thoroughly Roman. History as recorded in literature replaces myth; Cicero replaces Socrates as the man who can answer questions; and his (potential) literary activity replaces Socrates' (potential) intellectual activity. What is left out at this point is the characteristic project of "knowing oneself." But that topic has merely been reserved for the end of the Book, where Cicero discusses "knowing oneself," which is treated as the wisdom (*sapientia*) one seeks in stages corresponding to the "parts" of philosophy, and he adds a personal confession of his debt to philosophy (1.58–63). So, even in this regard, he turns out to be more like Socrates than the reader might at first have suspected.

There is also some intertextual play with Plato's *Laws*. The path Marcus proposes to his companions is explicitly compared to that of the interlocutors in the *Laws* (1.15; 625a–b), just after Atticus has adduced Plato's *Laws* as a precedent for the kind of thing he would like to see Marcus do. The change of scene recommended (by Atticus?) in the fr. from book 5 to take advantage of the more adequate shade of tall alders is also reminiscent of that passage of the *Laws* (625b4: ἐν τοῖς ὑψηλοῖς δένδρεσιν).

It is an advantage that Cicero has chosen to set *Leg.* in the countryside of his native Arpinum that he knows well and can describe vividly and with warm appreciation. The result is a homage to his own roots, but not a naive one. The setting is carefully calculated to thread into the themes of the dialogue (Book 1), to make certain points about the loyalties of a *municipalis*, and to provide a fit counterpart for the settings of Plato's dialogues (Book 2; cf. *ad* 2.5–6).

Leg. is unique among Cicero's dialogues in including no fixed chronological point,[78] though possibly this occurred in a part now lost or was meant to be added later. Various indices enable us to fix the fictive date fairly closely, however. It was certainly set before the deaths of Servius Sulpicius (43) and of Pompey (48), both of whom are referred to as living (1.8, 2.6, 3.22 and 26; 1.17). On the other hand, it must have taken place after September 58, the date of the death of Atticus' uncle Q. Caecilius (Nep. *Att.* 13.2; Cic. *Att.* 3.20.1), for the *domus Tamphiliana* that he thereby inherited is already in his possession (1.3). Additional upper termini are 53/52, when Cicero was elected to the board of augurs as successor to P. Crassus, killed at the battle of Carrhae (at 2.32 Atticus refers to Marcus' membership of the college), and 18 January 52, when Clodius was killed at Bovillae (his death is clearly referred to at 2.42), and the description of his followers as *distracti ac dissipati* (2.42 with note) would fit the aftermath. *Leg.* may, when written, have been set in the future, for the publication of *Rep.* (April 51) is presupposed (1.15 and 21); see § 2a *supra*. Several references suggest a date not beyond the 50s: Cicero's exile counts as an event that is still *ante oculos* (2.41), and he is kept from writing history by preoccupation with "work,"

---

78. Cf. Ruch, 252.

surely the work of the courts (1.8), which would apply to the 50s but not thereafter. An argument from silence, but, I think, a rather telling one, can be drawn from his failure to mention having governed Cilicia, as he does at *Div.* 1.2 and as one would have expected at 2.33 (a pointer also to date of composition; see § 2a).

6. The Characterization of the Participants[79]

This is not the place for a full assessment of the life of Cicero's friend T. Pomponius **Atticus**.[80] *Leg.* represents Cicero's first attempt to inscribe him in one of his dialogues. He went on to be one of the interlocutors in *Brut.* (46). In early July 45 Cicero mooted his inclusion as a speaker in the revised version of *Ac.* and received reassurances (*Att.* 13.22.1).[81] He would also be the dedicatee of *Sen.* and *Amic.* One wonders how the cautious man would have reacted to playing a rôle in this political dialogue and indeed to having quite decided political views attributed to him (3.26 and 37).[82] If Cicero raised the question, we are prevented from knowing the answer by the gap in the friends' correspondence between November 54 and Cicero's departure for Cilicia in early May 51.

In any case, Atticus is the catalyst and motor of this dialogue, and without him it would have been very different indeed. It is a common pattern of Cicero's dialogues that younger or less distinguished figures visit the estate of a senior statesman and ask him to expound his views on some set theme, which he, after a show of reluctance, proceeds to do.[83] Whereas *de Orat.* and *Rep.* have each a fairly large cast of characters, *Leg.* anticipates the technique of most of the later dialogues by reducing the number to three.[84] Under this economy Atticus takes on the rôle of the questioner assigned to Sulpicius and Cotta in *de Orat.* or Laelius in *Rep.* So from the very beginning of the dialogue Atticus sets the topic, in fact, several topics leading up to the one that will occupy the burden of the dialogue: first the identity of

---

79. Cf. in general Schmidt, 1959, 170–72 n. 1, and, from the standpoint of dating, 1969, 53–69; Haury, 162–64.

80. Cf. Shackleton Bailey, *Att.* 1, 5–58; Perlwitz; R. Feger, *RE* Suppl. 8 (1956), 503.27 ff.

81. Cf. Schmidt, 1969, 63–64.

82. Cf., however, Nep. *Att.* 6.1: *in republica ita est versatus ut semper optimarum partium et esset et existimaretur . . .*

83. Cf. M. Griffin, "The Composition of the *Academica*: Motives and Versions" in Inwood-Mansfeld, 18–20.

84. *Viz., Brut., Ac., Sen.,* and *Amic.;* add *N.D.*, where Cicero, though present, is essentially a κωφὸν πρόσωπον. The reduction is carried still further in *Div.* and *Fat.* with two speakers each.

the oak mentioned in Cicero's *Marius,* then the possibility of Cicero's writing a history, and finally the *ius civile,* which, it is agreed, should be approached from a philosophical angle by analogy to Plato's *Laws* (1.1–16). Moreover, it is his consent, hedged with a humorous reference to the natural environment, that enables the discussion to take the course it does and not become instead a dialogue *de natura deorum* (1.21; see *ad loc.*). Once having set the dialogue in motion, Atticus takes on the rôle of moderator. As such, at critical points he steers the conversation in a certain direction (2.5, 24, 32), keeps a sharp eye on the coherence of the unfolding argument, asks for clarification as needed (1.1, 4, 22, 63; 3.33), provides summaries of arguments (1.17 and 35), and comments on their nature or consequences (1.28, 45, 62). At 2.1 he assumes the rôle of stage-manager and suggests a place for the interlocutors to sit (sim. fr. from Book 5? See *ad loc.*). To be sure he must occasionally, for variety's sake, share such responsibilities with Quintus.[85]

But beyond this function of providing the topic and giving shape and structure to the argument and some clues as to how to interpret it, Atticus' presence and his give-and-take with Marcus lend a liveliness and vitality to this dialogue that make it scenically the most attractive of all of Cicero's contributions to the genre. To heighten the drama, this should not be simply a routine visit. Instead, it is represented as being Atticus' first visit to Arpinum, the birthplace of both Marcus and Quintus.[86] Nor is the focus so much on the estate itself, Cicero being all too well aware of the *invidia* that could be provoked (cf. 3.30), as on the charms of the surrounding country-side (cf. especially 2.2). When he does come to speak of the family house, it is to emphasize the smallness of the original villa built by his grandfather, in which he had been born (2.3). It is Atticus' sympathetic presence that enables Marcus to speak of these personal matters.[87] It is Atticus, who knows his friend so well, who is represented as having noticed his change in oratorical style in recent years (1.11). In the course of the dialogue Atticus presents his friend with a series of compliments: his potential to create in Latin a historiography able to challenge comparison with the Greeks (1.5–7), the citation of Pompey's praise of Cicero (2.6), and his hint that Cicero can excel in both learning and statecraft (3.14). Atticus receives in return complimentary references to his houses at Rome and Athens (1.3),[88] Quintus'

---

85. See p. 28 and n. 96 *infra.*

86. Two passages in the letters (*Att.* 2.16.4; 2.17.1) show that a visit to Arpinum was planned by Atticus ca. May 59 but not that it actually occurred.

87. Note his reaction at 2.4: . . . *ipse, vere dicam, sum illi villae amicior modo factus atque huic omni solo, in quo tu ortus et procreatus es.*

88. On the importance of his estate for a great man's public image cf. *ad* 2.3.

praise of the beauty of Atticus' estate in Epirus (2.7), and Marcus' recognition of the importance of the work *de Potestatibus,* which M. Junius Congus
Gracchanus dedicated to Atticus' father (3.49). But above all there is the
glowing tribute to Atticus' combination of *gravitas cum humanitate* at 3.1.
This may be a clue that *Leg.* was meant to be dedicated to Atticus in
recognition not least of his loyal support during Cicero's exile (see *ad loc.*).
One would, however, have expected the dedication to be made explicit in a
preface attached to the beginning of the work explaining *inter alia* the
circumstances of Atticus' visit to Arpinum (see pp. 52–53 *infra*).

Finally, Atticus adds to a dialogue on rather weighty themes a much-
needed pinch of Attic salt, in this respect playing a rôle similar to that of
Catulus in *de Orat.*[89] He needles Marcus for allowing himself, although an
Academic skeptic and thus ostensibly free to do as he pleases, to have his
procedure dictated to him by others (1.36). With tongue in cheek he cites L.
Gellius' earnest but misguided effort to reconcile the philosophical schools
of Athens (1.53). He puns wittily on Antiochus' nearly successful attempt to
convert him from Epicureanism: *me ex nostris paene convellit hortulis*
(ibid.). His humor becomes sardonic, however, at 3.29, when he, as the
eques among the interlocutors, opines that the misdeeds of the senatorial
order would exhaust the efforts of the censors and all judges.

It is, then, above all the presence of Atticus that makes *Leg.* a real dialogue; and the banter between Atticus and Marcus strikes one as the most
natural and unforced in the entire corpus of Ciceronian dialogues, whereas
the "Heraclidean" dialogues involving historical reproduction and projec-
tion onto other figures of the social relations he knew at first hand show
inconsistencies or other infelicities.[90]

According to the distinction drawn in his letters,[91] *Leg.* is an "Aristotelian" dialogue in the sense that the author takes the leading part in
the discussion. Though the contributions of the other two speakers are more
important than has sometimes been allowed (see above and below),[92]

89. Cf. Leeman et al. on *de Orat.,* v. 2, 204–5.

90. Cf. A.R. Dyck, "Cicero the Dramaturge: Verisimilitude and Consistency of Characterization in Some Ciceronian Dialogues," in *Qvi Miscvit Vtile Dvlci: Festschrift Essays for Paul
Lachlan MacKendrick,* ed. Gareth Schmeling and Jon D. Mikalson (Wauconda, Ill., 1998),
151–64; for the term *Heraclidean* see the next note.

91. *Q. fr.* 3.5.1 (cited § 2b *supra*); *Att.* 13.19.4 (28 June 45): *hoc in antiquis personis
suaviter fit, ut et Heraclides in multis et nos in sex de republica libris fecimus. . . . quae autem
his temporibus scripsi* Ἀριστοτέλειον *morem habent, in quo ita sermo inducitur ceterorum ut
penes ipsum sit principatus.*

92. Busuttil, p. 28, for instance, thought that *Leg.* "can more appropriately be called a
monologue rather than a dialogue."

Marcus is the center of attention from the very beginning, whether the topic be details of his poem *Marius,* his possible contribution to historiography, or—the topic finally settled upon—his views on law. In Book 1 the unfolding of the philosophical argument is in his hands, in Books 2 and 3 the formulation of his legislation and the main commentary thereon. But what are the features of his personality as he constructs it in *Leg.*? He is the one member of the group who is of consular rank, and, well aware of his dignity, he is careful to see that the subject is framed in such a way as to be worthy of him (1.14–17). We are also meant to see him as a devoted enthusiast of philosophy in general, Plato in particular. It is when the present project is defined as one analogous to Plato's *Laws* that Marcus is won over (1.15, including Marcus' admiration for Plato); this will give him the opportunity to play the rôle of Socrates. His prefaced remarks on the origins of *ius* provoke wonderment (1.28: *Di immortales, quam tu longe iuris principia repetis!*). Nor is he content with a sweeping account *philosophorum more . . . veterum* but insists on pursuing the issues *separatim distincte⟨que⟩* in the manner of more recent philosophical discourse (1.36). When he digresses on the *finis bonorum,* he finally exhausts his listeners' patience and has to be reined in (1.52–57), even though he would gladly have continued (*at ego huc declinabam, nec invitus:* § 57). Moreover, Book 1 concludes with Marcus' encomium on *sapientia* and the "parts" of philosophy interpreted as stages in the quest for *sapientia* and his confession of a personal debt to the pursuit of *sapientia* (§§ 58–63). Elsewhere we are, thanks to the intimate circle in which we see him, vouchsafed personal glimpses of Marcus such as hardly emerge in other dialogues: he introduces to Atticus the house where he was born and speaks of the importance to him of his native place (2.3: *haec est mea . . . germana patria*); he discusses in personal terms his own exile and recall (2.41–43) and also analyzes the political forces that drove him into exile (3.25–26). In addition, we see him reflecting on his career in the courtroom, his use of his leisure, and possible occupations for his old age (1.8–12). Cicero was, throughout his literary career, to a considerable degree his own best subject. Insofar as he creates here a framework in which he can comfortably reveal a bit more of his personality,[93] *Leg.,* together with *Brut.,* can rank as the most introspective work he intended for the public and as his finest achievement in self-presentation.

The brothers Cicero were never closer than in the immediate aftermath of Marcus' exile, **Quintus** having exerted himself ceaselessly both before the

---

93. And not just show himself "on good behavior": cf. *ad Off.* 2.51.

senate and the people for his brother's restoration.[94] Indeed he found himself in danger of his life when on 23 January 57 he was attacked by a mob of Clodiani and left for dead (cf. *ad* 3.22). The public praise his brother lavished upon him after his return was well earned (*Red. Sen.* 37; *Red. Pop.* 8; *Scaur.* 35). But Marcus' return was not the end of their difficulties. On 3 November 57 a band of Clodiani interrupted the rebuilding of Marcus' house on the Palatine and set fire to Quintus' nearby house as well (*Att.* 4.3.2; *Cael.* 78; *Mil.* 87; *Fam.* 1.9.5). During the exile Quintus went surety with Pompey for his brother's "good behavior" vis-à-vis Caesar, Pompey, and Crassus (*Fam.* 1.9.9 and 10.12; Plut. *Pomp.* 49.3), and his service as legate of Pompey in Sardinia (mid-December 57 to June 56) and Caesar in Gaul (April 54 to the end of 52) can be seen in the context of diplomacy between the Tullii Cicerones and the "triumviri": at the same time Quintus obtained posts in which he could demonstrate his usefulness (with a view perhaps to an eventual consular candidacy; cf. Wiseman, 1987, 34–40), and Marcus was relieved of the pressure to accept such a post himself. The dedication of both of the great works published in the 50s, *de Orat.* and *Rep.*, to Quintus attests the closeness of the bond at this time.

Quintus' rôle as a speaker in *Leg.* thus comes as no surprise. A similar tone to the *post reditum* speeches is struck, but only once and with specific reference to the events surrounding Marcus' exile, which Quintus had attributed to the machinations of tribunes but Marcus sees differently (3.25: *optime et dulcissime frater*). Quintus also contributes to the personal characterization of the Tullii Cicerones by citing a bit of family history at 3.36. In general, Quintus' depiction in the dialogue accords with what is known of the personality of the historical Quintus. It is noticeable that, though all three had been students together in Athens in 79 (*Fin.* 5.1) and Atticus and Quintus had been brothers-in-law since at least November 68 (*Att.* 1.5.2), Marcus Cicero is the pivot on which the relation among the three men turns. He is familiar in advance with Quintus' views (cf. *ad* 1.21: *nam Quinti novi sententiam*), and the dialogue of Books 1 and 2 is mostly conducted, in an occasionally bantering mode,[95] between Marcus and Atticus. As a poet, Quintus is allowed some general reflections on the relation of "Dichtung und Wahrheit" and also praise of his brother's *Marius* (1.2) before Atticus turns to Marcus himself for clarification of the relation of the impressively aged oak tree now before them and the one mentioned in that poem (1.1–3), and Quintus reports the brothers' disagreement on the proper starting point

---

94. Documentation provided by F. Münzer, *RE* 7A2 (1948), 1293.21 ff.

95. See above.

for a history of Rome (1.8). Quintus of the dialogue is a man of opinions and is sometimes contradicted by his elder brother (rather sharply, it seems, at 1.18a and 3.17; more gently at 2.43). His interest in philosophy being, apparently, limited, he shows a bit of impatience with his brother's plan to offer separate proof of the proposition *ius esse natura* (1.34: *tu vero iam perpauca licet*). Later in the same Book he calls a halt altogether to his brother's digression on the *finis bonorum* and by putting his concrete expectations on the table sets the discussion back on track (1.56–57). He sometimes takes on Atticus' rôle in reacting to and commenting on Marcus' points.[96]

It is natural that in Book 3 Quintus, as the other interlocutor who has pursued a political career, should take a larger rôle. Here irreconcilable differences between the brothers emerge on tribunician power, which Quintus would decisively curb, and on the secret ballot, which he would eliminate altogether. In both cases the positions attributed to Quintus are those of the extreme optimates, whereas Marcus espouses a more moderate line, seeing the tribunes as a necessary check on consular power and proposing an odd compromise on voting whereby votes shall be in writing but yet "known to the optimates" (cf. *ad* 3.33–39). By framing the dialogue this way, Cicero is able to bring the grumblings of the optimates to the surface and present counter-arguments. Whether the historical Quintus held these positions is unknown. But Quintus of the dialogue is not alone, for Atticus, too, takes the optimate line on ballot laws (3.37). This fact, the lack of a resolution, and the length at which these issues are discussed suggests that the point is not to discredit the optimate position but to win over optimate sentiment (in the interest, presumably, of the *concordia ordinum*).[97]

7. The Reconstruction of the Whole

The extant portion of *Leg.* begins with a Book devoted to the general grounding of *ius* in nature and the defense of that position against criticisms from the angle of egocentric utilitarianism. Then follows Marcus' promulgation and justification of laws in several areas ordered according to their importance in holding the state together (2.69), the two extant sets of laws being on religious observance (Book 2) and magistrates (Book 3); the order could also be justified by the traditional Roman view that divine cult takes precedence over magisterial power (cf. V.Max. 1.1.9). After Marcus' ideal laws (*leges quibus*

---

96. 1.57–58, 2.9 and 23, 3.12.
97. Cf. *ad* 3.33–39.

civitates regi debeant), there is to follow a discussion of the enactments of individual peoples (*iussa et iura populorum:* 1.17); and this plan is carried out in connection with religious law at 2.46 ff. (see the introduction to Book 2). At 3.48 Atticus requests that Marcus similarly dilate *de potestatum iure.* Marcus has just agreed to do so and received further encouragement from Atticus when the text breaks off (3.49). It seems clear therefore that Book 3, like Book 2, was meant to end with a treatment of its subject from the point of view of the *iura populorum* and that this material has been lost through physical damage to our text as the last member of the Leiden corpus (see further *ad* 3.49).

Cicero wrote, however, at least two further books, as we know from the fr. from Book 5 (see *ad loc.*). Thanks to Marcus' over-eagerness to reach the next topic at 3.47, we know that Book 4 was to deal with *iudicia*. Certainly corrupt courts were much on Cicero's mind at the time of writing (cf. 1.40, 2.43), so a full treatment of how integrity could be restored to them is à propos. Marcus also promised at 1.23 a consideration of the distinction in status of families by relation through the paternal line (*agnatio*). Such distinctions were, of course, critical in the law of inheritance (see *ad loc.*). This fact suggests that topics from the civil law received attention.[98] It is a problem whether the criminal law was also dealt with. Riggsby, 168 and 228 n. 54, thinks that it was sufficiently handled in Book 3, which, however, has not a word to say about the *iudicia publica* (see *ad* 3.8.1 and 11.10); were they to be eliminated or merely reserved for Book 4? If the introductory part of Book 4 framed very broad issues of crime and punishment, then the latter may have been the case; for it has been suggested that Cicero's preface to Book 4 included general reflections on human character such as are found in fr. ex inc. lib. 1 (*pravitate dissentiunt*)[99] as well as the eight types of punishment that Augustine attributes to Cicero (*civ.* 21.11).[100] There is also the reference at 3.29 to *educatio . . . et disciplina,* which Marcus proposes to discuss if the topic can be accommodated; Atticus replies encouragingly (3.30), but it is unclear whether the relatively brief remarks at 3.30–32 are all that was intended, or if Cicero had a more extensive treatment in view; if so, it could easily have formed the theme of an entire Book of *Leg.* (Book 5?), though one wonders how it would have been differentiated from the treatment of education at *Rep.* 4 (see *ad* 3.29).

98. In Book 6? So Schmidt, 2001, 15; but he assigns the discussion *de iure potestatum* to Book 4, rather than the appendix to Book 3; see *ad* 3.49.

99. So Schmidt, 1965, 319–20; cf. *ad loc.*

100. The passage is attributed to *Leg.* (as fr. 4) in Baiter and Halm's 1861 ed.; sim. Schmidt, *loc. cit.*

Finally there is the question of the total number of books Cicero planned
to write. One might have expected at least six, to equal the number of *Rep.*,
even if only five could be executed, but hard evidence eludes us.

8. Influence through the Centuries

References to *Leg.*, even in antiquity, are sporadic. The absence of such a
reference in any of Cicero's other works, including the catalogue of his philosophical writings at *Div.* 2.1–4, makes it very likely that it remained unpublished during his lifetime.[101] But not long after Cicero's death Cornelius
Nepos seems to refer to our work, *viz.* at fr. 58 Marshall, expressly assigned to
the *de Historicis Latinis* section of the *de Viris Illustribus;* this is preserved as
a prefatory note to the cod. Gudianus 278 (g) of Cicero's *Philippics:*

> *non ignorare debes unum hoc genus Latinarum litterarum adhuc non*
> *modo non respondere Graeciae, sed omnino rude atque inchoatum morte*
> *Ciceronis relictum. ille enim fuit unus qui potuerit et etiam debuerit*
> *historiam digna voce pronuntiare, quippe qui oratoriam eloquentiam*
> *rudem a maioribus acceptam perpoliverit, philosophiam ante eum in-*
> *comptam Latinam sua conformarit oratione. ex quo dubito, interitu eius*
> *utrum respublica an historia magis doleat.*

The passage is very similar in tenor to Atticus' evaluation of the state of
Roman historiography at *Leg.* 1.5–7, in particular the critique of earlier
writers as lacking polish (*quibus nihil potest esse ieiunius . . . quid tam exile
quam isti omnes? . . . habuitque vires agrestes . . . atque horridas sine nitore
ac palaestra* etc.). In *Leg.* Cicero's ability to correct these deficiencies is assumed based on the character of the genre as *opus . . . oratorium maxime,*
whereas Nepos spells out Cicero's contributions to oratory and philosophical
writing. Common to the two passages is the idea of Cicero's both being able to
produce and "owing" a history (*qui potuerit et etiam debuerit historiam
digna voce pronuntiare: . . . mihi videris . . . patriae debere hoc munus . . .
potes autem tu profecto satis facere in ea . . .*).[102] It seems only natural to

---

101. One might also have expected a reference to *Leg.* 1.41 ff. as a fuller exposition of the
doctrine that *utilitas* is a false value at *Fin.* 2.59; but instead Cicero simply says *deque his rebus
satis multa in nostris de republica libris sunt dicta a Laelio;* this fact suggests that by the
summer of 45 Cicero had abandoned any thought of publishing *Leg.* See also § 2b *supra.*

102. For comparison of the two passages cf. Edward A. Robinson, "Cornelius Nepos and
the Date of Cicero's *De Legibus*," *TAPhA* 71 (1940), 524–31, although his inferences about
the dating of *Leg.* (ibid. 529–31) are misguided; cf. Schmidt, 1959, 402 ff.

suppose that at the death of Marcus and Quintus Cicero a copy of *Leg.* either was in or passed into Atticus' possession and that he called Nepos' attention to this passage relevant to the preface of a work *de Historicis Latinis*. In view of Nepos' evident dislike of philosophy[103] it may be doubted that he turned the manuscript up on his own, let alone edited it.[104] Since Nepos had access to unpublished Ciceroniana in Atticus' hands, namely the letters to Atticus (cf. Nep. *Att.* 16.3), his knowledge of a passage of *Leg.* would not necessarily show that it was already published, though one suspects that, if anyone, Atticus would have seen to publication.

We must wait roughly a century for the next reference to *Leg.*, when it was consulted for its antiquarian lore by the elder Pliny. Within the section of Book 7 of the *Historia Naturalis* devoted to human life from birth to death, Pliny paraphrases Cicero's observations about the altered burial practice of the *gens Cornelia* from inhumation to cremation, which resulted from Sulla's fear that his remains might be disturbed, just as he had disturbed those of his enemy C. Marius; Pliny has also adapted the following definition of the terms *sepultus* and *inhumatus* (2.56–57 : *Nat.* 7.187). There is, however, no citation of *Leg.* by title; Cicero is merely given as one of the source-authors in the Index to this Book (1, p. 22 Mayhoff). It is surprising that Pliny failed to make more extensive use of the valuable information on Roman cult and government contained in *Leg.* 2–3.[105] Nor, to judge by the absence of reference to the work by Quintilian, did *Leg.* share in the popularity that the orations and rhetorical treatises enjoyed in the schools of rhetoric. The jurists, too, are conspicuously silent about *Leg.*[106] Plutarch seems to have known the work, however (cf. *ad* 2.54 and 58).

The fourth century offers the richest vein of ancient citation of *Leg.*,

---

103. Cf. *Att.* 16.5.5: *Nepotis epistulam exspecto. cupidus ille meorum, qui ea quibus maxime* γαυϱιῶ *legenda non putat*, where, in light of Lact. *inst.* 3.15.10 = fr. 39 Marshall, where Nepos disparages philosophy as a guide to life, *ea quibus maxime* γαυϱιῶ is often read as the philosophical works; cf. Shackleton Bailey *ad Att.* 410.5; Horsfall *ad* Nep. *loc. cit.*

104. The latter is suggested with a query by Schmidt, 1965, 325 n. 10. Likewise, the comparison of the ties between Cicero and Atticus on the one side and Cicero and Quintus on the other at *Att.* 16.2–3 (sim. *Att.* 5.3) need not point to *Leg.* in particular, since Nepos merely refers generally to published books as well as to the letters to Atticus as proof (Schmidt, ibid., 302, states that *Leg.* "als Beweis für die . . . Feststellung des Nepos dienen konnte").—There are points of contact between the preface of Sallust's *Historiae* and *Leg.* 1.5b–7 (see *ad loc.*), but it is not clear that this is a case of direct dependence; cf. Scanlon, 202–3.

105. Cf. Schmidt, 1965, 303–5.

106. Cf. D. Nörr, "Cicero-Zitate bei den klassischen Juristen," *Ciceroniana* n.s. 3 (1978), 111–50, esp. the conclusion (p. 143): "Die rechtsphilosophischen Partien des (im gewissen Sinne) juristischen Hauptwerkes Ciceros, der Bücher *de legibus*, blieben für die Jurisprudenz anscheinend folglos."

including the one ancient author who shows a grasp of the work's overall purpose, namely the man known since late antiquity as the "Christian Cicero," Lactantius (cf. Schmidt, 1965, 327 n. 19). Presenting Cicero as *non tantum perfectus orator, sed etiam philosophus* (*inst.* 1.15.16), he describes Cicero's achievement in *Leg.* this way: *Platonem secutus leges voluit ponere, quibus putaret usuram esse iustam et sapientem civitatem* (ibid. 1.15.23; cf. *Leg.* 3.29). Despite this degree of acquaintance and understanding, if Lactantius' ten express citations of *Leg.* were our only evidence, we would have a very one-sided picture of the work, for they are dictated by the author's theological agenda. Five are drawn from the anthropology of 1.22–28,[107] an important influence on Lactantius, especially the description of the human being (1.22)[108] with upright posture (1.26) and the concept of the *notitia dei* as a human monopoly (1.24), even though Lactantius conceded animals some forms of intelligence (cf. *ad loc.*). Three other express citations refer to the sacral laws of Book 2;[109] here he approves of Cicero's requirements of *castitas* and *pietas* and the removal of wealth from divine cult (2.19.1 cited at *inst.* 5.20.3) but has much to criticize in the list of licit deities a little later in the same chapter (*inst.* 1.15.23 and 20.19). One citation has with probability been assigned to Book 4 (see on fr. ex inc. lib. 1), another (fr. dubium) may belong in the lacuna at 2.28, and a third probably belongs rather to *de Consolatione* (see on fr. ex inc. lib. 2).

Far from always interpreting Cicero's words in light of their context, Lactantius is prepared, if it suits his purpose, to tear them out of context in such a way as to give them an altogether different meaning. A striking example occurs in the discussion of the creation at *inst.* 2.11.1 ff. Here Lactantius cites (anonymously) the words at *Leg.* 1.24 about the earth being in process of time prepared to receive the seeds of the human race; but in Lactantius' text it is not a *maturitas . . . serendi generis humani* but a *maturitas . . . animalium serendorum*. This is not a simple lapse of memory but is adjusted to the origin of animals as described at Lucr. 5.783 ff., which Lactantius now quotes and paraphrases. But a little later (§ 14) he cites with approval and explicit mention of author and work the description of the human being from *Leg.* 1.22.[110] Or, again, at *inst.* 6.25.1 Lactantius cites Plato's view, quoted by Cicero at *Leg.* 2.45, that ivory is an unsuitable gift

---

107. 1.22 at *inst.* 1.5.24 and 2.11.16; 1.27 at *opif.* 1.13; 1.28 at *inst.* 6.24.9 and *ira* 14.4.

108. In particular the words . . . *hominem, praeclara quadam condicione generatum esse a supremo deo* fit well with the Christian doctrine of the special grace of the creation; cf. Zielinski, 1929, 123.

109. 2.19 at *inst.* 1.15.23, 1.20.19, and 5.20.3.

110. Cf. Schmidt, 1965, 307–8; he discusses a similar phenomenon at 313.

for the gods and then goes on to criticize precious textiles as likewise unsuitable without mentioning the restrictions Plato imposes, in the same context, on allowable expense for such items.[111] From such examples it is clear with how much caution Lactantius' citations need to be used when the full text is not available as a control (i.e., fr. ex inc. lib. 1 and 2).

Though *Leg.* had nothing like the impact of the *Hortensius* upon St. Augustine, its influence is seen clearly in the wording of some passages, though Augustine tends to give similar terms a different meaning in accord with his very different overall system. Above all the definition of Augustine's basic concept, the *lex aeterna*, is clearly adapted from *Leg.*: *lex vero aeterna est ratio divina vel voluntas dei ordinem naturalem conservari iubens, perturbari vetans* (c.Faust. 22.27 = CSEL 25.6.1, 621.13–15);[112] cf. *Leg.* 2.8: . . . *legem . . . esse . . . aeternum quiddam . . . ita . . . legem . . . mentem esse . . . omnia ratione aut cogentis aut vetantis dei*; sim. 1.18: . . . *lex est ratio summa insita in natura, quae iubet ea quae facienda sunt, prohibetque contraria.* At the same time, however, the structure of Augustine's thinking about the *lex aeterna* and its relation to positive law is different from Cicero's view of the relation of natural and positive law since for Augustine they comprise two separate categories but not for Cicero.[113]

It would, of course, be of great interest if Augustine provided material useful for the reconstruction of portions of *Leg.* now lost. Schmidt, 1965, 320, has very plausibly suggested that Augustin. *civ.* 21.11, citing Cicero for eight types of punishment specified in laws[114] derives from a passage of Book 4, *de iudiciis*; cf. § 7 *supra*. Possibly another passage in Augustine may help us to understand the tenor of a passage in one of the preserved books that is marred by a lacuna. In question is Augustin. *lib. arb.* 1.48 (CSEL 74.6.3): *quid? illa lex quae summa ratio nominatur, cui semper obtemperandum est et per quam mali miseram, boni beatam vitam merentur . . . potestne cuipiam intellegenti non incommutabilis aeternaque videri?*[115] Perhaps we might look here for a part of the thought missing in the lacuna at the beginning of *Leg.* 1.40; for this idea of the happiness of those who obey *summa ratio* (for the term see *Leg.* 1.18, cited above) and unhappiness of those who do not is

---

111. Ibid., 315.

112. Schmidt, 1965, 323, first called attention to this passage as likely to derive from *Leg.*

113. See further K.M. Girardet, "Naturrecht und Naturgesetz: eine gerade Linie von Cicero zu Augustinus?" *RhM* 138 (1995), 266–98.

114. *Octo genera poenarum in legibus esse scribit Tullius, damnum, vincla, verbera, talionem, ignominiam, exilium, mortem, servitutem.*

115. Maurice Testard, *Saint Augustin et Cicéron* (Paris, 1958), 2, 17, called attention to the passage, albeit in connection with *Leg.* 1.18, not 1.40.

otherwise unexpressed in this direct form in *Leg.*, but the examples at 1.40–41 clearly imply the idea.[116]

Beyond its uses for Christian apologetic literature, *Leg.* was among the texts ransacked by grammarians in search of parallels for Vergil's language and matter. In his comment on *A.* 6.611 (*nec partem posuere suis*) Servius notes that one was expected to give to one's relations; he then paraphrases and somewhat simplifies Cicero's prohibition of *stips* and its rationale from *Leg.* 2.40. For *pectore toto* (*A.* 9.276) the Danieline Servius offers a citation of *Leg.* 1.49 to show that this is a proverbial phrase (*ubi illa sancta amicitia, si non ipse amicus per se amatur toto pectore, ut dicitur?*).[117]

Two otherwise unknown fragments of *Leg.* are cited by Macrobius.[118] In his treatise *de Verborum Graeci et Latini Differentiis vel Societatibus* Macrobius cites as an example of indicative for subjunctive the sentence from *Leg.* 3: *qui poterit socios tueri, si dilectum rerum utilium et inutilium non habebit?* Vahlen rightly inserted this in the lacuna at 3.17 as part of the commentary on the law *sociis parcunto* (3.9.4).[119] Our sole fragment from beyond Book 3, the fr. from Book 5, comes via Macr. *Sat.* 6.4.8 and is one of three passages cited to show that *umbraculum* (*Ecl.* 9.42) was not a Vergilian coinage; in view of grammarians' penchant for citing from the beginnings of Books as well as parallels to the beginning of Book 2, the passage is likely to be from the beginning of Book 5.[120] Thus in the early fifth century one could still read as many as five Books of *Leg.*

The medieval transmission of *Leg.* is discussed at pp. 40–42 *infra*. Once published (1471), the essay found admirers, among the earliest and most ardent of whom was the Spanish Christian humanist influenced by Erasmus, Juan Luis de Vivès (1492–1540).[121] In a preface to the work published in

116. Ibid., 2, 73, attention is drawn to the parallel of *quaest. hept.* 3.20 (CSEL 28, 249.2–4) to *Leg.* 1.19 (etymology of *lex*), though Cicero is not specifically cited (merely *Latini auctores*); however, Cicero appears to be unique among Augustine's predecessors in interpreting, like Augustine, *lego* in this etymology as "choose," rather than "read"; cf. Maltby s.v. *lex*.

117. Schmidt, 1965, 322.

118. For the dating of his literary activities to the 430s cf. Alan Cameron, "The Date and Identity of Macrobius," *JRS* 56 (1966), 25–38. The two citations of sentence-fragments from *Leg.* in the work of the early-fifth-century lexicographer Nonius Marcellus (for the date cf. Schmidt, 2000, 107) need not show personal acquaintance with the text, for *Leg.* is not one of the works he has systematically excerpted in a set order; rather, they seem likely to derive from a repertory of lexicographical examples. In question are Non. p. 307M s.v. *facessere* (*Leg.* 1.39: *paulisper facessant rogemus*); Non. p. 347M s.v. *molle* (*Leg.* 2.38: *in animos teneros atque molles influere quam varios canendi sonos*); cf. Schmidt, 1965, 321 and 331 n. 65.

119. See further on the fr. from Book 3.

120. So Schmidt, 1965, 321.

121. For Petrarch on *Leg.* see p. 42 and notes 149–50 *infra*.

1519, he praises *Leg.* highly, applying Pliny's encomium of *Rep., Off.,* and *Cons.* (*Nat. praef.* 22), that no other work (of pagan authors, he adds) is more worthy of being read, re-read, and learned by heart. While granting *Off.* superiority in quantity, he classes the two works together as occupying the apex which unaided human wisdom can attain.[122]

In the meantime the reception of the *lex naturalis* as defined in *Leg.* had taken place,[123] but it was the Christian deists of the seventeenth and eighteenth century for whom the content of Cicero's philosophical works had special significance. Starting from the view that natural religion alone was sufficient for salvation and developing a critique of revealed religion, the deists found in Cicero support for both their projects, on the negative side in *N.D.* and *Div.,* on the positive side in *Leg.*[124] Thus the founder of English deism, Edward Herbert, Lord Cherbury, praises *Leg.* as a "religionis veterum compendium" containing natural religion in its pure form[125] and cites it extensively.[126] Similarly, citing *N.D.* 1.84 on the benefits of acknowledging ignorance on the title page of the *Essay concerning Human Understanding,* John Locke demolishes the *consensus gentium* argument for the existence of God but leaves the cosmological argument standing with specific citation of *Leg.* 2.16 (*quid est verius—nulla ratione moveri putet?*).[127] The first publication of John Toland (1670–1722), *Christianity not Mysterious* (1696), exaggerating some ideas of Locke, brought its author notoriety. But a new phase of his philosophy is marked by the *Letters to Serena* (1704), the monarch addressed being Sophia Charlotte, queen of Prussia. He explains in the preface that the first letter had its origin when he showed the learned lady

---

122. Ioannis Lodovici Vivis Valentini *Praefatio in Leges Ciceronis et Aedes Legum,* ed. Constantinus Matheeussen (Leipzig, 1984) at *Praef. in Leg.* 22–24, esp. 24: "atque in hanc ipse opinionem adductus sum ut credam nullam humanam sapientiam viribus suis absque peculiari dei beneficio et munere ea quae in his Legum atque Officiorum libris scribuntur consequi potuisse."

123. Cf. Thomas Hobbes, *Opera philosophica quae Latinè scripsit omnia* (Amsterdam, 1568), no. 5, c. 2: "Est igitur lex naturalis, ut eam definiam, dictamen rectae rationis circa ea, quae agenda vel omittenda sunt ad vitae membrorumque conservationem, quantum fieri potest, diuturnam," where the combination of *Leg.* 1.18 and 23 with a version of the doctrine of οἰκείωσις ("ad vitae membrorumque conservationem . . ."; cf. *ad Off.* 1.11–17) is notable.

124. Cf. Günter Gawlick, "Cicero and the Enlightenment," *Studies on Voltaire and the Eighteenth Century* 25 (1963), 657–82 at 660; my treatment of deism owes much to Gawlick's paper.

125. *De religione gentilium* (Amsterdam, 1663), 184.

126. Ibid. 17: 2.37; 96: 2.40; 150: 242; 185 and 192: 2.28; 192: 2.27; 193: 2.21; 197: 1.40; 198: 2.22.

127. John Locke, *An Essay concerning Human Understanding* (orig. 1690), ed. Peter H. Nidditch (Oxford, 1975, based on ed. London, 1700), IV.10.6.

Leg. 1.47 (*sensus nostros—non cernimus satis*). She replied that she thought she *could* disabuse herself of prejudice but asked him to expound the subject in writing. The letter that resulted, "The Origin and Force of Prejudice," Toland considered to be the key to all his other works.[128] His last work, the *Pantheisticon* (1720), with its liturgical rituals of pantheists mocking those of the church, stirred scandal on a similar scale to his first; here the influence of our work is palpable in the description of the morally perfect man quoted verbatim from *Leg.* 1.59–62.[129]

Across the Channel *Leg.* was much studied, especially for its political implications, by the French *philosophes*. Montesquieu cites the work six times in his masterpiece, the *Esprit des lois* (1748),[130] but was, in spite of his warm admiration for Cicero, too original a thinker to be dominated by him to the degree that Toland was.[131] But it is in *Des droits et des devoirs du citoyen* of the abbé Gabriel Bonnot de Mably (1709–85) that the influence of *Leg.* reaches its apogee. The work is a series of dialogues between the author, who had defended the absolute monarchy in his *Parallèle des Romains et des Français* (1740), and an English friend, Lord Stanhope. The opening dialogue borrows from *Leg.* a peripatetic conversation in which the natural environment is the initial topic with a gradual shift to weightier matters, the "duties of the citizen," a phrase dropped as if by chance, coming to be the focus. In the final dialogue there is an explicit reference to the scenery of *Leg.*[132] The interlocutors agree on the point made at *Leg.* 3.2 that the magistrate has power over the citizen and the laws over the magistrate, but for the English-man an absolute duty of obedience could perpetuate evils. The first conversa-tion ends in disagreement, with the shaken author returning home and seek-ing guidance in his text of *Leg.*, where he comes upon the denunciation of unjust laws at 1.42. The following day he shows the passage to Stanhope, and

128. Unpublished letter of 28 December 1709 quoted by F.H. Heinemann, "John Toland and the Age of Reason," *Archiv für Philosophie* 4 (1952), 42. Cf. John Toland, *Letters to Serena*, ed. Günter Gawlick (facsimile rp. of 1704 ed.; Stuttgart-Bad Cannstatt, 1964); at pp. 4–8 Toland dilates on the themes of the Ciceronian passage.

129. John Toland, *Pantheisticon sive Formula celebrandae sodalitatis Socraticae* (Cosmo-poli, 1720), 83–85.

130. Montesquieu, *De l'esprit des lois*, ed. Gonzague Truc, 2 vols. (Paris, 1949): 2.2 : *Leg.* 3.34–37; 5.11 : *Leg.* 3.23; 12.19 : *Leg.* 3.44; 23.22 : *Leg.* 3.19; 24.13 : *Leg.* 1.40; 29.16 : *Leg.* 2.59.

131. Cf. Zielinski, 1929, 254.

132. Gabriel Bonnot de Mably, *Des droits et des devoirs du citoyen*, ed. Jean-Louis Lecercle (orig. Kell, 1789; Paris, 1972), 213: ". . . je me croyois transporté à Tusculum, je croyois me promener avec Cicéron sur les bords du Liris . . ." (a lapse of memory: the Liris is near Arpinum, not Tusculum!).

the conversation resumes. As in the case of Toland, a passage of *Leg.* serves as the basis for a decisive break with the past, in this case Cicero's critique of positive law calling into question any duty of absolute obedience to laws made by human beings. Mably, thus converted, provided in his turn arguments for the revolutionaries of France.[133]

But *Leg.* could not long sustain this position at the center of a discourse on the mutual rights and obligations of citizen and state. Several nineteenth-century developments diminished Cicero's influence in general and that of *Leg.* in particular. Cicero's position as one of the *auctores* ("authors" but shading into "authorities") who were read in school and whose views could be expected to play a part in educated discussion of almost any topic, a position maintained throughout the Middle Ages, the Renaissance, and the Enlightenment, was being challenged both by historians, like Wilhelm Drumann and Theodor Mommsen, who found Cicero to play a much smaller rôle in the historical process than his writings, taken at face value, might suggest,[134] and also by students of ancient philosophy, keen to uncover the Hellenistic Greek sources underlying Cicero's philosophical treatises. In light of this latter research Cicero would never again be described, as by Toland, as the "greatest philosopher."[135] A blow to *Leg.* in particular as the major source of Cicero's views on political philosophy was the discovery and publication in 1822 from a Vatican palimpsest of the fragments of *Rep.* by Angelo Mai. To the tantalizing *Somnium Scipionis* section, which survived the Middle Ages in the manuscript tradition of Macrobius' commentary, were now added substantial new materials, perhaps all the more fascinating because of their fragmentary state of preservation and unexpected rediscovery. Thus though over the last century and a half progress has been made in analyzing the textual tradition of our work,[136] it was *Rep.*, not *Leg.*, that was destined to occupy center stage in discussions of Cicero's political philosophy.[137]

---

133. The revolutionary assemblies adopted laws inspired by Mably's ideas; cf. Aldo Maffey, "Il Mably e la Rivoluzione francese," *Studi francesi* 20 (1963), 248–57, esp. 251 ff.; Georg Müller, *Die Gesellschafts- und Staatslehren des Abbés Mably und ihr Einfluß auf das Werk der Konstituante* (Berlin, 1932), ch. 5; Nippel, 1980, 156 n. 66, wrongly denies any influence to Cicero's constitutional theory because of the loss of most of *Rep.* until its discovery by Mai.

134. On this approach of historians to Cicero, by no means a thing of the past, cf. Christian Habicht, *Cicero the Politician* (Baltimore and London, 1990), 3–8.

135. John Toland, *Life of John Milton* (London, 1699), 147: "John Locke . . . must be confessed to be the greatest philosopher after Cicero in the universe"; and Cicero is "summus philosophus" at John Toland, *Collection of Several Pieces*, 1 (London, 1726), 232.

136. See § 10 *infra*.

137. See p. vii and n. 4.

9. Language and Style

De Legibus combines two basic types of material, each of which calls for a different stylistic treatment: there are (1) the dialogues among Marcus Cicero, his brother Quintus, and Atticus and (2) the laws themselves, set out in a moderately archaizing Latin. Within (1) there are further subdivisions: (a) the urbane framing conversations about Arpinum and the local landscape and legends; (b) the exposition of the doctrine of natural law in Book 1, for which Marcus adopts two different styles, so that it is first conducted *fuse ac libere,* then *articulatim distincte⟨que⟩,* though this description conceals rather than elucidates the nature of the distinction (1.36 with note); (c) the explanation and justification of the laws, mostly handled in a businesslike, down-to-earth style but occasionally, especially when the activities of P. Clodius become the focus, rising to emotional peaks (2.42–44; 3.21–22 and 25–26); embedded here, as in *Rep.,* are translations or paraphrases from Plato and Xenophon (2.45, 56, 67–68) as well as of Athenian laws (2.64). There is thus much more stylistic variety in *Leg.* than a categorization within the *aequabile et temperatum orationis genus* of philosophical writing (*Off.* 1.3) might suggest.

The reader of *Leg.* encounters a wider range of forms, vocabulary, and syntactic phenomena than appears in the speeches. The archaizing morphology is striking in the laws proper, where we find an abundance of "future" imperatives as well as such museum specimens as *ollos* for *illos, endo* for *in* (2.19.7), *escunt* for *erunt* (3.9.2), and third declension nom. pl. *-is* (3.6.5); there is even the unique form *appellamino* (3.8.2), whether a pseudo-archaism of Cicero's own invention or a corruption resulting from a double reading in the archetype (see *ad loc.*). Here, too, the archaic conjunction *ast* plays a rôle (3.9.2 etc.), and *nec* is used in the archaic fashion as equivalent to *non* (2.22.1). There are some archaic spellings, e.g., *duellum* (2.21.2, 3.9.2 and 4), *loedis* (2.22.2), *coeret* (3.10.7); in our manuscripts this is not consistently carried through, however; cf. *bella* (2.21.7) and *ludorumque* and *curatores* (3.7.1). But in one case outside the laws Cicero uses a form he elsewhere eschews in prose, namely the third-person plural perfect in *-ere,* in imitation of the style of the historians he is discussing (*successere:* 1.6; see *ad loc.*);[138] and *duellum* appears, not only in his own laws (see above) but also to lend archaic color to the translation from Plato's *Laws* at 2.45.

In his commentary on the laws Cicero shows himself a keen observer of

---

138. It is not clear why he uses *sequare* at 1.36, rather than *sequaris,* in spite of his preference elsewhere for the *-ris* forms in the second-person singular present.

usage and includes notes on the meanings of such words as *humatus* and *lessus* (2.57 and 59). This sensitivity is on display in his own vocabulary in this treatise, enriched by poeticisms, e.g., *catus* (1.45), *delubrum* (in the law at 2.19.5 but also in the translation from Plato at 2.45), *opaco* (fr. from Book 5), possibly *fatidicus*, though it is not attested in earlier poetry (cf. *ad* 2.20.5). The poetic and archaic may overlap, as in the case of *suboles* (3.7.3). In its archaic diction *Leg.* is sometimes comparable to *Rep.*, as in the use of *proles* in both works (3.7.3; *Rep.* 2.40); the archaic *sepse* at 1.34a may be a reminiscence of the earlier dialogue (see *ad loc.*). There are also apparent coinages of new words: *coangusto, commendatrix, compositor, conciliatrix, deducta* (as a substantive), *diiudicatio, effatum* (as a substantive), *emendatrix, obtemperatio, perturbatrix, saepimentum,* and *temperamentum* all appear here for the first time.[139] The two new substantivized participles (*deducta, effatum*) also show Cicero's tolerance for technical terms from the sphere of commercial and augural law, respectively.[140] To the former sphere also belong Greek loan-words such as *syngrapha* (3.18), also admitted in the speeches, or *astu* (2.5); nor does Cicero avoid calling the νομοφύλακες by their Greek name (3.46); he likewise cites, and translates, the Solonic word τύμβος (2.64) and does not hesitate to use the Greek-derived *prooemium*, which he earlier avoided (cf. *ad* 2.16).[141] There are also new metaphorical usages, as Cicero strives to expand the Latin vocabulary to match the demands of the content, often dictated by Greek sources.[142] Here we meet for the first time *intellegentiae* as an equivalent for the ἔννοιαι of the Stoa (cf. *ad* 1.26b), but the term is introduced unobtrusively, without the fanfare of *Fin.* 3.3–5. In addition I would single out *aequalitas*, first used at 1.49 of equality of rights under law; see further the Index of Grammatical and Stylistic Features s.vv. "Coinages" and "Metaphor." Generally he succeeds in concealing the gaps in Latin, as in his rendering of Plato's μονόξυλον without needing to use a compound (cf. *ad* 2.45).

The syntax of the laws is also consciously archaizing, with its use of *-que* as the predominant sentence-connector (cf. *ad* 2.19.9), as well as the archaic *-que . . . -que* coordination (cf. *ad* 2.21.2); the archaic organization with relative clause preceding main clause, sometimes with a single word drawn

---

139. See the Index of Latin Words s.vv.

140. At 2.45 *exemplum* occurs in a technical legal sense; and *cado* used with *in* plus ablative may also be based on legal usage; see *ad* 2.19.9.

141. On Greek loanwords in *Leg.* see further Päivo Oksala, *Die griechischen Lehnwörter in den Prosaschriften Ciceros* (Helsinki, 1953), 136.

142. By 45 he could claim: *quo in genere* [sc. the expression of ideas] *tantum profecisse videmur, ut a Graecis ne verborum quidem copia vinceremur* (*N.D.* 1.8; cf. *Fin.* 3.5).

out of the relative clause and placed in front, is striking, e.g. at 2.19.2: *qui secus faxit* (see *ad loc.*). There is also some innovative syntax on the Greek model, including the adnominal dative (*obtemperatio scriptis legibus*: 1.42). Though Cicero's translations from Greek show an expected reduction in the use of the participle (see *ad* 2.67–68), there is some adumbration of the fuller exploitation of its verbal properties characteristic of his later style: cf. 3.35: . . . *Lucio Cassio . . . dissidente a bonis atque omnes rumusculos populari ratione aucupante.*

As one expects from Cicero, the various registers of the Latin language are all played with great virtuosity. The range is wide, from the teasing exchanges between Marcus and Atticus (esp. 1.21 and 36), written in a *sermo urbanus* not dissimilar to that of the correspondence and marked by such features as intensification with the *per-* prefix rather than the fussier suffixes,[143] to the full-throated encomium of *sapientia* at 1.58–62; there is even a mini-philippic denouncing P. Clodius *tacito nomine* at 2.42–43. The whole armory of Ciceronian rhetoric is brought forward as appropriate, including diminutives expressive of contempt, personifications, puns, *praeteritio,* tricola, the effect capped by resonant clausulae; see the Index of Grammatical and Stylistic Features s.vv.; Index of Latin Words s.v. *per-*. On the other hand, it must be said that there are patches that are not as carefully worked up as one expects in a publicly circulated Ciceronian work, and this appears not only in a less well thought through content[144] but also in the style, e.g., 3.19b: . . . *cuius . . . ortum . . . procreatum videmus.* On occasion it is difficult to know whether we should be emending away the roughness of Cicero's draft; see, e.g., *ad* 1.46, 2.28.

10. The Text

The centuries following the fifth exacted a heavy price from *Leg.* as from the Latin classics generally. The archetype of our surviving medieval codices (Powell's ω = Schmidt's x) emerged in the ninth century; it was, as shared errors and lacunae show, a single, badly mutilated manuscript, written already in minuscule characters; it may also have contained double readings; cf. *ad* 1.33, 2.20.1, 29, 62a, 2.15b; p. 448 n. 22; 3.8.2, 33; Zelzer, 2001, 198 and 209–10.

---

143. On Cicero's special fondness for *per-* cf. J. André, "Les adjectifs et adverbes à valeur intensive en *per-* et *prae-*," *REL* 29 (1951), 121–54, esp. 141–47; cf. also Parzinger, 120–22; Powell *ad Sen.* 3. The omission of *quam* with a comparative at 3.9 has been attributed to the influence of the spoken language; cf. *ad loc.*

144. See the Index of Topics s.v. "Incompleteness or Lack of Final Polish."

De Legibus belongs to the so-called Leiden corpus of nine Ciceronian philosophical/rhetorical works named after the Dutch city that houses several of the principal witnesses, including the two earliest codices of *Leg.*, Voss. F.84 (A) and 86 (B), both written in France in the mid-ninth century. As the last item in the Leiden corpus *Leg.* is, not surprisingly, mutilated at the end, with the loss of the conclusion of Book 3 and at least two additional Books.[145] At the next level, there were two hyparchetypes: one manuscript, B, forms a hyparchetype by itself, its independence shown by its unique preservation of ⟨es⟩se debeat through enumerare sententias at *N.D.* 1.1–2, whereas the other branch (y) needs to be reconstructed from two other witnesses, one (Powell's ε) the exemplar of the three fifteenth-century witnesses E (Leid. Periz. F 25), R (Rouen, Bibl. Mun. 1041), and S (Paris, BN Lat. 15084). It has been suggested that ε may be identical with another member of the Leiden corpus, Vindobonensis 189 (V, also of the ninth century), which survives for other works, but not for *Leg.* The other branch of y, namely w, is reconstructed from another Leiden manuscript (Leid. BPL 118 = H, eleventh century) and L (London, Burn. 148, 13th century). The third Leiden manuscript of *Leg.*, A, has been, on grounds of its age, much overrated in the past; it appears to offer a text contaminated from the B and y traditions.[146]

A famous name in the transmission of the Latin classics is associated with the ninth-century copies of *Leg.*: A and B both passed through the hands of Hadoard of Corbie, and he may be the author of the corrections designated by Powell A^a;[147] and Corbie was the center from which copies of *Leg.* spread. Especially influential was F (= Laur. Marc. 257, 9th century), an amalgam of A and B; and F^2 is the source of some notable conjectures. After F, already

---

145. For the end of Book 3 cf. *ad* 3.49; for the (at least) two additional books see § 7 above.

146. Cf. in general Schmidt, 1974, summarized by Schmidt, 1973, as well as the Praefatio to Powell's edition. Powell goes beyond Schmidt in arguing (6.5) that common errors of A and B can be ascribed to contamination (he cites a telling example from 1.26, where B's *formaultioris* is evidently the source of A's *formatioris*, whereas ESRHL have *formavit oris*) and that there is no reason to deny that the true readings of ESRHL may derive from the archetype, rather than from conjecture, as Schmidt, 1974, 95–96, suggested. Powell adds that there appears to be no passage of *Leg.*, not even at the end of Book 3, where B and H are missing, where A alone preserves the true reading. A different view of the history of the text is offered at Zelzer, 2001, doubting that scribes of the ninth and tenth century engaged in much conjectural emendation and challenging the existence of the Leiden corpus as such; for *Leg.* they posit a Late Antique archetype and three lines to it represented, respectively, by AB, H, and FK; these arguments will be dealt with elsewhere.

147. Cf. Schmidt, 1974, 142 ff.; for skepticism of such conjectural activity on Hadoard's part cf. Zelzer, 2001, 211–12.

containing the F^2 conjectures, was copied in western Franconia (M = Monacensis Univ. 528.4), it came to be lodged in the Strasburg cathedral.

Although *Leg.* was not a school text in the Middle Ages,[148] in the twelfth century a special edition of the work, p, was created apart from the rest of the Leiden corpus; its main representative is P (Berlin, Phillipps. 1794, end of the twelfth century; cf. Schmidt, 1974, 201 ff.); this witness is in the line of ε, though possibly with some influence from B and A (cf. Powell's Praefatio, 6.6). Circulated at first in France, southern Germany, and England, a text of the p type arrived in Italy with Petrarch's help ca. 1350, and this was soon the dominant form of the text there. Petrarch twice cites from *Leg.* 2 in a letter of consolation on the misfortune of a friend who died and remained unburied.[149] In one of the letters addressed to Cicero he complains that *Leg.*, together with *de Orat., Ac.,* and some unnamed speeches, has survived in so mutilated a state that it were almost better had they perished altogether![150] During the Council of Constance Poggio discovered F on a journey up the Rhine and created his own text (Vat. Lat. 3245) based on comparison of F with a codex of the p type; he also marked almost all of the lacunae recognized by modern editors and reassigned the parts to the appropriate speakers;[151] the result was a much more readable text than the one Petrarch had complained of. Versions of Poggio's text spread widely, and the *editio princeps* (Rome: Sweynheym and Pannartz, 1471) stands in that tradition.

The figure on page 43 is Powell's stemma (after Schmidt) illustrating the major relations but does not attempt to represent the chronology.

Citations of *Leg.* in ancient authors hold out the possibility of seeing beyond the confines of the tradition preserved in the archetype, but the material is less rich than one might have hoped. There are at most only four fragments that go beyond the scope of the medieval text: the fr. from Book 3, which evidently belongs in the lacuna at 3.17; the fr. from Book 5

148. Cf. Ernst Robert Curtius, *Europäische Literatur und lateinisches Mittelalter,* 3d ed. (Bern-Munich, 1961), 59 = *European Literature and the Latin Middle Ages,* tr. Willard R. Trask (London, 1953), 49–50; Schmidt, 2000, 105 ff.; Günter Glauche, "Die Rolle der Schulautoren im Unterricht von 800 bis 1100," in *Settimane di studio del centro italiano di studi sull'alto medioevo* 19.2 (1972), 617–36, esp. 630.

149. Petr. *Fam.* 2.2.16 (*Leg.* 2.57) and 19 (*Leg.* 2.58: the exception to burial within the city-walls granted for outstanding achievement; Petrarch wrongly assigns the passage to Book 3).

150. Ibid. 24.4.14: "Quin et superstitum librorum magnas partes amisimus, ut velut ingenti prelio oblivionis et ignavie superatis, duces nostros non extinctos modo sed truncos quoque vel perditos sit lugere. Hoc enim et in aliis multis, sed in tuis maxime oratoriis atque achademicorum et legum libris patimur, qui ita truncati fedatique evaserunt, ut prope melius fuerit periisse" (the fuller recension of *de Orat.* was, of course, discovered later).

151. Cf. Schmidt, 1974, 285, and 2000, 27; for the earlier confusion cf. *ad* 1.1.

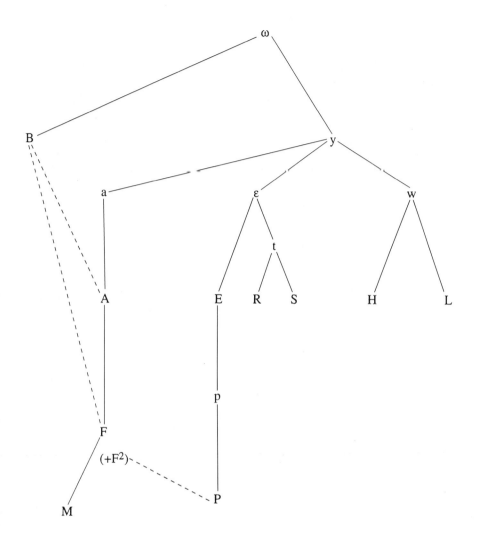

(= Macr. 6.4.8); fr. ex inc. lib. 1 (= Lact. *inst.* 5.8.10), belonging either to the lacuna at 1.33–34 or to Book 4; and fr. dubium, possibly from a lacuna in 2.28; the other fragment claimed for *Leg.* probably derives from *Cons.*; see *ad* fr. ex inc. lib. 2.

Relevant citations, all deriving from Lactantius,[152] rarely provide help in emending the preserved text. Though he sometimes alludes to and cites *Leg.* at length, the variant readings are few. Given that he is probably relying on memory, not much weight can be attached, e.g., to his variations in word order. Thus at *ira* 14.4 he cites *Leg.* 1.28 with the order *doctorum hominum* rather than *hominum doctorum*, as in the manuscripts of *Leg.*; but at *inst.* 6.25.9 he cites the same passage with *hominum doctorum*.[153] Some passages are more paraphrase than exact quotation, such as the treatment of 1.24 at *inst.* 2.11.1. There are also, of course, syntactical adjustments to the new context, as in the quotation of *Leg.* 2.19.1–2 at *inst.* 5.20.3. Of interest to the editor of *Leg.* are *inst.* 1.15.23, where the citation of 2.19.7 includes the reading *locaverunt* restored by Powell for ω's *vocaverint; inst.* 3.10.7–8, where Lactantius' *haberi* seems preferable to *habere*[154] transmitted at *Leg.* 1.24; and in the same passage his omission of the second *agnoscat* seems likely to be right; see *ad loc.*

Current editions of *Leg.* are not based on the stemma indicated above, which is primarily the result of the work of P.L. Schmidt. Though he provided no stemma, Vahlen had already founded his first edition of the text (1871) closely on A and B; in his second edition, while insisting in the preface on the correctness of his previous practice, he added the readings of H to his apparatus. In his Heidelberg text (1949, 1963) Ziegler treats A, B, and H (whose agreement is designated as V) as equal partners in constituting the "echte Überlieferung" (p. 13), whereby, inevitably, too little weight is given to B and too much to H and (especially) A.[155] In revising Ziegler's edition, though acquainted with Schmidt, 1974, Görler (1979) made it his principle "so wenig wie möglich von der bis jetzt gesicherten Tradition (B, A und H) abzuweichen" (p. 115); the possible is reduced to instances where the trans-

---

152. For Lactantius' use of *Leg.* cf. pp. 31–33 *supra*; Schmidt, 1965, 305–21.

153. Cf. also the change of order in the citation of 1.22 at *inst.* 4.4.6: *hominem praeclara quadam condicione a supremo deo esse generatum* vs. *hominem praeclara quadam condicione generatum esse a supremo deo* (*Leg.* mss.).

154. There is another Lactantian passive for an otherwise attested active (*consecrari* for *consecrare*) at *inst.* 1.20.16 (paraphrase of *Leg.* 2.28; see *ad loc.*).

155. On the inflated traditional estimate of A see p. 41 and n. 146 *supra*. For difficulties with the selection of mss. in the other recent edition of *Leg.*, that of de Plinval, cf. Schmidt, 1974, 395–96.

mitted text is incomprehensible and the correction open to no intelligent doubt (p. 17). In practice that means that the text has been relieved of many of Ziegler's unnecessary changes but at the price, at times, of a degree of awkwardness not found in Cicero's other works. Görler's justification is that this work never received the *summa manus;* therefore "Unebenheiten sind . . . geradezu zu erwarten" (p. 17).

Ziegler, 1953, 303, argued that, since *Leg.* is a corrupt text, the editor should be granted greater freedom to change the transmission. This Görler denies (pp. 16–17). Ziegler's argument needs to be restated in terms of the state of the manuscript tradition: if the tradition itself is weak, resting, as in the case of *Leg.*, essentially on a single pillar (ω), then the transmitted text needs to be scrutinized very critically and with reference to the author's practice in other works. We cannot know in what state Cicero left his manuscript (though there are phenomena that can be taken as signs of a lack of final polish; see the Index of Topics s.v. "Incompleteness"), but even letters quickly dashed off and not polished for publication show elegance of expression, not awkwardness (cf. *Fam.* 3.11.5: *si, ut scribis, eae litterae non fuerunt disertae, scito meas non fuisse*). It is also true that *Leg.* has not been much studied of late even by professional Latinists, so that solutions for some cruces may be attainable.

A new edition of *Leg.* has been prepared by J.G.F. Powell and should appear in about a year's time. He gives a full inventory of the stemmatically significant readings; readers should also refer to this edition for a full explanation of manuscript sigla and the like. Readings are cited here according to Powell's edition, which he very kindly made available to me prior to publication; we have discussed the textual problems in detail (hence the use in the commentary of the first-person plural of textual decisions), as is shown by the textual notes in the commentary, where, with his generous permission, his views are often cited. The text may be called "moderately reformist," i.e., the transmitted text is subjected to rigorous scrutiny with a view to bringing it up to the stylistic level of Cicero's other works without resorting to an implausible degree of rewriting. In the process the character of the archetype has been borne in mind, including the possibility that it contained double readings, and the types of errors scribes were likely to fall into, especially saltation errors (see the Index of Topics s.vv. "Archetype, suspected double readings in"; "Haplography"; "Saltation error"), as well as Cicero's rhythmical preferences.

Commentary on Book 1

atqui nos legem bonam a mala nulla alia nisi naturae norma dividere possumus.

—Cic. *Leg.* 1.44

Within the economy of *de Legibus* Book 1 performs several essential functions.[1] It indicates the reason Cicero is providing, after *de Republica*, a second work on political philosophy, and it establishes the status of *ius* and of the laws that will be put forward in the subsequent Books. This work is to stand in relation to *Rep.* as Plato's *Laws* to his *Republic* (§ 15; cf. 2.14), and Cicero's laws are to be adapted to the kind of state espoused by Scipio in the earlier work (§ 20), i.e., a mixed constitution. The approach to be taken also needs to be clarified. After the setting of the scene and a bow to Atticus' historical interests, Cicero defines the subject so as to clear away possible misunderstandings: the reader is not to look for a treatment, as in earlier Roman legal literature, of the *ius civile* or its parts; rather, the subject is more broadly defined as *ius ipsum* or *ius civitatis,* and this is going to be explored from a philosophical angle, i.e., it will be traced back to its source

---

1. The text is that of the OCT of J.G.F. Powell, whence also derive all reports of manuscript readings; see p. 45 *supra;* since I am not printing a full critical apparatus, my lemmata make a more extensive use of brackets than he does in order to alert the reader to departures from the archetype. Capitalization is used in lemmata for the beginning of a speech or the initial letter of a paragraph; the speaker's initial is indicated only if there is a change from the speaker of the preceding lemma. In general "Marcus" is used of the dialogue speaker, "Cicero" of the author or historical figure. *Delenda* are enclosed within { } since square brackets are used to mark the end of lemmata. I have used "—" in lemmata for an ellipsis to indicate that the intervening words are also included but " . . . " when the reference is only to the cited words and not the omitted matter. Sections of the particular book of *Leg.* under discussion are referred to simply with "§" preceding the paragraph number, with book number preceding for the other books. When there is a paragraph break within a section (or other break in sense which I expressly indicate), I have, for greater precision, often referred to section numbers with "a" or "b" attached to indicate matter before or after the break. All dates are B.C. unless otherwise indicated. My commentary on *de Officiis* is cited without author's name. The most detailed and subtlest interpretation of *Leg.* is that of P.L. Schmidt; I have in general preferred to cite the 1959 dissertation rather than the 1969 printed version, in which much of the detailed interpretation has been excised.

(§§ 14–17), though there will be some scope for comment on the *iura et iussa populorum,* including the Roman *ius civile* (§ 17).

After an *exordium* on the implications of the Greek and Latin terms for "law" (§§ 18b–19), Cicero goes on to provide a "preliminary fortification" for the project (cf. § 34b: *quae praemuniuntur omnia reliquo sermoni disputationique nostrae*) by undertaking to show, based on a survey of the qualities of the human being, that *ius* is in accord with human nature (§§ 20–34a). This argument is basically an adaptation of the old Stoic doctrine of the community of sages, who were said to have a law based not on written enactments but on right reason shared by all. At some point[2] this concept of natural law was broadened to include all human beings, and it is in this form that Cicero uses it. The second argumentative section comprising §§ 40–47, the *refutatio* (Schmidt, 1959, 221), argues against the contrary view that *ius* is by convention only (and thus can be circumvented when it is in the individual's interest to do so); here, too, the central point is human nature, in particular the predisposition to love one's fellow humans (§ 43: *haec nascuntur ex eo quia natura propensi sumus ad diligendos homines, quod fundamentum iuris est*). Law is to be judged by the *naturae norma* (§ 44) and thus legitimated through ethics, the ethics of "life according to (human) nature." Approached in this way, the philosophy of law is a philosophy of the human being; hence Book 1 as a whole can be called Cicero's anthropology[3] or, more precisely, anthropology in the service of the thesis that justice is by nature.[4] An appendix (§§ 48–52a) argues that the virtues are to be sought for their own sake. In transitional passages placed before and after the *refutatio* (§§ 36–39 and 52b–57) Cicero seeks to establish a broad front of philosophical schools in good standing that can be expected to agree with this position and whose differences on the *finis bonorum* are said to be trivial (cf. Perelli, 116); the strategy is comparable to the kind of *consensus bonorum omnium* that has marked Cicero's political thinking since *Sest.* (Mehl, 137–38). This Book, which has emphasized a philosophical approach to its topic (cf. § 17: ... *penitus ex intima philosophia hauriendam iuris disciplinam putas?*), concludes with (1) an encomium of *sapientia* based on the precept "know thyself," which, as explored in Pl. *Alcib. I,* formed the introduction to philosophy in the Academy, and including a

2. The guesses have included Chrysippus, Antiochus, and Cicero himself; cf. *ad* §§ 28b–34a and 23 and p. 50 n. 6 *infra.*

3. Cf. Richard Harder, *Kleine Schriften,* ed. Walter Marg (Munich, 1960), 399–400; Boyancé, 1970, 265.

4. Compare the concise, goal-oriented treatment of this theme from late antiquity that survives at [Alex. Aphr.] *de An.* 2 (= Suppl. Aristot. 2) 156–59.

survey of the three traditional "parts of philosophy" (see *ad* §§ 58–62), and
(2) Cicero's personal confession of its importance to him and its rôle in
forming his own character (§ 63). The contents may be outlined as follows
(cf. Schmidt, 1959, 229):

I. Frame, leading to the definition of the subject (1–17)
   A. The putative "Marian oak" and the relation of "Dichtung und
     Wahrheit" (1–5a)
     1. Atticus' guess that a certain oak tree must be the one men-
       tioned in Cicero's *Marius* (1a)
     2. The question parried by Quintus and Marcus (1b–5a)
   B. Historiography as a field for potential cultivation by Marcus
     (5b–12)
     1. Atticus' report of the state of the genre (5b–7)
     2. Problems of the scope of the work (8) and of the time re-
       quired (9–12)
   C. The definition of the subject (13–17)
     1. Atticus' query (13)
     2. Marcus' reservations (14)
     3. Philosophical contextualization (15)
     4. Plan of treatment in Book 1 (16)
     5. Definition of the subject and plan for the whole treatise (17)
II. The *principia iuris* (18–35)
   A. *Exordium:* terms for "law" in Greek and Latin (18–19)
   B. Establishment of premises (20–21)
     1. Relation of the *leges* to *Rep.*
     2. Atticus concedes divine government of the world (in contra-
       diction of Epic. κυρ. δοξ. 1)
   C. *Praemunitio* on the derivation of *ius* from human nature (22–34)
     1. Relation of the human being to the deity (22–28)
       a. *Ratio* in the human being as basis for the relation to god
         (22–23)
       b. Creation of the human being as a proof of the relationship
         (24–25a)
       c. Proof from the gifts of Nature (25b–27)
     2. The similarity of human beings as an indicator of a natural
       community of law (28–35)
       a. Equivalence of community of law and similarity (28–29)
       b. Proof of similarity (30–32) based on
         1. A shared definition (30a)

Unlike his practice in some other works (notably *Off.* 1.6–7), Cicero is not forthcoming about naming his source(s) in *Leg.* (cf. the vague *doctissimis viris . . . placuit:* § 18). Hence the various theories on the subject. In spite of Cicero's having modeled the idea of writing *Leg.* as a sequel to *Rep.* on his view of the relation of Plato's *Laws* to his *Republic* (cf. § 15), Plato himself was not the source of *Leg.* 1, as Turnebus showed, pointing rather to Chrysippus' definition of law (p. 750; cf. *ad* § 18b). This position remained standard through most of the nineteenth century until it was challenged by du Mesnil (p. 9), who inferred from 3.14 that Cicero regarded the older Stoa as barren on these issues and was likely to have turned instead to Diogenes of Babylon and Panaetius. On the basis of the same passage, apparently independently, Thiaucourt, 28, concluded that Cicero must have followed Panaetius here, and the point was argued vigorously by Schmekel, 47–54. Another Stoic candidate, Posidonius, was put forward by Heinemann, 2, 225–77, as the source of *Leg.* as a whole, limited by Reesor, 51, to Book 1 only. The claim of the Academy to be Cicero's source was revived, however, by Hoyer, who, on the basis of the *Carneadea divisio,* attributed to Antiochus of Ascalon and found at §§ 37–39 as well as *Fin.* 2.35, assigned the whole of Book 1 to Antiochus. Reitzenstein supported this position with new arguments, and it has won the backing of Theiler, Luck, Philippson, 1939, 1121.18–19, and, most recently, Boyancé (followed by Schmidt, 1969, 173–74). It remained for Finger to offer the syncretistic solution whereby in Book 1 Cicero followed Panaetius, Antiochus, and Posidonius in turn.

The lack of consensus on the question of the source or sources suggests an incommensurability of means and ends. Source-criticism as traditionally practiced seldom yields satisfactory results for Cicero,[5] for it is based on the premise that a single source is being followed fairly closely. But, far from being a philosophical hack, Cicero was widely read and fully capable of doing his own excerpting of points of interest to him,[6] formulating his own critique of philosophical arguments,[7] and adapting them to context (cf. *ad* §§ 58–62). Moreover, the Hellenistic texts among which his source(s) would have been found have survived, if at all, in a highly fragmentary state. Large inferences from limited evidence, such as those cited in the last paragraph, are nowadays viewed with considerable skepticism. Thus Barnes,

---

5. An exception is *Off.* 1–2, where there are clear guidelines; cf. Dyck *ad Off.,* p. 19, but also, with modifications well worth considering, esp. for Book 2, Eckard Lefèvre, *Panaitios' und Ciceros Pflichtenlehre* (Stuttgart, 2001).

6. Cf. Jonathan Barnes, "Cicero's *de Fato* and a Greek Source," in *Histoire et structure. À la mémoire de Victor Goldschmidt,* ed. J. Brunschwig, C. Imbert, and A. Roger (Paris, 1985), 230–32. Thus Mehl, 131, 147–49, and 282, argues that Cicero himself has patched the argument of *Leg.* together from Stoic and Platonic sources.

7. As, presumably, in the refutation of Cratippus' argument for divination at *Div.* 2.107–9.

1989, concludes that "the large claims which *Quellenforschung* has made on [Antiochus'] behalf are unproven and improbable" (89). A sober approach to possible sources should begin by differentiating clearly between the literary frame of *Leg.* 1 and the literary model for the plan of *Leg.* on the one side and the doctrines argued for in the body of Book 1 on the other.

One of the most attractive features of *Leg.* is the care Cicero has lavished on the literary frame. For our Book he has drawn upon the mise-en-scène to Plato's *Phaedrus* with a nod to Plato's *Laws* as well; see the Introduction § 5. But, if Plato has provided both a respectable peg on which Cicero can hang a second work on political philosophy after already having written *Rep.* and an attractive frame for this first Book, the contained doctrines can be called Stoic or Stoicizing, whereby "Stoicizing" is a periphrasis for Antiochus of Ascalon, *qui appellabatur Academicus, erat quidem si perpauca mutavisset, germanissimus Stoicus* (*Luc.* 132), though the difference may have appeared to others greater than it did to Cicero (or to Antiochus himself; cf. *N.D.* 1.16). In the body of the Book there is some language reminiscent of Plato or the Academy, *viz.*, the image of the "sowing of souls" at § 24 or the reference to pleasure being like a natural good in § 31—signs either that Cicero's source has already added some Platonic features to the essentially Stoic doctrine of natural law[8] or that Cicero himself added minor Platonic touches to what he found in a Stoic source.[9]

As a Skeptic, Cicero is, in fact, chary of identifying his argument too closely with any of the dogmatic schools. As in politics he sought a *consensus bonorum omnium*, so here he is at pains, rather, to create a broad front of schools in good standing against the positions he excoriates (§§ 37–39). The line taken on the *finis bonorum* could qualify as either Old Academic or Stoic (cf. *ad* § 56 and the similar strategy at *Off.* 3.33); and the reference to Antiochus at § 54 is distancing rather than endorsing.[10] Similarly, Cicero is reluctant to associate the opponents he criticizes at §§ 40 ff. with any school. As Inwood points out *(per litt.)*, this is not merely out of politeness to his Epicurean interlocutor, Atticus; rather, "he wants to have a broadly conceived utilitarian whipping boy and a broadly conceived position which uses law as central to ethics. And this latter position has to be broad, since he needs to exploit both Platonic and Stoic elements to construct the anti-utilitarian

---

8. Girardet, 1983, emphasizes the contrast between Cicero's view of natural law and that of the Stoa; but cf. *ad* § 17.

9. Görler, 1995, 86, speaks of Cicero's work as "an amalgam of Stoic and Platonic elements"; see the introduction to Book 2 for the Platonic elements there.

10. Vander Waerdt, 1994, 4871, perhaps makes the matter too simple when he supposes that the praise of Antiochus at § 54 "provides a clear source citation"; see further *ad loc.*

position on the nature of law which he is aiming at." Nor is it an accident that the version of the Stoic τέλος-formula Cicero cites stands close to Antipater (§§ 56 and 59); as the author of three books arguing that, according to Plato the καλόν is the only good (*SVF* 3, 252.31–32), he was a natural mediator between the Stoic and Platonic positions. The criticism of the Stoa at §§ 55–56 suggests, however, that the Academy (i.e., Antiochus) lies at the bottom (of this section only, or of the whole Book?).

Finally, some special problems of Book 1 need to be considered, namely the lack of a personal preface, the peculiar nature of some of the philosophical argumentation, and the state of the transmitted text.

Unlike *de Orat., Rep., N.D., Fin., Tusc., Sen.,* and *Amic., Leg.* lacks a personal preface. There has been considerable discussion of whether the author would have added one prior to publication.[11] Robinson has pointed out that *Leg.* and *Part.* alone among Cicero's dialogues lack a non-dramatic preface.[12] It has been argued by Schmidt, 1969, 45–49, and accepted by Rawson, 1991, 129–30, that it is unnecessary to assume that a preface was planned, since most of the matter in such prefaces, *viz.*, the scene and list of characters, is indicated in the opening lines of the dialogue and such personal concerns as an author might address in a preface[13] are interwoven at §§ 5–12. Moreover, Cicero's model, Plato's *Laws*, has no preface; Cicero might be engaged in an experiment under Plato's influence.[14] But it may be objected to this theory that one would expect the dramatic date and the identity of the dedicatee to be clarified in the preface. To take the latter point first: an analogue might be sought in *Div.*, a dialogue likewise without a formal dedication but with Quintus as interlocutor and, implicitly, dedicatee; cf. Pease *ad Div.* 2.150 and pp. 15–16; similarly, *Part.*, with Marcus jr. as interlocutor and implicit dedicatee. But doubts have also been expressed about the completeness of *Div.*,[15] and *Leg.*, with its three interlocutors, would seem to require a preface to clarify the dedicatee's identity. Schmidt notes that the full title of the work is not transmitted; it might have

---

11. Cf. literature at Schmidt, 1969, 45 n. 40.

12. Edward A. Robinson, "Did Cicero Complete the *De Legibus?*," *TAPhA* 74 (1943), 109.

13. Cf. Tore Janson, *Latin Prose Prefaces: Studies in Literary Conventions* (Stockholm, 1974), 35, with reference to the reflections at *de Orat.* 1.1–3 on the possibility of a statesman obtaining the *otium* needed for literary pursuits.

14. Schmidt, 1969, 48, sees the influence of *Laws* on the scenery of *Leg.* as stronger than that of the *Republic* on *Rep.* The point is true in itself (cf. *ad* 1.15 and 2.1 and 3, though the influence of *Phaedr.* on the scenery of *Leg.* is more important; see the Introduction § 5); but this would not necessarily imply a change in Cicero's dedicatory practice.

15. Cf. G. Sander, *Quaestiones de Ciceronis libris quos scripsit De divinatione* (diss., Göttingen, 1908), 5 ff.

included the dedicatee's name, as did, e.g., the title of *Fin.* and *Brut.*[16] Perhaps the dedicatee was indicated in the original title, but it is also unparalleled for the dedicatee's name to be transmitted in the title alone and not also clarified in the text. The lack of a fixed dramatic date is generally admitted to point to the incompleteness of *Leg.*[17] The lack of a personal preface in a work without a clear dedicatee may have been another gap Cicero meant to fill in; it was sometimes his practice to add the preface after the composition of a work was already under way.[18] One might also have expected some explanation of Atticus' trip to Arpinum, just as Cicero is careful to sketch the background to the meeting at Crassus' Tusculan estate at *de Orat.* 1.24–27.[19] It cannot be excluded, however, that some of these matters were handled in lacunae in our text.

If Cicero was able to adapt some topics and modes of analysis learned in his philosophical studies to courtroom use (cf. *ad* § 63), so too he imports into his philosophical writing some of the vigor and energy of the practicing advocate. This feature is particularly in evidence in our Book in the rhetoric of the *refutatio* and the transitional passages on either side. Cicero does not scruple to use personal invective against the Epicureans (*sibi autem indulgentes et corpori deservientes . . . :* § 39), to ridicule his opponents or reduce their claims to absurdity (esp. §§ 49–52)—in stark contrast to the ordinarily placid discourse of philosophy. This is not an accident or an isolated occurrence. As a reader of philosophical writing, Cicero came to the conclusion that many philosophers—especially Stoics—provided an excessively jejune *patrocinium* for their case, and he aimed to show how it could be done better. *Leg.* 1 is an early example of the technique.[20]

Finally, like the other extant Books of *Leg.*, Book 1 is disfigured by lacunae. These occur after §§ 33, 39, and 57. There is no way to ascertain the extent of the losses with certainty, in spite of some efforts to do so (cf. *ad* § 40). The last lacuna is particularly unfortunate since in it some of the procedural plans for the essay seem to have been lost (see *ad loc.*).

1–13 In the tradition of the Socratic dialogue the characters are introduced

---

16. Schmidt raised this possibility in private discussion.

17. Also by Schmidt, 1969, 52.

18. *Att.* 16.6.4 (25 June 44).

19. Sim. Reid: "Cicero has . . . not imitated the *Phaedrus* in one respect, for there are in it several pages leading up to the πλάτανος scene. One would expect an explanation of how Atticus took the journey to Arpinum." For Atticus as possible dedicatee of *Leg.* cf. the Introduction § 6; *ad* 3.1.

20. See further Walter Englert, "Bringing Philosophy to the Light: Cicero's *Paradoxa Stoicorum*," *Apeiron* 23 (1990), 117–42.

in a specific setting and, in imitation of actual conversation, only gradually focus on the major topic of discussion. Prior to that, several subjects are broached, with the original impetus arising from the dialectic of nature and poetry in the mind of Atticus as he seeks confirmation for his hunch that a certain very old tree is the oak referred to in Cicero's poem, *Marius* (§ 1). From there the discussion expands to the difference between poetic and historical truth (§§ 3–5a), to the current state of Roman historiography and the possibility of Marcus' coming to its rescue (a possibility rejected on grounds of lack of time: §§ 5b–8), and finally to the giving of legal advice as an occupation for Marcus' old age (§§ 10–12). Then Atticus has the bright idea of using the "leftover" time now available for a discussion of the *ius civile*, a topic of interest both to himself and Marcus since the days when they sat at the feet of Scaevola the Augur (§ 13). Marcus himself is the unifying force that holds this discussion together: his poetry, his possible contributions to historiography, his use of his leisure are the topics. By setting the scene in the countryside of Arpinum near his ancestral home and assigning parts to his best friend Atticus, his brother Quintus, and himself, Cicero contrives to make this conversation look unforced. The prologue exists here, as in other dialogues, to establish the character and relations of the interlocutors: Marcus at the center; Atticus, sympathetically engaged with Marcus' work; Quintus, a man of opinions capable of disagreeing with his brother (§ 8; cf. 3.26 and 33). The prologue also serves to explain why Cicero has not tackled historiography, in spite of demands that he do so (*postulatur a te iamdiu, vel flagitatur potius, historia*, Atticus reports [§ 5b]). It also provides a plausible background for Atticus' request in § 13 that introduces the main subject.

1–5a The opening chapters of *Leg.* display Marcus on his native soil, surrounded by his best friend and his brother, the center of his own intellectual world (cf. Schmidt, 1959, 140 ff.). The initial conversation turns upon his poem *Marius*, his potential contribution to historiography, his use of his leisure, etc. Even the order of speakers is so arranged that the secondary characters precede and prepare the way for the protagonist (Pohlenz, 1938, 104 = 412). As it has come down to us (but see the introduction to this Book), the dialogue has its starting point in a concrete object, an oak tree supposed by Atticus to be the oak mentioned in Cicero's *Marius*. As a boy, Marius caught in his cloak an eagle's nest containing seven young, an incident the soothsayers interpreted as portending that he would attain the consulate seven times (cf. Plut. *Mar.* 36.8; App. *BC* 1.61). Atticus' attempt to construe a one-to-one correspondence between the natural and the literary oak is rebuffed first by Quintus, then by Marcus, the former on grounds of the independence of poetic creations from real prototypes, the latter with reference to legends not to be taken seriously. This opening then leads to Quintus' comparison of poetic and historical truth, further elaborated by Marcus (§ 5a), and to historiography as a field for Marcus' potential cultivation (§§ 5b–12) before the actual topic of the dialogue is finally broached. **1** As the guest, Atticus is given the first word. He is seen visiting Arpinum for the first time (cf. *ad* 2.2 and 4); one such visit was planned in early May 59 (*Att.* 2.16.4; 2.17.1).[21] In the early 80s he had been a fellow student with Marcus of Scaevola the Augur (§ 13) and with both brothers in Athens in 79 (*Fin.* 1.16 and 5.1), and he was the brother-in-law of Quintus by November 68 (*Att.* 1.5.2); hence an earlier visit, though unattested, could easily have occurred.

The setting in Arpinum is clearly a homage to Cicero's roots; cf. Gasser, 49. Hirzel, 1895, 475, sees the Marian oak as a symbol of Roman history, from which Cicero's ideas about the polity and law arise. On the other hand, Becker, 29, denies a connection between the proems and contents of the individual Books, since the argument of Book 1 proceeds from nature, whereas Book 2, which begins with a description of nature, is more historical in orientation. But this is a bit too schematic: the oak pointed to by Atticus at the beginning of Book 1 is a natural object, though its historical status remains in doubt, and the historical evolution of the Italian communities and their relation to Rome is one of the topics of the proem to Book 2. Nevertheless, it seems doubtful that Cicero meant for the setting to have a general symbolic function of this type (cf. the detailed arguments of Gasser, 38 ff. and 46[22]).

Perhaps the connection between the Marian oak and the content of *Leg.*

---

21. On the fictive date of the dialogue see § 5 of the Introduction.

22. The same objections apply to the theory of Ulrich Eigler, "Von der Platane im 'Phaidros' zur Eiche des Marius—vergangene Zukunft in Ciceros 'De Legibus,'" in: M. Flashar, H.-J. Gehrke, E. Heinrich, eds., *Retrospektive. Konzepte von Vergangenheit in der griechisch-römischen Antike* (Munich, 1996), 139, that the constructed rural setting may be meant to suggest an ideal past which Marcus' legislation should help to instantiate. On the other hand, Benardete, 295, sees the "Marian oak," with its unclarified historical status, as an emblem of *Leg.* itself, "meant to supply the legislation for a regime that no longer exists except in speech," i.e., the regime of the dictator Scipio Aemilianus forestalled by his sudden death in 129 (cf. *Rep.* 6.12; that such a rôle was actually weighed for Scipio is the thesis of Claude Nicolet, "Le *De Republica* [VI, 12] et la dictature de Scipion," *REL* 42 [1964], 212–30; Lehmann, 40, is rightly skeptical). But the laws of *Leg.* 2–3 are never brought into relation to a putative regime of Scipio Aemilianus, merely, as § 20 shows, to the ideal state sketched in *Rep.* without reference to such an eventuality (for Scipio's name in *Leg.* as mostly a code for *Rep.* cf. the introduction to Book 3). Cicero expresses the purpose of this discussion generically, not with reference to a single state: *ad respublicas firmandas . . . omnis nostra pergit oratio* (§ 37).

should be sought at a different level. It raises the general problem of the relation of *opinio* to *natura, opinio* in this case being the construction Atticus places upon a particular oak tree, *natura* the tree itself. Marcus will revert to this question in the course of the following dialogue (with a tree used as an example: § 45). Indeed, the whole foundation of the system of law that he propounds will rest upon situating judgments of value *(honestum, turpe)* on the side of *natura* rather than *opinio*. Thus the deceptiveness of *opinio*, suggested already in the introductory scene, will play a rôle in the coming argument; cf. §§ 29, 31, and 47. In addition, the Marian oak was "planted" by Cicero the poet and gives rise to general questions about the relative durability of natural and poetic planting (cf. § 1: *seminari, serunt*) of a stem or trunk *(stirps)*. The project of this Book is to find the *stirps* of right and involves the "planting" of morals *(serendi etiam mores)*: § 20; cf. *ad loc.* The success of Cicero the poet in "planting" and insuring the longevity of the Marian oak is perhaps a challenge to Cicero the lawgiver to create something just as durable in *Leg.*[23]

A. Lucus quidem ille et haec Arpinatium quercus agnoscitur, saepe a me lectus in Mario.] Modern editors, after Poggio, distinguish three speakers and designate them as Atticus, Quintus, and Marcus (though to label the first speaker "Titus" would be more consistent; in the dialogue he is called by both names). In general, attributions of parts appear in the manuscripts only from the twelfth century onward and carry no authority; thus Poggio had to lay to rest the confusion of the p recension (to which one of his codices belonged; see *supra* p. 42, which distinguished as speakers Titus, Quintus, Atticus, and Pomponius (!); cf. Schmidt, 1974, 285; 2000, 27.—This first sentence economically sets the scene and establishes the first topic of discussion. It is, as Gasser, 32, observes, an original means of launching a dialogue to have a character recognize a place on the basis of a literary reminiscence. The inclusion here of the word *Arpinatium* pays homage to Cicero's native city—a nice touch if this was meant to be the opening sentence of the work (see the introduction to this Book). *Quercus* can be limited by an ethnic, as in the phrase *quercus Dodonaea* at *Att.* 2.4.5; that oak had, of course, quasi-proverbial

---

23. The comparison of the farmer and his seeds to the person possessing knowledge of the just, the beautiful, and the good at Pl. *Phaedr.* 276b ff. shows a similar concern with the durability of planting, though there the suggestion is that oral transmission is better suited to the task than written; on this passage cf. Szlezák, 12–16; on the relation of our passage to the *Phaedrus* see the Introduction § 5.—Gasser, 34, emphasizes that "im ersten Buch haftet den Naturbeschreibungen etwas Mechanisches an"; certainly they are not there for their own sake, *pace* those (cited ibid., 32) who have seen the setting as an expression of Cicero's connection with nature and his native place.

status; *Arpinatium quercus* seems to imply the same for the tree mentioned in the *Marius.*—Located ca. sixty miles southeast of the capital, Arpinum was a Volscian city that Rome seized from the Samnites in 305; it received the *civitas sine suffragio* two years later and the *civitas cum suffragio* in 188 (Liv. 10.1.3 and 38.36.7); since the Social War it had the status of a *municipium* (cf. 2.5–6; *ad* 3.36); cf. Hülsen, *RE* 2.1 (1895), 1218.36 ff.— For *haec Arpinatium quercus agnoscitur* cf. the query Phaedrus addressed to Socrates: ὁϱᾷς οὖν ἐκείνην τὴν ὑψηλοτάτην πλάτανον; (*Phdr.* 229a8). Phaedrus goes on immediately to explain the practical advantages—shade, a moderate breeze, and grass on which to sit. No such practical considerations but only literary interest prompts Atticus' remark, however,[24] even though *Leg.,* like the *Phaedrus,* is set on a hot summer day (cf. *ad* 2.3). The plane tree in the *Phaedrus* gives rise to the dialogue in the sense that it provides beneath its shade a venue for carrying on a discussion. The Marian oak, on the other hand, provides both the venue and the subject-matter for the first stage of conversation in *Leg.,* but these will soon be superseded.—The chiastic arrangement (a natural one in Latin; see Berry *ad Sul.* 2.2) of nouns and demonstratives leads the reader from the more remote to the nearer, from the undifferentiated mass to the specific individual that will form the first topic of discussion.—The use of the passive voice *(agnoscitur)* seems a bit stilted; one might have expected *lucum . . . illum et hanc . . . quercum agnoscere videor, saepe a me lectum . . .*

Saepe a me lectus in Mario: for the common idiom *lego* with accusative instead of the preposition *de* cf. Reid *ad Luc.* 3 *(quos legisset).*—For the reference of *lectus* to *lucus* over the intervening *et haec Arpinatium quercus agnoscitur* cf. parallels at S. Lundström, *Vermeintliche Glosseme in den Tusculanen* (Uppsala, 1964), 47 ff.—Atticus was a keen student of Cicero's works; indeed, he was normally their first recipient, for he rendered Cicero a service by reading and criticizing his drafts prior to general circulation and seeing that his works were copied by trained slaves and circulated.[25] The orator relied on his judgment in matters of literary propriety and proper Greek; he also consulted his friend as an expert on historical questions; cf. R. Feger, *RE* Suppl. 8 (1962), 512.62 ff.

This phrase, as well as the citation of Scaevola in § 2, bears upon the date of Cicero's *Marius,* which is controversial. In contention are a date in the 80s (advocated by E. Koch, 60–63, and Pietro Ferrarino, "La data del

---

24. Contrast in this regard the allusion to the plane tree at *de Orat.* 1.28.

25. Cf. E.J. Kenney in *The Cambridge History of Classical Literature,* ed. E.J. Kenney and W.V. Clausen, 2 (Cambridge, 1982), 20; R. Sommer; Shackleton Bailey, *Att.* 1, Introduction, p. 13; Murphy, 495 and 499.

Marius Ciceroniano," *RhM* 88 [1939], 147–64) and one in the 50s (the latter argued for in most detail by Gnauk, 49 ff.). Those who argue for the early date claim a reference here to Scaevola the Augur, whose granddaughter Licinia (*RE* s.v. Licinius no. 184) married the younger C. Marius; but there are chronological difficulties,[26] and that Scaevola is not known to have written poetry. Those who favor the later date see a reference rather to the poet attested at Plin. *Ep.* 5.3.5, possibly the same as a Scaevola mentioned in Cicero's correspondence. Courtney *ad* Cic. frr. 15–16 points out that the verse *canescet saeclis innumerabilibus* is echoed by Cinna (fr. 1.2 Courtney), whose fame for *cana saecula* was prophesied by Catullus (95.6), so that it looks as though the verse of our Scaevola belongs in a context of neoteric encomium. The proponents of the early date also point to the words *in montis patrios et ad incunabula nostra / pergam* cited at *Att.* 2.15.3 (late February 59) = fr. 13 (dubium) Courtney; if they derive from the prologue to the *Marius*,[27] a later date would be excluded; cf. Pohlenz, 1938, 109 = 417. But those words, echoed at Verg. *A.* 3.105 *(mons Idaeus ubi et gentis cunabula nostrae)* and possibly at *Leg.* 2.4 *(gaudeo igitur me incunabula paene mea tibi ostendisse)*, might rather be Ennian; cf. Shackleton Bailey *ad Att.* 35.4. Finally, the metrical technique of the fragments is more mature than that of the *Aratea* (cf. Büchner, *RE* 7A1 [1939], 1264.46 ff.), but the sample is small. On balance, the late dating seems more probable.

sin manet illa quercus, haec est profecto; etenim est sane vetus.] It is a question of whether the present oak *(haec)* can be identified with the famous one *(illa)*.—*Etenim*, as often, in part proof, adducing a telling index or sign (cf. *TLL* s.v., 918.79 ff.). *Sane* often adheres to *est*, particularly when there is a predicate adjective: *Cat.* 2.21: *quartum genus est sane varium; Phil.* 2.59: *difficilis est sane reprehensio; Leg.* 3.27 (where restoration of *est* is very likely; see *ad loc.*); *Lael.* 62; *Off.* 1.65; *Fam.* 2.4.1; *OLD* s.v. *sane* 8a.—Oak was a tough wood, *robur,* the generic term (of which *quercus* is a species), being a metaphor for strength and hardiness; cf. *OLD* s.v. *robur.* Similarly long rooted in the Arpinate soil is Cicero's own family: *hinc enim orti stirpe antiquissima sumus* (2.3). The oak also had patriotic associations

---

26. It is doubtful that Scaevola the Augur, who is last attested opposing Sulla's demand that Marius be declared a *hostis* (V.Max. 3.8.5) and probably died early in 87 (so F. Münzer, *RE* 16.1 [1933], 435.37–40), lived long enough to see the return of Marius to Rome (probably toward the end of 87: Weynand, ibid., Suppl. 6 [1935], 1416.59–60), let alone a poem written to celebrate that event.

27. Or might these words, rather, express Marius' decision, at the crisis, to flee for safety to his native district (cf. *Pis.* 43)?

since the *corona civica* awarded for saving the life of a fellow citizen was woven from its leaves; cf. Haebler, *RE* 4.2 (1901), 1639.28 ff.

Q. Manet vero, Attice noster, et semper manebit; . . .] One might have expected the reply to come from the poet himself, but instead Quintus intervenes—the somewhat awkward result of the transference from a two-person dialogue (the *Phaedrus*) to a dialogue among three speakers. This procedure does, however, enable the encomium of the *Marius* to be spoken by someone other than the poet (cf. *ad* 3.14: *Puto posse, et quidem aliquem de tribus nobis*); it also establishes the rôles of the minor characters, followed, after a certain small amount of suspense, by the first intervention of the main speaker (cf. *ad* §§ 1–5a).—With *manet* Quintus takes up Atticus' *manet* and transfers it from the physical to the literary plane; cf. the similar transference of the plane tree of the *Phaedrus* at *de Orat.* 1.28 (quoted in the next note). Quintus' reply is surely not a "misunderstanding" of Atticus (so Benardete, 296) but a conscious correction.—This form of address for T. Pomponius is not found in the body of Cicero's letters until 50 (cf. Adams, 1978, 159–60; Shackleton Bailey, 1995, 26–27) and may be a factor in the dating of the dialogue; see the Introduction § 2a. Cf. *Fin.* 5.4: *ita enim se Athenis collocavit ut sit paene unus ex Atticis, ut id etiam cognomen videatur habiturus.* The *praenomina* of Atticus and Quintus, but not of Marcus, appear in this work; indeed in none of the dialogues in which he represents himself as a character do any of the other interlocutors address him by name; cf. the detailed discussion by Dickey, 1997, who sees no particular point in the phenomenon; Adams, 1978, 162, refers it to "the common delicacy which deters a man from mentioning his own most intimate name"; ibid., he comments on the absence from *Leg.* of *mi* with the vocative. In the solemn conclusion of this Book Marcus uses the more formal *Pomponi*; cf. *ad* § 63.—*Et semper* with repetition of the verb in a different tense is a formula for emphasizing continuity found ten times in Cicero's speeches and essays; for the shift from present to future cf. *Planc.* 89 *(est et semper erit)*; ibid. 94 *(quod ego et facio . . . et semper faciam)*; *Phil.* 1.14 *(licet et semper licebit)*; sim. Plin. *Ep.* 2.1.11: *vivit enim vivetque semper;* the shift from present to future is also found without *semper;* cf. Wills, 302 and n. 21; Woodman and Martin *ad* Tac. *An.* 3.12.5.

sata est enim ingenio. nullius autem agricolae cultu stirps tam diuturna quam poetae versu seminari potest.] "*Sata est enim ingenio* looks to me very unlike Cicero, who would write *est enim ingenio sata* or *sata enim ingenio est*" (Reid); his apparent premise is that the "banal" collocation *sata est* (cf. Adams, 1994, 40) should be broken up. But focused word + *esse* often precedes *enim* (see examples at Hand, 2, 401 ff.), and, if the second *i* of *ingenio* is treated as a glide (cf. *ad* § 22 *fin.*), the clausula is cretic + iamb.— The comparison of "Dichtung und Wahrheit" is reminiscent of the remarks about the plane tree of the Platonic *Phaedrus* that set the stage for the conversation in *de Orat.* (1.28; Scaevola to Crassus): *nam me haec tua platanus admonuit quae non minus ad opacandum hunc locum patulis est diffusa ramis quam illa cuius umbram secutus est Socrates, quae mihi videtur non tam ipsa acula quae describitur quam Platonis oratione crevisse* . . . Both passages emphasize the greater power of literature in insuring, in the one case, growth, in the other, permanence.—This is the second attestation of *semino* and the earliest in what was surely the original sense, "to plant"; cf. *OLD* s.v.

A. Quo tandem modo, Quinte, aut quale est istuc quod poetae serunt? mihi enim videris fratre laudando suffragari tibi.] Request for an explanation combined with a suspicion that his brother-in-law, also a poet (see Courtney, pp. 179–81), may be paying himself a backhanded compliment.—With *quo tandem modo* understand *seminant poetae*. Atticus' *serunt* then takes up and varies Quintus' *seminare*. Atticus pursues the matter further with the poet himself at § 3 *(tuine versus hanc quercum severint?).*—*Fratre* (B¹) is preferable to *fratrem* (BᵃAᵃPHLε) in point of Latinity (cf. Kühner-Stegmann, 1, 752).—A favorite word of Cicero, *suffragor* has the sense "auxilio sum, commendo, iuvo, obsequor" (Forcellini s.v., 2, citing our passage); as Reid observes, "flatter" is often, as here, the best English rendering.

2 Q. Sit ita sane {verum}; verum tamen, dum Latinae loquentur litterae, quercus huic loco non deerit quae Mariana dicatur, . . .] *Sit ita sane* grants a concession, followed immediately by the strong adversative *verum tamen;* for the pattern cf. *Luc.* 139 (with the order *sit sane ita*); Reid compares the Greek pattern with εἶεν . . . δέ (cf. LSJ s.v. εἶεν).—The dittography of *verum* was removed already by S (Paris. lat. 15084, s. xv).—*Loquor* with literature (as here; *OLD* s.v. *littera* 8b; also *Dom.* 86; *Luc.* 5), monuments (*Brut.* 181) or the like as subject appears to be a Ciceronian innovation (*OLD* s.v. *loquor* 1c; *TLL* s.v., 1660.83 ff.). Translate "as long as Latin literature shall have a voice" (Reid), i.e., exist.

. . . eaque, ut ait Scaevola de fratris mei Mario, 'canescet saeclis innumerabilibus'; . . .] This is probably the man who was tribunus plebis in 59; cf. *ad* § 1; F. Münzer, *RE* 16.1 (1933), 447.29 ff. (Mucius no. 23); ibid. 446.27 ff. he infers from *Q.fr.* 1.2.13 that this Scaevola was in Quintus' *cohors amicorum,* but this is implausible, given the other names listed there; see Shackleton Bailey *ad loc.* The fragment = no. 1 (p. 186) Courtney. The durability of poetic creations was a *topos* of Greek poetry; cf. Kiessling-

Heinze *ad* Hor. *Carm.* 3.30.2; Eduard Fraenkel, *Horace* (Oxford, 1957), 302 and n. 3.

nisi forte Athenae tuae sempiternam in arce oleam tenere potuerunt, aut quod Homericus Ulixes Deli se proceram et teneram palmam vidisse dixit, hodie monstrant eandem.] On Atticus' residence in Athens *(Athenae tuae),* probably dating from ca. 86, his capture of the goodwill of the Athenians (albeit he also served as advisor to Sulla in his theft of artworks), but refusal of Athenian citizenship cf. R. Feger, *RE* Suppl. 8 (1956), 505.18 ff.—Just as the Greeks and Romans generally prized things of great antiquity, so ancient trees were connected with saga and closely watched for omens; besides the cases mentioned in our text cf. Str. C 598 (the oak that marked the outer limit of Hector's advance when Achilles was in the fray, according to *Il.* 9.352–54); Tac. *Ann.* 3.61.1 (an olive tree at Ephesus clinging to which Latona was thought to have given birth to Apollo and Diana); ibid. 13.58 (withering of the *ficus Ruminalis* interpreted as an omen; cf. Fest. 169M as restored by Müller; Plin. *Nat.* 15.77); cf. also the sign of the bees alighting on the eponymous laurel tree of Laurentum at Verg. *A.* 7.59 ff.—The longevity of the putative "Marian oak" challenges comparison with two famous Greek trees. The sacred olive of the acropolis was thought to have been planted by Athena in her contest with Poseidon for status as the tutelary deity of the place and to be the source of all the olives of Attica; when burned by the Persians, it was said to have put forth new shoots the following day; it is supposed to have survived to the second century A.D.; cf. A. Schulten, *RE* 17.2 (1937), 2016.62 ff. (s.v. Ölbaum); Burkert, 1985, 85.— *Quod* = "in regard to the fact that"; Turnebus changed *quod* to *quam,* but *quam . . . palmam* would be a single-noun phrase, and it would be odd for it to be interrupted by another focused element, namely *Deli,* shown to be such by the position of *se.*[28]—Addressing Nausicaa, Odysseus compares her to a φοίνικος νέον ἔρνος (Cicero's *teneram; proceram* is perhaps inferred from the following ἀνερχόμενον) seen beside the altar of Apollo on Delos (*Od.* 6.162–63); there are problems with the botany, however, since the true palm is not indigenous to the northern Aegean, and the young plant should be short and squat, not tall and thin; cf. Hainsworth *ad loc.*

multaque alia multis locis diutius commemoratione manent quam natura stare potuerunt.] This generalizes and summarizes Quintus' point about the greater longevity of cultural constructs as compared with products of nature.

quare 'glandifera' illa 'quercus', ex qua olim evolavit 'nuntia fulva Iovis,

---

28. I am grateful to J.G.F. Powell for clarification of this point.

miranda visa figura', nunc sit haec; . . .] *Glandifera* and *nuntia—figura* are respectively frr. 15 and 16 at p. 174 Courtney; Cicero economically conjures up the whole scene for the reader familiar with the poem. Another portent narrated in the *Marius* is the description of the eagle's battle with a snake at fr. 17 p. 175 Courtney (modeled on *Il.* 12.200 ff.), an omen of Marius' massacre of Sulla's followers, seen upon his return to Italy from Africa. Such touches place the *Marius* in the category of works containing *fabulae* (cf. § 5). Cf. E. Koch, 64–65.—*Glandifer,* formed on the analogy of βαλανηφόρος, is a poetic epithet for an oak also at Lucr. 5.939 *(glandiferas inter curabant corpora quercus)* and Ov. M. 12.328 *(glandiferam quercum).* On compounds in *-fer* cf. in general Françoise Bader, *La formation des composés nominaux du latin* (Paris, 1962), 107 ff.; on their relation to compounds in -φορος cf. J.C. Arens, "*-fer* and *-ger,*" *Mnem.* 3 (ser. 4) (1950), 241 ff.—The yellow of *fulvus* shades sometimes more toward red or brown, sometimes even to green (cf. Gel. 2.26.11); it is an epithet applied in poetry to subjects as varied as rivers, mud, and, notoriously, olive branches (Verg. *A.* 5.309).—*Visa* may be used of omens; cf. Luc. 1.635: *di visa secundent;* cf. φαίνομαι used of epiphanies, e.g., at *Il.* 1.197–98 (of Athena): στῆ δ' ὄπιθεν, ξανθῆς δὲ κόμης ἕλε Πηλείωνα, / οἴῳ φαινομένη . . . —Reid found *nunc sit haec* "a most unusual ending," but this order enables a cretic rhythm to follow the quotation, and, as Adams, 1994, shows (summarized p. 89), the copula may be expected to follow an emphatic word (*nunc* here refers to discourse time; translate: "for present purposes" or the like; cf. Risselada, 117–18); *haec sit* may have been felt as too abrupt.

sed cum eam tempestas vetustasve consumpserit, tamen erit his in locis quercus, quam Marianam quercum vocent.] *Vocant* is transmitted; Klotz had conjectured *vocabunt* in accord with Kühner-Stegmann, 1, 144–45 ("In Nebensätzen wird das Futur gebraucht, wenn die Handlung mit einer zukünftigen Handlung des Hauptsatzes gleichzeitig ist," etc.). Manutius' *vocent,* however, is likelier; cf. Kühner-Stegmann, 2, 304–5, on Cicero's preference for subjunctive in such instances where other authors would use indicative; hence the ease of corruption.

3 A. Non dubito id quidem. sed haec iam ⟨non⟩ ex te, Quinte, quaero, verum ex ipso poeta: tuine versus hanc quercum severint, an ita factum de Mario ut scribis acceperis?] Not satisfied with Quintus' answer, simply an amplification of his previous claim of the poet's power of conferring greater longevity than nature, the skeptical Atticus[29] turns to "the poet himself" to inquire whether his account rests upon tradition or poetic fancy; this emphasizes

29. Cf. Haury, 163.

slightly the oddity of Quintus' intervention at § 1 (cf. *ad loc.*).—The omission or corruption of negatives is not uncommon in the transmission of this work[30] (*non* is supplied in PH^N); besides the two instances in this chapter cf. § 54, 2.29, 42, 57, and 3.39.—A form of *fieri* accompanied by *de* and a personal object is relatively uncommon in Cicero and probably has its roots in the sphere of legal procedure and legislation, as is suggested by *Inv.* 2.113 (. . . *eo praemium postulet, uti de se praeiudicium factum esse videatur*) or *Fam.* 12.25.1 (*factum de te senatus consultum honorificum;* sim. *Att.* 3.26.1); cf. *Ver.* 3.45: *quod quidem   nullo umquam de homine factum est, ut . . . ; Att.* 15.1.1: *o factum male de Alexione!* Cf. also 3.45: *nihil omnino actum esse de nobis.*

M. Respondebo tibi equidem, sed non antequam mihi tu ipse responderis, Attice: . . .] For the tactic of dictating the order of questions cf. Pl. *Gorg.* 463c, where Socrates insists that Polus should ask him ὁποῖον μόριον τῆς κολακείας . . . εἶναι τὴν ῥητορικήν before he will say whether he regards it as καλόν or αἰσχρόν.

certen⟨e⟩ non longe a tuis aedibus, inambulans post excessum suum, Romulus Proculo Iulio dixerit se deum esse et Quirinum vocari, templumque sibi dedicari in eo loco iusserit; . . .] *Certen* is the reading of AB, whereas H offers *certe non;* the interrogative particle is needed, but not in the comic form *certen* (but cf. *viden* at *Fam.* 9.22.3); hence Powell's *certen⟨e⟩.*— Cicero's response is to reduce the question *ad absurdum* by citing tales that, though traditional, are wildly improbable; cf. Benardete, 298: "Cicero's question implies that tradition does not differ from a poet's free invention," i.e., both bear the same relation to the truth. He shows his urbanity, however, by connecting his points with complimentary references to Atticus' houses; cf. *ad* 2.5 (*ut vestri Attici*); cf. the critique of Epicurean tenets tied to a recital of the deeds of Torquatus' famous ancestors at *Fin.* 1.23–24.—In question is the *domus Tamphiliana* that Atticus came into on the decease of his uncle Q. Caecilius in September 58, which is thus a *terminus post quem* for the fictive date of the dialogue (see the Introduction § 5); cf. Nep. *Att.* 13.2; Cic. *Att.* 3.20.1. The house was on the Quirinal between the temples of Quirinus and Salus; hence Cicero's joke about Caesar's statue (*Att.* 12.45.2; mid-May 45): *de Caesare vicino scripseram ad te . . . eum* σύνναον *Quirino malo quam Saluti;* cf. Richardson s.v. Domus Pomponii; W. Eck, *LTUR* s.v. Domus: T. Pomponius Atticus.—Romulus' epiphany to Proculus Julius was the foundation legend of the cult of Quirinus. Cicero narrates it in greater detail at *Rep.* 2.20, where he calls the witness *homo agrestis* (cf.

---

30. Or in general; cf. Shackleton Bailey, 1997, index s.v. negatives (omitted by scribes).

D.H. 2.63.3: γεωργικὸς ἀνήρ) but adds that he spoke up *impulsu patrum*, who were eager to avert the suspicion of having gotten rid of the king by foul play (sim. Plut. *Rom.* 28.1 ff.). Cicero and Livy avoid a difficulty by omitting the tradition that he came from Alba Longa, for the *gens Iulia*, along with other Albans, settled in Rome only under Tullus Hostilius (see Ov. *Fast.* 2.499; Plut. *Rom.* 28.1; implied also in the descent from Ascanius noted at D.H. 2.63.3; cf. Münzer, *RE* 10.1 [1918], 106.5–13). In view of the poeticisms in Livy's version of Proculus' speech (1.16.6–8), on which see Ogilvie *ad. loc.*, Skutsch suggested that Enn. *Ann.* 1.**lxii *(Romulus in caelo cum dis genitalibus aevom / degit)* was spoken by Proculus (see *ad loc.*). This need not, however, imply that the cult originated in the third century, rather than the first, B.C. (for the problem cf. *ad Off.* 3.41); cf. Classen, 179. C. Koch, 35–36, sets its origin into the context of Marius' political exploitation of Romulus; Classen, 191 ff., argues, more convincingly, for an innovation of Julius Caesar as pontifex maximus.[31] The Augustan understanding of Rome's mission appears in the injunction to cultivate the arts of warfare, added in some versions to the instructions about the cult (Liv. 1.16.7; Ov. *Fast.* 2.508). On the legend of Proculus cf. in general C. Koch, 34–37; on Quirinus in general Beard, 1998, 1, 15–16, with literature at n. 42.

et verumne sit ⟨ut⟩ Athenis, non longe item a tua illa antiqua domo, Orithyiam Aquilo sustulerit? sic enim est traditum.] Atticus' house in Athens is referred to also at the very end of *Fin.* (5.96: ... *in oppidum ad Pomponium perreximus omnes*). The Athenians localized Boreas' abduction of Orithyia on the bank of the Ilissus river, as mentioned at Pl. *Phaedr.* 229b–c; cf. also Hdt. 7.189.3; Paus. 1.19.5; Eva Frank, *RE* 18.1 (1939), 954.30 ff. Benardete, 298, works out the analogy of the *Phaedrus* passage to our context as follows: "Socrates' curt denial that the place which Phaedrus reasons might be where Boreas raped Orithyia prompts him to ask whether Socrates is convinced τὸ μυθολόγημα is true (229c1–5). Phaedrus' inference from the charming, clear and transparent waters of the Ilissus, that, since they would afford a suitable spot for girls to play near, it could be the place,

---

31. Stefan Borzsák, "Cicero und Caesar. Ihre Beziehungen im Spiegel des Romulus-Mythos," in A. Michel and R. Verdière, eds., *Ciceroniana. Hommages à Kazimierz Kumaniecki* (Leiden, 1975), 22–35, esp. 29–32, argues that the different tone of our passage from that of *Rep.* 2.20 points to its having been inserted after the civil war. In fact, however, the difference is not so striking, for at *Rep.* 2.20 Cicero does not commit himself to the veracity of the tale (*sed profecto tanta fuit in eo vis ingeni atque virtutis, ut id de Romulo Proculo Iulio ... crederetur ...*); no need, then, to assume that our passage is a late addition to the text; cf. also Lehmann, 11 n. 21.

recalls Atticus' own inference *etenim est sane vetus*, that led him to ask whether *illa quercus* was *haec quercus.*"

4 A. Quorsum tandem {aut cur} ista quaeris?] Atticus makes it his business in this Book to keep an eye on the coherence of the unfolding argument; cf. his previous question *quo tandem modo, Quinte, aut quale est istuc ... ?* (§ 1); § 22: *... id quod tibi concessi quorsus pertineat exspecto;* and his final question of the Book: *sed quorsus hoc pertinet?* (§ 63).—*Quorsum* = "to what end? with what in view?" (*OLD* s.v., 2b); in light of that Maas (to Watt *per litt.*) suspected *aut cur*, which Powell deletes; the words may originate either in a gloss on *quorsum*, relatively rare in such usage, or be a corruption of *atticus*, a stray indication of speaker.—Here and in Marcus' reply *iste* appears—unusually in this work—with a slightly contemptuous undertone; cf. *OLD* s.v., 3.

M. Nihil sane, nisi ne nimis diligenter inquiras in ea quae isto modo memoriae sint prodita.] For *memoriae prodi* cf. Caes. *Gal.* 1.13.7, 5.12.2, and 6.25.5; sim. *posteris prodi* (*Rep.* 6.23) with Zetzel *ad loc.*

A. Atqui multa quaeruntur in Mario, fictane an vera sint; et a nonnullis, quod et in recenti memoria et in Arpinati homine versere, veritas a te postulatur.] Atticus attempts to save his question by claiming that this is one of a number of ζητήματα in the *Marius* raised by several individuals *(a nonnullis)*, not himself only. He adds two factors that would set this material apart from Cicero's examples: the poem deals with the recent past and with a native son of Cicero's own Arpinum (cf. 2.6). The intense scrutiny of the *Marius* suggested in this passage is not otherwise attested; the poem was appealed to by the false C. Marius in requesting Cicero's *patrocinium* (cf. *Att.* 12.49.2: 20 May 45); that is the only contemporary reference apart from Cicero's own. This response is evidently a ploy designed so that Cicero's riposte will be diffused and not directed specifically at Atticus.—*Versor* is used with *in* to denote a field of activity; its unusual use with a person is softened by the parallel *et in recenti memoria* that precedes; cf. *Balb.* 14: *... cum in tanta re publica versere ... ; Phil.* 2.57: *scio me in rebus celebratissimis omnium sermone versari.*—For *postulo* cf. *ad* § 5b.

M. Et mehercule ego me cupio non mendacem putari. sed tamen 'nonnulli' isti, Tite noster, faciunt imperite, qui in isto periculo non ut a poeta sed ut a teste veritatem exigant; ...] Plato does not scruple to say that poets lie (ψεύδεσθαι: *Rp.* 377d, with following argument; cf. also *ad* § 47); and Zoilus of Amphipolis had attacked Homer in similar terms; cf. U. Friedländer, *De Zoilo aliisque Homeri obtrectatoribus* (Königsberg, 1895), 83; Luc. *Ver. Hist.* offers a clever parody of the πολλὰ τεράστια καὶ μυθώδη told by poets, historians, and philosophers (1.2). The view that the content of a poem is a view taken by the poet maintained itself (with difficulty) while epic, elegy, and lyric were the principal forms, but drama, with its different speakers often enunciating opposite points of view, posed a challenge and led to the concept of poetic fiction famously formulated by Arist. *Poet* 1451a36–37: φανερὸν δὲ . . . ὅτι οὐ τὸ τὰ γενόμενα λέγειν, τοῦτο ποιητοῦ ἔργον ἐστίν, ἀλλ᾽ οἷα ἂν γένοιτο . . . ; cf. Wolfgang Rösler, "Die Entdeckung der Fiktionalität in der Antike," *Poetica* 12 (1980), 283–319, esp. 308–12. Similarly, Cicero is at pains to create space for a different type of poetic truth; his remark to Tiro *ego certe singulos eius* [sc. *Euripidis*] *versus singula testimonia puto* (*Fam.* 16.8.2) is, of course, jocular; cf. Ov. *Am.* 3.12.19: *nec tamen ut testes mos est audire poetas.* Lucian (*Hist. conscr.* 8) would later emphasize the greater freedom of the poet vis-à-vis the historian.—Atticus is addressed by his *praenomen* here, as one expects in so close a friendship (cf. Dickey, 2002, 66), though he is so addressed in the letters only twice (*Att.* 2.16.3; 9.6.5); cf. T.A. Dorey, "The Use of *praenomina* in Cicero's Letters," *Humanitas* 9/10 (1957–58), 36.—*Imperitus/-e,* occurring more than one hundred times in the speeches, essays, and letters, is as harsh a characterization of opponents and their procedures as Cicero usually allows himself; as applied to the plebs, it implies that they allow themselves to be deceived by unscrupulous leaders; cf. Achard, 133–34; Morstein-Marx, ch. 2 n. 3; in other contexts it applies to laypersons not specially versed in a given subject, such as philosophy at *Mur.* 61 and *Fin.* 4.74 or, as here, literature.[32]—Forcellini s.v. *periculum* 2 explains the phrase *in isto periculo* as follows: "in isto carmine, quod Cicero in C. Marii honorem scripserat, quoque periculum virium suarum fecerat." This explanation, however, implies the sense "test-piece," "Probestück" unattested elsewhere; cf. Gnauk, 54, who daggers the word. The phrase *'nonnulli' isti* ("those *nonnulli* of yours") suggests that *istum periculum* may mean "that trial of yours," i.e., the adjudication, as proposed by Atticus, of the truth or falsehood of the incidents narrated in the Marius, the metaphor being continued in *ut a teste.* Cf. *TLL* s.v., 1462.43 ff. (with a query); cf. also 1459.58. Watt, 1997, 241–42, revives the humanist conjecture *opusculo*; D.R. Shackleton Bailey suggests *(per litt.) ista particula.*

nec dubito quin idem et cum Egeria collocutum Numam, et ab aquila Tarquinio apicem impositum putent.] After the reference to Romulus (§ 3) two further incidents from the saga of the Roman kings such as inexperienced persons (*imperiti;* cf. the previous note) believe; these did not rate a mention in *Rep.* According to tradition, Numa gave it out that his sacral

---

32. Contrast the flattering reference to *hoc concursu hominum litteratissimorum* at *Arch.* 3.

laws were inspired by the advice of the nymph Egeria, whom he met by night (Liv. 1.19.5 and 21.3); Juv. 3.12 burlesques these meetings as lovers' assignations *(ubi nocturnae constituebat amicae).*—The incident of the eagle interfering with the headgear of Tarquinius Priscus—and thus providing an omen of kingship—was already narrated at Enn. *Ann.* 3.iii. Though the word can denote any point, *apex* in reference to headgear indicates the rod cut from olive wood affixed to the cap *(pilleus)* of a priest; by synecdoche the term then comes to designate the priest's cap itself.[33] In Cicero, as (presumably) in Ennius,[34] this is a supernatural occurrence: the eagle swoops down and places the *apex* upon Tarquin's head, the *apex* itself being the symbol of kingship.[35] Liv. 1.34.8 (or his source) seems to have misunderstood the meaning of *apex* and, since Tarquinius Priscus was not a priest, to have substituted *pilleus* for *apex* and reinterpreted the incident (this interpretation is also found at D.H. 3.47.3 and *Vir. ill.* 6.3). In this version the eagle removes and replaces the felt cap *(pilleus;* πῖλος: D.H.) on Tarquin's head *(pilleum aufert . . . capite apte reponit:* Liv.). The essential difference between the two tales has evidently not been seen (cf. Cicero's use of *impono* versus Livy's *repono).* The historians present a rationalizing version in which Tarquin is wearing an ordinary cap *(pilleus),* and it is the raising of the cap to a great height that has symbolic value. For an eagle's intervention symbolizing rule cf. the story of the eagle alighting on Claudius' right shoulder (Suet. *Claud.* 7); for a pragmatic account of Tarquin's rise to power cf. *Rep.* 2.35.

5a Q. Intellego te, frater, alias in historia leges observandas putare, alias in poemate.] In formulating the underlying principle, Quintus lets drop, for the first time in the dialogue, the word *leges* (for *leges historiae* cf. also *Fam.* 5.12.3). But this is merely a teaser; a digression on historiography will supervene before the interlocutors settle down to what is to be the major topic (§§ 10 ff.). The digression on historiography is appropriate as a bow to Atticus' interests (cf. Münzer, 1905; but Quintus, too, wrote history; cf. *ad* § 8) before going on to philosophical positions that, as an Epicurean, he could hardly share (cf. § 21).—The difference between poetry and history is implicit at Thuc. 1.21.1 (. . . οὔτε ὡς ποιηταὶ ὑμνήκασι περὶ αὐτῶν ἐπὶ τὸ μεῖζον

---

33. Cf. Habel, *RE* 1.1 (1894), 2699.47 ff. with references; for a sculptural portrait from the Vatican collection of a flamen wearing a *pilleus* with *apex* cf. Th. Schäfer, "Zur Ikonographie der Salier," *JDAI* 95 (1980), 358.

34. Skutsch *ad* Enn. *Ann. loc. cit.* observes that Ennius, like Cicero, is likely to have used the term *apex.*

35. "(Worn as a sign of kingship or greatness) a diadem or crown": *OLD* s.v., 1b, citing our passage.

κοσμοῦντες . . .) and 22.4 (καὶ ἐς μὲν ἀκρόασιν ἴσως τὸ μὴ μυθῶδες αὐτῶν ἀτερπέστερον φανεῖται . . .), insofar as what is lacking in his history (τὸ μυθῶδες and the quality of being pleasing to the hearing) is associated with poetry. The difference was formulated abstractly by Arist. *Poet.* 1451b4 ff.: . . . τούτῳ διαφέρει, τῷ τὸν μὲν τὰ γενόμενα λέγειν, τὸν δὲ οἷα ἂν γένοιτο. διὸ καὶ φιλοσοφώτερον καὶ σπουδαιότερον ποίησις ἱστορίας ἐστίν· ἡ μὲν γὰρ ποίησις μᾶλλον τὰ καθόλου, ἡ δ᾽ ἱστορία τὰ καθ᾽ ἕκαστον λέγει. For the idea of contrasting generic "rules," if not laws, cf. Luc. *Hist. conscr.* 8: . . . ποιητικῆς μὲν καὶ ποιημάτων ἄλλαι ὑποσχέσεις καὶ κανόνες ἴδιοι, ἱστορίας δὲ ἄλλοι. A common source for *Leg.* and Lucian, posited by R. Reitzenstein, *Hellenistsche Wundererzählungen* (Leipzig, 1906), 2–3, need not be implied, however.—*Frater* is the form of address invariably used by Quintus for Marcus in the dialogue (cf. §§ 18, 52, 56; 2.8, 17, 43, 69; 3.12, 19, 28, 34; for the tone ["mildly polite"] cf. Dickey, 2002, 123), never *Marce* (cf. *ad* § 1; cf. *Fam.* 16.16: *mi Marce*), whereas there is greater nuance in the way Marcus addresses his brother: *Quinte* (§ 5, 2.43, 3.17, 23, 33, 39), *o Quinte frater* (3.26), and even *optime et dulcissime frater* (3.25); see on the last two passages; Shackleton Bailey, 1995, 101–3, and 1996, 62.

M. Quippe, cum in illa ad veritatem ⟨omnia⟩, Quinte, referantur, in hoc ad delectationem pleraque; . . .] In view of Cicero's tendency toward balanced clauses, editors since Camerarius have been inclined to insert or substitute a subject for the prior clause, rather than taking *pleraque* as subject of both; a word for "all" would likewise effect a sharper contrast with the following adversative *(quamquam et apud Herodotum . . .).* Camerarius' substitution of *cuncta* for *Quinte* is probably not the solution, however: surely Marcus' first address to Quintus should be marked with the vocative (see the previous note). Ziegler's *Quinte, ⟨cuncta⟩* lacks euphony; Ernesti inserted *omnia* after *referantur,* a position from which, however, it is unlikely to have dropped through mechanical causes; more convincing is Powell's placement before *Quinte,* the two rounded letters *o* and *q* being similar enough to have prompted the saltation error; the vocative will have been so placed as to highlight the emphatic word.—Cicero, both here and in the following lemma, clearly means to emphasize the importance of veracity in the writing of history, even though the rest of the passage focuses on the literary qualities (or lack thereof) of the historians discussed, Cicero being obviously equipped, so it is assumed, to remedy such deficiencies; cf. Antonius' remarks at *de Orat.* 2.36 *(historia vero testis temporum, lux veritatis . . .)* and 2.62 (quoted below). Cf. (on the similar emphasis of *de Orat.* but applicable *mutatis mutandis* to *Leg.* as well) Brunt, 1979, 313–15 and 321–22.—The denigration of the τερπνόν in historiography can be traced back to Thucydides (1.22.4 [quoted above]) and was a point specially emphasized by Polybius; cf. Petzold, 265 and n. 37. In *de Orat.* the Ciceronian Antonius cast his net wider: while asking *nam quis nescit primam esse historiae legem, ne quid falsi dicere audeat?* (2.62), he seems to allow that pleasure is a legitimate goal of historiography; cf. 2.55: *tanta est eloquentia* [sc. *Herodotus*] *ut me quidem . . . magno opere delectet . . .* ; sim. 2.59: *. . . horum libros . . . delectationis causa, cum est otium, legere soleo.* The letter to Lucceius also speaks favorably of the *delectatio* and *voluptas* afforded by historiography (*Fam.* 5.12.4–5); cf. also *Fin.* 5.51: *nec vero sum nescius esse utilitatem in historia, non modo voluptatem.* Affording *delectatio* gradually came to be accepted as a legitimate aim even of a senator writing history; see Wiseman, 1987, 250; id., "Lying Historians: Seven Types of Mendacity," in *Lies and Fiction in the Ancient World,* ed. Christopher Gill and T.P. Wiseman (Exeter, 1993), 139 and n. 56. On the influence of Cicero's view of historiography in general cf. Rambaud, 121 ff.—It was presumably so as not to spoil the *delectatio* that, as described at Cic. *Man.* 25, poetic accounts of Roman history tended to pass over the defeats.

quamquam et apud Herodotum, patrem historiae, et apud Theopompum sunt innumerabiles fabulae.] = *FGrHist* 115 T 26a. For Herodotus' status as the founder of the genre cf. *de Orat.* 2.55: *Herodotum illum, qui princeps genus hoc ornavit . . .* The famous description of Herodotus as the "father of history" is a characteristically Roman way of constructing literary or intellectual history as a genealogy ordered under a *paterfamilias;* cf. 3.14: *ab hac familia magis ista manarunt Platone principe; de Orat.* 2.10: *. . . ille pater eloquentiae . . . Isocrates;* cf. also *ad* § 55 *(familia); N.D.* 1.93: *Socraten . . . parentem philosophiae* (sim. *Fin.* 2.1). *Imitatio* fits into this scheme[36] insofar as a son might well be expected to imitate his father (cf. *Off.* 1.116 and 121).[37]—*Fabula* is here "a story told for entertainment, instruction, etc., tale" (*OLD* s.v., 4a, citing our passage), implicitly with primary reference to criteria other than truth (at *Sen.* 3 Cicero speaks of there being *parum . . . auctoritatis in fabula*). Thucydides' strictures on the μυθῶδες and recommendation of τὸ μὴ μυθῶδες (1.21.1 and 22.4) come to mind, though it is not clear that he was thinking of Herodotus in particular as opposed to a general tendency of his predecessors; cf. Gomme *ad* Thuc. 1.22.4. On Herodotus' veracity or lack thereof cf. *Div.* 2.116; Plut. *Hdt. mal.;* Luc. *Ver. Hist.* 2.31. The topic has been raised again by D. Fehling, *Die Quellenangaben bei Herodot* (Berlin, 1971) = *Herodotus and His "Sources,"* tr. J.G. Howie

---

36. Cf. Sisenna's *imitatio* of Clitarchus at § 7.

37. I owe this point to Christina S. Kraus.

(Leeds, 1989), who poses a fundamental challenge to Herodotus' commitment to veracity; cf. the assessment by John Marincola, "A Selective Introduction to Herodotean Studies," *Arethusa* 20 (1987), 26–33.—A.D. Momigliano, "The Place of Herodotus in the History of Historiography," *History* 43 (1958), 1 = *Studies in Historiography* (London, 1966), 127, reflects on the irony of these two juxtaposed assertions about Herodotus.—Elsewhere Cicero mentions Theopompus of Chios above all as a pupil of Isocrates (*de Orat.* 2.57 and 94; *Orat.* 151; cf. ibid. 207), sometimes in contrast with his slower colleague and fellow-pupil Ephorus (*Att.* 6.1.12; *de Orat.* 3.36; *Brut.* 204); his name was also a byword for vituperative history (cf. *Att.* 2.6.2: *itaque* ἀνέκδοτα *a nobis . . . Theopompio genere aut etiam asperiore multo pangentur*); on his style cf. *Brut.* 66. Was Cicero aware that Theopompus had produced an epitome of Herodotus (*FGrHist* 115 T 1) and hence led to associate the two? In one passage Theopompus boasted that he could tell μῦθοι better than Herodotus and others (ibid., F 381); and Book 8 of his Φιλιππικά was sometimes designated as τὰ θαυμάσια (ibid., 64–84; Richard Laqueur, *RE* 5A2 [1934], 2212.9 ff.). On his historiography in general cf. Michael A. Flower, *Theopompus of Chios: History and Rhetoric in the Fourth Century B.C.* (Oxford, 1994).

5b–12 This is a bridge passage leading to the choice of the subject of the essay. Here the topic shifts from a past work of Marcus (*viz.,* the *Marius*) and its truth-value to a possible future historical work mooted by Atticus, who bolsters his case with a critical survey of earlier Roman historians (§§ 5b–7). This possibility was already a subject of debate between the brothers, namely whether such a work should start at the beginning of Roman history, as Quintus suggests, or deal only with contemporary events, as Marcus prefers (§ 8). Though Atticus approves of the proposed reduction in scope (ibid.), Marcus nonetheless pleads lack of time as a hindrance to any such project, since it would demand more than the "leftover time" *(subsiciva tempora)* he has so far allotted to producing literature (§ 9). Though he does not crave a "free embassy," i.e., a purely honorific post that would leave him free for other occupations, Marcus expects in old age to find time for writing history as for giving legal advice (§ 10). Each of these possibilities is, as L. Troiani, "Per un'interpretazione delle 'Leggi' Ciceroniane," *Athenaeum* 70 (1982), 317, has pointed out, an outgrowth of his work as an orator (cf. § 5 à propos historiography: . . . *opus . . . unum hoc oratorium maxime*). Neither is allowed to stand as a serious possibility, however, the former for lack of the right kind of time in view of work [sc. at the bar], the latter because the change of Cicero's oratorical style opens the possibility that he can continue pleading indefinitely; even an "experiment" in doing both in tandem, as proposed by Quintus (§ 12), is rejected out of hand. The centrality of oratory in Marcus' life is thus established as well as the requirement that any additional project must fit that framework. The mention of legal advice is at first incidental, as an occupation for Cicero's old age alongside historiography (§ 11). In the sequel Atticus seizes upon the law as the topic for the present discussion (§ 13).

5b–7 Postulatur—nisi quid Quinto videtur secus.] The argument is carefully structured beginning with the thesis *(postulatur a te . . . historia)*. Atticus asserts the need *(abest . . . historia litteris nostris)* as well as Cicero's ability to satisfy it *(potes autem tu profecto satis facere in ea . . .)* and then restates the request *(quamobrem aggredere, quaesumus, . . .)*. The *argumentatio* then offers a potted history of Roman historiography *(post annales pontificum maximorum . . . Fanni . . . aetati coniunctus . . . ecce autem successere huic . . . Sisenna, eius amicus, . . .)*. In focusing exclusively on the rhetorical side of historiography and in its structure, this section resembles *de Orat.* 2.51 ff.: in both there is a "primitive" stage much influenced by the dry reportage of the pontifical annals, with Coelius Antipater marking the transition to a more polished style. The critique of earlier historians in our passage has thus not evolved primarily out of reading done in connection with *Rep.* (the supposition of Rawson, 1991, 64), though that may have provided some detail. Atticus concludes with a restatement of the *propositio (quare tuum est munus hoc)* with a request for confirmation from Quintus appended for politeness' sake. Cf. Atticus' similar rôle in debunking earlier orators (to Cicero's advantage) at *Brut.* 292–300. Similar to our passage in reviewing past historians by name is the preface to Sal. *Hist.* esp. fr. 4 with specific mention of Cato and Fannius, two of Cicero's examples at § 6, though Sallust comments on content as well as style; cf. Scanlon, 202–3.

The relation of this conversation to the following dialogue about law is not straightforward. One wonders if there was a widespread demand for a history from Cicero's pen; apart from our passage and Nepos fr. 58 (quoted p. 30 *supra*), our evidence shows the demand flowing only in the reverse direction, from Cicero to others; cf. his attempts to persuade first the poet Archias, then the historians Posidonius and L. Lucceius to write a narrative of his consulate, though, in spite of some promises, nothing materialized.[38] Might Cicero be giving a broad hint that this dialogue itself is to be a kind of substitute for a history? It will enable him to comment on the recent past but without the need to narrate all events systematically and in order as a

38. Archias: *Arch.* 28; Posidonius: *Att.* 2.1.2 = T 34 and F 82 E.-K. = *FGrHist* 87 F 82; L. Lucceius: *Fam.* 5.12; Lucceius' promise is reported at *Att.* 4.6.4 (ca. 19 March 55). Cf. on § 7 and in general Beretta, ch. 3.

historian would; instead, as in his poem *Marius,* he clothes his observations about events in a fictitious form with resulting ambivalent relation of "Dichtung und Wahrheit"; and to have the freedom to comment on such matters selectively and under a veil of fiction was one of Cicero's motives for writing *Leg.* (see Introduction § 2b).

5b A. Postulatur a te iamdiu, vel flagitatur potius, historia; . . .] *Postulo* is generally used of that to which one is entitled (*OLD* s.v., 1a; cf. Atticus' previous *veritas a te postulatur* [§ 4]; § 56, where *natura* is the subject), if only in one's own opinion (cf. *TLL* s.v., IAc), whereas *flagito* emphasizes the vehemence or insistence of the action without regard to the justification (*OLD* s.v., 3a; *TLL* s.v., *init.*; cf. also Berry *ad Sul.* 35). The *correctio* thus emphasizes the intensity of the demand. In the sequel Marcus seems to accept the justice of the claim (*intellego equidem a me istum laborem iamdiu postulari:* § 8).—The *topos* is taken up at Plin. *Ep.* 5.8.1: *suades ut historiam scribam, et suades non solus: multi hoc me saepe monuerunt . . .*

Whether or not there was such a demand for a history from Cicero's pen, having failed to enlist anyone else to write a history of his consulate (see the previous note), he contemplated a Latin work of this kind (he actually wrote a ὑπόμνημα on the subject in Greek; cf. fr. phil. pp. 86 ff.). Atticus seems to have revived this request in the hope of providing Cicero with a diversion during Antony's hegemony; cf. *Att.* 14.14.5 (28 or 29 April 44): *et hortaris me ut historias scribam, ut colligam tanta eorum scelera a quibus etiam nunc obsidemur!;* ibid. 16.13a.2 (10 November); *ad* § 8. On Cicero's plans to write history cf. Häfner, 83 ff.; Aloysius P. Kelley, *Historiography in Cicero* (diss., University of Pennsylvania, 1968), 152 ff.

sic enim putant, te illam tractante effici posse ut in hoc etiam genere Graeciae nihil cedamus.] The emphatically placed *te,* together with its limitation *tractante,* encompasses the referent for historiography *(illam)* in much the way it is assumed that Cicero will dominate the Latin genre.—Cicero was fond of constructing such Greco-Roman generic comparisons to highlight the achievements either of his countrymen (*Tusc.* 1.1: *. . . meum semper iudicium fuit omnia nostros aut invenisse per se sapientius quam Graecos aut accepta ab illis fecisse meliora . . .*) or of himself, existing or possible (the deficiency in historiography noted in our passage contrasts with oratory, where there were such great practitioners down to Cicero's time *ut non multum aut nihil omnino Graecis cederetur: N.D.* 1.5). It was left to later authors to place such comparisons on a more systematic and less self-serving basis, as in the σύγκρισις Δημοσθένους καὶ Κικέρωνος of Caecil. Calact. (frr. 153–54 Ofenloch) or Quint. *Inst.* 10.1. By Quintilian's time the defect had been remedied, or so he claims: *at non historia cesserit Graecis. nec opponere*

Thucydidi Sallustium verear, nec indignetur sibi Herodotus aequari Titum Livium . . . (10.1.101).—Cicero's ability to elevate Latin historiography is inferred from his oratorical skill, as is clarified in the sequel: *potes autem tu— unum hoc oratorium maxime* and (of Sisenna) *is tamen neque orator in numero vestro umquam est habitus:* § 7; cf. David S. Potter, *Literary Texts and the Roman Historian* (London–New York, 1999), 136. Perhaps influenced by our passage, Nepos fr. 58 Marshall made a similar point; cf. p. 30 *supra*; Schmidt, 1965, 302–3.

. . . **mihi videris . . . patriae debere hoc munus, ut ea quae salva per te est, per te eundem sit ornata.**] The chiastic arrangement of attributes and prepositional phrases *(salva per te—per te . . . ornata)* reinforces the parallelism of the two acts. The anaphora of *per te* is reminiscent of a prayer to a deity; for the "'Du'-Stil" in Roman prayers cf. Norden, 1913, 149 ff. In addition, Cicero reverses the normal order of elements of the compound verb to effect the cretic plus trochee clausula, which, at 16.2 percent frequency, was his clear favorite (De Groot's figure at Shewring, 15).—The adornment of the city with spoils of victory was the typical grand gesture of the general returning in triumph; Cicero's adornment of Rome should, in Atticus' view, rather take literary form.—On writing as a patriotic act cf. *N.D.* 1.7: . . . *magni existimans interesse ad decus et ad laudem civitatis res tam graves tamque praeclaras Latinis etiam litteris contineri.*—The claim of having saved the state and/or its citizens was, of course, raised several times in *Cat.* 3–4 (e.g., 3.25: . . . *ita me gessi . . . ut salvi omnes conservaremini . . .*), formed the content of the oath Cicero swore on leaving the consulate (Plut. *Cic.* 23.3) and was his constant refrain thereafter.

abest enim historia litteris nostris, . . .] Cf. Antonius' remark at *de Orat.* 2.55: *minime mirum si ista res* [sc. *historia*] *adhuc nostra lingua illustrata non est . . . ; Brut.* 288: *genus hoc scriptionis* [sc. *historia*] *nondum est satis Latinis litteris illustratum.* The premise is that the dry pontifical annals have cast their shadow over the genre so as to stunt its development as literature; cf. Petzold, 262; Peter Kuklica, "Cicero als potentieller Historiker," *GLO* 15–16 (1983–84), 25–46 at 26.—The emphatic initial position of the verb, contrary to normal Latin placement at the end of the sentence, is more characteristic of Cicero's speches than the *philosophica*; cf. von Albrecht, 1983, 61 and 82 = Engl. tr. 42 and 61.—*Litteris nostris* is dative; *absum* would require a preposition *(ab, ex)* if used with the ablative; cf. *OLD* s.v., 1.

. . . **quippe cum sit opus (ut tibi quidem videri solet) unum hoc oratorium maxime.**] The same assumption underlies Antonius' question *qualis oratoris et quanti hominis in dicendo putas esse historiam scribere?* (*de Orat.* 2.51); ibid. 2.62: *videtisne quantum munus sit oratoris historia?* Indeed, our lemma is perhaps a citation of the latter passage; cf. Pohlenz, 1938, 110 = 418. The *orator* is *par excellence* the one able to work up raw materials into artistic form. After discussing the shaping of raw materials in the plastic arts, Luc. *Hist. conscr.* 51 remarks: τοιοῦτον δή τι καὶ τὸ τοῦ συγγραφέως ἔργον εἰς καλὸν διαθέσθαι τὰ πεπραγμένα καὶ εἰς δύναμιν ἐναργέστατα ἐπιδεῖξαι αὐτά. In this passage he draws some useful distinctions between historian and orator: historians must find not what to say, but how to say it (οὐ τί εἴπωσι ζητητέον αὐτοῖς ἀλλ᾽ ὅπως εἴπωσιν: § 50), i.e., not *inventio* but *dispositio* and *elocutio* will be their concern; nor need they indulge in a *captatio benevolentiae* such as orators use (§ 53). He might have added that the *narratio* dominates, with *argumentatio* and *refutatio* subordinate to it. For a generic σύγκρισις of history and oratory cf. Plin. *Ep.* 5.8. Cicero, however, seems to measure historiography, like philosophical writing, primarily by stylistic criteria (on the latter cf. Philippa R. Smith in Powell, 1995, 301 ff.). Cicero's characterization does not imply, as some have suspected, any deviation from truthfulness, which he described as the *prima lex* of historiography (*de Orat.* 2.62), but, rather, greater attention to the stylistic clothing *(ornatus)* of narrative; cf. Leeman, 188–90; Fleck, 32 ff.; Alexandru Cizek, "Antike Rhetoren als Theoretiker der Historiographie und dichtende Historiker," in T. Pekáry, H.-J. Drexhage, and J. Sünskes, eds., *Migratio et Commutatio: Studien zur alten Geschichte und deren Nachleben* (St. Katharinen, 1989), 289. The *orator* is also, as Cicero makes clear in *de Orat.*, both trained in philosophy and experienced in affairs of state and thus able to provide, not merely a factual report, but a penetrating analysis of the causes of events; in this respect Cicero's conception of the historian approaches that of Polybius; cf. Petzold, 270–72.—The addition of *maxime* effects a fine double cretic clausula; nevertheless, it is not likely to have been placed so emphatically if it were empty of meaning (*pace* Brunt, 1979, 325 n. 30a, according to whom it "should not be taken too seriously"); it is presumably deployed to help with the task of persuasion. Translate "to the highest degree" or the like ("in allerhöchstem Grade": Büchner); cf. *OLD* s.v., 1.

6 quamobrem aggredere, quaesumus, et sume ad hanc rem tempus, quae est a nostris hominibus adhuc aut ignorata aut relicta.] For *aggredere* cf. Tac. *Hist.* 1.2.1: *opus adgredior opimum casibus,* where, however, Ruperti's *tempus* is often substituted for the transmitted *opus.*—The archaic spelling seems to have remained standard in the first-person plural of *quaeso*: cf. *OLD* s.v., *init.*—Similar was the state of philosophical writing as described at *Tusc.* 1.5: *philosophia iacuit usque ad hanc aetatem nec ullum habuit lumen litterarum Latinarum.*

nam post annales pontificum maximorum, quibus nihil potest esse ieiunius, si aut ad Fabium aut ad eum qui tibi semper in ore est, Catonem, aut ad Pisonem aut ad Fannium aut ad Vennonium venias, quamquam ex his alius alio plus habet virium, tamen quid tam exile quam isti omnes?] Davies proposed ⟨in⟩iucundius for the transmitted iucundius. Iniucundus is a favorite Ciceronian word (cf. OLD s.v.) and might be thought to be a more likely source of the transmitted text. Yet the comparative form is very sparsely attested (cf. TLL s.v., 1664.11–13). For that reason and in light of the following characterization quid tam exile quam isti omnes?, like most recent editors, we prefer Ursinus' ieiunius.—The pontifex maximus posted notices of events on a bronze tablet (album or tabula) at his house (the Regia) for the benefit of the public; in this form they must have been quite difficult to read and hence went largely unexploited except by early historians, though Atticus must have studied them in detail in writing his own Liber Annalis. They provided a year-by-year account of events allegedly starting ab initio rerum Romanarum and ending with P. Mucius Scaevola Pontifex; cf. Gregory S. Bucher, "The Annales Maximi in the Light of Roman Methods of Keeping Records," AJAH 12 (1987 [1995]), 2–61. They were published in the Augustan age in an eighty-book edition; it is presumably from this that Verrius Flaccus cited (Fest. pp. 189 and 354M). Cf. Cato, fr. 77; de Orat. 2.51–52 (whence the quoted words); Serv. auct. ad Aen. 1.373; editions: hist. 3–4 and Martine Chassignet, L'Annalistique Romaine, 1: Les Annales des pontifes et l'annalistique ancienne (fragments) (Paris, 1996); cf. B.W. Frier, Libri Annales Pontificum Maximorum: The Origins of the Annalistic Tradition, PMAAR, 27 (Rome, 1979); S.P. Oakley, A Commentary on Livy Books VI–X, 1 (Oxford, 1997), 24–27; Walt, 119–21; on Cicero's use of the work cf. Giovanni D'Anna, "La testimonianza di Cicerone sugli Annales Maximi," Ciceroniana n.s. 7 (1990), 223–30; Fleck, 92–97. On the early annalists in general cf. Rawson, 1991, 245–71.—The order of names suggests that Fabius refers to the first of the Roman annalists, the senator Q. Fabius Pictor. He wrote in Greek (fragments at hist. 5–39 and FGrHist 809), but Latin annals were sometimes attributed to him (cf. hist. LXXVII ff.), possibly a Latin translation; cf. Douglas ad Brut. 81; J. Briscoe in OCD[3] s.v.—For the Romans Cato was historiae conditor (Quint. Inst. 12.11.23). Cicero expresses his admiration of Cato's Origines at Brut. 66 (spoken in his own person): iam vero Origines eius quem florem aut quod lumen eloquentiae non habent? The sequel shows, however, that subsequent stylistic developments left him isolated in this view (amatores huic desunt... Catonis luminibus obstruxit haec posteriorum quasi exaggerata altius oratio). He continues of Cato's style in general and its difference from the style current in his own day: *antiquior est huius sermo et quaedam horridiora verba. ita enim tum loquebantur. id muta, quod tum ille non potuit, et adde numeros et, ⟨ut⟩ aptior sit oratio, ipsa verba compone et quasi coagmenta . . . : iam neminem antepones Catoni* (ibid. 68). He concludes (§ 69) by commending Cato's richness in metaphors and figures (σχήματα). Atticus, however, offers criticism from the modern point of view (ibid. 293–94), e.g., . . . *his* [sc. *Philisto et Thucydidi*] *tu comparas hominem Tusculanum nondum suspicantem quale esset copiose et ornate dicere.* For the fragments cf. *hist.* 51–97; Caton, *Les origines (fragments),* ed. Martine Chassignet (Paris, 1986); cf. also Wilt Aden Schröder (ed. and comm.), M. Porcius Cato, *Das erste Buch der Origines* (Meisenheim am Glan, 1971); Walt, 69–71, gives an overview of recent scholarship. For Cicero's relation to Cato the historian see further Fleck, 109–15.—On the style of L. Calpurnius Piso Frugi (cos. 133) cf. *Brut.* 106: . . . *isque orationes reliquit, quae iam evanuerunt, et annales sane exiliter scriptos* . . . *Hist.* fr. 27 (on the curule aedileship of Cn. Flavius), compared with the dependent passage Liv. 9.46.1–10, shows why his style failed to please Cicero. Fleck, 122–29, takes the field against attempts to overrate the influence of Piso's histories on Cicero. For the fragments cf. *hist.* 120–38; Gary Forsythe, *The Historian L. Calpurnius Piso Frugi* (Lanham, Md., 1994), who reprints the fragments, with more context than Peter and English translation but no critical apparatus, in an appendix. K. Latte, *Der Historiker L. Calpurnius Frugi,* Sb. d. Deutschen Akademie der Wissenschaften zu Berlin, Kl. für Sprachen, Literatur un Kunst 1960, no. 7 = *Kleine Schriften,* ed. O. Gigon, W. Buchwald, and W. Kunkel (Munich, 1968), 837 ff., complains of Piso's tendentiousness; a more positive view is taken by Forsythe, *loc. cit.,* but a cautionary note is rightly sounded by Gary D. Farney, *BMCR* 7 (1996), 673–77.—There were two cousins named C. Fannius, one C.f., the other M.f.; in Cicero's day it was disputed which was the anti-Gracchan historian (*Att.* 12.5b); cf. G.V. Sumner, *The Orators in Cicero's Brutus: Prosopography and Chronology* (Toronto, 1973), 170–74; *MRR* 3, 89–90 (at *Brut.* 101 Cicero assumes it was the son of Marcus); for the remains *hist.* 139–41. Cicero passed a tepid judgment on the work: *eius omnis in dicendo facultas historia ipsius non ineleganter scripta perspici potest, quae neque nimis est infans neque perfecte diserta* (*Brut.* 101; cf. 118).—In spite of the judgment passed here, ca. May or June 46 Cicero expressed annoyance at not having Vennonius' book (*Att.* 12.3.1); cf. P.T. Pütz, *De M. Tulli Ciceronis bibliotheca* (diss., Münster, 1925), 85. The one fragment is printed at *hist.* 142.—*Quid tam exile quam isti omnes?* Models that might have pointed the way to a fuller treatment did not yet exist; cf. the comment on orators and poets at *Fin.* 1.10: *quando enim nobis, vel dicam aut oratoribus bonis aut poetis, postea quidem quam fuit quem imitarentur, ullus orationis vel copiosae vel elegantis ornatus defuit?*

Fanni autem aetati coniunctus Antipater paulo inflavit vehementius, . . .] Transmitted is *Fanni . . . aetate coniunctus;* the choice lies between *Fannio* (Turnebus) and *aetati* (quidam apud Turnebum). The available parallels provide more support for the latter (*viz., Brut.* 174: *horum aetati prope coniunctus I. Gellius . . .*; ibid. 226: *coniunctus . . . Sulpici aetati P. Antistius fuit*). *Brut.* 264 might suggest that the construction of the person would not be plain dative (. . . *qui fuit cum Sicinio aetate coniunctus*); but see *Brut.* 317: *itaque cum Hortensio mihi magis arbitrabar rem esse, quod et dicendi ardore eram* [sc. *ei*] *propior et aetate coniunctior.*—The rare name Antipater was reduced, by trivializing error, to *pater,* corrected by the *recentiores.* Ziegler assumes that an additional saltation error eliminated *Coelius* as well; this is possible, especially after *coniunctus,* but cf. *de Orat.* 2.54, where our historian is identified by cognomen alone.—The phrase *paulo inflavit vehementius* looks like an allusion to Lucil. 999M = 1012K: *continuo simul ac paulo vehementius aura / inflarit, fluctus erexerit extuleritque,* where the subject is perhaps the wife, and the prelude to a domestic storm is being described; cf. *TLL* s.v. *inflo* 1465.5–8 and 23–25; but Cicero is also playing on *inflo* as used in a transitive metaphorical sense of style; ibid. 1467.24 ff.—Besides *hist.* CCXI ff. and 158–77 cf. Wolfgang Hermann, *Die Historien des Coelius Antipater. Fragmente und Kommentar,* Beiträge zur Klassischen Philologie 104 (Meisenheim am Glan, 1979). For Cicero's relation to Antipater cf. Fleck, 134 ff.

. . . habuitque vires agrestes ille quidem atque horridas . . .] For *horridus* ("rough, rude, uncouth": *OLD* s.v., 4) used of style cf. *Brut.* 238 (of C. Macer): *non erat abundans, non inops tamen; non valde nitens, non plane horrida oratio; Orat.* 152: *orationes illae ipsae horridulae Catonis.*

. . . sine nitore ac palaestra, . . .] Similar contrast at *Brut.* 238 (previous note); for the metaphors from athletics cf. *ad Off.* 1.130. Greek historians are surely the implicit standard of comparison. Philosophical writing as described by Antonius at *de Orat.* 1.81 has precisely these qualities: *nitidum quoddam genus est verborum et laetum, et palaestrae magis et olei quam huius civilis turbae ac fori.*

. . . sed tamen admonere reliquos potuit ut accuratius scriberent: . . .] Does *accuratius* apply to style only or might the content be implicated as well (cf. Liv. *praef.* 2: . . . *novi semper scriptores aut in rebus certius aliquid allaturos*

se aut scribendi arte rudem vetustatem superaturos credunt)?[39] The whole
tenor of the argument suggests that style is meant (cf. *ad* § 5a), and this is no
surprise since most of the attestations of the adjective *accuratus* are with
reference to style (under "t.t. de oratione . . .": *TLL* s.v., 342.74 ff.); cf.
Scanlon, 191 and n. 19 and 203 ("Cicero's exclusively stylistic approach").
**ecce autem successere huic Gellius, Claudius, Asellio, nihil ad Coelium, sed
potius ad antiquorum languorem et inscitiam.**] In vivid narrative *ecce autem*
introduces "a new event, usually a sudden or surprising one"; ellipsis of the
verb is possible but optional (*OLD* s.v. *ecce* 4a); cf., e.g., *Orat.* 30: *ecce
autem aliqui se Thucydidios esse profitentur—novum quoddam imperitorum et inauditum genus!*—*Successere* here and *dedere* at *Fam.* 10.19.2 are
counted by Neue-Wagener, 3, 191, as the only certain instances in Ciceronian prose of -*ere* as the termination of the third-plural perfect, a form of
which he disapproved (cf. *Brut.* 76; *Orat.* 157; sim. Quint. *Inst.* 1.42–44).[40]
He may have adopted the form in our passage in imitation of the style of the
annalists; cf. Liv. 8.12.4: *successere consules Ti. Aemilius Mamercinus* ⟨*Q.*⟩
Publilius Philo . . . ; the word is likewise used to narrate historical stages at
Plin. *Nat.* 6.58, Quint. *Inst.* 3.1.13, and Tac. *Hist.* 2.95; cf. von Albrecht,
1973, 1253.14–18.—Those who, like Vahlen, retain *belli* (transmitted for
Gellius), a word of praise in stylistics = κομψοί (cf. Krostenko, 111–14),
interpret the remark as ironic. But a study of all the occurrences of *bellus* in
Cicero's *philosophica* and *rhetorica,* where the word is not otherwise used
ironically, indicates caution; cf. also Pohlenz, 1938, 111 = 419 n. 11; Görler
ad loc. Likewise Pohlenz's *novelli,* a word Cicero uses elsewhere only of
trees (see on the fr. from Book 5), can hardly be right. We have adopted
Passerat's *Gellius,* the one plausible solution so far offered. If that is right,
the reference is to Cn. Gellius, whose *Annals,* in ninety-seven books if the
figure is correctly transmitted, carried Roman history from the founding to
at least 146 B.C.; cf. *hist.* CCIV and 148. Wiseman, 1979, 20–22, sees him,
like Geoffrey of Monmouth in his *History of the Kings of Britain,* as having
filled out an annalistic structure of bare names with events of his own
inventing; for a more cautious view of Gellius' sources see Badian, 12.—The
next name is transmitted as Clodius; we have either, in spite of the sequence,
which implies a second-century date, a reference to Claudius Quadrigarius

---

39. A third possibility, that *accuratus* refers to content alone, favored by H. Henze,
Quomodo Cicero de historia eiusque auctoribus iudicaverit quaeritur (diss., Jena, 1899), 65, is
surely ruled out by the context.

40. Now, however, editors tend to read Orelli's *dederunt* in the latter passage, with the
transmitted termination possibly anticipated from the immediately following *quam com-
plectere obsecro.*

(whose omission is otherwise surprising) or to some otherwise unknown
historian named Clodius or Claudius (probably not Clodius Licinus cited in
the transmitted text of Liv. 29.22.10[41]). The former is assumed by Marga-
rete Zimmerer, *Der Annalist Q. Claudius Quadrigarius* (diss., Munich,
1937), 2–3, and Walt, 143 n. 632; on this assumption I have substituted,
with Powell, *Claudius* for the transmitted *Clodius* (perhaps resulting from a
confusion with Cicero's enemy P. Clodius).—A military tribune who served
with Scipio during the siege of Numantia (134/33: *MRR* 1, 491), Sempronius Asellio concentrated on the history of his own time (whether Cicero's
projected history should confine itself in this way or go back to the origins
are debated alternatives at § 8); for his *res gestae* cf. *hist.* CCXLII ff., 179–
84. Gentili and Cerri, 52 ff., discuss his observations on method (*hist.* 179–
80 frr. 1–2), which place him close to Polybius, and emphasize that Cicero's
damning comment in our passage (*ad antiquorum languorem et inscitiam*)
relates purely to style. Cf. further Fleck, 147–49.—For *nihil ad Coelium* cf.
de Orat. 2.25: . . . *scripsit* [sc. Lucil.: fr. 592M = 594K] *'Persium non curo
legere' (hic fuit enim, ut noramus, omnium fere nostrorum hominum doctissimus) 'Laelium Decumum volo,' quem cognovimus virum bonum et non
illitteratum sed nihil ad Persium. Ad* has two different senses here: the first
"in comparison with, measured against," the second "so as to agree with,
according to" (*OLD* s.v., 38 and 35, respectively).

**7 nam quid Macrum numerem? cuius loquacitas habet aliquid argutiarum,
nec id tamen ex illa erudita Graecorum copia, sed ex librariolis Latinis; . . .]**
If Antipater could warn others to write more carefully (*accuratius*: § 6), the
strength of C. Licinius Macer (pr. 68) lay in his *mira accuratio* and *diligentia* (*Brut.* 238). Macer wrote a history of Rome from the origins in at
least sixteen books; cf. *hist.* CCCL, 298; new edition by Walt. In saying that
Macer's "cleverness in the use of words" (*argutiae: OLD* s.v., 1a) derives
from *librarioli Latini*, Atticus is surely referring to Macer's rhetorical training, perhaps at the feet of such *rhetores Latini* as those against whom
Cicero had been warned in his youth (cf. his letter cited at Suet. *Gram.* 26.1
= fr. ep., p. 167); see further Walt, 145–47; Fleck, 159. To call his Latin
masters *librarii* (= scribes, copyists; cf. *OLD* s.v. *librarius*[3] 1) would imply
their lack of originality; to substitute the diminutive *librarioli* adds, as at
Balb. 14 *(quod librarioli . . . scire se profiteantur),* a note of contempt.[42]

---

41. S.P. Oakley, "Livy and Clodius Licinus," *CQ* n.s. 42 (1992), 547–51, argues powerfully against the authenticity of this chapter. Cf. *hist.* CCXXXVIII–IX; Badian, 20.

42. The text has been suspected by R. Sommer, 391. But the points he objects to, the
limitation *Latinis* and the construction of *ex* with a person are explicable: the *librarioli Latini*
form a contrast to *illa erudita Graecorum copia,* and the parallelism is reinforced by the

The comparison with the Greeks is explicit, the poverty and tralaticiousness of the sources of Macer's cleverness contrasting sharply with the learned *copia* of Greek rhetoricians;[43] cf. also Sal. *Cat.* 8.5 (in contrast to the Greeks): *at populo Romano numquam ea copia fuit, quia prudentissumus quisque maxume negotiosus erat.*

in orationibus autem multas ineptias, et adeo summam impudentiam.] Transmitted is *in orationibus autem multas ineptus datio summam impudentiam* (!). The first point to establish is the reference of *in orationibus:* surely these are the speeches inserted in Macer's history, not his own forensic speeches. If that is so, then *Brut.* 238, referring to the latter, need not be a safe guide to the emendation of our passage; hence Kenter's argument that the reading *multas ineptias* (LERS) introduces a harsher criticism than in the *Brutus* lacks force; cf. Walt, 144. *Datio* is a *vox nihili* in need of replacement. The choice lies between the fifteenth-century conjecture *elatio* (R), accepted by most editors, and Zumpt's *et adeo*, revived by J.G.F. Powell. The former has its attractions: it is a technical term likely to have been unfamiliar to scribes[44] and could easily have yielded the transmitted *datio.* If, however, one reads *elatio*, the resulting text is very awkward, for *loquacitas* would continue as subject through *multas ineptias* but then would follow an abrupt change of subject; cf. Walt, 145. This problem could be obviated by adopting Mommsen's *multa sed inepta elatio, summa inpudentia,* but the accusatives seem too firmly rooted in the tradition to be removed. Hence Zumpt's *et adeo* deserves preference: it allows *loquacitas* to continue as subject through to the end and makes it clear that the critique reaches its climax with *summam impudentiam.*[45]—Macer's extant fragments provide no sufficient basis for a stylistic judgment independent of Cicero's; cf. Walt, 147–48.—The one case Cicero is known to have handled as praetor was that in which Macer was convicted *de repetundis* with his suicide resulting; cf. *Att.* 1.4.2; Alexander no. 195.

Sisenna, eius amicus,—ab optimo tamen abesset.] The influential *Histories*

---

repetition of the preposition *ex;* it is hard to see how *ex commentariolis Latinis* (his suggestion) could have been corrupted to *ex librariolis Latinis.*

43. An alternative interpretation would be that *librarioli Latini* refers to Macer's historical sources and that Cicero's contempt is thus related to the plebeian slant of his work. But then the contrast to the learned *copia* of the Greeks remains obscure; and Atticus' argument tends to be framed in terms of style rather than content (cf. *ad* § 5a).

44. *Elatio* is stylistic elevation; cf. *Brut.* 66, explaining the eclipse of Philistus, Thucydides, and Cato by later authors: *nam ut horum* [sc. *Philisti, Thucydidis*] *concisis sententiis . . . officit Theopompus elatione atque altitudine orationis suae . . . , sic Catonis luminibus obstruxit haec posteriorum quasi exaggerata altius oratio; TLL* s.v., 326.38 ff.; Ernesti s.v.

45. Zumpt himself, however, read *multus et ineptus et adeo summa impudentia.*

of L. Cornelius Sisenna (pr. 78) encompassed at least twelve books with emphasis on the period 90 to 82; Sallust continued them (cf. his judgment at *Jug.* 95.2: . . . *L. Sisenna, optume et diligentissume omnium qui eas res dixere persecutus, parum mihi libero ore locutus videtur*), and Varro entitled one of his *Logistorici Sisenna de historia;* cf. *hist.* CCCXXXIV ff., 276–97; Rawson, 1991, 363–88; Fleck, 154–59.

Our passage acknowledges Sisenna's superiority to his predecessors, and his oratory receives a generally favorable notice at *Brut.* 228: . . . *L. Sisenna, doctus vir et studiis optimis deditus, bene Latine loquens, gnarus reipublicae nec satis versatus in causis.* Yet, in Clitarchus, a companion of Alexander who wrote a history of his reign,[46] he chose a model liable to criticism on grounds both of substance[47] and style, though in our passage the focus is evidently on the latter; cf. *ad* § 5a. For strictures on Clitarchus' pretentious style cf. Demetr. *Eloc.* 304; [Longin.] 3.2; Phld. *Rhet.* 1, 180.24–25 Sudh.; ibid. 152.1–2 there is a reference to "the Clitarchian" (τοῦ Κλειταρχείου) in the context of imitation, albeit a preceding lacuna makes the exact sense unclear; on his style see further M. Schmidt, *Clitarchi Reliquiae* (Berlin, 1842), 21–22.—The transition by means of the phrase *eius amicus* keeps the exposition conversational in tone.

. . . **(nisi qui forte nondum ediderunt, de quibus existimare non possumus) . . .**] This qualification was hardly needed. Cicero was surely thinking of some specific individual, perhaps L. Lucceius, a good friend of the orator who turned to historiography and whom Cicero tried to persuade to write a history of his consulate (*Fam.* 5.12: ca. 12 April 55; see Shackleton Bailey's introductory note to this letter = no. 22 of his Cambridge ed.). Cf. Leeman, 184, and Münzer, *RE* 13.2 (1927), 1557.2 ff., with William C. McDermott, "De Lucceiis," *Hermes* 97 (1969), 233–46, esp. 243–44, distinguishing the historian as L. Lucceius Q. f. as opposed to M. f. On the other hand, Wiseman, 1979, 117–21, followed by Walt, 143, thinks of Valerius Antias, conspicuously absent from Cicero's list and possibly having published later.

is tamen neque orator in numero vestro umquam est habitus, et in historia puerile quiddam consectatur, ut unum Clitarchum neque praeterea quemquam de Graecis legisse videatur, . . .] *Vestro* does not mean "yours and Quintus' " (cf. *de Orat.* 2.10) but "yours and that of your colleagues": cf.

---

46. Fragments at *FGrHist* 137.

47. Cf. the critique at *Brut.* 42 (Atticus *ridens*): . . . *concessum est rhetoribus ementiri in historiis . . . ut enim tu nunc de Coriolano, sic Clitarchus, sic Stratocles de Themistocle finxit;* on the irony of *concessum est . . . ementiri* cf. Boyancé, 1970, 138–39; Brunt, 1979, 331; cf. also Quint. *Inst.* 10.1.74: *Clitarchi probatur ingenium, fides infamatur.*

2.32 (with reference to the board of augurs: *in collegio vestro*); *Fam.* 2.14:
novi ego vos magnos patronos.—For *unum Clitarchum neque praeterea
quemquam de Graecis* cf. the proverbial phrase *unus e multis* (A. Otto, 358;
Brut. 274: *sed de M. Calidio dicamus aliquid, qui non fuit orator unus e
multis* . . . ; *de Orat.* 3.136, cited p. 95 n. 54 *infra*); he does not spell out
that the Greeks are many; that may be implied in the preceding phrase *illa
erudita Graecorum copia.*

quare tuum est munus hoc, a te exspectatur; nisi quid Quinto videtur secus.]
A summarizing formula and polite nod to the third interlocutor (cf. *ad
§§ 5b–7*), this, too, a feature of Plato's dialogues; cf., e.g., *Gorg.* 458b5–6
(Gorgias is the speaker): ἴσως μέντοι χρῆν ἐννοεῖν καὶ τὸ τῶν παρ-
όντων.—*Tuum . . . a te* takes up again the " 'Du'-Stil" of Roman prayers; cf.
ad § 5b.

**8 Q. Mihi vero nihil; et saepe de isto collocuti sumus, sed est quaedam inter
nos parva dissensio.—ut ea complectatur quibus ipse interfuit.**] *Mihi vero
nihil:* sc. *videtur secus.*—As Reid notes, *isto* for *ista re* results from the
preceding *munus hoc.*—Bendlin's ⟨non⟩ *parva* may be unnecessary if *parva*
is understood as ironic.—The historical Quintus carried his interest in historiography to the point of composing annals that he wanted his brother to
correct and publish; cf. *Att.* 2.16.4 (30 April or 1 May 59): *ita rursus remittit ut me roget ut annales suos emendem et edam;* nothing further is
known about the project.—This point of disagreement between the brothers
highlights two of the three approaches characteristic of Roman historiography of the time. The traditional approach was the history *ab urbe condita*,
but, in light of Sempronius Asellio and Sisenna, dealing with one's own
times alone was now an available option. Cicero leaves unmentioned world
history, recently cultivated by Cornelius Nepos in his *Chronica.* See Wiseman, 1987, 246–48.—It looks as though Cicero is preparing opinion for a
monograph on his own times. The significant change since the discussion of
historiography in *de Orat.*, and possibly resulting from work on *Rep.*, is not
so much the evaluation of the historians' stylistic qualities (cf. *ad § 5a
supra*), the main lines of which were adumbrated in the earlier work (though
there, to avoid anachronism, Cicero had to limit the *status quaestionis* to the
literature available in 91), as the specific hint that Cicero may be preparing
to do something about it. To be sure any such hint in *de Orat.* would have
had to be broadly formulated, as was the hint of the possibility of a "better
Crassus" at 1.95. Cf. Rambaud, 12. On the position of such a work between
encomium and history cf. Petzold, 274. The impulse to write such a work—
with Atticus' encouragement—ultimately found expression in the *Expositio
consiliorum suorum*; it was originally meant for Atticus' eyes only (*Att.*

2.6.2), later for posterity (cf. phil. fr., pp. 89–90 = Dio 39.10); cf. Rawson, 1991, 408–15.

ego enim ab ultimis censeo, quoniam illa sic scripta sunt ut ne legantur quidem; . . .] Quintus thus appropriates for his argument the essence of Atticus' critique of earlier historiography (§§ 6–7). By Tacitus' time the position seemed completely different: *sed veteris populi Romani prospera vel adversa claris scriptoribus memorata sunt* (*Ann.* 1.1).

ipse autem aequalem aetatis suae memoriam deposcit, ut ea complectatur quibus ipse interfuit.] "He himself demands a record coterminous with his own lifetime so that it may embrace the affairs in which he himself participated." For *memoria* = "record" cf. *OLD* s.v., 8; sim. 3.46: *memoriam publicam nullam habemus. Aetatis suae* depends on *aequalis;* cf. 2.9: . . . *vis . . . aequalis illius caelum atque terras tuentis et regentis dei.*—To take as one's subject *quibus ipse interfuit* can enhance accuracy as at Thuc. 1.22.2: . . . οὐδ' ὡς ἐμοὶ ἐδόκει, ἀλλ' οἷς τε αὐτὸς παρῆν . . . The specimen reconstruction of early history Cicero provides at *Rep.* 2 shows a much more critical approach than Livy would later take; cf. Brunt, 1979, 322; J.L. Ferrary, "L'archéologie du De re publica (2, 2, 4–37, 63): Cicéron entre Polybe et Platon," *JRS* 74 (1984), 87–98.

A. Ego vero huic potius adsentior; sunt enim maximae res in hac memoria atque aetate nostra.] For *haec memoria* = "living memory" cf. *Off.* 3.5 with note. Herodotus (7.20.2–21.1) and Thucydides (1.1.2) similarly attributed their historical vocation to the magnitude of the events they described; cf. Marincola, 34–36; this then becomes a topos in the prefaces of later Greek and Roman historians; cf. the material collected by Elmar Herkommer, *Die Topoi in den Proömien des römischen Geschichtswerks* (diss., Tübingen, 1968), 164–71.

tum autem hominis amicissimi Gnaei Pompei laudes illustrabit; . . .] Pompey is alive and flourishing, a sure sign of a dramatic date prior to 48. Cicero inserted notable encomia of Pompey at *Man.* 27 ff. and 61 ff. and *Balb.* 13 ff.—Eduard Meyer, *Caesars Monarchie und das Principat des Pompejus,* 3d ed. (Stuttgart and Berlin, 1922), 182–91, thought Cicero so attached to Pompey that he had him in mind in formulating the rôle of the *rector* or *moderator reipublicae* at *Rep.* 5–6. But, if *Leg.* contains a set of laws for the type of constitution depicted in *Rep.* (cf. § 20; 2.14; 3.4), then Cicero can hardly have meant the *rector reipublicae* to be a governmental post, merely a type of statesman he would like to see at work within the framework of the Republic, conceived along traditional lines; cf. Richard Heinze, "Cicero's 'Staat' als politische Tendenzschrift," *Hermes* 59 (1924), 73–94 = *Vom Geist des Römertums*[3] (Darmstadt, 1960), 141–59; sim. Rawson, 1991,

141–42; J.G.F. Powell, "The *rector rei publicae* of Cicero's *De Republica*," *SCI* 13 (1994), 19–29.—By the date of composition of *Leg.* (52–51), Cicero's relations with Pompey, strained by the defense of Milo and the successful prosecution of T. Munatius Plancus Bursa, were less close than formerly; cf. Johannemann, 76–77; Rawson, 1982, 706. The references to Pompey in *Leg.* seem to adumbrate, however, Cicero's choice of sides in the civil war; cf. Riemer, 65–66.

incurret etiam in illum memorabilem annum suum; . . .] To see the achievements of his consulate properly set forth for posterity was a major concern of Cicero (see on §§ 5b–8); this prospect, if anything, was what could induce him to write history.

quae ab isto malo praedicari quam, ut aiunt, de Remo et Romulo.] *Quae* is summarizing: "all which things"; *praedico* changes construction in mid-sentence from transitive to use with *de.*—*De Remo et Romulo*[48] [sc. *loqui* or the like] was apparently a proverbial expression (found only here) for speaking of the remote and/or hackneyed; cf. A. Otto, 302. The joke lies in the fact that the proverbial phrase would apply literally if Cicero were to write a history *ab urbe condita*.

M. . . . quem [sc. laborem] non recusarem, si mihi ullum tribueretur vacuum tempus et liberum.] If this response was meant to be Cicero's "excuse auprès du publique" (Leeman, 186), it may also be, at this point in his life,[49] the true reason; cf. *Att.* 2.6.1 (April 59), where Cicero announces that he is abandoning the writing of a geographical work in view *inter alia* of the difficulty of reconciling conflicting sources, or ibid. 4.16.2, where he complains of the demands of writing *Rep.: rem . . . magnam complexus sum et plurimi oti, quo ego maxime egeo.* Wiseman, 1987, 249, notes a trend in the first century away from distinguished statesmen writing history and concludes that "modern Hellenized literary taste demanded a more erudite, elaborate and sophisticated type of history than a senior statesman's leisure could easily accommodate."—*Vacuum tempus* is time "not taken up with other activities or affairs, unoccupied, idle" (*OLD* s.v. *vacuus* 10; cf. Forcellini s.v., II.3: "minime occupatus, otiosus"), whereas *liberum tempus* is time that one is free to arrange at will, not subject to the claims of others ("respicitur status arbitrio aliorum obnoxius": *TLL* s.v. *liber* 1287.18 with examples cited at 26 ff.). For the sake of *variatio* Cicero at first uses a

48. For this order, possibly implying that Remus was the elder, cf. T.P. Wiseman, *Remus: A Roman Myth* (Cambridge, 1995), 203 n. 48.

49. Later on, of course, there were other hindrances: besides the political difficulty of writing such a work under Caesar's dictatorship (see below), there was the loss of mental balance resulting from his divorce and remarriage and the death of Tullia; cf. Plut. *Cic.* 41.

paraphrase *(vacuum tempus et liberum)*, to which Atticus responds with *tempus vacuum*, rather than the *mot juste (otium)*, reserved for Cicero's next speech, taken up in turn by Atticus' paraphrase *cessationem liberam atque otiosam*. With a similar regard for placing business first, Cicero's dialogues on philosophy and rhetoric are set during festivals; cf. Becker, 12–13; Philip Levine, "Cicero and the Literary Dialogue," *CJ* 53 (1958), 147. On Cicero's position, caught between maintaining his *dignitas* in politics and desiring to have and exploit *otium*, cf. in general Jean-Marie André, *L'otium dans la vie morale et intellectuelle romaine des origines à l'epoque augustéenne* (Paris, 1966), 284 ff. But, even when Caesar's dictatorship freed him from most public duties, he chose to write instead on rhetoric and philosophy. This situation reflects a new, complex set of realities: an unvarnished version of the past from Cicero's viewpoint would have offended Caesar (cf. Leeman, 186–87); and, with the institutions of the republic suspended and most of the men who had sustained them passed from the scene, the dynamic of civic life was altered, and the point of historiography as a spur to achievement of youth by glorifying the deeds of the past must have seemed blunted. It was only after Caesar's assassination, in November 44, that he turned with a vengeance to the writing of history (*Att.* 16.13a.2; see *supra* on *est quaedam inter nos parva dissensio*).

neque enim occupata opera neque impedito animo res tanta suscipi potest; utrumque opus est, et cura vacare et negotio.] The obstacles are arranged chiastically, with *cura* referring back to *impedito animo* and *negotio* to *occupata opera*.—For the transmitted *occupata* Davies suggested *occupato*, agreeing with *animo*, but such attractions are possible; cf. Reid *ad Luc.* 89 *(incitato furore)*.—By "work" *(opera, negotium)* Cicero evidently means pleading in the forum—a clear pointer to a dramatic date in the 50s, rather than the 40s; cf. the complaints at *Fam.* 7.1.4 (September 55); *Planc.* 84: *nam quod in eo me reprehendisti quod nimium multos defenderem, utinam et tu, qui potes, et ceteri, qui defugiunt, vellent me labore hoc levare!*—Plin. *Ep.* 5.8.7 describes a similar dilemma: *dices: 'potes simul et rescribere actiones et componere historiam.' utinam!*

9 A. Quid ad cetera, quae scripsisti plura quam quisquam e nostris, quod tibi tandem tempus vacuum fuit concessum?] Cicero took a certain pride in his literary productivity (cf. *Off.* 1.3: . . . *magnopere te hortor, mi Cicero, ut non solum orationes meas sed hos etiam de philosophia libros, qui iam illis fere se aequarunt, studiose legas*), as well as the efficient use of time that made it possible (see the next lemma).

M. Subsiciva quaedam tempora incurrunt, quae ego perire non patior; ut si qui dies ad rusticandum dati sint, ad eorum numerum accommodentur quae

scribimus.] This looks like a fairly accurate description of the writing habits not only of Cicero but of Roman statesmen generally since the Elder Cato (*hist.* fr. 2 *apud Planc.* 66): *clarorum virorum atque magnorum non minus oti quam negoti rationem exstare oportere;* cf. Cicero's preceding remark: *nam quas tu commemoras, Cassi, legere te solere orationes cum otiosus sis, has ego scripsi ludis et feriis ne omnino umquam essem otiosus.* The use of time in the country corresponds, for instance, to his writing at several Italian villas of philosophical works, including *Off., Am.,* and a third book as well as *Phil.* 2 in fall, 44 (cf. *Att.* 16.11.1–3; *ad Off.* 2.23–29).—*Subseco* (= "cut away") may be used of the dividing off of boundaries (cf. *OLD* s.v.). Derived from it is the adjective *subsicivus,* evidently a term from surveying,[50] which refers to land "left over at the end of an allotment," hence "odd" or "spare" (ibid. s.v., 1). Our passage is the earliest instance of *subsicivus* used metaphorically of time (ibid. s.v., 2); Lucil. 762M = 776K had, however, already referred to *subsiciva opera;* Atticus' *ut ais* in repeating the expression (§ 13) shows that it was felt to be bold.

historia vero nec institui potest nisi praeparato otio, nec exiguo tempore absolvi. et ego animi pendere soleo, cum semel quid orsus {si} traducor alio; neque tam facile interrupta contexo quam absolvo instituta.] Cicero differentiates between historiography and other genres in that the former requires a greater amount of free time, presumably because of the systematic coverage entailed, though it might be argued that such works as *de Orat.* and *Rep.* likewise required systematic handling of subject-matter.—*Animi* is "genitive of the sphere"; cf. Hofmann-Szantyr, 74 ff. ("Genitiv des Sachbetreffs"); translate *animi pendere* as "to be unsettled" (Reid).—The textual choice is between (a) *et ego animi pendere soleo, cum semel quid orsus ⟨sum⟩* (Nizolius s.v. *ordior*) *si traducor alio . . .* and (b) *cum semel quid orsus {si} traducor alio* (the *recentiores*), in either case a conjecture.—The tendencies described here might help to account both for Cicero's displeasure at being posted as governor to Cilicia when he had already embarked on *Leg.* (cf. *Fam.* 3.2.1; *Att.* 5.10.3 and 11.1; Stockton, 1971, 227) and, ironically, for his apparent inability to complete the work later on; see pp. 10–12 *supra.*

10a A. Legationem aliquam nimirum ista oratio postulat, . . .] "Those words of yours [i.e., about the need for *praeparatum otium,* not merely *subsiciva tempora*][51] surely call for some embassy," i.e., an appointment as

---

50. Cf. Var. R. 1.10.2: *. . . mensores non numquam dicunt in subsicivum esse unciam agri aut sextantem . . .*

51. *Ista oratio* is sometimes taken to refer to "istud scribendi genus aut compositionis" (Bake), i.e., the writing of history as conceived by Cicero; but the interpretation given in the text is perhaps the more natural in dialogue form; cf. § 52: *libenter enim, frater, quo ducis ista oratione, tecum prolabebar* (for the reading see *ad loc.*).

legatus that would, however, leave the recipient free of official responsibility. A *libera legatio* is envisioned, as the following clause clarifies; cf. Ulp. *dig.* 50.7.15: *qui libera legatione abest, non videtur reipublicae causa abesse; hic enim non publici commodi causa, sed sui abest,* as well as other passages cited by *TLL* s.v. *legatio* 1102.36 ff. Marcus makes it clear in his reply that this is not what he had in mind, and indeed he generally disapproved of such *legationes* and would as consul have abolished them altogether but for a tribune's veto (cf. *ad* 3.18). For Cicero's declination of a *libera legatio voti causa* offered by Caesar cf. *Att.* 2.18.3 (June 59); *Prov.* 41. In 44 he spoke publicly of having *ius legationis liberum* in connection with his planned trip to Greece, though, in fact, it was a *legatio* granted by Dolabella; cf. *Att.* 15.8.1 and 15.11.4; *Phil.* 1.6 with Denniston's note.

. . . **aut eiusmodi quampiam cessationem liberam atque otiosam.**] *Cessatio* is a "relaxation from business, rest" (*OLD* s.v., 1); similar is *secessus* at Ov. *Tr.* 1.1.41: *carmina secessum scribentis et otia quaerunt.*

10b–11 Rejecting Atticus' interpretation of his need for greater leisure as a call for a *libera legatio*, Marcus sets the problem rather into the context of his adaptation to old age, when the physical demands of oratory might be excessive; cf. *Sen.* 28: *orator metuo ne languescat senectute; est enim munus eius non ingenii solum, sed laterum etiam et virium.* Atticus worries, however, that a more moderate oratorical style—presumably both in terms of colon-lengths and vehemence of delivery—may enable Marcus to continue pleading indefinitely and thus militate against the writing of any historical work.

10b M. Ego vero aetatis potius vacationi confidebam; . . .] "I was relying rather on an exemption by reason of age." *Vacatio* is a legal term applied originally to military service, later generalized (cf. Ernout-Meillet s.v. *vaco*); it is sometimes used, as here, with a genitive denoting the cause of exemption; cf. *OLD* s.v., 1.

cum praesertim non recusarem quominus more patrio sedens in solio consulentibus responderem, senectutisque non inertis grato atque honesto fungerer munere.] That old age should not be *iners* was a precept put forward by Cicero in his own person (*nihil autem magis cavendum est senectuti quam ne languori se desidiaeque dedat: Off.* 1.123) and by characters in his dialogues. He has Crassus describe the rôle of *iuris interpretatio* in old age in similar terms at *de Orat.* 1.199; and the Ciceronian Cato spends his old age *inter alia* by helping friends in court cases and by writing history (*Sen.* 38). Cicero also describes his own attempts to avoid such inertia (. . . *nec eam solitudinem languere patior: Off.* 3.3) and to fill his leisure with honorable activities (. . . *nec me angoribus dedidi . . . nec rursum indignis homine docto voluptatibus:* ibid. 2.2). Writing history and other works intended for Atticus (*Am.* and *Sen.* would be dedicated to him) thus fits with his view of how one should spend old age or other leisure.—For Marcus' picture of himself *cum . . . non recusarem quominus more patrio sedens in solio consulentibus responderem*, cf. *de Orat.* 2.143 (Antonius on Crassus' reduction of the *ius civile* to an art): *tum a Crasso discemus cum se de turba et a subselliis in otium, ut cogitat, soliumque contulerit.* On the *solium*, a high seat with back- and arm-rests and a footstool *(scamnum)*, cf. Hug, *RE* 3A1 (1927) s.v.—For Cicero as a jurisconsult cf. *iur. anteh.*, pp. 127–30, together with Emilio Costa, *Cicerone giureconsulto*, 2d ed., 2 vols. (Bologna, 1927–28).

sic enim mihi liceret et isti rei quam desideras, et multis uberioribus atque maioribus, operae quantum vellem dare.] Under *uberiores atque maiores (res)* Cicero understands writing on philosophy, as all interpreters agree. If that is so, then the difference should be one of quality, not quantity, and *multo*, proposed (for *multis*) by Emil Orth, "Cicero: de legibus I 3, 10," *Philologische Wochenschrift* 42 (1922), 287–88, has much to recommend it.

11 A. Atqui vereor ne istam causam nemo noscat, . . .] *Causa* is here an alleged ground, excuse, or pretext: cf. *OLD* s.v., 5a. In such combination *nosco* means "accept as valid, true": ibid. s.v. *nosco* 6; cf. *Att.* 11.7.5 (17 December 48): *quod te excusas, ego vero et tuas causas nosco et mea interesse puto te istic esse . . . ; Fam.* 4.4.1 (to Ser. Sulpicius, Sept.–Oct. 46): *illam partem excusationis . . . nec nosco nec probo.*

et eo magis quod te ipse mutasti, et aliud dicendi instituisti genus; . . .] Cf. *de Orat.* 1.254 (following upon the passage quoted in the next note): *quod si ille* [sc. Roscius], *adstrictus certa quadam numerorum moderatione et pedum, tamen aliquid ad requiem senectutis excogitat, quanto facilius nos non laxare modos, sed totos mutare possumus?* The nature of this change is defined in the sequel; see the note after next.

ut quemadmodum Roscius, familiaris tuus, in senectute numeros in cantu leniverat, ipsasque tardiores fecerat tibias, sic tu . . . cotidie relaxes aliquid, . . .] Transmitted is the tautological *numeros in cantu cecinerat.* Cf. *de Orat.* 1.254: *. . . solet idem Roscius dicere se, quo plus sibi aetatis accederet, eo tardiores tibicinis modos et cantus remissiores esse facturum.* In light of this parallel Lambinus' *remiserat* for *cecinerat* is generally accepted. Other suggestions are *cautius* for *in cantu* (Urlichs, 154) and Hermann's *leniverat*, here adopted.[52]—The taste and tact of Q. Roscius Gallus, the greatest actor of his age, are celebrated by Cicero in a number of passages of *de Orat.*; cf. also Plut. *Cic.* 5.4–5. Cicero's earliest preserved speech is the defense undertaken at his instance of his nephew P. Quinctius (81); a part of Cicero's

---

52. Büchner's *lentaverat* is poetic.

defense of the actor himself against prosecution by C. Fannius Chaerea is also extant; cf. Von der Mühll, *RE* 1A1 (1914), 1123.28 ff. (Roscius no. 16); F. Warren Wright, *Cicero and the Theatre* (Northampton, MA, 1931), 16–20; on the date of the latter speech (ca. 76) cf. Gelzer, 26. At *Brut.* 325 ff. Hortensius is criticized for *not* changing his manner of speaking with advancing years (though there the reference is to style rather than delivery). . . . sic tu a con⟨ten⟩tionibus quibus summis uti solebas cotidie relaxes aliquid, ut iam oratio tua non multum a philosophorum lenitate absit.] *Contentio est oratio acris et ad confirmandum et ad confutandum adcommodata* (*Rhet. Her.* 3.23); cf. *ad Off.* 2.48. Cf. Cicero's description of his youthful style of speaking at *Brut.* 313: . . . *hoc eos quibus eram carus commovebat, quod omnia sine remissione, sine varietate, vi summa vocis et totius corporis contentione dicebam;* on Cicero's natural equipment for oratory and training of voice and body cf. also Plut. *Cic.* 3.7 and 4.4–7. At *Sen.* 28 (where see Powell's note) he remarks: *est decorus seni sermo quietus et remissus.*— Atticus' observation of Cicero's change in oratorical practice seems to be partially confirmed by the chronological study of relative colon-lengths in the speeches conducted by B.D. Frischer, "How to Do Things with Words per Strong Stop: Two Studies in the *Historia Augusta* and Cicero," *Aspects of Latin: Papers from the Seventh International Colloquium on Latin Linguistics, Jerusalem, April, 1993,* Innsbrucker Beiträge zur Sprachwissenschaft 86 (Innsbruck, 1996), 593 ff., the orator's weakening lungs being accommodated by shorter colons. Presumably Atticus will have in mind such speeches as *pro Plancio* and *pro Rabirio Postumo* (both from the year 54); cf. *Planc.* 72: *respondebo tibi nunc, Laterensis, minus fortasse vehementer quam abs te sum provocatus . . .* —For *philosophorum lenitas* cf. *Orat.* 64: *mollis est enim oratio philosophorum et umbratilis . . . nihil iratum habet, nihil invidum, nihil atrox, nihil miserabile, nihil astutum; Off.* 1.3: *te hortor, mi Cicero, ut non solum orationes meas sed hos etiam de philosophia libros . . . studiose legas; vis enim maior in illis dicendi, sed hoc quoque colendum est aequabile et temperatum orationis genus.*
12 Q. At mehercule ego arbitrabar posse id populo nostro probari, si te ad ius respondendum dedisses; . . .] *Mehercule* (also at 2.5b; cf. *hercle:* 2.8, 3.1) is an interjection ordinarily used only by men; created by a crossing of *hercle* and *mehercules* (the latter *for ita me Hercules iuvet ut*), it was Cicero's preferred form of the interjection (cf. *Orat.* 157); cf. Hofmann, 136–38.—Though *respondeo* is ordinarily intransitive, it can have either a neuter pronoun or *ius* as a direct object; if the latter, the sense is "to pronounce one's ruling on a point of law" (cf. *OLD* s.v., esp. 4c).—For *do* used with *ad* rather than the dative cf. examples at *OLD* s.v., 20a and c.

quamobrem, cum placebit, experiendum tibi id censeo.] Transmitted is *tibi censeo. id si . . .*, which Turnebus emended to *id censeo. si* with resulting double cretic clausula; for the word order cf. *Att.* 4.16.4: *gratum enim tibi id esse intellego.*

M. . . . sed vereor ne dum minuere velim laborem augeam, . . .] Marcus expresses fear not merely of an unintended consequence but of the very opposite of the result desired; cf. *Luc.* 5: *ac vereor interdum ne talium personarum cum amplificare velim, minuam etiam gloriam.*

. . . atque ad illam causarum operam, ad quam ego numquam nisi paratus et meditatus accedo, . . .] Cf. *Quinct.* 39: *. . . cum paratus meditatusque venisses . . .* ; *Ver.* 1.103: *. . . crimina . . . quae notiora sunt his qui adsunt quam nobis qui meditati ad dicendum paratique venimus;* criticism of the prosecutor C. Erucius for inadequate preparation at *Sex. Rosc.* 42, 54, 59, 61, 72. Such preparation belongs to the advocate's *fides* toward his client; cf. Freyburger, 160 ff.

. . . adiungatur haec iuris interpretatio, quae non tam mihi molesta sit propter laborem, . . .] Cicero well knew the long hours success as a legal advisor could entail (*Mur.* 22 [addressed to Servius Sulpicius]: *vigilas tu de nocte ut tuis consultoribus respondeas*); he often emphasized his own hard work, e.g., in foiling Catiline's conspiracy (*Cat.* 4.1 and 23).

. . . quam quod dicendi cogitationem auferat, sine qua ad nullam maiorem umquam causam sum ausus accedere.] This practice corresponds to Antonius' advice at *de Orat.* 2.99–103. At *Off.* 1.73 Cicero urges careful preparation before any action.

13–15 The subject of conversation has meandered from the writing of history, including the lack of an adequate treatment of Roman history in Latin and the possibility of Cicero's filling that gap, to the means of spending the *otium* of old age, also to be used for the traditional giving of legal advice to clients. Here the discussion takes a decisive turn: Atticus has the bright idea that at present they have some "leftover time" *(subsiciva tempora)* such as Cicero uses for his literary projects (§ 9); Cicero could fill it by explaining his views of law, which the two of them had learned about in their youth from Scaevola the Augur. This way of introducing the subject connects it with Atticus' interests and provides a Roman precedent for the project in the *responsa* of great men of the past (cf. § 17); at the same time, it forestalls the excuse Cicero had used for not writing history. The choice of topic is the prerogative here, as at *Rep.* 1.30 ff., of the guest who is at the same time the close friend of the major speaker. For the conversation to take this turn is, however, a little surprising in view of the intensity with which Atticus has just introduced the topic of historiography (*teneo quam opta-*

bam occasionem neque omittam: § 5). In any case, Marcus is chary of the topic as first introduced (*de iure civili quid sentias:* § 14) as being at too humble and utilitarian a level. Atticus clarifies, offering the precedent of Plato's *Laws* produced as a sequel to his *Republic* (§ 15). The definition of the subject is continued in §§ 16–17.

13 A. Quin igitur ista ipsa explicas nobis, his subsicivis (ut ais) temporibus, . . .] Here the subject of *Leg.* is defined, but the formulation is rather casual and has given rise to misunderstandings. Kenter *ad loc.* is probably right to see in *ista ipsa* a loose reference to *iuris interpretatio* and hence implicitly to the *ius civile;* the following justification *(nam)* is based upon Cicero's long acquaintance with the latter; *aliter* Girardet, 1983, 41, who sees a reference to the *parari, meditari,* and the *dicendi cogitatio* just described by Cicero.—For *subsicivus* cf. ad § 9.—*Ais:* Vahlen restored *aiis* from *aliis* (BAᵃ)[53] on the assumption that it preserves a trace of the Ciceronian spelling; cf. Quint. *Inst.* 1.4.11; W.S. Allen, 39; Leumann, 127.

. . . et conscribis de iure civili subtilius quam ceteri?] Benardete, 300–301, interpreting these words as a paraphrase of the previous question *(quin igitur ista ipsa explicas nobis . . . ?),* sees this as a first instance of the confounding of the categories of oral and written. But, as Reid notes, "*nobis explicas* above may refer to a speech—to be expanded into a book." In the sequel Marcus will refer to Atticus' request as one for both an oral account *(In longum sermonem me vocas, Attice* [§ 13]) and a written work *(quamobrem quo me vocas . . . ? ut libellos conficiam . . . ?* [§ 14]). On the other hand, at § 15, citing Plato's precedent and Cicero's already written *Rep.,* Atticus remarks: *. . . consequens esse videtur ut scribas tu idem de legibus,* and Marcus takes this as an invitation to conduct the current discussion *isdem de rebus.* There is, in other words, a certain sliding back and forth between the categories of oral and written as Cicero seeks to place this conversation vis-à-vis Plato's and his own previous writing. The phenomenon can also be viewed as a piece of metatheater: the characters will have nothing to say unless Cicero writes.—Cicero once projected but never completed a work *de Iure Civili in Artem Redigendo;* cf. fr. phil., 27–28 and 93–94; Häfner, 21 ff.; Ferdinando Bona, "L'ideale retorico ciceroniano ed il 'ius civile in artem redigere,'" *SDHI* 46 (1980): 282–382, esp. 366 ff.; H.L.W. Nelson, "Ciceros Vorschläge für eine neues juristisches Lehrbuch. Betrachtungen über *De oratore* I, 185–192," *WZRostock,* 34.1 (1985), 37–39.—*Subtilius* is ambiguous; Atticus perhaps means "in a more refined, cultivated way" (Reid), but Marcus takes this to mean ἀκριβέστερον

53. *Ais* is the reading of HLER.

("more minutely") and in the sequel professes to be shocked at the prospect of writing *libelli de stillicidiorum ac de parietum iure*, especially when many have done so *diligenter* (§ 14); cf. 3.49 à propos the *ius potestatum*.

nam a primo tempore aetatis iuri studere te memini, cum ipse etiam ad Scaevolam ventitarem; . . .] Cicero narrates at *Am.* 1 his transfer to the care of Scaevola the Augur (cos. 117; *RE* s.v. Mucius no 21; Bauman, 1983, 312–40) upon assumption of the *toga virilis* (cf. Gelzer, 5); at *Brut.* 306 he describes Scaevola's method: *ego autem in iuris civilis studio multum operae dabam Q. Scaevolae Q. f., qui, quamquam nemini se ad docendum dabat, tamen consulentibus respondendo studiosos audiendi docebat.* Atticus' legal studies with Scaevola are not elsewhere attested. For Cicero's later studies with Scaevola the Pontifex cf. *ad* 2.47 and 49.—*Ventitare* corresponds to Greek φοιτᾶν (Reid); the subjunctive *ventitarem* is an example of attraction of mood in the presence of *oratio obliqua* even though the *cum*-clause is purely temporal; cf. Kühner-Stegmann, 2, 205–6.

neque umquam mihi visus es ita te ad dicendum dedisse, ut ius civile contemneres.] For *te ad dicendum dedisse* cf. *ad* § 12 *si te ad ius respondendum dedisses.*—Cf. *ad* § 10b.

M. In longum sermonem me vocas, Attice; quem tamen, nisi Quintus aliud quid nos agere mavult, suscipiam, et quoniam vacui sumus, dicam.] For the alternation of terminology for oral and written discourse cf. *supra* on . . . *et conscribis de iure civili subtilius quam ceteri?*—The phrasing is reminiscent of the legal formula *in ius vocare* for citation before a court: cf. *Lex XII* 1.1 (cited at 2.9). Similarly, *agere* is the verb for pleading in court (*OLD* s.v. *ago* 44) and *suscipere causam* is used for taking on a client's case (ibid. s.v. *suscipio* 8c).—The third interlocutor, Quintus, needs to be consulted for politeness' sake; cf., e.g., *Ac.* 1.14: *sed videamus idemne Attico placeat fieri a me quod te velle video.*—*Quoniam vacui sumus:* time must not be taken away from the business of governing the state; cf. *ad* § 8 (. . . *quem* [sc. *laborem*] *non recusarem*—).

Q. Ego vero libenter audierim; quid enim agam potius, aut in quo melius hunc consumam diem?] Cf. Atticus' response following upon the query just quoted from *Ac.*: *mihi vero, quid est enim quod malim . . . ?* Quintus' *audierim* contrasts with the preceding *dicam;* indeed, Marcus will do almost all the speaking, the longest contribution by either of the other interlocutors being Quintus' speech at 3.19b–22.—For *quid . . . agam potius* cf. *Div.* 2.6: . . . *cum in armis civilibus nec tueri meo more rempublicam nec nihil agere poteram nec quid potius . . . agerem reperiebam.*—This remark is the first indicator of the duration of this dialogue; cf. *ad* 2.7. Similarly, Plato's *Laws* is set on one long summer day, as noted at § 15; cf. also *Gorg.* 458d

(Callicles is the speaker): . . . κἂν τὴν ἡμέραν ὅλην ἐθέλητε διαλέγεσθαι, χαριεῖσθε.

14–15 Now that Atticus has chosen the general subject, it needs to be more clearly defined, both negatively and positively. Cicero dismisses as too humble the *ius civile* as practiced by the *iuris consulti*. This is contrasted with the larger themes *ius civitatis* and *universum ius*. The project is meant to stand in relation to *Rep.* as Plato's *Laws* to his *Republic* (but the actual relation of *Republic* and *Laws* is more complex than Cicero indicates; see further *ad* § 15); hence the discussion will have greater scope than forensic practice allows. The subject is thus contextualized within philosophical discourse, not discourse on the *ius civile* as it has previously existed; cf. Introduction § 1.

14 M. Quin igitur ad illa spatia nostra sedesque pergimus?] Here Cicero indicates how the dialogue will be formally staged, divided between walking and sitting. As in § 15 *spatia* refers to any circular way (cf. *OLD* s.v. *spatium* 2); cf. the setting of *Fin.* 5, the *Academiae nobilitata spatia* (§ 1). The walk will continue to the end of this Book; in Book 2 and what remains of Book 3 the wayfarers continue the discussion while taking their rest on the island in the Fibrenus near its junction with the Liris (2.6). Then, as the day progresses, the afternoon sun forces the interlocutors to seek the shade of the alders along the bank of the Liris: cf. on the fr. from Book 5; Becker, 26–27.

ubi, cum satis erit ambulatum, requiescemus, nec profecto nobis delectatio deerit aliud ex alio quaerentibus.] Cicero is careful to provide his interlocutors with a balance of walking and sitting; cf. 2.1; *Div.* 2.8: *nam cum de divinatione Quintus frater ea disseruisset . . . satisque ambulatum videretur . . .* —For *aliud ex alio quaerentibus* cf. the philosophers' inquiries at Pl. *Tht.* 172d: . . . τοῖς μὲν [sc. φιλοσόφοις] τοῦτο ὃ σὺ εἶπες ἀεὶ πάρεστι, σχολή, καὶ τοὺς λόγους ἐν εἰρήνῃ ἐπὶ σχολῆς ποιοῦνται· ὥσπερ ἡμεῖς νυνὶ τρίτον ἤδη λόγον ἐκ λόγου μεταλαμβάνομεν, οὕτω κἀκεῖνοι, ἐὰν αὐτοὺς ὁ ἐπελθὼν τοῦ προκειμένου μᾶλλον καθάπερ ἡμᾶς ἀρέσῃ . . . ; § 52 (*ut ex alio alia nectantur*).

A. Nos vero, et hac quidem ad Lirem, si placet, per ripam et umbram.] With *nos vero* supply *pergamus* from Marcus' *pergimus*.—*Hac* refers forward to the route *per ripam et umbram*, where the different objects require different translations of *per* ("along" and "through," respectively).—*Ad Lirem* is Bake's correction for *adire(m)*; the accusative of the mixed inflection is transmitted at 2.6, but the *i*-stem *Lirim* in the fr. from Book 5; cf. Meiser § 97.4.— The gentle Liris was celebrated in Latin poetry (Hor. *C.* 1.31.6–7: *non rura quae Liris quieta / mordet aqua taciturnus amnis*; Sil. 4.348–50: *et Liris nutritus aquis, qui fonte quieto / dissimulat cursum ac nullo mutabilis imbri /*

perstringit tacitas gemmanti gurgite ripas). The bank of the river will afford shade and attractive views; cf. *Att.* 15.16a (where the location described is uncertain): *et tamen haec* ῥωπογραφία *ripulae videtur habitura celerem satietatem.* The parallel to the Ilissus of *Phaedrus* 230b is explicit at 2.6 (cf. Hirzel, 1895, 475 n. 2).

sed iam ordire explicare, quaeso, de iure civili quid sentias.] *Explicare* takes up *Quin igitur ista ipsa explicas . . .* (§ 13).

M. Egone? summos fuisse in civitate nostra viros qui id interpretari populo et responsitare soliti sint; sed eos magna professos in parvis esse versatos.] *Egone:* sc. *ordiar.* "Shall I?" or "Meinst du?" (Zumpt). *-ne* is commonly attached to the first-person pronoun in a diffident reply to a request: cf. *OLD* s.v. *-ne* 7b; *Leg.* 2.32; 3.47; *Luc.* 148; *N.D.* 1.16; *Fin.* 3.11; *Tusc.* 2.42.— There is a similar emphasis on the standing of the practitioners by Pomponius: *iuris civilis scientiam plurimi et maximi viri professi sunt* (*dig.* 1.2.2.35). The phrase *magna professos* is reminiscent of Servius Sulpicius' alleged exaggeration of the importance of legal knowledge (*Mur.* 21). The contrast of Servius with the general Murena at *Mur.* 19 ff. underlines, through use of the same verbs for both sets of activities, the pettiness of the lawyer's work, e.g., *tu caves ne tui consultores, ille ne urbes aut castra capiantur; ille tenet et scit ut hostium copiae, tu ut aquae pluviae arceantur . . .* (§ 22); *res enim sunt parvae, prope in singulis litteris atque interpunctionibus verborum occupatae* (§ 25). Cicero gives more examples in the sequel (*ut libellos conficiam de stillicidiorum ac de parietum iure?* etc.). Cf. also Antonius' contemptuous description of the jurisconsult at *de Orat.* 1.236: *ita est tibi iuris consultus ipse per se nihil nisi leguleius quidam cautus et acutus, praeco actionum, cantor formularum, auceps syllabarum . . .* ; sim. Maternus' plan to cultivate poetry and be rid of *forensium causarum angustiae* (Tac. *Dial.* 4.2). On Cicero's attitude toward the *iuris consulti* in general cf. *ad* 2.47 and further literature at Girardet, 1983, 42 n. 9.—The frequentative *responsito* is appropriate for the activity of the jurisconsult; it first appears at *Rep.* 5.4, where Cicero makes the point that the *rector* should study law *sed se responsitando et lectitando et scriptitando ne impediat;* cf. *OLD* s.v.

quid enim est tantum quantum ius civitatis?] For *ius civile*, used in Atticus' request *(sed iam ordire explicare, quaeso, de iure civili quid sentias)*, is substituted *ius civitatis* to make the subject generic; cf. 2.35: *non enim populo Romano, sed omnibus bonis firmisque populis leges damus;* in fact, in Books 2–3 a fair amount of Greek material is introduced by way of precedent, positive or negative. The definition of *respublica* as *res populi* at *Rep.* 1.39 is a similar deconstruction; cf. Girardet, 1983, 42 n. 10; Benardete, 300.

quid autem tam exiguum quam est munus hoc eorum qui consuluntur,

quam⟨quam⟩ est populo necessarium?] See the note before last. Cicero could, however, if it suited his purpose, emphasize the importance of the service; cf. *Caec.* 70; *Off.* 2.65: *nam in iure cavere, consilio iuvare atque hoc scientiae genere prodesse quam plurimis vehementer et ad opes augendas pertinet et ad gratiam.*—*Quam* is the reading of BAPH^N, *quod* of H¹L; *quam* could be the result of haplography; hence *quamquam* of the *recentiores;* the alternative would be to assume that *quam est* is a perseverative error from above; in that case, however, it is difficult to know what might have dropped out. **nec vero eos qui ei muneri praefuerunt universi iuris fuisse expertes existimo; sed hoc civile, quod vocant, eatenus exercuerunt, quoad populo praestare voluerunt; . . .**] Here the concept of *universum ius* makes its first appearance in *Leg.*;[54] it will reappear in § 17; in both passages there is a contrast with the *ius civile,* which is only a part of *universum ius.*[55] The law applying to all people is, as Kenter points out, a philosophical, rather than a juridical, concept. Cicero is prepared to allow that the *iuris consulti* have some share in *universum ius,* although this does not appear in their practice, which is geared to the so-called *ius civile* and even within that smaller sphere to the special needs of clients; sim. Mehl, 115.—For *hoc civile quod vocant* cf. § 17: *hoc civile quod dicimus . . . quae vocantur iura civilia.* The implication is that the name is undeserved; cf. Schmidt, 1959, 152: "es ist als Privatrecht nur ein Teil des 'ius civitatis' . . ."—*Praesto* should be taken as "make available, furnish," or the like (*OLD* s.v., 9a; *TLL* s.v. 2. *praesto* 14.70 ff.), with *id munus* to be supplied as its object. The alternative interpretation with *praesto* taken as "be superior to, excel" (*OLD* s.v., 2a; *TLL* s.v. 1. *praesto*), adopted by du Mesnil *ad loc.,* Merguet, *Phil.* s.v. *praesto,* and Girardet, 1983, 44, is less probable; criticism of the *iuris consulti* as promoting their interests through obscurantism is phrased very cautiously at 2.47; cf. Schmidt, 1959, 152 n. 2. The rise of the jurists was connected with the legal disadvantages suffered by *equites* and others from the Italian municipalities; it was natural for *equites* to cultivate it; cf. Frier, 256–60. By Cicero's day *iuris scientia,* though cultivated by the *principes* in former times, was mostly in the hands of *equites* and even some freedmen; cf. Wolfgang Kunkel, *Herkunft und soziale Stellung der römischen Juristen*² (Graz-Vienna-Cologne, 1967), esp. 366; Crook, *CAH* 9², 553–54, adds

---

54. But cf. already *de Orat.* 3.136 (Crassus is the speaker): *nunc contra plerique ad honores adipiscendos . . . nudi veniunt . . . nulla cognitione rerum, nulla scientia ornati. sin aliquis excellit unus e multis, effert se, si unum aliquid adfert . . . aut iuris scientiam, ne eius quidem universi.*

55. *Pace* Girardet, 1983, 43, who thinks that *universum ius* is used here as a synonym for *ius civile/civitatis;* see further *ad* § 17.

some restrictions, noting the fluid line between senate and *equites*. At the time of the composition of *Leg.* it was rare for a jurist to hold the consulship (for a possible reference to Ser. Sulpicius' consulship in 51 see *ad* § 17; the previous instance was Q. Mucius Scaevola [cos. 95]). Indeed it seems doubtful that *iuris scientia* ever conferred per se the kind of preeminence that the second interpretation assumes.

id autem in cognitione tenue est, in usu necessarium.] "As far as science is concerned,[56] it is slight, but in practice it is essential."—On the ease with which knowledge of the subject could be obtained cf. *de Orat.* 1.185–90 (Crassus is the speaker, in part quoting Scaevola). For the indispensability of the *ius civile* in civil society cf. *Caec.* 70–75.

quamobrem quo me vocas, aut quid hortaris? ut libellos conficiam de stillicidiorum ac de parietum iure, an ut stipulationum et iudiciorum formulas componam?] Marcus effects a *reductio ad absurdum* of the request to deal with the *ius civile*[57] by citing patently inappropriate examples. Benardete, 300, emphasizes the oddity of the response given that the request was that he speak, not write, about the *ius civile*; cf. *ad* § 13.—These sets of examples are drawn respectively from the sphere of private *(ut libellos—parietum iure)* and procedural law *(ut stipulationum—componam)*. *Stillicidia* and *parietes* are examples of servitudes, the former involving the right of drainage onto a neighbor's property (cf. Watson, *Property,* 176), the latter the rights and obligations involved in the building and maintenance of an individual or party wall; they are among the causes of litigation listed by Crassus at *de Orat.* 1.173 and illustrate matters too minute for a pontifex to know about at *Leg.* 2.47.—The *stipulatio* was a verbal contract creating an actionable obligation and including the question of the *stipulator* (e.g., *sestertium X milia mihi dari spondesne*) and the answer of the *promissor* *(spondeo)*; cf. Pompon. *dig.* 45.1.5.1: *stipulatio . . . est verborum conceptio, quibus is qui interrogatur daturum facturumve se quod interrogatus est responderit*; Kaser, 1, 538 ff. A *formula* was "a written document by which in a civil trial authorization was given to a judge *(iudex)* to condemn the defendant if certain factual or legal circumstances appeared proved, or to absolve him if this was not the case *(si paret . . . condemnato, si non paret, absolvito)*. Introduced by the lex Aebutia, . . . the formulary procedure replaced almost completely the former procedure of *legis actiones*" (Berger s.v. *formula*); cf. also Greenidge, 49 ff. and 164–65; Watson, *loc. cit.,* 96, and *Law Making,* 31 and 120; Girardet, 1983, 49 n. 43; Wieacker,

---

56. Reid's rendering of *in cognitione*.
57. Cf. his procedure in dealing with Atticus' query at § 3.

1988, 447 ff.; Kaser-Hackl, 237. Cicero holds such *formulae* up to ridicule at *Mur.* 26.

quae et scripta a multis sunt diligenter, et sunt humiliora quam illa quae a nobis exspectari puto.] *Diligenter* = "minutely" (Reid); cf. Atticus' use of *subtilius* at § 13.—Corresponding to the shift from *legis actiones* to formulary procedure was a change in the focus of legal literature from works commenting on the *ius civile*[58] to works dealing with *actiones;* hence Cicero can truly say that these matters *scripta a multis sunt diligenter.*—Though the legal literature prior to Justinian is highly fragmentary (see Wieacker, 1988, 110), it is clear that the great jurists of Cicero's day did not ordinarily deal with minor cautelary questions; their major task was rather to draft carefully thought through formulas; cf. ibid. 559 and n. 40. In our passage, however, Cicero makes no distinction between the two tasks; for him both minor cautelary problems *(stillicidia, parietes)* and formulary law *(stipulationum et iudiciorum formulae)* are too humble. See *supra* on *nec vero eos qui ei muneri praefuerunt—*. Marcus does not deny that he is capable of doing the work of the jurisconsult (indeed in § 10 he reserves this for his *senectus*), only that this is appropriate for the current discussion (in fact, at 2.46–53 he will give a specimen of his juridical thinking). Similar to his construction of his own *dignitas* here is Crassus' indignant response when Sulpicius asks him whether he considers oratory an art (though the point of contrast is different): *quid? mihi nunc vos tamquam alicui Graeculo otioso et loquaci et fortasse docto atque erudito quaestiunculam de qua meo arbitratu loquar ponitis?* (*de Orat.* 1.102). Scaevola's clarification that the younger members of the party are not asking as one would a loquacious Greek or seeking a school catechism (ibid. 2.105) clears the way for Crassus' response (Cicero plays further on the relation of the dialogue to school instruction, ibid. 2.13 and 28).

15 A. Atqui si quaeris ego quid exspectem, . . .] Previous wishes regarding Marcus' literary plans were formulated in the passive voice (*postulatur a te iam diu vel flagitatur potius historia . . .* : § 5), but Atticus' personal wish is more difficult for him to brush aside.—*Quaeres* is transmitted, but Rath's *quaeris* is smoother with the following *videtur.*[59]

. . . quoniam scriptum est a te de optimo reipublicae statu, . . .] Cf. Laelius' request that Scipio explain what he holds to be the *optimus status civitatis* (*Rep.* 1.33; cf. 1.46), as well as 3.4 (*quaeque de optima republica sentiremus in sex libris ante diximus . . .*). To be more precise, *de optimo*

---

58. Cf. pp. 3–4 *supra.*

59. Cf. Reid: "*quaeris* seems necessary."

statu civitatis and *de optimo cive;* this description at *Q.fr.* 3.5.1, though formulated with a nine-book version in mind, still holds, with the first day (Books 1–2) devoted to the *optimus status civitatis,* the third day (5–6) to the *optimus civis,* and the second day (3–4) to "the ethical and human foundations of the *optimus status* and of the *optimus civis*"; cf. Ferrary, 1995, 49–51 (the quoted words at 50).—In mid-July 51 Atticus is evidently reading *Rep.* with a friend (the name is corrupt: *Att.* 5.12.2).

... consequens esse videtur ut scribas tu idem de legibus. sic enim fecisse video Platonem illum tuum, quem tu admiraris, quem omnibus anteponis, quem maxime diligis.] *Consequens* (= "consistent") is a word of which Cicero was fond (cf. Reid *ad Ac.* 1.19: *consentiens*).—The anaphora of *quem* (sim. the encomium of Plato at *Tusc.* 1.79) suggests a hymn of praise, often characterized by a piling up of relative clauses; cf. Norden, 1913, 168 ff.—The analogy of *Rep.* to Plato's *Republic* already appears at *Att.* 4.16.3 (ca. 1 July 54): *feci idem quod in* Πολιτείᾳ *deus ille noster Plato.* Cicero does not address the characterization of the state of Plato's *Laws* as second best (*Lg.* 739e; cf. 875a–d) but treats the relation of *Republic* and *Laws* as a difference of subject matter; cf. also § 20. Another ancient view was that the *Laws* dealt with the contingent state (περὶ . . . τοῦ ἐξ ὑποθέσεως), whereas the *Republic* dealt with the ideal state (περὶ . . . τοῦ ἀνυποθέτου).[60] Recent scholarship defines the differences between the two dialogues as a result either of the evolution of Plato's thought or his attempt to reach a broader, no longer purely philosophical, audience or some combination of the two; cf. Stalley, 8–10 with literature. Cf. most recently André Laks, "Legislation and Demiurgy: On the Relationship Between Plato's *Republic* and *Laws,*" *CA* 9 (1990), 209–29, esp. 223, who sees the relation in similar terms to Cicero's (cf. *ad* 2.14b), i.e., that the laws of the *Laws* are for the state of the *Republic,* but considers that they add some important qualifiers about what a true constitution entails and about the need for constraint.—Cicero's relation to Plato would merit a monograph. He much admired Plato both as a stylist (cf. *ad* 2.14b) and as a philosopher. Throughout his life he declared his allegiance to the Academy (cf. *ad* § 39), to which he acknowledged a debt even in his oratory (cf. *Orat.* 12 cited *ad* § 36). Cf. Thelma B. DeGraff, "Plato in Cicero," *CPh* 35 (1940): 143–53; P. Boyancé, "Le platonisme à Rome. Platon et Cicéron. Rapport," *Association G. Budé: Actes du Congrès de Tours et de Poitiers, 3–9 septembre 1953* (Paris, 1954), 195–222; Burkert, 1965; Lévy, 68–70 with literature; Long, 1995b, 43–52.

---

60. *Prolégomènes à la philosophie de Platon,* ed. L.G. Westerink, tr. J. Trouillard, with collaboration of A.P. Segonds (Paris, 1990), 26.57–58.

M. Visne igitur, ut ille Crete cum Clinia et cum Lacedaemonio Megillo, aestivo (quemadmodum describit) die in cupressetis Gnosiorum et spatiis silvestribus,—tum autem residentes, . . .] For the form of the request see the fr. from Book 5 with note. Cicero, like *hyp. ad Lg.*, assumes that the Athenian Stranger is identical with Plato himself (the reason given there: αὐτὸς γὰρ ὁ ᾿Αθηναῖος ξένος . . . λέγει ὅτι ἤδη αὐτῷ δύο πολιτεῖαι προηγνύσθησαν).[61] Some of what the Stranger says of himself does not fit Plato, however, so once again we have a constructed *persona*, albeit the disguise seems to be thinner than usual; cf. Morrow, 74–75.—Cicero commonly places ethnics in front of their nouns (*Crete cum Clinia et cum Lacedaemonio Megillo*); see Powell *ad Sen.* 13.—The carefully described route leads the wayfarers from Cnossus to the cave and sanctuary of Zeus. Like the way suggested by Marcus, it affords ample shade and charm for the eye and resting-places en route (*Lg.* 625b). The parallelism of the setting and procedure[62] corresponds to a parallelism of the subject matter (*isdem de rebus*).— For *residentes* cf. 2.1: *visne . . . sermoni reliquo demus operam sedentes?* with note.

. . . quaeramus eisdem de rebus aliquid uberius quam forensis usus desiderat?] Oratorical practice is the point of comparison, given its centrality to Cicero's activities (cf. *ad* §§ 5b–12); similarly, at *Arch.* 32 Cicero confesses having said *a foro aliena iudicialique consuetudine* (cf. §§ 3 and 18). *De Orat.* 2.109 illustrates the difference: Antonius recommends omitting definitions of terms from courtroom speeches as being too pedantic and easily disputed. *Usus forensis* was the sole point that Scaevola was prepared to concede the orator in *de Orat.*, and Crassus argues against this position (esp. 1.59, where the phrase occurs), later taken up by Antonius (ibid. 1.260). **16** After Atticus and Quintus have given assent, Marcus offers a précis of what he means by an inquiry "in fuller form than forensic practice requires" (*uberius quam forensis usus desiderat:* § 16). Given that a philosophical treatment is envisaged (see *ad* §§ 14–15), it will not merely describe surface phenomena but will seek the source (*fons iuris et legum*). This is connected with four points: (1) the endowment of the human being by nature, (2) the qualities of the human mind, (3) the duties (or tasks) for the sake of which human beings are born, (4) human society. These items, though presented in a "thoroughly rhetorical" fashion (Reid) in a series of balanced clauses, are clearly linked, with the prior two and the latter two forming pairs. There is an implicit process of reasoning from nature's provision (1), though only the

---

61. D.L. 3.52 shows knowledge of the identification but rejects it.

62. Note the parallel participial phrases *crebro insistens, interdum adquiescens . . . in viridi opacaque ripa inambulantes, tum autem residentes . . .*

special quality of the human mind, *viz.*, reason, is specified here (2), to the formation of society (4) and proper behavior toward society and its members, especially parents and children (3). Thus one would expect points (3) and (4) to be reversed, the existence of society being basic, duties performed within its framework secondary; and, in fact, when the plan is executed (§§ 33–34), these two points appear in the expected order, i.e., (4), then (3), though the recapitulation at § 35 displays the same sequence as our paragraph.[63] The execution of the plan, then, is organized as follows: (1) corresponds to §§ 22–27; (2) to §§ 28–32; (3) to § 34; (4) to § 33. The discussion of *lex*/νόμος in §§ 18b–19 is omitted both here and in the summary of § 35; on its special character see *ad loc.* In light of this "preview," the emphasis on the gods at §§ 22–27 is unexpected. The argument appears stripped down to essentials (and without reference to the gods) at *Off.* 1.11–12. This exposition reinforces that the discussion is to be philosophical in nature, as Atticus at once notes (§ 17). Cf. Pohlenz, 1938, 114–16 = 422–24.

nam sic habetote, nullo in genere disputandi honest⟨ior⟩a patefieri: quid sit homini a natura tributum, . . .] Cicero uses *habeto(te)* alone as imperative of *habere* in the sense "know"; cf. Kühner-Stegmann, 1, 199. This is the first of the "future imperatives" that will play a large rôle in the archaic language of Cicero's legislation; cf. Wilhelms, 26 and 110–11; Pascucci, 1968, 34 ff. Only the forms in *-to* were inherited, the plural in *-tote* formed by analogy to the present imperative; cf. Meiser § 143.3. Passages such as Plaut. *Ps.* 20 or 647, where present and "future" imperative forms are juxtaposed, suggest that the latter refer to a more remote future; cf. Leumann, 571–72; Wackernagel, 1, 217 ff.; Lebreton, 199; Powell *ad Sen.* 81. Most recently Rodie Risselada, *Imperatives and Other Directive Expressions in Latin: A Study of the Pragmatics of a Dead Language* (Amsterdam, 1993), 122 ff., esp. 128 and 130, notes the frequency of the *-to* imperative in legal texts (cf. also Daube, 87 ff.) and explains that these "express directives whose realization is required only when the appropriate circumstances obtain" (129). She goes on to reject (130) the distinction drawn by Vairel-Carron, 249–50 and 258–61, between second person *-to* occurring in ordinary language and the third person *-to* in juridical language. The *-to* imperatives in legal texts would repay further study.—Büchner, 1970, 28, defends *disputando* (BAHLε) against *disputandi* (PHᴺ) but yet renders (both *loc. cit.* and in his 1969 Reclam translation) "in keiner anderen Art der Erörterung," as if he had, in fact, read *disputandi*. Since *disputo* is hardly used transitively in "good prose" (cf. *OLD* s.v., 2), *disputando* would have to be taken as a gerund: "by engaging in discussion in

---

63. For a comparison of the wording of our paragraph with § 35 cf. Schmidt, 1959, 191.

no other category." In fact, *disputandi* seems an all but certain correction, *genus* being often limited by such a gerund; cf., e.g., *Off.* 1.133: *in illo ipso forensi genere dicendi; Luc.* 92: *interrogandi genus.*[64]—*Honesta* has been daggered (Görler) and variously replaced.[65] But these attempts are perhaps on the wrong track. One concern at the outset of Cicero's rhetorical and philosophical works is to establish the importance and standing of the theme; cf. *Inv.* 1.2: *ac si volumus huius rei, quae vocatur eloquentia, . . . considerare principium, reperiemus id ex honestissimis causis natum atque optimis rationibus profectum; N.D.* 1.1: *cum multae res in philosophia nequaquam satis adhuc explicatae sint, tum perdifficilis . . . et perobscura quaestio est de natura deorum, quae et ad cognitionem animi pulcherrima est et ad moderandam religionem necessaria;* in still more detail *Off.* 1.4: *nam cum multa sint in philosophia et gravia et utilia accurate copioseque a philosophis disputata, latissime patere videntur ea quae de officiis tradita ab illis et praecepta sunt. nulla enim vitae pars neque publicis neque privatis neque forensibus neque domesticis in rebus, neque si tecum agas quid neque si cum altero contrahas, vacare officio potest . . .* This same function falls in *Leg.* to our passage, where Cicero is outlining and characterizing the topics that will be handled. Though he evidently does not yet regard an elaborate apologia as necessary (as he does in the *philosophica* of 45–44), he does want to establish that the handling of such material is worthy of his *persona* (cf. § 14; *Fin.* 1.11: . . . *quis alienum putet eius esse dignitatis quam mihi quisque tribuat quid in omni munere vitae optimum et verissimum sit exquirere?*). Hence the importance for Cicero of establishing that the topics of the present discussion are *honesta.*[66] To keep the transmitted text one will need to provide a point of comparison; this is most elegantly achieved by Powell's *honest⟨ior⟩a*, with a dash or colon placed after *patefieri*; for added weight one might contemplate *honest⟨iora proposit⟩a.* Translate: "In no type of discussion do more honorable matters come to light— . . . "—The human being's endowment of qualities by Nature is a Stoic doctrine elaborated by Cicero at § 22; see *ad loc.* and

---

64. I am grateful to J.G.F. Powell for clarification of this point.

65. Urlichs, 154, proposed *non ista*, but the pronoun, either contemptuous or referring to an item possessed by or associated with the interlocutor, is wrong; Vahlen wrote *posse ita*, but *posse* seems otiose (*posse patefieri* has a special point at *Balb.* 54); Ziegler has adopted the variant *magis* (PH[N]), but this, too, is a conjecture. Watt, 1986, 265, writes *tam manifesto*, which gives fair sense but seems rather remote from the *ductus litterarum*. Schmidt, 1959, 155 n. 1, brackets *honesta* as a gloss, as does Pohlenz, 1938, 116, but with *si ullo* for *nullo* and addition of *oportere* or *debere* after *patefieri*.

66. This praise of the subject-matter continues in § 28: *sed omnium quae in hominum doctorum disputatione versantur, nihil est profecto praestabilius, quam plane intellegi nos ad iustitiam esse natos . . .*

ad Off. 1.11–14 and 105.—Before *natura* the preposition *a* is added in HL[67] in accord with Cicero's usage when *natura* is strongly personified, as here with *tribui*; cf. *Off.* 1.11: *principio generi animantium omni est a natura tributum . . .* ; for loss of *a* cf. § 19 and 3.8.2; for loss of small words in general *ad* § 23.

. . . **quantam vim rerum optimarum mens humana contineat, . . .**] *Vis* has here the sense "the total sum, the whole range or stock of," or the like, a usage first attested in Cicero (cf. *OLD* s.v., 8c; Forcellini s.v., B.I.2.a.). The reference to the "range of the best things" contained in the human mind is left vague at this point; later he singles out reason for praise, which, as right reason, is made equivalent to *lex* (§§ 22–23); cf. also *Ac.* 1.20: . . . *virtus, quasi perfectio naturae omniumque rerum, quas in animis ponunt, una res optima.*

. . . **cuius muneris colendi efficiendique causa nati et in lucem editi simus, . . .**] Here Cicero is content to suggest that there is a higher purpose. Only at § 28 does he indicate clearly what this is: . . . *nos ad iustitiam esse natos* . . . When discussing human society Cicero was fond of citing the similar point at [Pl.] *Ep.* 9.358a (to Archytas): . . . *non sibi se soli natum meminerit, sed patriae, sed suis, ut perexigua pars ipsi relinquatur* (*Fin.* 2.45; sim. *Off.* 1.22).

. . . **quae sit coniunctio hominum ⟨cum dis⟩, quae naturalis societas inter ipsos.**] *Cum dis* was supplied by Powell; it is the natural antithesis to *inter ipsos.* The *hominum inter ipsos societas coniunctioque* of § 28 is different since it "comes after he has discussed the *coniunctio cum dis* and is now moving on to discuss the *coniunctio hominum inter ipsos*" (Powell, *per litt.*). For the latter point cf. *Fin.* 3.65 = *SVF* 3, 83.38: *quodque nemo in summa solitudine vitam agere velit ne cum infinita quidem voluptatum abundantia, facile intellegitur nos ad coniunctionem congregationemque hominum et ad naturalem communitatem esse natos; ad Off.* 1.12 and 154–55, 3.21–28.

his enim explicatis fons legum et iuris inveniri potest.] The metaphorical sense of *fons* in Latin was probably influenced by the similar use of the Greek πηγή; cf. LSJ s.v., 2; *TLL* s.v. *fons* IIB. Certainly Cicero connected the two; cf. *Rep.* 6.31 = *Tusc.* 1.53: *quin etiam ceteris quae moventur hic fons, hoc principium est movendi* = Pl. *Phaedr.* 245c: ἀλλὰ καὶ τοῖς ἄλλοις ὅσα κινεῖται τοῦτο πηγὴ καὶ ἀρχὴ κινήσεως.—For *fons iuris* cf. Liv. 3.34.6 and

---

67. Powell points out *(per litt.):* "In 1.16, *a natura* is peculiar to H and L; it is omitted both in B (and in A and P) and in ERS. There are quite a few other passages, however, in which HL have a correct reading against B(AP)ERS. This may mean that the reading of HL in such cases is a conjecture, but there is no reason why we should not accept it as such. For example, in 1.9 HL have the correct *concessum* against *concensus* BAPERS; 1.19 *quod si ita* HL against *quo sit ita* BAPERS; 1.38 *cum* HL against *dum* BAPERS; etc."

Ruperti's conjecture at Tac. *An.* 3.27.1 (cf. Woodman and Martin *ad loc.*).—*Lex et ius:* a virtual hendiadys (cf. Girardet, 1983, 48: "Recht in Gesetzesform"); on their relation cf. *ad* § 23.

17 This chapter provides essential orientation for the understanding of the whole essay. It includes a definitive statement of the subject (*tota causa . . . universi iuris ac legum*) and the tripartite plan that will be followed in the sequel (cf. Schmidt, 1959, 156–57), with the order of topics under II. determined, as we are told only at 2.69, by their relative importance in constituting the *respublica:*

   I. *natura . . . iuris explicanda nobis est, eaque ab hominis repetenda natura* = 1.18 ff. and 2.7–14;

  II. *considerandae leges quibus civitates regi debeant*
     A. *de religione:* 2.19 ff.
     B. *de magistratibus:* 3.6 ff.
     C. *de iudiciis* (announced 3.47)
     D. *de educatione/disciplina* (announced 3.29–30; see *ad loc.*)

  III. *tum haec tractanda quae composita sunt et descripta iura et iussa populorum* = 2.47 ff. (the execution in Book 3 is lost in the lacuna at the end).

This chapter is also the basis for Girardet's interpretation of *Leg.*, whereby the codex of laws proposed by Cicero in Books 2 ff. comprises natural law (Girardet, 1983, esp. 52–54). His argument, briefly stated, is that previous interpreters have been wrong to view the philosophical arguments of §§ 18 ff. as a working out of natural law on which the "optimal laws" of Books 2 and 3 are based, for this view ascribes to Cicero a dichotomy between natural and positive law for which the text provides no support.

Although Girardet's interpretation of *Leg.* is problematic in some other respects,[68] this analysis seems likely to be correct. In spite of its lacunose transmitted state, there would surely be some clue in the extant text of *Leg.* if Cicero had intended his proposed laws to have some intermediate status between natural law and positive law.[69] In addition—though this is denied

---

68. Especially in his supposition that Cicero intended the laws of *Leg.* as a political program that should actually be implemented (cf. the Introduction § 4) and his use of an alleged fragment of *Rep.* preserved in an anonymous Byzantine treatise mentioning a board of ten men with "regal powers" as a possible means of implementing his laws (cf. *ad* 3.4); cf. also *ad* 2.62a.

69. This is the suggestion of Miriam Griffin, "When Is Thought Political?" *Apeiron* 29 (1996), 272–73, who locates the laws of *Leg.* at the same level as the *ius gentium*, which at *Off.* 3.69 is the model for the *ius civile*, different on the one hand from the *fons legum et iuris* (§ 16)

by Girardet—, *Leg.* stands in a Stoic tradition of writing about natural law.[70] Thus Obbink, 1999, has argued convincingly that, when Chrysippus in *On Republic* described the city of sages, he was describing what he conceived to be an actually existing world-order, not a utopia.[71] Cicero's text takes over this approach but, as elsewhere,[72] broadens the constituency to include in this world-order the entire human race along with the gods. What a Chrysippus or a Cicero purports to describe is the true world-order in accord with nature. The obvious difficulty is that some elements in Cicero's legislation are clearly contingent without any possible claim to a fixed place in the order of nature, e.g., that there should be two consuls or ten tribunes of the plebs (3.8.2; 3.9.6). But perhaps Cicero would reply that this is a too literal reading and that he is merely filling in the kind of detail his Roman readers would expect; if so, these considerations have caused Cicero to introduce positive law where it is least wanted.[73]

A. Non ergo a praetoris edicto, ut plerique nunc, neque a Duodecim Tabulis, ut superiores, sed penitus ex intima philosophia hauriendam iuris disciplinam putas?] Atticus describes the subject as Marcus has worked it out so far, the key word being *philosophia*. The *iuris disciplina* (= "the science of law"[74]) is to be derived, not from particulars, but from philosophical investi-

---

and on the other from the *iura et iussa populorum* of our passage; but the exchange between Marcus and Quintus at 2.14 seems to place Marcus' laws on the same level as the law of nature; see *ad loc.*; cf. also *Har.* 32, where the *lex naturae* seems to be equivalent to the *commune ius gentium.*—Cicero does, of course, have a way of referring to positive law (the *iussa populorum* of our passage; cf. also the *leges hominum*); it is just that this is not, except marginally (see above on the *iussa populorum*), the subject of *Leg.*

70. Cf. Girardet, 30 ff., 73–74, 82 ff., and 90. Here he focuses too narrowly on what he sees as a difference between the Stoics and Cicero on the status of *leges scriptae.* But Cicero uses different terminologies in Books 1 and 2, and there is not enough Stoic evidence on this point to afford clarity, especially since the Stoics were not always sticklers for their own preferred terminology (cf. *SVF* 3, 33.19 ff.). In the meantime, the Stoic origin of natural law theory has been sufficiently clarified; cf. *ad* §§ 18a and 40–41.

71. Cf. Obbink, 1999, 186: "According to Philodemus, Chrysippus was describing not a utopia of sages and gods that might under the best circumstances one day come into being, but a σύστημα that already exists in the nature of the world."

72. Cf. *ad* § 25.

73. I owe this observation to Brad Inwood.—Stephan Podes, "Die Krise der späten römischen Republik und Ciceros Rechtsphilosophie *(de legibus),*" *Archiv für Rechts- und Sozialphilosophie* 77 (1991), 84–94 at 86–87, taxes Girardet with reintroducing a dichotomous system of the type he has criticized and merely altering the point at which the dividing line is drawn; this may be so, but nonetheless Girardet's insight is an important one that there is no real distinction between the natural law of Book 1 and the *leges* put forward in the subsequent books.

74. Watson, *Law Making,* 31 and 120; other references at Girardet, 1983, 49 n. 43.

gation; cf. Mehl, 94–95: "He is not starting from the Twelve Tables or the praetor's edict, because he is attempting to establish a new code of laws, which might of course contest the present *ius civile*. It is logical, therefore, and even necessary that he begin by establishing a new foundation. Otherwise he would only be instigating a debate of jurisprudential interpretation." Marcus' following speech elaborates this vision, revolutionary at Rome; cf. V.-A. Georgescu, "'Nihil hoc ad ius, ad Ciceronem!' Note sur les relations de M.T. Cicéron avec la *iurisprudentia* et la profession de *iuris consultus*," *Mélanges de philologie, de littérature et d'histoire anciennes offertes à J. Marouzeau* (Paris, 1948), 200. On the inadequacy of written law as a basis for such an undertaking cf. §§ 42–47.—*A praetoris edicto:* the praetors were Rome's chief judicial officers; for the origin and history of the office cf. *ad* 3.8.1. At the beginning of his year of office the praetor issued an edict indicating to which types of accusation he would grant an action at law. The *ius praetorium* thus served, especially after the procedural reform of the second-century lex Aebutia, to fill in gaps in the XII Tables; cf. Papin. *dig.* 1.1.7.1: *ius praetorium est quod praetores introduxerunt adiuvandi vel supplendi vel corrigendi iuris civilis gratia . . .* ; Berger s.v.v. *Edicta magistratuum, Ius praetorium,* as well as the reconstruction by Lenel. On the corresponding shift in the form of legal literature from commentaries on the XII Tables to ones on the praetor's edict or sections thereof (*ut plerique nunc . . . ut superiores*) cf. *ad* § 14 *(quae et conscripta a multis sunt diligenter—).—OLD* s.v. *intimus* classes our passage under no. 4: "most abstruse, recondite, or profound."

M. Non enim id quaerimus hoc sermone, Pomponi, quemadmodum caveamus in iure, aut quid de quaque consultatione respondeamus.] Marcus thus names two of the three practical tasks of the jurisconsult (*cavere* and *respondere,* the third being *agere)* and refuses to allow his approach to be determined by them. This is in contrast to the general run of jurists, whose scope of activity was to a considerable degree determined by these three tasks; cf. Wieacker, 1988, 574 ff. This approach also marks a contrast to the activity of giving legal advice he had envisioned for himself in old age (§ 10) and reinforces the sharp line drawn in § 13 between the current approach and that of the jurisconsults.

sit ista res magna, sicut est, . . .] For the form of expression cf., e.g., *Sex. Rosc.* 22: *quamvis ille felix sit, sicut est, . . .* ; *Luc.* 69 (cited *ad* § 54: *Vir iste fuit ille ⟨quidem⟩ prudens—); Phil.* 2.68: *. . . quamvis sis, ut es, violentus et furens . . .* ; *Fam.* 7.32.3.

. . . quae quondam a multis claris viris, nunc ab uno summa auctoritate et scientia sustinetur; . . .] The reference is to Servius Sulpicius Rufus, on whom cf. Dyck *ad Off.* 2.65; further literature at Wieacker, 1988, 602 n. 45. Might the reference to *summa auctoritas* imply that he has held, or been elected to, the consulate (which he held in 51)? Since he is referred to as living, our passage entails January, 43 (his death), as a *terminus ante quem* for the dramatic date; see further the Introduction § 5.

sed nobis ita complectenda in hac disputatione tota causa est universi iuris ac legum, ut hoc civile quod dicimus in parvum quendam et angustum locum concludatur {naturae}.] The so-called *ius civile*, the subject Atticus originally proposed (§§ 13–14a), is cut down to proper size in relation to the totality of right and laws (*tota causa . . . universi iuris ac legum*; cf. already Marcus' reply at § 14b), which is now declared to be the topic.— *Causa* has the sense "subject matter, problem": cf. *OLD* s.v., 15; *TLL* 685.67 ff. (our passage cited at 686.44–45).—For *universum ius* cf. § 14; the attempt of Girardet, 1983, 51 n. 52, to distinguish *universum ius* as used in our passage from its use in § 14 is to be rejected; cf. Schmidt, 1959, 156; Mehl, 115.—For the *iunctura* cf. *Off.* 1.53: *. . . in exiguum angustumque concluditur.*—*Naturae* was rightly expelled by R. Stephanus. F. Sommer, 122–23 and n. 9, attempts to defend it with reference to Aristotle's division of political justice into natural and legal species (*EN* 1134b18 ff.); but, if that is what Cicero had in mind, he would surely have had to elaborate the thought. The word evidently resulted from a dittography of the following *natura* and was then altered to genitive to provide a specious connection to this sentence.

natura enim iuris explicanda—quae vocantur iura civilia.] Here Cicero announces the bipartite plan of the treatise: first to explain the nature of right and derive it from human nature (Book 1) and formulate laws in accord with nature and discuss actual enactments (Books 2 ff.; cf. headnote to this section).—For the spelling *descripta* cf. *ad* § 23.—*Iussa populorum* is an evident paraphrase for statutes, i.e., positive law (cf. *Vat.* 8, *Balb.* 38, *Phil.* 1.16, and other parallels cited by Wieacker, 1988, 280 n. 58). The idea of "commanding" and "forbidding" is common to both natural law and positive law; cf. § 18b (for the Stoic background see *ad loc.*): *iubet ea quae facienda sunt, prohibetque contraria*; 2.9: *iussa ac vetita populorum.*—For the status of the *leges quibus civitates regi debeant* see the headnote to this section.

18a–34a This discussion of the *fons legum et iuris* (§ 16) aims to show that *ius in natura esse positum* (§ 34); it thus turns the tables on sophists such as Callicles in the *Gorgias* who would claim that nature sanctions the pursuit of self-interest; cf. Mehl, 122–23. The argument is conducted *uberius quam forensis usus desiderat* (§ 15), indeed *fuse . . . ac libere* according to the method of the *veteres philosophi* (§ 36). Its extent elicits an exclamation of wonderment from Atticus: *Di immortales, quam tu longe iuris principia repetis!* (§ 28). The first step is an exordium on *lex* (§§ 18b–19); next Cicero proceeds to ground *ius* (= just dealing) in human nature; only in § 23 does he clarify the place of *lex* in this argument, i.e., that *ratio* is *lex* and since human beings possess it they also must possess *ius*; on the relation of *lex* and *ius* see further Mehl, 144–49. The possession of these forges the link between god and man. The similarity of human beings to one another is also argued at length so as to establish a basis for the human community; cf. the detailed outline on pp. 48–49. Nor is the argument brought to a close at § 34a; rather, in view of the importance of the subject (cf. § 37 *init.*), this treatment is reinforced by an additional argument that law is by nature, which, however, is not freestanding and is mostly a refutation of utilitarianism (cf. *ad* § 36 and § 42 [*est enim unum ius*—]).

18a Q. Alte vero et ut oportet a capite, frater, repetis quod quaerimus; . . .] The sense "fountain head, origin" for *caput* (*OLD* s.v., 12) is confirmed by the paraphrase *a fonte* (§ 20; cf. § 16: *fons legum et iuris*). Cf. *Sex. Rosc.* 74: *nonne his vestigiis ad caput maleficii perveniri solet?; Planc.* 18: *etenim ad caput et ad fontem generis utriusque veniamus; Leg.* 2.46; *Top.* 39: *cum autem a genere ducetur argumentum, non erit necesse id usque a capite arcessere. saepe etiam citra licet . . .* Quintus' *repetis* takes up his brother's *eaque* [sc. *natura iuris*] *ab hominis repetenda natura;* cf. § 28 (Atticus): *Di immortales, quam tu longe iuris principia repetis!* as well as *Rep.* 3.18 (Philus): *noster hic populus, quem Africanus hesterno sermone a stirpe repetivit . . .* This description of Marcus' procedure (*a capite . . . repetis*) corresponds to that of Socrates in dialogues in which he responds to definitions or questions put forward by others and thus must go back ἐξ ἀρχῆς to find a more solid basis for discussion; cf. Pl. *Euthphr.* 15c; Vicaire *ad* Pl. *La.* 184d.—*Quod quaerimus* denotes the subject of discussion; cf. *quem quaerimus eloquentem* at *Orat.* 14; sim. ibid. 100: *tenemus igitur . . . quem quaerimus; Tusc.* 3.11: *id quod quaerimus;* a little different *Fin.* 3.29: *atque iste vir altus et excellens . . . quem quaerimus . . .*

M. Non ita est, Quinte, ac potius ignoratio iuris litigiosa est quam scientia; . . .] Reid finds this contradiction "rather brusque"; sim. 3.17 (cf. also the implicit correction at 2.43; Quintus disagrees at 3.26 and 33).—On Cicero's preference for *ignoratio* over *ignorantia* cf. Reid *ad Ac.* 1.42.—For an example of *ignoratio iuris* at court cf. *de Orat.* 1.168–69 (a counsel's ignorance of proper use of an *exceptio*).—An example of ignorance of the law leading to litigiousness is that of Sex. Aebutius, who thought that, by driving Caecina away from the disputed estate so that the formal ejection could not take place, he had won his case, when, in fact, even on a strict construction of the law, he had lost his *sponsio* since he had not restored Caecina "whence he had ejected him," as Aebutius alleged (*Caec.* 82–84). **sed hoc posterius; nunc iuris principia videamus.**] For the formula for postponement cf. *Div.* 2.7: *sed haec alias pluribus; nunc ad institutam disputationem revertamur.* The point is taken up at § 42: *quam* [sc. *legem*] *qui ignorat, is est iniustus.*—Like the Greek ἀρχή, *principium* can denote either the origin or the guiding principle or basis; cf. *OLD* s.v., 6 and 8. Although in line with Quintus' formulation (*a capite . . . repetis*) one thinks initially of the former meaning, the latter proves to be implicated as well. Cicero could have cited Platonic precedent for a digression grounding law in first principles; cf. *Lg.* 891d ff. with Szlezák, 72–78. Sim. to our passage Tac. *An.* 3.25.2: *ea res admonet ut de principiis iuris . . . altius disseram.*

18b–19 The distinction between the projects announced at § 18a (*nunc iuris principia videamus*) and § 20 (*visne ergo ipsius iuris ortum a fonte repetamus?*) is not prima facie clear. It does not hinge, e.g., on a subtle distinction between *principium* and *ortus* or between *ius* and *ius ipsum*, as one might at first suppose. Paragraphs 18b–19 are twice described as an *exordium* and once referred to by means of the verb *proficisci*: this is evidently to be the starting point for thinking about *ius*, but it leads to a close consideration of the term *lex*, rather than *ius*, or, more importantly, to the Greek equivalent of *lex*, νόμος. This material gives a preview of the broadening of the discussion to include philosophical propositions that we have been led to expect since §§ 16–17 but will not be the foundation for the whole system of *ius* constructed in this Book; cf. *ad* § 16 and Schmidt, 1959, 168–69; it does, however, enable Cicero to begin his treatment with a rhetorical flourish culminating in the encomium *ea* [sc. *lex*] *est enim naturae vis, ea mens ratioque prudentis, ea iuris atque iniuriae regula* (§ 19).

18b Igitur doctissimis viris proficisci placuit a lege, . . .] For *igitur*, like the German *also*, often as the first word, introducing an account, particularly when, as here, the plan has just been enunciated, cf. 2.14; Hand, 3, 195–96; *TLL* s.v., 270.10 ff.; *OLD* s.v., 4; on its initial position cf. Madvig *ad Fin.* 1.61.—For *docti* or *doctissimi* = *philosophi* cf. §§ 28b and 52. For Cicero's vagueness about naming his source(s) see the introduction to this Book.— *Lex* is not the actual goal, only the starting point; *ius* resumes the center of attention by the middle of § 19. The detour via *lex* enables Cicero to bring in νόμος as theorized by the Greeks, in particular the Stoics,[75] and thus broaden the basis of discussion *a limine*; cf. Schmidt, 1959, 164.

75. Cf. Theiler, 45: "Typisch stoisch ist das Vordrängen der *lex* gegenüber *ius* im Hauptteil."

... **si modo, ut idem definiunt, lex est ratio summa insita in natura, quae iubet ea quae facienda sunt, prohibetque contraria.**] *Si modo* means "provided that" (*OLD* s.v. *si* 8) and carries no implication of doubt.—It now becomes clear why Cicero has been so careful to set his project into a philosophical context (§§ 14b and 17): this is not the type of definition Roman readers would have expected; see Ateius Capito fr. 24 Strz. = Gel. 10.20.2: *lex est generale iussum populi aut plebis rogante magistratu.*— Early Greek writers did not speak of gods as lawgivers, but Plato saw the law of Sparta and Crete as derived from Apollo and Zeus respectively (*Lg.* 624a, 632d, 634a); cf. Burkert, 1985, 248 and 444 n. 26. Aristotle had defined νόμος as a τάξις (*Pol.* 1287a18 and 1326a30) or as ἄνευ ὀρέξεως νοῦς (*Pol.* 1287a32; cf. also Pl. *Leg.* 714a, cited *ad* § 19). It is typical of the Stoa to redefine terms. Cicero's definition[76] comprises three elements, all of Stoic provenance (hence our passage = *SVF* 3, 78.1 ff.): 1) the identification of law with supreme reason, whereby Cicero, at first deliberately avoiding technical terms, substitutes *ratio summa* for *recta ratio,* which appears at § 23 (see *ad loc.*); cf. *SVF* 2, 4.2–3 (Chrysippus): . . . ὁ νόμος ὁ κοινός, ὅσπερ ἐστὶν ὁ ὀρθὸς λόγος διὰ πάντων ἐρχόμενος; other parallels at Frank, 346;[77] 2) its characterization as embedded in nature *(insita in natura);* cf. *Rep.* 3.33, cited *ad* § 23; *N.D.* 1.36 = *SVF* 1, 42.35: *Zeno autem ... naturalem legem divinam esse censet* ...;[78] 3) its function of commanding and forbidding; ibid. 3, 79.40: λόγος δέ ἐστι [sc. ὁ νόμος] φύσεως προστακτικὸς μὲν ὧν πρακτέον, ἀπαγορευτικὸς δὲ ὧν οὐ πρακτέον; sim. ibid. 81.23 ff., 158.11 and 18 ff.; Phil. *vit. Mos.* 2.4. In περὶ νόμου Chrysippus offered a similar doctrine to Cicero's (*SVF* 3, 42.4 ff.): καὶ μὴν ἡ ὁρμή, κατά γ᾽ αὐτόν [sc. Χρύσιππον], τοῦ ἀνθρώπου λόγος ἐστὶ προστακτικὸς αὐτῷ τοῦ ποιεῖν, ὡς ἐν τῷ περὶ νόμου γέγραφεν. οὐκοῦν καὶ ἡ ἀφορμὴ λόγος ἀπαγορευτικὸς καὶ ἡ ἔκκλισις· ... The Stoic definition can be seen as a reaction to the Aristotelian view. The Stoics retained the idea of impartial intelligence from Aristotle's definition (ἄνευ ὀρέξεως νοῦς: see above) by substituting their own concept of transcendent λόγος. This change enabled the Stoics to claim, in contrast to Aristotle (ibid.

---

76. Cf. the paraphrase at Lact. *inst.* 6.24.29: *illa lex dei ... praeclara et divina, semper quae recta et honesta iubet, vetat prava et turpia.*

77. Schofield, 1991, 69, explains the significance of this move: the Stoics do not want to tie law to the state at this stage of the argument, as in a conventional definition of law (like that of Ateius Capito cited above); rather, "the point of their equation of law with right reason is to identify an alternative source for its authority ... Its effect is to internalize law, making it something like the voice of conscience ..."

78. In his περὶ τοῦ καλοῦ Chrysippus affirmed that law and right were by nature (D.L. 7.128 = *SVF* 2, 76.4–5); cf. other test. *SVF* ind. s.v. νόμος.

1257b10–11 and Plato *Gorg.* 482e, etc.), that law is in accord with, rather than contrary to, nature; on the difference between Aristotle and the Stoics on natural law cf. Perelli, 116–17. For the Stoics as originators of the concept of natural law cf. Striker, with Inwood, 1987, tying the concept to categories of action in Stoic ethics; Vander Waerdt, 1994a, sees the concept of natural law as having been developed by Zeno to describe the relations of sages in his Republic; cf. also Mitsis, 1994, 4812–50, esp. the critique of Vander Waerdt, 4841–43; Forschner, 7 ff., esp. 14–16 (on Cicero's dependence on the Stoic view).—Advocates in court often spoke of the law as commanding or forbidding certain actions, e.g., Aeschin. 3.249: τὰς βεβαιώσεις τῶν κτημάτων ὁ νόμος κελεύει ποιεῖσθαι; ibid. 203: ἀλλὰ πρῶτον μὲν τοὺς νόμους ἐπέδειξα ἀπαγορεύοντας μὴ στεφανοῦν τοὺς ὑπευθύνους. Hence the Stoic description.

18b–19 eadem ratio cum est in hominis mente confirmata et perfecta, lex est; itaque arbitrantur prudentiam esse legem cuius ea vis sit ut recte facere iubeat, vetet delinquere.] This follows a bit oddly upon the previous definition; one would expect *etiam* prior to *lex est:* not only the λόγος distributed throughout the universe (cf. Pohlenz, *Stoa*, 1, 73) but also perfect λόγος within the human being deserves the name "law"; see further *ad* §§ 22–23, 2.11, and 3.2. For the Stoic definition of φρόνησις (= *prudentia*) cf., e.g., *SVF* 2, 297.13: ἐπιστήμη ποιητέων τε καὶ οὐ ποιητέων; sim. *Off.* 1.153. This definition of law and the preceding one, though located at different levels (respectively the whole of nature and the human being), are materially identical (*eadem ratio* referring back to *ratio summa*). Perhaps Cicero has introduced *prudentia* here in order to forge a link with the conception of *lex* as related to *legere* (see below on *nam ut illi aequitatis, sic nos delectus vim in lege ponimus*—).—The restriction *cum est . . . confirmata et perfecta* is needed in view of the undeveloped *intellegentiae* given at birth and the corrupting influences to which human beings are subject (cf. §§ 26 and 29).—Vahlen's *perfecta* seems preferable to the transmitted *confecta,* in accord with Ciceronian usage elsewhere in this dialogue (§§ 22, 27 [cf. *ad loc.*]; 2.11), in spite of *N.D.* 1.26 and 2.16, cited by Görler *ad loc.* Change in authors' vocabularies over time is in the meantime a well studied phenomenon even though the rationale often eludes us; cf. Adams, 1972, 350–51 and n. 6. *Confecta* may have arisen under the influence of the preceding *confirmata.*

19 eamque rem illi Graeco putant nomine ⟨a⟩ suum cuique tribuendo appellatam, . . .] The Stoics were generally fond of adducing etymologies in support of their arguments, a fact that Cicero notes and imitates at *Off.* 1.23; cf. also *N.D.* 2.64 ff. The underlying theory is that language is as it is φύσει, with the first sounds imitating the things of which they form the designation; cf. *SVF* 2, 44.40–43.—*Illi* are still the *doctissimi viri* referred to at the beginning of the paragraph.—The connection of νόμος and νέμειν occurs at [Pl.] *Min.* 317d–18a; cf. Carl Werner Müller, "Cicero, Antisthenes und der pseudo-platonische 'Minos' über das Gesetz," *RhM* N.F. 138 (1995), 263; cf. *Lg.* 713b–714a: ἀλλὰ μιμεῖσθαι δεῖν ἡμᾶς οἴεται . . . τὸν ἐπὶ τοῦ Κρόνου λεγόμενον βίον . . . τὴν τοῦ νοῦ διανομὴν ἐπονομά- ζοντας νόμον; *SVF* 2, 295.30: οὐδὲ ἔστι μὲν νέμεσις, οὐκ ἔστι δὲ νόμος; Plut. *Qu. conv.* 644c: . . . οἱ νόμοι τῆς ἴσα νεμούσης εἰς τὸ κοινὸν ἀρχῆς καὶ δυνάμεως ἐπώνυμοι γεγόνασιν. For giving to each his own as a just act cf. Simonides *PMG* 642 *apud* Pl. *Rp.* 331e: τὸ τὰ ὀφειλόμενα ἑκάστῳ ἀποδιδόναι δίκαιόν ἐστι.—For loss of *a* cf. § 16; 2.26; 3.8.2: . . . *iique ⟨a⟩ praeeundo iudicando consulendo praetores iudices consules appellamino*; for loss of small words in general *ad* § 23.

. . . **ego nostro a legendo; . . .**] Romans seem to have agreed in deriving *lex* from *lego* but to have differed as to the sense of the verb; Cicero assumes "choose" (*OLD* s.v., 6), as the sequel makes clear. This allows scope for the operation of reason, whereas the alternative interpretation would lay stress on the written form, contrary to Cicero's emphasis; cf. *Var. L.* 6.66: *legere . . . hinc . . . etiam leges, quae lectae et ad populum latae quas observet* with other passages cited by Maltby s.v. *lex*; above p. 34 n. 116; below on . . . *et appellare eam legem quae scripta sancit quod vult*—.— Here Cicero does not include an object for *legere*; but cf. 2.11.

nam ut illi aequitatis, sic nos delectus vim in lege ponimus. et proprium tamen utrumque legis est.] While claiming that both features posited by the etymologies of the Greek and Latin terms are proper to law (*proprium . . . utrumque legis est*), Cicero does not specify how, if at all, the two are meant to relate to each other. *Suum cuique tribuere* is Cicero's paraphrase for *aequitas*, which is the principle underlying the commands and prohibitions of law (*ut recte facere iubeat, vetetque delinquere*), i.e., it determines what constitutes *recte facere*. If, on the other hand, *legere* refers to the selection of actions to go under each category (cf. 2.13: *est lex iustorum iniustorumque distinctio*), the features posited by the two etymologies would be related as guiding principle and the application of principle to particulars—the two necessary points in the lawmaking process. For a different attempt to define the relation cf. Benardete, 299.—*Aequitas* is introduced on the basis of the Stoic etymology of νόμος and given equal validity to the Latin etymology of *lex*. It was adopted as a legal principle under the influence of rhetoric and Greek philosophy but does not appear in the extant writings of republican jurists; cf. Wieacker, 1988, 506–7. The defense of A. Caecina and its publication shows that *aequitas* was a principle important to Cicero; cf. Frier. On the other hand, *lex* as *delectus* relates to the previous definition of it as *prudentia*, since Cicero associates *prudentia* with the choice *(delectus)* between goods and evils *(Fin.* 5.67; *Off.* 3.71).

quodsi ita recte dicitur, ut mihi quidem plerumque videri solet, a lege ducendum est iuris exordium; . . .] *Ut mihi quidem videtur* is used to flag a personal opinion; cf., e.g., *Ac.* 1.18: *abundantia quadam ingeni praestabat, ut mihi quidem videtur, Aristoteles . . .* The addition of the equivocating *plerumque* (= "for the most part") may hint at skeptical reservations (so Görler, 1995, 103); certainly at § 39 Cicero shows awareness that the doctrines of this Book may be vulnerable to skeptical attack.—For the *iunctura ducere exordium* cf. *Fin.* 5.18: . . . *ut illa prudentia . . . in earum trium rerum aliqua versetur a qua totius vitae ducat exordium.*

ea est enim naturae vis, ea mens ratioque prudentis, ea iuris atque iniuriae regula.] The introduction of the concept of *lex* concludes with this tricolon articulated by anaphora of hymnic type *(ea . . . ea . . . ea . . .)* and capped by a double cretic clausula.—According to the Stoics, there were two basic principles, ὕλη and δύναμις (= *vis*), which interpenetrates matter and is identified with god (*SVF* 2, 308.37–38); in the phrase *naturae vis, natura* has the sense of "the physical world" (*OLD* s.v., 7), i.e., ὕλη. Law as *naturae vis* takes up the idea of it as *insita in natura* (§ 18); the further implication that law is identical with the mind of god, with the entailed identification of law with the legislator, is made explicit only at 2.8 (see *ad loc.*); cf. also *N.D.* 1.36 with Pease's note.—For *mens ratioque prudentis* cf. Plut. *Stoic. rep.* 1038a: εἰ δ᾽ οὐκ ἄλλο τι νόμος ἐστὶν ἢ ὁ τοῦ σοφοῦ λόγος . . .—*Regula* is a "rule" or "standard" (*OLD* s.v., 2) and corresponds to the Greek κανών. Again Cicero's text amounts to a translation of Chrysippus: δεῖ δὲ αὐτὸν [sc. τὸν νόμον] . . . κανόνα . . . εἶναι δικαίων καὶ ἀδίκων . . . (*SVF* 3, 77.35–37, quoted from the beginning of the περὶ νόμου); sim. Sen. *Ben.* 4.12.1: . . . *legem dicimus iusti iniustique regulam esse . . .*; cf. Herbert Oppel, ΚΑΝΩΝ. *Zur Bedeutungsgeschichte des Wortes and seiner lateinischen Entsprechungen (regula-norma)*, Philologus, Suppl. 30.4 (Leipzig, 1937), 55–56.

sed quoniam in populari ratione omnis nostra versatur oratio, populariter interdum loqui necesse erit, . . .] This was the approach used by such Stoic philosophers as Chrysippus and Panaetius; cf. *ad Off.* 2.35.—*Popularis ratio* is ordinarily a political term for "the popular cause"; but here *ratio* has the more general sense "affair, concern, business" (cf. *OLD* s.v. *ratio* 11c and 9), and *popularis* is, of course, without political reference; on Cicero's use of this word see further *ad* 3.26a.

... et appellare eam legem, quae scripta sancit quod vult aut iubendo ⟨aut vetando⟩, ut vulgus appellat; ...] *Eam* for *id* results from assimilation in gender to the following *legem*.—In this "popular" version of *lex* there is emphasis on the written form rather than the relation to reason (see *supra* on ... *ego nostro a legendo* ...); certainly the description *sancit quod vult* allows for arbitrary legislation; the following description of *summa lex* and *scripta lex* further limits the place of the "popular" concept. Cicero will criticize such notions of law at § 42 and 2.11; cf. Girardet, 1983, 57. On the other hand, there is no reason why the *summa lex* could not be written down, and the idea that it could be is sometimes seen as a Ciceronian innovation (cf. *ad* § 42); cf. also 3.46, a proposal for new and better means to preserve writen laws.—After *aut iubendo* the negative correlate has fallen out (for the thought cf. § 18a); the choice is between Baiter's *aut prohibendo* or *aut vetando* of the *recentiores*. The latter deserves preference on grounds of the handsome ditrochaic clausula; sim. 1.33 *(et vetando)*, 2.10 *(ad vetandum)*, and 3.35 *(ac vetandis)*.—For B's *appellaret*[79] the preferable substitute is Manutius' *appellat*, which yields a clausula of the *omne debetur* type, whereas the rhythm of *appellare* ⟨*sole*⟩*t*, proposed by H.A. Koch, is distinctly inferior.

constituendi vero iuris ab illa summa lege capiamus exordium, quae saeclis multis ante nata est quam scripta lex ulla, aut quam omnino civitas constituta.] The *iunctura summa lex* appears to occur elsewhere in classical Latin only at 2.11 and *Fin.* 4.11;[80] for the likewise unusual *supremus deus* cf. *ad* § 22; for *suprema lex* cf. 3.3 and 8.2. For the following phrase cf. *Phil.* 5.35: *a Bruto ... capiamus exordium*.—*Communibus*, transmitted after *saeclis*, is clearly impossible. Ascensius' *omnibus* is usually preferred on palaeographical grounds; cf. Zelzer, 1981, 228. In view of the loose use of *saecula* in expressions "denoting a long or indefinite period" (*OLD* s.v. *saeculum* 9a), it is conceivable that Cicero wrote *saeclis omnibus ante nata est* meaning "was born infinitely before," but there is no Ciceronian parallel for the expression (*Fat.* 37 being merely a pseudoparallel [cf. *Fat.* 27]). Down to this point Cicero has been speaking of *lex* in general without any epithet added; in this sentence he refers to it for the first time as *illa summa lex*. This corresponds, of course, to the κοινὸς νόμος of the Stoics (see *ad* § 18b). Might *communibus* have started its existence as *communi*, a variant to *summa* as epithet for *illa ... lege* (perhaps an author's variant; see *ad* § 53), which then entered the text in the wrong place with adjustment to agree

79. *Appellare et* HLε.
80. Based on search of PHI 5.3.

with *saeclis*, thus ousting the original epithet?[81] If so, choice of the epithet need not be guided by the *ductus litterarum* of *communibus;* the simple *multis*, the common epithet in such cases (Powell; cf. Merguet, *Phil.*, 1, 205), is here supplied *exempli gratia;* Powell suggests *hominum multis* (cf. *Rep.* 6.28) or *iam multis* as further possibilities.—For this lofty conception of law and the limitations of *scripta lex* see *ad* § 42.

20–21 These chapters mark a new beginning: the emphasis henceforth will be, not on the *summa lex*, but on *ius* and its relation to nature; cf. *ad* §§ 18b–19; Schmidt, 1959, 168. They also serve to clear the ground for what follows by clarifying the relation of this discussion to *Rep.*, publication of which is assumed, and by securing the assent of Atticus, despite his adherence to Epicurus' school, to the proposition that the gods govern the universe.

20 Visne ergo ipsius iuris ortum a fonte repetamus?] *Ipsum ius* is *ius* per se, an abstraction (cf. *ad* § 48); this approach sets Cicero's program apart from the activities of the *iuris consulti;* cf. § 14 and Girardet, 1983, 58.—For the procedure cf. *Div.* 2.50: *ortum videamus haruspicinae; sic facillime quid habeat auctoritatis iudicabimus.* Cf. also *ad* § 18a (*a capite*).

quo invento non erit dubium quo sint haec referenda quae quaerimus.] For *quo sint haec referenda* cf. Wilkins on *de Orat.* 1.145 (*quo quidque referat:* "the standard he is to use in each case"); *OLD* s.v., 10. *Referri* corresponds to ἀναφέρεσθαι in Stoic writing on ethics (the corresponding substantive is ἀναφορά); cf. this definition of the τέλος: ἐφ' ὃ πάντα τὰ ἐν τῷ βίῳ πραττόμενα καθηκόντως τὴν ἀναφορὰν λαμβάνει, αὐτὸ δ' ἐπ' οὐδέν (*SVF* 3, 3.18–20; cf. ibid. 17.9); cf. also § 52b.—For *quae quaerimus* cf. *ad* § 18a (*quod quaerimus*).

A. Me quoque adscribi⟨to⟩ fratris sententiae.] Manutius' *adscribito* is to be preferred to *adscribe* of the *recentiores* both as the likelier source of the transmitted text *(adscribi)* and as agreeing with the language of the dialogue in general (cf. *ad* § 16: *habetote*).[82] Cf. Pl. *Rp.* 450a3: καὶ ἐμὲ τοίνυν, ὁ Γλαύκων ἔφη, κοινωνὸν τῆς ψήφου ταύτης τίθετε.

Quoniam igitur eius reipublicae, quam optimam esse docuit in illis sex libris Scipio, tenendus est nobis et servandus status, omnesque leges accommodandae ad illud civitatis genus, . . .] Cicero thus defines the relation of the current project to *Rep.* For *status civitatis* as constitution or form of government cf. Zetzel *ad Rep.* 1.33. Does the stipulation that the legislation must

81. Cf. de Plinval's conjecture *communis omnibus.* As J.G.F. Powell points out *(per litt.) saeclis tout court* in the sense "for ages" appears at Plin. *Nat.* 22.115 but does not appear to be Ciceronian usage; he adds that *communibus* may be a dittography of *commodius.*

82. So Reid.

be adapted to the type of commonwealth of *Rep.* mean that the laws are for a mixed constitution, or does *Rep.* control the drafting of laws in *Leg.* in some stronger sense?[83] In any case, this policy is in potential conflict with nature as the norm of legislation (§ 44; see the introduction to Book 2). The state of *Rep.* is, of course, an idealized version of the Roman state, and the first comment on the laws drafted by Cicero emphasizes their similarity to Roman laws (2.23 and 3.12), which, in their turn, are claimed to be "adapted to nature" (*gaudeo nostra iura ad naturam accommodari:* 2.62). In mediating between Stoic philosophy and Roman institutions, Cicero seems to assume that the norms of the one can be brought into line with those of the other. This is perhaps the most problematical aspect of *Leg.*: in practice the legislation of Books 2 and 3, oriented on Roman institutions, tends to stultify the *universum ius* set up as the ideal in Book 1 with its potential for providing a thoroughgoing critique of existing law.[84]

. . . **serendi etiam mores nec scriptis omnia sancienda, repetam stirpem iuris a natura, qua duce nobis omnis est disputatio explicanda.**] Elsewhere *serere* is ordinarily used metaphorically of negative qualities, trouble, cares, war, etc. (cf. the passages cited by *OLD* s.v. *sero*[1] 4), so Cicero was bold in using it of the *respublica* at *Rep.* 2.5 (*qui diuturnam rempublicam serere conatur;* cf. *propagare* with *multa saecula reipublicae* as object at *Cat.* 2.11) and here of morals; he could, however, point to Plato's analogy at *Phaedr.* 276b ff.; see p. 56 n. 23 *supra;* cf. also *Tusc.* 1.31 (after citing Caecil. com. 210: *serit arbores, quae alteri saeclo prosint*): *ergo arbores seret diligens agricola, quarum aspiciet bacam ipse numquam; vir magnus leges instituta rempublicam non seret?* Justice is seen as a plant-like growth; the botanical metaphor is continued with the following *repetam stirpem iuris a natura.*—The legislator's work in relation to *mores* resembles the project of the *rector* as described at *Rep.* 3.3: *hanc* [sc. *verecundiam*] *ille rector rerum publicarum auxit opinionibus, perfecitque institutis et disciplinis, ut pudor cives non minus a delictis arceret quam metus;* a similar extension of the statesman's work into the moral sphere is the advice *comprimendae libidines* given to Caesar at *Marc.* 23; cf. Lintott, 1999, 226 n. 48; § 57 *(leges vivendi)* and *ad* 2.10.—The point *nec scriptis omnia sancienda* confirms the implication of § 19 that written form is not a *proprium* of true *lex;* cf. § 42; 2.11. On the limitations of positive law cf. Arist. *EN* 1137b11 ff.: ποιεῖ δὲ τὴν ἀπορίαν ὅτι τὸ ἐπιεικὲς δίκαιον μέν ἐστιν, οὐ τὸ κατὰ νόμον δέ, ἀλλ᾽ ἐπανόρθωμα

---

83. Cf. J.G.F. Powell, "Were Cicero's *Laws* the Laws of Cicero's *Republic*?" in Powell-North, 17–39.

84. Cf. Cancik, 1995, 66–68; *ad* 2.62a.

νομίμου δικαίου; *Off.* 3.68–69. Similarly, Cicero praised Solon for declining to make a special law for the then supposedly unheard of crime of parricide *ne non tam prohibere quam admonere videretur* (*Sex. Rosc.* 70).— *Repetam stirpem iuris a natura* does not necessarily contradict the earlier declaration *a lege ducendum est iuris exordium* (§ 19), given that *lex* is the *vis naturae* and thus interpenetrates nature (cf. *ad* § 19).—For following nature as a Stoic project cf. Gisela Striker, "Following Nature: A Study in Stoic Ethics," *OSAP* 9 (1991), 1 ff. = *Essays on Hellenistic Epistemology and Ethics* (Cambridge, 1996), 221 ff..; examples of *natura* as *dux* also at Dyck *ad Off.*, p. 24 n. 48; for the personification of *natura* cf. Zellmer, 23 ff.—*Explico* = "unfold" (*OLD* s.v., 8).

A. Rectissime; et quidem ista duce errari nullo pacto potest.] This formula would in itself be unobjectionable to an Epicurean, for whom ἡδονή is the σύμφυτον or φυσικὸν τέλος (cf., e.g., *Epicurea* 274.25: ... οἱ Ἐπικούρειοι δεικνύναι νομίζουσι φύσει αἱρετὴν εἶναι τὴν ἡδονήν), but the Stoic and Epicurean conceptions of φύσις are in sharp conflict, with the Stoics emphasizing the "higher nature" of the human being, i.e., *ratio* (see the previous note; *ad Off.* 1.131; *ad* §§ 42 [*ita fit ut*—] and 54 [*Parvam vero controversiam dicis*—]), so Atticus can only agree in a certain sense. The text, however, conceals rather than emphasizes this point.—For *ista duce errari nullo pacto potest* cf. *Off.* 1.100: ... *quam* [sc. *naturam*] *si sequemur ducem numquam aberrabimus* ...

21 M. Dasne igitur hoc nobis, Pomponi (nam Quinti novi sententiam), deorum immortalium vi, natura, ratione, potestate, mente, numine,— naturam omnem regi? nam si hoc non probas, ab eo nobis causa ordienda est potissimum.] Cicero presents this "postulate" as required in order for the discussion to advance; otherwise it will be necessary to take a detour and begin the discussion *ab eo*, i.e., the rôle of the gods in the universe.[85] The theological emphasis of the following paragraphs could have been avoided, however; the argument could have been stated in terms of nature, as at § 16 (see *ad loc.*). But once law has been defined as *ratio summa, insita in natura* (§ 18), it has assumed the place-value of the deity in the Stoic system, and there is little to be gained by suppressing this fact, though it is made explicit only at § 23 and 2.8. In fact, the definition of law and the divine government of the universe are the two unargued premises that ground the following argument (on the use of postulates in *Leg.* 1 cf. Moatti, 165). The stronger,

---

85. This is, in fact, the starting point of *N.D.*; cf. 1.2: *quod vero maxime rem causamque continet, utrum nihil agant nihil moliantur omni curatione et administratione rerum vacent, an contra ab iis et a principio omnia facta et constituta sint et ad infinitum tempus regantur atque moveantur* ...

theologically based form of the argument has rhetorical advantages, an important point *in philosophicis* as elsewhere (cf. *ad Off.* 3.20). It elevates the human being, through having a share, like the gods, in reason, to a godlike level and thus facilitates the argument that law is "by nature," i.e., in accord with the true, higher nature of the human being.[86] Cf. also Mehl, 125, who points out that, though the gods are not needed for this argument, they are generally helpful in combatting those who make self-interest the basis for action; cf. 2.15–16. For the connection of the following argument with Stoic theology cf. *ad* §§ 22–27.

Atticus' suspension of disbelief is merely a technical device to enable the dialogue to proceed on the previously agreed topic; it does not imply that even "Atticus" of the dialogue has permanently abandoned his Epicurean principles (cf. § 54; 3.1; cf. also his portrayal at *Fin.* 1.3; for the historical Atticus cf. *Fam.* 13.1.5; Perlwitz, 90 ff.). Cicero's silencing of the doubts of an Academic Skeptic at § 39 is similar in function, though it has sometimes been mistaken for a philosophical volte-face; cf. Haury, 162; Görler, 1995, who cites other examples (on our passage 87). It is only much later, at *N.D.* 1, that Cicero will tackle the Epicurean view of the gods.

Cicero does not need to direct such a question to his brother, as he adds parenthetically, *nam Quinti novi sententiam,* thus suggesting that Quintus is in agreement; for Marcus' prior knowledge of Quintus' views cf. also 3.33. In *Div.* 1 Quintus has the rôle of promoting a belief in divination by means of Stoic arguments, but this need not mean that the historical Quintus was a Stoic;[87] a preference for Antiochus' philosophy is attributed to him at *Fin.* 5.96. In both cases the author's convenience, rather than historical accuracy, is being served.[88] One also needs to bear in mind Cicero's disinclination to draw sharp lines between the Academy/Peripatetos on the one side, the Stoa on the other (cf. *ad* § 38).

"Strictly speaking *summi dei* ought to be written by Cicero for *deorum immortalium,* but the distinction between the *summus deus* and inferior gods is not always strictly expressed": Reid. While the Stoa emphasized a

---

86. Cf. also *Rep.* 3.27, where the rôle of god is to invent and establish the law, teach it, etc.—Du Mesnil *ad loc.* suggests that Cicero emphasizes the theological dimension here because some legislation was devoted to the regulation of the state cult; but that would not necessarily have entailed theological argument at this level.

87. As F. Münzer, *RE* 7A2 (1948), 1305.25 ff., seems to imply: ". . . daß er nicht ohne Grund und ohne die Zustimmung des Q. in späteren Dialogen, in denen er das tat, gerade ihm gewisse Anschauungen in den Mund legte, wie . . . die Vertretung der stoischen Divinationslehre (div. I 9–132)"; cf. also Schmidt, 1969, 60.

88. Cf. Malcolm Schofield, "Cicero for and against Divination," *JRS* 76 (1986), 60–61; cf. also *ad* 2.33.

single supreme intelligence directing the operations of the universe (cf. § 22: . . . *generatum esse a supremo deo*), it did not deny polytheism and spoke of a plurality of gods in the context of the shared community of gods and men (cf. *ad* § 23). Difficulty arises, however, through the contrast of our passage, where it appears that the gods jointly govern the universe, and § 23 *(parent autem huic caelesti descriptioni mentique divinae et praepotenti deo . . .)*, where humans and lesser deities apparently obey the supreme deity; cf. Mehl, 124–25.

In the series *deorum immortalium vi, natura, ratione, potestate, mente, numine,* Lambinus deleted *natura* since *naturam omnem* is the object influenced by these agencies. Once *natura* is removed we have two pairs of opposites *(vi/ratione, potestate/mente)* capped by the summarizing *numine;* cf. 2.15: *iudicio ac numine;* N.D. 2.16: *quod . . . mens quod ratio quod vis quod potestas;* ibid. 1.26: *vi ac ratione.*[89] *Nutu* for *natura,* cited by J. Tunstall, *Epistola ad C. Middleton* (Cambridge, 1741), 177 and n., as the proposal of a learned friend,[90] and revived by Zelzer, 1981, 229, though, especially with *ratione* following, palaeographically attractive, fails to carry conviction; Watt, 1986, 265–66, points out that *nutus* (= "a person's nod as a symbol of absolute power": *OLD* s.v., 2b) would anticipate *numen* ("divine power as controlling events, divine will or sanction": *OLD* s.v., 3a). Watt's own suggestion, *motu,* cannot claim, however, to be a quality of the gods on the same level as these other terms. But perhaps the transmitted text can stand after all: *vis et natura divina* or *deorum* is so common in Cicero (*Tusc.* 1.30, 5.70, *N.D.* 1.32, 49, 122) and his striving here for comprehensiveness so patent that this may be a simple instance of hasty formulaic writing of the kind often encountered in *Off.* (see the Index of Grammatical and Stylistic Features s.v. "Formulaic Writing").—For this Stoic doctrine cf. also *N.D.* 1.4 and 2.73–153; *Fin.* 4.12; in general *SVF* 2, 322 ff.—*Sive quod est aliud verbum quo planius significem quod volo:* the adequate description of the deity's means of acting upon the world challenges even Cicero's formidable powers of expression; cf. 2.3: . . . *inest nescioquid et latet in animo ac sensu meo . . . ; Fam.* 13.63.1: *non putavi fieri posse ut mihi verba deessent . . .*

A. Do sane, si postulas; etenim propter hunc concentum avium strepitumque fluminum non vereor condiscipulorum ne quis exaudiat.] For Atticus in the circle of his fellow-students cf. *Fin.* 5.1 ff. His mock face-saving comment that the singing of birds and noise of the rivers (sc. the Liris and the Fibrenus, of

---

89. Cf. *Ac.* 1.29, where there is a focus on the two terms *vis* and *mens.*

90. Perhaps J. Chapman, the author of the essay on the chronology of *Leg.* appended to Tunstall's book?

which the former is quite gentle, the latter more agitated; cf. *ad* § 14 and 2.6) will prevent his fellow-students' noticing his "treason" is one of the rare instances in which the setting, once established, is invoked within a Ciceronian dialogue; cf. Becker, 27–28; Gasser, 34; it also enables the discussion to proceed on track (see the previous note). On Atticus' character as sketched in *Leg.* in general cf. the Introduction § 6.—For *sane* adhering to the repeated word in an agreement to a request cf. *OLD* s.v., 6; hence the use of *sane* by itself as an affirmation (ibid., 2).—*Concentus,* perhaps a Ciceronian coinage (so *TLL* s.v., 19.69), first occurs in *de Orat.* (3.21 and 196) and recurs in *Rep.* (2.69, 6.10); our passage is its first use of the singing of birds; cf. Sen. *Ep.* 56.11: *nullus hominum aviumque concentus interrumpet cogitationes bonas; TLL, loc. cit.,* 20.17.—In *exaudiat* the prefix "conveys the idea of catching a distant or faint sound": Reid ad *Luc.* 20; sim. Tarrant *ad* Sen. *Thy.* 114.

M. Atqui cavendum est; solent enim, id quod virorum bonorum est, admodum irasci, . . .] *Atqui* introduces a mock-serious warning: "and yet [i.e., in spite of the aviary interference] one must be on one's guard"; here Marcus pokes a bit of gentle fun at the Epicureans.—*Id quod virorum bonorum est* is urbane (cf. *Tusc.* 3.50: *Epicurei, viri optimi* and 2.44: *venit Epicurus, homo minime malus vel potius optimus vir;* sim. *Fin* 2.80–81 and 99), but also, in this context, mildly ironic/patronizing;[91] on their intemperance in debate cf. *N.D.* 1.93–94; at *Tusc.* 3.38 Zeno the Epicurean is referred to as *ille acriculus . . . senex.* The favorable construction placed on anger *(id quod virorum bonorum est)* is characteristic of the Peripatos; cf. Ar. *Rhet.* 1367a38 (. . . τὸν ὄργιλον καὶ τὸν μανικὸν ἁπλοῦν . . .); *EN* 1108a4–5 and 1125b30–32;[92] this adds, as Inwood points out *per litt.,* "a further wrinkle in a complex bit of inter-school fun-poking."

. . . nec vero ferent si audierint te primum caput viri optimi prodidisse, in quo scripsit nihil curare deum nec sui nec alieni.] *Caput* here is a paragraph or section of a literary work (*OLD* s.v., 18); cf. *Luc.* 101: *ex uno Epicuri capite,* with Reid's note.—The reference is to the first of Epicurus' κύριαι δόξαι: τὸ μακάριον καὶ ἄφθαρτον οὔτε αὐτὸ πράγματα ἔχει οὔτε ἄλλῳ παρέχει . . . = *quod beatum et immortale est id nec habet nec exhibet cuiquam negotium* (*N.D.* 1.85); cf. *Div.* 2.40: *illius* [sc. *Epicuri*] *enim deus nihil habens nec sui nec alieni negoti . . . ;* there is also an echo at Phld. *Piet.* 1 P.Herc. 1077, col. 19, 530–33. Cf. in general Matthias Baltes, "Zur Nachwirkung des Satzes Τὸ μακάριον καὶ ἄφθαρτον οὔτε αὐτὸ πράγματα ἔχει . . . , " in *Epikureismus in der späten Republik und der Kaiserzeit,* ed.

---

91. Cf. Reid *ad Luc.* 115.
92. Cf. Hor. *S.* 1.3.53: *caldior est: acres inter numeretur.*

M. Erler (Stuttgart, 2000), 93–108.—*Caput viri* is the correction of Aldus'
grandson. J.G.F. Powell explains the corruption this way *(per litt.):* "B's
capulli is explicable as deriving from *cap.uIrI;* B has a lot of trouble with *I*
and *L*. The other MSS had *capituli: u > it, ir > ul,* plus the attempt to make
a sensible word."

22–27 This matter comprises a "preparation" in three stages for the actual topic (cf. Atticus' words at § 28: . . . *ipsa illa quorum haec causa
praeparantur*):

     I. The commonwealth of gods and men based upon partnership in
       reason (§§ 22–23)
    II. The special relation of gods and men, as seen in the origins of human
       beings, their possession of the same virtue, their *cognatio,* and na-
       ture's provident provision for human needs (§§ 24–26a)
   III. The qualities of human beings, with particular reference to those that
       bring them closer to the gods and separate them from the beasts,
       including powers of communication and reasoning (§§ 26b–27).

The argument amounts to a précis of Stoic theology; cf. Balbus' outline at
N.D. 2.3 (sim. *Div.* 1.117): (1) *primum docent esse deos,* (2) *deinde quales
sint,* (3) *tum mundum ab his administrari,* (4) *postremo consulere eos rebus
humanis.* The gods' existence (1) is challenged by none of the interlocutors,
so that only one proof is offered in passing, namely that from the universal
notitia dei (§§ 24–25; see *ad loc.*). The qualities of the gods (2) are not
systematically presented, but Cicero establishes the ones important for his
purpose, namely the possession of *ratio* (§ 23) and the benevolent care for
human beings (= [4]: §§ 22 and 24 ff.). For an Epicurean like Atticus the
sticking point is the gods' government of the universe (3), but this hurdle has
already been cleared by his acceptance of Marcus' postulate at § 21, so that
Marcus is now free to dilate on the subject without having to provide proof
(§§ 22–23).

22–23 These chapters, comprising the argument for a law and polity valid
in different places, correspond to *SVF* 3, 89.41 ff. The doctrine of the cosmic
city of gods and men was a broadening of Zeno's conception in his *Republic,* for Aristo of Chios and Chrysippus found that it made no sense to
confine the community of goods to neighbors only or membership to humans; cf. *ad* § 23; Schofield, 1991, 102. As developed in our passage, the
community of gods and men includes three elements not found elsewhere in
this combination: (1) right reason, (2) obedience to the same authorities,
and (3) kinship. The closest parallel, involving points (1) and (2), is *SVF* 2,

169.26 ff.: . . . ὁ κόσμος οἰονεὶ πόλις ἐστὶν ἐκ θεῶν καὶ ἀνθρώπων συνεστῶσα, τῶν μὲν θεῶν τὴν ἡγεμονίαν ἐχόντων, τῶν δ' ἀνθρώπων ὑποτεταγμένων. κοινωνίαν δ' ὑπάρχειν πρὸς ἀλλήλους διὰ τὸ λόγου μετέχειν, ὅς ἐστι φύσει νόμος. For (1) cf. *N.D.* 2.154: *est enim mundus quasi communis deorum atque hominum domus aut urbs utrorumque; soli enim ratione utentes iure ac lege vivunt;* for (2) *Fin.* 3.64: *mundum autem censent regi numine deorum, eumque esse quasi communem urbem et civitatem hominum et deorum . . . ;* for (3) *SVF* 3, 82.6 ff. (quoted in full *ad* § 23: *quibus autem haec sunt inter se communia*), where the familial relation is simile rather than fact (ὡς παῖδες σὺν ἀνδράσι λέγονται μετέχειν πόλεως: 9–10). Cf. also Sen. *Ot.* 4.1, quoted *ad* 2.5. M. Aurel. 4.4.1–2 offers a more modest form of the argument, i.e., a cosmic city without reference to the gods.

22 A. Perge, quaeso; nam id quod tibi concessi quorsus pertineat exspecto.] Such questions from Atticus drive the conversation forward at various points in this Book; cf. §§ 1, 4, and 63.

M. Non faciam longius.] *Facio* here draws its content from Atticus' *perge;* cf. *OLD* s.v., 26: "(absol.) To perform the action indicated by another verb in the context, do so"; cf. *Fin.* 3.16; see further Harm Pinkster, *Latin Syntax and Semantics* (London and New York, 1990), 11–12. In the sequel Cicero will use verbs of motion to describe the unfolding dialogue: *longius progredi* (§ 27); *labebar longius* and *tecum prolabebar* (§ 52).

animal hoc providum, sagax, multiplex, acutum, memor, plenum rationis et consili, quem vocamus hominem, praeclara quadam condicione generatum esse a supremo deo; solum est enim ex tot animantium generibus atque naturis particeps rationis et cogitationis, cum cetera sint omnia expertia.] This passage is cited word for word from *Leg.* 1 at Lact. *inst.* 2.11.16.— *Animal* can have the broader sense of "a living creature" (*OLD* s.v., 1; *TLL* s.v., I 1), in our passage referring, of course, specifically to the human being, as is clarified by the added clause *quem vocamus hominem* (ibid. 78.73); *animans* would have been possible and is used for variety in the next sentence, as in § 27.—All the attributes listed have to do with mental faculties which, according to the Stoa, set the human being apart from animals; cf. Sorabji, 20 ff.; for a similar list of the qualities of the human mind including *sagacitas* and *memoria* cf. *Tusc.* 1.67.—*Providus* = "exercising foresight, provident" (*OLD* s.v., 2); it is used in preference to *prudens,* which, though also related to *provideo,* detached itself semantically as well as phonetically and assumed the broader sense "knowledgeable in"; cf. Ernout-Meillet s.v. *Providentia* (= πρόνοια) is a quality often associated with the deity (cf. *N.D.* 2.58 and 77), and the sharing of mental powers between god and man will, in fact, turn out to be the point of this inventory.—Our passage is only the second attestation of *sagax* as applied to intellect (*OLD* s.v., 2) and the first in which *multiplex* is applied directly to a human being (ibid. s.v., 6b; *TLL* s.v., 1592.68–70); cf., however, *Cael*. 14: *hac ille* [sc. *Catilina*] *tam varia multiplicique natura* . . . ; at *ad Brut*. 1.1.1 Cicero finds that making pronouncements about others is *periculosum propter occultas hominum voluntates multiplicisque naturas*. Cf. also Arnob. *nat*. 2.7: . . . *potest quisquam explicare mortalium* . . . *homo quid sit aut unde sit, anceps varius mobilis pellax multiplex multiformis* . . . ? Synes. *Regn*. 10 (p. 21, 3–6 Terzaghi): εὖ γὰρ ἴσθι τοῦτο, ὡς οὐχ ἁπλοῦν τι χρῆμα οὐδὲ μονοειδὲς ἄνθρωπος ἀλλὰ συνῴκισεν ὁ θεὸς εἰς ἑνὸς ζῴου σύστασιν ὄχλον δυνάμεων παμμιγῆ τε καὶ πάμφωνον; cf. also Reid *ad Ac*. 1.17.—Like *sagax*, *acutus* earlier referred to the powers of the senses and has been transferred to mental powers (cf. *OLD* s.v., 5 and 8).—*Ratio et consilium* comprise reason both in the abstract and as applied concretely; cf. the description of *ratio* at *N.D*. 3.69 (. . . *motum istum celerem cogitationis acumen sollertiam, quam rationem vocamus* . . .) and of *consilium* at *Inv*. 1.36 (*consilium est aliquid faciendi aut non faciendi excogitata ratio*).—*Praeclara quadam condicione*: besides the mental qualities listed here, other advantages of the human condition are indicated at §§ 25–26. For *quadam* cf. *ad* 3.1.—For human origin from the supreme being cf. Arat. 5: τοῦ γὰρ καὶ γένος εἰμέν; sim. Cleanthes' hymn to Zeus, ll. 4–5; the process is described at § 24.

Boyancé, 1970, 297–98, sees Plut. *Qu. Plat*. 1000f (Τί δήποτε τὸν ἀνωτάτω θεὸν πατέρα τῶν πάντων καὶ ποιητὴν προσεῖπεν; referring to *Tim*. 28c3–4: τὸν μὲν οὖν ποιητὴν καὶ πατέρα τοῦδε τοῦ παντός) as similar to Cicero's *supremus deus* and suggests that such an exegesis of *Tim*. 28c would have been known to Cicero through his Academic studies (a similar phrase recurs, he points out, at Phil. *Spec. leg*. 2.165[93]) and his phrase a translation of it. Certainly there are some Platonic echoes in the passage (cf. *ad* §§ 24 and 31), but the Stoa too was inclined to emphasize a supreme deity, identified with Zeus and with right reason; cf. *ad* § 23; and indeed the following sentence strongly suggests that that is what Cicero has in mind (cf. also *summa lex* in § 19): *quid est autem, non dicam in homine, sed in omni caelo atque terra, ratione divinius?*[94]—The *iunctura supremus*

---

93. εἰ δ' ἔστιν, ὃν μιᾷ γνώμῃ πάντες ὁμολογοῦσιν Ἕλληνες ὁμοῦ καὶ βάρβαροι, ὁ ἀνωτάτω πατὴρ θεῶν τε καὶ ἀνθρώπων καὶ τοῦ σύμπαντος κόσμου δημιουργός, . . . ἔδει . . . πάντας ἀνθρώπους ἀνῆφθαι ⟨τούτου⟩ . . .

94. Schmidt, 1965, 307, reads these words in light of § 23: ". . . hier [sc. in our passage] ist der höchste Gott König im Staat der Götter und Menschen" (this, of course, need not be at odds with the interpretation of the *supremus deus* as the Stoic λόγος).

deus is not previously attested; but cf. Pl. *Capt.* 426 and 976 and *Ps.* 628: *supremus Iuppiter* in various case-forms; Acc. *trag.* 143 *(Antigona): deum supremus rex;* for *summus deus* cf. Caecil. *com.* 259 (of Cupid); *Rep.* 6.21 *(summus . . . deus);* Luc. 126: *Zenoni et reliquis fere Stoicis aether videtur summus deus . . . ; summus Iuppiter* in a verse translated from Greek at *Div.* 2.25; for *praepotens deus* cf. § 23.—Lact. *inst.* 1.5.24 fastens on the phrase *supremus deus* in our passage as an adumbration of Christian monotheism; cf. Schmidt, 1965, 307.

Solum est enim ex tot animantium generibus atque naturis particeps rationis et cogitationis, cum cetera sint omnia expertia: for *ratio* as the *differentia specifica* between man and beast cf. *Fin.* 2.45; *N.D.* 2.16 = *SVF* 2, 302.4; *Off.* 1.11; § 30 *(ratio qua una praestamus beluis);* Sen. *Ep.* 76.9 = *SVF* 3, 48.20–21: *in homine quid proprium est? ratio: hac antecedit animalia, deos sequitur; SVF* 2, 236.10–11; Cleanthes was led to ponder this precept after observing ants exchange a grub for the corpse of one of their tribe; cf. *SVF* 1, 116.5 ff. After considering the claims of animals to *signa rationis,* Lact. *inst.* 3.10.5 concludes, in conscious variation of our passage: *incertum igitur est utrumne illa quae homini tribuuntur communia sint cum aliis viventibus, religionis certe sunt expertia;* cf. Schmidt, 1965, 309–10.— The use of *particeps,* as of μετέχειν in Greek sources, suggests that reason is not the peculiar possession of the human being but is shared [sc. with the gods].—*Genera* and *naturae* are more or less synonymous here (= εἴδη); cf. Reid *ad Ac.* 1.39 *(quintam naturam).*—*Ratio et cogitatio* = λόγος καὶ διάνοια (Reid).

quid est autem . . . ratione divinius?] Cf. *N.D.* 1.37: *. . . nihil ratione censet* [sc. Cleanthes] *esse divinius;* sim. Chrysippus quoted ibid. 2.16: *. . . ratio, qua nihil potest esse praestantius,* as well as *nihil est ratione melius* in the sentence after next.

quae cum adolevit atque perfecta est, nominatur rite sapientia?] At § 18b *lex* is described in very similar terms *(eadem ratio cum est in hominis mente confirmata et perfecta, lex est);* the content of both will be the *recta ratio* of the Stoic sage; cf. Inwood, 1987, 99–101. Cf. Sen. *Ep.* 89.4: *sapientia perfectum bonum est mentis humanae,* as well as the encomium of *sapientia* at §§ 58–62. Our sentence is, however, an aside; *ratio* continues to be the functional term within the developing argument.—On the maturing process within the human mind cf. 2.11; *Tusc.* 5.39: *hic igitur si est excultus et si eius acies ita curata est, ut ne caecaretur erroribus, fit perfecta mens, id est absoluta ratio . . .* On the conflict in the sources as to whether, in the Stoic view, reason was complete after the first or second seven years of life cf. Schofield, 1991, 33–34 n. 21.—For *nominari rite* cf. *Fin.*

2.37: . . . *divinarum humanarumque rerum scientia, quae potest appellari rite sapientia* . . . —In our sentence the resonant word *sapientia* is reserved for the emphatic final position; if its second *i* is treated as a glide,[95] the clausula is of the *debuerat omne* type.

23 est igitur—civitatis eiusdem habendi sunt; . . .] A chain syllogism, in which four points are claimed as shared by gods and men with a single *civitas* as the consequence: *ratio, recta ratio, lex, ius.* The odd step in the argument is not, as Schmidt, 1959, 174, supposed, from *lex* to *ius*,[96] but, rather, from *ratio* to *recta ratio*, since one would expect the presence of the weaker term to be inferred from that of the stronger, rather than vice versa; see the note after next. Cf. in general Schofield, 1991, 69, who notes that "having seemingly extruded all reference to the city or community or state from their account of law [cf. *ad* § 18], they [sc. the Stoics] now try to reinstitute a connection"; he goes on to show (p. 72) that this move is facilitated by a concept of "prescriptive reason instructing them [i.e., human beings] how to treat each other as social animals."—A similar argument about qualities shared between gods and men appears at *N.D.* 2.78–79, where the shared state is that of the gods alone (though both gods and men are said to share reason and law); the pont of that passage is the gods' possession of reason and their use of it *in maximis et optimis rebus,* i.e., the government of the world.

est igitur, quoniam nihil est ratione melius, eaque ⟨est⟩ et in homine et in deo, prima homini cum deo rationis societas.] *Quoniam nihil est ratione melius:* cf. *N.D.* 2.38: *nihil autem est mente et ratione melius* (in the proof that the *mundus* has these attributes); *ad* § 22 *(quid est autem . . . ratione divinius?).*—*Eaque ⟨est⟩ et in homine et in deo:* cf. SVF 3, 58.37: ἀρετῇ τε γὰρ οὐχ ὑπερέχειν τὸν Δία τοῦ Δίωνος . . .—The omission of small words like *est* (also 3.19 and 27), *et* (§ 24, 2.41 and 51 [⟨et⟩si]), *a* (§§ 16 and 19, 3.8.2), *se* (3.23), or *-que* (§§ 24, 34, 35, 37, 42) is a marked feature of the transmission of *Leg.* (as well as being common generally).—*Societas* follows from both groups' having a share of *ratio;* cf. *ad* § 22 *(particeps rationis)* and Wegner, 30–31.—*Prima*, in light of the justification *quoniam nihil est ratione melius,* refers to hierarchy, whereas *prima societas in ipso coniugio est* (*Off.* 1.54) is a stage in the reconstruction of the history of society.

inter quos autem ratio—inter eos communio iuris est.] The key point is the identification of *recta ratio* and *lex.* This was already implicit at § 18, though there a descriptive clause substitutes for the technical term *recta*

---

95. Cf. W.S. Allen, 38; *ad* 3.7b.

96. He says, *loc. cit.*, that it was "von Cicero geformt"; but the Stoics had established a relation of νόμος to τὸ δίκαιον; cf. SVF 3, 77.35–37, quoted *ad* § 19: *ea est enim naturae vis—*.

ratio: eadem ratio cum est in hominis mente confirmata et perfecta, lex est.
Recta ratio is an attribute of the gods and of the Stoic sage; in that sphere
also *lex* and *ius* would be, as Reid notes, identical (= τὸ δίκαιον). The
argument was probably originally framed with gods and sages in mind and
then adapted to human beings generally (the same argument is applied to
human beings alone at § 33); in that case the odd step of reasoning from
ratio to *recta ratio* (the former applying to human beings generally, the latter
to sages and gods; see the note before last and the next note) would have
been imposed on this context superficially at a later date.

inter quos autem ratio, inter eosdem etiam recta ratio {et} communis est; quae
cum sit lex, lege quoque consociati homines cum dis putandi sumus; . . .] For
recta ratio (= ὀρθὸς λόγος) as law cf. D.L. 7.88 = SVF 1, 43.1–3 = 3, 4.2–4:
ὁ νόμος ὁ κοινός, ὅπερ ἐστὶν ὁ ὀρθὸς λόγος διὰ πάντων ἐρχόμενος, ὁ αὐτὸς
ὢν τῷ Διί, καθηγεμόνι τούτῳ τῆς τῶν ὄντων διοικήσεως ὄντι; *Rep.* 3.27 (=
SVF 3.80.20 ff.): *est quidem vera lex recta ratio, naturae congruens, diffusa in*
omnes, constans, sempiterna . . . ; Phil. 11.28: *est enim lex nihil aliud nisi*
recta et a numine deorum tracta ratio, imperans honesta, prohibens con-
traria;[97] cf. also *SVF* 3, 79.40, cited *ad* § 18a; § 42. Vander Waerdt, 1994b,
4875, sees this step in the argument as a reinterpretation, perhaps after Antiochus, of the old Stoic concept of κοινὸς νόμος, which originally applied, like
ὀρθὸς λόγος, only to sages (Mehl, 131, attributes the change to Cicero himself). This is the source of the sage's special freedom; cf. *SVF* 3, 146.8–9: . . .
καὶ πάντα τὸν σοφὸν εἶναι ἐλεύθερον, ἐξουσίαν αὐτοπραγίας ἀπὸ τοῦ
θείου νόμου εἰληφότα· καὶ τὴν ἐξουσίαν δὲ ὁρίζονται νομίμην ἐπιτροπήν;
see also the previous note.—The *cum deo rationis societas* of the preceding
sentence now becomes a partnership in law *cum dis;* Schmidt, 1959, 175,
finds the Stoic argument weakened here by being overlaid with Roman polytheism. But Greek Stoic sources, too, refer to a plurality of gods when describing the κόσμος as a divine πόλις (see *SVF* 2, 169.26 ff., cited *ad* §§ 22–23), to
which the community of *ius* in our passage is leading; cf. the first note *ad* § 21.
inter quos porro est communio legis, inter eos communio iuris est.] A relation of *ius* and *lex* is assumed whereby *lex* is constitutive of *ius* (cf. § 42: *est*
enim unum ius, quo devincta est hominum societas, et quod lex constituit
una . . .). Under *ius* the Roman understood the set of traditional legal acts
and powers that were, in the event of a dispute, adjudicated in court, with
lex as their authoritative formulation. Historically, the relation was not
simple, however. The *leges* of the Twelve Tables represented the first step in

97. For a defense of this passage as referring to an exceptional emergency situation cf.
Klaus M. Girardet, "Die Rechtsstellung der Caesarattentäter Brutus und Cassius in den Jahren
44–42 v.Chr.," *Chiron* 23 (1993), 227–32.

the process of bringing the old *ius* into line with the demands of the *civitas*, whereby there was often a resistance of those with positions based on *ius* against changes effected by *lex;* cf. Max Kaser, "Die Beziehung von Lex und Ius und die XII Tafeln," *Studi in memoria di Guido Donatuti*, 2 (Milan, 1973), 523–46; Wieacker, 1988, 282 ff.—*Communio* is first attested in Cicero (*Sex. Rosc.* 63); for the *iunctura communio iuris* cf. *TLL* s.v. *communio* 1962.57.—*Communio legis* and *communio iuris* are made the condition for the existence of a *civitas;* cf. Scipio's famous definition (*Rep.* 1.39): *est igitur res publica res populi; populus autem non omnis hominum coetus quoquo modo congregatus, sed coetus multitudinis iuris consensu et utilitatis communione sociatus.* A shared justice that would exclude tyranny or other inequalities in rights is implied in both passages; cf. also Arist. *Pol.* 1253a37–39 (part of the argument that πᾶσα πόλις φύσει ἐστίν and ἄνθρωπος φύσει πολιτικὸν ζῷον: ibid. 1252b30 and 1253a2–3): ἡ δὲ δικαιοσύνη πολιτικόν· ἡ γὰρ δίκη πολιτικῆς κοινωνίας τάξις ἐστίν· ἡ δὲ δίκη τοῦ δικαίου κρίσις; *Rep.* 1.49; *Fin.* 3.67: *quoniamque ea natura esset hominis ut ei cum genere humano quasi civile ius intercederet . . . ;* Schofield, 1995, 72. For the idea of a shared polity of gods and men cf. also *SVF* 3, 82.6 = D.Chr. 36.23: μίαν γὰρ δὴ ταύτην καθαρῶς εὐδαίμονα πολιτείαν εἴτε καὶ πόλιν χρὴ καλεῖν, τὴν θεῶν πρὸς ἀλλήλους κοινωνίαν, ἐάν τε καὶ ξύμπαν τὸ λογικὸν περιλάβῃ τις, ἀνθρώπων σὺν θεοῖς ἀριθμουμένων, ὡς παῖδες σὺν ἀνδράσι λέγονται μετέχειν πόλεως . . . ; *Fin.* 3.64: *mundum autem censent regi numine deorum, eumque esse quasi communem urbem et civitatem hominum et deorum . . . ; ad* § 61.—The argument glances at *ius* here, but only briefly (cf. *N.D.* 2.79, where the same argument appears without reference to *ius*); this preparatory material continues to the end of § 27; then the discussion will focus on the topic . . . *neque opinione sed natura constitutum esse ius* (§ 28; cf. *ad* §§ 22–27).

quibus autem haec sunt {inter eos communi} ⟨ . . . ⟩ et civitatis eiusdem habendi sunt; . . .] The transmitted *inter eos* was suspected both by Reid and by Kühner-Stegmann. Discussing our passage in the context of how *inter se* and other such formulaic phrases can refer to an oblique correlate, Kühner-Stegmann, 1, 604–5, remark that our passage is "ganz vereinzelt und vielleicht verdorben"; sim. Lebreton, 120. To write *inter se* for *inter eos*,[98] and adopt *communia* (AHL) for B's *communi* and Bake's *ei* for *et* might appear attractive at first glance. But, as J.G.F. Powell points out *(per litt.),* it

---

98. Cf. *Fin.* 5.25: *nihil enim prohibet quaedam esse et inter se animalibus reliquis et cum bestiis homini communia; Off.* 1.53: *multa enim sunt civibus inter se communia,* in both of which passages, as in ours, the grammatical subject is neuter plural, but the personal idea prevails.

is "odd to say 'those who have A have B; but then those who have A and B have C'. Why not just say 'those who have A have B and C?'" One could instead assume, with Powell, that *inter eos communi* was simply repeated from the previous line and then "corrected" to *communia*. If that is so, then, in default of parallels from other Stoic sources, we simply have to indicate a lacuna and the intrusive character of the transmitted text.

si vero eisdem imperiis et potestatibus parent, multo iam magis.] *Imperia* and *potestates* are abstract for concrete (= "authorities, magistrates"): for the former cf. *TLL* s.v. *imperium* 570.69 ff; for the latter *ad* 3.6.2: . . . *ni par maiorve potestas populosve prohibessit*—; the next sentence provides further clarification.—Editors vary between *multo iam magis* (BAHLε) and *multo etiam magis* (P). The former, besides being the transmitted text, deserves preference for its superior clausula (type *omni debebitur*); *multo etiam magis* is never found before a full-stop or a pause marked by comma or semi-colon in modern editions of Cicero's corpus.[99] Cf. also *Rep.* 1.49: *multo iam id in regnis minus; Tusc.* 1.98: *id multo iam beatius est. Multo iam magis* distinguishes a shared *civitas* in a stronger sense from the weaker one preceding—a polity with not only the same law-code but also the same ruler(s).

parent autem huic caelesti descriptioni mentique divinae et praepotenti deo, . . .] For the general idea cf. *SVF* 1, 43.1–3, cited above on *inter quos autem ratio;* ibid. 42.23–24: *Zeno rerum naturae dispositorem atque artificem universitatis* λόγον *praedicat . . . ;* also Cleanthes' hymn to Zeus (ibid., 121.33 ff.) 1–2: . . . παγκρατὲς αἰεί, . . . νόμου μέτα πάντα κυβερνῶν . . . ; *Ac.* 1.29: *quam vim animum esse dicunt mundi eandemque esse mentem sapientiamque perfectam, quem deum appellant, omniumque rerum quae sunt ei subiectae quasi prudentiam quandam, procurantem caelestium maxime, deinde in terris ea quae pertinent ad homines;* Velleius' summary of Stoic doctrine at *N.D.* 1.22: . . . *cum omnes naturae numini divino, caelum ignes terrae maria, parerent.*—Repetitions, such as that of *parent* in our sentence, are a common structural device in Latin prose from Cato onward; cf. von Albrecht, 1983, 32–33 = Eng. tr. 16–17.—*Caelestis* is often, as here, conjoined with *divinus,* with which it is in practice often synonymous; cf. *TLL* s.v., 71.4 ff.; for *caelestis* as a substantive cf. *ad* § 24 *(agnatio nobis cum caelestibus).*—*Descriptio* here has the sense "certa constitutio, ordo" (perhaps a rendering of διοίκησις in a text such as *SVF* 1, 43.3 [cited above on *inter quos autem ratio*—]); "design" is perhaps the best English rendering; cf. *N.D.* 1.26; *TLL* s.v., IID (with note on spelling); on

---

99. Based on a search of PHI 5.3.

the other hand, *discriptio* (cf. A's *discriptione*) would mean "distributio" (*TLL* s.v.); the case for *descriptio* here and elsewhere is argued in detail by Vahlen *ad* 3.12.—Obedience to the *caelestis descriptio* might be taken to imply astrological influence;[100] cf. *Fat.* 8, perhaps a reply to a claim by Chrysippus that the *astrorum affectio* influences all things; it remains unclear, however, to what degree astrology was part of the mainstream Stoa's interest in divination; cf. A.A. Long, "Astrology: Arguments pro and contra," in *Science and Speculation: Studies in Hellenistic Theory and Practice,* ed. Jonathan Barnes et al. (Cambridge-Paris, 1982), 165–92, esp. 167–69 (on *Fat.* 8 cf. 169 n. 12). But in our passage the *caelestis descriptio* seems to be an equivalent of *mens divina* and *praepotens deus,* i.e., the Stoic λόγος, so that the astrological interpretation is unnecessary.—The inclusion of *mens divina* follows from what is said in § 22 about *ratio* (sim. § 24 à propos *animus* as a link between gods and men), with which it is virtually synonymous in this argument; cf. § 19: *mens ratioque prudentis.* For a short introduction to the divine intellect in Aristotle, Stoicism, Middle Platonism, and Plotinus cf. Dominic J. O'Meara, *Plotinus: An Introduction to the Enneads* (Oxford, 1993), 33–35.—*Praepotens* first occurs in a burst of comic alliteration at Pl. *Poen.* 1182 *(praepotentes pulchre pacisque potentes, soror, fuimus).* It is chronologically the first of the adjectives with *prae-* as an intensifier (as an alternative to comparative or superlative) formed by analogy to verbs compounded with *prae-;* cf. Leumann, 400–401; *OLD* s.v. *prae-; TLL* s.v. *praepotens.* Cicero's post-exilic work shows a fondness for it. In most oblique forms followed by an iambic word beginning with a consonant it effects a double cretic clausula.—At this point a deity is distinguished at a different level from the gods who share in law and thus form a community with human beings *(lege . . . consociati homines cum dis putandi sumus);* this is for the sake of accommodating the idea of obedience, which, in Cicero's thought, is closely bound up with the functioning of the world-order in general and states in particular (cf. 3.3–5); elsewhere the supreme god in Stoic contexts mediates between stricter Stoic and more popular conceptions; cf. *N.D.* 2.4: *. . . Iovem . . . praesentem ac praepotentem deum; Div.* 2.42: *. . . ea efficere rerum omnium praepotentem Iovem;* cf. also the first note *ad* § 21.

. . . ut ⟨sit⟩ iam universus hic mundus una civitas communis deorum atque hominum existimanda; . . .] *Sit* was added after *existimanda* by Turnebus but moved before it by Ziegler so as to improve the clausula; it is placed after *ut* by Powell, whence it can easily have dropped out through saltation error, so as to

---

100. The possibility was raised at the Cambridge seminar by G.E.R. Lloyd.

preserve the ditrochaic clausula; for the word order cf. *Tusc.* 1.2: . . . *ut sit cum maioribus nostris comparanda.*—For the attraction of the verb to the gender of the predicate noun cf. Kühner-Stegmann, 1, 40.—For the idea cf. *SVF* 3, 79.38–40: ἡ μὲν γὰρ μεγαλόπολις ὅδε ὁ κόσμος ἐστὶ καὶ μιᾷ χρῆται πολιτείᾳ καὶ νόμῳ ἑνί; sim. ibid. 82.17–19 and 29–31; *Rep.* 1.19; *Fin.* 3.64; *N.D.* 2.154. In Zeno's conception this community seems only to have included humans (*SVF* 1, 61.1–5); the gods were added by Aristo of Chios, but with a significant restriction: . . . μίαν εἶναι κοινὴν πολιτείαν τῶν καθαρῶν ψυχῶν πρὸς τοὺς θεούς . . . (ibid. 87.1 11). There is also an allusion to the doctrine at § 61 (. . . *seseque non {omnis} circumdatum moenibus {populare} alicuius {diffinitio} loci, sed civem totius mundi quasi unius urbis agnoverit . . .*).—One might have expected Cicero to develop the implications of the common polity of gods and men or use it as a point of reference in the following discussion of justice; but his closest subsequent approach to this theme is the argument at *N.D.* 2.154: *mundus deorum hominumque causa factus est.*

et quod in civitatibus ratione quadam, de qua dicetur idoneo loco, agnationibus familiarum distinguuntur status, id in rerum natura tanto est magnificentius tantoque praeclarius, ut homines deorum agnatione et gente teneantur.] *Quod* is the conjunction (= "the fact that": OLD s.v., 4); *id* has as its antecedent the entire previous clause. The sentence involves a brachylogy whereby an encomium of the second item usurps the place of the comparison proper; Feldhügel paraphrases: "et quod fit in civitatibus ratione quadam, ut agnationibus familiarum distinguantur status, idem fit in rerum natura in eaque est tanto magnificentius, ut homines deorum agnatione et gente teneantur"; for a similar shift of emphasis within a comparison cf. *ad Off.* 1.97–98.—*De qua dicetur idoneo loco:* such a passage, discussing the distinction in the status of families by blood relationship through the male line *(agnatio),* is not extant. This was an important topic in the law of inheritance and would have been dealt with as such by Varro in his *de gradibus libri (iur. anteh.* p. 127) and by Paulus in his *liber singularis de gradibus et adfinibus et nominibus eorum;* cf. Dahlmann, *RE* Suppl. 6 (1935), 1255.10 ff. Du Mesnil suggested that Cicero treated the topic under the *ius civile;* cf. the Introduction § 7.—Authors seldom make descent of the human race from the deity a point of pride, but cf. Pi. *N.* 6.1–2, where the link is sought, not through the male line *(agnatio),* but through the common mother, Earth: ἓν ἀνδρῶν, ἓν θεῶν γένος· ἐκ μιᾶς δὲ πνέομεν / ματρὸς ἀμφότεροι; cf. also the use of the broader term *gentilis,* referring to all who share a *gens,* at *Tim.* 41: . . . *qui tales creantur ut deorum immortalium quasi gentiles esse debeant, divini generis appellentur . . . ,* as well as *N.D.*

1.91: *deorum cognationem agnoscerem non invitus;* cf. also *ad* § 22 *(animal hoc providum, sagax, multiplex,—).*

24–26a—sollerter consecuta est.] The preceding claims about the human possession of reason and the consequent relation to the deity are asserted rather than demonstrated. Here Cicero provides justification *(nam)* with reference to human origins. Broadly speaking, the previous passage was Stoic in tenor (cf. *ad loc.*), whereas our passage is an amalgam: the mind/body dualism and some of the phrasing shows contact with Platonism (see the following notes);[101] the *consensus omnium* about the existence of the deity is an adaptation of an Epicurean argument (cf. *ad* § 24); the continuous rotation of the earth upon its axis and the origin of the human being from seeds scattered on the earth, Nature's provision for human needs, and the development of *artes* in imitation thereof are inspired by the Stoa (cf. the following notes).

24 Nam ⟨ea quae⟩ cum de natura omni quaeritur disputari solent, nimirum ita sunt ut disputantur: perpetuis cursibus—ingeneratum a deo: . . .] Formally this material is an explanation *(nam)* of the familial connection between gods and men just delineated.—Powell adds *ea quae* and substitutes *quaeritur* for the transmitted *quaeruntur* and thus obviates four changes of verb from plural to singular as well as the addition of *et.*—For *omni* R. Stephanus' *hominis* is often adopted, but, as J.G.F. Powell points out *(per litt.),* the general perspective goes back to the *Timaeus,* where the subject is indeed "all nature."—This stately period begins with an indication of the general topic and that he is reporting received views *(⟨ea quae⟩ . . . disputari solent);* Cicero then adds his personal affirmation *(nimirum ita sunt ut disputantur).*[102] The background in cosmic time is sketched in an ablative absolute *(perpetuis cursibus . . . caelestibus)* before the critical event is pinpointed *(exstitisse quandam maturitatem serendi generis humani).* The final part of the first half of the indirect statement concludes with a relative clause focusing on the divine element in the process *(quod . . . divino auctum sit animorum munere).* The second half describes a similar movement and emphasis from the perishable parts of the human being, described as background in a *cum*-clause, to the *animus* and its divine origin, reserved for the emphatic final position. Without elision the clausula is of the *omne debuit* type.

---

101. Thus Finger, 171, assigns §§ 24–27 to Antiochus, the preceding section to Posidonius.

102. On Cicero's "opining"—particularly striking when he is being ostensibly skeptical—cf. W. Görler, "Cicero's Philosophical Stance in the *Lucullus*," in *Assent and Argument: Studies in Cicero's Academic Books*, ed. Brad Inwood and Jaap Mansfeld (Leiden, 1997), 36–57, esp. 38 and 46.

. . . perpetuis cursibus conversionibus⟨que⟩ caelestibus exstitisse quandam maturitatem serendi generis humani, quod sparsum in terras atque satum, divino auctum sit animorum munere; . . .] This striking passage has been variously claimed as (1) Platonic, (2) Peipatetic, or (3) Stoic. The imagery of sowing *(serendi . . . sparsum . . . satum),* though reminiscent of Plato, is differently applied; the continuous movement of the world is Stoic, and the image of human beings rising from the soil is paralleled in Zeno, though our passage omits the agency of the Stoic divine fire and seems to differ in the timing.

(1) Festugière, 430 and n. 2, found an echo of *Tim.* 41e (δέοι δὲ σπαρείσας αὐτὰς [sc. τὰς ψυχάς] εἰς τὰ προσήκοντα ἑκάσταις ἕκαστα ὄργανα χρόνων φῦναι ζῴων τὸ θεοσεβέστατον) and connected the temporal indication with Pl. *Pol.* 272a (ἐπειδὴ γὰρ πάντων τούτων χρόνος ἐτελεώθη καὶ μεταβολὴν ἔδει γίγνεσθαι). But in our passage, as Festugière rightly notes, it is not the souls, but the human race that is sown (for the sowing of souls cf. rather *Sen.* 77[103]), with the soul added afterward (note perfect tense *sparsum . . . atque satum*), so that we have at most a vague and much altered reminiscence of the Platonic passage. Furthermore it is far from obvious that Cicero's reference to *perpetuis cursibus conversionibus⟨que⟩ caelestibus* (paraphrased by Festugière as "temps révolu") must have been inspired by ἐπειδὴ γὰρ πάντων τούτων χρόνος ἐτελεώθη (which is a teleological description without the element of revolutions in a circuit); Cicero's *maturitas* would be closer. Also unlikely is the notion of Boyancé, 1970, 294 ff., that Cicero's *in perpetuis cursibus conversionibus⟨que⟩ caelestibus* is based on a misunderstanding of the words εἰς τὰ προσήκοντα ἑκάσταις ἕκαστα ὄργανα χρόνων of the *Timaeus*. He cites Plut. *Qu. Plat.* 8 (1006b), D.S. 1.6.3, and Calcidius' translation together with Cicero's own to suggest that there is underlying each an interpretation of the *Timaeus* passage going back to Antiochus of Ascalon. Ἐν χρόνῳ of Plut. *Qu. Plat.* 8 can easily have been based, however, on the attested variant reading ἐν χρόνῳ in the *Timaeus* (as Boyancé, *loc. cit.,* 298, admits), and Calcidius' translation *certis legitimisque temporum vicibus* can have been influenced by Cic. *Tim.* 43 *(certis temporum intervallis)* (in spite of Calcidius' speaking in the preface of the *spem proventuri operis intemptati ad hoc tempus*). Different again is D.S. 1.6.3 (οἱ δὲ γεννητὸν καὶ φθαρτὸν εἶναι νομίσαντες, ἔφησαν ὁμοίως ἐκείνῳ τοὺς ἀνθρώπους τυχεῖν τῆς πρώτης γενέσεως ὡρισμένοις

---

103. *Sed credo deos immortales sparsisse animos in corpora humana.*

χρόνοις), where we have a hypothesis of cyclical coming to be and passing away including the origin of human beings at fixed points in the cycle, whereas in our passage there is no indication that human beings arose more than once. Thus Boyancé's theory that this and the other passages cited derive from Antiochus lacks cogency.

(2) The view of Luigi Alfonsi, "Su un passo delle 'Legge' Ciceroniane," *P.P.* 18 (1962), 59–61, that *perpetuis cursibus conversionibus⟨que⟩ caelestibus* corresponds to the *replicatio mundi* referred to by Aristotle in *de Philosophia* 3 = fr. 26 Walzer = *N.D.* 1.33 also seems unlikely. For *replicatio mundi* there refers to the ἀνείλιξις or contrary motion of the universe (cf. Pease *ad loc.*; *OLD* s.v. *replicatio* 1). In our passage, however, the phrase *perpetuis cursibus* suggests continuous motion in a single direction, as does Cicero's usage elsewhere of *conversio;* cf. attestations at *TLL* s.v., 854.25 ff.

(3) Our passage is printed by von Arnim at *SVF* 2, 210.39 ff.; Stoic doctrine on the subject is briefly summarized at *Div.* 2.119: *divinos animos censent esse nostros, eosque esse tractos extrinsecus . . .*; sim. ibid. 1.110; § 28; *Tusc.* 1.56 (cited *ad* § 59) and 65. The continuous movement of the world on its own axis is Stoic; cf. *N.D.* 2.15, 46, 49, 84. Zeno's view that human beings arose from the soil with the aid of divine fire [sc. to provide the soul] shows some points of contact: *Zeno Citieus . . . principium humano generi ex novo mundo constitutum putavit, primosque homines ex solo, adminiculo divini ignis, id est dei providentia, genitos: SVF* 1, 35.20 ff. Here the phrase *ex novo mundo* poses a problem, since Cicero's text implies that the new earth was not suitable to give rise to human beings. Also, the doctrine of the divine fire is absent from our passage, and the idea of sowing is absent from Zeno. Closer to our passage is the reference to the σπερματικοὶ λόγοι at Origen, *Cels.* 1.37 = *SVF* 2, 211.6–7: . . . ἀνάγκη τοὺς πρώτους [sc. ἀνθρώπους] μὴ ἐκ συνουσίας γεγονέναι, ἀλλ᾽ ἀπὸ γῆς, σπερματικῶν λόγων συστάντων ἐν τῇ γῇ; the rôle of the σπερματικοὶ λόγοι in cosmogony (without specific reference to the origin of human beings) is described at D.L. 7.136; cf. ibid. 148; Pohlenz, *Stoa,* 1, 373.[104]

Quod sparsum in terras atque satum, divino auctum sit animorum munere: for *sparsum . . . atque satum* cf. *Tim.* 43: *satis autem et quasi sparsis animis fore uti certis temporum intervallis oreretur animal quod esset*

---

104. The Epicureans held a similar doctrine of the origins of the human race (cf. Lucr. 2.991–98), criticized by Cotta at *N.D.* 1.91.

ad cultum deorum aptissimum, where Plato (*Tim.* 41e4) has σπαρείσας alone.—*Munus* here has the sense "gift"; *animorum* is a defining genitive; cf. *TLL* s.v. *munus* 1665.5–6, where our passage is cited.

cumque alia quibus cohaererent homines e mortali genere sumpserint, quae fragilia essent et caduca, animum esse ingeneratum a deo: . . .] The description *quibus cohaererent homines* makes the human being a compound entity, in terms of the Stoic threefold division of bodies a ἡνωμένον (cf. *SVF* 2, 124.10–11).—*Mortale genus* is the "domain of perishable things" (Reid).—For the fragility of the human body cf. *Rep.* 6.30 (. . . *sic fragile corpus animus sempiternus movet*); *N.D.* 1.98. What we have is, strictly speaking, not the doctrine of the preexistence of the soul (*pace* Finger, 168) but of the preexistence of the non-mortal material of which the soul is made, and this is the point critical for the following argument (§ 25: *ex quo efficitur illud, ut is agnoscat deum, qui unde ortus sit quasi recordetur*).—For *fragilia . . . et caduca* cf. *Fin.* 2.86: *quis enim confidit semper sibi illud stabile et firmum permansurum quod fragile et caducum sit?*

ex quo vere vel agnatio nobis cum caelestibus vel genus vel stirps agnosci potest.] The transmitted text (with *appellari* for *agnosci*) presents three alternative ways of designating something *(vel agnatio . . . vel genus vel stirps)* but fails to specify the entity to which these predicates apply. The usual explanation is brachylogy (= "ex quo vere ea, quae nobis cum diis intercedit necessitudo vel agnatio vel genus vel stirps appellari potest": Feldhügel *ad loc.*). Schmidt, 1959, 176 n. 1, recommends retention of the transmitted *stirpis* and change of *genus* to *gentis*. But one expects the genitive with *agnatio* to define the person with whom the relation subsists, as in § 23 above *(deorum agnatione)*. Powell's *agnosci* is preferable; it also yields a clausula of the *omni debebitur* type; despite the good double cretic clausula Davies' *adrogari* seems too weak in light of § 23 *(. . . ut homines deorum agnatione et gente teneantur)*.—*Caelestes* appears as a synonym for *dei superi* in affective or elevated style; cf. 2.19.7 and 3.5; other examples at *TLL* s.v. 67.64 ff.; *OLD* s.v. *caelestis*[2].—After *stirps* Ziegler's clarifying *communis* is worth considering but not absolutely necessary.

24–25 itaque ex tot generibus—quasi recordetur.] This passage, with omission of *itaque* and of *agnoscat* after *recordetur,* is cited with approval *(Ciceronis vera sententia est)* by Lact. *inst.* 3.10.7–8, though he does allow animals a share of reason (ibid. 6).

24 itaque ex tot generibus nullum est animal, praeter hominem, quod habeat notitiam aliquam dei; . . .] *Genera* = species; cf. *de Orat.* 1.189.—For *notitia* (and later, in §§ 26, 27, 44, and 59, *intellegentia*) as equivalent to ἔννοια in the Stoic sense of a conception "arrived at by the conscious and purposely applied efforts of reason" cf. Reid *ad Luc.* 30; on the equivalence cf. also *Fin.* 3.21: *simul autem cepit intellegentiam vel notionem potius, quam appellant* ἔννοιαν *illi . . .* ; Hartung, 80–82; and the next note.— Going as far back as Socrates (cf. X. *Mem.* 1.4.13), the ancients generally excluded animals from a knowledge of god. There were some dissenting voices, however; cf. the previous note and Sorabji, 90 (for testimonies notes 90–91) and 202.

ipsisque in hominibus nulla gens est neque tam mansueta neque tam fera, quae non, etiamsi ignoret qualem haberi deum deceat, tamen habendum sciat: . . .] From the assertion that no other animal than the human being has the *notitia dei* Cicero now moves ahead to the (empirical) observation that every human *gens* believes in the deity; cf. also *Tusc.* 1.30: *ut porro firmissimum hoc adferri videtur cur deos esse credamus, quod nulla gens tam fera, nemo omnium tam sit immanis cuius mentem non imbuerit deorum opinio . . . ;* N.D. 2.12. There are prima facie two ways of reading this: (1) the universality implicitly results from the presence of the *notitia dei* in the human being; (2) the two juxtaposed assertions (note the connector *-que*) are unrelated, the second merely reproducing Epicurus' argument for the existence of god *e consensu omnium* (cf. *N.D.* 1.43–45 and 62; cf. also *Div.* 1.2: *gentem quidem nullam video neque tam humanam atque doctam neque tam immanem tamque barbaram, quae non significari futura et a quibusdam intellegi praedicique posse censeat*). Of these, (1) seems more likely in light of the sequel related to our sentence as effect to cause *(ex quo efficitur illud, ut is agnoscat deum, qui unde ortus sit quasi recordetur).*[105] In other words, Cicero seems to want the universality of a belief in god not merely to stand on its own as a proof of the existence of god but also to be a pointer to the link between the human being and the deity. If that is so, then Cicero may have combined the doctrine of *consensus omnium* with that of the Stoic ϰοιναὶ ἔννοιαι; cf. Vander Waerdt, 1994b, 4876 with attached notes: ". . . here [sc. in our passage] as elsewhere (e.g., De Nat. Deorum 1.43–44) Cicero employs the *consensus omnium* argument in a way that suggests confusion with the much different doctrine of *koinai ennoiai:* while these are often supposed to be common to all mankind, there is in fact no example among the early scholarchs of a *koine ennoia* which necessarily is shared by all mankind (or of an argument which relies upon *consensus omnium* to establish that an *ennoia* is *koine*), but many counter-examples of *koinai ennoiai* which are by no means common opinion."—The wording

---

105. *Ex quo efficitur* and the like can, however, be used very loosely; cf. Dyck *ad Off.* Index of Grammatical and Stylistic Features s.v. "Connection of thought, careless, loose, or lacking."

etiamsi ignoret qualem habere deum deceat is likewise Epicurean: "for the Epicureans . . . every normal person agrees that there are gods, but disagrees as to what the gods are like" (Obbink, 1992, 201, with references).—*Habeo* in the sense of religious belief is wanted here (cf. *TLL* s.v., 2409.41 ff., esp. 47 [our passage; cf. also the law at 2.19.3]); as parallel to the following passive *habendum,* Lactantius' *haberi* is adopted in preference to ω's *habere.*—*Decet* contains an implicit thrust at the Egyptian theriomorphic deities; see further *ad* § 32.

25 ex quo efficitur illud, ut is agnoscat deum, qui unde ortus sit quasi recordetur {agnoscat}.] *Ex quo efficitur* = "the conclusion drawn from which is" (Reid); see the preceding note.—The recognition of divinity on the basis of similarity would follow from the origin of the human being as described in § 24. The comparison to recollection *(quasi recordetur)* implies no connection with Plato's doctrine.—The second *agnoscat* was omitted by Lactantius and bracketed by Davies. Manutius' *ac noscat* provides a connector and yields a good clausula; but deletion of *agnoscat* gives the same clausula (type *omne debetur*); and *ac noscat* seems anticlimactic and, with *agnoscat* preceding, betrays a poverty of expression uncharacteristic of Cicero.[106] More probably *agnoscat* has been repeated from earlier in the sentence or inserted as a gloss on *recordetur.*

iam vero virtus eadem in homine ac deo est, neque alio ullo in genere praeterea; est autem virtus nihil aliud nisi perfecta et ad summum perducta natura; naturalis est igitur homini cum deo similitudo.] The transitional formula *iam vero* (= "to proceed": Reid) calls attention to the following point; cf. *de Orat.* 1.58: *iam vero de legibus tuendis . . . dicant . . . Graeci;* Kroon, 319–25, esp. 322.—Ἀρετή could per se have reference to animals, parts of the body, etc. (cf. § 45). Aristotle had already laid it down that ἡ ἀρετὴ τελείωσίς τις (*Met.* 1021b20–21; cf. *SVF* 3, 61.38: ἡ δ' ἀρετὴ τελειότης ἐστὶ τῆς ἑκάστου φύσεως). Given the way *ratio* has been described at §§ 22–23, it is clear that only it could claim to be the *perfecta et ad summum perducta natura* and as such common and exclusive to gods and men; the point is made explicit at § 45 *(est enim virtus perfecta ratio);* sim. the Academic/Peripatetic definition at *Ac.* 1.20 (. . . *virtus, quasi perfectio naturae;* see Reid *ad loc.*); *Fin.* 4.35 and 5.37; *Tusc.* 5.39; Boyancé, 1970, 275 and n. 1. In our passage, then, *natura* is virtually a synonym for

---

106. In view of the Indoeuropean tendency for compound verbs to be taken up by simple ones in the same context (on which cf. Calvert Watkins, "An Indo-European Construction in Greek and Latin," *HSPh* 71 [1966], 115–19; Jaan Puhvel, "An 'Indo-European Construction' in Arcadian," *CPhil* 65 [1970], 50–51), *agnoscat* and *noscat* would be assumed to bear the same sense.

ratio; cf. Frank, 352–53. The sameness of virtue in the deity and in the human being was disputed by Aristotle[107] but accepted by the Stoa.[108] Vander Waerdt, 1994b, 4876, interprets our passage as a departure from the early Stoa, which attributed such perfection and hence similarity to god only to the sage (who was seen as alone having attained *virtus*).[109]

quod cum ita sit, quae tandem esse potest propior certiorve cognatio?] *Cognatio* is evidently used in the sense "relationship, affinity, kinship" (*OLD* s.v., 3); cf. the stronger claim of *agnatio* made at §§ 23 and 24.

Itaque ad hominum commoditates et usus tantam rerum ubertatem natura largita est, ut ea quae gignuntur donata consulto nobis, non fortuito nata videantur; . . .] *Itaque* has been regarded as a very hard transition (Theiler, 45); the coherence depends upon the assumed identity of *natura* and *deus* (cf. their similar function in endowing the human being at §§ 16 and 22), with the *cognatio* of gods and men, inferred from their *similitudo*, leading to abundant provision for human needs. The deity's care for the human being is argued in detail at *N.D.* 2.154 ff., esp. the similar argument from the abundance of the earth's bounty at 156 ff. The number of harmful things could, however, be adduced as a difficulty (cf. *Luc.* 120).—The handsome chiastic arrangement *donata consulto . . . non fortuito nata* helps to emphasize the purposeful nature of the phenomenon; cf. *N.D.* 2.58: . . . *natura . . . non artificiosa solum sed plane artifex ab eodem Zenone dicitur, consultrix et provida utilitatum opportunitatumque omnium.*

nec solum ea quae frugibus ⟨onusta⟩ atque bacis terrae fetu profunduntur, sed etiam pecudes, quas perspicuum sit partim esse ad usum hominum, partim ad fructum, partim ad vescendum procreatas.] The phrase *ea quae . . . terrae fetu profunduntur* highlights the lack in classical Latin of a generic noun for plantlife; cf. Madvig *ad Fin.* 4.13; add to his examples *N.D.* 1.4 and 2.156 and *Off.* 2.11.—Watt, 1986, 266, deleted *frugibus atque bacis* as a gloss on *fetu* interpreted as "produce" rather than "productiveness": contrast, respectively, *OLD* s.v. *fetus* 4 and 2; he notes that Cicero uses *fetus* in the former sense in prose only metaphorically. In addition, *frugibus atque bacis* in apposition with *fetu* present genus and species juxtaposed in asyndeton—and with examples of the species preceding the

---

107. Cf. *EN* 1145a25–27: . . . ὥσπερ οὐδὲ θηρίου ἐστὶ κακία οὐδ᾽ ἀρετή, οὕτως οὐδὲ θεοῦ, ἀλλ᾽ ἡ μὲν τιμιώτερον ἀρετῆς ἡ δ᾽ ἕτερόν τι γένος κακίας.

108. Cf. *SVF* 1, 129.9–10: . . . οἱ [sc. Chrysippus and Cleanthes] φάσκοντες εἶναι τὴν αὐτὴν ἀρετὴν καὶ ἀλήθειαν ἀνδρὸς καὶ θεοῦ; sim. ibid. 11–12; our passage = 12–14; cf. ibid. 3, 58.35–59.24, cited in part in the second note to § 23.

109. Sim. already H.C. Baldry, *The Unity of Mankind in Greek Thought* (Cambridge, 1965), 196.

genus—, contrary to Cicero's usual manner of creating clear hierarchies. The solution may lie in the insertion of some connecting word, e.g., *onusta* (Powell).—*Quas perspicuum sit:* Davies' *quas* for the transmitted *quod* provides the needed subject for the accusative-infinitive clause; *quod* will have arisen through assimilation in gender and number to the following *perspicuum sit.* Madvig, 1826, 9–10, already showed, with reference to *deceat* at *Fin.* 3.64,[110] that it is unnecessary to restore *est* for *sit;* for the subjunctive in the relative causal clause (motivating *consulto*) cf. in general Kühner Stegmann, 2, 292 93. *Partim esse ad usum—procreatas:* cf. the similar list at *Tusc.* 1.69. *Usus* would encompass the transport of burdens, *fructus* such products as milk, cheese, honey, etc. For use of animals as food cf., e.g., *Fin.* 5.38 = *SVF* 2, 206.14 ff. (where other testimonies are given): . . . *ut non inscite illud dictum videatur in sue, animum illi pecudi datum pro sale, ne putesceret.*

26a artes vero innumerabiles repertae sunt docente natura, quam imitata ratio res ad vitam necessarias sollerter consecuta est.] For art as an imitation of nature cf. Arist. *Mete.* 381b6: μιμεῖται γὰρ ἡ τέχνη τὴν φύσιν . . . ; Sen. *Ep.* 65.3: *omnis ars naturae imitatio est.*—On the personification of *natura* cf. *ad* § 20.—*Ratio* here refers to human intelligence (cf. *ad Off.* 2.14); Seneca discussed the invention of the arts in detail at *Ep.* 90, where he differs from Posidonius in this regard: *omnia ista ratio quidem, sed non recta ratio commenta est* (§ 24) and thus denies that the progress of civilization hinged upon the intervention of sages *(sapientes).*

26b–27 Ipsum autem—et perficit.] A catalogue of the qualities of the human being, which might have been expected following the second sentence of Marcus' speech in § 22 (. . . *generatum esse a supremo deo*). Completeness is not intended here; the focus is on the *differentia specifica* of the human being. The human body, however, is not merely described as ephemeral, as in § 24, but is treated, rather, *more Stoico,* as an appropriate vessel for the contained mental powers (cf. parallels in *N.D.* 2 cited in the following notes). Though some topics may have been suggested by a Stoic inventory of human attributes such as is found in *N.D.* 2, Cicero selects so as to empha-size the communicative powers of the eyes and voice, a foreshadowing of the social implications explored at §§ 28 ff. Cf. Schmidt, 1959, 177. The goal of the argument is the development of reason (last sentence of § 27).

26b Ipsum autem hominem eadem natura non solum celeritate mentis ornavit sed ⟨ei⟩ et sensus tamquam satellites attribuit ac nuntios, . . .] For the human senses as an endowment of divine providence cf. *N.D.* 2.140 ff.; for

---

110. There the subjunctive ending is firmly attested albeit with variation in the verb stem.

the phrase *sensus tamquam satellites attribuit ac nuntios,* ibid. 140: *oculi tamquam speculatores.* The idea of the senses as guards recurs at Phil. *Leg. all.* 3.115; it may be doubted, however, whether both passages should, with Boyancé, 1963, 110, be traced to the reference to the heart being placed εἰς τὴν δορυφορικὴν οἴκησιν at Pl. *Tim.* 70b.—*Ornavit* = "equipped" (Reid); so also in § 27 *(generavit et ornavit deus).*—For *celeritas mentis* cf. *Ac.* 1.20: *naturae celeritatem ad discendum et memoriam dabant, quorum utrumque mentis esset proprium et ingeni.*—The other passages of "good prose" listed along with ours by *TLL* s.v. *attribuo* 1164.61 ff. (under 5: "adiungere aliquem alicui comitem") suggest that the dative must be expressed unless there is a preceding dative which can be understood in the clause with *attribuo* (as at Liv. 24.46.2); with our passage cf. Caes. *Gal.* 6.32.6: *ei legioni castrisque Q. Tullium Ciceronem praeficit ducentosque equites ei attribuit,* where *ei* is inserted because the referent had previously been (as in our passage) in the accusative case. Hence we have adopted Ziegler's ⟨*ei*⟩ before *et,* a position from which it could easily have dropped out, like so many little words in the transmission of this work; cf. *ad* § 23.—For *et* = *etiam* cf. § 33: *ergo et lex.*

. . . et rerum plurimarum obscuras nec satis enodatas intellegentias quasi fundamenta quaedam scientiae.] These words pose problems of both text and interpretation. Here and in three other passages (*viz.,* §§ 27, 30, and 59) Cicero uses the term *intellegentiae* (like *notitia* in § 24) of the ἔννοιαι, half-formed thoughts that develop through use of the senses; cf. *Fin.* 3.21; *SVF* 2, 33.14–16 = Augustin. *civ.* 8.7: . . . *a corporis sensibus eam* [sc. *sollertiam disputandi*] *ducendam putarunt, hinc asseverantes animum concipere notiones, quas appellant* [sc. *Stoici*] ἐννοίας . . . In addition, at § 44 he speaks of *communis intellegentia* = κοινὴ ἔννοια. The doctrine was evidently developed as an alternative to the Platonic doctrine of ἀνάμνησις in response to the paradox of the *Meno* and *Phaedo* that one can only investigate something if one already knows what it is (cf. Obbink, 1992, 198 ff.). The doctrine was originally formulated by Epicurus, using the term πρόληψις (cf. *N.D.* 1.44), but adopted by the Stoics, usually substituting ἔννοια (Sandbach, 30–31; Scott, 165–68).[111] The reference to ἔννοια (assumed as the counterpart to *intellegentia*) in the representation of Antiochus' doctrines at *Fin.* 5.59 has led some to suppose that Antiochus reshaped the term; cf. Theiler, 41; Boyancé, 1975, 25. On the other hand, Pohlenz, 1940, 97–99, and *Stoa,* 1, 244–45, and 2, 126–27, citing *Part.* 123 and *Top.* 31 (see

---

111. On the general problem of whether the early Stoics were innatist or empiricist cf. Scott, 201–10 (arguing for the former).

below), thought that Cicero has taken over a rhetorical doctrine formed under the influence of Chrysippus' theory of ἔννοια and πρόληψις; he accordingly assumes that *Fin.* 5.59 is a reminiscence of *Leg.* But *Part.* itself derives from an Academic source (§ 139; *Top.* is said to have been composed from memory: § 5). It is therefore easier to assume that Antiochus, dependent in turn on Chrysippus, is the source of both *Part.* 123 and *Fin.* 5.59; our passage could therefore conceivably derive either from Antiochus or Chrysippus; see further the introduction to this Book.

The text is transmitted in the form . . . *obscuras nec satis intellegentias enodavit* (H: *enudavit* AB). An epithet is needed for *intellegentias,* and the verb *enodo* is wrong. *Enodo* in the sense "unravel, explain the difficulties of" (*OLD* s.v., 2) is attested at *N.D.* 3.62 *(in enodandis autem nominibus quod miserandum sit laboratis).* What nature does to the half-formed *intellegentiae* is not, however, to "unravel" or "explain" them (this is done by the rational individual; cf. *Off.* 3.81: *explica atque excute intellegentiam tuam*) but rather to "impress" (cf. § 30) or "implant" them (cf. *SVF* 2, 29.5 ff.: *et intellectui occurrat universale aliud, quod deus prius non fecerit, <u>menti inserens fecunditatem, quae optime est apta ad admovendum sibi singula,</u> occurrentibus signis vel antea conceptis pro naturis inquirendis).*

At *Top.* 31 Cicero defines the phenomenon this way: *notionem appello quod Graeci tum* ἔννοιαν *tum* πρόληψιν. *ea est insita et animo praecepta cuiusque cognitio enodationis indigens.* One suspects that *obscuras nec satis* ⟨ . . . ⟩ corresponds in sense to *enodationis indigens* in *Top.* In line with that assumption, Boyancé, 1970, 260 n. 6, suggested that the original reading was *enodatas intellegentias inchoavit,*[112] with *enodatas* omitted in transcription and then rewritten so as to appear to follow *intellegentias* and the nonsensical *enodatas inchoavit* reduced to *enodavit.* This is possible, but it is perhaps more plausible to assume, with Powell, that the original was simply *nec satis enodatas intellegentias,* with *attribuit* understood from the preceding clause. A reader assuming that a verb was needed wrote *enodavit* as a variant for *enodatas,* and the former was inserted in the text in the wrong place.[113]

112. Auratus' conjecture; cf. the cross-reference at § 30 to *quaeque in animis imprimuntur, de quibus ante dixi,* <u>inchoatae</u> *intellegentiae;* cf. also § 44: . . . *natura . . . eas* [sc. *intellegentias*] . . . *in animis nostris inchoavit; Fin.* 5.59. Vahlen objected, however, that *inchoavit* is no proper midpoint between *attribuit* and *dedit.*

113. Other proposals: Vahlen suggested *nec satis ⟨inlustratas ingenuit⟩ intellegentias et donavit (donavit* having been proposed by Krause). But Pohlenz, 1940, 98 n. 2, criticized the coordination of the empty *donavit* with *ingenuit;* Zwierlein, 122, added that the doubling of the verb destroys the parallelism of four balanced members. Zwierlein's conjecture

Quasi fundamenta quaedam scientiae: for a fuller account of the Stoic view, including the step of *comprehensio* (= κατάληψις) elided here, cf. *Ac.* 1.42: *sed inter scientiam et inscientiam comprehensionem . . . collocabat* [sc. Zeno] etc.; ibid. 1.32.

figuramque corporis habilem et aptam ingenio humano dedit; . . .] The advantages of the human *figura corporis* are delineated in the sequel; the point is argued in detail at *N.D.* 2.140 ff.; see especially the remarks on the hand, ibid., 150–52; cf. also *Fin.* 5.35.

nam cum ceteras animantes abiecisset ad pastum,—ut in ea penitus reconditos mores effingeret; . . .] For the rare sense of *abicio* "to make prostrate in form" (clarified by the contrasting verbs *erexit . . . excitavit*) cf. *OLD* s.v., 2c; *Parad.* 14: *tu, cum tibi sive deus sive . . . natura dederit animum . . . sic te ipse abicies atque prosternes ut nihil inter te atque inter quadripedem aliquam putes interesse?*—For the upright posture distinguishing men and beasts cf. passages cited *ad Off.* 1.105, to which add X. *Mem.* 1.4.11: οἳ [sc. οἱ θεοί] πρῶτον μὲν μόνον τῶν ζῴων ἄνθρωπον ὀρθὸν ἀνέστησαν; Sal. *Cat.* 1.1: *omnis homines qui sese student praestare ceteris animalibus summa ope niti decet ne vitam silentio transeant, veluti pecora quae natura prona atque ventri oboedientia finxit*; Cato Pythag. *apud* Stob. 2.8 (= 2, 158.6 ff. W.-H.) with implicit etymology of ἄνθρωπος: καὶ διὰ τοῦτο ἀναθρῷσκοντα αὐτὸν ἐποίησεν εἰς τὸν ὠρανὸν καὶ αὐτὸ νοατὸν καὶ ὄψιν αὐτῷ ἐνέφυσε τοιαύταν, τὸν προσαγορευόμενον νόον, ᾧ τὸν θεὸν ὀψεῖται; Pl. *Rp.* 586a6 describes some humans as beastlike and thus focused downward rather than upward: . . . βοσκημάτων δίκην κάτω ἀεὶ βλέποντες καὶ κεκυφότες εἰς γῆν καὶ εἰς τραπέζας . . . ; *Crat.* 399c6: etymology of ἄνθρωπος < ἀναθρῶν ἃ ὄπωπε.—For *ad caeli quasi cognationis domiciliique pristini conspectum excitavit* cf. *Tusc.* 1.68–69: . . . *cum videmus . . . hominem . . . ipsum quasi contemplatorem caeli ac deorum cultorem . . . ;* the implications of this orientation toward the heavens are developed at § 61. For the influence of this idea on Lactantius cf. Schmidt, 1965, 310–11 with literature at 328 n. 35.—*Domicilium pristinum*, like *unde ortus sit quasi recordetur* (§ 25), glances back at the divine origin of the *animus* (§ 24).

27 nam et oculi nimis arguti quemadmodum animo affecti simus loquuntur, et is qui appellatur vultus, qui nullo in animante esse praeter hominem potest, indicat mores; cuius vim Graeci norunt, nomen omnino non habent.]

commodavit, accepted by Görler, as a synonym of the following *dedit*, seems flat. Sichirollo wanted to insert *expressas* as the missing adjective, since Cicero frequently contrasts *expressus* and *adumbratus*; cf. *Tusc.* 3.3: *est enim gloria solida quaedam res et expressa, non adumbrata* with other examples at Zwierlein, 121 n. 2.

For the eyes in general cf. *N.D.* 2.142–43.—This use of *nimis* in the colloquial sense ("very, exceedingly"), though elsewhere rare in Cicero (cf. *OLD*
s.v., 3), is probably right (similar phenomena cited at Dyck *ad Off.* Index of
Grammatical and Stylistic Features s.vv. "Colloquialism," *Sermo Cotidi-
anus*); cf. *Fam.* 1.5b.1: *nimium magno silentio,* where the transmitted
nimium is now retained by Shackleton Bailey (in the Loeb edition).—
Ziegler's "correction" *argute* (cf. his apparatus) is clearly wrong: *argutus*
means "expressive, eloquent" (*OLD* s.v., 5a; sim. *TLL* s.v., 557.52, both
citing our passage), whereas *argute* should mean "cleverly" or the like (ibid.
558.61 ff.).—For the expressiveness of the *vultus* cf. 3.37: *quantum e vultu
eius intellego; de Orat.* 3.221: *animi est enim omnis actio et imago animi
vultus, indices oculi. nam haec est una pars corporis, quae, quot animi
motus sunt, tot significationes et commutationes possit efficere;* sim. ibid.
2.149; *Pis.* 1: *vultus . . . qui sermo quidam tacitus mentis est; Rab. Post.* 35
(*vultus* as an indicator of the veracity of witnesses; cf. *Cat.* 3.13); *Tusc.* 3.31
(of M. Crassus [pr. 105]): *iure autem erat semper idem vultus, cum mentis, a
qua is fingitur, nulla fieret mutatio;* Sen. *Phaed.* 363–64: *proditur vultu
furor; I erumpit oculis ignis . . . ;* Quint. *Inst.* 11.3.66: *. . . ex vultu in-
gressuque perspicitur habitus animorum;* Isid. *or.* 11.1.34: *vultus vero
dictus eo quod per eum animi voluntas ostenditur.* Reading the *vultus* was,
of course, a project of the physiognomists; cf. Cic. *Fat.* 10. This art seems to
have originated in the East and been introduced at Athens by a Syrian magus
named Zopyrus, who predicted a violent death for Socrates: Arist. fr. 32
Rose = D.L. 2.45; *Scriptores Physiognomici,* ed. R. Foerster, 1–2 (Leipzig,
1893): 1, vii–viii, and 2, ind. s.v. *vultus.* The characterization *cuius vim
Graeci norunt, nomen omnino non habent* turns the tables on the Greeks,
usually thought to have the richer vocabulary (cf. Pease *ad N.D.* 1.8; *Fin.*
3.51; *ad Off.* 1.142). Though the Greek spoken in Cicero's day may have
lacked a word corresponding to *vultus* in the sense "the facial expression"
(*OLD* s.v., 1), πρόσωπον does have an equivalent sense in poetry (cf. LSJ
s.v., II). Gel. 13.30.2 reports a similar doctrine with *facies* substituted for
*vultus: sicuti quidam faciem esse hominis putant, os tantum et oculos et
genas, quod Graeci* πρόσωπον *dicunt;* perhaps such considerations led Cicero to translate πρόσωπον as *os* at *Tim.* 49. Thus, as Reid observes,
πρόσωπον combines the senses of *os* and *vultus.* The implications of this
passage and its sequel, establishing norms of nature in the physical realm,
are well analyzed by Corbeill, 30–34.

**omitto opportunitates habilitatesque reliqui corporis—humanae maxime
societatis . . .]** *Habilitas* is surely a Ciceronian coinage; ours is the unique
occurrence of the word in this number and sense (= "aptitudo") in classical

Latin; cf. *TLL* s.v. Here and at *Amic.* 37 *(cum conciliatrix amicitiae virtutis opinio fuerit)* Cicero is the first to use *conciliatrix* in a good sense, rather than as = "procuress, bawd" (for which as a metaphor see *N.D.* 1.77); cf. *TLL* s.v. For speech as the bond that holds society together cf. *Inv.* 1.2–3; *N.D.* 2.148; *Off.* 1.50.

. . . (neque enim omnia sunt huius disputationis ac temporis, . . .] Cf. *Rep.* 1.38 (Scipio is the speaker): *nec enim hoc suscepi, ut tamquam magister persequerer omnia . . .*

. . . et hunc locum satis, ut mihi videtur, in eis libris quos legistis expressit Scipio): . . .] These words are cited by Lact. *opif.* 1.13.—A beginning was evidently made at 4.3 ff. The next sentence, too, with its parenthetical *ne omnia disserantur,* suggests abridgement of a fuller treatment; even so Atticus' reply (§ 28) emphasizes the length at which Cicero has discussed the *iuris principia.*—*Quos legistis:* though Quintus and Atticus may have read the work privately prior to general circulation (cf. the Introduction § 2b; *ad* 1.1), these words suggest a dramatic date near April 51. For Atticus' familiarity with *Rep.* cf. § 15.

nunc quoniam hominem, quod principium reliquarum rerum esse voluit, ⟨ita⟩ generavit et ornavit deus, perspicuum est illud . . .] *Nunc* = *ut nunc se res habet* or "as the matter stands" (Reid); *OLD* s.v., 10; Risselada, 113–14. With this word the focus returns to what is relevant for present purposes, namely the perfection of reason (cf. §§ 22–23).—*Principium* is the "occupier of first place" (cf. *Fin.* 5.8 and *OLD* s.v., 7a), and *quod principium* could have been expressed less abstractly as *quem principem* (Reid).—The insertion of *ita* before *generavit* (Reitzenstein) makes explicit the connection with the preceding and can easily have dropped out after *voluit.*—I have written *perspicuum est* for the transmitted *perspicuum sit,* which does not occur in a main clause in Cicero's *philosophica* (Ziegler's *perspicuum fit* is also unparalleled); perhaps the phrase has been repeated from § 25 above; for confusion of *sit* and *est* cf. Zetzel *ad Rep.* 2.42; possibly in our passage the corruption arose from a misunderstanding of a phonetic spelling *perspicuumst.*[114]

. . . ipsam per se naturam longius progredi, quae etiam nullo docente, profecta ab eis quorum ex prima et inchoata intellegentia genera cognovit, confirmat ipsa per se rationem et perficit.] The perfection of reason had been mentioned (as *lex*) in § 18b[115] and (as *sapientia*) in § 22; here we discover how this comes about. The recognition of kinds is the first step in the development of concepts (cf. *SVF* 2, 29.9 ff.: τῶν νοουμένων τὰ μὲν κατὰ

---

114. I owe this suggestion to David Blank.

115. In particular, *confirmat . . . et perficit* takes up the phrasing *cum est in hominis mente confirmata et perfecta* used there with reference to *ratio* (for the reading see *ad loc.*).

περίπτωσιν ἐνοήθη, τὰ δὲ καθ᾽ ὁμοιότητα); the *prima et inchoata in-tellegentia* forms the starting point (*ex*; cf. *ad* § 26). The process is described in detail (after Antiochus' defense of Stoic epistemology) at *Luc.* 21 = Long-Sedley 39C; cf. also *Fin.* 5.43, where the subject is treated from an ethical angle.—The last phrase hints at the Stoic definition of *virtus* as *perfecta ratio* described at § 25 (Reid); see *ad loc.* (*iam vero virtus eadem—*).

28a A. Di immortales, quam tu longe iuris principia repetis!] The exclamation is both amusing and apt: since § 22 the focus has been on the gods and their provision for the human being. Marcus has gone on at length in spite of the promise at § 22 *(non faciam longius)*. The *principia iuris* were the theme announced at § 18, somewhat varied at § 20: *visne ergo ipsius iuris ortum a fonte repetamus?* Cf. *Off.* 1.50: *sed quae natura principia sint communitatis et societatis humanae, repetendum videtur altius.*

atque ita ut ego non modo ad illa non properem, quae exspectabam a te de iure civili, . . .] *Ad . . . non properem* = "I am in no hurry to get to" (Reid).—Atticus appears to adhere to his original understanding of the subject matter (sc. *ius civile*: § 13) in spite of Marcus' attempt to redefine it in § 14; however, at § 34b Marcus himself accepts the *ius civile* as the agreed topic; see *ad loc.*

. . . sed facile patiar te hunc diem vel totum in isto sermone consumere; . . .] Atticus thus echoes Quintus' comment at § 13 (see *ad loc.*) and restricts its scope to just the *iuris principia.*

sunt enim haec maiora . . . quam ipsa illa quorum haec causa praeparantur.] Atticus finds a reversal of the usual hierarchy by which *minora* are discussed for the sake of *maiora* (on *maiora* as the preferable topic cf. *Rep.* 1.30–31); cf. *Fam.* 3.13.1 (to Appius Claudius Pulcher; ca. August 50): *haec mihi ampliora multo sunt quam illa ipsa propter quae haec laborantur.* But is he still perhaps thinking too much of the traditional picture of *ius civile*, rejected by Marcus as an unworthy topic at § 14 (see the note before last)? In any case, Marcus is prepared to concede only that the preceding topics are *magna*, not that they are *maiora* than the proper theme.

28b–34a With the statement of the main thesis *nos ad iustitiam esse natos, neque opinione sed natura constitutum esse ius* Cicero's strategy becomes clearer. The foregoing inventory of qualities shows that human beings share a similar endowment. Proceeding to further arguments in favor of human similarity, he immediately confronts the difficulty that it does not seem to be so. (He does not indicate what is at stake here; but clearly the notion of individual differences and hence differences in interests could be an entering wedge for injustice: much of the argumentation of Philus' speech at *Rep.* 3.6–19 and of *Off.* 3 is directed at this point). He blames this state of affairs on the *opinionum vanitas* and reaffirms the similarity on the basis of (1) the common definition of the *genus* of human beings, (2a) the fact that nature provides all human beings a similar stock of *inchoatae intellegentiae,* (2b) the similarity of the stimuli that impinge upon the senses, and (3) similar tendencies *in pravitatibus.* Cicero goes on to invoke friendship among the Stoic *sapientes,* apparently as a survival of the original state of human society before perceived differences in interest arose. Vander Waerdt, 1994a, 286, citing D.L. 7.124,[116] and 1994b, 4873, suggests that the argument from similarity as the basis for natural law was originally formulated in Zeno's *Republic* with reference to sages and has been transferred, with some implausibility, to the human race generally by a later Stoic (Chrysippus?). The state of our sources leaves the chronology a bit vague, but there are several indices that speak against Vander Waerdt's reconstruction, namely the tendencies (ἀφορμαί) to the virtues shared by all human beings (*SVF* 1, 129.18–19; cf. Mitsis, 1994, 4842 n. 81) and Zeno's view that his *Republic* applied to the times and places in which he lived (cf. Obbink, 1999, 183). 28b–30 = *SVF* 3, 84.12–30.

28b M. . . . sed omnium quae in hominum doctorum disputatione versantur, nihil est profecto praestabilius, quam plane intellegi nos ad iustitiam esse natos, neque opinione sed natura constitutum esse ius.] The words *sed omnium—natos* are cited twice by Lactantius: *ira* 14.4 and *inst.* 6.25.9, in the former with the order *doctorum hominum.*—For *docti* = *philosophi* cf. *ad* § 18b.—Of the two juxtaposed points (connected with the *-que* of *neque*), the former follows from the preceding description of the human being as a social animal possessing reason and virtue,[117] justice being preeminently the quality that holds society together (cf. *Fin.* 5.65, cited in the next note), whereas the latter forms the topic of the following discussion. Cicero returns to the former point at § 35 as well as *Off.* 1.12 and 157–58.— *Neque opinione sed natura constitutum esse ius:* cf. *SVF* 3, 76.4–6 = D.L. 7.128: φύσει τε τὸ δίκαιον εἶναι καὶ μὴ θέσει, ὡς καὶ τὸν νόμον καὶ τὸν ὀρθὸν λόγον, καθά φησι Χρύσιππος ἐν τῷ περὶ τοῦ καλοῦ; *Inv.* 2.160– 61: *eius* [sc. *iustitiae*] *initium est ab natura profectum . . . natura{e} ius est, quod non opinio genuit, sed quaedam in natura vis insevit . . . ; Fin.* 3.71: *ius autem . . . esse natura . . . Ius* is attested well before Cicero as the equivalent of *aequitas,* τὸ δίκαιον, or the like (cf. *TLL* s.v., 684.41 ff.; *OLD* s.v., 7) and would not necessarily imply the *ius civile,* which, indeed, Marcus, at least in the ordinary sense, has rejected as the topic of the present discussion

---

116. Λέγουσι δὲ καὶ τὴν φιλίαν ἐν μόνοις τοῖς σπουδαίοις εἶναι, διὰ τὴν ὁμοιότητα.
117. Cf. also § 62: *cumque se* [sc. *homo*] *ad civilem societatem natum senserit . . .*

(§ 14). The assertion about *ius* in our passage is assisted, in a general way, by what was said of νόμος and *aequitas* at § 19[118] as well as the development of reason and formation of concepts as described in §§ 26b and 27.—For *opinio* cf. *Ac* 1.41: *quod autem erat sensu comprehensum, id ipsum sensum appellabat* [sc. Zeno], *et si ita erat comprehensum, ut convelli ratione non posset, scientiam: sin aliter, inscientiam nominabat: ex qua exsisteret etiam opinio, quae esset imbecilla et cum falso incognitoque communis.*

id iam patebit, si hominum inter ipsos societatem coniunctionemque perspexeris.] The assumption is that human *societas* and *coniunctio* must rest upon a shared sense of justice. Cf. *Fin.* 5.65: *quae animi affectio suum cuique tribuens atque hanc quam dico societatem coniunctionis humanae munifice et aeque tuens iustitia dicitur . . .* On the relation in general of the *societas generis humani* to justice in Cicero's works cf. Reijnders, 57 ff.

29 Nihil est enim unum uni tam simile, tam par, quam omnes inter nosmet ipsos sumus; . . .] This is a strong claim; cf. Corbeill, 33 ("This natural state, he seems to think, requires that all persons had once resembled one another") and 34 ("Cicero refuses to speculate how his hypothetical 'universal similarity' [*similitudo omnium*] would express itself in terms of physique").[119] Though unproven (cf. Moatti, 294), it has been partially prepared for by the preceding remarks on the natural gifts of *sensus, inchoatae intellegentiae*, etc.; cf. Schmidt, 1959, 191. In the sequel Cicero merely shows that human beings are similar enough to be comprised under a single definition and *genus*. The unstated premise is evidently that *similitudo* promotes *coniunctio* (cf. the connection with *enim*). Cf. the argument at § 25 about human *similitudo* with the gods, with emphasis on *cognatio*.[120]

quodsi depravatio consuetudinum, si opinionum vanitas non imbecillitatem animorum torqueret et flecteret quocumque coepisset, sui nemo ipse tam similis esset quam omnes sunt omnium; . . .] Here Cicero offers a theory to reconcile the phenomena with his thesis of human similarity without abandoning an essentialist standpoint. Presumably the *depravatio consuetudinum* arose, in spite of the similar endowment of *inchoatae intellegentiae* and similar sensory input (§ 30), because of the *imbecillitas animorum*. But this is implied, rather than stated; we are merely given a description of its further

118. So much can be conceded to Schmidt, 1959, 180, who thought that *ius* in this passage is equivalent to νόμος rather than τὸ δίκαιον and concluded that Cicero is aiming to provide a justification in nature for the Roman *ius civile* and also to broaden and deepen the concept *ius*.

119. Cf. also Vander Waerdt *loc. cit. ad* §§ 28b–34a.

120. In epistemology arguments from similarity had a different rôle, being invoked by skeptics against the dogmatists' claim of accurate sense perception; cf. the dogmatist's reply at *Luc.* 54.

progress. Cf. *ad* § 47, where Cicero paints a detailed picture of the process of corruption.—R. Stephanus' *varietas* for *vanitas* may seem tempting in light of § 32 *(si opiniones aliae sunt apud alios)* and § 47 *(sed perturbat nos opinionum varietas hominumque dissensio . . .)*, *sed nil mutandum:* elsewhere, too, the Stoa associated *vanitas* (= τῦφος) with the non-sage; cf. *SVF* 1, 69.26–27 = D.L. 7.22; Sen. *Ep.* 90.28; for its invocation in this type of argument cf. *Tusc.* 3.2: . . . *nunc* [sc. *natura*] *parvulos nobis dedit igniculos, quos celeriter malis moribus opinionibus depravati sic restinguimus ut nusquam naturae lumen appareat . . . ita variis imbuimur erroribus ut vanitati veritas et opinioni confirmatae natura ipsa cedat.* For *opinio* cf. *Ac.* 1.41 (quoted *ad* § 28b).—*Quodsi depravatio consuetudinum, si opinionum vanitas non imbecillitatem animorum torqueret et flecteret quocumque coepisset:* "if the corruption of behavior, if the vanity of opinions were not twisting and turning weak minds in whatever direction it had begun [sc. to turn them]." But our text may be thought to place an odd emphasis on the starting point of the process *(quocumque coepisset)*. Kenter *ad loc.* promoted Davies' *cupisset*[121] for *coepisset* in order to express the idea that "these bad habits and false beliefs turn man's mind . . . from the path it had originally taken." But "the soul" can hardly be understood as the subject of *quocumque cupisset;* we must rather assume that *opinionum vanitas* continues as subject, as did Davies, comparing § 47 (of insidious influences): *inficiunt et flectunt ut volunt.* A sense like that posited by Kenter can be obtained by reading ⟨*ab eo*⟩ *quocumque coepisse*⟨*n*⟩*t* (Inwood); but, as J.G.F. Powell points out *(per litt.)*, this would also require emendation of *quocumque*, for "there would be no sense in saying 'from wherever they started from', since according to this passage, our minds all started from the same point." The transmitted text can stand; but if it is to be changed, *cupisset*, as interpreted by Davies, would be a possibility. Corbeill, 33, points out that such language *(depravatio, torqueret, flecteret)* is typical of invective against physical deformities.—*Sui nemo ipse tam similis esset quam omnes sunt omnium:* contrast the emphasis on the variety of human character at *Off.* 1.108–9 or human differences in general at *Fat.* 8.—*Sunt* is the transmitted text, often changed with Ascensius to *essent*, unnecessarily.

itaque quaecumque est hominis definitio, una in omnes valet.] *Itaque:* i.e., in view of the basic similarity prior to the onset of *depravatio consuetudinum* and *opinionum vanitas.*—Cicero goes no more deeply into the theory of definition here than he has to; he operates merely with the terms *definitio* and (in the next sentence) *genus;* he could have pointed out that what

---

121. Revived by de Plinval.

constitutes a single *genus* is a common οὐσία (cf. Arist. *Met.* 1037a29: ἡ γὰρ οὐσία ἐστὶ τὸ εἶδος τὸ ἐνόν . . .)[122] or that a single *genus* might encompass several *differentiae* (cf. *Top.* 31: *genus est notio ad pluris differentias pertinens*). At this stage he claims as a purely formal point that any definition, if accepted, is based on *similitudo* applying to the entire human race; hence he leaves open for the moment the definition of man *(quaecumque est hominis definitio)*, a favorite example of Aristotle (cf. *Top.* 103a27, 130a26, b8, 133a3, 22, etc.). It would be possible, however, to construct a definition of man that is common to all and yields an essence but does not help Cicero's argument that human commonality leads to a society in the stronger sense of the *civitas* of § 23—e.g., "a biped with limbs turned in, rather than out like those of birds" (G.E.R. Lloyd at the Cambridge seminar). Hence the shared definition alone does not carry the argument very far; a content needs to be added involving shared rationality, and this Cicero proceeds to supply *(etenim ratio . . .)*.—For *valeo* in the sense "hold good, apply" or the like (sometimes, as here, with *in* + accusative to indicate the sphere of application) cf. *OLD* s.v., 9b (citing our passage).

30 quod argumenti satis est nullam dissimilitudinem esse in genere; . . .] A bit ambiguous: at the level of the *genus* there is uniformity, though *differentiae* may lead to the positing of species within the *genus* (see the previous note).—For the phrase *argumenti satis* cf. *Fin.* 5.31; *Tusc.* 2.60; *Div.* 1.10.

etenim ratio, qua una praestamus beluis, . . .] *Etenim* introduces an instance supporting a general assertion (*OLD* s.v., d), in this case that of human *similitudo*. The sequel distinguishes first the positive, then the negative traits uniting the human race (§ 31: *nec solum in rectis . . .*); cf. the concluding formula toward the end of § 32: *quibus ex rebus cum omne genus hominum sociatum inter se esse intelligatur . . .*—On the human possession of *ratio* cf. *ad* § 22; for the denial of reason to animals by Aristotle and the Stoics cf. Sorabji, 12 ff. and 20 ff.; *de Orat.* 1.33 (Crassus is the speaker): *. . . quis hoc non iure miretur . . . ut quo uno homines maxime bestiis praestent, in hoc hominibus ipsis antecellat?* (sim. *Inv.* 1.5); *Fin.* 2.45; *Off.* 1.107; Sen. *Ep.* 76.9 (= *SVF* 3, 48.20): *in homine quid est optimum? ratio: hac antecedit animalia, deos sequitur. ratio ergo perfecta proprium bonum est, cetera illi cum animalibus satisque communia sunt.*

. . . per quam coniectura valemus, argumentamur, refellimus, disserimus, conficimus aliquid, concludimus, . . .] This account of the functions of *ratio* presupposes the double sense of λόγος as both reason and speech (see

---

122. Thus he might have observed that the quality of being capable of laughter, though peculiar to the human being (cf. Arist. *PA* 673a8 and 28), does not bear on the essence and hence is not a true definition.

below) but is not paralleled in extant Stoic sources; it is thus not clear that, as Reid suggested, it was "taken straight from the Greek";[123] it could be a Ciceronian dilation on a favorite theme (see below).—*Coniectura valeo* is set in parallel with a series of verbs evidently because *conicio*, although it can have at this period the sense "form a conclusion about, conjecture" (cf. *OLD* s.v. 13), would have been ambiguous. *De Orat.* 3.113 offers a brief discussion; more detail at *Top.* 82; Cicero may be rendering the attribute στοχαστικός found in Greek sources from Pl. *Gorg.* 463a7 on. The first item and the last *(concludimus)*[124] are most closely related to *ratio* in the sense "reason," the others to speech, though all play a part in the training of the orator. *Argumentatio* and *refutatio*, represented by the verbs *argumentamur* and *refellimus*, as parts of a speech, are antithetical; both are subsumed under the general term *disserimus*. In this context *conficimus aliquid* surely refers to the orator's work of persuasion; cf., e.g., *Orat.* 86: *accedit actio non tragica nec scaenae sed modica iactatione corporis, vultu tamen multa conficiens.*

. . . **certe est communis, doctrina differens, discendi quidem facultate par.**] *Ratio* appears here as a kind of base line, with *doctrina* (= education) added to it in different degrees; on the latter cf. H. Altevogt, *Der Bildungsbegriff im Wortschatze Ciceros* (diss., Münster-Emsdetten, 1940), 12–18. The equal distribution of reason (*ratio . . . par*) accords with the original similarity of humans prior to the onset of *depravatio* (§ 29: . . . *sui nemo ipse tam similis esset quam omnes essent omnium*) and seems to adumbrate *cuncta paria* as a description of the state of friendship in § 34. The equal *discendi facultas* may also seem to be overstated[125] but is in accord with the Stoic view that virtue is an intellectual achievement (cf. *SVF* 1, 129.21–23; 2, 30.36–37; 3, 52.17–20) and that all have an equal capacity, starting with the *inchoatae intellegentiae*, to attain it (cf. *ad* § 26; the last sentence of this section).

nam et sensibus eadem omnium comprehenduntur, et ea quae movent sensus, itidem movent omnium; quaeque in animis imprimuntur, de quibus ante dixi, inchoatae intellegentiae, similiter in omnibus imprimuntur; interpresque mentis oratio verbis discrepat, sententiis congruens; . . .] *Omnium* is Reitzenstein's conjecture for *omnia*; it is needed in view of the

---

123. The letters to Atticus amply demonstrate Cicero's ability to think in Greek terms; cf. George E. Dunkel, "Remarks on Code-Switching in Cicero's Letters to Atticus," *MH* 57 (2000), 122–29.

124. On this cf. *Top.* 53 ff.

125. Cf. *ad* § 29: *nihil est enim unum uni tam simile, tam par, quam omnes inter nosmet ipsos sumus.*

following *itidem movent omnium . . . similiter in omnibus imprimuntur.*— *Comprehendo* corresponds to καταλαμβάνω in the sense "perceive," just as *comprehensio* does to κατάληψις; cf. *Ac.* 1.41 with Reid's note; *Luc.* 17; Pease *ad N.D.* 2.147; *Fin.* 3.17.—*Ea quae movent sensus:* only later will Cicero coin the technical term *visa* for the φαντασίαι; cf. *Luc.* 18; *Ac.* 1.40.— On the *intellegentiae* cf. *ad* § 26; for the idea of their being impressed on the mind *(imprimere)* cf. *Luc.* 18 with Reid's note and *Ac.* 1.42.—For the *interpres mentis oratio* cf. D.L. 7.49 = Long-Sedley 39A2: . . . ἡ διάνοια ἐκλαλητικὴ ὑπάρχουσα, ὃ πάσχει ὑπὸ τῆς φαντασίας, τοῦτο ἐκφέρει λόγῳ; for the *iunctura Hort.* fr. 112: *vates . . . divinae mentis interpretes . . .*—*Verbis discrepat, sententiis congruens* will refer, as Reid suggests, to differences of language; cf. the following reference to *quisquam gentis ullius.* This doctrine poses a potential challenge to the previous understanding of law as authoritatively formulated in a single language.

nec est quisquam gentis ullius, qui ducem nactus ad virtutem pervenire non possit.] PF[rec.]·H[rec.] insert *naturam* after *nactus,* unnecessarily. The idea is that a teacher may be needed to guide one to virtue. On virtue as teachable see the note before last.

31 This chapter continues the analysis of the similarity of human beings with reference to false choices made in ignorance *(inscitia),* including the choice of pleasure and avoidance of death and pain on the assumption that these are *maxima mala.* Cicero thus takes the opportunity to dilate on ethical themes and score some points against a view similar to that of the Epicureans (albeit not identified as such). He will later return to the problem of death and pain at *Tusc.* 1–2.

Nec solum in rectis, sed etiam in pravitatibus insignis est humani generis similitudo; . . .] If it had looked as though the remarks on its *similitudo* would amount to another encomium of the human race, that impression is now dispelled. *Rectum* and *pravitas* are antonyms not only in their literal senses "straight" vs. "crooked," but also as applied metaphorically to "correct" and "incorrect" judgments and behaviors. Here *recta* are presumably those corresponding correctly to sensory inputs (cf. §§ 23 and 42: *recta ratio*), *pravitates* incorrect judgments based on ignorance, not instances of moral depravity (see the following examples as well as *OLD* s.v. *pravitas* 3 vs. 4).[126]

nam et voluptate capiuntur omnes, quae etsi est illecebra turpitudinis, tamen habet quiddam simile naturali bono; . . .] The *et* correlates with the *-que* of

---

126. Schmidt, 1959, 182–83, interpreting *recta* and *pravitas* as moral qualities, finds the antithesis forced.—For Cicero's use of abstract nouns like *pravitas* in the plural cf. Lebreton, 32 ff.; for nouns in *-tas* in particular, ibid., 65–67.

similique (Reid).—For *voluptate capi* cf. *Off.* 1.105; *OLD* s.v. *capio* 17b ("take hold of, delight, charm"); *TLL* s.v. 341.32 ff.—Since, as is clear from the context, *voluptas* pertains to the body, the *naturale bonum* presupposed here appears to be in line with the Academic/Peripatetic division of goods taught by Antiochus (cf. *Ac.* 1.19–21, where the phrase *naturale bonum* recurs; *Fin.* 5.68). It will be like "*a* natural good," but not, of course, the *summum bonum* itself. For the characterization *habet quiddam simile naturali bono* cf. § 47 *(imitatrix boni voluptas)*. The similarity will reside in both providing enjoyment *(gaudium)* in accord with the doctrine at *Fin.* 5.69.[127]— The phrase *illecebra turpitudinis* could be a translation of Plato's ἡδονὴ κακοῦ δέλεαρ (*Tim.* 69d); sim., with citation of Plato, *Hort.* fr. 84 *(illecebrae . . . atque escae malorum)*, *Sen.* 44 *(esca malorum)*, where see Powell's note with further references.

levitate est enim et suavitate delectans; sic ab errore mentis tamquam salutare aliquid asciscitur; . . .] Pleasure can be said to be *levis* as opposed to *dolor . . . cum sua asperitate* (below). Originally these were meant as descriptions of the physical processes productive of pleasure and pain; thus the Cyrenaics identified the former as a λεία κίνησις, the latter as a τραχεῖα κίνησις.[128] The Epicureans kept the distinction, now explained by means of Democritean physics; cf. the report of Epicurus' position at *Tusc.* 5.73: . . . *neque quicquam ad nos pertinere nisi quod aut leve aut asperum in corpore sentiatur.* Cicero, in turn, uses these striking images but without reference to the underlying physical theories both here and at *Fin.* 1.39 (cf. 37): *nam si ea sola voluptas esset quae quasi titillaret sensus, ut ita dicam, et ad eos cum suavitate adflueret et illaberetur . . .*—Transmitted is *levitatis est enim et suavitatis delectans,* changed by Vahlen (after Turnebus) to *levitate est enim et suavitate delectans.* The present participle is rare in Cicero as a predicate; cf., however, *de Orat.* 2.364: *nemo umquam tam sui despiciens fuit . . . ; Fam.* 3.8.4: *neque enim eram tam desipiens . . . ; Orat.* 41: *est enim . . . his ipsis verbis loquens Socrates; Fin.* 3.27: *illud autem perabsurdum, bonum esse aliquid quod non expetendum sit, aut expetendum quod non placens . . . ; N.D.* 1.110: *et deus vester nihil agens* [sc. *est*]; see further H. Blase *apud* Landgraf, 256; Powell *ad Sen.* 26. Hence R. Stephanus proposed *lenitate enim et suavitate delectat;* but *est,* though added above the line in A and changed from *es* in B, must count as the transmitted text and is likely to be correct. A less

127. I am grateful to J.G.F. Powell for help in interpreting this passage.
128. D.L. 2.86 = *Cirenaici* 1 B 1.86 = *Socr.* IV A 172.86 = Aristippus fr. 197A Mannebach; the point about pleasure is also repeated ibid. frr. 197B–C and 198. For the terminology *smooth* and *rough,* cf. Voula Tsouna, *The Epistemology of the Cyrenaic School* (Cambridge, 1998), 9–10.

invasive change would be *levitatis est enim et suavitatis delectatio;* for the objective genitive with *delectatio* cf. *Parad.* 10: . . . *aut amoenitatum ad delectationem* . . . ; other examples at *TLL* s.v., 420.29 ff.—*Ab* = "as a result of"; cf. *OLD* s.v., 15.—*Ascisco* is a *variatio* for *expeto* or *appeto;* cf. *Fin.* 3.17. **similique inscitia mors fugitur quasi dissolutio naturae, vita expetitur quia nos in quo nati sumus continet; dolor in maximis malis ducitur, cum sua asperitate, tum quod naturae interitus videtur sequi; . . .**] A carefully organized tricolon, with the guiding word *inscitia* placed to the front for emphasis, in turn the leading idea of each of the subdivisions is likewise fronted: *mors, vita, dolor,* and to each is added a verbal complement *(fugitur, expetitur, in maximis malis ducitur)* as well as explanatory material *(quasi dissolutio naturae, quia nos in quo nati sumus continet, cum sua asperitate, tum quod naturae interitus videtur)* according to the law of increasing members. The whole is capped by a fine double cretic clausula.—*Expeto* and *fugo* are often opposed as technical terms in ethics for choosing and avoiding; cf. *OLD* s.v. the former 3a.—According to Epicurus, death is the dissolution of one's personal nature but not of nature as a whole; hence he would agree that the fleeing of death is based on ignorance (cf. *Epicurea* 226.21 ff.; Lucr. 3); on the other hand, he would regard this valuation of pain as correct (cf. *Epicurea* 288.15 ff., esp. 291.17–18 = *Tusc.* 2.44). However, the Academic or Stoic must reject both the underlying premises, *viz.,* that death is the dissolution of the individual's identity (and therefore an evil)[129] or that pain is *in maximis malis;* hence *inscitia* is said to motivate them.—For *dissolutio naturae* etc. cf. *Fin* 5.31: . . . *hoc quidem est in vitio, dissolutionem naturae tam valde perhorrescere (quod idem est reprehendendum in dolore)* . . .—*Vita expetitur* is the starting point of the doctrine of οἰκείωσις, on which see *ad Off.* 1.11–14.—*Dolor—sequi: dolor* clearly refers here to physical pain (*OLD* s.v., 1), not mental distress, as sometimes elsewhere (ibid. 2); cf. *Fin.* 5.94: *hic* [sc. Dionysius Heracleotes] *si Peripateticus fuisset, permansisset, credo, in sententia, qui dolorem malum dicunt esse, de asperitate autem eius fortiter ferenda praecipiunt eadem quae Stoici;* on the avoidance of pain see above.—*Sua asperitate* is causal ablative in parallel with the explanatory clause *quod naturae interitus videtur sequi* (note the *cum* . . . *tum* structure); cf. the previous note.

32 propterque honestatis et gloriae similitudinem beati qui honorati sunt videntur, miseri autem qui sunt inglorii.] Cicero is careful to speak of the

---

129. The *Phaedo* teaches that death is the separation of body and soul, but this is not a *dissolutio naturae,* since Socrates refutes Cebes' claim that the soul is scattered at death (cf. 77b ff.); for the Stoic at death the πνεῦμα of the individual soul remains together until the ἐκπύρωσις and then dissolves into the matter of the universe (cf. Pohlenz, *Stoa* 1, 92–93).

similarity rather than the identity of *honestas* and *gloria* (cf. the relation of *voluptas* and the *naturale bonum* in the previous section); cf. *Fin.* 5.69: *non perfecti homines . . . excitantur saepe gloria, quae habet speciem honestatis et similitudinem*, as well as the warning against *gloriae cupiditas* at *Off.* 1.68 and just action as the prerequisite for *vera gloria* (ibid. 2.43; *gloria* is defined from an idealistic and from an empirical point of view at *Tusc.* 3.3 and *Off.* 2.31 respectively). *Honestas* was for the Roman implicitly *laudabilis* (cf. *ad Off.* 1.14); derived from *honos* (= honor, public office; cf. Ernout-Meillet s.v. *honos*), *honestas* could in practice all too easily slip from the praiseworthy to what is, in fact, praised; cf. Long, 1995a, 216–17. Cicero himself was not immune to this way of thinking; certainly he was never more miserable than when, public favor withdrawn, he was forced into exile; cf. Gelzer, 140 ff., esp. 146; Mitchell, 1991, 141 ff.

molestiae, laetitiae, cupiditates, timores similiter omnium mentes pervagantur; . . .] Cicero personifies and affirms the universality of the four πάθη of the orthodox Stoa, with *molestiae* = λῦπαι, *laetitiae* = ἡδοναί, *cupiditates* = ἐπιθυμίαι, and *timores* = φόβοι; cf. *SVF* 3, 92 ff.; Inwood, 1985, 127 ff. For wandering passions cf. *Off.* 1.102 *(qui appetitus longius evagantur)*. Again a topic of Cicero's later philosophical writing (*Tusc.* 3–4) is anticipated.—*Pervagantur: Per-*, like other transitivizing prefixes corresponding to prepositions governing the accusative, has its origin in sentences in which the accusative denoted the goal of motion or extent of space, e.g., *moenia circum eo;* cf. Hofmann-Szantyr, 33.

nec si opiniones aliae sunt apud alios, idcirco qui canem et felem ut deos colunt non eadem superstitione qua ceterae gentes conflictantur.] For the Egyptian theriomorphic gods cf. Burkert, 1985, 64 and 371 n. 85.—*Si . . . idcirco* is a fairly common pattern, in which *si* takes on a causal coloring; cf. Kühner-Stegmann, 2, 427; hence *si . . . apud alios* = "in light of the fact that there are different views among different peoples"—at first sight a contradiction of the idea of *similitudo*. *Nec* and *non* cancel each other out; hence translate: "those who worship the dog and cat as gods are buffeted by the same superstition as other peoples." Wyttenbach inserted *non* before *colunt*, unnecessarily. As J.G.F. Powell points out *(per litt.)*, "it is banal to say 'non-cat-worshippers are just as superstitious as cat-worshippers are.' What Cicero is actually arguing is: 'it may look as though cat-worshippers have a special, exotic kind of superstition all their own; but in fact it is essentially no different from the common-or-garden superstition that other races suffer from.'"—Our passage suggests that *superstitio* "began to denote the religious practices of particular foreign peoples" well before the early second century A.D. *(pace* Beard, 1998, 1, 221). At *N.D.* 2.72 Cicero takes *su-*

perstitiosus to imply excessive fear (sim. Var. *ARD* fr. 47); Lact. *inst.* 4.28.6 found the distinction from *religiosus* unsatisfactory because the same beliefs were involved: *haec interpretatio quam inepta sit, ex re ipsa licet noscere. nam si in isdem diis colendis et superstitio et religio versatur, exigua vel potius nulla distantia est.* Cf. in general Denise Grodzynski, "Superstitio," *REA* 76 (1974), 36–60; Maurice Sachot, "Religio/superstitio," *Revue de l'histoire des religions* 208 (1991), 355–94; older literature at Pease *ad N.D.* 1.45.—By using *conflicto* (= "distress, torment": cf. *OLD* s.v., 2) Cicero depicts the process as violent.

quae autem natio non comitatem, non benignitatem, non gratum animum et benefici memorem diligit?] Here and in the following lemma we finally come to the kinds of shared qualities that prepare the way for the community Cicero sketched in §§ 22–23. Thus, in spite of § 31 *(nec solum in rectis, sed etiam in pravitatibus . . .),* the argument turns back to the good qualities of the human being, but this was inevitable, given Cicero's goal (see also the note after next on the *recti vivendi ratio*); it need not be taken, as by Bake, XXVI, as a sign of incompleteness; cf. Schmidt, 1959, 183 n. 2.—Here and in the following sentence Cicero merely claims the right attitude toward social and anti-social behavior, whether or not such views are put into practice.—For *comitas* and *benignitas* as synonyms cf. *Balb.* 36: *comes, benigni, faciles, suaves homines esse dicuntur . . . 'comiter' . . . benigne;* for *comis/comitas* in general cf. Karl Heinz Heuer, *Comitas—facilitas—liberalitas. Studien zur gesellschaftlichen Kultur der ciceronischen Zeit* (diss., Münster, 1941), 24 ff. For *benefici memor* cf. Norden *ad Aen.* 6, p. 36 n. 2.— The inclusion of *gratus animus* in this series shows the lack of an abstract noun for "gratitude" (Reid).

quae superbos, quae maleficos, quae crudeles, quae ingratos non aspernatur, non odit?] The *superbi* clearly offend against *comitas,* and the *ingrati* lack a *gratus animus et benefici memor;* the *malefici* and *crudeles* could both be seen, in their separate ways, as embodying the opposite of *benignitas* (Reid).—According to the Stoics, the base man is ungrateful (Stob. *Ecl.* 2, 104.6–9 W.-H.), a point elaborated by Seneca (*Ep.* 81.8–14 and *Ben.* 5.12–17); cf. Brad Inwood, "Politics and Paradox in Seneca's *De beneficiis,*" in Laks-Schofield, 249 ff.—For vigorous rejection expressed by the piling up of verbs at the end of the sentence cf. *N.D.* 2.74 (Balbus): *non decet, non datum est, non potestis* (with reference to Epicurean mockery of the Stoa); *Off.* 3.119: *non recipit istam coniunctionem honestas, aspernatur repellit.*

quibus ex rebus cum omne genus hominum sociatum inter se esse intellegatur, illud extremum est, quod recte vivendi ratio meliores efficit.] *Quibus ex rebus* summarizes the positive and negative features shared by the human race that have been enumerated since § 30 *(etenim ratio . . .)*. The last point at the end of this chain of similarities *(extremum)*[130] is the assertion that there is a *recte vivendi ratio* that can improve humans; this corresponds to the Stoic τέχνη περὶ βίον (= φρόνησις) combatted at S.E. *P.* 3.239 ff. Cicero uses the phrase *vivendi ratio* as early as *Inv.* 2.131; it recurs in our work at §§ 35 and 55 and 2.36. Elsewhere he modifies it with *bene* (*de Orat.* 1.212; *Fin.* 5.68 [restored]), *optime* (ibid. 5.36), or *beate* (ibid. 5.16), but not *recte*. The use of this term is typical of *Leg.*, however, where the function of law is to command *recte facere* (§ 19), law is defined as *recta ratio* (§§ 23, 33, 42, 2.10), *recta* are correct responses to sensory inputs (§ 31), and the *rectum* is a synonym for the *honestum* (§ 37; 3.2) (though *recte vivendi ratio* is different, of course, from *recta ratio*, since *recte* modifies *vivendi*). The content of the *recte vivendi ratio* is not at issue here and is left open (cf., however, § 57, where Quintus calls for *leges vivendi et disciplinam*).—People can be said to be *sociati* in several senses (see, e.g., the definition of *populus* at *Rep.* 1.39, cited *ad* § 23); the most recent examples have taken existing political entities as a given *(quae autem natio . . .)*; the various *nationes* may be *sociatae* in the sense of sharing attitudes or qualities, but at this point it remains unclear how the stronger bond of *eadem civitas* (§ 23) is to be achieved.—What is the appropriate final term *(extremum;* cf. *Fam.* 4.13.7 and 15.4.16) to this series of arguments? Philippson, 1929, 979, proposed *similiores* for the transmitted *meliores;*[131] certainly it is the similarity of human beings that has been the point ever since § 29, including the origin of apparent differences; *sed nil mutandum:* one has a right to expect the *recte vivendi ratio* to make humans not merely more similar but better. Some add, with Reifferscheid, *omnes* before *meliores,* but *homines* can be understood from the preceding *genus hominum.*

quae si approbatis, pergam ad reliqua; sin quid requiritis, id explicemus prius. A. Nos vero nihil, ut pro utroque respondeam.] Bake conjectured *pergam⟨us⟩;* in spite of § 14 *(pergimus)*, this is unnecessary; cf. § 22 *(perge, quaeso)*.—For Atticus' reply *pro utroque* cf. Pl. *Lg.* 896e4–5: ἐγὼ ὑπὲρ σφῷν ἀποκρινοῦμαι; Tac. *Dial.* 16.3: *pro duobus . . . promitto.*

33 If the argument since § 29 has established a human *societas* in a weaker sense (see *ad* § 32), Cicero now begins to argue for the stronger sense expected since the mention of *una civitas* at § 23, i.e., he brings the anthropology developed since § 22 to bear on the problem of *ius* in such a way as

---

130. Different is the use of *extremum* of the logical *summa* drawn from the preceding; cf. *Off.* 3.27.

131. J. Simon, *CR* n.s. 3 (1953), 173, calls this "an almost certain correction"; Powell conjectures *coniunctiores.*

to show that *ius* is natural to the human being. At the same time, however, he must account for the all too human tendency in the other direction. But this argument is not presented with as much attention to logical sequence as one might have expected. Indeed, the sharing of justice among all is attached to the preceding argument with *sequitur igitur* but does not follow logically (see the next note); it would have been more convincing as a sequel to the series of syllogisms toward the end of the paragraph *(quibus enim ratio—ius igitur datum est omnibus)*. In addition, it is odd that *utilitas* is suddenly introduced within an example as a principle opposed to *ius* (in addition to *mala consuetudo)*; only at §§ 40–41 will Cicero discuss the problem in detail. Cf. Schmidt, 1959, 184–86.

Sequitur igitur, ad participandum alium cum alio communicandumque inter omnes ius nos naturā esse factos . . .] *Sequitur igitur:* this is not a logical consequence of the foregoing argument but "follows" merely in the sense of being the next point to be expounded; see the preceding *pergam ad reliqua.*—The text is controverted, with these possibilities: *ab alio* B¹PLεH: *alio* BˣA: *cum alio* Huschke. *Participo* means "share or participate with others in" or "cause to participate in" *(OLD* s.v.). What is shared is not clarified until the noun *ius.*[132] It is a question of whether to take *participandum* as (1) a gerundive or (2) a gerund (cf. *TLL* s.v. *participo* 504.64 ff.).[133] If the former, then one would read *ab alio* and render "for giving one after another a share [sc. *iuris:* of justice]"; if the latter, then *ius* is the object of the gerund in both clauses; in that case insert *cum* and render "for sharing justice one with another" (it would thus fall under *TLL* IB1a). The choice between these alternatives is not easy: (1), as the transmitted text, is preferred by Schmidt, 1974, 117;[134] Görler *ad loc.;* van Leijenhorst, *TLL loc. cit.* But if (1) is correct, this is the sole example of *participo* with an animate object in "good prose" cited in either *OLD* or *TLL* s.v., whereas the *aliquid cum aliquo* construction is found at Liv. 3.12.5 *(Lucretius consul . . . suas laudes participare cum Caesone).* Moreover, (2) with *ius* functioning in both clauses as object of the gerund, seems more natural;[135] furthermore *cum* can

---

132. Though even *ius nos* has had to be restored (by Davies) for *iustos* BAHLε : *ius hos* P.

133. The third possibility *ad participandum alium alio* "id est, ad alium alio bono et commodo, si quo possimus, impertiendum," favored by *OLD* s.v. *participo* and Madvig, 1887, 513 (whence the quoted paraphrase), is subject to the same objection on grounds of construction as *participare ab alio.*

134. In conversation, however, Schmidt now suggests to me that the difference between the two actions should correspond to that between "teilgeben" and "teilnehmen," respectively—a distinction that would be achieved by *cum alio.*

135. It is adopted among recent editors by de Plinval and Powell.

easily have dropped out by saltation following *alium*. Finally, what would be the point of saying *ad participandum alium ab alio* [sc. *iuris*]? Why should the sequence "one after the other" be so emphasized? Surely the point of the first half of the sentence is the sharing *with* each other, that of the second half the involvement of all *(inter omnes)*. For the behavior described here as a periphrasis of *iustitia* cf. Girardet, 1983, 35.

. . . **(atque hoc in omni hac disputatione sic intellegi volo, cum dicam naturā esse ⟨ius⟩), . . .**] *Quod dicam* and *naturam* are transmitted. *Ius*, inserted prior to *quod dicam* in some *recentiores,* is commonly accepted and with it Turnebus' *naturā* for *naturam* (both readings approved by Madvig *ad Fin.* 3.71). However, Reitzenstein, 14 n. 2, objected that this sentence connects neither with the preceding nor the following one, both of which contain the word *ius* (albeit in the former sentence conjecturally restored). He adds that it makes no sense for the *probandum* to be repeated as if it were an explanation of itself. Supposing a definition of *natura* needed, he went on to propose (14–15) *sic intellegi volo, quom dicam naturam ⟨rectam me dicere rationem summumque deum. ab hoc igitur dico iustitiae omniumque virtutum nobis semina tributa⟩ esse, tantam autem esse corruptelam . . .* De Plinval, on the other hand, thinks to mend the problem merely by writing . . . *sic intellegi volo, quom dicam naturam {esse};* but the preceding can hardly stand as a definition of *natura,* and one still feels the need of a clause to contrast with *tantam autem esse corruptelam . . .* Cicero surely means rather that the statement *naturā esse ius* implies the described behavior of human beings; to arrive at this sense one need merely adopt J.G.F. Powell's enclosure of this matter in parentheses and assume (with Reitzenstein and de Plinval) corruption of *quom* to *quod* (an easy mistake after *hoc;* the same error at 2.50) and (with Turnebus) of *naturā* to *naturam;* for the phrase *cum dicam 'naturā esse'* cf. 3.3: *quod cum dico, legem a me dici intellegi volo.* In addition, Powell inserts *ius* but after *esse* so as to effect the molossus + cretic clausula: the repetition of *ius* is surely inoffensive here, where it is a major topic, and the failure to use it to connect sentences not a decisive objection.

. . . **tantam autem esse corruptelam malae consuetudinis ut ab ea tamquam igniculi exstinguantur a natura dati, exorianturque et confirmentur vitia contraria.**] *Mala consuetudo* (for which *ea* stands) is personified as an agent; cf. the *depravatio consuetudinum* of § 29. Later in this section it appears that notions of one's *utilitas,* like *mala consuetudo,* can have the function of diverting the human being from the ethical path; though the relation is unexplained, we are surely to understand that *mala consuetudo* is formed under the influence of perceived *utilitas.*—Our passage is the earliest attestation of *igniculus* (first used in the literal sense at *Att.* 12.1.2 [November 46]); cf. *TLL* s.v.; hence *tamquam*, apologizing for the bold expression. The *igniculi . . . a natura dati,* endangered by *mala consuetudo* and opposite to the *vitia,* must be some form (or pre-form?) of the virtues; cf. § 25: *est autem virtus nihil aliud nisi perfecta et ad summum perducta natura. Scintilla* is similarly used; cf. *Fin* 5.19: *quorum* [sc. *primorum secundum naturam*] *similia sunt prima in animis, quasi virtutum igniculi et semina;* ibid. 5.43: . . . *in pueris virtutum quasi scintillas videmus, e quibus accendi philosophi ratio debet . . . ; Tusc.* 3.2: *nunc parvulos nobis dedit* [sc. *natura*] *igniculos . . . sunt enim ingeniis nostris semina innata virtutum, quae si adolescere liceret, ipsa nos ad beatam vitam natura perduceret;* Sen. *Ep.* 94.29: *omnium honestarum rerum semina animi gerunt, quae admonitione excitantur non aliter quam scintilla flatu levi adiuta ignem suum explicat;* Plut. ὑπὲρ εὐγενείας *apud* Stob. 4, 722.13–14 W.-H.: . . . οὐκ οἴονται [sc. οἱ σοφισταί] λεληθυίας τινὰς ἀρχὰς καὶ σπέρματα ἀρετῆς συγκαταβάλλεσθαι τοῖς γεννωμένοις . . . Panaetius used ἀφορμαί as a non-metaphorical designation; cf. *ad Off.* 1.11–14. The use of the diminutive suggests their frailty; cf. Sen. *Tranq. an.* 1.3: *non est quod dicas omnium virtutium tenera esse principia, tempore illis duramentum et robur accedere.* Heinemann, 2, 236, points out that the *igniculi* would fit with the incipient *intellegentiae* of § 26 (cf. also § 59): such *intellegentiae* are the *igniculi* as seen from an epistemological perspective.

quodsi, quomodo est naturā, sic iudicio homines 'humani' (ut ait poeta) 'nihil a se alienum putarent', coleretur ius aeque ab omnibus.] Here *iudicium* substitutes for *opinio,* previously used of the human view when it diverges from nature (§§ 28 and 32).—On the meaning of Terence's famous tag (*Hau.* 77) in context cf. H.D. Jocelyn, " 'Homo sum: humani nil a me alienum puto,' " *Antichthon* 7 (1973), 14–46 at 29 ff. The insertion of the parenthetical *ut ait poeta* at this point emphasizes the separated elements *humani* and (especially) *nihil;* cf. Lausberg §§ 716 and 860.

quibus enim ratio—ius igitur datum est omnibus.] The relations of *ratio, recta ratio,* and *lex,* restated from § 23, are here reduced to syllogistic form (cf. 2.12); for the association of *iubere* and *vetare* with *lex* cf. *ad* § 19. The point is to establish the universality of *ius.* Hence this argument might have been expected to stand at the beginning of this paragraph; see the headnote to this section.—For *ius . . . datum est omnibus* cf. αἰδώς τε καὶ δίκη given to all human beings according to the myth at Pl. *Prot.* 322c1–d5.—*Ius* is potentially given to all (cf. the last sentence of § 30), but only the sage has achieved *recta ratio;* hence this sentence is the basis for the introduction of the *vir* *sapiens* at § 34. Cf. *Fin.* 3.71: *ius autem, quod ita dici appellarique possit, id esse naturā, alienumque esse a sapiente non modo iniuriam cui facere verum etiam nocere.*

⟨ . . . ⟩ **recteque Socrates exsecrari eum solebat qui primus utilitatem a iure seiunxisset; id enim querebatur caput esse exitiorum omnium.**] *A iure* is Davies' needed correction for the transmitted *naturae* (see the reference to τὸ δίκαιον in the passage from Clem. Al. quoted below). This is the third time that the critical word *ius* has been lost or corrupted in the transmission of this single paragraph.—Bake bracketed *recteque—locus* as an interpolation. But the reference to Socrates is à propos, for it focuses on the point at which a *ius datum omnibus* came to be perceived as sometimes not in one's interest; see also the next note. Moreover, the content receives external confirmation at *SVF* 1, 127.20 ff. = Clem. Al. *Strom.* 2.131: διὸ καὶ Κλεάνθης ἐν τῷ δευτέρῳ περὶ ἡδονῆς τὸν Σωκράτην φησὶ παρ᾽ ἕκαστα διδάσκειν, ὡς ὁ αὐτὸς δίκαιός τε καὶ εὐδαίμων ἀνήρ, καὶ τῷ πρώτῳ διελόντι τὸ δίκαιον ἀπὸ τοῦ συμφέροντος καταρᾶσθαι, ὡς ἀσεβές τι πρᾶγμα δεδρακότι· ἀσεβεῖς γὰρ τῷ ὄντι οἱ τὸ συμφέρον ἀπὸ τοῦ δικαίου τοῦ κατὰ νόμον χωρίζοντες.[136] Marcus had already rejected the view that *ius* is constituted *opinione*, rather than *naturā* (§ 28). The argument here with regard to *ius* is thus similar to that of *Off.* with regard to the *honestum*, where a separation from the *utile* is ruled out *a limine*. Cf. *Off.* 2.9–10 and 3.11 and *supra* on . . . *tantam autem esse corruptelam* . . . The introduction of *utilitas* without further explanation seems abrupt, however; hence the lacuna posited before *recteque* by one of the participants in the Cambridge seminar.—The transmitted *exitiorum* ("destructions"), used in a physical or political sense (cf. *OLD* s.v. *exitium*), is, as Reid notes, odd (cf., however, § 39: *nimias edet ruinas*; 3.22: *sed ille quas strages edidit! Fin.* 1.18: *illae Epicuri propriae ruinae;*); one might expect something like *caput . . . vitiorum omnium* ("the fountain head of all vices").

⟨ . . . ⟩ **unde enim illa Pythagorea vox?** ⟨ . . . ⟩ {*de amicitia locus.*}] *Pythagoraeia* is the reading of A and perhaps B¹. Accordingly Vahlen conjectured *ia⟨m trita⟩*, which could have dropped out through *saut du même au même* and for which he compares *Fin.* 2.52: *hoc tritum vetustate proverbium.* Cicero alludes elsewhere to Pythagoras' saying (3 and 4: see below) but does not refer to it as well worn, and there is no allusion to it in earlier Latin literature; cf. A. Otto, 25–26. The explanation of the phenomena is prob-

---

136. Dependent upon Clement is Theodoret. *Gr. aff. cur.* 11.11: . . . ὁ Σωφρονίσκου Σωκράτης οὐ τὸν πλούτῳ περιρρεόμενον καὶ ἐξ οὐρίων φερόμενον, ἀλλὰ τὸν δικαιοσύνῃ κοσμούμενον εὐδαίμονα εἰώθει καλεῖν· καὶ ἀσεβεῖς ὠνόμαζε τοὺς τὸ ξυμφέρον τοῦ δικαίου χωρίζοντας· μόνον γὰρ εἶναι ξυμφέρον τὸ δίκαιον ἔλεγεν.

ably rather that A and B show traces of a double reading *Pythagorae/Pythagor(e)ia,* either of which would be possible.

There are four relevant Pythagorean pronouncements on friendship: (1) κοινὰ τὰ φίλων (D.L. 8.10, quoting Tim. *FGrHist* 566 F 13b);[137] (2) φιλίαν ἰσότητα (D.L. *loc. cit.* = Stob. 2, 257.3 W.-H.; cf. *P.T.* 236.25); (3) that in friendship *unus fiat e pluribus (Off.* 1.56; see *ad loc.*); (4) that a friend is an *alter idem (Amic.* 81; Porph. *vit. Pyth.* 33; A. Otto, 26). Of these Reitzenstein, 16 and n. 1, followed by Schmidt, 1959, 188 n. 1, thought (2) referred to in our passage. But (2) is never cited by Cicero or indeed, to judge from its absence at A. Otto s.v. *amicitia,* any Latin author. The preference for (2) is based on the question in § 34 *quid enim est quod differat cum sint cuncta paria?* Φιλίαν ἰσότητα means, however, that the friends are equal in status (thus Sen. *Ben.* 2.13.3 argues against pride *quae in odium etiam amanda perducat,* i.e., by placing itself at a higher level it destroys any possible friendship). That "all things are equal," i.e., that a friend would not seek to gain something at a friend's expense, would rather follow from (1), (3), or (4), any of which would be possible; I use (1) in my tentative reconstruction; see below.

If in friendship one arises out of many and/or goods are held common, then friendship preserves a remnant of the original unity of *ius* and *utilitas* (and of the human race; cf. § 29), disrupted, according to Socrates, by the first man to separate the two. One can, then, reconstruct a coherent pattern of thought from the transmitted text, but what we have is elliptical and lacks a transition to § 34 *(ex quo perspicitur, hanc benevolentiam),* so that some matter must have been lost in transmission.

The supplements so far proposed fail to carry conviction. Thus after *amicitia* Vahlen would add ⟨*nimirum huic communioni est in hominum societate, non solum in amicitia*⟩ *locus.* But this leaves a very oblique allusion to Pythagoras' saying, which would probably not have sufficed to identify the phrase for most Roman readers (see above),[138] and leaves the question *unde* etc. unanswered. De Plinval inserts *ut unus fiat ex pluribus* from *Off.* 1.56 and deletes *de amicitia locus* as a paraphrase of the content added by a scribe (but then he should insert *in amicitia* after *ut* in the quotation).

Though any attempt to fill the lacuna must, in default of information about its extent, be highly speculative,[139] some inferences can be drawn

---

137. For Latin parallels cf. A. Otto, 20.

138. Similarly, one doubts that *illa* alone would be a sufficient identifier (Schmidt, 1959, 189 n. 1).

139. For another theory cf. *ad* § 40.

from the context. The deictic *hanc* attached to this phrase suggests that *benevolentiam tam late longe⟨que⟩ diffusam* (§ 34) was introduced. I would expect something like the following sense (examples supplied from *Off.* 1.52): *unde enim illa Pythagorea vox ⟨ut in amicitia omnia sint communia? inde scilicet quod omnes homines inter se tam arte coniuncti sunt ut alter alteri vel ignoto beneficia quaedam sponte conferat, ut non prohibere aqua profluente, pati ab igne ignem capi, consilium si qui velit deliberanti dare fidele.⟩*[140] Such an argument would provide a point of reference for *hanc benevolentiam tam late longe⟨que⟩ diffusam.* If this, or something like it, is correct, then § 34 continues the exploration of Pythagoras' saying (and therefore should not be set off as a new paragraph). In addition, something of the kind needs to be established before the point in § 35 that *omnes inter se naturali quadam indulgentia et benevolentia . . . contineri.* We follow S²'s deletion of the words *de amicitia locus,* which look like a marginal guide to the content that crept into the text in subsequent copying.[141]

Finally, if there is, as suggested above, a close connection of § 34 with Pythagoras' view of friendship, then following *locus* may not be the place to insert, as Ziegler proposed, the fragment preserved at Lact. *inst.* 5.8.10, which deals with the bonds of the human community and their disruption by *pravitas.*[142]

34a If something like the reconstruction mooted in the previous note is correct, the exchange of smaller *beneficia* among human beings adumbrates *(ex quo perspicitur)* the complete equality of self-love and love for the other as practiced among sages, which thus fulfills Pythagoras' description of friendship. Moreover, the entry of the slightest difference in the relation *(quodsi interesse quippiam tantulum modo potuerit)* destroys the friendship. The concept of friendship *(amicitia)* is thus taken in a strong sense and modelled on the relation of Stoic sages; see the next note.

ex quo perspicitur, cum hanc benevolentiam tam late longe⟨que⟩ diffusam vir sapiens in aliquem pari virtute praeditum contulerit, . . .] This is the Stoic notion of friendship among sages (cf. *SVF* 1, 54.3–8 and 3, 161.7–8; *N.D.*

---

140. For a different suggestion cf. Schmidt, 1959, 189 and n. 2.

141. Were they added by a reader at a prearchetypal stage? Philippson, 1929, 979, suggests that with these words a scribe replaced Cicero's Greek quotation of Pythagoras; but this might be expected in a private letter rather than an essay. Might they, instead, have been a note Cicero wrote to remind himself what was to be filled in later?—Schmidt, 1974, 105, argues against striking *de amicitia locus* on grounds that the suspect text could have either preceded or followed the lacuna. I find it difficult to picture these words in either function, but any solution must remain tentative and subject to correction if new evidence comes to light.

142. Schmidt, 1965, 319–20, assigns it rather to the fourth book, *de iudiciis;* see *ad* fr. inc. sed. 1.

1.121: *censent* [sc. *Stoici*] *autem sapientes sapientibus etiam ignotis esse amicos*[143]), here invoked as an illustration that justice *(ius)* is by nature. For the community of sages in Zeno's *Republic*, of which our text is a reflex, cf. Schofield, 1991, 22 ff.—For the reference of *hanc benevolentiam tam late longe⟨que⟩*[144] *diffusam* see the last note on § 33.

. . . **tum illud effici quod quibusdam incredibile videatur, . . . : uti nihilo sepse plus quam alterum diligat.**] *Quibusdam* glances at the Epicureans, whose utilitarian view of friendship is criticized at *N.D.* 1.122; cf. also *Amic.* 31 and the note after next.—*Uti nihilo sepse plus quam alterum diligat:* cf. *Fin.* 1.70: . . . *foedus esse quoddam sapientium ut ne minus amicos quam se ipsos diligant; N.D.* 1.121; sim. but without reference to the *sapientes Fin.* 1.67 and *Off.* 1.56; see also the late note *ad* § 33 à propos *alter idem.*—Baiter's *sepse,* an archaic form found at *Rep.* 3.8 (cf. Leumann, 471), is the likely correction for *sepe* (ERHL) or *sese* (BˣAᵃP; the original reading of B and A has been erased); it is the probable reading also at *N.D.* 1.110 (ci. Plasberg). Though *Leg.* is a contemporary, not a historical, dialogue, and, apart from the laws proper and the embedded translations from Plato, its language is not archaic (cf. *ad* 2.19.5), the archaic form can be defended here as a reminiscence of *Rep. loc. cit.* (. . . *eam virtutem quae est una . . . maxime munifica et liberalis, et quae omnes magis quam sepse diligit . . .*).[145]

quid enim est quod differat, cum sint cuncta paria?] The relations of sages endowed *pari virtute* thus culminate in the perfection of human *similitudo;* cf. § 29; Schmidt, 1959, 189; *Amic.* 31 (of those who seek the type of friendship he is defining): . . . *fruantur et moribus sintque pares in amore . . .* For the possible relation of this text to the citation of Pythagoras cf. *ad* § 33.

quodsi interesse quippiam tantulum modo potuerit, iam amicitiae nomen occiderit, cuius est ea vis ut simul atque sibi aliquid alter maluerit ⟨quam alteri⟩, nulla sit.] "If there could be some distinction, however tiny, in friendship, the name of friendship would already be gone; for the essential feature of friendship is that, the moment one partner prefers to have something for himself rather than for the other, it vanishes" (tr. Rudd). The text incorporates Powell's modification (chiefly *clausulae causa*) of Vahlen's supplement;[146] cf. *Fin.* 3.70: . . . *in amicitia alii dicant aeque caram esse sapienti*

---

143. The same terminology *(bonus, sapiens)* appears at *Amic.* 18 and 65, though Cicero denies *(Amic.* 18–19) that he is using it in the strong sense of the Stoic sage.

144. Correction of AᵃP.

145. I am grateful to J.G.F. Powell for advice on this point; he has also restored the form at *Sen.* 28.

146. Vahlen wrote *alter ⟨quam alteri⟩ maluerit;* Cratander had proposed *⟨quam⟩ alter⟨i⟩ maluerit;* in Powell's version the missing matter can be attributed to saltation error.

rationem amici ac suam . . . This is a slap at any view of friendship which, like that of the Epicureans, has self-interest as a component; cf. § 49; *Epicurea*, p. 324.16–17 = Lact. *inst.* 3.17.42: *dicit Epicurus . . . neminem esse, qui alterum diligat nisi sua causa;* in general ibid. 324–25, esp. 325.5–7 = *Fam.* 7.12.1–2 (to Trebatius; February, 53); *ad Off.* 1.56 and 118 (denial of the name of friendship to societies based on *utilitas*); on Epicurus' belief "that we can value something for its own sake apart from its instrumental contribution to our satisfaction" and the resulting tensions with his basic hedonism cf. Mitsis, 1988, 98–128 (the quoted words at p. 128).— For *nullus* in the predicate used "hyperbolically of something that does not fully qualify for the name applied to it" cf. *OLD* s.v., 5.

34b–37 We now move from the preliminaries (*quae praemuniuntur:* § 34b) to the main argument. Marcus announces the plan to show *ius in natura esse positum*—briefly, he emphasizes, in order to forestall objections—before going on to the *ius civile*. His interlocutors protest that the point is already well established. Marcus persists, however, in his plan. The doctrine *ius in natura esse positum* has so far been argued *fuse . . . ac libere* (§ 36) in the manner of the *veteres philosophi*, but he wants now to handle the subject *separatim* (ibid.) according to the more recent style of philosophical discourse. The reason for this special caution is that the stakes are high: *ad respublicas firmandas—⟨id⟩ e⟨s⟩t ad stabiliendas {vi}res, sanandos⟨que⟩ populos—omnis nostra pergit oratio* (§ 37).

34b Quae praemuniuntur omnia reliquo sermoni disputationique nostrae, . . .] Originally a military term, *praemunio* was taken over as a technical term in rhetoric for "fortifying one's position in advance" (i.e., in preparation for an anticipated attack); cf. Rufin. 32: προυπεργασία *vel* προπαρασκευή: *praemunitio, qua ante utimur, ut confirmetur id quod subiecturi sumus; ut si testem producturi sumus, ante necesse est ei fidem habendam esse doceamus* with other testimonies at Lausberg § 854; *OLD* s.v. *praemunio* 1; cf. *praeparantur* (§ 28). Our text might perhaps be more elegant with the jussive *praemuniantur.*—As Schmidt, 1959, 190, pointed out, *reliquus sermo* refers not merely to the rest of this Book, but to the whole remainder of *Leg.*[147]

de quo cum perpauca dixero, tum ad ius civile veniam, ex quo haec omnis est nata oratio.] A reference back to Atticus' query at § 13 about the *ius civile*, which started the conversation. I take it that Marcus understands the *ius civile* in the broader sense of the *ius civitatis* (cf. § 14) and that he plans

---

147. Misunderstanding the reference of *quae* and of *reliquo sermoni*, Theiler, 44, thinks that the *praemunitio* in question consists of the discussion of natural law in Book 1 and the beginning of Book 2.

to handle this topic by proposing his own legislation, as he does, in fact, in Books 2 and 3.

Q. Tu vero iam perpauca licet; ex eis enim quae dixisti, ⟨etiamsi aliter⟩ Attico, videtur mihi quidem certe ex natura ortum esse ius.] *Dicas* is to be supplied with *tu vero* from Marcus' *dixero.*—*Perpauca licet* is Powell's conjecture for *perpaucas valet licet* BF², *perpauca sua licet* AεHL, or *perpauca si licet* P. He explains the error thus *(per litt.):* "The meaningless *sua* might be the remnant of a gloss, *s[cilicet] u[erb]a* on *perpauca*. If this is right, then the intrusive letters can just be removed, and we are left with my conjecture *perpauca licet*. We would then explain B's reading as follows: *perpaucasualicet* misread as *perpaucas ualicet* and then *ualicet* expanded to *ualet licet* by a combination of dittography and striving towards sense."—A certain impatience is apparent both here and in Quintus' interventions in §§ 52 *(quo tandem?)*, 56 *(iam nunc . . . exspecto)*, and 57 *(licebit alias)*; cf. *ad locos.*—Quintus' mention of Atticus for politeness' sake before giving his own opinion draws him into the discussion again (§ 35); thus a solution to the textual problem like Haupt's *effici* for *Attico* that deletes his name altogether is unlikely. Schiche's supplement, *videaturne nescio,* though possible in sense, is awkward in wording and sound. De Plinval proposed ⟨*etsi aliter*⟩, but how can Quintus already know Atticus' reaction? Better ⟨*etiamsi aliter*⟩ *Attico* (Powell), which via *aliter* forges a link to Atticus' reply *an mihi aliter videri possit . . . ?*

35 In his reply Atticus gives a précis of the preceding argument beginning with the divine endowment of the human being (§§ 22–27), continuing with reason, shared among humans (§§ 28–32), and their natural tendency to form bonds of kindness and justice (§§ 33–34, in reverse order; cf. *ad* § 16). Cf. Schmidt, 1959, 190. The points are recapitulated systematically *(primum . . . , secundo . . . loco . . . , deinde . . . , tum . . .)* without any attempt made to delineate the logical nexus among them (ibid., 188 n. 2).

A. . . . primum quasi muneribus deorum nos esse instructos et ornatos, . . .] In spite of his concession at § 21, Atticus places the discussion on a pragmatic footing once again, as in § 16 and in contrast to § 24, where *divino . . . munere* is stated without the equivocating *quasi.* For the thought cf. §§ 26–27.

. . . deinde omnes inter se naturali quadam indulgentia et benevolentia, tum etiam societate iuris contineri?] Perhaps we are meant to understand that the *societas iuris* is based both on the natural human *indulgentia/benevolentia* and on shared reason, which could be inferred to recommend a *societas iuris* as in everyone's interest; society, then, would spring from a combination of self-interest and natural tendency, as in *Off.* 2.73 (see *ad loc.*); cf. Schofield, 1995, 71.

36 M. Recte dicis, et res se sic habet; verum philosophorum more—dispu-tarint.] Atticus has just concluded his speech with a rhetorical question *(. . . qui iam licet nobis a natura leges et iura seiungere?)*. Marcus reacts with agreement but sounds a cautionary note that one should not leap to conclusions.

Cicero contrasts two groups of philosophers and their methods. On the one side are *veteres illi* by whom matters *fuse olim disputabantur et libere*,[148] on the other those *qui quasi officinas instruxerunt sapientiae* and who handle matters *articulatim distincte⟨que⟩*. Under the *veteres*[149] Cicero no doubt has in mind Plato and Aristotle of the dialogues; cf. *Ac.* 1.16: Socrates' *sermones . . . ab his qui illum audierunt perscripti varie copioseque sunt*; similarly Plato is called *varius et multiplex et copiosus* ibid. 17; cf. *Orat.* 5, where his *amplitudo* is praised; for Aristotle cf. *Luc.* 119: *cum enim tuus iste Stoicus sapiens syllabatim tibi ista dixerit, veniet flumen orationis aureum fundens Aristoteles qui illum desipere dicat*; and the Academics and Peripatetics together are said to be *Platonis ubertate completi* (*Ac.* 1.17); cf. the similar contrast of styles at Tac. *Dial.* 32.5 and 39.2; Schmidt, 1959, 21–22.[150]

The list of titles attested for Chrysippus illustrates what Cicero surely had in mind under speaking *articulatim distincte⟨que⟩* (*SVF* 2, 4–10).[151] Though Cicero tends to associate this style with the Stoics,[152] it was no doubt a

---

148. *Fuse . . . et libere* is a virtual ἓν διὰ δυοῖν with *fuse* pointing to abundance (cf. Ernesti s.vv. *fundere, fusus*), *libere* to lack of constraint; cf. *de Orat.* 2.23: *libere volitare* of birds; ibid. 3.124: *libere vagari*; for a similar application to style of discourse cf. *Arch.* 3: *. . . quaeso a vobis ut . . . detis hanc veniam . . . ut me . . . patiamini de studiis humanitatis ac litterarum paulo loqui liberius.*

149. Cf. § 54 *(antiqui)*.

150. The presocratics, though mentioned as *veteres* in discussions of fate (*Fat.* 39) or epistemology (*Ac.* 1.44; *Luc.* 14), are surely not in question here (*pace* Schmidt, 1959, 200).

151. *Articulatim* is attested as early as Pl. *Epid.* 488 and *trag. inc.* 167 (*apud* Cic. *N.D.* 3.67); the metaphorical sense appeared previously at Pl. *Boeot.* fr. 3; apart from the tragic quotation, the word is found only here in Cicero; cf. *TLL* s.v. *Distincteque* is P's correction for *distincte* εHL: *distincta* Bˣ (*deticta* B¹): *detecta* Aᵃ (A¹ eras.). Moser's change to *dissecta* is implausible: this would be the earliest attestation of *disseco* (otherwise first found at Var. *R.* 1.59.3) and the only one in "good prose": *TLL* s.v., esp. 1451.53–55.

152. Cf. (with similar contrast to Cicero's own style) *Luc.* 112: *cum sit enim campus in quo exultare possit oratio, cur eam tantas in angustias et Stoicorum dumeta compellimus?*; *Tusc.* 3.13: *et primo, si placet, Stoicorum more agamus, qui breviter astringere solent argumenta; deinde nostro instituto vagabimur*; cf. also *de Orat.* 2.159 (of Diogenes of Babylon): *. . . genus sermonis adfert non liquidum, non fusum ac profluens, sed exile, aridum, concisum ac minutum . . .* ; *Fin.* 4.6: *. . . hominum non spinas vellentium, ut Stoici, nec ossa nudantium, sed eorum qui grandia ornate vellent, enucleate minora dicere.*

general trend initiated by the dogmatic sects to reduce vulnerability to Carneadean-style critique[153] and also a natural one in view of the proliferation of philosophical literature. The metaphor of the *officinae sapientiae* ("wisdom factories") here bears a pejorative tone; cf. Aristophanes' φροντιστήριον (*Nu.* 94); *Orat.* 12: . . . *fateor me oratorem . . . non ex rhetorum officinis sed ex Academiae spatiis extitisse,* with a similar contrast of the confined to the free; but there is also a more positive use of *officina* with reference to the efficient production of men trained in rhetoric at *de Orat.* 2.52 and *Brut.* 32 (both with reference to Isocrates' school) and *Orat.* 40; and at *Fin.* 5.7 the Academy is referred to as an *officina* because of its roster of distinguished pupils.

There is a similar contrast of styles of philosophical discourse at *Fin.* 3.14, where Cato announces *non respondebo ad singula,* and 4.10: *aliud est enim poetarum more verba fundere, aliud ea quae dicas ratione et arte distinguere;* sim. *N.D.* 2.98; *Tusc.* 3.13 and 4.9.

Do the two methods correspond to the ones actually employed in the two "halves" of *Leg.* 1, i.e., can §§ 18–34 be said to argue *fuse ac libere* in the manner of the *veteres,* and do §§ 40–52 consider the ethical problem separately from the broad context of nature and the human being's place in it? This characterization of the arguments is true in broad outline, the previous argument presenting a system of the entire cosmos and the place of *ius* and the human being in it somewhat in the manner of the Platonic dialogue that most gripped Cicero's imagination, the *Timaeus;* on the other hand, the following section (through § 52) argues individual points within this conception against a possible alternative view: see the outline on pp. 48–49 *supra.*[154] What may come as a surprise, particularly if the following is meant to appease the Skeptical Academy (cf. § 39), is the kinds of arguments used; for §§ 40–52 contrast with the preceding, not by their close argumentation, but rather by their highly rhetorical character (cf. *ad loc.*), whereas §§ 18–34 present theses supported by proofs in the traditional manner of philosophical disputation; cf. p. 53 *supra.*

nec enim satisfieri censent huic loco qui nunc est in manibus, nisi separatim hoc ipsum, naturā esse ius, disputarint.] *In manibus esse* or the like originally refers to one's reading of or working on a book; cf. *Ac.* 1.2 (Varro is speaking of *de Lingua Latina*): *sed habeo opus magnum in manibus;* from

---

153. Balbus sees it just the other way around, however, at *N.D.* 2.20: *atque haec cum uberius disputantur et fusius, ut mihi est in animo facere, facilius effugiunt Academicorum calumniam; cum autem, ut Zeno solebat, brevius angustiusque concluduntur, tum apertiora sunt ad reprendendum.*

154. Cf. also Schmidt, 1959, 202–3.

there it becomes a way of referring, as here, to a topic that is being treated; sim. *N.D.* 3.19: *sed ab hac ea quaestione quae nunc in manibus est separantur;* OLD s.v. *manus* 12 and 13.—*Separatim* is frustratingly vague: separately from what? Theological premises? Cf. also p. 184 below.

A. Et scilicet tua libertas disserendi amissa est, aut tu is es qui in disputando non tuum iudicium sequare, sed auctoritati aliorum pareas?] The *et* is used to join an indignant question (cf. OLD s.v., 15a), and Cicero frames his reply as to a question (*Non semper, Tite; . . .*), so the query is needed at the end of the sentence (as in Powell's edition), though other recent editors use an exclamation point (Ziegler, Keyes, de Plinval, Nickel) or a period (Vahlen); cf. Ter. *Hau.* 705–7 (Clinia): *et scilicet iam me hoc voles patrem exorare ut celet / senem vostrum?* [Quint.] *Decl.* 12.19: *et scilicet speras ut tantam sceleris invidiam ab animis nostris duplae pecuniae strepitus avertat?* The misunderstanding of this idiom led Lambinus to substitute *aut* for *et.*—For the ironic use of *scilicet* pointing to an impossible or absurd position cf. OLD s.v., 4a ("to be sure, doubtless").—Cicero valued the *libertas disserendi* that the Skeptical Academy provided (cf. *Tusc.* 4.7: *nos institutum tenebimus nullisque unius disciplinae legibus adstricti quibus in philosophia necessario pareamus, quid sit in quaque re maxime probabile semper requiremus; Off.* 3.20 [with note]) and held that the following of authorities was not what philosophy is about (*N.D.* 1.10: *non . . . tam auctoritatis in disputando quam rationis momenta quaerenda sunt*); see also Görler, 1995, 103, with references; idem, 1997, 53–54. Atticus' question assumes that Cicero is an Academic skeptic and calls attention to the irony that he, of all people, should allow his approach to be dictated to him by others. At *Luc.* 62 Lucullus is made to rail (on different grounds) against Cicero's skepticism.—*Sequare:* in the present indicative Cicero has a marked preference for the passive/deponent ending in *-ris,* perhaps to avoid confusion with the infinitive ending, whereas *-re* is more common in other tenses and moods; cf. Neue-Wagener, 3, 204, with examples cited ibid. 204–9.

37 M. Non semper, Tite; sed iter huius sermonis quod sit vides: . . .] Sc. *auctoritati aliorum pareo* (Reid). Cicero does not challenge the premise of Atticus' question (i.e., that as a skeptic he should not be following the authority of others). He goes on to argue rather that the use of extra caution[155] seems warranted since the goal is such an important one.—The ὁδὸς λόγων or the like is a favorite Pindaric metaphor (cf. W.J. Slater, *Lexicon to Pindar* [Berlin, 1969] s.v. ὁδός b), imitated by Plato (*Lg.* 688e3–4: ὁδὸς τοῦ

---

155. See the following *vereor committere ut non bene provisa et diligenter explorata principia ponantur.*

λόγου), whence Cicero has perhaps picked it up both in our passage and at *de Orat.* 2.234 *(iter disputationis meae);* for similar locutions in later authors cf. *TLL* s.v. *iter* 543.12–14.

ad respublicas firmandas—⟨id⟩ e⟨s⟩t ad stabiliendas {vi}res, sanandos populos—omnis nostra pergit oratio.] The importance of this project is taken for granted here, perhaps in view of *Rep.;* cf. 1.2: . . . *virtus in usu sui tota posita est. usus autem eius est maximus civitatis gubernatio;* ibid. 1.12: *neque enim est ulla res in qua propius ad deorum numen virtus accedat humana, quam civitates aut condere novas aut conservare iam conditas.* Our text could stand as the theme of *Rep.* and *Leg.* together, never stated with such clarity in the remains of the former work.—For the *iunctura rempublicam firmare* cf. *Att.* 1.16.6 (July 61, with reference to the Bona Dea trial): *reipublicae statum illum quem tu meo consilio, ego divino confirmatum putabam . . . elapsum scito esse de manibus uno hoc iudicio.* Similar wording might have been found in the inscription in honor of Cato the Censor in the temple of Salus; cf. Plut. *Cat. mai.* 19.3: ὅτι τὴν Ῥωμαίων πολιτείαν ἐγκεκλιμένην καὶ ῥέπουσαν ἐπὶ τὸ χεῖρον τιμητὴς γενόμενος χρησταῖς ἀγωγαῖς καὶ σώφροσιν ἐθισμοῖς καὶ διδασκαλίαις εἰς ὀρθὸν αὖθις ἀποκατέστησε.—For the clearly impossible *stabiliendas vires* Ursinus' *stabilienda iura* is usually substituted. The *iunctura iura stabilire,* however, is unparalleled in classical Latin;[156] it should mean "stabilize rights," as was done, e.g., at Rome by the XII Tables (cf. *ad* 3.19: *deinde cum esset cito necatus—*); but this would presumably only apply to communities that had no previous written law and seems to leap over the stage of establishing what *ius* is, which is the topic of the current discussion (§ 17). What needs to be stabilized? *Res* is surely needed for *vires* (so Powell, also changing *et* to *id est*): *Off.* 2.73 and 78 show that Cicero regarded the securing of property as a prime function of the state (2.79 goes on to argue the folly of a policy that would take from some and give to others).—The "healing" of peoples is presumably to be understood in the sense of the reform of character hinted at by Quintus at § 57 *(leges vivendi et disciplina).* For the metaphorical application of *sano* cf. *Cat.* 2.11; *Att.* 1.18.2 (of his action in the Bona Dea trial): . . . *non odio adductus alicuius sed spe . . . sanandae civitatis;* ibid. 2.1.7: *quin etiam si mihi nemo invideret, si omnes, ut erat aequum, faverent, tamen non minus esset probanda medicina quae sanaret vitiosas partes reipublicae quam quae exsecaret.*

37–38 quocirca vereor committere—eis omnibus haec quae dixi probantur.] This long period connects the procedure to be followed with the previously

---

156. Based on a search of PHI 5.3; cf., however, § 62: *qua stabiliat leges.*

stated goal *(quocirca)*. It is first defined negatively in terms of what Cicero seeks to avoid *(vereor committere ut . . .)*. There is a further negative clause to forestall misunderstandings *(nec tamen ut omnibus probentur)*. Then he proceeds to define the groups to whom his premises *(principia;* see next note) should appeal, first in terms of their position on the *finis bonorum (sed ut eis qui omnia recta—sua sponte posset),* then in terms of school affiliation *(eis omnibus sive in Academia vetere—ponerent).* Then he recapitulates *eis omnibus haec quae dixi probantur.* The extent of intervening matter leads to the anacoluthon by which the indicative *(probantur)* is substituted for the expected subjunctive (after *nec tamen ut omnibus probentur . . . sed ut eis qui . . .).*

37 quocirca vereor committere ut non bene provisa et diligenter explorata principia ponantur; . . .] Here *principium* is the "premiss or starting-point of an argument" *(OLD* s.v., 8b); the word is used in a different sense in § 18 (cf. *ad loc.).* The plan is evidently to subject the *principia* to rigorous examination (cf. *articulatim distincte⟨que⟩* [§ 36]) of a kind not inherently congenial to Cicero.

nec tamen ut omnibus probentur . . . sed ut eis qui omnia recta atque honesta per se expetenda duxerunt, et aut nihil omnino in bonis numerandum nisi quod per se ipsum laudabile esset, aut certe nullum habendum magnum bonum nisi quod vere laudari sua sponte posset.] Cicero does not propose to debate at present with the Epicureans or other hedonists[157] or the Skeptics (cf. *ad* § 39), but he hopes to carry with him the Stoics *(qui . . . duxerunt . . . nihil omnino in bonis numerandum nisi quod per se ipsum laudabile esset)*[158] and the Older Academics/Peripatetics *(qui . . . duxerunt . . . certe nullum habendum magnum bonum nisi quod vere laudari sua sponte posset);* cf. the similar elimination of opposed opinion at *Off.* 1.5–6; *ad Off.* 3.18 and 33. For Cicero's tendency to lump together the views of these groups on the *finis bonorum* cf. *ad* §§ 38 and 55.[159]—*Recta atque honesta* stands for the morally good here (cf. *Tusc.* 2.43, where Cicero refers to the usage by which *omnes rectae animi affectiones* are called virtues); *honesta* alone might have served, as it often does in *Off.,* but the use of *rectus* is characteristic of *Leg.;* cf. *ad* § 32 *(quibus ex rebus cum omne genus hominum—).*—For the inclusion of the "natural advantages" in the *sum-*

---

157. Cf. § 39: *nihil enim opus est hoc loco litibus.*

158. On the Stoic classification of goods cf. *SVF* 1, 49.19 ff.; ibid. 3, 17.3 ff.; Pohlenz, *Stoa,* 1, 119 ff.; no. 60 Long-Sedley.

159. Cf. Klaus M. Girardet, " 'Naturrecht' bei Aristoteles und bei Cicero *(De legibus):* Ein Vergleich," in Fortenbaugh-Steinmetz, 127, who concludes that Cicero's claim only makes sense as regards Aristotle if it refers to the doctrine of goods (as indeed it does).

mum bonum by the Old Academy and Peripatos cf. *Luc.* 131; the "balance of Critolaus" is a striking example of the view of the latter school; cf. *ad* § 52a.—*Sua sponte* is a *variatio* for the preceding *per se ipsum.*

38–39 Marcus offers a potted history of philosophical sects designed to show that most will find his approach acceptable (see the introduction to this Book). The criterion is the relation of the *honestum* to the *summum bonum.* His case will appeal to those prepared to allow the *honestum* a large rôle in constituting the τέλος, if not indeed the sole rôle, for *ius,* in the sense of justice, is a part of the *honestum,* so that to establish that the *honestum* is "sought by nature" is virtually the same as establishing that *ius* is by nature. For the basic dichotomy of virtue and pleasure that runs through Cicero's ethical writings cf. Algra, 116–18 (on our passage 117 n. 31). Cicero (or his doxographical source) distinguishes two Academies, the Old and the New (i.e., the Skeptical), the former represented by the first three heads following Plato (named in order: Speusippus, Xenocrates, and Polemo), the Peripatos by the first two heads, Aristotle and Theophrastus, and the Stoa by its first head, Zeno, and a notable dissenter, Aristo of Chius (see the note after next); Arcesilas and Carneades appear for the New Academy (see further *ad* § 39). The position of the Epicureans is paraphrased *(sibi autem indulgentes—),* but they are rather roughly dismissed *(paulisper facessant rogemus;* see below) and not dignified with a philosopher's name (though the phrase *in hortulis suis iubeamus dicere* identifies them clearly enough). In fact, §§ 40–52 will mount a sustained attack on an ethical and political doctrine that roughly corresponds to the Epicurean position but is not identified as such (see *ad* § 39). The Skeptical Academy, on the other hand, is bidden to hold silence *(exoremus ut sileat);* while acknowledging the destructive potential of the neo-Academic approach *(nimias edet ruinas),* Cicero brackets it out of the present discussion. This is one of a group of passages in which he clears the way for positive doctrine; it has, however, sometimes been misunderstood as expressing hostility to the Skeptical Academy; cf. *ad* § 39 *(perturbatricem autem harum omnium rerum—).*

38 . . . sive in Academia vetere cum Speusippo Xenocrate Polemone manserunt, sive Aristotelem et Theophrastum (cum illis congruentes re, genere docendi paulum differentes) secuti sunt, . . .] = Speusippus fr. 106 I.P. = 58e L. = 78d T.; Xenocrates fr. 245 I.P. = 88 H.; Polemo fr. 137 G.; Theophr. F 500 F. Cicero characteristically sees the Academic scholarchs as curators of a legacy at *Ac.* 1.34: *Speusippus autem et Xenocrates, qui primi Platonis rationem auctoritatemque susceperant, et post eos Polemo et Crates unaque Crantor, in Academia congregati, diligenter ea quae a superioribus acceperant tuebantur.* The lumping together of Academy and Peripatos in terms of doctrine is very often met with in Cicero; cf. the next note and *ad* §§ 37 and 55. *Genere docendi . . . differentes* glances at the contrast of Platonic dialectic and Aristotelian lecture; cf. Düring, 5 and 9.

. . . sive ut Zenoni visum est, rebus non commutatis immutaverunt voca-bula, . . .] For Zeno's view of the *finis bonorum* cf. *SVF* 1, 45.15 ff. For Cicero's tendency, after Carneades (*Fin.* 3.41) and Antiochus, to interpret this as a mere verbal discrepancy cf. *N.D.* 1.16; *Fin.* 3.5 (*Zenoque . . . non tam rerum inventor fuit quam verborum novorum*) and 5.74; *Luc.* 15; *Ac.* 1.37; *Tusc.* 4.6; Görler, 1974, 198 ff.; Glucker, 64 n. 81.

. . . sive etiam Aristonis difficilem atque arduam, sed iam tamen fractam et convictam sectam secuti sunt, ut virtutibus exceptis atque vitiis, cetera in summa aequalitate ponerent—. . .] = *SVF* 1, 84.33; cf. also § 55. Our passage describes one of Aristo's positions, the refusal to distinguish between the two classes of "indifferents" (ἀδιάφορα), namely the προηγμένα (the "preferred") and ἀποπροηγμένα (the "non-preferred"); cf. *SVF* 1, 83.6 ff.; 58F-G Long-Sedley with commentary; Anna Maria Ioppolo, *Aristone di Chio e lo stoicismo antico* (Naples, 1980), 162 ff. Aristo also taught— though Cicero does not mention this—that an attitude of indifference (ἀδιαφορία) toward the ἀδιάφορα is the *summum bonum* (*SVF* 1, 79.6–7 = 58G Long-Sedley). When speaking in an Antiochean mode, Cicero mentions Aristo eleven times in company with Pyrrho and/or Herillus as a means of marginalizing him; Aristo appears separately when Cicero is speaking in a Stoic mode (*Fin.* 3.50; *Tusc.* 5.33) or quoting from a Stoic debate (*Fin.* 4.68–72); our passage, with its desire to have Aristo on his side, albeit tempered by criticism of his doctrine as passé, suggests the possibility of a Stoic source modified by reminiscence of Antiochus.[160]—For the description of Aristo's position as "broken and refuted" cf. *Fin.* 2.35 and 5.23, *Tusc.* 5.85, *Off.* 1.6 (see *ad loc.*), all collected at *SVF* 1, 83.37 ff.; *Fin.* 4.47 = *SVF* 1, 84.18–20.—The epithets *arduam* and *fractam* suggest a bastion being crushed militarily, whereas the other two adjectives clarify that these are metaphors for intellectual posture and activity; *tamen* shows the adversative relation of the two pairs of epithets; for *fractam et convictam* cf. *Tusc.* 2.48: *saepe enim videmus fractos pudore qui ratione nulla vincerentur.*

. . . eis omnibus haec quae dixi probantur.] The reference (*haec quae dixi*) is not merely to the Stoic/Academic/Peripatetic valuation of goods, but to the views on law and society put forward since § 18; that these are at issue is also made clear in § 39 *fin.* (*nam si invaserit in haec, quae satis scite nobis instructa et composita videntur, . . .*).

---

160. I owe this argument to D.N. Sedley.

39 sibi autem indulgentes et corpori deservientes, atque omnia quae sequan-tur in vita quaeque fugiant voluptatibus et doloribus ponderantes,—paulis-per facessant rogemus.] = *Epicurea*, p. 94.28 ff.; sim. already Timon of Phlius (*Suppl. Hell.* no. 781). In spite of Atticus' adherence to the school (cf. *ad* § 21), Marcus ventures a surprisingly unflattering portrait of the Epicure-ans as morally weak *(sibi ... indulgentes et corpori deservientes*[161]); the Epicurean view of the *summum bonum* is dismissed with similar contempt at § 52 (see *ad loc.*).[162] With *etiamsi vera dicunt* and *nihil enim opus est hoc loco litibus* Marcus seeks to forestall a debate over the substance of the Epicurean position; for the phrase cf. *Fin.* 2.103.—*Pondero* (= "form a considered opinion of, weigh up, appraise": *OLD* s.v., 2), like *metio* in § 41 (see *ad loc.*), gives expression to the Epicurean calculus of pleasure and pain, on which cf. *Epicurea*, pp. 288 ff.—The diminutive *hortulus (in hortulis suis iubeamus dicere)* carries in this context a note of contempt; cf. *N.D.* 1.120 (Cotta): *... Democritus ... cuius fontibus Epicurus hortulos suos irriga-vit ...* ; Hanssen, 194–95; however, on Atticus' lips (§ 54) it suggests, rather, familiarity and fondness.—*Paulisper facessant rogemus* = "let us bid them take a short holiday" (Sedley). *Facesso* is used in the sense "go away, depart" (*OLD* s.v., 3; *TLL* s.v., II.1; cf. the Greek phrase χαίρειν ἐῶ), often of a curt or insulting order, as in the haughty response of the senate of Veii that led to war, as reported at Liv. 4.58.7: *ni facesserent propere urbe finibusque, daturos quod Lars Tolumnius dedisset;* cf. *Hort.* fr. 39: *facessant igitur omnes qui docere nihil possunt, quo melius sapientiusque vivamus.* Cf. the similar dismissal of pleasure at *Fin.* 3.1: *quare illam quidem* [sc. *voluptatem*] *dimittamus et suis se finibus tenere iubeamus, ne blanditiis eius inlecebrisque impediatur disputandi severitas.* It is a bit odd that Cicero bids the Epicureans do what they wanted to do anyway—and what he criticizes them for in the proem to *Rep.* (cf. Zetzel *ad Rep.* 1.3)—namely to keep clear *ab omni societate reipublicae;* however, there were circumstances in which an Epicurean sage might feel the need to participate in politics,[163] and some Roman Epicureans did so.[164]—The Epicureans are not expected to accept the following argument; they seem to be dismissed as though their opinions

---

161. The *de-* prefix in *deservio* presumably adds the notion of thoroughness or complete-ness (cf. *OLD* s.v. *de-*).

162. On Cicero's oft repeated characterization of Epicurus as "the philosopher of the body" cf. Leonhardt, 191 ff.

163. Cf. Sen. *Ot.* 3.2: *Epicurus ait: 'non accedet ad rempublicam sapiens, nisi si quid intervenerit.'*

164. L. Calpurnius Piso Caesoninus (cos. 58) is a famous instance; see further D.N. Sedley, "The Ethics of Brutus and Cassius," *JRS* 87 (1997), 45–47.

do not matter; but what Cicero does not say is that some of the positions they hold will, in fact, be the target of polemic in §§ 40–52. It is curious that Epicurus and the Epicureans are never mentioned by name in *Leg.* (though they are referred to clearly enough both here and in § 21). Is this the philosophical equivalent of Cicero's criticism of political opponents *tacito nomine* (P. Clodius is not mentioned by name in *Leg.* either: cf. *ad* 3.25 [*cum illa tum peste*] and 26a [*tribunicia vis*]; see also *Parad.* 6 [Crassus]; *ad Off.* 3.41)? Or is the omission dictated by sensitivity to Atticus' feelings? See Inwood, cited *supra* p. 51, and *ad* § 42 *(idem)*.

perturbatricem autem harum omnium rerum, Academiam hanc ab Arcesila et Carneade recentem, exoremus ut sileat: nam si invaserit in haec, quae satis scite nobis instructa et composita videntur, nimias edet ruinas; . . .] I.e., Cicero acknowledges that the structure he has erected (note the perfects: *instructa, composita*) is vulnerable to such attack; cf. Görler, 1995 (refuting the notion that this passage is evidence of a change of school-affiliation on Cicero's part, as argued by Glucker and P. Steinmetz, "Beobachtungen zu Ciceros philosophischem Standpunkt," in Fortenbaugh-Steinmetz, 1–22); Lévy, 515; Leonhardt, 85 and 87.—*Perturbatrix* is a ἅπαξ, and *perturbator* is not attested until the fifth century (Sulp. Sev. *chron.* 2.49.2); cf. Forcellini s.vv.—*Hanc . . . recentem* clearly sets the Skeptical New Academy apart from the earlier phase of the school (Antiochus distinguished his school by calling it the "Old Academy"; cf. *ad* § 53). Notice that *hanc* may denote both personal connection ("this of mine") and nearness (here in terms of time). Cf. Lévy, 116: "De cette Nouvelle Académie Cicéron parle comme d'un adolescent trop turbulent que l'on préfère preventivement écarter d'objets précieux, sans qu'une telle précaution diminue nécessairement l'affection qu'on lui porte." Cicero takes a similar view of the New Academy at *Fam.* 9.8.1 (letter dedicating *Ac.* to Varro; 15 July 45): *misi autem ad te quattuor admonitores non nimis verecundos: nosti enim profecto os illius adulescentioris Academiae.*—Arcesilas was a pupil of Polemo (*de Orat.* 3.67), with whom the list of the scholarchs of the Academy given at § 37 ended. He is likewise described as the pioneer of a new direction for his school at *de Orat.* 3.68 *(hinc haec recentior Academia manavit)*, S.E. *PH* 1.220, and D.L. 1.14; on his thoroughgoing skepticism cf. *de Orat.* 3.67 and *Ac.* 1.45. In general cf. Görler, 1994, 786 ff.—Carneades' brand of skepticism was particularly congenial to Cicero, who confesses *ego vero ipse et magnus quidem sum opinator* (*Luc.* 66; cf. p. 130 n. 102 *supra*), because he held *licebat . . . nihil percipere et tamen opinari* (ibid. 78); Cicero praises him as being *divina quadam celeritate ingeni dicendique copia* (*de Orat.* 3.68). Cf. Görler, 1994, 849 ff.—Atticus' Epicureanism and Marcus' New

Academicism are thus placed simultaneously on the sidelines, a parallelism that might have occasioned comment in the following lacuna (so D.N. Sedley).

quam quidem ego placare cupio, summovere non audeo.] Here Marcus takes a more respectful approach than for the Epicureans (contrast the preceding *paulisper facessant rogemus*): he does not dare to move them roughly aside.[165] He uses a similar strategy of trying to "placate" *(placare)* some critics and confute others at *N.D.* 1.5: *qua quidem in causa* [sc. his philosophical writing] *et benivolos obiurgatores placare et invidos vitupera-tores confutare possumus, ut alteros reprehendisse paeniteat, alteri didicisse se gaudeant.* In both cases those whom Cicero seeks to "placate" are poten-tial allies, and indeed in later philosophical works he will present with some force skeptical arguments on epistemology, theology, and ethics. Two ways of reading this statement have been proposed: (1) Cicero treats the skeptics respectfully because he is in accord with them on other issues (so Busuttil *ad loc.*); or (2) skeptical doubts remain, and Cicero is not necessarily commit-ted to the argument that follows (so Görler, 1995, 97). In fact, the preceding sentence *(nam si invaserit in haec, quae satis scite nobis instructa et com-posita videntur, nimias edet ruinas)* shows Cicero aware of the vulnerability of his edifice, so that interpretation (2) seems appropriate.—For *quam . . . ego placare cupio* see also the next note.

40–52 The demonstration that law is not merely by convention is the essen-tial component of natural law theory. In Greek the same word (νόμος) denotes both "law" and "convention," a fact that may, as Inwood, 1987, 95–96, suggested, have retarded the development of the theory. Here "by nature" has the sense of "the nature of the thing itself . . .—something would be just by nature if it were just always and in all contexts, that is, absolutely and not relatively" (Striker, 82). Cicero argues this point for the goods in general at §§ 45–46.

This section is to execute the plan to consider the problem of *ius separatim* so as to conform to the current style of philosophical discourse (§ 36) and satisfy the New Academy (*quam . . . ego placare cupio:* § 39). It aims to show that a utilitarian approach fails to provide adequate grounding for values in general, justice in particular. Any reader who expects this sequel to be reasoned more closely than the preceding argument will be disappointed, however.[166] Instead of building a case from the ground up,

---

165. *Submoveo* is the verb used of the lictors' clearing of the way for magistrates (*OLD* s.v., 1b).

166. Cf. Schmidt, 1959, 220: "Wenn wir aber danach suchen, worin eigentlich die Argu-mente von Teil II bestehen, bleibt uns fast nichts in den Händen."

Cicero relies on conventional assumptions that murder, robbery, etc., are bad, generosity, patriotism and the like good, even though such an argument would hardly satisfy an advocate of egotistical utilitarianism like Plato's Callicles; cf. Mehl, 135. With few exceptions, such as §§ 44b–46, Cicero bases his argument on instinctive reactions (§§ 40, 48, 51), the absurd consequences of the opposing theories (§§ 40, 41, 42 ff., 49), and invective[167] in lieu of strict proof. Here, without any theoretical justification, two contrasting human types, the *impii* and the *boni,* are set up and their behavior analyzed—all this in sharp contrast to the human similarity argued for at §§ 28–32; cf. Mehl, 136–37. Moreover, the argument cannot really stand on its own apart from what was previously established (cf. *ad* § 42). This section is likewise marked by a lack of sequential, goal-oriented argument, with Cicero reverting to the starting point of his argument at §§ 41 and 48–49, including verbal repetitions (see the next note), and altering or omitting the expected conclusion of the argument (§§ 41, 44, 46, 52). Schmidt concludes that, if §§ 18–35 comprised the *argumentatio,* our section can be called the *refutatio;* it also betrays more clearly than the preceding section the lack of final polish. This is, in fact, the first Ciceronian experiment in using political rhetoric to enliven philosophical discourse; see *supra* p. 53 and n. 20.

40–41 The lacuna may have brought the preceding delineation of school positions to a conclusion (see *ad* § 39: *perturbatricem autem harum omnium rerum*—). Possibly it included the general point that those who obey the *summa ratio* will be happy and those who do not miserable; see pp. 33–34 *supra*. Immediately prior to the preserved text one would have expected a distinction of expiable and inexpiable crimes as well as mention of the appropriate punishments for the latter (see the next two notes and on *sed eos agitant insectanturque Furiae*—). When the text resumes, Cicero is arguing that nature is the most effective deterrent to crime, and, in view of the inadequacy of the criminal justice system in meting out punishment, apart from the influence of nature (i.e., conscience), crime would be much more rampant than it is; the argument bears some similarity to the Epicurean view of justice at *Fin.* 1.51 (though in our passage Cicero combats the notion that the fear of punishment should deter crime [cf. *Fin.* 1.50]). Cicero wants to establish a *consensus omnium* for the natural character of justice by eliciting agreement even from the behavior of the *impii.* He adds the argument that,

---

167. *O rem dignam in qua non modo docti sed etiam agrestes erubescant!* (§ 41), *stultissimum* (§ 42), *dementis est* (§ 45), *quid dici potest stultius* (§ 46), *quo quid potest dici immanius?* (§ 49), *me istorum philosophorum pudet* (§ 50); cf. Schmidt, 1959, 220–21, esp. 221 n. 1.

if justice is based on advantage rather than nature, moral distinctions vanish. In the third and sixth sentences of § 40 the verbal repetition is striking: *quodsi homines ab iniuria poena, non natura, arcere deberet, quaenam sollicitudo vexaret impios sublato suppliciorum metu?* vs. *quodsi poena, si metus supplicii, non ipsa turpitudo deterret ab iniuriosa facinerosaque vita . . . ;* cf. Schmidt, 1959, 209 n. 2. The two *quodsi* clauses mark the onset of two different arguments, namely (1) from the behavior of the *impii* and (2) from the collapse of moral distinctions (see above). The argument from instinctive behavior *(o rem dignam . . . erubescant!)* is conventional; see *ad loc.*

40 Though the extant manuscripts show no damage at this point, editors since Davies mark a lacuna at the beginning of this chapter. As in the case of the lacuna before § 34, the extent is uncertain. Reitzenstein, 16 n. 2, supposing that our lacuna and that before § 34 were found on two outside sheets of a quire, both lost, thought that it comprised one folio of the archetype; this is a possibility, but loss of matter, e.g., by saltation is by no means excluded. Presumably what is lost is at the very least the beginning of the separate argument *naturā esse ius* promised at § 36.[168] Perhaps the argument *ius esse naturā* began with the instinctive revulsion of the *vir bonus* at wrongdoing (the allusion to *noster . . . hic naturā iustus vir ac bonus* at § 41 implies that he was previously mentioned) and elicited an argument from the instinctive feeling even of wrongdoers (the words *itaque poenas luunt* and *eos agitant insectanturque Furiae* imply a previous reference to them) about crime and punishment as a sign that "Nature" has established deterrents to crime (cf. the question *quodsi homines ab iniuria poena, non natura, arcere deberet . . . ?* [§ 40]).[169] When the text resumes, Cicero is arguing that nature is a more potent deterrent to crime than legal penalties (opposing the view that *homines ab iniuria poena, non natura, arcere deberet*) as evidenced by the guilt a person feels after committing a crime and the search for means of expiation.

⟨ . . . ⟩ **nam et in eis sine illius suffimentis expiati sumus.**] *Illius* has been emended to *ullius* (Turnebus), *ullis* (Camerarius), and *illis* (Vahlen, app.); but the loss of preceding matter indicates caution, for the full text might well have provided an antecedent. The word has been referred to Epicurus (Turnebus, on the assumption that the fear of death is in question and that *in eis* refers to the Eleusinian mysteries; but *suffimenta,* without *quasi* or *ut ita dicam,* will be

---

168. For several unsatisfactory suggestions as to what stood in the lacuna cf. Schmidt, 1959, 207 n. 4; see also the next note.

169. For other possible thoughts to be restored in the lacuna see the Introduction, pp. 33–34, *ad* § 39, the next note, and on *at eos agitant insectanturque Furiae*—.

used literally, not metaphorically) or the Vestal virgin;[170] de Plinval *ad loc.*, followed by Kenter, regarded *suffimenta* as Pythagorean purifications, but there is no parallel for *suffimentum* with such reference. *Suffimentum* is a "substance used to fumigate" (*OLD* s.v.); the word is attested in classical Latin limited not by a personal genitive but a genitive of the unclean thing removed; cf. *OLD* s.v., citing Plin. *Nat.* 15.135: . . . *quia* [sc. *laurus*] *suffimentum sit caedis hostium et purgatio*. In view of the following contrast *(at vero . . .)*, *illius* should refer to some lesser offense than *scelera in homines* or *in deos impietas* that can be expiated without agents of fumigation (note the parallel construction of limiting genitives: *illius suffimenta—scelerum . . . atque . . . impietatum . . . expiatio*). An example would be the shedding of blood in war, for which, according to Pliny *loc. cit.*, there was no need of a *suffimentum;* hence, he argues, the burning of laurel branches in a general's triumph must have some different significance; hence *in eis = in bellis* and *illius = caedis* would be one possible set of referents. In the lacuna one would expect immediately prior to this point a distinction between *scelera expianda* and *punienda* and possibly one or more other examples of the former type; the antecedents of the pronouns *eis* and *illius* will also have appeared.[171]

at vero scelerum in homines atque in d⟨eos imp⟩ietatum nulla expiatio est; . . .] *At vero* introduces a sharp antithesis between the expiable and inexpiable.—The two categories of wrongdoing reappear at *Ver.* 1.6: *multa . . . et in deos et in homines impie nefarieque commisit; N.D.* 3.84: *ita ad impietatem in deos in homines adiunxit iniuriam* [sc. Dionysius of Syracuse]; *Fin.* 4.66: . . . *nihil est quod tam miseros faciat quam impietas et scelus . . .* Contrast the right behavior toward these two groups as described at § 43: *in homines obsequia . . . in deos caerimoniae religionesque . . .* See further *ad* 2.22.1.—The text incorporates the needed supplement proposed by Reifferscheid, 287. On Cicero's fondness for using abstract nouns in the plural *(impietates)* see p. 149 n. 126 *supra*.

itaque poenas luunt, non tam iudiciis (quae quondam nusquam erant, hodie multifariam nulla sunt, ubi sunt tamen persaepe falsa sunt), . . .] Cicero combines a picture of a golden age before there was any need of courts (cf. Nörr, 27 and n. 82) with a critique of conditions of his own day, when

---

170. Schmidt, 1959, 207 n. 5; he evidently has in mind the *suffimenta* distributed to individual households by the Vestal Virgins during the Parilia; cf. Wissowa, 200 and 399. Thereby he takes *in eis* as = *in sceleribus;* but such a reference of *in eis* would destroy the contrast with the following *scelerum;* and why "die Vestalin" (singular)?

171. Cf. Schmidt, 1959, 209, who notes that the relation of *expiato* and *poena* is not clarified in the extant text and suspects that this may have been handled in the lacuna.

courts are needed but are nonexistent in many places *(multifariam nulla sunt)*[172] or, if they do exist, often render false verdicts *(persaepe falsa sunt)*. The point is that wrongdoing would be far more rampant if the legal system were the sole check. Corrupt courts are alluded to also at 2.43; providing remedies for them was no doubt a major theme of Book 4 *(de iudiciis;* cf. 3.47; *ad fr. ex inc. lib.* 1).—The clausulae are double cretic *(multifariam nulla sunt)* and cretic plus iamb *(persaepe falsa sunt);* cf. rhythmical analysis of this and the following lemma by Hutchinson, 1995, 498.

... sed eos agitant insectanturque Furiae, non ardentibus taedis sicut in fabulis, sed angore conscientiae fraudisque cruciatu.] We adopt Zumpt's *sed* for *ut.*—The anacoluthon (a new main clause in lieu of the expected *quam Furiis)* enables Cicero to describe the punishment in vivid and drastic terms *(agitant insectanturque)* while holding the identity of the agent in reserve to the end of the clause for effect; likewise, the following twofold description of the modality, the mythic and the actual, reserves for the end the torment Cicero wants to emphasize *(angore conscientiae fraudisque cruciatu;* on the form and sense see below).—For the *iunctura agitant insectantur* cf. *Mur.* 21; *Div.* 2.144; Tac. *Dial.* 4.1.

The Furies, goddesses of vengeance (cf. *N.D.* 3.46) equipped with torches, were depicted on the Roman stage in Ennius' play on the saga of Alcmaeon (cf. *trag.* pp. 20–21 [esp. v. 25: *unde haec flamma oritur?* and 27: *flammiferam hanc vim*]; cf. the similar play of Accius, ibid., 165–66); it is unclear that a pre-Ciceronian Roman play on the saga of Orestes included this detail (ibid. Index Fabularum s.vv. *Agamemnonidae, Orestes*). Cicero alludes to such depictions and offers a similar psychological interpretation in two speeches (similar phrasing to our passage is underlined): *videtisne quos nobis poetae tradiderunt patris ulciscendi causa supplicium de matre sumpsisse, cum praesertim deorum immortalium iussis atque oraculis id fecisse dicantur, tamen ut eos agitent Furiae neque consistere umquam patiantur ... ? ... nolite enim putare, quem ad modum in fabulis saepenumero videtis, eos qui aliquid impie scelerateque commiserint agitari et perterreri Furiarum taedis ardentibus (Sex. Rosc.* 66–67); *nolite enim ita putare, patres conscripti, ut in scaena videtis, homines consceleratos impulsu deorum terreri furialibus*

---

172. This critique of the courts echoes some of the rhetoric of the Verrine speeches, e.g., *Ver.* 43: *nulla in iudiciis severitas, nulla religio, nulla denique iam existimantur esse iudicia;* sim. ibid. 3.132 (Verres' behavior predicated on the assumption that there were no courts at Rome); still more pessimistic the letter written to Plancus in September 44: *quae potest enim spes esse in ea republica ... in qua nec senatus nec populus vim habet ullam nec leges ullae sunt nec iudicia nec omnino simulacrum aliquod ac vestigium civitatis? (Fam.* 10.1.1).

taedis ardentibus; sua quemque fraus, suum facinus, suum scelus, sua audacia de sanitate ac mente deturbat; hae sunt impiorum furiae, hae flammae, hae faces (*Pis.* 46).

The horrific equipment of the Furies is reinterpreted in psychological terms, but their gruesome quality is no less present *(cruciatu)*. This aspect is reserved for impact to the end of the sentence, the final words assuming, in contrast to the content, an orderly chiastic arrangement of nouns and limiting genitives and a fine clausula (type *debuerat omne*). *Fraudis . . . cruciatu* = "the torment resulting from wrongdoing"; cf. *OLD* s.v. *fraus* 3; for the idea cf., besides *Pis.* 46, cited above, *Ver.* 1.6: *. . . quorum scelerum poenis agitatur et a mente consilioque deducitur.*

Cicero describes the effects of guilty conscience in 2.43 and, in greater detail, *Tusc.* 2.53; cf. also *N.D.* 3.85. Though in these cases guilty conscience appears only after the fact, rather than in time to deter the crime (cf. Schmidt, 1959, 208), Cicero may in the lacuna have framed the argument to show that conscience ordinarily deters crime altogether or, if it does not, provides its own punishment.

Quodsi homines ab iniuria poena, non natura, arcere deberet, quaenam sollicitudo vexaret impios sublato suppliciorum metu?] The *impii* lack, *ex vi termini,* fear of punishment by the gods, indeed, according to *N.D.* 1.63 (Cotta), they implicitly deny their existence; if fear of punishment by human agencies were also removed *(sublato suppliciorum metu),* there would be no deterrent to crime. Here Cicero combats the view that fear of punishment is sufficient to prevent wrongdoing, a position associated elsewhere with the Epicureans; cf. *Fin.* 2.53–54; Sen. *Ep.* 97.15 = *Epicurea* 321.3: *illic dissentiamus cum Epicuro ubi dicit nihil iustum esse natura et crimina vitanda esse quia vitari metus non posse.*—Like German *denn, -nam,* follows upon the interrogative word in lively or impatient questions (cf. *OLD* s.v., 7).— For the relation of this point to the overall argument see the headnote to this section.

quorum tamen nemo tam audax umquam fuit quin aut abnueret a se commissum esse facinus, aut iusti sui doloris causam aliquam fingeret, defensionemque facinoris a naturae iure aliquo quaereret.] I.e., the suspect will either confess, as the five captured Catilinarian conspirators did (*Cat.* 3.10 ff.), or appeal to some standard of natural right, however bogus the claim (cf. the instances at V.Max. 8.1.amb.1–2). Similarly at Pl. *Euthphr.* 8b–e Socrates argues that no one would be bold enough to claim that wrongdoing should go unpunished. For an argument from the behavior of criminals cf. also *Ver.* 3.195: *hoc vero quid est? quam habet rationem non quaero aequitatis, sed ipsius improbitatis atque impudentiae? neque enim*

est fere quicquam quod homines palam facere audeant in magistratu quam-
vis improbe, quin eius facti si non bonam, at aliquam rationem adferre
soleant; Fin. 3.36; in general Quint. *Inst.* 3.8.44: *neque enim quisquam est*
tam malus ut videri velit.—*Naturae* is the (needed) correction of the *re-*
centiores for *natura* of ω. The *ius naturae* appealed to would be, of course,
revenge.

quae si appellare audent impii, quo tandem studio colentur a bonis!] *Quae*
for *quod* (referring back to *ius*) is generalizing.—*Appello* is ordinarily used
of appeals for help to a person (*OLD* s.v., 2).—This is an a fortiori argument from the behavior of the *impii* to that of the *boni:* if even the former
appeal to the *ius naturae* . . .

Quodsi poena, si metus supplicii, non ipsa turpitudo deterret ab iniuriosa
facinerosaque vita, nemo est iniustus, atque incauti potius habendi sunt
improbi; . . .] If the category of the morally bad *(turpitudo)* is removed, an
"Umwertung aller Werte" is entailed such that the person who is *incautus*
(i.e., because caught in wrongdoing) is called *improbus,* and the *callidus*
usurps the name of *vir bonus;* cf. Thucydides' famous analysis of the effect of
στάσις on Greek usage (3.82); a similar shift of categories was argued for by
Thrasymachus at *Rp.* 343a ff., summarized thus by Socrates at 348e1: . . .
τόδε ἐθαύμασα, εἰ ἐν ἀρετῆς καὶ σοφίας τιθεῖς μέρει τὴν ἀδικίαν, τὴν δὲ
δικαιοσύνην ἐν τοῖς ἐναντίοις.—Ernesti's *atque* is adopted here; the alternative is to take the transmitted *aut* in a weak, almost copulative sense; cf.
Kühner-Stegmann, 2, 102–4.—*Incauti:* for caution to avoid public disgrace
or punishment cf. § 41 *(ne emanet, id est ne malum habeat)* and § 51
(infamia).

41 tum autem qui non ipso honesto movemur ut boni viri simus, sed utilitate
aliqua atque fructu, callidi sumus, non boni.] The utilitarian approach to
justice allots a new meaning not only to *iniustus* but also the positive counterpart, *bonus vir.* In the sequel this alternate set of values is referred to not
only as *utilitas* (§ 42; cf. already § 33), *fructus* (§ 49), or as a view to a *res*
fructuosa (§ 42), but also as a search for *emolumenta* (§ 49 *bis*), *praemium*
(ibid.), or *merces* (§§ 48 and 49). Cf. also *Fin.* 2.60: *perspicuum est enim,*
nisi aequitas fides iustitia proficiscantur a natura, et si omnia haec ad
utilitatem referantur, virum bonum non posse reperiri; sim. *Off.* 1.63, citing
Pl. *Mx.* 246e, *La.* 197b; at *Off.* 2.42 considerations of interest are allowed
to play a rôle supporting *iustitia,* albeit not by themselves; in *Off.* 3, however, Cicero redefines the *utile* so as to agree with the *honestum;* cf. Dyck *ad*
Off., pp. 491–94.—*Callidus* need not be, but often is, used in a pejorative
sense; cf. *TLL* s.v., I; *OLD* s.v., 3; for the contrast with *bonus* cf. *Att.* 7.2.4.
nam quid faciet is homo—in qua non modo docti sed etiam agrestes

erubescant!] Two hypothetical cases in which despoiling another could be concealed, one involving darkness, the other a vulnerable person *(imbecillus atque solus)* met in a deserted place. These scenarios serve to contrast the behavior of two human types, the *iustus vir ac bonus* on the one side, the person who acts purely for selfish motives on the other. Like the latter, Thrasymachus at Pl. *Rp.* 348d5 ff. approves of purse-snatching if it is undetected (λυσιτελεῖ μὲν οὖν, ἦ δ᾽ ὅς, καὶ τὰ τοιαῦτα, ἐάνπερ λανθάνῃ). At *Off.* 3.39 Cicero makes similar use of the case of Gyges' ring with its power of making the bearer invisible; there is a similar argument also at *Fin.* 2.52–53 and 3.38. For comparison of philosophers with ordinary persons or their capacities cf. also *Off.* 3.77; *N.D.* 1.61, 101, 109.

nam quid faciet is homo in tenebris, qui nihil timet nisi testem et iudicem?] *In tenebris:* cf. the proverbial designation of an honest person, *quicum in tenebris mices,* invoked at *Fin.* 2.52 and *Off.* 3.77. Cato makes a similar point at *Fin.* 3.38.—*Testem et iudicem:* on Cicero's fondness for the singular as a collective cf. Lebreton, 78–82.

quid in deserto quo loco nactus quem multo auro spoliare possit imbecillum atque solum?] Supply *faciet* as the main verb.—On *quo* for *aliquo* cf. Kühner-Stegmann, 1, 634, citing *inter alia* our passage.—The points that make him vulnerable *(imbecillum atque solum)* are postponed to the emphatic sentence-final position with resulting ditrochaic clausula; cf. *Sex. Rosc.* 20: *huius* [sc. *Sex. Rosci*] *inopia et solitudo commemoratur.*

noster quidem hic natura iustus vir ac bonus etiam colloquetur, iuvabit, in viam deducet; . . .] I.e., he will provide those services *quae sunt iis utilia qui accipiunt, danti non molesta* (*Off.* 1.52).—*Noster . . . hic natura iustus vir ac bonus* seems to refer to a category previously established (presumably in the lacuna at the beginning of § 40; see *ad loc.*). Here, as at §§ 48–49 and *Off.* 3 (see *ad* 3.18), this Roman construct substitutes for the Stoic sage as the model of behavior. *Iustus . . . ac bonus* is a ἓν διὰ δυοῖν since *iustitia* is really constitutive of moral virtue; cf. *ad Off.* 1.20.—*Quidem* introduces the first half of a contrast (cf. Solodow 30 ff. and 123).—The expression is a bit elliptical; hence Vaucher wanted to transpose *etiam* to follow *colloquetur, sed nil mutandum.* Cicero means *non solum non spoliabit sed etiam colloquetur . . .*—For *deduco* used of taking a person to a destination cf. *OLD* s.v., 8.

is vero qui nihil alterius causa faciet et metietur suis commodis omnia, videtis, credo, quid sit acturus; . . .] The verbs of the relative clause have been corrupted; transmitted is *facti et mentietur* (B¹) and *faciet emetietur* (HLES). Both verbs should be in the same tense; either present or future is possible.[173] The choice lies between (1) *facit et metitur* (Manutius) and (2) *faciet et metietur* (P). It is merely a question of *uter in utrum?* (in either case *ment-* must be emended to *met-*). Probably *faciet et* is both the more difficult reading and the one more likely to have yielded what is in the manuscripts, becoming *facti et* in B (and thence variously "corrected" to *faciet* B[x]R: *facit et* A[a]) and *faciet e-* in HLES; and there is no reason why the straightforward *-itur* ending should have been corrupted to *-ietur* (*mentietur* or *emetietur*), especially when the preceding verb was no longer read as a future.—For corrective *et* cf. *ad* 2.53.—*Metio* here and in § 42 corresponds to μετρῶ in some Greek testimonies for Epicureanism (cf. also *ad* § 39 [*ponderantes*]); cf. *Epicurea*, p. 289.18 ff.: καίπερ γὰρ ἀξιοῦντες ἅπασιν ἡδονὴν ἀγαθὴν εἶναι καὶ πᾶσιν ἀλγηδόνα κακόν, ὅμως οὐκ ἀεί φασι δεῖν τὴν μὲν αἱρεῖσθαι, τὴν δὲ φεύγειν, μετρεῖσθαι γὰρ αὐτὰ τῷ πόσῳ καὶ οὐ τῷ ποιῷ; cf. *Pis.* 68: *audistis . . . dici philosophos Epicureos omnis res . . . voluptate metiri;* sim. *N.D.* 1.113: *ventre metiri; commodis metiri* also characterizes the Epicurean position at *Off.* 1.5 and 3.18; cf. also *voluptate metiri* at *Fin.* 2.56 and 5.93.—The *credo* is, of course, ironic (*OLD* s.v., 8c: "doubtless, I suppose, presumably"); Seyffert-Müller *ad Amic.* 24 (p. 174).

quodsi negabit se illi vitam erepturum . . . , numquam ob eam causam negabit quod id natura turpe iudicet, sed quod metuat ne emanet, id est ne malum habeat: . . .] What the hypothetical utilitarian is afraid of is "becoming known, attracting attention" (= German "auffallen"; cf. *OLD* s.v. *emano* 3) with all the consequences thereof.[174] *Malum habeo* is colloquial = "get into trouble"; cf. *Fin.* 2.71 as well as *malum dare* (= "make trouble for": *OLD* s.v. *malum* 1c).

o rem dignam in qua non modo docti sed etiam agrestes erubescant!] This takes up the theme of brazenness (cf. § 40: *nemo tam audax umquam fuit quin . . .*). For feelings of shame playing a rôle in ethical argument cf. Pl. *Rp.* 350d3 (Thrasymachus' blush); sim. *Gorg.* 482d1 ff. (Polus' claim that Gorgias' answer was dictated by shame); *Fin.* 2.7 (*'quasi vero me pudeat' inquit* [sc. Torquatus] *'istorum. . . .'*); ibid. 2.28: *deinde ubi erubuit (vis enim est permagna naturae) . . .* ; 2.69; 2.76–77; 4.2; *N.D.* 2.69. For the comparison with rustics cf. *Sen.* 75: *quod igitur adulescentes, et ei quidem non solum indocti sed etiam rustici contemnunt, id docti senes extimescunt? Off.*

---

173. For the gnomic future in such expressions cf. Kühner-Stegmann, 1, 143, citing *inter alia* Cat. *Agr.* 31.2: *quae materies semen non habebit, cum glubebit, tempestiva erit;* cf. also § 42: *. . . is qui sibi eam rem fructuosam putabit fore.*

174. The subjunctives in the *quod*-clauses indicate grounds alleged by those holding these positions.

3.77: *haec non turpe est dubitare philosophos, quae ne rustici quidem dubitent?*

42–44a This section continues the argument begun in § 40 that *ius* is by nature, not by convention *(opinio)*, the implicit target being those who, like the Epicureans, hold that *utilitas* is the criterion of action. The previous section handled the stronger version of that claim, namely that one can engage in wrongful acts if one is certain to escape detection. Here Cicero goes on to the weaker version, according to which just dealing consists merely in obedience to existing statutes.[175] He opposes to this view the argument that actual legislation reflects *ius* only very imperfectly. He offers historical examples, one Greek, one Roman, *viz.*, the laws of the Thirty at Athens and the powers granted to Sulla under the lex Valeria. Mehl, 136, points to the function of this argument within Cicero's overall plan: "he needs to invalidate actual laws that will give way to his own"; but, as Mehl goes on to show, this kind of proof from consensus is brittle because, as Cicero admits (§ 47), opinions on such matters vary. In addition, Marcus doubts these opponents' commitment to law; he suspects that they will break the law if opportunity offers. He asserts contrariwise the general human propensity to kindness and good deeds. The polemical tone continues from the previous section with references to his opponents as *stultissimi*, legislation as *stultorum sententiae*, and impassioned questions *(ubi enim liberalitas, ubi patriae caritas . . . ?* etc.). In addition, the argument meanders from one topic to another and back again: (1) the opponents' theory of legislation as sufficient guarantor of morality, (2) the two counter-examples, (3) Marcus' own position, (4) the consequences of the opposing theory for human relations and religious institutions, (5) the limitations of legislation; cf. Schmidt, 1959, 212.

42 Iam vero illud stultissimum, existimare omnia iusta esse quae scita sint in populorum institutis aut legibus. etiamne si quae leges sint tyrannorum?] = *SVF* 3, 79.5–7. Here Cicero turns to attack the notion that laws are just because they are laws, i.e., that justice is merely conventional in the sense of the sophistic controversy over whether values are νόμῳ or φύσει. At X. *M.* 1.2.43–44 the young Alcibiades traps his guardian Pericles in contradiction when he first answers that what a tyrant prescribes is νόμος and then that it is ἀνομία. Cf. also Laelius' speech in defense of justice at *Rep.* 3.27: *est quidem vera lex recta ratio . . . nec vero aut per senatum aut per populum solvi hac lege possumus . . .*—The ellipsis of a form of *sum* in the main

---

175. That he has in mind specifically the Epicureans is one interpretation of § 42: *et si (ut idem dicunt) utilitate omnia metienda sunt;* see *ad loc.*

clause *iam vero illud stultissimum* creates an emphatic nominal sentence containing a value-judgment; cf. 3.42; Dyck *ad Off.*, p. 50.—*Scita* of the *recentiores* is clearly needed for the transmitted *sita;* for *scita . . . in populorum institutis aut legibus* cf. 2.13: *multa pestifere sciscuntur in populis.*— The prior *sint* is subjunctive in indirect discourse; the second *sint* is in the protasis of a future less vivid conditional; cf. Kühner-Stegmann, 2, 393– 94.—As the sequel shows, *populorum instituta* need not imply popular enactment of the laws, merely that they are in place; contrast *Rep.* 1.39 and 3.35, where emphasis is laid on the involvement of the properly constituted *populus.*—The emphatic word *tyrannorum* is held in reserve to the end of the second sentence and underlined by a clausula of the cretic plus trochee type.

si triginta illi Athenis leges imponere voluissent, aut si omnes Athenienses delectarentur tyrannicis legibus, num idcirco eae leges iustae haberentur?] The misrule of the Thirty at Athens (404–3) figures as an example of oligarchy at *Rep.* 1.44 and ibid. 3.35 as a type of regime which does not qualify as a *respublica* because the people have been deprived of their rights (cf. also the anecdote of Theramenes' death at *Tusc.* 1.96). Was the example of the Thirty already so used in Alcidamas' *Messenian Speech* (see the note after next)?— *Athenis* is locative, not dependent on *imponere.*—*Aut si* is transmitted, for which Zumpt proposed *etsi* (better perhaps *etiam si*[176]). The transmitted text is possible if one understands *tyrannicae leges* as laws granting tyrannical powers (like the lex Valeria at Rome; see below); with *etsi* or *etiamsi* the sentence would clarify that procedure was not at issue in the case of the laws of the Thirty.[177]—On "railroading" *num* in rhetorical questions showing that the speaker anticipates a negative answer ("surely . . . not . . ." or the like) cf. *OLD* s.v., 3.

nihilo, credo, magis illa quam interrex noster tulit, ut dictator quem vellet civium vel indicta causa impune posset occidere.] For ironic *credo* cf. *ad* § 41.—Supply in the main clause *lex iusta habenda est.*—*Noster* here does not indicate personal attachment (cf. *ad* 2.6: *Magnus ille noster*) but simply marks the transition from an *exemplum externum* to an *exemplum domesticum* (for the practice in general of adding domestic to foreign examples cf. *ad Off.* 2.26b).—The interrex in question was L. Valerius Flaccus (censor 97), also alluded to simply as interrex at *Att.* 9.15.2. As flamen Martialis he was able to steer a safe course through the treacherous political shoals of the 80s. Though Marius' colleague in the consulate of 100, as *princeps senatus*

---

176. So Powell *(per litt.)*.

177. Cf. Socrates' refusal to obey their order to apprehend Leo of Salamis (Pl. *Ap.* 32c–d).

in 85 he proposed a reconciliation of the warring factions. Then, with the consuls Marius (the younger) and Cn. Papirius Carbo killed in the wake of Sulla's victory, as interrex he carried the law naming Sulla dictator *legibus scribendis et reipublicae constituendae* (the lex Valeria: 82; cf. Rotondi, 348–49), criticized by Cicero here and at *Ver.* 3.81 and *Agr.* 3.5 *(hic rei publicae tyrannum lege constituit);* cf. Diehl, 149–50. App. *BC* 1.459 reports that the senate hoped Valerius would hold consular elections. Indeed, it was a novelty for an interrex to carry a law for appointing a dictator, rather than for the dictator to be appointed by a consul;[178] cf. Jahn, 161–65. On the interrex in general, ibid., 11 ff. In the sequel Sulla appointed Valerius magister equitum. By 63 he was no longer alive (*Rab. perd.* 27). On Valerius cf. Münzer, *RE* 8A1 (1955), 22.60 ff.—Cicero is describing here the effect of the law, rather than its content; cf. François Hinard, *Les proscriptions de la Rome republicaine* (Rome, 1985), 68–69. On the lack of legal protections under Sulla *(indicta causa)* cf. in general Mommsen, *Staatsr.* 2, 736; Duncan Cloud in *CAH* 9, 496.

est enim unum ius, quo devincta est hominum societas, et quod lex constituit una, quae lex est recta ratio imperandi atque prohibendi. quam qui ignorat, is est iniustus, sive est illa scripta uspiam sive nusquam.] = *SVF* 3, 79.7–10. This is a reprise of themes sounded in Laelius' reply to Carneades' argument on justice as presented by Philus in *Rep.* 3. Cf. 3.26: . . . *nec erit alia lex Romae, alia Athenis, alia nunc, alia posthac, sed et omnes gentes et omni tempore una lex et sempiterna et immutabilis continebit* . . . In our work the relations of *ius, lex, recta ratio,* and human *societas* were established at §§ 22–23; as Mehl, 135, points out, the reference back to the previous discussion highlights that this argument cannot really stand on its own in spite of the claim put forward (§ 36) of making a case *separatim* for *ius* being by nature. Here the divine element, prominent in the earlier passage, is omitted for the moment but will return in § 43. For the conception of *unum ius* cf. the κοινὸς νόμος of *SVF* 1, 43.1–3, cited *ad* § 23 *(inter quos autem ratio—).* The idea can be traced further back; cf. Antigone's famous declaration of the priority of unwritten divine law over human decree: οὐ γάρ τί μοι Ζεὺς ἦν ὁ κηρύξας τάδε, / οὐδ' ἡ ξύνοικος τῶν κάτω θεῶν Δίκη / τοιούσδ' ἐν ἀνθρώποισιν ὥρισεν νόμους, / οὐδὲ σθένειν τοσοῦτον ᾠόμην τὰ σὰ / κηρύγμαθ' ὥστ' ἄγραπτα κἀσφαλῆ θεῶν / νόμιμα δύνασθαι θνητά γ' ὄνθ' ὑπερδραμεῖν (S. *Ant.* 450–55); Pl. *Min.* 316b5 (Socrates is the speaker), where "being" corresponds to the *unum ius* of our passage: ὃς ἂν ἄρα τοῦ ὄντος ἁμαρτάνῃ, τοῦ νομίμου ἁμαρτάνει; Arist. *Rh.* 1375a31 ff. (cf. 1375b3–5), citing *inter alia*

---

178. At 3.9.2, however, Cicero gives this power to the senate.

Ant. 456–58 and the famous fragment of Alcidamas' *Messenian Speech* (=
no. 3 Avezzù): ἐλευθέρους ἀφῆκε πάντας θεός· οὐδένα δοῦλον ἡ φύσις
πεποίηκε.[179] As a "philosophical orator" (cf. *ad* § 63), Cicero glances at such
concepts when he speaks of the right of self-defense at *Mil.* 10: *est igitur
haec . . . non scripta, sed nata lex, quam non didicimus, accepimus, legimus,
verum ex natura ipsa adripuimus, hausimus, expressimus, ad quam non docti
sed facti, non instituti sed imbuti sumus . . .—Quo devinctus:* there were
several competing ancient theories about the origin of society (cf. *ad Off.*
2.73), including that of the Epicureans that the wise consented to laws to
protect themselves against wrongdoing (*Epicurea* 320.27–28: οἱ νόμοι
χάριν τῶν σοφῶν κεῖνται, οὐχ ὅπως μὴ ἀδικῶσιν ἀλλ᾽ ὅπως μὴ
ἀδικῶνται); cf. Mitsis, 1988, 89. As in *Rep.*, Cicero rejects this view and
claims, rather, that what holds society together is a shared sense of justice; cf.
Rep. 1.39 (following the definitions of *respublica* and *populus;* cf. *ad* § 23):
*eius autem prima causa coeundi est non tam imbecillitas, quam naturalis
quaedam hominum quasi congregatio . . .* ; ibid. 1.49 and 6.13.—*Quam qui
ignorat, is est iniustus, sive est illa scripta uspiam sive nusquam:* this sentence
clarifies the relation of justice to natural law: justice consists in obedience to
natural law but is not its content; cf. Girardet, 1983, 34–35 and n. 56; 139.
Ignoro covers two cases, that of "having no knowledge of" and "acting as if
in ignorance of, ignoring": cf. *OLD* s.v., 1 and 4. There is no better evidence
than our passage that *uspiam* and *nusquam* were felt as opposites (*sive . . .
uspiam sive nusquam* = "whether . . . somewhere or nowhere"). Thus natural law *can* be written down (cf. Girardet, 1983, 72); indeed allowing for the
possibility of written natural law may be one of Cicero's innovations vis-à-vis
traditional Stoicism (ibid., 83). The legislation put forward in Books 2 ff. will
be his version of natural law; see further *ad* § 17. This point, taken together
with the definitions of law preceding and following (§§ 18–19, our passage,
and esp. 2.8: *ratio mensque sapientis*), would mean that only the sage is just
and all fools are criminals; cf. *SVF* 3, 73.18 ff.

**quodsi iustitia est obtemperatio scriptis legibus institutisque populorum, et
si (ut idem dicunt) utilitate omnia metienda sunt, negleget leges easque
perrumpet, si poterit, is qui sibi eam rem fructuosam putabit fore; . . .]** A
standard attack upon egotist utilitarians: the false premises *(quodsi . . . et
si . . .)* lead, according to Cicero, to illegal action in this instance as surely as
to immoral action in the cases discussed in § 41. His objection is, however,
not well formulated: if justice is obedience to written laws, even if advantage

<hr/>

179. Cicero restricts the idea to the Roman people at *Phil.* 6.19: *populum Romanum
servire fas non est, quem di immortales omnibus gentibus imperare voluerunt. . . . aliae nationes servitutem pati possunt, populi Romani est propria libertas.*

is the measure of all things (including laws)[180] and the laws are perceived as disadvantageous, the result should not be violation of laws but an attempt to repeal them. Cicero needed to qualify the first premise in such a way as the Epicureans did, for whom justice consists in obedience to *just* written laws; that would provide an escape from the duty of absolute obedience.— *Obtemperatio* is used only here in classical Latin (cf. *OLD* and *TLL* s.v.); the adnominal dative is unusual[181] and possibly modeled on the usage of Greek, where the verbal properties of verbal nouns are more strongly felt (so du Mesnil *ad loc.;* for the general tendency cf. Parzinger, 140; for parallel Greek material cf. Guy L. Cooper III, *Attic Greek Prose Syntax after K.W. Krüger,* 1 [Ann Arbor, 1998], 48.12.4), though Friedrich Haase at C.K. Reisig, *Vorlesungen über die lateinische Sprachwissenschaft,* 3: *Syntax* (Berlin, 1890), 524 n. 511, sees the usage, rather, as derived "aus dem nach möglichster Präzision [I would add: und Kürze; cf. *ad* 2.18] ringenden juristischen Kurialstil der Römer."—The second protasis *(si [ut idem dicunt] utilitate omnia metienda sunt)* suggests that Cicero may be thinking of a specific group who hold both doctrines. The Epicureans come to mind, for Cicero often speaks of them as measuring value by their own advantage; cf. *ad* § 41. But the first protasis fits the Epicureans less well (see above). There are two possibilities: either (1) Cicero has carelessly reproduced his source but really meant to target the Epicureans; or (2) Cicero is here constructing a generic group of opponents to serve as a "straw man." If (1), then the two protases may be directed at the two halves, as it were, of the Epicurean theory of justice: (a) that it is a contract by which Epicureans can protect themselves against those who do not share Epicurean ideals (see the previous note); (b) that it is pursued for the sake of one's own peace of mind; cf. *Epicurea,* pp. 323–25; Mitsis, 1988, 59–97.—*Utilitate omnia metienda sunt: omnia* will, of course, include laws. But whose advantage is being served—that of society in general or of a tyrant? A distinction is drawn at *Rep.* 3.35.—*Negleget leges easque perrumpet:* the point appears to have been argued in detail by Laelius in *Rep.* (cf. *Fin.* 2.59; Ferrary, 1974, 754–60); cf. *ad* 2.43; *Fin.* 2.53–59; *Off.* 3.36. For the *iunctura perrumpere leges* cf. Luc. 1.322; for the thought cf. *Cat.* 1.18: *tu non solum ad neglegendas leges et quaestiones, verum etiam ad evertendas perfringendasque valuisti.*— Cicero rounds off the period with a fine double cretic clausula.

ita fit ut nulla sit omnino iustitia, si neque naturā est, ⟨et⟩ ea quae propter

---

180. On advantage as a possible criterion of laws cf. also Pl. *Tht.* 172b and 177d.

181. The other Ciceronian examples are *Top.* 28 *(abalienatio est eius rei quae mancipi est aut traditio alteri nexu aut in iure cessio)* and possibly *N.D.* 1.96 *(similitudo deo,* though Müller's *similitudo deorum* is commonly adopted).

utilitatem constituitur, utilitate illa convellitur.] *Ita fit ut nulla sit omnino iustitia . . . :* for the introductory formula cf. *ad Off.* 1.101. Here *iustitia* is the virtue, destroyed, for Cicero, by the operation of an egotist utilitarianism with constantly fluctuating goals. Cf. Pl. *Cri.* 50b ff., according to which to disobey a single law is, in intent, to destroy all the laws of the state.— Cicero's double protasis *(si neque . . . et . . .)* rests on the disjunctive premise that law is either by nature or set up for some utilitarian purpose. But, if this is meant to be an attack on the Epicureans (see the previous note), further clarification is needed, for the Epicureans also regarded justice as "by nature," just as its criterion, the "useful," is by nature, i.e., in accord with the natural tendencies of the human being; cf. Hor. *S.* 1.3.98: *utilitas, iusti prope mater et aequi; Fin.* 1.30.—⟨Et⟩ *ea quae propter utilitatem constituitur utilitate illa convellitur:* ⟨et⟩ *ea quae* is Manutius' correction of transmitted *aeaquae* (B), which, as J.G.F. Powell notes *(per litt.),* suggests *et ea quae* as the original reading, or *eaque* (PLε). For *utilitate illa* referring back to *utilitatem* cf. TLL s.v. *ille* 357.83. The antonyms *constituo* and *convello* stand contrasted. For the general idea cf. *Off.* 1.31: *ea cum tempore commutantur, commutatur officium et non semper est idem.*—The whole argument since § 40 has tended to show that *utilitas* does not necessarily provide for *iustitia;* cf. also *Fin.* 3.70: *minime vero probatur huic disciplinae de qua loquor* [sc. *sectae Stoicorum*] *aut iustitiam aut amicitiam propter utilitates adscisci aut probari. eaedem enim utilitates poterunt eas labefactare atque pervertere;* for the argument applied to *amicitia* alone ibid. 2.78: *. . . si utilitas amicitiam constituet, tollet eadem.* Cicero took a different approach to the problem in *Off.,* denying that *utilitas* and *honestum* could diverge, but forced in the process to give *utilitas* a meaning different from that in ordinary use; cf. *ad* § 41.

43a Atque si natura confirmatum ius non erit,—quae est homini cum deo conservandas puto.] = *SVF* 3, 84.31–38.

Atque si natura confirmatum ius non erit, tollantur ⟨. . . necesse est⟩.] *Si natura confirmatum ius non erit: confirmatum* is the reading of Bˣ, rightly set in the text by Powell, rather than *confirmatura* (PL), the double future being unnecessary: "if right will not stand confirmed by nature . . ."—It does not necessarily follow from the preceding argument that to sever *iustitia* and *natura* would eliminate all the other virtues as well, as claimed by those who, with the *recentiores,* insert *virtutes omnes* in the lacuna, nor is this position supported by the following explanation *(enim),* which adduces instances only of the social virtues. Possibly Cicero may be assuming the doctrine of the interconnectedness of the virtues (ἀντακολουθία τῶν ἀρετῶν) and have chosen to provide only partial illustration, as at § 45 *infra* (see *ad loc.: nam si opinione universa virtus, eadem eius etiam partes probarentur*). Or one might assume, with J.G.F. Powell, the loss of a line of the archetype with the following sense: *tollantur ⟨omnia humanae societatis vincla necesse est⟩* (*necesse est* was part of Vahlen's insertion); another alternative would be to read with G. Striker ⟨*iustitia omnis*⟩ *tolla{n}tur*. In any case one can dispense with Ziegler's *utque* for *atque* and the rather unwieldy sentence entailed thereby.

ubi enim liberalitas, ubi patriae caritas, ubi pietas, ubi aut bene merendi de altero aut referendae gratiae voluntas poterit exsistere?] Two reciprocal pairs constituting major bonds that hold a community together: *patriae caritas* finds a response in *pietas; liberalitas* is virtually the same as *bene merendi de altero . . . voluntas;* its counterpart is the *referendae gratiae voluntas;* together these two qualities kept in motion the cycle of benefits on which ancient society depended; see further *ad Off.* 2.63. For *liberalitas* as a species of justice cf. *ad Off.* 1.42–60 (gratitude also may be considered as such; cf. the detailed analysis of ingratitude at Sen. *Ben.* 3); for *pietas* as a kind of justice toward the gods cf. *ad* § 60. Since these attributes require a commitment to something outside the self, they are assumed to be endangered by the egotist utilitarian view. Cicero is thus arguing from values generally accepted as good and worthy of preservation.[182]

nam haec nascuntur ex eo quia natura propensi sumus ad diligendos homines, quod fundamentum iuris est.] The propensity to love one's fellow human being was argued at §§ 33–34 (see *ad loc.*).—*Qui* of B¹APLε points to *quia* (H¹) as the likely original ("corrected" to *quod* in Bᵀ or *quo* Hˣ); cf. *Tusc.* 1.42: *quod ex eo sciri potest, quia corpora nostra terreno principiorum genere confecta ardore animi concalescunt.*

neque solum in homines obsequia, sed etiam in deos caerimoniae religionesque tolluntur; quas non metu sed ea coniunctione quae est homini cum deo conservandas puto.] *In homines obsequia . . . in deos caerimoniae:* the adnominal prepositional phrases appear without linking participle; cf *ad* 2.45 *(tum ebur, exanimi corpore extractum, haud satis castum donum deo).* For *in homines obsequia* cf. Liv. 1.35.5: *obsequio et observantia in regem;* sim. ibid. 29.15.3; *obsequium* appears with the objective genitive at Tac.

---

182. Cf. the similar argument with respect to *pietas* at N.D. 1.3–4: *in specie autem fictae simulationis sicut reliquae virtutes item pietas inesse non potest; cum qua simul sanctitatem et religionem tolli necesse est, quibus sublatis perturbatio vitae sequitur et magna confusio; atque haud scio an pietate adversus deos sublata fides etiam et societas generis humani et una excellentissima virtus iustitia tollatur;* this is, of course, a subsidiary argument (cf. Schmidt, 1959, 211: "Daß Tugend und Religionsausübung in utilitaristischer Sicht ihres Sinnes entkleidet würden, ist ja an sich kein Beweis für das Naturrecht . . .").

Dial. 41.3.—*Caerimoniae religionesque: caerimonia*, though first attested in Cicero (*Inv.* 2.66 and 161), seems likely to be an old word. The suffix -*monium* points to a quality, rather than an action; hence "holiness" will be the basic meaning. The origin of the word is obscure (an Etruscan connection is sometimes invoked). It is often used, as in our passage, in connection with another term from the religious sphere (cf. 2.55: *totaque huius iuris compositio pontificalis magnam religionem caerimoniamque declarat;* more examples of the phenomenon at *TLL* s.v., 100.29 ff.). Cf. in general Karl-Heinz Roloff, "Caerimonia," *Glotta* 32 (1953), 101–38.—*Non metu:* Epicurean theology aimed to relieve humans of fear of the gods (*N.D.* 1.45 and 56 [Velleius]); but the Skeptic Cotta claims that few believe in any case that the terrors of nature have a divine cause (ibid. 3.16). Here as elsewhere (cf. *Off.* 3.102) Cicero regards fear of the deity as inappropriate.—For the *coniunctio* of gods and men cf. *ad* § 23.

43b–47 quodsi populorum iussis,—non cernunt satis.] M. Untersteiner, "La dottrina di Protagora e un nuovo testo dossografico," *Riv. di Filologia Classica* n.s. 22–23 (1944–45), 21–99, argues that the view that Cicero opposes here ultimately goes back to Protagoras mediated via Panaetius and in turn via Antiochus; see esp. 87–88 for his reconstruction with parallels to Protagoras attached in footnotes. But as parallels Untersteiner mixes both fragments of Protagoras and materials from the Platonic *Protagoras*. In spite of some points of contact between the view attacked by Cicero and the relativity of Protagoras, it will hardly be possible to reach the doctrines of the sophist through so many layers of tradition; cf. Dyck *ad Off.*, pp. 358–59, on attempts to locate fragments of Democritus there.

43b quodsi populorum iussis, si principum decretis, si sententiis iudicum iura constituerentur, ius esset latrocinari, ius adulterare, ius testamenta falsa supponere, si haec suffragiis aut scitis multitudinis probarentur.] Cicero names three means of establishing *ius* at Rome: (1) *populorum iussa*, which may be expressed through (a) *suffragia* or (b) *scita*, (2) *principum decreta*,[183] (3) *sententiae iudicum*; a similar list of constituents of the *ius civile* at *Top.* 28 adds *iuris peritorum auctoritas* and *edicta magistratuum*, as well as *mos* and *aequitas*; on the whole topic cf. Watson, *Law Making*; Peter Stein, "The Source of Law in Cicero," *Ciceroniana* n.s. 3 (1978), 19–31.—*Ius* determined in such ways might well come into conflict with morality. *Latrocinari, adulterare,* and *testamenta falsa supponere* are given as egregious examples of wrongful acts; cf. similar lists at *Off.* 1.128, 3.36, and

---

183. He could have written *senatus decreta;* cf. the lack of expected reference to senators at 3.10.6, where he speaks of balloting being *optimatibus nota* (not *senatoribus*).

73.—*Falsa* is, of course, redundant; but such pleonasm is sometimes found, e.g., *Q. Rosc.* 51: *falsum subornavit testem Roscius Cluvium; Caec.* 71: *fictus testis subornari solet.*—The protasis with which the sentence begins provides the major premise, the last clause *si haec suffragiis—probarentur* the minor one.

44a quodsi tanta potestas est stultorum sententiis atque iussis ut eorum suffragiis rerum natura vertatur,—bonum eadem facere non possit ex malo?] The two rhetorical questions, underlining the impossibility of legislating morality, constitute a *reductio ad absurdum* of the conventionalist position.—In speaking of legislative acts as *stultorum sententiae* Cicero speaks as a philosopher rather than a senator or a pleader at court, as in the Stoic way of referring to non-sages; cf. *SVF* 4 s.vv. ἄφρων, φαῦλος.[184] Cf. also the philosophical detachment of *Div.* 2.142: . . . *nec mihi magis umquam videor, quam cum aut in foro magistratus aut in curia senatum video, somniare.*

atqui nos legem bonam a mala nulla alia nisi naturae norma dividere possumus.] Our sentence is perhaps the clearest formulation of the central point of Book 1; cf. *ad* 2.2. Nature, i.e., the human being's natural feeling for what is right or wrong, is to be the criterion for judging, not only right and wrong (as argued in §§ 45–46), but also legislation (cf. Girardet, 1983, 65) and will form, implicitly, the basis for the laws to be put forward beginning in Book 2. At 2.13, however, Cicero introduces a different terminology, according to which bad laws do not even deserve to be called laws; Girardet, 1983, 80 n. 63, concludes that the distinction in our passage between *lex bona* and *mala* is thus shown to have been provisional; but there is nothing in our passage to suggest that Cicero is speaking provisionally. The explanation will rather be found at § 19, where Cicero states *populariter interdum loqui necesse erit*, our passage being an instance of law in the "popular" sense.—The Epicureans would agree on nature as the criterion for judging laws but disagree on the implications (cf. *ad* § 42: *ita fit ut nulla sit omnino iustitia—*).

44b–46 Nec solum ius et iniuria naturā diiudicatur—ad naturam referenda sunt.] The attempt to establish that *ius* is by nature led Marcus to consider deterrence to crime as an effect of some kind of natural law (§§ 40–41); he then went on to consider the status of actual laws and to find that enactment alone does not secure them the status of natural law; rather nature (= φύσις) is to be the criterion for judging them (§§ 42–44a). At this point he broadens the discussion to include the *honestum* and *turpe*, the larger categories within which respectively *ius* and *iniuria* fall. The new argument is self-contained and should comprise a separate paragraph. We are told that on

---

184. Cf. also ἀνόητοι of the unenlightened at Pl. *Gorg.* 493a7.

the epistemological level the *communes intellegentiae* distinguish *honestum* and *turpe* as belonging respectively to virtue and vice. Marcus offers a series of supporting arguments of different types: (1) the argument from analogy to the natural world, an argument evidently translated from Greek since he hesitates to apply *virtus* to a horse or tree: if *virtus* is by nature here, so too the *honestum* in the case of humans; (2) the argument from the evaluation of *virtus* and its constituent parts, *prudentia* in particular; judgment is formed on the basis of the nature of the thing itself *(sua sponte, non aliena; sua natura)*; so virtue, too, is judged *sua natura*; (3) a partially mutilated argument, a variant, apparently, of nos. (1) and (2): the *ingenia* of young persons is judged by nature; if so, then virtue and vice, which arise from *ingenium*, are likewise so judged and *honestum* and *turpe* as well; (4) an argument from the most inclusive terms, *bonum* and *malum*: if they are by nature, so too the *honestum* and *utile*.

In our section, despite some residue of the previous invective *(ea . . . in opinione existimare . . . posita dementis est; . . . quo quid dici potest stultius?)*, we find some attempt at close reasoning. There are, however, problems with the argument, chiefly having to do with the term *nature*, that Cicero evidently does not see. The starting point is nature as a criterion of judgment *(naturā diiudicari*, used first of *ius* and *iniuria*, then of *honesta* and *turpia* in general): the original argument will have been that what is in accord with φύσις is δίκαιον, ἀγαθόν, etc., what is not is ἄδικον, αἰσχρόν, etc.; the "nature" in question will be the general human propensity to love our fellow humans (§ 43, argued for at §§ 33–34). To suppose that such things lie *in opinione* rather than *in natura* is called the view of a madman.[185] In this way we have made the transition from "judging" to "existing"—from epistemology to ontology. Hence the further argument that *virtus,* as *perfecta ratio,* is *in natura.* But existing *in natura* (= καθ᾽ἑαυτό) is not truly relevant to the criteria for judging *ius* and *iniuria.* Yet a third matter is to judge a thing with reference to "its own nature," variously expressed as *sua natura, sua sponte,* or *ex ipsius habitu* and opposed to *ex aliqua re externa* or *aliena sponte.* Here we are once again in the realm of φύσις, but this time the nature of the given thing. But this point would only help if Cicero meant to argue that *ius* and *iniuria* are judged by their own nature, when, in fact, he wants to show that they are judged by human nature. So we must burden Cicero, or possibly his source, with some fairly serious misunderstandings in this sector (cf. Schmidt, 1959, 213). Further problems: why is Marcus so confident in no. (1) that the *virtus* of a

185. See further *ad* § 45.

tree or a horse is not *in opinione?* Are such matters never subject to dispute? He also seems not to realize the difficulties entailed by the term *laudabile* (4); for praise is something bestowed or not bestowed by human beings, and human views of any kind are subject to disagreement; indeed there was, contrary to Marcus' implication, disagreement among philosophers as to what persons deserve the predicate *beati*.

44b Nec solum ius et iniuria naturā diiudicatur, sed omnino omnia honesta et turpia; . . .] This is likewise the position of Panaetius, followed by Cicero in *Off.* 1–2; contrast Hor. *S.* 1.3.113: *nec natura potest iusto secernere iniquum.*

nam ita communes intellegentia⟨s⟩ nobis natura efficit easque in animis nostris inchoat, ut honesta in virtute ponantur, in vitiis turpia: . . .] This is among the passages of *Leg.* involving multiple corruption. Transmitted is: *nam et communis intellegentia nobis notas res efficit . . .* It is helpful, however, that the context shows the function of this material in the argument: Cicero is going back to the doctrine of the *communes intellegentiae* (cf. § 26b) to establish a basis in nature for judgments about the morally good and bad; note the emphasis of the preceding and following sentences: *nec solum ius et iniuria naturā diiudicatur sed . . . omnia honesta et turpia; ea autem in opinione existimare non in natura posita dementis est.* Cf. *SVF* 2, 28.19–21: τῶν δὲ ἐννοιῶν αἱ μὲν φυσικῶς γίνονται . . . αἱ δὲ ἤδη δι' ἡμετέρας διδασκαλίας καὶ ἐπιμελείας . . . ; ibid. 3, 17.12–15: τὸν περὶ ἀγαθῶν καὶ κακῶν λόγον . . . συμφωνότατον εἶναί φησι τῷ βίῳ καὶ μάλιστα τῶν ἐμφύτων ἅπτεσθαι προλήψεων. We therefore agree with those scholars who, beginning with Bake, want to find a place for *natura* in our sentence, the obvious possibility being its substitution for *notas res*. The relation of *natura* to *communis intellegentia* is, as indicated clearly enough—in spite of the corruption of that text—in § 26, that of the creator to the thing created; hence Bake's *ita communis intellegentia⟨s⟩* (for *et communis intellegentia*) also seems to be needed—an easy enough corruption given the prima facie tendency to take *communis* as singular.[186] This conjecture has the added benefit of making *communes intellegentia⟨s⟩* the object of *inchoare*; cf. § 27: *. . . ex prima et inchoata intellegentia genera cognovit, confirmat ipsa per se rationem et perficit.* The distinction of good and evil is the desired outcome of the whole process. But how was the transition effected? Powell adopts P's *inchoat ut* and

---

186. Cf., with J.G.F. Powell, Thom. *S. th.* Iª 79.8: *intelligere enim est simpliciter veritatem intelligibilem apprehendere, ratiocinari autem est procedere de uno intellecto ad aliud, ad veritatem intelligibilem cognoscendam,* a view of *intelligere* as the beginning of a process of understanding that might help explain how a medieval scribe could have fallen into the text as transmitted.

change of the transmitted *ponuntur* to *ponantur*;[187] but the transition may have been subtler, the lacuna more extensive. For the general thought cf. Sen. *Ep.* 120.3–4: *nunc ergo ad id revertor . . . quomodo ad nos prima boni honestique notitia pervenerit. hoc nos natura docere non potuit: semina nobis scientiae dedit, scientiam non dedit . . . nobis videtur observatio collegisse et rerum saepe factarum inter se conlatio; per analogian nostri intellectum et honestum et bonum iudicant.*

45 ea autem in opinione existimare, non in natura posita, dementis est.] There was, in fact, an ancient debate on whether καλά and αἰσχρά are relative (πρός τι κατηγορούμενα) or absolute terms (κατὰ τὴν ἰδίαν φύσιν λεγόμενα). The position Cicero ascribes to a madman was espoused by Diogenes of Sinope and, to a degree, Zeno of Citium; cf. *ad Off.* 1.126–32a; sim. *Off.* 1.148. The third Epicurean scholarch, Polystratus, sided with the conventionalists in his treatise περὶ ἀλόγου καταφρονήσεως.[188]

nam nec arboris nec equi virtus quae dicitur (in quo abutimur nomine) in opinione sita est, sed in natura; . . .] For the argument cf. *ad* §§ 44b–46 and the next note.—The catachresis is inferred from the etymology: *appellata est . . . ex viro virtus* (*Tusc.* 2.43); *virtus ut viritus a virilitate* (Var. *L.* 5.73); cf. other passages cited by Maltby, 649. Though Cicero chooses to emphasize the oddity of the expression, *virtus* was broadly used in Latin from an early date; cf. *OLD* s.v. *virtus* 5. Similarly, the Greeks felt no difficulty in speaking, e.g., of the ἀρετή of a horse (Hdt. 3.88.3); Plato takes the opportunity to apply the term to the capacities of the eyes, ears, horses, dogs, and the soil; cf. Paul Friedländer, *Plato*, 2: *The Dialogues: First Period* (New York, 1964), 277.

quod si ita est, honesta quoque et turpia naturā diiudicanda sunt.] An argument of the form "what applies to the containing term does so also to the contained term." The moral categories *honesta* and *turpia,* applied to human beings, are treated as a special case of the *virtus* or its opposite of animals and plants (see also *universa virtus* in the next sentence), the difference being that plants (and animals according to most ancient analyses; cf. *ad* § 22) cannot choose. Hence if the *virtus* of animals and plants is "by nature," then the *honestum* (and its opposite) in human beings must be also. The point is argued again in § 46, where the species of the *bonum* is the *honestum* rather than *virtus* (as a result of the use of two different sources?).

iam si opinione universa virtus, eadem eius etiam partes probarentur.] *Iam* (Powell) is for transmitted *nam.*—"Parts" suggests a unitary concept of

187. If this is right, then Bake's *ita* for the *et* prior to *communes intellegentias* is well worth considering. Görler *ad loc.* provides a full list of previous suggestions.

188. Polystratus XXIV–XXVI Indelli.

virtue; cf. *ad* §§ 42–43a and *ad Off.* 1.15a and 152–61 and, for relevant Stoic doctrine, 61C–F Long-Sedley with M. Schofield, "Ariston of Chios and the Unity of Virtue," *Ancient Philosophy* 4 (1984), 83–96. Cicero infers the nature of the parts from the whole; in the sequel he might have been expected to go through all the virtues, but he contents himself with *prudentia* alone.

quis igitur prudentem et, ut ita dicam, catum, non ex ipsius habitu sed ex aliqua re externa iudicet?] *Ut ita dicam* apologizes for the poetic word *catus*, first used in extant prose in our passage (used without apologetic formula at *Luc.* 97 and *Tusc.* 2.45). For the equivalence with *prudens* cf. Aug. *gen. ad litt.* 12.18 p. 407.6: . . . *cum me quisque interrogat* . . . *quid sit catus et respondeo 'prudens vel acutus'* . . .—*Habitus* without other limitation usually refers to physical state in Cicero; cf., e.g., *Inv.* 2.159: *virtus est animi habitus;* but cf. *TLL* s.v., 2483.54–57, citing *Arch.* 15: *homines* . . . *naturae ipsius habitu prope divino* . . . *et moderatos et graves extitisse.*

est enim virtus perfecta ratio, quod certe in natura est; igitur omnis honestas eodem modo.] Sc. *iudicabitur* (Reid). Cf. § 22, where *sapientia* receives the predicate *perfecta ratio;* § 25: *est autem virtus nihil aliud nisi perfecta et ad summum perducta natura; Tusc.* 5.39: *hic igitur* [sc. *humanus animus*] *si est excultus* . . . *fit perfecta mens, id est absoluta ratio, quod est idem virtus; Fin.* 5.38: . . . *virtus* . . . , *quae rationis absolutio definitur* . . . Here, contrary to the usage of *Off.* (where they are equivalent; cf., e.g., 2.1; *ad* 2.18), *honestas* is contained within *virtus.* Marcus wants to be clear that the conclusion applies to *omnis honestas,* not just *prudentia.*—For initial *igitur* cf. *ad* § 18b.

nam ut vera et falsa, ut consequentia et contraria sua sponte, non aliena iudicantur, . . .] An unusual contrast of *sua sponte* and *aliena* [sc. *sponte*] in the sense "inherently" and "judged by external criteria" respectively; cf. *OLD* s.v. *spons* 6a. The examples are odd, however, since they are of antithetical terms, i.e., from Aristotle's category πρός τι, so in a sense they are what they are—*pace* Cicero—"judged by external criteria."

. . . sic constans et perpetua ratio vitae, quae virtus est, itemque inconstantia, quod est vitium, sua natura probabitur.] The same problem as in the prior half of the argument (see the previous note). The *constans et perpetua ratio vitae* is a paraphrase of the original τέλος-formula of the Stoics, τὸ ὁμολογουμένως ζῆν, perhaps to be understood in the etymological sense of "to live in accord with reason"; cf. *SVF* 1, 45.24–25: the exegesis of τὸ ὁμολογουμένως ζῆν as καθ᾽ ἕνα λόγον καὶ σύμφωνον ζῆν; *ad Off.* 3.13a. But taken on its own a *constans et perpetua ratio vitae* looks like a characteristic rather than a true definition of virtue; similar the relation of *inconstantia* to *vitium.* Nor does Cicero clarify the relation of this formulation to the definition of *virtus* just given *(perfecta ratio)*.—We follow Goerenz's change of *probavit* to *probabitur*. Madvig restored an argument similar to no. (1) (see *ad* §§ 44b–46): ⟨*iudicabitur. an arboris aut eculei*[189] *ingenium natura*⟩ *probabimus* (for *probavit nos*). But Cicero does not use *ingenium* elsewhere except of persons or personified concepts; cf *TLL* s.v. 1534.42 ff., esp. 1535.41–42 (*Tusc.* 3.69 with reference to philosophy).

⟨ . . . ⟩ **nos ingenia iuvenum non item?**] If *nos* is sound, then the preceding matter should have included a different subject for contrast. But possibly *nos* has been corrupted from the *-mus* suffix (see the preceding note), e.g., ⟨*haec ita probabimus*⟩, *ingenia iuvenum non item?* In any case, the argument seems to be that we pass judgment on persons not fully mature with reference to their own nature, including their potential for growth; we do not merely pass the negative judgment that they are not large enough; in this sense we can be said to judge them *sua sponte, non aliena*.

46 an ingenia natura, virtutes et vitia, quae exsistunt ab ingeniis, aliter iudicabuntur?] Here the argument becomes a bit slippery. In light of the preceding points one is inclined to read *natura* as a brachylogy for *sua natura*. In fact, the *sua* disappears at this point in the argument and never returns (cf. *non <u>ad naturam</u> referri necesse erit? . . . ipsum enim bonum non est opinionibus sed <u>natura</u> . . . honesta quoque et turpia . . . <u>ad naturam</u> referenda sunt*). Clearly judging a thing by *its own nature* is a different matter from judging it *with reference to nature itself,* and the judgment of values with reference to nature—the goal of the argument—should have been differently grounded; cf. *ad* §§ 44b–46.

⟨ . . . ⟩ **quod laudabile bonum est, in se habeat quo{d} laudetur necesse est; ipsum enim bonum non est opinionibus sed natura; . . .**] The transmitted text presents a hard transition.[190] Moreover, the proof that the *honestum* belongs to the *bonum*, which is the concluding point of this paragraph (see the note after next), has not been satisfactorily conducted. The first link in the chain was the establishment that *ingenium* was judged "by nature"; next comes the point that *virtutes et vitia, quae exsistunt ab ingeniis*, are so also, where the proof is provided by the relative clause. The *honestum* also requires proof, and this is provided in our sentence. In addition, in view of the following *ipsum bonum* it is clear that *laudabile* must limit *bonum*, rather than functioning as predicate. Thus *honestum* is likely to be the subject; and indeed the view that the *honestum* is a *laudabile bonum* is well attested; cf. *Fin.* 3.14; Klose, 109–10. Probably one should insert in the

---

189. For *eculeus* cf. *Hort.* fr. 98.
190. Schmidt, 1959, 213–14 n. 3, suggested insertion of *itaque* before *quod*.

lacuna *honestum enim,* which can easily have dropped out after *necesse erit.* Finally we adopt Zumpt's *quo* for the second transmitted *quod,* possibly carelessly repeated: "must have in itself that on account of which it is to be praised" is more precise than the alternative "must have in itself something to be praised," since the praise accrues to the *laudabile bonum* itself, not merely a portion of it.

nam ni ita esset, beati quoque opinione essent; quo quid dici potest stultius?] The *beati* are, implicitly, those in enjoyment of the *bonum.* Cicero's argument presupposes a commonsense consensus as to the *finis bonorum,* but this, of course, was not to be had even in antiquity.

quare cum et bonum et malum naturā iudicetur, et ea sint principia naturae, certe honesta quoque et turpia simili ratione diiudicanda et ad naturam referenda sunt.] Here Cicero argues from the position of the *honestum* and *turpe* within the larger categories *bonum* and *malum,*[191] which are said to be, in an ethical sense, the *principia naturae,* where *principia* evidently means "elements" (cf. *OLD* s.v. *principium* 6). The important move was somehow to connect *bonum* and *malum* with nature. In fact, all of the proofs have pertained to *bona* rather than *mala,* just as Cicero's *De Finibus Bonorum et Malorum* is really concerned with the *summum bonum.*

47 Marcus has just laid down *ipsum . . . bonum non est opinionibus, sed natura; nam ni ita esset, beati quoque opinione essent; quo quid dici potest stultius?* Perhaps, but the whole controversy over the *finis bonorum* shows that there was a variety of opinion on the topic. He therefore feels the need to add this section, an appendix explaining why this is so, i.e., why people's minds *quae natura bona sunt . . . non cernunt satis.* He distinguishes between the *sensus* and the *animus,* both of which are implicated, the former as the seat of *voluptas,* the latter as vulnerable to external influences. He thus offers a version of Chrysippus' account of the origin of vice; cf. *SVF* 3, 54.19 ff. = D.L. 7.89: διαστρέφεσθαι δὲ τὸ λογικὸν ζῷον ποτὲ μὲν διὰ τὰς τῶν ἔξωθεν πραγμάτων πιθανότητας, ποτὲ δὲ διὰ τὴν κατήχησιν τῶν συνόντων· ἐπεὶ ἡ φύσις ἀφορμὰς δίδωσιν ἀδιαστρόφους; sim. ibid. 55.1–4; cf. Pohlenz, *Stoa,* 1, 124. Our text, like the testimonies cited, offers a short version of the process without going into full epistemological detail about how false assents may arise (presumably from the other πάθη as well, not just pleasure). For the influence of this passage on John Toland see pp. 35–36 *supra.*

Sed perturbat nos opinionum varietas hominumque dissensio, . . .] Cf. *Tusc.* 4.23: *. . . pravarum opinionum conturbatio et ipsarum inter se repugnantia sanitate spoliat animum morbisque perturbat.*

---

191. See the note before last, also *ad* § 45, where they are species of *virtus.*

. . . et quia non idem contingit in sensibus, hos natura certos putamus, illa quae aliis sic, aliis secus, nec eisdem semper uno modo videntur, ficta esse dicimus.] Cicero draws a clear line of demarcation between the evidence of the senses and other matters on which opinions vary and which are called *ficta*.[192] The text reflects the Stoa's generally positive evaluation of the evidence of the senses; cf. 40 Long-Sedley; *SVF* 2, 33 ff.; Pohlenz, *Stoa* 1, 54 ff. Contrast *Luc.* 79–90, where Cicero argues the limitations of the senses in an Academic vein.

quod est longe aliter; nam sensus nostros non parens, non nutrix, non magister, non poeta, non scaena depravat, non multitudinis consensus abducit a vero; . . .] Here Cicero moves on to other sources of error that affect not the senses but the soul. The nurse, the parents, teachers, and the multitude recur as a source of *pravitas opinionum* at *Tusc.* 3.2. Chrysippus was much exercised by the rôle of the nurse; cf. Quint. *Inst.* 1.1.4 = *SVF* 3, 184.1: *ante omnia ne sit vitiosus sermo nutricibus, quas, si fieri posset, sapientes Chrysippus optavit, certe quantum res pateretur optimas eligi voluit;* sim. ibid. 16 = *SVF* 3, 183.36–37; ibid. 1.10.32; Lucr. 5.229–30; Tac. *Dial.* 29.1. Cicero's denial that the poets are to blame would be, of course, but for the next sentence, an implicit criticism of Plato's analysis (*Rp.* 377d ff.; cf. also *ad* § 4). The stage is criticized at *N.D.* 3.69: . . . *scaena . . . referta est his sceleribus . . .* ; further testimonies at Bernstein, 243 n. 83.—*A vero* is the reading of B^{X}A^X, *ad vero* that of B^1 and possibly A^1, *at vero*, after a stop, PHLε. Some editors (Vahlen, de Plinval) have preferred to end the sentence with *abducit* and begin the next with *at vero*. But when *abduco* occurs in the sense "entice" (with moral implications) the place or thing from or to which one is enticed needs to be specified (unless it is chastity or the like); cf. *OLD* s.v., 3b; *TLL* s.v., 62.75 ff.; nor is the conjunction needed here (see the next note).

animis omnes tenduntur insidiae, . . .] Following the previous denial, Cicero emphatically puts his finger on the target of these baneful influences, the *animi*, highlighted through asyndeton and initial position (thus contrasting with *sensus nostros*, emphatically placed in the previous sentence). For the sentence-division see the previous note.

. . . vel ab ea quae penitus in omni sensu implicata insidet, imitatrix boni voluptas, malorum autem mater omnium; . . .] An artful description: the descriptive relative clause placed in advance sounds a warning of the insidious

---

192. The failure of Panaetius to draw such a clear distinction is criticized by Scipio at *Rep.* 1.15: . . . *non nimis assentior in omni isto genere nostro illi familiari; qui, quae vix coniectura qualia sint possumus suspicari, sic affirmat ut oculis ea cernere videatur, aut tractare plane manu.*

nature of the phenomenon *(quae penitus in omni sensu implicata insidet)* followed by the appositional *imitatrix boni,* which will make it even more difficult to root out; notable the chiastic arrangement of the antithetical *imitatrix boni . . . malorum . . . mater* and the emphatic position of *omnium.* Cf. also *Inv.* 1.3: *commoditas quaedam, prava virtutis imitatrix.*—Especially in his theoretical works Cicero was fond of feminine agent-nouns in *-ix* (cf. § 27: *conciliatrix;* § 39: *perturbatrix;* von Albrecht, 1973, 1254.58–61) and may well have coined *imitatrix* (first attested *Inv.* 1.3: cf. *TLL* s.v.).—For *imitatrix boni voluptas* cf. *ad* § 31 *(quae* [sc. *voluptas*] *. . . habet quiddam simile naturali bono).*

cuius blanditiis corrupti, quae natura bona sunt, quia dulcedine hac et scabie carent, non cernunt{ur} satis.] For *blanditiis corrupti* cf. *Fin.* 1.33: *. . . qui blanditiis praesentium voluptatum deleniti atque corrupti quos dolores . . . excepturi sunt . . . non provident.*—Our passage is the first metaphorical use of *scabies* ("morbid itch," i.e., a strong yearning; cf. *OLD* s.v., 3); its juxtaposition with *dulcedo* effects a nice oxymoron.—The subject is the *animi* (cf. above: *animis omnes tenduntur insidiae*); hence *cernunt* of the *recentiores.*

48–52a At §§ 37–39 Cicero had postulated as the basis for further discussion that virtue is the sole or principal value. But here, surprisingly, he argues for this position nonetheless. He begins by establishing that *ius* and *omne honestum* is sought for its own sake. *Omne honestum* is then analyzed into its components, *aequitas et ius ipsum, liberalitas,* and *modestia/ temperantia/verecundia,*[193] and the same established for each (for the technique cf. Lausberg § 813). Chapter 49 essentially repeats the argument of § 48 (on *liberalitas* and related qualities) with an expanded set of examples. Chapters 50–51 (dealing with *modestia* and the like) consist almost exclusively of rhetorical questions.[194] The aim is to show that judging an action purely based on its consequences does not go to the root of the problem; *turpitudo* can inhere in the act itself. Chapter 52 argues from the hierarchy of goods: doing act A for the sake of B implies for B a superior position in the hierarchy; the tacit assumption is that virtue must be supreme and thus a virtuous act cannot merely be performed for the sake of some other end. Finally, virtue and pleasure are said to be antithetical concepts; only by rejecting pleasure can one attain virtue. At the end of § 52 Marcus restrains himself from continuing this dilation on the virtues as absolute values, not really required by the main argument that justice is by nature (he stresses the loose connection by calling it a *series rerum sententiarumque)* since at

193. The cohort of virtues is reduced, as it sometimes is, to those of the human being in society, with *fortitudo* omitted; cf. *ad Off.* 3.24.
194. For Schmidt, 1959, 221, § 51 represents "einen Höhepunkt der Polemik."

§§ 42–46 he has already tried to show that standards for justice are objective, not conventional. He has evidently not settled on a dialectical strategy. In revision he surely would have wanted to clarify the premises and scope of the argument, if not eliminate this section altogether, since the two groups set aside at § 39, the Epicureans and the Academic Skeptics, will still not be convinced (cf. *ad* § 52a: *quae et cum adsunt perparva sunt*—).

48 Sequitur—ut conclusa mihi iam haec sit omnis oratio—id quod ante oculos ex eis est quae dicta sunt: et ius et omne honestum sua sponte esse expetendum.] Certainly the bad effects of supposing that the *honestum* is to be sought for the sake of *utilitas* have been illustrated (§§ 42–43), and it has been argued that values should be judged "on their own terms" (*sua sponte:* §§ 45–46), but the general point has not been argued so much as presupposed from the outset by limiting the discussion to those *qui omnia recta atque honesta per se expetenda duxerunt* (§ 37). For the weak use of *sequitur* to link the next point in the argument cf. § 33.—The aside *ut conclusa mihi iam haec sit omnis oratio* is a tactic for keeping the audience's attention toward the end of a lengthy presentation; cf. *Sest.* 136: *sed ut extremum habeat aliquid oratio mea . . . concludam illud de optimatibus . . . ; Fin.* 4.73: *nos paucis ad haec additis finem faciamus aliquando;* ibid. 4.78: *itaque—iam enim concludatur oratio—hoc uno vitio maxime mihi premi videntur tui Stoici, quod se posse putant duas contrarias sententias optinere.—Ante oculos* is a metaphor for the evident; for the *iunctura* cf. 2.41; *TLL* s.v. *oculus* 446.19 ff.—*Ius* is placed at the front of its clause for emphasis, but Marcus wants to establish the same for the *honestum* and its other "parts" as well. By raising the topic of what is to be sought and for what reason, he steers the discussion toward the problem of the τέλος, which will occupy §§ 52–57; cf. Schmidt, 1959, 211 n. 1.

etenim omnes viri boni ipsam aequitatem et ius ipsum amant, nec est viri boni errare et diligere quod per se non sit diligendum; per se igitur ius est expetendum et colendum.] For justice (i.e., the cultivation of *aequitas et ius*) as the essential quality of the *vir bonus* see *ad* § 41.—The two instances of *ipse* belong to the type "describit aliquem (aliquid) ita, ut spectentur natura, qualitates ingenitae": cf. *TLL* s.v. *ipse* 337.62–63; examples in a context of moral doctrine (including our passage) ibid. 338.64 ff.; cf. also § 20 *(ipsius iuris ortum . . . repetamus).*

quodsi ius, etiam iustitia; . . .] *Ius* and *iustitia* are scarcely distinguishable here (cf. *OLD* s.vv. 7 and 1, respectively); the terminological shift accommodates the commonly accepted cardinal virtue and thus effects a transition to the argument that the same applies to all the virtues (*aliter* Mehl, 158 n. 26, seeking to find a distinction); see also the previous note.

sin ea, reliquae quoque virtutes per se colendae sunt.] This would follow from the unitary conception of virtue assumed here; cf. *ad* § 45 *(nam si opinione universa virtus, eadem eius etiam partes probarentur)*. The argument down to the end of § 52a comprises essentially variations on this theme.

quid liberalitas?—officium, non fructum sequatur.] Both here and in the similar argument at §§ 43 and 49 *liberalitas/beneficentia* is the first virtue cited because the idea of *liberalitas mercennaria* or *conducta* is patently absurd. Cf. Sen. *Ben.* 6.14.3: *illos ex toto praeteribo quorum mercennarium beneficium est quod qui dat non computat cui sed quanti daturus sit quod undique in se conversum sit.*—Ziegler wrote *si ⟨quis⟩ sine praemio benignus est, gratuita,* perhaps rightly; but the transmitted text can stand if *vir bonus* can be extrapolated from the preceding *viri boni.*—The words *nec est dubium—fructum sequatur* are cited at Lact. *inst.* 6.11.14; the only variant is the inferior *benignusque* for *-ve;* cf. Schmidt, 1965, 329 n. 43.—For the *iunctura officium sequi* cf. *Sex. Rosc.* 1, *Fin.* 2.58, and *Div.* 1.27.

ergo item iustitia nihil exprimit praemi, nihil preti; per se igitur expetitur, eademque omnium virtutum causa atque sententia est.] *Exprimo* has the sense "elicit, extort, extract": cf. *OLD* s.v., 4a (*expetit* of the *recentiores* is unnecessary).—*Sententia* is the "sense" of the virtues (cf. *Dom.* 53, quoted *ad* 3.11.8; *OLD* s.v., 7), i.e., that they are sought for their own sake is part of the definition; cf. *Fin.* 2.48: . . . *ait eos* [sc. Epicurus] . . . *neque intellegere nec videre sub hanc vocem honestatis quae sit subicienda sententia; ad Off.* 2.42a; Nep. *Paus.* 1.3.

49 Atque etiam si emolumentis, non suapte ⟨natura⟩ virtus expenditur, una erit virtus, quae malitia rectissime dicetur.] *Atque etiam,* loosely stringing arguments together, becomes a mannerism in *Off.;* cf. *Off.* 1.8, 37, 90–91, and 2.21–22.—*Emolumentum* was probably originally "the output from a mill" (from *emolo* = "grind out"); cf. *OLD* s.vv. Though the English derivative has become specialized as "pay," the Latin word could be used broadly, as here, for "advantage" or "benefit" (= Greek ὠφέλημα; cf. *Fin.* 3.69).—Löfstedt, 2, 251–52, followed by von Albrecht, 1973, 1261.24–26, sought to defend the transmitted *suapte* by reference to Apul. *Met.* 9.25, but there *noxa* can be understood from the context (so already Oudendorp); Halm's *sua sponte* for *suapte* (based on H²'s correction of the latter to *sponte*) is followed by de Plinval; but *sponte* for *suapte* is likely to have been suggested to the scribe by the occurrence of *sponte* earlier in this paragraph. Moser's *suapte ⟨vi⟩* is adopted by Vahlen, Ziegler, and Görler but is improbable. *Suapte* in Cicero is almost always followed by *natura* (*de Orat.* 2.98; *Orat.* 164; *Fin.* 1.54, 5.36, 5.61; *Fat.* 42; cf. Acc. *Atr.* 234 at *Tusc.* 2.13); the exceptions are *de Orat.* 3.10 *(suapte interfectum manu)* and *Fat.* 43 *(suapte vi et natura);* this last passage suggests that *suapte vi* would not have sufficient weight to stand on its own; hence Minutianus' *suapte natura,* here adopted.—In light of *suapte natura* it becomes possible to retain *expenditur* (= "is weighed") of the archetype (so Powell), rather than, as is usually done, substitute P's *expetitur.*—Halm's *illa* for *una* (an easy corruption) is well worth considering: the word in this position must bear considerable weight; yet this is not an argument for the unity of virtue but for its having a certain content; a scribe could easily have mistaken the point and thought a contrast intended with *omnium virtutum* of the previous sentence.—If, as for the Epicureans (cf. §§ 41 and 42), *emolumenta* are the goal, then *malitia* (= injustice[195]), as the straightest route to that goal, usurps the place of *virtus* in value-judgments on human action, and we have a similar "transvaluation of values" to §§ 40–41; cf. *ad* § 40 *(quodsi poena—);* similarly, *malitia* is described as some people's equivalent of *sapientia* at *Off.* 2.10.

ut enim quisque maxime ad suum commodum refert quaecumque agit, ita minime est vir bonus; ut qui virtutem praemio metiuntur nullam virtutem nisi malitiam putent.] The *ut . . . ita* construction sets up an inverse proportion between the use of self-interest as a basis of conduct and worthiness of the name *vir bonus; ut . . . putent* is the result that flows from that relation. For *qui virtutem praemio metiuntur* cf. *ad* § 42.

ubi enim beneficus, si nemo alterius causa benigne facit?] Whether the epithet *beneficus* (or in the next sentence *gratus*) is deserved depends on the agent's state of mind. One is disqualified by conferring a benefit for the sake of one's own interest, rather than truly with an eye for the well-being of the other party (cf. *ad Off.* 2.69–70).

ubi gratus, si non eum respiciunt grati cui referunt gratiam?] This is the second of three rhetorical questions all of which presumably emphasize that selfishness negates the various social values, *beneficentia, gratia,* and *amicitia* being illustrated in turn. Transmitted is *. . . si non eum ipsi cernunt grati . . .* Previous solutions are listed by Görler *ad loc. Ipsi* is a problem; if it is to be read, it should refer to the object, rather than the subject.[196] The best solution so far proposed is Powell's change of the transmitted *ipsi cernunt* to *respiciunt:* "where is gratitude to be found, if grateful people do not have regard for those to whom they repay thanks." Less convincing is the change of *cernunt* to *spernunt* and deletion of *non* (Philippson, 1929, 979), even if one also changes *ipsi* to *ipsum,* since *spernunt* seems too harsh in this

195. *Malitia* is differently defined (= *versuta et fallax ratio nocendi*) at *N.D.* 3.75.
196. Cf. Watt, 1997, 242, proposing *ipsum* or, rather, with A.E. Housman, *The Classical Papers,* ed. J. Diggle and F.R.D. Goodyear, 2 (Cambridge, 1972), 873–74, *eumpse.*

context, and the deletion of *non* is a further disadvantage.[197] For the thought
cf. *Fin.* 2.117: *tollitur beneficium, tollitur gratia, quae sunt vincla concordiae. nec enim cum tua causa cui commodes, beneficium illud habendum
est sed faeneratio, nec gratia deberi videtur ei qui sua causa commodaverit.*

**ubi illa sancta amicitia, si non ipse amicus per se amatur toto pectore, ut
dicitur?**] *Sancta amicitia* occurs only here and at Catul. 109.6 *(aeternum hoc
sanctae foedus amicitiae)*. *Illa* points an ironic thrust at the Epicurean view
of friendship (Schmidt, 1959, 215 n. 7). At *Amic.* 56 ff. Cicero repudiates
the view that friendship should be carefully managed with an eye on equality
of benefit; cf. also § 34 and the polemic against the Epicurean view of
friendship at *Fin.* 2.78 ff.; ibid. 3.70: *minime vero probatur huic disciplinae
[sc. Stoicorum] de qua loquor aut iustitiam aut amicitiam propter utilitates
adsisci aut probari.* *Toto pectore* is a proverbial phrase (= "heart and
soul"): see *TLL* s.v. *pectus* 915.57 ff.; *OLD* s.v., 4b; A. Otto, 270.

**qui⟨n⟩ etiam deserendus et abiciendus est desperatis emolumentis et fructi-
bus; quo quid potest dici immanius?**] *Qui⟨n⟩* is Davies' correction.—The
gerundives make these actions in form duties (cf. *Off.* 1.103 with note);
hence the strong reaction.—For *emolumentum* see the first note on this
section.—*Immanis* (= "savage, brutal": *OLD* s.v., 1) is often expressive of
a viscerally negative reaction.

**quodsi amicitia per se colenda est, societas quoque hominum et aequalitas et
iustitia per se expetenda; . . .**] A similar argument to the one that apparently
stood at §§ 33–34.—Society was postulated by the Stoa as something naturally sought by human beings (cf. *ad Off.* 1.12 and 2.72–85); therefore it is
odd to see it lumped together with *aequalitas* and *iustitia* as something that
ought to be sought per se.—*Aequalitas* is evidently used here of equality of
rights under law (ἰσοτιμία); cf. *TLL* s.v. 1003.26 (where our passage is cited
as the first use in this sense).—Lambinus' insertion of *est* before *expetenda* is
unnecessary; cf. Kühner-Stegmann, 1, 14.

**quod ni ita est, omnino iustitia nulla est; id enim iniustissimum ipsum est,
iustitiae mercedem quaerere.**] This looks like a thrust at the Epicurean account of justice, emphasizing its psychic benefits as relieving one of the fear
of punishment for wrongdoing; cf. §§ 40–41; Mitsis, 1988, 76–79.

**50 Quid vero de modestia, quid de temperantia, quid de continentia, quid
de verecundia pudore pudicitiaque dicemus?**] This continues the argument
broached at the beginning of § 48 that *omne honestum*, including all of the
virtues, is to be sought for its own sake: upon the treatment of *liberalitas*

---

197. Watt, *loc. cit.*, has proposed *cernuntur grati quoi referunt gratiam*, glossed as "if
people are not seen to be grateful to the man himself to whom they repay a favour." But the
idea of "being seen to be grateful" places an unwelcome emphasis on the subjective element.

and *iustitia* (§§ 48–49) now follows that of *temperantia*.—As elsewhere, Cicero uses a congeries of synonyms for σωφροσύνη; cf. *Tusc.* 3.16; *ad Off.* 1.93. Most of these nouns or their adjectival or verbal correlates will recur in the following discussion *(continentia–continentes; verecundia–verecundi; pudor–pudet).—Pudor* and *pudicitia* are distinguished as mental state and a state of bodily purity respectively; cf. *OLD* s.vv.; on *pudor* see further Robert Kaster, "The Shame of the Romans," *TAPhA* 127 (1997), 1–19, who promises a detailed study of the subject; on *pudicitia* cf. Mueller, csp. (on Cicero) 239 and n. 68.

infamiaene metu non esse petulantes, an legum et iudiciorum?] Sc. *dicemus. Petulantia* is the opposite of *pudor;* cf. *Cat.* 2.25: *ex hac enim parte pudor pugnat, illinc petulantia;* for Cicero's conception of *petulans/petulantia* see further *ad Off.* 1.127.

innocentes ergo et verecundi sunt ut bene audiant, et, ut rumorem bonum colligant, erubescunt?] A *reductio ad absurdum* of the opposing position; especially striking is the instinctive blush seen as part of a calculated plan *(ut rumorem bonum colligant).*

pudet iam loqui de pudicitia; . . .] *Pudet iam* is Madvig's correction for *pudi etiam* (B¹: *pudet etiam* BˣAˣ). The *iam* indicates that while Marcus may not mind discussing *pudicitia* per se, he is ashamed to go on treating it in this vein (for it degrades the subject of discussion).—This is a nice instance of παρονομασία; cf. parallels at Holst, 77–78.

ac me istorum philosophorum pudet, qui †ullum iudicium vitare nisi vitio ipso mutatum† putant.] Marcus' general shame over this topic is probably continued and intensified in his shame over these philosophers' attitude; hence *ac* (ω) need not be altered with Zumpt to *at.*—Various solutions have been put forward for this *locus conclamatus* (see list provided by Görler *ad loc.* and now Watt, 1997, 242), none of them convincing. Cicero's "shame" surely results from the attitude of the philosophers whom he has been criticizing, who posit that the virtues should be cultivated with a view to external benefits and vice only avoided if it carries a penalty or stigma. If that is so, then I would expect something like: *qui volunt aliorum*[198] *iudicium vitare nec crimen vitio ipso notatum*[199] *putant,* i.e., they wish to avoid a (negative) judgment (cf. *infamiae metu,* both above and in § 51) and do not consider a misdeed to have been branded as infamous by the vice itself (cf. § 51: . . . *cuius turpitudo ex ipsis vitiis facillime percipi potest);* J.G.F. Powell suggests *qui quemquam pudicum vocari nisi vitio ipso intactum putant.*—For shame as a factor in philosophical discussion cf. *ad* § 41.

198. *Ullum* Aε : nullum PHL : *illum* B.
199. *Notatum* HLSR : *nutatum* B¹E : *mutatum* Bˣ AP.

51 quid enim? possumus eos qui a stupro arcentur infamiae metu pudicos dicere, cum ipsa infamia propter rei turpitudinem consequatur?] *-ne* need not be attached to *possumus* since the question is signaled by the preceding *quid enim?*—Here Marcus puts his finger on the problem with using *infamia* as a criterion, namely that *infamia* in the ordinary sense of social stigma can be avoided by the careful criminal; hence he distinguishes this from *ipsa infamia*, linked to *rei turpitudo*. Cf. *ad Off.* 3.35 *(poena ipsius turpitudinis)*; Garnsey, 191 n. 1.—On *stuprum* cf. *ad* 2.10.

nam quid aut laudari rite aut vituperari potest, si ab eius natura recesseris quod aut laudandum aut vituperandum putes?] To call someone *pudicus*, as in the previous sentence, is, of course, a *laudatio*. Praise and blame are associated with *temperantia* and *libido* but also with the virtues and vices generally, so that, though particular virtues have been discussed since § 48b *(quid liberalitas?—)*, the topic broadens here once again. Now praise and blame are dealt with by rhetoric as well,[200] under precepts for the proper subject of encomium; cf. *Inv.* 1.94 (on faults of argumentation): ... *aut si qui, cum aliquem volet laudare, de felicitate eius, non de virtute dicat ...* ; on *virtus* as the proper subject of *laudatio* cf. *Part.* 70–71; on actions undertaken *sine emolumento et praemio* as the ones to which *gratissima laus* accrues cf. *de Orat.* 2.346. But a philosophical treatment, as in our passage, goes to the level of the motive of an act and denies the name of the virtue altogether if the right motive (a part of the *natura* of the virtue) is missing. Similar to our lemma are some of the arguments at §§ 45–46 about things being judged by their own nature or by alien criteria (see *ad* §§ 44b–46).

an corporis pravitates, si erunt perinsignes, habebunt aliquid offensionis, animi deformitas non habebit, ...] An a fortiori argument from the body to the mind, a form of which Cicero was fond (cf. *ad Off.* 1.14); sim. 2.24. Roman invective did not scruple to target physical deformities; cf., e.g., *de Orat.* 2.262 and, in general, Corbeill, 20 ff. *Inv.* 2.178, however, recommends targeting *animus* and not *fortuna.*—*Perinsignis* is a ἅπαξ; cf. *TLL* s.v. On Cicero's fondness in philosophical dialogue for adjectives compounded with the "urbane" prefix *per-* cf. p. 40 n. 143 *supra.*—Our passage is the first use of *deformitas* of mental qualities, though the way had been prepared by its use with reference to speech at *de Orat.* 1.156 and 2.236; cf. *TLL* s.v., 370.11 ff.

... cuius turpitudo ex ipsis vitiis facillime percipi potest?] Either *percipio* or *perspicio* can be used with *ex* in this way (cf. for the former *Ver.* 33,

---

200. Cf. *Part.* 70: *laudandi vituperandique rationes, quae non ad bene dicendum solum sed etiam ad honeste vivendum valent ...*

1.57; for the latter § 34). We therefore stick with the transmitted text rather than adopt *perspici* of the *recentiores* (attributed to Poggio by Schmidt, 1974, 284).

quid enim foedius avaritia, quid immanius libidine, quid contemptius timiditate, quid abiectius tarditate et stultitia dici potest?] These are vices corresponding to the four cardinal virtues: *avaritia* to *iustitia/liberalitas*, *libido* to *temperantia, timiditas* to *fortitudo,* and *tarditas* and *stultitia* to *sapientia;* they reappear at *Fin.* 3.39. Each of them provokes a distinct negative reaction. For *avaritia* cf. the definition at *Tusc.* 4.26 and the visceral reaction at *Off.* 2.77 (*nullum vitium taetrius est . . . quam avaritia . . .).* For *immanius* cf. *ad* § 49; *libido* corresponds to ἐπιθυμία, one of the four passions recognized by the Stoa; cf. *SVF* 3, 96.14 ff.; *ad* § 32; it is distinguished from *voluntas* at *Tusc.* 4.12. For *quid contemptius timiditate?* cf. *Off.* 1.61; for the last in the series ibid. 1.94: *. . . falli errare labi decipi tam dedecet quam delirare et mente esse captum . . .*

eos qui singulis vitiis excellunt aut etiam pluribus, propter damna aut detrimenta aut cruciatus—in virtute dici potest.] Much of Plato's *Republic* is given over to arguing this point in response to the revival at the beginning of Book 2 by Glaucon and Adimantus of Thrasymachus' position that the virtue or vice of an act is to be judged on the basis of its consequences; cf. in particular the example of the just man with a reputation for injustice and vice versa at 361c–d, imitated in Philus' speech at *Rep.* 3.13.

quod item ad contrariam laudem in virtute dici potest.] Cf. *de Orat.* 2.349: *iam vituperandi praecepta contrariis ex vitiis sumenda esse perspicuum est.*—For *in* = "in the matter of," virtually equivalent to *de*, cf. OLD s.v., 42; Wilkins on *de Orat.* 2.96.

52a Postremo, si propter alias res virtus expetitur, melius esse aliquid quam virtutem necesse est.] Cf. the classification of goods at Pl. *Rp.* 357b4 ff. or the hierarchy whereby the activity that includes its own τέλος ranks above the one pursued for the sake of a product (ἔργον) at Arist. *EN* 1094a3 ff.; *ad* §§ 48–52a.

pecuniamne igitur, an honores, an formam, an valetudinem?] The construction of *melius esse . . . necesse est* carries over from the previous clause. Of the four examples the former two fall into the class of external goods, the latter two are goods of the body.

quae et cum adsunt perparva sunt, et quam diu adfutura sint certum sciri nullo modo potest.] The underlying assumption is the stability of εὐδαιμονία; cf. Arist. *EN* 1100b2–3: *. . . διὰ τὸ μόνιμόν τι τὴν εὐδαιμονίαν ὑπειληφέναι καὶ μηδαμῶς εὐμετάβολον . . .* This could argue against the Epicurean doctrine that pleasure is the *summum bonum,* and Epicurus sought to counter it with the assertion that what matters is the overall pleasantness of one's life, not the duration of individual pleasures; cf. *Fin.* 1.63 and 2.87 ff.; Mitsis 1988, 24–25.—This valuation of the external goods and those of the body is found most famously in the "balance of Critolaus"; cf. Critol. frr. 19–24 with Wehrli's note. A similar line was, according to Plut. *Comm. not.* 1065a, taken by Xenocrates (fr. 249 I.P. = 92 H.) and Speusippus (fr. 107 I.P. = 59 L.); an Epicurean would, of course, hardly accept this view (cf. § 39).—*Perparvus* of value rather than size apparently occurs first here in classical Latin (cf. also 2.47); cf. *OLD* s.v.; for *per-* compounds in general cf. p. 40 n. 143 *supra.*—*Certum scire* is fairly commonly used for *pro certo scire*: cf. *OLD* s.v. *certus* 4b.

an—id quod turpissimum dictu est—voluptatem? at in eā quidem spernendā et repudiandā virtus vel maxime cernitur.] Cicero's argument shows that *virtus* and *voluptas* are irreconcilable goals[201] but does not establish the priority of *virtus;*[202] for this he evidently relies upon societal norms as well as the way the discussion has been framed at §§ 37–39. Here the Epicurean view of the *summum bonum* is dismissed with a similar contempt to that shown at § 39; cf. also *Fin.* 2.37; *Parad.* 14; *Amic.* 32.—The *quidem* is emphatic with some contrasting force; cf. Solodow, 97.

Sed videtisne quanta series rerum sententiarumque sit, atque ut ex alio alia nectantur? quin labebar longius, nisi me retinuissem.] Cf. *N.D.* 1.9 (a description of the various subdivisions of philosophy): *est enim admirabilis quaedam continuatio seriesque rerum ut alia ex alia nexa et omnes inter se aptae colligataeque videantur.* As Busuttil *(ad loc.)* points out, *series* points to sequence, *ex alio alia nectantur* to interrelations; cf. *Fin.* 3.74 (Cato on the consistency of Stoic doctrine): *quid non sic aliud ex alio nectitur ut, si unam litteram moveris, labent omnia?* The implication seems to be that Marcus could go on in this vein indefinitely. Yet it is he, rather than one of his interlocutors, who wants to rein in the argument, whereas Quintus is willing to see his brother continue. The dramatic incoherence at this point mirrors an incoherence of plan, whereby the argument has proceeded since § 48 by free association (cf. *ad* §§ 48–52a). It is Quintus who, at § 56, will finally put an end to this process of sliding from point to point *(labebar)* and call the conversation back to the stated topic.—*Ut ex alio alia nectantur*: cf. *ad* §14 *(aliud ex alio).*—*Quin labebar longius, nisi me retinuissem* is a

---

201. On this dichotomy cf. *ad* §§ 38–39.

202. Cf. Schmidt, 1959, 217. For the relation of virtue and pleasure cf. also *Fin.* 2.117: *maximas vero virtutes iacere omnis necesse est voluptate dominante.* Here, as sometimes elsewhere, Cicero neglects the Stoic distinction between mental and physical pleasure, the latter allowed in moderation; cf. *Off.* 3.119 with note.

formula for returning to the subject after a digression; cf. *Div.* 2.79: *sed labor longius; ad propositum revertar;* sim. *Fam.* 9.10.3; *Pis.* 33: *sed perge porro; N.D.* 2.92: *sed ad maiora redeamus; Fin.* 2.104: *ut ad propositum;* J. Colin Davies, "*Reditus ad rem*: Observations on Cicero's Use of *Digressio*," *RhM* 131 (1988), 305–15, classifies different types of linkages between *digressio* and argument in the speeches.—For the imperfect indicative *(labebar)* denoting an act in progress interrupted by the contrafactual subordinate clause cf. Kühner-Stegmann, 2, 404–5, citing our passage.

Q. Quo tandem?] Sc. *labebaris.* Quintus' *tandem* implies impatience to know where this is leading; cf. Atticus' queries *Quorsum tandem {aut cur} ista quaeris?* (§ 4) and *sed quorsus hoc pertinet?* (§ 63).

libenter enim, frater, quo d⟨ucis⟩ ista oratione, tecum prolaberer.] *Quod istam orationem* is the reading of the archetype (B¹A¹HLε), corrected to *cum ista oratione* (BˣAˣ). But *cum* is not wanted twice in this clause with two quite different objects; and, if *cum ista oratione* were correct, one would expect coordination following, i.e., either *tecumque* or *et tecum;* nor does *oratio* fall into the possible semantic categories for ablative of accompaniment with *cum* (cf. Kühner-Stegmann, 1, 407 ff.). An improvement on Ziegler's *quo duces* is J.G.F. Powell's *quo ducis;* he explains *per litt.* that he assumes "that this was first contracted to *quoducista oratione,* then the beginning read as *quod,* and the *uc* deleted as meaningless."—The *recentiores* supply the needed imperfect subjunctive *prolaberer* (= "I would gladly continue gliding forward"); it was truncated to *prolaber* in B¹PεHL.[203] The meandering course of this conversation is described with the verb *declino* at § 57.

52b–57 This excursus on the problem of the *finis bonorum* is similar in tendency to § 37 in that both aim to reduce the distance between the Stoa and the Academy/Peripatos, whereas § 52a discusses related issues without attaching school labels. Our passage barely gets beyond a report of the principal positions before Quintus interrupts and steers discussion firmly back to the subject previously agreed upon. Atticus lightens the tone with the mention of L. Gellius' well intended but misguided attempt to reconcile the philosophical schools, and the interlude concludes with Marcus' pun on *fines* in the technical philosophical and in the ordinary sense.

52b–56 The question whether the virtues are to be sought for their own sake, dealt with in §§ 48–52a, forms part of the larger problem of the *finis bonorum,* on which Cicero now digresses (cf. § 57: *at ego huc declinabam, nec invitus*); cf. the systematic survey of relevant doctrines at *Fin.* 5.15–28

---

203. Cf. *testificare* A¹R for *testificarere* A² P at *Fin.* 2.51.

and *Tusc.* 5.84–85. Just as in politics Cicero endeavored to establish and maintain a *concordia ordinum* and later, when civil war threatened in early 49, tried to reconcile Caesar and Pompey, so here he offers himself as an arbiter between the disputing parties. Now a dispute can be resolved either by judging one of the parties the winner or by showing that there was no real disagreement in the first place. Cicero's approach to the dispute between Zeno and the Old Academy on the *finis bonorum* is a combination of the two: first he suggests that their disagreement is *verbis* and not *re* (§ 54), but then he seems to declare the Old Academy the winner by right of prior possession (§ 55). Quintus intervenes to move discussion back to its proper subject (§ 56) before the issue has been fully clarified.

52b M. Ad finem {tecum} bonorum, quo referuntur et cuius a⟨dipi⟩scendi causa sunt facienda omnia: . . .] *Tecum*, evidently repeated from the previous sentence, was already deleted by B^x and A^x (and omitted in P).—*Quo referuntur . . . omnia:* cf. *Fin.* 1.29 and 42; ibid. 5.16; *ad* § 20.—*A⟨dipi⟩scendi*, proposed by Schmidt, 1974, 118, for *ascindi* of ω is surely needed here; Victorius' *a⟨pi⟩scendi* was favored by editors prior to Görler. But if *a⟨di⟩piscendi* is correctly read at *Att.* 8.14.3,[204] *apiscor* is an archaism nowhere used by Cicero; cf. Shackleton Bailey, 1997, 333 and n. 1; Woodman and Martin *ad* Tac. *An.* 3.31.2. For *adipiscor* cf. § 59; for a similar *iunctura* cf. *Fin.* 4.46: . . . *ut is qui eam* [sc. *summam bonorum*] *adeptus sit nihil praeterea desideret.*—*Cuius a⟨dipi⟩scendi causa sunt facienda omnia* is a second paraphrase of the technical term *finis bonorum*, on which Cicero will pun (§ 55 *fin.*).

. . . controversam rem et plenam dissensionis inter doctissimos, sed aliquando tamen iudicandam.] The point *controversa res et plena dissensionis inter doctissimos* is found in skeptical arguments for ἐποχή in light of unsettled disagreement;[205] it is thus surprising for an Academic Skeptic like Cicero to follow it up with *sed aliquando tamen*[206] *iudicandam.* Marcus' legal metaphor *(iudicandam)* causes Atticus to think of Gellius, who, as Reid observes, treated the controversy among philosophical schools as if it were a lawsuit (cf. § 53: *quodsi essent eo animo ut nollent aetatem in litibus conterere* . . .).

53 A. Qui istuc fieri potest, Lucio Gellio mortuo?] L. Gellius (b. ca. 136; pr.

---

204. *Ait enim Lepidus eum* [sc. *Domitium*] *nescio quo penetrasse itineribus* ⟨*occultis*⟩, *occultandi sui causa an maris a⟨di⟩piscendi . . . (adipiscendi* Pδ : *apiscendi* Ω).

205. Sim. *Fin.* 1.11; *Tusc.* 5.83; *N.D.* 1.1 and 94; in the first and third of these passages there is likewise reference to the *doctissimi* (cf. also § 18); at *Tusc.* 5.83 they are *dissentientes philosophi.*

206. *Tamen* is the reading of PHL for *tam* of B^{1}ε and *iam* B^{x}A^x.

94, cos. 72, cens. 70) was a *familiaris* of Cicero, as our passage indicates (cf. also *Brut.* 105).[207] He was an unlucky opponent of Spartacus and of the agrarian law carried during Caesar's consulate, as well as a legate in Pompey's war with the pirates. He was unstinting in his praise of the firm handling of the Catilinarian conspirators by his fellow *homo novus* (*Pis.* 6). His last years were clouded when his son by his first marriage fell under grave suspicion of having committed adultery with his stepmother and of plotting his father's murder; Gellius, however, acquitted him in a family court (V.Max. 5.9.1); however, Wiseman, 1974, 119–29, esp. 127, suggests that, contrary to V.Max., the man who acquitted his son in family court was the son of the censor. L. Gellius was still in the senate in 55 (*Pis.* 6). At the time of the composition of our passage (ca. 52) his death must have been fairly recent. Cf. Münzer, *RE* 7.1 (1910) s.v. Gellius no. 17.

Quia me Athenis audire ex Phaedro meo memini,—si posset inter eos aliquid convenire.] The incident will have occurred in 93 when Gellius was en route to or from the eastern province he was assigned as proconsul following his praetorship and thus before Atticus took up residence in Athens in 86 (cf. *MRR* 2, 15; R. Feger, *RE* Suppl. 8 [1956], 505.17 ff.). Hence the attribution of the story to Phaedrus. On Atticus' special closeness to the Epicurean philosopher *(ex Phaedro meo)* cf. *Fin.* 1.16 and 5.3; *Fam.* 13.1.5. Atticus clearly cites the incident with tongue in cheek (see the next note); and in the same spirit Cicero offers himself as a successor to this would-be Roman mediator *(sed ego plane vellem me arbitrum . . .).—Quodsi essent eo animo ut nollent aetatem in litibus conterere:* Gellius' mistake was that, as a hard-headed Roman, he assumed that this activity was merely distracting them from matters they would rather be getting on with; cf. the depiction of the philosopher's life at *Fin.* 5.57 (similar phrasing to Gellius' supposition is underlined): *tantaque est vis talibus in studiis ut eos etiam qui sibi alios proposuerunt fines bonorum, quos utilitate aut voluptate derigunt, tamen in rebus quaerendis explicandisque naturis aetates conterere videamus.*—Noting the repetitiveness of *posse rem convenire* and *si posset inter eos aliquid convenire,* Powell *ad loc.* suspects that in revision Cicero would have canceled one of these versions unless perhaps, as Bake mooted, he meant to convey some of the flavor of Gellius' speech.

M. Ioculare istuc quidem, Pomponi, et a multis saepe derisum.] Were the

---

207. The cognomen Poplicola sometimes attributed to him evidently stems from a confusion with his adopted son, L. Gellius Poplicola (cos. 36); cf. E. Badian, "The Clever and the Wise: Two Roman *cognomina* in Context," in *Vir bonus discendi peritus: Studies in Celebration of Otto Skutsch's Eightieth Birthday,* ed. Nicholas Horsfall, *BICS* Suppl. 51 (London, 1988), 8 n. 11.

many *(multi)* laughing with Gellius at the philosophers or at Gellius? Translators and interpreters have taken both views.[208] Note the adverbial phrase *magno opere* in the narrative of his actions: there is no hint of a twinkle in his eye; he had taken pains to convene the philosophers to a single place and was exerting himself in earnest to persuade them; it was just that, in treating the dispute as if it were a piece of litigation (see above), he completely misunderstood its nature and so was laughed at (and this is the only possible meaning of *derideo* here [cf. *OLD* s.v., 1a], whereas *iocularis* means "humorous" in a neutral sense without indicating whether the humor was intentional or not [ibid., s.v.]). But in spite of its having been laughed at so widely (*a multis saepe derisum* [sc. in learned circles]), the incident will hardly have been a factor in the long interval between Gellius' tenure of the praetorship and the consulate, *pace* Münzer, *RE* 7.1 (1910), 1002.15 ff.; rather there was a backlog of qualified consular candidates following the disordered conditions of the 80s (Sal. *Hist.* 1.86, a request that Curio stand down from candidacy for 77, is a symptom).

sed ego plane vellem me arbitrum inter antiquam Academiam et Zenonem datum.] With these words Marcus returns to his point that in spite of its contentiousness the dispute about the highest good must be resolved (*aliquando tamen iudicandam:* § 52). Here he follows Carneades (fr. 137 W. = *Tusc.* 5.120), who offered himself as an *honorarius arbiter* of the controversy *de finibus* and went on to make a similar point about a verbal discrepancy underlying the dispute (on which cf. *ad* § 38); sim. Chrysippus at *Fat.* 39. Setting Marcus' "wish" beside the behavior of the inept Gellius tempers any implied claim to wisdom on his part.—An *arbiter* could be chosen by agreement between the disputants in an extra-legal procedure *(ex compromisso)* or assigned *(datus)* by the presiding magistrate at a trial to settle a disputed point requiring specialized knowledge; in view of *datus* the latter is Cicero's model here; cf. Berger s.vv. *arbiter, arbiter datus, arbiter ex compromisso;* M. Wlassak, *RE* 2.1 (1895), 408.34 ff. The procedure was commonly used in boundary disputes; see further *ad* § 55.—Antiochus called his school the "Old Academy" (*vetus Academia:* testimonies at Görler, 1994, 942), but Cicero is not using *antiqua Academia* in this technical sense, as the sequel shows (§ 55: . . . *valde a Xenocrate et Aristotele et ab illa Platonis familia discreparet* . . .).

A. Quo tandem istuc modo?] Sc. *dicis.* Cf. 1.1.

54 M. Quae quidem ad rem pertineat, una: . . .] "(There is) one point of

---

208. Contrast, e.g., "Yes, that was a joke, Pomponius, and it has caused many a laugh" (Rudd) and "Das ist freilich lustig, Pomponius, und von vielen oft belacht worden" (Büchner). Cf. also the view of Görler, 1974, 202, that Gellius' offer was made "im Scherz."

disagreement such as to concern the substance": *res* as opposed to *verba*, the contrast made explicit in Marcus' next reply. A limiting force for *quidem* is best established on the basis of its use in relative clauses such as this; cf. Solodow, 108–9; Kühner-Stegmann, 2, 307–8. For subjunctive in a consecutive relative clause ibid. 296.

quippe cum antiqui omne quod secundum naturam esset, quo iuvaremur in vita, bonum esse decreverint, hic nisi quod honestum esset ⟨nihil⟩ putarit bonum.] The view of the philosophers of the Academy/Peripatos *(antiqui)* is contrasted with that of Zeno; cf. *Fin.* 5.21: ... *antiquis, quos eosdem Academicos et Peripateticos nominavimus; ad* § 38. For the doctrine cf. *Sen.* 71 with Powell's note.—We have adopted Bake's *omne* for *omnes* and Turnebus' *nihil*, the latter on the assumption that the error came about through the scribe's eye skipping from the *hasta* of the *t* of *esset* to the *hasta* of the *l*; Vahlen's *nihil esse* or Ziegler's *non* would also be possible.

A. Parvam vero controversiam dicis, at tamen eam quae dirimat omnia.] "That is a small point of disagreement, but nevertheless such as to cause a complete split." The text incorporates Powell's *at tamen* (= *attn.*) for the transmitted *at non* (= *atn.*). The traditional text develops the conversation in a problematic way, for Marcus' *Probe quidem sentires, si re ac non verbis dissiderent* is no intelligible response to *at non eam quae dirimat omnia*. *Probe quidem sentires* ... is framed as a reply to the idea that the controversy is a large matter or has large consequences, but this can hardly be inferred from *Parvam ... omnia*. Nor is there any sign that Atticus is speaking, or that Marcus understands him as speaking, ironically.—On the doctrine of goods as the dividing line among the philosophical schools cf. *Luc.* 132: ... *omnis ratio vitae definitione summi boni continetur, de qua qui dissident, de omni vitae ratione dissident; ad Off.* 3.12.

M. Probe quidem sentires, si re ac non verbis dissiderent.] In spite of his previous assertion that there was one point of disagreement in substance *(quae quidem ad rem pertineat, una)*, Marcus now adopts the position of Carneades (*Fin.* 3.41) that even this disagreement is purely verbal (cf. § 55: *non rerum sed verborum discordia*); cf. Fladerer 48–49 with literature at n. 166. Kraus, 305, would read *Probe quidem sentis* and then insert *tum enim magnopere dissentirent*. But Atticus has not acknowledged that the disagreement is merely *verbis* and not *re*; as an Epicurean, he may not have regarded it as significant even if *re*.—Cicero was no stranger to disputes centered on *verba*; indeed he makes the verbal dispute a major theme in his defense of A. Caecina: cf. Susanne Dagmar Mühlhölzl, *Cicero "pro A. Caecina"* (diss., Munich, 1992), 79 ff.

A. Ergo adsentiris Antiocho, familiari meo ('magistro' enim non audeo

dicere), **quocum vixi et qui me ex nostris paene convellit hortulis, deduxit-que in Academiam perpauculis passibus.**] Antiochus of Ascalon broke with Philo of Larissa and started his own school (the "old Academy" in Cicero's terminology; cf. *ad* § 53) headquartered in the Ptolemaeum, an elegant gymnasium outside Athens. In 79 he counted Cicero, Quintus, their cousin Lucius, Atticus, and M. Pupius Piso among his students (*Fin.* 5.1). On his life, doctrines, and works cf. Görler, 1994, 938 ff.—Atticus' loyalty to Epicureanism (cf. *ad* § 21 and *Fin.* 5.3) hinders him from calling Antiochus his *magister* in spite of the close personal connection described in our passage.—Atticus offers a witty pun *(me ex nostris paene convellit hortulis)*; for *convello* used of uprooting plants or trees cf. *TLL* s.v., 817.82 ff.; *paene* tones down the hyperbole (cf. *OLD* s.v., 2): "he all but uprooted me." For the diminutive *hortulus* as a way of referring to Epicurus' school cf. *ad* § 39; *nostris* attached to *hortulis* indicates Atticus' school affiliation; sim. Cicero's references to *Academia nostra* at *Tusc.* 3.7 and 12; *Off.* 3.20.—*Deduxitque in Academiam perpauculis passibus:* du Mesnil *ad loc.* explained *perpauculis passibus* as "ablativus intervalli"; but in classical Latin this construction is confined to a fixed group of verbs which does not include *deduco* (cf. Kühner-Stegmann, 1, 364 ff.). Hence, Watt, 1997, 242, inserted *exceptis* after *perpauculis* to clarify that Antiochus brought Atticus (meta-phorically) within a few steps of the Academy. On the other hand, Powell *(per litt.)* explains the transmitted text this way: "I would take *perpauculis passibus* as a sort of instrumental ablative 'by means of a few paces,' i.e., by walking a few paces, *perpaucos passus ambulando.*" Now Atticus' house was, according to § 3 (our sole testimony for its location), close to the place where Aquilo abducted Orithyia, i.e., near the Ilissus River, which was outside the city walls of Athens on the south, whereas the Academy was likewise outside the city walls, but on the northwest: the two were too distant to be described, even by a Roman, as separated by but a few paces. The reference of *nostri hortuli* must be rather to Epicurus' Garden (see above), which was located in the deme Melite (D.L. 10.17), which bordered the Ceramicus;[209] the Academy, on the other hand, was located in the Outer Ceramicus near the Colonus Hippius:[210] so surely *perpauculis passibus* em-phasizes the geographical proximity of the two.[211] *Deduxit in Academiam* = "brought me into the Academy" [sc. for instruction]; cf. *OLD* s.v. *deduco*

209. Honigmann, *RE* 15.1 (1931), 541.44–46.

210. Cf. John Travlos, *Pictorial Dictionary of Ancient Athens* (New York, 1980), 42.

211. Cf. plan at Long-Sedley, 1, 4; maps 1 and 3 in John S. Traill, *The Political Organiza-tion of Attica: A Study of the Demes, Trittyes, and Phylai, and Their Representation in the Athenian Council,* Hesperia Suppl. 14 (Princeton, 1975).

10c; for Atticus' attendance at Antiochus' lectures see above.—*Perpauculus*, in which the idea of smallness is doubly intensified, both by the "urbane" *per-* prefix (cf. p. 40 n. 143 *supra*) and the diminutive ending, occurs nowhere else in Cicero.

M. Vir iste fuit ille ⟨quidem⟩ prudens et acutus et in suo genere perfectus, mihique, ut scis, familiaris; cui tamen ego adsentiar in omnibus necne, mox videro; . . .] While expressing esteem for Antiochus, Cicero at first avoids a direct response to Atticus' supposition. In fact, it will turn out in §§ 55–56 that Cicero agrees with Antiochus (and Carneades; see above) that the difference among the schools on this point is inconsequential.—*Vir iste* = "that man of yours," "that man you mention" (a conversational stance, since he was a *familiaris* of Cicero as well as Atticus).—*Quidem* is expected beside the otherwise superfluous *ille* with contrasting clause following and was supplied by the *recentiores*.—*Prudens* is not a common epithet of philosophers, but cf. *N.D.* 1.34: *nec vero eius condiscipulus Xenocrates in hoc genere prudentior est* as well as *uter . . . est prudentior?* in a comparison of philosophers in the corrupt passage *Luc.* 132; *Div.* 2.11: *unusne mundus sit an plures, quae sint initia rerum ex quibus nascuntur omnia: physicorum est ista prudentia* (where *prudentia* seems virtually equivalent to *sapientia*). In post-Carneadean philosophy *prudentia* in forestalling opposing arguments could be a great asset!—For *acutus* see *ad* § 55 *(depasci veterem possessionem—).*—*In suo genere*: sc. *philosophiae* (Reid); cf. *Luc.* 4: *cum autem e philosophis ingenio scientiaque putaretur Antiochus . . . excellere . . .*—*Mox videro*[212] has been variously referred to *Luc.* 132 (but it is most unlikely that Cicero had already conceived this work at the time when *Leg.* was composed; see the Introduction § 2a), to *Fin.* 5.76 ff. (but the same objection applies; cf. Schmidt, 1959, 352 ff.), or to a later lost passage of our work (e.g., the discussion of education; cf. *ad* 3.29); cf. Philippson, 1939, 1118.37 ff. Görler, 1974, 202–3, thinks the reference to § 55 and that there Cicero admits the identity of views among the schools but in a different sense from Antiochus; but, if that is what Cicero had in mind, he would surely have had to add clarification (see above). In fact, *mox videro* postpones a topic without necessarily implying a definite plan to take it up again; cf. *Fam.* 8.13.2 (Cael.); with the simple future *Fam.* 3.9.4; *Att.* 10.7.1; Wilkins on *de Orat.* 2.33.—Boyancé (1970, 264; 1975, 24 and n. 12; sim. Vander Waerdt: cf. p. 51 n. 10 *supra*) supposes that our passage expresses unqualified approval of Antiochus, but cf., *contra*, Schmidt, *loc. cit.*, 223, citing the words *in suo genere perfectus*: "sein Urteil

---

212. For the phrase cf. Kühner *ad Tusc.* 2.26; for the sense of the future perfect (= "I shall see"), Lebreton, 200–202.

[ist] nicht uneingeschränkt positiv." Antiochus is praised at *Brut.* 315 and *Luc.* 113 and called *acutus* at *N.D.* 1.16, but Cicero's reservations surface at *Luc.* 69: *sed prius pauca cum Antiocho, qui . . . scripsit de iis rebus acutissime . . . quamvis igitur fuerit acutus, ut fuit, tamen inconstantia levatur auctoritas,* alluding to Antiochus' break with the Skeptical Academy, on which cf. John Glucker, *Antiochus and the Late Academy* (Göttingen, 1978), 13 ff. For Cicero's relations with Antiochus in general cf. testimonies at Luck, 17.

55 Quia si, ut Chius Aristo dixit solum bonum esse quod honestum esset, malumque quod turpe, ⟨ita Zeno dixisset⟩ ceteras res omnes plane pares, ac ne minimum quidem utrum adessent an abessent interesse, . . .] Our passage = *SVF* 3, 84.36 ff.—The subject must be Zeno (the *hic* of the following sentence and the appropriate point of contrast with representatives of *Platonis familia*), and the translators (Keyes, de Plinval, Nickel, and Rudd) insert his name in their versions. But surely we need both a pluperfect subjunctive to indicate that the hypothesis is unreal and, for clarity, the name of Zeno, who has not been mentioned since § 53. Madvig merely changed *dixit* to *dixisset,* but the immediately following doctrine *(solum bonum esse quod honestum esset)* is the one Zeno actually held (the same objection applies to de Plinval's insertion of *dixisset* after *esse* or the insertion by Kraus, 304, of Zeno's name immediately after *Aristo*). Powell more convincingly inserts *ita Zeno dixisset* prior to the doctrine he did not hold, namely *ceteras res . . .* and compares for the structure *Rep.* 1.58: *si ut Graeci dicunt, omnes aut Graios esse aut barbaros . . .* Another possibility would be to add ⟨*cum*⟩ *before dixit* to indicate that the equivalence of *bonum* and *honestum* as well as of *malum* and *turpe* are points held in common by Aristo and Zeno.—The hypothesis is that Zeno, like Aristo of Chius, rejects the distinction between "preferred" and "non-preferred" indifferents (προ-ηγμένα vs. ἀποπροηγμένα): only in that case would there be a major inter-scholastic difference, rather than a merely verbal one. In fact, our sources attribute the distinction to Zeno (cf. *SVF* 1, 47.31 ff.) with the result that what Zeno calls προηγμένα are for the Peripatos ἀγαθά—in Cicero's eyes a mere verbal discrepancy (but see below on *sentit idem quod Xenocrates*).—On the heterodox position of Zeno's pupil Aristo of Chius cf. *SVF* 1, 83.9 ff. = 58F Long-Sedley (with their commentary, 1, 358–59) and the dismissive allusion to him at § 37.

. . . valde a Xenocrate et Aristotele et ab illa Platonis familia discreparet, esset⟨que⟩ inter eos de re maxima et de omni vivendi ratione dissensio.] Cicero pioneered the use of *familia* of a school of philosophy—perhaps a characteristically Roman conception, like that of Herodotus as *pater historiae* (§ 5), with clear lines of authority and dependence; cf. *OLD* s.v. *familia* 5 (to the examples there given add both our passage and *Fin.* 4.49); Fladerer, 5–6.—*Essetque* is the reading of B^xA^aP, *esset* that of B¹Lε; Halm's ⟨*et*⟩ *esset* would also be possible.

nunc vero, cum decus—divitias valetudinem pulchritudinem commodas res appellet, non bonas, paupertatem debilitatem dolorem incommodas, non malas; . . .] Quintus' summary of views on the *finis bonorum (vita modica et apta virtute perfrui aut naturam sequi et eius quasi lege vivere* (§ 56; see below) likewise assimilates the Academy/Peripatos to the Stoa, as does *Fin.* 5.21–22, on which cf. Görler, 1974, 104–5.—*Nunc vero* is a formula for introducing a factual statement in contrast with what precedes; cf. Risselada, 113–14.—*Decus* or *decorum* is a *variatio* for the *honestum* (cf. *Fin.* 2.35: *una simplex* [sc. *formula de fine bonorum*] *cuius Zeno auctor, posita in decore tota, id est ⟨in⟩ honestate; ad Off.* 1.94), and *dedecus* corresponds to the *turpe.*—*Divitias valetudinem pulchritudinem* represent the external goods and goods of the body; cf. *ad* § 52a.

sentit idem quod Xenocrates, quod Aristoteles, loquitur alio modo.] = Xenocrates fr. 246 I.P. = 89 H. For the distinction between *loqui* and *sentire*—a potentially hazardous one for authors now dead—cf. *ad Off.* 1.147; for a similar criticism of Zeno for unnecessary change of terms cf. *Fin.* 4.3 and 12–13. Surely there was a difference—and one that was important to Zeno— between *commoda* and *bona* and between *incommoda* and *mala* (or rather the Greek equivalents: προηγμένα–ἀγαθά; ἀποπροηγμένα–κακά); cf. the response to such criticism at *Fin.* 3.44 and 4.2 (Cato) and *N.D.* 1.16 (Balbus) with Barnes, 1989, 88–89; for other equivalents for the Greek terms cf. *Fin.* 3.15. For Aristotle's doctrine of goods cf. *EN* 1098b12 ff.

ex hac autem non rerum, sed verborum discordia, controversia est nata de finibus; . . .] Cf. *Fin.* 3.5: . . . *Zenoque . . . non tam rerum inventor fuit quam verborum novorum.* On Cicero's tendency, after Antiochus, to lump together the Stoic and Academic/Peripatetic views of the *finis bonorum* as a mere verbal discrepancy cf. § 54; Görler, 1974, 198 and n. 27, and 1989, 252. The phrase *controversia de finibus* is the starting point for an elaborate pun on *finis*, equivalent in *Leg.*, as in other philosophical texts, to the τέλος, the goal of human activity (cf. *Fin.* 3.26), but in common parlance denoting the boundary of property; cf. Caes. *Gal.* 6.13.5 *(si . . . de finibus controversia est).*

. . . usus capionem XII Tabulae intra quinque pedes esse noluerunt, . . .] = *Lex XII* 7.4. Between two fields there had to be a strip of land five feet wide.

That strip could be easily erased in plowing with resulting *controversia de finibus*. The provision of the Twelve Tables that *usucapio*[213] does not apply within five feet of the boundary was designed to protect this bordering strip. Cf. Kübler, *RE* 13.1 (1926), 959.26 ff. (s.v. *locus*).

... **depasci veterem possessionem Academiae ab hoc acuto homine non sinemus; nec Mamilia lege singuli, sed e XII tres arbitri fines regemus.**] = *Lex XII* 7.5. Ter. *Hau.* 498–500 speaks of a single arbiter in a boundary dispute; but it is unclear whether this reflects Roman realities rather than Athenian. In any case, the lex Mamilia Roscia Peducaea Alliena Fabia allowed *inter alia* a single arbiter to decide such disputes; cf. Kroll, *RE* 12.2 (1925), 2397.1 ff., who dates the measure to the tribunate of Mamilius Limetanus in 109 (*RE* s.v. Mamilius no. 8; *MRR*, 1, 546); cf. also M.H. Crawford, "The Lex Iulia Agraria," *Athenaeum* n.s. 77 (1989), 183 and 190; older literature at Rotondi, 388–89. Going back to the older law enables all three participants to serve as arbiters of the "boundary dispute" (Crawford, *loc. cit.*, suspects that *Lex XII* provided for two or more arbiters, not precisely three, the number three being invoked because there are three interlocutors in our passage), though, in fact, only Marcus will pronounce a verdict.—Cicero would later find another philosophical use for the metaphor of disputed possession; cf. *Luc.* 132 (Cicero is the speaker on the subject of his own philosophical preferences): *erit igitur res iam in discrimine; nam aut Stoicus constituatur sapiens aut veteris Academiae—utrumque non potest; est enim inter eos non de terminis sed de tota possessione contentio . . .—Hic acutus homo* is, of course, Zeno, in spite of the similar characterization of Antiochus (*acutus et prudens:* § 54); cf. *Fin.* 4.56: *postea tuus ille Poenulus (scis enim Citieos, clientes tuos, e Phoenica profectos), homo igitur acutus, causam non obtinens repugnante natura verba versare coepit . . . ; Luc.* 77: *hic Zenonem vidisse acute nullum esse visum quod percipi posset . . . ,* as well as the allusion to *Zenonis . . . brevis et acutulas conclusiones* at *N.D.* 3.18 (cf. 3.22); sim. also *Fam.* 9.22.1. *Acutus* is elsewhere used of both philosophers and jurisconsults (cf. material at *TLL* s.v. *acuo* 464.72 ff. and 465.7 ff.); it may form part of an unfriendly characterization of the latter; cf. *de Orat.* 1.236 (quoted *ad* § 14: *Egone? summos fuisse*—).

56 A. Quamnam igitur sententiam dicimus?] The attribution to Quintus, adopted in most recent editions, goes back to Poggio; but *ceteris paribus* no change of interlocutors should be assumed; cf. Schmidt, 1974, 285. As J.G.F. Powell remarks *(per litt.)*, the indicative is appropriate in a question

---

213. Cf. Watson, *Property*, 21: "*Usucapio* is the acquisition of ownership of a thing through possessing it without interruption for a certain period of time." See further *ad* 2.48b.

requiring an immediate decision, as in Dido's *en quid ago?* (= "what do I do now?" *Aen.* 4.534).

M. Requiri placere terminos quos Socrates pepigerit, eisque parere.] Here we have the judgment held in prospect in § 52 *(. . . aliquando . . . iudicandam)* of the interscholastic controversy over the *finis bonorum,* though because of Quintus' immediate intervention the point is merely postulated rather than argued in detail. The Stoa's relation to the Academy is conceived (presumably after Antiochus) not merely as a tampering with boundaries but as a wholesale appropriation of property at *Fin.* 5.74: *ei quidem* [sc. *Stoici*] *non unam aliquam aut alteram ⟨rem⟩ a nobis, sed totam ad se nostram philosophiam transtulerunt.* This apparently Antiochian view appealed to Cicero as a Roman with a strong sense of historical continuity and as a conservative in questions of property rights, particularly since he did not take the differences among the schools that seriously (§ 55). Burkert, 1965, 199, sees our statement as a symptom that Cicero's view of the Socratic method differs radically from the original: "Indem Cicero Skeptiker bleibt und sich festzulegen vermeidet [sc. in the question of the *summum bonum* and the status of the "natural advantages"], glaubt er die Offenheit des sokratischen Fragens zu bewahren; doch ist dies nicht ein freies Forschen angesichts der Fülle des Seienden, sondern ein Lavieren auf eingefahrener Bahn zwischen Mauren, die nicht angetastet werden." Ibid., n. 66, he sees the phrase *terminos pangere*[214] in our passage as an expression of typically Roman fixity that influences the way the Socratic enterprise is conceived. Certainly it is not the skeptical but the dogmatic side of the Academy that is emphasized here, but Cicero is merely considering the doctrine of goods, and he has hinted at some skeptical reservations at § 39; the skeptical component of Academic teaching is highlighted in some of his later works.—Perhaps Socrates is invoked here as a figure around whom both Stoics and Academics could rally; for his influence on Hellenistic philosophical debate cf. A.A. Long, "Socrates in Hellenistic Philosophy," *CQ* 38 (1988), 150–71 = *Stoic Studies* (Cambridge, 1996), 1–33 (with Postscript 1995, ibid., 34).

Q. Praeclare, frater! iam nunc a te verba usurpantur civilis iuris ac legum, quo de genere exspecto disputationem tuam.] The legal terms used in the wake of Marcus' punning reference to the *controversia de finibus,* namely *terminos pangere, usucapio, possessio, lex Mamilia,* and the XII Tables, enable Quintus to give a pointed reminder of the subject from which the discussion has digressed (cf. § 52 *fin.* and § 57 *init.*). *Iam nunc* and *exspecto* constitute another hint of impatience; cf. § 52 *(quo tandem?)*.

---

214. Cf. *Pis.* 37: *. . . finibus eis quos lex . . . pepigerit.*

nam ista quidem magna diiudicatio est, ut ex te ipso saepe cognovi.] *Diiudicatio* is first attested here (*TLL* s.v.; *OLD* s.v.; see the following *diiudicari*); it is a *variatio* for the preceding *controversia*; cf. also § 52: *aliquando tam⟨en⟩ iudicandam.* No doubt the brothers discussed such matters, as they did historiography (§ 8) and rhetoric (*de Orat.* 1.5), but it is a bit surprising that Quintus is represented as knowing about this from his brother, for Quintus, too, enjoyed a philosophical education and at *Fin.* 5.1 is among the company who have listened to Antiochus' lecture in the Ptolemaeum and then pursue a related discussion. Quintus goes on to describe two positions that had been taken up on the *finis bonorum* and concludes that the matter is insoluble or, if soluble, would require more time than is available if the goal of the present discussion is to be reached. The *nam* therefore is a narrative use of the particle introducing a detailed account; cf. Hand, 4, 5.

sed certe ita res se habet, ut ex natura vivere summum bonum sit, id est vita modica et apta ⟨e⟩ virtute perfrui; aut naturam sequi et eius quasi lege vivere, id est nihil (quantum in ipso sit) praetermittere quominus ea quae natura postulet consequatur, quod item hoc valet, virtute tamquam lege vivere.] In view of his apparent impatience to return to the topic at hand, it is surprising that Quintus allows himself this further digression on the *finis bonorum*. Moreover, his presentation of the two alternative views is such as to emphasize their closeness rather than their difference, a fact that might suggest that the dispute *could* be settled (see below), in contrast to the following assertion: *quapropter hoc diiudicari nescio an numquam.* Hence Halm's deletion of this entire lemma. But if *nam ista quidem magna diiudicatio est . . .* immediately preceded *quapropter hoc diiudicari nescio an numquam,* it would be odd for *ista . . . diiudicatio* to be taken up by *hoc.*[215] Hence the lemma surely represents the draft as the author left it, though the possibility that he would have revised it later is by no means excluded.—Quintus' alternatives are the τέλος formulas respectively of the Academic/Peripatetic and the Stoic schools, with an explanation appended to each with *id est;* cf. Reitzenstein, 24–26 n. 1. The salient differences are the *vita modica,* which involves the Peripatetic mean, and *eius quasi lege vivere,* which points to the natural law of the Stoa with its commands and prohibitions; cf. *ad* § 18b. For the Stoic definition cf. also 63B–C and 64C Long-Sedley = Stob. 2, 75.11–76.8 and D.L. 7.87–89; 59D Long-Sedley = *Fin.* 3.17 and 20–22; *Fin.* 4.14. The distinction between *ex natura vivere* and *naturam sequi et eius quasi lege vivere* does not prima facie look so very great, so that Quintus'

---

215. I owe this point to J.G.F. Powell.

formulation implicitly supports Marcus' view that the controversy *de finibus* is *non rerum sed verborum discordia* (§ 55).—In the phrase *vita modica et apta virtute perfrui, virtute* was altered by Orelli to *virtuti,* for which there appears to be no parallel. Görler *ad loc.* defends the transmitted text by citing *Luc.* 31: . . . *virtutem* . . . *ex qua re una vita omnis apta sit. Perfruor* with ablative of means in addition to the usual ablatival complement appears, however, to be unparalleled (cf. *TLL* and *OLD* s.v.); hence the adoption of A.W. Zumpt's ⟨e⟩ *natura.*—*Id est nihil (quantum in ipso sit) praetermittere quominus ea quae natura postulet consequatur:* this "explanation" of the Stoic τέλος formula is along lines suggested by Antipater of Tarsus, who, evidently to obviate criticisms of Carneades, emphasized that one does everything in one's power to obtain the natural advantages; cf. *SVF* 3, 252.39–253.2: πᾶν τὸ καθ' αὑτὸν ποιεῖν διηνεκῶς καὶ ἀπαραβάτως πρὸς τὸ τυγχάνειν τῶν προηγουμένων κατὰ φύσιν; Gisela Striker, "Antipater, or the Art of Living," in *The Norms of Nature: Studies in Hellenistic Ethics,* ed. M. Schofield and G. Striker (Cambridge-Paris, 1962), 185–204; further bibliography at Long-Sedley, 2, 508–9. The implication is that the Stoic source used by Cicero or his source is at the stage of Antipater; see also *ad* § 59.—The concluding phrase, transmitted as *quod iter hoc velit virtute tamquam lege vivere,* was deleted by Davies; but sense can be restored by du Mesnil's changes of *iter* to *item* and of *velit* to *valet.* Quintus' point will be that the two formulas amount to the same thing, namely living in accord with virtue.

quapropter hoc diiudicari nescio an numquam, sed hoc sermone certe non potest, . . .] Concluding that the adjudication is either impossible or too lengthy to be handled within the scope of the current conversation (but see the previous note), Quintus brings to an end the discussion of the controversy *de finibus* begun by Marcus at § 52b (just when he had promised to stop digressing!).

57 M. At ego huc declinabam, nec invitus.] The attribution of parts in the mss. of *Leg.* carries no authority per se; cf. *ad* § 1. Poggio's attribution to Atticus against the manuscripts' to Marcus has been generally accepted by editors but recently questioned (Schmidt, 1974, 285, followed by Görler *ad loc.*), since there is no explicit indication of a change of speaker here.—For *declinabam* cf. *labebar* § 52).

Q. Licebit alias; nunc id agamus quod coepimus, cum praesertim ad id nihil pertineat haec de summo malo bonoque dissensio.] After his apparent complaisance about the drifting course of conversation (§ 52: *libenter enim, frater, quo ducis ista oratione, tecum prolabebar*), Quintus now, with the rather abrupt *licebit alias,* calls a firm halt to the topic of the *finis bonorum.* The historical Quintus could be impatient and unpredictable (cf. McDermott,

717; F. Münzer, *RE* 7A2 [1948], 1291.59 ff. and 1300.63–64), qualities captured here for posterity. On Quintus' character in general cf. D.R. Shackleton Bailey, *Cicero* (London, 1971), 184; Elizabeth Rawson, *Cicero: A Portrait* (London, 1975), 7: "Quintus was in fact something of a caricature of his brother, whose mobility of temperament and sense of humour in him took the form of an uncertain temper and a biting tongue . . ."—For use of *nunc* as a marker of a phase of discourse cf. Risselada, 117–22.—*Cum praesertim ad id nihil pertineat* . . . : taking Quintus' comment at face value, Reid concludes that "the whole episode is put in merely to shew off Cicero's knowledge of the subject." But perhaps here, as at the beginning of this phase of the argument (§§ 37–39), Cicero is concerned to portray a united front of the Stoa and Peripatos/Academy against the utilitarian position he has been combatting. **M. Prudentissime, Quinte, dicis. nam quae a me adhuc dicta sunt ⟨ . . . ⟩— leges vivendi et disciplinam daturum.**] Lambinus saw that Marcus' speech must be truncated (though his own supplement is unconvincing); Vahlen was first to recognize that the beginning of Quintus' reply has also been lost. He proposed this conclusion for Marcus' speech: *parva pars est institutae disputationis, si quidem nobis sunt* [the following repeated from § 17] *considerandae leges, quibus civitates regi debeant, tum haec tractanda quae composita sunt et descripta iura et iussa populorum, in quibus ne nostri quidem populi latebunt quae vocantur iura civilia.* He thought that Quintus' reply would have begun *neque ⟨vero ego a⟩ te Lycurgi leges* etc. (on the *nec* [B^{X}A^{b}P] or *neque* [HL] as an attempt to cover up the lacuna [*te* is the reading of B^{1}A^{1}ε before correction] cf. Schmidt, 1974, 81). Some such sense seems likely. For other possible losses at this point cf. *ad* 2.8 and 17.—The four named are the legendary or semi-legendary early lawgivers of the Greek states (7th to 6th c.): Lycurgus of Sparta, Solon of Athens, Charondas of Catana (but also lawgiver for other cities, notably Rhegium), and Zaleucus of Locri Epizephyrii; cf. Szegedy-Maszak, 1978; Gagarin, 1986, 58–62 and 129–30. Examples of historical lawgivers are cited and dismissed as belonging to a different category both here and at 2.14 (see *ad loc.*). Marcus' own laws are being requested; hence the modesty of his response in both passages (§ 58: *utinam esset etiam facultatis meae!* 2.18: *expromam equidem ut potero* . . .).—Down to this point *ius* has been the primary subject;[216] *lex* has been defined within the *iuris exordium* (§§ 18b–19);[217] and *lex* or *leges* have otherwise tended to appear in conjunction with *ius*.[218] We were, how-

---

216. *Iuris disciplina* and *natura iuris* (§ 17); *iuris principia* (§§ 18 and 28), *stirps iuris* (§ 20), *fundamentum iuris* (§ 43), as well as the general thesis *naturā esse ius* (§ 35).

217. The definition established there is repeated with minor variation in §§ 33 and 42.

218. *Fons legum et iuris* (16); *causa . . . universi iuris ac legum* (17); *unum ius . . . quod lex constituit una* (42).

ever, put on notice that there would be a discussion of *leges quibus civitates regi debeant* (§ 17), so the reference to *leges* here is not wholly unexpected. But the term is given a new twist by the limitation *vivendi* and the juxtaposition with *disciplina*, which hark back to Quintus' previous phrase *eius* [sc. *naturae*] *quasi lege vivere* (§ 56). He seems to have ethical precepts as well as legislation in mind, and, in fact, Marcus' law code will include both elements; cf. the Introduction § 3. The *disciplina* [sc. *vivendi*] is reminiscent of the Stoic τέχνη περὶ βίον, on which see *ad* § 32.

58–62 This passage[219] begins by emphasizing, in light of Quintus' request in § 57, the rôle of law in providing an ethical basis for living, then advances to an encomium of wisdom *(sapientia),* which includes philosophy as the *amor sapientiae* (in § 63 Atticus understands the whole passage as an encomium of *sapientia). Sapientia,* in fact, plays a double rôle here as both the guiding deity (= σοφία)[220] and the goal of human development.[221] The instruction to "know oneself" forms the starting point. The process of self-discovery begins with an inventory of human qualities similar to that at §§ 22–23 but now seen as *instrumenta . . . ad obtinendam adipiscendamque sapientiam* (§ 59), which thus brings *sapientia* within reach of human beings. There is a brief reference to the theory, already alluded to at §§ 26 and 30, of the *intellegentiae,* faint at first but illuminated under the guidance of *sapientia.* The final stage in the process of self-discovery occurs when the individual is fully mature and recognizes that he is a *vir bonus* and therefore *beatus.* The individual's further progress corresponds to the well known threefold division of philosophy (Xenocrates fr. 82 I.P. = 1 H.) or of philosophical discourse (the Stoics; cf. Ierodiakonou, 57–62),[222] here arranged in the order ethics, physics, logic. By a kind of ring-composition, at the end the whole argument is made to reflect back on knowing oneself and on *sapientia* as the final point in the process (§ 62 *fin.*).

It has been assumed that Cicero found this conglomerate in a single source.[223] But the threefold division of philosophy is put to quite different

---

219. For its use by John Toland see above, p. 36 and n. 129.

220. Cf. § 59: *sapientia duce.*

221. Cf. § 18: *eadem ratio cum est in hominis mente confirmata et perfecta, lex est;* Schmidt, 1959, 225 n. 3.

222. S.E. *M.* 7.17 states that Plato was potentially (δυνάμει) the first to use the threefold division of philosophy since he dealt with all three parts but that Xenocrates and others expressly adopted it.

223. Thus Heinemann, 2, 316–17, pointed out the similarity of our passage to *Tusc.* 5.68 ff. and wanted to claim both for Posidonius (Wilamowitz already held a similar position; cf. *"Sed serviendum officio . . .": The Correspondence between Ulrich von Wilamowitz-Moellendorff and Eduard Norden [1892–1931],* ed. William M. Calder III and Bernhard

uses at *Tusc.* 5.68 ff., where it provides content for the *vita contemplativa* and thus helps to buttress the case that virtue alone is sufficient to insure happiness. This and other evidence suggests that Cicero was capable on his own of selecting, recombining, and changing the emphasis of philosophical arguments.[224] As to the *partes philosophiae* in particular, there was no standard order. Xenocrates and most Stoics placed physics first, then went on to ethics and logic,[225] probably corresponding to the areas explored in successive stages of the history of philosophy by the presocratics, Socrates, and Plato. Our passage places ethics first, as was done by some Stoics (cf. *Fin.* 3.71–73) and at *Ac.* 1.19b ff. (Varro; cf. Ierodiakonou, 68–69), whereas at *Luc.* 114 the order is, as in Xenocrates, physics, ethics, logic; cf. Barnes, 1997, 140 and n. 4. Boyancé, 1971, and, more briefly, 1975, argues that our passage and *Ac.* 1.19b ff. reflect Antiochus' re-ordering of the parts and that, on the other hand, *de Orat.* 1.41 ff., *Luc.* 114 and 116, and *Tusc.* 5.68 and 70–72 show Philo's order (the same as that of Xenocrates and most Stoics). But we should not lose sight of the function of this material in our particular context: in the individual's progress toward *sapientia,* development as an ethical person forms the essential foundation for all else, and the contemplation of nature provides, as in the *Somnium Scipionis,* perspective on the human condition, but the full flowering appears in the ability to deploy *ratio* and, especially, *oratio* for the benefit of the community. Perhaps Antiochus is the ultimate inspiration for Cicero's emphasis,[226] but our passage should probably be seen as a case similar to the so-called *Chrysippea divisio* of views on the τέλος as analyzed by Algra (esp. 109 and 127–28): Cicero is not slavishly copying sources but responding to the exigencies of the given argument.

Huss [Hildesheim, 1997], 20 and 58; Wilamowitz, 179). Theiler, 45 ff., acknowledged the similarity (46 n. 2) but claimed our passage for Antiochus (albeit as a kind of default position [46]: "... aber doch drängen keine entscheidenden Gründe zur Annahme, daß Cicero hier nicht mehr Antiochus folgt"); sim. R. Müller, 227–28; Boyancé, 1975, promoted this analysis with further argument.

224. Cf. p. 50 nn. 6–7 *supra.*

225. Chrysippus, however, favored the order logic, ethics, physics, so that theology forms the culmination (sim. Tac. *Dial.* 30.4); cf. Jacques Brunschwig, "On a Book-Title by Chrysippus: 'On the Fact That the Ancients Admitted Dialectic along with Demonstrations,'" *OSAP* Suppl. 1991: *Aristotle and the Later Tradition,* ed. Henry Blumenthal and Howard Robinson (Oxford, 1991), 81–95 at 91 ff. (with a defense against Plutarch's charge of self-contradiction in this respect).

226. The emphasis in our passage on epistemology and lack of interest in physics seems to correspond to Antiochus' point of view; cf. Görler, 1994, 949.

Is this passage a mere digression unconnected with the general theme of
Leg. 1? In fact, a clear connection is not at first established; hence Atticus'
question in § 63: *sed quorsus hoc pertinet?* and Marcus' retrospective clarification (see *ad loc.*). Schmidt, 1959, 228, sees strong connections between
this passage and what precedes in terms of doctrinal echoes and via the idea
that the legislator must be philosophically trained. Certainly there is some
repetition of doctrine here (in particular, the endowment of the human being
by Nature and its development [§ 59]; cf. §§ 22 ff.). Drafting laws is one of
the activities that the philosophically trained man described here engages in
when he returns—to use the Platonic image—to the cave from the outer
world (*qua stabiliat leges:* § 62), but only one, and this is by no means the
main focus of the passage.[227] The parallels just discussed indicate that the
arguments preexisted *Leg.*: the meditation on knowing oneself was inspired
by Cicero's Academic studies,[228] the threefold division of philosophy perhaps by Antiochus in particular;[229] § 59, probably supplied by Cicero for
this place, takes "knowing oneself" in the direction of the anthropology
developed at §§ 22–27; and the latter part of § 62 *(cumque se ad civilem—
sempiternis monumentis prodere)* is probably a Ciceronian appendix to
dialectic aiming to link verbal skills with the work of the statesman, which
was a point of special interest to himself and his readers.[230] Cicero, then, has
grafted preexisting material onto his argument and adapted it to a degree. Its
presence here enables him to round off this Book with a full-blown encomium of the philosophic life followed by a personal confession of faith in
philosophy (cf. § 63). This fits with the main theme of this Book since he has
reframed the source of *ius* as a philosophical issue (cf. §§ 14–16). In addition, this passage, together with Marcus' following remarks (§ 63), serves to
buttress his authority, not merely to speak on *ius* (this was already established at § 13), but to do so in a philosophical vein.

Finally, Cicero has contrived to organize the introductory section on
knowing oneself (§ 59 = a) and most of the matter under the three following
"parts" of philosophy in stately periods: § 60: ethics (= b); § 61: physics (=
c); § 62: the Ciceronian addition to the topic of dialectic (= d; see above),
with (a) and (b) concluding with the blessedness of the human condition, (c)

227. The title "Preis der sapientia des Gesetzgebers" given to our passage by Schmidt,
1959, 229, is thus one-sided; cf. also *ad* § 62.
228. *Alc. 1* was often the first of the Platonic dialogues studied; cf. A.J. Festugière, "L'ordre
de lecture des dialogues de Platon aux Ve/VIe siècles," *MH* 26 (1969), 281–96, esp. 281–82
and 285–87.
229. See the previous paragraph and n. 226 *supra.*
230. Cf. Wilamowitz, 180.

with the despising of commonly accepted values, (d) with the transmission in eternal monuments of the deeds and policies of the wise and brave. As expected, the rhythm receives careful attention: the clausula of (a) is double cretic, (b) cretic plus iamb, (c) double cretic; for (d) see *ad loc.*

58 This chapter forms a bridge between Quintus' request for *leges vivendi et disciplina* and the following encomium of *sapientia* by connecting *sapientia* with *lex*. The point was already implicit in the description of *lex* as *ratio summa* at § 18b and of *sapientia* as *perfecta ratio* at § 22.

sed profecto ita se res habet, ut quoniam vitiorum emendatricem legem esse oportet commendatricemque virtutum, ab ea vivendi doctrina ducatur.] *Sed profecto* ("but assuredly") contrasts with the immediately preceding *atque utinam esset etiam facultatis meae:* i.e., whether or not the task is within my power, at any rate . . .—Cf. the similar view at *de Orat.* 1.194 (Crassus is the speaker): . . . *docemur . . . auctoritate nutuque legum domitas habere libidines, coercere omnes cupiditates, nostra tueri, ab alienis mentes, oculos, manus abstinere.*—For the relation of law and philosophy cf. Xenocrates fr. 256 I.P. = 3 H. *apud* Cic. *Rep.* 1.3: *quin etiam Xenocratem ferunt . . . , cum quaereretur ex eo quid adsequerentur eius discipuli, respondisse 'ut id sua sponte facerent quod cogerentur facere legibus'.*—Both the positive and negative sides of law have been emphasized from the beginning; cf. § 18b: *lex . . . quae iubet ea quae facienda sunt, prohibetque contraria;* in light of §§ 42–46 this can now be stated in terms of moral categories (*vitiorum emendatricem . . . commendatricemque virtutum:* a handsome chiasmus with its attributes surrounding the midpoint *legem*).—Cicero was fond of agent nouns; both *emendatrix* and *commendatrix* are first used in this sentence; *emendator* itself may have been a Ciceronian coinage (*Balb.* 20); but *commendator* is not attested until Plin. *Ep.* 6.23.5; cf. *TLL* s.vv. *emendator, emendatrix, commendator, commendatrix.*—Perhaps the law should play this rôle *(oportet)*, but can it really? Cicero saw a more complex relation of law and morals at *Off.* 3.67 *(sed huiusmodi reticentiae iure civili comprehendi non possunt);* see *ad loc.*—The entailed *vivendi doctrina* accommodates Quintus' expectation of *leges vivendi et disciplina* (§ 57; see *ad loc.*), though *doctrina* represents a subtle shift, with Marcus placed implicitly in the rôle of teacher.

ita fit ut ⟨ . . . ⟩ mater omnium bonarum rerum sapientia . . .] What had started as an encomium of *lex* thus becomes one of *sapientia* personified; the connection between *sapientia* and *vivendi doctrina* is understood; for *sapientia* as (1) knowledge of things divine and human and (2) an *ars vivendi* cf. *Fin.* 2.37 and *Off.* 1.153 (1) and *Fin.* 1.42 (2); Homeyer, 307. At the very least a subjunctive verb has been lost (*sit* is commonly supplied before *sapientia*). But the transition is abrupt, the lacuna probably more extensive. Schmidt, 1959, 225 n. 1, would insert *lex sit* after *sapientia;* Theiler, 45, would read *ita fit ut mater omnium bonarum rerum ⟨sit lex quae cum sit ratio perfecta eadem est⟩ sapientia* (cf. § 22: [*ratio*], *quae cum adolevit atque perfecta est, nominatur rite sapientia*); Powell (after *ita fit ut*) *⟨eodem lex habenda sit honore quo⟩; and indeed lex* and *sapientia* should be on the same level if *lex* is perfect reason (cf. §§ 18, 33, 42). Or is Cicero rather thinking of *lex* as one of the *bonae artes* of which *sapientia* is the mother *(ita fit ut mater ⟨et legis sit et⟩ . . .)? Mater omnium bonarum rerum sapientia:* for the metaphor of "mother" cf. § 47: *voluptas, malorum autem mater omnium;* at § 62 *fin. sapientia* is called *parens;* sim. with reference to philosophy *de Orat.* 1.9: *neque enim te fugit laudandarum artium omnium procreatricem quandam et quasi parentem eam quam* φιλοσοφίαν *Graeci vocant ab hominibus doctissimis iudicari . . .* The "good things" of which *sapientia* is the mother include the blessings of self-knowledge as described in the sequel; cf. below on *haec enim una nos—.*

. . . (a cuius amore Graeco verbo philosophia nomen invenit), . . .] The etymology (also at *Off.* 2.5) probably figured in the *Hortensius;* cf. Aug. *conf.* 3.8: *amor autem sapientiae nomen Graecum habet philosophiam, quo me accendebant illae litterae* [sc. the *Hortensius*]; other references at Maltby s.v. *philosophia.*

. . . qua nihil a dis immortalibus uberius, nihil florentius, nihil praestabilius hominum vitae datum est.] *Philosophia* must be the antecedent of *qua* because the gods have given it and not *sapientia* to human beings;[231] cf. Pl. *Tim.* 47b1–2: . . . φιλοσοφίας γένος, οὗ μεῖζον ἀγαθὸν οὔτ᾽ ἦλθεν οὔτε ἥξει ποτὲ τῷ θνητῷ γένει δωρηθὲν ἐκ θεῶν, rendered in similar terms by Cicero (*Tim.* 52): . . . *philosophiam . . . quo bono nullum optabilius, nullum praestantius neque datum est mortalium generi deorum concessu atque munere neque dabitur.* This was a favorite passage that Cicero cites or imitates at *Ac.* 1.7, *Tusc.* 1.64, and *Fam.* 15.4.16 (to Cato); cf. Boyancé, 1970, 241 n. 2.— For other Ciceronian encomia of philosophy cf. *Tusc.* 5.5 (on which cf. Hildebrecht Hommel, *Ciceros Gebetshymnus an die Philosophie, Tusculanen V 5,* SHAW, philos.-hist. Kl. [Heidelberg, 1968], no. 3) and *Off.* 2.5—Cicero was fond of the anaphora of *nihil;* cf. Pease *ad N.D.* 1.75.

haec enim una nos cum ceteras res omnes, tum quod est difficillimum docuit: ut nosmet ipsos nosceremus, cuius praecepti tanta vis et tanta sententia est, ut ea non homini cuipiam sed Delphico deo tribueretur.] *Haec* surely refers back to *philosophia,* the preceding characterization of which is

---

231. The gods give *ratio,* which must mature into *sapientia;* cf. §§ 22 and 59.

hereby justified (*enim*); *sapientia* is the end of the process, though it also helps mortals along the way (§ 59: *sapientia duce*).—The project of "knowing oneself" connects the conclusion of this Book with the *Phaedrus* passage that served as the model for the opening dialogue on the problem of mythopoetic and actual truth: in the *Phaedrus* Socrates explains that he has not the leisure to deal with the truth-value of myths since he is still occupied with the project of knowing himself (229e).—"Knowing oneself" similarly comes down to knowing one's soul and its divine nature at Pl. *Alc. 1* 129a ff., esp. 130e and 133c; cf. also *Tusc.* 5.70: *haec tractanti animo et noctes et dies cogitanti existit illa ⟨a⟩ deo Delphis praecepta cognitio, ut ipsa se mens agnoscat coniunctamque cum divina mente se sentiat . . .*—The transmitted text is *tanta aut sed tanta sententia est* B¹ or *tanta sententia est* LERS, corrected to *tanta vis et tanta sententia est* Bˣ, whence also in AP (*tanta vis et* in ras. Aᵃ). Cf. *de Orat.* 1.196 (cited in full *ad* 2.3): *cuius rei tanta est vis ac tanta natura,* followed, as here, by the imperfect subjunctive.²³² As J.G.F. Powell suggests (*per litt.*), the two passages present a kind of hendiadys standing for *tanta vis naturae* and *tanta vis sententiae* respectively, these expressions being avoided because there is already a genitive limiting the entire phrase; for the latter cf. Gel. 11.13.5: *sed enim, cum eadem ipsa verba saepius petentibus nobis lectitarentur, admoniti a Castricio sumus, ut consideraremus, quae vis quodve emolumentum eius sententiae foret;* similarly Quintilian speaks of *validae sententiae* (*Inst.* 10.1.60) or of giving force (*vires*) to a *sententia* (ibid. 4.1.65).—*Ea* for the expected *id* (referring to *praeceptum*) is a synesis under the influence of the intervening *vis* and *sapientia*.—At Pl. *Charm.* 164e–165a the words γνῶθι σεαυτόν are interpreted as a divine greeting to visitors of the temple (they were inscribed in the *pronaos*). Our passage is reminiscent of Pl. *Alc. 1* 129a, where Socrates' question implies the difficulty of the process and the character of the author is inferred from the nature of the precept: πότερον οὖν δὴ ῥᾴδιον τυγχάνει τὸ γνῶναι ἑαυτὸν καί τις ἦν φαῦλος ὁ τοῦτο ἀναθεὶς εἰς τὸν ἐν Πυθοῖ νεών . . . , to which Alcibades replies: ἐμοὶ μέν, ὦ Σώκρατες, πολλάκις μὲν ἔδοξε παντὸς εἶναι, πολλάκις δὲ παγχάλεπον. Cf. also *Fin.* 5.44: *quod praeceptum quia maius erat quam ut ab homine videretur, idcirco assignatum est deo;* Plut. *Dem.* 3.2: . . . εἰ παντὸς ἦν τὸ "γνῶθι σεαυτὸν" ἔχειν πρόχειρον, οὐκ ἂν ἐδόκει τὸ πρόσταγμα θεῖον εἶναι. Paus. 10.24.1, however, ascribes the precept, not to the god, but to the "Seven Wise Men."

---

232. The sequence of tenses (*est* followed by *tribueretur*) is to be explained by the imperfect making itself felt even in the subjunctive (for *tribuebatur*); cf. Kühner-Stegmann, 2, 186–87, citing our passage.

On the difficulty of the task cf. *Fin.* 5.41: *nunc vero a primo quidem mirabiliter occulta natura est nec perspici nec cognosci potest. progredientibus autem aetatibus sensim tardeve potius quasi nosmet ipsos cognoscimus.*—For the characterization *tanta vis* cf. Plut. *Pyth. or.* 408e, who finds in this instruction and the equally famous μηδὲν ἄγαν πυκνὸς καὶ σφυρήλατος νοῦς.

59 This chapter forms the basis (cf. *nam*) for attributing to the precept "know thyself" *tanta vis et tanta sententia.* An epistemological process is described with parallels on the moral plane: one sees one's own resources, including a godlike *ingenium* such as is delineated at §§ 22–23, but these now take on a new aspect as the *instrumenta . . . ad obtinendam sapientiam.* There is a brief reference to the theory of the *intellegentiae* as the starting point of knowledge. The final step in the process of self-discovery, which is at the same time a process of maturation, is the recognition of one's moral status as a *bonus vir* and therefore one who is *beatus.* The parallel moral plane also appears earlier in the description *tantoque munere deorum semper dignum aliquid et faciet et sentiet.*

Nam qui se ipse norit, primum aliquid se habere {sentiet} divinum, ingeniumque in se suum sicut simulacrum aliquod dicatum putabit;. . .] At *Tusc.* 1.52 Cicero makes the point that the Delphic precept calls for introspection: *cum igitur 'nosce te' dicit, hoc dicit: 'nosce animum tuum'.* For the idea *aliquid se habere sentiet divinum* see *ad* § 24; for the wording cf. *Tusc.* 1.56: *. . . inesse in animis hominum divina quaedam.*—Powell deletes *sentiet* because *putabit* suffices and to restore the cretic + trochee clausula.— *Ingenium* corresponds to Greek νοῦς; cf. *Tusc.* 1.70: *. . . vim divinam mentis adgnoscito;* Courcelle, 114–15; *ad Off.* 3.44.—Powell remarks *(per litt.):* "*in se* was postponed to the Wackernagelian position in the second clause because of the awkwardness of *aliquid se in se habere divinum,* which is what the sense really needs."—*Simulacrum* is not limited by *dei* since a *simulacrum* is usually of a god (cf. *OLD* s.v., 3). The soul is described in terms similar to Alcibiades' comparison of Socrates to statues of Silenus, οἳ διχάδε διοιχθέντες φαίνονται ἔνδοθεν ἀγάλματα ἔχοντες θεῶν (*Smp.* 215b2–3),[233] where θεῶν is specified though it need not have been (cf. LSJ s.v. ἄγαλμα 3). As a Stoic parallel Jean Pépin, *Idées grecques sur l'homme et sur dieu* (Paris, 1971), 8, cites Epict. 2.8.18–19, where the human being is compared to an ἄγαλμα and is said to have been created by Zeus. The famous

---

233. It is not clear, *pace* Boyancé, 1963, 109, that Philo had this passage in mind at *Op. mundi* 69, where à propos Ge. 1.26 (*. . . ποιήσωμεν ἄνθρωπον κατ᾿ εἰκόνα ἡμετέραν καὶ καθ᾿ ὁμοίωσιν κτλ.*) he uses ἀγαλματοφορεῖν to describe the relation of the human being to the deity, for ἄγαλμα may simply be a *variatio* for εἰκών.

deum te . . . scito esse of *Rep.* 6.30 offers the idea in pithier form.—By omission of *esse* Cicero achieves a clausula of the *omnibus debiturus* type.

tantoque munere deorum semper dignum aliquid et faciet et sentiet, . . .] There is a similar reference to doing something worthy of the "divine endowment" of the human being immediately following a lacuna of four folios at *Rep.* 3.5: [***] *quorum animi altius se extulerunt et aliquid dignum dono, ut ante dixi, deorum aut efficere aut excogitare potuerunt.* Whether or not in that passage a discussion of the "Entwicklung der Philosophie im Sinne der *ratio vivendi*" preceded (so Büchner *ad loc.*), there must have been at least some reference to the soul *(ut ante dixi).* Cf. also *Fin.* 1.23: *quod* [sc. the Epicurean valuation of pleasure and pain] . . . *eiusmodi esse iudico ut nihil homine videatur indignius; Off.* 1.106: *ex quo intellegitur corporis voluptatem non satis esse dignam hominis praestantia . . .*—For an example of the opposite behavior to that described here cf. *Parad.* 14 (cited *ad* § 26b).

. . . et cum se ipse perspexerit . . .] Courcelle, 114, believes that this text corresponds to the analogue of the mirror at *Alc. 1* 132e–133a; but in that passage the point is to find some object, looking at which the eye will see itself (εἰς ὃ βλέπων ὁ ὀφθαλμὸς ἔμελλεν αὐτὸν ἰδεῖν: 132d7–8), whereas in our passage there is no such external object.

. . . intelleget quemadmodum a natura subornatus in vitam venerit, quantaque instrumenta habeat ad obtinendam adipiscendamque sapientiam, . . .] See *ad* §§ 58–62 and the headnote to this section.—For the human endowment by Nature cf. §§ 22–23; for the personification of *natura* (here as an agent) cf. *ad* § 26. Similarly at *Luc.* 31 the mental faculties are called *instrumenta vel ornamenta vitae.*—Cf. Madvig *ad Fin.* 2.71: "apud Cic. Legg. I.59 in verbis *ad obtinendam adipiscendamque sapientiam* aut durissima hysterologia est aut scriptura mendosa; nam obtinemus, quod iam adepti sumus . . ."

. . . quemadmodum a natura subornatus—quasi adumbratas intellegentias animo ac mente conceperit; . . .] *Intellegentiae* is one of Cicero's equivalents for the ἔννοιαι or προλήψεις of Hellenistic epistemology; cf. *ad* § 26b. The process leading from the ἔννοιαι to *sapientia* is described in greater detail at *Luc.* 30.—The *iunctura adumbratae intellegentiae* does not occur elsewhere in Cicero; for a possible equivalent cf. *ad* § 26b.

quibus illustratis sapientia duce, bonum virum et ob eam ipsam causam cernat se beatum fore.] That the process leads to self-knowledge needs to be shown, not necessarily that the individual is *beatus;* nevertheless this point is established both here and in § 60 *(quid eo dici aut cogitari poterit beatius?);* sim. *Tusc.* 5.68 ff., where, however, this topic connects with the overall thesis of the Book, *viz., virtutem ad beate vivendum se ipsa esse contentam*

(5.1; cf. § 70: *ex quo insatiabili gaudio compleatur;* § 71: *efficitur . . . ut virtus ad beate vivendum sit se ipsa contenta*). It seems likely that both in our passage and at *Tusc.* 5.68 ff. Cicero has added an argument that once served different ends (in the latter passage, apart from the postulate of a *praestans vir optimis artibus* [5.68], *virtus* does not come into the matter).— For both the Stoa and the Old Academy, virtue is a sufficient condition for happiness (for the former cf. *Tusc.* 5; for the latter *Fin.* 5.68–72). The wording of our passage is reminiscent of the Stoic doctrine, combatted by Plutarch (*mor.* 75b ff.: *Quomodo quis suos in virtute sentiat profectus*), that one may become wise without even knowing it.

60 The conjunction *nam* shows that this material justifies the connection just drawn between goodness and happiness. The person who has understood the virtues *(cognitis perceptisque virtutibus)* now proceeds to instantiate them, as Cicero describes; he concludes with the rhetorical question: *quid eo dici aut cogitari potest beatius?* In fact, only three of the four virtues are included (*temperantia, iustitia* as proper behavior toward humans and the gods, and *prudentia*), *fortitudo* being omitted (see p. 198 n. 193 *supra*).

. . . a corporis obsequio—omnemque mortis dolorisque timorem effugerit, . . .] This account of the virtue of *temperantia* describes the eradication of three of the four πάθη (ἡδονή, φόβος, λύπη) recognized by the orthodox Stoa, with the fourth, ἐπιθυμία, omitted; cf. *ad* § 32 *(molestiae, laetitiae, cupiditates,—).*

. . . a corporis obsequio indulgentiaque discesserit, . . .] A similar mind/body dualism to § 24 *(. . . cumque alia quibus cohaererent homines e mortali genere sumpserint, quae fragilia essent et caduca . . .).* The Epicureans, as described at § 39 *(sibi autem indulgentes et corpori deservientes)*, have failed to reach this stage; see *ad loc.*

. . . voluptatemque sicut labem aliquam dedecoris oppresserit, . . .] Cicero is the first known to have used *labes* in the non-physical sense so widespread in later authors; cf. *TLL* s.v., 770.9 ff. Cf. *Parad.* 33: *refrenet primum libidines, spernat voluptates, iracundiam teneat, coërceat avaritiam, ceteras animi labes repellat . . .*

. . . omnemque mortis dolorisque timorem effugerit, . . .] The Epicureans would differentiate between the unwarranted fear of death and the justified avoidance of pain; cf. *ad* § 31; and for them the order is reversed, the contemplation of nature (§ 61) liberating one from the fear of death (cf. *Fin.* 1.63 [Torquatus]).

. . . societatemque caritatis coierit cum suis, omnesque natura coniunctos suos duxerit, . . .] A short version of the doctrine of οἰκείωσις; sim. *Fin.* 3.62; *Off.* 3.28; cf. in general *ad Off.* 1.11–14.

. . . **cultumque deorum et puram religionem susceperit, . . .**] *Pietas* falls, as
sometimes elsewhere, under justice (cf. Pl. *Euthphr.* 12e; *N.D.* 1.116;
Boyancé, 1975, 28–29); *aliter Part.* 78 and G. Romaniello, reply to Boyancé,
Ciceroniana n.s. 2 (1975), 40–42.—The *iunctura pura religio* does not occur
elsewhere in Cicero or indeed in classical Latin. Cicero seems to mean religion
free of superstition and immorality (cf. *ad* § 32; Schmidt, 1959, 226). Cicero
implicitly draws a line at *impura religio* in the prohibition of a cult of vices
(2.19.7), of women's nocturnal sacrifices (2.21.11), and the restrictions on
stipes and offerings by *impii* (2.22.8 and 4); cf. also on 2.19.3. For Cicero
impura religio was represented above all by Clodius and his violation of
religious rites (cf. 2.37); he is called an *impura belua* at 3.22; he lectures
Clodius on proper religious observance in *Dom.* (cf., e.g., *Dom.* 134, cited
infra ad 2.19.1).

. . . **et exacuerit illam ut oculorum, sic ingeni aciem ad bona seligenda et
reicienda contraria (quae virtus ex providendo est appellata prudentia), . . .**]
Acies mentis occurs for the first time at *de Orat.* 2.160; hence the metaphor
is still fresh; cf. *Hort.* fr. 115: . . . *nobis . . . acuentibus . . . intellegentiam
quae est mentis acies,* as well as the reference to *acies animorum nostrorum*
at *Fin.* 4.37; *OLD* s.v. *acies* 5; *TLL* s.v., 402.19 ff.; sim. *mentis oculi* at *Sen.*
42.—The selection of the "natural advantages" *en bloc* is reminiscent of
Chrysippus' formulation of the τέλος (cf. *Fin.* 3.31); however, Antipater
both incorporated that point and laid stress, as in our passage, on "exercising" one's faculties to that end; cf. *SVF* 3, 252.37 ff.; literature cited *ad Off.*
3.13a; for the presence of Stoic material at the stage of Antipater cf. also *ad*
§ 56.—The etymology is repeated from *Rep.* 6.1 = Non. 42.3 (cf. Heck,
1966, 164): *totam igitur exspectas prudentiam huius rectoris, quae ipsum
nomen hoc nacta est ex providendo;* cf. also *Hort.* fr. 96: *id enim est sapientis, providere, ex quo sapientia est appellata prudentia.* For the definition
cf. [Pl.] *Def.* 411d: φρόνησις . . . διάθεσις καθ᾽ ἣν κρίνομεν τί πρακτέον
καὶ τί οὐ πρακτέον; sim. Chrys. *SVF* 3, 297.13: ἐπιστήμη ποιητέων τε καὶ
οὐ ποιητέων; closer to our wording ibid. 3, 156.2: . . . φρόνησιν, ἐπιστήμην . . . ἀγαθῶν καὶ κακῶν καὶ οὐδετέρων. For the element of selection cf.
Hort. fr. 110: *ne prudentia quidem egeremus, nullo delectu proposito
bonorum et malorum.*

61 This stately period begins with a long *cum*-clause and concludes with
four exclamations in asyndeton capped by a double cretic clausula. It summarizes the message of the *Somnium Scipionis* that knowledge of the universe tempers human ambitions. It is at first unclear how the contemplation
of the universe relates to the previous subject, *idemque* [sc. *animus*] provid-

ing but a superficial link, but finally *quam se ipse noscet* clarifies that this activity is being pursued for the sake of Apollo's injunction. Our passage presents not so much a study of physics as an edifying vision of the universe, possibly a reflection of Antiochus' emphasis;[234] also a vision, but with more physical detail, is the version at *Tusc.* 5.69.

Idemque cum caelum terras maria, rerumque omnium naturam perspexerit, . . .] The list comprises three of the four elements, the fourth, fire, being alluded to obliquely in the next clause; cf. the list of *omnes naturae* at *N.D.* 1.22.

. . . eaque unde generata, quo recur⟨sur⟩a, {quando} quomodo obitura, . . .] In view of the cosmological context Sprey, 81, is surely right to connect this with the conflagration which, according to the Stoics, punctuates the end of each world-cycle; cf. no. 46 Long-Sedley; contrast Schmidt, 1959, 226 n. 2, who takes our lemma in a general sense.—*Recur⟨sur⟩a* is Vahlen's correction; Reid suggested *recasura* and bracketing *quando—obitura* as a gloss on the rare word *recasura,* but the alleged gloss is hardly equivalent in sense. Powell more plausibly brackets *quando* alone, since Stoic sources give no hint that a human being can know when the ἐκπύρωσις will occur.

. . . quid in eis mortale et caducum, quid divinum aeternumque sit viderit, . . .] Cf. *ad* § 24.

. . . ipsumque ea moderantem et regentem ⟨deum⟩ paene prenderit, . . .] This appears to be the earliest metaphorical use of *pre(he)ndo* for understanding (*TLL* s.v., 1165.32–34; *OLD* s.v., 7b), softened a bit by *paene* (cf. *ad* § 54). After *regentem* Ziegler inserted *deum,* for which he cited 2.9 (*tuentis et regentis dei,* a double cretic). For the *iunctura* cf. *de Orat.* 1.226: . . . *cui populus ipse* moderandi et regendi *sui potestatem . . . tradidisset; Rep.* 6.30: . . . *si quidem est deus . . . qui tam* regit et moderatur *et movet id corpus cui praepositus est, quam hunc mundum ille princeps deus.*

. . . seseque non {omnis} circumdatum moenibus {populare} alicuius {diffinitio} loci, sed civem totius mundi quasi unius urbis agnoverit: . . .] Cosmopolitanism had its origin in the assertion of Diogenes of Sinope that he was a κοσμοπολίτης; cf. Schofield, 1991, ch. 3 and app. H; *ad* § 23 *supra; Parad.* 18: *exilium autem* [sc. *terribile est*] *illis quibus quasi circumscriptus est habitandi locus, non iis qui omnem orbem terrarum unam urbem esse ducunt;* Sen. *Tr. an.* 4.4: *ideo magno animo nos non unius urbis moenibus clusimus sed in totius orbis commercium emisimus patriamque nobis mundum professi sumus . . .*—The text is difficult. Neither *omnis* (BA) nor

---

234. Cf. p. 222 n. 226 *supra.*

hominis (HLε) yields any sense, nor is any of the proposed substitutions convincing;[235] hence Powell's deletion. *Popularis* in this sense and with genitive of place seems not to be otherwise attested until Gel. 5.3.3: cf. *OLD* s.v. *popularis*² 2; *populare*, along with *alicuius diffinitio*,[236] was ejected already by Davies. Powell suggests *ad loc.* that the transmitted text resulted from piecemeal insertion of a marginal annotation *hominis popular[is] definitio;* indeed, order is restored once these three words are removed.

. . . **quam se ipse noscet (quod Apollo praecepit Pythius),** . . .] Certainly self-knowledge includes, or can include, the contemplation of nature[237] and acceptance of cosmopolitanism; nevertheless, the reversion to self-knowledge seems a rather narrow conclusion to so wide-ranging a survey—perhaps a visible seam in the connection of the *partes philosophiae* with the topic of self-knowledge (cf. *ad* §§ 58–62).[238]—*Quam se ipse noscet:* De Plinval's *qualem* (for *quam*) might seem at first sight attractive, but it destroys the fourfold anaphora of *quam.*—*Quod Apollo praecepit Pythius:* according to § 58 it was *haec* (= *philosophia;* see *ad loc.*) that taught this, and the attribution to the god was merely to account for *tanta vis et tanta sententia*. These words might thus be thought to be an insertion by a reader keen to show off knowledge; hence de Plinval deleted them. But these objections are perhaps too pedantic.

. . . **quam contemnet, quam despiciet, quam pro nihilo putabit ea quae vulgo dicuntur amplissima!**] Sc. honors and wealth; cf. § 52; *Rep.* 6.24 ff.; *Luc.* 127; *Off.* 2.37.

62 Dialectic receives a brief, jejune description, rhetoric a full, resonant one, Cicero's style reflecting in each case the qualities of the subject; cf. *Orat.* 113: *Zeno . . . manu demonstrare solebat quid inter has artis interesset. nam cum compresserat digitos pugnumque fecerat, dialecticam aiebat eiusmodi esse; cum autem diduxerat et manum dilataverat, palmae illius similem eloquentiam esse dicebat* with Catherine Atherton, "Hand over Fist: The Failure of Stoic Rhetoric," *CQ* 38 (1988), 392–427.

Atque haec omnia, quasi saepimento aliquo, vallabit disserendi ratione—et quid sit cuique contrarium.] Cicero uses *disserendi ratio* both of λογική and

---

235. Ziegler's *omnino* "has the air of a desperate conjecture," as Powell notes *(per litt.),* and Büchner's *humanis* is likewise improbable; P's *unius* forestalls and weakens the following contrast *totius mundi–unius urbis*.

236. The reading of BA : *definiti* SHL.

237. Cf. also *Fin.* 5.44: *intrandum est igitur in rerum naturam et penitus quid ea postulet pervidendum; aliter enim nosmet ipsos nosse non possumus.*

238. § 61 is also hard to square with the following summary (§ 62): *quae cum tot res tantaeque sint, quae inesse in homine perspiciantur . . .*—Contrast *Tusc.* 5.70, where physics is more convincingly connected with the topic of self-knowledge.

of one of its subdivisions, διαλεκτική, though more frequently of the latter; cf. *TLL* s.v. 2. *dissero* 1462.47 ff. But as a member of the three-fold analysis of philosophy or its discourse (cf. *ad* §§ 58–62) *disserendi ratio* is here equivalent to λογική (cf. Boyancé, 1971, 153 n. 3, where our passage is misidentified). On the other hand, in our passage it functions as dialectic in the analysis of formal argument *(ars quaedam intellegendi quid quamque rem sequatur et quid sit cuique contrarium)*; cf. Barnes, 1997, 141 and n. 8. For the claim that it is also a *veri et falsi iudicandi scientia* cf. D.L. 7.42: αὐτὴν [sc. τὴν διαλεκτικήν] ὁρίζονται [sc. οἱ Στωικοί] ἐπιστήμην ἀληθῶν καὶ ψευδῶν καὶ οὐδετέρων; *Brut.* 152: *quod numquam* [sc. Ser. Sulpicius] *effecisset ipsius iuris scientia nisi eam praeterea didicisset artem quae doceret . . . habere regulam qua vera et falsa iudicarentur et quae quibus propositis essent quaeque non essent consequentia . . . Dialecticam mihi videris dicere, inquit* [sc. Brutus]; *Tusc.* 5.68: *. . . tertius in iudicando quid cuique rei sit consequens quid repugnans, in quo inest omnis cum subtilitas disserendi, tum veritas iudicandi*; *Top.* 6.: *iudicandi enim vias diligenter* [sc. *Stoici*] *persecuti sunt ea scientia quam* διαλεκτικὴν *appellant . . .* In our passage, however, Cicero brings *disserendi ratio* into the picture not as part of the process of self-discovery but only afterward in order to protect the insights won *(haec omnia, quasi saepimento aliquo, vallabit . . .)*; cf. *Ac.* 1.34 (cited *ad* § 38); *ad* § 56.—*Saepimentum* is first attested here.[239] This function of dialectic was first described by Plato: ἆρ᾽ οὖν δοκεῖ σοι, ἔφην ἐγώ, ὥσπερ θριγκὸς τοῖς μαθήμασιν ἡ διαλεκτικὴ ἡμῖν ἐπάνω κεῖσθαι, καὶ οὐκέτ᾽ ἄλλο τούτου μάθημα ἀνωτέρω ὀρθῶς ἂν ἐπιτίθεσθαι . . . (*Rp.* 534e2–4), where θριγκός has the sense "topmost course of stones in a wall, coping" (LSJ s.v., I); the word shades into the sense "*wall, fence* of any sort" (ibid. II); cf. Alcin. 7 *fin.*: ἐπεὶ δὲ ἡ διαλεκτικὴ ἰσχυρότατον τῶν μαθημάτων, ἅτε καὶ περὶ τὰ θεῖα καὶ βέβαια γινομένη, διὰ τοῦτο καὶ ἀνωτέρω τῶν μαθημάτων τάττεται, ὥσπερ θριγκός τις ὑπάρχουσα ἢ φυλακὴ τῶν λοιπῶν; the latter meaning alone at Clem. Al. *Strom.* 6.81.4 (= p. 472.17–18 St.): οἷον θριγκὸς γάρ ἐστι διαλεκτική, ὡς μὴ καταπατεῖσθαι πρὸς τῶν σοφιστῶν τὴν ἀλήθειαν. The metaphor was taken up in the Stoic comparison of philosophy to a garden with logic as the enclosure (ὁ περιβεβλημένος φραγμός), the fruits as ethics, and the land or trees as physics (D.L. 7.40 and, dependent on Stoic sources, Phil. *Agr.* 14). Cicero's use of the image thus corresponds to that of the Stoics and Middle Platonists; cf. Boyancé, 1971, 144–47.

---

239. *OLD* s.v. lists Var. *R.* 1.14.1 first, but that work dates to 37; cf. H. Dahlmann, *RE* Suppl. 6 (1935), 1185.8–9.

**cumque se ad civilem societatem natum senserit, non solum illa subtili dispu-
tatione sibi utendum putabit, sed etiam fusa latius perpetua oratione, . . .]**
Cumque se ad civilem societatem natum senserit: the point follows somewhat oddly upon the preceding cosmopolitanism; cf. Kretschmar, 62. The
topic occurs also at *Tusc.* 5.72 *(transeat idem iste sapiens ad rempublicam
tuendam . . .)* but without an emphasis on cosmopolitanism in the same
context (the difficulty there is the conclusion *quid haec tandem vita
desiderat, quo sit beatior?* juxtaposed with the *vita activa,* notoriously ex-
posed to worries, etc.). For the claim of the *patria* upon one see also *ad* § 16
(. . . cuius muneris colendi efficiendique—).—In view of the parallel with
Tusc. 5.72, Theiler, 46 n. 2, followed by R. Müller, 228, sees the topic of
political oratory as derived from Cicero's source. Possibly so; but surely the
topic of dialectic was capable of triggering more than once in Cicero's mind
an association with the public uses of rhetoric; cf. the contrast at *Tusc.* 3.22
between the dialectic of the Stoics and a fuller style of discourse more apt to
persuade.

Two styles of discourse are contrasted here, one of them the *genus tenue*
or *subtile* (cf. *de Orat.* 3.177), associated elsewhere with philosophers such
as Socrates (ibid. 3.60; *Brut.* 31) or the Stoics (*de Orat.* 3.66) or with proof
in forensic speeches (*Orat.* 69), the other a fuller style suited to other public
uses. Only later, at *Orat.* 91–96, did Cicero develop the concept of the
Middle Style; cf. M. Winterbottom, "Cicero and the Middle Style," *Studies
in Latin Literature and Its Tradition in Honour of C.O. Brink, PCPhS,*
Suppl. 15 (Cambridge, 1989), 125 ff. Similar to the distinction of our passage is § 36 or *Off.* 1.3, where Demetrius of Phalerum is called *disputator
subtilis, orator parum vehemens;* cf. the contrast of Sulpicius and Cotta at
de Orat. 3.31 and of Lysias and Demosthenes at *Brut.* 35. On Lysias as a
subtilis orator who succeeded at the bar cf. *Orat.* 30.

. . . qua regat populos, qua stabiliat leges . . .] These characteristics are
placed at the beginning of the list since they connect with the theme of this
work; cf. § 37; for a similar process of reasoning from social obligation to
political activity cf. *Fin.* 3.68: *cum autem ad tuendos conservandosque
homines hominem natum esse videamus, consentaneum est huic naturae ut
sapiens velit gerere et administrare rempublicam . . .*—What is the subject's
qualification? Presumably his status as a *vir bonus,* in whatever sense (see *ad*
§ 59); Schmidt, 1959, 226,[240] would add *et sapiens,* but this has not been
said, merely that *sapientia* is guiding (§ 59), educating, and giving rise to the

---

240. Sim. ibid., 227: "es geht um die 'sapientia' des einzelnen"; see also p. 223 and n. 227
supra.

qualities of this individual (§ 62); see also *ad* § 63 *(eam cuius studio teneor—).*

... **factaque et consulta fortium et sapientium cum improborum ignominia sempiternis monumentis prodere.**] Here Cicero has in mind what he elsewhere calls *monumenta rerum gestarum* (*de Orat.* 1.201), i.e., history (cf. *OLD* s.v. *monumentum* 5b); the topic broached at the beginning of the dialogue (§§ 5–8) thus finds an honorable place in the life of the statesman after all.—One expects one of Cicero's favorite *clausulae* as at the end of the other periods of this section (cf. *ad* §§ 58–62 and the following note). Forms of *sempiternus* often perform the function of providing a ditrochaic sentence-ending; might *sempiternis* have been displaced in transmission?

quae cum tot res tantaeque sint, quae inesse in homine perspiciantur ab eis qui se ipsi velint nosse, earum parens est educatrixque sapientia.] This sentence neatly summarizes the preceding and draws together the theme of knowing oneself and the encomium of wisdom (= *sapientia*); with synizesis of the final *-ia* a favorite Ciceronian clausula is effected (type *debuerat omne*); for the license cf. §§ 1 *(ingenio)*, 22 *fin.*, and *ad* 3.7.3.—For the characterization as *parens* cf. *ad* § 58.—*Educatrix* first occurs in our passage—its only metaphorical application to something inanimate in classical literature; *educator* is also first attested in Cicero (*Planc.* 81); cf. *TLL* s.vv.

63 Atticus praises the encomium but is puzzled about its relevance. Heinemann, 2, 239, takes Atticus' query as an indicator "daß diese *peroratio* zu Ciceros Thema nicht paßt." Certainly the relevance is not prima facie clear and requires explanation, which Marcus proceeds to give. The answer is in two parts (marked by *primum . . . deinde . . .*) on two different levels: (1) pertaining to the subject; (2) pertaining to Marcus himself, as befits this most personal of Cicero's extant philosophical dialogues. Under (1) we now discover that the preceding amounts to an indirect encomium of *ius:* the grandeur of *ius* is in proportion to that of its source, philosophy; the passage thus provides at the same time a finale to Book 1, which dealt essentially with *ius* in relation to philosophy, and an overture to the rest of the essay focused on *ius* itself as embodied in *leges*. No less important to Cicero (and thus placed on the same level as [1]) is the personal motive of paying tribute to philosophy.

A. Laudata quidem a te graviter et vere; sed quorsus hoc pertinet?] *Laudata:* sc. *sapientia.* Once again it is Atticus who raises the question of relevance; cf. §§ 1 and 4.

M. Primum ad ea, Pomponi, de quibus acturi iam sumus, quae tanta esse volumus.] The formal mode of address marks the solemn conclusion of the

Book, as at *Off.* 3.121; contrast the more familiar forms used at *Sen.* 1 as well as §§ 1 and 3 *(Attice)* and § 5 *(Tite)*.—*Quae tanta esse volumus:* the significance of the topic has come under discussion at §§ 16 and 28a; cf. *ad locos. Volo* = "claim, maintain"; cf. *OLD* s.v., 18.

non enim erunt, nisi ea fuerint unde illa manant amplissima.] It is fitting for Marcus' final speech to include a reference to sources and derivatives (the size of the derivative implying that of the source, according to a common rhetorical topos: cf. Arist. *Rh.* 1363b27 ff.), since the search for the source of *ius* has been the project of this Book; cf. § 16: *fons legum et iuris;* § 18: *iuris principia;* § 28: *quam tu longe iuris principia repetis!*

. . . eam cuius studio teneor, quaeque me eum quicumque sum effecit, non possum silentio praeterire.] *Studium sapientiae,* like *amor sapientiae* (cf. § 58), is equivalent to *philosophia* (cf. *Off.* 2.5); *quae* refers back to *eam* (= *sapientiam*). In saying that *sapientia* made him what he is Cicero is not implying that it made him wise (indeed at *Luc.* 66, speaking in his own person, he says *non . . . sum sapiens*), merely that it has improved his mind.— "Jamais Cicéron n'a affirmé plus solennellement son attachement à philosophie et sa dette envers elle . . ."; ". . . ces pages du *De legibus* sont la première manifestation publique et d'une solennité quasi religieuse d'un Cicéron philosophe" (Boyancé, 1975, 21 and 38, respectively); to the latter point I would add: if not actually the first public manifestation (because not published during his lifetime), these pages were, when written, intended to be such.—For Kretschmar, 63, these words signal a change in Cicero's relation to philosophy and rhetoric, with the former now occupying the center of his interest. This impression is deceptive, however. Cicero had a lifelong interest in both (for his lifelong interest in philosophy see M. Griffin, "Philosophical Badinage in Cicero's Letters to His Friends," in Powell, 1995, 325–46) and did not sharply distinguish the two; thus philosophy, as here defined, subsumes rhetoric (cf. *ad* § 62), as it does in the list of his philosophical books at *Div.* 2.1 ff.—*Quaeque me eum quicumque sum effecit:* this can be taken, together with *Orat.* 12 (cited *ad* § 36[241]), as evidence that Cicero regarded himself as a "philosophical orator." He pays tribute, albeit vaguely, to the *persons* who made him what he was at *Off.* 1.155.

A. Re⟨cte⟩ vero facis et merito et pie, fuitque id, ut dicis, in hoc sermone faciendum.] Atticus' reply, with which this Book concludes, is thus rightly printed in recent editions, including *recte vero* (Feldhügel), the needed response to Cicero's *ut spero recte,* for *revero* of B¹(A¹?), *revera* BˣAˣ, *vero*

---

241. Note the similar formula of modesty: *quicumque sim;* sim. also *Off.* 1.155: *nosque ipsi, quidquid ad rempublicam attulimus . . .*

PHL, *ne vero* ε, and Vahlen's *pie* for *ipse* of ω.[242]—There is no external marker of the end of this Book. Similar in this regard is the conclusion of *Rep.* 1, where the conversation likewise continues on the same day. *Rep.* 1 is also similar in concluding with an expression of diffidence on the part of the main speaker and a confirmation by the main interlocutor that all is well. In *Leg.* the transition from one Book to the next corresponds to a change of procedure insofar as Atticus proposes (2.1) that they have walked enough and can sit through the next part of the discussion. On problems of closure in the dialogues in general cf. Becker, 29–30.

---

242. It follows that *vero* functions as usual in a confirmatory response ("certainly, indeed"), as one expects with a repeated word (note the implied question in *ut spero recte*), not in the literal sense "in accordance with the truth, honestly" (at *OLD* s.v., our passage is to be categorized under 4a, rather than 1); cf. also Kroon, 291–98 ("*vero* in reactive moves").

Commentary on Book 2

Ex patriis ritibus optuma colunto.
—Cic. Leg. 2.22.3

There is between Book 1 and the rest of *Leg.* an odd dichotomy. The Stoic premise of Book 1 is that law is perfect reason (1.18, 23, etc.), the moral voice within; for the Stoics the sage is the only human being to possess this, and natural law could be realized only in a community of gods and sages. One might, then, have expected the rest of *Leg.* to be a plan to educate human beings to achieve, or approximate, perfect reason. Cicero speaks of a community of gods and men (not sages) at 1.23 and offers the formula *inter quos autem ratio, inter eosdem etiam recta ratio* (ibid.), but, in fact, it is not so simple to progress from ordinary human being possessing reason to sage possessing perfect reason, and much of Middle Stoic ethical teaching was devoted to the problem. The move from the embrace of Stoic theory in Book 1 to the drafting of legislation for human communities in Books 2 ff., though held the prospect as early as 1.17,[1] is thus deeply problematic in ways Cicero either did not see or chose not to grapple with. The project would not have been expected to result in laws for human communities, still less in laws resembling actual Roman legislation (cf. §§ 23 and 62; 3.12).[2] The plan for the drafting of laws in Books 2 ff. goes back, then, not so much to the "source" of law as described in Book 1, namely nature,[3] as to *Rep.* or,

---

1. . . . *considerandae leges quibus civitates regi debeant;* . . .

2. Cf. Büchner, 1961, 89: ". . . konnte nach dem ersten Buche nicht eine Interpretation der römischen Gesetzeswelt erfolgen, sondern da hätte ein Naturrecht prinzipiellerer Art aufgestellt werden müssen . . ."; on the difference in approach between Books 1 and 2 ff. cf. also Anselmo, 665 ff.; Mehl, 141; Farrell, 24; but cf. Moatti, 294–95, who argues for unity.

3. There is no consistent process of reasoning from nature to the laws of 2–3, as one would have expected in light of 1.44. The usual criteria are tradition (e.g., §§ 23, 40, esp. 54–68: see below), promotion of the state interest (cf. §§ 26 and 30), and considerations of practicality (§§ 29, 45, 61) or morality (§§ 28, 35–36). References to nature as a criterion occur at §§ 2, 59, and 61. But § 2 is merely a cross-reference to 1.44 (*itaque ut tu paulo ante de lege et de iure disserens ad naturam referebas omnia*); and at § 62 the conformity of the XII Tables to Nature is merely postulated, not argued (*haec habemus in XII, sane secundum naturam, quae norma legis est,* followed by Atticus' remark *gaudeo nostra iura ad naturam accommodari*); only in

238

rather, to *Rep.* seen in light of what Cicero thought Plato was doing in his *Laws*—providing as a sequel to his *Republic* a separate treatise containing the laws for his state (cf. § 14); at 1.20 Cicero speaks a bit more vaguely about providing laws for the *kind* of state described in *Rep.* A conflict between these two criteria—suitability for the state or kind of state of *Rep.* and conformity with right reason—is never raised as a possible problem.[4]

Various scholars have observed the difference in approach between Books 1 and 2 ff., with a resulting theory, first formulated by Reitzenstein, of the separate composition of Book 1. Reitzenstein's point of departure was the repetition at the beginning of Book 2 of ideas from Book 1. In view of its preoccupation with Antiochus and the problem of the *finis bonorum* Reitzenstein argued that Book 1 ought to have been written later than the spring of 45 as part of the same phase of philosophical writing that yielded the reproduction of Antiochus' doctrines in *Ac.* and *Fin.*;[5] but there is, of course, nothing binding in this, since Cicero was familiar with Antiochus' doctrines much earlier (cf. *Fin.* 5.1, set in 79; Plut. *Cic.* 4.1; the Introduction § 2a). Büchner, 1961, reargued the case for a late date of Book 1 based on criteria of style, rather than content. He sees the repetition of ideas not as superfluous but as understandable on the assumption that Book 2 was composed first and then, after Book 1 had been written, was adjusted to accommodate the different perspective. He focuses on peculiarities of §§ 7–10, including Quintus' request *Ordire igitur; nam hunc tibi totum dicamus diem* (§ 7), where, in light of Book 1, one would have expected *ceterum*, not *totum*; Marcus' reply '*A Iove Musarum primordia*', which looks like the beginning of an exposition; the fact that the ideas about natural law are repeated from Book 1 with only the most superficial reference back to what was established there[6] and in less developed form.[7] P.L. Schmidt has recently argued for this theory in a modified form. For Schmidt Book 2 was composed before Book 1, but Book 1 still dates to the late 50s, rather than 45–44. Taking as his starting point *Q.fr.* 3.5.1–2 with its disclosure of an earlier plan whereby *Rep.* was to be divided into nine books staged on nine days, he argues that *Rep.* as originally conceived included Books 1, 2, 4, and 5 as well as five books of *Leg.* and that Books 3 and 6 of *Rep.* as well as *Leg.* 1 were

---

§ 59 is a connection established between what is natural and a particular law (of Solon); cf. also *ad* 1.20; the introduction to Book 3.

4. Thus, for instance, Ar. *Pol.* 1296b13 ff. recognizes that the best constitution per se may not be the best for a particular group.

5. Reitzenstein, esp. 26–28.

6. § 8: *videamus igitur rursus* . . . ; § 9b: *Aliquotiens iam iste locus a te tactus est.*

7. Büchner, 1961, esp. 84–88.

written later, after Cicero had changed his plan.[8] Schmidt's theory accommodates Büchner's observations; it is also more satisfying than Büchner's in that it explains the point that Büchner had left open, namely why, if in Laelius' speech at *Rep.* 3 Cicero had used similar arguments to *Leg.* 1, he waited until 45–44 to write the latter. Schmidt's theory cannot, however, be strictly demonstrated[9] and requires the assumption that Books 2–3 of *Leg.* were originally conceived (and written?) with the speakers of *Rep.* in mind, which is, to say the least, difficult to picture. An alternative explanation of the phenomena would be: (1) *hunc tibi totum dicamus diem* in § 7 is a true (present progressive) statement: "we are dedicating this whole day to you"; there is no need to assume that it was written for a version in which our Book 2 was the beginning; (2) '*a Iove Musarum primordia*' is an appropriate beginning for the portion of the treatise dealing with the *leges* proper, since ancient law-codes often began with the gods (cf. *ad* § 15); (3) when Cicero began work on Book 2 he did not have a fully formed dialectical strategy and only settled on it in the course of writing; hence he begins with a theory of law along the lines of Book 1, which he has just written, but comes to prefer a broader justification which incorporates utilitarian considerations as well (see *ad* §§ 8–9a; for a similar phenomenon in Book 1 see *ad* 1.48–52a; sim. also the handling of Plato's doctrines: cf. *ad* §§ 39 and 45).

Cicero has chosen to present his views in the form of laws, a palpable influence of Plato's *Laws* upon the form of our work; the diction is, however, as befits Roman laws, archaizing—an attenuated imitation of the Twelve Tables (§ 18). Like Zaleucas, Charondas, and Plato he prefaces an encomium of law (§ 14, executed at §§ 15b–16). This turns out to be a brief case, along Stoic lines, for the existence of god and the divine government of the universe as the foundational beliefs of an ordered human society. The following procedure imitates the Roman legislative process, albeit several different events are telescoped into a single session. The bill was presumably read aloud at promulgation and then posted in public; it would be read again, in whole or in part, at any *contiones* summoned to discuss it and in full prior to the final vote.[10] Our text includes Marcus' reading out of his proposals and then his recommendation of them, as if in a *contio*.[11] Cicero

---

8. Schmidt, 2001; cf. pp. 7–10 *supra*.

9. It is not clear, for instance, that there were, or were meant to be, five books of *Leg.* in addition to Book 1.

10. Cf. M. Crawford, "The Laws of the Romans: Knowledge and Diffusion," in *Estudios sobre la Tabula Siarensis,* ed. J. Gonzalez and J. Arce (Madrid, 1988), 132, with references.

11. For using persuasion and not attempting, in the manner of a tyrant, *omnia vi ac minis cogere,* there was also Platonic precedent (§ 14).

thus produces a commentary on his own laws,[12] a commentary of widely varying proportions that may omit a law altogether, focus on a single element in a law, treat the subject of the law from the ground up, or indulge in lengthy digressions (cf. *ad* 3.49). The persuasive process is preliminary to voting (cf. § 24; 3.11.8),[13] and the interlocutors' comments on Marcus' election law are tantamount to a rejection (he refers to them as "rejecting" his measure by oral vote: *vos quidem ut video legem antiquastis sine tabella* [3.38]). An appendix supplies an assessment of relevant provisions of the pontifical law and the *ius civile* (§§ 46–57 and 58–68). The overall structure of Book 2 can be outlined as follows (see the notes on the individual sections for the organization of material under each):[14]

I. The introductory dialogue (1–7a)
II. Philosophical preliminaries to the laws (7b–14a)
III. The *prooemium legis* (14b–16)
IV. Some further preparatory remarks (17–18)
   A. Relation to Plato
   B. The language of the laws
V. The laws proper (19–22)
   A. Manner of approach to the gods (19:—*vindex erit*)
   B. Licit gods and their shrines (*Separatim nemo—neve ulla vitiorum*)
   C. Sacred rites, their timing, and their manner of celebration (*Sacra sollemnia—20 providento*)
   D. Religious functionaries (*Divisque ⟨alii⟩ aliis sacerdotes—21 obstita pianto*)
     1. The priests
       a. Those who preside over public ceremonies
       b. The *quindecimviri*
     2. The augurs
     3. The fetials
     4. The haruspices
   E. Miscellaneous provisions (*Nocturna mulierum—22*)
     1. Prohibition of women's nightly festivals
     2. Expiations
     3. Public games
     4. Selection of the best ancestral rites
     5. Restriction on alms-giving

12. For the commentary form see further *ad* §§ 23–45.
13. Cf. Cancik, 1995, 299.
14. See Schmidt, 1959, 54; Cancik, 1995, 298–99.

This Book represents a substantial and original intellectual achievement. It is true that Cicero did not, as Varro recommended for one founding a new state, make a thoroughgoing attempt to create a new religious system from the ground up *ex naturae formula* (*ARD* fr. 12); he did, however, select those parts of the Roman tradition to which he wished to attach exemplary value (part V.) and explain those choices (part VI.). The arrangement of the laws is fairly straightforward except for the large group designated as "miscellaneous provisions." Here it is not a priori clear why Cicero treats as separate items "expiations" and "violations of divine law" (E.2. and 7., respectively). Possibly he held *violatum ius* ⟨*divinum*⟩ (if that is the right reading; cf. *ad* § 22.10) in reserve for rhetorical effect in order to conclude the commentary on his laws with a denunciation of Clodius in that connection (§§ 41b–44), since what follows is a quotation from Plato (§ 45) and then (§§ 46–68: no. VII.) material of ambivalent status. This latter material could have been subsumed under VI. as the commentary on the last laws (V.E.9–10), *Sacra privata perpetua manento* and *Deorum Manium iura sancta sunto,* etc., which indeed are otherwise without commentary. This material is, however, rather different from the preceding commentary, which is framed mostly in terms of what is best per se (see pp. 238–39 n. 3 *supra*); here Cicero proposes some laws such as Rome had not seen before: regulation of music (§§ 22.2, 38–39) and against the consecration of arable land (§§ 22.11, 45); cf. Schmidt, 1959, 96. On the other hand, the following section, especially §§ 54 ff., is largely antiquarian, i.e., tradition, Roman and Greek, becomes the basis for argument (cf. Schmidt, 1959, 89); after all, on Cicero's view, establishing the antiquity of a practice can be a step in promoting its claim to be best (cf. § 40); there is innovation in this section as well, however, in the proposal for limits on expenditure for tombs (implicit in

§ 66). Since 1.17 we have been expecting a treatment of *quae composita sunt et descripta, iura et iussa populorum,* including those of the Roman people; and 3.48 cross-refers to 2.46–53 as a discussion of the *ius populi Romani* on the analogy to which Marcus is now (upon completion of his commentary on the *leges de magistratibus*) bidden to provide a corresponding discussion *de potestatum iure.* Hence §§ 46–58 are doing double duty here, both as commentary on Cicero's last laws and as a discussion of relevant points of the *pontificium ius et . . . civile* (cf. the exchange of Atticus and Marcus at §§ 15 *fin.* 16 *init.*), a fact that becomes fully clear to the reader, however, only in light of Book 3; cf. Bögel, 1911, 309.

The fundamental tendencies of Cicero's approach emerge clearly. He is not concerned with providing exhaustive lists of gods, priesthoods, or festivals; indeed in a set of laws purporting to be "by nature" such contingent details should be reduced to a minimum; cf. *ad* 1.17. Cicero is trying rather to save core elements of Roman religion by tying religion closely to morality and reducing the rôle of wealth, with its potential both to impoverish through excessive expenditures and to corrupt. As he writes, Cicero is much occupied with the Bona Dea scandal and the frustrated effort to obtain sanctions against Clodius in the sequel, as well as Clodius' attempt to use religion to shield and make permanent his seizure of Cicero's house by erecting a temple of Liberty on the site (§§ 41–44; also alluded to at §§ 36 and 37). Cicero's religious laws aim *inter alia* to guard against such abuses in future. Cicero wants to insure that religious observance cannot provide cover for (§§ 35–37a) or promote (§§ 38–39) immorality, and he wants to direct the power of the *publicus sacerdos* against those guilty of gross violations (§ 37b). When he sets down rules as to which abstract entities can properly receive temples (§ 19.7), he perhaps has Clodius' Libertas (Licentia, as he calls it in § 42) in view. Another concern is that religion should not impoverish the productive community: thus he bans alms (with one exception: § 40), forbids the consecration of (especially arable) land (§§ 22.11, 45, 67), and wants strict limits set to expenditures on funerals and tombs (§§ 54 ff.). He would also like to see the augurate, of which he himself was now a member (§ 31), restored to its old powers and dignity (§§ 30–33); if properly respected, it, too, can serve to protect state institutions against adventurers like Clodius (cf. *ad* § 14). In accord with optimate political rhetoric, Marcus presents his reforms not as an innovation, but as a return to Roman tradition (§§ 23, 40a, etc.).

A *non liquet* appears to be the appropriate current verdict about the relation of overlappings of opinion or doctrine discussed in the following notes with Varro's *Antiquitates Rerum Divinarum.* The dedication of the work to

Julius Caesar as pontifex maximus points to a date between 63 and 44.[15] It thus remains unclear whether similar views of the two authors should be explained through Cicero's dependence on Varro or as views held generally by intellectuals of the time; the similarities include the definitions of religion and superstition (§ 30), the classification of *augurium* as a species of *divinatio* (§ 32), the dangers of neglect of religious rites and practices (§ 33), and the shared disapproval of the Bacchanalia (§ 37). In addition, the distinction of four types of Fortuna in § 28 has been thought to be an antiquarian list *more Varroniano* (cf. Bögel, 1907, 12), albeit no corresponding material of the *ARD* has been preserved.[16]

If the content of Cicero's sacral laws mostly derives from Roman tradition, Greek philosophy and institutions provide a basis for selection and supplementation. The Greek sources used have been discussed in the case of *Leg.* 2 as of other philosophical books of Cicero; the problem is a complex one. The grounding of the concept of *lex* at §§ 8–13 echoes some features of the essentially Stoic concept of natural law from Book 1 but also, *more Platonico*, abstracts from individual laws a general "power" of law (cf. *ad* § 9b) and adds utilitarian considerations reminiscent of Epicurean contract theory (cf. *ad* §§ 9b–13). Again, the case for belief in the gods at § 16 is largely Stoic (see parallels from *N.D.* 2 cited *ad loc.*) but includes utilitarian elements as well. It is clear, however, that Plato, together with a Pythagorean redaction of the laws of Zaleucus and Charondas, inspired the idea of providing a proem to the legislation (cf. *ad* § 14b).

Some of the innovations vis-à-vis Roman tradition are inspired by Plato (cf. *ad* §§ 19–22 and §§ 68–69). Interesting, though, that in two places Cicero begins with an endorsement of Plato's view only to modify it in the sequel (§§ 38–39 and 45); this suggests some Platonic influence on the topics discussed, but that, as elsewhere, Cicero reserves himself the (Academic) freedom to select, modify, or reject; cf. § 17 (with reference to Plato's influence being restricted to the *orationis genus*); *Luc.* 99; *N.D.* 1.12; *Off.* 2.7–8. In addition, Athenian laws of Solon and Demetrius of Phalerum serve as starting points (cf. *ad* §§ 54–68, 59, and 64), and he also draws

15. Cf. Cardauns, Var. *ARD*, pp. 132–33; H.D. Jocelyn, "Varro's *Antiquitates Rerum Diuinarum* and Religious Affairs in the Late Roman Republic," *BRL* 65 (1982), 148–205, esp. 164–77, seeks to narrow the date of composition to 62–55, perhaps rightly.

16. Varro should be factored into the discussion of similarities of the doctrines of *Leg.* 2 with the religious reforms under Augustus (cf. Dörrie, 1973, 240, who compares the proposals of Cicero with the reforms of Augustus without considering the possible influence of Varro on the latter); cf. *ad* § 19.3. For a comparison of Cicero's constitutional theory with the practice of Augustus cf. Cambeis, 258–60.

inspiration from Theophrastus' works on piety, laws, and legislators (cf. *ad* §§ 15a, 19, 66; cf. also 3.13–14). The idea that Cicero followed Posidonius as his single source for the doctrines of *Leg.* 2 but sought to conceal that dependency seems an inadequate explanation for a work that subtly combines strands of Roman and Greek tradition.[17]

The composition of this Book also calls for general comment. The project itself entails a variety of styles—the urbane banter of the three interlocutors, the archaizing style of the laws themselves, and a down-to-earth expository style in the commentary on the laws. But certain sections within the commentary are clearly still at the rough draft stage and would have required further polish. This is particularly noticeable in the latter part of § 28, where Cicero seems to fall into composition by keywords. In other places there are overlappings of material: §§ 8–9a vs. 9b ff.; §§ 58 and 60; at § 54 topics are listed as if they are not to be treated in detail but then are in fact handled at § 57. Chapters 39 and 45, where he begins with unreserved praise of Plato but then tempers his agreement, show, like §§ 8 ff., that the dialectical strategy may not have been fully thought through. The commentary is highly uneven, sometimes isolating a single aspect of a law, sometimes attacking the underlying problem in a fundamental way; expected cross-references are missing; cf., e.g., *ad* § 26 *init.* This state of the text, together with the unreliable manuscript tradition, poses difficulties for the editor, who needs to determine just how smooth a text to restore (see *supra* pp. 44–45).

1–7a—hunc tibi totum dicamus diem.] This proem to Book 2 is the most frequently cited passage of *Leg.* It is justly admired for its appreciation of natural beauty, the delicate drawing of a tightening bond of friendship between Cicero and Atticus, and Cicero's confession of his special attachment to his own birthplace.[18] Here a transition between major subjects, the philosophical perspective on law in Book 1 and the concrete legislation put forward in Books 2 ff., coincides with a change of scene.[19] Cicero seems more inclined than Plato in his *Laws* to allow room for the exercise of

---

17. Heinemann, 2, 251 ff., and Dörrie, 1973, 225 and 239, see Posidonius behind *Leg.* 2, but the surviving fragments of Posidonius περὶ θεῶν (F 20–23 E.-K.) are too scanty to provide any real foundation for the idea; cf. Turpin, 1885 ff.; for the possibility that Posidonius is the source for individual doctrines cf. *ad* §§ 8 and 62b–66 and 3.4.

18. Cf., e.g., Theiler, 46: "nach der szenischen Einleitung von Buch 2—der schönsten, die ihm gelungen ist, in der sich an Plato geübte Kunst, römische Staatsgesinnung und allgemein menschliches Fühlen zu harmonischem Ganzen zusammenschließt— . . ."

19. For the function of a change of scene in Cicero's dialogues cf., in general, Becker, 25 ff. A further change of scene—a descent to the Liris in search of shade—is indicated in the fragment from Book 5.

private religion.[20] As Cicero finds his own roots in the simple house built by his grandfather in the Italian countryside, so the roots of the best religion lie in the simple rites observed by the Roman ancestors. Hence the very first law admonishes *pietatem adhibento, opes amovento* (§ 19.1), Atticus' first reaction emphasizes the similarity to the laws of Numa (§ 23), and Cicero cites with approval the Pythia's response that one should cling to those cult practices that are *in more maiorum* (§ 40).

The opening dialogue can be arranged under the following headings:

    I. Atticus' reaction to Cicero's native place (§§ 1–4)
    II. The question of two *patriae* (§§ 5–6a)
    III. The setting of the following dialogue (§ 6b)
    IV. The beauty of Atticus' estate at Buthrotum (§ 7a).

The conversation follows a ring pattern, moving from the scene before the speakers (I) to the theoretical problem of the dual identity of *municipales* and its solution by Cicero and Marius (II), then back to a description of the visible landscape (III). In order to avoid an impression of onesidedness, a comparison with Atticus' Buthrotan estate is added at the end (IV).

As in Book 1, the discussion takes its starting point from the natural environment, and again it is Atticus who takes the initiative, this time with the suggestion that they continue the conversation resting on the island in the Fibrenus that has come into view (§ 1). Praising the natural beauties of the place, he declares that he now understands Marcus' fondness for it, which he had not grasped from his speeches and verses (§ 2). Marcus' feelings thus move to the center of interest, as in the prologue to Book 1. Marcus offers that his attachment to Arpinum is of a personal nature, for it contains the house where he was born and thus has a claim to be his and Quintus' *germana patria* (§ 3). In Atticus' reply his process of οἰκείωσις with Arpinum is completed. The revelation of Marcus' relation to this place causes him to become *amicior* to the villa and in general to love the place (*amabo . . . locum*). This is in accord with the general human tendency to

<hr/>

20. Contrast *Lg.* 909d7–8: ἱερὰ μηδὲ εἷς ἐν ἰδίαις οἰκίαις ἐκτήσθω and § 19.4: *Privatim colunto quos rite a patribus ⟨cultos acceperit⟩* as well as the explicit sanctioning of the *Larum sedes* and the *ritus familiae* (ibid.); cf. Turpin, 1891 and n. 67; Burkert, 1987, 11 and 138 n. 57, formulates too generally when he speaks of Cicero as advocating "repression of private cults" (on the basis of § 21.11 *Nocturna mulierum sacrificia ne sunto* etc.); he contrasts Plato in his *Laws* as being "willing to allow some tolerance" (on the basis, apparently, of Plato's disinclination to restrict dances connected with the mysteries at *Lg.* 815c–d); but Cicero, too, makes an exception for the mysteries (§ 36).

be moved by places associated with great men, to whom Cicero is implicitly assimilated (§ 4). Atticus, still in control of the course of the discussion, now steers it back to the concept of *duae patriae* implicit in Marcus' characterization of Arpinum; Marcus replies by comparing Theseus' συνοικισμός of Attica and subjoins a σύγκρισις of his relations to Arpinum and to Rome (§ 5). To illustrate the successful blending of loyalties, Atticus cites Pompey's encomium of Cicero and Marius as two men who, though from the *municipium* of Arpinum, preserved Rome. He then turns to describe the charming landscape before them, namely the island in the Fibrenus where they have now arrived and which will form the scene of the following dialogue (§ 6). Marcus adds a complimentary reference, based on reports from Quintus, to another lovely river, the Thyamis, near Atticus' estate at Buthrotum. This draws Quintus into the conversation for the first time with confirmation and a request to proceed with the agreed subject from the point at which it had been left (§ 7a).

Apart from the somewhat forced premise that Atticus had not known that the brothers were born in Arpinum prior to this visit (cf. Dörrie, 1978, 209), this prologue, with its movement, reminiscent of Plato's *Symposium*, from an attractiveness based on external beauty to one based on internal qualities and its affectionate setting of the scene, provides a charming backdrop for the discussion of philosophy and law that follows. By placing Arpinum and Rome in parallel and showing the depth of Cicero's feeling for the former, he underlines his still stronger attachment to Rome (*pro qua mori et cui nos totos dedere et in qua nostra omnia ponere et quasi consecrare debemus:* § 5). Through adroitly placed allusions Cicero also contrives to keep Greek culture in view (§§ 3, 4, 5, and 6b [twice]), so thoroughly is even this description of Cicero's native place embedded in Greek parallel and precedent.

1 A. Sed visne—sermoni reliquo demus operam sedentes?] The book-division here is unconventional. That *aliud dicendi initium* is needed at this point follows from Quintus' intervention and Marcus' response at 1.57–58. The praise of *sapientia* at 1.58–62 was said to be relevant to the grandeur of the following subject (1.63) and, as a kind of protreptic, might have been expected to lead to it directly, but instead Book 1 draws to a close, and the beginning of Book 2 returns the reader to the dialogue's fictitious frame. One might wonder whether this unusual way of dividing up the material may be related to a need to accommodate an already written Book 2—the thesis of Reitzenstein, which Büchner, 1961, more plausibly reargued (see the introduction to this Book). Division of a conversation without a change of day also occurs, however, at *de Orat.* 2.367, where the host Crassus says

*surgendum censeo et requiescendum; post meridiem, si ita vobis est com-
modum, loquemur aliquid . . . ;* cf. Becker, 29–30. Here the transition is
marked by the change Atticus proposes from walking to sitting (cf. *ad* 1.63).
Similarly the actual framing of legislation in Plato's *Laws* begins when the
speakers have reached a "lovely resting place" (722c8–9: ἐν ταύτῃ παγκάλῃ
ἀναπαύλῃ τινὶ γεγόναμεν).—For the alternation of walking and sitting cf.
ad 1.14; *Brut.* 24: *sed quo facilius sermo explicetur, sedentes . . . agamus;
Fin.* 3.8: *'sed residamus' inquit 'si placet'.*

**. . . locum mutemus, et in insula quae est in Fibreno—nam ⟨id⟩, opinor, illi
alteri flumini nomen est—sermoni reliquo demus operam sedentes?**] At 1.14
Atticus had not hesitated over the name of the Liris, but he does over that of
illud alterum flumen, the smaller and less famous Fibrenus,[21] which joins the
Liris less than three miles from Arpinum. The *insula quae est in Fibreno*
corresponds to the modern Carnello; it is probably identical with the *insula
Arpinas* later considered by Cicero as a possible site for the shrine to Tullia
(*Att.* 12.12; 16 March 45). After some additional walking the three inter-
locutors reach their goal (§ 6b: *sed ventum in insulam est*). Cf. Bunbury;
O.E. Schmidt, 9 ff.

M. Sane quidem; . . .] Assenting *sane* (*OLD* s.v., 6), emphasized by *quidem*
(ibid. s.v., 1a). The formula is first attested at Ter. *An.* 195:[22] SI. *nempe ergo
aperte vis quae restant me loqui?* DA. *sane quidem.* This is its first use by
Cicero; it recurs at § 8 and 3.1; cf. also *Brut.* 292; *Tusc.* 1.78; Reid *ad Ac.*
1.14 (*sane istud*). Later the formula is used as an emphatic *quidem;* cf., e.g.,
Gel. 6.3.8: *Tiro autem Tullius, M. Ciceronis libertus,* <u>*sane quidem*</u> *fuit
ingenio homo eleganti et hautquaquam rerum litterarumque veterum indoc-
tus . . . sed profecto plus ausus est, quam ut tolerari ignoscique possit.*

**nam illo loco libentissime soleo uti, sive quid mecum ipse cogito sive aut
quid scribo aut lego.**] This was especially so when Cicero sought to escape
the heat; cf. *Q.fr.* 3.1.1 (September 54): *ego ex magnis caloribus (non enim
meminimus maiores) in Arpinati summa cum amoenitate fluminis me refeci
ludorum diebus . . . ,* where the *flumen* referred to is the Fibrenus (cf. § 6b
infra);[23] he complains of his inability to do this in a letter of 26 June 45: *nos
cum flumina et solitudines sequeremur quo facilius sustentare nos possemus,
pedem e villa adhuc egressi non sumus; ita magnos et adsiduos imbris
habebamus (Att.* 13.16.1); cf. also *Tusc.* 5.74 (quoted below on § 3).—The

---

21. Cf. § 6; named elsewhere only by the later owner of Cicero's property (Mart. 11.48),
Silius Italicus (8.399: *Fibreno miscentem flumina Lirim*).

22. Based on a search of PHI 5.3.

23. The passage is cited, for instance, by Sir Archibald Geikie, *The Love of Nature among
the Romans* (London, 1912), 249–50 n. 4.

phrase *sive quid mecum ipse cogito* is a variant of an introductory formula found in other Ciceronian works; cf. *Inv.* 1.1: *saepe et multum hoc mecum cogitavi* with other parallels adduced by Hildebrecht Hommel, "Saepe et multum mecum cogitavi," in *Beiträge zur altitalischen Geistesgeschichte. Festschrift Gerhard Radke zum 18. Februar 1984,* ed. R. Altheim-Stiehl and Manfred Rosenbach (Münster, 1986), 139–40.

2 A. Equidem qui nunc potissimum huc venerim, satiari non queo, magnificasque villas et pavimenta marmorea et laqueata tecta contemno.] In describing himself as *qui nunc potissimum huc venerim* Atticus clearly indicates that this is his first visit to the site; cf. also his observation at 1.1, matching his reading with what he now sees (*lucus quidem ille et haec Arpinatium quercus agnoscitur, saepe a me lectus in Mario*; cf. *ad loc.*), and the exchange with Marcus at §§ 3–4.—Though temporarily laid aside at 1.21, a bit of Atticus' Epicureanism comes to the surface in this encomium of the beauties of nature as superior to those of culture. Cf. Lucr. 2.22–31: . . . *delicias quoque uti multas substernere possint / gratius interdum, neque natura ipsa requirit, / si non aurea sunt iuvenum simulacra per aedes / lampadas igniferas manibus retinentia dextris, / lumina nocturnis epulis ut suppeditentur, / nec domus argento fulget auroque renidet / nec citharae reboant laqueata aurataque templa, / cum tamen inter se prostrati in gramine molli / propter aquae rivum sub ramis arboris altae / non magnis opibus iucunde corpora curant . . .* ; Cicero commends the Epicurean valuation of nature at *Fin.* 2.90.—There is a similar ranking of nature and culture at Juv. 3.18 ff.: *quanto praesentius esset / numen aquis, viridi si margine cluderet undas / herba nec ingenuum violaret marmora tofum*; cf. Juvenal, *Satires: Book 1,* ed. S.M. Braund (Cambridge, 1996), *ad* 3.17, who sees the setting of that poem as a parody of that of Plato's *Phaedrus* or our work. In our context one thinks of the contrast between natural law and positive law developed at 1.40 ff.—The theme of the superiority of simplicity over wealth is taken up in the sequel; cf. the very first of the *leges sacrae: Ad divos adeunto caste; pietatem adhibento, opes amovento* (§ 19.1).

ductus vero aquarum, quos isti Nilos et Euripos vocant, quis non cum haec videat irriserit?] *Isti* presumably refers to the owners of the villas so equipped, but to use so vague a referent is not Cicero's usual way; one might have expected *luxuriosi.*—*Nilus* is first used of an artificial canal at *Q.fr.* 3.7.7 (December 54; *OLD* s.v., 2), where Cicero reports progress in construction on his brother's *Arcanum* near Arpinum (cf. Shackleton Bailey *ad Att.* 1.6.2 [= 2.2 of his commented edition]). *Euripus* is so used for the first time in our passage; cf. *TLL* s.v., 1077.42. The most famous (or notorious) construction of the kind was at Lucullus' Neapolitan villa; cf. Plin. *Nat.* 9.170 (with

Shatzman, 380 n. 644): *Lucullus exciso etiam monte iuxta Neapolim maiore inpendio quam villam exaedificaverat euripum et maria admisit, qua de causa Magnus Pompeius Xerxen togatum eum appellabat.*—As Farrell, 21, points out, "it would seem that the main fault of those other estates is that they use cultural means to counterfeit nature, whereas at Arpinum nature has been improved by culture," to which one might add that the "Marian oak" of 1.1–4 is an example of the latter.

itaque ut tu paulo ante de lege et de iure disserens ad naturam referebas omnia, sic in his ipsis rebus, quae ad requietem animi delectationemque quaeruntur, natura dominatur.] With *tu paulo ante—referebas omnia* Atticus summarizes the purport of Book 1 (cf. his summary of the preceding argument at 1.35); the position is formulated *in nuce* at 1.44: *nos legem bonam a mala nulla alia nisi naturae norma dividere possumus*, where *ius* may be assumed as the underlying principle embodied in *lex* (cf. 1.42: *est enim unum ius, quo devincta est hominum societas et quod lex constituit una*); cf. Girardet, 1983, 66 and n. 3.—*Requies animi* and *delectatio*, his primary goals, are where the Epicurean sees the power of nature (*natura dominatur*): Atticus thus appropriates the theme of the preceding discussion and gives it an Epicurean twist.

. . . nihil enim his in locis nisi saxa et montes cogitabam, itaque ut facerem et orationibus inducebar tuis et versibus . . .] Wyttenbach conjectured *narrationibus* for *orationibus.* The latter can be defended, however, with reference to *Planc.* 20 and 22 (Cn. Plancius came from Atina, a little east of Arpinum, both not far from the Abruzzi): *quorum honoribus agri ipsi prope dicam montesque faverunt; . . . tota denique nostra illa aspera et montuosa et fidelis et simplex et fautrix suorum regio;* cf. Schmidt, 1959, 129 n. 2, and Görler *ad loc.* Certainly in the dialogue Marcus and Atticus are represented as friends, and we are meant to suppose that there has been prior communication between them (cf. 1.5: *ut . . . ex te persaepe audio*). Though it may seem a bit artificial for Atticus to have heard of Arpinum only from Cicero's writings and not in personal communications,[24] it may be that Cicero wanted the prior impressions of "Atticus" to have been obtained through a literary filter, given the following *in versibus* and the rôle of the "Marian oak" at the beginning of Book 1. And indeed the historical Atticus was an avid reader of Cicero's speeches (cf. *Att.* 2.1.3). Under "verses" Atticus will be thinking of the *Marius,* in which the narration of the sign of the eagle will have provided the opportunity for an ἔκφρασις of the landscape; cf. *ad* 1.2; Büchner, *RE* 7A1 (1939), 1253.46–48.

---

24. Contrast *Div.* 1.58 (Quintus to Marcus): *saepe tibi meum narravi, saepe ex te audivi tuum somnium.*

3 M. Ego vero, cum licet plures dies abesse, praesertim hoc tempore anni, et amoenitatem hanc et salubritatem sequor; raro autem licet.] *Vero* here, as often, adheres to the pronoun (Kühner-Stegmann, 1, 798) and is used in a mildly adversative context (ibid., 2, 80; *OLD* s.v., 7a); cf. also Kroon, 327.—That the conversation is set in summer has not been explicitly said but is implied in Atticus' suggested route (. . . *et hac quidem ad Lirem, si placet, per ripam et umbram:* 1.14) and the problem of adequate shade raised in the fragment from Book 5. It is also suggested by the plan to imitate Plato's *Laws* (2.69), which, like his *Phaedrus,* is set on a long summer day (*Lg.* 625b; *Phdr.* 229a); cf. also 3.30 (*longitudo diei*) and *ad* § 1. For the attraction of Arpinum in summer cf. *Tusc.* 5.74: . . . *si quis aestuans, cum vim caloris non facile patiatur, recordari velit sese aliquando in Arpinati nostro gelidis fluminibus circumfusum fuisse.* Though he did so *raro,* he did allow himself to retreat to Arpinum, for instance, in June 45, while recovering from the blow of Tullia's death; cf. Marinone, 225–27.

sed nimirum me alia quoque causa delectat quae te non ita attingit.] As his *germana patria* the place holds an additional source of pleasure for Marcus, as he now proceeds to explain.—*Attingo* has the sense "concern, relate to": cf. *OLD* s.v., 12b, where our passage is cited.—The relative clause is transmitted as *quae te non attingit ita,* which Powell has altered to the expected order *quae te non ita attingit* (to which the hiatus is no obstacle); cf. Hand, 3, 497–98;[25] presumably *ita* fell out by saltation and was added in such a way that it appeared to follow rather than precede *attingit.* The alternative is Gulielmius' *Tite* for *ita* (for *Tite* at the end of a sentence when the second person pronoun has preceded cf. § 34: *at vero quod sequitur, quomodo aut tu adsentiare* ⟨*aut*⟩ *ego reprehendam sane quaero, Tite*). In favor of the transposition is the resulting rhythm, *viz.,* with elision, a clausula of Cicero's favorite type (*omne debetur* vs. *omni debebitur* of the transmitted text or Gulielmius' conjecture).

Quia si verum dicimus, haec est mea et huius fratris mei germana patria; . . .] The *iunctura germana patria* occurs only here and in § 5 in classical Latin.[26] Cicero's feeling of connection to his native place found expression, e.g., in his having his son put on the *toga pura* there (*Att.* 9.19.1; ca. 1 April 49) and later having his son and nephew stand for aedile of the *municipium* (*Fam.* 13.11.3; 46).

hinc enim orti stirpe antiquissima sumus, hic sacra, hic genus, hic maiorum multa vestigia.] A sonorous encomium divided into two parts, the first

---

25. Hand suggested either (a) *item* for *ita* or (b) transference of *ita* to Atticus' response (*ita*⟨*ne*⟩? *quae tandem ista causa est?*); Davies deleted *ita.*

26. Based on a search of PHI 5.3.

concluding with the equivalent of a double cretic, the second with the equivalent of cretic plus iamb, two of Cicero's favorite clausulae. The second part is a tricolon with alliteratively dilated final element. Unity is achieved by anaphora of the deictic adverb (the emphatic deixis continues in the sentence after next: *hanc . . . hic*).—Although some later authors assigned him an ancestry from Volscian royalty (Suet. fr. 50 Reiff.: *ex regio Volscorum genere;* Plut. *Cic.* 1.2: οἱ δ᾽ εἰς Τύλλον Ἄττιον ἀνάγουσι τὴν ἀρχὴν τοῦ γένους, βασιλεύσαντα λαμπρῶς ἐν Οὐολούσκοις καὶ πολεμήσαντα ῾Ρωμαίοις οὐκ ἀδυνάτως), deformed in some traditions to an ancestry from Tullus (Hostilius) (Sil. 8.404–11;[27] *Vir. ill.* 81; Cicero jokes about the similar name at *Tusc.* 1.38; sim. about M'. Tullius [cos. 500]: *Brut.* 62), Cicero's own information about his ancestors does not extend beyond his grandfather; cf. F. Münzer, *RE* 7A1 (1939), 822.35–42 and 824.42–48; *ad* 3.36b.—*Hic sacra:* although he felt keenly the importance of familial rites and shrines (cf. §§ 47–53; *Off.* 1.55: *magnum est enim eadem habere monumenta maiorum, isdem uti sacris, sepulcra habere communia*), Cicero provides no information about his own except the claim at *Red. Sen.* 27 that the day of his return from exile would be celebrated in perpetuity by the Tullii Cicerones; cf. Gasser, 43.

hanc vides villam ut nunc quidem est, lautius aedificatam patris nostri studio, . . .] His father, also named M. Tullius Cicero, is known to us only from Cicero's references; cf. F. Münzer, *RE* 7A1 (1939), 824.49 ff. (Tullius no. 28). Marcus' evident pride in his father's elegant refurbishment is in line with the Roman aristocrat's general concern with image expressed in domestic architecture; cf. Andrew Wallace-Hadrill, "The Social Structure of the Roman House," *PBSR* 56 (1988), 44–47; Anne Leen, "Cicero and the Rhetoric of Art," *AJPh* 112 (1991), 229–45, esp. 237 ff.; Dyck *ad Off.* 1.138–40; Susan Treggiari, "The Upper-Class House as Symbol and Focus of Emotion in Cicero," *JRA* 12 (1999), 33–56. The source of financing for the enlargement is unclear (his wife Helvia's dowry?).—Cicero was seldom enthusiastic about the enlargement of buildings; cf. *Off.* 1.138 and *Fin.* 5.2 (with Dörrie, 1978, 214 n. 22), where Piso says that in the senate house he could picture Scipio, Cato, Laelius, and his own grandfather but adds *Hostiliam dico, non hanc novam, quae minor mihi esse videtur posteaquam est maior.*

. . . qui cum esset infirma valetudine, hic fere aetatem egit in litteris; . . .] In view of the encouragement his grandfather had received from M. Scaurus (3.36b), Cicero's father might have been expected to pursue a political

---

27. Besides the ancestor mentioned here, who supposedly fought at Cannae, another *clarum Volscorum Tulli decus* appears at Nola (Sil. 12.175).

career; but *infirma valetudo* provides an excuse for failing to do so; cf. *ad Off.* 1.71.

sed hoc ipso in loco, cum avus viveret et antiquo more parva esset villa, ut illa Curiana in Sabinis, me scito esse natum.] Cicero, himself the owner of a number of splendid villas (cf. O.E. Schmidt), could participate in the legend of Roman austerity only through the circumstances of his birth. M'. Curius Dentatus, four times consul and censor (272), was renowned for his simple way of life.[28] Cf. *Sen.* 55 (Cato is the speaker): *ergo in hac vita* [sc. cultivating the soil] *M'. Curius, cum de Samnitibus de Sabinis de Pyrrho triumphavisset, consumpsit extremum tempus aetatis. cuius quidem ego villam contemplans (abest enim non longe a me) admirari satis non possum vel hominis ipsius continentiam vel temporum disciplinam;* for Cato on Curius cf. also *Rep.* 3.40. Similar thoughts occurred to Seneca as he contemplated the villa of Scipio Africanus (*Ep.* 86).—For Cicero's grandfather, also named M. Tullius Cicero, see *ad* 3.36b.

quare inest nescioquid et latet in animo ac sensu meo, quo me plus hic locus fortasse delectet, . . .] On Cicero's untypically being at a loss for words here in describing his most personal feelings (*inest nescioquid . . .*) cf. Dörrie, 1978, 209, and *ad* 1.21.

. . . siquidem etiam ille sapientissimus vir, Ithacam ut videret, immortalitatem scribitur repudiasse.] Homer never provides so pointed a formulation, but Cicero's inference is justified: Calypso tells Hermes that she has offered Odysseus immortality (*Od.* 5.135–36), and there are several descriptions of his unhappiness on her island and longing for home (1.58–59; 5.81–84 and 151–53).—*Sapientissimus* may be Cicero's rendering of Odysseus' standing epithet πολύμητις (*Od.* 5.214 etc.; cf. *de Orat.* quoted below). Certainly *Ithacam* provides sufficient identification, and *sapientissimus vir* is highlighted by the absence of the name and thus strongly ratifies Odysseus' preference (the statement is underlined by a clausula of the *debuerat omne* type).—*De Orat.* 1.196 offers an expanded version with Rome, not the "smaller homeland," as the equivalent of Ithaca (Crassus is the speaker; similar wording to our passage is underlined): *ac si nos, id quod maxime debet, nostra patria delectat, cuius rei tanta est vis ac tanta natura ut <u>Ithacam illam in asperrimis saxulis tamquam nidulum adfixam sapientissimus vir</u> immortalitati anteponeret, quo amore tandem inflammati esse debemus in eius modi patriam, quae una in omnibus terris domus est virtutis, imperii, dignitatis?* Cf. Bonjour, 81.—At *Att.* 2.11.2 (ca. 24 April 59) Cicero applies

---

28. Schwering, *TLL* Onom. 762.74–77, wrongly refers our passage to the M'. Curius, who ca. 91 was the adversary of M. Coponius in a famous court case (on the *causa Curiana* cf. *ad Off.* 3.67).

to Arpinum Odysseus' description of Ithaca: τρηχεῖ’, ἀλλ’ ἀγαθὴ κουρο-
τρόφος, οὔτ’ ἄρ’ ἔγωγε / ἧς γαίης δύναμαι γλυκερώτερον ἄλλο ἰδέσθαι
(*Od.* 9.27–28).

**4 A. Ego vero tibi istam iustam causam puto, cur huc libentius venias atque
hunc locum diligas; . . .**] For *ego vero* cf. *ad* § 3. The first point, Atticus'
acceptance of Cicero's frequent visits to Arpinum, had been forestalled in
§ 2; hence the emphasis placed (through use of *atque*) on the second point,
that Cicero's love for this place is seen to be just.

**quin ipse (vere dicam) sum illi villae amicior modo factus, atque huic omni
solo in quo tu ortus et procreatus es.**] As Farrell, 19, observes, "the expected
reply to Cicero's encomium of his birthplace would be, 'Yes, I feel just the
same way about my own home town.' Instead, Atticus inscribes himself
within a triangular erotic relationship: Cicero's love for Arpinum produces
in Atticus, who loves Cicero, a similar love for Arpinum." He goes on to
argue that Atticus' "acculturated love" for Arpinum is fundamentally different from the natural love felt for the place by Cicero himself.—As in *tibi
dicam*, the future in *vere dicam* shades toward a modal meaning ("I will tell
the truth," virtually equivalent to "let me tell you the truth"); cf. Hofmann-
Szantyr, 310–11.—The phrase *amicior modo factus*, together with his previous allusion to Cicero's speeches and verses as the sources of his information
about the place (§ 2), indicates clearly that this is meant to be Atticus' first
visit to Arpinum and to the house where Cicero was born; cf. *ad* § 2 and
Dörrie, 1978, 209.—*Ortus et procreatus* is a striking example of ὕστερον
πρότερον; for another cf. *ad* 1.59.

**movemur enim nescioquo pacto locis ipsis in quibus eorum quos diligimus
aut admiramur adsunt vestigia.**] Atticus' *nescioquo pacto* seems to echo
Marcus' *nescioquid*. The addition of *aut admiramur* widens the topic from
personal to intellectual affinity and thus creates space for the examples
Atticus is about to adduce. Cf. *Fin.* 5.2: *'naturane nobis hoc' inquit* [sc. Piso]
*'datum dicam an errore quodam, ut, cum ea loca videamus in quibus
memoria dignos viros acceperimus multum esse versatos, magis moveamur
quam si quando eorum ipsorum aut facta audiamus aut scriptum aliquod
legamus?'*

**me quidem ipsae illae nostrae Athenae non tam operibus magnificis
exquisitisque antiquorum artibus delectant, quam recordatione summorum
virorum, ubi quisque habitare, ubi sedere, ubi disputare sit solitus; stu-
dioseque eorum etiam sepulcra contemplor.**] Cicero is implicitly assimilated
to the *summi viri*, whose dwellings, places of activity, or tombs are deserving
of keen contemplation (*studiose . . . contemplor*). The house where Cicero
was born thus becomes the counterpart to the first topic of conversation in

Book 1, the "Marian oak"; cf. Dörrie, 1978, 209–10; the pairing of the two men becomes explicit in § 6a. The structure of this sentence (*non tam . . . quam*) suggests a scale of value on which works of art rank behind historical monuments; cf. Guilelmus Goehling, *De Cicerone artis aestimatore* (diss., Halle, 1876), 28–29 and 31.—For Atticus' connection with Athens (*illae nostrae Athenae*) cf. *ad* 1.2.—This is the first and, in classical prose, unique example of *ars* in the sense "work of art"; cf. *OLD* s.v., 8b; *TLL* s.v., 673.9–12.—For the two final items in the tricolon (*ubi sedere, ubi disputare*) cf. *Fin.* 5.2: *venit enim mihi Platonis in mentem, quem accepimus primum hic disputare solitum; . . . hic . . . Polemo, cuius illa ipsa sessio fuit quam videmus.*—For the interest in *sepulcra* cf. *Tusc.* 5.64: *cuius* [sc. *Archimedis*] *ego quaestor ignoratum ab Syracusanis, cum esse omnino negarent, saeptum undique et vestitum vepribus et dumetis indagavi sepulcrum.*

quare istum ubi tu es natus plus amabo posthac locum.] The hyperbaton of *istum . . . locum,* separated by the two units *ubi tu es natus* and *plus amabo posthac* enfolds both Cicero and Atticus together in this place; this word order also yields a cretic clausula (double cretic with shortening of the *o* of *amabo*).[29]

M. Gaudeo igitur me incunabula paene mea tibi ostendisse.] This seems to echo the verse *in montis patrios et ad incunabula nostra* cited in *Att.* 2.15.3; cf. *ad* 1.1; Ov. *Met.* 8.99: *Iovis incunabula, Creten.* In the sequel Cicero's *gaudeo . . . me . . . ostendisse* finds its counterpart in Atticus' *me cognosse . . . gaudeo.*—In real life Cicero was not keen to show this modest place to his sophisticated friend; cf. *Att.* 2.11.2; 2.14.2; 2.16.14; Gasser, 39 and n. 46.—This is only the second occurrence of *incunabula* referring to a cradle; the first was at *Ver.* 4.107: *. . . in his locis vestigia ac prope incunabula reperiuntur deorum . . . ,* though both are metaphorical as indicated respectively by *paene* and *prope*; cf. *TLL* s.v., 1077.77 ff.—For *paene* cf. *ad* 1.54.

5 Usually the topic of conversation unfolds linearly, but here for once Atticus reaches back to explore the implications of a phrase Marcus used a bit earlier (*quod paulo ante dixisti*), namely the reference to the brothers' *germana patria*. Cicero thus takes the opportunity to broach a theme that is likely to have concerned many of his generation. Much of Italy was now, since the Social War, possessed of double voting rights, both at Rome and in local communities.[30] The evidence of coins and inscriptions suggests a continuing identification of such "double citizens" with their smaller homeland, the

---

29. For shortening of the -o in first singular verbs, guaranteed in verse from the time of Horace and Ovid on, cf. Leumann, 110.

30. Arpinates possessed full voting rights at Rome (in the Cornelian tribe) from 188 onward; cf. Liv. 38.36.7–9.

source of the family's landed wealth and the natural base of its social prestige and political influence; yet at the same time they were gaining in influence at Rome itself; cf. Gasser, 15, 23, and 27; *RRC,* 728. This situation inevitably entailed the question of primary allegiance. Cicero knew only too well that origin in a *municipium*[31] could be a liability for a Roman politician; thus, in defending P. Sulla, he had faced the sneer of alien status (*consulem peregrinum*) from the aristocratic prosecutor L. Torquatus (cf. Berry *ad Sul.* 23.2), and more recently P. Clodius had launched the provocative question that Cicero quotes at *Har.* 17: *cuius essem civitatis;*[32] on *municipalis origo* in Roman politics generally cf. Wiseman, 1971, ch. 2. Exploring the implications in terms of law and personal allegiance, Marcus argues that, in spite of his use of the phrase *germana patria,* origin as a *municipalis* need not dilute loyalty to Rome, or, as Atticus puts it in concluding the topic, the "smaller homeland" also has a claim to the title *patria* (*ut iam videar adduci, hanc quoque quae te procrearit esse patriam tuam*). To help establish this case, Marcus cites the extension of Athenian citizenship to residents of Attica following the συνοικισμός (see below). He does not cite the Athenian cleruchy or the development in fourth-century Greece of the possibility of holding citizenship of several states simultaneously (isopolity, compared by Mason Hammond, "Germana Patria," *HSPh* 60 [1951], 147–74, esp. 148–51), for Cicero's ἰσοπολιτεία is not juridical, but, though based on a Greek *topos,* purely sentimental; cf. Bonjour, 83–84; Gasser, 14 ff.

The Stoics viewed the question of *duae patriae* from a different angle; cf. Sen. *Ot.* 4.1: *duas respublicas animo complectamur, alteram magnam et vere publicam qua di atque homines continentur . . . alteram cui nos adscripsit condicio nascendi; haec aut Atheniensium erit aut Carthaginiensium aut alterius alicuius urbis quae non ad omnes pertineat homines sed ad certos.*[33] Cicero had, of course, seen recognition of one's status as a *civis totius mundi* as a stage in the process of achieving self-knowledge at 1.61. A Stoic might object that legislating for a state, as Cicero envisages in *Leg.* (cf. 1.37), is no legitimate enterprise, since a state is an artificial construct. Perhaps Cicero

---

31. On Arpinum as a *municipium* cf. *ad* 3.36b.

32. *Hospitem Capitolinum* (Shackleton Bailey for *hostem Capitolinum*), which should probably read at *Dom.* 7 (*aliter* W. Jeffrey Tatum, "*Hospitem* or *Hostem*?" *RhM* 139 [1996], 358–60), is a similar Clodian jibe at Cicero's municipal origin. Cicero himself was, of course, not above using non-Roman ancestry as grist for his own vituperative mill; cf. aspersions cast on Piso's ancestry (*Pis.* frr. 9, 14, 15, 16), particularly odd since he had married his daughter to a Calpurnius Piso (apparently he found some excuse in the corrupt fr. 13); cf. also *Phil.* 11.4: *praemisso Marso nescio quo Octavio, scelerato latrone et egenti . . . consecutus est Dolabella.*

33. See further Vander Waerdt, 1994a, 290; Mark Morford, "The Dual Citizenship of the Roman Stoics," in Byrne-Cueva, 147–64.

aims to counter that point by showing that a state of the Athens/Rome type is a composite of smaller, natural *patriae*.[34]

Ulrich Knoche, "Ciceros Verbindung der Lehre vom Naturrecht mit dem römischen Recht und Gesetz," in *Cicero, ein Mensch seiner Zeit,* ed. Gerhard Radke (Berlin, 1968), 59, sees a symbolic significance in this comparison of the "smaller homeland" to the "larger homeland": "die Rechtsordnung Roms, baut man sie nur auf absolut gerechten Gesetzen auf, hat demnach die Chance, Weltenrecht im gültigsten Sinne zu werden" [sc. just as the "larger homeland" has absorbed the smaller]; but the analogy is faulty in that the same entity, Rome, is the "larger homeland" in relation to Arpinum but the "smaller homeland" in relation to the world; the "smaller homeland" should be absorbed by the "larger," not vice versa; other objections are raised by Gasser, 46.

A. . . . sed illud tamen quale est quod paulo ante dixisti, hunc locum (id est, ut ego te accipio dicere, Arpinum) germanam patriam esse vestram?] *Id est ut* was the proposal of Vahlen[1] for the transmitted *idem.*—Given the general tone, this question is surely ingenuous, not insidious (*pace* Haury, 163 and n. 8).

quid? vos duas habetis patrias? an est una illa patria communis?] Though the Stoics had developed the idea that a human being is born into two communities, one natural, the other conventional (see above), the notion of *duae patriae,* sounded strange to Roman ears; the *iunctura* occurs elsewhere in classical Latin only at Serv. *G.* 3.121,[35] where the possibility is ruled out; the passage deals with the need to cull an old horse ruthlessly, whatever its merits may have been: . . . *quamvis saepe fuga versos ille egerit hostis, / et patriam Epirum referat fortisque Mycenas / Neptunique ipsa deducat origine gentem* (3.120–22); the preserved comment (presumably on *-que* as equivalent to *vel*): *patriam Epirum referat *** non enim potest unus equus duas patrias habere.* Atticus himself was a native of Rome (Nep. *Att.*1.1) and had declined Athenian citizenship when it was offered to him for fear of losing his Roman citizenship; cf. ibid. 3.1: *quo factum est ut huic* [sc. Attico] *omnes honores, quos possent, publice haberent civemque facere studerent: quo beneficio ille uti noluit quod nonnulli ita interpretantur amitti civitatem Romanam alia ascita* (where *quod—ascita* is sometimes

---

34. Cf. also Farrell, 21, who points out in discussing our passage that "Cicero's claim throughout the dialogue [is] that the basis of human law and culture lies in nature. This exposition takes place under an ideological assumption that the cultural institution being discussed is grounded in nature, while the specific terms in which the discussion is framed relegate nature to a clearly inferior position *vis à vis* the cultural force of law."

35. Based on a search of PHI 5.3.

deleted as an interpolation, wrongly; cf. Madvig, 1871–84, 3, 207); hence his difficulty with the concept of *duae patriae;* cf. R. Feger, *RE* Suppl. 8 (1956), 505.67–506.13; Rawson, 1991, 457; Gasser, 24–25 n. 49.—A similar paradox was Ennius' claim to have *tria corda* because he could speak *Graece . . . Osce . . . Latine* (op. inc. fr. i Skutsch = Gel. 17.17.1); cf. Werner Suerbaum, *Untersuchungen zur Selbstdarstellung älterer römischer Dichter: Livius Andronicus, Naevius, Ennius,* Spudasmata 19 (Hildesheim, 1986), 140–42.

nisi forte sapienti illi Catoni fuit patria non Roma sed Tusculum.] For the epithet *sapiens* Cicero often attributes to Cato see Powell *ad Sen.* 5; for the content see the note after next.

M. Ego mehercule et illi et omnibus municipibus duas esse censeo patrias, unam natur⟨ae, alter⟩am civitatis; . . .] For *mehercule* see *ad* 1.12. Cf. *IG* II² 3, 11169.9–10 (grave of one Dionysius; Ceramicus; mid-4th cen.): δισσαὶ δ' αὖ πατρίδες σ' ἢ μὲν φύσει, ἢ δὲ νόμοισιν / ἔστερξαν πολλῆς εἵνεκα σωφροσύνης. Cicero reformulates the distinction between nature and convention below: . . . *habuit alteram loci patriam, alteram iuris; . . .* The *recentiores* already supplied the missing matter. E.T. Salmon, "Cicero, Romanus an Italicus Anceps," in *Cicero and Virgil: Studies in Honour of Harold Hunt,* ed. J.R.C. Martyn (Amsterdam, 1972), 75–86, argues that this claim, as regards *omnes municipes,* is overstated and that this degree of Roman patriotism existed throughout Italy only beginning with Octavian's triumviral rule.

ut ille Cato, cum est Tusculi natus, in populi Romani civitatem susceptus est.] Cato made no secret of his origin in the *municipium* of Tusculum; he seems, for instance, to mention with local patriotic pride *lucum Dianium in nemore Aricino Egerius Laevius Tusculanus dedicavit dictator Latinus* (*hist.* fr. 58). Though associated in the public mind with his place of origin (cf. *Planc.* 20), he seems to have escaped criticism on such grounds (*Sul.* 23).— Tusculum was among the first, if not the first, *municipium* to receive Roman citizenship; this occurred, according to the historical tradition, ca. 381; cf. G. McCracken, *RE* 7A2 (1943–48), 1467.55 ff. By Cicero's day it had produced more consular families than all the other *municipia* combined (*Planc.* 19).

ut vestri Attici, priusquam Theseus eos demigrare ex agris et in astu, quod appellatur, omnes se conferre {se} iussit, et sui erant idem et Attici, . . .] The illustration is chosen to involve Atticus, long-time resident of Athens (*vestri Attici;* cf. *ad* 1.2); cf. 1.3: ⟨non⟩ *longe a tuis aedibus;* § 36 (*Athenae tuae*). The result is that "the modern custom is justified, not by an appeal to nature, as Cicero's derivation of the legal order from the natural order might suggest, but by a paradigm drawn from another culture" (Farrell, 20). The history, however, is flawed: the συνοικισμός welded the communities of Attica into a unified state but did not involve resettlement of all the citizens *ex agris in astu*, which only occurred, with disastrous consequences, during the Peloponnesian War; cf., in general, Kahrstedt, *RE* 4A2 (1932), 1435.61 ff. (s.v. Synoikismos); Robert Parker, *Athenian Religion: A History* (Oxford, 1996), 10–17. The process is likely to have been more gradual than Cicero's words suggest, as our earliest source for the συνοικισμός, Thuc. 2.15–16, already indicates; cf. II. Herter, *RE* Suppl. 13 (1973), 1212.8 ff. (s.v. Theseus).—The Greek-derived *astu*, though taken over into Latin as early as Ter. *Eu.* 987, is still qualified with the apologetic *quod appellatur* here, though Nepos felt no such need (*Them.* 4.1; *Alc.* 6.4); cf. *TLL* s.v. For use of Greek terms in *Leg.* cf. p. 39 *supra; ad* 3.46.—The *recentiores* already correct the repetition of *se*.

. . . sic nos et eam patriam ducimus ubi nati, ⟨et illam qua excepti⟩ sumus.] The words *et illam qua excepti* first occur in P; they are nonetheless needed in order to complete the terms of the comparison,[36] with *et sui erant* corresponding to *et eam patriam ubi nati* and *et Attici* corresponding to *et illam a qua excepti sumus.*

sed necesse est caritate eam praestare ⟨e⟩ qua reipublicae nomen ⟨et⟩ universae civitatis est, pro qua mori et cui nos totos dedere et in qua nostra omnia ponere et quasi consecrare debemus; . . .] After having tempered the significance of the *patria* by acknowledging *duae patriae,* Cicero now goes about rehabilitating the *patria,* but he does so in an unexpected way. One would have thought, given what Cicero has just said about Arpinum (*germana patria:* 3), that this would take precedence *caritate,* but in fact this place is reserved for Rome, and the damage must again be repaired in the sequel (*dulcis autem non multo secus est ea quae genuit quam illa quae excepit*). For the criterion of *caritas* cf. Bonjour, 63–64; for the expression of willingness to die for the *patria* cf. *ad Off.* 1.57 (there add reference to *Att.* 8.2.2 [17 February 49]: . . . *qui* [sc. *Pompeius*] *urbem reliquit, id est patriam, pro qua et in qua mori praeclarum fuit*).—We adopt Bake's ⟨e⟩ as well et Lambinus' ⟨et⟩, a more plausible solution than du Mesnil's deletion of *reipublicae* and substitution of *civitati* for *civitatis.* Translate: "from which derives the name of the republic and of the entire state" [sc. of which we are a part].—This is perhaps the first use of *consecro* in the sense "devote," "dedicate to" (note the *quasi*): cf. *OLD* s.v., 5; *TLL* s.v., where our passage would belong at 382.67.—The sentence concludes with a

---

36. *Pace* Schmidt, 1974, 212–13, and Görler.

quasi-hymnic piling up of relative clauses (cf. Norden, 1913, 168 ff.) and a fine clausula consisting of cretic plus trochee.

itaque ego hanc meam esse patriam prorsus numquam negabo, dum illa sit maior, haec in ea contineatur.] For the emphatic particle *prorsus*, often adhering to negatives, whether preceding or postponed, cf. *OLD* s.v. *prorsus*[1] 2b; Hand, 4, 619; Madvig *ad Fin.* 2.17.—The proviso is needed to exclude the possibility of a conflict of loyalties. Nicolet, 1966–74, 1, 412, tries to connect *maior* here with the juridical concept of the *maiestas populi Romani*, unconvincingly.—After these words the following text is transmitted: *habet civitatis, et unam illam civitatem putat.* This is often emended to ⟨. . . *duas*⟩ *habet civitates, sed unam illas civitatem putat* on the assumption that *omnis municeps* or the like has fallen out as the subject (*duas* add. Ziegler after Ascensius; *sed unam illas* Vahlen). But as Schmidt, 1969, 266, has shown, our passage does not recognize the possibility of two *civitates,* the term *civitas* being reserved for the *urbs* (cf. *cum ortu Tusculanus esset, civitate Romanus*). Schmidt, *loc. cit.*, n. 11, suggests ⟨*patriam*⟩ *habet civitatis* (cf. above: *duas . . . patrias, unam natur⟨ae, alter⟩am civitatis*). But perhaps the best solution is the simple deletion already effected by S[2]: the statement *itaque ego . . .* forms an effective conclusion to the topic of *duae patriae;* it is hard to see how it could be improved upon by these words, however supplemented; and, as J.G.F. Powell points out (*per litt.*), Atticus' reply is framed as to the more personal conclusion *itaque ego . . . in ea contineatur.* Perhaps the words *habet civitatis, et unam illam civitatem putat* derive from a reader's conclusion or summary extrapolated from the first sentence of Marcus' speech.

6 Atticus' speech falls into two parts, distinguished in modern editions by paragraph division, the first concluding the previous topic of *duae patriae* by reference to the services to Rome of the two great Arpinates, Cicero and Marius, the second resuming from § 2 his enthusiastic reaction to the natural environment.

6a Besides his ancestors and associated rites and monuments (cf. *ad* § 3), another tie that bound Cicero to his birthplace was his great fellow-Arpinate (and distant relative) C. Marius (Atticus assumed at 1.4 that on grounds of their common place of origin Cicero must have expert knowledge about Marius' biography); cf. *Sest.* 50: *. . . divinum illum virum atque ex isdem quibus nos radicibus natum ad salutem huius imperi, C. Marium . . .* On Cicero's complex relation to Marius and his legacy cf. Gnauk; T.F. Carney, "Cicero's Picture of Marius," *WS* 73 (1960), 83–122; Mitchell, 1979, 6–9.

A. Recte igitur Magnus ille noster, me audiente, posuit in iudicio, cum pro Ampio tecum simul diceret,—ut iam videar adduci, hanc quoque quae te procrearit esse patriam tuam.] Cicero was aware of the pride with which

Pompey bore this *cognomen,* conferred by his troops in 81 and confirmed by Sulla; cf. Plut. *Pomp.* 13.4–5; Plin. *Nat.* 7.96. He uses *Magnus* alone in show of affection (real or apparent) or intimacy, albeit rarely after 59; for another example cf. *Mil.* 68, where the more formal reference by means of *praenomen* plus *nomen* has appeared not long before (§ 67): *te, Magne, tamen ante testaretur, quod nunc etiam facit;* cf. Adams, 1978, 160–61; Shackleton Bailey, 1992, 78. For *Magnus . . . noster,* emphasizing the shared tie, cf. *Pompeium . . . nostrum* at 3.22; Shackleton Bailey, 1995, 80–81. In letters to Atticus, however, he also exploits the ironic potential of the cognomen; cf. Corbeill, 81. For Cicero's relations with Pompey down to his departure for Cilicia, cf. Johannemann; cf. also Allen M. Ward, "The Early Relationship between Cicero and Pompey until 80 B.C.," *Phoenix* 24 (1970), 119–29, and "Cicero and Pompey in 75 and 70 B.C.," *Latomus* 29 (1970), 48–71.—T. Ampius Balbus (tr. pleb. 63; pr. 59) was a partisan of Pompey. Proconsul of Asia in 58, he was probably transferred thence to Cilicia (when Gabinius was assigned Syria as his province instead of Cilicia) and superseded there by Lentulus Spinther at the end of 57 or beginning of 56; cf. Shackleton Bailey *ad Fam.* 3.7.5 (= 71.5); *MRR* 3, 15. If the charge was *repetundae,* 56 would be the likely trial date. Gruen, 1974, 314, places the trial in 55, after Ampius' failed consular campaign. But, as J. Crawford, 175, notes, *ambitus* charges were unlikely to be filed against the loser. For collaboration of Cicero and Pompey in defense cf. *Balb.* from early 56.—Cicero had bracketed himself with Marius as a "preserver" of Rome in reply to Torquatus' criticism of his municipal roots at *Sul.* 23 (quoted *ad* 3.23). Here he makes the point doubly indirect as a statement of Pompey quoted by Atticus; in this way Cicero may hope to deflect to a degree criticism for self-praise; for Cicero as a target of such criticism cf. Plut. *de Laude Ipsius* 540f.; *Comp. Cic. et Dem.* 2; Fuchs, 2, ties this trait of the orator to his inability to find a historian willing to write about his consulate (cf. *ad* 1.5b–8). That may be a factor, but the causes surely lie deeper and have to do with his insecurity as a *novus homo;* further material at Graff, 77 ff.; other palliative factors are adduced by Walter Allen, Jr., "Cicero's Conceit," *TAPhA* 85 (1954), 121–44. For another Pompeian encomium on Cicero cf. *ad Off.* 1.78. For Cicero and Marius as the two great Arpinates cf. *Planc.* 20.—*Ut iam videar adduci:* sc. *credere* (Reid).—Atticus' concession that Marcus' birthplace *also* (*quoque*) can count as his *patria* is, as Farrell, 21, remarks, to the modern mind "a jarring paradox."

6b With its three different similes Atticus' description of the natural setting "load[s] the island with a variety of overdetermined cultural markers" (Farrell, 22); see below. It also raises some points about dualities suggestive of

the previous theme: the island divides the Fibrenus into two parts which
then flow into one; and the Fibrenus in turn flows into the Liris. The shifting
and merging identities of nature seem to mirror the condition of humans in
relation to their *patria(e)*. In addition, as the infusion of the Fibrenus has a
significant impact on the Liris by making it colder, so citizens from the
"smaller homelands," like Marius and Cicero, may have a significant impact
on Rome, though the larger river remains dominant, just as Rome does. The
comparison to human institutions is explicit: *et quasi in familiam patriciam
venerit, amittit nomen obscurius.*

Sed ventum in insulam est; . . .] With these words Atticus announces the
completion of the plan formed at § 1 to rest on the island of the Fibrenus,
the modern Carnello.

hac vero nihil est amoenius. ut enim hoc quasi rostro finditur Fibrenus, . . .]
This is one of a number of enthusiastic appreciations of nature deriving from
Cicero's pen; they include *Luc.* 80 and *Q.fr.* 3.1.14; cf. in general A.
Foucher, "Cicéron et la nature," *BAGB* 1955.3, 32–49.—Atticus' praise of
the site chosen for rest is more elaborate than Socrates' simple exclamation
at *Phaedr.* 230b2: νὴ τὴν Ἥραν, καλή γε ἡ καταγωγή; cf. also Pl. *Lg.*
722c8–9 cited *ad* § 1.—This first use of *rostrum* with reference to the part
of an island projecting into the current of a river is qualified by *quasi*, clearly
a development of the use of *rostrum* of the prow of a ship that cleaves the
water; cf. *OLD* s.v., 2b and c. Farrell, 23, sees an allusion to the *rostra*
captured in the Roman naval victory over Antium in 338 that adorned the
speaker's platform at Rome; the civic center of Rome thus conjured would
be an appropriate backdrop to Cicero's legislative project.

. . . et tantum complectitur quod satis sit modicae palaestrae loci!] It is a
mistake to regard these words with their sober indication of dimensions as
disturbing (*pace* Gasser, 34, who, however, admits that the description as a
whole "wirkt . . . warm und lebendig"): Cicero is intent on creating for
Romans at leisure an appropriate correlate of the settings of Plato's dialogues; cf. Gasser, 40. The Greek *palaestra* was used for instruction as well
as athletics (cf. *de Orat.* 2.21: *cum omnia gymnasia philosophi teneant,
tamen eorum auditores discum audire quam philosophum malunt;* in general, Willi Göber, *RE* 18.2 [1942], 2492.56 ff.) and is the setting, e.g., of
Plato's *Charmides.* Hence it seems as though nature has created this space
for the use to which the friends will put it (*tamquam id habuerit operis ac
muneris ut hanc nobis efficeret sedem ad disputandum*).—The hyperbaton
of *tantum . . . loci* instantiates a fine double cretic clausula.

**quo effecto . . . statim praecipitat in Lirem, et quasi in familiam patriciam
venerit, amittit nomen obscurius . . .**] The reference is to adoption, by

which, in its traditional form, the adoptee would assume the name of the adoptive father with addition of his former *gentilicium* as an *adnomen* with the *-anus* suffix; cf. Bruno Doer, *Die römische Namengebung. Ein historischer Versuch* (Stuttgart, 1937), 74 ff., esp. 80; there was, however, some variation in the late Republic; cf. Shackleton Bailey, 1991, 53 ff., esp. 55–56. On the obscurity of the Fibrenus cf. *ad* § 1.

. . . Liremque multo gelidiorem facit: . . .] For the accusative *Lirem* see *ad* 1.14. Besides the headnote to this section cf. Bunbury, 898: "[The Fibreno's] whole course does not exceed seven or eight miles in length; but, like many rivers in limestone country, it rises all at once with a considerable volume of water, which forms, in the first instance, a deep and clear pool, or little lake, from whence its waters flow in a channel of ten or twelve yards in breadth, but of great depth and remarkable clearness . . . The Fibreno is still remarkable for its extreme coldness, a quality common to many rivers which rise under similar circumstances."

nec enim ullum hoc frigidius flumen attigi, cum ad multa accesserim; ut vix pede temptare id possim, quod in Phaedro Platonis facit Socrates.] Cicero has, of course, had Plato in mind all along; but it is only here, at the end of the scene, that he shows his cards (cf. Farrell, 24); he follows a different strategy in Book 3, which alludes to Plato right at the beginning.—At *Phaedr.* 229a Phaedrus notes that he is barefoot (ἀνυπόδητος), as Socrates habitually is, so that they can wet their feet in the Ilissus. At 230b Socrates reports the result of the experiment: ἥ τε αὖ πηγὴ χαριεστάτη ὑπὸ τῆς πλατάνου ῥεῖ μάλα ψυχροῦ ὕδατος, ὥστε γε τῷ ποδὶ τεκμήρασθαι.— Cicero's upper-class Romans are less inclined to expose themselves to possible discomfort than Socrates' circle in Plato's dialogues; cf. *de Orat.* 1.29, where Crassus sends for pillows so that his guests can be more comfortable sitting beneath a plane tree (contrast *Phaedr.* 230b, where the interlocutors seat themselves beneath a plane tree without this refinement).—It is difficult to write a true dialogue among three characters; having set the stage, Atticus now recedes into the background and will not speak again until § 24.

7a M. Est vero ita; sed tamen huic amoenitati, quem ex Quinto saepe audio Thyamis Epirotes tuus ille, nihil, opinor, concesserit.] The Thyamis (= the modern Kalamas) forms the northern boundary of the Thesprotian plain; cf. Smith s.v.; Rudolf Herbst, *RE* 6A1 (1936), 656.54 ff. It is, however, twenty-five kilometers south of Buthrotum. Hence Perlwitz, 68–70, suggests that Cicero is referring to one of its tributaries of the same name originating near modern Konispoli and flowing from north to south (hence perhaps the designation as *Thyamis Epirotes tuus ille*).—After travelling to Italy without stopping at Buthrotum, Cicero writes: *Q. Ciceroni obsisti non potuit quo* *minus Thyamin videret* (*Att.* 7.2.3; ca. 25 November 50; cf. *Fam.* 16.7). It has been supposed that the lapse of five months' correspondence with Atticus from February to September 57 should be explained by the friends' having spent most of this time together at Atticus' estate at Buthrotum (certainly Cicero had been invited: cf. *Att.* 3.7.1: 30 April 58), but our passage (as well as *Att.* 7.2.3, already quoted) suggests that he had not yet visited there; cf. Shackleton Bailey *ad Att.* 3.27 (= 72) and *ad Q.fr.*, p. 255.

Q. Est ita ut dicis; cave enim putes Attici nostri Amalthio platanisque illis quicquam esse praeclarius.] The Amaltheum was apparently a temple and grove dedicated to the nymph Amalthea on Atticus' Buthrotan estate; cf. *Att.* 1.13.1 (= 13.1) with Shackleton Bailey *ad loc.*; *Att.* 1.16.15 and 18; Perlwitz, 69 n. 210. Her association with the cornucopia was proverbial; cf. Zenob. 2.48 (᾿Αμαλθείας κέρας) with Leutsch-Schneidewin *ad loc.* So the dedication will have been motivated by the estate's real or hoped for productiveness; cf. also Wiseman, 1974, 144. *Amalthium* in our passage and elsewhere is apparently used by synecdoche for the estate as a whole: Perlwitz, 67–68 and n. 203.

sed, si videtur, considamus hic in umbra, . . .] At this point there is no foreboding of the insufficient shade that will cause them to change position later (on the assumption that no other change of place has intervened before Book 5; see its preserved fragment).

. . . atque ad eam partem sermonis ex qua egressi sumus revertamur.] Atticus first suggested the topic (1.13), but since 1.56–57 Quintus has been keeping the discussion on track.—For *egredior* = *digredior* cf. *TLL* s.v., 285.35 ff.; *OLD* s.v., 3.

M. Praeclare exigis, Quinte (at ego effugisse arbitrabar!), et tibi horum nihil deberi potest.] Marcus' *at ego effugisse arbitrabar!* adds a realistic conversational touch; cf. § 45: *at mihi ista exciderant; Fin.* 2.44: . . . *accedam ad omnia tua, Torquate, nisi memoria forte defecerit;* the actual content to be covered is at first left vague (*horum*) for nearer specification later (§ 8); cf. Schmidt, 1959, 111.

Q. Ordire igitur; nam hunc tibi totum dicamus diem.] In this context *ordire igitur* clearly takes up *ex qua egressi sumus revertamur.* Cf. 1.13 (Quintus; cf. also *ad* § 69): . . . *in quo melius hunc consumam diem?*—Büchner, 1961, 84, points out that *totus dies* is not the same as *ceterus dies* and that the discussion of natural law in Book 1 must have used up considerable time; he uses this fact as one indicator pointing to separate composition of Book 1; but see the introduction to this Book.

7b–18 'A Iove Musarum primordia',—] Here begins matter preliminary to the individual laws (cf. § 8: *priusquam aggrediamur ad leges singulas*).

Revisiting some basic points about law dealt with in a similar, but not identical, way in Book 1, Marcus clarifies the *vis legis* and clears away misunderstandings that might arise from *lex* in popular usage in preparation for the sacral laws. The following are the major divisions of the argument:

    I. Force and proper usage of "law"
       A. Characteristics of true law: eternality, *(recta) ratio, mens sapientis,* origin in *mens dei* (§§ 8–9) or the *rerum natura* (§ 10a)
       B. Historical examples of prescribed and forbidden acts (§ 10b)
         1. Horatius Cocles at the bridge
         2. Sextus Tarquin's rape of Lucretia
       C. "Law" to be used in a strict sense only (§11)
       D. Law as a good and constitutive of the *civitas* (§ 12)
       E. Status of harmful legislative acts (§§ 13–14a)
    II. Precedents for supplying a proem for laws (§§ 14b–15a)
   III. The proem itself (§§ 15b–16)
   IV. Cicero's method
       A. The relation to Plato (§ 17)
       B. The diction of the laws (§ 18)

The *vis* of law is abstracted from individual enactments (§ 9b) but stands above and prior to them all. Cicero then adds an empirical approach based upon the earliest lawgivers, their goals, and professions (§ 11b: *quae sunt autem varie—*). He thus has both a transcendent and an empirical basis for criticizing actual legislation. He follows this up in § 12 with a syllogism defining the quality of law in relation to its function in the state. Thus armed, he proceeds to deny the name of law to enactments specified by type and by name, for which purpose the criterion of eternality is also emphasized (§§ 13–14a).

Finally, Cicero clarifies both the relation to Plato, who is imitated only in terms of the *genus orationis,* not the content (§ 17, though this statement is, in fact, misleading; see the introduction to this Book), and the style to be used for the laws, which is to be, for the sake of *auctoritas* and in spite of the familiar environment and company, moderately archaic (§ 18).

7b M. 'A Iove Musarum primordia', sicut in Aratio carmine orsi sumus.] = fr. I Soubiran, rendering Arat. 1: ἐκ Διὸς ἀρχώμεσθα (= Theoc. 17.1). For another Latin version, clearly mediated by Cicero in its use of *Musae* as a limiting genitive, cf. Verg. *Ecl.* 3.60 (*ab Iove principium Musae*). At *Rep.* 1.56 Scipio similarly remarks at the beginning of his exposition *imitabor ergo Aratum, qui magnis de rebus dicere exordiens a Iove incipiendum* *putat;* hence the reference serves to bind the two works together; cf. also Quint. *Inst.* 10.1.46; Schmidt, 1959, 111 n. 3. Cf. Pl. *Lg.* 712b4–5: θεὸν δὴ πρὸς τὴν τῆς πόλεως κατασκευὴν ἐπικαλώμεθα. Proponents of the prior composition of Book 2 have seized on our passage as evidence; cf. Büchner, 1961, 84; but there was precedent for beginning legislation with a preamble concerning the gods; cf. *ad* § 15.—*Primordia,* a poetic and post-Augustan word for "beginnings" (cf. *OLD* s.v. *primordium* 1a), also appears at Q. Cicero v. 4 Courtney, from a poem influenced by his brother's *Aratea* (cf. Courtney, p. 181).

Q. Quorsum istuc?] The verse baffles Quintus, much the way the dilation on knowing oneself and the "parts" of philosophy had Atticus, who asked *sed quorsus hoc pertinet?* (1.63); cf. also Atticus' query at 1.4.

M. Quia nunc item ab eodem ⟨Iove⟩ et a ceteris dis immortalibus sunt nobis agendi capienda primordia.] *Nunc* functions here as the discourse marker; cf. Risselada, 117–22. ⟨*Iove*⟩ is Powell's supplement.—*Ago* probably has here the general sense "speak about, discuss," etc., rather than its technical legislative sense "decree, enact" (for the two senses cf. *OLD* s.v., 40 and 41b), for a discussion of general principles precedes the actual legislation; *aliter* Schmidt, 1959, 111 n. 3 and 112.—In the sequel the *mens . . . dei* will form the basis for legislation (§ 8); ibid.

8–9a—Q. Aliquotiens iam iste locus a te tactus est.] This material oddly repeats the sequel: Marcus moots as the initial subject *vis naturaque legis* and, with Quintus' consent, proceeds to supply a treatment of the theme; then Quintus notes that his brother has already dealt with this matter several times (*aliquotiens*); but instead of pressing his brother to broach the real subject of this book, the *leges singulae,* he asks for an explanation of the *vis istius caelestis legis*—the same subject once again! Cf. Büchner, 1961, 86; sim. but with somewhat different boundaries at Bögel, 1907, 7, followed by Theiler, 47. Moreover, Marcus' doctrine is the same in essentials: law is eternal (*aeternum quiddam:* § 8; *aequalis illius . . . dei:* § 9b; *orta . . . est simul cum mente divina:* § 10) and is the mind of god or the like (*mentem esse . . . dei:* § 8; *ratio est recta summi Iovis:* § 10). The difference is that § 8 is dogmatic, based upon the *sapientissimorum sententia,* whereas §§ 9b–13 are inductive, abstracting the *vis legis* from what Quintus and Marcus had been taught to call "law" (§ 9b), the practice of legislators (§ 11: *eosque qui primum eiusmodi scita sanxerint . . .*), and Quintus' own responses to questions about the relation of laws to the state (§§ 12–13). The two passages, §§ 8–9a and 9b–13, are, then, a doublet, offering two different approaches to the *vis legis.* Surely Cicero could not have meant for them to stand side by side in the published version but would have canceled one or the other.

Which that would have been is not hard to discern, since it is §§ 9b–13 that issue in a definition of *lex* that leads on to the following application to specific laws, differentiation of the *leges* Marcus is about to propose, etc. It is also clear that the explanations of § 8 follow the same method as Book 1, whereas §§ 9b–13 follow a different approach, closer to utilitarianism. Büchner, *loc. cit.*, argued that §§ 8–9a were added later to connect this Book with Book 1. A more plausible explanation is that Book 1 was, in fact, written first but that when he reached this point Cicero realized that he was going to have to follow a different approach in Book 2; §§ 8–9a would thus represent a failed effort to adapt the doctrines of Book 1 to the needs of Book 2; see also the introduction to this Book.

8 M. Videamus igitur rursus, priusquam aggrediamur ad leges singulas, vim naturamque legis, ne cum referenda sint ad eam nobis omnia, labamur interdum errore sermonis, ignoremusque vim rationis eius qua iura nobis definienda sint.] *Igitur* follows, not upon Marcus' previous statement (*Quia nunc—primordia*), but Quintus' assent; *aliter* Schmidt, 1959, 112.—*Priusquam* with present subjunctive is from Cicero's time onward commonly used to express a future action; cf. Kühner-Stegmann, 2, 369.—The *singulae leges* fulfill the plan of 1.17: *considerandae leges quibus civitates regi debeant.* Defining terms at the outset of discussion is a procedure Cicero favors elsewhere; cf. *Rep.* 1.38; *ad Off.* 1.7a. The subject of the *vis naturaque legis* was already discussed at 1.18–19; hence *videamus . . . rursus.* Büchner, 1961, 85, has taken the return to this topic as an indicator that Book 2 was composed before 1. But, besides the *rursus,* Cicero also alludes to the repetition at § 9a (*aliquotiens iam iste locus a te tactus est*); see the introduction to this Book.—On the definition given in this chapter as the criterion for the following *leges* cf. Girardet, 1983, 71.—For the sense of *vis* cf. *ad* § 9b; for *vis legis* cf. 1.19; for *cum referenda sint ad eam nobis omnia* cf. *ad* 1.20.—Following *ignoremusque* the archetype appears to have read *uimsermonieius* B¹(?A¹) ES corrected to *materiam sermoni eius* (R) or *vim sermonis eius* (AªP); HL have *eius* alone, omitting *ignoremusque vim sermoni.* The clearly impossible *sermoni(s)* is simply deleted by Büchner; Vahlen substitutes *rationis,* de Plinval *nominis* (also with following *quo*). Of these solutions that of Vahlen seems the most plausible. Both Büchner and de Plinval assume that Cicero is referring to *lex* here. But, as Powell points out (*per litt.*), "if we simply supply the idea of *lex,* Cicero is repeating himself inanely. *Rationis* adds something desirable—the idea of a rational method or form of reasoning which enables us to deduce *iura* from the *summa lex.* Before we can do that, we have to know not only what the *summa lex* is but also its relationship to positive *iura.* That seems to me to fit the context not only equally well, but better, and in a way exactly analogous to the use of the phrase *vim rationis eius qua* in *de Orat.* 3.21."

Q. Sane quidem hercle, et est ista recta docendi via.] For *sane quidem* cf. *ad* § 1, for the interjection *hercle ad* 1.12; for critique of a defective teaching method cf. § 47.

M. Hanc igitur video sapientissimorum fuisse sententiam, legem neque hominum ingeniis excogitatam nec scitum aliquod esse populorum, sed aeternum quiddam quod universum mundum regeret imperandi prohibendique sapientia.] This amounts to a précis of the major points of Book 1, with the *sapientissimi* substituted for the *doctissimi viri* of 1.18b: for the law as eternal and independent of particular enactments cf. 1.42–44a; for its universality cf. 1.23; for its function of commanding and forbidding cf. 1.18b; for *sapientia* as constitutive cf. 1.22.

ita principem legem illam et ultimam mentem esse dicebant omnia ratione aut cogentis aut vetantis dei.] Here, apparently presupposing the assent given at 1.21 (see *ad loc.*), Marcus launches in on theological doctrine at odds with Atticus' Epicureanism.—The *princeps lex et ultima* is evidently another designation for what Cicero elsewhere calls the *summa lex* (1.19; § 11), the *caelestis lex* (§ 9a), or the *lex vera atque princeps* (§ 10).—Cicero has spoken of law as "perfect reason" (1.18b); in view of the association of *mens* with *ratio* (cf. Frank, 357), the identification of law with the *mens dei* does not greatly surprise (cf. also § 10: *mens divina*). For the divine mind interpenetrating the universe cf. Chrysipp. *SVF* 2, 192.1 ff. = Posidon. F 21 Ed.-K. = 345 Th. = D.L. 7.138; Heinrich Dörrie, *Von Platon zum Platonismus,* Rheinisch-Westfälische Akademie der Wissenschaften, Vorträge G 211 (Opladen, 1976), 25 and n. 53, who attributes this entire section (§§ 8–12) to Posidonius (but see the introduction to this Book); see also *ad* 1.19 (*naturae vis*). The Stoics appear ordinarily to have spoken of "god" as "mind" (*SVF* 1, 40.5 and 42.7–8 and 13; 2, 306.14–15 and 24–25) rather than of the "mind of god"; cf., however, the reference to the *mens divina* at 1.23, with note.—For the attributive participles ("*a* god who . . .") cf. Laughton, 65.

ex quo illa lex quam di humano generi dederunt recte est laudata; est enim ratio mensque sapientis ad iubendum et ad deterrendum idonea.] Transmitted is *ex qua,* usually explained as "derived from which," i.e., from the *mens . . . dei.* But this idea, if expressed, should surely have been elaborated. Davies' *ex quo* yields a more convincing sequence: "as a result of which [i.e., the status of the first and last law as the mind of god] the law given to humans is rightly praised," i.e., because it corresponds in microcosm to the position in the universe as a whole, the mind of the *sapiens* being to the human sphere what the mind of god is to the universe (cf. 1.18).—*Recte est laudata:* presumably by the *sapientes* previously mentioned, who praised the law as eternal, etc.[37]—This is the first reference to praise of law; Cicero goes on to say that law should be praiseworthy (§ 11); in the sequel the procedure is that praise of the law precedes the law itself (cf. 3.1).

9a Q. Aliquotiens iam iste locus a te tactus est. sed antequam ad populares leges venis, vim istius caelestis legis explana si placet, ne aestus nos consuetudinis absorbeat et ad sermonis morem usitati trahat.] For *Aliquotiens— tactus est* cf. *ad* §§ 8–9a.—In political contexts Cicero uses *populares leges* to refer to laws put forward by those claiming to be *populares;* cf. *Agr.* 1.24 and 2.15; *Luc.* 13; *Amic.* 96; Schmidt, 1959, 115 n. 1; on the *populares* in general cf. Tatum, 1999, 1–11 with literature. Quintus seems to be alluding to a plan of procedure previously established (cf. the reference to *leges singulae* at § 8); cf. 1.37 (*ad respublicas firmandas—⟨id⟩ e⟨s⟩t ad stabiliendas {vi}res, sanandos populos*) and 57 (*. . . sed te existimo cum populis tum etiam singulis hodierno sermone leges vivendi et disciplinam daturum*). Probably, then, *popularis* here has the sense "of or concerned with the organization of a people" (so *OLD* s.v., 8, citing our passage); *aliter* Schmidt, *loc. cit.*—Quintus refers to Marcus' concept as *ista caelestis lex* because of his association of it with the deity; the phrase is adumbrated by the *caelestis descriptio* of 1.23.—*Aestus* used in a metaphorical sense appears to be a Ciceronian innovation; cf. *Mur.* 35: *. . . quantos aestus habet ratio comitiorum!* Sim. (also with reference to elections) *Planc.* 15: *. . . sic effervescunt quodam quasi aestu . . .* ; cf. other Ciceronian passages (including ours) cited at *TLL* s.v., 1121.59 ff. and *OLD* s.v., 9b. The *aestus consuetudinis* and *sermonis mos usitati* pose an obstacle to the understanding similar to the *error sermonis* referred to by Marcus in § 8; cf. the similar function of the *depravatio consuetudinum* and *opinionum varietas* (1.29 and 49, respectively). For *lex* in the popular sense cf. 1.19.

9b–13 Here we have an explanation of *ius* on a different basis from the preceding or from that encountered in Book 1: it is inductive and largely dispenses with theology;[38] it assumes that laws must be good for the citizens and is thus close to the utilitarianism of the Epicureans, on which cf. Mitsis, 1988, 79 ff.; cf. *ad* §§ 8–9a and the following notes. Contrast 1.40–47, which was essentially doing the same work of establishing *lex* as *iustorum iniustorumque distinctio* (§ 13) but with a strong anti-utilitarian bent.

9b M. A parvis enim, Quinte, didicimus 'Si in ius vocat', atque alia eius-

---

37. I owe this point to Andreas Bendlin.

38. The exceptions are *orta autem est simul cum mente divina* and *ratio est recta summi Iovis* (§ 10 *fin.*) and *illa divina mens* (§ 11 *init.*).

modi, leges {alias} nominare.] For use of *enim* at the beginning of an exposition expected in the light of previous discussion cf. Hand, 2, 180.—Cicero
cites the beginning of the first law of the first of the Twelve Tables: *si in ius
vocat, ⟨ito⟩. ni it, antestamino: igitur em capito.* ("If plaintiff summons
defendant to court, he shall go. If he does not go, plaintiff shall call witness
thereto. Then only shall he take defendant by force": tr. Warmington); cf. *ad*
§ 64.—The text *alia eiusmodi leges* is Baiter's correction for *at eiusmodi
leges alias*, transmitted with only trivial variants, whereby *at* is an evident
dittography which will have displaced the true reading, *alia*, perhaps added
in the margin and then reinserted in the wrong place in the text and adjusted
to agree with *leges*. Here the point is that Cicero and his brother learned to
call the Twelve Tables and other such things *laws*, not that they learned to
recite them (cf. § 59).

**sed vero intellegi sic oportet, et hoc et alia iussa ac vetita populorum vim
habere ad recte facta vocandi et a peccatis avocandi, quae vis non modo
senior est quam aetas populorum et civitatum, sed aequalis illius caelum
atque terras tuentis et regentis dei.**] *Vetita populorum* could not stand on its
own; it is through being so closely tied to *iussa* that it can be treated as a
substantive; cf. Madvig *ad Fin.* 5.44.—Cicero abstracts from individual
laws a general power (*vis*). What he has just referred to (§ 8) as *imperandi
prohibendique sapientia* now becomes specifically *vis . . . ad recte facta
vocandi et a peccatis avocandi*. His description of this construct as "older
than the age of the peoples and states" [sc. who have enacted legislation]
and coeval with the deity suggests a Platonic "idea," but functioning as a
lodestar to guide conduct, rather than a sole reality. The treatment of the
orator in *Orat.* and of the *vir bonus* in *Off.* 3 is similar; cf. Klaus Reich,
"Die Tugend in der Idee," in *Argumentationen. Festschrift für Josef König,*
ed. H. Delius and G. Patzig (Göttingen, 1964), 209. That these principles
exist prior to legislative enactments but nonetheless deserve obedience is the
point of the historical examples of § 10; a similar idea surely underlies 1.19:
quae [sc. *summa lex*] *saeclis multis ante nata est quam scripta lex ulla aut
quam omnino civitas constituta.*—For the final phrase cf. *N.D.* 1.33:
Aristoteles [fr. 25,1 Gigon] . . . *ei* [sc. *deo*] . . . *eas partis tribuit ut replica-
tione quadam mundi motum regat atque tueatur; Sen.* 81: . . . *deos verentes
qui hanc omnem pulchritudinem tuentur et regunt* . . . The clausula is a fine
double cretic.

**10 neque enim esse mens divina sine ratione potest, nec ratio divina non
hanc vim in rectis pravisque sanciendis habere.**] By virtue of its placement
esse is not merely a copula but denotes existence; cf. Adams, 1994, 69–
76.—*Mens* as the "facultas intellegendi" (*TLL* s.v., 715.65) implies *ratio* as

a basis (for the association of the two cf. *ad* § 8). *Ex vi termini ratio divina* must make the correct discrimination between right and wrong acts, and thus its legislative prescriptions (*sancio* = "prescribe by law": OLD s.v., 3a, citing our passage; cf. Fugier, 123) must have *haec vis*, i.e., the force of law as described in the previous sentence.—Here *recta* and *prava* clearly have moral content (cf. 1.19: . . . *legem, cuius ea vis sit ut recte facere iubeat, vetet delinquere*), whereas 1.31 offers a different sense (cf. *ad loc.*).—Coherence is improved with *habere*, attested for *habet* only in P.

nec quia nusquam erat scriptum ut contra omnes hostium copias in ponte unus assisteret a tergoque pontem interscindi iuberet, idcirco minus Coclitem illum rem gessisse tantam fortitudinis lege atque imperio putabimus; . . .] This is Cicero's most detailed account of Horatius' exploit (for full discussion cf. *ad Off.* 1.61). In this entire passage Cicero consistently keeps in view the two sides of law, its prescriptions and prohibitions, and hence offers both positive and negative illustrations from Roman history. There was no statute precisely specifying what Horatius should do in the particular circumstances in which he found himself. He had to extrapolate from a general understanding of *recta* and *prava*. To the modern mind, accustomed to distinguish between legislation and morality, it may be surprising for Horatius' action to be discussed in terms of law, but Cicero's subject is *leges vivendi et disciplina* in the widest sense (cf. 1.57), and the ancients tended to believe that the laws do not merely forbid wrongdoing but enjoin virtuous action; cf. Ar. *EN* 1129b19 ff.: προστάττει δ' ὁ νόμος καὶ τὰ τοῦ ἀνδρείου ἔργα ποιεῖν . . . ; *Fin* 2.94: *fortitudinis quaedam praecepta sunt ac paene leges* . . . ; cf. also the rendering of the famous epigram for the dead at Thermopylae at *Tusc.* 1.101, where *sanctae leges* is Cicero's interpretation of the Greek ῥήματα: *dic, hospes, Spartae nos te hic vidisse iacentis, / dum sanctis patriae legibus obsequimur.*

nec si regnante ⟨Lucio⟩ Tarquinio nulla erat Romae scripta lex de stupris, idcirco non contra illam legem sempiternam Sextus Tarquinius vim Lucretiae Tricipitini filiae attulit.] ⟨*L.*⟩ *Tarquinio* is Turnebus' correction to distinguish from the following *Sex. Tarquinius* (cf. *uel Tarquinio* of εL).— *Stuprum* appears here in the wider sense of any illicit intercourse (cf. OLD s.v., 2a), not the narrower juristic sense in which *stuprum* pertained to virgins or widows, *adulterium* to married women (ibid. 2b); cf. Pfaff, *RE* 4A1 (1931), 423.25 ff.; Berger s.v. *stuprum;* cf. in general Fantham, esp. 269–71; O.F. Robinson, 58. The action of Sex. Tarquin (and the entailed fall of the Roman kingship) was, of course, well before Rome's first written law, the Twelve Tables (450). Cicero had alluded to these events at *Rep.* 2.46 (*itaque cum maior eius filius Lucretiae, Tricipitini filiae, Collatini uxori vim*

attulisset, . . .). On the historical tradition cf. Ogilvie *ad* Liv. 1.57–59.—
Cicero had championed the unwritten law at 1.42; it can now be called *lex
sempiterna* in view of § 8 (*aeternum quiddam*).

**erat enim ratio, profecta a rerum natura, et ad recte faciendum impellens et a
delicto avocans, . . .**] Cf. 1.18b: . . . *lex est ratio summa insita in natura,
quae iubet ea quae facienda sunt, prohibetque contraria,* with note; sim.
1.33: *quibus enim ratio ⟨a⟩ natura data est, eisdem etiam recta ratio data est;
ergo et lex, quae est recta ratio in iubendo et vetando* . . . —The participles
profecta, impellens, and *avocans* personify *ratio.*—Here we have *rerum
natura* for *natura* previously used; the two were more or less interchange-
able, as in Lucretius' *de Rerum Natura,* a title presumed to translate περὶ
φύσεως of Epicurus; cf. Bailey *ad* Lucr., p. 583; cf. also § 16: *cum . . .
nefasque sit dicere ullam rem praestare naturae omnium rerum.*

**. . . quae non tum denique incipit lex esse cum scripta est, sed tum cum orta
est; orta autem est simul cum mente divina.**] These points are implicated in
§ 8 (*principem legem illam et ultimam mentem esse dicebant . . . dei*) and §
9b (*quae vis . . . aequalis illius caelum atque terras tuentis et regentis dei*);
sim. already 1.19.

**quamobrem lex vera atque princeps, apta ad iubendum et ad vetandum,
ratio est recta summi Iovis.**] The hyperbaton calls attention to the technical
term *recta ratio*; cf. *ad* 1.23 (*ratio mensque sapientis* at § 8 amounts to the
same thing); it alone would suffice to characterize true law, as it does in that
passage; the addition of *summi Iovis* effects ring-composition (cf. § 7b: 'A
Iove Musarum primordia') as well as a fine double cretic clausula. Though
the Stoics sometimes preferred a more vague formulation (cf. *ad* 1.22 à
propos *supremus deus*), Chrysippus seems not to have been averse to naming Zeus explicitly in such contexts; cf. *SVF* 2, 315.8 ff. = Phld. *Piet.* 2 P.
Herc. 1428 col. 4, 30ff.: . . . καὶ ο[ὕ]τως συνά[γε]σθαι τὸν Δία καὶ τὴν
κοινὴν πάντων φύσιν καὶ εἰμαρμένην καὶ ἀνάγκην· καὶ τὴν αὐτὴν εἶναι
καὶ Εὐνομίαν καὶ Δίκην . . . ; ibid. 316.35–36 = col. 7, 6–8: . . . τὸν Δία
νόμον φησὶ⟨ν⟩ εἶναι . . . ; ibid. 316, 8–9 = *N.D.* 3.40: *idemque* [sc. Chrysip-
pus] *etiam legis perpetuae et aeternae vim, quae quasi dux vitae et magistra
officiorum sit, Iovem dicit esse* . . . ; cf. also *Phil.* 11.28 (on this passage see
further *ad* 1.23: *inter quos autem ratio, inter eosdem etiam recta ratio*—):
*qua lege, quo iure? eo quod Iuppiter ipse sanxit, ut omnia quae reipublicae
salutaria essent legitima et iusta haberentur.*

**11 Q. Adsentior, frater, ut quod est rectum verumque ⟨aeternum quoque⟩ sit,
neque cum litteris quibus scita scribuntur aut oriatur aut occidat.**] Something is clearly needed to complete the sense; Vahlen's supplement *aeternum*

quoque fills the bill neatly in terms of sense and palaeography (less satisfying is du Mesnil's *lex idem*). The essential point was forestalled at § 8: . . . *legem . . . nec scitum aliquod esse populorum, sed aeternum quiddam . . .* **M. Ergo ut illa divina mens summa lex est, item, cum in homine est, perfecta ⟨est⟩ in mente sapientis.**] After *perfecta* the *est* appears in P alone; this is the easiest solution. More involved is Vahlen's suggestion: *item cum in homine est perfecta ⟨ratio, lex est: ea vero est perfecta⟩ in mente sapientis* (he compares 1.18: *eadem ratio cum est in hominis mente confirmata et perfecta, lex est;* and 1.22: *quae [sc. ratio] cum adolevit atque perfecta est, nominatur rite sapientia* and might have added § 8: *illa lex . . . est . . . ratio mensque sapientis*). Büchner's attempt (*ad loc.*) to defend the transmitted text as an instance of the σχῆμα καθ' ὅλον καὶ μέρος is unconvincing.

quae sunt autem varie et ad tempus descriptae populis, favore magis quam re legum nomen tenent.] For *describo* as the preferable spelling when the reference is, as here, to the writing out or prescribing of laws by a lawgiver cf. *OLD* s.v., 5; further *ad Off.* 1.124 and Powell *ad Sen.* 59; for the corresponding problem of *descriptio/discriptio* cf. *ad* 1.23.—*Favor* is first used by Cicero; in our passage it has its basic meaning, "enthusiasm" or the like; cf. *TLL* s.v., 383.45–52.—*Legum nomen* reverts to the starting point of Marcus' explanation, namely the use of the term *laws* (*A parvis enim, Quinte, didicimus 'si in ius vocat' atque alia eius modi leges nominare:* § 9b). He has so far abstracted the *vis legis* and argued that it does not matter whether it is written down or not. Here he moves on to the point that there are legislative enactments that do not deserve the name *law*.

11–12 omnem enim legem, quae quidem recte lex appellari possit,—Necesse est igitur legem haberi in rebus optimis.] = *SVF* 3, 78.33–79.4.

11 omnem enim legem, quae quidem recte lex appellari possit, esse laudabilem, ⟨ . . . ⟩ quibusdam talibus argumentis docent: . . .] A law that is identical to the *divina mens* and stands in some relation to the *mens sapientis* (see the next to last note) must be good and thus *laudabile* (cf. 1.37 and 46); the following arguments are meant to establish the point.—It is difficult to find a subject for *docent*, as well as an antecedent for *illi* in the first sentence of § 12. Wissowa wanted to substitute *quidam* for the transmitted *quibusdam*, but this seems too vague. We probably need to posit a lacuna before *quibusdam* and suppose that something like *qui ista subtilius quaerunt* (Powell, comparing *Amic.* 7 and 18) has dropped out by saltation.

constat profecto ad salutem civium civitatumque incolumitatem vitamque hominum quietam et beatam inventas esse leges, . . .] Here Cicero makes it clear in what sense *Leg.* complements *Rep.* (cf. 1.15): good laws will protect the state (*ad . . . civitatum . . . incolumitatem*).[39] Cf. 1.37: *. . . iter huius sermonis quod sit vides: ad respublicas firmandas*—⟨*id*⟩ *e*⟨*s*⟩*t ad stabiliendas* {*vi*}*res, sanandos populos*—*omnis nostra pergit oratio; Off.* 2.15: *. . . ex quo leges moresque constituti, tum iuris aequa discriptio certaque vivendi disciplina . . . . effectumque* [sc. *est*] *ut esset vita munitior atque ut dando et accipiendo mutuandisque facultatibus et commodis nulla re egeremus.*— Here for the first time Cicero juxtaposes *quieta* and *beata* as epithets of *vita;* cf. *Fin.* 1.71 (Torquatus). Elsewhere he contrasts the *quieta vitae ratio* with (and admits it may be *beatior* than) the *civilis* [sc. *vita: Rep.* 3.5; cf. also the report of Peripatetic views at *Fin.* 5.11]. He probably means by the *vita quieta* a life undisturbed (cf. *OLD* s.v. *quietus* 4), i.e., the kind of life possible in a community with ordered personal and property relations, not subject to vendetta or other forms of rough justice (cf. *Off. loc. cit.*).

. . . eosque qui primum eiusmodi scita sanxerint, populis ostendisse ea se scripturos atque laturos, quibus illi ascitis susceptisque honeste beateque viverent, quaeque ita composita sanctaque essent, eas leges videlicet nominarent.] If down to this point Cicero has established the nature of law by abstracting the essential features and situating them on a metaphysical plane, he now shifts to an empirical approach with reference to the legendary first lawgivers, on whom cf. 1.57 with note. The result looks like a combination of Stoic doctrine with utilitarian views characteristic of the Epicureans.[40] The clause *quibus illi ascitis susceptisque honeste beateque viverent* essentially repeats the point *ad . . . vitam . . . hominum quietam et beatam inventas esse leges.* In general the Greeks were at pains to name "inventors" for the various arts and disciplines; cf. Adolf Kleingünther, Πρῶτος εὑρετής. *Untersuchungen zur Geschichte einer Fragestellung,* Philol. Supplbd. 26.1 (Leipzig, 1933); K. Thraede, *RAC* s.v. Erfinder.—For *sancta* cf. *ad* § 10.

ex quo intellegi par est—ut perspicuum esse possit, in ipso nomine legis interpretando inesse vim et sententiam iusti et veri legendi.] Cicero denies the name of *lex* to the enactments of those *qui perniciosa et* ⟨*in*⟩*iusta populis iussa descripserint.* This accords with the doctrine of 1.42–44a, where he cites specific examples from Greek and Roman history. Similarly, in *Rep.* he denies the name of *respublica* to a state not managed in the public interest; cf. Schofield, 1995, 73–77.—*Cum contra fecerint quam polliciti professique*

---

39. The orderly relations of the society he envisions seem to be mirrored in the chiastic arrangement of nouns and limiting genitives in the phrase *ad salutem civium civitatumque incolumitatem.*

40. There is nothing here that points clearly to the sophists, although de Plinval mentions them beside the Epicureans *ad loc.*

sint gives the reason for the denial of status as *lex*. This is a somewhat compendious way of referring to the profession of the early lawgivers as described in the previous sentence: *populis ostendisse ea se scripturos atque laturos* . . . ; cf. Solon's defense of his work as lawgiver: "I carried out as I had promised" (διῆλθον ὡς ὑπεσχόμην: F 36.17 West). Cicero seems to assume (though he has not said) that the same is true of *all* lawmakers and thus should apply to those *qui perniciosa et ⟨in⟩iusta populis iussa descripserint* as well.— *Quidvis potius tulisse quam leges*: this contradicts what Marcus and Quintus had once learned (*a parvis enim, Quinte, didicimus* . . . : § 9b), which was the starting point.—The last clause of this sentence reverts to and fills out the etymology of *lex a legendo* mooted at 1.19 (see *ad loc.* and *ad* § 13); that passage is, on the other hand, richer in discussing both the Greek and Latin terms for law; cf. Büchner, 1961, 86. In philosophical writing an argument is usually justified by means of an etymology, rather than, as here, vice versa.— For *sententia* cf. *ad* 1.48.—*U(er)i legendi* is the reading of HL, rightly set in the text by Powell, for *uim legendi* of ε, *curilendi* of B¹, *iuris colendi* of BᵃAᵃ(A¹ eras.) or *uirulenti* (!) of P; Turnebus' *iuris legendi* is usually adopted.

12 Quaero igitur a te, Quinte, sicut illi solent: . . .] Turnebus took *illi* to refer to the Stoics, and this view is often repeated (e.g., by Bake and du Mesnil *ad loc.* and Schmidt, 1959, 120 n. 1). But the Stoics are nowhere mentioned in this context, nor does the reference to the *sapientissimi* at § 8 suffice to establish the connection. Cicero may, however, have omitted explicit reference to the Stoics here so as to avoid the impression that he is merely arguing for sectarian views (so Powell, *per litt.*); cf. also the introduction to Book 1; or the antecedent may have been lost in the lacuna in § 11 (see *supra* on *omnem enim legem*—).—Cicero seems to be continuing the policy announced at 1.36 of using two different methods of argumentation—one more discursive, the other more concise—to arrive at the same result; cf. *ad loc.*

quo si civitas careat—Necesse est igitur legem haberi in rebus optimis.] Cicero here reproduces a syllogism associated with Diogenes the Cynic at D.L. 6.72: περί τε τοῦ νόμου ὅτι χωρὶς αὐτοῦ οὐχ οἷόν τε πολιτεύεσθαι· οὐ γάρ φησιν ἄνευ πόλεως ὄφελός τι εἶναι ἀστείου· ἀστεῖον δὲ ἡ πόλις· νόμου δὲ ἄνευ πόλεως οὐδὲν ὄφελος· ἀστεῖον ἄρα ὁ νόμος; cf. Marie-Odile Goulet-Cazé, "Un syllogisme stoïcien sur la loi dans la doxographie de Diogène le Cynique. À propos de Diogène Laërce VI 72," *RhM* 125 (1982), 222–23; Schofield, 1991, 139–40. The issue is whether the predicate "good" applies to *lex*. This was already implicitly answered in § 11, where *lex* was established as praiseworthy, but is now spelled out with reference to the rôle of *lex* in the *civitas*, whereby *civitas* implicitly has the same relation to *lex*, as defined here, as *respublica* does to organization so as to serve the public interest in *Rep.*; cf. the last note to § 11. For fully worked out syllogisms in Cicero cf. 1.33; *ad Off.* 2.10; Paul MacKendrick, *The Philosophical Books of Cicero* (New York, 1989), Index s.v. "Syllogism(s)."

Lege autem carens civitas estne ob ⟨id⟩ ipsum habenda nullo loco?] Cf. Pl. *Cri.* 53a5: τίνι γὰρ ἂν πόλις ἀρέσκοι ἄνευ νόμων;—*Id* is Lambinus' supplement, approved by Madvig *ad Fin.* 2.93.

Q. Prorsus assentior.] Here and in § 17, where the same formula recurs, *prorsus* lends strong emphasis to what follows it (cf. § 5; § 23: *immo prorsus ita censeo; Att.* 4.12: *prorsus id facies*), sometimes to what precedes (*N.D.* 3.21: *nullo modo prorsus adsentior*); sim. 3.49: *sic prorsum censeo*. Cf. *OLD* s.v., 2; Hand, 4, 617–18.

13 M. Quid quod multa perniciose, multa pestifere sciscuntur in populis, quae non magis legis nomen attingunt quam si latrones aliquas consessu suo sanxerint?] This represents a change of terminology since Book 1, which was more oriented toward popular usage; cf. 1.19 and *ad* 1.44. Cf. also the strictures on terminology at *Rep.* 1.50, where the subject is evidently the democrats (cf. Zetzel *ad loc.*): *** *ceteras vero respublicas ne appellandas quidem putant iis nominibus quibus illae sese appellari velint.*—For the *latrones* (Turnebus' certain correction for *latores*) as a culture outside the norms of civilized society and from whom any sort of barbarity could be expected cf. Shaw. Cicero often branded his political enemies, such as Catiline, Clodius, and their followers, as *latrones;* cf. *TLL* s.v. *latro*[2] IIA1b; Ilona Opelt, *Die lateinischen Schimpfwörter und verwandte sprachliche Erscheinungen. Eine Typologie* (Heidelberg, 1965), 132–33; Shaw, 23 and n. 56; Achard, 328–29; Thomas N. Habinek, *The Politics of Roman Literature: Writing, Identity and Empire in Ancient Rome* (Princeton, 1998), 69–87.—*Consessu* is Gulielmius' emendation of the transmitted *concessu:* in Cicero's view some legislation is comparable to what an assembly of bandits might enact.

nam neque medicorum praecepta dici vere possint, si quae inscii imperitique pro salutaribus mortifera conscripserint, neque in populo lex cuicuimodi fuerit illa, etiamsi perniciosum aliquid populus acceperit.] The formulation is ambiguous: these could be called *medicorum praecepta* in the sense of "instructions of (some) physicians" but not in the sense of "instructions of physicians (in general)"; they could not, moreover, be called *medicinae praecepta,* since they are the mistakes of particular practitioners, not of the art itself. The premise is the perfection and incorruptibility of art, regardless of the mistakes of practitioners, as argued at Pl. *Rp.* 342a–b, Cic. *Div.* 1.24 and 118, and S.E. *M.* 2.12. Cf. also Plato's comparison of lawgivers to physicians at *Lg.* 720a ff. Cicero aims to create in this way a category for *lex* independent of actual usage (see the preceding and following notes).— *Cuicuimodi,* used fourteen times by Cicero,[41] is based on an archaic genitive *quoi* or *cui;* cf. Leumann, 479.

ergo est lex iustorum iniustorumque distinctio, ad illam antiquissimam et rerum omnium principem expressa naturam, ad quam leges hominum deriguntur, quae supplicio improbos afficiunt, defendunt ac tuentur bonos.] This artful sentence places *lex* and its definition in the foreground; to the predicate is added a participial modifier (*ad illam—expressa naturam*), which is then expanded by a relative clause (*ad quam leges hominum diriguntur*), to which in its turn a relative clause is attached with chiastic arrangement of verbs and objects. The whole is capped with a fine double cretic clausula. The sentence describes a movement from *lex* as a principle to its embodiment in legislation (*leges hominum*).—*Ergo* draws an inference from the preceding medical analogy: if you accept that law is a τέχνη like medicine, then it follows . . . —"Choosing the just and the true" (*iustum et verum legere:* § 11) also implies the eschewing of the unjust, as the formulation here makes clear (cf. also *ad* 1.19).—For *exprimo ad* in the sense "model on (a pattern)" cf. *OLD* s.v. *exprimo* 6d.—The last clause *quae supplicio improbos afficiunt, defendunt ac tuentur bonos* indicates that law in this sense does the work of moral teachings, as had been suggested by Quintus' expectation *te existimo . . . leges vivendi et disciplinam daturum* (1.57); cf. also *ad* 1.58 (Xenocrates); Tac. *Ger.* 19.2: . . . *plusque ibi boni mores valent quam alibi bonae leges.*

Q. Praeclare intellego, nec vero iam aliam esse ullam legem puto non modo habendam sed ne appellandam quidem.] For the change of terminology cf. *supra* on *Quid quod multa perniciose—?*

14a M. Igitur tu Titias et Apuleias leges nullas putas? Q. Ego vero ne Livias quidem.] Upon the declaration of principle follows its application to specific cases (with initial *igitur:* cf. *ad* 1.18b). The three examples all come from the 90s, a period Cicero had recently studied to provide background for *de Orat.,* and all involve invalidation of legislation on grounds that it had been passed contrary to auspices. The basis was the *leges Aelia et Fufia,* dating from before 133, which regulated the announcement of unfavorable omens (*obnuntiatio*) in the assemblies; cf. G.V. Sumner, "Lex Aelia, Lex Fufia," *AJPh* 84 (1963), 337–58, distinguishing the laws and dating them to 132; *contra* Astin, 1964, esp. 437–40, suggesting the laws were a reaction to the election of Scipio Aemilianus to the consulate in 148; cf. also Luca Fezzi,

---

41. According to a search of PHI 5.3.

"Lex Clodia de iure et tempore legum rogandarum," *SCO* 45 (1995), 305–10; Lintott, 1999, 62 and n. 95. This method of optimate control had come to the fore during the year 59, when the tribunician veto was evidently no longer a practicable option (cf. *ad* 3.24); but in that year the consul M. Bibulus was hindered by force from reporting adverse omens at an assembly; thereafter he took refuge in his house and repeatedly announced (evidently via his lictors) that he had been watching the sky (*de caelo servasse*). Bibulus' tactic was ultimately ineffective (cf. Vanderbroeck, 156 and n. 51), but it did leave lingering doubts about the validity of legislation passed by his colleague Julius Caesar. The following year Clodius modified these laws so as to clarify that the mere announcement *de caelo servasse* was insufficient to disband an assembly; a report of adverse omens (*obnuntiatio*) had to be made in person. Cf. Mommsen, *Staatsr.* 1, 111–12 n. 4; Rotondi, 288–89 and 397; H. Benner, 51; W. Jeffrey Tatum, "Roman Religion: Fragments and Further Questions," in Byrne-Cueva, 280–82. Our passage mirrors concerns Cicero had already expressed both privately and publicly; cf. *Att.* 2.9.1 (16 or 17 April 59): *festive . . . et minore sonitu quam putaram orbis hic in republica est conversus . . . id culpa Catonis, sed rursus improbitate istorum, qui auspicia, qui Aeliam legem . . . neglexerunt, qui omnia remedia reipublicae effuderunt . . . ; Red. sen.* 11; *Har.* 58; *Pis.* 9: . . . *a fatali portento prodigioque reipublicae lex Aelia et Fufia eversa est, propugnacula murique tranquillitatis atque oti . . . ; Sest.* 33.

Several Titii were authors of legislation (cf. *MRR*, 2, 473), and Sex. Titius, tr. pl. 99, may have sponsored more than one law (ibid., 2, 2), but the *cause célèbre* (and the one invalidated by the senate) was his agrarian law (Rotondi, 333), a continuation of the policies of the dead L. Appuleius Saturninus (tr. pl. 100). Invalidation of legislation by the senate appears to be a post-Gracchan innovation (cf. Burckhardt, 233) and was used exclusively on religious grounds (cf. Heikkilä and below). In this case invalidation followed upon a decree of the college of augurs (cf. § 31), albeit Obseq. 46 attributes the decision to the haruspices; cf. Lintott, 1968, 140; Linderski, 1986, 2165 n. 54. The lex Caecilia Didia passed by the senate the following year (98) may *inter alia* have reasserted the invalidity of legislation passed contrary to auspices; cf. Rotondi, 335; Lintott, 1999, 62 and n. 95; Burckhardt, 215 (somewhat skeptical). Probably that same year Titius was tried, perhaps *maiestatis*,[42] and condemned, primarily for keeping a bust of Saturninus; cf. *Rab. Perd.* 24–25. Cicero represents Antonius' testimony at his trial at *de Orat.* 2.48 and (probably) 265. Even Titius' oratorical delivery

---

42. Cf. Duncan Cloud in *CAH* 9², 519 n. 139; Alexander no. 80 with further references.

did not escape Ciceronian censure (... *tam solutus et mollis in gestu ut saltatio quaedam nasceretur, cui saltationi Titius nomen esset: Brut.* 225). Cf. F. Münzer, *RE* 6A2 (1937) s.v. Titius no. 23; Andrew Lintott in *CAH* 9², 101–2.

Paired with this, appropriately enough, is the agrarian law of Saturninus himself, which provided for the distribution, by allotment, of land in Cisalpine Gaul (100; Rotondi, 331; *MRR*, 1, 575–76). There was thunder during the assembly at which it was voted, and Saturninus' opponents used this omen to argue against its validity, the first known invocation of the *leges Aelia et Fufia*. Cf. Lintott, 1968, 99–100. Cicero had, of course, argued the legality of the murder of Saturninus and his followers by an armed mob in spite of a guarantee given by the consul Marius, acting under a *senatus consultum ultimum*, in *Rab. Perd.* (esp. 28).

The *ne ... quidem* construction evinces somewhat greater sympathy for the legislation of M. Livius Drusus (tr. pl. 91), in whom, according to *de Orat.*, the moderate senatorial circle around L. Licinius Crassus reposed its hopes. The struggle between Drusus and the consul, L. Marcius Philippus, forms the dark backdrop for that dialogue (cf. 1.24–25). At least some of Drusus' laws, the agrarian/grain law and the equal division of the courts between senators and *equites* (Rotondi, 336–38), were carried *per vim* (Liv. *per.* 71; for procedural details cf. Lintott, 1968, 142–43) and, after the death of his leading supporter, Crassus (cf. *de Orat.* 3.2 ff.), invalidated on the motion of Philippus (cf. § 31), who had been elected to the board of augurs by 93 (*MRR* 2, 16 and 17 n. 9). Cic. *Dom.* 41 claims a violation of the lex Caecilia Didia (... *iudicavit senatus M. Drusi legibus, quae contra legem Caeciliam et Didiam latae essent, populum non teneri*), probably in order to construe an analogy to Clodius; a religious violation seems much more likely; cf. Heikkilä, 136–37. Drusus' assassination followed while he was still in office. Cf. *MRR* 2, 21–22; Burckhardt, 193–95; E. Gabba in *CAH* 9², 111–13.

M. Et recte, quae praesertim uno versiculo senatus puncto temporis sublatae sint; ...] The ephemeral character of the legislation is emphasized both by the manner and speed of its abrogation (*uno versiculo senatus puncto temporis*). *Versus* is older, but the diminutive *versiculus* first appears in Cicero (*Ver.* 1.98: *audistis quaestoriam rationem, tribus versiculis relatam*); cf. *OLD* s.vv., esp. *versiculus* 1; Hanssen, 206.—*Sublatae sint*: this is a technical expression for the repeal of laws (cf. *OLD* s.v. *tollo* 14b) and as such synonymous with *abrogo* (cf. *TLL* s.v. *abrogo* 137.11–12 and 37–40); the subjunctive is causal.

lex autem illa, cuius vim explicavi, neque tolli neque abrogari potest.] This is the clearest indicator, that, as Girardet, 1983, esp. 80–84, has argued in detail, the laws of *Leg.* are conceived as the *leges naturae* and not merely *ad tempus descriptae* (§ 11). Though by implication he is writing *studi et delectationis . . . causa,* not *reipublicae causa* (see below), Plato, by contrast, provides for a period of testing before his laws become unalterable (*Lg.* 957b), and Solon's laws were to have force for one hundred years (Plut. *Sol.* 25.1 = fr. 541 M.).—For *neque tolli neque abrogari* cf. the previous note.

14b–18 This introductory section comprises (1) a case that belief in the deity and in the deity's concern for the human being is foundational for laws in general and a justification of this emphasis (§§ 14b–16) and (2) remarks on the relation of his laws to Plato's and on the style of the laws (§§ 17–18). The initial impression is that this matter is meant to apply to all the following laws, not just those of Book 2 (cf. Schmidt, 1959, 61); however, at 3.1 a new *laus legis* is introduced specifically for the laws on magistrates; hence (1) may apply, in fact, only to the *constitutio religionum* of Book 2; the matter is never fully clarified in the extant text; §§ 46–68 have a similarly ambiguous status; cf. pp. 242–43 and *ad loc.* Perhaps a revision would have clarified.

14b sed ut vir doctissimus fecit Plato atque idem gravissimus philosophorum omnium, qui princeps de republica conscripsit, idemque separatim de legibus eius, id mihi credo esse faciendum, ut priusquam ipsam legem recitem, de eius legis laude dicam; . . .] *Princeps* refers to writing both *de republica* and *de legibus* and implies that Cicero himself is Plato's successor; cf. Schmidt, 1959, 54 n. 2.—The legislation of Plato's *Laws* was not designed necessarily for the ideal state constructed in his *Republic*. Cicero did have in mind, however, that the laws of *Leg.* should fit the type of state constructed in *Rep.* (cf. 1.20), and he may well have understood Plato's project in a similar sense. Hence, though *eius* was deleted by Ziegler, this may be a correction of the author (cf. also Lehmann, 4 n. 4). The plan to preface "praise of the law" follows Platonic precedent, as indicated at *Lg.* 722e–723b.—Cicero praises Plato in similar terms at *de Orat.* 1.47: *principi longe omnium in dicendo gravissimo et eloquentissimo, Platoni; Orat.* 10: *ille non intellegendi solum sed etiam dicendi gravissimus auctor et magister Plato;* ibid. 62: *exstitit et gravitate ⟨et suavitate⟩ princeps Plato; Rab. Post.* 23: *virum unum totius Graeciae facile doctissimum, Platonem;* cf. *Q.fr.* 1.1.29: *atque ille quidem princeps ingeni et doctrinae Plato;* indeed, he is *paene philosophorum deus* according to *Hort.* fr. 84. Cf. also the first mention of Plato at 1.15.

quod idem et Zaleucum et Charondam fecisse video, cum quidem illi non studi et delectationis sed reipublicae causa leges civitatibus suis scrip-

serint; . . .] A προοίμιον to the laws of Zaleucus is attested also at Stob. vol. 4, p. 123, 12 ff. W.-H. (summarized at D.S. 12.20.2–3), but this material may be contaminated with Pythagorean doctrine; cf. Gagarin, 1986, 62; Delatte, 177 ff. It did, however, influence Cicero (via Aristoxenus?): cf. *ad* §15a and 3.5. The idea of a preamble to laws is, however, even older than Cicero indicates and probably goes back to Near Eastern models. The famous code of Hammurabi of Babylon (1792–50) can now be set into a broader context of earlier and later enactments of similar type, including the laws written in Sumerian and attributed to Lipit Ishtar of Isin (1934–24), the laws of Eshnunna written in Akkadian and possibly antedating Hammurabi's, a "stele of righteousness" set up at about the same time by Attakhushu, prince of Elam, and a code promulgated by Ammisaduqa, Hammurabi's fourth successor. They were often tralaticious from previous enactments. A prologue and epilogue serve to advertise their authors' commitment to justice; cf. C.J. Gadd, *CAH* 1.2³, 634–35 and ibid. 2.1³, 187–89.—*Quidem* contrasts with the following *sed* (the adversative force, is, I think, guaranteed by the superfluous *illi* that follows; cf. Solodow, 38–39); *aliter* Feldhügel *ad loc.*—Cicero contrasts two types of lawmaking, one *studi et delectationis . . . causa,* the other *reipublicae causa.* He places Plato in the former category, Zaleucus and Charondas in the latter. Since Plato is the model for Cicero's own project (cf. 1.15), it surely follows that he, too, is writing *studi et delectationis . . . causa* even if his laws are drafted with free states in view and with the intent of strengthening them (if they choose to adopt his legislation: cf. 3.29); cf. Introduction § 4; 1.37, § 35, and 3.4. He has no state commission to draft legislation as did Zaleucus and Charondas and so can hardly be said to be doing so *reipublicae causa* in the same sense as they. Cf. Keyes, 1921, 310; *aliter* Schmidt, 1959, 56 n. 1, and Girardet, 1981, 8–10, 98, and 164.—Du Mesnil pleads at length for the retention of the transmitted indicative (*scripserunt*) and is followed in this by Görler. But the former's view of the relation of ideas as temporal ("und zwar haben jene in diesem Falle, die in diesem Falle, während sie") is unconvincing, as is the latter's apparent interpretation of it as causal. We see the relation of ideas as adversative (the similarity in procedure being in spite of the different goals) and thus accept, with most editors, R. Stephanus' *scripserint;* cf. Kühner-Stegmann, 2, 348–49.

quos imitatus Plato videlicet hoc quoque legis putavit esse, persuadere aliquid, non omnia vi ac minis cogere.] The laws are not laws if they do not serve the common good; hence persuasion, not force, is the legislator's appropriate mode. Cf. Aristox. fr. 33: . . . ὑπήκοον αὐτὸν κατασκευάζειν μὴ πλαστῶς ἀλλὰ πεπιστευμένως; Pl. *Lg.* 660a4 ff.: . . . ὁ ὀρθὸς νομοθέτης ἐν τοῖς καλοῖς ῥήμασι καὶ ἐπαινετοῖς πείσει τε, καὶ ἀναγκάσει μὴ πείθων, . . . ὀρθῶς ποιεῖν; sim. 718b, 723a; cf. *Rp.* 536e1–2: οὐδὲν μάθημα μετὰ δουλείας τὸν ἐλεύθερον χρὴ μανθάνειν . . . Plato did not, however, see his practice as an imitation of predecessors, quite the contrary: πρὸς τοῦτο δὲ <u>οὐδεὶς</u> ἔοικε διανοηθῆναι πώποτε <u>τῶν νομοθετῶν</u>, ὡς ἐξὸν δυοῖν χρῆσθαι πρὸς τὰς νομοθεσίας, πειθοῖ καὶ βίᾳ, καθ' ὅσον οἷόν τε ἐπὶ τὸν ἄπειρον παιδείας ὄχλον, τῷ ἑτέρῳ χρῶνται μόνον (*Lg.* 722b4 ff.). Plato often plays on the opposition of force and persuasion; cf., e.g., *Rp.* 327c; *Tim.* 70a.—There was a different relation of citizens not only to the laws but also to the magistrates under Charondas' system; cf. 3.2.

15a Q. Quid quod Zaleucum istum negat ullum fuisse Timaeus?] = *FGrHist* 566 F 130a. Some have been reluctant to take these words at face value. Thus Bake *ad loc.* supposed that Timaeus merely denied that the historical Zaleucus was the lawgiver. Jacoby, assigning this fragment to the excursus on the Locrians leading up to the treatment of Pythagoras in Book 9 of the *Histories,* wonders (*ad loc.*) whether Timaeus had merely disputed Zaleucus' alignment with the Pythagorean school (as claimed by Aristoxenus and his Pythagorean sources; cf. Delatte, 28), rather than his existence, but then one must assume that Cicero misrepresented his source on two separate occasions (see the next note). Oldfather, *RE* 13.2 (1927), 1318.50–54, supposes that Timaeus' doubts stemmed from the confused reports about the lawgiver; cf. Arist. *Pol.* 1274a28–31 on confusions in chronology regarding Zaleucus and Charondas; Szegedy-Maszak, 1978, 199 and n. 3. Such doubts have been revived in modern times by Bentley and Beloch: cf. von Fritz, *RE* 9A2 (1967), 2299.54 ff. with literature.

At ⟨ait⟩ Theophrastus, auctor haud deterior mea quidem sententia (meliorem multi nominant); . . .] = F 598C F. (perhaps from the νομοθέται [F 589.16 F.]). We follow Müller's insertion of *ait* after *at, aio* forming the expected contrast with *nego*, as at *Rab. Post.* 35, *Luc.* 104, and *Fin.* 2.70; Schiche's *non negat* after *nominant* is another possibility. De Plinval's *adseverat* after *at* may be too emphatic since the fact is not known to have been disputed prior to Timaeus, who evidently attacked Theophrastus (cf. *FGrHist* 566F12 = Polyb. 12.11.5). Cf. *Att.* 6.1.18 (20 February 50): *quis Zaleucum leges Locris scripsisse non dixit? num igitur iacet Theophrastus* (fr. 598B F.) *si id a Timaeo* (*FGrHist* 566F130b), *tuo familiari, reprehensum est?*[43]—Timaeus' critics included Istrus, Polemo of Ilium, and, above all, Polybius; cf. Truesdell S. Brown, *Timaeus of Tauromenium* (Berkeley, 1958), ch. V ("Timaeus and His

---

43. For this reason I am not convinced that Theophrastus περὶ νομοθετῶν is Cicero's source here, as, for instance, Regenbogen, *RE* Suppl. 7 (1940), 1519.30–32, suggests as a possibility; cf. Rawson, 1991, 136 with literature cited at n. 31.

Critics"); for Polybius' critique cf. G. Schepens, "Polemic and Methodology in Polybius' Book XII," in *Purposes of History: Studies in Greek Historiography from the 4th to the 2nd Centuries B.C.*, ed. H. Verdin, G. Schepens, and E. de Keyser (Leuven, 1990), 39–61, esp. 51 ff. Another critic was Demetrius of Scepsis; cf. fr. 27 Gaede = *FGrHist* 566 F 129.

commemorant vero ipsius cives, nostri clientes, Locri.] The Locrians probably belonged to the *clientela* of the Tullii since the time of the Verrine prosecution (cf. Oldfather, *loc. cit.* next to last note, 1342.6–10), and indeed the citation is reminiscent of Cicero's appeal to the testimony of relevant communities in the Verrine speeches. At *Planc.* 97 he represents *omnia illa municipia quae sunt a Vibone ad Brundisium* as being under his patronage. For Cicero's attitude toward the *patrocinium* of foreign peoples in general cf. Meyer, 211 ff.

sed sive fuit sive non fuit, nihil ad rem; loquimur quod traditum est.] Cicero will not attempt to decide the question; the acceptance of tradition here contrasts with the attitude at 1.3–4 but is similar to *Off.* 1.150 (*sic fere accepimus*) and §§ 54 ff.; cf. the introduction to this Book and *ad* § 40.

15b–16 Here Marcus offers his *legis prooemium* (cf. § 16 *fin.*), a procedure inspired by Zaleucus, Charondas, and Plato (cf. *ad* § 14b). It consists of the affirmation of: (1) the divine government of the universe in general (cf. Atticus' concession of the point at 1.21) and the gods' concern for human beings in particular; (2) the existence of the gods, based upon the idea that a *ratio* permeating the universe accounts for the regular patterns of nature and that the superior being must possess *ratio;* (3) the utility of such beliefs as a foundation for organized society. Of these points, (1) and (2) are well known Stoic positions argued with greater detail and nuance in *N.D.* 2 (see parallels cited in the following notes); on the other hand, (3) is a personal conviction that Cicero enunciates at *N.D.* 1.3–4; it is similar to the idea he expresses in *Div.* 2 that divination should be cultivated *reipublicae causa*.

Our passage is one of several pieces of evidence cited by Wiseman, 1994, in arguing, after Liebeschuetz, for a connection between religion and morality at Rome; sim. W. Jeffrey Tatum, "Ritual and Personal Morality in Roman Religion," *Syllecta Classica* 4 (1993), 13–20. Certainly Cicero thinks it desirable for such a connection to exist in people's minds; hence this exhortation and the following law *nocturna mulierum sacrificia ne sunto . . .* (§ 21.11 with commentary at §§ 36–37). An original focus on ritual purity seems to have broadened, as among the Greeks (cf. Parker, 322 ff.), to include considerations from the sphere of law and ethics; cf. *ad* § 22.1.

15b Si⟨t⟩ igitur hoc iam a principio persuasum civibus, dominos esse omnium rerum ac moderatores deos, . . .] *Sit* is the correction of the *recentiores* for transmitted *si*.—At Pl. *Lg.* 887b8–c2 Clinias states that a proof of the existence of the gods would be the most apt προοίμιον for all laws; in § 16 Cicero contents himself with a rudimentary proof (see below). His prooemium begins in the traditional way; cf. D.S. 12.19.1–2: . . . ἤρξατο πρῶτον [sc. Zaleucus] περὶ τῶν ἐπουρανίων θεῶν. εὐθὺς γὰρ ἐν τῷ προοιμίῳ τῆς ὅλης νομοθεσίας ἔφη δεῖν τοὺς κατοικοῦντας ἐν τῇ πόλει πάντων πρῶτον ὑπολαβεῖν καὶ πεπεῖσθαι θεοὺς εἶναι . . . ; Stob. vol. 4, p. 123.13 W.-H.: τοὺς κατοικοῦντας τὴν πόλιν καὶ τὴν χώραν πάντας πρῶτον πεπεῖσθαι χρὴ καὶ νομίζειν θεοὺς εἶναι . . . This point and the following lemma both appear at Pl. *Lg.* 903b ff. with summary at 907b5 ff. Plato's third point, that the gods are incorruptibly just, is implied by Cicero's law *Impius ne audeto placare donis iram deorum* (§ 22.8).—This doctrine is, of course, contrary to Atticus' Epicureanism (cf. Schmidt, 1959, 57), but the obstacle has already been cleared away at 1.21 (see *ad loc.*). See also *ad* § 32.

. . . eaque quae gerantur eorum geri iudicio ac numine; . . .] Contrast 1.21, where Cicero seemed to have difficulty finding the right word to describe the modality of divine government.—The wording is reminiscent of Lucr. 1.127 ff. (sim. 1.568): *quapropter bene cum superis de rebus habenda / nobis est ratio, solis lunaeque meatus / qua fiant ratione, et qua vi quaeque gerantur in terris* . . .—The transmission of the first of the divine attributes is corrupt, with *iudicione* B¹A¹ (? *-no* A¹), evidently going back to a double reading of the archetype (*iudicio/dicione*), separated as *iudicio ne* in ES¹RHL⁴⁴ and corrected to *iudicio* in BˣAˣS² but to *dicione* in P. Cicero uses *dicio*, however, only of human sovereignty; the first datable use with reference to the gods comes from the year 362 (*Paneg.* 11.28); it thereafter becomes fairly frequent in Christian authors (see *TLL* s.v., 962.43 ff.); hence the corruption. There is no obstacle to *iudicium* being limited by *deorum*; cf., e.g., *N.D.* 3.82; on the gods as *iudices* cf. also *ad* § 16.

eosdemque optime de genere hominum mereri, . . .] Cf. *ad* 1.25 (*Itaque ad hominum commoditates et usus—*).

. . . et qualis quisque sit, quid agat, quid in se admittat, qua mente, qua pietate colat religiones intueri; piorumque et impiorum habere rationem.] *Admitto* (sometimes, as here, with *in se*) is used of "becoming guilty of, committing," or "perpetrating" a crime; cf. *OLD* s.v., 13a.—The deity's concern with the individual's piety is the foundation of cult (cf. *N.D.* 1.3). A clear statement of this can be found at Crit. *Sis.* 43.19.16 ff. Sn.-Kn.; further Greek parallels at Marx *ad* Pl. *Rud.* 15; cf. Pl. *Capt.* 313–15 and *Rud.* 9–

---

44. J.G.F. Powell notes (*per litt.*) that the space suggests that *ne* may have been a supralinear addition in the archetype or may point to an attempt to write *iurisdictione*.

12; Liv. 1.21.1 (on Numa): . . . *et deorum adsidua insidens cura, cum interesse rebus humanis caeleste numen videretur, ea pietate omnium pectora imbuerat ut fides ac ius iurandum pro nimio* [Walters; *proximo* mss.] *legum ac poenarum metu civitatem regerent;* cf. C. Koch, 181–82.—Whether Cicero himself believed in the deity's concern with the individual's piety or merely regarded such a conviction as a part of *religio utilis civitatibus* (cf. § 26) may be left open; Seneca lacked not only a belief in the gods' concern with the individual's pious state of mind in performing cult acts but also in the efficacy of the rituals themselves: *quae omnia* [sc. cult acts] *sapiens servabit tamquam legibus iussa, non tamquam diis grata* (F 71 Vottero).

16 his enim rebus imbutae, mentes haud sane abhorrebunt ab utili aut a vera sententia.] The *utile* and the *verum* should underlie legislation, as was made clear in § 11. The rest of this chapter will be devoted to establishing these points (in reverse order): (1) *quid est enim verius—confitendum est;* (2) *utiles esse autem has opiniones quis neget*—, the former on the basis of Stoic arguments paralleled in *N.D.* 2 (see the following notes), whereas the latter emphasizes the gods' rôle as guarantors of social contracts and might be Epicurean in origin.

quid est enim verius, quam neminem esse oportere tam stulte arrogantem, ut in se rationem et mentem putet inesse, in caelo mundoque non putet; . . .] The *a minore ad maius* argument reappears in *N.D.*; cf. 2.16: *esse autem hominem qui nihil in omni mundo melius esse quam se putet desipientis arrogantiae est; ergo est aliquid melius* (cf. 3.26); 2.18 ff., esp. 2.21 (Zeno): *quod ratione utitur id melius est quam id quod ratione non utitur; nihil autem mundo melius; ratione igitur mundus utitur.* Cf. ibid. 2.97; see also the note after next.

aut ut ea quae vix summa ingeni ratione ⟨comprehendat, nulla ratione⟩ moveri putet?] The supplement is that of Manutius.—Cf. *N.D.* 2.43 (with Pease's note): *sensum autem astrorum atque intellegentiam maxime declarat ordo eorum atque constantia (nihil est enim quod ratione et numero moveri possit sine consilio), in quo nihil est temerarium nihil varium nihil fortuitum.*

quem vero astrorum ordines,—hunc hominem omnino numerari qui decet?] For such regularities of nature as a sign of the existence of the gods cf. *N.D.* 1.100, 2.15, 97, and 132; this last passage is also a parallel for the *dierum noctiumque vicissitudines.* The teleological view of the world as created for human good is developed in detail at *N.D.* 2.154 ff.—For *hunc hominem omnino numerari qui decet?* cf. *N.D.* 2.97: *quis enim hunc hominem dixerit, qui, cum tam certos caeli motus tam ratos astrorum ordines tamque inter se omnia conexa et apta viderit, neget in his ullam inesse rationem eaque casu fieri dicat, quae quanto consilio gerantur nullo consilio adsequi possumus?*

cumque omnia quae rationem habent praestent eis quae sint rationis expertia, nefasque sit dicere ullam rem praestare naturae omnium rerum, rationem inesse in ea confitendum est.] Another argument from the container
and the contained; see the second note on this chapter and for the form of
argument *ad* 1.45. Cf. also *N.D.* 2.136: *quorum igitur causa quis dixerit*
effectum esse mundum? eorum scilicet animantium quae ratione utuntur; hi
sunt di et homines; quibus profecto nihil est melius, ratio est enim quae
praestet omnibus . . . Cicero also shows awareness of the weakness of this
argument, however, since "being better" (*praestare, melius esse*) can apply
to any number of different things but should not be used as a blank check to
allow the introduction of unproven predicates; cf. *N.D.* 3.20–23.—For
nefas see *ad* § 21.5.

utiles esse autem has opiniones quis neget,—dis immortalibus interpositis
tum iudicibus, ⟨tum⟩ testibus?] The appeal to expedience is in line with the
Epicurean justification of the social contract; cf. *ad* §§ 9b–13. Cicero lists
four areas in which belief in the gods is expedient: (1) oaths; (2) treaties; (3)
fear of divine punishment as a deterrent to crime (cf. 1.40; Stob. vol. 4, p.
125.14–17 W.-H.); (4) relations of citizens in a community.—For *sancta*
societas, denied, according to Ennius, when kingship is involved, cf. *ad Off.*
1.26.—The second *tum* was added by Minutianus to complete the coordination. The gods are witnesses of oaths and treaties and judges of their proper
observance or otherwise as well as of right or wrong behavior in general; on
their *iudicium* and the sphere of its exercise cf. also § 15; the view that the
fear of the gods is the only guarantee that oaths would be kept was widespread in antiquity; cf. Burkert, 1985, 252.—After *testibus* the mss. have
the puzzling notation (*h*)*i*(*i*)*s*.

Habes legis prooemium; sic enim haec appellat Plato.] For the concluding
formula cf. *ad Off.* 1.15a.—One might expect *legum,* rather than *legis,* in
accord with Pl. *Lg.* 722d1–2: τὰ δ' ἔμπροσθεν ἦν πάντα ἡμῖν προοίμια
νόμων, unless the singular is used as a collective for the whole body of
legislation that will follow (a usage not recognized by *OLD* or *TLL* s.v. *lex,*
but cf. *ad* 1.41).—*Prooemium* first enters Latin as a technical term of rhetoric for one type of opening of a judicial speech (*Rhet. Her.* 1.6; Cic. *Inv.* 1.20
avoids the Greek word and uses instead *principium*); Cicero used the term of
the prefatory matter to a clause in the praetor's edict at *Ver.* 1.111 (*cum abs*
te caput illud tam multis verbis mercennarioque prooemio esset ornatum)
and often, in various applications, thereafter; cf. *OLD* s.v.

17–18 To prepare the reader for the laws themselves Cicero includes clarification of their relation to the *Laws* of Plato, which have twice been invoked
as a precedent (1.15 and § 14b), and of the diction used. One should not

expect a verbatim rendering of Plato; this could have been done but for Cicero's desire to be his own man (*nisi plane esse vellem meus*). The language will, for the sake of *auctoritas*, be moderately archaizing, but not carried so far as in the Twelve Tables (albeit even they had been updated a bit in orthography; cf. Wieacker, 1967, 316).

17 Q. Habeo vero, frater, et in hoc admodum delector, quod in aliis rebus aliisque sententiis versaris atque ille; . . .] Marcus' conclusion with the name of Plato inevitably suggests a comparison. In spite of Quintus' assertion of his brother's independence, Rawson, 1991, 136, suspects that Cicero might have been influenced by the repeated references to the deity at *Laws* 4.716 ff.; see the next note.—*Delector* is usually construed with plain ablative in Cicero; cf. examples at *TLL* s.v. *delector* 426.55 ff., as well as § 2 (*mirabar . . . te tam valde hoc loco delectari*) but with *in* followed by ablative in our lemma as well as at *Fam.* 6.4.4 (. . . *tamen in hac inani prudentiae laude delector*) and *Fin.* 1.39 (. . . *quae manus significet illum in hac rogatiuncula delectatum*); cf. Madvig on the latter passage.

nihil enim tam dissimile quam vel ea quae ante dixisti, vel hoc ipsum de dis exordium; . . .] *Quae ante dixisti* comprise Stoic elements with some points of contact with Epicureanism: see *ad* § 16; the *de dis exordium* itself seems to have been inspired by reports about Zaleucus' legislation: see *ad* §§ 14b and 15b.

unum illud mihi videris imitari, orationis genus. M.: Velle fortasse: quis enim id potest aut umquam poterit imitari?] Cf. *ad* § 14b and Burkert, 1965, 182–83 with literature.

nam sententias interpretari perfacile est; quod quidem ego facerem, nisi plane esse vellem meus; quid enim negoti est eadem prope verbis eisdem conversa dicere?] *Interpretari* and cognates are generally used of a close, literal translation; cf. § 45 and J.G.F. Powell in Powell, 1995, 278; similar to our passage is Varro's claim of originality at *Ac.* 1.8 (*Menippum imitati, non interpretati*).—For translation as an exercise for the orator in training cf. *de Orat.* 1.155 (Crassus): *postea mihi placuit eoque sum usus adulescens ut summorum oratorum Graecas orationes explicarem. quibus lectis hoc adsequebar ut, cum ea quae legeram Graece Latine redderem, non solum optimis verbis uterer et tamen usitatis, sed etiam exprimerem quaedam verba imitando, quae nova nostris essent . . .* Cicero's youthful version of Xenophon's *Oeconomicus* (fr. phil., pp. 65 ff.) is an example. *De Orat., Rep.,* and *Leg.,* all from the 50s, clearly aim to be more original (cf. *nisi plane esse vellem meus*). The *philosophica* of 44–43 may have lowered this standard if *Att.* 12.52.3 refers to them and is to be taken at face value (ἀπόγραφα *sunt, minore labore fiunt; verba tantum adfero, quibus abundo*; the reference is unclear, however), though *Off.* 1.6 emphasizes the use of his own judgment and *Off.* 3 lays claim to originality (*nullis adminiculis, sed, ut dicitur, Marte nostro:* 3.34). Cf. in general R. Poncelet, *Cicéron traducteur de Platon* (Paris, 1957); D.M. Jones, "Cicero as a Translator," *BICS* 6 (1959), 22–33; Mario Puelma, "Cicero als Platon-Übersetzer," *MH* 37 (1980), 137–78; J.G.F. Powell, *loc. cit.,* 273–300.

Q. Prorsus adsentior; . . .] Cf. *ad* § 12.

sed iam exprome, si placet, istas leges de religione.] Since § 8 we have been expecting *singulae leges.* The *ius sacrum* formed a part of the *ius publicum* (cf. Wissowa, 380; Kaser, 1986, 57–58) and is thus expected per se, but how does Quintus know that sacral laws will be the first category? They appeared only in the tenth of the Twelve Tables (cf. § 64), and the fact hardly follows from the *de dis exordium.* Moreover, Marcus' remark at § 45 (*O miram memoriam Pomponi tuam!*) suggests that an explicit *divisio* was somewhere given but has been lost (in the lacuna of 1.57?). The alternative is to regard *istas leges de religione* without identifiable referent as a sign of incompleteness, as did Henricus Schwarz, *Miscellanea critica* (diss., Tübingen, 1878), 29–30.

18 M. Expromam equidem ut potero; et quamquam et locus et sermo familiaris est, legum {leges} voce proponam.] Rath's *quamquam* for *q(uonia)m,* revived by Watt, 1986, 286, is an easy change and deserves acceptance, in spite of Cicero's use of the archaic *reri* in the correspondence with Atticus, by means of which Lebek, 31 and n. 40, seeks to buttress the transmitted text. De Plinval's arbitrary treatment of this passage is sufficiently refuted by Pascucci, 1968, 3 n. 1.—We follow Halm's deletion of *leges,* perhaps the inept insertion of a scribe or other reader who thought the object needed clarification. Certainly one expects *legum* to limit what immediately follows, as in all other instances in this essay: *legum nomen* (§ 15), *legum verba* just below, *legum scriptoribus* (§ 63), and *legum custodiam* (3.46); cf. also *Fin.* 3.62: *naturae ipsius vocem videmur audire.* The hyperbaton merely creates confusion by making *legum* at first seem to limit *leges.* Hence the unfortunate attempt of Turpin, 1884 ff., to interpret *legum leges* with the former limiting the latter (how would she take *voce?*); cf also 3.43: *legis voce.* Another alternative would be Moser's transposition: *leges legum.*

Sunt certa legum verba, Quinte, neque ita prisca ut in veteribus XII sacratisque legibus, et tamen, quo plus auctoritatis habeant, paulo antiquiora quam hic sermo est.] Here Cicero carefully defines the stylistic level of the following laws as a mean between the language of the Twelve Tables and *sacratae leges* on the one hand and *hic sermo,* the style of the dialogue,[45] imitative of elevated conversation, on the other. The reason given is a gain in *auctoritas*. Though Cicero does not use this term when he discusses archaic language in *de Orat.* 3 (cf. Lebek, 34 with literature), cf. Quint. *Inst.* 1.6.39: *verba a vetustate repetita . . . adferunt orationi maiestatem aliquam non sine delectatione: nam et auctoritatem antiquitatis habent et, quia intermissa sunt, gratiam novitati similem parant;* Pascucci, 1968, 5 and n. 2. For the language of Cicero's laws, which corresponds to the language used in legislation of his own time with only a small percentage of archaisms, cf. Jordan, esp. 228; Wilhelms, esp. 128–31 (and the summary, "Is the Language of the Ideal Laws in Cicero's *De Legibus* Truly Archaic?" *CJ* 38 [1942–43], 458–59); Pascucci, 1970.—For *legum verba* cf. 1.56: *iam nunc a te uerba usurpantur ciuilis iuris et legum;* for the *leges sacratae* cf. *ad Off.* 3.111; for *et tamen* in Cicero cf. Powell *ad Sen.* 1.

eum morem igitur, cum brevitate, si potuero, consequar.] Cicero's *brevitas* also imitates a feature of legal language; cf. *Mur.* 28 (denigrating the importance of the *iuris periti*): *difficilis res ideo non putatur quod et perpaucis et minime obscuris litteris continetur;* Wieacker, 1967, 328, speaks of the "lapidare Konzentration" of the Twelve Tables deriving from cult tradition; cf. also Pascucci, 1968, 6–7. It is precisely their brevity that Atticus and Quintus remark upon after hearing the two extant sets of laws (§ 23 and 3.12, respectively; cf. on the former).

leges autem a me edentur non perfectae—nam esset infinitum—sed ipsae summae rerum atque sententiae.] Cicero will not strive for completeness, an impossible task; instead he will offer *ipsae summae rerum atque sententiae.* Here *ipse* has restrictive force, separating from the mass (for parallels cf. *TLL* s.v., 334.69 ff., esp. 335.37 ff.). *Summa* evidently means τὸ σύμπαν (Forcellini s.v., 9), "the whole" (*OLD* s.v., 5a), as limited by *sententiae* "the general sense or drift, the substance, gist" or the like (ibid. 7b), though this sense seems not to be paralleled in the plural. *Summa sententiae* would be akin to what Thucydides claimed to be offering in relation to the speeches delivered by the participants in his *Histories:* ἡ ξύμπασα γνώμη (1.22.1). Perhaps translate the phrase "only the essence of the content and thought"; see the phrase *constitutio religionum* (§ 23). The reduction of wide-ranging matter to *una sententia* is what Cicero thinks the jurisconsults should do; cf. § 47, where *sub fin.* he offers an example of such compression. Similarly, as he embarks on the topic of education at *Lg.* 788a–c, Plato emphasizes the difficulty of providing detailed legislation for every point and speaks of using "samples" (δείγματα).

---

45. Ziegler's *hic sermo* ⟨*noster*⟩ is not needed to yield this meaning.

19–22 Plato had sought, through an admixture of philosophy, to purify and rationalize the traditional religion of his day; cf. Dodds, ch. VII. The relation of Cicero's sacral laws to Roman religious tradition is similar.[46] *Ex patriis ritibus optima colunto* (§ 22.3) could stand as the motto of Cicero's *constitutio religionum* as a whole. Plato's influence on some of the legislation is palpable: moderation in musical performance (§ 22.2 with § 38), the exclusion of the *impius* from sacrifice (§ 22.8 with § 41), and licit types of dedication (§ 22.12 with literal rendering of a *locus Platonicus* at § 45); cf. H. Müller, 49–50. There is a moralizing tendency in the prohibition of women's nightly sacrifices (§ 21.11), whereas hard-headed practicality underlies the limitation on almsgiving (ibid.). A Roman predecessor lies behind the notion that a species of *sacrum commissum* can be expiated (presumably if involuntary, as in Scaevola's ruling); cf. *ad* § 22.1; the restrictions on expense in connection with the cult of the dead (§ 22.16) are, as the corresponding commentary (§§ 54 ff.) shows, inspired partly by the Twelve Tables, partly by legislation of Solon and Demetrius of Phalerum. Cicero's own observations of the use and abuse of religion in the Roman state of his day form the basis for his laws for maintaining the calendar and the authority of the augurs (§§ 20.1 and 20.6–21.6), and some earlier practices, the use of the fetials (§ 21.7) and possibly the *augurium canarium*, if that is meant by *vineta virgetaque* (§ 21.1; see *ad loc.*), are to be revived. Much stress is laid on "control from the top," in terms both of licit cults (*Separatim nemo habessit deos,* etc.: § 19.3) and of cult practice (*Quoque haec privatim et publice modo rituque fiant, discunto ignari a publicis sacerdotibus:* § 20.4; *quique non paruerit, capital esto:* §21.6; *si senatus iussit:* § 21.8; . . . *publici sacerdotes expianto:* § 22.1). For the plan of this section see the introduction to this Book.

19.1–2 Ad divos adeunto—vindex erit.] Cited as from *Leg.* at Lact. *inst.* 5.20.3; cf. Schmidt, 1965, 315.

19.1 Ad divos adeunto caste; . . .] The first of the *leges de religione* regulates contact with the gods. The *castitas* demanded is ritual but also moral, as Cicero's commentary on this law makes clear (cf. *ad* § 24; Liebeschuetz, 48–49); for the thought cf. *N.D.* 2.71: *cultus autem deorum est optimus idemque castissimus atque sanctissimus plenissimusque pietatis, ut eos semper pura integra incorrupta et mente et voce veneremur;* Gel. 4.9.9, who, after citing Masurius Sabinus' etymology *caerimonia a carendo,* comments: *secundum hanc Sabini interpretationem templa quidem ac delubra, quae non vulgo ac temere, sed cum castitate caerimoniaque adeundum, et reve-*

---

46. Cf. Paul Wendland, *Die hellenistisch-römische Kultur in ihren Beziehungen zu Judentum und Christentum*[2] (Tübingen, 1912), 141 and n. 4.

renda et reformidanda sunt magis quam invulganda. It is, however, *castus,* not *caerimonia,* that is related to *careo;* see P. Schrijver, *The Reflexes of the Proto-Indoeuropean Laryngeals in Latin* (Amsterdam-Atlanta, 1991), 101 (against the view of Ernout-Meillet s.v. that the two senses of *castus* have different origins). Cicero translates εὐαγές with *castum* in § 45. The requirement of ritual purity serves to separate the divine from the human sphere. This is most pronounced in the case of the Vestal Virgins, committed to thirty years of chastity (Wissowa, 508 and n. 5; cf. § 29). This provision was blatantly violated, Cicero claims, in the rite by which a junior member of the college of pontiffs acting in Clodius' interest sought to consecrate Cicero's house as a temple of Libertas; cf. *Dom.* 134: *... si dixit aliquid verbis haesitantibus postemque tremebunda manu tetigit, certe nihil rite, nihil caste, nihil more institutoque perfecit.* For *caste* elsewhere in Cicero cf. *TLL* s.v., 570.50 ff. Cf. Suet. *Aug.* 6: *huc* [i.e., the *nutrimentorum locus Octavii*] *introire nisi necessario et caste religio est,* and in general the provisions at *Leg. sac.* nos. 84–89; Latte, 1960, 49–50.—The two stems *deus* and *divus* both originate in **deivos.* Walther Schwering, "*Deus* und *divus,*" IF 34 (1914–15), 1–44, corrected the view that in classical times *deus* functions as a noun, *divus* as an adjective. During the Republic, *deus* tended to drive out the more archaic *divus* as the word for "god,"[47] but *divus* proved to be useful as the designation for the divinized emperor. Thus though *deus* is the form previously met in this essay (e.g., 1.21, 23), *divus* is appropriate to the more archaic language of the laws (cf. § 18). In the following sentence, however, Cicero reverts to *deus,* perhaps for *variatio;* cf. § 20.2 *cuique divo;* Ernout-Meillet s.v. *deus;* Wilhelms, 61–62. For a different sense of the word cf. *ad* § 22.15.—In *adeunto* the third person plural *-to* imperative is used impersonally (the usage is continued in the following *adhibento . . . amovento . . . colunto*); the singular is often so used in *Lex XII;* cf. Daube, 57 ff.; Wackernagel, 1, 220; *ad* 1.16.

. . . pietatem adhibento, opes amovento.] Cf. *N.D.* 1.3: *haec* [*sc. pietas, sanctitas, religio*] *. . . omnia pure atque caste tribuenda deorum numini . . . sunt . . .* with Pease's note. *Pietas,* like the *impius* or *impii* of 1.40 or § 22.8, remains undefined here (cf. Mehl, 197); in fact, the concept will take on a moralizing tincture in §§ 24–25 and will be a major weapon deployed in Cicero's effort to judge and classify political figures of his time (cf. the references to the *impii,* i.e., Clodius, at § 43); cf. Mehl, 180.—*Opes amovento* accords with the simplicity of the oldest stratum of Roman religion as

---

47. Cf. Var. *L.* 3, fr. 2: *ita respondeant cur dicant deos cum ⟨de⟩ omnibus antiqui dixerint divos.*

Cicero conceived it; cf. *Rep.* 2.27 with Zetzel's note (Atticus remarks the general similarity to Numa's legislation at § 23): *sacrorum . . . ipsorum diligentiam difficilem, apparatum perfacilem esse voluit* [sc. Numa]; *nam quae perdiscenda quaeque observanda essent, multa constituit, sed ea sine impensa.* The sumptuary laws in § 22.4, 12 and 16, restricting alms-giving, precious donations, and excessive funeral expenditures, give effect to this provision, as do the restrictions on funerals and tombs at §§ 55–68.—Here Cicero may be influenced by Laelius' speech *de Collegiis,* which he else-where praises highly (*N.D.* 3.5 and 43); it emphasized simplicity of cult (e.g., *orat.* fr. 16: . . . *simpuia pontificum dis immortalibus grata sint Sami-aeque . . . capudines*); cf. Rawson, 1991, 137.

19.2 Qui secus faxit, deus ipse vindex erit.] Improper treatment of the gods is punished by the gods themselves; cf. § 22.6: *Periurii poena divina exitium, humana dedecus.*—The sentence *qui secus faxit, deus ipse vindex esto* illus-trates several aspects of the handling of relative and main clause shared by Latin and Hittite: (1) the order relative clause, main clause; (2) the fact that the correlative word in the main clause is optional rather than obligatory, even in oblique cases (cf. omission of the oblique antecedent, e.g., at Pl. *Mil.* 156). At an earlier linguistic stage the sentence would be understood as "A certain man will have done otherwise; the god himself will be the punisher," with the relative retaining its original indefinite force; the word order is dictated by the order of actions. Cf. Heinrich Hettrich, *Untersuchungen zur Hypotaxe im Vedischen* (Berlin–New York, 1988), 504–5, with literature; for the origin of the relative pronoun in the indefinite cf. already W. Kroll, "Der lateinische Relativsatz," *Glotta* 3 (1910), 1–18; on such clauses in the XII Tables cf. Wieacker, 1967, 322–24. Relatives and conditionals are the only forms of subordination found in these laws, dominated by parataxis (cf. *infra* on § 19.9).—The usual account of *faxo, -it,* is that it is in origin an athematic aorist subjunctive, properly future in sense, that has come to be used as equivalent to future perfect by Cicero's time; cf. Kühner-Holzweis-sig, 797; Leumann, 573–74 and 622–23; Sihler § 502; Helmut Rix, "Bemerkungen zu den lateinischen Verbformen des Typs *faxo faxim,*" in *Mír Curad: Studies in Honor of Calvert Watkins,* ed. J. Jasanoff, H.C. Melchert, and L. Oliver (Innsbruck, 1998), 619–34; but the subjunctive is ordinarily thematic, whereas the Sabellian *s*-future, similar to our form, is athematic; hence Meiser § 121.8 now interprets it as desiderative; for the semantics of the form cf. ibid. § 122.1.—Cicero is apparently the first to use *vindex* in the sense "one who punishes (an offense)": cf. *Inv.* 2.104; *OLD* s.v., 3a.—The asyndeton, reminiscent of Cato, lends an archiac quality; cf. von Albrecht, 1983, 49 = Eng. tr. 30; Hofmann-Szantyr, 830.

19.3 Separatim nemo habessit deos, neve novos neve advenas, nisi publice adscitos.] The two poles of this sentence are the adverbs *separatim* ("apart from the rest": OLD s.v. 1) and *publice*. That public worship is in question is clear from the following contrastive *privatim*.—This aims to codify the *mos maiorum* (cf. § 23) and seems to be in line with the prayer uttered at the beginning of Roman assemblies (see the next note). The Athenian attitude was similar, as evidenced most famously by the charge against Socrates: Σωκράτη φησὶν [sc. Meletus] ἀδικεῖν τούς τε νέους διαφθείροντα καὶ θεοὺς οὓς ἡ πόλις νομίζει οὐ νομίζοντα, ἕτερα δὲ δαιμόνια καινά (Pl. *Ap.* 24b6–8; cf. 26b5); cf. Eudore Derenne, *Les procès d' impiété intentés aux philosophes à Athènes au Vᵐᵉ et au IVᵉᵐᵉ siècles avant J.-C.* (Liège-Paris, 1930), 139–40 and 217 ff.; cf., however, the skeptical review of evidence for such trials by K.J. Dover, "The Freedom of the Intellectual in Greek Society," *Talanta* 7 (1975), 24–54. Cicero perhaps means by this provision to draw a dividing line against superstition; cf. Fest. p. 289M: *religiosi dicuntur qui faciendarum praetermittendarumque rerum divinarum secundum morem civitatis dilectum habent, nec se superstitionibus implicant.*[48]— Famous instances of the public recognition of foreign deities at Rome include Ceres (cf. *ad* § 21.11), Aesculapius (see *infra* on § 19.7), and the Magna Mater (*Har.* 27; Liv. 29.10.4–14; cf. Wissowa, 317 ff.; Scullard, 97 ff.; Beard, 1998, 1, 96–98, with literature at 97, n. 89), the latter two in time of war and on advice from the Sibylline books; these three are grouped together at Fest. p. 237M s.v. *peregrina sacra.* On the other hand, there were instances of strict senatorial restriction on cults, as in the suppression of the Bacchanalia in 186 (see *ad* § 37) or that of the cult of Isis and Sarapis, on which cf. Sarolta Takács, *Isis and Sarapis in the Roman World* (New York, 1995), 56 ff.; in connection with a temple to the (Celtic?) deity Alburnus the senate decreed that no general could dedicate a temple to any deity without its prior approval; cf. Var. *ARD* fr. 44; Wissowa, 45 and n. 2. Cotta's argument at *N.D.* 3.47 emphasizes the difficulty of knowing where to draw the line: *quid autem dicis, si di sunt illi quos colimus et accepimus, cur non eodem in genere Serapim Isimque numeremus? quod si facimus, cur barbarorum deos repudiemus?* Cf. further *ad* § 26 (*nam ⟨a⟩ patribus acceptos deos ita placet coli—*). On the enlargement of the Roman pantheon cf. in general Wissowa, 43 ff. Augustus' policy was in line with Cicero's injunction; cf. Suet. *Aug.* 93: *peregrinarum caerimoniarum sicut veteres ac praeceptas reverentissime coluit, ita ceteras contemptui habuit;* Beard, 1998, 1, 228–29.—In *habessit* the double *s* is a problem variously explained: it

---

48. See further *ad* 1.60.

presumably originates within Latin, perhaps to *amassem* on the analogy of *deixem : deixim*; cf. Leumann, 624; Sihler § 502 *sub fin.*; Meiser § 122.1; cf. also E. Benveniste, "Les futurs et subjonctifs sigmatiques du latin archaïque," *Bulletin de la Société de Linguistique* 23 (1922), 32–63, esp. 53–54, who suspects that the gemination was expressive and to avert rhotacism (besides being influenced by the subjunctive type *amassem*). The perfect subjunctive expresses aorist aspect in prohibitions (Kühner-Stegmann, 1, 189), and our form, though historically distinct, approximates that sense; cf. Powell *ad Sen.* 1. For the sense of *habere* cf. *ad* 1.24.

19.4 Privatim colunto quos rite a patribus ⟨cultos acceperint⟩.] Here Cicero takes a more liberal approach than Plato, who forbade private shrines altogether (see *ad* §§ 1–7a and n. 20 *supra; ad* § 41).—A private, indeed secret, rite, the Bacchanalia, was the cause of a crisis in 186 (cf. *ad* § 37). Similar to our injunction is the opponents' argument as presented at Liv. 39.15.2–3: *nulli umquam contioni, Quirites, tam non solum apta sed etiam necessaria haec sollemnis deorum comprecatio fuit, quae vos admoneret hos esse deos quos colere venerari precarique maiores vestri instituissent, non illos, qui pravis et externis religionibus captas mentes velut furialibus stimulis ad omne scelus et ad omnem libidinem agerent.*—The text incorporates Madvig's generally accepted supplement.—For the asyndeton cf. the note before last.—For the impersonal *colunto* cf. above on § 19.1 (*Ad divos adeunto caste . . .*).

19.5 ⟨In urbibus⟩ delubra habento. lucos in agris habento et Larum sedes.] *In urbibus* is clearly needed to contrast with *in agris* (cf. the commentary on this law at §§ 26–27, where the contrast recurs); R. Stephanus already inserted the words, albeit after *delubra*. Feldhügel's placement before *delubra* provides a palaeographical reason for the omission (saltation: *patribus—urbibus*).—*Delubrum* is "often used affectively" (*OLD* s.v.). Recurring at § 45, *delubrum* there is a sign that the embedded translations from Plato strive for an archaic dignity. The word also occurs in *Rep.* (1.41), an indicator that our laws are on a similar stylistic plane to that work. With the injunction *delubra habento* contrast the policy of the Persians (§ 26).— For the *lucorum leges* cf. *Leg. sac.* nos. 1–12.—The characteristically Roman gods called Lares were basically gods of a specific place, where their power was thought to be centered. The *Lar familiaris* was originally the god who protected landed property,[49] with a shrine on the road dividing two farms (the *compita*); hence Cicero's placement of their cult out of doors (*in agris* in our passage; cf. § 27: *posita in fundi villaeque conspectum religio*

---

49. Cf. the reference to the *lares praediorum* at *CIL* VI.455.

Larum . . .). The *Compitalia,* celebrated in late December / early January, was an occasion when the slaves received greater than usual license; cf. Scullard, 58–60. When slaves began to play a larger rôle as domestic staff, they brought the worship of the *Lares* with them indoors, and sacrifice was made to them on family occasions, such as the marriage, death, or arrival home from a trip of one of the family members. Cf. Wissowa, 166 ff., and for the Augustan and later development of the cult Beard, 1998, 1, 184–87.

19.6 Ritus familiae patrumque servanto.] The mention of the *Lares* may have prompted thought of the *ritus familiae* in general; these are, of course, private rites, whereas the later stipulation *Ex patriis ritibus optuma colunto* (§ 22.3) is in a context of public observance. This provision was one of the matters of concern to the censor; cf. Cato *orat.* fr. 72.

19.7 Divos et eos qui caelestes semper habiti sunt colunto, et ollos quos endo caelo merita locaverunt, Herculem Liberum Aesculapium Castorem Pollucem Quirinum, . . .] These words are cited at Lact. *inst.* 1.15.23, whence Powell restores *locaverunt* for the transmitted *vocaverint* (*vocaverunt* P); Feldhügel had proposed *locaverint,* but the indicative can stand in a purely descriptive relative clause (cf. the parallel *habiti sunt;* Kühner-Stegmann, 2, 304–5).—The groups distinguished are (1) those who have always held divine status and (2) heroes who have been elevated to such. There is a similar distinction at Var. *ARD* fr. 32*: *deos alios esse qui ab initio certi et sempiterni sunt, alios qui immortales ex hominibus facti sunt;* this is used, among other passages, by Bögel, 1907, 13, to show that Cicero had used *ARD,* though Agahd, 74 n. 1, posited instead a common Greek source; see the introduction to this Book. Cicero soon adds a third category of divinized virtues. The threefold classification certainly derives from Greek theory (it is implicit in the Stoic analysis at *N.D.* 2.61–62); cf. Schmidt, 1959, 66.—For *divos* cf. on *Ad divos adeunto caste;* for *caelestes* on 1.24. The equivocation *et eos qui caelestes semper habiti sunt* is necessitated by the religious practice of the ancients, which accorded cult to a variety of different demigods, heroes, abstractions, etc., but not to others who would have seemed equally qualified; cf. Cotta's *sorites*-type argument at *N.D.* 3.39 ff.—*Olle,* the original form, was altered to *ille,* when preceded or followed by a stress-accent, a development favored by the other pronominal forms *is, ipse.* The older form survives as an archaism in hexameter verse and some formulas, including laws. As our passage shows, Cicero, unlike the poets, does not confine the *oll-* forms to those with *i* in the ending. Cf. Skutsch *ad* Enn. *Ann.,* pp. 64–66; Leumann, 470; *TLL* s.v., 569.46 ff. and 70 ff. (legal attestations); for a different view of the origin of *ille* cf. Sihler § 377.4.—The archaic preposition *endo* for *in* derives from Proto-Indo-European full-grade **en,* seen also in Greek ἐν; cf. Leumann, 45–46; for a different suggestion ("may be nothing more than the hesitation between *e* and *i* which is common in OL epigraphy") cf. Sihler, § 41.2.a. The second element of the compound is the deictic particle **de, *do, *dē, *dō;* cf. H. Eichner, "Reklameiamben aus Roms Königszeit," *Sprache* 34 (1988–90), 229 n. 58. For use of *endo* in legal language see *Lex XII* 3.3: *ni iudicatum facit aut quis endo eo in iure vindicit, secum ducito . . .*

The deities listed were all well established members of the Roman pantheon by Cicero's day; the pontifex Q. Mucius Scaevola even thought it harmful to speak publicly of their human origin (*iur.* 20–21 fr. 20 = Augustin. *civ.* 4.27). The views of Cicero and Scaevola are contrasted by Francesca Fontanella, "L'interpretazione ciceroniana del culto degli eroi e delle virtù: un contributo delle *leges de religione* alla formazione morale della *élite* repubblicana," *RSI* 107 (1995), 5–19; cf. also Aldo Schiavone, "Quinto Mucio teologo," *Labeo* 20 (1974), 342 ff. Hercules was regarded as divine as early as *Od.* 11.602–4, albeit these verses were suspected even in antiquity (see Allen's critical apparatus *ad loc.*); for his cult in Italy cf. J. Bayet, *Les origines de l'Hercule romain* (Paris, 1926); Beard, 1998, 1, 68. For Hercules and Liber as benefactors of the human race cf. *Fin.* 3.66 (Hercules alone at *Off.* 3.25). Liber was an Italian fertility god associated in cult with Ceres and Libera, with whom he shared a temple dedicated in 493 (cf. Orlin, 97); save for his identification with the Greek Dionysus, his inclusion in this list would be odd (cf. Mehl, 207); cf. *N.D.* 2.62 (*hunc dico Liberum Semela natum, non eum quem nostri maiores auguste sancteque Liberum cum Cerere et Libera consecraverunt*); Wissowa, 297 ff.; Orlin, 100–101. Aesculapius clearly also belongs to the category of benefactors; for his introduction at Rome cf. Liv. 10.47.7; Wissowa, 306–9; Beard, 1998, 1, 69–70; Orlin, 106–8, who interprets this move as a bid for support in Magna Graecia on the eve of the Third Samnite War. The oldest temple dedicated to foreign deities at Rome was that of Castor and Pollux in the forum (484); it had been vowed fifteen years earlier by the dictator A. Postumius during the battle of Lake Regillus. The cult may have been introduced via Tusculum, where, in contrast to Rome, the *pulvinaria*, doubtless originally part of the twins' Greek worship, were still used. The dedication to the twins on a thin bronze lamina discovered near Lavinium in 1958 and dated to the middle to late sixth century provides early evidence of the cult: *ILLRP* 1271a; Arthur E. Gordon, *Illustrated Introduction to Latin Epigraphy* (Berkeley–Los Angeles–London, 1983), 76–77. Cf. in general Wissowa, 268–71. For the cult of Quirinus cf. *ad* 1.3 and in general Beard, 1998, 1, 15–16, with literature at 16 n. 42.

. . . ast olla propter quae datur homini ascensus in caelum, Mentem Virtutem Pietatem Fidem; earumque laudum delubra sunto, neve ulla vitiorum.] Lactantius cites these words at *inst.* 1.20.19 with *neve ulla vitiorum*
omitted for the sake of the point that one should cultivate the virtues rather
in one's heart, though this idea is not so alien to Cicero as Lactantius'
polemic might suggest; cf. Schmidt, 1965, 317–18.—Turnebus proposed to
substitute *et* for the transmitted *ast*, which, used without adversative force,
would have to be defended as a false Ciceronian archaism; cf. Pascucci,
1968, 31–32, cf. *ad* § 60 and 3.8.2.—For the divinization of such entities at
Rome cf. in general J. Rufus Fears, "The Cult of the Virtues and Roman
Imperial Ideology," *ANRW* 2.17.2 (1981), 827–948. Cf. *N.D.* 2.79, where
the same list appears, with the substitution of Concordia for Pietas, as part
of an argument for the divine government of the universe. All the entities
named had, in fact, temples in Rome (cf. § 28), so Cicero is proposing no
innovation. Further detail at *N.D.* 2.61 (on which see Pease's note): . . . *res*
ipsa, in qua vis inest maior aliqua, sic appellatur ut ea ipsa vis nominetur
deus, ut Fides ut Mens, quas in Capitolio dedicatas videmus proxime a M.
Aemilio Scauro, ante autem ab A. Atilio Calatino erat Fides consecrata.
vides Virtutis templum . . . The cult of <u>Mens</u> originated in 217 in the aftermath of the Roman defeat at Lake Trasimene; the foundation followed
advice of the decemviri and the Sibylline oracles when, in light of the
amentia of Flaminius, Rome did indeed need *mens* in her conduct of the war
(*pace* Wissowa, 313–15, there was no real counterpart in Greek cult; cf.
Orlin, 102 and n. 100). <u>Virtus</u> appeared first in the circle of Mars and with
military application; cf. Wissowa, 149 ff.; Weinstock, 230–33. <u>Fides</u> was
originally a quality of Jupiter (*Dius fidius*) and later became independent,
her temple dedicated during the First Punic War; ibid. 133 ff.; Weinstock,
168–69; Giulia Piccaluga, "Fides nella religione romana di età imperiale,"
ANRW 2.17.2 (1981), 703–35; Freyburger, 282 ff.; Orlin, 102. The worship of <u>Pietas</u> was relatively young; her temple was vowed by M'. Acilius
Glabrio on the eve of the battle of Thermopylae (191), a vow executed ten
years later by his son of the same name; cf. Wissowa, 331; Weinstock, 248
ff.; Orlin, 46–47 and 180–81. The true force of this law is to exclude
temples to the *vitia*; cf. § 28; *N.D. loc. cit.: quarum omnium rerum quia vis*
erat tanta ut sine deo regi non posset, ipsa res deorum nomen optinuit. quo
ex genere Cupidinis et Voluptatis et Lubentinae Veneris consecrata sunt,
vitiosarum rerum . . . For the deification of trivial entities cf. Pl. *Bac.* 115 ff.;
for the *aedes Libertatis* (Cicero calls it *Licentiae*) that Clodius erected on the
site of Cicero's house cf. *ad* § 42.—Cicero is the first to use *ascensus*
metaphorically, elsewhere of a political career; cf. *TLL* s.v., 761.17 ff.; for

our *iunctura* cf. V.Max. 8.15 pr.: . . . *cui ascensus in caelum patet* . . . — *Laudes* has here, as often, the sense of "praiseworthy qualities" (*OLD* s.v. *laus* 3b).—*Neve ulla vitiorum*: for Cicero's moralizing interpretation of religion and ritual cf. *ad* § 22.1.

19.8 Sacra sollemnia obeunto.] For the sense of *sacra* cf. *ad* § 22.1; for Seneca's reservations about such rituals cf. *ad* § 15b.

19.9 Feriis iurgia ⟨a⟩movento, easque in famulis operibus patratis habento; idque ut ita cadat in annuis anfractibus descriptum esto.] For the Romans *feriae* were days set aside for the deity and implied rest from work, originally agricultural work; cf. Scullard, 38 ff. (for participation of slaves and cessation of courts, 39); in general Rüpke, 1995, 464–67 and ch. 12.—*Iurgium* is used in the technical sense of a controversy before a judge or arbiter;[50] cf. *TLL* s.v., 667.3 ff. In the exordium of *Cael.* Cicero, in an attempt to win favor with the jurors, complains of the trial taking place *diebus festis ludisque publicis, omnibus forensibus negotiis intermissis* (§ 1; cf. Austin *ad loc.*).—Though *moveo* can be used with plain ablative in the sense of *amoveo*, this usage seems to be confined to a small number of fixed expressions; cf. *Cat.* 2.1: *loco ille* [sc. Catiline] *motus est* (sim. *N.D.* 2.92: *mota loco*) or the censors' action *tribu movere* (cf. *OLD* s.v., 7; *TLL* s.v., 1540.47 ff.); hence P's *amovento* is commonly substituted for *movento* of BAε (H and L have *inavento*). À propos the transmitted text. J.G.F. Powell poses the query (*per litt.*): "How would we know except by common sense that *feriis iurgia movento* did not mean 'let them start quarrels on feast days'?"— Watt, 1986, 266, wonders whether we do not need *cum* instead of *in* before *famulis* and compares Hor. *C.* 3.17.14 ff.: *cras genium mero / curabis et porco bimenstri / cum famulis operum solutis. In = inter* can be paralleled in Cicero, however; cf. *Ac.* 3 (p. 25, 1 ff. Plasberg): *digladiari autem semper, depugnare in facinorosis et audacibus quis non cum miserrimum tum etiam stultissimum dixerit?* Cf. *TLL* 776.25 ff. Its occurrence in our passage is also protected by the paraphrase at § 29: *feriarum festorumque dierum ratio in liberis requietem habet litium et iurgiorum, in servis operum et laborum;* cf. Wilhelms, 63, pointing out that *famulus,* though not archaic, is rarer than the equivalent *servus.*—*Patro* ("carry through, bring to completion": *OLD* s.v., 1) is a verb frequently used by the historians except Tacitus; cf. *TLL* s.v., 772.62; other *iuncturae* with *opera* are found ibid. 773.18–20. The parataxis is notable here, with *feriis* taken up in the following clause by *easque.* It lends a naive, archaic quality in sharp contrast to Cicero's usual periodic

---

50. This is confirmed by the paraphrase in § 29: . . . *in liberis requietem habet litium et iurgiorum* . . .

style; cf. von Albrecht, 1983, 42 = Engl. tr. 25; Gonda, esp. 185–94.—
Idque is Cratander's correction for *itaque* (*itque* already B¹). The predominant sentence connector in the Twelve Tables and in the old prayer quoted at Cat. *Agr.* 141, *-que* occurs frequently in these laws; see the next note.—The *anfractus* is "the circular motion or course of a heavenly body" (*OLD* s.v., 2a; cf. *TLL* s.v., 43.47 ff.). The *annui anfractus* of our passage are equivalent to *solis anfractus reditusque* of *Rep.* 6.16 (cf. Macr. *somn.* 1.6.83).—*Cado in* with ablative rather than the expected accusative may be characteristic of legal language; cf. Gai. *dig.* 44.7.1.5: *magnam . . . neglegentiam placuit in doli crimine cadere; TLL* s.v. *cado* 31.67 ff.

19.10 Certasque fruges certasque bacas sacerdotes publice libanto.] The products mentioned represent the *primitiae* of the harvest; such were the offerings of private cult, Cicero's apparent model for reforming state cult on the principle *opes amovento;* cf. Wissowa, 35 and 409 ff. For the *iunctura fruges (terrae)/bacae (arborum)* cf. *Div.* 1.116; *Sen.* 5.—This is the first sentence (according to the punctuation of modern editions) to be connected with *-que;* of the next eight sentences from this point on, six will have such connection, with only two instances of *autem* interrupting the series. This kind of λέξις εἰρομένη is characteristic of the XII Tables, with the laws presented as individual units in sequence; see also the preceding note.

20.1 Hoc certis sacrificiis ac diebus, itemque alios ad dies ubertatem lactis feturaeque servanto; . . .] *Hoc,* though deleted by Ernesti and Ziegler, is retained by Vahlen, Görler, and Powell; *faciunto* is to be supplied; for parallels cf. Vahlen *ad loc.*—*Itemque alios ad dies ubertatem lactis feturaeque servanto:* sc. by offerings of the *primitiae* of these types of products. The *do ut des* principle[51] exemplified here is found in all religious systems; cf. Burkert, 1996, 136 ff.; for its place in Roman cult cf. Wissowa, 23–27.—By zeugma *ubertas* ("copious flow, abundance [of milk; also, of other liquids]": *OLD* s.v., 2) is joined with *fetura* as well as *lac.*—On offerings of milk cf. Wissowa, 411 and n. 6.—*Fetura* developed beside and largely replaced the older *fetus* as a technical term in animal husbandry; the semantic development leads from the desired outcome to the concrete product (the latter the sense in our passage); cf. Zellmer, 200–201; *TLL* s.v., A and B; *OLD* s.v.

idque ne committi possit, ad eam rem {rationem} cursus annuos sacerdotes finiunto.] *Committo* here has the sense "falsely or defectively observe" (of religious ceremonies), as at § 22.1 or *Har.* 21: . . . *vosque pontifices, ad quos epulones Iovis optimi maximi, si quid est praetermissum aut commissum,*

---

51. An apt summary of the ancient attitude, albeit not a Roman technical expression; cf. literature at Burkert, 1996, 225 n. 44.

adferunt . . . , as Vahlen showed *ad loc.;* Kiessling's *omitti* is thus redundant; cf. also *TLL* s.v., 1911.21 ff. Problems could arise, for instance, if the calendar grew out of phase with the cycle of nature so that young animals were unavailable at the prescribed time. Proper counting of the months per year and intercalation have been a stumbling-block for many peoples; cf. Martin P. Nilsson, *Primitive Time-Reckoning* (Lund, 1920), ch. 9.—With the fussiness of legal or religious language *idque ne committi possit* is taken up by *ad eam rem;* cf. Cat. *Agr.* 141.3 (a prayer): *harumque rerum ergo.* For further examples with the relative cf. Landgraf *ad Sex. Rosc.* 8; Kühner-Stegmann, 2, 283–84; Hofmann-Szantyr, 563–64; Pascucci, 1968, 12 ff.— The transmitted *rationem* is difficult. *Finio* should mean "lay down as a limit, appoint, prescribe, specify (a number, date, etc.)": *OLD* s.v., 5a; *TLL* s.v., 783.68 ff. (our passage is cited at 784.8–9); but *rationem* is not an apt object beside *cursus annuos.* Turnebus changed to *ratione,* but, as J.G.F. Powell points out (*per litt.*), one would expect the ablative adjacent to the verb, and the formulation is not very legal (though on occasion Cicero introduces extralegal concepts, e.g., *Iusta imperia sunto:* 3.6.1); perhaps better to assume *rem rationem* to be a double reading of the archetype and bracket the latter (with Powell).

20.2 Quaeque cuique divo decorae grataeque sint hostiae, providento.] On *divus* for *deus* cf. *ad* § 19.1.—Selecting the proper victim for the occasion and the deity was of great importance, with the fundamental division being by sex: male victim for gods, female for goddesses (at § 29 Cicero makes it clear that he does not intend any innovations in this regard); cf. Wissowa, 413 ff.; Latte, 1960, 392, who contrasts the complex Roman rules, which require the advice of a priest (cf. just below: . . . *discunto ignari a publicis sacerdotibus;* sim. Liv. 1.20.5–6, partly quoted below on *quoque haec privatim ac publice*—), with the relatively simple Greek ones (cf. Burkert, 1985, 95); Beard, 1998, 1, 36–37, with literature at 36 n. 102.

20.3 Divisque ⟨alii⟩ aliis sacerdotes, omnibus pontifices, singulis flamines sunto; . . .] "The several gods shall have their several priests, the gods all together their pontiffs, and the individual gods their flamens" (Keyes).—*Alii* was inserted by Ascensius after *aliis* and transposed by Powell to follow *Divisque.*—The *sacerdotes* form the genus,[52] the *pontifices* and *flamines* the species. The pontifical college took over the sacred responsibilities of the Roman kings; it was composed of the *pontifices,* who numbered fifteen at the time of the composition of *Leg.,* the *rex sacrorum,* who assumed the

---

52. Beard in Beard-North, 46–47, claims that *sacerdos* achieved this generic status rather late and through Hellenistic influence; the paucity of earlier evidence makes this hard to establish, however; cf. A. Bendlin et al., review of Beard-North, *Numen* 40 (1993), 85.

king's priestly functions, the *flamines,* and the Vestal Virgins; cf. Mommsen, *Staatsr.* 2, 21 ff.; Wissowa, 502–4; Beard in Beard-North, 35–39. The flaminate was also very old (at *Rep.* 2.26 Cicero attributes it to Numa, as had Ennius [*Ann.* 116–18 Sk. = 122–24 V.]). *Flamen* refers not to a priesthood but to the function of performing sacrifice. The fifteen *flamines* belonged to the *collegium pontificum,* each assigned to the cult of a particular deity (cf. *singulis flamines sunto*). Of these, three were *maiores* (the Dialis, Quirinalis, and Martialis) and twelve *minores.* Though they were obliged to obey the pontifex maximus, the three *maiores* outranked him—a further sign of their antiquity—and were inferior only to the *rex sacrorum;* cf. Samter, *RE* 6.2 (1909), 2485.15 ff.; Ogilvie *ad* Liv. 1.20; Beard, 1998, 1, 19 and 28–29. Cf. in general Wissowa, 479 ff. (on the *flamines* 482–83 and 504 ff.).—Though in theory Cicero's goal is to indicate the kinds of religious institutions that would be in accord with nature (cf. §§ 13 and 18), the similarity to Roman institutions is striking and becomes still more so in the sequel (cf. Atticus' comment at § 23).

virginesque Vestales in urbe custodiunto ignem foci publici sempiternum.] The many archaic features shared between the Vestal Virgins and the flamen Dialis suggest that these were perhaps the oldest functions of the Roman state cult; cf. Koch, *RE* 8A2 (1958), 1737.40 ff. The activity of the Vestals presumes a sympathetic connection between the burning of the public hearth and the well-being of the state. The interpretation of the Vestals as having taken over the functions of the womenfolk of the royal family is dubious on various grounds; cf. Beard, 1980, and 1998, 1, 52; note, too, that the Vestals are attested at Alba for the period of the Roman kingship: Koch, *loc. cit.,* 1742.52 ff., esp. 1743.19 ff.—*In urbe* might seem superfluous, but the phrase emphasizes that this was the Vestals' sphere of power; cf. Plin. *Nat.* 28.13: *Vestales nostras hodie credimus* <u>*nondum egressa urbe*</u> *mancipia fugitiva retinere in loco precatione*... Their privilege of being buried within the city also points to a special connection; cf. *ad* § 58; Koch, *loc. cit.,* 1735.65 ff.—The sacred fire was kept inside the *aedes Vestae,* a circular building of modest proportions between the forum and the Velia; adjacent to the sacred fire was the *penus,* where the Vestalian *sacra* were kept, the rescue of which during several fires was an oft told tale (cf., e.g., *Scaur.* 48). There were in Cicero's time six Vestals, previously four; there is some evidence that they operated in teams of two each so that there would always be a pair of Vestals watching the sacred fire (Koch, *loc. cit.,* 1733.1 ff.) while others slept or attended to other matters, such as fetching water from the spring of the Camenae (cf. Wissowa, 508 and n. 8). Cf. in general Koch, *loc. cit.,* 1732.24 ff. and *Religio,* 1–16.—*Sempiternum* with its double trochee lends gravity and emphasis; cf. *Cat.* 4.18: . . . *supplex . . . patria communis . . . vobis illum ignem Vestae sempiternum . . . commendat.*

20.4 Quoque haec privatim et publice modo rituque fiant, discunto ignari a publicis sacerdotibus.] Probably *modo* refers to *privatim* and *ritu* to *publice,* moderation (*modus*) in private cult being stressed in the sequel,[53] whereas in public cult what matters is that ceremonies are performed according to proper ritual (*ritu*).[54]—For *fio* of the performance of a sacrifice cf. *OLD* s.v., 13b. Again *sacerdos* is the generic term; cf. the note before last.—*Publici sacerdotes, publici augures,* and the like are recurrent phrases in our work (§§ 20.6, 22.1, 37; 3.11.7 and 43) and serve to emphasize "the priests' religious authority with respect to the public interpretation of religion on behalf of the community as a whole" (Bendlin, 1998, 86, where see parallels cited at n. 98).—For the priests' oversight over private as well as public rites cf. Liv. 1.20.6: *cetera quoque omnia publica privataque sacra pontificis scitis subiecit* [sc. Numa], *ut esset quo consultum plebes veniret, ne quid divini iuris neglegendo patrios ritus peregrinosque adsciscendo turbaretur;* further testimonies at Wissowa, 400 n. 8, and 401 n. 1.

20.5 Eorum autem genera sunto duo: unum quod praesit caerimoniis et sacris, alterum quod interpretetur fatidicorum et vatium effata incognita, quom senatus populusque ⟨it⟩a sciverit.] The *sacerdotes* are distinguished this time not by name but by function: (1) the priests previously named, who are charged with expiations; (2) the board for consulting the Sibylline books, which, at the time of the composition of *Leg.,* consisted of fifteen men (hence called the *quindecimviri,* a name that continued in use even after the board was expanded by Caesar and Augustus); cf. Wissowa, 534 ff.; Gerhard Radke, *RE* 24 (1963), 1114.53 ff., esp 1142.17 ff. (s.v. *Quindecimviri*); Bernstein, 132 n. 70.—The numeral is variously transmitted: *generas otriunum* B[1], corrected by the same hand to *genera sunto triunum; genera sunt otriunum* LESR; *genera sunto tria unum* (*in rasura*) H; *genera sunto duo, unum* A; *duo genera sunto, unum* P; the latter two readings are conjectures but may be right nonetheless. Peter Cohee, "Is an Augur a Sacerdos? (Cic. *Leg.* 2.20–21)," *Philologus* 145 (2001), 79–99, esp. 96–99, argues convincingly that A's *duo* should be adopted here even though there is evidence for Cicero's classing the augur as a (kind of) *sacerdos* (*Fam.* 3.10.9; *ad Brut.* 1.5.3). In a Ciceronian *partitio* any other member beyond the first two is also introduced with an ordinal; cf. *Ver.* 4.129, *de Orat.* 2.235, *Part.* 70, *Fin.* 1.45 and 2.16, *Tusc.* 3.47, *Att.* 16.11.4, *Tim.* 35; I have

---

53. Cf. § 62a: *sed cedo ut ceteri sumptus sic etiam sepulcrorum modum;* § 66: *sepulcris . . . novis finivit modum;* cf. also *ad* 3.40.

54. Cf. § 22.1: *Sacrum commissum quod neque expiari poterit impium esto.*

not found any counter-example. In addition, the *autem* of the following lemma should mark a transition on the same level as the one in our lemma, i.e., should lead into the next subject. Possibly *duo* fell out by saltation error after *sunto,* and *tria* was introduced by a reader who wanted to restore the same threefold division as in *N.D.* 3.5 (sim. Var. *ARD* fr. 4); see further *ad* § 30.—First attested here, *fatidicus* is a chiefly poetic word (coined for the hexameter by Ennius?); its other preaugustan occurrence is as an adjective at *N.D.* 1.18, where Velleius sneers at *anum fatidicam Stoicorum Pronoeam.* Cf. *TLL* and *OLD* s.v. Cicero thought it unfamiliar enough to require the exegetical expansion *et vatium,* which also obviates the etymological jingle *fatidicorum effata.*—The substantive *effatum* (= "pronouncement by a soothsayer") also appears here for the first time; cf. *OLD* s.v.; *TLL* s.v. (*effor*) 199.54. *Ex* followed by *f* yields *ecf-,* later assimilated to *eff-;* P already corrected the transmitted *etfata.* The unusual word was corrupted in § 21.4 as well (*efflata,* corrected by Minutianus); cf. Wilhelms, 78. The word is a technical term from augural procedure; cf. Var. *L.* 6.53: *hinc effari templa dicuntur; ab auguribus effantur qui in his fines sunt.*—*Quom senatus populusque ⟨it⟩a sciverit: quom* is the correction of H. Usener, *Kleine Schriften,* 1 (Leipzig-Berlin, 1912), 353–54, for *quorum; ita sciverit* is Powell's emendation for *asciverit.* This is evidently Cicero's way of generalizing the status of the Sibylline books; it is also in line with the principle of "control from the top" (cf. *ad* §§ 19–22). The alternative is to assume ellipsis of *effata* in the relative clause; less satisfactory to take *quorum* as an instance of assimilation to the case of the antecedent, a Greek construction without parallel in good Latin, or to adopt Moser's *quae eorum;* cf. Vahlen *ad loc.;* Wilhelms, 125–26; Hofmann-Szantyr, 566–67.

20.6 Interpretes autem Iovis Optimi Maximi, publici augures, signis et auspiciis poste⟨r⟩a vidento, disciplinam tenento, . . .] The common view is that *augurium* was originally a prayer for an increase in power (< *augere*) and had no necessary connection with the observance of birds; cf. Latte, 1960, 66–67; Skutsch *ad* Enn. *Ann.* 1.73.[55] But this interpretation has both formal and semantic defects, as Günter Neumann, "Zur Etymologie von Lateinisch 'augur'," *Würzburger Jahrbb.* N.F. 2 (1976), 219–29, has shown; he suggests instead a connection with *avi* and the IE root **geus-,* which can mean "choose" or "perceive." Cicero assumes that the augurs' function is to read signs from the sky. They are accordingly the servants of the sky-god, not as sacrificial priests, but, like the *fetiales,* as bearers of special knowledge, and

---

55. Sim. also Di Moreno Morani, "*Augurium augur augustus:* una questione di metodo," *Glotta* 62 (1984), 65–71, who sees the augurs as the "confirmers" (< **augos* "strength").

have their *arx* on the Capitoline hill; cf. Wissowa, 199; Beard in Beard-North, 39–40, and 1998, 21–24. Cf. 3.32 and *Phil.* 13.12: *utrum . . . augurem Iuppiter Optimus Maximus, cuius interpretes internuntiique constituti sumus, . . . sanciet, Pompeiumne an Antonium?* For the augurs' rôle cf. also Arn. *nat.* 4.35: *sedent interpretes augures divinae mentis et voluntatis.*[56] On the basis of an old decree of the augural college, however, any bird could be seen to be the *interpres . . . Iovis* (cf. *Div.* 2.73; sim. 72).—Divine names appear very sparingly in the laws, Jupiter only here; otherwise there are the divinized heroes and virtues of § 19.7 and Ceres and the Idaean Mother as exceptions at §§ 21.12 and 22.4; cf. Mehl, 207. For Jupiter's association with bird-signs cf. fr. 17.1 Courtney; *Div.* 2.78. Mention of the name is perhaps part of the project developed at §§ 31–33 of lending prestige to the augurs (the use of the cult title argues against the suggestion of Mehl, 213, that Cicero means to suggest, *more Stoico,* the "all-pervasive reason of nature").— *Postera* is the correction of "Lambinus" for the transmitted *postea.* The other suggestions, *ostenta* (Orelli) and *portenta* (Feldhügel), do not fit the context. *Postera vidento,* which effects a clausula of the *debuerat omne* type, is most naturally taken to indicate that they foresee the future (see *OLD* s.v. *video* 13). Though Cicero denies this at *Div.* 2.70 (*non enim sumus ii nos augures qui avium reliquorumve signorum observatione futura dicamus*), the idea can be defended by § 33: *ex augurum praedictis multa incredibiliter vera cecidisse;* cf. Linderski, 1986, 2149 n. 7. Wilhelms, 70, objects: "*Postera . . .* is condemned . . . through the appearance nowhere else of the phrase *postera videre.* The normal Ciceronian expression is *in posterum providere*[57] or *in posterum prospicere*"; cf. also *futura prospicere* at *Fam.* 15.15.3. But in these laws, with their special diction (§ 18), one would not necessarily expect "the normal Ciceronian expression."—*Disciplinam tenere* is to uphold the augural law (Linderski, 1995, 488); this could be difficult in several senses, either (1) as a functioning element of the Roman state (cf. Cicero's complaint at *N.D.* 2.9: *sed neglegentia nobilitatis augurii disciplina omissa veritas auspiciorum spreta est, species tantum retenta*) or (2) as a body of knowledge which had to be memorized by successive generations of augurs; cf. Fest. p. 16M: *arcani sermonis significatio trahitur sive ab arce, quae tutissima pars est urbis; sive a genere sacrificii, quod in arce fit ab auguribus, adeo remotum a notitia vulgari ut ne litteris quidem mandaretur, sed per memoriam successorum celebretur . . . ; ad* § 33; Linderski, 1986, 2254–55; for the sense of *disciplina* under (2), ibid. 2240. Possibly, as Gelzer conjectured (*RE* 22.1

---

56. For *interpretes deorum* in a proof of the existence of the gods cf. *N.D.* 2.12.
57. Cf. 3.44.

[1953], 127.60–62), such concerns were already expressed in Cato's speech *de auguribus* (*orat. fr.* 220).

21.1 . . . {sacerdotesque} vineta virgetaque et salutem populi auguranto . . .] This sentence is carefully structured. It consists of four actions enjoined upon the augurs, each in asyndeton with a *-to* imperative at the end of the clause (*vidento . . . tenento . . . auguranto . . . praemonento*), then the change of subject clearly marked with pronoun and sentence-connector (*ollique*); for the pattern (without change of subject) cf. 3.6.5 and 7.3 (*minoris magistratus—agunto; censores populi—relinquonto*); see also *infra* on § 2.1.2 (*quique . . . quique . . .*). Given that, *sacerdotesque* is a problem. It cannot be a new subject, for the following list continues the functions of the augurs (cf. Linderski, 1986, 2151 and 2215 ff.). Surely *vineta virgetaque* form a compound unit, like *vineta virgultaque* at Cato *Agr.* 141.3 and annexed to it with *et* as the second object of *auguranto* is *salutem populi;* and one expects this injunction, like the others, to be in asyndeton (see above). There is, then, no place for *sacerdotesque,* and, given that no convincing emendation has been offered,[58] it should be deleted. It will be an insertion by a reader who misunderstood the structure and was unfamiliar with the matter.[59]—*Vineta virgetaque* form an alliterative pair characteristic of Latin liturgical and legal language: cf. 3.6.2; Norden, 1939, 16 ff.; Hofmann-Szantyr, 702–3. *Virgetum* ("a place full of brushwood or withies": *OLD*) is an apparent ἅπαξ (our passage is the sole citation in *OLD* or Forcellini); its formation, however, from *virga* = "twig" conforms to a well known type, with the *-etum* suffix added to a plant-name to denote the place where the plant grows; cf. *vepretum, dumetum, oletum, arboretum,* etc.; Leumann, 335; *OLD* s.v. *-etum;* Ivy J. Livingston, *A Linguistic Commentary on Livius Andronicus* (diss., Cornell, 1997), 28 ff. It is likely to have been borrowed from, or formed in imitation of, an archaic liturgy (see Cat. *loc. cit.*). The augural ceremony relating to *vineta virgetaque* is obscure; Wissowa, *RE* 2.2 (1896), 2328.38 ff., followed by Pierangelo Catalano, *Contributi allo studio del diritto augurale,* 1, Università di Torino, Memorie dell' istituto giuridico 2.107 (Turin, 1960), 353, connects it with the *augurium canarium,* involving the sacrifice of a dog, the purpose of which was to protect the grain against the summer heat; however, Rawson, 1991, 137–38, points out that the *augurium canarium,* defunct in Cicero's day, would have had to be revived. If the identification is correct, he may have known of the ritual from the augural books, on which cf. Wissowa, *loc cit.,* 2323.26 ff.; Linderski, 1995, 496 ff. Cf. also Latte, 1960,

---

58. E.g., Bake writes *sacerdotibus,* de Plinval inserts *docento* after *sacerdotesque.*
59. My thinking about this passage has benefited from comments by J.N. Adams.

66–67.—Cicero clearly distinguishes from the foregoing the *augurium salutis*. This rite, an auspication by the augurs followed by a prayer for the *salus publica*, required the Roman world to be at peace; though rarely performed, it did occur in 63; cf. *Div.* 1.105; Dio 37.24; Rawson, 1991, 137 and n. 36; cf. in general Wissowa, 133 and 525–26; Linderski, 1986, 2253 ff.; Rüpke, 1990, 141–43.

21.2 . . . quique agent rem duelli quique popularem, auspicium praemonento, ollique obtemperanto.] Supply *eos* as the antecedent of *qui* (cf. *TLL* s.v. *praemoneo* 721.55); for the structure cf. *ad* § 19.2. The augurs continue as the subject of *praemonento* (= "give previous warning of, announce in advance": *OLD* s.v. *praemoneo* 1a, where our passage is cited; sim. *TLL loc. cit.*); the shift to a different subject is signaled by *olli*. As concerns those presiding at assemblies, our law is duplicated at 3.11.7: *qui agent auspicia servanto, auguri publico parento;* see *ad loc.* The use of -*que* . . . -*que* instead of *et* . . . *et* to connect relative clauses is an archaism; our passage either eluded or was otherwise interpreted by Kühner-Stegmann, who claim that the construction is found only in prose of Augustan or later date (2, 35); cf. also Gonda, 185 and n. 4; *noctesque diesque* at *Fin.* 1.51 and elsewhere is generally viewed as a reminiscence of Enn. *Ann.* 336 Sk. = 334 V.; see Powell *ad Sen.* 1; von Albrecht, 1973, 1263.11 ff.—Our work contains the only Ciceronian occurrences of *duellum* (cf. § 45 and 3.9.2 and 4; restored later in our chapter), obsolete in his time; cf. *TLL* s.v., 2181.26 ff. and 69 ff.; Leumann, 131; Sihler § 185.1; Meiser § 77.2.—The phrase *res duelli* has caused difficulties. Its opposed term (*res*) *popularis* ("of or belonging to the people": *OLD* s.v. *popularis* 1b, citing our passage; cf. also 3.11.2 [of a senator]: *Causas populi teneto*) is of some help; it suggests that we have a variant of the polar expression *domi militiae*, on which see *ad* § 31. À propos our passage Linderski, 1986, 2199, remarks (see also his attached note 189): "If Cicero has in mind regular military operations, then he assigns to the augurs a function which they did not perform in his time. The difficulty would, however, disappear if we interpret the phrase *rem duelli* as referring to actions and ceremonies which concerned the *res militares* but were performed *domi*, like *dilectus* and departures for war." But this interpretation would destroy the antithesis of *res duelli* - (*res*) *popularis*. In the recent past promagistrates with *imperium* had brought personal haruspices with them to interpret omens (cf. Wissowa, 548; Rawson, 1991, 304 ff.), but at *Div.* 2.76 Cicero complains: *bellicam rem administrari maiores nostri nisi auspicato noluerunt; quam multi anni sunt, cum bella a proconsulibus et a propraetoribus administrantur, qui auspicia non habent;* cf. Mommsen, *Staatsr.* 1, 101; Beard in *CAH* 9, 744 (*aliter* Rüpke, 1990, 47). Cicero reforms this situation by providing the consuls, not promagistrates, with *militiae summum ius* (3.8.2; see *ad loc.*). Moreover, at § 31 the words *nihil domi, nihil militiae per magistratus gestum sine eorum* [sc. *augurum*] *auctoritate posse cuiquam probari?* certainly suggests auspication in the field.—There were auguries that were "asked for" before undertaking a mission (*impetrativa*) and others that offered themselves (*oblativa*) and were reported (*obnuntiari*) independent of the wishes of the presiding magistrate; cf. Don. *Ad.* 547 (on *obnuntio*); for the distinction Serv. *A.* 6.190; Mommsen, *Staatsr.* 1, 77 and n. 4. If, as has generally been assumed, (*augures*) *auspicium praemonento* refers to "impetrative auspices which the augurs would have consulted in place of the magistrates" (cf. Wissowa, 529–30 n. 7), Cicero is attributing to the augurs a power they never possessed in historical times (though he may have thought they once possessed it); cf. also Wissowa, *RE* 2.2 (1896), 2337.18 ff.; Linderski, 1986, 2199 (whence the quoted words, paraphrasing Wissowa's view), who goes on to argue that *praemonento* may refer rather to the augural right to announce oblative signs (2200–2201); but *praemoneo* is more naturally taken to refer to impetrative auspicies and is often so used elsewhere (cf. *OLD* and *TLL*, cited above); and Cicero's laws do not, of course, necessarily reflect historical realities; cf. Mehl, 209 and 217–18 n. 53.

21.3 Divorumque iras providento, sisque apparento.] *Divorum irae* were expressed by *prodigia*, unnatural occurrences thought to have been provoked by some flaw in ritual or other slight to a deity; they called for speedy atonement; the idea could be expressed as a violation of the *pax deorum*; cf. Wülker, 1; Rüpke, 1990, 125 ff.; Rosenberger, 21–22.—*Providento* has been variously interpreted as (1) "sie sollen . . . abwenden" (Ziegler) or (2) "the priests shall foresee" (Keyes); contrast *OLD* s.v. *provideo* 2a and 3a. The technical term for (1) was *procurare* in the sense "attend to in advance" (i.e., before the full force of divine anger is felt; see *infra* on § 21.10). But Cicero surely does not mean to supersede the senate's authority to decide the means of expiation; cf. Wülker, 29 ff. Cicero specifies the augur's rôle at *Div.* 1.29 (where *dirae* = *divorum irae* of our passage; cf. Serv. *Aen.* 4.453; Paul. *Fest.* p. 69M): *etenim dirae, sicut cetera auspicia, ut omina, ut signa, non causas adferunt cur quid eveniat, sed nuntiant eventura nisi providetis.* Cf. Linderski, 1986, 2201–2 and n. 198, and 1995, 477: "The augural sign was not a disclosure of an inflexible verdict of fate, nor was its announcement by the augur a prediction of the future. It was only a warning. However, it is possible to argue that the warning given by the *auspicium infaustum* or *malum* was also a premonition disregard of which would result in calamity. Thus a negative sign could be held to offer a glimpse of the future, to function as a qualified prediction . . ." In that limited sense the augur could be said to "foresee" (meaning 2) the divine wrath.—*Sisque* is the transmitted reading, (*i*)*isque* a correction (PB^XA^X). The *lectio difficilior,* from the archaic demonstrative pronoun *sum,* is to be retained as a feature of legal language; cf. Fest. p. 371M = *Font. iur.,* p. 27 (*ad* VII.7): *viam muniunto: ni sam delapidassint qua volet iumento agito; OLD* s.v. *sum²*; Skutsch *ad* Enn. *Ann.,* p. 64.—*Appareo* appears here in the sense "give heed to, obey, be amenable to"; cf. *OLD* s.v., 6.

21.4 Caelique fulgura regionibus ratis temperanto, urbemque et agros et templa liberata et effata habento.] *Fulgura* are "flashes of lightning" as opposed to the *fulmina* "bolts that strike": cf. *TLL* s.v. *fulgur* 1518.11 ff. The relation of the augurs to them differs from that of the haruspices described below: whereas the latter are to expiate them (*fulgura atque obstita pianto*), the augurs are to "maintain [them] in a state of balance or moderation, control, regulate [them]" by means of their system of defined regions (of the sky): *OLD* s.v. *tempero* 9; cf. Forcellini s.v., 5–6; Wilhelms, 64–65.—*Libero* refers to the removal from a place of all earlier sacral obligations and ties which might hinder its use for augury; cf. Wissowa, 528. Similarly, *effor* has the technical sense "to demarcate by word of mouth (areas within which signs might be observed, or their boundaries)": see above on § 20.5. For *urbemque—habento* cf. St. Weinstock, *RE* 5A1 (1934), 483.60 ff. (s.v. Templum); Latte, 1968, 103; Linderski, 1986, 2157 n. 31; Daniel J. Gargola, *Lands, Laws, and Gods: Magistrates and Ceremony in the Regulation of Public Lands in Republican Rome* (Chapel Hill, 1995), 41–49.—For the perfect periphrastic *templa liberata et effata habento* as characteristic of juridical Latin cf. de Meo, 99.

21.5 Quaeque augur iniusta nefasta vitiosa {dira} dixerit, irrita infectaque sunto.] For the asyndeton cf. *ad* § 19.1.—*Vitium* is the technical term in augury; *nefas,* on the other hand, is not strictly a term of sacral law; its early and specific usage is with reference to the calendar, a *dies nefastus* being one on which public business was prohibited; cf. Rüpke, 1995, 270; *OLD* s.v., 1; *iniustus* states the matter in general terms (cf. § 13: *est lex iustorum iniustorumque distinctio*); cf. Linderski, 1986, 2203–5 with literature at n. 208; Dorothy Paschall, "The Origin and Semantic Development of Latin *Vitium,*" *TAPhA* 67 (1936), 219–31, proceeds from the assumption that the augural sense ("hindrance") is original and that "defect" is a later development.—*Dira* is different from the other items in this list, as Linderski, 1986, 2211, points out: ". . . *dira dicere* refers above all to signs, whereas *iniusta* (*nefasta, vitiosa*) *dicere* seems to refer above all to questions of the ritual";

cf. ibid. 2234 ff. Insofar as they were not notorious, unnatural occurrences were reported by the augurs to the senate, either on request from that body or on their own initiative; the transmitted text telescopes both that situation and the *nuntiatio* of omens at assemblies (the singular of our passage according with the latter case; cf. Mommsen, *Staatsr.* 1, 115–16 and 116 n. 2; in general ibid. 3, 364 ff.), perhaps wrongly; Powell deletes *dira,* which may have resulted from a rewriting of *defixerit* as *dixerit,* the latter restored by Cratander (also possible is Turnebus' *deixerit,* with the older spelling; cf. *TLL* 967.15 ff. and 27 ff.), or have been added as a variant to *vitiosa;* cf. *Div.* 1.28: *itaque sinistra dum non exquirimus in dira et in vitiosa incurrimus.*

21.6 Quique non paruerit, capital esto.] Failure to obey the augurs was not a capital offense at Rome, but Cicero clearly thinks that it should be (*capitale esto* is P's reading, *caritalesto* that of the archetype [B¹HL]; see below); cf. *Div.* 2.71: *nec vero non omni supplicio digni P. Claudius L. Iunius consules* [sc. of 249], *qui contra auspicia navigarunt? parendum enim religioni fuit nec patrius mos tam contumaciter repudiandus. iure igitur alter populi iudicio damnatus est, alter mortem sibi ipse conscivit.* Claudius' trial for *perduellio* was suspended due to a storm, but he was heavily fined on another charge; for details cf. Linderski, 1986, 2176–77; Rosenstein, 90 and n. 122. Rawson, 1991, 140, sees our passage as implying that Caesar's acts of 59 deserved capital punishment. Whatever political ramifications he may have had in mind, Cicero reinforces the importance of obedience to the augurs—much neglected in recent years (cf. *ad* § 14a)—not only here but also at § 31, 3.11.7 and 43.—Here is another example of relative *qui* with suppressed oblique antecedent; cf. *ad* § 19.2.—*Capital* was substantivized as early as Plautus from the adjective *capitalis,* usually with substitution of the substantival ending *-al* for *-ale,* in the sense "a crime punishable by death"; cf. *OLD* s.v., 1.

21.7 Foederum {pacis belli} indutiarum ratorum fetiales iudices nun⟨tii⟩ sunto, duella disceptanto.] This sentence poses a number of problems. It is transmitted as follows: *foederum pacis belli indotiarum oratorum fetiales iudices non sunto, bella disceptatio.* The spelling *indotiae* is odd. Elsewhere we find only *indutiae* (cf. *TLL* s.v., 1277.77). Vine finds this spelling suspect in view of *ū/ō* alternations being virtually unheard of outside dialectal contexts (e.g., Praenestine *losna* for *lūna*). He notes that the best derivation appears to be from the IE root meaning "to extend" (**duh₂* > Lat. *dū-,* as in *dūdum,* **dūro-* "far", the denominative verb *dūrāre,* etc.). Possibly the spelling with *o,* if correct, might have been influenced by popular etymology (cf.

Don. Ter. *Eun.* 60, who suggests *in dies otium* as the source).[60] For *non sunto* Vahlen proposed *nontii sunto*,[61] though he thereby posits a unique form; *nontii* could, at a pinch, be supported with reference to *nontiata* at CIL I² 586.5 and *nondinae*. But given that it is in any case a conjecture, better simply to write *nuntii*. Vahlen sees a chiastic balance of *foederum pacis* and *belli indutiarum;* but, as Powell points out (*per litt.*), the chiasmus seems odd, especially when *bella/duella disceptanto* follows; hence his deletion of *pacis belli* so as to create a smooth run of plural genitives limiting *iudices nuntii.*[62] Finally, *oratorum,* whether taken (as by Vahlen *ad loc.*) as the participle of *oro* or (as by Rawson[63]) as a substantive, is unlikely. Our sentence should surely reflect the spheres of the fetials outlined in § 34 (*in quo* [sc. *bello*] *et suscipiendo et gerendo et deponendo*); the wrongs done to ambassadors (*oratorum*) are evidently not on the same level of importance as these. If that is so, then the otherwise missing element in our sentence is the valid decision to go to war, and this is expressed by Urlichs' *ratorum:* the fetials are the judges and heralds of "matters that have legal validity" (cf. OLD s.v. *ratus* 2a), i.e., the valid decision to go to war.—*Duella* is Powell's correction for the transmitted *bella* in accord with the archaizing diction elsewhere (cf. earlier in this chapter; § 45: *duelli instrumenta;* 3.9.2 and 4).—For *disceptanto* (Ascensius' necessary correction of *disceptatio*) in the sense "judge" cf. OLD s.v., 3; TLL s.v., 1295.16 ff.; on *Off.* 1.34–40.

21.8–9 Prodigia portenta ad Etruscos et haruspices, si senatus iussit, deferunto. Etruriaque principes disciplinam doceto.] In spite of some ancient attempts to draw distinctions, *prodigia* and *portenta* are really synonymous terms; cf. TLL s.v. *portentum* 15.62 ff. and 16.13 ff., esp. 20–23 and 28.

---

60. *Indutiarum* has been challenged, however, by Rawson, 1991, 138 n. 39, who notes that "we do not hear of fetials being concerned in truces," whereas the fetials were involved in cases of wrongs done to ambassadors; she therefore retains *oratorum* and supposes either that *indutiarum* is a corruption of *iniuriarum* or that the latter has dropped out following *indutiarum*. But it is not necessarily a question of what Roman practice actually was; the fetials were after all defunct in Cicero's day. I suspect that Cicero had in mind a case like that of Mancinus, in which, when a truce had been entered into improperly, the fetials handed over the offending commander to the enemy (cf. further *ad Off.* 3.109); in this sense they could be regarded as *indutiarum . . . iudices.* Furthermore the *uter in utrum?* test points to *indutiarum* rather than *iniuriarum* as the probable original.

61. For this description of the fetial cf. Liv. 1.32.6: *ego sum publicus nuntius populi Romani.* Görler, however, still prints †*non* in the text. *Consultores sunto* proposed by Latte, 1960, 419, for *non sunto* is contrary to the tenor of the passage; cf. Behrends, 1970, 21 n. 63; Watt, 1997, 242, proposes ⟨*populi*⟩ *nomine.*

62. Otherwise one must assume that the familiar contrast *pacis/belli* overrode Cicero's desire for archaism here (cf. *duelli* just above).

63. See n. 60 *supra.*

For the alliterative pair cf. *supra* on *vineta virgetaque*.—The haruspices were and remained Etruscan, the Romans never having learned this recondite discipline, which was, at least in some cases, passed down from father to son (*Fam.* 6.6.3); hence the *et* of *Etruscos et haruspices* will be epexegetic (Turnebus' deletion of *et* is unnecessary). It is not clear whether in Cicero's time, as in that of the Emperor Claudius, there was already a formal *ordo haruspicum*. In any case, some haruspices were available, under the supervision of the *xvviri sacris faciundis,* to be consulted by the senate on such matters as objects struck by lightning; Cicero's law keeps them, as in the past, under strict senatorial control (*si senatus iussit*). Cf. Rawson, 1991, 302–12 (including a nuanced picture of their possible political affiliations in the late Republic); John North in Beard-North, 49 ff.; Thulin, *RE* 7.2 (1912) 2441.6 ff.; Wissowa, 543 ff.; Latte, 1960, 158 and 396–97.—On the future perfect *iussit* (= *iusserit*) cf. *ad* § 19.2 (*faxit*).—There is a slight awkwardness in that the subject of the verb *deferunto* is clearly not the preceding subject, the *fetiales,* but, rather, "the people" or the like. But the harshness is mitigated since this has been the general practice throughout these laws (beginning with the very first: *Ad divos adeunto caste:* § 19.1; cf. *ad loc.*).—The latter provision is a generalized form of a senatorial decree; cf. *Div.* 1.92: *quocirca* [sc. because of their proficiency in interpreting omens; see the next note] *bene apud maiores nostros senatus tum cum florebat imperium decrevit ut de principum filiis X singulis Etruriae populis in disciplinam traderentur ne ars tanta propter tenuitatem hominum a religionis auctoritate abduceretur ad mercedem atque quaestum;* sim. V.Max. 1.1.1; another such effort to maintain the haruspices was undertaken on the initiative of the Emperor Claudius; cf. Tac. *Ann.* 11.15.—For vividness Cicero personifies: *Etruria . . . doceto.*

21.10 Quibus divis creverint procuranto, idemque fulgura atque obstita pianto.] For Romans this function of the haruspices was an inextricable part of the ancestral religion; cf. *Har.* 18: *. . . portentorum expiationes Etruscorum disciplina contineri* [sc. *maiores nostri*] *putaverunt.*—Apart from the legal phrase *hereditatem cernere, TLL* s.v. *cerno* cites the word in the sense "decerno" in Cicero only from our work, elsewhere in poetry or prose of Augustan or later date (864.66 ff.). Perhaps he thought of it as an archaism appropriate here.—*Procuro* is used in a variety of constructions, including the accusative or dative of the thing or person. It is also used with the dative of the deity in the *senatusconsultum* of 99 *apud* Gel. 4.6.2: *. . . censuerunt uti M. Antonius consul hostiis maioribus Iovi et Marti procuraret . . .* Cf. *OLD* s.v. The simplex *curo* is also used with dative in the sense "care about, heed": ibid. s.v., 8b; *TLL* s.v., 1502.83 ff. The impersonal plural continues as subject; as the cited *senatusconsultum* shows, it was ordinarily a consul who was mandated by the senate to carry out the *procuratio* (cf. also Rüpke, 1990, 126).—Even the ancients disputed the sense of *obstitum*: cf. Fest. p. 220M: *obstitum Cloatius* [*gram.* p. 472, fr. 13] *et Aelius Stilo* [*gram.* p. 64, fr. 24] *esse aiunt violatum attactumque de caelo. Cincius* [*gram.* p. 379, fr. 24] *... cum qui deo deaeque obstiterit, id est qui viderit quod videri nefas esset.* Clearly, Cincius' interpretation will not serve our passage; the close connection with *fulgura (atque)* recommends the alternative view of Cloatius and Aelius Stilo (on the latter see further *ad* § 59); cf. *TLL* s.v.: "genus ostenti, ut vid." For the various methods by which the haruspices expiated lightning strikes cf. Thulin, *loc. cit.* previous note, 2446.43 ff.—More common than *pio* is the compound with perfective prefix *expio,* but the two are used more or less interchangeably; cf. Fugier, 340 and 356–58.

21.11 Nocturna mulierum sacrificia ne sunto, praeter olla quae pro populo rite fient.] Though nocturnal sacrifices were sometimes associated with magic (cf. Paul. *Sent.* 5.23.15), this prohibition aims to curb licentiousness, as §§ 36–37 show. Versnel, 228–29, sets this law into the context of Roman restrictions on women.—Sacrifices conducted *pro populo* would include the annual festival of the Bona Dea, an ancient fertility goddess, held on 3 December; cf. *ad* § 36. Cicero does eliminate, however, another mystery cult, the Bacchanalia, banned by senatorial decree in 186; cf. *ad* § 37.

21.12 Neve quem ini⟨ti⟩anto nisi ut adsolet Cereri Graeco sacro.] Although this is generally phrased, Cicero has in mind the initiation of women in particular, as his commentary at § 37 shows; cf. Spaeth, 105.—The worship of Ceres *Graeco sacro* was annexed to her preexisting local cult, presumably in 217, and celebrated in the same temple according to a different ritual, conducted in Greek, in which, for instance, unlike the original one, the drinking of wine was banned; the officiating priestess was a Roman citizen from an allied community of Magna Graecia; cf. *Balb.* 55; Paul. *Fest.* p. 97M; Wissowa, 60 and 300–301; Le Bonniec, 423–38; Burkert, 1987, 93–95; John Scheid, "*Graeco ritu:* A Typically Roman Way of Honoring the Gods," *HSPh* 97 (1995), 23–24.[64]—The correction *initianto* for *in(h)ianto* already appears in the *recentiores.*

22 These provisions are, in their different ways, designed either to maintain, or restore after a breach, the *pax deorum* or to hold expenditures within bounds (restrictions on the collection of alms or dedications of precious materials).

---

64. The contrast at Var. *ARD* fr. 49 (*nostro ritu sunt facienda quam †his civilibus Graeco castu*) remains obscure (for one interpretation cf. Wissowa, 59 n. 1).

22.1 Sacrum commissum quod neque expiari poterit, impium est⟨o⟩; quod expiari poterit, publici sacerdotes expianto.] *Sacrum* surely has the same sense as previously in these laws, namely "religious observance, ceremony, or rite": cf. *OLD* s.v., 3; *sacra sollemnia obeunto* (§ 19.8); *unum quod praesit caerimoniis et sacris* (§ 20.5); *nisi ut adsolet Cereri Graeco sacro* (§ 21.12), not the sense "Religionsfrevel" posited by Ziegler *ad loc.* (but contradicted already by Görler *ad loc.*); sim. Fugier, 345, comparing Cat. *Agr.* 139, where, however, *sacrum* can be taken from *sacer* in the sense "consecrated to a deity, sacred". *OLD* s.v., 1. For *committo* in the sense "falsely or defectively observe" cf. *ad* § 20.1.—For archaic *neque/nec* = *non*, common in juridical and religious language, cf. Hofmann-Szantyr, 448–49; Pascucci, 1968, 22 ff.; de Meo, 91.—Originally, there was no means of expiating a *sacrum commissum*, cf. W. Ehlers, *RE* 20.1 (1941), 1183.9 ff. (s.v. Piaculum). But at some point a distinction was introduced based on intent; cf. Var. *L.* 6.30 (= *iur.* p. 19, fr. 10): *praetor qui tum fatus est, si imprudens fecit, piaculari hostia facta piatur; si prudens dixit, Q. Mucius aiebat eum expiari ut impium non posse;* sim. Macr. *sat.* 1.16.10; cf. the catalogue of expiable and inexpiable offenses at Scheid, 121 ff. The transmitted *impie commissum* (prior to *esto*) has been suspected by Bendlin; the passage just quoted suggests that we need simply *impium esto; commissum* was presumably repeated by someone who misunderstood the technical term and changed *impium* to *impie* accordingly.—*Est⟨o⟩* is Lambinus' correction.—For the rôle of the priests, cf. Ehlers, *loc. cit.*, 1184.28 ff.; for the *iunctura publici sacerdotes* cf. *ad* § 20.4.

22.2 Loedis publicis, quae sive curriculo et certatione corporum, sive cantu et fidibus et tibiis fiat, popularem laetitiam moderanto, eamque cum divum honore iungunto.] Like other legislators, Cicero caters for the people's need for relaxation; on the construction of leisure in Greek political philosophy cf. Solmsen, 2, 1 ff.; cf. also Sen. *Tr. an.* 17.7: *legum conditores festos instituerunt dies, ut ad hilaritatem homines publice cogerentur, tamquam necessarium laboribus interponentes temperamentum . . .* —For the epigraphically attested spelling *loid-/loed-* cf. *TLL* s.v. *ludus* 1783.16 ff.; but cf. *ludorum* (3.7.1); Wilhelms, 81; see further *ad* 3.10.7.—*Loedis publicis* is taken out of the relative clause for emphasis; cf. 3.9.6: *Plebes quos pro se contra vim auxilii ergo decem creassit . . .* ; *ad Off.* 1.129; Watkins, 541 and n. 2. It thus serves to announce the general activity to be regulated by the following law. The games are properly called "public" since they are financed from the *aerarium* and conducted by magistrates; cf. Bernstein, 14.—The text *quae—laetitiam* has been restored by Madvig, Bake, and Powell. Transmitted is *quod sine curriculo et sine certatione corporum fiat,*

314 A Commentary on Cicero, *De Legibus*

popularem laetitiam in cantu et fidibus et tibiis. The starting point for understanding this sentence must be Cicero's own interpretation at § 38 (for the text see *ad loc.*): *iam ludi publici quoniam sunt cavea circoque divisi, sint corporum certationes cursu et pugillatu et luctatione curriculisque equorum usque ad certam victoriam circo constitutis, cavea cantu vigeat ⟨ac⟩ fidibus et tibiis* . . . Thus there is a bipartite division of *ludi,* one involving musical entertainment, the other athletic competition (*cavea circoque divisi*); Bake restored this organization (*sive - sive*). The word transmitted after *loedis publicis* is *quod*; this clause has been taken as a relative clause with limiting force (type *quod sciam*); so Wilhelms, 121–22 (sim. Feldhügel and Görler *ad loc.*); but this seems not to fit the usual pattern of such clauses as a brief parenthetical qualification (cf. Kühner-Stegmann, 2, 307–8). Better to read *quae* with Powell so that we have relative clause anticipating its antecedent (*popularem laetitiam*), as is characteristic of archaic Latinity (cf. Hofmann-Szantyr, 563–64; *ad* § 19.2); the transmitted *quod* will be a case of perseveration from the preceding sentence; the subjunctive should be taken as conditional (cf. Kühner-Stegmann, 2, 309). Translate: "Let them control the popular merriment, whether it take the form of the race-course and physical competition, or of singing and harps and flutes, by means of public games."—Did Cicero think of these musical performances as competitive, like the Pythian games (*certatio corporum* used of the other class of games leaves open the possibility of another type of *certatio* as a counterpart)? In any case, we know of separate musical contests at Rome only beginning with the reign of Domitian (cf. Walther Vetter, *RE* 6A1 [1936], 811.51 ff. [s.v. Tibia]; Wille, 353), though they formed part of the Neronia (Suet. *Ner.* 12.3). Music did, however, after the Greek model, accompany various Roman cult activities; cf. Ihm, *RE* 6.2 (1909), 2286.18 ff. (s.v. Fidicines); Wille, 26 ff.; the *tibicines,* for instance, were organized into a *collegium* to be available for *sacra publica;* cf. Wissowa, 254. The emphasis rests upon *moderanto;* see further *ad* § 38.—On *divus* for *deus* cf. *ad* § 19.1.

22.3 Ex patriis ritibus optuma colunto.] Marcus has already laid down *Privatim colunto quos rite a patribus ⟨cultos acceperint⟩* (§ 19.4). As the commentary at § 40 shows, our law is meant to provide guidance in the event of conflicting traditions; cf. *ad* §§ 19–22.

22.4 Praeter Idaeae Matris famulos, eosque iustis diebus, ne quis stipem cogito.] Though the procession of priests begging and collecting alms was an ancient tradition (Burkert, 1985, 97 and 388 n. 21), Plato disapproved of the ἀγύρται (*Rp.* 364b–c; *Lg.* 909b); similarly at *Div.* 1.132 Quintus declines to recognize those who prophesy for money; disapproval is also implied by the decree of the Roman senate which D.H. 2.19.5 alleges prevented Romans from participating in the mother goddess's procession and collection of alms. The custom of collecting alms in small coin (*stips*) was widespread in Italy and by no means confined to the cult of the Magna Mater, though Ovid traces the origin of the alms-giving to the collection made by a Metellus for the rebuilding of her temple in 111 (*Fast.* 4.349 ff.; it is not clear which Metellus is meant; cf. Fantham *ad Fast.* 4.348). Cicero is evidently concerned to curb superstition that could be financially ruinous to families. Hence this law designed to keep the collection of *stips* within the fixed bounds of a single cult and the officially licit days (as well as to restrain superstition: cf. *ad* § 40). Restriction on collection of *stips* from the poor was, in fact, legally enacted at Rome some time prior to Septimius Severus: cf. Latte, 1960, 252–53 and n. 5. Scullard, 99, finds Cicero's exception for the Magna Mater "curious"; perhaps the explanation lies in the embrace of the cult by the aristocrats, who formed special *sodalitates* in her honor; even Cato the Censor was a member (*Sen.* 45; cf. Wissowa, 64 and n. 1), and Cicero treats the cult with great respect at *Har.* 22–24; however, Bernstein, 191 n. 414, sees the permission to collect *stips* as a sign that the cult was partitioned into an official Roman one and a Phrygian one without state support; cf. Burkert, 1985, 101–2. Cf. in general ibid., 177–79; Wissowa, 317 ff., esp. 320; Scullard, 97–100; Hug, *RE* 3A2 (1929), 2538.55 ff. (s.v. Stips). The problem with Cicero's law is that many cults could not survive without *stips;* cf. Bendlin, 1998, 90–92.— *Eosque iustis diebus:* for a specification joined with *et is* or the like cf. parallels at Kühner-Stegmann, 1, 619.

22.5 Sacrum sacrove commendatum qui clepsit rapsitve, parricida esto.] "Whoever steals or carries off what is sacred or a thing entrusted to what is sacred shall be a parricide" (Keyes' translation, slightly modified). On the consecration of property cf. in general Kaser, 1949, 47. Temples might receive, not only donations, but also deposits of private or public property. The two examples Cicero cites at § 41 are Greek (cf. in general Walter Burkert, "The Meaning and Function of the Temple in Classical Greece," in *Temple in Society,* ed. Michael V. Fox [Winona Lake, Ind., 1988], 27–47), and Greek temple treasures are generally well documented; cf., e.g., Diane Harris, *The Treasures of the Parthenon and Erechtheion* (Oxford, 1995). Italian temples had the same function; thus the Roman state treasury (*aerarium*) was on deposit at the temple of Saturn on the Capitoline; see further Stambaugh, 585–86. The *sacro commendata* were not *sacra* but profane;[65] Cicero nevertheless treats them the same way as *sacra* since they

---

65. Cf. Bendlin, 1998, 261 (with attached n. 4): "Following pontifical decision, a dedication *in loco publico* which had not been authorized by the city-state was not *sacrum.*"

are under the protection of a deity. Schmidt, 1959, 77, thinks that Cicero may have introduced the distinction with some actual event in mind; the "borrowing" of temple property in time of war would fall under this ban (later documented during the civil war: Caes. *BC* 2.21.3 and 3.105.1; cf. also Luc. 3.112 ff., where opprobrium attaches to Caesar's raid on the temple of Saturn). It is not clear that this provision reflects early Roman legal thinking; Cicero may have been influenced by Plato's punishment of the temple-robber with death (*Lg.* 854e) and by the well known topic for debate in rhetorical schools whether theft of private property stored in a temple is *sacrilegium* or *furtum;* cf. Cic. *Inv.* 1.11; T. Mommsen, *Römische Forschungen,* 2 (Berlin, 1879), 447 n. 69, with further references.—For *parricida esto* cf. the law of Numa cited at Paul. *Fest.* p. 221M: *si qui hominem liberum dolo sciens morti duit, paricidas esto* (Yan Thomas, "Parricidium," *MEFR* 93 [1981], 643–715, esp. 659–79, wants to throw out this testimony, an obstacle to assuming that "parricide" is the original sense of *parricida*); sim. the report at Plut. *Rom.* 22.4 that Romulus πᾶσαν ἀνδροφονίαν πατροκτονίαν προσειπεῖν. *Parricida* is used of various noxious individuals, often by way of abuse; cf. *TLL* s.v. 440.25 ff. One might have expected the commoner formula *sacer esto* (perhaps avoided for *variatio* after *sacrum sacrove commendatum*), on which cf. Kaser, 1949, 48 ff., and Moreno Morani, "Lat. 'sacer' e il rapporto uomo-dio nel lessico religioso latino," *Aevum* 55 (1981), 40–41. A. Magdelain, "*Paricidas*" in *Du châtiment dans la cité. Supplices corporels et peine de mort dans le monde antique,* Collection de l'École Française de Rome 79 (Rome, 1984), 569, thinks our text was influenced by Greek commonplaces assimilating sacrilege to murder, but Cicero could have found precedent for his classification as *parricidium* of this type of crime in the case cited at V.Max. 1.1.13: *Tarquinius . . . rex M. Atilium duumvirum, quod librum secreta rituum civilium sacrorum continentem, custodiae suae commissum corruptus Petronio Sabino describendum dedisset, culleo insitum in mare abici iussit, idque supplicii genus multo post parricidis lege inrogatum est, iustissime quidem, quia pari vindicta parentum ac deorum violatio expianda est.* If Cicero reflects old usage here, one wonders whether *parricida esto* might not be comparable to the early Greek ἄτιμος ἔστω, which in turn is similar to the concept of "outlawry" in Anglosaxon and Icelandic law; cf. Mogens Herman Hansen, *Apagoge, Endeixis and Ephegesis against Kakourgoi, Atimoi and Pheugontes* (Odense, 1976), 75 ff.; Michael Gagarin, *Drakon and Early Athenian Homicide Law* (New Haven and London, 1981), 119. If that is so, then the later concept of *parricidium* may perhaps have been influenced by folk etymology (see Pompeius Maurus, *GL* 5, 306.19: *parricida est qui parentem occidit*).[66] The alternative is to suppose, with J.D. Cloud, "*Parricidium:* from the *lex Numae* to the *lex Pompeia de parricidiis,*" *ZSS* 88 (1971), 12, that Numa's law adds "to the class of kin-murderers a further category of criminal, namely those who kill a citizen with malice afore-thought"; sim. Kunkel, 139 n. 476: "der Dieb oder Räuber von *res sacrae* soll wie ein Mörder, oder gar wie ein Vatermörder bestraft werden." In any case, the archaic punishment of the *parricida* by enclosure in a sack and immersion in water (cf. V.Max. *loc. cit.*) was no longer used, even for murderers of relatives, in late Republican Rome (cf. Mommsen, *Strafr.,* 922–23; Cloud, *loc. cit.,* 1–66), though as governor of Asia Q. Cicero inflicted it on provincials (*Q.fr.* 1.2.5); on the penalty and its later revival cf. F. Egmond, "The Cock, the Dog, the Serpent, and the Monkey. Reception and Transmission of a Roman Punishment . . . ," *IJCT* 2 (1995), 159–92. In later practice *peculatus* involving temple property was subsumed under *sacrilegium* so that capital punishment could be inflicted on temple person-nel in the event of malfeasance; cf. Plin. *Nat.* 34.38; Bendlin, 1998, 264.

22.6 Periurii poena divina exitium, humana dedecus ⟨esto⟩.] *Esto* is Lambi-nus' supplement.—This is the oft repeated Roman view; cf. Tac. *Ann.* 1.73.4: *ius iurandum perinde aestimandum quam si Iovem fefellisset: deorum iniurias dis curae;* Cod. Iust. 4.1.2: *iurisiurandi contempta religio satis deum ultorem habet;* Marx ad Pl. *Rud.* 13–20 (pp. 56–57); Latte, 1968, 376; Cornell, 29–30. False testimony in court would result, however, in the perjuror's being hurled from the Tarpeian rock (*Lex XII* 8.12); Cicero surely did not mean to alter that; cf. Rawson, 1991, 139. Perjury for purposes of self-enrichment was also punishable; cf. Mommsen, *Strafr.,* 681. *Humana* [sc. *poena] dedecus:* perhaps, as Mommsen, *Staatsr.,* 2, 380 n. 2, suggests, Cicero has in mind some equivalent of the censorial *nota* (and indeed the censorship will be strengthened: cf. 3.7.3 and 11.13–14).

22.7 Incestum pontifices supremo supplicio sanciunto.] *Incestum* was origi-nally any violation of ritual purity (*fas;* cf. Cicero's first law [§ 19.1]: *Ad divos adeunto caste*). The term later became specialized in the sexual sphere and could cover either unchastity by a Vestal Virgin or intercourse between blood relatives (incest); cf. Latte, 1960, 49. Alleged *incestum* by a Vestal was tried by the pontifical college, presided over by the pontifex maximus (an exception was the scandal of 114–13, when two of three Vestals accused of *incestum* were acquitted by the pontifical court and a bill of the tribune Sex.

---

66. Mommsen, *Strafr.,* 528 n. 2, speculates that *parricida esto* implies that the matter is to be tried by the quaestor in charge of murder cases and that in legal language his mandate was referred to as *parricidium;* but Cicero's archaizing laws need not reflect so closely the legal procedure and terminology of his own time.

Peducaeus then set up a court to retry the case). If found guilty, she was buried alive; her seducer was beaten to death under the *furca*, a punishment otherwise reserved for slaves (cf. Mommsen, *Strafr.*, 919 n. 1). Incest, i.e., marriage to a person within the sixth grade of blood relationship, was probably originally also viewed as an offense against the gods. In historical times, however, this crime was not tried before the pontiffs, though they might perform *piacula;* cf. Tac. *Ann.* 12.8.1, where the reference to a law of King Tullus suggests the revival of an old ritual: *die nuptiarum Silanus mortem sibi conscivit . . . Calvina soror eius Italia pulsa est. addidit Claudius sacra ex legibus Tulli regis piaculaque apud lucum Dianae per pontifices danda, inridentibus cunctis, quod poenae procurationesque incesti id temporis* [i.e., on the day of Claudius' marriage to his niece Agrippina] *exquirerentur.* Cicero offers no comment on this law at § 41; hence scholars have tried to guess whether he meant to cover both forms of *incestum* or only one and, if so, which: Carl Koch, *RE* 8A2 (1958), 1749. 37 ff. argues that both types are implicated; Cornell, 33, suspects that Cicero had in mind only *incestum* by a Vestal Virgin; Rawson, 1991, 139–40 (against Koch, *loc. cit.*, 1749.12 ff.), suggests that the crime of Clodius at the rites of the Bona Dea, classified as *incestum* by the senate, is implicated. Cf. in general Mommsen, *Strafr.* 682–84, esp. 682–83 n. 1; Klingmüller, *RE* 9.2 (1916), 1246.47 ff., esp. 1247.23 ff. (s.v. Incestus); Treggiari, 37–39 and 281 and n. 105, and O.F. Robinson, 54–57 (on *incestum* in marriage, often dealt with leniently if ignorance could be shown); Cornell, 27–37 (on the court established by Sex. Peducaeus, 36–37).—*Supremum supplicium* seems to be a *variatio* for *summum supplicium* or *ultimum supplicium*,[67] usually an aggravated form of the death penalty; see above as well as Mommsen, *Strafr.* 908 n. 1; Garnsey, 122–25.

22.8 Impius ne audeto placare donis iram deorum.] In contrast to the naive notion that the gods can be appeased by incense, prayers, libations and the smell of fat (*Il.* 9.499–501), the *impius* is here excluded from cult, as in the mystery religions (cf., e.g., Suet. *Ner.* 34.4: *peregrinatione quidem Graeciae et Eleusinis sacris, quorum initiatione impii et scelerati voce praeconis summoventur, interesse non ausus est*); sim. Plato, cited *ad* § 15b; cf. also

67. One of these three expressions (perhaps *ultimum supplicium*) was presumably used by D. Junius Silanus, the consul-designate, when, at the senate meeting of 5 December 63, he was the first to be asked his view of the appropriate punishment for the captured Catilinarian conspirators: Plut. *Cic.* 20.4: εἶπε τὴν ἐσχάτην δίκην δοῦναι προσήκειν (sim. *Cat. min.* 22.4; App. *BC* 2.19), commonly understood to mean the death penalty (Cic. *Cat.* 4.7 and 11; Sal. *Cat.* 51.16 ff.), though, under the influence of Caesar's speech, he claimed he had merely meant imprisonment (Plut. *Cic.* 21.3).

Dom. 107: *nec est ulla erga deos pietas nisi honesta de numine eorum ac mente opinio, cum expeti nihil ab his quod sit iniustum aut inhonestum arbitrare.* The *piaculum* restoring the *pax deorum* must be offered by priests; cf. Ehlers, *RE* 20.1 (1941), 1181.26 ff.; for the *ira deorum* see further *ad §* 21.3.—On the basis of our passage Mommsen, *Staatsr.*, 2, 52–53 n. 4, supposed that the priests intervened to exclude worshippers. But our text includes no enforcement mechanism; it may be a case similar to perjury; cf. the next to last note and *ad §* 41; Schmidt, 1959, 77 n. 2; Wissowa, 400 and n. 7; sim. lack of a penalty at 3.11.1–2 (senatorial absence).

22.9 Caute vota reddunto.] The Roman *votum*, a promise to a god often expressed in legalistic language to give it solemn force, was taken very seriously, being regularly fulfilled in times good and bad, if not by the person who made the vow, then by the legal successor; cf. *dig.* 50.12.2 pr. (Ulpian): *si quis rem aliquam voverit, voto obligatur;* Latte, 1960, 46–47; Werner Eisenhut, *RE* Suppl. 14 (1974), 964.29 ff. I take *caute* in the sense ἀκριβῶς (cf. *TLL* s.v. *caveo* 644.20) or *diligenter* (cf. the paraphrase at § 41), i.e., so as not to provoke divine wrath through some flaw. Du Mesnil *ad loc.* interprets differently: "d.h. ohne Schmälerung anderer Rechte"; he goes on to relate this to Clodius' dedication of a temple of Libertas on the site of Cicero's house, alluded to in § 42. But Clodius is mentioned there in connection with the following law, *Poena—esto; votum reddere* is to "discharge a vow" (*OLD* s.v. *reddo* 9c); but it is not clear that Clodius made any vow in connection with his temple.

22.10 Poena violati iuris ⟨divini divina⟩ esto.] The commentary on this passage (§§ 41–43) indicates that Cicero is really discussing divine punishments; cf. esp. § 43: *non . . . recte existimamus quae poena divina sit;* hence Powell's supplement *divini divina.* If this is right, we have a forerunner of the Tacitean Tiberius' principle (see above on *Periurii poena divina*—).— Powell explains the relation of this text to other laws about *sacra* as follows (*per litt.*): "I suppose that *sacrum commissum* and (later in § 22.5) *Sacrum . . . qui clepsit rapsitve* are both fairly specific offences, the one relating to interference with a religious ritual, the other to theft of sacred property. Perhaps Cicero felt that he needed to put in a more general provision at the end to cover cases not coming under either of these: in that case, it would not be necessary to suppose a sharp distinction between *violata religio/ violatum sacrum* and *sacrum commissum;* it would merely be that the latter was a subset of the former."—This point is illustrated (§§ 41–44) with reference to P. Clodius' construction of a temple of Libertas (Licentia, as Cicero calls it) on Cicero's Palatine property, a matter discussed in similar terms in the *post reditum* speeches (see parallels cited *ad loc.*); our lemma can thus be seen as "put[ting] into legal language his rhetorical condemnation of his enemies" (Mehl, 203).

22.11–12 {Quocirca} Ne quis agrum consecrato. Auri argenti eboris sacrandi modus esto.] The connective, deleted by Puteanus, is not wanted here, these laws being composed in an apodictic, not an argumentative style; it may, as Madvig suggested, have been inserted from § 45 (*quocirca ne quis iterum idem consecrato*).—These laws derive, as § 45 states, from Pl. *Lg.* 955e, the assumption being that *all* land is sacred to the gods. The sumptuary provision is in accord with the general principle *opes amovento* (§ 19.1; see *ad loc.*).

22.13 Sacra privata perpetua manento.] The Romans drew a sharp distinction between *sacra publica* and *sacra privata,* the latter including rites of families, clans, and corporate bodies; cf. Wissowa, 398 and n. 6. Providing for the continuity of *sacra privata* had become tricky in Cicero's day; cf. *ad* §§ 48–49. In *Dom.* Cicero casts the confusion of *sacra* in Clodius' teeth in connection with his adoption: he neither became a Fonteius nor assumed new familial *sacra* in exchange for the Claudian *sacra* he had relinquished (cf. *Dom.* 34: *quid? sacra Claudiae gentis cur intereunt, quod in te est?* and 35, esp. the phrase *perturbatis sacris*). But given the nature of Cicero's commentary at §§ 46–53, it is hard to credit that our law is "primarily directed against Clodius' adoption," as is claimed by Mehl, 191–92, though this may have been one motive.

22.14 Deorum Manium iura sancta sunto.] The *deorum Manium iura* comprise the survivors' duties to the departed, discussed at §§ 55–57; cf. Wissowa, 238–40; Cumont, ch. 1; Hopkins, 226–35.—For *sancta* cf. *ad* § 10.

22.15–16 Suos leto datos divos habento. Sumptum in ollos luctumque minuunto.] The first word is transmitted as *nos,* but this seems too personal for the tenor of these laws; one expects generalized provisions (cf. *ad* § 20.5; 3.9.4: *populi sui gloriam augento*). Urlichs' ⟨bo⟩nos is also doubtful insofar as it establishes a moral category: not just the good, but all the dead were divinized; cf. § 55 (. . . *nisi maiores eos qui ex hac vita migrassent in deorum numero esse voluissent*); W.F. Otto, 68–69. Perhaps the best solution is Davies' *suos,*[68] the cult of the dead being preeminently a family cult (ibid.; cf. § 55); for the corruption cf. *Rep.* 3.15.[69] For the thought cf. *Sen.* 81, translated, with altered emphasis, from X. *Cyrop.* 8.7.22.—*Leto datum* =

---

68. The more archaic equivalent *sos* has also been proposed (Goerenz and an anonymous scholar cited by Creuzer), but this form may be too archaic for these moderately archaizing laws (cf. § 18). Huschke's *sepultos* is sometimes adopted (e.g., by de Visscher, 170 n. 26).

69. I owe this parallel to J.G.F. Powell.

"deceased" is a solemn formula from funeral rites; cf. Var. *L.* 7.42: . . . *in funeribus indictivis, quo dicitur 'ollus leto datus est'* . . . and other passages cited at *TLL* s.v. *letum* 1189.40 ff.—Legislation limiting funeral expenses is first attested for Solon (F 72 R. = 470 M.; sim. Dem. Phal. fr. 135 W. = 53 S.O.D. = §§ 63–66 [see below]) and was taken up in the Twelve Tables (*Lex XII* 10.2–3 and 5–6). The periodic renewals of such legislation suggest their ineffectiveness; cf. Kübler, *RE* 4A1 (1931), 901.45 ff. (s.v. Sumptus); *ad* §§ 59–60, 62b–66, 64.—For the form *olle* cf. *ad* § 19.1.

23–45 This portion of the essay consists of Atticus' request for Marcus to state the case for his laws and the latter's compliance. His presentation follows the order of the laws he has just put forward (cf. *ad* §§ 19–23):

 I. Atticus' request that Marcus plead the case for his laws (§ 23)
 II. Marcus' advocacy of his laws (§ 24b)
   A. Right relations with the gods
     1. In worship *castitas* to be used, riches to be eschewed (§ 25a)
     2. New or alien gods (§ 25b)
     3. Sacred places in the city and country (§ 26b)
     4. Preservation of ancestral rites (§ 27)
     5. Additions to the pantheon, licit and illicit
     6. Holidays (§ 29a)
   B. Religious functionaries
     1. Vestal Virgins (§ 29b)
     2. Priests (§ 30)
       a. Those who preside over public ceremonies
       b. The *quindecimviri*
     3. Augurs (§ 31)
     4. Fetials (§ 34)
     5. Haruspices
   C. Miscellaneous provisions (§ 35)
     1. Banning of nocturnal mysteries
     2. Expiation and its limits (§ 37b)
     3. Appropriate music for the *ludi publici* (§ 38)
     4. Observance of ancestral laws (§ 40a)
     5. Alms forbidden except for the Magna Mater
     6. Sacrilege (§ 40b)
     7. Impious excluded from cult (§ 41)
     8. Penalty for violated religious rites, including digression on Clodius
     9. Arable land not to be consecrated (§ 45)

This passage is an early example of a commentary. There was already a tradition at Rome of writing commentaries on the Twelve Tables, several of which Cicero cites at § 59 (see *ad loc.*), so legal text plus commentary was a form familiar to Romans of his day. The commentator faces the technical problem of establishing a link with the base text. This Cicero achieves not by use of lemmata but of key words or phrases, usually syntactically integrated into the commentary (cf. § 19.1: *pietatem adhibento, opes amovento* with the corresponding commentary at § 25: *quod tamen pietatem adhiberi, opes amoveri iubet*; § 19.2: *deus ipse vindex erit*, with § 25: *quod autem non iudex sed deus ipse vindex constituitur . . .*), but sometimes not (*sic enim a me recitata lex est de suffragiis: 'optimatibus nota, plebi libera sunto'*: 3.38). Cf. Bögel, 1911, 313–14; Cancik, 1995, 301. Movement from law to law is often marked by use of transitional formulas (*deinde sequitur*: 3.40; *deinceps sunt*: 3.42, etc.), but sometimes there is asyndeton; cf. Bögel, 1911, 312–13; *ad* § 24. The presentation takes the form not of question and answer as in *Part.* or of a legal consultation, but of a conversation among colleagues (cf. § 59: *nostis quae sequuntur. discebamus enim pueri XII ut carmen necessarium . . .*)[70] or the explication of a law in the course of a *suasio* in a *contio*; cf. *Agr.* 2.16–75, explaining Rullus' law point by point; Bögel, 1911, 319–20. The depth of coverage varies considerably, with some points dealt with at length, others very briefly or not at all; cf. *ad* 3.49.

23 Q. Conclusa quidem est a te, frater, magna lex sane quam brevi; . . .] *Quidem* sets up the contrast with the sequel (*sed . . . non multum discrepat . . .*).—*A te, frater* is Vahlen's correction for *alter* (A¹B¹) or *altera* (HLERS); *a te tam* of the *recentiores* is no less a conjecture; Ziegler changed to *a te* and thus made Atticus the interlocutor until § 43. But Vahlen's solution both accounts for the transmitted *-ter* and is in line with the principle that the interlocutor remains the same unless there is an explicit change, since Quintus was the interlocutor at § 18. Thus the next comment (*immo prorsus ita censeo*) should likewise be given to Quintus and Atticus' interventions begin with *suade igitur . . .* (§ 24), indicated by Marcus' *ain tandem, Attice?*—Quintus confirms that Marcus has succeeded in his goal of setting forth the laws *cum brevitate* (§ 18; see *ad loc,*) and sets this treatment in contrast with the *magnitudo* of the content; cf. *Ac.* 1.43 (Cicero in response to Varro's exposition of Antiochus' epistemology): *breviter sane minimeque obscure exposita est . . . Brevitas* was among the virtues of narration (cf. Lausberg §§ 294 and 297 ff.), and knowing when βραχυλο-

---

70. Cancik, *loc. cit.*, 302, compares the discussion which Cicero and C. Trebatius Testa conducted *inter scyphos* about *furtum* (*Fam.* 7.22).

γίαι are appropriate is a mark of full mastery of the art of rhetoric at Pl. *Phaedr.* 272a.

sed . . . non multum discrepat ista constitutio religionum a legibus Numae nostrisque moribus.] *Constitutio religionum* could be rendered as "system of religious practices" (*OLD* s.v. *constitutio* 2 and *religio* 8b); "religiöses Rahmengesetz" (Cancik, 1995, 302).—Roman tradition built up Numa— perhaps in part because of a folk-etymological connection of his name with *numen* (cf. sch. Pers. 2.59: . . . *Numa dictus est eo quod numinibus deser-viret*)—into a kind of second founder of Rome with special responsibility in the sacred sphere corresponding to Romulus' in the secular and military. In the process many institutions of later origin were retrojected to his reign, such as the cult of Fides (cf. Ogilvie *ad* Liv. 1.21.3) or intercalation (cf. § 29). Hence for Cicero's legislation to accord with (1) the laws of Numa and (2) *nostri mores* amounts to the same thing and is implicitly treated as such in Marcus' reply. On the ancestral Roman constitution as the best generally cf. *Rep.* 1.70.

M. An censes—non necesse esse optimae reipublicae leges dare consen-taneas?] I.e., *optimas.* Cf. 1.15: *de optimo reipublicae statu* with note. On the difference of the relation of Cicero's *Republic* and *Laws* from Plato's cf. *ad* § 14b. The superiority of *nostra vetera respublica* rested upon the proper blend of the three constitutional elements, monarchy, oligarchy, and democ-racy; cf. *Rep.* 2.42: *itaque ista aequabilitas atque hoc triplex rerum pu-blicarum genus videtur mihi commune nobis cum illis populis fuisse; sed quod proprium sit in nostra republica, quo nihil possit esse praeclarius, id persequar si potero subtilius; quod erit eiusmodi, nihil ut tale ulla in repu-blica reperiatur.*

Ergo adeo exspectate leges—tamen erunt fere ⟨quae olim fuerunt⟩ in more maiorum, qui tum ut lex valebat.] *Adeo* often serves, like the Greek γέ, to emphasize the preceding word (cf. *TLL* s.v., 614.43 ff.; *OLD* s.v., 8) but is unusual with a conjunction; it also can lend liveliness to a command (cf. Ter. *Andr.* 759: *propera adeo;* Hand, 1, 148). Perhaps it colors *exspectate,* and the word order is in the interest of the ditrochaic clausula.—The transmitted *erunt* has caused difficulty: Minutianus changed to *erant,* Ziegler to *fuerunt;* but *erunt* matches *rogabuntur,* and the time indicated by *tum* should be specified; hence Powell's supplement.—It may seem odd that the sacral laws are justified as either corresponding to historical legislation or the *mos ma-iorum,* when the reader has been led to believe that nature is to be the criterion (cf. *ad* 1.17; pp. 238–39 n. 3 *supra*) and put on notice of the different status of literary and historical truth (1.1–5). Cicero, however, is consciously concealing his originality; cf. Keyes, 1921, 322; Schmidt, 1959,

62 n. 2. For the *mos maiorum* as the equivalent of *lex* but with weakening power in Cicero's day (cf. *tum* presumably referring to *vetera nostra respublica*) cf. Roloff, 90–91; for its special significance in the religious sphere ibid., 110–11. At *Phil.* 5.47 Cicero similarly cites the practice of the *maiores* to help justify an exception to existing law (see further *ad* 3.9.1).

24 A. Suade igitur, si placet, istam ipsam legem, ut ego 'uti {tu} rogas' possim dicere.] At § 14 Marcus had cited Plato's view that it was the function of law *persuadere aliquid, non omnia vi ac minis cogere*. But the text of the law cannot perform the whole work of persuasion; the legislator must advocate his law as well (cf. *OLD* s.v. *suadeo* 2); hence Atticus' request.—When legislation was proposed, the voters were given two tablets marked respectively V.R. (= *uti rogas*) and A. (= *antiquo*); cf. Shackleton Bailey *ad Att.* 1.14.5 (= 14.5 ed. Cantabr.); Mommsen, *Staatsr.* 3, 402 and nn. 2–3. *Tu* was rightly deleted by Turnebus as an intrusion in the formula. **Prorsus maiorem quidem rem nullam sciscam aliter; in minoribus, si voles, remittam hoc tibi.]** Atticus is saying that he will approve (cf. *OLD* s.v. *scisco* 2b) no weighty matter otherwise [sc. than by listening to a reasoned argument (*suasio*)], though in minor matters he is prepared to give Cicero this (*hoc* = *uti rogas*, i.e., his assent) without such process; cf. Schmidt, 1959, 63 n. 1. Watt, 1986, 267, assigns *in minoribus, si voles remittam hoc tibi* to Cicero, who would thus be giving permission to Atticus to vote otherwise [sc. than himself] in minor matters; but one expects *in minoribus* to be the continuation by the speaker who spoke of *maiorem . . . rem*, evidently with the distinction already in mind.

Q. Atque ea quidem ⟨mea⟩ sententia est.] The text is Powell's; transmitted is *Atque mea quidem sententia est. Atque . . . quidem* is a formula for emphasizing an added element (sim. καὶ . . . δή as described by Denniston, 157); cf. examples at Hand, 1, 502–3. The emphatic point should be the item enclosed by *atque . . . quidem*. *Mea* (supplied by Moser) could have been omitted after *quidem* and then added in such a way as to appear to be a correction of *ea*. The alternative would be to adopt Madvig's insertion of *eadem* prior to *sententia*. This speech should be given to Quintus; hence Marcus' following address to both interlocutors: *at ne longum fiat videte.* **Caste iubet lex adire ad deos,—nec amnibus ullis elui potest.]** With these words Marcus begins the commentary on his first law. The asyndeton is notable: just as the laws themselves are justaposed in asyndeton, so the comments on the individual laws often are; cf. *Delubra esse in urbibus censeo* (§ 26), *Feriarum festorumque dierum ratio* (§ 29), *Stipem sustulimus* and *Sacrilego poena est* (§ 40), *Donis impii ne placare audeant deos* and *⟨De⟩ diligentia votorum satis in lege dictum* (§ 41). Finally, each law is clearly identified by key words, as here *caste adire ad deos,* repeating with change of order and of syntax *Ad divos adeunto caste.* The commentary precisely follows the order in which the laws were presented. Cf. Cancik, 1995, 301.—Taken on its own the stipulation *Ad divos adeunto caste* is unremarkable. Only in this explanation does Cicero's intent to reform the "inherited conglomerate"[71] emerge. Euripides called attention to the conflict between ritual purity and moral judgments (fr. 266, cited *ad* § 45) and thus prepared the way for Plato's proposed reforms; cf. Dodds, 222–23. Cicero's project to reform Roman religion is similar and is constructed on the Platonic mind-body dualism with emphasis here, as elsewhere, on the mental constituent (*cum multum animus corpori praestet;* see below); cf. the inscription on the temple of Asclepius at Epidaurus *apud* Theophr. F 584A.19.5: ἁγνεία δ' ἐστὶ φρονεῖν ὅσια.

. . . animo videlicet, in quo sunt omnia; . . .] Cf. 1.16: *. . . quantam vim rerum optimarum mens humana contineat . . .* , an idea developed at 1.22 and 24; Mueller, 239 n. 68.

. . . observeturque ut casto corpore adeatur, . . .] Sc. *ad deos.*—*Observo* has the sense "observe, respect (laws, rules, etc.)": *OLD* s.v., 4a; cf. *ad* 3.46.

. . . multo esse in animis id servandum magis; . . .] For the a fortiori argument from the body to the mind cf. *ad* 1.51; for the phrasing cf. 1.23: *multo iam magis.*

nam illud vel aspersione aquae vel dierum numero tollitur, animi labes nec diuturnitate evanescere nec amnibus ullis elui potest.] This bipartite anaphoric sentence substitutes *animi labes* for the expected *hoc* and thus clarifies that *illud* stands for *corporis labes;* for the *hic - ille* structure cf. Hofmann-Szantyr, 182 with literature. Cicero's careful organization also appears in the chiastic arrangement of nouns and limiting genitives in the first clause and the parallelism of ablatives and infinitives in the following one.—For use of water in Greek purification rituals cf. Parker, 226–27 and 371. The reference to "number of days" presumably refers to a fixed number of days prior to a sacrifice during which the officiating priest must have abstained from sexual intercourse; ibid., 85–88; similar restrictions applied to one officiating at a magical rite (specified in some sources as three days); cf. Hopfner, *RE* 14.1 (1928), 360.4 ff., esp. 35 ff. (s.v. Mageia).—For *labes* cf. *ad* 1.60; for the *iunctura animi labes* cf. *Parad.* 5.33; sim. the *conscientiae labes* which Julius Caesar had *in animo* according to *Off.* 3.85 (where see note). For the irreversibility of moral stain cf. Aesch. *Ch.* 519–21; *Eu.*

---

71. Gilbert Murray, *Greek Studies* (Oxford, 1946), 66–67, a phrase taken up by Dodds, 179.

261 ff.; Hor. *Carm.* 3.5.27–28 with Kiessling-Heinze *ad loc.*; Sen. *Phaed.* 715–18 (Hippolytus is the speaker): *quis eluet me Tanais aut quae barbaris / Maeotis undis Pontico incumbens mari? / non ipse toto magnus Oceano pater / tantum expiarit sceleris* (cf. Shakespeare, *MacB.* 2.2.58 ff.: "Will all great Neptune's ocean wash this blood / Clean from my hand? No, this my hand will rather / The multitudinous seas incarnadine . . .").

25 quod autem pietatem adhiberi, opes amoveri iubet, significat probitatem gratam esse deo, sumptum esse removendum.] Cicero now moves on to the next clause: *pietatem adhibento, opes amovento.*—Sim. Theophr. περὶ εὐσεβείας F 584A.154–55 F.: δεῖ τοίνυν καθηραμένους τὸ ἦθος ἰέναι θύσοντας, τοῖς θεοῖς θεοφιλεῖς ταύτας ⟨τὰς⟩ θυσίας προσάγοντας, ἀλλὰ μὴ πολυτελεῖς.—*Autem* is Manutius' correction for the transmitted *tamen*, too strong an adversative.—As Latte, 1960, 39–40, points out, *pius* originally had the sense "ritually correct," as can be seen in the formula *pihom estu = pium esto* on the Volscian bronze tablet from Velletri (Vetter § 222.3), and *piare* and *piaculum* have preserved this sense both in Latin and in the Italic dialects. But from an early date the word was broadened to encompass correct behavior not only toward the gods but also those to whom one was bound by ties of kinship; in Ciceronian times, under Greek influence, the concept was further enlarged to include the *patria;* cf. C. Koch, *RE* 20.1 (1941), 1222.3 ff. (s.v. Pietas). Hence in our passage Cicero simply glosses *pietas* as *probitas* (though Bake *ad loc.* queries whether *pietatem* should not be read twice in this sentence); cf. § 41, where the *impii* are to the gods as the *improbus* to the *bonus,* and in general *ad* § 19.1 (*pietatem adhibento*).

paupertatem cum divitiis etiam inter homines esse aequalem velimus, . . .] Zumpt's insertion of *cum* before *paupertatem* is well worth considering unless one thinks that in this work "Unebenheiten sind . . . geradezu zu erwarten" (see p. 45 *supra*).—Cicero was far from egalitarian in his politics: he did not think that the votes of the wealthy and poor should carry equal weight (*Off.* 2.79 with note) and certainly had no sympathy for policies aiming at an *aequatio bonorum* (ibid. 2.73); on his political base cf. *Att.* 1.19.4, quoted *ad* 3.29; for his services to the *equites* in particular cf. Jochen Bleicken, *Cicero und die Ritter,* Abhandlungen der Akademie der Wissenschaften, philol.-hist. Klasse, 3.213 (Göttingen, 1995), esp. 113–14. Nevertheless Cicero favors strict equality in religious rites (cf. also § 45 and § 59 *fin.: quod quidem maxime e natura est, tolli fortunae discrimen in morte*); this is in accord both with the universalism of Book 1, where the similarity of human beings one to another is emphasized (1.29–32), and with the early Roman view. In Roman religious practice of Cicero's time and later, however, it was open to the wealthy to put their *pietas* on display through financing temples, offering rich dedications and sacrifices, building elaborate grave monuments, etc.; cf. Mehl, 192–93.

. . . cur eam sumptu ad sacra addito deorum aditu arceamus? . . .] This supplies the rationale for the policies of Numa described, but not explained, at *Rep.* 2.27: . . . *religionibus colendis operam addidit, sumptum removit.* The sentence concludes with a fine ditrochaic clausula. The *impius* is an exception (§ 22.8).

. . .—praesertim cum ipsi deo nihil minus gratum futurum sit, quam non omnibus patere ad se placandum et colendum viam.] Cf. Theophr. περὶ εὐσεβείας F 584A.142–44 F.: τὸ δὲ εὐδάπανον καὶ εὐπόριστον πρὸς συνεχῆ εὐσέβειαν συντελεῖ καὶ πρὸς τὴν ἁπάντων with following supporting argument.—The *impius* is an exception; cf. § 22.8.

quod autem non iudex sed deus ipse vindex constituitur, praesentis poenae metu religio confirmari videtur.] The topic is now the sanctioning clause: *qui secus faxit, deus ipse vindex erit.*—Cf. *ad* 1.40, where Cicero reinterprets the *Furiae* as *angor conscientiae fraudisque cruciatus.*

Suosque deos aut novos aut alienigenas coli confusionem habet religionum et ignotas caerimonias nos⟨tris⟩ sacerdotibus.] With *aut novos aut alienigenas* Cicero clearly signals that he is now dealing with the next law: *Separatim nemo habessit deos, neve novos neve advenas, nisi publice adscitos* (§ 19.3).—Translate *habet* as "involves"; cf. *OLD* s.v., 14a; the following word order is a bit rough; I would have expected *et caerimonias nos⟨tris⟩*[72] *sacerdotibus ignotas.*—This explanation needs to be read in conjunction with § 20.4: *Quoque haec privatim et publice modo rituque fiant, discunto ignari a publicis sacerdotibus.* Introduction of foreign gods would place proper observance in the hands of foreign priests, a prospect a Roman could not—with the single exception of the haruspices—contemplate with equanimity;[73] and introduction of private gods by individuals would involve a similar loss of control by Roman priests; possibly the banning of astrologers in 139 was motivated by such considerations; cf. Beard, 1998, 1, 161. On strengthened "control from the top" as characteristic of these laws cf. *ad* §§ 19–22 and the introduction to Book 3.

26 nam ⟨a⟩ patribus acceptos deos ita placet coli, si huic legi paruerint ipsi patres.] The phrase *a patribus acceptos* connects this explanation with the law *privatim colunto quos rite a patribus ⟨cultos acceperint⟩* (§ 19.4).— *Nam* is used in an *occupatio*, forestalling the objection that Cicero has

---

72. Davies' correction.

73. Cf. *ad* § 21.11 for the grant of Roman citizenship to priestesses from allied communities performing ceremonies *Graeco ritu.*

recognized family cults (*viz.*, the cult of the Lares and of dead ancestors at §§ 19.5 and 22.14–15; cf. also the general injunction: *ritus familiae patrumque servanto* [§ 19.6]); cf. Hand, 4, 16–17.—*A* was added by Manutius; cf. the first note *ad* 1.19.—The idea that the gods are to be worshipped (*coli*) is simply taken for granted; Cicero might have included a reference to the idea that the gods take cognizance of *qua pietate* [sc. *quisque*] *colat religiones* (§ 15b); cf. Bögel, 1907, 12. That the inactive gods of the Epicureans destroy the basis of cult is the criticism leveled at *N.D.* 1.115 ff. (cf. 1.3, where the point is stated in generic terms, without specific reference to a school).— The *si*-clause has a causal coloring, as often when correlated with *ita;* cf. Kühner-Stegmann, 2, 387.—Contrary to what Cicero implies, the gods the Romans accepted from their fathers were, as far back as our evidence allows us to see, themselves an amalgam of deities, native and foreign; cf. Beard, 1998, 1, 12. However unhistorical the Romans' picture of their own pantheon, Cicero is likely to be in touch with the feelings of his audience when, e.g., he inveighs against *inaudita ac nefaria sacra* (*Vat.* 14); for the Romans' attempts to draw a line between acceptable and unacceptable religious practices cf. in general *ad* 1.32; Beard, 1998, 1, 214–27.

Delubra esse in urbibus censeo, nec sequor magos Persarum, quibus auctoribus Xerxes inflammasse templa Graeciae dicitur, quod parietibus includerent deos quibus omnia deberent esse patentia ac libera, quorumque hic mundus omnis templum esset et domus.] The key word *delubra* marks the transition to the next law: ⟨*in urbibus*⟩ *delubra habento* (§ 19.5). Whereas the preceding commentary had focused on particular points (*castitas,* the removal of *opes,* the problem of *novi dei*), here Cicero raises the fundamental question whether there should be temples at all. His answer to that question may seem at first sight surprising, especially in light of Book 1 with its view of the deity as immanent in the world (*insita in natura:* 1.18b); certainly Zeno drew the consequence that no shrines should be built in cities (*SVF* 1, 62.10–12); Cicero's solution is, however, in line with his concept of *religio utilis civitatibus* (cf. below and § 16).—*Censeo* is the technical term for a senator's "recommending" of a course of action; cf. *OLD* s.v., 4.— Open-air shrines are characteristic of an early stage of cult among many peoples, including the Romans; cf. Latte, 1960, 79–80, on the early cult of Jupiter, centered on mountain peaks, including an open-air altar on the Capitoline preceding the erection of the temple.—Hdt. 1.131 remarks that the Persians did not use temples or images of the gods; they worshipped instead natural phenomena, including the vault of heaven as Zeus, and they sacrificed to the sun, the moon, earth, fire, water, and the winds; he describes the burning of the acropolis at 8.53.2; cf. also 8.109.3 (Themistocles describing Xerxes): . . . ἐμπιπράς τε καὶ καταβάλλων τῶν θεῶν τὰ ἀγάλματα. Our passage repeats *Rep.* 3.9 (Philus' speech): *eamque unam ob causam Xerxes inflammari Atheniensium fana iussisse dicitur, quod deos, quorum domus esset omnis hic mundus, inclusos parietibus contineri nefas esse duceret.*[74] But Xerxes may have acted on political rather than religious principle here; cf. Mary Boyce, *A History of Zoroastrianism*, 2 (Leiden-Cologne, 1982), 169: "He allowed the destruction of the temples of those who showed themselves hostile, but respected the holy places of those who aided him." On the limitations in general of Herodotus' information on Persian religion cf., ibid., 179 ff. His observation about the lack of temples is not contradicted, however, by archaeological evidence (ibid., 21–22, 89, 99, 175), and there is no literary evidence for them until the reign of Darius II (ibid., 201–2).—At *N.D.* 1.115 Xerxes' destruction of religion *manibus* is paralleled with Epicurus' overturning of temples and altars *rationibus.*

melius Graii atque nostri, qui ut augerent pietatem in deos easdem illos urbes, quas nos, incolere voluerunt.] A rare instance in which a foreign custom is given preference to the *mos maiorum* (cf. § 23). Cicero surely does not mean that the Greeks and Romans held that the gods lived *only* in cities; he might have phrased this differently to avoid confusion and apparent contradiction of § 27 *init.* (see *ad loc.*).—*Graii* was restored by Vahlen for *g(ra)ti* B¹A¹PεHL (corrected to *Graeci* at BˣAˣ). The form *Graius* is, as *OLD* s.v., 1 notes, "chiefly poetic" (cf. also Forcellini, *Onom.* s.v.), but Cicero uses it in contrasts at *Inv.* 1.35 (*Graius an barbarus*) and *Rep.* 1.58 (*Graeci dicunt omnes aut Graios esse aut barbaros*); cf. also Pac. *trag.* 90 = *N.D.* 2.91.—For the sense of *volo* cf. *ad* 1.63.

adfert enim haec opinio religionem utilem civitatibus, si quidem et illud bene dictum est a Pythagora . . . 'tunc maxime et pietatem et religionem versari in animis cum rebus divinis operam daremus', . . .] The preference for this view is based on its being beneficial to states (*utilis civitatibus*). The *utile* is expected as a standard in light of §§ 11 and 16, the latter passage explaining specifically how a *societas civium inter ipsos* benefits from belief in the gods; a corollary is the utility of temples as a visible reminder of the gods and their worship; Cicero may also be thinking of the link commonly accepted in antiquity between the success of a state and the piety of its citizens; cf. Mehl, 188–89. However, the sayings of Pythagoras and Thales cited in support do not make the connection with state interests (cf. Schmidt, 1959, 65) but speak rather of the benefits individuals derive from participation in cult.

---

74. Cf. the view Tacitus attributes to the Germans: *ceterum nec cohibere parietibus deos neque in ullam humani oris speciem adsimulare ex magnitudine caelestium arbitrantur: lucos ac nemora consecrant . . . (Ger.* 9.2).

Cicero no doubt means for the reader to infer that the state is stronger for having citizens of this type.—Seneca (*Ep.* 94.42) seems to have the same maxim in mind: *Pythagoras ait alium animum fieri intrantibus templum deorumque simulacra ex vicino cernentibus et alicuius oraculi opperientibus vocem;* cf. Plut. *Superst.* 169e: . . . τὸν Πυθαγόρου λόγον . . . εἰπόντος ὅτι βέλτιστοι γιγνόμεθα πρὸς τοὺς θεοὺς βαδίζοντες; sim. *Def. orac.* 413b. See also the note after next.

. . . et quod Thales, qui sapientissimus in septem fuit, 'homines existimare oportere omnia ⟨quae⟩ cernerent deorum esse plena; . . .] Cf. 11A23 D.-K. = Aët. 1.7.11: Θαλῆς νοῦν τοῦ κόσμου τὸν θεόν, τὸ δὲ πᾶν ἔμψυχον ἅμα καὶ δαιμόνων πλῆρες· διήκειν δὲ καὶ διὰ τοῦ στοιχειώδους ὑγροῦ δύναμιν θείαν κινητικὴν αὐτοῦ and *N.D.* 1.25: *Thales enim Milesius . . . aquam dixit esse initium rerum, deum autem eam mentem quae ex aqua cuncta fingeret.* In most versions of the ἀγών of the Seven Wise Men the tripod was first given to Thales (with the implication that he was considered *sapientissimus*), who thought himself unworthy and passed it along to the next until it had come back to him; he then dedicated it to Apollo; some gave this rôle, however, to Bias or Solon; cf. the short version at *Luc.* 118; Barkowski, *RE* 2A2 (1923) 2250.21 ff. (s.v. Sieben Weise). There is play on the contrast between the conventional designation and the content of doctrine at *Fin.* 3.76 (Cato): . . . *quod ille unus e septem sapientibus non sapienter Croesum monuit.* Cicero hedges the epithet *sapientissimus* by adding *in septem;* the title *sapientissimus Graeciae vir* is reserved for Plato at § 39; see *ad loc.*—⟨*Quae*⟩ *cernerent* was restored by Carolus Stephanus (quoted by Davies); the transmitted readings are *cerneret* (BAES), *cernent* (R), and *cernere* (PHL).

fore enim omnes castiores, veluti cum in fanis essent maxime religiosis'.] Cf. *N.D.* 2.71: *cultus autem deorum est optimus idemque castissimus atque sanctissimus plenissimusque pietatis, ut eos semper pura integra incorrupta et mente et voce veneremur.*—*Cum* is H's correction for *quo; in fanis essent* that of Turnebus for *infans esset; religiosis* that of "Lambinus" for *religiosus* BAᵡP or *religiosos* A¹εHL.

est enim quaedam opinione species deorum in oculis, non solum in mentibus.] An aniconic period at the beginning of the history of Roman religion was famously posited by Varro (*ARD* fr. 18), though the discovery (on the likely site of the Volcanal) of a sherd of Athenian black figure pottery depicting Hephaestus casts some doubt on our ability to penetrate so far back; cf. Coarelli, 1, 161–78, with fig. 48; J.A. North in *CAH* 7.2, 579–80. Cicero, of course, takes anthropomorphic representations of the gods for granted.—Watt, 1986, 267, suggested that some modifier may have been lost before *opinione*, such as *hominum, vulgi*, or *communi* (*omnium?*); this would also provide a subject for the following *habent*.

27a eandemque rationem luci habent in agris; . . .] *In agris* contrasts with *in urbibus* both in § 26 (*Delubra esse in urbibus censeo . . .*) and in the text of the underlying law (⟨*In urbibus*⟩ *delubra habento, lucos in agris habento et Larum sedes:* § 19.5).—This point apparently contradicts the Greeks' policy (*Graeci . . . easdem illos* [sc. *deos*] *urbes quas nos, incolere voluerunt:* § 26; see *ad loc.* and Schmidt, 1959, 65 n. 2). But the Greeks, too, had sacred mountains, groves, springs, etc. (cf. Burkert, 1985, 26–28, 86), a fact that Cicero surely did not mean to deny.

neque ea quae a maioribus prodita est cum dominis tum famulis, posita in fundi villaeque conspectu, religio Larum repudianda est.] *Larum* is Turnebus' necessary correction for the transmitted *parum*.—*Religio* with genitive of a divine name is the cult of that deity; cf. *OLD* s.v., 9. For the Lares see *ad* § 19.5 (*Larum sedes*). The violation of the *religio Larum* will be the basis of the bitter complaint launched against Clodius at § 42.

Iam ritus familiae patrumque servare, id est, quoniam antiquitas proxime accedit ad deos, a dis quasi traditam religionem tueri, ⟨decet⟩.] *Iam* marks the transition to the next law: *Ritus familiae patrumque servanto* (§ 19.6).—The present infinitives active and passive being much confused (cf. 1.24: *haberi*; §§ 28, 31, and 38 and 3.34 below), we adopt *servare* of the *recentiores* for the better attested *servari* (note that the underlying law has the active voice). Görler explains the text as a crossing of two expressions: (1) . . . *ritus familiae . . . servare* [sc. *censeo;* cf. § 26: *Delubra esse in urbibus censeo*], *id est . . .* ; (2) . . . *ritus familiae patrumque servare est . . . a dis quasi traditam religionem tueri.* Powell more plausibly posits a lacuna and supplies *decet* after *tueri*.—For the notion that the ancients were closer to the gods cf. Pl. *Phil.* 16c7: καὶ οἱ μὲν παλαιοί, κρείττονες ἡμῶν καὶ ἐγγυτέρω θεῶν οἰκοῦντες, ταύτην φήμην παρέδοσαν . . . ; *Tusc.* 1.26: . . . *antiquitate, quae quo propius aberat ab ortu et divina progenie, hoc melius ea fortasse quae erant vera cernebant;* § 40 below; S.E. M. 9.28: τῶν δὲ νεωτέρων Στωικῶν φασί τινες τοὺς πρώτους καὶ γηγενεῖς τῶν ἀνθρώπων κατὰ πολὺ τῶν νῦν συνέσει διαφέροντας γεγονέναι, ὡς πάρεστι μαθεῖν ἐκ τῆς ἡμῶν πρὸς τοὺς ἀρχαιοτέρους ⟨συμβλήσεως⟩, καὶ ἥρωας ἐκείνους ὥσπερ τι περιττὸν αἰσθητήριον σχόντας τὴν ὀξύτητα τῆς διανοίας ἐπιβεβληκέναι τῇ θείᾳ φύσει καὶ νοῆσαί τινας δυνάμεις θεῶν. Cf. Roloff, 109, who, however, ignores the *quasi* of our passage. The idea that the ancients were morally better is found at *Rep.* 6.27: . . . *qui ante nati sunt, qui nec pauciores et certe* *meliores fuerunt viri* and elsewhere. A character in a Ciceronian dialogue may, however, state a different view; cf. *Div.* 2.70: *errabat enim multis in rebus antiquitas.*

27b–28 quod autem ex hominum genere—a gignendo. †comestum ⟨ . . . ⟩.] This material explicates § 19.7: *Divos et eos qui caelestes semper habiti sunt—neve ulla vitiorum.* There are four essential points in that passage: (1) continuation of the cult of the traditional gods; (2–3) recognition of the cults of divinized heroes and of positive qualities that lead to divinization; (4) rejection of any cult of faults. Of these, (1) is passed over as too obvious to need explanation; (2) is restated; (3) is praised (*bene vero quod . . .*); (4) is elaborated with examples both foreign (Athenian shrines of Ὕβρις and Ἀναίδεια) and domestic (altars of Febris and Mala Fortuna); shrines should be dedicated instead to positive qualities, examples of which are given. Cicero lists Roman phenomena in an antiquarian mode; it was left to Fronto to voice the criticism *quis autem ignorat rationem humani consilii vocabulum esse, Fortunam autem deam dearumque praecipuam, templa, fana, delubra passim Fortunae dicata, at rationi nec simulacrum nec aram usquam consecratam?* (p. 4, 22 ff. van den Hout²). If he has not banned Fortuna, however, Cicero has at least provided for a cult of Mens.

27b . . . indicat omnium quidem animos immortales esse, sed fortium bonorumque divinos.] Cicero would later argue in detail for the immortality of the soul at *Tusc.* 1.—The divinity of the brave and the good was an important personal tenet of Cicero; cf. *Rep.* 6.17 (with reference to heaven): *harum* [sc. *civitatum*] *rectores et conservatores hinc profecti huc revertuntur;* Fuchs, 2 ff. The divinity of the soul was sometimes less restricted, both in Roman religious tradition and in Greek, especially Platonic, thought; see *ad* §§ 22.15–16 and 28 (. . . *ut illas qui habeant—*).

28 In this critique of religious naming-practices Cicero repeatedly gives his own value judgments (*bene . . . vitiosum . . . decet . . . recte . . . sit*), as in the personal affirmations of §§ 54–68 (see *ad loc.*); cf. the claim to originality at § 17.

bene vero quod Mens Pietas Virtus Fides consecratur {manu}, quarum omnium Romae dedicata publice templa sunt, . . .] The verb agrees with the nearest subject, as often; cf. Kühner-Stegmann, 1, 45; no need to change to *consecrantur* (Bake).—*Manu* was deleted by Schütz; Feldhügel's *humana* is often adopted, a restriction that is not wanted; the next clause explains that these are divine qualities that can reside in the human mind.—For the content cf. *ad* § 19.7 (. . . *et olla propter quae datur homini ascensus in caelum* . . .).

. . . ut illa qui habeant (habent autem omnes boni) deos ipsos in animis suis

collocatos putent.] The divinity of the soul is not always restricted this way; cf. 1.24 (... *divino auctum sit animorum munere* ...); 1.59 (*qui se ipse norit, primum aliquid se habere sentiet divinum* ...); *ad Off.* 3.44.

nam illud vitiosum Athenis, quod Cylonio scelere expiato, Epimenide Crete suadente, fecerunt Contumeliae fanum et Impudentiae; ...] Punctuation after *vitiosum* (so Ernesti, Wagner, Bake) gives undue emphasis to Athens, as if what happened there were specially relevant (so already Feldhügel *ad loc.*).—For Cylon's conspiracy and the murder of the participants contrary to the right of asylum (in an Olympiad year soon after 640) cf. Andrewes, *CAH* 3.3, 368–70.—Our passage is printed, together with the parallel account at Clem. Al. *Protr.* 26 = p. 19, 25 St. and sch. *ad loc.*, among the testimonies for Epimenides at *FGrHist* 457T4e; cf. esp. sch. Clem. Al., p. 196, 189 Marc. (= p. 305, 6 St.): οὗτος [sc. Ἐπιμενίδης] καὶ Ὕβριν καὶ Ἀναίδειαν ὑπέλαβεν εἶναι θεούς, καὶ νεὼς καὶ βωμοὺς αὐταῖς ἱδρύσατο Ἀθήνησι, καὶ θύειν παρεκελεύετο; Theophrastus (F 646 F.) will have been Cicero's source. He no doubt sees here a parallel to the temple of Licentia he attributes to Clodius (§ 42). On the Cretan holy man Epimenides and the tradition about him the best account is still Dodds, 141–46.

virtutes enim, non vitia consecrari decet.] *Consecrari* for *consecrare* is Goerenz's correction after Lact. *inst.* 1.20.16.[75] For confusion of active and passive infinitives cf. *ad* § 27 (*Iam ritus familiae patrumque servare*—).— For *decet* in such a context cf. *N.D.* 1.26: ... *cum* ... *deum non modo aliqua sed pulcherrima specie deceat esse* ...

araque vetus⟨ta⟩ in Palatio Febris, et altera Esquiliis Malae Fortunae, detestanda, atque omnia eiusmodi repudianda sunt.] *Vetusta in* is Madvig's correction for *uetustin* B¹(A¹?); see Powell's apparatus for other variants; Halm's *detestanda atque* is adopted for the transmitted *detestatque* (B¹AεHL); Madvig has already proposed *detestandae atque.*—For evils conceived as gods cf. Dodds, 41–42; Burkert, 1996, 152. At *N.D.* 3.63 Cicero refers to a sacred site on the Palatine as the *Febris fanum;* cf. F. Coarelli, *LTUR* s.v. Febris, templum. The dedications comprised *remedia quae corporibus aegrorum adnexa fuerant* (V.Max. 2.5.6). The underlying belief was evidently that the evil could be contained by having its own place (cf. Aesch. *Eu.* 804 ff.). For the *ara Malae Fortunae* on the Esquiline cf. J. Aronen, *LTUR* s.v. Fortuna Mala. The church fathers took up Cicero's critique of sacred places dedicated to malignant powers; cf. Wissowa, 246 n. 1.

quod si fingenda nomina, Vicae Potae potius vincendi atque potiundi, Statae standi, cognominaque Statoris et Invicti Iovis, rerumque expetendarum

---

75. ... *adiecit virtutes enim oportere, non vitia consecrari.* See further *infra* on fr. dubium.

nomina Salutis Honoris Opis Victoriae, . . .] The elliptical main clause should probably be filled out as follows: *Vicae Potae potius nomen fingendum, vincendi atque potiundi* [sc. *numen* or *dea*],[76] *Statae standi, cognominaque Statoris et Invicti Iovis* [sc. *fingenda*]; cf. Vahlen *ad loc.;* less plausible to regard *Vicae Potae* and *Statae* as generalizing plurals, *fingendae* as the verb to be supplied and *a nomine* as omitted with the gerunds. One suspects that this passage is a draft that never received the final polish; cf. Schmidt, 1959, 68 n. 3.—Vica Pota was an ancient goddess later identified with Victoria (cf. Asc. *Pis.* 12). The interpretation of her name is correct; it belongs, like Panda Cela and others, to the class of postverbals, formed from verbal stem plus suffix; cf. St. Weinstock, *RE* 8A2 (1958), 2014.26 ff. and 2015.6 ff. She had a temple on the Velia and a festival on 5 January; ibid., 2014.12 ff.; cf. Wissowa, 140 and 244; Scullard, 60; Ogilvie *ad* Liv. 2.7.12.—In the forum stood an image of Stata Mater, the deity in charge of quenching fire (cf. Fest. p. 317M); inscriptions of Augustan date attest the decentralization of her worship to the individual *vici*, possibly connected with the reorganization of the fire brigade; cf. Wissowa, *RE* 3A2 (1929), 2167.10 ff.—Jupiter Stator[77] had two temples, one at the Porta Mugonia, the other by the Circus Flaminius; the former, though retrojected to Romulus, was vowed by M. Atilius Regulus during the Third Samnite War (294); cf. Wissowa, 122–23; Orlin, 55. Cicero invoked the name of the deity to potent effect at *Cat.* 1.11 and esp. 33; cf. Goar, 36–37; Vasaly, 41 ff.—For the old Italian goddess Salus cf. Wissowa, 131 ff.—Honos was usually paired in cult with Virtus and understood in a military sense; thus the most famous temple of Honos was located in front of the Porta Capena near the temple of Mars; it had been vowed during a battle with the Ligurians by Q. Fabius Maximus Verrucosus (233; for the characteristic Roman practice of founding a temple based on some specific event cf. Stambaugh, 557–58); its restoration was vowed and begun by M. Claudius Marcellus, who added a nearby temple of Virtus (after his request to lodge the two deities under a single roof was refused by the pontifices; cf. Beard, 1998, 1, 105); the building project was completed by his son (cf. *N.D.* 2.61 with Pease's note; Orlin, 170); C. Marius added a new temple to the two divinities together; cf. Wissowa, 149 ff.; Orlin, 193; see further *ad* § 58.—Ops Mater was the personified bounty of the harvest: Wissowa, 203–4.—Victoria grew up as an independent goddess

---

76. Cf. Var. *apud* Don. in Ter. *Ph.* 49: *initiari pueros Educae et Poticae et Cubae divis edendi et pontandi et cubandi* . . . (cf. *gram.* p. 246, fr. 172).

77. Cf. Var. *gram.* pp. 236–37, fr. 137: *dixerunt eum* [sc. *Iovem*] . . . *Statorem* . . . *quod haberet* . . . *statuendi stabiliendi* . . . *potestatem* . . . ; for the formation Ernout-Meillet s.v. **-stano*.

replacing Vica Pota and beside Jupiter Victor, perhaps under the influence of Greek cults of Nike; often the name of the particular general was added in the genitive; she received a temple at Rome in 294; ibid. 139–41; Weinstock, 91 ff.; Beard, 1998, 1, 69; Richardson, s.v. Victoria, Aedes, and P. Pensabene, *LTUR* s.v.—On the text: *vincendi atque potiundi* and *standi* were deleted by Goerenz. Wissowa, *RE* 3A2 (1929), 2168.23 ff., thought that *standi* (instead of *sistendi*) must either be a gloss or that Cicero had confused Stata with Statina, the goddess corresponding to Statanus/Statilinus, the god who presides over children's ability to stand upright. The following reference to Jupiter Stator has evidently been provoked, however, by association with the preceding term, an argument for the authenticity of *Statae*. Moreover, *sto* can mean "stop moving, come to a standstill" (cf. *OLD* s.v., 10b) and thus describe the action produced by the goddess.

. . . quoniamque exspectatione rerum bonarum erigitur animus, recte etiam Spes a Caiatino consecrata est; . . .] The temple, vowed by A. Atilius Caiatinus (cos. 258, 254; censor 247) during the First Punic War, stood in the Forum Holitorium; its dedication was celebrated on 1 August; cf. F. Coarelli, *LTUR* s.v. Spes, aedes; Orlin, 102. On Caiatinus cf. Klebs, *RE* 2.2 (1896), 2079.68 ff. (Atilius no. 36); K.-L. Elvers, *NP* s.v. Atilius I 14; he also dedicated a temple of Fides (*N.D.* 2.61). For the poorly attested cult of Spes cf. Wissowa, 329–31.

Fortunaque sit, vel Huiusce Diei (nam valet in omnes dies), vel Respiciens ad opem ferendam, vel Fors in quo incerti casus significantur magis, vel Primigenia a gignendo. †comestum ⟨ . . . ⟩] In contrast to the Greeks, who treated Τύχη as an all-encompassing force, the Romans tended to divide Fortuna up into individual aspects (cf. Plut. *Qu. Rom.* no. 74), as in the Fortuna Huiusce Diei and Fortuna Respiciens of our passage; cf. Wissowa, 261–62. Bögel, 1907, 12, suggests that this list of four different species of Fortuna has been lifted from an antiquarian collection, such as Var. *ARD* (among the fragments of which, however, no corresponding material is preserved); for the relation to Varro see in general pp. 243–44 *supra*.—Fortuna Huiusce Diei is the deity to whom good fortune is owed on a particular day (for the deictic local adverb *-ce* cf. Leumann, 468–70). As in Greek references to a δαίμων, the divine agent is left vague so as not to offend any power; cf. Burkert, 1985, 180–81. During the battle of Vercellae (30 July 101), Q. Lutatius Catulus vowed a temple to Fortuna Huiusce Diei and fulfilled the vow with the dedication of a shrine on the Campus Martius on the anniversary date some years later (in any case before his suicide in 87). There may have been an earlier temple to this deity on the Palatine. Cf. Wissowa, 262; P. Gros, *LTUR* s.v. Fortuna Huiusce Diei, aedes; F. Coarelli,

ibid. s.v. Fortuna Huiusce Diei, aedes (in Palatio).—The epithet Respiciens
ad opem ferendam suggests that this type of Fortuna saves one *in extremis*.
It is a difficulty that Plut. *Fort. Rom.* 323a, according to the generally
accepted emendation, sites the temple of Τύχη Ἐπιστρεφομένη on the
Esquiline, whereas other evidence points to the Palatine; see further L.
Anselmino–M.J. Strazzulla, *LTUR* s.v. Fortuna Respiciens; Wissowa, 262
and n. 12.—We hear of an early temple of Fors Fortuna outside the city on
the right bank of the Tiber; it was vowed by Sp. Carvilius Maximus (cos.
293) during a battle with the Samnites and built with the spoils of victory;
ibid., 256–57; Orlin, 31, 123–24, and 135. It is odd, however, to see Fors
placed on the same level as these particular aspects of Fortuna (cf. Bögel,
1907, 12); for theories on the significance of the double name cf. Francis M.
Lazarus, "On the Meaning of Fors Fortuna: A Hint from Terence," *AJPh*
106 (1985), 359–67, with literature.—Fortuna Primigenia or, as designated
more fully in an early inscription of Praenestine origin, *Fortuna Diovo fileia
primogenia* (= *Fortunae, Iovis filiae, primigeniae*: CIL XIV.2863), had her
main temple in Praeneste, a city open to Greek influences, where worshipers
received oracles inscribed on pieces of oak (for the foundation legend cf.
Div. 2.85). Though the Romans long rejected this alien cult, during the
stress of the Second Punic War P. Sempronius Tuditanus as consul in 204
vowed a temple to Fortuna Primigenia prior to the battle of Croton; it was
dedicated on the Quirinal in 194. This figure seems to combine several
different conceptions: a goddess of childbirth worshiped by *matres* (cf. *Div.*
2.85) and a Greek-style Τύχη who controls and can predict the future; cf.
Wissowa, 257–59; Orlin, 64–65; Beard, 1998, 1, 89 and n. 58 with
literature.—On the text: Vahlen interpreted *a gignendo comes* as "quae nos
a primo ortu comitatur"; but he presupposes a passive sense of *gigno* only
attested much later; cf. *TLL* s.v. 1985.21 ff. The etymology *Primigenia a
gignendo* "from giving birth" may be sound, but the following *comestum*
(AH) or *cumestum* (B) may be remnants either before, after, or on either side
of a lacuna (Manutius has *cum est* with following lacuna; sim. S²)—possibly
an extensive one: Bake *ad loc.* expected some commentary on the next law,
Sacra sollemnia obeunto (§ 19.8), not otherwise discussed; Cicero may also
have prefaced some general remarks on the necessity and utility of holidays
(cf. Bögel, 1907, 13); see the next note.

29a With this paragraph Cicero passes on to the law *Feriis iurgia ⟨a⟩mo-
vento* etc. (§ 19.9), his commentary centering on three points: (1) the festivals themselves, (2) the timing of sacrifices, and (3) the types of victims for
each deity. Under (1) Cicero provides for a rest (*requies*) from the labors
appropriate to the two social groups, the free and the slaves. Furthermore he

makes it clear that, in contrast to Aristotle's ideal state, σχολή is not the τέλος (cf. Solmsen, 2, 1 ff.); rather, *requies* is to be provided for in such a way that the completion of work is not endangered (*quas compositor— operum rusticorum*). Such may have been the principle behind, e.g., the scheduling of the Saturnalia and Compitalia in December / early January when farm work was at a minimum; cf. Scullard, 58 ff. and 205 ff.; Arist. *EN* 1160a25–28 finds this principle underlying the timing of Greek festivals. Point (2) forms the basis of a warning of the need for care in intercalation. *Pace* Cicero, who attributes it to Numa, the Decemviri of 450 seem to have established the first law *de intercalando;* cf. Michels, 126–30; Rüpke, 1995, 230 ff. This was followed by the publication of the *fasti* by Cn. Flavius as curule aedile in 304 (Michels, 108–18; Rüpke, 1995, 245 ff.). By the late Republic an intercalary month of twenty-seven days was inserted after 23 or 24 February (depending on the length of intercalation needed); there is no scholarly consensus as to the frequency of intercalation; on the whole question cf. Michels, 145–72. Partly through negligence, partly through machinations for political or other gain (though Cicero here ignores this latter point[78]), the months and seasons sometimes fell seriously out of sync until Caesar's reform of the calendar in 46; cf. Michels, 168 with sources cited; Libero, 53–54; *MRR* 2, 293; Rüpke, 1995, 369 ff. Number (3) amounts to a warning against changing practices established by the pontifices and haruspices.

Feriarum festorumque dierum ratio in liberis requietem habet litium et iurgiorum, in servis operum et laborum. quas compositor anni conferre debet ad perfectionem operum rusticorum; . . .] For the distinction between *feriae* (official days of rest, though possibly because of mourning) and *dies festi* (days of pleasurable celebration including religious ceremonies) cf. Michels, 69–71, 82–83, and 85; Rüpke, 1995, 504 n. 61. Michels, 71, notes that in our passage "Cicero seems curiously uninterested in the physical work of the free man, and seems to visualize his only occupation as that of the courts." But, as elsewhere, Cicero is thinking in terms of himself and others of his social class (cf. *ad Off.* 1.18–19 and 150).—The operative distinction is between slave and free, not between citizens and non-citizens,

---

78. Laser, 56 n. 58, infers from this that intercalation was not a usual political strategy (it is not treated as such by Burckhardt). Cicero gives a particularly flagrant example (albeit not involving the Roman calendar) at *Ver.* 2.128–30, namely Verres' removal of a month and a half from the calendar at Cephaloedium so as to exclude Herodotus from candidacy for the major priesthood; on the other hand, Cicero appeals to Atticus to exert influence to hinder any intercalation that would lengthen his term as governor of Cilicia (*Att.* 5.9.2 and 5.13.3); cf. in general Taylor, 1949, 78–79.

who were presumably not excluded; cf. Beard, 1998, 1, 261 n. 51. It has been debated whether or to what degree slaves actually enjoyed freedom from work on such days; cf. Rüpke, *loc. cit.*, with literature.—The archetype reads *compositior*, a *lectio impossibilis*, the result either of a double reading *compositio/compositor* or *compositio* corrected to *compositor*. *Compositor* is the reading of the *recentiores*, *compositio* of H. As the subject of an action (*conferre debet*) *compositor* deserves preference, as Vahlen already saw. Our passage would be the earliest attestation of the agent noun, next found at *Orat.* 61 (cf. *TLL* s.v.).—*Perfectio* is first attested in Cicero (*Inv.* 1.36); cf. *TLL* s.v., 1349.60 and 1350.18.

quod ⟨ad⟩ tempus ut sacrificiorum libamenta serventur . . .] *Ad* is Klotz's supplement; with *quod ad tempus* understand *attinet* and translate "as to the dates" (Rudd). Feldhügel understood *ad tempus* in the sense "on time, punctually" (cf. *OLD* s.v. *tempus* 8e) but then had to eliminate *quod* and read *adque tempus.*—Attested as early as Var. *Men.* 568, *libamenta* appears here in the proper sense of "offerings"; cf. *Rep.* 2.44 with Zetzel's note.[79] The phrase *sacrificiorum libamenta* (suspected by Bake, who wanted to delete *sacrificiorum*) has the sense "ea quae in sacrificando libantur" (Feldhügel).

. . . diligenter habenda ratio intercalandi est; quod institutum perite a Numa, posteriorum pontificum neglegentia dissolutum est.] The calendar of the Republic had months of 28, 29, or 31 days and a total of 355 days per year, the odd number being considered lucky; such attention to numbers was associated with the Pythagoreans; hence the traditional attribution to the "Pythagorean" Numa; cf. Rüpke, 1995, 203–4. Cicero accepts this attribution even though he rejects on chronological grounds the possibility of Numa having been a Pythagorean (*Rep.* 2.28–29; cf. *Tusc.* 4.2), for it fits with Numa's introduction of other early priestly institutions (*Rep.* 2.26); cf. also *ad* § 23. Here, as often elsewhere, Cicero's law aims to curb recent excesses; see the headnote to this section and Rüpke, 1995, 370.—On the pontifical control of the calendar until its publication by Flavius in 304 cf. Wieacker, 1988, 310 and n. 5; Michels, 8–9, 20, 53, 115, 117, and 210, as well as the cautionary note sounded by Rüpke, 1995, 238.

iam illud ex institutis pontificum et haruspicum non mutandum est, quibus hostiis immolandum cuique deo: cui maioribus, cui lactentibus; cui maribus, cui feminis.] Serv. *G.* 2.380 propounds the theory *victimae numinibus aut per similitudinem aut per contrarietatem immolantur.* This is, however, not

---

79. Its counterpart *libamen* was initially poetic and is first attested in Vergil; cf. *TLL* s.vv. *libamen, libamentum;* Jean Perrot, *Les dérivés latins en -men et -mentum* (Paris, 1961), 110 and 130.

a sacral law, and our passage suggests that the matter was complex and not easily summarized; cf. Georg Rohde, *Die Kultsatzungen der römischen Pontifices* (Berlin, 1936), 169 and 171.

29b Plures autem deorum omnium, singuli singulorum sacerdotes et respondendi iuris et conficiendarum religionum facultatem adferunt.] Cicero now takes up his next law: *Divisque ⟨alii⟩ aliis sacerdotes, omnibus pontifices, singulis flamines sunto* etc. (§ 20.3).—For the polyptoton cf. *Dom.* 44: . . . *ut singuli cives singulis versiculis e civitate tollantur.*—In speaking of the priests' capacity for giving legal responses, Cicero makes no distinction between *ius sacrum* and *civile,* for both originally fell to the *pontifices;* cf. *ad* § 47. The other priestly function specified is, however, strictly religious, namely that of bringing religious rites to completion (*conficiendarum*[80] *religionum*).

cumque Vesta quasi focum urbis (ut Graeco nomine est ⟨Ἑστία⟩ appellata, quod nos prope idem {Graecum interpretatum} nomen tenemus) complexa sit, ei colendae virgines praesint, ut advigiletur facilius ad custodiam ignis, et sentiant mulieres {in} naturam feminarum omnem castitatem pati.] Powell adds Ἑστία, which can easily have dropped out after *est;* the Greek name should surely have been cited if it is to be discussed to this extent; cf. *N.D.* 2.67: *nam Vestae nomen a Graecis (ea est enim quae ab illis* Ἑστία *dicitur).* *Vesta* in Cicero's day denoted only the hearth-goddess; hence the *ut*-clause explains the connection to *focus* based upon the fact that Vesta is equivalent to Ἑστία, which, as a common noun in Greek, means "hearth."[81] The relation of the Greek and Latin nouns is problematic because of the lack, with one exception, of Ϝ in the Greek dialect forms; cf. Frisk and Ernout-Meillet s.vv.; however, Sihler § 188 cites considerable evidence for PIE *w-* (almost always followed by *s*) corresponding to Greek spiritus asper.—The *focus* is properly the "domestic hearth or fireplace" (*OLD* s.v., 1); hence the application of the term to a city is metaphorical (*quasi*). Just as the atrium of the house was the center of the worship of the *Lar familiaris,* so the *atrium Vestae,* in particular the inner part of the temple, called the *penus,* was the center of the worship of the *Penates populi Romani* (cf. Tac. *Ann.* 15.41); it contained the sacred fire and the sacred objects of the Vestals, including the Penates, the Trojan Palladium, and the holy phallus; cf. Koch, *RE* 8A2 (1958), 1729.66 ff. The position of the temple of Vesta on the border between the Velia and the forum also raises problems since that would imply that it was not within the Palatine *pomerium* (a contradiction of *quasi*

---

80. *Conficiendarum* is the reading of the *recentiores* for transmitted *confitendarum;* Lipsius proposed *cum fide tuendarum.*

81. Cf. LSJ and *OLD* s.vv.; Davies deleted *Graecum interpretatum.*

focum urbis complexa sit); but more recent stratigraphical research suggests that it belongs, in fact, to the oldest regnal plastering of the forum, ca. 575; cf. Koch, *loc. cit.*, 1726.10 ff.; Coarelli, 1, 65–67.—Wissowa added the number VI prior to *virgines*, whence it can easily have fallen out, on grounds that the number accounts for the following *ut advigiletur facilius ad custodiam ignis* (on the number of Vestals cf. Koch, *loc. cit.*, 1732.24 ff.); but their status as virgins without familial responsibilities would sufficiently explain the phrase.—The concluding motivation supplied by Cicero *ut . . . sentiant mulieres {in}*[82] *naturam feminarum omnem castitatem pati* interprets the Vestals as an ethical model; one suspects, however, that the sense of the virgin priesthood was that the priestesses should be wholly given over to the service of the goddess without interference of any other ties; cf. Parker, 90–93; Beard, 1980, discusses the earlier literature on the problem. Cicero's remark also counters the charge of lewdness levelled against women in the mysogynistic literature of antiquity from the time of Semonides of Amorgus (fr. 7.48–49 West) onward; cf. the remarks of Judith P. Hallett, "Women as *Same* and *Other* in [the] Classical Roman Elite," *Helios* 16 (1989), 60–61.
30–31 The functions of the *sacerdotes* are described in four lines in the edition of Görler-Ziegler, whereas those of the augurs claim thirteen and a half; these proportions are especially striking since historically the pontiffs tended to gain power and influence at the augurs' expense. One suspects that, in spite of his denial, Cicero's membership of the board of augurs has influenced this emphasis; cf. Schmidt, 1969, 54–55.
30 Quod sequitur vero non solum ad religionem pertinet, sed etiam ad civitatis statum, ut sine eis qui sacris publice praesint, religioni privatae satis facere non possint; . . .] The state has not been forgotten in the preceding paragraphs (cf. *ad* § 26: *religionem utilem civitatibus*). But the following connects even more closely with the topic of *Rep.*, defined at 1.15 as *de optimo reipublicae statu*. Cicero is preparing the way for his encomium of the powers of the augurate. For *ut sine eis—possint* cf. *ad* § 25 (*Suosque deos—*).
continet enim rempublicam, consilio et auctoritate optimatium semper populum indigere.] *Continet* = "it is the cornerstone" (Reid). This "holding together" of the state through binding its constituents in mutual dependency was a major goal of Cicero's political philosophy, just as the binding together of human beings in general was of his ethics.[83] This is the general

---

82. Deleted by Ascensius.
83. Cf. *Off.* 1.22: *. . . communes utilitates in medium adferre, mutatione officiorum, dando accipiendo, tum artibus, tum opera, tum facultatibus devincire hominum inter homines societatem.*

function of laws,[84] and their contribution to this end was the criterion used to determine the areas of legislation to be dealt with in *Leg.* and their order; cf. § 69: *. . . dicam de magistratibus. id enim est profecto quod constituta religione rempublicam contineat maxime* (cf. 3.12).—*Consilio et auctoritate optimatium semper populum indigere:* this refers to the provision *Quoque haec privatim et publice modo rituque fiant, discunto ignari a publicis sacerdotibus* (§ 20.4), whereby Cicero assumes that the *publici sacerdotes* of § 20.4 are *optimates,* a term he uses with considerable latitude (cf. p. 14 n. 60 *supra*). Patrician status was originally a requirement for holding a priesthood, but the office had long been open to the plebs (cf. Wissowa, 491–92); it is safe to assume, however, that in Cicero's day priests were overwhelmingly drawn from the senatorial/aristocratic class; cf. Szemler, 28–33;[85] even P. Clodius, as quoted at *Dom.* 4, assumed optimate sentiments among the pontiffs. In assuming that the *populus* will benefit from the *consilium* and *auctoritas* of the optimates, Cicero takes a leaf from the book of his political mentor L. Licinius Crassus, who argued at length the benefits that the senators conferred upon the community (cf. *orat.*, pp. 243–45); this same principle seems to underlie Cicero's plan to restore optimate oversight over votes cast; see further *ad* 3.33–39. For influence of L. Crassus on *Leg.* cf. also *ad* 3.19b–26 and 42.

descriptioque sacerdotum nullum iustae religionis genus prae⟨ter⟩mittit; nam sunt ad placandos deos alii constituti qui sacris praesint sollemnibus, ad interpretanda alii praedicta vatium, neque multorum (ne esset infinitum), neque ut ea ipsa quae suscepta publice essent quisquam extra collegium nosset.] At § 20.5 these two types of priesthood had been distinguished.[86] Here Cicero states the underlying principle and gives fuller detail about the functions of each. The first serves *ad placandos deos,* i.e., to maintain or reestablish the *pax deorum* (cf. *ad* § 22.1), the second *ad interpretanda . . . praedicta vatium*. There follow two restrictions set to this activity (*neque . . . neque*): first, *only* the *praedicta vatium,* not those of every single person, are to be considered;[87] second, the public business is to be held in strict

84. Cf. *Off.* 3.23: *. . . legibus populorum, quibus in singulis civitatibus respublica continetur.*

85. A new prosopography of the priests of the city of Rome is being prepared by Jörg Rüpke.

86. *Disscriptio* is the reading of B, *descriptio* that of APεHL. It is a "division" (*di-*) or a "system" (*de-*) of priests that is in question? Either would be conceivable and require justification (*nam*); *descriptio* is usually adopted here (e.g., by Vahlen; Vetter, *TLL* s.v. *descriptio* 667.16; Powell) in view of *descriptio magistratuum* at 3.12; see also 1.24 and § 11.

87. At § 20.5 he had restricted more closely, insisting on official standing: *vatium effata . . . cum senatus populusque ⟨it⟩a sciverit.*

confidence (*ut—nosset:* a consecutive clause with limiting force).—The phrase *iusta religio* draws a line, presumably before *superstitio;* sim. *pura religio* at 1.60; see *ad loc.* and *ad* § 26 (*nam ⟨a⟩ patribus acceptos deos—*). Cicero's apparent exclusion of the augural law from *iusta religio* is mitigated by the loose apposition (*autem*) in which he sets the two concepts (so Cohee, *loc. cit. ad* § 20.5).—The concept of *ius(tus)* itself originated in the religious sphere; cf. *ad* § 36 (*qua licentia Romae data—*).—Because the XVviri handled the potentially explosive Sibylline prophecies, keeping the business of the *collegium* secret was particularly important; cf. Wissowa, 536 and n. 2, and on the Sibylline books generally H.W. Parke, *Sibyls and Sibylline Prophecy in Classical Antiquity,* ed. B.C. McGing (London, 1988), esp. ch. 7. A breach of secrecy had occurred in 56 when the XVviri were persuaded by the tribune C. Cato, an ally of Clodius, to divulge a prophecy that they connected with the planned restoration of Ptolemy XII to the Egyptian throne (cf. Dio 38.15; Tatum, 1999, 200–201); possibly Cicero had this or a similar incident in mind.

31 Here Cicero offers, not a commentary on the augurs' functions specified at §§ 20.6–21.6, but an encomium of the augural law itself. This digression is built upon a thesis, followed by a denial that it is personally motivated; the thesis is then bolstered by a series of rhetorical questions implying that nothing else could be superior in each of several respects (*quid . . . maius . . . quid gravius . . . quid magnificentius . . . quid religiosius . . . ?*). Bögel, 1907, 15, suggested that this material could have been more closely integrated with the whole by including a cross-reference to the *prooemium legis* (§§ 15b–16); but there the case is made for the general community-building function of belief in the gods, but not for its rôle in the state as such, which is the point in our passage (*maximum . . . et praestantissimum in republica ius est augurum . . .*).

Maximum autem et praestantissimum in republica ius est augurum cum auctoritate coniunctum; . . .] Correct auspication before electoral and other assemblies at which decisions were taken was considered to insure the *pax deorum* and hence the community's continued good fortune; hence Cicero often emphasized the importance of the augurs for the proper running of the state; cf. evidence collected from the speeches by Linderski, 1995, 479 ff. The augurs could not, however, act independently of the magistrates (for their procedure see below on *quid magnificentius quam posse decernere—*), so Cicero's description of their *ius* as *maximum . . . in republica* is over-stated (unless *maximum* is in comparison merely with other religious officials), though he saves his strongest argument for the last sentence of this paragraph.

neque vero hoc quia sum ipse augur ita sentio, sed quia sic existimari nos est necesse.] This passage yields 53/52 as the likely *terminus post quem* both for the composition and the fictive date of *Leg.*, since it was probably then that Cicero was elected to the board of augurs as successor to P. Licinius Crassus, slain at Carrhae; cf. *MRR* 2, 233; J. Linderski, "The Aedileship of Favonius, Curio the Younger and Cicero's Election to the Augurate," *HSPh* 76 (1972), 190 ff. = (1995), 240 ff. (with 651–52).—Vahlen preferred *existimare* of the *recentiores* to *existimari* of the archetype; but Powell rightly defends the transmitted text (*per litt.*): " 'It is necessary that we should be thought of in this way' (exclusive 'we') seems to have more point than 'it is necessary for us to take this view' (generalising 'us' = everyone)."—The alteration of the usual order (*necesse est*) yields a handsome ditrochaic clausula.

quid enim maius est, si de iure quaerimus, quam posse a summis imperiis et summis potestatibus comitiatus et concilia vel instituta dimittere, vel habita rescindere?] Examples follow. On this right of the augurs cf. I.M.J. Valleton, "De iure obnuntiandi comitiis et conciliis," *Mnemosyne* 19 (1891), 75–113 and 229–70; Wissowa, *RE* 2.2 (1896), 2330.44 ff.; Linderski, 1986, 2162 ff.; Libero, 56–64.—*Imperia* and *potestates* are abstract for concrete; cf. *ad* 1.23 and 3.9.4.

quid gravius quam rem susceptam dirimi, si unus augur 'alio ⟨die⟩' dixerit?] Turnebus rightly restored the augural formula for dissolving an assembly; cf. *Phil.* 2.82: *confecto negotio bonus augur—C. Laelium diceres—'alio die' inquit*; Mommsen, *Staatsr.* 1, 109–10 and 110 n. 1. The action of the individual augur in our sentence contrasts with that of the *collegium* as a whole to take certain actions as described in the following sentence; cf. Linderski, 1986, 2152.

quid magnificentius quam posse decernere ut magistratu se abdicent consules?] The consuls for 162, P. Cornelius Scipio Nasica and C. Marcius Figulus, had already departed for their provinces when the consul of the previous year, Ti. Sempronius Gracchus, who was also an augur, reading in the augural books, recalled a flaw in his taking of electoral auspices; he wrote a letter explaining this point to the board of augurs, who determined that there had been a *vitium* and referred the matter to the senate, which decreed that the new consuls should abdicate; cf. *N.D.* 2.10–11; *Div.* 1.33 (the case as an example of the *auspiciorum auctoritas*) and 2.74–75; other testimonies at *MRR* 1, 441–42; Linderski, 1986, 2160–61; on the procedure cf. Mommsen, *Staatsr.* 1, 115–16.

quid legem, si non iure rogata est, tollere, ut Titiam decreto collegi, ut Livias consilio Philippi consulis et auguris; nihil domi, nihil militiae per magistratus

gestum sine eorum auctoritate posse cuiquam probari?] On the *leges Titiae et Liviae* cf. ad § 14.—*Non iure rogata* is nontechnical for *vitio* or *contra auspicia lata;* cf. Asc. 60–61C. In fact, the *collegium* did not possess such power but had to refer the matter to the senate for action, as in Cicero's own account of the lex Titia at § 14; cf. *ad loc.* and Heikkilä, 121. It is doubtful that Cicero meant for even informal pronouncements of augurs (such as those made before a *contio* in 58 about the validity of Caesar's legislation: *Dom.* 40; *Har.* 48; cf. on § 30) to have binding force, as Mehl, 211–12, argues; the reference in our passage to the lex Titia, albeit inaccurate, suggests that Cicero does not envision an expansion of augural power beyond what existed in the past.—For the paired procedures cf. Linderski, 1986, 2165 n. 54: "Cicero both juxtaposes and places on the same legal level the *decretum conlegi* and the *consilium Philippi consulis et auguris.* As Asconius explains (*in Corn.* 68–69 C.), *Philippus consul . . . obtinuit a senatu ut leges eius* [i.e., of Livius Drusus] *omnes uno S.C. tollerentur.* Marcius Philippus advised the senate to nullify the Livian laws, and the college of augurs advised the senate by their decree to annul the lex Titia. It is quite characteristic that in the case of the *leges Liviae* the college of augurs apparently passed no decree; the senate probably did not refer the question to them. It decided to act on the advice of the consul who at the same time was a prominent augur." For Philippus' election to the college by 93 cf. *MRR* 2, 16–17 and n. 9; for his consulate (91), ibid., 20. That Cicero must go so far back for invalidation of a law on grounds of defective auspices foreshadows his point that the art has fallen into desuetude (§ 33).—*Militiae* is R. Stephanus' correction for *familiae* (!); for the polar expression *domi militiae* cf. *OLD* s.v. *militia* 1b; cf. also § 21.2.—For Roman military divination cf. Rüpke, 1990, 244.

32 Two Claudii, both acquaintances of Cicero, were members of the augural college and had written treatises on the discipline. Atticus now constructs them as representatives of opposing tendencies and tries to induce Marcus to commit to one side or the other. Wissowa, *RE* 2.2 (1896), 2315.20 ff., takes this difference of opinion as an indicator that the augurs of Cicero's day were no longer clear about the foundations of their discipline; it might, rather, be viewed as an attempt by Appius to expand the augural practice of his day beyond the narrow uses which had become traditional (cf. *Div.* 2.70 and the note after next).—C. Claudius Marcellus (pr. 80) was a great-great-grandson of the conqueror of Syracuse. Following his praetorship he was allotted Sicily as his province; the *patrocinium* of Sicily being a family tradition, he exerted himself to be a just administrator, for which the Sicilians showed themselves grateful. He was later an assessor of the praetor M'.

Acilius Glabrio, the presiding officer in the trial of Verres, as well as a juror in the trial. Cicero's comparison of Verres' misrule with the moderate conquest of M. Claudius Marcellus (*Ver.* 4.115 ff.) will have been meant not least for his descendant's ears. At *Fam.* 15.8, written in the prior half of September, 51, Cicero addresses him as *collega* with reference to their joint membership of the board of augurs. At *Div.* 2.75 "Marcus" indicates agreement with Marcellus' viewpoint on augury after a detailed recital of the abdication of the consuls of 162 (cf. *ad* § 31), a fact which suggests that this was among the examples cited in his treatise; see further the first note *ad* § 33. The use of the past tense there with reference to Marcellus and Appius (*qui ambo mei collegae fuerunt*) indicates that both had died in the meantime. Cf. Münzer, *RE* s.v. Claudius no. 214.—Appius Claudius Pulcher (*RE* s.v. Claudius no. 297), the eldest brother of Cicero's enemy P. Clodius, is attested as augur as early as 63 (*MRR* 2, 171). The family tie explains why, in 57, he was the only praetor to oppose Cicero's recall from exile. Pompey took pains to reconcile Appius with the orator upon his return.[88] As consul of 54, he was tainted by electoral scandal but nonetheless received Cilicia as his province the following year. He conducted a detailed and in part acrimonious correspondence with his successor in this office, Cicero (*Fam.* 3). Upon his return to Rome he faced prosecution *maiestatis* and *repetundarum* by Cicero's later son-in-law Dolabella. He was, however, with Cicero's support, acquitted and elected censor for 50, in which capacity *inter alia* he expelled C. Ateius from the senate for falsification of auspices prior to the battle of Carrhae (cf. *Div.* 1.29–30). Initiation in the mysteries may have led him to vow as consul the renovation of the small propylaea at Eleusis; he was probably also responsible for work on the sanctuary of Amphiaraus near Oropus. During the civil war, on advice of the Delphic oracle, he withdrew from the Pompeian forces to Euboea but died prior to the battle of Pharsalia. He began a work on augury dedicated to Cicero (*Fam.* 3.4.1) but probably did not complete it (ibid. 3.9.3, and 3.11.4);[89] the sparse fragments are found at Fest. p. 197, 297, and 298M. s.vv. *oscines, sonivium tripu⟨dium⟩*, and *sollistimum*. Keenly interested in various forms of divination, including necromancy (cf. *Tusc.* 1.37; *Div.* 1.132), Appius interpreted the augur's mandate very broadly (*disciplina vestra quasi divinari videatur*

---

88. One of Appius' daughters would later marry Pompey's eldest son, an event that has been variously dated; see most recently W. Jeffrey Tatum, "The Marriage of Pompey's Son to the Daughter of Ap. Claudius Pulcher," *Klio* 73 (1991), 122–29, who argues for 56 against the traditional dating to 54.

89. It is not clear that the dedication was offered "teasingly" (*neckischerweise*), as Gelzer, 337, thinks.

posse; see the note after next). At *Brut.* 267 Cicero mentions that Appius was the addressee's father-in-law and accords him a favorable obituary notice. Cf. Münzer, *RE loc. cit.;* Constans; Oppermann, 248–52.

A. . . . sed est in collegio vestro inter Marcellum et Appium, optimos augures, magna dissensio (nam eorum ego in libros incidi), . . .] Bake *ad loc.* inferred from *Fam.* 3.4.1 (ca. 4 June 51 from Brundisium) that Appius' book on augury came into Cicero's hands only after his departure for Cilicia. But the book is named in that passage among the points which convinced Cicero of Appius' high regard for him *iam antea* and which, in his reply, Appius dismissed as *ex alto repetita* (ibid. 3.5.1). Moreover, the evidence suggests that, despite his claim to the contrary, Appius was seeking to avoid a meeting with Cicero in summer, 51 (Constans, pt. 2, ch. 1); this would hardly have been the case if he had just dedicated a book to him. The first book of the work on augury will have been presented shortly after Cicero's election to the board of augurs (cf. *ad* § 31: *neque vero hoc quia sum ipse augur—*) and before his defense of Milo; cf. Constans, 50 n. 5.

. . . cum alteri placeat auspicia ista ad utilitatem esse reipublicae composita, alteri disciplina vestra quasi divinari videatur posse.] Historical Roman augury was narrower than Greek μαντική since it was not predictive but merely sought to ascertain divine approval or disapproval of a contemplated action; cf. Beard, 1986, 41. That augury should be practiced *reipublicae causa* was the accepted Roman view (cf. *Div.* 2.28, 43, 70, 74, and 75); the question in our passage is whether it should be pushed further (cf. *Div.* 1.105 [Quintus, speaking approvingly of App. Claudius]: *solus enim multorum annorum memoria non decantandi augurii sed divinandi tenuit disciplinam;* at 2.70, however, Marcus denies that the Roman augur has any such scope); Appius may be called a "traditionalist" (as is done by A. Wardman, *Religion and Statecraft among the Romans* [London, 1982], 46–47) but in the sense that he wanted to substitute still more ancient traditions for ones that had in his time been in place for many years.—For *utilitas reipublicae* cf. Dyck *ad Off.*, p. 492.—The usual order of complement-verb has been altered, surely for the sake of the clausula, but which? Cicero perhaps thought of this as equivalent to a double cretic, with the *e* of *videatur* treated as a glide[90] and one of the *s*'s of *posse* failing to make position on the analogy of *s* after short final vowel.[91]

90. Sim. the suspected synizesis of *i* in *pecunias* at 3.7.2 (see *ad loc.* and *ad* 1.62).

91. Cf. W.S. Allen, 36–37; Robin Nisbet, "Cola and Clausulae in Cicero's Speeches," in "*Owls to Athens*": *Essays on Classical Subjects Presented to Sir Kenneth Dover,* ed. E.M. Craik (Oxford, 1990), 359: ". . . when I read 'ipse sceleratus' before a pause (*Pis.* 28), I hear *esse videatur*"; cf. Nisbet *ad Pis.* 70.9; Berry *ad Sul.* 42.3.

M. Egone? divinationem, quam Graeci μαντικήν appellant, esse sentio, et huius hanc ipsam partem quae est in avibus ceterisque signis {quid} disciplinae nostrae.] Marcus affirms the existence of divination (*divinationem . . . esse*) and that this very art (*hanc ipsam*) is part (*partem* [sc. *esse*]) of it which consists in the birds and other signs of "our discipline." He thus replies to the point *disciplina vestra quasi divinari posse*. This response may appear to create a *praeiudicium* in favor of one of Atticus' alternatives, but Cicero will add a distinction of theory and practice at the end of § 33.—For *egone?* cf. *ad* 1.14. Cicero similarly treats *divinatio* and μαντική as equivalent at *N.D.* 1.55 and *Div.* 1.1. *Augurium* appears here as a division of *divinatio* as in Serv. *auct. ad Aen.* 3.359 (Varro did too if Servius has interpreted him correctly): *Varro [ARD app. ad lib. III] autem quattuor genera divinationum dicit: terram, aerem, aquam, ignem: geomantis, aeromantis, pyromantis, hydromantis. Vergilius tria genera complexus est: per lauros geomantis, per sidera pyromantis, per praepetes aeromantis.* Cf. *Var. Cur.* 42.—We follow Cratander's deletion of *quid*, which could, as Madvig, 1887, 2, 149, pointed out, be a dittography of the following *dis-*.

si enim deos esse concedimus, eorumque mente mundum regi, et eosdem hominum consulere generi, et posse nobis signa rerum futurarum ostendere, non video cur esse divinationem negem.] Stoic premises, laid down already at 1.21 and § 15b; cf. *N.D.* 1.6: *sunt autem alii philosophi—et hi quidem magni atque nobiles—qui deorum mente atque ratione omnem mundum administrari et regi censeant, neque vero id solum, sed etiam ab isdem hominum vitae consuli et provideri* . . . The case is argued in detail in *N.D.* 2: 4–44: existence of the gods; 73–153: their government of the world; 154–68: their providential care for human beings (divination figures as an argument for the gods' existence at 2.7 ff and as part of the case for divine providence at 2.162–63). The fact of divine providence was the basis for Chrysippus' argument for μαντική: cf. *SVF* 2, 342.19–343.16, albeit this step is omitted in the simple syllogism at *Div.* 2.41 (= *SVF* 2, 343.19–20): *si di sunt, est divinatio; sunt autem di; est ergo divinatio*; sim. *Div.* 1.9 and 82–83 ("Quintus"; the latter passage with explicit attribution to the Stoics). "Marcus" attacks this argument at *Div.* 2.101–6 on grounds that the premises are neither proven nor universally agreed; cf. Linderski, 1995, 473.

33 Here Cicero buttresses the argument based upon philosophical premises with examples, foreign and domestic,[92] meant, no doubt, to establish a kind of *consensus omnium* in favor of divination; then follows the answer to Atticus' query. Cicero names a series of legendary seers, then a series of

---

92. Cf. *ad* 1.42: *nihilo, credo, magis illa quam interrex noster tulit—*.

peoples in Asia Minor associated with a belief in divination. The testimony of Asian witnesses could, however, be easily impeached in court (cf. *Flac.* 90 ff. with Vasaly, 198 ff.); hence perhaps the emphasis on *vetustas* and the shift to *exempla Romana*,[93] with Romulus and Attus Navius produced as crown witnesses to confirm the marvels attributed to the foreign seers.[94] The result is an answer to Atticus' query mediating between Marcellus and Appius. This position contrasts, of course, with the thoroughgoing skepticism of "Marcus" in *Div.* 2 (cf. esp. 2.75, where he clearly takes sides *pro Marcello, contra Appium*). But the views of a dialogue speaker should not necessarily be identified with those of the author, nor should one expect the same speaker to hold the same position from dialogue to dialogue, each dialogue being autonomous and having a different method and goal; on the problem cf. further Beard, 1986. Leonhardt, 73, contrasts the two dialogues as exhibiting different forms of skepticism, ἐποχή in our work and doubt in *Div.* For Cicero's views on divination see further C.W. Tucker, "Cicero, Augur, *de iure augurali*," *CW* 70 (1976), 171–77.

iam vero permultorum exemplorum et nostra est plena respublica et omnia regna omnesque populi cunctaeque gentes, ⟨ex⟩ augurum praedictis multa incredibiliter vera cecidisse.] Cf. the examples cited at *Div.* 1.25–30.—*Ex* was supplied by an anonymous scholar cited by Creuzer; translate "in accordance with"; cf. *OLD* s.v., 20a.—*Cado* has the sense "turn out" or the like; for such use with an adj. cf. *OLD* s.v., 17b.

neque enim Polyidi—nisi vetustas ea certa esse docuisset; . . .] The six seers Cicero lists break down into three pairs: (1) legendary early seers: the significant name Polyidus (< πολ- + *εῖδω: "the much-knowing");[95] Melampus, from whom he was descended; (2) the founders of famous oracles: Mopsus, founder of Claros, the oracle of Apollo at Colophon, and Amphiaraus, who had an incubation-shrine in Attica near Oropus; (3) Calchas and Helenus, figures from either side of the Trojan War, the former said to have disputed preeminence in prophecy with Mopsus (Str. C 675). The archive at Mari on the Euphrates provides documentation of oracular shrines dating from as early as the eighteenth century; cf. G. Dossin, "Sur le prophétisme à Mari," in *La divination en Mésopotamie ancienne et dans les régions voisines*, XIVe

---

93. Cf. *Rep.* 1.58 (Scipio is the speaker): *** *sed si vis, Laeli, dabo tibi testes nec nimis antiquos, nec ullo modo barbaros.*

94. Contrast *Div.* 2.70, where "Marcus," while accepting that Romulus practiced augury, does not believe in it but concedes that it should continue in use out of regard for the *opinio vulgi* and *utilitates reipublicae;* cf. Linderski, 1995, 473.

95. Cf. *Div.* 1.89: *quid, Polyidum Corinthium nonne Homerus* [sc. *Il.* 13.663 ff.] *et aliis multa et filio ad Troiam proficiscenti mortem praedixisse commemorat?*

Rencontre Assyriologique Internationale (Paris, 1966), 77–86. The belief in oracles, firmly rooted in Asia Minor, may have spread thence to mainland Greece (cf. Dodds, 69–70). Cicero associates it with Anatolia's rough and mountainous parts, incompletely Hellenized. Certainly Phrygia was a center of ecstatic religion well known to the Romans through the importation of the Magna Mater in 204; cf. *ad* § 19.3. Amphilochus, son of Amphiaraus, and Mopsus were said to have founded Mallus in Cilicia;[96] their tombs were pointed out at Megarsus near the Pyramus (Str. C 676), and Mopsuestia took its name from the latter. The Phrygians, Pisidians, and Cilicians reappear, together with the Arabs, as cultivators or possible founders of augury at *Div.* 1.92 and 94 and 2.80.—If this passage had been written after 50, one would have expected a reference to Cicero's term as governor of these peoples, as at *Div.* 1.2: *Cilicum autem et Pisidarum gens et his finitima Pamphylia, quibus nationibus praefuimus ipsi . . .* —As an Academic skeptic, Cicero cannot, of course, accept that there are *certa;* cf. *ad Off.* 2.7–8.

nec vero Romulus noster auspicato urbem condidisset, . . .] For the famous augury cf. Enn. *Ann.* 72–91 Sk. = 77–96 V. = Cic. *Div.* 1.107–8; H.D. Jocelyn, "*Urbs augurio augusto condita,*" *PCPhS* 17 (1971), 44–51; cf. also *ad* § 40.—*Auspicato* is an impersonal passive in an ablative absolute ("upon taking of the auspices" or the like, with the implication that they were favorable); cf. Kühner-Stegmann, 1, 777–78. Cf. *Rep.* 2.5: . . . *urbem auspicato condere . . . ; N.D.* 3.5: . . . *mihique ita persuasi Romulum auspiciis Numam sacris constitutis fundamenta iecisse nostrae civitatis . . . ; Div.* 1.3: *Romulus non solum auspicato urbem condidisse . . . traditur;* ibid. 2.70: . . . *credo Romulum, qui urbem auspicato condidit.*

. . . neque Atti Navi nomen memoria floreret tam diu, nisi omnes hi multa ad veritatem admirabilia dixissent.] With the name of Attus Navius (consisting of a Sabine *praenomen* and an apparently Etruscan *nomen*) was associated a *puteal* on the comitium. It was said to contain a whetstone which the augur had cut with a knife. Its antiquity caused him to be placed under the Tarquins, with Tarquinius Superbus as the taskmaster.[97] He is also said to have opposed the king's plan to alter the names of the three groups of *equites* (*Rep.* 2.36); cf. the renaming of the Dorian tribes by Cleisthenes of Sicyon with addition of one of his own (Hdt. 5.68). Another miracle was added to his legend, that of a bunch of grapes of marvelous size that he found upon repeated augural division of a vineyard and dedicated to the god who enabled him to find a lost pig. Cicero narrates Attus' miracles most

---

96. Cf. *Div.* 1.88: *Amphilochus et Mopsus Argivorum reges fuerunt sed iidem augures, iique urbes in ora maritima Ciliciae Graecas condiderunt.*

97. By apparent lapse of memory Cicero associates him with Tullus Hostilius at *N.D.* 2.9.

fully at *Div.* 1.31–32 (see Pease *ad loc.*); cf. ibid. 2.80; *N.D.* 2.9 and 3.14. Cf. Kroll, *RE* 16.2 (1935), 1933.7 ff.; Ogilvie *ad* Liv. 1.36.2.

sed dubium non est quin haec disciplina et ars augurum evanuerit iam et vetustate et neglegentia.] Cicero complains of the neglect of augury by the nobles of his day at *N.D.* 2.9, cited *ad* § 20.6; cf. Linderski, 1986, 2152 ff. The ancient forms must have seemed increasingly irrelevant as the auspices were regularly overridden by force or falsified; cf. *ad* §§ 14a and 32. Hence the difficulty of the injunction *disciplinam tenento* (§ 20.6).—Anxiety about old institutions slipping away is found in various Ciceronian passages; cf. *Rep.* 5.1: *nostra vero aetas cum rempublicam sicut picturam accepisset egregiam sed iam evanescentem vetustate, non modo eam coloribus eisdem quibus fuerat renovare neglexit, sed ne id quidem curavit ut formam saltem eius et extrema tamquam liniamenta servaret; ad Off.* 3.44. Varro shared this concern for Rome's traditional religion; cf. *ARD* 1.2a: *se timere ne pereant* [sc. *dei*], *non incursu hostili, sed civium neglegentia . . .*

ita neque illi adsentior qui hanc scientiam negat umquam in nostro collegio fuisse, neque illi qui esse etiamnunc putat.] Here finally is Cicero's response to Atticus' query. His historically differentiated approach places him between Marcellus (*qui hanc scientiam negat umquam in nostro collegio fuisse*) and Appius (*qui esse etiamnunc putat*) on the divinatory power of augury; *aliter* Linderski, 1995, 447, who, on the basis of § 21.3, thought that Cicero adopted the view of Appius; but that law does not go beyond current Roman state practice; cf. *ad loc.*

quae mihi videtur apud maiores fuisse duplex, ut ad reipublicae tempus nonnumquam, ad agendi consilium saepissime pertineret.] I.e., both types of augury were found in early Rome, the type pertaining to conditions of the state (*ad reipublicae tempus:* cf. *OLD* s.v. *tempus* 11a), emphasized by Marcellus, and the type that involved forming a plan of action (*ad agendi consilium*), advocated (and acted upon[98]) by Appius. Attus Navius performed auguries of both types: the counsel against renaming the tribes involved a contemplated state measure; the augury that led to the discovery of the wondrously large cluster of grapes, guidance in an action (see above). See further *ad* 3.43.

34 Reddam vero, et id si potero brevi.] *Brevitas* is a stylistic virtue, not only of the laws themselves (cf. *ad* §§ 18 and 23), but also of the commentary (cf. § 44) and in general (cf. 3.40).

sequitur enim de iure belli,—essent lege sanximus.] Cf. *ad* § 21.7 and *ad Off.* 1.34–40.

---

98. For his consultation of the Delphic oracle and its sequel cf. *ad* § 32.

iam de haruspicum religione, de expiationibus et procurationibus satis esse plane in ipsa lege dictum puto.] I.e., as in the case of perjury (cf. § 41), no explanation is needed; see the Index of Topics s.v. "Commentary."—For *iam* marking a transition to the next law cf. § 27 (*Iam ritus familiae patrumque servare* etc.).

A. Adsentior, ⟨et⟩ quoniam omnis hac in religione versatur oratio ⟨tua, quam omnes habemus in manibus, nihil amplius dicendum puto⟩.] With the text as transmitted Atticus' logic is hard to grasp. As Powell points out (*per litt.*), "*hac in religione* would surely have to refer in this context to *haruspicum religio,* and it is absurd to say that the whole discussion has been about that"; nor is it any improvement to read *haec* with the *recentiores.* Powell's solution is that *oratio* refers, not to the current discussion, but to Cicero's speech *de Haruspicum Responso;* hence his clarifying supplement; for Atticus as a reader of Cicero's speeches see *ad* § 2; for *in manibus habere* cf. *ad* 1.36.

M. At vero quod sequitur, quomodo aut tu adsentiare aut ego reprehendam sane quaero, Tite.] For the transition cf. § 30: *Quod sequitur vero non solum ad religionem pertinet . . .* —Marcus senses storm clouds looming over the next stage of conversation, for what follows is the prohibition of women's nocturnal sacrifices (*Nocturna mulierum sacrificia ne sunto, praeter olla quae pro populo rite fient:* § 21.11), which Atticus, as an initiate in the Eleusinian mysteries, is expected to defend. If so, Marcus, himself an initiate, may have difficulty mustering a plausible refutation. In fact, Cicero is preparing a surprise: instead of objecting, Atticus readily assents, and instead of attacking the Eleusinian mysteries Marcus will offer an encomium of them. Partly as a result of this pretended battle, the prohibition of women's nightly festivals and of initiations receives, at thirty-five lines in the edition of Görler-Ziegler, one of the longest commentaries.

35 Quid ergo aget Iacchus Eumolpidaeque nostri et augusta illa mysteria, si quidem sacra nocturna tollimus?] Marcus teases his friend by picking two names prominently associated with the Eleusinian mysteries and wondering about their fate under this law. Iacchus was the god whose image was carried in procession from his temple in Athens to Eleusis on 19 Boedromium; in the festival songs he was called upon as leader of the procession of initiates (Ar. *Ran.* 398 ff.); sometimes identified with Dionysus, he owes his origin to the cry ἴαχος sounded during the procession; cf. Fritz Graf, *Eleusis und die orphische Dichtung Athens in vorhellenistischer Zeit* (Berlin–New York, 1974), 46 ff.; Kevin Clinton, *Myth and Cult: The Iconography of the Eleusinian Mysteries* (Stockholm, 1992), 64–71. The Eumolpidae were the noble family of Eleusis who supplied the hierophants: Graf, *loc. cit.,* 18 and

n. 68.—*Nostri*, the reading of the mss. here, should not be tampered with; it points to the interlocutors' shared connection with the Eleusinian mysteries (see the note after next); Ascensius' conjecture *vestri*, which would highlight, unnecessarily, Atticus' connection with Attica (cf. *ad* 1.2; § 67: *Athenienses tui*), has been accepted (without discussion) by Pease *ad N.D.* 1.119, who finds, accordingly, the inference that Cicero had been initiated "unsafe."—Cicero applies the epithet *augusta* to Eleusis itself at *N.D.* 1.119 (cited *ad* § 36).—The *quidem* is emphatic, and *si quidem* appears, as usual, with the indicative; cf. Solodow, 127–28.

non enim populo Romano, sed omnibus bonis firmisque populis leges damus.] Cicero's position has been that the laws are to be in accord with the *optimus reipublicae status* delineated in *Rep.* (cf. 1.15, § 23); they would thus be eligible for adoption by any people of the kind described, weak peoples being unable either to throw off a monarch or sustain a *respublica;* cf. also 3.4; *Off.* 2.74.

36 A. Excipi⟨e⟩s, credo, illa quibus ipsi initiati sumus.] *Excipi⟨e⟩s* is Powell's correction to match the following *excipiam.*—*Credo* is best translated "presumably," albeit it is used here without irony; cf. *ad* 1.41.—The initiation is generally placed during the residence ca. 79 of Cicero, Quintus, and their cousin Lucius in Athens, a time lovingly recalled at the beginning of *Fin.* 5; see, for example, E.G. Sihler, *Cicero of Arpinum* (New Haven–London–Oxford, 1914), 57; Marinone, 59.

M. Ego vero excipiam.—sed etiam cum spe meliore moriendi.] Marcus makes the exception as readily as Atticus allowed the general law. Similarly, in A.D. 364, as governor of Achaea, Vettius Agorius Praetextatus gained an exception from the prohibition of nocturnal sacrifices issued by Valentinian I so as to allow the mysteries to continue: Zosim. 4.3.2–3; Beard, 1998, 1, 374 and n. 30.—Marcus next launches in on an encomium loosely modelled on Isoc. 4.28–29 of the inventions of Athens in general (tactfully connected with Atticus: *Athenae tuae;* cf. *ad* § 5 and *ad* 1.3) and the Eleusinian mysteries in particular (the topic forms the starting point for praise of Epicurus at Lucr. 6.1 ff.). Part of the encomium would be applicable to any civilizing *ars* or *artes* (cf. *quibus ex agresti immanique vita exculti ad humanitatem et mitigati sumus*); sim. *Inv.* 1.2 ff. (of rhetoric), *Off.* 2.15 (of human cooperation); in Isocrates it refers to Demeter's gift of grain, but it may have had larger significance in the context of the cult; cf. Spaeth, 17: "this transition [*viz.*, from barbarism to civilization] does not have merely a historical or societal significance, but also a personal mimetic meaning. By becoming initiated into the mysteries of the goddess, the individual is tamed and cultivated." There is a play on two meanings of *initia*, both "initiatory rites, mysteries" and "first principles" (= *principia*): cf. *OLD* s.v. *initium* 8 and 7, respectively (Isocrates has his own pun on τελετή/τελευτή: see below). The specific appeal of the mysteries is held in reserve for the end: . . . *neque solum cum laetitia vivendi rationem accepimus, sed etiam cum spe meliore moriendi,* sim. to Isoc.: Δήμητρος . . . δούσης . . . τὴν τελετήν, ἧς οἱ μετασχόντες περί τε τῆς τοῦ βίου τελευτῆς καὶ τοῦ σύμπαντος αἰῶνος ἡδίους τὰς ἐλπίδας ἔχουσιν . . . ;[99] cf. Burkert, 1987, 21–23. Even the skeptic Cotta speaks respectfully of the mysteries at *N.D.* 1.119 (*omitto Eleusinem sanctam illam et augustam, 'ubi initiantur gentes orarum ultimae'* [*trag. inc.* 43]) but adds that they contribute rather to a knowledge of nature than of the gods.

quid autem mihi displiceat in nocturnis, poetae indicant comici; . . .] As at *Fam.* 9.22.1, Cicero cites illustrative matter from comedy (that letter, a *jeu d'esprit,* presents the Stoic argument—which he does not endorse—that there is no obscenity since it resides neither in the matter nor the words). Similar to the disapproval of our passage is the view at *Rep.* 4.20a: *numquam comoediae, nisi consuetudo vitae pateretur, probare sua theatris flagitia potuissent;* contrast *Sex. Rosc.* 47, where he defends the realism of comedy.—Here Cicero alludes to the comic plot in which a young man has impregnated a woman at an all-night festival, with complications upon the birth of the child; cf. Pl. *Aul.* 35–36: *adulescentis illius . . . / qui illam stupravit noctu Cereris vigiliis;* Gel. 2.23.15 (describing the plot of the *Plocium* of Menander and Caecilius): *filia hominis pauperis in pervigilio vitiata est.* Refusal to participate in orgiastic rites or those of Cybele is taken as a mark of a woman's good character at *PT* 152.22–23 and 154.6–8 = Lefkowitz-Fant, 104–5. Plato, however, had planned that procreation by the Guardians should take place at festivals (*Rp.* 459e–460a).

qua licentia Romae data quidnam egisset ille qui in sacrificium cogitatam libidinem intulit, quo ne imprudentiam quidem oculorum adici fas fuit?] A *locus a minore ad maius* citing events of 3 December 62, when, wearing women's clothing, P. Clodius intruded on the rites of the Bona Dea, which were for women only. When the orator's court testimony destroyed his alibi, Clodius transferred to the plebs and, as tribune, procured the orator's exile; cf. Scullard, 199–201; Gelzer, 110–13 and 135 ff.; Mitchell, 1979, 226, and 1991, 125 ff.; Philippe Moreau, *Clodiana religio. Un procès politique en 61 av. J.-C.* (Paris, 1982); Tatum, 1999, ch. 3.[100] On the sense of *bonus* in the name Bona Dea ("beneficent," not "good") cf. J. Marouzeau, "'Iuppiter

---

99. Cf. the reminiscence of Isoc. 3.26 at *Rep.* 1.56; Smethurst, 229 n. 19.

100. This is the standard interpretation; for H. Benner's different view cf. *ad* 3.21 (*quis umquam tam audax—*).

Optimus' et 'Bona Dea'," *Eranos* 54 (1956), 227–31 (esp. 230); for relevant archaeological finds Adolf Greifenhagen, "Bona Dea," *Mitteilungen des Deutschen Archaeologischen Instituts,* Römische Abteilung 52 (1937), 227–44; on the Bona Dea in general cf. Scullard, 116–17; Wiseman, 1974, 130–37; H.H.J. Brouwer, *Bona Dea: The Sources and a Description of the Cult* (Leiden, 1989), esp. 363–70 (the celebration on 3 December 62); Versnel, 228–88, interprets the festival in light of the Greek Thesmophoria. In his first criticism of a Greek institution Cicero implies that the *licentia* of Greek nocturnal festivals gives greater scope for abuse than any Roman counterpart.—For *cogitata libido* cf. Cicero's claim that Clodius would not have left Rome on 18 January 52 unless he were hastening to a *cogitatum facinus* (*Mil.* 45). Cicero is warming for the attack on Clodius at §§ 42–43.—*Imprudentiam oculorum adici* involves replacement of an adjective by an abstract substantive for emphasis (instead of *imprudentes oculos adici*); cf. *Agr.* 2.25: *cum ad omnia vestra pauci homines cupiditatis oculos adiecissent . . . ;* Hofmann-Szantyr, 152. The distinction between *imprudentia* and *libido* probably carries over into § 37; cf. *ad loc.*—For *fas* indicating licit action according to religious law cf. Latte, 1960, 38; on the trend of usage to confine *ius* to secular relations with a concomitant broadening of *fas* in the religious sphere cf. Riccardo Orestano, "Dal *ius* al *fas*," *Bullettino dell'Istituto di Diritto Romano "Vittorio Scialoja"* 46 (1939), 194–273, esp. 271; Behrends, 1970, 24–25.

A. Tu vero istam Romae legem rogato, nobis nostras ne ademeris.] Following upon Marcus' differentiation, Atticus envisions regional variations, even though Marcus has declared that his laws are for all strong and free peoples (*non enim populo Romano, sed omnibus bonis firmisque populis leges damus:* § 35).—For perfect subjunctive in prohibitions cf. *ad* § 19.3.

37 M. . . . quibus [sc. legibus] profecto diligentissime sanciendum est ut mulierum famam multorum oculis lux clara custodiat, initienturque eo ritu Cereri quo Romae initiantur.] Sc. *Graeco ritu;* cf. *ad* § 21.12; our passage is among the testimonies that suggest that the initiations and other cult acts in honor of Ceres were for women only; cf. Spaeth, 105–7.

quo in genere severitatem maiorum senatus vetus auctoritas de Bacchanalibus et consulum exercitu adhibito quaestio animadversio(que) declarat; . . .] Cicero cites the suppression of the Bacchanalia in 186 as an example of the severity of the senate in guarding the chastity of women, which might be endangered at secret rituals performed at night. The tone of Varro *ARD* fr. 93 is sharper: *sic Bacchanalia summa celebrantur insania; . . . a Bacchantibus talia fieri non potuisse nisi mente commota. haec tamen postea displicuerunt senatui saniori et ea iussit auferri.* The phrase *severitas maiorum* suggests that standards had been relaxed in the meantime; cf. Matthias Gelzer, "Die Unterdruckung der Bacchanalien bei Livius," *Kleine Schriften*, ed. H. Strasburger and C. Meier, 3 (Wiesbaden, 1964), 268; the greater acceptability of the cult is also a possible interpretation of the decorative program of the Villa of the Mysteries in Pompeii (dated 60–50); cf. Beard, 1998, 1, 161–64. The main sources are the preserved *S.C. de Bacchanalibus* (*CIL* I² 581) and Livy's narrative (39.8 ff.); detailed analysis of the latter, distorted by late annalistic expansion, at Gelzer, *loc. cit.*, 256–69, who also shows that our passage and Varro probably depend upon an early annalist. The senate treated the matter as a conspiracy *contra rempublicam* and delegated to the consuls a *quaestio extra ordinem* to deal with it (Liv. 39.14.6; cf. 39.16.12; Mommsen, *Staatsr.* 3, 1066–69); the consuls were in a position to use the full weight of their office, including *imperium* (the reference to *consulum exercitus*). Though the suppression was no doubt severe, figures, such as the seven thousand men and women who are said to have joined the conspiracy (Liv. 39.17.6), are suspect; cf. Gelzer, *loc. cit.*, 264. References in Plautus and archaeological evidence for a Bacchic cult-grotto at third-century Volsinii make it clear that the cult was no sudden discovery; cf. Beard, 1998, 1, 93. Livy's account thus seems overdramatized; indeed P.G. Walsh, "Making a Drama Out of a Crisis: Livy on the Bacchanalia," *G & R* 43 (1996), 188–203, argues that it was based on a dramatic treatment of the subject. Of the considerable literature the following are fundamental: Mommsen, *RG* 1, 870, and *Strafr.* 579; Wissowa, 64 and 303, and *RE* 2.2 (1896), 2721.14 ff. (s.v. Bacchanal); Georges Méautis, "Aspects religieux de l' 'affaire' des Bacchanales," *REA* 42 (*Mélanges Radet*) (1940), 476–85; Latte, 1960, 270 ff.; Burkert, 1985, 109; J.-M. Pailler, *Bacchanalia: la répression de 186 av. J.-C. à Rome et en Italie* (Rome, 1988); A.E. Astin, *CAH* 8, 186; Erich Gruen, *Studies in Greek Culture and Roman Policy* (Leiden, 1990), ch. 2, who sees the senate's intervention as designed to increase Rome's authority over the affairs of its Italian allies; Beard, 1998, 1, 91–96 with further literature.—*que* is Cratander's supplement.

atque omnia nocturna (ne nos duriores forte videamur) in media Graecia Diagondas Thebanus lege perpetua sustulit.] Interesting use of a Greek example to bolster a line taken by the senate. Diagondas is not otherwise known; Meurs wanted to restore *Pagondas*, the Boeotarch of 424 responsible for the crushing Athenian defeat at Delium; on him cf. Lenschau, *RE* 18.2 (1942), 2313.12 ff.

novos vero deos et in his colendis nocturnas pervigilationes sic Aristophanes facetissimus poeta veteris comoediae vexat, ut apud eum Sabazius et quidam

alii di peregrini iudicati e civitate eiciantur.] Our passage = test. ii K.-A. under Aristophanes' ῞Ωραι (there is a reference to Sabazius in fr. 578); Kaibel *apud* Kassel-Austin *ad loc.* suggests that Cicero is offering a plot-summary and that the expulsion of the foreign gods will have been the outcome of an ἀγών, part of which is preserved in fr. 581.—Lane Cooper, *An Aristotelian Theory of Comedy* (New York, 1922), 91–92, and Wright (*loc. cit. ad* 1.11 supra), 81–82, discuss Cicero's fondness for Aristophanes. **Publicus autem sacerdos imprudentiam consilio expiatam metu liberet, audaciam in committendis ⟨sacris⟩ religionibus⟨que⟩ foeda⟨ndi⟩s damnet atque impiam iudicet.**] This brief three-line comment on the expiatory rôle of the *publici sacerdotes*[101] contrasts with the thirty-five-line comment on the previous law (cf. *ad* § 34 *fin.*).—Following *liberet* the transmitted text is badly corrupt: *audaciam inet inmittendas religionibus foedas*. Various solutions have been offered. Vahlen proposed *audaciam ⟨ad libid⟩ines inmittendas religionibus foedas,* which is problematic because of the construction of *audacia* with *ad* and the gerundive; one expects *in* plus ablative (cf. *TLL* s.v. *audacia* 1243.74–81).[102] Hence the solution adopted here: *audaciam in committendis ⟨sacris⟩ religionibus⟨que⟩ foeda⟨ndi⟩s* (Powell-Dyck). In any case there is doubtless a reference to Clodius; cf. the mention of his *cogitata libido* (§ 36); *Dom.* 125: *quid te impurius, qui religiones omnes pollueris aut ementiendo aut stuprando? Mil.* 87: *polluerat stupro sanctissimas religiones.*—As Schmidt, 1959, 75, points out, the distinction here is based upon intent (*imprudentia : audacia*), as one expects in the sphere of law or ethics. In traditional Roman religion, however, the concern was with preserving the forms of ritual purity; a reform along such lines seems to date to Q. Mucius Scaevola the Pontifex; see further *ad* § 22.1.

38–39 These chapters take up the next law, regulating the *loedi publici* (§ 22.2), and continue the critique of music evidently begun at *Rep.* 4 (cf. Aristid. Quint. 2.6 [p. 61 W.-I.], cited by Powell among test. to *Rep.* 4.23). Here Cicero shows familiarity with Platonic doctrine on the subject from both the *Republic* and the *Laws* (see below), perhaps also, for the incident of Timotheus, a treatise on music similar to, but not identical with, the extant [Plut.] *Mus.* He thus buttresses his argument both from the philosophical and the historical side (cf. Schmidt, 1959, 76), though he leaves the last point of the law, *eamque* [sc. *popularem laetitiam*] *cum divum honore iungunto,* without commentary.

---

101. For the *iunctura* cf. *ad* § 20.4.

102. Similarly, Ziegler proposed *audaciam ⟨libid⟩ines inmittendi religionibus foedas,* but the construction of *audacia* plus genitive of the gerund seems not to be attested in Cicero: cf. *TLL* s.v. *audacia* 1243.71–74.

38 Iam ludi publici quoniam sunt cavea circoque divisi, sint corporum certationes cursu et pugillatu et luctatione, curriculisque equorum usque ad certam victoriam circo constitutis, cavea cantu vigeat ⟨ac⟩ fidibus et tibiis, . . .] For the interpretation cf. *ad* § 22.2.—The reading of ABH is *pugilla ueluctatione*, corrected in AB to *pugillatione luctatione*, in H to *pugilla uel luctatione;* the archetype will have had *pugillatione uel lucta* with the ending of the latter to be supplied; cf. Zelzer, 2001, 209–10; *pugillatio* being unattested in this sense, Vahlen's *pugillatu et luctatione* is to be adopted, thus restoring running, boxing, and wrestling, which were already among the funeral games celebrated in honor of Patroclus in *Il.* 23; they are given as the basic forms of athletic competition at Ar. *Rh.* 1361b23–25; cf. D.H. 7.73.3.—*Ad certam victoriam* = "until victory declares itself" (Reid).—The second verb is variously transmitted as *vice ad* (B¹Lε), *vice ac* (BˣAˣP), *viceat* (H¹), or *vigeat* (Hª), which, as the closest reading to the *ductus litterarum* that yields sense, has been adopted by Hoffmann (without knowing it to be a ms. reading), Vahlen, and Görler (*gaudeat* was conjectured by H.A. Koch to provide a correlate to the *popularem laetitiam* of § 22.2). Büchner, probably rightly, follows this with *ac*[103] so as to yield a demarcation of terms similar to that in § 22.2 (*cantu et fidibus et tibiis*).

adsentior enim Platoni, nihil tam facile in animos teneros atque molles influere quam varios canendi sonos, quorum dici vix potest quanta sit vis in utramque partem; . . .] Pl. *Lg.* 653d: φησὶν δὲ [sc. a widespread theory] τὸ νέον ἅπαν ὡς ἔπος εἰπεῖν τοῖς τε σώμασι καὶ ταῖς φωναῖς ἡσυχίαν ἄγειν οὐ δύνασθαι, κινεῖσθαι δὲ ἀεὶ ζητεῖν καὶ φθέγγεσθαι . . . ; for the response to music among humans from an early age cf. also Diog. Bab. *SVF* 3, 222.14–17.—The penultimate close *in animos teneros atque molles* is rhythmic and emphatic, whereas *influere* is unrhythmic; cf. Hutchinson, 1995, 492.—*In utramque partem* is here used in the pregnant sense "for good or ill"; cf. *OLD* s.v. *uterque* 1d.

namque et incitat languentes et languefacit excitatos, et tum remittit animos tum contrahit.] The effects are arranged chiastically (*a-b-b-a*); the *a-b* pattern recurs alone at 3.23 (of the *vis populi*): *at aliquando incenditur: et quidem saepe sedatur.*—For Plato the rousing modes (*incitare, contrahere*), suitable for military action, are the Dorian and Phrygian, whereas the Ionian and certain Lydian modes relax the mind (*languefacere, remittere*); cf. *Rp.* 398e ff.; [Plut.] *Mus.* 1136c ff. Here Plato probably follows the musical theorist Damon of Athens (cf. *Rp.* 400b–c), an associate of Pericles, Prodicus, and Socrates, who was active as early as the 440s; his essay connecting

---

103. This can easily have fallen out after *-at;* see also the reading of BˣAˣP.

the musical modes with morals took the form of an address to the Areopagus Council and urged careful regulation of musical education; frs. at no. 37 D.-K.; cf. Andrew Barker, *Greek Musical Writings*, 1 (Cambridge, 1984), 168–69; Robert W. Wallace, "Damone di Oa ed i suoi successori: un' annalisi delle fonti," in *Harmonia Mundi. Musica e filosofia nell' antichità*, ed. R.W. Wallace and B. MacLachlan (Rome, 1991), 30–53, esp. 45–46; M.L. West, *Ancient Greek Music* (Oxford, 1992), 246 ff.

civitatumque hoc multarum in Graecia interfuit antiquum vocum conservari modum; . . .] *Conservari* is Bake's correction for *conservare* (B^{X}A^{b}P) or *conserva* (B^{1}A^{1}εHL); for confusion of active and passive infinitive endings cf. *ad* § 27.

quarum mores lapsi ad mollitias pariter sunt immutati cum cantibus, . . .] For the Roman view of effeminacy (*mollitia*) cf. Catharine Edwards, *The Politics of Immorality in Ancient Rome* (Cambridge, 1993), ch. 2; Maud W. Gleason, *Making Men: Sophists and Self-Presentation in Ancient Rome* (Princeton, 1995), 62 ff.; Craig A. Williams, *Roman Homosexuality: Ideologies of Masculinity in Classical Antiquity* (Oxford, 1999), General Index s.v. *mollitia*. Greek moralists made similar use of the term μαλακός/-ία; Plato speaks of harmonies as μαλακαί (*Rp.* 398e9 and 411a7–8) and connects them with the corresponding human type; cf. also *ad* § 39 *fin*. For Cicero's response to a charge of personal μαλακία (= *mollitia*) cf. Plut. *Cic.* 7.8.

. . . aut hac dulcedine corruptelaque depravati, ut quidam putant,—etiam huic mutationi locus.] The issue is whether the change of musical style is the cause or effect of the change in morals. *Ut quidam putant* refers to Plato, cited in the note after next.

39 quamobrem ille quidem sapientissimus Graeciae vir longeque doctissimus valde hanc labem veretur; . . .] This encomium of Plato (cf. *ad* § 14) is a prelude to a subtler position of his own; see the note after next. The characterization *sapientissimus Graeciae vir* clearly puts Plato ahead of Thales, *sapientissimus in septem* (cf. § 26); *ille sapientissimus vir* used of Ulysses at § 3 may be elative.—One might have expected *Graecorum* rather than *Graeciae*, but the Romans were accustomed to use the collective as an administrative entity[104] and hence generally; cf. *Off.* 2.60: . . . *Periclem, principem Graeciae, vituperat . . .*

negat enim mutari posse musicas leges sine mutatione legum publicarum; . . .] *Rp.* 424c: εἶδος γὰρ καινὸν μουσικῆς μεταβάλλειν εὐλαβητέον

---

104. Cf., e.g., Enn. *Ann.* 324 Sk. = 329 V. (of the allocation of provinces for 200): *Graecia Sulpicio sorti data, Gallia Cottae.*

ὡς ἐν ὅλῳ κινδυνεύοντα· οὐδαμοῦ γὰρ κινοῦνται μουσικῆς τρόποι ἄνευ πολιτικῶν νόμων τῶν μεγίστων, ὥς φησί τε Δάμων καὶ ἐγὼ πείθομαι. He argues the case in detail at *Lg.* 700a–701d (of which 701b5 ff. is cited, somewhat inaccurately, at 3.5; see *ad loc.*). In Cicero Plato's μουσικῆς τρόποι harden into *musicae leges* (cf. *ad* § 10 à propos *Tusc.* 1.101).

ego autem nec tam valde id timendum nec plane contemnendum puto.] Cicero had seen changes of musical style without fundamental changes in the Roman constitution and thus has reason to find Plato's worries on this score excessive, but he is concerned about such changes (see the next note and Wille, 435–36).

illud quidem ⟨video⟩: quae solebant quondam compleri severitate iucunda Livianis et Naevianis modis, nunc ut eadem exsulte⟨n⟩t ⟨et⟩ cervices oculosque pariter cum modorum flexionibus torqueant.] After *quidem* Vahlen inserted *video*, Ziegler *videmus;* the former deserves preference since it avoids a rather abrupt shift to plural; cf. *N.D.* 1.75: *illud video pugnare te* . . . For *video* followed by *ut* cf. *Sex. Rosc.* 66: *videtisne . . . ut eos agitent Furiae;* ibid. 135: *videtis . . . ut omnes despiciat;* Powell *ad Sen.* 26. We adopt Halm's *et,* which can easily have dropped out after *exsultent,* which the *recentiores* have changed from *exsultet* to agree with *torqueant* (Ziegler keeps *exsultet,* changes *solebant* to singular, and inserts *cavea* and a lacuna after *exsultet*).—The *iunctura cervices torquere* is not found elsewhere in Cicero or indeed, according to PHI 5.3, in classical Latin; the zeugma with *oculos torquere* is striking. Görler thought the text unsound and daggered *illud quidem—cervices.* But surely, though bold, the text as emended can stand. For *oculos torquere* cf. *Luc.* 80: *itaque Timagoras Epicureus negat sibi umquam cum oculum torsisset duas ex lucerna flammulas esse visas.* Rolling the eyes, also expressed by *oculos volvere,* is often a symptom of dementia; cf. *Aen.* 4.642–43: *effera Dido / sanguineam volvens aciem,* with Serv. *ad loc.*: *sanguineam aciem: more suo ostendit eam furentem vultu, gestu, voce;* similarly, the crazed Amata at *Aen.* 7.399: *sanguineam torquens aciem.* Twisting the neck (and thus turning the head) is a sign of antipathy; cf. Karl Sittl, *Die Gebärden der Griechen und Römer* (Leipzig, 1890), 82 and 84; Andrea de Jorio, *Gesture in Naples and Gesture in Classical Antiquity,* tr. Adam Kendon (Bloomington-Indianapolis, 2000), 291–92 and 309.—What is the source of Cicero's characterization of the "Livian and Naevian modes"? The whole context, with its distinction of entertainments of the circus and the *cavea,* seems to point to music accompanying performances of tragedy. At *Brut.* 71, however, Cicero says *Livianae fabulae non satis dignae quae iterum legantur,* whereby *legantur* may point to Livius' no

360 A Commentary on Cicero, *De Legibus*

longer being part of the repertory. On that basis it is usually assumed that the reference to a performance of *Equus Troianus* in connection with the opening of Pompey's theatre in September 55 (*Fam.* 7.1.2), must be to the Naevian, rather than the Livian play of that title. Goldberg observes: "The formula found in the Terentian *didascaliae, modos fecit Flaccus Claudi tibiis duabus dextris* and the like, implies that a play's musical settings were the responsibility of the *tibicen,* not the dramatist. The music was therefore unlikely to be preserved with the text." It is conceivable that, given the conservatism of religious ritual,[105] cult-hymns such as that composed by Livius in 207 (cf. Liv. 27.37.7 and 31.12.10; Fest. p. 333M) were still used on occasion; the impression thus formed, projected to the theater, might be the basis for Cicero's characterization (*severitas iucunda*).

graviter olim ista vindicabat vetus illa Graecia,—quos plures quam septem haberet, in Timothei fidibus in⟨ci⟩di.] At *Pers.* 219 ff. Timotheus refers to his dispute with the Spartans, situates himself as successor to Orpheus and Terpander, and praises his own innovations (241–43: νῦν δὲ Τιμόθεος μέτροις / ῥυθμοῖς τε ἑνδεκακρουμάτοις / κίθαριν ἐξανατέλλει); cf. also Su. τ 620: . . . τὴν ι′καὶ ια′χορδὴν προσέθηκε καὶ τὴν ἀρχαίαν μουσικὴν ἐπὶ τὸ μαλακώτερον μετήγαγε. The incident is also recounted at Plut. *Inst. Lac.* 238c–d, D.Chr. 33.57, and Paus. 3.12.10. This was, however, a "floating anecdote" and also attached itself to Phrynis (Plut. *Apoph. Lac.* 220c, where see Babbitt's note) and to an anonymous musician performing at Argos ([Plut.] *Mus.* 1144f). Though Plut. *Inst. Lac. loc. cit.* says an ephor was responsible, Cicero prefers to personify *illa severa Lacedaemo;* his admiration for Sparta is on display esp. in *Rep.;* cf. Elizabeth Rawson, *The Spartan Tradition in European Thought* (Oxford, 1969), 102–4. For his general lack of sympathy for lyric poets cf. his remark (*apud* Sen. *Ep.* 49.5) that even a double lifetime would not provide sufficient leisure for reading them.—For *Graecia* (personified) see *supra* on *sapientissimus Graeciae vir.*—*Incidi* is Paulus Manutius' correction.

40 Deinceps in lege est ut de ritibus patriis colantur optima.] For use of *deinceps* in Cicero's commentary as a transitional formula to the next law see 3.27: *Deinceps igitur omnibus magistratibus*—; the reference is to § 22.3.

de quo cum{que} consulerent Athenienses Apollinem Pythium, quas potissimum religiones tenerent, oraculum editum est: 'eas quae essent in more maiorum'.] *-que* was already deleted by A^x and P.—Cf. X. *Mem.* 4.3.16:

---

105. D.H. 7.72.5 remarks on the use of an old-fashioned *aulos* in the procession of the *ludi Romani*.

ὁρᾷς γὰρ ὅτι ὁ ἐν Δελφοῖς θεός, ὅταν τις αὐτόν ἐπερωτᾷ πῶς ἂν τοῖς θεοῖς χαρίζοιτο, ἀποκρίνεται· Νόμῳ πόλεως; sim. 1.3.1: ἥ τε γὰρ Πυθία νόμῳ πόλεως ἀναιρεῖ ποιοῦντας εὐσεβῶς ἂν ποιεῖν . . . ; Xenophon gives no indication that the query was put by Athenians; Cicero may have inferred this from the sequel of the latter passage: . . . Σωκράτης τε οὕτω καὶ αὐτὸς ἐποίει καὶ τοῖς ἄλλοις παρῄνει . . . ; sim. Zaleuc. ap. Stob. 4, 126.1–2 W.-H. (following a corrupt sentence[106]): πάτρια δὲ εἶναι τὰ κάλλιστα. It is interesting that, though νόμος can be either "custom" or "law," Cicero unhesitatingly renders νόμος πόλεως as *mos maiorum* even though the sen ate had from time to time legislated on the subject by admitting the cult of the Magna Mater (cf. *ad* § 19.3), forbidding that of Dionysus (cf. *ad* § 37), etc. As Bendlin, 1998, 241, notes, "the *mos maiorum* was . . . an extremely flexible category which did not necessarily entail the definition of a binding core of religious behaviour"; hence the following attempt at clarification.

quo cum iterum venissent maiorumque morem dixissent saepe esse mutatum, quaesissentque quem morem potissimum sequerentur e variis, respondit 'optimum'.] This sequel is not found in the extant Greek sources but supplies the Pythia with a characteristically ambiguous answer. The idea of frequent changes is at odds, however, with Cicero's usual concept of the *mos maiorum* as the set of traditions that his own time must strive to preserve en bloc (see Roloff, 128 ff.); hence *lex civitatis* might have been a better translation of νόμος πόλεως; see the previous note. As a guide to decision-making, the response is not very helpful (cf. Schmidt, 1959, 76); hence Cicero elaborates in the sequel.

et profecto ita est ut id habendum sit antiquissimum et deo proximum quod sit optimum.] This is Cicero's gloss on the anecdote, whereby *antiquissimum* is equivalent to *optimum*. This interpretation suggests that the solution may be found through antiquarian research. For antiquity as closest to god cf. *ad* § 27 *supra;* a similar view without the theology at Posid. F 284 E.-K. = 448 Th. = Sen. *Ep.* 90.5: *illo ergo saeculo quod aureum perhibent penes sapientes fuisse regnum Posidonius iudicat.* This view may help account for Cicero's tendency to project major features of later Rome, including the senate, to the earliest stages of the kingship; cf. Zetzel *ad Rep.* 2.15; Liv. 1.8.7. In this way, however, he nullifies to a degree the "developmental" scheme of *Rep.* and obscures why he denied that period the character of a mixed constitution and thus status as the ideal (cf. *Rep.* 1.69). On the other hand, Cicero's attribution to Romulus of the augural college will have

---

106. I would expect (after Meineke): πάντας δὲ τιμᾶν τοὺς κατοικοῦντας τὴν πόλιν καὶ τοῖς ἄλλοις νομίμοις πατρίοις ⟨πεπεισμένους⟩ τοὺς θεούς.

served to enhance the plausibility of the rôle of augury in the founding of the city as well as the general prestige of the augurate, which once stood so high; cf. Wissowa, *RE* 2.2 (1896), 2316.43–53 and 2321.13 ff.

Stipem sustulimus, nisi eam quam ad paucos dies propriam Idaeae Matris excepimus; implet enim superstitione animos et exhaurit domos.] For introduction of a law in asyndeton cf. *ad* § 24 (*Caste iubet lex adire ad deos*—); for the content cf. *ad* § 22.4. In his ethics Cicero regularly takes account of such practical considerations (*exhaurit domos*); cf. *ad Off.* 1.44 and 59 and 2.55. At Serv. *Aen.* 6.611 the citation of our passage is evidently either meant as a paraphrase or from memory: *Cicero ait in libris legum 'stipem prohibeo: nam auget superstitionem et exhaurit domos'*.

Sacrilego poena est, neque ei soli qui sacrum abstulerit, sed etiam ei qui sacro commendatum, . . .] For the asyndetic transition to the next law see the previous note.—The emendation *sacro* (P) for *sacrum* follows inevitably from the wording of the law (§ 22.5: *Sacrum sacrove commendatum qui clepsit . . .*); see *ad loc.*

41 . . . quod etiam nunc multis fit in fanis. Alexander in Cilicia deposuisse apud Solenses in delubro pecuniam dicitur, . . .] For the *exemplum* introduced in asyndeton cf. *ad Off.* 1.36 (though Madvig inserted *et* prior to *Alexander*); Powell *ad Sen.* 21.—This fact is not elsewhere attested. Possibly the reference is to the fine of two hundred silver talents levied on Soli for supporting the Persians (Arr. 2.5.5; Curt. 3.7.2); but E.I. McQueen *apud* Rudd-Powell, 212, doubts that Alexander, at this time acutely short of money, would have left a large sum on deposit in a temple.—Might this allusion, as well as § 33, point to reading Cicero undertook in preparation for his term as proconsul of Cilicia (cf. *MRR* 2, 243)? He knew of the appointment by February or March 51 (cf. Shackleton Bailey *ad Fam.* 65 [= 3.2]) and left Rome by 1 May (cf. Gelzer, 225). This connection would also account for his thinking of his predecessor in office, Appius Claudius (§ 32), with whom he was corresponding at this time (*Fam.* 3.2).

. . . et Atheniensis Clisthenes Iunoni Samiae, civis egregius, cum rebus timeret suis, filiarum dotes credidisse.] The epithet *Atheniensis* distinguishes him from his maternal grandfather of the same name, the tyrant of Sicyon; for the order epithet-proper name cf. 1.15 with note. On his father's side he was a member of the aristocratic clan of the Alcmeonidae; the sum for the dowry will thus have been substantial. The disposition of it, or indeed the fact that he had daughters, is not elsewhere attested; nor has any son of his been identified with certainty; cf. J.K. Davies, *Athenian Propertied Families* (Oxford, 1971), 375–76. The reference is presumably to the year of the archonship of Isagoras (508/7), when Cleisthenes fled Athens before Cleomenes and the Spartan army; cf. Busolt, 2, 402–5, with sources cited.—The temple of Hera at Samos contained many distinguished dedications and suffered depradations accordingly (cf. v. Geisau, *RE* 1A2 [1920], 2197.20 ff.), including those of Verres (*Ver.* 1.50, 52, 61; 4.71; 5.184).

Iam de periuriis, de incesto nihil sane hoc quidem loco disputandum est.] These topics may have been reserved for treatment in the context of *iudicia* in Book 4, possibly with further reference to Clodius' trial of 61; cf. Schmidt, 1959, 77.—*Sane* sometimes adheres to *nihil* as to other negatives (cf. *OLD* s.v. *sane*, 1); it apologizes for a categorical assertion without diminishing its force (= "actually").

donis impii ne placare audeant deos, Platonem audiant, qui vetat dubitare qua sit mente futurus deus, cum vir nemo bonus ab improbo se donari velit.] Once again a law is introduced in asyndeton (cf. *ad* § 24).—Cf. *Lg.* 716e: ἀκάθαρτος γὰρ τὴν ψυχὴν ὅ γε κακός, καθαρὸς δὲ ὁ ἐναντίος, παρὰ δὲ μιαροῦ δῶρα οὔτε ἄνδρ' ἀγαθὸν οὔτε θεὸν ἔστιν ποτὲ τό γε ὀρθὸν δέχεσθαι; sim. 905d; likewise, Plato's prohibition of private shrines is to prevent the impious from seeking to gain secret favor (ibid. 910a–b); cf. Zaleuc. *apud* Stob. vol. 4, p. 124.7 W.-H. (= *PT* p. 226.30): ὡς οὐ τιμᾶται θεὸς ὑπ' ἀνθρώπου φαύλου οὐδὲ θεραπεύεται δαπάναις οὐδὲ τραγῳδίαις τῶν ἀναλισκομένων καθάπερ μοχθηρὸς ἄνθρωπος ...—Schmidt, 1959, 77, sees in our law an intrusion of ethical distinctions, but the terms *pius/impius* do not imply that; the reference to the *bonus* and *improbus* is merely an *a minore ad maius* argument to establish the attitude of the deity.—At *Off.* 2.69 Cicero gives a sample of reactions to supposedly unworthy benefactors.

⟨de⟩ diligentia votorum satis in lege dictum; est autem votum sponsio qua obligamur deo.] Another asyndetic transition.—The reference is to the provision *Caute vota reddunto* (§ 22.9), with *diligentia* of the lemma corresponding to *caute* in the law.—The text is Powell's restoration of the transmitted *diligentiam votorum satis in lege dictum est ac votis sponsio qua obligamur deo*. One wonders, however, whether the explanation of *votum* may not be a gloss that has crept into the text.

Poena vero violatae religionis iustam recusationem non habet.] He thus begins discussion of the law *Poena violati iuris ⟨divini divina⟩ esto*: § 22.10 (for the text see *ad loc.*) by asserting its justice. This commentary will achieve surprising length (forty-four lines in the edition of Görler-Ziegler) because it includes a digression on Clodius' career, including his seizure of Cicero's property on the Palatine and use of a part of it as a site for a temple of Libertas, as well as his death.

quid ego hic sceleratorum utar exemplis, quorum plenae tragoediae? quae

ante oculos sunt, ea potius attingam, . . .] The supposition of Sprey, 107 n. 1, that a lacuna should be posited before *quid ego* to accommodate a discussion of human punishment is sufficiently refuted by Schmidt, 1959, 78 n. 2.—Juv. 15.30–32 also aligns a contemporary event with tragedy, but by making the former (an act of cannibalism) far worse: *nam scelus, a Pyrrha quamquam omnia syrmata volvas, / nullus apud tragicos populus facit. accipe nostro / dira quod exemplum feritas produxerit aevo.*—The phrase *quae ante oculos sunt* (on which cf. *ad* 1.48) certainly suggests that his own exile and the attendant circumstances are fresh and fits much better with the late 50s than with 46 as the dramatic date. Cf. Introduction § 5.

. . . etsi haec commemoratio vereor ne supra hominis fortunam esse videatur; tamen, quoniam sermo mihi est apud vos, nihil reticebo, . . .] The topic raises delicate questions of the literary πρέπον, i.e., of the appropriateness of matter to speaker (cf. *ad Off.* 1.97–98), judgment of the fulfillment of human vows being the gods' prerogative, hence *supra hominis fortunam.* Cicero invokes the audience as an extenuating circumstance, as he does at *Off.* 1.78: *licet enim mihi, Marce fili, apud te gloriari . . .*

. . . volamque hoc quod loquar dis immortalibus gratum potius videri quam grave hominibus.] The *iunctura deo/dis gratum* apparently does not recur until Itala Phil. 4.18: *sacrificium gratum deo;*[107] cf., however, *Man.* 47 (of his way of speaking of Pompey's *felicitas*): *. . . ne aut invisa dis immortalibus oratio nostra aut ingrata esse videatur.* Ordinarily, of course, it was the human reaction that was of concern to the orator; cf., e.g., *Sex. Rosc.* 142: *. . . optimo et nobilissimo cuique meam orationem gratissimam esse oportet.* The language here (in an attractive chiastic arrangement of nouns and adjectives) underlines the earnestness of Cicero's view of Clodius' acts; cf. Dyck, 1998, 221.—Taking *grave* in the sense ἐπαχθές [sc. because of the self-praise], Vahlen deleted *hominibus;* but surely Cicero's point is that the following is calculated more for a divine than for an ordinary human audience; the latter may judge the sequel as *grave* (= "having weight or authority": *OLD* s.v. *gravis* 13b) or not, as they wish; the important point is that it is *dis immortalibus gratum.*

42 Cum perditorum civium scelere, discessu meo, religionum iura polluta sunt, . . .] The chiastic arrangement of nouns and modifiers continues, setting the two background factors in opposition, albeit an unbalanced one, with *perditorum civium scelere* overpowering *discessu meo* in number of syllables, just as Clodius and followers were too strong for Cicero to resist.

---

107. Based on a search of PHI 5.3.

For *perditi,* often used by Cicero of enemies of the state, cf. *TLL* s.v. *perdo* 1275.70 ff. His departure took place during the first third of March, 58; cf. Gelzer, 139 and n. 60. For the *iunctura discessu meo* cf. *Pis.* 21: *itaque discessu tum meo omnes illi nefarii gladii de manibus crudelissimis exciderunt* . . . ; for *religionum iura* cf. *Dom.* 127: . . . *disce ab homine religionibus dedito* [sc. *Clodio*] *ius totum omnium religionum; Sest.* 56: *mitto eam legem quae omnia iura religionum* . . . *delevit.*

. . . **vexati nostri Lares familiares, . . .**] This explains what Cicero meant by the pollution of religious rights (he was careful to affirm the sanctity of the *Larum sedes* in § 19.5; see *ad loc.*); but see *ad* § 58. In fact, Cicero's house on the Palatine was plundered and burned on the day following his departure, the same day on which was passed Clodius' law banning anyone who had put a citizen to death without a trial; cf. *Sest.* 53–54.—*Lar familiaris* becomes a synonym for "home" (cf. *OLD* s.v. *Lar* 2a), but, as our passage shows, the religious connotations are still alive (see also the next note).

. . . **in eorum sedibus exaedificatum templum Licentiae, . . .**] Cicero had formidable resources, especially the backing of the *equites* (cf. *ad* § 25). That Clodius nonetheless proceeded, in spite of assurances previously given, to attack the consular can be explained either by personal enmity (cf. *ad* § 36), Clodius' own ambition, or (best) some combination of the two; cf. Tatum, 1999, 151–52. He had moreover detected that the orator was vulnerable because of popular unhappiness over the execution of the Catilinarian conspirators; hence Clodius' first law touching Cicero, the lex Clodia *de capite civis Romani* was framed so as to banish from Rome anyone who had put a Roman citizen to death without a trial.[108] Then followed the *lex de exilio Ciceronis* apparently providing for the construction, on a portion of Cicero's property on the Palatine, of an *aedes Libertatis;* this was meant to symbolize the reassertion of the lex Sempronia *de capite civis Romani* violated by Cicero in the Catilinarian matter; cf. Philippe Moreau, "La lex clodia sur le bannissement de Cicéron," *Athenaeum* 75 (1987), 465–92; *ad* 3.26; the clear implication was that Cicero had acted tyrannically. On the whole incident and on liberty and tyranny as slogans in Rome at this period cf. W. Allen and (on *libertas*) Bleicken, 1972, 34 ff., and Vanderbroeck, 105–7; cf. also Tatum, 1999, 156–58 (on the measure); on Clodius' building program cf. ibid., 159–66, and Beverly Berg, "Cicero's Palatine Home and Clodius' Shrine of Liberty: Alternative Emblems of the Republic in Cicero's *De domo*

---

108. Vell. 2.45.1; Liv. *per.* 103; Dio 38.14.4; Cicero was not the only citizen who, at least potentially, fell within the scope of the law; cf. Tatum, 1999, 153–54.

sua," in *Studies in Latin Literature and Roman History,* ed. C. Deroux, 8 (Brussels, 1997), 122–43; on the *aedes Libertatis* as a master stroke of political propaganda cf. H. Benner, 54–55.—Sim. with pathetic embellishment *Dom.* 108–9: *ista tua pulchra Libertas deos penates et familiares meos Lares expulit, ut se ipsa tamquam in captivis sedibus conlocaret? quid est sanctius, quid omni religione munitius quam domus unius cuiusque civium? hic arae sunt, hic foci, hic di penates, hic sacra, religiones, caerimoniae continentur* . . . In our passage Cicero uses what later rhetoric called a *color* (cf. Lausberg §§ 329 and 1061). This denigration of the dedication is foreshadowed at *Dom.* 112 (especially with Markland's supplement): . . . *signum de busto meretricis ablatum isti* [sc. *Clodio*] *dedit* [sc. his brother App. Claudius], *quod esset signum magis istorum* ⟨*licentiae*⟩ [suppl. Markland; cf. § 131] *quam publicae libertatis.* Similarly, the voting law proposed by L. Cassius, viewed by the *populus* as a question of *libertas,* was feared by the *principes* as *licentia* (*Sest.* 103; see further *ad* 3.35).

. . . **pulsus a delubris is qui illa servarat, . . .**] Cicero's position has already been described at the beginning of the sentence (*discessu meo*) but is restated in stronger form here to cap the series of outrages.

circumspicite celeriter animo—et iustis exsequiarum caruerunt.] For the structural similarity to Lact. *mort.* 1.5 cf. Eberhard Heck, ΜΗ ΘΕΟΜΑΧΕΙΝ *oder: Die Bestrafung des Gottesverächters,* Studien zur klassischen Philologie, 24 (Frankfurt a.M., 1987), 222–23.

. . . **(nihil enim attinet quemquam nominari) . . .**] The technique of criticism *tacito nomine* is used to good effect here and elsewhere by Cicero when his target cannot be mistaken: cf. the critique of Crassus at *Parad.* 6; *ad Off.* 3.41 and 82b–85; Adams, 1978, 163–64.

nos qui illam custodem urbis, omnibus ereptis nostris rebus ac perditis, violari ab impiis passi non sumus, eamque ex nostra domo in ipsius patris domum detulimus, . . .] "Cicero was not the man to be outdone in a contest of phrases and symbols" (W. Allen, 8); hence both here and in *Dom.* he sets his own patron goddess in opposition to Clodius' Libertas. As tutelary goddess of Rome, corresponding to Athena Polias at Athens, Minerva received, jointly with Jupiter and Juno, the dedication of the temple on the Capitoline that was the center of Roman cult (cf. Wissowa, 41 and 254). In his invocation of the three dedicatees of that temple at *Dom.* 144, Cicero represents her both as tutelary goddess of the city (*custos urbis*), as in our passage,[109] and as his

---

109. This corresponds to the Greek epithet πολιοῦχος, though Plut. *Cic.* 31.6 and Dio 38.17.5 give a literal backtranslation of the Latin ('Ρώμης φύλαξ and φυλακίς, respectively). For the relevant archaeological evidence cf. Henner von Hesberg, "Minerva Custos Urbis—

own special patroness: . . . *et tu, custos urbis, Minerva, quae semper adiutrix consiliorum meorum, testis laborum exstitisti* . . . [110] Plut. *Cic.* 31.6 narrates the dedication of the statue just prior to Cicero's departure from the city: . . . τὸ μὲν ἄγαλμα τῆς Ἀθηνᾶς, ὃ πολὺν χρόνον ἔχων ἐπὶ τῆς οἰκίας ἱδρυμένον ἐτίμα διαφερόντως, εἰς Καπιτώλιον κομίσας ἀνέθηκεν, ἐπιγράψας "Ἀθηνᾷ Ῥώμης φύλακι" . . . ; sim. Dio 45.17.2–3. Clodius sneered at this solicitude; cf. *Dom.* 92: . . . *me dicere solere esse me Iovem, eundemque dictitare Minervam esse sororem meam.* After his return from exile Cicero seems to have sought to purchase a replacement from the collection (or agents) of App. Claudius Pulcher (on whom cf. *ad* § 32; cf. *Fam.* 3.1.1). The original statue, damaged in a storm in March 43, was to be restored according to a decree of the senate (*Fam.* 12.25.1); this incident was later interpreted as an omen of Cicero's death (Dio *loc. cit.*).—The placement of the ablative absolute (*omnibus ereptis nostris rebus ac perditis*) keeps *illam custodem urbis* separate from the designs of Clodius (*violari ab impiis*) in the economy of this sentence, as Cicero did in life, with his own intervention reserved for emphasis to the end of the clause (*passi non sumus*). Du Mesnil notes (*ad loc.*), that *omnibus ereptis nostris rebus atque perditis* was not yet true at the time of the dedication; this highlights the absence from classical Latin of a future passive participle, in which function the gerundive appears only in late Latin; cf. Hofmann-Szantyr, 139.

. . . iudicia senatus, Italiae, gentium denique omnium conservatae patriae consecuti sumus; . . .] Cicero's account of his misfortune and triumph skips over the seventeen bitter months of exile—no doubt painful for him to relive even in the telling (cf. *Planc.* 99 [on his first meeting with Plancius in Macedonia]: *o acerbam mihi, iudices, memoriam temporis illius et loci . . .*); at *Pis.* 21 he refers to it as *non meum solum sed patriae funus*; cf. also *Dom.* 97: *accepi, pontifices, magnum atque incredibilem dolorem; non nego neque istam mihi adscisco sapientiam quam nonnulli in me requirebant, qui me animo nimis fracto esse atque adflicto loquebantur*; in general Graff, 31 ff. For Cicero's hesitancy in general to speak of unpleasant occurrences cf. J.P.V.D. Balsdon, "Cicero the Man," in *Cicero*, ed. T.A. Dorey (London,

zum Bildschmuck der Porta Romana in Ostia," in *Imperium Romanum. Studien zu Geschichte und Rezeption. Festschrift für Karl Christ zum 75. Geburtstag*, ed. P. Kneissl and V. Losemann (Stuttgart, 1998), 370–78.

110. Minerva was evidently described by Cicero as his instructor in the arts in *de Consulatu suo* 1: cf. Quint. *Inst.* 11.1.24; S.J. Harrison, "Cicero's 'De Temporibus suis': The Evidence Reconsidered," *Hermes* 118 (1990), 460–62. For the general conception of outstanding individuals owing their achievements to divine aid (within a proof of the gods' providential care for human beings) cf. *N.D.* 2.165–66.

1964), 196.—Cicero took great pride in the decrees in his favor leading to his restoration: cf. *Dom.* 44, 73, and 75; *Pis.* 35 and 41; for a full citation of sources cf. Gelzer, 148–49.—The three groups are carefully arranged, in both number of syllables and content, according to the "law of waxing members." The limitation *conservatae patriae* rather than, e.g., *civitatis nostrae* suggests that his services in quashing the Catilinarian conspiracy were the basis for recall; the entities which so "judged" thus nullify the exile imposed on grounds of Cicero's rôle in the execution of the conspirators.

quo quid accidere potuit homini praeclarius?] Cf. *Red. Sen.* 24: *quid enim magnificentius, quid praeclarius mihi accidere potuit quam quod illo* [sc. the consul Lentulus] *referente vos decrevistis ut cuncti ex omni Italia qui rempublicam salvam vellent ad me unum, hominem fractum et prope dissipatum, restituendum et defendendum venirent?*—As a *novus homo* without the security of ancestry to fall back on, Cicero felt the need for, and indulged in, such acts of public self-validation; cf. *ad* § 5. The effect may be mitigated somewhat in that the immediate audience consists of his brother and his brother's brother-in-law (cf. *ad* § 41).

quorum scelere religiones tum prostratae adflictaeque sunt, partim ex illis distracti ac dissipati iacent; . . .] *Quorum—adflictaeque sunt* summarizes the impiety against Cicero's *Lares familiares* described at the beginning of the paragraph. *Partim ex illis* stands, by a common kind of *constructio ad sententiam* for *pars ex illis*; cf. *Vat.* 16: *e quibus partim plane tecum sentiebant . . .* ; *Phil.* 8.32: *. . . cum partim e nobis ita timidi sint . . .* ; cf. also *Man.* 18: *partim eorum*; Kühner-Stegmann, 1, 433–34.—The Clodiani had their difficulties: even before their ringleader's death, L. Sergius and Se(r)vius were convicted in court (*Dom.* 13; *Q.fr.* 2.5.4); and in the flood of trials that followed in the wake of the "Battle of Bovillae" (see the next note), both Sex. Cloelius and Plaguleius were condemned *de vi*. But, as early as 49, Cicero had forebodings of their recall (*Att.* 10.8.3), and the former was, in fact, recalled by Antony in 44; cf. H. Benner, 155 ff. These indicators point to the late 50s as the likely dramatic date; see § 5 of the Introduction.

qui vero ex eis et horum scelerum principes fuerant et praeter ceteros in omni religione impii, non solum ⟨nullo in⟩ vita cruciatu atque dedecore, verum etiam sepultura et iustis exsequiarum caruerunt.] The departure from the expected *partim . . . partim* structure calls special attention to this point; for such *variatio* cf. *Rep.* 4.1; *N.D.* 1.66; *Div.* 1.93.—Cicero continues his policy of criticism *tacito nomine* (see *supra* on *nihil enim attinet quemquam nominari*). In contrast to the outcome (*exitus*) favorable to Cicero is that of Clodius, unhappy both in life and death.—Clodius' impiety *in omni religione* suggests above all the violation of the rites of the Bona Dea (cf. *ad* § 36), but at *Mil.* 85 Cicero lays great stress on his desecration of sacred places on the Alban Mount (cf. Dyck, 1988, 235 ff.); he frequently ridicules Clodius as *sacerdos* (cf. Tatum, 1999, 312 n. 103).—*Nullo in* is Halm's (necessary) supplement.—The phrase *in vita cruciatus* will refer to his violent death at the hands of Milo and his followers on 18 January 52 in the "Battle of Bovillae." In his defense of Milo Cicero thrice cites Clodius' disorderly funeral as either a personal disgrace or, through the burning of the senate-house, a symbol of his danger to the state (§§ 33, 86, 90); in particular § 86 of the speech is similar to our passage in seeing Clodius' death as condign punishment for his impiety. One reason Cicero is so keen to impute *impietas* may be Clodius' claim to be the defender of strict observance of religious rituals in the controversy over the *aedes Libertatis;* cf. *Dom.* 127 with Tatum, 1999, 191; ibid. 215 ff.—*Iustis exsequiarum:* the phrase recalls the original reference of *ius(tus)* to the sacred sphere; cf. *ad* § 36 (*qua licentia Romae data*—).—For the formation of *sepultura* cf. *ad* § 56.

43 Q. Equidem ista agnosco, frater, et meritas dis gratias ago; sed nimis saepe secus aliquanto videmus evadere. M. Non enim, Quinte, recte existimamus quae poena divina sit, sed opinionibus vulgi rapimur in errorem nec vera cernimus.] The inability of human beings to see the workings of divine justice is a problem with which moralists have wrestled from early times. Thus most of Plato's *Republic* is an attempt to find an answer to Glaucon's query at the beginning of Book 2 about the utility of justice (cf. *ad* 1.51). Balbus offers a Stoic answer to the problem of the suffering of the good at *N.D.* 2.167. At *Mil.* 87 Cicero represents himself as having doubted divine justice in view of Clodius' successes; cf. Dyck, 1998, 233 ff. The *opinionum varietas* is made responsible for error at 1.29 and *Tusc.* 3.2–3. The opinion of the masses is often deprecated in Socratic and Stoic writings (cf. *ad Off.* 1.118), and such an attitude is easy for an optimate politician like Cicero to adopt.

morte aut dolore corporis aut luctu animi aut offensione iudicii hominum miserias ponderamus, . . .] "We estimate the unhappiness of men on the basis of death . . ." (Keyes); cf. *OLD* s.v. *pondero* 2; for its use with the ablative of means cf. 1.39: *omnia . . . voluptatibus et doloribus ponderantes . . .* For the fear of death and physical or emotional pain cf. *ad* 1.31; these were among the conditions for which the Stoics tried to provide therapy. The first two were treated in *Tusc.* 1 and 2, respectively, the third in the *de Consolatione;* cf. Stephen A. White, "Cicero and the Therapists," in Powell, 1995, 219–46. *Offensio iudicii* is a special case of emotional pain, perhaps suggested to Cicero in this context by the recent conviction of Milo.

sceleris est poena tristis, et praeter eos eventus qui sequuntur per se ipsa maxima est.] The penalties of conscience have been described already at 1.40. For *praeter eos eventus qui sequuntur* see the note before last.

vidimus eos qui nisi odissent patriam numquam inimici nobis fuissent, ardentes tum cupiditate, tum metu; {tum} conscientia quid agerent modo timentes, vicissim contemnentes religiones; perrupta ab eis quidem iudicia hominum, non deorum.] We seem to have a composite portrait of Cicero's enemies, both the Catilinarians and the Clodians.[111] Cupidity would fit both groups. The fear and pangs of conscience describe the Catilinarian conspirators confronted with the evidence against them (*Cat.* 3.10 ff.). The despising of religious scruples and frustration of the judicial process applies to Clodius; for the former point cf. *ad* § 42 (*qui vero ex eis et horum scelerum principes fuerant*); for the latter, the Bona Dea scandal and its aftermath (cf. *ad* § 36) and Milo's prosecution of him *de vi* in 57, frustrated by a *iustitium* imposed by Clodius' political allies (cf. H. Benner, 94 and n. 334); for the heckling of a pleader at the bar by the Clodiani cf. Cic. *Q.fr.* 2.3.2 (Milo's trial *de vi*: 7 February 56); such behavior was repeated at Milo's more famous trial beginning on 4 April 52; cf. Gelzer, 209; H. Benner, 91 ff.; it must be added, however, that in the former case Milo's followers, under massive provocation, were the first to resort to physical violence; cf. Tatum, 1999, 202–3.—Powell rightly deletes the *tum* prior to *conscientia,* which should not be connected with *ardentes* and placed in parallel with the πάθη *cupiditas* and *metus* (cf. *ad* 1.32).—The final part of the sentence is transmitted as follows: *iudicia perrupta ab isdem corrupta hominum non deorum.* But *perrupta* and *corrupta* are not both wanted here, the rarer *perrupta* likely to be original (cf. *Ver.* 1.13: *confringat iste sane vi sua consilia senatoria, quaestiones omnium perrumpat . . . artioribus apud populum Romanum laqueis tenebitur;* sim. thought also at *Cat.* 1.18, cited *ad* 1.42). Halm saw this and deleted *corrupta.* The rhetorical balance of the sentence is enhanced by Powell's *ab eis quidem* for *ab isdem* (for the corruption he compares *vosdem* for *vos quidem* at 3.38) and transposition of *iudicia* to precede *hominum* (presumably *iudicia* will have been omitted in transcription and reinserted in the wrong place); *quidem solum* may be followed by adversative asyndeton (cf. *ad* § 53); cf. *Har.* 38 (also with reference to Clodius): *hominum poenas deesse adhuc, non deorum;* § 45: *duelli instrumenta, non fani; Luc.* 80: *opinionis . . . esse mendacium, non oculorum.*— For Cicero's construction of Clodius as metaphorically blinded by viewing the rites of the Bona Dea cf. *Har.* 48; for the *lex curiata* sanctioning his adoption as the force that released him from bonds cf. *Sest.* 16.

---

111. Surely not Marc Antony, *pace* Reitzenstein, 29–30.

44 Reprimam iam me, non insequar longius, eoque minus quo plus poenarum habeo quam petivi.] These words mark the end of the personal digression and return the conversation to its proper theme; cf. *ad* 1.52.—The concluding clause suggests that Cicero would have been content with a judicial verdict forcing Clodius into exile, which was, however, frustrated (see the previous note); he makes it a point of pride that he returned from exile with Clodius alive (⟨te⟩ *vivo: Dom.* 87, where *te* is the generally accepted reading of the *recentiores*); at *Mil.* 47 he deals with the suspicion that he had suborned Milo to murder Clodius; cf. also *Fam.* 7.2.2 (to M. Marius; perhaps January 51, à propos Clodius' end): *iudicio malo quam gladio.*

tantum ponam brevi: duplicem poenam esse divinam, quod constet et ex vexandis vivorum animis, et ea fama mortuorum ut eorum exitium et iudicio vivorum et gaudio comprobetur.] *Ponam brevi* is Lambinus' conjecture for *poenammerebi* B, *poenam erebi* Aᵃ,[112] *p(o)ena merui* εHL, *penam merui* P. The adopted text motivates the following indirect statement and is fairly close to the *ductus litterarum*. It is easy to understand how *ponam* could have become *poenam* in this context, but the corruption of so common a word as *brevi* (if that is the correct solution) is puzzling; cf. *Fam.* 1.9.13: *tantum dicam brevi.* For Cicero's striving for *brevitas* in commentary cf. § 34. *Constet et* is the correction of the *recentiores* for *constaret* (*constaret et* F).—The digression on Clodius now complete, Cicero returns to the exposition of the law *poena violati iuris* ⟨*divini divina*⟩ *esto* (§ 22.10), which he cited at § 41. He defines two types of divine punishment, namely the mental torment of the malefactor (for which he might have been expected to refer to 1.40) and in terms of the *fama mortuorum*. This latter point, though generally phrased, may still have Clodius primarily in view: this is the sentiment Cicero was counting on at *Mil.* 79, where he uses the hypothesis of Clodius' resurrection to uncover the hypocrisy of those who publicly deplored his death but were privately relieved by it.

45 After the lengthy discussion of the penalty for violating religious law (cf. *ad* § 41), Cicero passes to his next laws: *Ne quis agrum consecrato. Auri argenti eboris sacrandi modus esto* (§ 22.11–12). At Rome the consecration of land came within the purview of the censors as overseers of the *ager privatus* and changes in its extent; cf. Mommsen, *Staatsr.* 2, 389–90; such questions evidently underlie Cato *orat.* fr. 90: *citer ager alligatus ad sacra erit;* for the laws governing dedications at Rome cf. W. Jeffrey Tatum, "The *Lex Papiria de dedicationibus*," *CPh* 88 (1993), 319–28, esp. 322–24. Here, however, Cicero seeks support, not from Roman tradition, but a passage from Plato's *Laws* (955e) enacting specific limitations on

112. The original reading is erased but involved *ui.*

dedications, some without any known historical precedent; cf. Morrow, 469 n. 225. As Cicero makes clear at the end of the paragraph,[113] the aim is to maintain a strong rural economy by keeping arable land in cultivation and curbing competitive spending on funerals and grave goods; in this way wealth and goods will be recycled for the benefit of the living, not withdrawn for the benefit of the dead.[114] Toward the end of the paragraph he makes it clear, however, that, though he accepts the general principle, he does not subscribe to all of Plato's detailed provisions (*cetera non tam restricte praefinio*).

Agri autem ne consecrentur, Platoni prorsus adsentior, qui (si modo interpretari potuero) his fere verbis utitur: . . .] Cicero had included several fairly close renderings from Plato in *Rep.*: *Rp.* 562c at 1.66–67 and *Phaedr.* 245c at 6.30–31, neither explicitly acknowledged; there is also an indirect rendering of Pl. *Lg.* at §§ 67–68; cf. J.G.F. Powell, "Cicero's Translations from Greek," in Powell, 1995, 279–80; Susanne Widmann, *Untersuchungen zur Übersetzungstechnik Ciceros in seiner philosophischen Prosa* (diss., Tübingen, 1968), 310; *ad* § 17. On Cicero's use of *interpres/interpretari* cf. Powell, *loc. cit.,* 278. H. Müller, 50, finds Cicero producing here a closer rendering than elsewhere (he does, however, vary the connecting particles, in contrast to Plato's prevalent δέ: ibid., 51); he attributes this fact to Cicero's willingness to tolerate a divergence from his normal style because he is accommodating the language of laws; see *infra* on *iam aes atque ferrum duelli instrumenta, non fani*.—The ringing endorsement (*prorsus adsentior*) is tempered in the sequel (*haec illi placent, sed ego . . .*); see the previous note.
'Terra igitur, ut focus domiciliorum, sacra deorum omnium est; . . .] The hearth was regarded as sacred, and offerings were brought there; cf. Carl Koch, *RE* 8A2 (1958), 1760.61 ff. (on the problematic relation of this private ritual with the public cult of Vesta).—Cicero accepts the idea of the sacredness of the earth, in contrast to Roman sacral laws, which set aside individual places as sacred (and are thus implicitly in violation of the following *ne quis iterum idem consecrato*); among the Greeks, too, Γαῖα/Γῆ had a very limited rôle in cult (cf. Burkert, 1985, 175); hence Plato's justification.—In rendering the Greek γῆ μὲν οὖν ἑστία τε οἰκήσεως ἱερὰ πᾶσι πάντων θεῶν, Cicero has sacrificed the polyptoton, perhaps for clarity; cf. Pascucci, 1981, 421.

---

113. *Terrae cultum segniorem suspicor fore si ad eam tuendam ferroque subigendam superstitionis aliquid accesserit.*

114. A similar motive lay behind English legislation designed to prevent land from falling into the "dead hand" of the Church or other corporations with resulting loss of feudal incidents; cf. R.E. Megarry, *Encyclopaedia Britannica* (New York, 1972), s.v. Mortmain.

aurum autem et argentum in urbibus, et privatim et in fanis, invidiosa res est; . . .] A literal rendering except that Cicero omits ἐν ἄλλαις πόλεσιν [sc. other than the city being constructed by the interlocutors]. Both here and in the clause *color autem albus praecipue decorus deo est* Cicero includes the copula, as in the Greek; cf. H. Müller, 50. This provision is in line with the general principle stated at the outset *pietatem adhibento, opes amovento* (§ 19.1).

tum ebur, exanimi corpore extractum, haud satis castum donum deo; . . .] *Exanimi corpore extractum:* the Platonic phrase is ἀπὸ λελοιπότος ψυχὴν σώματος; transmitted is *ex inani;* but *inanis* is poetic and postaugustan in the sense "sine vita, exanimis" (cf. *TLL* s.v. *inanis* 823.42 ff.). Paulus Manutius conjectured *ex inani⟨mo⟩* in view of the Ciceronian *inanimus* (cf. *TLL* s.v., 819.69 ff.) or *ex inanimi,* the solution favored by Pascucci, 1981, 420. Better is Powell's *exanimi,* which clarifies the meaning "dead," rather than merely "inanimate," a necessary point, since death is the polluting agent (cf. Parker, ch. 2), even though the word is not otherwise attested for Cicero, and *extraho* with plain ablative is also unique in his corpus (cf. *TLL* s.vv. *exanimis, extraho*): these poetic touches may be in keeping with the elevated diction of this rendering from Plato (see the next note).—Cicero has added the participle (*extractum*), which serves, as often with prepositional phrases used adnominally, to clarify the referent; cf. Kühner-Stegmann, 1, 216 ff., esp. 218.—*Castum* is Cicero's rendering of εὐαγές; thus *castitas* is the criterion of the proper offering, as of the proper approach to the gods in general, as indicated at § 19.1. For the secondary application of *castus* to inanimate objects cf. Fugier, 27.—*Deo* is Cicero's own addition, effecting a clausula of the *omni debebitur* type; Plato was content to leave the recipient implicit.—Lactantius refers to these words at *inst.* 6.25.1 (*ebur inquit Plato non castum donum deo*) and goes on to criticize that *picta et texta pretiosa* are allowed, but without noting the restrictions indicated later in the passage (e.g., *tincta vero absint nisi a bellicis insignibus*); cf. Schmidt, 1965, 313.

iam aes atque ferrum duelli instrumenta, non fani.] Compared with Plato's σίδηρος . . . καὶ χαλκός, Cicero inverts the order of metals, perhaps for rhythm and to yield a consistent progression from more to less precious materials (*aurum, argentum, ebur, aes, ferrum, lignum*); cf. H. Müller, 51. The use of *duelli* (in spite of *bellicis* in the sentence after next) shows that Cicero finds the moderately archaizing "language of laws" appropriate here (cf. § 18; § 21.2: *rem duelli*); see also *infra* on *delubris. Non fani* is Cicero's addition for rhetorical emphasis.—The view that the *duelli instrumenta* are unfit offerings is a moralizing critique of cult practice found already in Euripides; cf. Eur. fr. 266 (Auge addresses Athena, angered over her having given birth in her shrine): σκῦλα μὲν βροτοφθόρα / χαίρεις ὁρῶσα καὶ νεκρῶν ἐρείπια / κοὐ μυσαρά σοι ταῦτ᾽ ἐστίν, εἰ δ᾽ ἐγὼ ἔτεκον, / δεινὸν τόδ᾽ ἡγῇ; with Parker, 34.

ligneum autem quod quis voluerit uno e ligno ⟨di⟩cato, itemque lapideum, in delubris communibus, . . .] The Greek: ξύλου δὲ μονόξυλον ὅτι ἂν ἐθέλῃ τις ἀνατιθέτω καὶ λίθου ὡσαύτως πρὸς τὰ κοινὰ ἱερά . . . Cicero adroitly obviates the lack of a Latin compound corresponding to μονόξυλον (he ventured *unigena* as a translation of μονογενής at *Tim.* 12); he recreates the effect of the Greek by placing the generic *ligneum* in emphatic first position to correspond to the partitive ξύλου. *Uno e ligno* limits *ligneum,* but Cicero postpones it for balance; he does not add a participle as he did above (see the note before last); the *lign-* root itself provides a connection; cf. also Kühner-Stegmann, 1, 214.—*Quod quis* is Lambinus' correction of the transmitted *quodque.*[115]—For *delubrum* cf. *ad* § 19.5.—The "future imperative" *dicato,*[116] like the preceding *consecrato* and following *sunto,* imitates the language of the Twelve Tables; cf. *ad* 1.16; H. Müller, 51.

. . . textile ne operosius quam mulieris opus menstruum.] A close rendering of the Greek (. . . ὑφὴν δὲ μὴ πλέον ἔργον γυναικὸς μιᾶς ἔμμηνον) except that Cicero has regularized the compendious comparison by adding *operosius,* which together with *opus* forms a *figura etymologica,* and omitted the specification of a single woman (μιᾶς; contrast *ab uno pictore* below); or has *unius* been lost before *mulieris?* Considerations of balance surely led Cicero to place the small word *opus* between *mulieris* and *menstruum,* contrary to the Greek order (possibly influenced by the epic formula ἔργα γυναικῶν); cf. Pascucci, 1981, 421–22.

color autem albus praecipue decorus deo est, . . .] Plato's χρώματα λευκά suggests "bright colors" and may refer to the ritual requirement of clean clothing (cf. Parker, 68; similarly, the corpse is buried in clean robes, usually white or red: ibid., 35).—For *decorus* = πρέπων cf. Dyck *ad Off.,* p. 242.— With *deus* Cicero substitutes the singular for Plato's plural; Latin sometimes has the word in the henotheistic sense "the supreme being" (cf. *OLD* s.v., 4); cf. *supremus deus* at 1.22 and the assumed identification of *deus* and *natura* in 1.25.

tincta vero absint nisi a bellicis insignibus.] Cicero's adoption of the apotropaic formula *absint* represents a gain in elegance compared with Plato's more direct βάμματα δὲ μὴ προσφέρειν . . . ; cf. Pascucci, 1981, 421.— With *bellicis* contrast the preceding *duelli instrumenta.*

---

115. Müller's *quod ⟨quis⟩que* is favored by Pascucci, 1981, 420.
116. This is Halm's correction of *cato* (*cauato* P).

divinissima autem dona aves et formae ab uno pictore uno absolutae die, . . .] Here Cicero achieves greater compression than his model (at the price of a bit of nuance) by substituting the participial construction for the conditional relative clause (ὅσαπερ ἂν ἐν μιᾷ ζωγράφος ἡμέρᾳ εἰς ἀποτελῇ); cf. H. Müller, 50. The placement of *absolutae* gives a sense of Plato's interlocking word order and also effects a fine double cretic clausula.

. . . cetera huius exempli dona sunto'.] "Other gifts should be of this type." *Exemplum* here has a technical legal sense; cf. Ulp. *dig.* 27.10.1: . . . *solent hodie praetores . . . curatorem ei* [sc. *prodigo*] *dare exemplo furiosi;* OLD s.v., 6a.

sed ego cetera non tam restricte praefinio, vel hominum vitiis vel subsidiis temporum victus; . . .] Cicero demurs only at the restriction of *cetera* [sc. *dona*] in the preceding sentence.—First used at Ter. *Hec.* 94 (*nam illi haud licebat nisi praefinito* [sc. *tempore*] *loqui / quae illi placerent*), *praefinio* is common in legal contexts in Cicero and elsewhere (e.g., *Sex. Rosc.* 130: . . . *quare aliquanto post eam diem venierint quae dies in lege praefinita est . . .*); it is rare in poetry (but cf. Lucr. 1.618); cf. TLL s.v.—*Hominum vitiis— subsidiis temporum* forms a handsome chiasmus, and there is a fine clausula consisting of cretic plus trochee.—*Subsidiis temporum victus:* increasing wealth created competitive pressures in dedications, as in other matters; cf. the striving for grand funerary monuments illustrated by that of C. Figulus (§ 62) or the later graves of the Ceramicus (§ 64); sim. the *splendor aedilitatum* discussed at *Off.* 2.57.

terrae cultum segniorem suspicor fore—superstitionis aliquid accesserit.] See the headnote to this section. For *superstitio* as *religio* taken to excess cf. Nigidius *gram.* p. 162, fr. 4; cf. in general *ad* 1.32.

A. Habeo ista; nunc de sacris perpetuis et de Manium iure restat.] It was Atticus who had mooted the general topic of law (1.13). However, Quintus suggested the continuation of the discussion (§ 7) and first mentioned the topic of sacral law (§ 17). Here Atticus continues his rôle of propelling discussion forward, begun in § 24 when he asked for a case to be made for the sacral laws (*suade igitur si placet istam ipsam legem . . .*).—*Habeo* appears in the sense "have knowledge of, be in possession of (facts, information)": OLD s.v., 11a; *nunc* is the discourse marker; cf. Risselada, 117–22.—The commentary on the last of Cicero's sacral laws (§ 22.13–16: *Sacra privata perpetua manento* and *Deorum manium iura sancta sunto* etc.) still remains, which Cicero manages to combine with the promised treatment of the *iura et iussa populorum* (1.17; cf. the introduction to this Book). The last two sacral laws are related insofar as a major part of family cult had to do with rites in honor of the dead, including a feast at the tomb on the day of the funeral, on

376 A Commentary on Cicero, *De Legibus*

the ninth day thereafter, and subsequently on the anniversary of the death. Other observances in honor of deceased ancestors included the Parentalia in February and the decoration of the tombs at the Rosalia in May. For *sacra* and their classification cf. Macr. *sat.* 1.16.4 ff.; Geiger, *RE* 1A2 (1920), 1656.37 ff. (s.v. Sacra); Wissowa, 398 ff.; on the *feriae familiares* in general cf. Rüpke, 1995, 502–3. In the sequel (§§ 48 ff.) the discussion will be confined to rites in honor of the dead, on which cf. Cumont, 53 ff.; on the Parentalia in particular Scullard, 74–75; Wissowa, 232–33.

M. O miram memoriam, Pomponi, tuam! at mihi ista exciderant.] The exclamatory accusative without interjection is frequent in old Latin and still well represented in Cicero but later rare; cf. Hofmann-Szantyr, 48–49.—*At mihi ista exciderant* [sc. *e memoria*], like *at ego effugisse arbitrabar* at § 7a (see *ad loc.*), adds a realistic touch; cf. Quint. *Inst.* 4.5.4. The device appears in Plato's dialogues, e.g., *Rp.* 449c.

46–68 At 1.17 Marcus had promised that the *leges quibus civitates regi debeant* would be followed by an examination of *quae composita sunt et descripta iura et iussa populorum*. Atticus remembers this promise (*memini*: § 46) and asks for its fulfillment with respect to both pontifical law and the *ius civile*; this now follows at §§ 46–57 and 58–68, respectively, though this material can also be seen as Marcus' commentary on his final laws; cf. *ad* § 45 and the introduction to this Book.

46–53 Starting from Atticus' juxtapositon of *pontificium ius* and *ius civile* (§ 46), Marcus argues that only a tiny part of the *ius civile* is relevant to pontifical law; moreover, the latter has suffered from distinctions imported into it from the former. In particular, the Scaevolae have wrongly assimilated the law regulating rites for the dead to the law of succession;[117] see *ad* §§ 48b–49. The critique of the Scaevolae is similar to that directed at the *iuris consulti* in general at *Mur.* 27: *nam, cum permulta praeclare legibus essent constituta, ea iure consultorum ingeniis pleraque corrupta ac depravata sunt.* Cicero's point seems to be that the modifications of the Scaevolae endanger the perpetuity of the *sacra*. But the effect may have been the opposite, since they increased the chances that the *sacra* would be the responsibility of family members, rather than of a *heres extraneus*; cf. *ad* § 53 (*quid si hoc qui testamentum faciebat cavere noluisset?*). Cf. the critique by A. Momigliano, "The Theological Efforts of the Roman Upper Classes in the First Century B.C.," *CPh* 79 (1984), 206–7: ". . . Cicero was aware of contradictions between *ius civile* and *ius pontificium*. But he never puts the problem in sufficiently general terms to

---

117. On the Roman law of succession and strategies used by families to preserve their property cf. Saller, ch. 7.

make it an important argument for reform," as well as the detailed study of our passage by Gennaro Franciosi, *Usucapio pro herede. Contributo allo studio dell'antica hereditas*, Pubblicazioni della Facoltà Giuridica dell'Università di Napoli 74 (Naples, 1965), 74–130.

46 A. Ita credo! sed tamen hoc magis eas res et memini et ⟨ex⟩specto, quod et ad pontificium ius et ad civile pertinent.] The *ius civile* was the subject Atticus mooted at 1.13, and Marcus accepted it with some broadening and clarification. It, together with the *pontificium ius*, comprised the *ius publicum* (cf. Wissowa, 380; Kaser, 1986, 57 58). The two remaining topics bring these two areas together. The digression on *ius* here provides the model for that in Book 3, now lost (cf. 3.48: . . . *si de sacrorum alienatione dicendum putasti cum de religione leges proposueras, faciendum tibi est ut magistratibus lege constitutis, de potestatum iure disputes*). Though some material from the *ius civile* is adduced prior to these digressions (§§ 29, 37; 3.44), it is mostly reserved for this place; cf. Schmidt, 1959, 83.—*Exspecto* is Manutius' correction.

M. Vero: et a peritissimis—a quo sit capite repetendum.] Cicero consents to Atticus' request but, as at 1.14, makes it clear that he does not propose to descend to details. This sentence places in parallel the previous literature on the subject, which is considerable and learned (*et a peritissimis sunt istis de rebus et responsa et scripta multa*), and Cicero's own different approach (*et ego . . .*); this latter is developed rather amorphously, with two prepositional phrases followed by the verb and object, explicated by a consecutive clause with restricting force, followed by a purpose clause with a contained relative clause and capped with a *cum*-clause; nor is the clausula a good one. Marcus proposes to familiarize his interlocutors with the *caput* of each part of *ius* so that, whatever subject arises, they will be in possession of the *ius* relevant to it. *Caput* here is evidently used in a way similar to 1.18a (= "the source, fountainhead, origin"; cf. *ad loc.* and § 51) but equivalent to *locus* also used in this sentence, as well as in rhetorical teaching, where the recognition of the relevant *locus* can obviate learning a host of details and make possible the *inventio* of arguments even on obscure subjects (cf. *Top.* 7). On the relation of the Ciceronian *loci* to Aristotle's τόποι cf. Solmsen, 2, 197–98.—*Vero* is of the type used in a confirmatory response to a command or exhortation (= "certainly, indeed"); cf. *Mur.* 65 '*in sententia permaneto*'. *vero, nisi sententiam sententia alia vicerit melior; OLD* s.v., 4b; Kroon, 291 ff.

. . . quod ad cumque legis genus me disputatio nostra deduxerit, tractabo . . . ; sed ita, locus ut ipse notus sit ex quo ducatur quaeque ⟨p⟩ars iuris, ut non difficile sit qui modo ingenio sit mediocri, quaecumque nova causa consultatiove acciderit, eius tenere ius, . . .] *Pars* for *ars* of BAˣ is Ranconnet's conjecture reported by Turnebus.—*Qui modo* was proposed in a note in Turnebus' second edition for *qui domo* (B¹A¹εHL) or *qui homo* (BˣAᵇP).— *Ingenio sit mediocri* is Davies' correction for *ingenio possit moveri* of BA; for minor variants see Powell's apparatus.

47 The essential point of this criticism is the disproportion of the subject-matter of the *ius pontificium*, as conceived by the Scaevolae, with the true state of affairs: *quam magnum illud Scaevolae faciunt,* . . . *'pontificem bonum neminem esse, nisi qui ius civile cognosset'.—totumne?* . . . *id autem quantulum est!* . . . *cur igitur haec tanta facimus cum cetera perparva sint, de sacris autem, qui locus patet latius, haec sit una sententia* . . . In Cicero's view, a knowledge of the whole *ius civile* is, *pace* the Scaevolae, hardly necessary for the pontiff; the points of contact between the *ius civile* and the *pontificium ius* are limited; even the largest area, *de sacris*, can be reduced to a single *sententia*.

sed iuris consulti, sive erroris obiciendi causea quo plura et difficiliora scire videantur, . . .] An attack on the obscurantism of the *iuris consulti*, who, according to *Mur.* 26, profited from others' ignorance of legal technicalities: *quae dum erant occulta, necessario ab eis qui ea tenebant petebantur; postea vero pervulgata atque in manibus iactata et excussa, inanissima prudentiae reperta sunt, fraudis autem et stultitiae plenissima.*

. . . sive (quod similius veri est) ignoratione docendi . . .] An apparent thrust at his teacher Scaevola (cf. *ad* § 49); on the other hand, he clearly admired the method of another teacher of his, Molon of Rhodes (cf. *Brut.* 316). In general, the Roman aristocrat tended to despise teaching as an occupation for slaves or freedmen (cf. Cicero's qualified defense of learned occupations, including teaching, as *iis quorum ordini conveniunt honestae* at *Off.* 1.151). Crassus' scruples on the subject have to be overcome in *de Orat.* (cf. *ad* 1.14 *supra*), and Cicero argues against this attitude at *Orat.* 143–44.[118] Instead of immersion in particulars Cicero would rather see the principles explained (see the second note *ad* § 46).—For *ignoratio* cf. *ad* 1.18a.

. . .—nam non solum scire aliquid artis est, sed ⟨est⟩ quaedam ars etiam docendi— . . .] This is the one instance of the *iunctura ars docendi* in classical Latin (according to a search of PHI 5.3). Cf. also Quint. *Inst.* 1 pr. 23: *his omnibus admiscebitur, ut quisque locus postulabit, docendi ratio quae non eorum modo scientia quibus solis quidam nomen artis dederunt studiosos instruat* . . . —*Est* was supplied (after *ars*) by Lambinus but moved to this position for emphasis by Powell.

---

118. Indeed he gave rhetorical instruction himself to Hirtius in 46 and 44; cf. *Fam.* 7.33.1; 9.16.7 and 18.3; Gelzer, 277 n. 89 and 329.

... saepe quod positum est in una cognitione, id ⟨in⟩ infinita dispertiuntur; velut in hoc ipso genere: quam magnum illud Scaevolae faciunt, pontifices ambo et idem iuris peritissimi!] *Cognitio* has here the sense "notion, idea" (cf. *OLD* s.v., 1c; syn. *sententia* at the end of this chapter): the increased number of distinctions *in hoc ipso genere* (i.e., the *sacra perpetua*: cf. § 45) compared to the earlier system (from three to five) will constitute the essence of Cicero's critique in §§ 48–49; *id ⟨in⟩*[119] *infinita dispertiuntur* is, of course, rhetorically exaggerated. Cicero claims at the end of this chapter that he can reduce the matter to *una sententia* (see below).—Here and at Liv. 3.10.9 a deponent *dispertior* is attested; cf. *OLD dispertio/-or* b.— *Velut* = "as for example" (*OLD* s.v., 1).—The reference is to P. Mucius Scaevola and Q. Mucius Scaevola, father and son (*RE* s.v. Mucius nos. 17 and 22, respectively). The son, in fact, succeeded the father in the *collegium* of pontiffs on his death in 115; cf. F. Münzer, *RE* 16.1 (1933), 437.44–47; *MRR* 1, 532; both served as pontifex maximus, the father from 130 on, the son from 89 on; ibid. 2, 37; Münzer, *loc. cit.,* 440.31–33. Both are fairly characterized as *iuris peritissimi*: the elder Scaevola was rated in antiquity as the youngest of those *qui fundaverunt ius civile* . . . (Pompon. 38 *dig.* 1.2.2.39–40). The sparse surviving testimonies about his juristic writings and *responsa* (*iur.,* pp. 7–9 = *iur. anteh.* 58–104) make it difficult for moderns to form a just estimate; cf. Wieacker, 1988, 547–48 with literature. We have a somewhat clearer picture of his son, "der bedeutendste Jurist der Republik" (ibid., 549); testimonies at *iur.* 17–19 = *iur. anteh.* 48 ff.; cf. Wieacker, 549–51 and 596–600.—Cicero's critique goes to the very root of the method of the Roman jurists, which he proposes to reform after a Greek philosophical model (cf. *ad* 2.9); cf. Franz Blatt, "Written and Unwritten Law in Ancient Rome," *C & M* 5 (1943), 145 ("Cicero . . . criticised the Roman juridical literature which was so hostile to abstractions"); Ulrich von Lübtow, "Cicero und die Methode der römischen Jurisprudenz," *Festschrift für Leopold Wenger,* 1 (Munich, 1944), 224–35, esp. 233 ff. A similar concern, though at a more practical level, underlies the goal formulated by Crassus at *de Orat.* 1.185–90 of creating an *ars* wherein the *ius civile* would be divided into categories for ease of learning by the advocate in training and later executed, at least in part, by Cicero in his work *de Iure Civili in Artem Redigendo;* cf. *ad* 1.13. The subsuming of particulars under categories was also useful for the orator; cf., e.g., *Pis.* 85–86.

'sae⟨pe⟩', inquit Publi filius, 'ex patre audivi, pontificem bonum neminem esse, nisi qui ius civile cognosset.'] *Saepe* is Turnebus' correction.—The

---

119. Already inserted in P.

younger Scaevola's reliance on the authority of his father appeared also in his defense of the *summum ius* in the famous *causa Curiana;* cf. *de Orat.* 1.244: *paterni iuris defensor et quasi patrimonii propugnator sui;* sim. *Brut.* 197: *quam ille multa de auctoritate patris sui, qui semper ius illud esse defenderat?* Cf. Wieacker, 1988, 549 n. 136. Hence it is only natural for Cicero to treat the two of them together as a unit (*Scaevolae . . . pontifices ambo* etc.; cf. the reference to *Scaevolae* at §§ 50 and 52).—Sacred and profane law were gradually differentiated during the Republic. The elder Scaevola's view, though traditional, no longer prevailed in Cicero's day, as is suggested not only by the following critique but also Capito's relative neglect of sacred law; cf. Fritz Schultz, *Principles of Roman Law* (Oxford, 1936), 26 with literature.—*Publi filius* does not differentiate son from father, since the latter was also *Publi filius,* but does distinguish him from his homonymous cousin, the Augur (*RE* s.v. Mucius no. 21), who was *Quinti filius.*

—**Totumne? quid ita? . . .**] A lively rejoinder suggestive of an *altercatio* in court. This is a feature of the diatribe style often used by Cicero to dramatize a clash of ideas; cf. Dyck, 1998, 231 and n. 54.

quid enim ad pontificem de iure parietum aut aquarum, aut ullo omnino ⟨ni⟩si eo quod cum religione coniunctum est?] The *ius parietum* and *ius aquarum* already appeared in 1.14 as examples of trivial topics; cf. *ad loc.* For the transmitted *ullo omnino* Turnebus conjectured *lumine* to restore the name of yet another servitude (cf. Watson, *Property,* 194–95), unnecessarily.—*Nisi eo* is Madvig's correction of *si ego.*

de sacris, credo, de votis, de feriis et de sepulcris, et si quid eiusmodi est.] This list constitutes a rough delineation of the pontiffs' sphere of responsibility; cf. in general Richard L. Gordon, *NP* s.v. Pontifex.—Here *credo* is used, as in § 36, without irony; contrast 1.41 and 42.—With *si quid eiusmodi est* supply *de eo.*

cur igitur haec tanta facimus cum cetera perparva sint, . . .] *Haec* are the points just listed, covered by the *pontificium ius; cetera* are opposed to the *sacra,* the significant subgroup.

. . . de sacris autem, qui locus patet latius, haec sit una sententia, ut conserventur sem⟨per⟩ et deinceps familiis prodantur, et ut in lege posui, perpetua sint sacra?] This refers, of course, to § 22.13: *Sacra privata perpetua manento.* Cicero shows that this corresponds to his method of providing laws that are *non perfectae . . . sed ipsae summae rerum atque sententiae* (§ 18). For *haec . . . una sententia* see the headnote to this section; the point is taken up in the sequel: *hoc uno posito, quod est ad cognitionem disciplinae satis . . . —Semper et* is P's correction for *semet* of BAHL, reduced to *et* in ε.

48a haec iura pontificum auctoritate consecuta sunt, ut ne morte patris familias sacrorum memoria occideret, eis essent ea adiuncta ad quos eiusdem morte pecunia venerit.] Before *haec iura* the words *haec positae* are transmitted in the other witnesses but omitted in B, which is equal to the others in weight; thus they need not have been in the archetype, and there is no obstacle to their omission (cf. Schmidt, 1974, 78). Perhaps the error resulted from *saut du même au même* and is a rewriting of *hoc uno posito*, with which the following sentence begins.—*Sacra,* understood from the previous clause, should be taken as the subject of *consecuta sunt:* "The ritual acts [*sacra*] have, through the authority of the pontiffs, obtained the following legal rights . . ."; less convincing to separate *haec* from *iura* (so, e.g., Nickel), especially in view of the Ciceronian pattern whereby a form of *hic,* as object of *consequor,* forms the link to a defining *ut*-clause: cf. *TLL* s.v. *consequor* 409.22 ff.—The responses of pontiffs to queries from magistrates or private persons were kept on file in the *Regia* but had influence only in proportion to the *auctoritas* of the individual respondent; cf. Bruck, 2–3; hence Cicero's emphasis on this factor.—For *venerit* one expects *venisset;* for vividness Cicero shifts to the tense in which the rule was originally framed; cf. Kühner-Stegmann, 2, 194–95; du Mesnil *ad loc.*

hoc uno posito,—quibus implentur iuris consultorum libri.] Cf. the headnote to § 47.

48b–49 Quaeruntur enim qui astringantur sacris.—proinde habeatur quasi eam pecuniam ceperit.] *Quaeruntur—sacris:* for the form of expression cf. 1.4: *multa quaeruntur in Mario, fictane an vera sint.*—*Astringo* is "to bind" (here legally) by some obligation, commonly expressed in the ablative; cf. *OLD* s.v., 8a; *TLL* s.v., 963.25 ff. and esp. (in the language of jurists) 74 ff.

The original form of Roman testament was one entered into before the army or a citizen assembly; property would ordinarily be passed down within the family and along with it the familial religious rites (*sacra*). When the comitium testament was replaced by the private testament, the possibility arose that the property of the deceased would pass to a *heres extraneus* but that family members would still be responsible for performing the *sacra gentilicia.* The aim of the pontiffs was to see that the *sacra* were properly observed (cf. *Dom.* 37: *sacra . . . quorum custodes vos* [sc. the *pontifices*] *esse debetis*). But would this goal be better achieved by entrusting the *sacra* to relatives of the deceased, however impecunious, or to the inheritors of the property? In early times the performance of familial *sacra* was regarded as such a solemn obligation that, according to V.Max. 1.1.11, it was undertaken by members of the *gens Fabia* even amidst a besieging enemy in time of war. At some fairly early date, however, the pontiffs assumed the *sacra* to be more likely to be performed by the heir, and they established purely pontifical laws on the subject giving the heir this responsibility—an innovation unknown in other Italian communities; cf. Cato *hist.* fr. 61: *si quis mortuus est Arpinatis, eius heredem sacra non secuntur.* In the late Republic the performance of *sacra privata* was increasingly felt as a great burden, as is indicated by the proverbial expression for an unalloyed blessing, *sine sacris hereditas* (cf. Fest. p. 290M; A. Otto, 163). The policy of the Scaevolae shows a change of perspective, related, no doubt, to a change of *mores*: they provided loopholes to enable heirs to evade the *sacra*, apparently because they viewed the family as more likely to be conscientious in their performance. Cicero chooses to criticize the Scaevolae for corrupting pontifical law by an admixture of categories from the *ius civile;* but the older pontiffs had already taken that step by modeling the transfer of the *sacra* on that of property (see above); the Scaevolae merely carried the trend further (and were guided by a different purpose). Cf. Mommsen, *Staatsr.* 3, 20–22; Bruck, 4; de Visscher, 97 and 131.[120]

Our passage lists the five groups obliged, according to the doctrine Cicero learned from the younger Scaevola, to perform *sacra*. He also gives (§ 49b) the earlier set of rules (*ita descripta ab antiquis*). According to both systems the underlying principle is that the *sacra* follow the property. The two sets of rules may be summarized as follows (cf. Bruck, 4):

antiqui	Scaevola
(1) the heirs	(1) the heirs
(2) the *usucaptor* of most of the property	(3) the *usucaptor* of most of the property
(3) the legatee of most of the property if he has accepted any of it	(2) he who by virtue of the death or by testament receives as much as all the heirs together
	(4) in the absence of an heir or legatee, the creditor who receives the greatest part of the estate
	(5) in the absence of an heir or legatee, the debtor freed from obligation by the death.

120. Francesca Fontanella, "*Ius pontificium, ius civile* e *ius naturae* in *De Legibus* II, 45–53," *Athenaeum* 84 (1996), 254–60, thinks that Cicero regarded the *ius pontificium* at the prior stage as a close approximation of the *ius naturale*; possibly so, but he has not chosen to express the matter in such terms; one would have thought that a closer approximation of the *ius naturale* would be for both *sacra* and property to be passed down within the family.

Scaevola's innovation consists in further specifications under (3) of the earlier system (= no. 2 of the new one) and in the added points (4) and (5). The force of the change in (3) of the older system was (a) to recognize the *donatio mortis causa* (i.e., a gift agreed upon during the life of the benefactor to be valid in the event of his death) as equivalent to a legacy and (b) to make the burden of *sacra* depend upon actually receiving the majority of the estate, rather than the provision of the will, i.e., a legatee can avoid the *sacra* by declining to accept a majority of the estate—an impossibility under the older system. Items (4) and (5) are, as is argued in the notes below, an extrapolation from (2) of the older system and intended to meet the more complex circumstances of the later Republican economy. The purpose of the reform of (3) under the ancient system was surely to see to it that the *sacra* would not pass to non-relatives who had no desire to perform them by giving such persons a way out. The point of the Mucian reform was clearly to protect the continuity of the rites by increasing the chances that they would be performed by interested relatives (reform of [3]) or by adding other beneficiaries of the death to the list of those responsible under (4) and (5). The reform thus sought to combat one manifestation of the neglect of religious rites characteristic of the late Republic; cf. Var. *ARD* 1.2a, cited *ad* § 33 *supra;* Mary Beard, *CAH* 9, 742–45. See also the note after next.

48b tertio loco, si nemo sit heres, is qui de bonis quae eius fuerint cum moritur usu ceperit plurimum possidendo; . . .] Roman law recognized in *usucapio* a primitive method of establishing possession of property by use, i.e., the possessor was freed from having to prove ownership after a certain time had elapsed; cf. Kaser, 1971, 418 ff. (§ 101); Berger s.v. *Usucapio*. Here, too, possession of the greater part of the property entails responsibility for the *sacra* both in the Mucian system and its predecessor (where it is method no. 2). On the whole subject cf. Gennaro Franciosi, *Usucapio pro herede. Contributo allo studio dell' antica hereditas.* Pubblicazioni della Facoltà Giuridica dell' Università di Napoli 74 (Naples, 1965).

quarto, si {qui} nemo sit qui ullam rem ceperit, ⟨qui⟩ de creditoribus eius plurimum servet.] Here and in the following provision Scaevola goes beyond the older system by making the creditor occupy the same position as the functionally equivalent *usucaptor.* The new system thus does greater justice to the growing complexity of economic life in the late Republic, as de Plinval, 1969, 305, points out. The new realities are reflected, for instance, in Cicero's own extensive lists of creditors and debtors; cf. Shatzman, 416–20. This and the following rule also provide for non-family members to perform the rites—a need that arose as aristocratic families died out, a process accelerated by the civil war of the 80s (cf. Friedrich Münzer, *Römische*

Adelsparteien und Adelsfamilien [Stuttgart, 1920], 302 = Engl. tr. 278). However, insofar as Scaevola *père* was involved in drafting the rule (at § 50 Cicero again speaks of *Scaevolae*), it must have predated the civil war.—On the text: *quarto si* of S² corrects the transmitted *quarto si qui* (*quarto qui si:* P). In view of the loss of *qui* later in the sentence (inserted by the *recentiores*), one suspects that the word was overlooked in transcription and falsely reinserted.

49 extrema illa persona est, ut si quis ei qui mortuus sit pecuniam debuerit, nemini {qui} eam solverit, proinde habeatur quasi eam pecuniam ceperit.] The debtors of the deceased are, in the absence of an heir, the beneficiaries of the death and thus are treated the same way as the *usucaptores* and creditors; see the previous note.—*Si quis* is the reading of the *recentiores* for *si is qui* (BAε) or *si his qui* (HL); Halm deleted the *qui* following *nemini.*

haec nos a Scaevola didicimus. non ita discripta sunt ab antiquis; . . .] For the summarizing formula with *haec* cf. § 61: *Haec habemus in XII;* § 67: *haec igitur Athenienses tui.*—After the death of the Augur in 87 (cf. *ad* 1.13), Cicero and others turned to the Pontifex for further training; cf. *Amic.* 1; F. Münzer, *RE* 16.1 (1933), 440.36–41.—*Discripta sunt* (Powell) is probably right for *descriptas* ES¹RHL or *descriptis* B¹; the sense should be "were classified, set in order" (cf. *OLD* s.v. *discribo* 1c and 2); Bˣ already presents *descripta sunt;* see Powell's apparatus for further detail and for the distinction between the two verbs *ad* § 11.

nam illi quidem his verbis—si inde quippiam ceperit'; . . .] See *ad* §§ 48b–49. **. . . aut, si maior pars pecuniae legata est, si inde quippiam ceperit'; . . .]** "The phrase *si inde quippiam ceperit . . .* apparently was intended to defeat attempts by the legatee of the greater part of the legacy to escape liability for the *sacra* by accepting only a minor part. In this case, too, he was to be held liable for the *sacra*" (Bruck, 5).

50 videtis igitur omnia pendere ex uno illo, quod pontifi⟨ces⟩ cum pecunia sacra coniungi volunt, isdemque ferias et caerimonias adscribendas putant ⟨ad quos pecunia pervenerit⟩.] Cicero has abstracted from these rules the single principle *quod pontifi⟨ces⟩ cum pecunia sacra coniungi volunt,* i.e., they aimed to balance the expensive obligation of performing the *sacra* with benefits from the estate.—*Pontifi⟨ces⟩ cum* is Madvig's correction for *pontificum* (after R. Stephanus, who had simply substituted *pontifices* for *pontificum*).—Mommsen substituted *hereditates* for *ferias,* but the latter are surely the holidays on which the rites were to be performed; cf. *ad* § 45 (*Habeo ista; nunc de sacris perpetuis—*). But the sense he had in view can be restored by the addition of *ad quos pecunia pervenerit,* suggested *exempli gratia* by Powell.

Atque etiam dant hoc Scaevolae, cum est partitio, ut si in testamento deducta scripta non sit ipsique minus ceperint quam omnibus heredibus relinquatur, sacris ne alligentur.] The loose connector *atque etiam* is found also at 1.39 and 49 (cf. on the latter). Ziegler, after du Mesnil, conjectured *hoc docent* for *dant hoc* so as to make this point an addition to Scaevola's teaching as previously described (*haec nos a Scaevola didicimus:* § 49). It is not, however, so much an addition to the previous points as a method of obviating Scaevola's point (2). It was probably a response to a request for advice in a particular case (*si in testamento deducta scripta non sit*). Do here surely has the sense "give, grant (a position, right, or other immaterial object)"; cf., e.g., *Fin.* 2.86; it is sometimes so used, as here, with an *ut*-clause; cf. *OLD* s.v., 2a.—*Cum* (or *quom*) is Davies' generally accepted correction for the transmitted *quod*; for the same error cf. *ad* 1.33; sim. *quorum* transmitted for *cum* at § 22.5.—*Partitio* stands for *partitio legata*, "a legacy by which a fraction of an estate is left to the legatee (*legatarius partiarius*) who shares the inheritance with the heirs instituted in a testament" (Berger s.v. *Partitio legata*).— *Deducta* (= *deductio*) appears here for the first time as a substantive; cf. *TLL* s.v. *deduco* 283.10; a similar perfect participle substantivized as a feminine is *collecta* = "a contribution" (*de Orat.* 2.233). The word refers to a nominal sum, typically one hundred *nummi* (cf. § 53), deducted from his share in order to relieve the legatee of the burden of the *sacra*. In this case, though the testator had neglected the point, the pontiff allows the legatee to renounce a small share of the legacy in order to avoid the *sacra;* we can call this variant (2a) in Scaevola's system; cf. Bruck, 7.

(in donatione hoc idem secus interpretantur, et quod pater familias in eius donatione qui in ipsius potestate est approbavit, ratum est; quod eo insciente factum est, si id is non approbat, ratum non est.)] The reference is to the *donatio mortis causa,* a gift effective on the owner's death (cf. Berger s.v.). Scaevola's point (2) treats such a gift as equivalent to a legacy (*qui morte testamentove eius tantundem capiat . . . :* § 48) for purposes of assigning the *sacra.* This is evidently another *responsum* of Scaevola, in another case (cf. the previous note): he allows the *donatio,* with its entailed *sacra,* to be voided by the *pater familias* of the beneficiary; we can denote this as variant (2b) of Scaevola's doctrine. This is an unsurprising finding given the general control of the *pater familias* over his dependents and their financial dealings; cf. Kaser, 1971, 345–50 (§ 83); Berger s.v. *Pater familias.*

51 his propositis, quaestiunculae multae nascuntur; quas qui {nascuntur} intellegat, non, si ad caput referat, per se ipse facile perspiciat?] This is the second appearance in extant Latin of *quaestiuncula;* the diminutive also implies contempt at *de Orat.* 1.102, quoted on 1.14. Cf. Hanssen, 137, 186 and 192.—The second *nascuntur,* an evident dittography, was omitted already in Pε.—*Intellego* is intransitive here (= "have or exercise powers of understanding"); cf. *OLD* s.v., 7.—For *si ad caput referat* cf. *ad* § 46.

—veluti si minus quis cepisset—solum sine coheredibus sacris alligari.] Cicero introduces this scenario as an illustration (*veluti*) of his view that the detailed arguments all flow from a grasp of the general principle (*caput*). The case begins with situation (2a) above, i.e., the voluntary renunciation by legatee A of a portion of the legacy in order to avoid the *sacra.* One of the heirs, B, claimed not only the portion of the legacy passed over by A but also another portion so that his total share came to more than that of all the other heirs: B was then bound to perform the *sacra* without the participation of his co-heirs.

quin etiam cavent ut—quasi ea pecunia legata non esset.] This is the third way Scaevola provided of evading the *sacra* (2c) and involves collaboration of the legatee and the heirs. The old legal ceremony *per aes et libram,* performed before five Roman citizens as witnesses and a man holding the scales (*libripens*), and involving a set form of words, frees the heirs of the obligation of paying the legacy (*nexi liberatio*). At the same time, as Cicero mentions in § 53, the legatee receives a *stipulatio* from the heirs that they will pay the amount in question. The transaction thus becomes, formally, the fulfillment of a *stipulatio* rather than the payment of a legacy, and the *sacra* are thus the responsibility of the heirs, rather than the erstwhile legatee; cf. Bruck, 7, and for the legal forms Berger s.vv. *Nexum* and *Per aes et libram; ad* 1.14.

52 Hoc ego loco multisque aliis quaero a vobis, Scaevolae, . . .] This imitation of debate continues the diatribe style from § 47; see *ad loc.* (*totumne? quid ita? . . .*). For the Scaevolae treated as a unit ibid. (on '*sae⟨pe⟩*', *inquit Publi filius,* '*ex patre audivi . . .*').

civilis enim iuris scientia pontificium quodam modo tollitis.] This is the burden of Cicero's criticism, restated more provocatively in the sequel (*itaque si vos . . .*), namely that the Scaevolae have essentially annexed the *ius pontificium* to the *ius civile;* see *ad* §§ 48b–49.

nam sacra cum pecunia pontificum auctoritate, nulla lege coniuncta sunt; . . .] Cf. § 50 (*videtis igitur omnia pendere ex uno illo, quod pontifi⟨ces⟩ cum pecunia sacra coniungi volunt . . .*); the principle was already latent in the previous pontifical findings (cf. § 49) and was refined by the Scaevolae. For the rôle of *pontificum auctoritas* cf. *ad* § 48a.

itaque si vos tantummodo pontifices essetis, pontificalis maneret auctoritas, sed quod idem iuris civilis estis peritissimi, hac scientia illam eluditis.] *Eludo* here has the sense "frustrare, irritum reddere, tollere" or perhaps rather the weaker sense "infirmare, infringere": cf. *TLL* s.v., 430.52–58 (citing our passage). In Cicero's view, to descend to such distinctions as the Scaevolae have drawn about responsibility for the *sacra* is unworthy of *pontifices;* cf. § 47: *quid enim ad pontificem de iure parietum aut aquarum, aut ullo omnino nisi eo quod cum religione coniunctum est?* The distinctions also serve to weaken the basic principle that the *sacra* follow the money (§ 50). **placuit P. Scaevolae et Ti. Coruncanio pontificibus maximis, itemque ceteris, eos qui tantundem caperent quantum omnes heredes, sacris alligari.]** This is, then, as § 49 suggested, a traditional view of *pontifices* going back well before Scaevola (– *iur.* 8, 3 = *iur. anteh.* 33, 8a). Ti. Coruncanius (cos. 280) became in 254 the first plebeian pontifex maximus: *MRR* 1, 210; our passage is one of only two preserved fragments (*iur.* 1, 2). By Cicero's time little was known of his personality and views; cf. Münzer, *RE* 4.2 (1901), 1663.47 ff., esp. 1664.6 ff.; on Coruncanius as a jurist cf. Jörs, ibid. 1664.25 ff., and Wieacker, 1988, 535.

habeo ius pontificium: . . .] For *habeo* cf. *ad* § 45 (*habeo ista*). The implication, as at § 50, is that this single principle is all one needs.

53 partitionis caput scriptum caute: ut centum nummi deducerentur, . . .] The *partitionis caput* is the clause or section of the will providing for the division of property between legatee and heirs (cf. *OLD* s.v. *caput* 18; for *partitio ad* § 50). For the doctrine cf. *ad* §§ 48b–49.—*Ut* introduces a proviso (*OLD* s.v., 31).

quid si hoc qui testamentum faciebat cavere noluisset? admonet iuris consultus hic quidem, ipse Mucius, pontifex idem, ut minus capiat quam omnibus heredibus relinquatur . . .] This is variant (2a) described *ad* § 50 *supra*. At § 47 the description of the Scaevolae as *pontifices ambo et idem iuris peritissimi* seemed benign; here, however, the two rôles seem to conflict, the *iuris consultus* finding ways to evade rights that the pontifex maximus ought to be enforcing. In fact, however, the effect of Scaevola's refinements is to give the legatee the chance to opt out of the *sacra* and thus leave them in the hands of family members, who would be more likely to discharge them conscientiously (the legatee being likely to be burdened by familial *sacra* of his own); cf. Bruck, 9; *ad* §§ 48b–49.—*Quid si* is the reading of APεHL, *qui si* that of B; R. Stephanus' *quod si* is often adopted, unnecessarily.— Contrasting *quidem solum* adheres, as often, to a pronoun (*hic*), with adversative asyndeton following; cf. Solodow, 36 and 67 ff.; § 43 above. **. . . (super⟨iores⟩ dicebant, quidquid cepisset, astringi): rursus sacris liberatur.]** This refers to no. (3) of the doctrine of the *antiqui* (cf. *ad* §§ 48b–49): *si maior pars pecuniae legata est, si inde quippiam ceperit* (§ 49), where no provision is made for the legatee to accept a smaller share on his own initiative, whereas Scaevola allows this to occur (2a). *Rursus*, i.e., in addition to the method just mentioned of deducting one hundred *nummi* from the amount of the legacy.—*Superiores* (Turnebus[2]) is the needed correction of *super;* for the usage, not uncommon, of persons cf. *OLD* s.v. *superior* 4b; Görler *ad loc.* tries to revive *supra* of Turnebus[1], but cf. Watt, 1986, 267. Watt conjectures *semper,* but surely the subject must be clearly stated.

hoc vero nihil ad pontificium ius et e medio est iure civili,—sitque ea non 〈. . .〉] This is variant (2c); only here does Cicero provide full detail as to the legatee's compensation via a *stipulatio;* cf. *ad* § 51.—For *et* in the corrective sense cf. 1.41: *nihil alterius causa facit et metitur suis commodis omnia* and *TLL* s.v., 893.56 ff.—The following lacuna was first detected by Turnebus; see the next note.

54–68 When the text resumes after the lacuna, Cicero has evidently concluded his critique of the Scaevolae for mixing the *ius civile* with the *ius pontificium* and thus endangering the perpetuity of the *sacra* (cf. *ad* §§ 46–53).[121] Since there is no change of topic between §§ 54 and 55, we must assume that § 54, too, belongs under the heading *quae sint in pontificio iure* [sc. *de iure Manium*]; cf. § 45 and § 58 *init.* On the basis of the words *eadem illa de immortalitate animorum* at § 68, Vahlen, du Mesnil, and others have supposed that the topic of the *ius Manium* was introduced with a digression on the immortality of the soul (cf. Schmidt, 1959, 94). But the words *eadem illa* would not suffice to connect § 68 with a discussion of the soul's immortality preceding at such a great interval, and our context does not require such a discussion; cf. also on fr. ex inc. lib. 2. The lacuna must have contained the conclusion to the treatment of the *sacra* and transition to the new topic of the *ius Manium.* Beyond that, one can speculate that there might have been some discussion of the concept of the *di Manes,* including the beginning of the argument continued in § 55 that the *maiores* divinized the dead.[122] One might also have expected an explanation of the fact that, though such matters are *sacra privata,* they fall within the jurisdiction of the *pontifices*[123] and/or of the definition of *religio* or of a *locus religiosus,* on which much of the following discussion turns (cf. § 55: *tanta est religio sepulcrorum;* the distinction at § 58 when Cicero goes on to the next topic,

121. Thus I doubt that the Scaevolae should be understood as the subject of *negent* at the beginning of § 55, as Schmidt, 1959, 87, thinks possible; the subject is more likely to be the *pontifices* in general. The statement *totaque huius iuris compositio pontificalis magnam religionem caerimoniamque declarat* (§ 55) suggests that Cicero has by now passed from a critique of the Scaevolae to a general discussion of the pontifical law of burials; cf. also Atticus' summarizing comment *video quae sint in pontificio iure* (§ 58).

122. Cf. the words *nec vero tam denicales . . . quam ceterorum caelestium quieti dies, 'feriae' nominarentur, nisi maiores eos qui ex hac vita migrassent in deorum numero esse voluissent.*

123. On this cf. Bendlin, 1998, 264 and n. 7; 300 and n. 91.

the relevant provisions of *leges: sed ea <u>non</u> tam ad religionem spectant quam ad ius sepulcrorum;* de Visscher, 144). Cicero seems likely to have indicated what would or would not fall within the scope of his treatment, with D. Brutus' eccentric celebration of the Parentalia in December, rather than February, perhaps cited (§ 54) merely as an example of matters too minor to be discussed in detail (note the words *<u>neque</u> necesse est edisseri a nobis* . . . : § 55). The following are the main subdivisions of the argument:

    I. *Quae sint in pontificio iure* (§§ 54–57)
      A. Regarding festivals of the dead (§ 54)
      B. Regarding burial (§§ 55–57)
   II. *Quid sit in legibus* (§§ 58–62a)
  III. *Sepulcrorum modus* (§§ 62b–68).

It is noticeable that the first two main divisions are based on the sources used, the final one on a topic (§ 62: *sed cedo ut ceteri sumptus sic etiam sepulcrorum modum*). In fact, it will turn out that, since Rome offers no precedents for limitation on expenditures for tombs, Cicero turns here to Greek sources, both historical and literary (cf. Schmidt, 1959, 92). Nor does he confine himself to expenses for tombs but adds Greek material on method of burial, restrictions on mourning, etc., already touched on in the Roman context. The result is a crossing of two sets of categories, but there is no real difficulty in following the argument, discursive though it sometimes is; cf. ibid. 93 and 95.

    The two different approaches suggest, however, several different sources or sets of sources somewhat hastily combined: (1) a commentary on the pontifical books, perhaps consulted by Cicero also in connection with *Dom.* (cf. p. 390, n. 126); (2) an explication of the Twelve Tables on funerals and burials; (3) a source for Greek (mostly Athenian) legislation on the same topics; of these (2) may well be a work of L. Aelius Stilo (see *ad* §§ 58–62a) and (3) a work of Demetrius of Phalerum (cf. *ad* § 64). For the hypothesis that Posidonius was used for §§ 62b–66 see *ad loc.* Cicero injects some comments bearing on the politics and mores of his own day (Marius and Sulla [§ 56]; the tomb of C. Figulus [§ 62b]). Some of the points are introduced with a subjective coloring[124] that suggests that these are Cicero's own inferences from the data; cf. Siewert, 334; Rawson, 1991, 67–68 and 137 and n. 35.

---

124. *Sed mensem <u>credo</u> extremum anni* . . . *sequebatur:* § 54; *ac mihi quidem antiquissimum sepulturae genus illud fuisse <u>videtur</u>* . . . ; *quod <u>haud scio an</u> timens* . . . : § 57; *<u>credo</u> vel propter ignis periculum:* § 58; *<u>credo</u> quod erat factitatum* . . . *quod ne fieret lege sanctum est:* § 60.

The passage is of interest for its setting of Greek and Roman materials on the same level: the oldest burials, Cyrus, known from Xenophon, and Numa (§ 56); the laws of Solon compared with the XII Tables (§§ 59 and 64), including one word from Solon's code, τύμβος, translated by *bustum,* a word from the XII Tables (§ 64); *nenia,* said to be a term for a dirge in both languages (§ 62); luxurious burials equally prevalent in the Athens of Demetrius of Phalerum and in Rome of Cicero's day (§ 66); the Greek and Latin designations for the hexameter verse, the latter quoted from Ennius (op. inc. fr. 20) in a citation of Plato (§ 68); cf. Siewert, 336–37. As in the citation of foreign examples elsewhere in this Book (§§ 26, 28, 33, 35, 37–39) the aim is to construct a cult practice that incorporates the best of native and foreign traditions or rather that purifies the native by reference to the foreign ones: *Ex patriis ritibus optima colunto* (§ 22.3). Part of the strategy involves upgrading the Romans' view of Greek traditions (note the "ennobling" effect of the Ciceronian translations cited above). Thus the view of Solon's laws in *Leg.* contrasts sharply with that of Crassus at *de Orat.* 1.197.[125]

If in *Leg.* we see something of Cicero's antiquarian interests, it is not merely that he was intent on turning to account *paralipomena* gathered in connection with *Rep.*[126] The antiquarian approach is controlled by Cicero's conception of antiquity as closest to the gods (§ 26) and of the oldest as best (§ 40). It is thus notable that, although various pieces of sumptuary legislation for funerals are attested subsequent to the Twelve Tables (see the list at Engels, 170 n. 55), Cicero's discussion of Roman legislation on the subject confines itself exclusively to the Twelve. For the Roman ways of dealing with death at this period cf. in general Hopkins, ch. 4.

54 ⟨. . .⟩ doctum hominem sane, cuius fuit Accius perfamiliaris; . . .] On the probable contents of the lacuna see the previous note.—The man characterized as *doctus* and a friend of Accius is D. Junius Brutus Callaicus (cos. 138), as Plut. *Qu. Rom.* 34 makes clear: διὰ τί τῶν ἄλλων Ῥωμαίων ἐν τῷ Φεβρουαρίῳ μηνὶ ποιουμένων χοὰς καὶ ἐναγισμοὺς τοῖς τεθνηκόσι Δέκιμος Βροῦτος, ὡς Κικέρων ἱστόρηκεν, ἐν τῷ Δεκεμβρίῳ τοῦτ' ἔπραττεν; ἦν δ' οὗτος ὁ Λυσιτάνειαν ἐπελθὼν καὶ πρῶτος ἐπέκεινα στρατῷ διαβὰς τὸν τῆς Λήθης ποταμόν. This description of his exploits may have been drawn by Plutarch from our passage prior to its mutilation. On this man, awarded a

---

125. . . . *quantum praestiterint nostri maiores prudentia ceteris gentibus, tum facillime intellegetis, si cum illorum Lycurgo et Dracone et Solone nostras leges conferre volueritis. incredibile est enim quam sit omne ius civile praeter hoc nostrum inconditum ac paene ridiculum* . . .

126. Here Cicero may also be calling upon the close study of pontifical law he undertook in preparation for *Dom.*; cf. esp. *Dom.* 136 = *FLP* 41–42; *ad* § 58.

triumph for subjugation of the Lusitani and Callaici in campaigns of 138–37 (whence the *adnomen*), cf. Münzer, *RE* 10.1 (1918), 1021.17 ff., esp. 1024.32 ff. The relation to Accius was clear from the Saturnian epigrams he commissioned from the poet to adorn the vestibule of the temple of Mars he built in the Campus Martius (cf. *Arch.* 27; sch. Bob. *ad loc.* [p. 179 St.]; E. Stärk in W. Suerbaum, ed., *Die archaische Literatur von den Anfängen bis Sullas Tod,* Handbuch der lateinischen Literatur der Antike, ed. R. Herzog and P.L. Schmidt, 1 [Munich, 2002], 164–65); Accius is also supposed to have written a book under Brutus' name—or is this perhaps a confused reference to the praetexta *Brutus* celebrating his ancestor's expulsion of the Tarquins (sch. Bob. *loc. cit.:* . . . *sub eius nomine Acci, poetae tragici, exstat liber;* frr. at *trag.* pp. 328–31)?—For the prefix of *perfamiliaris* cf. p. 40 n. 143.

sed mensem credo extremum anni, ut veteres Februarium, si⟨c⟩ hic Decembrem sequebatur.] In context and in light of Plut. *loc. cit.* this will refer to the time of the celebration of the yearly rites in honor of the dead, the Parentalia, which began on 13 February (cf. *ad* § 45). Cicero supposes that Brutus transferred these rites to December because he meant to celebrate them in the last month of the year (*mensem . . . extremum anni . . . sequebatur*). Cicero evidently connects this change with the reform whereby, beginning in 153, the consular year began on 1 January, rather than 1 March, so that December, not February, became its last month (*ut veteres Februarium, si⟨c⟩ hic Decembrem sequebatur*); cf. Mommsen, *Historische Schriften,* 1 (Berlin, 1906) = *Gesammelte Schriften,* 4 (rp. Berlin-Dublin-Zurich, 1965), 102 and n. 24; *Staatsr.* 1, 600 n. 1; this brought the consular year into line with the calendar year; cf. Michels, 97 ff. But Cicero's interpretation is suspect: it is hard to see why Brutus should have oriented his familial rites on the consular year, when the calendar year was the basis for religious festivities generally. Wissowa, 233, thinks that Brutus chose to celebrate the rites just after the Larentalia (23 December); or perhaps he thought time could be more easily spared for the festival at mid-winter; cf. the headnote to § 29a. Plut. *loc. cit.* in the previous note offers further alternative explanations.—*Sic* is Minutianus' correction.

hostia autem maxima parentare pietatis esse adiunctum putabat.] The offerings at the Parentalia were simple, reminiscent of the earlier economy (bread is attested at Cat. 59; cf. also Ov. *Fast.* 2.535: *parva petunt Manes*); cf. Wissowa, 410. Brutus evidently adduced the availability of large victims as an argument for celebrating the Parentalia in December.—*Parento,* the technical term for "making offerings at the tombs of the dead" esp. in the context of the Parentalia, is attested from the second century onward, e.g., Cornelia fr. 4 Cugusi: *parentabis mihi et invocabis deum parentem;* ours is the earliest attestation with instrumental ablative (*hostia maxima*); cf. *TLL* s.v.; *OLD* s.v., 1.—As Ziegler saw, *adiunctum* is a substantive here, so Bake's deletion of the word is unnecessary; cf. *coniunctum* as a substantive at *de Orat.* 2.166 and *Top.* 53. There is, however, no unambiguous instance of *adiunctum* with genitive in Cicero (at *Ac.* 1.21 *vitae* can be dative), whereas *Inv.* 1.41 shows the dative (*adiunctum negotio*); cf. *TLL* s.v. *adiungo* 712.31 ff. One might therefore contemplate *pietati esse adiunctum*.

55 iam tanta religio est sepulcrorum, ut extra sacra et gentem inferri fas negent esse, idque apud maiores nostros A. Torquatus in gente Popillia iudicavit.] The basic distinction was between *sepulcra familiaria* and *sepulcra hereditaria*, with our passage clearly in the former sphere; cf. Mommsen, *Juristische Schriften*, 3 (Berlin, 1907) = *Gesammelte Schriften*, 1 (rp. Berlin-Dublin-Zurich, 1965), 204; Kaser, 1978, 43; Rüpke, 1995, 196. Few tombs containing family members of more than one generation have been found; cf. Hopkins, 205–6.—The subject of *negent* is presumably the *pontifices* in general (so de Visscher, 145; our passage was not, however, included in *FLP*); cf. p. 388 n. 121 *supra*. The aim of this ruling is clearly to prevent appropriation or other alienation of tombs; cf. Lenel, 226; Paul. *Sent.* 1.21.6 (sim. 9): *qui sepulchrum alienum effregerit vel aperuerit eoque mortuum suum alienumve intulerit, sepulchrum violasse videtur;* de Visscher, 55 ff.; Behrends, 1978, 93 and n. 34; on such risks and strategies for avoiding them cf. Paul Veyne, "Monumentum rude ex ascia," *RPh* 56 (1982), 189–90.—This A. (Manlius) Torquatus is otherwise unknown but must have attained praetorian rank; cf. Münzer, *RE* 14.1 (1928), 1194.18 ff. (Manlius no. 75), who wonders whether he may be identical with no. 73 or 74 or whether we may have a confused reference to T. Torquatus (no. 83; cos. 165), a known expert on sacred and secular law. Any of these would qualify chronologically, the *maiores* ordinarily being two generations or more older than Cicero (cf. Roloff, 131).—*In gente* = "in the case of the family"; for *in* virtually equivalent to *de* cf. *ad* 1.51.—The *Popillii* were a plebeian *gens* first attested after the Licinian-Sextian laws; the branch that bore the *cognomen Laenas* was prominent in the middle Republic; its last known representative lived under Tiberius; cf. Volkmann, *RE* 22.1 (1953), 50.33 ff.

nec vero tam denicales, quae a nece appellatae sunt quia residentur mortuis, quam ceterorum caelestium quieti dies, 'feriae' nominarentur, . . .] The family polluted by the death must first insure the corpse a proper burial and then pass a liminal period of nine days (the *feriae denicales*) before resuming normal activity; cf. Paul. *Fest.* p. 70M: *denicales feriae colebantur cum hominis mortui causa familia purgabatur. Graeci enim* νέκυν *mortuum* *dicunt;* Samter, *RE* 5.1 (1903), 219.59 ff. (s.v. Denicales feriae); de Visscher, 144–45; Toynbee, 50; the note after next.—Cicero's etymology (evidently < *de nece*) is accepted by *TLL* and *OLD* s.v. *denicalis;* more reserved Ernout-Meillet: "Formation obscure: dérivé de *de nece?* Cf. *parentalis, lustralis.*" Rüpke, 1995, 511–12 and n. 92, interprets differently: he compares the propitiation following a rain of stones or an earthquake, each involving *feriae novemdiales,* as well as the forbidden naming of chthonic divinities, likewise atoned for by *feriae* (Macr. *sat.* 1.16.8). Similarly, the disturbance of the earth, or the powers beneath the earth, entailed by burial would require propitiation (see further *ad* § 57: *porcam heredi esse contractam*—). If that is so, then, *pace* Cicero, the *feriae denicales* would presumably derive from *deni* "ten each" (= nine by the earlier inclusive method of counting); cf. also *ad* § 3.7.3.—*Quia residentur mortuis* = "because they are passed in idleness for the dead," a rare instance of the transitive use of this verb (here passive); cf. *OLD* s.v. *resideo* 1c. The prohibition of work on the *feriae denicales* extended to the harnassing of mules (Col. 2.21.5 = *FLP* 32B) and the watering of a meadow (Serv. auct. *G.* 1.272 = *FLP* 32A); they even provided a valid excuse for suspending a soldier's oath of obedience (Gel. 16.4.4).—On the *feriae* in general cf. *ad* §§ 19.9, 29a, and 45.

. . . nisi maiores eos qui ex hac vita migrassent in deorum numero esse voluissent; . . .] The status of the *denicales* as *dies feriae* is used to undergird the divinization of the dead (cf. § 22.15: *Suos leto datos divos habento*), perhaps mistakenly: see the previous note. The *religiosa iura* established for the dead by the ancestors is offered as a proof of the soul's immortality at *Amic.* 13.

eas in eos dies conferre ius, ut ne ipsius neve publicae feriae sint.] "The law requires that these days of purification should be fitted into the religious calendar in such a way that they do not clash with other private or public holidays" (Rudd). *Eae* = *denicales,* previously referred to as feminine (*quae a nece appellatae sunt*), whereas *ei dies* are *ceterorum caelestium quieti dies.*—*Feriae* can be used with the genitive either of the celebrant or the honorand; cf. *TLL* s.v., 503.84 ff. But *ipsius* here is reflexive (so Madvig *ad Fin.* 1.67; cf. in general *TLL* s.v. *ipse* 302.65 ff.) and hence refers to the former.—*Ne . . . neve* is Powell's correction for *nec . . . neque.*—The *denicales,* themselves *feriae,* are to be kept separate from the other family festivals and from public festivals.[127] As Samter, *loc. cit.* note before last, 229.28 ff., pointed out, our passage shows that the timing of the *feriae denicales* was discretionary, albeit the family would certainly want to be purified as

---

127. *Ut* thus introduces a consecutive clause with limiting force.

soon as possible; the day of the funeral itself could not be counted as part of the *denicales*, however (Gel. 16.4.4). A similar restriction applied to the date of the *funus*: Col. 2.22.4 = *FLP* no. 36: *feriis publicis hominem mortuum sepelire non licet.*

totaque huius iuris compositio pontificalis magnam religionem caerimoni-amque declarat.] Our passage certainly suggests that pontifical law dealt with the subject at length, in spite of our meager surviving testimonies; cf. *N.D.* 1.84: *deinde nominum* [sc. *divinorum*] *non magnus numerus ne in pontificiis quidem nostris* [sc. *libris*]; de Visscher, 44.—*Hoc ius pontificale* merely refers to the *ius feriarum denicalium;* hence our passage should not be used to try to prove a general early competence of the pontiffs in regard to burials; cf. ibid. 146 and n. 25.—For *religionem caerimoniamque* cf. *ad* 1.43.

neque necesse est edisseri a nobis, quae finis funestae familiae, quod genus sacrificii Lari vervecibus fiat, . . .] For the impurity attaching to the corpse cf. Parker, ch. 2; de Visscher, 33–35. The period of mourning concluded with one of the oldest cult practices at Rome, the propitiatory sacrifice of wethers (*verveces*) to the Lar familiaris, purifying the family and marking the transition back to normal life; cf. Wissowa, 411; Latte, 1960, 102.— The use of *finis* as feminine is unusual: cf. *Fam.* 12.1.1; *OLD* s.v.; Hans Bauer, "Das Geschlecht von *finis*," *Glotta* 10 (1920), 122–28, thinks that the feminine *finis* spread from adverbial *ea*, by later misunderstanding expanded to *ea fine.*—For Marcus' refusal to descend to details cf. 1.14; contrary to the implication of our lemma, however, he does discuss some such details in § 57.

. . . quemadmodum os resectum terra obtegatur . . .] This practice implies that inhumation was the original mode of burial and had to be used for at least a token part of the body even after cremation was prevalent; cf. Latte, 1960, 100–101; *ad* § 56. Cf. Paul. *Fest.* p. 148M: *membrum abscidi mortuo dicebatur, cum digitus eius decidebatur, ad quod servatum iusta fierent reliquo corpore combusto.* This is sometimes held to refer to the treatment of the corpse of one who died abroad (cf. Var. *L.* 5.23: *. . . si os exceptum est mortui ad familiam purgandam . . .* ; Latte, 1960, 101 n. 1, with literature); this would be one application of the doctrine but not the only one; cf. *ad* § 57.

. . . quaeque in porca contracta iura sint, quo tempore incipiat sepulcrum esse et religione teneatur.] These points are dealt with more fully in § 57; see *ad loc.*

56 Ac mihi quidem antiquissimum sepulturae genus illud fuisse videtur, quo apud Xenophontem Cyrus utitur: . . .] *Ac* is Lambinus' correction for *at.*— For the antiquity of inhumation cf. also § 63. Pliny, too, held inhumation to be earlier than cremation (*Nat.* 7.187: *ipsum cremare, apud Romanos non* *fuit veteris instituti: terra condebantur*); he goes on to give the exhumation of those who died abroad as the motive for change. The archaeological evidence on priority in Rome is ambivalent, though by 400 B.C. cremation was the general practice; cf. Toynbee, 39–40.—Cicero had translated Xenophon's *Oeconomicus* at an early age (cf. *ad Off.* 2.87) and was aware of the younger Scipio's admiration for the *Cyropaedia* (*Q.fr.* 1.1.23 and *Tusc.* 2.62).—The deverbative *sepultura* is not part of the early sacral vocabulary but belongs to the series of technical terms from various disciplines formed in -*ura*, it is attested from *Rhet. Her.* onward; cf. Zellmer, 269–71.

redditur enim terrae corpus, et ita locatum ac situm quasi operimento matris obducitur.] A summarizing paraphrase of Cyrus' famous concluding speech from the *Cyropaedia* (8.7.25): τὸ δ᾽ ἐμὸν σῶμα, ὦ παῖδες, ὅταν τελευτήσω, μήτε ἐν χρυσῷ θῆτε μήτε ἐν ἀργύρῳ μήτε ἐν ἄλλῳ μηδενί, ἀλλὰ τῇ γῇ ὡς τάχιστα ἀπόδοτε. τί γὰρ τούτου μακαριώτερον τοῦ γῇ μιχθῆναι, ἣ πάντα μὲν τὰ καλά, πάντα δὲ τἀγαθὰ φύει τε καὶ τρέφει, whereby the justification (τί γὰρ τούτου μακαριώτερον—) is omitted;[128] cf. Pascucci, 1981, 423. Cyrus' practice reinforces the laws of Plato and Cicero against luxurious burials; cf. § 45.—*Operimentum*, transparent in its formation from *operire* (cf. Var. *L.* 5.167), is attested from Cato onward (cf. *TLL* s.v. *operimentum*, esp. 681.1–3). The *quasi* refers to the metaphorical designation of the earth as *mater* (cf. Serv. Verg. *G.* 2.268, *A.* 3.96, 12.209), a considerable compression of Xenophon's relative clause ἣ πάντα . . . τρέφει.

eodemque ritu in eo sepulcro quod ⟨haud⟩ procul a Fontis ara est, regem nostrum Numam conditum accepimus; . . .] Here, as so often in the later *philosophica*, Cicero finds a Roman example to pair with a Greek one (or, to be more precise for our passage, a Persian one known via a Greek source); cf. *ad* 1.42.—*Haud* is Grotius' insertion; there is a similar omission of an expected negative before *procul* at *Rep.* 1.1; cf. Zetzel *ad loc.*—Solin. 1.21 places Numa's tomb *sub Ianiculo;* Plut. *Num.* 22.2 records a similar tradition: πυρὶ μὲν οὖν οὐκ ἔδοσαν τὸν νεκρὸν αὐτοῦ κωλύσαντος, ὡς λέγεται, δύο δὲ ποιησάμενοι λιθίνας σοροὺς ὑπὸ τὸ Ἰάνοκλον ἔθηκαν, τὴν μὲν ἑτέραν ἔχουσαν τὸ σῶμα, τὴν δὲ ἑτέραν τὰς ἱερὰς βίβλους . . . For the localization see further Richardson s.v. *Fons* (or *Fontus*), *Ara;* J. Aronen, *LTUR* s.v.—*Ara est* is Zumpt's correction for *aras.*

gentemque Corneliam usque ad memoriam nostram hac sepultura scimus esse usam.] As one of the oldest patrician families, which gave its name to the *tribus Cornelia* and celebrated their own family festivals for centuries

---

128. There is a detailed rendering of a slightly earlier passage (8.7.17–22) at *Sen.* 79–81, where see Powell.

(Macr. *sat.* 1.16.7), the Cornelii might have been expected to be conservative in burial practice; cf. Münzer, *RE* 4.1 (1900), 1249.12 ff. The following chapter, with its citation of Ennius' epitaph for Africanus, gives further evidence of Cicero's familiarity with the family burials; see *ad loc.* Plin. *Nat.* 7.187 records the same fact and the same motive for change as our passage, on which he probably depends; see the Introduction § 8.—*Ad memoriam nostram* = "to our time"; sim. *haec memoria* at *Off.* 3.5 and elsewhere (cf. *OLD* s.v., 6).—For *sepultura* cf. *ad* § 55.

Gai Mari sitas reliquias apud Anienem dissipari iussit Sulla victor acerbiore odio incitatus quam ⟨si tam⟩ sapiens fuisset quam fuit vehemens; . . .] Cf. V.Max. 9.2.1 (*de Sulla agitur*): *sed mortuorum umbris saltem pepercit? minime: nam C. Marii, cuius, etsi postea hostis, quaestor tamen aliquando fuerat, erutos cineres in Anienis alveum sparsit;* Luc. 1.582–83: *tollentemque caput gelidas Anienis ad undas / agricolae fracto Marium fugere sepulchro.* To disturb the remains of a person laid to rest with solemn rites was a criminal offense (indeed, probably originally, as under the Roman Empire, a capital crime; cf. Behrends, 1978); cf. Paul. *Sent.* 1.21.4, cited *ad* § 57; de Visscher, 152; Toynbee, 51. This was one of a series of vengeful acts undertaken by Sulla against the memory of Marius, which included the toppling of the monuments of his victories over the Germans and Africans and the repeal of all his laws; cf. Fröhlich, *RE* 4.1 (1900), 1549.33 ff. In general the view prevailed: *Sulla . . . pulcherrimam victoriam crudelitate, quanta in nullo hominum fuit, inquinavit* (Liv. per. 88; cf. *Off.* 2.27; Diehl, 147–48); the restoration of Marius' trophies by Julius Caesar as aedile in 65 took on the character of a political demonstration; cf. *MRR* 2, 158. Sulla's action was not unprecedented, however: Tiberius Gracchus had been denied burial; cf. Plut. *Ti. Gracch.* 20.2; for the similar fate of P. Sulpicius cf. *ad* 3.20. For Greco-Roman folk wisdom on the folly of lashing out at the dead cf. *ad Off.* 3.82b–85.—*Incitatus: incitato* would also have been possible; cf. Reid *ad Luc.* 89 (*incitato*).—Understand *fuisset* after the prior *quam; si tam* was added in P, an easy saltation error.—For the characterization cf. *Phil.* 11.1: *L. Cinna crudelis, C. Marius in iracundia perseverans, L. Sulla vehemens.*

57 quod haud scio an timens ⟨ne⟩ suo corpori posset accidere, primus e patriciis Corneliis igni voluit cremari.] The qualification *primus e patriciis Corneliis* is needed since the name was exceedingly common; cf. fr. orat. *Corn.* 144: *. . . Cornelios vero ita multos ut iam etiam collegium constitutum sit.*—Lambinus added *ne.*—Sulla was also remarkable in being the first Roman to receive a public burial, i.e., one conducted by magistrates and paid for by the state; cf. App. *BC* 1.105; Mommsen, *Staatsr.* 3, 1188 and n. 4; Keaveney, 211–12.

declarat enim Ennius de Africano, 'hic est ille situs', vere, nam siti dicuntur ei
qui conditi sunt, . . .] = fr. 43 Courtney; the rest of the epitaph is supplied by
Sen. *Ep.* 108.33; the whole reads: *hic est ille situs cui nemo civis neque hostis /
quivit pro factis reddere opis pretium,* where *hostis* has its archaic sense
"foreigner": cf. Courtney *ad loc.*—*Enim* reaches over the immediately preceding sentence to justify the one before; cf. Schmidt, 1959, 89 n. 1.—Cicero's
observation on the usage of *situs* is correct and in accord with his own practice
in this passage: *redditur enim terrae corpus, et ita locatum ac situm quasi
operimento matris obducitur . . . Gai Mari sitas reliquias apud Anienem
dissipari iussit Sulla . . .* ; cf. *OLD* s.v., 1b.—On the tomb of the Scipios,
carved out of tufa near the Porta Capena, a much remarked monument in
ancient times that was rediscovered in the seventeenth and eighteenth centuries, cf. F. Zevi, *LTUR* s.v. Sepulcrum (Corneliorum) Scipionum.

. . . nec tamen eorum ante sepulcrum est quam iusta facta et porcus caesus
est.] *Iusta* appears here in the old sense "things which are due to the dead,
obsequies, funeral offerings, etc."; cf. *OLD* s.v. *iustus* 3b; for the original
reference of *ius(tus)* to the sacred sphere cf. *ad* § 36.—*Porcus* is Lübbert's
correction for *corpus.*—The sacrifice of a pig, the commonest and cheapest
of sacrificial victims (cf. Wissowa, 411),[129] conferred the legal status of a
grave; cf. Toynbee, 50. Cicero does not indicate to whom the pig is sacrificed
(perhaps to the quiet spirits disturbed by the burial rather than to Tellus; cf.
ad § 58 [*porcam heredi esse contractam*—]).

et quod nunc communiter in omnibus sepultis venit usu, ⟨ut⟩ humati
dicantur, id erat proprium tum in eis quos humus iniecta contexerat,
eumque morem ius pontificale confirmat; . . .] This together with the following lemma = *FLP* no. 59A. Cf. Var. *L.* 5.23, cited in the next note; Plin. *Nat.*
7.187: *sepultus vero intellegitur quoquo modo conditus, humatus vero
humo contectus,* a passage bracketed, however, by Mayhoff. For testimonies
for *humo* in the narrower and broader sense cf. *TLL* and *OLD* s.v.; our
evidence does not permit an independent assessment of the earlier semantic
development, but Cicero's view certainly has a priori plausibility.—*Ut* was
supplied by Turnebus.—*Is mos* refers to inhumation, confirmed by pontifical law insofar as it insists upon the *iniectio glebae* as prerequisite to a *locus
religiosus;* cf. the next lemma; de Visscher, 25.

nam prius quam in {e}os iniecta gleba est, locus ille ubi crematum est corpus
nihil habet religionis; iniecta gleba tum et iure 'humatus' est et gleba
⟨'humus'⟩ vocatur, ac tum denique multa religiosa iura complectitur.] *Os* is R.
Stephanus' correction for the trivializing *eos.* Is *os* here face or bone (*OLD*

---

129. Also the oldest according to Var. *R.* 2.4.9.

s.v. *os*[1] and [2], respectively)? Surely it must be the latter, since the corpse has
already been cremated (*locus ille ubi crematum est corpus*); see also the next
lemma; *aliter* de Visscher, 23, who, taking *os* as face, regards this as a
different ritual from the *os resectum* alluded to at § 55; but surely this is an
unnecessary duplication of rites of symbolic inhumation.—For the rite of the
iniectio glebae, a necessary preliminary to the purification of the family of the
deceased, cf. Var. *L.* 5.23: *et quod terra sit humus, ideo is humatus mortuus
qui terra obrutus; ab eo qui Romanus combustus est, si in sepulcrum eius
abiecta gleba non est aut si os exceptum est mortui ad familiam purgandam,
donec in purgando humo est opertam* (*ut pontifices dicunt* [FLP no. 59],
quod inhumatus sit), *familia funesta manet.* Our text has caused great difficulty. *Tum et illis* is the reading of εH, *tum et in illis* of L, *tumulis et* of B\u1d43A,
tum et illic of P. Turnebus proposed *tum et ille,* but it is hard to see how that
simple phrase could have been corrupted this way. It likewise seems difficult to keep *tum et illis* by abstracting the pontifices from the preceding
reference to the *ius pontificale:* "then in their eyes he has been buried";
perhaps rather *tum et iure* (Powell), who notes that it "gives the right emphasis, with the strongest word coming after *et.*" After *gleba* Powell adds *humus*
on the assumption that Cicero is making "a point about the technical use of
the word *humus* by the pontifices"; see the passage of Varro just quoted.[130]
For the tomb as a *locus religiosus* cf. in general de Visscher, 55 ff.

**itaque in eo qui in nave necatus, deinde in mare proiectus esset, decrevit P.
Mucius familiam puram, quod os supra terram non exstaret; . . .]** = *iur.* 8, 4
= *iur. anteh.* 33, 7 = *FLP* 62 (*—piaculum et ferias*). *Quod os supra terram
non exstaret* is an extrapolation from the general principle reported at Var.
L. 5.23, quoted in the previous note; Serv. *A.* 6.176: . . . *cum pontificibus
nefas esset cadaver videre, magis tamen nefas fuerat si visum insepultum
relinquerent. genus autem fuerat sepulturae inectio pulveris* . . . According
to Behrends, 1970, 17 n. 39, the underlying idea is that the impurity of the
family during the *feriae denicales* results from their dangerous proximity to
the dead, which does not apply in a case of burial at sea; cf. also de Visscher,
33 n. 44.

**porcam heredi esse contractam, et habendas triduum ferias et porco femina
piaculum pati; . . .]** Cf. Var. *VPR* fr. 104 = Non. p. 163M: *quod humatus*

130. Other proposals: R.G. Böhm, "Emendationen zu Cicero, *De Legibus* II," in *Sodalitas.
Scritti in onore di Antonio Guarino,* 2 (Naples, 1984), 920–21, would read *et gleba sepulcrum
vocatur,* but, as Powell points out (*per litt.*), "the question of what is a *sepulcrum* has already
been resolved above, and the Varro passage [cited above] indicates that there can be a
sepulcrum before the *iniectio glebae* (though he may be speaking non-technically)"; the deletion of *illis* and *gleba* (Heck) seems too radical.

non sit, heredi porca praecidanea suscipienda Telluri et Cereri. aliter familia pura non est. The heir incurs responsibility for offering a sow: cf. *OLD* s.v. *contraho* 8b; this corresponds to the offering of a *porcus* to give the burial legal force (see above); the three-day holiday would be an abridged form of the *denicales* (cf. *ad* § 55), still necessary because of the contact with death; cf. Rüpke, 1995, 512 n. 92.—*Pati* is commonly daggered (Görler, Heck) or emended (e.g., *faciundum* Halm; *piandum at si* Madvig; *fieri* Watt, 1986, 268), unnecessarily. The *piaculum* is conceived as a kind of penalty which the heir (*heredem* to be supplied from the preceding *heredi*) "undergoes"; cf *TLL* s.v. *patior* 730.44 ff.; *porco femina* will be instrumental ablative; cf. Verg. *Ecl.* 5.80: *damnabis tu quoque votis* ("i.e. to the fulfilment of vows": Page *ad loc.*).—Our passage suggests that the sow (*porca praecidanea*) may not be sacrificed to the power that owns the gravesite (i.e., Tellus) but rather to the quiet powers disturbed by the death itself, i.e., the *di inferi;* cf. Behrends, 1970, 17–18 n. 39, with critique of Latte, 1960, 101–2 (though Cicero [cf. § 63] and Varro [cited above] understood the earth as needing propitiation).

si in mari mortuus esset, eadem praeter piaculum et ferias.] The omission of the *piaculum* and *feriae* follow from the death having occurred not in human society but in a battle with the elements, so that there could be no question of pollution adhering to survivors; see the note before last.

58–62a Cicero relies here not only on his own memory of the text of the Twelve Tables, which he had once learned by heart (§ 59), but also on one or more commentators, whom he cites; that his direct source is the youngest of those cited, L. Aelius Stilo Praeconinus, is the plausible suggestion of Boesch, 13–14. Other arguments in favor of the hypothesis are the explanations of other individual words that Cicero includes (besides *lessus,* for which L. Aelius is expressly cited), *forum* and *neniae,* or the distinction of *sepelio* and *uro,* which seem to point to a philologist as source.[131] Born at Lanuvium in the mid-second century, L. Aelius was the most impressive interpreter of early Latinity; both Varro and Cicero studied with him; cf. *Brut.* 205–7; Kaster *ad* Suet. *Gram.* 3.1.

58 A. Video quae sint in pontificio iure, sed quaero ecquidnam sit in legibus.] As in § 45 it is again Atticus who expresses satisfaction with the handling of the preceding topic (*habeo ista* in the earlier passage) and moves the discussion along to the next one; cf. *ad* §§ 54–68 and 55 (*negent*).

---

131. Boesch omits *neniae* and claims L. Aelius as source only to the end of § 61.—Less persuasive is Boesch's argument from agreement of § 60 with Plin. *Nat.* 21.7 on the right of wearing the *corona:* both Pliny and Cicero merely cite the law; it is not a question of agreement in exegesis (see *ad loc.*).

M. Pauca sane, Tite, et ut arbitror non ignota vobis; . . .] For the polite *non ignota vobis* cf. Hutchinson, 1998, 7 n. 8; cf. also *Sen.* 16: *notum enim vobis carmen est* [sc. Enn. *Ann.*]. For the learning of the Twelve Tables by heart cf. § 59.

sed ea non tam ad religionem spectant quam ad ius sepulcrorum.] As Cicero launches into the second topic he thus alerts the reader that the *pontificium ius* and the *ius civile* will handle essentially different areas; cf. § 47: *quid enim ad pontificem de iure parietum aut aquarum, aut ullo omnino ⟨ni⟩si eo quod cum religione coniunctum est?*

'Hominem mortuum', inquit lex in XII, 'in urbe ne sepelito, neve urito'; credo ⟨vel . . .⟩ vel propter ignis periculum; . . .] = *Lex XII* 10.1; in fact, our passage provides versions of all of the preserved fragments of the tenth table. Serv. *A.* 11.206 contains a garbled reference to the same law: *et meminit antiquae consuetudinis; nam ante etiam in civitatibus sepeliebantur, quod postea Duellio consule senatus prohibuit et lege cavit, ne quis in urbe sepeliretur; unde imperatores et virgines Vestae, quia legibus non tenentur, in civitate habent sepulchra*, where, as Crawford suggests, the reference to the consul Duellius may confuse C. Duellius (cos. 260) with the decemvir K. Duellius. Otherwise it may be an instance of a new law reviving one that had fallen into desuetude; cf. Münzer, *RE* 6.2 (1909), 1937.54 ff., who sees a senatorial reaction against the posthumous honors given to the plebeian Fabricius (see below); Latte, 1960, 102.—The earliest Roman custom was to bury the dead at home; cf. Serv. *A.* 5.64 and 6.152; de Visscher, 60 n. 57. The Etruscans, however, had already established regular necropoleis for their dead, including streets, outside their cities; cf. Toynbee, 18 ff. The provision of the XII Tables was generally observed, with some exceptions, until Late Antiquity; cf. Paul. *Sent.* 1.21.3: *intra muros civitatis corpus sepulturae dari non potest vel ustrina fieri.* Burial in the Campus Martius outside the *pomerium*—the site, for instance, of the Mausoleum of Augustus—did not count as a violation; cf. Toynbee, 48; Engels, 165 n. 36.— Cicero would be expected to give a reason not only for the latter but also the former prohibition. Davies was the first to suppose our passage mutilated and, comparing Isid. *orig.* 15.11.1, suggested *propter cadaverum foetorem* as the missing reason; cf. also Engels, 165 n. 36.—Cicero clearly has no feeling for the fear of the dead that causes them to be safely contained in their own place well away from human habitation; cf. Schmidt, 1959, 90; W.F. Otto, 102–4.—In Athens religious law similarly forbade burials *intra urbem*; thus Ser. Sulpicius Rufus reports to Cicero a ruling of the Areopagus on the burial of M. Marcellus (*Fam.* 4.12.3): *ab Atheniensibus locum*

sepulturae intra urbem ut darent impetrare non potui quod religione se
impediri dicerent, neque tamen id antea cuiquam concesserant.[132]

quod autem addit 'neve urito', indicat non qui uratur sepeliri, sed qui
humetur.] In other words, Cicero sees *ne sepelito neve urito* as a polar expression for the available methods of disposal of the corpse, with *sepelior,* like the previously discussed *humo,* referring (originally) to inhumation alone; cf. *OLD* s.v. *sepelior* 1, accepting Cicero's view of *Lex XII* 10.1 and of the early semantics. He repeats the point at § 60 *fin.*

A. Quid qui post XII in urbe sepulti sunt clari viri?] This fictional Atticus shows himself attentive to details of chronology, just as his historical prototype was in the *Liber Annalis;* cf. Münzer, 1905.

M. Credo, Tite, fuisse aut eos quibus hoc ante hanc legem virtutis causa
tributum est, ut Publicolae, ut Tuberto, quod eorum posteri iure tenue-
runt, . . .] The families thus had *iura* antedating the XII Tables; for such clashes of *ius* and *lex* cf. *ad* 1.23; for this rare honor cf. Mommsen, *Staatsr.* 3, 1187–88, with 1188 n. 1.—According to tradition, P. Valerius with the *adnomen* Publicola held the consulate in the first year of the Republic (509). When his plan to build a magnificent house *in summa Velia* roused suspicion of kingly ambitions, he showed restraint by building at the foot of the Velia instead (Liv. 2.7.5–12). He was permitted burial on the Velia, and this became the family gravesite; cf. D.H. 5.48.3; Plut. *Qu. Rom.* 79; Volkmann, *RE* 8A1 (1955), 180.6 ff., esp. (on his burial) 186.61 ff.; Ogilvie *ad loc.*—Like Publicola, whose colleague he was in the consulate of 505, P. Postumius Tubertus adorned the early *acta triumphalia* (505, 503). The year of his death and location of his tomb are unknown; his only known descendant is a grandson or great-grandson A. Postumius Tubertus; cf. F. Münzer, *RE* 22.1 (1953) s.v. Postumius no. 64 (the elder) and 63 (the younger).

. . . aut {eos} si qui hoc, ut C. Fabricius, virtutis causa soluti legibus con-
secuti sunt.] More elegant without the *eos,* perhaps a dittography from above, deleted by Powell.—A cluster of anecdotes illustrated the probity of C. Fabricius Luscinus (cos. I 282), especially in dealing with Rome's enemy,

---

132. Using this passage as his starting point, Rodney S. Young, "Sepulturae intra urbem," *Hesperia* 20 (1951), 67–134, reviewed the archaeological evidence and concluded that the ban went into effect ca. 500 B.C. and included only the inhumation of adults, not of children or cremation. F.E. Winter, "*Sepulturae intra urbem* and the Pre-Persian Walls of Athens," *Studies in Attic Epigraphy, History and Topography Presented to Eugene Vanderpool,* Hesperia Suppl. 19 (Princeton, 1982), 199–204, notes, however, that it was only the Themistoclean wall that would have placed burials in the cemetery studied by Young *intra urbem* and concludes that this ban is likely to be of Themistoclean date.

Pyrrhus of Epirus; cf. *ad Off.* 3.86 and, in general, Münzer, *RE* 6.2 (1909), 1931.23 ff. Cicero clearly regards this as an *ad hominem* honor for Fabricius, not one inherited by his family (Plutarch's report [*Qu. Rom.* 79] that not only Valerius' but also Fabricius' honor applied to descendants is perhaps based on a misreading of our passage).

sed ⟨ut⟩ in urbe sepeliri lex vetat, sic decretum a pontificum collegio, non esse ius in loco publico fieri sepulcrum.] = *FLP* no. 63A.—*Ut* was added by Madvig.—The action of the pontifical college is presented as parallel to that of the legislators: both occupy a similar position vis-à-vis *ius* (cf. *supra* on *sed ea non tam ad religionem spectant*—). Here begins a small digression extending to the end of this chapter about the building of an *aedes* on the site of a graveyard—a conflict of a newly declared *locus publicus* with preexisting *ius*. It is an interesting case in showing that legal qualifications for a *locus religiosus* were not fulfilled by a private burial; cf. Watson, *Property*, 6–7.

nostis extra portam Collinam aedem Honoris:—statuit enim collegium locum publicum non potuisse privata religione obligari.] = *FLP* no. 63B; for the jurisdiction of the pontifices over whether land was sacred or profane cf. Mommsen, *Staatsr.* 2, 49 with n. 3; de Visscher, 145; Stambaugh, 559.— For illustrative matter introduced in asyndeton (*nostis extra portam Collinam . . .*) cf. *ad* § 41.—For the earlier history of the temple of Honos cf. *ad* § 28 (*quod si fingenda nomina*—); for its localization under the east wing of the Ministry of Finance cf. Richardson s.v. *Honos, Aedes;* D. Palombi, *LTUR* s.v. This area beyond the Esquiline was evidently the site of paupers' mass graves; cf. Var. *L.* 5.25; Engels, 165 n. 36; for paupers' graves in general cf. Hopkins, 207–11.—Cicero may well have studied this case for its implications about the site of his own house; was it perhaps adduced by P. Clodius in favor of his *aedes Libertatis* in order to meet Cicero's claim about the disruption of his private religious rites (cf. § 42)? On the case before the pontifices cf. in general Tatum, 1999, 187–92.

59 Iam cetera in XII minuendi sumptus sunt lamentationisque funebris, translata de Solonis fere legibus.] = Solon F 72b R. = 468 M.; for such legislation attempting to impose some rational limit on expense and expressions of grief for the dead cf. Burkert, 1985, 194. Cicero will deal in turn with excesses of mourning and expenditure at the funeral (§§ 59–62a) and with *modus sepulcrorum* (§§ 62b ff.).—As Siewert, esp. 332–37, has shown in detail, the connection with the laws of Solon will be Cicero's own inference, not a reproduction of a written source, such as a jurist, since the treatment here corresponds to the general antiquarian method of §§ 54–68; cf. *ad loc.* Thus the story (first found in Livy and Dionysius of Halicar-

nassus) of an embassy of the Decemviri to obtain a copy of Solon's laws
from Athens may have been spun out of our passage; cf. Siewert. The
alternative view is that of Michèle Ducos, *L'influence grecque sur la loi des
douze tables* (Paris, 1978), 37–41, who makes Cicero's statement about the
borrowing from Solon presuppose the legend of the embassy to Athens.
Wieacker, 1967, 337 ff., and 1988, 301–2, believes that Cicero's conclusion is correct insofar as it points to Greek influences (albeit they are likely
to have emanated from Magna Graecia, rather than Athens); sim. Delz,
esp. 78 ff. The method of our passage is adumbrated at *Rep.* 2.59, where
Cicero compares the Roman elimination of the *nexum* with Solon's corresponding legislation.

'hoc plus', inquit, 'ne facito; rogum ascea ne polito' . . .] = *Lex XII* 10.2. In
general the provisions of the XII Tables curbing costly funerals and burials
are the ones that yield the clearest picture of the material culture of the time
and hence a likely date; the graves at Tarquinii dated between 530 and 470
offer *conferenda* for the forbidden items; and imported Attic vases disappear at Rome in the second half of the fifth century; cf. Wieacker, 1967,
311–14 and 333. The quoted words must have been preceded by stipulation
of what the mourner *was* permitted to do. The expression *hoc plus ne facito*
is paralleled in funerary laws at Delphi and Ceus (*Leg. Gr. sac.* 74; *SIG* 3,
1218; sim. also Solon's law [see the note after next] and the law of Demetrius of Phalerum cited at § 66). Norden, 1939, 254–57, thus regarded
Greek models as likely; Crawford *ad loc.*, noting that the form of expression
is natural in both languages (for Latin prohibitions of this form in early laws
cf. Vairel-Carron, 244–45), thinks the content of the legislation may yet be
borrowed from Greek sources (see below). The point was to prohibit elaborate pyres; some had taken the form of altars or had been decorated with
pictures or tapestries; cf. de Visscher, 293; Engels, 184 and n. 105.—*Ascea*
is the spelling in the best codd. for the word for axe; cf. *TLL* s.v. *ascia*
762.35–39; cf. also *OLD* s.v. *ascia* 1.

**. . . (nostis quae sequuntur; discebamus enim pueri XII ut carmen neces-
sarium, quas iam nemo discit).]** The *carmen necessarium* was a poem assigned for compulsory memorization. H.I. Marrou, *Histoire de l'éducation
dans l'antiquité*, 6th ed. (Paris, 1965), 354 = Eng. tr. 324, sees such training
in legal texts as characteristic of Latin culture as opposed to Greek; but cf.
Ael. *VH* 2.39: Κρῆτες δὲ τοὺς παῖδας τοὺς ἐλευθέρους μανθάνειν ἐκέ-
λευον τοὺς νόμους μετά τινος μελῳδίας . . . Lucil. fr. 552–53M = 553–
54K mocks a schoolboy's efforts: *'si non it, capito', inquit, 'eum et si
calvitur'. ergo / fur dominum?* As our passage shows, this regimen had become obsolete, the model prevailing in which the *grammaticus* used poetic

texts as the basis; cf. Robert A. Kaster, *Guardians of Language: The Grammarian and Society in Late Antiquity* (Berkeley–Los Angeles, 1988), 12.

extenuato igitur sumptu tribus riciniis et tunicula purpurea et decem tibicinibus, . . .] These three examples of maximal expenditure constitute *Lex XII* 10.3 (though they might rather have been expected to precede 10.2: see the note before last). *Ricinium* required a gloss in commentaries on the XII Tables: *recinium omne vestimentum quadratum i qui XII interpretati sunt esse dixerunt* (Fest. p. 274M); see further *OLD* s.v. *ricinium*. It is a difficult and controverted problem whether the reference is to garments to be buried with the body or worn by the women in mourning. At § 64 Cicero connects this material explicitly with Solon: *nam de tribus riciniis et pleraque illa Solonis sunt . . .* , but Solon had laws applying to both: Plut. *Sol.* 21.5–6 = F 72c R. = 470 M.: ἐπέστησε δὲ καὶ ταῖς ἐξόδοις τῶν γυναικῶν καὶ τοῖς πένθεσι καὶ ταῖς ἑορταῖς νόμον ἀπείργοντα τὸ ἄτακτον καὶ ἀκόλαστον, ἐξιέναι μὲν ἱματίων τριῶν μὴ πλέον ἔχουσαν κελεύσας . . . ἐναγίζειν δὲ βοῦν οὐκ εἴασεν, οὐδὲ συντιθέναι πλέον ἱματίων τριῶν . . . Often adduced in this connection is Var. *VPR* fr. 49 = Non. p. 542M: *ricinium . . . palliolum femineum breve*. Varro . . . 'ex quo mulieres in adversis rebus ac luctibus, cum omnem vestitum delicatiorem ac luxuriosum postea institutum ponunt, ricinia sumunt', which certainly suggests that the *ricinium* was not a luxurious garment; it is thus the *number* of the garments that would entail excessive expenditure; it was surely the burial of more than this number of garments that caused concern, not the wearing of them. See also the *Lex Cea de funeribus* (*SIG* 3, 1218): κατὰ τάδε θάπτεν τὸν θανόντα· ἐν ἑματίοις τρισὶ λευκοῖς . . . μὲ πλέονος ἀξίοις τοῖς τρισὶ ἑκατὸν δραχμέων; Wieacker, 1967, 345–48; Baltrusch, 46–47 n. 53; Engels, 165 n. 37, with literature.—Funeral music was originally meant to charm the Manes and render them harmless. Depictions of musicians in Etruscan funerary paintings have been seen as carrying a twofold meaning and referring "partly to the jovialities enjoyed by the dead in Elysium and partly to the banquets, games and other shows that were held on the occasion of a death, or to honour the departed's memory" (Toynbee, 17). Ov. *Fast.* 6.663–64 attests aedilician enforcement of the restriction to ten flautists. For funeral music in Athens and Rome see in general Engels, 87, and Wille, 69 ff.

. . . tollit etiam lamentationem: 'mulieres genas ne radunto neve lessum funeris ergo habento'.] = *Lex XII* 10.4. Women's scratching of the face in mourning was originally an offering of blood to the dead; cf. Cumont, 51–52. *Lessus* was obscure even to the ancients but was probably a keening or wailing; see the next lemma. Both points were outlawed by Solon: ἀμυχὰς δὲ κοπτομένων καὶ τὸ θρηνεῖν πεποιημένα καὶ τὸ κωκύειν ἄλλον ἐν ταφαῖς ἑτέρων ἀφεῖλεν . . . (Plut. *Sol.* 21.6 = F 72c R. = 470 M.). The latter was forbidden by the funerary law of Ioulis on Ceos (*SIG* 3, 1218: . . . τὸν θανόντα [δὲ φέρεν κ]ατακεκαλυμμένον σιωπῇ μέχρι ἐπὶ τὸ σῆμα), as well as by Plato (*Leg.* 960a1–2: . . . θρηνεῖν δὲ καὶ ἔξω τῆς οἰκίας φωνὴν ἐξαγγέλλειν ἀπαγορεύειν . . .).—Powell, perhaps rightly, conjectures *leiium* for *lessum* on the basis of Sex. Aelius' etymology and Cicero's comment on its transparency (*ut vox ipsa significat;* cf. the following lemma).—The construction of *ergo* with genitive, found in archaic prayers[133] but already obsolete by Plautus' day, is imitated by Cicero, as also in 3.9.5: *rei suae ergo ne quis legatus esto* and 3.10.8: *consulum rogandorum ergo;* cf. Wilhelms, 96–97; de Meo, 150–51.

hoc veteres interpretes, Sex. Aelius L. Acilius, non satis se intellegere dixerunt, sed suspicari vestimenti aliquod genus ⟨esse⟩ funebris; L. Aelius lessum quasi lugubrem eiulationem, ut vox ipsa significat; . . .] *Esse* is Powell's supplement.—Sex. Aelius Paetus (cos. 198), praised as *catus* by Ennius (*An.* v. 329 Sk. = 331 V.), is the first recognizable professional jurist; his *Tripertita* included the text of the XII Tables with interpretative comment (our passage = *iur.* 1 no. 3 = *iur. anteh.* 16 no. 4); cf. F. D'Ippolito, *I giuristi e la città. Ricerche sulla giurisprudenza romana della repubblica* (Naples, 1978), 53–70; Wieacker, 1988, 535–38.—L. Acilius was another early interpreter of the XII Tables (our passage = *iur. anteh.* 18); Cicero also mentions him at *Amic.* 6 as one who, like C. Laelius, bore the sobriquet Sapiens (*quia prudens in iure civili putabatur*); cf. Klebs, *RE* 1.1 (1893), 252.8 ff.; Kunkel, 10.—On L. Aelius Stilo see *ad* §§ 58–60 (our passage = *gram.* p. 61, fr. 13). Cicero repeated Stilo's interpretation in citing *Lex XII* at *Tusc.* 2.55 (assuming Muretus' restoration of *lessus* there for the transmitted *fletus*).

quod eo magis iudico verum esse, quia lex Solonis id ipsum vetat.] Cf. Plut. *Sol.* 21.6, quoted in the note before last. One wonders whether Aelius Stilo already cited this passage to confirm his interpretation; cf. *ad* §§ 58–60. **Haec laudabilia, et locupletibus fere cum plebe communia; quod quidem maxime e natura est, tolli fortunae discrimen in morte.]** The provisions of the XII Tables win approval on grounds that they largely eliminate the distinctions between rich and poor and that this is *e natura;* cf. *ad* § 25

---

133. E.g., Cato *Agr.* 139: . . . *illiusce sacri coercendi ergo harumque rerum ergo . . . eius rei ergo . . . harumce rerum ergo . . .*

⟨*paupertatem cum divitiis etiam inter homines esse aequalem velimus*—⟩. This is the unique invocation of *natura* as a justifying norm within Cicero's commentary on his laws; cf. pp. 238–39 and n. 3 *supra*. For death viewed as "the great leveler" cf. Hor. *C.* 1.4.13–14: *pallida Mors aequo pulsat pede pauperum tabernas / regumque turris,* with Nisbet-Hubbard *ad loc.*

60 'Homini', inquit, 'mortuo ne ossa legito quo post funus faciat': ⟨credo quod erat factitatum ut uni plura fierent lectique plures sternerentur, {id} quod ne fieret lege sanctum est.⟩ excipit bellicam peregrinamque mortem.] = *Lex XII* 10.5. *Quo post: quoi* (Müller) is unnecessary, the final particle being quite suitable here; *pos,* the reading of B¹L, is printed by Görler-Ziegler and Courtney, 1999, 15; but *pos* appears elsewhere as an archaic form of the preposition *post,* not the adverb: cf. *OLD* s.v. *pos*².—Schoemann transposed Cicero's explanation, transmitted below after *lex impositam iubet.*—Powell deleted the *id* before *quod;* transmitted is *id quod* A¹, *id quodque* B¹H¹ε, or *id quoque* BˣAˣHˣL.—For *sanctum* cf. *ad* § 10.—The exception for death in war receives implicit confirmation at *dig.* 3.2.25.1 (Papinian): *si quis in bello ceciderit, etsi corpus eius non conpareat, lugebitur.*

haec praeterea sunt in legibus: de unctura, quod 'servilis unctura' tollitur 'omnisque circumpotatio', quae et recte tolluntur, neque tollerentur nisi fuissent; . . .] For *unctura,* a technical term which grew up beside *unctio,* cf. Zellmer, 288–89. *Servilis unctura* will refer to the anointment of the corpse by specially trained slaves (*pollinctores*); relatives were expected to do the anointing, as at Enn. *Ann.* 147 Sk. = 155 V.; cf. Baltrusch, 46. Cf. *Lex XII* 10.6 (wording reconstructed from Fest. p. 154M): *homini mortuo murratam potionem ne indato.* Cf. Blümner, 484, and, for a short history of anointing of the corpse in Greco-Roman antiquity, Hug, *RE* 1A2 (1920), 1857.11 ff. (s.v. Salben).—*Quod* is Courtney's correction of the transmitted *qu(a)e.*—Paulus Manutius' *tollitor* for the transmitted *tollitur* should be rejected; such imperative forms are otherwise exclusively attested with deponents; no need to invent another false archaism like *appellamino* (3.8.2), since Cicero is merely paraphrasing: so Courtney, 1999, 24.—*Circumpotatio* is usually explained as "the practice of drinking together by passing a cup round the company": (*OLD* s.v.); Courtney, 1999, 25, well compares Gk. περίδειπνον, "a meal consumed with the corpse placed in the middle" (though our word will not be a calque of the Gk. one). *Circumpotatio,* though a ἅπαξ (cf. *TLL* s.v.), should not be altered to *circumportatio* (as proposed by J.F. Houwing, *De Romanorum legibus sumptuariis* [Leiden, 1883], 25, cited by Baltrusch, 46 n. 49), for this would not fit with the other provisions in this context, which are clearly aimed at limiting expenditure. In spite of this prohibition, heavy drinking was characteristic of funeral banquets down to the end of antiquity; cf.

Cumont, 53 ff. The goal of this law was to transfer the *circumpotatio* and the associated funeral feast (*silicernium*) from the public space of the cemetery into private houses; cf. Engels, 166.—For the comment *neque tollerentur nisi fuisset* cf. *Sex. Rosc.* 70: *is* [sc. Solon] *cum interrogaretur cur nullum supplicium constituisset in eum qui parentem necasset respondit se id neminem facturum putasse. sapienter fecisse dicitur, cum de eo nihil sanxerit quod antea commissum non erat, ne non tam prohibere quam admonere videretur.* 'ne sumptuosa respersio', 'ne longae coronae', 'ne acerrae': praetereantur illa; iam significatio est laudis ornamenta ad mortuos pertinere, quod coronam virtute partam et ei qui peperisset et eius parenti sine fraude esse lex impositam iubet.] Cf. *Lex XII* 10.7. I follow Powell's punctuation after *illa*. The epithet *longae* has puzzled commentators;[134] for instance, Crawford thinks "it may be a literary flourish by Cicero"; but this passage is not marked by literary flourishes. *Longae coronae* will presumably be wreaths of unusual height and thus unusually expensive (hence the parallel to *sumptuosa respersio*), possibly as grave ornaments or to be carried in funeral procession; cf. Blümner, 485 and n. 19; Baltrusch, 46 n. 50.—For *acerra* cf. Paul. *Fest.* p. 18M: *acerra ara quae ante mortuum poni solebat, in qua odores incendebant. alii dicunt arculam esse turariam, scilicet ubi tus reponebant;* cf. Blümner, 485 and n. 18; for other interpretations Baltrusch, 46 n. 51.—The wearing of garlands was very strictly regulated in early Rome, as Plin. *Nat.* 21.7–9, citing *inter alia* our law, attests; Boesch, 13, moots that Pliny depends upon Varro here and both Varro and Cicero on L. Aelius Stilo (cf. *ad* §§ 58–60); this is possible but not binding, since the agreement with our text merely amounts to the two authors' paraphrasing the same law. Pliny's exegesis shows clearly that the phrase *coronam virtute partam* refers both to insignia won at the games and military decorations (cf. Bernstein, 70–71). Serv. *A.* 11.80 corroborates Cicero's information: *in antiquis disciplinis relatum est, quae quisque virtute ornamenta consecutus esset, ut ea mortuum eum condecorarent.* The force of the law will be to make such status symbols not venal but dependent on the estimation of one's peers; cf. Flower, 120; Cicero's revival of it is in line with the critique of the latterday nobility at *Rep.* 1.51 as owing their position to wealth and tradition rather than *virtus;* cf. Mehl, 195–96.—For the sentence transmitted immediately after this lemma see the first note on this section.
qua in lege cum esset 'neve aurum addito', ⟨videte⟩ quam humane excipiat altera lex {praecipit altera lege ut}: 'cui auro dentes vincti esunt ast im cum illo sepeliet uretve, se fraude esto'.] = *Lex XII* 10.8 (the law is not known

---

134. Reid proposed *lautae*.

from other sources). The Etruscans were relatively advanced in the art of creating dental appliances; hence the phenomenon was sufficiently prevalent at the time of the XII Tables to prompt this provision; cf. D.J. Waarsenburg, "*Auro dentes iuncti:* An Inquiry into the Study of the Etruscan Dental Prosthesis," in *Stips Votiva: Papers Presented to C.M. Stibbe,* ed. M. Gnade (Amsterdam, 1991), 241–47.—*Videte* is Vahlen's supplement; the words *praecipit altera lex ut* were deleted by R. Stephanus.—*Vincti* is the reading of B¹(?) A(?) Lε, *iuncti* of P(?)H; in favor of *vincti* is Celsus 7.12.1: *at si ictu vel alio casu aliquid labant dentes, auro cum iis, qui bene haerent, vinciendi sunt.*—Various solutions have been mooted for the next transmitted word, *essent,* which violates the sequence of tenses. Crawford *ad loc.* expresses preference for *essint,* a dubious form (cf. *OLD* s.v. *sum init.*). *Escunt* of Pithoeus is accepted by most recent editors (cf. *escunt* at 3.9.2 and *escit* in *Lex XII* 1.3); the inceptive form is used as a future (our form should match *sepeliet uretve*), but only from the third century B.C. onward, not yet in the XII Tables. In light of *Lex XII* 6.7 (*quandoc sarpta, donec dempta erunt* transmitted at Fest. p. 348M), Pascucci, 1970, 320–24, regards *escunt* in our passage (if the correct reading) as a false archaism. But, as Brent Vine observes, Festus' *erunt* is likely to be a modernized form; accordingly Courtney, 1999, 16 and 25, restores in the XII Tables *esont* after J. Raevardus' *esunt.*—For *ast* joining a double protasis cf. *ad* §19.7.—For *im,* masculine accusative of *is,* cf. *OLD* s.v. *is init.*

et simul illud videtote, aliud habitum esse sepelire et urere.] Cicero repeats this point from § 58; see *ad loc.*

61 nam quod rogum bustumve moliri vetat propius sexaginta pedes {adici} aedes alienas invito domino, incendium veretur aedium {vetat}; . . .] = *Lex XII* 10.9. The content is paralleled in part by *CIL* VI.3823.31577 = *Font. iur.* no. 44, a *senatusconsultum* from the Esquiline now in the Palazzo dei Conservatori, forbidding among other things *ustrinae* or *foci ustrinae causa;* this seems to be one of the matters under the jurisdiction of the plebeian aediles.—Order is restored in the prior part of the sentence by Powell's *moliri* for the transmitted *novum* and deletion of *adici* (for which Madvig had proposed *adigi*).—The accusative (*pedes*) is sometimes found for extent of space where one might have expected the ablative; cf. Liv. 1.23.3: *castra ab urbe haud plus quinque milia passuum locant,* with other passages cited at Kühner-Stegmann, 1, 283 n. 6.—After *incendium* the transmitted text is *veretura cebum vetat* (B¹) or *veretur acerbum vetat* (APEHL); see Powell's apparatus for other variants. The following *quod autem forum* (*id es vestibulum sepulcri*) *bustumve usu capi vetat, tuetur ius sepulcrorum* at least clarifies the structure. This militates against some solutions, such as de

Plinval's *vereri videtur; item acerram vetat,* with its combination of direct quotation and reporting. *Vetat* can hardly appear in both clauses; the main clause will explain the policy underlying the prohibition of the *quod*-clause. The second *vetat,* likely to be a dittography from above, was rightly bracketed by Vahlen; *veretur* can stand; cf. § 39; *aedium* is P. Manutius' correction for *(a)ce(r)bum;* cf. Powell's apparatus.

quod autem forum (id est vestibulum sepulcri) bustumve usu capi vetat, tuetur ius sepulcrorum.] Cf. *Lex XII* 10.10. On *usucapio* cf. *ad* §§ 48b–49. In general, a *locus religiosus* was inalienable; cf. Paul. *Sent.* 1.21.7: *vendito fundo religiosa loca ad emptorem non transeunt nec in his ius inferre mortuum habet.* Hence Crawford reconstructs *Lex XII* 10.10 as *forum bustumve religiosum esto,* with the ban on *usucapio* inferred (cf. Gai. 2.48: *item liberos homines et res sacras et religiosas usucapi non posse manifestum est).*—For *forum* in this sense cf. Paul. *Fest.* p. 84M: *forum sex modis intellegitur.... quarto, cum id forum antiqui appellabant, quod nunc vestibulum sepulchri dici solet;* Boesch, 13–14, suspects L. Aelius Stilo as the common source. For *bustum* cf. Paul. *Fest.* p. 32M: *bustum proprie dicitur locus in quo mortuus est combustus et sepultus, diciturque bustum quasi bene ustum; ... sed modo busta sepulcra appellamus. Bustum* in our passage is surely used in the latter sense, which is also the one attested earlier; cf. *OLD* s.v. *bustum;* Pascucci, 1981, 424.

Haec habemus in XII, sane secundum naturam quae norma legis est.] With the words *Haec habemus in XII* Marcus concludes his response to Atticus' query at § 58 *(quaero ecquidnam sit in legibus);* for the summarizing formula cf. *ad* § 49.—For *natura* as the *norma legis* cf. 1.44: *atqui nos legem bonam a mala nulla alia nisi naturae norma dividere possumus. Natura* appeared previously in the discussion of the XII Tables at § 59 *fin. (quod quidem maxime e natura est, tolli fortunae discrimen in morte).* See further *ad* § 62 and the introduction to this Book.

reliqua sunt in more: . . .] The discussion of funerary legislation concludes with a brief description of funerary customs; § 63 discusses the corresponding Athenian customs.

funus ut indicatur si quid ludorum, . . .] The announcement is thus de rigueur if games are to be held; cf. Ville, 68 and 353. For the *funus indictivum* cf. Paul. *Fest.* p. 94M: *indictivum funus ad quod per praeconem evocabantur.*—Ville favors an Osco-Samnite, rather than Etruscan origin of the gladiatorial games. They were introduced at Rome in 264 when M. and D. Junius Pera produced games in honor of their deceased father Decimus; ca. 100 a secularized version was introduced, but the games seem first to have been detached from an actual funeral by Julius Caesar, who in 46 celebrated games in honor of his daughter Julia, who had died in 54; cf. sources at Ville, 69–70.

. . . dominusque funeris utatur accenso atque lictoribus, . . .] *Dominus . . . funeris* is Paulus Manutius' correction of the transmitted *domus . . . funeris*. This man was the organizer of the funeral, ordinarily a professional; cf. *OLD* s.v. *dominus* 2a.—*Accensus* is a substantive here ("attendant, orderly"): cf. *OLD* s.v., 2.—The lictors were an Etruscan institution borrowed by the Romans; it was unusual for a private citizen to have lictors at his disposal (cf. Kübler, *RE* 13.1 [1926], 507.64 ff.). Mommsen, *Staatsr.* 1, 391 n. 6, restored Fest. p. 272M (s.v. *praetexta pulla*) so as to include a reference to the practice; cf. Kübler, *loc. cit.,* 516.54 ff.

62a . . . honoratorum virorum laudes in contione memorentur, . . .] Polybius already describes the panegyric of great men (ἐπιφανεῖς ἄνδρες) in the forum (6.53.1–2); cf. Mommsen, *Staatsr.* 1, 442 n. 2. Such speeches tended, however, toward a brief, unadorned recital of deeds, hardly the way to win a reputation as an orator; cf. *de Orat.* 2.341. On the Roman funeral oration see further George Kennedy, *The Art of Rhetoric in the Roman World, 300 B.C.–A.D. 300* (Princeton, 1972), 21–23; Wilhelm Kierdorf, *Laudatio Funebris: Interpretationen und Untersuchungen zur Entwicklung der römischen Leichenrede* (Meisenheim am Glan, 1980); Flower, ch. 5. Contrast the Athenian ἐπιτάφιος λόγος, a great public event (cf. *ad* § 65).

. . . easque etiam ut cantus ad tibicinem prosequatur cui nomen neniae, quo vocabulo etiam ⟨apud⟩ Graecos cantus lugubres nominantur.] The singing of the encomium was entrusted to a professional female vocalist called in early times the *praefica;* cf. Var. *VPR* fr. 110; see further Wille, 67. Our passage is the only evidence for a Greek word νηνία (cf. LSJ s.v.), though νινήατος is a Phrygian tune for the flute at Hippon. fr. 163 W. Greek etymologies for *nenia* are offered at Paul. *Fest.* p. 163M (<νέατον or νήτη).—*Ut* is Powell's correction for *et*, which had been deleted by R. Stephanus; *apud* was inserted by Wesenberg (Victorius had written *Graeci . . . nominant*).

A. Gaudeo nostra iura ad naturam accommodari, maiorumque sapientia admodum delector.] Vahlen rightly made Atticus the speaker here in view of § 67 (*Athenienses tui*), rather than Quintus, as in the earlier editions.—By *nostra iura* Atticus means the *pontificium ius* and *ius civile* as expounded since § 46, as is clear from the parallel mention of the *maiorum sapientia*. Girardet, 1983, 94–95, is keen claim that their being "accommodated to nature" means that they *are* "Naturrecht." But he also wants Cicero's own law code to be natural law (cf. *ad* 1.17). That these two are not on the same level is shown by 1.17, where there is a clear distinction between *tota causa . . . universi iuris ac legum* and the *iura et iussa populorum;* these latter are different from the *leges quibus civitates regi debeant,* though they may be relevant insofar as they lead the legislator toward *optimae leges;* that surely is the function of the Athenian and Roman examples cited in this sector. The statements that some (or all) of the Laws of the XII Tables are *secundum naturam* (§ 61) and that *nostra iura* are adapted to (*accommodari*) nature are problematic, however. How can the law of a particular state claim universal validity? At 1.42–44a and § 14 Cicero shows awareness of the limitations of positive laws, even those accepted as valid at Rome. The problem is broached by Cancik, 1995, 66–68, invoking Cicero's initiation in the Eleusinian mysteries (cf. §§ 35–36) as a motive. This position is probably the result of two tendencies, that of Cicero's political philosophy of the 50s to take the historical Roman state (at an earlier stage of its development) as a model and the tendency of *Leg.* 1 (esp. 1.44) to posit nature as a norm of law; these two, perhaps too hastily combined, result in the normative value of the *mos maiorum* and hence its status as "according to nature." Mehl, 153–56, thinks that the success of the Roman state in gaining territory provides implicit validation since "nature gives dominion to the best people" (189); but, in fact, *Leg.* is not imperialistic, as Moatti, 295–96, has shown. Moreover, Cicero recognizes that not all Roman laws have been just, so one would have expected some clarification of how one can distinguish usable early laws (one looks in vain for the answer at § 40).—For the *sapientia maiorum* cf. 3.24: *sed tu sapientiam maiorum in illo vide . . .* ; probably also the truncated passage *Rep.* 3.4; cf. Roloff, 68.

sed cedo ut ceteri sumptus sic etiam sepulcrorum modum.] Atticus' queries have guided the course of almost the entire discussion in this book (cf. §§ 23, 24, 32, 34–36, 45–46, 58), Quintus' sole intervention having been provoked by the allusion to Clodius (§§ 42–43); so now he raises the final topic of discussion, the curbing of expensive funerary architecture, a natural one after the previous discussion of restrictions on funerals (§§ 59–60).—*Cedo*(= "describe to me, explain to me": *OLD* s.v. *cedo*² 2) is the correction of Leo (*apud* Boesch, 10 n. 3) for *recedoquiro* AL, *recedo q(ue)ro* PℰH or *recedophyro* B, based evidently on a double reading *requiro/cedo* in the archetype, the former reading inferred from Marcus' reply *requiri⟨s⟩*.

62b–66 Here Cicero seeks support in Athenian legislation for the view of *nostrae legis interpretes* that excessive expenditure and grief should be removed from the cult of the *di Manes.* He accords to the Athenian laws the honor of antiquity (*a Cecrope, ut aiunt, permansit:* § 63) and of having been borrowed into the XII Tables (*quam legem eisdem prope verbis nostri Decemviri in decimam tabulam coniecerunt,* etc.: § 64); and in his translation of Solon's law on tombs he uses the word *bustum* also attested in the XII Tables (see *ad* § 64). He seems to want to suggest a close correspondence of the Athenian and Roman legislation as a basis for arguing that the Romans, by analogy to the Athenians, should have laws limiting expenses for tombs; cf. de Visscher, 149–50. Boesch, 14–17, claims this material, as well as §§ 56–57, for Posidonius on general grounds such as his personal connections with Cicero, his polymathy, and his post-Sullan date but without being able to indicate a specific occasion for such a discussion within his corpus. Scholars have in the meantime learned to be wary of claims made for Posidonius; for our passage Boesch raises a possibility, but nothing more, and §§ 56–57 seem more likely to derive from Cicero's own reading (Xenophon, Ennius) and antiquarian studies (the graves of the Cornelii Scipiones, the pontifical books). In general, Roman legislation against luxury reached its climax in the second century B.C.; cf. in general Ingo Sauerwein, *Die leges sumptuariae als römische Maßnahme gegen den Sittenverfall* (diss., Hamburg, 1970); Guido Clemente, "Le leggi sul lusso e la società romana tra III e II secola a.c.," in *Modelli etici, diritto e trasformazioni sociali*, ed. A. Giardina and A. Schiavone (Rome, 1981), 1–14. Cicero seeks not merely to revive but to expand that tendency.

62b M. Recte requiri⟨s⟩; quos enim ad sumptus progressa iam {esta} res sit, in C. Figuli sepulcro vidisse ⟨te⟩ credo.] *Requiri⟨s⟩* is Turnebus' correction.— *Esta* is the transmitted text (BAεH¹L), *ista* (PHˣ) a conjecture. Powell brackets, suspecting a dittography following *progressa*[135] and notes, *per litt.*, that its elimination yields idiomatic Latin (cf. *OLD* s.v. *res* 17a) and a good rhythm (cretic + trochee, Cicero's favorite clausula).—The reference is to C. Marcius Figulus (cos. 64), who supported Cicero's handling of the Catilinarian conspiracy and, along with the other consulars, voted for the execution of the captured conspirators. Cf. Münzer, *RE* 14.2 (1930), 1559.57 ff.; on his (very likely) identification with a Thermus mentioned at *Att.* 1.1.2 cf. Shackleton Bailey, 1992, 66. In order for his funeral monument still to be a current topic, his death must have been fairly recent. Figulus' mausoleum has not survived, but on the general trend toward large-scale funerary monuments at this period cf. Hopkins, 205–7.—Madvig added *te*.

nostrae quidem legis interpretes,—sepulcrorum magnificentiam esse minuendam.] These are presumably the commentators on the XII Tables, two of whom have already been cited in § 59.

63 nec haec a sapientissimis legum scriptoribus neglecta sunt, et Athenis iam in more sunt: a Cecrope, ut aiunt, permansit hoc ius terra humandi. quod

---

135. Perhaps less likely to be influenced by pronunciation, as in Spanish.

cum proximi fecerant obductaque terra erat, frugibus obserebatur, . . .] For
sumptuary legislation regarding funerary monuments Cicero uses foreign
examples, though there seems to have been Roman legislation on the subject, perhaps in the same lex Cornelia that limited funeral expenses; cf. *Att.*
12.35 and 36.1; Plut. *Sull.* 35.4; Rotondi, 354–55.—Prior to *Athenis* H¹
has *et* alone, the other witnesses *nam et;* but the examples are, in fact,
Athenian, Pittacus being cited in § 66 merely to confirm an observation
based on Athenian material; hence *et* should coordinate with the preceding
nec.—After *Athenis* the archetype had *iam illo mores* (B¹ϛHL; for other
variants see Powell), for which Powell suggests *iam in more sunt,* here
adopted. Müller's *iam ab illo Iᵐᵒ rege* seems to be based on the assumption
that Cicero's Roman readers would have needed some explanation of
Cecrops' identity; but *ut aiunt* shows that his name was a byword for
antiquity; cf. A. Otto, 79.—*Quod* is Turnebus' correction for *quam,* which
Vahlen tried to defend as a reference to *humationem* present in the author's
mind; sim. Löfstedt, 2, 146–47, citing Sal. *Cat.* 18.2, where *qua* seems to
refer back to *coniuratio,* to be supplied out of *coniuravere;* von Albrecht,
1973, 1264.24 ff., sought to connect our construction with the *diem quo die*
type.—R. Stephanus proposed *corpus* for *hoc ius,* but this change is unnecessary if *ius* is taken in the broad sense "condicio, status": cf. *TLL* s.v, 686.51
ff., esp. 687.45 ff.—Cecrops was a name to conjure with at Athens, whether
he was regarded as the successor to Erectheus in the kingship (Hdt. 8.44.2)
or more vaguely as one of the early kings (Thuc. 2.15.1); hence the poetic
designation of the Athenians as Κέκροπος παῖδες (Eur. *Ion* 272) and Athens itself as Κέκροπος γᾶ or χώρα (Ar. *Nu.* 301 [lyric], *Pl.* 773). An Athenian proverbial expression for antiquity corresponding to Cicero's *a
Cecrope* does not seem to be attested; cf. 1.8: . . . *praedicari . . . , ut aiunt,
de Remo et Romulo.*—Cf. Kurtz-Boardman, 145: "We know that there was
a ceremony of some sort conducted at the grave on the day of burial—*ta
trita*—and this traditional sowing of the land may have been a part of it."
. . . ut sinus et gremium quasi matris mortuo tribueretur, solum autem
frugibus expiatum ut vivis redderetur.] For the metaphor of the earth as
mother cf. *ad* § 56; for the notion that the earth must be expiated for
receiving the dead cf. *ad* § 57.
sequebantur epulae, quas inibant propinqui coronati, apud quos de mortui
laude cum si quid veri erat praedicatum (nam mentiri nefas habebatur) iusta
confecta erant.] The funeral feast (περίδειπνον) took place at the home
following the carrying out; cf. Kurtz-Boardman, 146. For the corresponding
Roman customs cf. §§ 61–62.
64 postea cum (ut scribit Phalereus) sumptuosa fieri funera et lamentabilia

coepissent, Solonis lege sublata sunt.] = fr. 135 Wehrli = 53 S.-O.-D. Demetrius is likely to be Cicero's main source for Athenian funerary customs,
which he augmented with his own observations of the tombs in the Ceramicus, reported at the end of this chapter. Our passage suggests that
Demetrius may have presented his own sumptuary legislation as a revival of
Solon's; see further *ad* § 66.—Görler *ad loc.* rightly defends the transmitted
text against Ziegler's insertion of *Demetrius* after *Phalereus* with reference
to *Div.* 2.96, *Brut.* 37, and *Orat.* 94.

quam legem eisdem prope verbis nostri Decemviri in decimam tabulam
coniecerunt;—de lamentis vero expressa verbis sunt: 'mulieres genas ne
radunto, neve lessum funeris ergo habento'.] For the supposition of borrowing by the Twelve Tables cf. *ad* § 59 *init.*—This passage, together with 2.9 (*a
parvis enim didicimus 'si in ius vocat'* . . .) for the First Table and D.H.
2.27.3 (the *patria potestas*) for the Fourth, constitutes our only positive
evidence for the organization of the XII Tables; cf. Wieacker, 1967, 319.—
For *exprimere verbis* = "iure, formulis, legibus concipere, definire" cf. *TLL*
s.v. *exprimo* 1793.1 ff., where our passage is cited.—For *lessum* and *funeris
ergo* cf. *ad* § 59.

de sepulcris autem nihil est apud Solonem amplius quam 'ne quis ea deleat
neve alienum inferat'; . . .] = F 72a R. = 469 M. A similar problem was the
placement of one's own corpse on a pyre built by another, for lack of
materials, during the plague (Thuc. 2.52.4); for the corresponding Roman
prohibition cf. § 55. Cf. Kaser, 1978, 43.

poenaque est 'si quis bustum' (nam id puto appellari 'tymbon') 'aut monumentum aliquod aut columnam violarit deiecerit fregerit'; . . .] This continues Solon F 72a R. = 469 M. *Bustum* and τύμβος can both be a grave
mound (cf. *OLD* s.v., 2; *LSJ* s.v., I.1.),[136] so there is no difficulty about the
rendering. Perhaps, in view of the occurrence of *bustum* in the XII Tables
(see § 61), its use here (instead of *tumulus;* for the distinction cf. Richardson
s.v. *Sepulcrum*) is a conscious archaism; so Siewert, 334 n. 8. Cicero expresses himself cautiously in view of Atticus' superiority in Greek, which he
acknowledged by asking him to correct solecisms in his Greek narrative of
his consulate (*Att.* 1.19.10). He does not indicate the Greek words he is
translating as *monumentum* and *columna;* presumably μνῆμα and κιών.
Under the latter he may have had in mind archaic votive statues consisting of
a small figure on an inscribed column (suggestion of R.R.R. Smith).—
Aliquod is Davies' correction for *inquit.*—*Violarit deiecerit* is a conjecture

---

136. For the grave mounds of the archaic Ceramicus cf. Ian Morris, *Burial and Society: The
Rise of the Greek City-State* (Cambridge, 1987), 128 ff.

(P²) but is generally accepted for the tangled transmission: B presents *uocaretacerit;* the source of AHLERS had either *uiolaritiacerit* or *uolariciacerit. D* may have been misread as *a* and *eie* lost before *cerit.* Such asyndeton is characteristic of legal Latin; cf. Pascucci, 1968, 39 ff.

sed post aliquanto, propter has amplitudines sepulcrorum quas in Ceramico videmus, lege sanctum est 'ne quis sepulcrum faceret operosius quam quod decem homines effecerint triduo'.] John K. Papadopoulos, "The Original Kerameikos of Athens and the Siting of the Classical Agora," *GRBS* 37 (1996), 107–28, argues that the original potters' quarter at Athens, including the burial grounds, was on the site of the classical agora; Cicero, however, is clearly referring, perhaps anachronistically, to the later Ceramicus, located to the northwest, outside the classical city wall; for the surviving graves there cf. in general Ursula Knigge, *Der Kerameikos von Athen* (Athens, 1988). Some notion of the dimensions of the grave markers of the archaic Ceramicus can be formed from the fifteen surviving painted tablets, dated ca. 540, by Exekias; each originally measured 43 × 37 cm. and probably fit into the rectangular wall of the monument; cf. Heide Mommsen, *Exekias I. Die Grabtafeln* (Mainz, 1997), 1.—Cicero describes, with less precision than the historian would wish (*post aliquanto*), a second stage of Athenian legislation with respect to burials with clear intent of limiting the costliness of graves.[137] In this way the new Athenian democracy aimed to limit demonstrative expenditure by powerful aristocratic families in defiance of the new egalitarian ethos; cf. Karen E. Stears, "The Demise of the Archaic Athenian Funerary Monument" (abstract), *AJA* 99 (1995), 309. Gisela M.A. Richter, *Archaic Attic Gravestones* (Cambridge, Mass., 1944), 90–92, connected this legislation with a change dated on the basis of associated pottery finds to the end of the sixth century to a simpler style of Attic gravestones, now consisting merely of a slab with a palmette; cf. Kurtz-Boardman, 90 (cf. 121–22). A somewhat later Themistoclean dating of the *post aliquanto* law was first proposed by V. Zinzerling, "Das attische Grabluxusgesetz des frühen 5. Jh.," *WZJena* 14 (1965), 29–34; Sarah P. Morris, *Daidalos and the Origins of Greek Art* (Princeton, 1992), 305–6, proposes a revision of the ceramic chronology such that "the apparent 'gap' in the monuments would coincide more closely with the decades after the construction of the Themistoclean wall" (p. 305); cf. Engels, 97–106 with literature, who leaves open whether the legislation was Cleisthenic (508/1) or Themistoclean (488/81) though he expresses a personal preference for the

---

137. At *Dom.* 102 *post aliquanto* refers to an interval of somewhat more than twenty years between the death of M. Fulvius Flaccus (121) and the building of Catulus' portico *de manubiis Cimbricis* (i.e., won in the Battle of Vercellae in 101).

latter alternative; sim. Stears, *loc. cit.*—The limitation by numbers of workers and days was imitated by Plato; cf. *ad* §§ 45 and 68.

65 neque id opere tectorio exornari nec hermas hos quos vocant licebat imponi, . . .] *Opus tectorium* is plaster work or stucco; cf. *OLD* s.v. *tectorius.* All the extant Ceramicus structures are covered with it; at the date of this legislation it must have been seen as a new and extravagant style of decoration; less convincing Kurtz-Boardman, 122, who interpret *opus tectorium* as some more elaborate style of plaster decoration than that seen in the extant Ceramicus.—*Hermas hos* is R. Stephanus' easy and obvious correction for the transmitted *hermasos,* confusions involving an initial aspirate commonly infecting the medieval transmission of Latin texts.—*Hermae* first appears in extant Latin at *Att.* 1.8.2 (after 13 February 67): *hermae tui Pentelici cum capitibus aëneis, de quibus ad me scripsisti, iam nunc me admodum delectant.* The apologetic *quos vocant* shows that the term is still new at Rome.—Herms might have been thought apposite grave markers in view of their function as guardian figures[138] and Hermes' rôle as ψυχοπόμπος; cf. Kurtz-Boardman, 241–42, who note that herms do not appear as grave markers until Hellenistic and Roman times; on the evidence cf. further Henning Wrede, *Die antike Herme* (Mainz, 1986), 43–44 with literature. Wrede quotes our passage in the form *hermas hos vocant,* calls it corrupt, and supposes that ἕρματα, referring to "plastische Grabaufsätze," stood in Cicero's source; similary Stears, *loc. cit.,* previous note, suggests that by *hermae* Cicero may mean *kouroi.* In fact, Wrede misstates the transmission, and there is an easier explanation of the corruption (see above). The only way to save Wrede's hypothesis would be to assume that Cicero himself mistranslated the term ἕρματα, but this (as well as Stears' hypothesis) seems unlikely in view of his familiarity with what are clearly *hermae* of the usual form (see above). It is, however, curious that, if this legislation was reacting against the use of *hermae* as grave markers, there are no extant examples from the early period.

. . . nec de mortui laude nisi in publicis sepulturis, nec ab alio nisi qui publice ad eam rem constitutus esset dici licebat.] This restriction on freedom of speech was evidently motivated by the fear that orators' rhetorical excesses—especially at the funerals of noble families—could incite rioting and thus endanger the state; cf. Engels, 99. This legislation cleared the way for the public funeral speech (ἐπιτάφιος λόγος) to become an important event at Athens (unlike Rome; cf. *ad* § 62). It probably dates from the time of the

138. On this cf. Detlev Fehling, *Ethologische Überlegungen auf dem Gebiet der Altertumskunde* (Munich, 1974), 7 ff.

Persian Wars (Diod. 11.33.3; D.H. 5.17.4; cf. Engels, 98 n. 3); the earliest
known example is Pericles' speech on the fallen in the Samian War in 439;
cf. Wankel *ad* Dem. 18.208 (τοὺς ἐν τοῖς δημοσίοις μνήμασι κειμένους)
with literature. Cf. also the discussion of extant examples by George Kennedy, *The Art of Persuasion in Greece* (Princeton, 1963), 154–66; for influence of the genre on the formation of Athenian civic ideology cf. Nicole
Loraux, *The Invention of Athens: The Funeral Oration in the Classical City*,
tr. Alan Sheridan (Cambridge, Mass., and London, 1986; orig. 1981).—For
sepultura cf. *ad* § 56.

**sublata etiam erat celebritas virorum ac mulierum, quo lamentatio minu-
eretur; auget enim luctum concursus hominum; . . .**] An acute observation.
Cf. the remarks of Canetti (an often insightful, albeit more impressionistic
than systematic, observer of mass behavior) on the "lamenting pack" ("Klage-
meute"), e.g., 117 = Engl. tr. 105: "Aber das Wesentliche ist die Erregung als
solche, ein Zustand, in dem alle zusammen etwas zu beklagen haben." For the
treatment of mass psychology in Latin literature in general cf. F.-F. Lühr, "Zur
Darstellung und Bewertung von Massenreaktionen in der lateinischen Literatur," *Hermes* 107 (1979), 92–114.—A law attributed to Solon and cited
at [Dem.] 43.62 = fr. 466 M. already restricted the number of (female)
participants in funerals.

66 quocirca Pittacus omnino accedere quemquam vetat in funus alienum.]
Pittacus (ca. 650–570) defeated the Athenian general Phrynon in a battle for
Sigeum, though the conflict was later mediated by Periander. After obtaining
supreme power in Mytilene upon the death of the tyrant Myrsilus, he was
attacked by the poet Alcaeus, who had hoped to restore the old aristocratic
government. Of his laws the best known is the one providing a double penalty
for crimes committed in drunkenness. He resigned his office after ten years
and came to be numbered among the "Seven Wise Men." A collection of his
sayings is preserved (1, 64 D.-K.; cf. *PMG* 542.10–13). Cf. Fritz Schachermeyr, *RE* 20.2 (1950), 1862.64 ff.; J.M. Cook in *CAH* 3.3, 201; Rosalind
Thomas, *OCD*[3] s.v.—Pittacus surely did not mean to ban funerals altogether,
merely attendance at the funerals of other clans; hence we adopt *alienum* of
the *recentiores* for *aliorum* of the archetype.—Schachermeyr, *loc. cit.*,
1868.66 ff., casts doubt upon the reliability of Cicero's report on grounds that
it sounds "wie eine Vergröberung der solonischen Bestimmungen gegen den
Begräbnisprunk." But Pittacus' law was probably quite different and directed
at aristocratic conspiracies that might be formed in emotionally charged
circumstances; it was thus similar rather to the post-Solonian Attic law
against speeches and large gatherings at private funerals (see the last two
notes); cf. also Engels, 50–51.—Pittacus' restriction will derive either directly

or via Demetrius of Phalerum (see next note) from Theophrastus' νόμοι or περὶ νόμων (F 589.17b–c F.).

sed ait rursus idem Demetrius—et huic procurationi certum magistratum praefecerat.] = fr. 135 Wehrli = 53 S.-O.-D. This passage is our major source for Demetrius' sumptuary legislation. Cicero is relying on a work by Demetrius himself (cf. § 64: *ut scribit Phalereus*); Wehrli leaves open whether this was περὶ τῆς δεκαετίας, ὑπὲρ τῆς πολιτείας, or Ἀθηναίων καταδρομή. In contrast to those who have seen Demetrius as influenced by philosophical doctrine, Plato's *Laws* in particular, Gehrke, 166 ff., argues that similarities to Plato should rather be explained by the reliance of both on Athenian tradition; sim. Gagarin, 2000, 354–56, and Hans B. Gottschalk, "Demetrius of Phalerum: A Politician among Philosophers, a Philosopher among Politicians," in Fortenbaugh-Schütrumpf, 367–80, esp. 380. Cf. also Wehrli *ad* fr. 135, who remarks that fiscal as well as ethical considerations were probably at play, for keeping wealth in the families would leave it accessible to taxation by the public fisc. Engels, 137 ff., finds a mixture of motives on different levels, religious, philosophical, socioeconomic, and political. For Demetrius' rule of Athens (317–307) cf. in general Christian Habicht, *Athens from Alexander to Antony*, tr. D.L. Schneider (Cambridge, Mass., 1997), 58–66.—Archaeological evidence shows that Demetrius' legislation on funerary monuments, though rigorously enforced in the third century, was relaxed in the second; cf. Johannes Kirchner, "Attische Grabstelen des dritten und zweiten Jahrhunderts v. Chr.," *Arch. Eph.* 100 (1937), 338–40; idem, "Das Gesetz des Demetrios von Phaleron zur Einschränkung des Gräberluxus," *Die Antike* 15 (1939), 96–97; idem, *IG* II–III, 3², p. V. Engels, 150–52, accounts for the observance of Demetrius' law so long after his fall from power in 307 by the supposition that there were alternative means available for the wealthy to display their status.

sed ait rursus idem Demetrius increbruisse eam funerum sepulcrorumque magnificentiam, quae nunc fere Romae est; . . .] Cicero has discussed Roman funerals with reference to sumptuary provisions of the Twelve Tables (§§ 58–60), but here he hints that funerals of his day have gone well beyond that level (cf. Flower, 115–26); that Roman tombs could now be of extraordinary size was implied in § 62 (C. Figulus).

. . .—fuit enim hic vir, ut scitis, non solum eruditissimus, sed etiam civis e republica maxime tuendaeque civitatis peritissimus—. . .] A notable encomium of Demetrius, with whom Cicero had several points of similarity (cf. *ad Off.* 1.3). One suspects that this is the kind of characterization to which he himself aspired. Cf. also 3.14 and *Rep.* 2.2 (in a series of great lawgivers who benefited Athens): . . . *postremo exsanguem iam et iacentem* [sc. *rem-*

publicam Atheniensium] *doctus vir Phalereus sustentasset Demetrius . . .*—
The phrase *e republica* (= "serving the national interest, patriotic," or the
like) could be applied to persons as also at *Fam.* 9.21.3: *praeter hunc C.
Carbonem . . . civis e republica Carbonum nemo fuit;* cf. in general *TLL* s.v.
ex 1110.46 ff.; *OLD* s.v. *respublica* 2.

. . . **is igitur sumptum minuit non solum poena sed etiam tempore, ante
lucem enim iussit efferri; . . .**] As noted by Kurtz-Boardman, 144–45, "restricting the *ekphora* to the early morning hours . . . encouraged a simple
family procession, not a sumptuous public cortège." The measure also had
the effect of confining the lamentations during the πρόθεσις to a single day,
rather than three days, as was previously common practice; cf. Engels, 81
and, on lengthy and elaborate προθέσεις as a demonstration of status, 85.
Solon already had such a provision ([Dem.] 43.62 = fr. 466 M.); it was
repeated by Plato (*Lg.* 960a) and was observed by Greeks generally; cf.
Gehrke, 167 and n. 90.

**sepulcris autem novis finivit modum, nam super terrae tumulum noluit
quid⟨quam⟩ statui nisi columellam tribus cubitis ne altiorem, aut mensam
aut labellum, et huic procurationi certum magistratum praefecerat.**] Engels,
93, suspects that Solon deliberately left the size of grave monuments unrestricted so as to provide an alternative to an expensive funeral.—*Quidquam*
is Lambinus' correction for *quod* of BAεHL (*quidem* P).—Demetrius' restriction to three cubits was evidently a reaction against such monuments of
the previous generation as the 30-cubit column attested for Isocrates' tomb
([Plut.] *Vit. X Orat.* 838c). Cicero's *columella* corresponds to the κιονίσκος
commonly found in Attic cemeteries of Hellenistic or Roman times; on
these and their decoration cf. Kurtz-Boardman, 166–68.—The tombs of
Isocrates and Lycurgus are said to have had monuments in the form of a
τράπεζα ([Plut.] *Vit. X Orat.* 838c and 842e), of which *mensa* would be the
obvious Latin translation. Demetrius evidently allowed this form to continue but on a reduced scale; cf. Kurtz-Boardman, 168–69, citing relevant
archaeological finds.—*Labellum* has caused great difficulty because, although south Italian vases depict washbasins used in a sepulchral context
(cf. Twele, 93 n. 6), no Attic examples have been found. Twele, 98, notes
that three types of *columellae* have been found in Attic cemeteries: (1) those
that were meant to be dug in the ground, (2) those intended for insertion
into a base, and (3) those with a trumpet-shaped foot because they were
made from a washbasin. To bring the archaeological evidence into line with
Cicero's text he therefore proposes rendering "Nothing should be built
above the mound of earth except a small column no more than three cubits
in height, either (supported by) a mensa or (re-using) a labellum." That

cannot, however, be gotten out of the Latin, which has the three types, *columella, mensa,* and *labellum,* on the same level. It is conceivable, however, either that Cicero's text is corrupt or that Cicero himself has misunderstood or obscured distinctions made in Demetrius' legislation.—The magistrate charged with enforcing the limits imposed by the state is commonly assumed to have been one of the γυναιϰονόμοι, an Athenian institution probably dating from the late Lycurgan period; cf. Gehrke, 162–63 n. 66; Engels, 88–89.

67 Haec igitur Athenienses tui; . . .] This formula concludes the previous topic of Athenian sumptuary legislation for funerals and tombs; cf. *ad* § 49.—For *Athenienses tui* cf. *ad* 1.2 (*nisi forte Athenae tuae*—); § 36: *nobis nostras ne ademeris.*

sed videamus Platonem, qui iusta funerum reicit ad interpretes religionum (quem nos morem tenemus); . . .] A somewhat abrupt transition, which, once effected, creates a bridge to the relevant provisions of Plato's *Laws* with which this Book concludes (§ 69) as well as the encomium of Plato at the beginning of Book 3; cf. H. Müller, 51. In our passage Plato serves as Cicero's crown witness for limiting expenditure on tombs. Cf. Pl. *Lg.* 958d3: περὶ τελευτήσαντος δή, εἴτε τις ἄρρην εἴτε τις θῆλυς ᾖ, τὰ μὲν περὶ τὰ θεῖα νόμιμα τῶν τε ὑπὸ γῆς θεῶν ϰαὶ τῶν τῆδε, ὅσα προσήϰει τελεῖσθαι, τοὺς ἐξηγητὰς γίγνεσθαι ϰυρίους φράζοντας· . . . The distinction between Platonic and Athenian handling of the matter is not, however, so clear-cut as Cicero's text suggests: Plato's ἐξηγηταί are modeled on the corresponding Athenian institution (on which see Oliver); for the relation cf. ibid. 53–46 and Morrow, 425–26. Cicero's *iusta funerum* is more broadly formulated than Plato's τὰ μὲν περὶ τὰ θεῖα νόμιμα. Cicero's *quem nos morem tenemus* evidently refers to the pontifices, nor was Cicero the only one to see such an analogy; the rôle of the *sacerdotes publici* at Rome is thought to have strengthened the position of the Athenian ἐξηγηταί; cf. Oliver, 52. The Romans also had, however, as Cicero has just explained (§§ 58–61), civil laws dealing with funerals and tombs. I think it would be fair to say that in §§ 67–68 we see Cicero hastening to bring this Book to a close.

de sepulcris autem dicit haec: . . .] With these words Cicero goes over to a report of Plato's law on tombs (he ignores that Plato presents it as the statement of the ἐξηγηταί). In spite of the indirect form, Cicero reproduces with a fair degree of precision; see the following notes.

vetat ex agro culto eove qui coli possit ullam partem sumi sepulcro, . . .] *Lg.* 958d6–7: θήϰας δ᾽ εἶναι τῶν χωρίων ὁπόσα μὲν ἐργάσιμα μηδαμοῦ, μήτε τι μέγα μήτε τι σμιϰρὸν μνῆμα . . . With the fussiness of legal language

Cicero spells out that ἐργάσιμα include not only *ager cultus* but *is qui coli possit*; cf. H. Müller, 52; Pascucci, 1981, 426. Instead of saying, as Plato does, that the size of the tomb is of no importance (this might seem to contradict the kinds of restrictions just discussed!), Cicero declares "any part" of the arable land off limits to burials; thus *sepulcrum* suffices with no need to vary the designations (Plato uses both θήκη and μνῆμα[139]).—Plato's prohibition is an ideal not necessarily reflected in the practice of Athenian cemetery-building; thus the cemetery of Anavyssos lies in the middle of prime agricultural land; cf. Engels, 42.

... sed quae natura agri tantummodo efficere possit ut mortuorum corpora sine detrimento vivorum recipiat, ea potissimum ut compleatur; ...] *Lg.* 958e1–3: ἃ δὲ ἡ χώρα πρὸς τοῦτ' αὐτὸ μόνον φύσιν ἔχει, τὰ τῶν τετελευτηκότων σώματα μάλιστα ἀλυπήτως τοῖς ζῶσιν δεχομένη κρύπτειν, ταῦτα ἐκπληροῦν ... Again a fairly close rendering down to the structure of relative clause with antecedent following. Cicero does, however, change the content of the relative clause so that "the land" is no longer the subject and said to "have a nature" tending "toward" certain ends (πρὸς τοῦτ' αὐτό); rather he speaks of "what the nature of the land is able to effect"; he has thus essentially substituted *efficere* for πρὸς τοῦτ' αὐτό. The definition of what the land or its nature "alone" can do appears in an *ut*-clause, rather than an infinitive phrase; likewise, the injunction is moved into an *ut*-clause (*ea potissimum ut compleatur*), rather than being expressed by an infinitive (ταῦτα ἐκπληροῦν). He then strengthens the pronoun (*ea* = ταῦτα) by addition of *potissimum*. Cicero refrains from rendering μάλιστα ἀλυπήτως as *sine ullo detrimento*, perhaps because of the preceding *ullam partem*. Cicero also omits and simplifies δεχομένη κρύπτειν to *recipiat*. In general the reduction of the rôle of participles is characteristic of renderings from Greek to Latin: besides the change of δεχομένη to a finite verb, *mortui* and *vivi* substitute for οἱ τετελευτηκότες and οἱ ζῶντες.

quae autem terra fruges ferre et ut mater cibos suppeditare possit, eam ne quis nobis minuat neve vivus neve mortuus.] *Lg.* 958e3–6: τοῖς δὲ ἀνθρώποις ὅσα τροφὴν μήτηρ οὖσα ἡ γῆ πρὸς ταῦτα πέφυκεν βούλεσθαι φέρειν, μήτε ζῶν μήτε τις ἀποθανὼν στερείτω τὸν ζῶνθ' ἡμῶν. Cicero drops τοῖς ἀνθρώποις: humans can be understood as the beneficiaries (the point is argued in detail at *N.D.* 2.154–68); πρὸς ταῦτα is also eliminated. Cicero preserves the structure with a very general relative (*quae* : ὅσα), defined more closely by apposition (*fruges, cibos* : τροφήν). He renders πέφυκεν with *possit*, omits βούλεσθαι (perhaps as too strong a personification), but

---

139. There is no semantic difference, *pace* Pascucci, 1981, 426.

doubles the idea of τροφὴν φέρειν (*fruges ferre et . . . cibos suppeditare*). Plato allows the earth as mother to stand as a simple metaphor, whereas Cicero adds *ut* (cf. *quasi* added to the earth's functioning as a mother in §§ 56 and 63). The surprise is that the antecedent of *quae* turns out to be not *ea* but *eam*, the diminution of the earth itself substituting for that of the fruits of the earth. Again the elimination of participles is striking, with τὸν ζῶνθ᾽ ἡμῶν becoming simply *nobis*, μήτε ζῶν μήτε τις ἀποθανών becoming *neve vivus neve mortuus*.

68 extrui autem vetat sepulcrum altius quam quod ⟨quinque homines⟩ quinque diebus absolverint, . . .] *Lg.* 958e6–7: χῶμα δὲ μὴ χοῦν ὑψηλότερον πέντε ἀνδρῶν ἔργον, ἐν πένθ᾽ ἡμέραις ἀποτελούμενον. The specification *quinque homines* has clearly fallen out through saltation, as Turnebus saw. The parameters are thus given in terms of manpower and duration of work, as in the Athenian law cited at § 64 *fin.* as well as *Lg.* 955e, translated in § 45. Cicero makes no attempt to imitate the cognate accusative χῶμα . . . χοῦν or to cultivate *variatio* through use, e.g., of *bustum*; rather, *sepulcrum/ sepulcra* occurs four times in §§ 67–68. Plato has ἔργον loosely in apposition with χοῦν, with a further specification attached by means of the participial modifier ἀποτελούμενον. Cicero regularizes the comparative construction (*quam quod . . .*); he thus eliminates ἔργον and substitutes a finite verb (*absolverint*) for the participle.

. . . nec e lapide excitari plus nec imponi quam quod capiat laudem mortui incisam ne plus quattuor herois versibus (quos longos appellat Ennius).] *Lg.* 958e8–10: λίθινα δὲ ἐπιστήματα μὴ μείζω ποιεῖν ἢ ὅσα δέχεσθαι τῶν τετελευτηκότος ἐγκώμια βίου μὴ πλείω τεττάρων ἡρωικῶν στίχων. To compensate for the lack of a noun corresponding to ἐπιστήματα Cicero doubles and adds specificity to the verb (*nec . . . excitari . . . nec imponi* : μὴ . . . ποιεῖν). Again *mortuus* substitutes for a participle (τετελευτηκώς). In the Greek the encomium is τῶν τετελευτηκότος (= "the deeds of the deceased" or the like; τῶν can hardly be taken with στίχων, *pace* England *ad loc.*); but this nuance is lost in the Latin *laudem mortui*, Cicero apparently regarding *laudem factorum* (or *rerum gestarum*) *mortui* or the like as too fussy. On the other hand, he feels it necessary to insert *incisam* to clarify the relation of encomium to monument. The citation of Ennius (*Op. inc. fr.* 20) provides a native equivalent for the Greek-derived *herous* but also implies that this legislation belongs alongside the most hallowed Roman traditions; cf. the use of *bustum* from the XII Tables to render τύμβος in Solon's law at § 64. **habemus igitur huius quoque auctoritatem de sepulcris summi viri, . . .]** The formula for concluding a section; cf. § 16; *ad Off.* 1.15a.—For Cicero's high opinion of Plato cf. *ad* 1.15.

... a quo ite{ru}m funerum sumptus praefinitur ex censibus a minis quinque usque ad minam deinceps.] The foregoing was in response to Atticus' query about legislation regarding *sepulcrorum modus* (§ 62a). Marcus adds that Plato also had views on the previous topic, *ceteri sumptus* (i.e., regarding funerals), which are now summarized from *Lg.* 959d3–6, where five minas are specified for the top property class, three for the second, two for the third, and one for the fourth.—*Item* is Wagner's correction of *iterum*.—For *praefinio* cf. *ad* § 45.—*Deinceps* is taken by previous editors with the following sentence, and indeed it is often first in its clause (e.g., *Inv.* 1.23: *deinceps dicendum*). The problem is that Cicero would then be professing to report what Plato "says next" (*deinceps dicit*), i.e., after the laws on funerary expenses (*Lg.* 959d3 ff.), when, in fact, the material on immortality precedes (959a4 ff.). The solution lies in punctuating after rather than before *deinceps,* which can be treated as an unemphatic word that can be postponed (e.g., 3.43: *sunt deinde posita deinceps; Inv.* 1.33: *nunc de confirmatione deinceps*).

dicit eodem loco de immortalitate animorum et reliqua post mortem tranquillitate bonorum, poenis impiorum.] *Eodem loco* is Powell's correction for the transmitted *eadem illa,* surely insufficient to point readers to material lost in the lacuna at § 53, as has been suggested (nor would one otherwise have posited such content for the lacuna; cf. *ad* §§ 54–68); nor, as Powell points out (*per litt.*) is *Lg.* 959a4 ff. one of Plato's more famous pronouncements on immortality, as *illa* might seem to imply. *Reliqua* seems to mean "future" or "for the remaining time to come" as at *Sest.* 73, where there is likewise a *iunctura* with *tranquillitas: L. Cotta dixit . . . declinasse me paulum et spe reliquae tranquillitatis praesentes fluctus tempestatemque fugisse* (compared by Powell).

69 This is the last stage of conversation in Book 2, in which Marcus formally concludes the commentary on his laws (*Habetis igitur explicatum . . .*); the two interlocutors express themselves satisfied (though there is no reversion to the language of voting with which Atticus introduced his request for an explanation at § 24) and beg him to continue to the next topic, magistrates.

Habetis igitur explicatum omnem, ut arbitror, religionum locum.] Another concluding formula (as in § 68: see *ad loc.*), this time for the entire subject of *Leg.* 2.

Q. Nos vero, frater, et copiose quidem. sed perge ⟨ad⟩ cetera.] Since it was he whose request gave rise to this discussion of religious law (§ 17 *sed iam exprome, si placet, istas leges de religione*), it is appropriate that Quintus expresses himself satisfied. Atticus' commendation at 1.63 (*laudata quidem a te graviter et vere!*) functions similarly. At the same time Quintus' *perge*

⟨*ad*⟩ *cetera* propels the conversation to its next stage.—*Copia dicendi* was the mark of an orator and, indeed, sometimes stands for eloquence in general; cf. *Inv.* 1.1; Ernesti s.v. *copia.*—*Ad* is added in Aᵇ alone.

M. Pergo equidem—uno aestivo die; . . .] For the summertime setting cf. *Lg.* 625b3: πνίγους ὄντος τὰ νῦν and the concern for shade in the same passage; cf. *ad* § 3. By Book 4 of *Lg.* it is already midday (722c8); the fragment from Book 5 shows a similar stage (*sol paululum a meridie iam devexus videtur*). Thus, so far as we can tell, Cicero carried out this plan.—For (*e*)*quidem* used with a repeated word in affirmation by a second speaker cf. Solodow, 111–12.

sic igitur faciam, et dicam de magistratibus; id enim est profecto quod constituta religione rempublicam contineat maxime.] For *faciam* cf. *ad* 1.22.—The logic of our passage becomes clearer in light of the definition of *respublica* at *Rep.* 1.39 (quoted *ad* 1.23 *quos porro est communio legis*—). If *religio* holds the state together at one level, the *magistratus* do at another: they interpret *ius* and articulate the common interest through the formulation of *leges*. For the *iudicia* and *leges* as foundations of the *respublica* in Cicero's thought cf. Diehl, 25–26.—The subject of Book 3 is only announced here; at 3.2 Marcus launches in on it without further elaboration.

Commentary on Book 3

ut enim magistratibus leges, ita populo praesunt magistratus; vereque
dici potest, magistratum legem esse loquentem, legem autem mutum
magistratum.

—Cic. *Leg.* 3.2

In Book 3 the scene continues as before, with the interlocutors seated in the *palaestra*-like space in the island of the Fibrenus (2.6). The topic of conversation now shifts, however, to magistrates, as announced at 2.69. Book 3 follows the same plan as 2, with an initial "praise of the law" followed by the text of the laws themselves in moderately archaizing Latin (2.18) and then by Marcus' commentary on the laws, interrupted by occasional objections from Quintus. At 3.48 Atticus calls for a separate discussion *de iure populi Romani*, just as Marcus had followed the commentary on his own legislation in 2 with a discussion of *pontificium ius et . . . civile* (2.46); but the text breaks off before the plan can be executed (see further *ad* 3.49). In addition, there is a lacuna at the end of chapter 17 that must have been very extensive, since it contained the conclusion of the discussion of magistrates as handled by Greek philosophers and the commentary on roughly the first half of the laws. The remains can be outlined as follows (see the commentary on each section for further detail):

  I. Plato to be followed (§ 1)
 II. Preliminary praise of the law (§§ 2–5)
III. The laws themselves (§§ 6–11)
 IV. Transitional dialogue on their originality (§ 12)
  V. Treatment of the theme by Greek philosophers (§§ 13–17 + lacuna)
 VI. Commentary on the laws (lacuna + §§ 18–47a)
VII. Transition to the appendix *de iure populi Romani* (§§ 47b–49 + lacuna).

From the legislator's point of view the magistrates and the citizens are the two essential elements in the state. The entire question of how the state is to be governed will thus depend on the arrangements made for magistrates

(§ 5: *quorum . . .* [sc. *magistratuum*] *descriptione omnis reipublicae mode-ratio continetur,* apparently argued in greater detail at §§ 15 ff.). Hence systematic provisions *de magistratibus* are an expected part of a constitu-tion.[1] The difference between magistrates and citizens lies in the *imperium* possessed by the former, which entails the obedience of the latter. These relations are so fundamental to Cicero's notion of a *civitas* that he maps them onto the community of gods and men.[2] Accordingly, the proem to Book 3 is a meditation on *imperium* and its function in nature and within the polity; under the latter Cicero comes to focus on the interchangeability of the rôles of magistrate and citizen in a free commonwealth (§ 5), the power inhering in the office, not the person.

Cicero has claimed that the *leges* he is putting forward can never be abrogated (2.14a), i.e., they are tantamount to natural law (1.42). Moreover, nature (i.e., the nature of the human being) is the norm against which they are to be judged (1.44). There is some discussion of the rôle of *imperium* in nature at § 3, a point of contact with the anthropology of Book 1 in the prescription for the relations of magistrates and citizens at § 5 (see *ad loc.*), and a possible reference to nature in the corrupt sentence of § 49, but nature plays no rôle in the discussion of the constitutional provisions themselves. What substitutes as a justification is (1) Roman tradition, a problematic move (see the introduction to Book 2) but expected insofar as these laws have been connected with the state of *Rep.* (1.15; 2.14), where an earlier (and idealized) form of the Roman state has been defined as the *optima civitas;*[3] or (2) practical exigencies: cf. §§ 26, 33, 46–47 (in this last passage Greek practice is held up as a norm: *Graeci hoc diligentius . . .*). Nevertheless, Cicero's treatment of the subject is rather different from the approach of previous Roman authors on magistrates, of whom C. Sempronius Tuditanus (cos. 129) and M. Iunius Congus Gracchanus are known to us by name (*iur.* 9–10 and 13–14, respectively): he is not concerned with the history of the offices but solely their functions and liberally includes, besides pure descrip-tion, moral precepts, beginning with the very first law: *Iusta imperia sunto* (§ 6.1). In practice, then, Cicero's "philosophical" approach to the subject

1. Cf. Pl. *Lg.* 735a and 751a–b; Ar. *Pol.* 1290a7–8: πολιτεία μὲν γὰρ ἡ τῶν ἀρχῶν τάξις ἐστί, . . .

2. 1.23: *si vero eisdem imperiis et potestatibus parent, multo iam magis* [sc. *eiusdem civitatis habendi sunt*]. *parent autem huic caelesti descriptioni mentique divinae et praepotenti deo . . .*

3. Cf. Sprute, 93: "Da die beste Staatsform die alte römische war, brauchte er nur die alten römischen Gesetze zu sammeln und sie gelegentlich ein wenig zu modifizieren."

amounts to the superimposition of a hortatory/moralizing element upon a description of functions.[4]

Besides its homage to Roman traditions, *Leg.* 3 connects with *Rep.* in another sense. There Cicero had argued the merits of the *genus temperatum* consisting of elements drawn from the three constitutional types, monarchy, oligarchy, and democracy (*Rep.* 1.69). In *Leg.* 3 there is a similar concern for the blending of different types (*temperatio,* applied to his laws in general at § 12), particularly in the context of the tribunate of the plebs, defended as a *modica et sapiens temperatio* (§ 17: sc. vis-à-vis the consuls, who are said to possess *regium imperium* [§ 8.2]) or a *temperamentum* (§ 24: sc. of the powers of the *principes*). As Lintott, 1999, 231, remarks, however, Cicero's treatment of blending is too superficial: he should have considered the effect on each of the constitutional elements of the powers granted to the others, in which case he might have described the consular power, for instance, in different terms (see further *ad* § 8.2).

Though in *Rep.* Cicero had adopted the age of Scipio as a convenient setting for a discussion of political forms in general (this was about the earliest date at which Greek influence on Roman political thinking was conceivable), the detailed discussion of constitutional arrangements in *Leg.* 3 is conducted with reference to perceived problems of Cicero's own day, including violence in assemblies, the corruption of the senatorial class, etc. Hence the criticism of Clodius *tacito nomine* is continued from Book 2 (2.37 and 42–44; §§ 21–22 and 25), and Cicero seeks to strengthen the *leges Aelia et Fufia* (2.21.5–6; § 11.7) and the censorship (§§ 7.3 and 11.13–14 with § 47) in the face of what he regarded as Clodius' attempts to weaken these institutions. Thus it is misleading to contextualize *Leg.* within "Cicero's idealization of the period of the Scipios, including the Roman government as constituted at that time" (Keyes, 1921, 322). "Scipio" appears in *Leg.* as a code-word for *Rep.* (1.20, 27; §§ 12 and 38); the historical Scipio's stand on election laws even encounters criticism from Quintus (§ 37). If in *Leg.* 3 Cicero does have in mind a particular past moment, it might be that critical political turning point of his own lifetime, the Sullan restoration. He is providing the kinds of laws Sulla *ought* to have enacted to establish a durable and harmonious state.

In spite of his description of the consuls as having *regium imperium* (§ 8.2), Cicero sees the essential balance of power as that between the senate

---

4. Cf. § 9.4: *duella iusta iuste gerunto, sociis parcunto . . . domum cum laude redeunto;* § 10.4–5 and 9: *is ordo vitio vacato. ceteris specimen esto . . . quae cum populo quaeque in patribus agentur modica sunto;* § 11.1–2: *loco {senator} et modo orato. causas populi teneto.*

and the people (§ 25). The aim of his legislation is to restore the former to its position as *dominus . . . publici consili* (§ 28). Cicero's approach to this problem involves three bundles of measures designed to (1) strengthen the senate's prestige and powers, (2) reform the personnel and proceedings of the senate, and (3) reform the popular assemblies:

(1) The Ciceronian senate is to consist entirely of those who have been elected to public office, with automatic censorial adlection of ex-quaestors eliminated (cf. *ad* §§ 10.1–2 and 27); it thus becomes a more compact, more elite, and more senior body.[5] It also reclaims its place as an independent legislative organ of government without any need for its decrees to be confirmed by any other body (*eius decreta rata sunto:* § 10.3; cf. § 28). It, not the consuls, will create a dictator to deal not only with foreign wars but also with domestic strife, as was the case, according to the annalists, in Rome's early history; the controversial *senatusconsultum ultimum* is thus rendered redundant (§ 9.2). Obedience to the senate is required of the minor domestic magistrates (§ 6.5).

(2) The senators are exhorted to moderate and orderly proceedings and are, in their lifestyle,[6] to set an example for the other classes (§§ 10.2–5; 11.1). In addition, the censors are to hold office continuously and to keep a close eye on the behavior of senators (*probrum in senatu ne relinquonto:* § 7.3).

(3) Violence is to be eliminated from the popular assemblies, and the presiding magistrate is to be held accountable in the event of its occurrence. The auspices and rights of intercessors are to be scrupulously observed (§ 11.3–7). Voting is to be secret, but the contents of ballots are to be made known to the optimates (§ 10.6).

The aim is to recreate and/or strengthen the bond between the senate and the rest of society, so that the senate can credibly speak for the whole once again, since its legislation is to have the force of law. As in Book 2, "strengthened control from the top" would be an apt summary of the program; cf. *ad* 2.19–22 and 25; Perelli, 132 ff.

Cicero's program can be challenged on two grounds: its feasibility and its adequacy as a solution to the problems of the Roman state of his time. Feasibility would not normally be an issue in discussing a set of laws that

---

5. Cf. *ad* § 6.5; many *novi homines* advanced no further than the quaestorship, as Rawson, 1991, 143, pointed out.

6. The polemic against egotistical self-aggrandizement, kept in general terms in Book 1 (§§ 40 ff.), is here given specific point (see esp. §§ 30–32).

deal not *his de hominibus qui nunc sunt, sed de futuris, si qui forte his legibus parere voluerint* (§ 29). "Marcus" does not, however, hold consistently to this position, but, for instance, praises Pompey's acceptance of the *necessarium* in his restoration of the tribunate (§ 26; cf. also §§ 22 and 34). Thus the *necessarium* could be invoked in favor of the voting laws as they then existed and against Marcus' reform, which would turn back the clock in a way doubtless wholly unacceptable to the plebs. Here, as elsewhere (cf., e.g., *Sest.* 97), he seems to brush aside too readily the possibility that different social classes might pursue quite different interests and by no means accept interference by others in their decision-making.

The causes for the fall of the Roman Republic are complex and multi-layered, and there is no consensus among historians as to how exactly they should be formulated.[7] Rawson, 1991, 147, assessing the adequacy of Cicero's analysis, argues that he has failed to address what she sees as the fundamental problem of the Roman state, namely the excessive concentration of power in the hands of generals in the provinces. Though much nuance has been lost along with the commentary on § 9,[8] it is clear that Cicero has carefully placed their appointment under the control of the senate and the people, an apparent confirmation of the lex Pompeia of 52 (cf. the Introduction § 2a) doing away with the automatic assignment of provinces to retiring consuls; he has also hedged provincial commanders about with restrictions (*duella iusta iuste gerunto, sociis parcunto, se et suos continento, populi sui gloriam augento, domum cum laude redeunto:* § 9.4), and their record in office is presumably subject to review by the censors (§ 47). Cicero's analysis of problems and prescription of remedies deserves to be given due weight as that of an articulate and intelligent observer who knew the governmental system of the Republic from the inside; and he has succeeded in embodying in his laws a vision of the Roman state consistent with but more concrete than the one set out in *Rep.* At the same time it must be said that he has not made the kind of use of nature as a criterion that might have been expected in light of 1.44 and thus seems to be pursuing his political ends under the cloak of philosophy; see § 4 of the Introduction.

---

7. For an introduction to the problem cf. P.A. Brunt, *The Fall of the Roman Republic and Related Essays* (Oxford, 1988), 1–92; see further Alfred Heuss, "Der Untergang der römischen Republik und das Problem der Revolution," *HZ* 182 (1956), 1–28; Gruen, 1974, 498–507; Karl Christ, *Krise und Untergang der römischen Republik* (Darmstadt, 1979), esp. 1–15, among many others.

8. The lack of reference to Caesar in our Book has sometimes been called a " 'beredtes' Schweigen" (Lehmann, 11; sim. Strasburger, 17), but he might have been alluded to (indirectly, if not by name) in the lost commentary on § 9; cf. also *infra* p. 491 and n. 62.

1 This introductory conversation fixes the spotlight, not on Cicero himself and his home and activities, as in the corresponding sections of Books 1 and 2, but on Plato and Atticus. Appropriately placed at the beginning of a Book dealing with constitutional issues is another encomium of Plato (cf. 2.14b) and a reaffirmation that Cicero is following him (albeit only in the general sense of 1.15 and 2.14b, not in terms of specific doctrine; cf. 2.17). When Atticus chimes in with his agreement, Marcus adds an encomium of his friend—possibly a sign that he was to be the dedicatee of *Leg.*; cf. p. 11 n. 46, p. 25, and the introduction to Book 1.

M. Sequar igitur, ut institui, divinum illum virum, quem quadam admiratione commotus saepius fortasse laudo quam necesse est. A. Platonem videlicet dicis.] There is no break in dialogue corresponding to the division of Books; rather, Book 3 begins with Marcus' reply to Atticus' request at the very end of Book 2: *Tu vero dic, et istam rationem quam coepisti tene.* Marcus "follows" Plato in the sense that, having written about the "best" state, he is adding a set of laws for it (cf. 1.15; 2.14); but he is imitating only the "type of discourse" (*genus orationis*), not specific doctrines (2.17); the approach to Plato was closer, however, at 2.45, translated verbatim from *Lg.* 955e; cf. also *ad* 2.67–68.—*Quadam admiratione* has been thought to need further specification; hence ⟨*nimia*⟩ *quadam* Goerenz, followed by Ziegler², or ⟨*incredibili*⟩ *quadam* Ziegler¹. *Sed nil mutandum.* Görler well compares *Amic.* 30 (Laelius is the speaker): *sed ego admiratione quadam virtutis eius* [sc. *Scipionis*] . . . with Seyffert-Müller *ad Amic.* 29 (pp. 210 ff.), who document the use of *quidam* to emphasize the extraordinary.

Tu vero eum nec nimis valde umquam nec nimis saepe laudaveris; . . .] The perfect subjunctive is permissive and has a present sense; cf. Kühner-Stegmann, 1, 185–86.

nam hoc mihi etiam nostri illi, qui neminem nisi suum laudari volunt, concedunt, ut eum arbitratu meo diligam.] *Nostri illi* are the Epicureans, jealous of the praise of anyone but the founder of their school. Cotta reports with consternation that Zeno the Epicurean has even called Socrates—using the Latin term!—a *scurra Atticus* (fr. 9 Angeli-Colaizzo = *N.D.* 1.93; cf. Dyck *ad loc.*). Atticus' Epicureanism has already surfaced at several points; cf. *ad* 1.21 and 2.2. He not only praises Plato here, but also parts company with Epicurus in approving of "Socratic irony" at *Brut.* 292; cf. Hirzel, 1877–83, 2, 367–69.

M. Bene hercle faciunt. quid enim est elegantia tua dignius? cuius et vita et oratio consecuta mihi videtur difficillimam illam societatem gravitatis cum humanitate.] For *hercle* cf. *ad* 1.12.—His polished manners and wit gave Atticus, an *eques Romanus*, entrée into circles of the top nobility of Rome;

cf. Shackleton Bailey, *Att.* (Cambridge ed.), vol. 1, 6 ff. In the businessman and sometime historian *humanitas* was superficially evident but also present in a deeper sense: he refused to abandon friends in adversity (cf. Perlwitz, 120–24); indeed, he provided substantial help to Cicero and his family during the exile (Shackleton Bailey, *loc. cit.*, p. 22). Though Cicero reproached him during that period with keeping silent at the decisive moment, he later admitted *tibi . . . eo plus debebo quo tua in me humanitas fuerit excelsior quam in te mea* (*Att.* 3.20.3; cf. Gelzer, 146); for *humanitas* cf. in general Powell *ad Sen.* 1. Under *gravitas* falls his acting on firm principle, as in his refusal to purchase auctioned goods of victims of the proscriptions (Nep. *Att.* 6.3). In view of the gap in the friends' correspondence from November 54 to May 51 (cf. Shackleton Bailey, *loc. cit.*, p. 25), their relations in the time immediately surrounding the composition of *Leg.* are not documented; cf. the Introduction § 2a. But as he writes *Leg.*, the events of his exile and return are still much on Cicero's mind, and the tribute to Atticus' *humanitas* and *gravitas* fits with that focus. On Atticus' character cf. also G. Boissier, *Cicéron et ses amis*[7] (Paris, 1884), 129 ff. = Engl. tr. 123 ff.; J.L. Strachan-Davidson, *Cicero and the Fall of the Roman Republic* (London, 1894), 67–77; Karl Büchner, "Humanitas. Die Atticusvita des Cornelius Nepos," *Gymnasium* 56 (1949), 100–121.

Laudemus igitur prius legem ipsam, veris et propriis generis sui laudibus? A. Sane quidem, sicut de religionum lege fecisti.] For *propriae generis sui laudes* cf. 1.54: *in suo genere perfectus;* for the procedure cf. *ad* 2.14b. For *sane quidem* cf. *ad* 2.1; for the apparent inconsistency of this treatment with that of Book 2 cf. *ad* 2.14b–18.

2–5 As just announced, Marcus prefaces to his laws an encomium of the relevant category of legislation; in practice this takes the form of a dilation on the basic concepts magistrate, authority, obedience. He clearly indicates *magistratus* as the subject and locates this in relation to the laws and the people (§ 2). But then he goes back to the underlying concept *imperium*, which he identifies as inherent in the order of the world (§ 3) and in human societies from the very beginning, where it took the form of the rule of kings, for whom, however, magistrates substitute in Cicero's laws, intended for *liberi populi* (§ 4). Command on the one side implies obedience on the other: in the sequel this reciprocal relation is worked out and the interchangeability of these two rôles in the free state (§ 5). Only at §§ 13–14 does he indicate possible sources of such theories, though contacts with Stoicism appear in § 3; see *ad loc.*

2 Videtis igitur magistratus hanc esse vim, ut praesit praescribatque recta et utilia et coniuncta cum legibus.] *Magistratus,* like *potestas* (cf. *ad* § 6.2), was

432 A Commentary on Cicero, *De Legibus*

originally an abstract and has been converted to the concrete sense "magistrate, official"; cf. Wackernagel, 2, 23. For the Roman concept of the *magistratus* Mommsen, *Staatsr.* 1, 8 ff., is still fundamental: the term denotes those entitled to use the insignia of office, such as the fasces, and the powers associated therewith, as determined by properly conducted elections; cf. also Bleicken, 1981b.—Cicero follows the same method as at 2.9–10 of abstracting the *vis* of a concept—there *lex,* here *magistratus,* announced as the subject of our Book at 2.69; cf. also §§ 12 and 13. The definitions at *Rep.* 1.39 are again fundamental (quoted *ad* 1.23 *quos porro est communio legis*—), as is the concept of the governing *consilium, Rep.* 1.41 (*consilio quodam regenda est, ut diuturna sit*). The magistrate, like the *moderator reipublicae* (ibid. 5.2), whose goal is the *beata civium vita,* "is at the head of" (*praesit*) [sc. the people; see next lemma]; he either constitutes or is a member of the *consilium.* The *rectum et utile*—not in opposition here—are implicitly the criterion of laws at 2.11; cf. also 2.16, where it is shown that belief in the deity is *verum* and *utile.* The *utile* is presumably such in relation to the *beata civium vita* (see above). For the *rectum* cf. further *ad* 1.31 and 32. The magistrate's prescriptions must be not arbitrary but *coniuncta cum legibus* since the populace is *iuris consensu . . . sociatus,* and the principle applies *inter quos . . . est communio legis, inter eos communio iuris est* (1.23) and, presumably, vice versa.

ut enim magistratibus leges, ita populo praesunt magistratus; vereque dici potest, magistratum legem esse loquentem, legem autem mutum magistratum.] For the doctrine that the laws are over the magistrates cf. Pl. *Lg.* 715c6–7: τοὺς δ᾽ ἄρχοντας λεγομένους νῦν ὑπηρέτας τοῖς νόμοις ἐκάλεσα . . . F. Sommer, 116, claims that our passage has a different sense in view of the definition of *lex* given below, but he is assuming a dichotomy of "natural" and "positive" law that does not apply to *Leg.* (cf. *ad* 1.17). Arist. *Pol.* 1292a32–33 formulates more abstractly: δεῖ γὰρ τὸν μὲν νόμον ἄρχειν πάντων, τῶν δὲ καθ᾽ ἕκαστα τὰς ἀρχάς . . .—The magistrate and the law have the same function; the difference is that the magistrate has a voice. But this does not mean that the magistrate merely enunciates what is contained in the law, i.e., interprets it: that would apply only to the praetor, not to magistrates in general. Given that *lex* has the sense *ius condicioque naturae* (§ 6), the magistrate assumes the position of the Stoic sage in being able to see (and enunciate) what this is. Cf. F. Sommer, 124–26. The relation of magistrates and the law is differently conceived at *Clu.* 146: *legum ministri magistratus . . .* (cf. Pl., cited above).—The description of the magistrate as a living law and of the law as a mute magistrate probably derives from Xenophon's *Cyropaedia,* already cited by Cicero at 2.56, albeit the latter has given it greater terseness and epigrammatic point: αἰσθάνεσθαι μὲν γὰρ ἐδόκει καὶ διὰ τοὺς γραφομένους νόμους βελτίους γιγνομένους ἀνθρώπους· τὸν δὲ ἀγαθὸν ἄρχοντα βλέποντα νόμον ἀνθρώποις ἐνόμισεν, ὅτι καὶ τάττειν ἱκανός ἐστι καὶ ὁρᾶν τὸν ἀτακτοῦντα καὶ κολάζειν (8.1.22). The idea was originally formulated with reference to a king rather than a magistrate; similar ideas were also available in Pythagorean sources such as Cicero had consulted for a version of the laws of Charondas (cf. *ad* 2.14b; cf. Diotogenes the Pythagorean, περὶ βασιλείας *apud* Stob. 4.7.61 (= vol. 4, p. 263.18–19 W.-H.): . . . ὁ δὲ βασιλεὺς ἤτοι νόμος ἔμ[ψη]χός ἐντι ἢ νόμιμος ἄρχων; similarly, Philo refers to Moses and the patriarchs as "living law" (*Vit. Mos.* 1.162 and *Abr.* 5; cf. *Vit. Mos.* 2.4: . . . τὸν μὲν βασιλέα νόμον ἔμψυχον . . .); for further references see *ad Off.* 1.89.

3 nihil porro tam aptum est ad ius condicionemque naturae (quod cum dico, legem a me dici intellegi volo) quam imperium, . . .] For *ius* and *condicio* as quasi-synonyms cf. *Ver.* 3.15: *hic primus* [sc. Verres] . . . *condicionem amicitiae, ius societatis convellere et commutare ausus est.*—*Imperium* appears here as "potestas, dominatio, principatus" in a very broad sense that goes, unusually, beyond the human sphere; cf. *TLL* s.v., 570.24 ff., esp. 33–36, where our passage is cited. For the development of the concept of *imperium* in general cf. Bleicken, 1981b, 287ff.

. . . sine quo nec domus ulla nec civitas nec gens nec hominum universum genus stare, nec rerum natura omnis nec ipse mundus potest; . . .] The different realms of operation of *imperium* are listed from narrowest to broadest, as in the typical presentation of the doctrine of οἰκείωσις (cf. *ad Off.* 1.53) except that this phenomenon is traced beyond the human sphere. The sentence is capped by a fine double cretic clausula.—W.K. Lacey, "*Patria potestas,*" in *The Family in Ancient Rome: New Perspectives,* ed. Beryl Rawson (Ithaca, 1986), 132 and 140, connects our passage (among others) with *patria potestas* as the major influence on the Romans' view of government; cf. *ad* § 5; Powell on *Sen.* 37.

nam et hic deo paret, et huic oboediunt maria terraeque, et hominum vita iussis supremae legis obtemperat.] The movement is reversed and now proceeds from broad to narrow. The comprehensiveness is underlined by the *et . . . et . . . et . . .* structure. Cicero cultivates variety by use of the three synonymous verbs *paret . . . oboediunt . . . obtemperat.* This is a more concrete version of the Stoic doctrine at 1.23: *parent autem huic caelesti descriptioni mentique divinae et praepotenti deo;* for *suprema lex* cf. *ad* 1.19 (*summa lex*). Once again the double cretic forms the conclusion.

4 atque ut ad haec citeriora veniam et notiora nobis, . . .] *Citerior* is used here, not in a geographical sense but, rather, as "closer to one's experience, 'nearer home'" (*OLD* s.v., 3; cf. *TLL* s.v. *citer* 1195.55 ff.), a usage first attested at *Rep.* 1.57: *quare, si placet, deduc orationem tuam de eo loco* [*de caelo*: Non. 289M] *ad haec citeriora.*—Cf. the similar transition from the cosmic to the human sphere at *Tusc.* 5.71: *haec* [sc. the causal links in the universe governed by *mens*] *ille intuens atque suspiciens vel potius omnes partes orasque circumspiciens quanta rursus animi tranquillitate humana et citeriora considerat!*

omnes antiquae gentes—ad homines iustissimos et sapientissimos deferebatur, . . .] Sim. Just. 1.1: *principio rerum gentium nationumque imperium penes reges erat, quos ad fastigium huius maiestatis non ambitio popularis sed spectata inter bonos moderatio provehebat.*

. . . omnes antiquae gentes regibus quondam paruerunt; . . .] Cicero states this conclusion apodictically without explaining the basis; at *Pol.* 1252b19 ff. Aristotle offers this account: διὸ καὶ τὸ πρῶτον ἐβασιλεύοντο αἱ πόλεις καὶ νῦν ἔτι τὰ ἔθνη· ἐκ βασιλευομένων γὰρ συνῆλθον. πᾶσα γὰρ οἰκία βασιλεύεται ὑπὸ τοῦ πρεσβυτάτου . . .

quod genus imperi primum ad homines iustissimos et sapientissimos deferebatur, . . .] This was the view of Posidonius F 284 (5) E.-K. = 448.5 Th. = Sen. *Ep.* 90.5, quoted *ad* 2.40. An instance is the case of Deioces discussed at *Off.* 2.41; cf. *ad loc.*

. . . id quod in republica nostra maxime valuit quoad ei regalis potestas praefuit; . . .] I.e., the kingship was based upon ability, not lineage; this applied down to Tarquinius Superbus, when the dynastic principle asserted itself with concomitant loss of quality, as recounted at *Rep.* 2.4 ff., esp. 44–46.—*Id quod* is Bake's correction for *idq; ut* BPεHL (*idque* + ras. Aˣ); Davies' *idque et* is often adopted.

deinde eorum deinceps posteris prodebatur, quod et in eis, etiam qui nunc regnant, manet.] *Eorum deinceps* is Powell's correction for *etiam deinceps* (BAHL) or *etiam qui nunc* ES¹R (*qui nunc* del. S²); the pronoun is needed to indicate that the royal power was passed down to the successors or descendants of the original kings, not just to posterity, as Powell notes *per litt.*—For *deinceps* "in turn" sometimes used with *inde* or *deinde* cf. *OLD* s.v. *deinceps*² 1; sim. § 43: *sunt deinde posita deinceps . . .* ; *Div.* 1.64: *. . . qui deinde deinceps moriturus esset.*—For *posteris prodere* cf. Zetzel *ad Rep.* 6.23 of his edition.—For the use of *in* with reference to *imperium* cf. *Rab. perd.* 3: *summum in consulibus imperium*, together with similar phrases cited at *TLL* s.v. *in* 772.55 ff.—*Etiam qui nunc* is for *qui etiam nunc*.

quibus autem regia potestas non placuit, non ei nemini sed non semper uni parere voluerunt.] The royal power (*regia potestas*) might be vested in a single individual, as in the Roman dictatorship, or divided up, as between the consuls, who have *regium imperium* according to § 8.2 (see *ad loc.*); cf. also §§ 15–16. In what connection Cicero may have contemplated a rôle for a board of ten "best men" in the putative fragment of *Rep.* (Book 5?) brought to light by C.A. Behr, "A New Fragment of Cicero's *De Republica*," *AJPh* 95 (1974), 141–49, esp. 148–49, must remain moot (cf. p. 103 n. 68 *supra*).

nos autem, quoniam leges damus liberis populis, quaeque de optima republica sentiremus in sex libris ante diximus, accommodabimus hoc tempore leges ad illum quem probamus civitatis statum.] That "free peoples" are the recipients was already stated at 2.35 and follows from the laws being adapted to the ideal state depicted by Scipio in *Rep.*; the premise that this is already published spares Marcus the need to discuss constitutional first principles; see the Introduction § 5; *ad* 1.15, 2.14b.

5 magistratibus igitur opus est, sine quorum prudentia ac diligentia esse civitas non potest, quorumque descriptione omnis reipublicae moderatio continetur.] *Igitur* draws an inference from the preceding: the need for magistrates follows from the need for authority both in general and in the state in particular as well as Cicero's legislating for *liberi populi,* not monarchies.— For *prudentia* cf. *Rep.* 2.67 (discussed *ad* § 23: *sed vis populi multo saevior*—). —For the sense of *descriptio* cf. *ad* 1.23 and 2.30. The *magistratuum descriptio* also occurs twice in § 12 and *ista descriptio* in Atticus' reply at § 13 refers back to it; in those three passages *discriptio* is commonly substituted for the ms. reading, however; see further *ad* § 12.—*Moderatio* is the "power of governing, control" (*OLD* s.v., 3b); at *Rep.* 5.2 Cicero describes the goals of the *moderator reipublicae.*

neque solum eis praescribendus est imperandi sed etiam civibus obtemperandi modus; . . .] *Eis* are, of course, the magistrates, contrasted with *civibus.* Both groups will need to have rules prescribed for them corresponding to their respective rôles in the state.

nam et qui bene imperat, paruerit aliquando necesse est, . . .] The premise, just stated, is that a *liber populus* is in question, though, as a child, even an heir apparent would have been subject to the orders of the reigning monarch. Cf. Lintott, 1999, 226: "The desire of those who disapproved of regal power was not to obey no one, but not always to obey the same man. Therefore, in the republican mixed constitution *imperium* must be retained but limits must be placed upon the magistrates' commands and the citizens' obedience."— Sim. Solon 133.10 M. = Stob. vol. 3, p. 114.12 W.-H.: ἄρχεσθαι μαθών, ἄρχειν ἐπιστήσῃ; Xen. *An.* 1.9.5 (of the education Cyrus and others received at court): εὐθὺς παῖδες ὄντες μανθάνουσιν ἄρχειν τε καὶ ἄρχεσθαι; Pl. *Lg.* 942c7–8 (sim. 762e): . . . τοῦτο ἐν εἰρήνῃ μελετητέον εὐθὺς ἐκ τῶν παίδων, ἄρχειν τε ἄλλων ἄρχεσθαί θ᾽ ὑφ᾽ ἑτέρων; Arist. *Pol.* 1277b11–13 cites it as a known saying: διὸ καὶ λέγεται καὶ τοῦτο καλῶς, ὡς οὐκ ἔστιν εὖ ἄρξαι μὴ ἀρχθέντα; sim. ibid. 1333a2–3: τόν τε γὰρ μέλλοντα καλῶς ἄρχειν ἀρχθῆναί φασι δεῖν πρῶτον; ibid. 1287a16–18, finding alternation of rule δίκαιον, and 1332b25–27, finding it ἀναγκαῖον; Sen. *Ir.* 2.15.4: *nemo autem regere potest nisi qui et regi.*

. . . et qui modeste paret, videtur qui aliquando imperet dignus esse.] *Modeste* is an ethical term (on *modestia* cf. *ad Off.* 1.93 and 142); a state can demand that its citizens obey, but hardly *modeste*; nonetheless Cicero goes on to enjoin such obedience at § 6.1. Our passage is the first hint that Cicero wants to place the relations of governing and governed on a new basis. This together with the directive to love the magistrates (see the note after next) gives force to the argument that Cicero conceives the relations of magistrate and citizen on the analogy of father and son (cf. *ad* § 3).—Some quality besides mere modest obedience would seem to be needed in a ruler, but here Cicero wants to consider the ability to play the rôle well, whatever it may be, as the major point.

itaque oportet et eum qui paret sperare se aliquo tempore imperaturum, et illum qui imperat cogitare brevi tempore sibi esse parendum.] This will give the citizen incentive to the "modest obedience" just mentioned, dampen any revolutionary designs, and at the same time make the magistrate proof against any temptation to commit tyrannical acts.

nec vero solum ut obtemperent oboediantque magistratibus, sed etiam ut eos colant diligantque praescribimus, ut Charondas in suis facit legibus.] For the surprising requirement to love the magistrates see the note before last. Cf. Charond. *apud* Stob. 4.44.2 (= vol. 4, p. 152.1–2 W.-H.): χρὴ δὲ καὶ πρὸς τοὺς ἄρχοντας εὔνοιαν διαφυλάττειν καθάπερ πατράσιν εὐπειθοῦντας καὶ σεβομένους . . . ; sim. Aristox. fr. 35: τοὺς ἄρχοντας . . . φιλανθρώπους δεῖν εἶναι, καὶ τοὺς ἀρχομένους . . . φιλάρχοντας; Wehrli (*ad* Aristox. fr. 36) suggests that Cicero has this citation via Aristoxenus; for the laws of Charondas used by Cicero cf. *ad* 2.14b.

noster vero Plato Titanum e genere statuit eos qui ut illi caelestibus, sic hi adversentur magistratibus.] Plato is *noster* in view of the interlocutors' shared studies in the Academy (cf. *ad* 1.54).[9] For vivid contrast to the citizen *qui modeste paret* [sc. *magistratibus*] Cicero alludes to Pl. *Lg.* 701b5 ff., a description of a series of stages of defiance of authority. As du Mesnil notes, however, Cicero paraphrases loosely: Plato does not say that such rebels were "from the clan of the Titans," merely that they display and imitate their nature; for the phrase cf. D.Chr. 30.10: ὅτι τοῦ τῶν Τιτάνων αἵματός

___

9. For *noster . . . Plato* cf. also *Fam.* 1.9.12 (to Lentulus), cited *ad* § 31.

ἐσμεν ἡμεῖς ἅπαντες οἱ ἄνθρωποι. Cicero misremembers Plato's text or adjusts it to the current context by making it speak of rebelling against magistrates, rather than against parents, elders, and the laws (though the change is somewhat mitigated by the concept of the magistrate as a *lex loquens* at § 2 as well as the terms in which the relations of magistrates and citizens have just been described):[10] . . . φεύγειν πατρὸς καὶ μητρὸς καὶ πρεσβυτέρων δουλείαν καὶ νουθέτησιν, καὶ ἐγγὺς τοῦ τέλους οὖσιν νόμων ζητεῖν μὴ ὑπηκόοις εἶναι, πρὸς αὐτῷ δὲ ἤδη τῷ τέλει ὅρκων καὶ πίστεων καὶ τὸ παράπαν θεῶν μὴ φροντίζειν, τὴν λεγομένην παλαιὰν Τιτανικὴν φύσιν ἐπιδεικνῦσι καὶ μιμουμένοις . . . The Giants were a similar rebel band (and the two groups were sometimes confused); *Sen.* 5 speaks of them in similar terms: *quid est enim aliud Gigantum modo bellare cum dis, nisi naturae repugnare?—Qui ut illi . . . sic hi:* for the relative pronoun taken up by following demonstratives cf. Reid *ad Luc.* 14. *Hi* are the *cives,* already contrasted with the magistrates in the sentence *neque solum iis praescribendus est imperandi, sed etiam civibus obtemperandi modus.*—For *caelestes = dei superi* cf. *ad* 1.24; Cicero means, of course, the Olympian gods, led by Zeus/Jupiter; their description is proleptic since the Titans, too, were *caelestes* until their defeat.

6–11 These chapters comprise the laws themselves, composed in a style imitative of early Roman legislation (cf. *ad* 2.18). Their lapidary quality has sometimes led to interpretive controversy (cf. *ad* § 10.3: *eius decreta rata sunto*). They may be analyzed as follows:

    I. Authority of magistrates and its limits (§ 6.1–4—*ius ratumque esto*)
        A. Their commands to be just
        B. Their powers of coercion
        C. Trials before the people
        D. *Provocatio* and its limits
    II. The magistrates (§§ 6.5–10.7: *Minoris magistratus—eique ius coerandi dato*)
        A. Minor magistrates (§ 6.5)
            1. Quaestors
            2. *Triumviri capitales*
            3. *Triumviri aere argento auro flando feriundo*
            4. *Decemviri stlitibus iudicandis*
        B. Major magistrates (§§ 7.1–9)
            1. Aediles (§ 7.1)

10. For a similar case of adjustment to context cf. *ad Off.* 1.25.

2. Censors
3. Praetors (§ 8.1)
4. Consuls
5. The *lex annalis*
6. The dictator and magister equitum
7. Interregnum
8. Mandates outside the capital
9. Tribunes of the plebs
10. Magistrates' possession of *auspicium* and *iudicium* (§ 10.1)
C. The senate
  1. Composition
  2. Validity of its decrees
  3. Example for the other orders
D. The ballot: written but accessible to the optimates
E. Extraordinary magistracies
III. Public meetings and legislation passed during them (§§ 10.8–11.10)
  A. Right of convening
  B. Rules of decorum
  C. Auspices to be observed
  D. No omnibus bill
  E. No capital trial except by "the greatest assembly"
IV. Miscellaneous provisions (§ 11.11)
  A. No gifts to be accepted
  B. New competence for the censors
    1. Oversight over public documents
    2. Audit of the acts of retiring officials.

Several aspects of the arrangement and presentation call for comment. To begin with the point *Iusta imperia sunto* and the magistrate's power of *coercitio* seems odd, perhaps an outgrowth of the immediately preceding discussion of the relations of citizens and magistrates (*bene imperare—modeste parere*: § 5). The minor magistrates are not separately named, merely described by function. Did Cicero mean for them to comprise a single board who shared these various tasks (so Lintott, 1999, 138)? The point may have been clarified in the lost commentary on this passage; as things stand, the possibility cannot be excluded. What of the aediles? Do they rank among the minor or major magistrates? Two points separate the aediles from the minor magistrates, namely the mention of their office by name and the placement of the phrase *quodque senatus creverit agunto* immediately after the description of the tasks of the domestic minor magistrates and before the aediles: the former are mere instruments of the senate's authority, not members of the senate itself, whereas the aedileship is said to provide *ad honoris amplioris gradum primus ascensus* (§ 7.2; cf. *ad loc.*). Another oddity is the placement of the censors between the aediles and the praetors, which has led to the inference that Cicero ranked them below the praetors (Lintott, 1999, 228 n. 54). But this is surely an example of the associative method of composition found elsewhere in these laws (see above and below), the aediles as *curatores urbis* prompting thought of the *cura urbis* in a different sense exercised by the censors (cf. *ad* § 7.3). Other oddities of placement cause no great difficulty: the *lex annalis* (§ 9.1) is appended to the office of consul since it is the iteration of the consulate that will ordinarily be in question; similarly, the magister equitum is appended to the dictator as an instrument of his power (§ 9.2); and the prohibition of *liberae legationes* forms a natural appendix to the discussion of licit foreign missions (9.4–5). The tribunes of the plebs occupy a special position, equal in *potestas* with a consul (§ 16) but lacking *imperium* (cf. Mommsen, *Staatsr.* 1, 23); the tribunate was also chronologically the latest, instituted when the other magistracies were already in place (§ 16; *Rep.* 2.57–58); hence it concludes the series of regular magistracies (§ 9.6).[11] Under Cicero's system membership of the senate depends upon election to office; hence perhaps rules for elections are appended to the rules for the constitution and competence of the senate and the moral character of its members (§ 10.6). Upon rules for conduct in meetings of the senate and the people follow two prohibitions of conduct toward individuals: a ban on *privilegia* and on bribes. The final provision giving the censors new duties to guard the laws (§ 11.13–14) might have been expected in the section on the censors' other duties (§ 7.3); it looks like an afterthought that might have been integrated with the earlier passage in final revision.[12]

6 This chapter begins by restating the relations of magistrates and citizens in terms of command and obedience as sketched in § 5 and then proceeds to delineate the powers available to magistrates to enforce obedience, namely *coercitio* (and the limits set thereto) and prosecution before the comitial court. The special case of military service is appended. Cf. Kunkel, 33.

---

11. Hardly an afterthought (cf. Lintott, 1999, 229: "At this point—almost, it seems, as an afterthought—Cicero introduces the tribunes . . ."); Lehmann, 21 n. 37, thinks that the placement of the tribunate is meant to underscore its exceptional position within the constitution; similarly, Thommen, 1988, 360, finds that this placement, in spite of the position of the tribunate in the *cursus honorum*, lends it "besondere Bedeutung."

12. The censors' custody of the laws evidently differs from that assigned to the praetor at § 8.1, the latter being confined to the *ius civile*.

6.1 Iusta imperia sunto. eisque cives modeste ac sine recusatione parento.]
The nature of *imperium* was the starting point for Cicero's justification of
magistrates in §§ 3–4; this key word is now taken up in the first law, albeit
in the concrete sense of "command" (so very often in the public sphere: cf.
TLL s.v., 568.56 ff.). It is characteristic that the first law demands not the
obedience of the subject but the ethical quality of an official act; only when
this has been laid down is obedience required in the next provision; the two
together create the stability on the basis of which Scipio preferred the mixed
constitution; cf. *Rep.* 1.45 and 69; Sprute, 164. Cf. Charond. *apud* Stob.
4.44.2 (= vol. 4, p. 152.6–8 W.-H.): χρὴ δὲ καὶ τοὺς ἄρχοντας δικαίως
προεστάναι τῶν ἀρχομένων καθάπερ τέκνων ἰδίων, ἔχθραν καὶ φιλίαν
καὶ θυμὸν ἐν τῷ κρίνειν κοιμίσαντας. Cf. *ad* 2.10; Keyes, 1921, 319–20:
"The element of the constitution which would perhaps seem strangest to the
modern legal mind is the occasional introduction of provisions of a moral
rather than a legal nature—provisions which could not be made into enforceable laws. . . . Cicero's love for the old spirit of republican patriotism, and
his desire for its restoration, must have suggested these exhortations to
political righteousness. Each one of them is a rebuke to one of the political
evils or abuses of the time, which was out of reach of the law." Some
historical edicts, however, were also general declarations (cf. M. Benner,
179), so Cicero could claim that his practice is supported by custom.—The
duty of "modest obedience" is surprising and would apply, e.g., to a child's
relation to a parental directive; this is, in fact, the analogy invoked by
Charondas; cf. *ad* § 5.

**6.2 magistratus nec oboedientem et {in}noxium civem multa vinclis verberi-
busve coerceto, . . .]** A magistrate's action to enforce his orders upon a citizen
was expressed under the Republic, as here, by the verb *coercere*.[13] Our
sentence refers to a magistrate's powers independent of a criminal process
(the latter being dealt with in the sentence following).[14] For the prominence
given to this feature in Cicero's law code cf. *ad* §§ 6–11; it might seem to
imply that "magistrates should be general law-enforcers, when in fact they
had neither the time nor the resources so to be" (Lintott, 1999, 227).—The
change of *innoxium* to *noxium*, effected in the *recentiores*, is accepted by all

---

13. *Coercitio* is attested as a legal abstraction only under the Empire; cf. Kunkel-Wittmann,
149; on *coercitio* cf. Mommsen, *Staatsr.* 1, 138; Berger s.v.; Nippel, 1995, 5–12.

14. Sim. *dig.* 1.2.2.16 (Pompon.): . . . *qui tamen* [sc. *consules*] *ne per omnia regiam
potestatem sibi vindicarent, lege lata factum est ut ab eis provocatio esset neve possent in caput
civis Romani animadvertere iniussu populi: solum relictum est illis ut coercere possent et in
vincula publica duci iubere;* cf. Mommsen, *Staatsr.* 1, 138–39 n. 2.—For archaic *nec* = *non* cf.
ad 2.22.1.

recent editors. Mommsen, *Strafr.*, 38 n. 1, however, keeps the transmitted text:[15] "Ebenso wird *coercitio* mehrfach Beamten beigelegt, die büssen und pfänden können, aber Criminalgerichtsbarkeit nicht haben . . . [citation of testimonies]. In diesem beschränkten Sinne wird hier das Wort technisch gebraucht." That is, in fact, the issue: whether the word is being used here in the legal sense (*noxius* = "one guilty of wrongdoing; [esp.] a convicted criminal": *OLD* s.v., 1, citing our passage) or the more general sense "harmful, injurious" (ibid., 2; cf. Kunkel-Witmann, 150 n. 191); if the former, the conjecture must be rejected for the reason stated by Mommsen; if the latter, it can be accepted. If *innoxium* were correct, however, one would have expected *nec oboedientem sed innoxium civem;* cf. Kunkel, 19 n. 37; ibid., 37, he emphasizes that the *noxius* of our passage acts against the state interest, not merely a private citizen; offenses against the latter were presumably handled in Book 4.—No *provocatio* (see the next note) was possible for a fine (*multa*) of less than 3,020 *asses;* cf. Mommsen, *Staatsr.* 3, 353; du Mesnil *ad loc.* thinks that our law is not meant to diminish the rights of magistrates in this regard.—For the alliterative pair *vinclis verberibusve* cf. 2.21.1 with note; Gai. *dig.* 47.9.9: *qui aedes acervumve frumenti iuxta domum positum combusserit, vinctus verberatus igni necari iubetur;* Pascucci, 1968, 41.— For the specification of coercive powers at the magistrate's disposal compare the Quinctian law on aqueducts (9 B.C.) at Fron. *Aq.* 129 = *Font. iur.* p. 113.16 ff., which is also the first formulation of the power as such (the underlined words; cf. Kunkel-Witmann, 151): . . . *eaque omnia ita, ut coercenda multa dicenda sunt, quicumque curator aquarum est erit, si curator aquarum nemo erit, tum is praetor, qui inter cives et peregrinos ius dicet, multa pignoribus cogito exerceto; eique curatori aut, si curator non erit, tum ei praetori eo nomine* cogendi coercendi multa⟨e⟩ dicenda⟨e⟩ {sunt} pignoris capiendi ius potestasque *esto;* for further parallels see Mommsen, *Strafr.*, 38 n. 1; Garnsey, 149 n. 7.—Cicero was not concerned to provide a complete and precise catalogue of the coercive measures at the disposal of magistrates (e.g., he fails to mention the *pignoris capio;* see above), and he assigns these means of coercion to the magistrates as a body though there were different types of coercion available to magistrates of different grades; for details cf. Kunkel-Witmann, 153 ff. The second century saw three leges Porciae, insufficiently distinguished in our sources; cf. Rotondi, 268–69; one of them, probably the law of 195, attributed to the Elder Cato, had banned the use of *verbera* for Roman citizens; cf. Santalucia 71–74 with literature. There are appeals to this law in Cicero's forensic speeches (e.g., *Ver.* 5.163; *Rab. Perd.* 8

---

15. He had accepted the emendation previously, at *Staatsr.* 1, 138 n. 2.

and 13; fr. orat. *Corn.* 1, 50), but these, of course, should not be taken for his true opinion (cf. *Clu.* 139). On the "symbolic potency" of *verbera* for Roman citizens, who were thereby implicitly assimilated to slaves, cf. Saller, 139–42. Cf. further Keyes, 1921, 319; Kunkel-Wittmann, 167 and n. 250; Lintott, 1999, 227.

. . . ni par maiorve potestas populosve prohibessit, ad quos provocatio esto.] Mommsen, *Staatsr.* 1, 156–57 n. 4, complains of Cicero's usage here ("Es sind hier sehr verschiedenartige Dinge unpassend in einander geschoben"), in particular, that the appeal [sc. for intercession] to a magistrate (usually a tribune) is normally called *appellatio* (ibid., 271 n. 1; cf. Berger s.v.), not *provocatio,* which refers to an appeal by a person condemned by a magistrate to one of the popular assemblies;[16] nor was there a *provocatio ad populum* on grounds of *vincula;* and, of course, the lex Porcia had removed *verbera* from the magistrate's arsenal of powers (see the previous note). Santalucia, 38 and n. 27, thinks that by a kind of brachylogy (he calls it a "costruzione zeugmatica") Cicero means to include both the intercession of a colleague and *provocatio* in its standard form. This is doubtful, however; more probably, he is speaking nontechnically (see above); nor is he attempting to give a precise description of the existing Roman system.—Here we have *potestas* in the concrete sense "a person possessing power or influence (esp. a magistrate)"; cf. *ad* § 9.4; *OLD* s.v., 5; Einar Löfstedt, *Vermischte Studien zur lateinischen Sprachkunde und Syntax* (Lund, 1936), 214–16 (with parallel material from Greek).—*Par maiorve potestas:* a consul could intercede against another consul but not against a censor or dictator; the tribune could intercede against any official except a dictator, etc.; for full detail cf. Kunkel-Wittmann, 208–9. Bleicken, 1981b, 284–87, suspects that the principle of collegiality (*par potestas*) was introduced into the Roman constitution as a way of dealing with the conflict of the orders and this development opened the way for *potestas* to become, beside *auspicia* and *imperium,* a concept of public law. For the phrasing cf. § 10.3: *ast potestas par maiorve prohibessit . . .*—*Populosue* (BAHL), if correct, reflects the older spelling of *o*-stems, preserved epigraphically; cf. Leumann, 275 and 423; Meiser § 94.2a; however, *populusve* is transmitted at § 8.1.—For *prohibessit* cf. *ad* 2.19.3.—*Ad quos* should be taken by *constructio ad sensum* as referring back to *populos,* not to "magistrates" supplied out of *par maiorve potestas.*—*Provocatio* derives from the verb *provoco,* a cry for help. At *Rep.* 2.54 Cicero argued that it had existed at

---

16. Cf. Berger s.v. Similar objections to Mommsen's at Lehmann, 13–14 n. 26. As Andrew Lintott points out (*per litt.*), however, Tac. *An.* 14.28.1 speaks of *provocatio* to the senate: . . . *qui a privatis iudicibus ad senatum provocavissent . . .* , and *provocatio ad principem* is used in the second and third centuries A.D.: *FJRA* 1, 296.17–18 and 452–53.4–5.

Rome as early as the monarchy, but it was, in fact, much younger; cf. A.R. Dyck, "On the Interpretation of Cicero, *De Republica,*" *CQ* 48 (1998), 566–68 with literature.—Lintott, 1972, 258, points out that *provocatio esto* is probably permissive rather than jussive, in line with his general point that, "if no *provocatio* was made or there was no response to it from the tribunes and people, then there was nothing to prevent a Roman citizen being executed" (ibid., 244).

6.3 cum magistratus iudicassit inrogassitve, per populum multae poenaeve certatio esto.] In question is procedure before *iudicia populi* ("trials in criminal matters before the popular assembly [*comitia*] when a Roman citizen has been condemned by a magistrate to capital punishment or to a fine . . . exceeding the legal maximum": Berger s.v.; cf. Santalucia, 69 ff.). *Irrogo* is used of the presiding magistrate's "demanding, proposing, or calling for" a given penalty; cf. *OLD* s.v., 1. The verb *iudico* paired with it has been taken in two different ways: (1) as more or less synonymous with *irrogo* (so Kunkel-Wittmann, 148, citing Liv. 26.3.8: . . . *quoad vel capitis vel pecuniae iudicasset privato;* Lintott, 1972, 258); (2) that it "means, or includes in its meaning, a decision by a magistrate in the early form of *quaestio,* such as that used for the Bacchanals . . . In this case Cicero's clause may provide for automatic review of such decisions by the assembly" (Lintott, 1999, 227; sim. Strachan-Davidson, 1, 173–78); but see Santalucia, 49 n. 8, who convincingly distinguishes *aliquid* (or *alicuius rei*) *alicui iudicare,* as in our passage or Liv. 26.3.8, from *aliquem iudicare.* See further *ad* § 27 (*Deinceps igitur omnibus magistratibus*—).—*Multa poenave* is the polar expression for punishment meted out by the courts (literally "a fine and [other forms of] punishment"); cf. Mommsen, *Strafr.* 14–15 n. 2. *Poenaeve* is Powell's emendation for *poe ue* B(?A¹) or *p(o)ene* AᵃPεHL.—On the *iudicium populi* as a contest (*certatio*) between the magistrate and the accused, with the magistrate defending his decision either to prosecute or to condemn, depending on whether *iudico* has meaning (1) or (2), cf. Mommsen, *Staatsr.* 3, 354 n. 6; *Strafr.* 164 n. 1; Greenidge, 345–47.

6.4 militiae ab eo qui imperabit provocatio nec esto; quodque is qui bellum geret imperassit, ius ratumque esto.] Whether in Cicero's day a soldier could invoke *provocatio* against the decision of a military tribunal or commander depends upon the interpretation of three pieces of evidence: (1) coins minted by P. Porcius Laeca; (2) the execution of the prefect Turpilius mentioned at Sal. *Jug.* 69.4 (Mommsen, *Strafr.* 31–32 n. 3, concluded that by 108 [the date of Turpilius' execution] a general's decision against a Roman citizen was subject to *provocatio* but not against a Latin); and (3) the proposal by C. Gracchus' rival Livius Drusus that Latins in military service be exempted from the lash (since it implies that Roman citizens were already exempt; cf. Santalucia, 73–74).

(1) The coins in question (*RRC* no. 301; there dated 110 or 109) depict a figure in a toga with his right forearm raised and a second figure wearing a *lorica* with his right hand extended above the other's head; a lictor carrying rods is to the right, and the legend reads *provoco*. Lintott, 1972, 250, convincingly interprets this as a scene outside the *pomerium* commemorating the Roman citizen's right to appeal against flogging even when a tribune's help is unavailable.

(2) Sal. *Jug.* 69.4 reads as follows: *Turpilius, quem praefectum oppidi unum ex omnibus profugisse supra ostendimus, iussus a Metello causam dicere, postquam sese parum expurgat, condemnatus verberatusque capite poenas solvit; nam is civis ex Latio erat.* Kunkel-Wittmann, 168, argue that *civis ex Latio* means that Turpilius was a Roman citizen resident in Latium: Plut. *Mar.* 8.1 indicates that he was *praefectus fabrum* in Metellus' army; such a responsible post would, according to Kunkel-Wittmann, not usually be entrusted to a non-citizen; and App. *Num.* 3 calls him ἄνδρα Ῥωμαῖον.

Turpilius' status is not determined by ἄνδρα Ῥωμαῖον in the Constantinian excerpt from Appian, which may merely identify Turpilius as a member of the Roman army, not necessarily as a Roman citizen (this account is dubious in any event since it claims that Turpilius "surrendered himself to the enemy in a suspect manner" [οὐκ ἀνυπόπτως ἑαυτὸν ἐγχειρίσαντα τοῖς πολεμίοις], whereas Sallust says that his fault was fleeing the enemy). With *nam is civis ex Latio erat* Sallust gives his explanation for Turpilius' treatment, which is clearly different from what a Roman citizen could ordinarily expect. There are two possibilities: either Sallust is claiming in an odd but perhaps Sallustian way that Turpilius was not a Roman citizen or that he was a Roman citizen but "from Latium," with the implication that Metellus downgraded him mentally because he would have lacked friends in aristocratic circles (and thus have been unlikely to succeed in any attempted appeal).

(3) Plut. *CG* 9.5: . . . τοῦ δέ [sc. Λιβίου], ὅπως μηδὲ ἐπὶ στρατείας ἐξῇ τινα Λατίνων ῥάβδοις αἰκίσασθαι γράψαντος ἐβοήθουν [sc. οἱ πολλοί] τῷ νόμῳ.

Provocatio must have been possible for Roman soldiers in the field in his day, or Cicero, in our passage, would surely not have made a point of banning it. In practice it would have applied to the degree that an offending officer might be prosecuted later; but, given the Roman promotion of *metus ex re militari* (*Ver.* 5.133), the prospects for a successful prosecution would have been slight; cf. Lintott, 1972, 252; sim. Bleicken *RE* 23.2 (1959), 2450.14 ff., citing the earlier literature; Brecht, 75 n. 2.[17]

For archaic *nec* = *non* cf. *ad* 2.22.1.—For *ius ratumque,* a typical characterization of laws since the third century, cf. Thomas, 194–98; for *ratus ad* § 10.3.

6.5 minoris magistratus partiti iuris ploeris in ploera sunto: . . .] "Let there be several minor magistrates of authority divided into several (parts)."—In the *fasti* magistrates elected by the centuries and endowed with *imperium* are designated as *maiores.* Thus, though the phrase *minores magistratus* first appears in our passage, the concept is implicit in previous usage.[18] One could question, however, Cicero's inclusion of the military tribunes; see the next note. The terminology was later codified in the tract *de Auspiciis,* which M. Valerius Messala Rufus (cos. 53) wrote after Caesar's assassination; cf. Rudolf Hanslik, *RE* 8A1 (1955), 168.63 ff. (Valerius no. 268); fragments at *iur.* 47–50. Cf. in general Mommsen, *Staatsr.* 1, 19–20, 118, and 544 n. 1; Bleicken, 1981b, 264 ff. In the sequel Cicero is careful to categorize them under key words (*militiae . . . domi . . .* ; for the polar expression cf. *ad* 2.31). To put the quaestors among the *minores* implies that membership of the senate no longer depends upon holding that office, as it had since Sulla; cf. Tac. *Ann.* 11.22.6; *ad* § 7.2.—Transmitted nom. pl. *minoris/ploeris* (cf. *censoris:* § 11.13): nom. pl. *-is* for *i*-stems is attested at Var. *L.* 8.66 as well as by some readings in Plautus and in inscriptions: the *i*-stem nom. pl. *-ey-es* yielded *-ēs,* which drove out the old consonant stem nom. pl. *-es.* The nom. pl. *-īs* has been explained as a hypercorrection to match acc. pl. *-īs* (so Leumann, 440; sim. Wachter, 253 n. 662, and Meiser § 96.8) or, since in inscriptions it alternates with *-eis,* as a result of syncopation (so Sihler § 307.1.a); only on the latter view would *-īs* continue a genuine old form. For the transfer to *r*-stems Leumann, *loc. cit.,* cites *CIL* I² 20: ⟨*prai*⟩*toris,* but in view of the fragmentary context the restoration remains quite uncertain; cf. Wachter § 212b. Thus Jordan, Müller, and Wilhelm, 81, may be right in restoring the *-es* nom. pl. in our passage.—The conception of *ius* as unitary but divisible is reminiscent of the *honestum* in

---

17. My discussion of this passage had benefited from comments by Andrew Lintott and Robert Morstein-Marx.

18. Contrast Lehmann, 15, who emphasizes that "ein fixierter Sprachgebrauch lag für den von Cicero hier fest umrissenen Begriff *minoris magistratus* wohl noch nicht vor . . ."

Off. (after ἀϱετή in Plato); cf. *ad Off.* 1.15a. The title *iuris partiti libri* is attested for Cicero's younger contemporary, the jurist A. Ofellius (*iur. anteh.* 346). But Powell *ad loc.* moots deleting *partiti iuris* as an interpolation meant to facilitate the following *ploeris in ploera.*—The *ploe-* of *ploeris*[19]/ *ploera* is probably not a genuine old spelling. Leumann, 496–97, suspects deverbative **ple-y-ōs-* becoming *pleōrēs*, with *ploirume* in the Scipionic eulogy (*CIL* I² 9) possibly from an ablaut variant *plō-is*, then with *oi > ū* *plūs, plūres, plūrimi;* cf. Sihler § 353.4; Meiser § 105.4; cf. also *ad* § 9.2 (*oenus*).—For the polyptoton of adjectives cf. Wills, 222 ff.; for our locution compare Ov. *AA* 1.756: *mille animos excipe mille modis.*

militiae quibus iussi erunt imperanto eorumque tribuni sunto; . . .] The *tribuni militum*, professional officers of the Roman army numbering six per legion, were as old as the army itself. Cicero takes for granted that they must exist, though here, as with other officials, he is careful to explain their function. Their classification as magistrates is doubtful, however, since they were paid for their services (cf. Mommsen, *Staatsr.* 2, 185–86, and 3, 540 n. 1), had, apart from the levying of troops, no powers in the city and held no independent command. Perhaps Cicero was guided by their election by the people; cf. Kunkel-Wittmann, 12–13, and, in general, Jaakko Suolahti, *The Junior Officers of the Roman Army in the Republican Period*, Annales Academiae Scientiarum Fennicae, ser. B, 97 (Helsinki, 1955), 35 ff. It is not clear why Cicero discusses them before the quaestors, who outranked them (cf. Kunkel-Wittmann, 13 n. 26) unless he had in mind, as Lintott mooted, that all the minor officials should form a single board; cf. *ad* §§ 6–11. This provision, taken together with the following *quodque senatus creverit agunto*, led Lehmann, 16, to suggest that Cicero may be aiming to strengthen senatorial control over the Roman armies in the provinces; but Mehl, 247, rightly points out that there is a clear division between magistrates who function *militiae* and *domi*, with the provision *quodque senatus creverit agunto* attached to the latter.

domi pecuniam publicam custodiunto, vincula sontium servanto, capitalia vindicanto, aes argentum aurumve publice signanto, lites contractas iudicanto, quodque senatus creverit agunto.] Here Cicero lists the functions of various minor urban magistrates (see the note before last). The guarding of the public money (and other public objects and papers on deposit in the *aerarium;* cf. Mommsen, *Staatsr.* 2, 545) was the responsibility of the *quaestores aerarii;* they probably had nothing to do with the *quaestores parricidii*, a private mechanism for punishing murder that died out at an early date; cf. Latte, 1968, 359 ff.; Kunkel-Wittmann, 511–12; A.

---

19. The mss. have *ploeres*, which is evidently modernized for *ploeris;* see above on *minoris*.

Drummond, *CAH* 7.2, 195; *aliter* Mommsen, *loc. cit.*, 2, 537–38. Cf. in general ibid. 2, 535 ff.; Kunkel-Wittmann, 515–24.

Cicero summarizes the responsibilities of three different boards comprising most of the *XXVIviri* elected by the comitia tributa with the praetor urbanus presiding; cf. Kunkel-Wittmann, 532. He omits, perhaps as too localized for his purposes, the *praefecti Capuam Cumas* (on whom cf. ibid. 540–47). Our information about the rôle of these posts in building a career and their social prestige (with the *tresviri monetales* uppermost) comes mainly from imperial sources.[20] Cicero identifies each group by function:

(1) *vincula sontium servanto, capitalia vindicanto:* this was within the scope of the *tresviri capitales,* though they did not execute the criminals with their own hands (Mommsen, *Strafr.,* 930 n. 6, correcting *Staatsr.* 2, 595 and n. 7). Their other responsibilities included overseeing the general security of the city, fighting fires, and punishing slaves or poor citizens at the *columna Maenia* in the northwest corner of the forum; cf. ibid. 2, 594 ff.; Kunkel-Wittmann, 533–34; Nippel, 22–26.—*Sons* (= "criminal, guilty"; cf. *OLD* s.v.), an archaic word, is first used here in Cicero's extant corpus; the other instances are *Fam.* 4.13.3 (July 46); *Tusc.* 2.41; *Off.* 1.82; *Phil.* 2.18;[21] the word tends to increase in frequency in Tacitus as well; cf. Lebek, 196; Adams, 1972, 357–58.

(2) *aes argentum aurumve publice signanto:* this all but quotes the name of the *tresviri aere argento flando feriundo,* an official title attested, however, only under the Augustan principate. Cicero hints at the name also in the joking advice to Trebatius (*Fam.* 7.13.2): *sed ut ego quoque te aliquid admoneam de vestris cautionibus, tresviros vites censeo. audio capitales esse; mallem, aere, argento, auro essent.* Cf. Mommsen, *Staatsr.* 2, 601–3 (on the title see further 602 n. 3); Kunkel-Wittmann, 547–51.

(3) *lites contractas iudicanto:* this was the responsibility of the *decemviri stlitibus iudicandis,* a board that existed from very early times, though our passage is the only Republican source defining their competence. The charge *lites contractas iudicanto* is so vague as to apply to any civil case, but, in fact, this board judged disputes over free status; cf. Mommsen, *Staatsr* 2, 605–8, esp. (on our passage) 606 n. 1; Kunkel-Wittmann, 536–40. Cicero's speech *pro muliere Arretina* involved such a case (cf. J. Crawford, 33–34), and he refers to their procedures at *Dom.* 78.

20. For details cf. Werner Eck, "Beförderungskriterien innerhalb der senatorischen Laufbahn, dargestellt an der Zeit von 69 bis 138 n. Chr.," *ANRW* 1.2 (1974), 173–77.

21. Based on a search of PHI 5.3.

The final injunction *quodque*[22] *senatus creverit agunto* is confined to the domestic minor magistrates; they are simply to be, as a body, agents of the senate, whereas the consuls, with their *regium imperium,* are to obey no one (*nemini parento:* § 8.2); cf. Lehmann, 17; Kunkel-Wittmann, 244 n. 502; Mehl, 247.—For *cerno* = "decerno" cf. *ad* 2.21.10.

7.1 Suntoque aediles curatores urbis annonae ludorumque sollemnium.] Cicero did not give precise names for all the minor magistrates, but he does from now on.—*Aedilis* derives from the stem of *aedes* with the adjectival suffix *-ilis* attached; it denotes them as responsible for the care of the *aedes* (*Cereris*), with the mandate gradually expanded to encompass temples and public buildings generally (cf. Var. *L.* 5.81: *aedilis qui aedis sacras et privatas procuraret; OLD* s.v.; Ogilvie *ad* Liv. 3.6.9; Le Bonniec, 348). For most of the Republic there were four aediles, two plebeian and two curule, the latter office open to plebeians by the later fourth century; cf. Mommsen, *Staatsr.* 2, 480–82; to this number Julius Caesar added two *aediles plebis Ceriales* (see below). Cicero lists three of their main responsibilities: (1) the *cura urbis,* including the upkeep and cleaning of the streets, walkways, and public buildings, general oversight over private buildings open to the public such as baths or bordellos, responsibility for maintaining and regulating access to conduits for water, and the general maintenance of public order during parades and the like; (2) the *cura annonae:* this was a part of the aediles' general supervision of public commerce; this most politically sensitive of their activities was first transferred by Caesar to the two newly created *aediles plebis Ceriales,* then by Augustus to other officials, and finally devolved upon the Emperor himself; (3) the *cura ludorum:* this item of the aedile's mandate could launch him on a trajectory to higher office by winning popular approval through lavish expenditure; cf. *Off.* 2.55b ff., esp. 2.57, with notes; other testimonies at Bernstein, 76 n. 304. On the aediles cf. in general Mommsen, *Staatsr.* 2, 470–522, esp. 505–17 (*cura urbis*); 502–4 (*cura annonae*), and 517–22 (*cura ludorum*); Kunkel-Wittmann, 481–89; Ogilvie, *loc. cit.;* further literature at Bernstein, 52 n. 171.—The agent noun *curator* often occurs with the genitive of the (usually public) responsibility; cf. testimonies at *TLL* s.v., 1477.69 ff., including our passage.—If the mss. are to be relied upon, Cicero was inconsistent in spelling *cur-* and *ludus:* cf. *coero* (3x) at § 10.7; *loedis* at 2.22.2; Wilhelms, 82.—For the coordination of items in this list cf. Pinkster, *loc. cit. ad* § 47a.

7.2 ollisque ad honoris amplioris gradum is primus ascensus esto.] In view

---

22. *Quodque* is Powell's emendation; there is much confusion in the mss. here (perhaps stemming from a double reading in the archetype): *quodcumque* PEF²H^N : *quod quodcumque* BASH¹L : *quodque quodque* R^ac : *quod quodque* R^pc.

of Cicero's regular use of *honor amplissimus* or the like of senate member-ship (cf. Landgraf *ad Sex. Rosc.* 2; *Red. Sen.* 2; *Dom.* 55; *Pis.* 17; *Rab. Post.* 16–17), it has been supposed that our passage designates the aedileship, rather than the quaestorship, as the first senatorial office; cf. Sprey, 239–41, followed by Rawson, 1991, 142–43 (sim. 1982, 706); sim. Lintott, 1999, 229; *aliter* Heuss, 236–37, who would place all the *minores magistratus* in the senate (cf. *ad* § 10.1). But this is unlikely to be right. In our passage *honos amplior* is surely used not in an absolute sense but relative to the aedileship itself, which is said to be the "first step [*OLD* s.v. *ascensus* 6] toward the rank [cf. *OLD* s.v. *gradus* 8] of higher office." Mehl, 261, thinks that with *ollis* Cicero indicates that "for the aediles, and them alone, . . . the aedileship is the first step on the ladder of higher office." This is possible, but in the absence of *tantum* with *ollis,* it may be that Cicero is insisting that the aedileship, which has been optional, be prerequisite to the praetorship. For disapproval of those who omitted the aedileship cf. *Off.* 2.58.[23]

7.3 The censors are, according to the classification of M. Messalla, *de Auspiciis iur.* 47 = Gel. 13.15.4, the first of the *maiores magistratus* handled by Cicero here, with the praetors and consuls following (for the order cf. *ad* §§ 6–11). For the office of censor Mommsen, *Staatsr.* 2, 331–469, remains fundamental; cf. also Suolahti, 20–79; Nicolet, 1980, 49–88; Kunkel-Wittmann, 391–471, with literature at 391. The origin of the censorship is narrated at Liv. 4.8.2, though that passage may reflect an unhistorical itera-tion of the work of the consuls of the previous year (444), L. Papirius Mugillanus and L. Sempronius Atratinus. The office evidently had its origin in the need to relieve the consuls of the burden of conducting the census, which may originally have entailed a full military review, retained in later times only for the *equites;* probably only in the fourth century was determi-nation of the composition of the senate added; cf. A. Drummond, *CAH* 7.2, 197. There has been some recent criticism of the censorship, especially in its function of regulating the behavior of the citizens, as a futile institution, but our passage, aiming to strengthen it, suggests otherwise; cf. A.E. Astin, "Cicero and the Censorship," *CPh* 80 (1985), 233–39.

7.3 Censoris populi aevitatis suboles familias pecuniasque censento; . . .] For *censoris* and *aevitatis* (the latter restored by Powell for -*es*) see *ad* § 6.5 (*minoris*).—The archaic spelling *aevitas* for *aetas* is in imitation of *Lex XII;* cf. 1.3: *si morbus aevitasve escit, iumentum dato . . .*.—For the archaic and poetic word *suboles* cf. *ad Off.* 1.54.—The first census is described at Liv. 1.43.1–8 and D.H. 4.15.6; for the procedure cf. ibid. 5.75.3 as well as Tab.

---

23. This note has benefited from the advice of Robert Morstein-Marx.

Heracl. in *RS* 1, 368.145–48 (probably of Caesarian date but largely tralaticious from earlier laws: cf. ibid. 360): . . . *censum ag⟨i⟩to; eorumque nomina praenomina patres aut patronos tribus cognomina et quot annos quisque eorum habe⟨bi⟩t et rationem pecuniae ex formula census, quae Romae ab eo, qui tum censum populi acturus erit, proposita erit, a⟨b⟩ ieis iurateis accipito.*—The age (*aevitas*) of the enrolled citizen was important since males between the ages of seventeen and forty-five were subject to military service and might be required to swear that they had come forward for the levy or would do (cf. Nicolet, 1980, 68); failure to do so could be punished severely. Thus in 209 the censors reduced to *aerarii* (taxpayers without voting rights) those who had been seventeen at the beginning of the Hannibalic War but had not served (ibid., 77).—Marrying and producing children (*suboles*) for the state was considered the duty of a good citizen; cf. P.A. Brunt, *Italian Manpower, 225 B.C.–A.D. 14* (Oxford, 1971), 559 and n. 6. A man might be required to swear that he had taken a wife (*de Orat.* 2.260; Gel. 4.20.3–6; cf. Treggiari, 58) and that he had done so for the sake of begetting children (Gel. 4.3.2 and 17.21.44). See *infra* on . . . *caelibes esse prohibento* . . .—Declaring the value of property in slaves and money (*familias pecuniasque*) was until its abolition in 167 essential to the collection of the *tributum,* which was levied on property, not income (cf. Nicolet, *loc. cit.,* 69–71); this aspect of the census was also the basis for the functioning of the Roman state since the citizen body was divided into groups according to income levels (see below). Cicero does not mention that debts also had to be declared, a fact that had caused considerable embarrassment to his friend Milo when campaigning for the consulate of 52; cf. sch. Bobb. 169 St.; Nicolet, *loc. cit.,* 70–71.

. . . **urbis ⟨sarta tec⟩ta, vias aquas, aerarium vectigalia tuento; . . .**] This mandate follows from the censors' rôle in establishing the list of citizens and hence the basis for taxation and the state budget; cf. Mommsen, *Staatsr.* 2, 424.—Transmitted is *urbistatem pla* (BAH[1]L) or *urbis templa* (PεF[2]H[N]), for which Bake conjectured *urbis tecta templa,* Huschke *urbis sarta tecta templa,* Powell, to create a series of pairs and on the assumption that *templa* may be a corruption of *tecta,* restored *sarta tecta* alone. *Sarta tecta* are repairs, especially of public buildings, for which the censors were responsible: cf. *OLD* s.v. *sartus;* Mommsen, *loc. cit.,* 450–53; not surprising that the technical term should have been truncated in transmission.—The censors were responsible for temples, roads, and aqueducts in a different sense from the aediles: whereas the latter were charged with their upkeep (see above), the former let contracts for their construction; cf. D.E. Strong, "The Administration of Public Building in Rome during the Late Republic and Early Empire," *BICS* 15 (1968), 97–109. Another function—not mentioned by Cicero—was to let public property for the use of individuals; cf. Mommsen, *Staatsr.* 2, 427–32. Although Cicero confines these activities to the city (*urbis*), until the Social War the Roman citizen communities throughout Italy depended on censorial approval for their public buildings; ibid., 429.—The *aerarium* was under the supervision of the quaestors (cf. *ad* § 6.5: *domi pecuniam publicam custodiunto*—). But Cicero, evidently dissatisfied with their stewardship especially of public records (cf. § 46), plans to transfer this mandate to the censors, an extension of their oversight over state property, on which cf. Mommsen, *loc. cit.,* 434 ff.—The *vectigalia* consisted of the income derived from state property; ibid. 2, 434 n. 3; *OLD* s.v. *vectigal* 1a.

populique partes in tribus discribunto, . . .] I.e., "populum partiunto et in tribus discribunto"; cf. *Flac.* 15 (on the voting procedure specified by the ancestors following discussion of a bill *in contione*): . . . *distributis partibus, tributim et centuriatim discriptis ordinibus, classibus, aetatibus, re multos dies promulgata et cognita iuberi vetarique voluerunt;* cf. also Mommsen, *Staatsr.* 3, 273. According to Roman tradition the first such division was part of the first census, performed by Servius Tullius: *quadrifariam enim urbe divisa collibus qui habitabantur, partes eas tribus appellavit, ut ego arbitror, ab tributo; nam eius quoque aequaliter ex censu conferendi ab eodem inita ratio est; neque eae tribus ad centuriarum distributionem numerumque quicquam pertinuere* (Liv. 1.43.13). These local tribes were later increased to twenty-one (495: Liv. 2.21.7; cf. D.H. 7.64.6) and then, upon the annexation of Veii, to twenty-five (387: Liv. 6.5.8); cf. T.J. Cornell, *CAH* 7.2, 246; by 241 the number had risen to thirty-five, where it would remain into the late Empire; cf. Mommsen, *Staatsr.* 3, 162–74.

. . . exin pecunias aevitatis ordines {partiunto} equitum peditumque; . . .] *Exin,* alternating with *exinde,* is used before consonants in the poets (e.g., 4x in Cic. *Arat.*), elsewhere in Ciceronian prose only at *Orat.* 153–54 (where the shortening of *deinde* and *exinde* is ascribed to euphony), *N.D.* 2.101 (where the codices are divided between *exin* and *exim*), and *Div.* 1.55 (in a citation of Coelius Antipater = *hist.* 1, 174, fr. 49); cf. *TLL* s.v. *exinde* 1506.54 ff. and 69–70 and for the form George Dunkel, "B. Delbrück and the Instrumental-Ablative in *-*m*" in *Berthold Delbück y la sintaxis indoeuropea hoy,* ed. E. Crespo and J.L. García Ramón (Madrid-Wiesbaden, 1987), 66–68. It has not been noticed that in our text *exin* also appears *metri causa,* for *exin— ordines* form an iambic trimeter (in spite of Cicero's disapproval of verse embedded in prose: *de Orat.* 3.175). The only license is the synizesis whereby the *i* of *pecunias* is treated as a glide. Synizesis involving -*i*- is well attested for the hexameter (cf. Leumann § 139a) but controversial for the Plautine trimeter; cf. Hans Drexler, *Einführung in die römische Metrik* (Darmstadt, 1967), 53–55, who, however, allows that some examples are certain. Cf. also F VIII.3 p. 278 Soubiran = VII.3 p. 107 Ewbank at *Tusc.* 3.67 (tr. from Eur. *Phrix.*): *esset dolendi causa: ut iniecto equulei.* For synizesis in Cicero's treatment of clausulae cf. Zielinski, 1904, 175–76.—As *exin* ("thereupon, next") clearly indicates,[24] this is a different division; money and age were the criteria Servius used to divide the citizen-body into five *classes* to form the basis for his army; cf. above on *Censores populi aevitatis suboles familias pecuniasque censento . . . Ordo* (= "social class": cf. *OLD* s.v., 4) was not an initial factor; but it came to play a large rôle in the army, originally divided perhaps into two groups, *classis* and *infra classem,* with patricians tending to monopolize the *classis* and push plebeians into the *infra classem;* cf. A. Momigliano, *CAH* 7.2, 103–4.—For the punctuation after *peditumque* rather than *partiunto* cf. Mommsen, *Staatsr.* 3, 253 n. 1, who, citing other testimonies, points out that money, age, and *ordines* correspond to the divisions of the Servian army; hence *equitum peditumque,* a paraphrase for the army as a whole, limits all three of the categories; for the *iunctura* cf. *Tusc.* 4.1. But then, as Powell points out (*per litt.*), the word order is a problem, since otherwise the verb comes at the end of its clause; hence his deletion of *partiunto,* which may have been inserted by a reader who misunderstood the relation of ideas; alternatively, it could be transposed so as to follow *peditumque.*

prolem describunto, caelibes esse prohibento, . . .] *Proles* is among the archaic words which, at *de Orat.* 3.153, are said to be more readily admissible to poetry than oratory (sim., probably, the corrupt passage Quint. *Inst.* 8.3.26); Cicero uses it in prose elsewhere at *Rep.* 2.40 (*. . . proletarios nominavit, ut ex eis quasi proles, id est {quasi} progenies civitatis, exspectari videretur*) and 6.27; cf. Lebek, 28–29; von Albrecht, 1973, 1256.15–18.— Children, except for orphans, were registered[25] under the name of the father; cf. Nicolet, 1980, 68–69.—For the Roman view of marriage see above on *Censoris populi aevitatis—.* In Cicero's time the Roman state did not attempt to curb bachelorhood in any systematic way, though precedent existed: there were sanctions against bachelors at Sparta (cf. Plut. *Lyc.* 15.1–3), and Plato had provided fines for them (*Lg.* 774a–b); according to D.H. 9.22.2 an "ancient law" at Rome compelled those who were of age to marry; the

---

24. Cf. *TLL* s.v. *exinde* 1507.34–35, where our passage is cited.

25. *Describo* = "record in writing" (*OLD* s.v., 2), transmitted in most mss., is the verb wanted, not *dis-* of PS(?L¹); cf. *ad* 2.11.

censors of 403 M. Furius Camillus and M. Postumius Albinus[26] are said to have imposed a fine on those who remained bachelors into old age (V.Max. 2.9.1; Plut. *Cam.* 2.4; cf. Paul. *Fest.* p. 379M s.v. *uxorium*);[27] and the censors often made it their business to inquire whether citizens had taken a wife; see *supra* on *Censoris populi aevitatis*—. As elsewhere in these laws,[28] Cicero fails to specify what penalties he has in mind.

. . . **mores populi regunto, . . .**] Cf. § 46 with reference to the νομοφύλακες of Greek states: . . . *facta hominum observabant, ad legesque revocabant.* Cf. *Clu.* 119: . . . *C. Getam . . . censorem esse ipsum postea factum et . . . populi Romani . . . moribus praefuisse;* ibid. 129: *hoc tu idem facies censor in senatu legendo? . . . tu es praefectus moribus . . . ;* Liv. 24.18.2 *censores . . . ad mores hominum regendos animum adverterunt castigandaque vitia . . . ;* [Asc.] *in Div. Caec.* 8 (p. 189.16 ff. St.): *etiam censorium nomen. regendis moribus civitatis censores quinto quoque anno creari solebant;* other passages cited at *TLL* s.v. *censor* 798.37 ff. For the means available to the censors cf. Astin, 1988, 15: "The censors' concern with *mores* manifested itself principally in the discharge of other responsibilities—in the *lectio senatus,* the *recognitio equitum* and the census itself; and in matters of *mores* virtually the only sanction open to them was to depose a person from a higher to a lower order or classification . . ." with following discussion. Cf. also Suolahti, 47–52; Nicolet, 1980, 73 ff., esp. 85–86; Baltrusch, 5 ff.; Nippel, 1995, 8–9.

. . . **probrum in senatu ne relinquonto; . . .**] *Probrum* ("disgrace, ignominy, shame": *OLD* s.v., 2) is the technical term for the delict punished by the censors; thus Sallust speaks of the conspirator Q. Curius as one *quem censores senatu probri gratia moverant* (*Cat.* 23.1); cf. Mommsen, *Staatsr.* 2, 382 n. 8. In our passage the meaning shades toward the concrete ("a source of disgrace, scandal"), as at *Phil.* 11.36: *an Antonios potius ornarem . . . Romani nominis probra atque dedecora?* (*OLD loc. cit.* 2b).

bini sunto, . . .] A collegial system modelled on the consulate, to which the censorial functions had belonged; see the headnote to this section. On the Roman collegial system of magistracies in general cf. Mommsen, *Staatsr.* 1, 30 ff.; *ad* § 6.2.

. . . **magistratum quinquennium habento, . . .**] The *lustrum* and census were to take place *quinto quoque anno* (Censorin. 18.13), originally interpreted as "every fourth year," later as "every fifth year," with resulting

---

26. For the date cf. *MRR* 1, 82.

27. Astin, 1988, 16, suggests, however, that this was probably not done by direct fine but by "adjustment of census assessments."

28. Cf. *ad* 2.22.8 and § 11.1–2.

discrepancies. Roman tradition held that the censors had originally served for five years but that this was curtailed to a year and a half by the lex Aemilia of 434; cf. Liv. 4.24.5–6 and 9.33–34; Rotondi, 211. The historical censors took office on 15 March and did their work in a year or at most eighteen months; the new lists took effect on the day of lustration, new contracts on the following 15 March; cf. Mommsen, *Staatsr.* 2, 341–50. Cicero could thus have appealed to the *mos maiorum* for maintaining the censors continuously in office; his reason emerges only later; cf. *ad* §§ 11.13–14 and 47. The lengthened censorship was evidently an idea whose time had come: in 46 Caesar became censor for three years, double the traditional length; in 19 Augustus assumed the *censoria potestas* for five full years (Dio 43.14.4 and 54.10.5).

... reliqui magistratus annui sunto; ...] This, the unmarked duration of office, is made explicit only here by way of contrast.

eaque potestas semper esto.] When these words were written, the institution was deeply troubled. Sulla, while not eliminating the censorship altogether, had provided other means of fulfilling its functions; cf. Mommsen, *Staatsr.* 2, 336–37 and n. 4; and between 70 and 50 no successful census was completed. Moreover, the censors' freedom of action had been curtailed by Clodius' law of 58, which required that formal hearings be conducted before both censors prior to any action being taken to exclude a member from the senate or to affix a *nota* beside a name (Asc. *Pis.* 8); this procedure was traditional in the census proper but not hitherto in the *lectio senatus*. Clodius' goal will have been to shore up a following among senators who thought themselves under threat of expulsion. In bitter opposition to the law, Cicero equated it with the abolition of the censorship: *vetus illa magistra pudoris et modestiae, censura, sublata est: Pis.* 9; sim. *Dom.* 131; *Sest.* 55. Cf. Rotondi, 398; Astin, 1988, 20 n. 25, finding Cicero's complaints about the law overstated; idem, "Censorships in the Late Republic," *Historia* 34 (1985), 175–90 at 187–88; H. Benner, 51–52; Tatum, 1990. After Clodius' death, the law was repealed by the lex Caecilia of 52 (Rotondi, 412). Possibly the lex Clodia came in for discussion in the treatment of *leges* requested by Atticus at § 48 but no longer extant.[29] Augustus conducted a census three times, each time as consul, though under his principate there were also censors who were not simultaneously consul; the last census occurred in A.D. 74; after the fall of Domitian, who had made himself censor for life, the office disappeared; cf. Mommsen, *loc. cit.*, 337–38.

---

29. It is misleading to say, as does Nicolet, 1980, 56, that our law calls for its repeal; it is unclear whether the law was still in force at the time Cicero wrote.

8.1 Iuris disceptator, qui privata iudicet iudicarive iubeat, praetor esto; is iuris civilis custos esto; . . .] The description of the function precedes the name of the office, as with military tribunes, but unlike the aediles and censors.—The *nomen agentis disceptator* is attested as early as Plautus and is equivalent to *iudex* (cf. the gloss cited at *TLL* s.v., 1292.71); cf. 2.21.7; Cod. Iust. 3.1.14.1: *. . . omnes . . . iudices Romani iuris disceptatores . . .*— In defining the praetor in terms of judicial functions, Cicero voices a widespread view of his own time and later; cf. Pompon. *dig.* 1.2.2.27: *cumque consules avocarentur bellis finitimis neque esset qui in civitate ius reddere posset, factum est, ut praetor quoque crearetur, qui urbanus appellatus est, quod in urbe ius redderet;* sim. Liv. 6.42.11. The praetor at Rome was, however, originally a military commander (< *praeeo;* see below), and some usages of the adjectival form retained the military connection; cf. Paul. *Fest.* p. 223M: *praetoria porta in castris appellatur, qua exercitus in proelium educitur, quia initio praetores erant, qui nunc consules, et hi bella administrabant, quorum tabernaculum quoque dicebatur praetorium.* The supreme official was distinguished as *praetor maximus* (cf. Liv. 7.3.5); there was also a distinction drawn between *praetor maior* and *praetor minor* (L. Caesar *iur.* 47, 4 = *iur. anteh.* 107, 2). The *praetor urbanus* was perhaps first created (367) to see to the affairs of the city, including its defense, while the *praetores maximi* were away on campaign. Dio, 1, p. 66 Boiss. = Zon. 7.19.1 connects the first use of the designation "consuls" (ὕπατοι) with the settlement of 449: οἱ δ᾽ ὕπατοι, τότε γὰρ λέγεται πρῶτον ὑπάτους αὐτοὺς προσαγορευθῆναι, στρατηγοὺς καλουμένους τὸ πρότερον . . . The *praetor peregrinus* seems to have been created to help the consuls with military duties. Only later (from 197 on) did these two praetors become specialized in adjudication of civil cases and of cases between Roman citizens and foreigners, respectively. For the office, its designation, and development cf. Mommsen, *Staatsr.* 2, 74–79; H. Stuart Jones in *CAH* 7¹ (1928), 437–38; Kunkel-Wittmann, 296–99 and 696–97 and n. 158; T. Corey Brennan, *The Praetorship in the Roman Republic,* 2 vols. (Oxford, 2000); for its designation in Greek, Hugh J. Mason, *Greek Terms for Roman Institutions* (Toronto, 1974), 155–59. For the praetorship in general cf. Mommsen, *loc. cit.,* 193–238; J.-C. Richard, "*Praetor collega consulis est:* Contribution à l'histoire de la préture," *RPh* 56 (1982), 19–31.—Cicero's *iudicare* here seems to be used in a nontechnical sense as the equivalent of *ius dicere;* otherwise, he is attributing to the praetors a function of deciding issues that was, in his day, reserved at Rome for the *iudices;* cf. Kunkel, 50–51; Kunkel-Wittmann, 142 and n. 163. Cicero imitates the phrasing of actual laws, e.g., *CIL* I² 592.I.16–17: *ita ius deicito iudicia dato iudicareque* *iubeto;* this and other parallels cited by Brent Vine, *Studies in Archaic Latin Inscriptions* (Innsbruck, 1993), 73, suggest that in our text *iudicareve* may be the correct reading (for confusions of active and passive infinitive endings see *ad* 2.27a: *Iam ritus familiae patrumque servare*—).—*Custos* implies a need to preserve the institution from corruption or decay; cf. 2.43; *ad Off.* 3.44.—Curiously, Cicero makes no mention of the praetor's function as president of *quaestiones*. In fact, Cicero's legislation makes no provision at all for the *quaestio perpetua*, only the *iudicium populi* (cf. *ad* § 6.3). This need not mean, however, that he disapproved of the institution, only that he saw no need for it in his ideal state (so Lintott, 1999, 228 and n. 53; but on the ambivalence of premise here cf. the introduction to this Book); similarly, Kunkel, 32, speaks of "einen starken Anachronismus und zugleich eine Idealisierung des Komitialprozesses." Another possibility is that this subject and indeed the whole topic of criminal justice, which receives little attention in this set of laws (Lintott, 1999, 231), is being held in reserve for Book 4, *de iudiciis;* cf. also Thommen, 1988, 374 n. 50; Rawson, 1991, 147–48; Riggsby, 168; *ad* § 11.10.

huic potestate pari, quotcumque senatus creverit populusve iusserit, tot sunto.] *Potestate pari* is ablative of description, and *huic* depends on *pari.* For *cerno* = "decerno" cf. *ad* 2.21.10.—In 197 six praetors were elected for the first time; Sulla increased the number to eight, four for the city, four for foreign service; cf. Kunkel-Wittmann, 297; Mommsen, *Staatsr.,* 2, 200–202. Cicero chose to leave the number unspecified, perhaps because he foresaw the need for an increase; cf. Rawson, 1991, 143 n. 55. With the number of provinces growing, Caesar would later raise the number successively to ten, fourteen, and sixteen; cf. Mommsen, *loc. cit.,* 202. Under Augustus the norm was twelve praetors, the number rising to fifteen during the reign of Tiberius; cf. Richard J.A. Talbert, *The Senate of Imperial Rome* (Princeton, 1984), 19.

8.2 regio imperio duo sunto, . . .] This description of consular powers by no means fits the reality of Cicero's day (cf. Kunkel-Wittmann, 245). It does correspond, however, to Polybius' analysis,[30] to Scipio's ideal in *Rep.* (*placet . . . esse quiddam in republica praestans et regale*: 1.69), and to the position in the early Republic (*temporibus illis*) as described at *Rep.* 2.56: *tenuit igitur hoc in statu senatus rempublicam temporibus illis . . . uti consules potestatem haberent tempore dumtaxat annuam, genere ipso ac iure*

---

30. Cf. 6.11.12: . . . ὅτε μὲν γὰρ εἰς τὴν τῶν ὑπάτων ἀτενίσαιμεν ἐξουσίαν, τελείως μοναρχικὸν ἐφαίνετ' εἶναι καὶ βασιλικόν . . .; ibid. 6.12.9; Liv. 2.1.7: *libertatis . . . originem inde magis quia annuum imperium consulare factum est quam quod deminutum quicquam sit ex regia potestate numeres.*

regiam (in our passage the limitation to one year has already been established at § 7.3); cf. also Liv. 8.32.3; V.Max. 4.1.1; and it is true that the consular power, like that of the kings, extended to all areas of government; cf. Mehl, 225. However, the minimum age is a restriction as is the prohibition of iteration within ten years (§ 9.1); the fact of collegiality imposes a severe constraint on the power of the individual consul, which is limited by the other's power of intercession, which Cicero maintains (§§ 6.2 and 11.4). In addition, it is hard to see how Cicero's conception squares with the tribunician veto, which he does not propose to tamper with (cf. §§ 9.6 and 23) and the limitation of which on consular power he himself emphasizes (§ 16); however, the strengthened mandate of the censors (§§ 7.3 and 11.13–14), emphasized by Sabine-Smith, 92–93, as a limitation on the consular power, is directed primarily at members of the senate. Cicero could not be referring to emergency situations here, since he has provided for a dictator to be appointed in the event of civil strife (§ 9.2). It looks as though Cicero attributes *regium imperium* to the consuls in order to satisfy the requirements of constitutional theory[31] and in accord with his picture of the situation in early Rome. But the real balance of power, as he sees it, is between the *principes* and the plebs (§ 25).

... iique ⟨a⟩ praeeundo iudicando consulendo praetores iudices consules appellamino; ...] Cicero adopts available etymologies: cf. Lucil. 1160M = 1178K: *ergo praetorum est ante- et praeire;* Carbo had derived *consul* from *patriae consulere (orat.* p. 155 = *de Orat.* 2.165; sim. Pompon. *dig.* 1.2.2.16: *dicti sunt ab eo, quod plurimum reipubicae consulerent);* cf. Acc. *praet.* 39: *qui recte consulat, consul cluat;* both etymologies together at Var. *VPR* fr. 68 = Non. p. 23M: *consulum et praetorum proprietas, quod consulant et praeeant populis, auctoritate Varronis ostenditur de Vita Populi Romani lib. II: quod idem dicebantur consules et praetores; quod praeirent populo praetores; quod consulerent senatui consules;* sim. Var. L. 5.80 (quoting Accius and Lucilius given above): *consul nominatus qui consuleret populum et senatum ... praetor dictus qui praeiret iure et exercitu ...* ; Cic. *Pis.* 23: *animo consulem esse oportet ... id quod vis nominis ipsa praescribit, rei publicae consulendo;* for later testimonies cf. Maltby s.vv.—For loss of *a* in an etymology cf. 1.19.—*Iudex* was an old designation of the consuls, as is shown by two formulas for summoning the citizen army cited by Var. L. 6.88: *omnes Quirites, inlicium vos ite huc ad iudices; omnes Quirites, ite ad conventionem huc ad iudices;* Kunkel, 19 n. 36, emphasizes

---

31. Cf. A. Drummond, *CAH* 7.2, 188: "Ancient writers, influenced by Greek political theory and anxious to emphasize the continuity of Roman political development, see the republican chief magistracy as heir to the power of the kings."

that *iudicando* merely makes the connection with that old designation. Liv. 3.55.12 claims that the consuls were called *praetores* before they were called *iudices;* see *supra* on *Iuris disceptator*—.—*Appellamino* is a unique form; if correctly read, it is evidently a contamination of the third-person plural present and future passive imperative endings -*mini* and -*nto;* cf. Pascucci, 1968, 36; *aliter* Leumann, 571; however, the possibility of a double reading in the archetype cannot be excluded.

militiae summum ius habento, . . .] This is ensured by Cicero's denial of *provocatio* to soldiers in the field (cf. *ad* § 6.4). Against the notion of Mommsen, *Staatsr.* 2, 94, that the consuls' military authority in Italy lapsed after Sulla cf. Lintott, 1999, 106.

. . . nemini parento; ollis salus populi suprema lex esto.] Keyes, 1921, 317, comments: "The only other possible interpretation—one which has been universally rejected as unthinkable—seems to be the literal one that Cicero actually intended to place the consuls above the law, thus making an exception to the first provision of his code. I believe, however, that this interpretation is the only reasonable one, and that Cicero here intends to give the consul extraordinary powers in cases of emergency, without the necessity of action by the Senate." This law would substitute, in other words, in Cicero's system for the *senatusconsultum ultimum,* giving the consuls whatever power they need to insure the *salus populi;* sim. Turnebus and Sichirollo *ad loc.;* Heuss, 210–11; Lintott, 1999, 227. It is doubtful that this interpretation is right, however, especially in light of § 2: *ut enim magistratibus leges, ita populo praesunt magistratus . . .* Cicero surely cannot have meant to abrogate that foundational tenet; nor does he exempt consuls from the review of retiring magistrates by the censors (and possible prosecution): cf. § 47. Moreover, the mechanism Cicero has provided for handling severe civil discord (as well as military crises) is the senate-appointed dictator (§ 9.2); this is the feature that replaces the *senatusconsultum ultimum* in his system (and the dictator would, of course, be exempt from *provocatio*[32] or veto by a colleague or tribune); cf. Lehmann, 28 and n. 48; to this degree the

---

32. Insofar as the dictator was appointed to deal with *duellum gravius* (§ 9.2), the military exemption would apply (§ 6.4: *militiae ab eo qui imperabit provocatio nec esto*). Would the same extend to police actions entailed by *discordiae civium?* Lehmann, 42 n. 69, thinks not; but, in fact, there is some evidence that dictators were not obliged to give way to *provocatio* or to tribunician intercession even in the city; cf. Liv. 2.18.8 and other passages cited by Mommsen, *Staatsr.* 2, 163 n. 1; Oakley *ad* Liv. 6.38.3–13; *aliter* A.N. Sherwin-White and A.W. Lintott, *OCD*[3] s.v. dictator, citing Liv. 27.6.5, where the threat of tribunician veto leads to a constitutional crisis finally settled by agreement of all parties to the senate's solution, and Liv. 8.33.8 (but see 8.35.5 with Oakley's note).

effect of Cicero's laws is to reduce the power of the consuls (cf. Mehl, 229). The difficulty lies perhaps in the tendency to take *lex* in this sentence too literally; the *suprema lex* is surely "the supreme principle" for their conduct of office; cf. *OLD* s.v. *lex* 6.[33] Finally, *pace* Keyes, this is hardly meant to be an exception to the first provision of the code, *Iusta imperia sunto;* see *ad loc.* Cf. also Sprey, 233–34; Lehmann, 29 n. 49; Mehl, 227 and 235–36.—*Nemini parento* stands in contrast to the stipulation for the minor magistrates *quodcumque senatus creverit agunto* (§ 6) and is in accord with Cicero's lofty conception of the consuls' *regium imperium;* see above.—For *ollis* cf. *ad* 2.19.7.—The principle *ollis salus populi suprema lex esto* is made explicit here for the first time, though one suspects that *Cat.* 4.9 is meant as a paraphrase of the consul's duty (*animum . . . saluti populi consulentem*); see the note before last.—The phrase *salus populi* (usually with *Romani* added, though sometimes understood, as at 2.21.1, *Cat.* 4.9, or *Agr.* 2.7) is virtually Ciceronian property, occurring 18x in the speeches, especially those delivered during and after the Catilinarian conspiracy (15x), as well as twice in the letters; there are also a couple equivalent phrases (*omnium civium salus: Mur.* 7; *salus vestra: Phil.* 4.4); Livy also picked up the phrase (2x).[34] For Cicero's conception of the *salus populi Romani*, its origins, and influence cf. Lorenz Winkler, *Salus vom Staatskult zur politischen Idee. Eine archäologische Untersuchung,* Archäologie und Geschichte 4 (Heidelberg, 1995), 30–35.

9.1 Eundem magistratum ni interfuerint decem anni ne quis capito; aevitatem annali lege servanto.] It is interesting that of all the regulations of the *cursus honorum* it is the ten-year interval that Cicero emphasizes. Iteration of a magistracy was allowed in the older period, the ten-year interval first stipulated by plebiscite in 342, though often ignored, especially in times of crisis; cf. Liv. 7.42: *aliis plebiscitis cautum, ne quis eundem magistratum intra decem annos caperet;* Mommsen, *Staatsr.* 1, 519; for exceptions cf. ibid. 519–20 n. 5.—For *ne quis capito* cf. *ad* 2.59: '*hoc plus*', *inquit,* '*ne facito*—'; for *aevitas* see *ad* § 7.3: *. . . exin pecunias aevitatis*—.—Liv. 40.44.1 records the lex Villia annalis as follows: *eo anno* [sc. 180] *rogatio primum lata est ab L. Vil⟨l⟩io tribuno plebis quot annos nati quemque magistratum peterent caperentque.* This passage, together with ours, makes it clear that minimum ages were specified (for the curule offices). With the Hannibalic War, continuation of patrician offices became exceptional; some period (length unspecified) had to intervene; from 191 on the minimal

---

33. Sim. Fontanella, 1998, 199; for *suprema lex* in a different sense cf. § 3.
34. Based on search of PHI 5.3.

interval is two years; hence Mommsen, *loc. cit.*, 523–63, esp. 529, supposed that the lex Villia annalis contained this prescription as well; Kunkel-Wittmann, 45, think that this may have been a provision of the lex Pinaria; however, Astin, *CAH* 8, 176, and *The Lex Annalis before Sulla* (Brussels, 1978), 7–19 and 45, prudently leaves open whether the lex Villia or another law of roughly the same date introduced the two-year interval; cf. also Rotondi, 278–79; other literature at Kunkel-Wittmann, *loc. cit.*, n. 29. At *Phil.* 5.47 Cicero argues that an exception be made to the *lex annalis* for Octavian on grounds of his *excellens eximiaque virtus;* he adds that it was for such reasons (*itaque*) that the *maiores* had no qualification laws but that the *ambitio* of candidates motivated their introduction.

9.2 Ast quando duellum gravius discordiae⟨ve⟩ civium escunt, oenus ne amplius sex menses, si senatus creverit, idem iuris quod duo consules teneto, . . .] For *ast* cf. *ad* 2.19.7; for *duellum ad* 2.21.2; for *escunt ad* 2.60.—*Duellum gravius* and *discordiae civium* are double subjects (*-ve*, which can easily have been lost by saltation, was added in the *recentiores*); our sources vary correspondingly in giving the motive for the appointment of T. Larcius Flavus, who usually figures as the first dictator; cf. Mommsen, *Staastr.* 2, 142 n. 4 with references. Which of these two factors lay behind the creation of the office has been debated by historians. The evidence at our disposal for early dictatorships, if reliable, suggests that the need for unified command in a difficult war may have been the *causa efficiens*,[35] whereas *discordiae civium* may have been emphasized in light of the experience of Sulla's dictatorship; cf. A. Drummond, *CAH* 7.2, 190–92. The senate-appointed dictator would thus substitute in Cicero's system for the grant of special powers to the consuls to handle civil disturbance under the problematic *senatusconsultum ultimum,* on which cf. Siegfried Mendner, "Videant consules," *Philologus* 110 (1966), 258–67; J. von Ungern-Sternberg, *Untersuchungen zum spätrepublikanischen Notstandsrecht* (Munich, 1970); Vanderbroeck, 156 ff.; Burckhardt, ch. 2; A. Duplá Ansuategui, "El *senatus consultum ultimum:* medida de salvación pública o práctica de depuración politica?" *Latomus* 49 (1990), 75–80; cf. also *ad* § 8.2.—*Oenus* is the certain correction of Gifanius or Lambinus for transmitted *ones*. The word bears considerable weight as an identifier in this sentence, as does *decem* in the description of the tribunes later in this chapter. Lat. *unus* is reconstructed from PIE **oin-;* hence the older spelling was *oi-* as in *oinuorsei = universi.* The spelling *oe-* for *oi-*, though it does not correspond to a phonological

---

35. The same conclusion follows from the title *magister populi*, as Kunkel-Wittmann, 675, point out (see the next note).

development, is often found in inscriptions of second century date and may represent a sort of graphical renewal of older *oi-*; cf. *ad* § 10.7 (*coerari*); sim. also *ploeres* in § 6.5. Cf. Leumann, 60–61; Sihler § 389.1.A.—For *ne* cf. *ad* 2.21.11; it limits *amplius sex menses,* not *teneto*; cf. Vairel-Carron, 297.— For *amplius sex menses* without *quam* cf. *Sex. Rosc.* 39 (*annos natus maior quadraginta*) with Landgraf *ad loc.*; Kühner-Stegmann, 2, 471; this should probably be seen, with von Albrecht, 1973, 1262.6 ff., as an influence from the spoken language.—In specifying a six-month limit, Cicero is harking back to the old, pre-Sullan form of the dictatorship,[36] which had not been used since 202, perhaps because the time limit made it unsuitable for waging wars outside of Italy; cf. Mommsen, *Staatsr.* 2, 169 and n. 4. Cicero may therefore have in mind primarily the handling of civil conflicts; see above and Lehmann, 37–38. The limit was evidently included in the appointment formula (cf. Liv. 23.22.11: *M. Fabium Buteonem . . . dictatorem in sex menses dicit*; other references at Kunkel-Wittmann, 670 n. 23) and relates to the dictator's original function as general in the field, it being assumed that this was the maximum duration of the campaigning season; however, dictators appointed for a specific task were expected to vacate office upon completion (cf. *ad Off.* 3.112). Though the dictator was required to abdicate after six months, the senate could, if necessary, grant an extension; cf. Mommsen, *Staatsr.* 2, 161; Kunkel-Wittmann, 670–72.—*Si senatus creverit* is an innovation, the dictator ordinarily having been appointed by a consul; there was recent precedent in the law carried by L. Valerius Flaccus as interrex for appointment of Sulla as dictator, albeit that law (though not the procedure) was specifically disapproved by Cicero (cf. 1.42 with note). Rawson, 1991, 142 and n. 54, thinks that Cicero has been influenced by the plan to appoint Scipio as dictator in 129 *reipublicae constituendae causa.* But that plan, if it existed,[37] was related to a special set of circumstances and did not necessarily imply appointment by the senate. Rather, this provision is an example of Cicero's wish to make the senate fully responsible for and in control of the

---

36. Pompey may have been guided by such considerations when in 52 after ca. six months as *consul sine collega* he had his father-in-law, Metellus Scipio, elected as his colleague; cf. *MRR* 2, 233–35; Lehmann, 37; on the other hand, Caesar's extension of his second dictatorship to twelve months roused opposition: *MRR* 2, 272; A. Drummond, "The Dictator Years," *Historia* 27 (1978), 570–71. Lehmann, 40, wrongly assimilates, however, the tasks of Cicero's *magister populi* to those of the Sullan dictatorship *reipublicae constituendae causa*: Cicero has in mind the handling of *duellum gravius discordiae⟨ve⟩ civium,* i.e., military and police actions (hence the six-month limit), whereas Sulla's dictatorship was entered upon to reform the constitution after completion of the military campaign and the onset of the proscriptions and did not have a time limit fixed in advance; cf. Robin Seager, *CAH* 9, 199; Keaveney, 159–63.

37. See p. 55 n. 22 *supra.*

state; cf. § 28a; Lehmann, 43.—For *cerno* = *decerno* cf. *ad* 2.21.10: *quibus divis creverint procuranto*—.—Cicero is careful to define the power accruing to the extraordinary magistracies, dictator and magister equitum, with reference to the regular ones; however, he saw the dictator's *genus imperii* as *proximum similitudini regiae* at *Rep.* 2.56; sim. Dio 1, p. 42 Boiss. = Zon. 7.13.12: δικτάτωρ . . . ἠδύνατο . . . πάντα ἐξ ἴσου τοῖς βασιλεῦσι; the description fits the dictator better than the consul (cf. § 8.2), because the former is not subject to collegial or tribunician intercession; cf. *ad* § 6.2; p. 458 n. 32 *supra*.

. . . **isque ave sinistra dictus populi magister esto, . . .**] By easy transference *avis* here is "an augury, omen, portent" (*OLD* s.v., 3b, citing our passage). The left is the lucky side in Roman augury; cf. Pease *ad Div.* 1.12 (*a laeva*) and 2.82 (*laevum*); Fordyce *ad Cat.* 45.8f.—The condition that the auspices must be favorable applies to all magistrates; but for the others, except the dictator and the interrex, the auspication coincides with that necessary for holding the electoral assembly; hence perhaps the special emphasis on the point here; cf. Mommsen, *Staatsr.* 1, 97–98 and 98 n. 1.—*Populi magister* was the older designation for the dictator (the equivalence is noted at *Fin.* 3.75), attested in the augural books,[38] and coordinate with magister equitum. Here *populus* may have the original sense, "army," suggested by the verb *populor* (= "ravage," if the original idea is that of loosing the army upon) or the use of *populus* as opposed to *plebs* (cf. *OLD* s.v. *populus* 2c); cf. Momigliano, *CAH* 7.2, 104. This may go back to a time when the two divisions of the army were the *populus* and the *equites,* the latter in a subordinate rôle. Even in antiquity it was mooted that the later title—the one in ordinary use in Cicero's day[39]—may have been borrowed from the dictator of the Latin league[40] (see Licinius Macer fr. 7** with Walt's note). Its original sense, in spite of Cicero's attempt to explain it,[41] remains obscure. On the dictatorship in general cf. Mommsen, *loc. cit.,* 141–72; Marianne Elizabeth Hartfield, *The Roman Dictatorship: Its Character and Its Evolution* (diss., Berkeley, 1982); Kunkel-Wittmann, 665–717, with literature at 665.

---

38. Cf. *Rep.* 1.63: . . . *in nostris* [sc. *auguralibus*] *libris vides eum, Laeli, magistrum populi appellari.*

39. Cf. Fest. p. 198M s.v. *optima lex:* *** *in magistro populi faciundo, qui vulgo dictator appellatur* . . .

40. Cf. Cato *hist.* fr. 58, cited *ad* 2.5 *supra.*

41. *Dictus* in our passage may hint at Cicero's etymology; cf. *Rep.* 1.63: *nam dictator quidem ab eo appellatur quia dicitur;* sim. Var. *L.* 5.82 and 6.61; others connect the word, more plausibly, with *dictare:* cf. Ernout-Meillet s.v. *dix.*

. . . equitatumque qui regat habeto pari iure cum eo quicumque erit iuris disceptator.] The expression is somewhat cumbersome: *equitatum qui regat* is a paraphrase of the usual title magister equitum; Cicero evidently does not care to repeat the word *magister*. On the other hand, *iuris disceptator* is chosen to avoid ambiguity, since Cicero has recently referred to the consuls as *praetores* (§ 8.2).—In creating this careful hierarchy Cicero may have been guided by a desire to avoid conflicts of the kind the annalists described under the year 217 between Fabius Maximus and his magister equitum M. Minucius Rufus (cf. Liv. 22.23–29).[42] Just as the dictator is *collega maior* of the consuls (Mommsen, *Staatsr.* 2, 153), so the magister equitum, one step lower in the hierarchy, is at the level of the praetor (ibid., 176). In lists of magistrates from the late Republic, however, the magister equitum occupies last place, behind the praetor; cf. Kunkel-Wittmann, 42 n. 11, and 666 n. 1. On the office in general cf. ibid. 675–76 and 717–19; Mommsen, *loc. cit.*, 173–80.—Huschke's transposition of *reliqui magistratus ne sunto* (see next lemma) to follow immediately after our lemma is certainly wrong; other magistrates did indeed function alongside the dictator and magister equitum; cf. Görler *ad loc.* and Kunkel-Wittmann, 278 n. 20.

9.3 Ast quando consules magisterve populi nec erunt, reliqui magistratus ne sunto, auspicia patrum sunto, . . .] The premise is that the well-being of the city was connected with the unbroken chain of favorable auspices going back to the founding. When the chain was broken through a vacuum in top leadership, this circumstance had to be repaired through a reversion of the auspices "to the fathers," i.e., the patrician members of the senate, who for five days each in alternation conducted the interregnum until new elections were held and the auspices returned to elected officials; cf. Mommsen, *Staatsr.* 1, 650 ff.; Kunkel-Wittmann, 34–35; Jahn, 11 ff.; Rolf Rilinger, *Der Einfluß des Wahlleiters bei den römischen Konsulwahlen von 366 bis 50 v.Chr.*, Vestigia 24 (Munich, 1976), 14–16; Magdelain, 341–83. This function was the chief patrician privilege to survive to the late Republic; cf. Linderski, 1995, 560 ff.; Lintott, 1999, 39 and n. 52. Lehmann, 20 n. 36, uses our passage to argue against the theory of Sprey, 244–45, that the provincial commands were to be held by regular magistrates possessing *imperium* and the right of auspication, *viz.*, because the reversion of the auspices to the *patres* would only be feasible if the relevant magistrates were in or near Rome; but Cicero seems to provide for auspication in the field (cf. *ad* 2.21.2); perhaps he wanted to keep this feature of the ancestral constitution in spite of practical difficulties. When

---

42. Cf. Lehmann, 37 n. 60; however, the version of Polyb. 3.103.3–4, according to which M. Minucius was also appointed dictator, is confirmed by an inscription; cf. Ernst Meyer, "Die römische Annalistik im Lichte der Urkunden," *ANRW* 1.2 (1972), 975–78.

both consuls, Hirtius and Pansa, were killed in early 43, there was the difficulty, alluded to by Cicero *ad Brut.* 1.5.4, that the magistrates were scattered throughout Italy, and the reversion could not occur until all had abdicated.— For archaic *nec* = *non* cf. *ad* 2.22.1.

. . . **ollique ex se produnto qui comitiatu creare consules rite possint.**] *Ex se* of BPε must count as the transmitted text here and is unexceptionable (*haec se* A : *exe* HL). Vahlen's *ec se* is often adopted; but *ec* is nowhere transmitted and remains doubtful, in spite of L. Müller's keenness to restore it in poetic texts; cf. *TLL* s.v. *ex* 1084.36–41; Neue-Wagener, 2, 868; Wilhelms, 78–79.—On the process see the previous note. Both here and in § 10.8 (*eique quem patres produnt consulum rogandorum ergo*) Cicero avoids the technical term interrex, which he had used in narrating the sequel to the death of Tullus Hostilius at *Rep.* 2.31, but merely describes the function. Did he regard the term as catachrestic when applied to a *liber populus* (§ 4), or did he want to indicate that this was not a magistracy in the sense of the others outlined here (the latter is the explanation of Kunkel-Wittmann, 283 n. 39)? That the interrex could still play an important rôle is shown by the fact that he was responsible for executing a *senatusconsultum ultimum* in 77, 53, and 52; cf. Lehmann, 38.

9.4 Imperia potestates legationes, cum senatus creverit populusve iusserit, ex urbe exeunto, . . .] A senatorial decree of 53 provided for an interval of five years between the holding of an urban magistracy and a provincial command (cf. Dio 40.46.2; Lehmann, 8–9 n. 15 with literature). Similarly, though without stipulating an interval, Cicero apparently seeks to break the automatic sequence of urban magistracy followed immediately by provincial command by placing foreign missions firmly under the control of the sovereign bodies, the senate and people (cf. Lehmann, 16–17, as well as the senatorial decree passed on Cicero's motion on 20 December 44 and cited at *Fam.* 12.22a.1); in the sequel Cicero underlines one corollary: *rei suae ergo ne quis legatus esto.*—*Imperia potestates legationes* are all abstract for concrete referring to the office-holding magistrates; cf. *TLL* s.v. *imperium* 581.53, *potestas* 319.1–2, *legatio* 1102.57 ff. *Imperium,* derived from and implying the power of military command but not necessarily the exercise of such, will refer to the higher magistrates, though in practice the dividing line is not altogether clear; cf. Mommsen, *Staatsr.* 1, 116–19.—For *creverit* cf. *ad* 2.21.10.

. . . **duella iusta iuste gerunto, sociis parcunto, se et suos continento, . . .**] For *duellum* cf. *ad* 2.21.2; for the concept *bellum iustum* cf. Brunt, 1990, 305–8; *ad Off.* 1.36; for the general principle *iuste gerunto,* given more specific content by the following *sociis—continento,* see the strictures on cruelty ibid.

1.35 and 3.46b.—*Sociis parcunto* anticipates Anchises' famous mandate *parcere subiectis* at Verg. *A.* 6.853; cf. also Brunt, *loc. cit.*, 316–22.

. . . **populi sui gloriam augento, domum cum laude redeunto.**] *Sui,* bracketed by de Plinval and Ziegler, is cogently defended by Watt, 1986, 268, on grounds that "here for once Cicero remembers that he is laying down laws not only for Rome but for virtuous and stable states in general . . . [citation of 2.35; 3.4]. In that case *sui* would be *Romani* appropriately generalized." For the thought cf. Brunt, 1990, 291–93 and 300–302.—Cicero insists that the Roman governor return with *laus,* presumably in the first instance that of the provincials under his rule; cf. *Q. fr.* 1.1, esp. 22–31 and 41–43a; his letters from Cilicia show his own keenness in this regard (e.g., *Att.* 5.16.3). The taking of booty would not necessarily be ruled out by this provision (as Lintott, 1999, 229 n. 59, suggests), but only if, e.g., it occurred in a conflict with hostile neighbors would the approval of the governed be assured.

9.5 rei suae ergo ne quis legatus esto.] *Rei suae ergo* imitates an archaic construction found in prayers and legal texts; cf. *ad* 2.59 (*funeris ergo*).— On the *libera legatio,* limited to one year but not abolished altogether by the lex Tullia of 63, see further *ad* § 18.

9.6 Plebes quos pro se contra vim auxili ergo decem creassit, ii tribuni eius sunto, . . .] *Plebes* is placed in front of the subordinate clause for emphasis; cf. *ad* 2.22.2; Watkins, 541 and n. 2. It thus serves to announce the general sphere of the following law. For the order relative clause-main clause cf. *ad* 2.19.2.—The numeral bears weight as an initial identifier as does *oenus* in the preceding description of the dictator.—*Auxili ergo:* see the previous note. Cicero is right to underline the provision of help for the plebs as the essential feature of the tribunate. The *auxilii latio* is likewise emphasized in Livy's account of the origin of the tribunate during the first secession of the plebs (2.33.1; sim. D.H. 6.87.3; Dio 1, pp. 47–48 Boiss. = Zon. 7.15.1); it continued uninterrupted under the Sullan constitution.[43] Even Quintus, though critical of the tribunician power in general, is prepared to concede the *auxilii latio* (§ 22). The implication of a limitation on consular power is brought out in the subsequent discussion (see *ad* § 16). See further Kunkel-Wittmann, 587–92. The tribunate becomes the subject of a detailed debate between the brothers at §§ 17 and 19b–26; cf. *ad loc.* Cf. in general Mommsen, *Staatsr.* 2, 272–330; from among the recent literature I single out Bleicken, 1981a; Thommen, 1989; Nippel, 1995, 9–12; Badian, 1996; Lintott, 1999, 121–28.

---

43. Instances are attested from 76 (Asc. *Tog.* 75: C. Antonius Hybrida) and 72/71 (Cic. *Tull.* 38 ff.: P. Fabius); cf. Thommen, 1988, 360 and n. 10; see also *ad* § 22.

... quodque ii prohibessint quodque plebem rogassint, ratum esto; ...] The *ius prohibendi* of tribunes was the modality by which they were able to provide help against the action of a magistrate; in such cases, with the sole exception of the dictator (cf. p. 458 n. 32 *supra*), the tribune counted as the *par maiorve potestas* (cf. § 6.2). Our text (*quodque ei prohibessint*[44]) is broadly formulated and could include not only actions of individual magistrates but also bills brought before or passed by the senate; cf. Kunkel-Wittmann, 592, and on this right of the tribunes in general ibid. 592–607.—The right of the tribunes to conduct a *rogatio* of the plebs is a species of the *cum populo ... agendi ius* of certain magistrates (§ 10.8). Originally the *plebiscita* were valid for the plebs alone, but after the lex Hortensia of 287 were so for the entire community. Cf. Rotondi, 238–41; Kunkel-Wittmann, 607–26.—For *ratum esto* see *ad* § 10.3.

sanctique sunto; ...] The sacrosanct status of the tribunes served to insure that their *auxilium* could not be challenged by force; cf. Lintott, 1968, 70. Its basis was an oath sworn by the plebs on the Mons Sacer during the secession of 449.[45] Liv. 3.55.6–7 attributes to the consuls of that year *leges sacratae* which will have been closely modeled on that oath. The allusion at Festus p. 318M to *lex tribunicia prima* suggests two *leges sacratae*, the one granting immunity to anyone who avenged harm done to a tribune, the second declaring the property of the man who did such harm forfeit to Ceres. Cf. Kunkel-Wittmann, 572–73.

... neve plebem orbam tribunis relinquunto.] Severe penalties were imposed for violating this principle; cf. Liv. 3.55.14 (under the year 449): *M. Duilius deinde tribunus plebis plebem rogavit plebesque scivit qui plebem sine tribunis reliquisset, quique magistratum sine provocatione creasset, tergo ac capite puniretur;* cf. Kunkel-Wittmann, 561 and 565. One corollary was that a tribune could not absent himself from Rome for a day (Gel. 3.2.11).— Cicero seems to have pioneered the application of *orbus* to the state or its constituents (first at *Flac.* 54: *... orba fuit ab optimatibus illa contio ...*); cf. *TLL* s.v., 927.30 ff.—The manuscripts (reflecting Cicero's own inconsistency?) give the archaic spelling *relinquonto* at § 7.3, but not here.

10.1–2 Omnes magistratus auspicium iudiciumque habento; exque eis senatus esto.] Bleicken, 1981b, 259–68, 276, and 294–95, sees *auspicia* as the earliest term for power exercised by a magistrate; see also Rüpke, 1990, 44–45. In any case, the *auspicium* of magistrates was not a general license to conduct the community's relations with the gods but provided the more

---

44. For *prohibessint* cf. *ad* § 6.2.
45. See, however, *ad* § 19b.

limited power to obtain auspices prior to meetings of the senate or the *populus* or before elections; so rightly, against Mommsen, Kunkel-Wittmann, 28–37; it was actually the senate that had general oversight of relations with the gods; cf. Beard, 1990, 30–34. Mommsen, *Staatsr.* 2, 284 n. 1, refers the *auspicium* of our passage to oblative auspices, not impetrative (for the distinction cf. *ad* 2.21.2), but, in fact, it refers to impetrative auspices alone; cf. Linderski, 1986, 2205. See further *ad* § 27.—Tribunes did not possess *auspicia;* Lehmann, 24, thinks that they must have them according to our passage, but the tribunes, though possessing magisterial powers, were not magistrates: cf. Mommsen, *Staatsr.* 2, 281 and n. 1.—The possession of *iudicium* by "all magistrates" is puzzling. Cicero provides some clarification at § 27: *iudicia ut ⟨ea⟩ esset populi potestas ad quam provocaretur . . .* Mommsen, *Staatsr.* 1, 167 n. 1, offers three explanations for *iudicium* in our passage: (1) it refers to such clauses as the one underlined in the lex Silia quoted at Festus p. 246M: *eum quis volet magistratus multare dum minore parti familias taxat liceto . . .* ; (2) it refers to trials before the consul or quaestor; or (3) it is merely a proposal of Cicero's own without any correlate in positive law. But no. (1), dealing with a magistrate's discretion to impose a fine, is not relevant here, since we need an instance of *iudicium* subject to *provocatio;* if Cicero had in mind trials before the consul or quaestor (2), why did he specify *omnes magistratus?* But we need not resort to Mommsen's no. (3) (as seems to be assumed by Jones, 3); the reference will be to the procedure described at § 6.3 (*cum magistratus iudicassit inrogassitve*), where such powers are said to be limited by *provocatio,* just as the *iudicium* of our law is said to be at § 27.—Does Cicero mean to include the minor magistrates of § 6.5 among *omnes magistratus* who are here said to have *auspicium iudiciumque* and to form the basis of the senate? Keyes, 1921, 313–14, argues that this is so apart from the members of the vigintivirate.[46] But that would redraw Cicero's distinction between major and minor magistracies. More consistent is Heuss, 235–36, who thinks that the minor magistrates are to enter the senate en bloc. But, as is argued above, the *iudicium* Cicero provides here includes or leads to presiding over a *iudicium populi* when the punishment of a citizen is at issue; when later in this paragraph Cicero lists the magistrates who have the *ius agendi cum populo,* he omits the minor ones (see on § 10.8); nor do the military tribunes, etc., have the right of auspices; cf. Lehmann, 21–26; Cambeis, 247; Rawson, 1991, 142–43; Lintott, 1999, 229 n. 58; *ad* § 7.2. Hence Cicero evidently has in mind the major magistrates only, and his

46. Cf. Dio 54.26.5 (of the vigintivirate under Augustus): . . . ὅθεν οὐκέτ᾽ οὐδεὶς αὐτῶν ἐς τὸ βουλευτήριον ἐσεγράφη . . .

senate would, like the pre-Sullan senate, be an elite body of ca. three hundred members, with the ex-quaestors excluded.—Cicero's doctrine that the senate should consist exclusively of ex-magistrates is a "popular" innovation, eliminating censorial adlection (cf. *ad* § 27).

10.3 eius decreta rata sunto; . . .] *Senatusconsultum* is the common term, perhaps for that very reason avoided here; but *senatus decretum* was also in use and the verb *decernere* for senatorial action quite common; cf. Kunkel-Wittmann, 185 n. 319.—*Ratus* means "having legal validity"; cf. *Dom.* 79; *OLD* s.v., 1; Thomas, 194 ff.; *rata sunto* or *ratum esto* is a well attested legal formula; cf. *quodcumque postremum populus iussisset, id ius ratumque esto* (Liv. 7.17.12, albeit falsely attributed to *Lex XII;* cf. Oakley *ad loc.*); *RS* Index of Latin Words s.v. *ratus.* Does the unqualified *rata sunto* of our passage imply that the senate's decrees are to be immune from tribunician veto? This has been argued by Thomas (cf. Achard, 383), and at § 27 Marcus recommends this measure as a strengthening of the senate's authority (*senatus lege nostra confirmatur auctoritas*). But against this notion is the equally unqualified provision *quodque ii* [sc. *tribuni plebis*] *prohibessint quodque plebem rogassint, ratum esto* (§ 9.6) as well as the following qualification *ast potestas par maiorve prohibessit, perscripta servanto* (see *ad loc.*). Surely the tribunician veto power over legislation proposed in the senate remains intact (so also Thommen, 1988, 359 n. 6; Lintott, 1999, 230); otherwise, Quintus would hardly have made so many objections to the tribunician power enshrined in Marcus' legislation (§§ 19b–22) or Marcus have admitted its *nimia potestas* (§ 23) and held out the hope of conflicts among the tribunes themselves (§ 24). In previous Republican terminology, what a tribune has vetoed cannot be called a *decretum;* it is merely a failed bill (*rogatio;* but see the next note).

A further problem is the relation of the senate's decrees to legislation passed in the popular assembly: how can a conflict be avoided between these two different paths of authority? Lehmann, 26–27, thinks that the senate's decrees are to have validity without any limitation on the legislative prerogative of the popular assembly (cf. § 8.1: *quotcumque senatus creverit populusve iusserit*), but he does not address the problem of a possible conflict. Perhaps Cicero thought that the enhanced optimate influence on elections (cf. *ad* § 10.6) plus the number of tribunes and the likelihood of optimate influence on at least one of them (cf. § 24) sufficient guarantee. Sprey, 231, adds the possibilities for preventing action before the popular assembly either through announcement of unfavorable auspices or intercession; the unrestricted legislative power granted by our law, taken together with this obstructive potential, would *de facto,* if not *de iure,* remove legislative competence from the popular assembly (as was to be done under Tiberius or shortly after his death: Mommsen, *Staatsr.* 3, 346).

ast potestas par maiorve prohibessit, servanto.] Some reference to the possibility of veto and what it entails was necessary after *eius decreta rata sunto;* for this reason and in view of its correct use of technical language our lemma can scarcely be an interpolation (*pace* Büchner); sim. already Mommsen, *loc. cit.*, 1, 281 n. 3.—For *ast = si* cf. *ad* 2.19.7.—For prohibition by a *par maiorve potestas* cf. § 6.2.—*Perscribo* appears here in the technical sense "to record [a resolution of the senate which has been vetoed by a tribune] with a view to bringing it forward at a later date"; cf. *OLD* s.v., 3b; for an example cf. *Fam.* 8.8.4 ff.; *aliter* Kunkel-Wittmann and Thomas, cited below. Such a bill was preserved as a *senatus auctoritas* and for possible future revival; cf. *Fam.* 1.2.4: *cui* [sc. *senatus auctoritati*] *cum Cato et Caninius intercessissent, tamen est perscripta;* Mommsen, *Staatsr.* 3, 997–98; Lintott, 1999, 3 and n. 6.—*Servanto,* taken by itself, is ambiguous: does Cicero merely mean that such decrees should be "put away, kept, stored" (for possible future revival) or that they should be "kept, observed" (cf. *OLD* s.v. *servo* 8b and 4a, respectively)? Kunkel-Wittmann, 602, assume the latter (they speak, à propos our passage, of "Beachtung auch der an tribunizischer Interzession gescheiterten Senatsbeschlüsse"; sim. Thomas, 193); but this would effectively nullify the power just given to the tribunes: *quodque ei prohibessint . . . ratum esto:* § 9.6; see the previous note.

10.4–5 is ordo vitio vacato; ceteris specimen esto.] *Vaco* with the ablative is a poetic construction adapted evidently by Cicero to prose for use of moral qualities; cf. *Fam.* 7.3.4: *sed tamen vacare culpa magnum est solacium;* Wilhelms, 75; *OLD* s.v., 3a.—*Specimen,* deverbative from *specio* with the concretizing suffix -*men,* meant originally "a thing put in evidence"; cf. Pl. *Cas.* 516: *specimen specitur.* From here the word comes to denote, as in our passage, a thing pointed to as a model, perhaps first at Lucr. 5.186 (sim. 1361): *si non ipsa dedit specimen natura creandi.* Cf. *OLD* s.v., 1–2.—Cf. the detailed commentary on this provision at §§ 28–32.

10.6 Creatio magistratuum, iudicia populi, iussa vetita cum suffragio consciscentur, optimatibus nota, plebi libera sunto.] "There are odd new provisions for popular voting, preserving the ballot but making it visible to the optimates" (Rawson, 1991, 142). A series of *leges tabellariae* was carried between 138 and 106 changing over from a simple oral vote to a written ballot in all the types of voting (cf. *ad* §§ 35–36); though these were hailed in anti-senatorial rhetoric as the *vindex libertatis* (cf. *ad* § 39), there was a strong desire in some senatorial circles to turn back the clock to the earlier status quo; Cicero's measure is intended as a compromise between these two views. See further *ad* §§ 33–39.—Though *creare* is common in classical times, *creatio* in the sense of "election" of magistrates does not recur until the third century (Mod. *dig.* 48.14.1: ... *ad curam principis magistratuum creatio pertinet* ...); cf. *TLL* s.v., 1. David Daube, *Roman Law: Linguistic, Social and Philosophical Aspects* (Edinburgh, 1969), 48, sees the use of *creatio* here as pompous. He might have pointed out that by use of the gerundive Cicero managed to express the same entities without the abstract noun in the remarks on the auspices at *Div.* 2.74: ... *quod quidem institutum reipublicae causa est, ut comitiorum vel in iudiciis populi vel in iure legum vel in creandis magistratibus principes civitatis essent interpretes.* The series in nominative virtually demands, however, the substantivization to parallel *iudicia populi, iussa vetita.*—For *iussa vetita* cf. *ad* § 35.—Vahlen's *co(n)sciscentur* is generally accepted for the transmitted *eoscincentur*. *OLD* s.v. *conscisco* declares *cosc-* an archaic form, but it is rather a variant pronunciation involving loss of the nasal before the sibilant; besides *coservae = conservae* at *CIL* IX.1445 and 2715, *cosol, cosentiont* (Scip. elog.: *CIL* I² 8 and 9.1), and *cosoleretur* (SC de Bacch.: *CIL* I² 581.7), cf. *cesoris* transmitted at § 11.13 (as well as *cesor* at *CIL* I² 8) and *cos.* as an abbreviation for *consul.* Cf. Vel. Long. *gram.* VII 78.21–79.2: ... *sequenda est vero non numquam elegantia eruditorum virorum, qui quasdam litteras lenitatis causa omiserunt, sicut Cicero, qui foresia et Megalesia et hortesia sine n littera libenter dicebat* ... One wonders whether the omission of the nasal both here and at § 11.13 may go back to Cicero's dictation; in any case, it is not an archaic spelling and should probably not be retained in modern editions. The sense will be "ordain" (*OLD loc. cit.*).—*Optimatibus nota, plebi libera:* the recent literature offers two conflicting interpretations: (1) a single voting process "known to the optimates, open to the plebs" (this is the traditional interpretation; cf. *OLD* s.v. *liber* 10b: "exercised or used at one's own discression"); or (2) that two modalities of voting are described, one for the optimates, the other for the plebs: voting is to be "known in the case of the optimates, but free [i.e., secret] in the case of the plebs"; see L. Troiani, "Sulla lex de suffragiis in Cicerone, de legibus III,10," *Athenaeum* 59 (1981), 180–84, and idem, "Alcuni considerazioni sul voto nell'antica Roma (a proposito di Cic. *Leg.* III, 10)," ibid., 65 (1987), 493–99, followed by Fontanella, 1998, 208. This latter interpretation is, however, excluded by § 39: ... *habeat sane populus tabellam quasi vindicem libertatis, dummodo haec optimo cuique et gravissimo civi ostendatur ultroque offeratur* ... Yakobson, 1999, 129, on the basis of the wording of the commentary (cf. *ultro:* § 39), argues that this display of ballots was optional; but the proviso clause (*dummodo* ...) makes the possession of this *vindex libertatis* contingent upon displaying the ballot, so the description *species libertatis* (ibid.) applies. The wording of the law is surprising since the optimates (glossed as *optimus quisque et gravissimus civis* [ibid.]) are not an organ of the Roman government; yet here they are given the right to know the contents of ballots. Such sociopolitical language could not be used in actual laws; cf. Keyes, 1921, 315 n. 20; Heuss, 205. Robert Morstein-Marx observes (*per litt.*): "This actually seems to match very nicely his general idea that the people should enjoy full *potestas* even as they are guided by the *auctoritas* of the senate. This ideal is indeed incapable of being reduced to legal language, since it is based on a notion of willing and consciously adopted deference that cannot really be described or defined in concrete, objective terms. But he tries in his commentary to give an idea of what this principle would 'look like' in practice."

10.7 Ast quid erit quod extra magistratus coerari oesus sit, qui coeret populus creato eique ius coerandi dato.] "But if anything needs to be attended to outside the scope of the magistrates, the people shall appoint someone to attend to it and shall confer on him the authority to do so" (tr. Rudd). Here Cicero explicitly grants to the *populus* the right to create, when circumstances demand, extraordinary commissions and thus insures them a place within his constitution; for P. Clodius' attempt to eliminate them cf. H. Benner, 125–27.—A magistrate's appointment bypassing the laws was in Roman terminology *extra ordinem*; cf. Mommsen, *Staatsr.* 1, 20–21 n. 2. The late Republic saw the development of a number of *curationes* outside the competence of the regular magistrates, including the *duoviri perduellioni iudicandae,* the officials appointed *agris dandis adsignandis* and *coloniae deducendae,* etc.; cf. Mommsen, *Staatsr.* 2, 613 ff.; such extraordinary *imperia* as that of Pompey for eliminating the pirates or his *cura annonae* would also be included here (ibid., 2, 613 n. 1); see further Gruen, 1974, 534–43; Ronald T. Ridley, "The Extraordinary Commands of the Late Republic: A Matter of Definition," *Historia* 30 (1981), 280–97. The fact that during the siege of Mutina (43) the senate decreed the abolition of the *cura annonae* assigned to a single individual (Dio 46.39.3) suggests that this Ciceronian *lex,* no less than those on the tribunate of the plebs and balloting, might have been challenged by optimates; cf. Lehmann, 46.—For *ast = si* cf. *ad* 2.19.7.—The diphthongal spelling of *coerari, oesus,* etc., is probably not a historical stage in the development from *oi* to *ū,* for it first appears in the form *coerauere* in dedications at Capua (e.g., *CIL* I² 678), none of which is prior to 113. Rather *oe* is likely to have been introduced as a spelling for *oi* under the influence of *oe* from preserved *oi;* cf. Leumann, 65; *aliter* Sihler § 58c, who sees *oe* in such Ciceronian forms as the retention of the older spelling; *ad* 2.22.2.—For the order of *qui coeret populus creato* and suppression of the oblique antecedent of the relative pronoun cf. *ad* 2.19.2.

10.8 Cum populo patribusque agendi ius esto consuli praetori magistro populi equitumque eique quem patres produnt consulum rogandorum ergo; tribunisque quos sibi plebes creassit ius esto cum patribus agendi; idem ad plebem quod oesus erit ferunto.] For the periphrasis for the interrex cf. *ad* § 9.3.—For *oesus* cf. the previous note.—The *cum populo . . . agendi ius* implies that the magistrate can place a *rogatio* before the *populus* for a vote and that, if passed, it has the force of law; it is thus different from merely holding a *contio;* cf. Gel. 13.16.2–3.—The magistrates' *ius agendi* both before the people and the senate was one of the basic means by which the Roman state functioned; cf. in general Mommsen, *Staatsr.* 1, 191 ff. Gel. 14.7.4 reports from Varro's εἰσαγωγικός (λόγος) the list of those entitled to call meetings of the senate: the dictator, the consuls, the praetors, the tribuni plebis, the interrex, and the praefectus urbi. The two lists diverge in that Cicero omits the praefectus urbi and Varro the magister equitum (the clause *tribunisque—ferunto* grants equivalent rights to the tribuni plebis; cf. Kunkel-Wittmann, 607 and 628). Cicero's omission of the praefectus urbi is understandable since, in Republican times, he is not properly an official but appointed ad hoc to replace a high official during his absence; cf. Mommsen, *Staatsr.* 1, 671–74. On the hand, the magister equitum, primarily a military official, would seldom have had occasion to summon a legislative meeting. Perhaps Cicero has included him for completeness' sake, for he has placed this official at the same level as the praetor (§ 9.2); cf. Kunkel-Wittmann, 12 n. 22 and 719. Mommsen, *loc. cit.,* 1, 209–10 n. 5, shows the dubious historicity of earlier assemblies said to have been summoned by the magister equitum;[47] but Marc Antony did convene the senate as magister equitum in 48 (Dio 42.27.2). Cicero's account thus generally corresponds to current Republican practice on these matters, though, in accord with the principle of 2.18 (*ipsae summae rerum atque sententiae*), he does not provide full detail (e.g., that the *comitia centuriata* will be led by the consuls or interrex or praetor[48]); cf. Kunkel-Wittmann, 246–47 n. 509, and, in general, 246–49.—It is striking that Cicero does not include the tribunes with the other magistrates given a general *cum populo patribusque agendi ius,* even though he has already

---

47. He dates the εἰσαγωγικός too late, however: it should be prior to Pompey's consulate of 70 and thus would hardly reflect disapproval of Caesar's deployment of the magister equitum; cf. Dahlmann, *RE* Suppl. 6 (1935), 1249.15 ff.

48. By the praetor only if elections for consul, censor, or praetor were not in question; cf. *Att.* 9.9.3 (17 March 49, voicing objections to an electoral procedure mooted by Caesar), where appeal is made to the (presumably augural) books (*nos in libris habemus . . .*).

(§ 9.6) spoken of *quod . . . plebem rogassint* [sc. *tribuni plebis*]; here their *cum populo ius agendi* is restricted rather opaquely (*quod oesus erit*); might this imply that the summoning of a popular assembly by the tribunes for legislative purposes would require preceding authorization by the senate (in effect a revival of the Lex Cornelia Pompeia[49])? Cf. Bleicken, 1955, 52–53; Thommen, 1988, 361–62.

10.9 Quae cum populo quaeque in patribus agentur, modica sunto.] Surely a continuation of the previous provisions in the sense of a limitation of the *cum populo patribusque ius agendi* just granted. As in the very first law *Iusta imperia sunto* (§ 6.1) and in the law on war (*duella iusta iuste gerunto*: § 9.4), he goes beyond purely formal enactments to specify a tone or content for the proceedings. Here he clearly aims to forestall inflammatory rhetoric of the type used by P. Sulpicius (cf. *ad* § 20: *quid iam de Saturnino, Sulpicio, reliquis dicam?*—) and more recently P. Clodius (cf. H. Benner, 84–85).[50]

11.1–2 Senatori qui nec aderit aut causa aut culpa esto; loco {senator} et modo orato; causas populi teneto.] These three *iussa* for the senator (cf. § 40) should still be part of the preceding provisions for legislative bodies.—Ryan, 13–51, argues that under the Republic the quorum (*frequens senatus*) was deliberately set low, at two hundred, and not required for all meetings. But given that the Ciceronian senate was to be reduced in scope (cf. *ad* § 10.1), attendance was correspondingly more important; a related provision is the ban on *liberae legationes* (§ 9.5); cf. Lehmann, 25. The senator's obligation to be present at meetings had always existed in theory (cf. *Dom.* 8: *primum dico senatoris esse boni semper in senatum venire . . .*), but the strictness with which absence was viewed apparently varied with the consuls, for Cicero alleges *ita sine cura consules sunt ut paene liberum sit senatori non adesse* (*Phil.* 1.12). A famous instance of failure to appear was Cicero's absence from the senate meeting called for 1 September 44; when Cicero excused himself, Antony demanded pledges to force his appearance (ibid.) and threatened to send workmen to destroy his house (ibid. 5.19); such measures were within a magistrate's powers of *coercitio* and were not subject to *provocatio*; cf. Mommsen, *Staatsr.* 1, 160–61. Cicero does not specify what sanction, if any, he had in mind for this *culpa*;[51] cf. ibid. 3, 916, 2; cf. *ad* 2.22.8.—Cicero's delineation of standards of decorum and competence for senatorial debate

---

49. On this cf. *ad* § 22.

50. *Cael.* 27 has been thought not to refer to him; cf. Austin *ad Cael.*, pp. 155–56; H. Benner, 167; *orat.*, p. 492; but cf. A.R. Dyck, "P. Clodius, amicus meus: Cic. Cael. 27," *Historia* (forthcoming).

51. It is thus unclear that Cicero's law amounts to "eine . . . drakonisch strenge Präsenzpflicht," as Lehmann, 25, calls it.

suggests there must have been a need.—For archaic *nec* = *non* cf. *ad* 2.22.1.—Powell deletes *senator,* possibly added as a key word by a reader to the margin.—*Teneo* has here the sense "grasp mentally, understand" (*OLD* s.v., 23a).

11.3–5 Vis in populo abesto; par maiorve potestas plus valeto. ast quid turbassitur in agendo, fraus actoris esto.] Corresponding to the preceding provision for decorum in senatorial debate is this one for conduct of assemblies of the *populus*. Measures were very seldom defeated by vote of an assembly (cf. *ad* § 35); accordingly, as the political agendas of the senate and the popular leaders diverged, obstructionist tactics became increasingly prominent; cf. Nippel, 1995, 47–50; Vanderbroeck, 146–53. Lintott, 1968, 69, describes the function of political violence this way: "Most violence took place in assemblies, held either for elections, legislation, and trials before the people, or as *contiones* to discuss matters. It was used to stop the proceedings or to force them to a favourable conclusion in face of a veto, religious obstruction or superior voting power." He then offers, ibid., 69–70, an inventory of means used; for violence in the *contio* in particular cf. Morstein-Marx, ch. 4. Though, as Lintott shows, there had been a tendency to resort to political violence for some decades during the late Republic, it was left to P. Clodius Pulcher to make violence a "standard weapon in the political armoury" (Lintott, 1968, 193); see further H. Benner, 116–19; on Clodian violence as different in character from that organized by a Sestius or a Milo cf. Tatum, 1999, 141–48; on public sentiment against *vis* provoked by the confrontations of Clodius and Milo cf. Riggsby, 112–19. Instead of violence, *par maiorve potestas* is to prevail, as previously for hindering *coercitio* by a magistrate (§ 6.2) and for the veto of senatorial decrees (§ 10.3). Surely the reference to *par maiorve potestas* should be taken seriously and refer to a general magisterial right of intervening, not just that of tribunes (the problem is raised by Mommsen, *Staatsr.* 1, 285–86 n. 4, arguing that there was originally such a right of magistrates but not claiming that Cicero wanted to reinstate it); cf. Gel. 14.7.6 (reporting Varro's εἰσαγωγικὸς λόγος): *postea scripsit de intercessionibus dixitque intercedendi, ne senatus consultum fieret, ius fuisse iis solis qui eadem potestate qua ii, qui senatus consultum facere vellent, maioreve essent;* Kunkel-Wittmann, 219. Elsewhere, in defending Milo's resort to force against Clodius, Cicero makes the point that if the courts are extinguished the rule of violence is inevitable (*Sest.* 92); cf. Lintott, 1968, 53–54. But this premise would not, of course, apply to the ideal state for which he sometimes claims to be legislating; cf. *ad* § 29.—For *ast* = *si* cf. *ad* 2.19.7.—*Fraus* clearly has here, as at 1.40, its sense "offense, crime" (cf. *OLD* s.v., 3).—For the sense of *actor* see on

§ 11.7 (*qui agent*). Cf. in general Mehl, 244: "The leaders . . . are the point of his [Cicero's] political theory. They represent the danger to the state insofar as their intentions are potentially self-serving. They are the ones who must be directed, restricted and controlled." One instance of a presiding magistrate being held accountable for disorder at an assembly is cited at § 42 (see *ad loc.*); another was the trial *de maiestate* from the year 95 of C. Norbanus, which Cicero recounts from several angles in *de Orat.* During his tribunate (103),[52] Norbanus inflamed the mob at a *iudicium populi* against Q. Servilius Caepio (cos. 106), accused of causing the Roman disaster at Arausio (in 105). In the course of the proceedings the tribunes L. Cotta and T. Didius had been forcibly ejected, and the *princeps senatus,* M. Aemilius Scaurus, had been wounded by a thrown rock (cf. P. Sulpicius, *orat.* pp. 280 ff.; Lintott, 1968, 7, 69, and 210). Nonetheless, a skilled, unorthodox defense by Norbanus' counsel, M. Antonius,[53] procured acquittal; cf. *orat.* pp. 229 ff.; J. Lengle, "Die Verurteilung der römischen Feldherrn von Arausio," *Hermes* 66 (1931), 302–16; Lintott, 1968, 69, 118 n. 2, and 210; on the political background Erich S. Gruen, "Political Prosecutions in the 90's BC," *Historia* 15 (1966), 43–44 and 46–47, and, more briefly, idem, *Roman Politics and the Criminal Courts, 149–78 B.C.* (Cambridge, Mass., 1968), 195–96; Udo W. Scholz, *Der Redner M. Antonius* (diss., Erlangen, 1962), 59 ff.; Rosenstein, 124–28; Alexander, no. 86. The fact that Norbanus was tried *de maiestate* suggests that there was no specific law dealing with orderly procedure in assemblies.

11.6 intercessor rei malae salutaris civis esto.] *Intercedo* is intransitive and used with the dative, just as Cicero uses *intercessorem esse* (= *intercedere*) with the dative at *Sul.* 65: . . . *L. Caecilius . . . agrariae legi . . . intercessorem se fore professus est . . .* Livy, however, uses *intercessor* with the genitive, and that is the way our passage and *Q.fr.* 3.6.6 (*intercessor dictaturae*) should be read; cf. *TLL* s.v., 2159.40 ff.—Such a man will be a *salutaris civis* in the sense that he has promoted the *salus populi*, the highest principle of statecraft (cf. § 8.2 of the consuls: *ollis salus populi suprema lex esto*). Cf. also the characterization of Demetrius of Phalerum at 2.66: *fuit enim hic vir . . . non solum eruditissimus, sed etiam civis e re publica maxime tuendaeque civitatis peritissimus.* The problem is that there was at this time no consensus as to what constituted a *res mala.*—The context suggests that Cicero means by *intercessor* one provided with *par maiorve potestas* [sc. vis-à-vis the presiding

---

52. For the date cf. F. Münzer, *RE* 17.1 (1936), 928.16 ff.; *MRR* 1, 565–66 n. 7.

53. This was imitated by Cicero in *Corn.* 1 to the degree that he included a digression on the historical benefit of the tribunate to the Roman state in spite of opposition of the nobles (fr. orat. *Corn.* 1, 47–53); he gives arguments for and against Norbanus' action at *Part.* 105.

officer; cf. § 6.2] who intervenes to block legislation in an assembly. Our lemma is thus, as Lintott, 1999, 231, observed, an encouragement to obstructionism. At *Har.* 60 Cicero lists problems of the state, including the concern *civem qui se pro patriae salute opponat invidiae frustra posthac requiretis.* Our passage speaks of interceding within the legislative process; Heuss, 209, suggested that it could be read more broadly as giving his stamp of approval to the murder of Ti. Gracchus and his followers by a mob led by Scipio Nasica as a private citizen (often approved by Cicero elsewhere; cf. *ad Off.* 1.109); Cicero alludes to the matter at § 24.

11.7 Qui agent auspicia servanto, auguri publico parento.] *Ago* here, as in the phrase *agendi ius,* refers to "transacting business" (with the people), i.e., calling and presiding over assemblies; the periphrasis may be for *variatio* since he has just used the corresponding *nomen agentis (fraus actoris esto)*; cf. *Ver.* 5.28: . . . *scitote oppidum esse in Sicilia nullum ex iis oppidis in quibus consistere praetores et conventum agere soleant* . . . and other testimonies at *TLL* s.v. *ago* 1387.51 ff.—*Servo* is "watch for the appearance of, look out for"; similar the phrase *de caelo servare,* where *auspicia* or the like are understood; cf. *OLD* s.v. *servo* 2b.—In case an omen is observed, the assembly must be dissolved, and any contemplated act must be taken up on another day. Any violation is a *vitium,* and it lies in the competence of the college of augurs to ascertain and report to the senate that a *vitium* has occurred; cf. *ad* 2.21.5.—This law is part of Cicero's campaign to restore the dignity and effectiveness of the augurate; the point was made with greater detail and specific sanction at 2.20.6–21.6; cf. *ad loc.* and *ad* 2.14.

11.8 Promulgata proposita in aerario co⟨ndunto, neve in⟩cognita agunto, . . .] For the concept *promulgare* cf. Paul. *Fest.* p. 224M: *promulgari leges dicuntur, cum primum in vulgus eduntur, quasi provulgari;* Mommsen, *Staatsr.* 3, 370–71.—Against the transmitted text is Serv. *Aen.* 8.322 (*acceptae a populo leges in aerario claudebantur*), a passage which suggests that the *aerarium* served as an archive but would have been unsuitable for the posting of public notices; cf. Fritz Freiherr von Schwind, *Zur Frage der Publikation im römischen Recht* (Munich, 1940), 27. Hence Powell's supplement, here adopted; he explains (*per litt.*): "(on the one hand) they are to keep the texts of rogations secure in the *aerarium,* and (on the other) are not to put measures to the vote unless their contents have been made public." Jordan had proposed *condita sunto,* but, as Powell observes, it is difficult to see how this simple expression could have yielded the transmitted text.—In early times official copies of senatorial decrees were kept in the temple of Ceres (cf. Liv. 3.55.13 with Ogilvie's note), later in the *aerarium;* cf. Mommsen, *Staatsr.* 2, 476–77 and 489–91; Phyllis Culham, "Archives and Alternatives in Republican Rome," *CPh* 84 (1989), 100–115. The lex Iunia Licinia of 62 was interpreted by Mommsen, *Staatsr.* 2, 546 and n. 2, to mean that even laws that had not yet been voted upon but only proposed and promulgated were deposited in the *aerarium* to prevent tampering. This view has been rightly challenged by Lando Landucci, *La pubblicazione delle leggi nell' antica Roma*, Atti Acc. Padova N.S. 12 (1896), 119–49; cf. also Schwind, *loc. cit.*, 28–32. In support of his position Mommsen appeals to sch. Bob. *in Sest.* 135 (p. 140.25 St.), our passage (which, however, cannot be used as evidence for actual legislation), Suet. *Jul.* 28.3 (an embarrassing omission of an exception for Caesar discovered and corrected only *lege iam in aes incisa et in aerarium condita*), and *Mil.* 87 (*incidebantur iam domi* [sc. *Clodi*] *leges quae nos servis nostris addicerent*), the latter to show that Suetonius can be referring to a promulgated bill. But in *Mil.* 87 we must reckon with Cicero's rhetorical exaggeration, and at Suet. *Jul.* 28.3 the point is strengthened by the assumption that the reference is to a law actually passed rather than just a promulgated bill. Sch. Bob. *in Sest.* 135 reads: . . . *Licinia vero et Iunia: consulibus auctoribus Licinio Murena et Iunio Silano perlata illud cavebat, ne clam aerario legem inferri* [Halm for *ferri*] *liceret, quoniam leges in aerario condebantur.* The emendation is necessary (*pace* Mommsen and *RS* 9) because *clam* would require the personal ablative; cf. *OLD* s.v., 2c; *TLL* s.v., 1247.51 ff.; *infero* (+ dat.) will mean "foist upon" *vel sim.*; it is so used of various evils, including *dolus;* cf. *TLL* s.v., 1384.66 ff. If that is so, then there is no clear reference to placing a bill in the *aerarium* before enactment. Nor does the general reference to violations of the lex Iunia Licinia at *Att.* 2.9.1 confirm Mommsen's interpretation, as Kunkel-Wittmann, 519 and n. 38, suppose. Thus, in calling for the deposit of a copy in the *aerarium* upon promulgation, Cicero seems to be innovating, not merely accepting a recent reform (as Rawson, 1991, 145 n. 63, following Mommsen, suggests).—In the sequel this and the following two provisions are passed over without commentary (§ 43: *deinde de promulgatione, de singulis rebus agendis, de privatis magistratibus audiendis*).

. . . nec plus quam de singulis rebus semel consulunto; . . .] This is two provisions in one. On the one hand there is to be no *satura* or omnibus bill combining disparate measures;[54] such a provision probably existed prior to the Gracchan period; cf. *orat.* p. 106, no. 5 (T. Annius Luscus); the Urbino *lex. repet.* 1.72 (. . . *extra quam sei quid in saturam feretur*); Lucil. 48M = 34K; Mommsen, *Staatsr.* 3, 336 n. 5. It was renewed by the lex Caecilia

---

54. Cf. Fest. p. 314M: *satura . . . lex multis aliis legibus conferta. itaque in sanctione legum adscribitur: 'neve per saturam abrogato, aut derogato'.*

Didia of 98, to which Cicero appeals at *Dom.* 53: *quae est, quaeso, alia vis, quae sententia Caeciliae legis et Didiae nisi haec, ne populo necesse sit in coniunctis rebus compluribus aut id quod nolit accipere aut id quod velit repudiare?* Cf. Rotondi, 335. On the other hand, a rejected proposal could not be revived by the same magistrate within his term of office; similarly, the same magistrate could not revive the same charge against a man accused before the *iudicium populi;* cf. Mommsen, *loc. cit.*, 3, 337 n. 1, and 356–57. **rem populum docento, doceri a magistratibus privatisque patiunto.**] As in his very first law (§ 6.1: *Iusta imperia sunto*, etc.), Cicero delineates the reciprocal rôles of the magistrates and the people. Our law refers to *contiones* assembled by magistrates for the purpose of discussing proposed laws; private persons might, at the magistrate's discretion, be admitted to speak as well; cf. fr. orat. *Corn.* 1, 30 = Asc. 71 (in a list of *loca intercessionis*): *dum privati dicunt.* A vivid picture of such a *contio* is painted in the narrative of the repeal of the lex Oppia in 195 at Liv. 34.1–8; cf. also Liv. 45.21 and 36, dealing, respectively, with the declaration of war on Rhodes and the triumph of L. Aemilius Paullus (both in 167). Cf. Kunkel-Wittmann, 249 n. 520; Morstein-Marx, ch. 4.

11.9 privilegia ne inroganto.] "[Cicero] goes to great lengths in his code of laws to reverse his own political decline" (Mehl, 256–57). A *privilegium* is "a legal enactment concerning a specific person or case and involving an exemption from common rules" (Berger s.v.; sim. *TLL* s.v., 1401.33–34). Cicero uses the word fifteen times (ibid., 29), mostly in the claim that he himself was the victim of a *privilegium* (the lex Clodia *de exilio Ciceronis:* cf. *supra* p. 17 n. 71). For the *iunctura* cf. *Dom.* 110: . . . *cum indemnatum* ⟨*me*⟩ *exturbares privilegiis tyrannicis inrogatis; Sest.* 65: . . . *cum et sacratis legibus et duodecim tabulis sanctum esset ut ne cui privilegium inrogari liceret* . . . The commentary at § 44 makes plain that Cicero regards this law as a reaffirmation of a provision of the Twelve Tables; see *ad loc.*

11.10 de capite civis, nisi per maximum comitiatum ollosque quos censores in partibus populi locassint, ne ferunto.] The phrase *maximus comitiatus* was not a technical term in the later Roman constitution; it is therefore unlikely to be a Ciceronian retrojection; cf. Wieacker, 1967, 304. E. Gabba, "Maximus comitiatus," *Athenaeum* 75 (1987), 203–5, argues convincingly that in the XII Tables this phrase does not refer to any of the comitia but simply means "the fullest gathering"; see further *RS* pp. 699–700; Lintott, 1999, 151 n. 13; A. Corbino, "'De capite civis nisi per maximum comitiatum ferunto': Osservazioni su Cic. 'de leg.' 3.4.11," *Index* 26 (1998), 109–15; *aliter* Magdelain, 313–39, who interprets *maximus* as "sovereign," followed by Humbert, 467 n. 101. Cicero, however, took the phrase to refer to the *comitia centuriata*; cf. *ad* § 44.—*Per . . . ollos . . . quos censores in partibus populi locassint* clarifies that the members of the *maximus comitiatus* (i.e., for Cicero, the *comitia centuriata*) must have been duly enrolled in one of the constituents of the citizen body by the censors; cf. § 7.3 (*. . . populique partes in tribus discribunto . . .*). Since Cicero's wording points to a division of the entire *populus*, not just the three upper classes, Lehmann, 32 n. 54, is surely wrong in referring this phrase to the jury-courts, rather than to the *comitia centuriata*; cf. Rawson, 1982, 706, who adds: "It may be surprising that Cicero should think that all capital cases should go, in what he supposes to be the ancient fashion, to the *comitia centuriata*. But *De rep.* II 61 shows that he did suppose that under the XII Tables ordinary murder cases went to that body . . . It is just conceivable . . . that Cicero was stressing in *De leg.* III that the only *assembly* that could deal with capital cases was the centuriate assembly, and that he would later on have dealt with capital (as well as noncapital) cases coming before the *iudicia publica*. But the praise of the system obtaining under the XII Tables at *De rep.* II 61 makes one wonder." Cf. also Riggsby, 168 and 228 n. 54, who doubts that Cicero dealt with the jury courts in the lost portions of *Leg.*, since our Book "already has regulations that correspond to laws on *vis, ambitus, repetundae,* and (perhaps) *peculatus*"; there are further arguments for a Ciceronian plan to abolish the *iudicia publica* at Jones, 3. But Richard A. Bauman, "Did Cicero Want to Abolish the Jury-Courts?" *Latomus* 59 (2000), 842–49, shows that it is very unlikely that Cicero intended to abolish the jury-courts.

11.11 Donum ne capiunto neve danto neve petenda neve gerenda neve gesta potestate.] In early times an official who accepted gifts offended against the Romans' sense of decency but not the law. This changed with the prosecution in 171 of a series of Roman governors of both Spanish provinces and was followed in 149 by L. Calpurnius Piso's plebiscite establishing an ongoing *quaestio de repetundis*. Next came the lex Iunia of uncertain date and a surviving *lex repetundarum* inscribed on a bronze tablet found at Urbino; on this and its possible relation to attested legislation on the subject by C. Gracchus and Servilius Glaucia cf. Lintott, 1992, 73–169, esp. 166 ff. with literature; further literature at *RS* 1, 39–40, where see also text and commentary for the Urbino law at 65–112.

11.12 Quod quis earum rerum migrassit, noxiae poena par esto.] For the relative clause cf. *ad* 2.19.2.—*Migro* has the metaphorical sense "set aside, evade (the law)" (cf. *OLD* s.v., 3b), whereas *noxia* means "injurious behaviour, wrongdoing" (*OLD* s.v., 1a). See further *ad* § 46.

11.13–14 Censoris fidem legum custodiunto. privati ad eos acta referunto,

nec eo magis lege liberi sunto.] Transmitted is *cesor-* with loss of the nasal before the sibilant; the form, though paralleled elsewhere (cf. *TLL* s.v. *censor* 797.28 ff.), is not otherwise found in these laws (cf. just above *censores*; § 7.3 *censoris populi . . . censento*). In our text the spelling should be regularized to *censor-*; cf. *ad* § 10.6 (*consciscentur*). For *censoris* as nom. pl. cf. *ad* § 6.5 (*minoris*).—Cicero admits that these provisions are innovations but justifies them as *reipublicae necessariae* (§ 46). This law helps to clarify why Cicero has provided the censors with a continuous term of office (cf. *ad* § 7.3: *magistratum quinquennium habento*). It turns out that he is remodeling them in part after the Greek νομοφύλαϰες; cf. further *ad* § 46. The clause *privati ad eos acta referunto* becomes clearer in light of the description in § 46 of the νομοφύλαϰες: *facta hominum observabant, ad legesque revocabant*. As he goes on to indicate, Cicero does not envision the censors superseding the existing courts;[55] presumably they will judge acts brought before them, as in the past, with reference to civil status (cf. *ad* § 7.3 *supra*).

Lex recitata est: discedere et tabellam iubebo dari.] Marcus concludes his recital of his laws with a witty resumption of the technical language of voting used by Atticus at 2.24 (*suade igitur, si placet, istam ipsam legem, ut ego 'uti {tu} rogas' possim dicere*). Appropriately, this is the formula pronounced by the presiding magistrate at an assembly calling for the vote: the people had to go to their tribes (*discedere*), receive the marked *tabellae* (cf. *ad* 2.24), choose the appropriate one, and drop it into the urn; cf. Mommsen, *Staatsr.* 3, 398 ff., esp. 398 n. 5 and 400 n. 4; Rilinger, 494.

12 This section consists of comment by Quintus and reply by Marcus parallel in function with the reactions to the sacral laws at 2.23, which are likewise praised for brevity and said to be similar to Roman tradition; Cicero then proceeds to set his laws into relation to the ideal state of *Rep.* The (no doubt deliberate) effect is to downplay the innovative element of the laws (though he was keen to assert his independence of Plato at 2.17); cf. Roloff, 74–75 n. 5; *ad* § 46.

Q. Quam brevi, frater, in conspectu posita est a te omnium magistratuum descriptio! sed ea paene nostrae civitatis, etsi a te paulum adlatum est novi.] Here Quintus speaks for the first time in this Book. He had propelled the discussion forward at 1.57–58 and at the resumption of the substantive conversation at 2.7a and 9a, then yielded this rôle to Atticus until 2.69 with the exception of a comment on the many apparent instances of wrongs left unpunished (2.43). Book 3 will see his most detailed interventions (*viz.*,

---

55. Indeed at *Clu.* 117–35, esp. 130, he was at pains to show that the expulsion of two men from the senate by the censors of 70 created no presumption of guilt; cf. Astin, 1988, 30 and n. 70.

§§ 19b–22, 34–37), as might have been expected from a man of definite opinions who had pursued a political career.—Quintus' response to the laws *de magistratibus* is virtually identical to that to the sacral laws (see the previous note).—*In conspectu* = "on view": cf. *OLD* s.v. *conspectus*[2] 1b.— *Magistratuum descriptio* = "the system of magistrates"; for this Book as a treatise *de magistratibus* cf. 2.69 and §§ 2 and 13.—The spelling *descriptio* is used here and in the other two occurrences of the word in this chapter and the next, since *compositio* is used as its synonym in Marcus' next speech; cf. *ad* 1.23; p. 341 n. 86 *supra*.

M. . . . haec est enim quam Scipio laudat in ⟨sex⟩ libris, et quam maxime probat temperationem reipublicae, quae effici non potuisset nisi tali descriptione magistratuum; . . .] As in Book 2, Marcus replies to his interlocutor's praise by emphasizing that the laws presented are in line with the ideal state depicted by Scipio in *Rep.* Here he singles out in particular the mixed constitution praised by Scipio at *Rep.*1.69 and 2.65.—*Illis* was Turnebus' addition, *sex* that of Powell, effecting a better rhythm; cf. 1.20: *in illis sex libris*.

nam sic habetote, magistratibus eisque qui praesint contineri rempublicam, . . .] This point is repeated from 2.69; see *ad loc.*

. . . et ex eorum compositione quod cuiusque reipublicae genus sit intellegi.] The point is developed at *Rep.* 1.42; cf. also *ad* § 15; for *compositio* in the sense "arrangement, structure" cf. *OLD* s.v., 5d.

quae res cum sapientissime moderatissimeque constituta esset a maioribus nostris, nihil habui ⟨aut⟩ sane non multum quod putarem novandum in legibus.] The reference to the admirable provision of the ancestors and consequently the need for only minimal changes is likewise paralleled in Cicero's responses at 2.23. Here, however, he does not claim that his innovations are modeled on ancestral practice.—*Aut* seems to fit better before the apologetic *sane* (Powell), rather than after it (Madvig), though *sane* can per se limit either *nihil* or *non*; cf. see *OLD* s.v. *sane* 4; for *nihil sane* see *ad* 2.41.

13a–17 These chapters begin to take the discussion in a similar direction to that followed in Book 2 (cf. 2.24), i.e., upon request from Atticus Marcus agrees to state the case for his proposed legislation. At this point Marcus puts in, however, that the topic has been handled by Greek philosophers; at Atticus' prodding a small doxographical digression follows culminating in Atticus' compliment that, like Demetrius of Phalerum, "one of us three" would be capable of excelling in both learning and statecraft. Marcus then highlights one of the philosophical issues, illustrated with reference to both Sparta and Rome, namely whether the chief magistracy should be absolute or subject to checks, with the tribunate of the plebs adduced as a curb on consular power (§ 16). This prompts Quintus to intervene with the complaint that the tribunician power has been the ruin of the optimates (§ 17). Marcus disagrees, seeming to suggest that history could have taken a different course, when the text breaks off. This lacuna must be very extensive, comprising not only the conclusion of the topic under discussion but also the resumption, after this digression, of the plan to provide commentary on the laws; indeed, more than the first half of that commentary is missing, for intelligible text resumes with the law *domum cum laude redeunto* (§ 9.4).[56] The text as preserved thus buttresses, by indication of his wide reading of Greek sources, Marcus' authority to speak on these issues (§§ 13–14); it then provides a preview, from the standpoint of constitutional principles, of the subsequent debate over the status of the tribunate of the plebs (§§ 15–17; cf. §§ 19b–26).[57]

13a A. Reddes igitur nobis,—quibus de causis maxime placeat ista descriptio?] Cf. Atticus' functionally equivalent words at 2.24: *suade igitur, si placet, istam ipsam legem, ut ego 'uti {tu} rogas' possim dicere.—Reddes =* "you will keep your promise" (Reid); cf. *OLD* s.v. *redo* 9 ("render [any thing considered as a debt, obligation, . . . etc.]").

M. Faciam, Attice, ut vis: et locum istum totum ut a doctissimis Graeciae quaesitum et disputatum est explicabo, et ut institui nostra iura attingam.] For *quaero* both here and in the next two lemmata in the sense "inquire into, examine, consider" cf. *OLD* s.v., 9a.—Ziegler, 1953, 315, proposed *adiungam* for the transmitted *attingam* (and subsequently printed the word in his text). But Marcus emphasizes the brevity of his treatment of the theme (§ 49: *Faciam breviter si consequi potuero*), so that "mentioning briefly, touching upon" *nostra iura* (cf. *OLD* s.v. *attingo* 9a) seems a more apt description of his procedure than "annexing" them. It is odd, however, that at § 48 Atticus asks Marcus to add remarks *de iure populi Romani* as he had in Book 2, with neither man showing any sign of remembering this promise (another indicator that the work lacks the *summa manus?*).

13b–14 Atqui pleraque—inveniri potest?] This doxographical digression serves essentially to clear the ground by showing that Marcus is fully conversant with the literature on the subject and thus qualified to speak; cf. 1.14: *quae . . . scripta a multis sunt diligenter,* though the topic is rejected; *Rep.*

56. The fact that a late antique source preserves one sentence from the otherwise missing commentary (see on the fragment from Book 3), as well as the truncated matter transmitted at the end of § 17 (cf. *ad loc.*), suggests that the fault lies in mechanical loss of matter rather than the author's incomplete draft.

57. The tribunate as a check on consular power plays no rôle, however, in the following discussion, as Thommen, 1988, 363, points out.

1.36 (Scipio): *sed neque eis contentus sum, quae de ista consultatione scripta nobis summi ex Graecia sapientissimique homines reliquerunt . . .*; *Off.* 3.34: *neque enim quicquam est de hac parte post Panaetium explicatum, quod quidem mihi probaretur, de iis quae in manus meas venerint.* In fact, the name of none of the Greek philosophers mentioned here will crop up later in the extant treatise.

13b Atqui pleraque sunt dicta in illis libris, quod faciendum fuit cum de optima republica quaereretur; . . .] Some relevant topics seem to have been handled in *Rep.* 5, including the origins of royal power (§ 3) and the qualities of the *rector* or *moderator reipublicae* (§§ 2, 4, 5).

sed huius loci de magistratibus sunt propria quaedam, a Theophrasto primum, deinde a Dio⟨ge⟩ne Stoico quaesita subtilius.] Our passage = Theophr. F 591 F. The later statement *Theophrastus vero . . . habitavit ut scitis in eo genere rerum* (§ 14) is understandable in view of his very extensive list of titles on political and legal subjects; cf. F 589 F.; Regenbogen, *RE* Suppl. 7 (1940), 1516.20 ff. It is correspondingly difficult to estimate which work or works in particular Cicero had in mind here (the νόμοι, the πολιτικά, both?).—Because of the transmitted *Dione* (corrected already by Turnebus) our passage was not included in the collection of Diogenes' fragments in *SVF* 3. There is now papyrus evidence for the political philosophy of Diogenes of Babylon; cf. Dirk Obbink and Paul A. Vander Waerdt, "Diogenes of Babylon: The Stoic Sage in the City of Fools," *GRBS* 32 (1991), 355–96.

14 A. Ain tandem? etiam a Stoicis ista tractata sunt?] *Ain* expresses doubt or surprise (cf. *OLD* s.v. *aio* 2), emphasized by *tandem* (ibid. 1b): "Do you really say so?" Other examples at *Fin.* 4.1; Apul. *Met.* 1.8.—The reference of *ista* is important in determining what has *not* been treated by other Stoic authors except Diogenes and Panaetius (cf. Frede, 95 n. 9); surely it refers to *huius loci de magistratibus . . . propria quaedam.* Atticus' incredulity is understandable; political topics are not prominent among the titles of Stoic treatises. For recent discussion of the evidence cf. Andrew Erskine, *The Hellenistic Stoa: Political Thought and Action* (London, 1990).

M. Non sane nisi ab eo quem modo nominavi, et postea a magno homine et in primis erudito, Panaetio; . . .] = Panaetius fr. 48 S. = 103A. For the high regard Cicero occasionally expresses for Panaetius cf. *ad Off.* 2.7a; Laelius invokes among Scipio's qualifications for discoursing *de republica* the conversations he conducted with Polybius and Panaetius (*Rep.* 1.34).—We are not well provided with titles for Panaetius' works; περὶ τοῦ καθήκοντος seems to have contained some relevant material; cf. *ad Off.* 1.88–89, 122–25, 124, and 144.

nam veteres verbo tenus acute illi quidem, sed non ad hunc usum popularem

atque civilem, de republica disserebant.] For a contrast of styles of discourse between the *veteres* and more recent philosophers to the advantage of the former cf. 1.36. For Panaetius' cultivation of a "popular" style of exposition cf. *ad Off.* 2.35. In this context the *veteres* surely are the *veteres Stoici,* as Turnebus, 747, already saw (see the next note); *aliter* Schmidt, 1959, 21 n. 5. For the characterization of their method cf. *Fin.* 4.7 (referring to the older Stoics): *pungunt . . . quasi aculeis interrogatiunculis angustis, quibus etiam qui adsentiuntur nihil commutantur animo et idem abeunt qui venerant. res enim fortasse verae, certe graves, non ita tractantur ut debent sed aliquanto minutius.* Cicero aimed, of course, to remedy this defect in *Parad.* (see *supra* p. 53 and n. 20).

ab hac familia magis ista manarunt, Platone principe; . . .] The asyndeton contrasts the Stoic school, just discussed, with the Academy, the source of teachings about magistrates.—Gruter cites the conjecture *ab Academia* for *ab hac familia,* transmitted with minor variants. But *familia* of a philosophical school is a usage Cicero pioneered (cf. *OLD* s.v. *familia* 5)[58] and is unlikely to have been introduced by mistake. That the Academy is in question is clear both from the first person *deixis* of *hac* (cf. Hofmann-Szantyr, 180–81) and the following *Platone principe.*—*Ista* are still the *huius loci de magistratibus . . . propria quaedam,* which have their beginning with Plato, in his teachings about the Guardians, the νομοφύλακες, etc.; for the primacy of the Academy in political philosophy cf. also *Fin.* 4.61.

post Aristoteles illustravit omnem hunc civilem in disputando locum, Heraclidesque Ponticus profectus ab eodem Platone.] Cicero is generally assumed not to have known the *Politics:* cf. Frede, esp. 81, who provides evidence in support of a *communis opinio* that still requires further argument. Here he may be thinking, rather, of the 158 Aristotelian πολιτεῖαι (D.L. 5.27).— Our passage = Heracl. Pont. fr. 143; the works that come into question are the περὶ ἀρχῆς and περὶ νόμων, both in dialogue form (respectively frr. 144–45 and 146–50). After some hesitation Cicero followed the Heraclidean model, set in the past, for *Rep.,* the alternative Aristotelian model, with the author speaking in his own person, in our work (cf. the Introduction § 2b). Heraclides was a pupil of both Plato and Aristotle: cf. fr. 3 = D.L. 5.86; for his studies with Plato cf. also frr. 4, 5, and 7.

---

58. This is perhaps a characteristically Roman conception placing all the philosophers of the school under the *potestas* of a single *pater;* cf. Lucr. 3.9 (of Epicurus): *tu pater es . . . ; N.D.* 1.93: *Socraten ipsum parentem philosophiae;* for the implications cf. Richard Heinze, "Auctoritas," *Hermes* 60 (1925), 362 = *Vom Geist des Römertums*[3] (Darmstadt, 1960), 55; cf. also 1.5 with note: *. . . apud Herodotum patrem historiae . . .*

Theophrastus vero institutus ab Aristotele habitavit, ut scitis, in eo genere rerum, . . .] For Theophrastus' relation to Aristotle as student and successor as head of the Peripatos cf. F 8–11 F. The hyperbolic use of *habito* of "spending all one's time, 'living' (in an occupation or study)" is characteristically Ciceronian; cf. *OLD* s.v., 5b, where Cicero is the only author cited; for the thought cf. *ad* § 13b *supra*.

. . . ab eodemque Aristotele doctus Dicaearchus huic rationi studioque non defuit.] = Dicaearch. fr. 67; for his study with Aristotle see also fr. 1 and 1I. Like his teacher, he seems to have written on various constitutions (a Σπαρτιατῶν πολιτεία is attested: fr. 1). Like Heraclides, he served as a possible model for Ciceronian political dialogues; cf. fr. 68 = *Att.* 13.30; p. 25 n. 91 *supra*. For a sober evaluation of what Cicero is likely to have learned from Dicaearchus, namely, directly or indirectly, the theory of the mixed constitution, cf. Smethurst, esp. 231–32.

post a Theophrasto Phalereus ille Demetrius, de quo feci supra mentionem, mirabiliter doctrinam ex umbraculis eruditorum otioque non modo in solem atque in pulverem, sed in ipsum discrimen aciemque produxit.] = Dem. Phal. fr. 72 Wehrli = 57 S.-O.-D.; for his study with Theophrastus see also frr. 2 = 1, 3 = 2, and 5 = 10. He was previously cited at 2.64–66. On the theoretical side the περὶ πολιτικῶν (or περὶ πολιτικῆς) and περὶ νόμων (frr. 126 and 127 Wehrli = fr. 1.68–69 S.-O.-D., respectively) come into question; for his discussions of his own reforms and his rule of Athens in general cf. *ad* 2.66.— "Sun" and "shade" are metaphors for the *vita activa* and *vita contemplativa*, as at *Mur.* 30: . . . *cedat . . . forum castris, otium militiae, stilus gladio, umbra soli.* Cf. further Kaster *ad* Suet. *Gram.* 9.5.—The description of Demetrius' handling of philosophy is reminiscent of the description of what "we" (i.e., Cicero and Cato) have done at *Fam.* 15.4.16: . . . *nos philosophiam veram illam et antiquam, quae quibusdam oti esse ac desidiae videtur, in forum atque in rempublicam atque in ipsam aciem paene deduximus.* Kretschmar, 64, has argued that our passage suggests that Cicero is insincere in the letter (". . . die Erwähnung Catos nur aus Höflichkeit geschehen ist"). But Cicero speaks in our passage of "governing the state" (*regenda civitas;* see next lemma), a position that Cato, who never achieved consular rank, could not claim, so one would not have expected Cato to be named here.—*Umbraculum* is a "shady retreat"; cf. *OLD* s.v., 1c; sim. *Brut.* 37 (also describing Demetrius of Phalerum): *processerat enim in solem et pulverem, non ut e militari tabernaculo, sed e Theophrasti doctissimi hominis umbraculis;* cf. also on the fragment from Book 5.—For the metaphorical application of *acies* to disputes cf. *Tusc.* 2.60: *ad philosophos me revocas, qui in aciem non saepe* *prodeunt*, with other passages cited at *TLL* s.v., 412.79 ff., to which add *Fam.* 15.4.16.

qui vero utraque re excelleret, ut et doctrinae studiis et regenda civitate princeps esset, quis facile praeter hunc inveniri potest? A. Puto posse, et quidem aliquem de tribus nobis.] A pregnant question. The ancients were aware that the praise of others similar to oneself was a strategy for removing some of the offensiveness of self-praise (cf. *Fam.* 6.7.3 : *impeditum se ipsum laudare, ne vitium adrogantiae subsequatur*; Plut. *de Laude ipsius* 542c); but seldom is the move quite so blatant as this; cf. *ad* 2.6 and *Off.* 1.3. For Cicero's devotion to letters and its fruits cf. *Arch.* 12: *ceteros pudeat, si qui ita se litteris abdiderunt ut nihil possint ex eis neque ad communem adferre fructum neque in aspectum lucemque proferre; me autem quid pudeat . . . ?* The idea receives poetic expression at fr. 10.71 ff. Courtney: *haec adeo penitus cura videre sagaci / otia qui studiis laeti tenuere decoris, / inque Academia umbrifera nitidoque Lyceo / fuderunt claras fecundi pectoris artis. / e quibus ereptum primo iam a flore iuventae / te patria in media virtutum mole locavit.*

15 M. Quaesitum igitur ab illis est, placeret⟨ne⟩ unum in civitate esse magistratum cui reliqui parerent.] *Igitur* is resumptive; Marcus returns, after the doxographical digression, to the plan stated in § 13 (note the underlined referent for *ab illis: locum istum totum ut a doctissimis Graeciae quaesitum et disputatum est explicabo*).—The *-ne* is already in P.—*Magistratus* has here the very broad sense which Marcus gave it at § 2.—*Qui esset optimus reipublicae status* is explicitly attested as one of Theophrastus' topics (F 590 F. = *Fin.* 5.11), while Dicaearchus' τριπολιτικός was the first work to set forth the theory of the mixed constitution; cf. Smethurst, 225. The problem is most easily formulated in terms of the number sharing supreme power— the *rex*, the optimates, or the *populus* (cf. § 12; *Rep.* 1.55). The hyperbaton underlines *unum . . . magistratum.*

quod exactis regibus intellego placuisse nostris maioribus; . . .] Contrast *Rep.* 2.46–52, esp. 52, according to which the Romans did not hesitate to throw out the monarchy along with the monarch; see *ad* § 16.

sed quoniam regale civitatis genus, probatum quondam, postea non tam regni quam regis vitiis repudiatum est, . . .] The kingship lasted at Rome 240 years according to *Rep.* 2.52; the phrase *probatum quondam* will apply with greatest force to the reign of Romulus and its immediate aftermath (ibid.). Paronomasia serves a rhetorical purpose in that the acoustic similarity of *regni* and *regis*[59] forces the reader to focus more sharply on the

---

59. This verbal play defeated the scribes: *regis* is a conjecture (P; cf. *regiis* A^X), *regnis* (BεL) the transmitted text.

difference of content; cf. parallels at Holst, 77. No such distinction was drawn in *Rep.*, however; see the previous note.

. . . nomen tantum videbitur regis repudiatum, res manebit, si unus omnibus reliquis magistratibus imperabit.] For the *iunctura* cf. Lucr. 3.58: *eripitur persona, manet res* (Laur. xxxv 31 : *manare* OQV).

16 quare nec ephori Lacedaemone sine causa a Theopompo oppositi regibus, nec apud nos consulibus tribuni; . . .] Here Cicero glosses over a difficulty in his argument. The Spartan kings were two, as were the consuls, to whom Cicero has attributed *regium imperium* (§ 8.2). But this arrangement is different from the monarchical principle as Cicero has defined it so far, *viz.*, the supremacy of a *single* magistrate (*unus magistratus*); for the collegial principle at Rome cf. *ad* § 7.3 (*bini sunto*).—The ephorate at Sparta was sometimes attributed to Lycurgus (e.g., Hdt. 1.65.5), but by Aristotle (*Pol.* 1313a25 ff.), as by Cicero (a misplaced passage transmitted at *Rep.* 2.58), to the eighth-century king Theopompus; at *Lg.* 692a3 Plato refers to him obliquely as the "third savior" of Sparta (ὁ . . . τρίτος σωτήρ). In *Rep.* (2.56), as in our passage, a reference had preceded to the "royal power" remaining in the hands of the consuls. In both passages Cicero seeks to defend the tribunate by pointing to a parallel in an admired Greek constitution, though in that passage he adds a reference, missing here, to the ten *cosmoe* in Crete; cf. Zetzel *ad Rep. loc. cit.*

nam illud quidem ipsum quod in iure positum est habet consul, ut ei reliqui magistratus omnes pareant, excepto tribuno, qui post exstitit ne id quod fuerat esset; . . .] This version of Roman constitutional history finds the real caesura not in the expulsion of the kings but in the establishment of the tribunate as an effective check on consular power—a considerable change in perspective since *Rep.*, where Cicero had accepted the conventional periodization with a new constitution following immediately upon the expulsion of the kings; cf. *ad* § 15. There is some truth in both of these interpretations: the consular system would insure that the *vitium unius* could not precipitate the fall of government, as in the case of the Tarquins (cf. *Rep.* 2.47 and *regis vitiis:* § 15), because, presumably, the other consul would stand in the way (cf. Q. Catulus' view cited at *Red. Sen.* 9: . . . *non saepe unum consulum improbum, duo vero numquam excepto illo Cinnano tempore fuisse*); but the government was still controlled by a single social group; the tribunate prevented the tyranny of one group over the other. But the emphasis on the rôle of the tribunes in our passage results in Cicero's neglecting the innovative character of the consular system.—The euphemistic *ne id quod fuerat esset* obviates a recital of abuses (though one might have expected a reference back to 2.10).

hoc enim primum minuit consulare ius, quod exstitit ipse qui eo non teneretur; deinde quod attulit auxilium reliquis non modo magistratibus sed etiam privatis consuli non parentibus.] For the tribune possessing *par maiorve potestas* than the other magistrates except the dictator and for the right of *auxilii latio* cf. *ad* § 9.6.—The late Republic knew instances, even apart from the *auxilii latio,* of tribunes blocking the plans of the consuls, though there were also cases in which one or both consuls used the tribunes to exert pressure on the majority of the senate; cf. Thommen, 1988, 363. **17 Q. Magnum dicis malum; nam ista potestate nata gravitas optimatium cecidit convaluitque vis multitudinis.**] Whereas Marcus had been describing constitutional arrangements in value-neutral language, Quintus now breaks into the conversation (for only the second time in this Book; cf. *ad* § 12) with a decided value judgment (*magnum dicis malum*). The portrait seems to be true to life, for impetuousness and irritability seem indeed to have left their mark on his (quite complex) character; cf. *ad* 1.57.—Quintus does not use neutral terms for the power of the two groups. The *gravitas optimatium* (cf. § 19b: *principum gravitas*) is clearly the "authority, influence, importance" of the optimates; cf. *OLD* s.v. *gravitas* 7a; for the term cf. further Hellegouarc'h, 279–90; for *gravitas* as the optimate trait par excellence cf. Achard, 392–99. Diametrically opposed to this (note the chiastic arrangement of substantives and verbs) is not the *gravitas* or *pondus* but, rather, the *vis* of the multitude. In a legal context *vis* suggests unlawful force (cf. *OLD* s.v., 3), in a political context, violence used to override established procedures (ibid., 4; cf. Lintott, 1968, 69, cited *ad* § 11.3–5 *supra*). Is this feature also true to life, i.e., was the historical Quintus an opponent of tribunician power? The evidence is slight and not altogether clear. Like his brother (cf. *ad* §§ 19b–26), he never sought the tribunate of the plebs. During his candidacy for aedile in 66, an epigram criticizing the Lex Aurelia of 75, which restored the tribunes' right to seek higher office, was circulated as his (*Q.fr.* 1.3.8; cf. B.A. Marshall, "Q. Cicero, Hortensius and the Lex Aurelia," *RhM* 118 [1975], 136); even if he was not the author, it would seem that anti-tribunician views could be plausibly ascribed to him.

M. Non est, Quinte, ita; non ius enim illud solum superbius populo et violentius videri necesse erat? . . .] The contradiction is similarly phrased at 1.18a: *non ita est, Quinte* . . . Marcus reminds his brother of the background to the establishment of the tribunate. *Ius . . . illud* is the *consulare ius* mentioned toward the end of Marcus' previous speech; *solum* in this context means, as in a monarchy, having no *par maiorve potestas* that could serve as a check. This and the following lemma make it clear that Marcus' support for the tribunate rests chiefly upon constitutional theory and the consideration that the tribunate forestalls worse excesses of the plebs; see further *ad* §§ 23–26a.

quo posteaquam modica et sapiens temperatio accessit ⟨. . .⟩.] *Temperatio* is the quality *par excellence* that Scipio was looking for in a constitution (*Rep.* 1.69 and 2.65, each time referring to the *genus temperatum* [sc. of the three pure forms]). The *modica et sapiens temperatio* is also reminiscent of *Rep.* 2.54: . . . *Lucique Valeri Potiti et M. Horati Barbati, hominum concordiae causa* sapienter *popularium, consularis lex sanxit ne qui magistratus sine provocatione crearetur;* sim. *Dom.* 77: *a maioribus nostris, qui non ficte et fallaciter populares sed vere et* sapienter *fuerunt;* cf. Hellegouarc'h, 538. He thus approves of checks to the unmitigated power of magistrates in Rome's early period, be it the tribunate or *provocatio,* as in the interest of *concordia* in the body politic—a kind of adumbration of his own *concordia ordinum.* Cf. also § 27 and *ad* § 24 (*inventum est temperamentum*).—After this lemma the manuscripts present the garbled matter *convertem* (for which Powell conjectures *autem* on the basis of E's compendium 9*u'tem*) *lex in omnis est;* if, e.g., *haec* preceded, this phrase would effect the expected transition to the next law (cf. *ad* 2.23–45), though the point of contrast (presumably some principle of merely partial application) remains obscure. Intelligible text resumes with the citation of the law from § 9.4 *domum cum laude redeunto* followed by the expected commentary on that law. A fragment cited as from Book 3 and dealing with the *socii* (and hence likely to derive from the commentary on *sociis parcunto* [§ 9.4]) is preserved at Macr. *diff.* 16.6 (see *infra* on the fr. from Book 3). It is thus clear that the archetype was incomplete[60] because of loss of matter in transmission (cf. *ad* §§ 13a–17). Büchner posited a lacuna after *convertem,* editors prior to Vahlen generally after *est,* but certainly we need to mark a lacuna after *accessit* (so already Vahlen). What one expects as a conclusion to this argument, at the very least, is the point that, though the tribunate started out admirably, it was later corrupted, since *posteaquam* suggests a distinction of different stages. For the lost discussion of the tribunate and for Quintus' theory of its deformation cf. *ad* §§ 19b–26 and 19b–22.

18–47 These chapters comprise the commentary on the laws in the order of their presentation. Coverage begins with *domum cum laude redeunto* at § 9.4, the commentary on the preceding laws (§§ 6 ff.) having been lost in the lacuna at the end of § 17. For the commentary form cf. *ad* 2.23–45.

18 ⟨. . .⟩ autem lex in omnis est. 'Domum cum laude redeunto': nihil enim praeter laudem bonis atque innocentibus neque ex hostibus neque a sociis

---

60. Cf. Schmidt, 1974, 101.

reportandum.] This is in the context of *imperia potestates legationes* despatched from the city at the pleasure of the senate and the people, whether in time of peace or war (§ 9.4). See *ad loc.* and the last note to § 17.

Iam illud apertum est profecto, nihil esse turpius quam {est} quemquam legari nisi reipublicae causa.] Minutianus already deleted *est.*—A senator who wanted to depart Italy was required to petition the senate for leave and state the reason; if leave was granted, he was said to be on a *libera legatio*, for which costs were borne by the state; cf. *ad* 1.10. Restrictions on travel outside Italy were later placed on senators' sons as well (cf. Suet. *Jul.* 42). In spite of Cicero's protest, the system continued in place under the Empire. Cf. Mommsen, *Staatsr.* 2, 690–91, and 3, 897 and 913 n. 1, who shows that the system was a means of control, albeit subject to abuses (his last-named passage correcting the emphasis of the first one).—There are many *turpia*, some so extreme that Cicero declined even to mention them (*Off.* 1.159). This line of argument is thus a typical exaggeration, taken up again in the sequel (*sed quaero, quid reapse sit turpius . . . ?*). This is no doubt a small sample of the kind of polemic used to recommend the lex Tullia *de liberis legationibus* (see below). Though our text argues on moral grounds, Cicero was also moved by complaints of the allies that such visits by Roman officials on private business were burdensome; cf. *Agr.* 2.45: *legatos nostros, homines auctoritate tenui, qui rerum privatarum causa legationes liberas obeunt, tamen exterae nationes ferre vix possunt* with the underlined matter quoted in the next note.

omitto quemadmodum isti se gerant atque gesserint, qui legatione hereditates aut syngraphas suas persequuntur; . . .] *Omitto* [sc. *dicere*] . . . is vintage Ciceronian *praeteritio;* cf. in general Lausberg §§ 882–86.—For repetition of the verb in present and perfect forms cf. Wills, 300–301; for another instance of a verb repeated in different tenses cf. 1.1.—*Syngrapha*, a technical term from commerce meaning "contract, promissory note," or the like, is one of the very few Greek words that Cicero admits even to his forensic speeches (e.g., *Ver.* 4.30); cf. *OLD* s.v. In Cicero's speeches and letters (and in later sources) it appears as a form by which a literal obligation could be entered into between Romans and peregrines, to whom the *stipulatio*[61] was originally not open; cf. Kunkel, *RE* 4A2 (1932), 1384.39 ff.; Berger s.vv. *syngraphe, stipulatio.*—For the use of a *libera legatio* to claim legacies cf. *Agr.* 1.8: *hereditatum obeundarum causa quibus vos legationes dedistis, qui et privati et privatum ad negotium exierunt non maximis opibus neque*

61. For the *stipulatio* cf. *ad* 1.14.

summa auctoritate praediti, tamen auditis profecto <u>quam graves eorum</u> *<u>adventus sociis nostris esse soleant</u>.* For exacting of debts as a motive cf. *Flac.* 86 (addressed to M. Lurco, who has given testimony against Flaccus): *an legationes sumere liberas exigendi causa, sicut et tu ipse nuper et multi viri boni saepe fecerunt, rectum est, quod ego non reprehendo, <u>socios video</u>* *<u>queri</u> . . .*

quod quidem genus legationis ego consul, quamquam ad commodum sena-tus pertinere videbatur, tamen approbante senatu frequentissimo, nisi mihi levis tribunus plebis tum intercessisset, sustulissem; . . .] One suspects that it was precisely because they knew a tribune was going to veto the measure that the senators voted for it so overwhelmingly; at any rate the failure to revive the bill in subsequent years suggests senatorial hypocrisy.—For the known tribunes of 63 cf. *MRR* 2, 167–68; which one vetoed the legislation is not attested.—The characterization as *levis* is characteristic of Cicero's essays rather than speeches; cf. Achard, 131–32.

minui tamen tempus, et quod erat infinitum, annuum feci; ita turpitudo manet diurnitate sublata.] The lex Tullia *de liberis legationibus* and the lex Tullia *de ambitu* constituted the orator's main legislative achievements as consul (cf. Rotondi, 379–80), though, as our passage shows, he was not altogether satisfied with the former. As dictator Caesar also carried a mea-sure limiting the duration of embassies (*Att.* 15.11.4; Rotondi, 419–20), but it is unclear whether it merely reaffirmed the annual limit or set a new term; the former is the presumption of Mommsen, *Staatsr.* 2, 692 n. 1.—The final clause reverts to the characterization implicit in the rhetorical question *sed quaero quid reapse sit turpius . . . ?*

Sed iam, si placet, de provinciis decedatur, in urbemque redeatur.] The phrase wittily marks the transition to the rest of the legislation, which will indeed be centered *in urbe.*

A. Nobis vero placet; sed eis qui in provinciis sunt minime placet.] Feldhügel *ad loc.* sees here a hit at Caesar's command in Gaul, the legal basis for which was undermined by Pompey's legislation of 52 (Rotondi, 411–12; cf. Gelzer, *Caesar,* 138–39 = Engl. tr. 152–53), the date and manner of his supersession being a major political topic from then on. Possibly Cicero had this in mind, but his concern is unlikely to be focused narrowly on this alone.[62] The remark suggests that the lost commentary on the immediately

---

62. His relations with Caesar were relatively good at the time of writing; *Prov.* (56) and Caesar's loan to Cicero of 800,000 sesterces (first attested at *Att.* 5.5.2: 15 May 51) were fairly recent; cf. in general Riemer, 45–57. Moreover, in *Leg.* Cicero tends to take the dead as his targets (e.g., Clodius; Lucullus in § 30), Quintus' criticism of Pompey (§ 22) being the exception.

preceding laws included a general excoriation of abuses in provincial administration; cf. Meyer, esp. ch 6 ("Patrocinium und praedia populi Romani bei
Cicero"), for a full discussion of Cicero's views on such matters.

**19a M. At vero, Tite, si parebunt his legibus, nihil erit eis urbe, nihil domo
sua dulcius, nec laboriosius molestiusque provincia.**] Activity in Rome
rather than the provinces was, according to Cicero, the way to political
success in general; cf. *Planc.* 13 and 66; cf. also *Fam.* 2.11.1 and 12.2 on his
longing to return from Cilicia. He expatiates on the difficulties of governing
a province at *Flac.* 87 and, most famously, *Q.fr.* 1.1; Ulpian would later
write a treatise *de Officio Proconsulis;* cf. Jörs, *RE* 5.1 (1903), 1452.33 ff.
Our text corresponds to his attitude as displayed both in his declination of a
province after his consulate and in his unhappiness with his appointment as
governor of Cilicia in 51; for the former cf. Walter Allen, Jr., "Cicero's
Provincial Governorship in 63 B.C.," *TAPhA* 83 (1952), 233–41; for the
latter, Gelzer, 211–12.—For *si parebunt his legibus* cf. *ad* § 29.

**Sed sequitur lex quae sancit eam tribunorum plebis potestatem quae ⟨est⟩ in
republica nostra; de qua disseri nihil necesse est.**] *Est* is added in the *recentiores* and can easily have fallen out between a word ending in *e* and one
beginning in *i.*—Especially after § 17, Marcus can hardly have supposed
that the subject required no commentary (*de qua disseri nihil necesse est*);
these words are surely spoken with tongue in cheek in full knowledge that
his brother will rise to the bait (cf. also 1.21: *nam Quinti novi sententiam;*
§ 33: . . . *in ista sum sententia qua te fuisse semper scio . . .*).

19b–26 The tribunate is debated at what might seem disproportionate
length, given that Marcus' proposal amounts essentially to a continuation of
the status quo; for a similar paradoxically long discussion cf. *ad* §§ 33–39.
The sentiment, here voiced by Quintus, for clipping its wings goes back to
Sulla, a reaction against the use of the office by P. Sulpicius (cf. *ad* §§ 20 and
22); the sentiment remained fresh in light of Clodius' recent tribunate (58).
How widely this view was shared in optimate circles must remain moot; the
argument *contra* reaches its climax in the misfortunes of the Tullii Cicerones
(§ 21), so that personal concerns seem to dominate here. At the very least the
tribunate provided a platform from which an ambitious *popularis* politician
could curry favor with the people by reform proposals, as a series of tribunes
had done, e.g., on the subject of the secret ballot (cf. *ad* §§ 35–36a). Cicero
himself has been thought to have "deliberately avoided the tribunate because
of his 'senatorial' sympathies" (Wiseman, 1971, 162 n. 1), but in practice
even activist tribunes (of whom there were few) were not expected to hew to a
consistently *popularis* policy; cf. Tatum, 1999, 13–16. Pointing out that L.
Crassus and his friends had held the office, Rawson, 1991, 31 n. 76, suspects

that the defense of the tribunate in our passage may reflect Crassus' influence and the expectation that the office could be used for optimate ends (for examples see Bleicken, 1981a, 95–98; Burckhardt, 159 ff.).

It is unclear how this material relates to the previous discussion of the tribunate (also including an intervention by Quintus: §§ 16–17), for we do not know how the subject was developed in the lacuna at § 17. The loss of matter brings the two passages closer together in our text than they would have been in Cicero's draft, but one still wonders whether the topic was really to be dealt with twice, once from the standpoint of constitutional theory and once from that of political practice, or whether the two versions would have been integrated in final revision.

19b–22 Here Quintus interrupts Marcus' expressed wish to pass swiftly to the next topic and launches a vehement denunciation of the tribunate, including:

(1) its origins and levelling tendency (§ 19b)
(2) its leading representatives (§ 20)
(3) its rôle in precipitating Marcus' own exile (§ 21–22a)
(4) its revival by Pompey in 70 after Sulla had limited its powers (§ 22).

Quintus clearly does not aim to provide a balanced history (otherwise, he would have had to discuss the abuses that gave rise to the reform efforts led by the named tribunes) but merely to make a rhetorically effective case *contra tribunatum*.[63] Nor is his speech a model of consistency: after at first seeming to deny the tribunate any legitimate *raison d'être* (*pestifera . . . in seditione et ad seditionem nata,* etc.), he later suggests that the office had been abused by the unscrupulous Clodius contrary to law (§ 22), and in the end he pleads not for its abolition, but merely for Sulla's attenuated version; cf. Thommen, 1988, 366. In his defense of the tribunate (§§ 23–26; cf. *ad loc.*), Marcus leaves (1) altogether aside (the origin of the tribunate *per seditionem* had been conceded at *Rep.* 2.59; see the next note) and replies selectively to (2), admitting the existence of some bad tribunes but emphasizing their paucity (§ 24); he devotes most attention to (3) (§§ 25b–26a) and then replies to (4) with a brief defense of Pompey (§ 26b).

19b Q. . . . nam mihi quidem pestifera [sc. ista potestas] videtur, quippe quae in seditione et ad seditionem nata sit.] At *Dom.* 2 Cicero had applied the epithet *pestifer* to the tribunate of Clodius: . . . *si illa labes ac flamma*

---

63. Cf. Marcus' reply: *Vitia quidem tribunatus praeclare, Quinte, perspicis; sed est iniqua in omni re accusanda praetermissis bonis malorum enumeratio vitiorumque selectio; . . .* (§ 23).

reipublicae suum illum pestiferum et funestum tribunatum . . . divina reli-gione defenderit . . . ; in our passage Quintus uses it for the tribunate in general. From an optimate point of view Quintus' strictures on the tribunate have much to recommend them; cf. Robin Seager, *CAH* 9, 227: ". . . the exploitation of the tribunate by Pompey, Caesar and Crassus was to do much to further that excessive growth of individual power which the oligar-chy saw, with some justification, as the greatest threat to its collective predominance."—*Quidem* here has limiting force; cf. examples at Solodow, 108–9.—Tradition held that the tribunate had its origin in a withdrawal of the plebs in 494 to the Aventine or the Sacred Mount or both successively (see the next note) and that the cause was oppressive debt resulting, under the system of *nexum* then in use, in the bonded servitude of the defaulting debtor. It is not clear, however, how the concession granted the following year by the senate, namely the election by the plebs of two tribunes from their number endowed with sacrosanctity and the power of interceding against magisterial action, relates to the problem of debt. Cicero provides a brief narrative at *Rep.* 2.58 (with 2.59: . . . *duobus tribunis plebis per sedi-tionem creatis . . .*); cf. the circumstantial one at Liv. 2.22–33.4 with Ogilvie *ad loc.* and *ad* 2.32.1; other sources at *MRR* 1, 15; for an introduction to the problems cf. A. Drummond, *CAH* 7.2, 212–17. If the characterization of the tribunate as *in seditione . . . nata* was uncontroversial for Romans, the idea that it was *ad seditionem nata* shows Quintus' political cards; certainly with the tribunate there was established a potentially counter-vailing force to the senate and the consuls, the full potential of which was not realized until much later. There is mention of *seditiosi tribuni* at § 44 and *Luc.* 144; cf. Achard, 285–86. Quintus does not appear to admit the possibility of *e republica seditiones* as argued by M. Antonius in his defense of Norbanus (cf. *de Orat.* 2.124; *ad* § 11.3–5).

cuius primum ortum si recordari volumus, inter arma civium et occupatis et obsessis urbis locis procreatum videmus; . . .] *Locus* has the sense of "a place chosen for military occupation, strategic position" (*OLD* s.v., 8). This description of events does not commit to a precise location, which was disputed between the Mons Sacer (fr. orat. *Corn.* 1, 48) and the Aventine (Piso *hist.* p. 129, fr. 22 = Liv. 2.32.3). At *Rep.* 2.58 Cicero tries to accom-modate both traditions: . . . *plebs montem Sacrum prius, deinde Aventinum occupavit.* Ogilvie *ad* Liv. 2.32.1 (p. 311) plausibly argues that the Aventine, the traditional plebeian hill, was the site and that the version involving the Mons Sacer arose as a false etymology for the *leges sacratae*. Quintus' account emphasizes the military aspect; for *inter arma civium* cf. *Corn. loc. cit.:* . . . *mons Sacer . . . , in quo armati consederant . . .* ; Caes. *BC*

1.7.5: . . . *in secessione populi, templis locisque editioribus occupatis;* Livy's allusion to the fortification of the Aventine at 2.32.4.—Cicero had used *procreo* in a more straightforward metaphor at 2.6: *hanc quoque, quae te procrearit, esse patriam tuam;* cf. OLD s.v., 2a. The metaphorical usage of *ortus* of entities of the polity was pioneered by Cicero at *Rep.* 2.49: *habetis . . . primum ortum tyranni;* sim. 1.20: *visne ergo ipsius iuris ortum a fonte repetamus?* Cf. *TLL* s.v., 1068.39 ff. But for *ortus* to function as effective object of *procreare* rather than the concrete product (*tribunatus*) is sloppy writing; presumably, the intervening matter caused Cicero to lose sight of the relations (cf. *ad Off.* 1.101).

deinde cum esset cito necatus, tamquam ex XII Tabulis insignis ad deformitatem puer, brevi tempore nescioquo pacto recreatus multoque taetrior et foedior natus est.] This sentence continues the metaphor of the tribunate as a child, procreation and birth now being succeeded by the murder of the deformed infant. Contrast the imagery of child-rearing at *de Orat.* 2.124 (Crassus): *tu vero, Antoni, perge, ut instituisti. neque enim est boni neque liberalis parentis quem procrearis et eduxeris, eum non et vestire et ornare . . .*—*Necatus* is Puteanus' conjecture for the transmitted *legatus.* Orelli's *leto datus* has recently been revived on palaeographical grounds by Crawford (on *Lex XII* 4.1), but this is an archaic and poetic formula used in a law at 2.22.15 but not otherwise by Cicero (cf. *TLL* s.v. *letum* 1189.40 ff.), and it means "dead," not "killed."—*Cito necatus* refers to the regime of the Decemviri, subject to no checks; cf. *Rep.* 2.62: . . . *erat penes principes tota respublica, praepositis decemviris nobilissimis, <u>non oppositis tribunis plebis</u>, nullis aliis adiunctis magistratibus, non provocatione ad populum contra necem et verbera relicta;* Liv. 3.33.9 (of the Decemviri: *sine provocatione creati*). Established to satisfy a demand of the plebs, the Decemviri codified the disabilities under which the plebs suffered and left them profoundly dissatisfied; the sequel was a second secession and the granting of new rights; cf. Ogilvie *ad* Liv. 3.33–42; W. Eder, "The Political Significance of the Codification of Law in Archaic Societies: An Unconventional Hypothesis," in *Social Struggles in Archaic Rome,* ed. K.A. Raaflaub (Berkeley, 1986), 262–300.—Crawford on *Lex XII* 4.1 (where further literature is cited) infers from our passage that the Twelve Tables granted immunity for exposure of a deformed child by some such formula as *se fraude esto.*—For *insignis ad* indicating "noteworthy, remarkable, signal for" some quality see OLD s.v. *insignis* 4a.—*Multoque taetrior et foedior natus est:* in the sequel Quintus expatiates on what he sees as the crimes of the latter-day tribunate.

quid enim ille non edidit? qui primum, ut impio dignum fuit, patribus omnem honorem eripuit, omnia infima summis paria fecit, turbavit,

miscuit; . . .] Quintus uses invective, as in a *contio;* for a similar style of argument cf. *ad* 1.40–52 and § 18.—*Quid* is Madvig's conjecture for *quem* of the archetype (the *recentiores* offer *quae*).—Optimates were quick to level the charge of *impietas* at their opponents; cf. Achard, 289 ff., and, with reference to opponents of the senate in particular, 300 ff. The use of the affective term *patres* for the optimates (cf. Hellegouarc'h, 429–30; Momm-sen, *Staatsr.* 3, 837 n. 2) provides a punning continuation of the imagery of child-rearing.—The complaint *omnia infima summis paria fecit* corresponds to the optimate critique of democracy at *Rep.* 1.53, including the point: *cum enim par habetur honos summis et infimis, . . . ipsa aequitas iniquissima est;* similar is the critique of Ser. Sulpicius Rufus' voting bill at *Mur.* 47.—For *turbare* (and other words from the same stem) and *miscere* applied to the opponents of the optimates cf. Achard, 286–87. For the piling up of syn-onyms cf. *ad Off.* 3.115. *Miscuit,* though an action less intense than *tur-bavit,* effects the better clausula (type *omni debebitur*).

cum adflixisset principum gravitatem, numquam tamen conquievit.] For *principum gravitatem* cf. *ad* § 17 (*gravitas optimatium*). On the excitability of the masses according to optimate rhetoric (references to *multitudo concitata* and the like) cf. Achard, 134–37.

20 Apart from the omission of C. Flaminius and C. Curiatius, *Har.* 41 and 43 present the same series of popular leaders but with different emphasis: § 41 dwells on their abilities and (perverted) potential, § 43 on personal motives for their defection from the cause of the senate.[64] On Cicero's greater candor in the treatises than in the speeches cf. Achard, 86 and n. 128 and 279–80; for the general image of the demagogic tribunes in Roman literature cf. Andrew Lintott, *CAH* 9, 9.

namque ut Gaium Flaminium atque ea quae iam prisca videntur propter vetustatem relinquam, . . .] For the *praeteritio* cf. *ad* § 18.—*Namque* is Bake's correction for the transmitted *an que* (Minutianus proposed *at-que*).—C. Flaminius (cos. I 223) appears as the first tribune in a list of *clari viri* of antiquity whom *seditiosi cives* assert to have been *populares* in Lucullus' speech at *Luc.* 13: . . . *C. Flaminium qui legem agrariam aliquot annis ante secundum Punicum bellum tribunus plebis tulerit invito senatu et postea bis consul factus sit* . . . Flaminius' name was kept alive by the build-ing projects he carried through as censor in 220, including the Via Flaminia leading to Ariminum and the Circus Flaminius, and, less happily, in the historical record by his debâcle at Lake Trasimene (23 June 217: Ov. *Fast.*

---

64. On the existence by Cicero's day of a fairly standard canon of *popularis* leaders cf. Lintott, *CAH* 9, 52.

6.767–68); hence his inclusion among the *clari viri*. His tribunate and agrarian law were variously dated to 232 (Polyb. 2.21.7–8, accepted by Broughton, *MRR* 1, 225 and n. 1) or 228 (Cic. *Sen.* 11[65]); the measure provided that the *ager Picenus et Gallicus*, won in the war with the Senones, be divided among Roman colonists; optimate opposition to the measure was intense (*invito senatu; Sen.* 11: *contra senatus auctoritatem*), perhaps because the territory was regarded as inadequately secured (so Kunkel-Wittmann, 612), and is reflected in Polybius' sharp criticism (*loc. cit.*). In *Div.* Quintus criticizes him for ignoring bad omens prior to Trasimene (1.77–78; cf. 2.21, 67, 71; *N.D.* 2.8;[66] Liv. 21.63 ff.; Rosenstein, 58, 77–78, and 90 n. 122). Cf. in general Münzer, *RE* 6 (1909), 2496.36 ff.; Z. Yavetz, "The Policy of C. Flaminius and the Plebiscitum Claudianum," *Athenaeum* n.s. 40 (1962), 325–44, who argues for a thread connecting the land distribution and his rejection of Fabian tactics.

. . . **quid iuris bonis viris Tiberi Gracchi tribunatus reliquit?**] The *boni* (*viri*) were, for Cicero, those of one's own persuasion, as in the "honest men" of earlier English usage, as opposed to subversives (the *improbi*). On the evolution of *boni viri* from an ethical to a social and political term cf. Hellegouarc'h, 484–93.—It is more typically the plebs who appealed to *ius* (as a constituent of *libertas*); cf. Hellegouarc'h, 546–47. But the *boni viri* could also feel their rights infringed.—Under the rights of the *boni viri* removed by Tiberius Gracchus' tribunate of 133 Quintus certainly understands above all

---

65. Powell *ad Sen.*, pp. 276–77, attempts to harmonize the two versions by the interpretation that Q. Fabius Maximus opposed the project in his second consulate not at the stage of passing the legislation but at that of dividing up the land (*Gaio Flaminio tribuno plebis quoad potuit restitit, agrum Picentem et Gallicum viritim contra senatus auctoritatem dividenti . . .*). But one must still assume that Cicero (or his source) was in error in calling Flaminius *tribunus plebis* at the time, and *dividenti* can be taken as conative ("trying to divide" [sc. through legislation]). More probable the assumption of Giovanni Niccolini, *I fasti dei tribuni della plebe* (Milan, 1934), 88–89, followed by Broughton (*MRR* 1, 225 n. 1), that there was a confusion by Cicero or his source of Fabius' two consulates, the prior of which would have overlapped with Flaminius' tribunate. Cf. now Rachel Feig Vishnia, "Cicero *De Senectute* 11, and the Date of C. Flaminius' Tribunate," *Phoenix* 50 (1996), 138–45, who argues that Cicero deliberately falsified the chronology so that the confrontation between Fabius and Flaminius over the latter's agrarian law would remind readers of Cicero's own confrontation with Rullus; Cicero may have seen such an analogy, but one doubts that he would have deliberately altered chronology in order to achieve it, especially in a work dedicated to so keen a student of chronology as Atticus (cf. *Brut.* 74; in general Münzer, 1905); there may well have been a confrontation between Flaminius and Fabius in the latter's first consulate (see above) and hence an honest mistake in chronology.

66. In the first and last passages cited Cicero refers to the account of Coelius Antipater = *hist.* pp. 163–64 frr. 20 and 19, respectively.

the senate's prerogative to initiate legislation and conduct foreign affairs, threatened respectively by the promulgation of his agrarian bill directly to the *concilium plebis* and the plan to make a similar use of the plebeian assembly in handling Attalus' legacy of his Pergamene kingdom to the Roman people. Cf. Stockton, 1979, 61–86, but also Klaus Bringmann, *Die Agrarreform des Tiberius Gracchus. Legende und Wirklichkeit* (Stuttgart, 1985).

etsi quinquennio ante, Decimum Brutum et Publium Scipionem consules (quos et quantos viros!) homo omnium infimus et sordidissimus tribunus plebis C. Curiatius in vincula coniecit, quod ante factum non erat.] Causes of friction between the tribune and consuls of 138 were the grain dole and the military levy for the war in the Iberian peninsula, though it was the latter, in particular the claim of Curiatius and another tribune, Sex. Licinius, to be able to exempt ten men, that resulted in the brief imprisonment of the consuls for failing to pay a fine; cf. A.E. Astin, *CAH* 8, 193–95; Kunkel-Wittmann, 576 and n. 79; J.K. Evans, "Resistance at Home: The Evasion of Military Service in Italy during the 2nd Century B.C.," in *Forms of Control and Subordination in Antiquity*, ed. T. Yuge and M. Doi (Leiden, 1988), 124–25. For D. Junius Brutus Callaicus cf. *ad* 2.54; for P. Cornelius Scipio Nasica Serapio *ad Off.* 1.109; for C. Curiatius, Münzer, *RE* 4 (1901), 1831.52 ff.—For the brief exclamatory characterization *quos et quantos viros!* cf. *Font.* 39 (of C. Gracchus' attacks on L. Calpurnius Piso Frugi): *at in quem virum!* sim. *N.D.* 1.72: *quem virum, dii immortales! Div.* 1.52: *Xenophon Socraticus (qui vir et quantus!).*—The epithet *sordidissimus* forms part of the standard lexicon of abuse hurled by optimates at their lower class opponents; cf. § 35; Achard, 139. On the other hand, *infimus* is a term used of persons of humble birth regardless of political allegiance; ibid., 376. Münzer, *loc. cit.*, 1831.61–64, suggests, implausibly, that the characterization may have been added to dissociate the tribune from the Curiatii of saga; rather, it contrasts sharply with that of the imprisoned consuls (*quos et quantos viros!*).—*Quod ante factum non erat:* precedent was thus set for the similar tribunician obstruction of the levy of 55; cf. *ad Off.* 1.25 with literature.

Gai vero Gracchi tribunatus, eis sicis quas ipse se proiecisse in forum dixit quibus digladiarentur inter se cives, nonne omnem reipublicae statum permutavit?] *Tribunatus* is Halm's emendation of the transmitted *ruinis*.—C. Gracchus may have referred to the *sica*, the gladiator's sword, more than once: first in defiant response to a threat of war from the senate over the judiciary law; cf. D.S. 37.9: κἂν ἀποθάνω, οὐ διαλείψω ⟨. . .⟩ τὸ ξίφος ἀπὸ τῆς πλευρᾶς τῶν συγκλητικῶν †διηρημένον (where a participle, e.g., βαστάζων, seems to have been lost, and one would expect ἀφ- for δι-); then in exultation upon passage of a law (topic unspecified) by a single vote, ibid. 34–35.27: τὸ μὲν ξίφος ἐπίκειται τοῖς ἐχθροῖς, περὶ δὲ τῶν ἄλλων ὡς ἂν ἡ τύχη βραβεύσῃ στέρξομεν; cf. Stockton, 1979, 184. In view of the corruption of the prior passage it is difficult to say whether Quintus has in mind one of these statements or yet a third.[67] Perhaps it was from C. Gracchus that Cicero learned to use *sica* in his speeches as a vivid metaphor for violence; cf. Achard, 339.—Cicero pioneered the metaphorical application of *digladior* to dialectical disputes, but here it has its literal sense (reflecting C. Gracchus' own usage?); cf. *TLL* s.v.—The view that C. Gracchus' tribunate resulted in a change of the Roman constitution (*reipublicae status*), i.e., presumably away from the mixed constitution and toward democracy, can find, of course, no reflection in *Rep.*, which is set before that event; but there Tubero observes: ... *mors Tiberi Gracchi, et iam ante tota illius ratio tribunatus, divisit populum unum in duas partes* (*Rep.* 1.31). Cicero attributes such an effect to Ti. Gracchus at *Har.* 41: *convellit statum civitatis.* For C. Gracchus and his tribunate cf. in general Münzer, *RE* 2A4 (1923), 1375.31 ff. (Sempronius no. 47); Stockton, 1979, 114 ff.; Andrew Lintott, *CAH* 9, 77–86.

quid iam de Saturnino, Sulpicio, reliquis dicam? quos ne depellere quidem a se sine ferro potuit respublica.] For Saturninus cf. *ad* 2.14a.—The last in Quintus' series of older tribunes, P. Sulpicius is called an imitator of Saturninus at Plut. *Mar.* 35.1 and placed in series between Saturninus and Marius in Philippus' speech (Sall. *Hist.* 1.77.7). In *de Orat.* he, together with C. Aurelius Cotta, represents the younger generation of orators. He handled his first case in 95 and the following year undertook the ambitious prosecution *de maiestate* of C. Norbanus, who won acquittal thanks to M. Antonius' skillful defense; cf. *ad* § 11.3–5. He was a close friend of the reform tribune of 91 M. Livius Drusus, who was killed by an assassin during his tenure of office (Vell. 2.14.1). Elected tribune for 88,[68] he displayed remarkable oratorical gifts *in contionibus*, and the young Cicero made a close study of his technique (cf. *Brut.* 306: *P. Sulpici in tribunatu cotidie contionantis*

---

67. Malcovati (*orat.* p. 189) recognizes no such distinction and has oddly chosen to print as the main text the colorless version at App. *BC* 1.92: φασὶ δὲ κυρωθέντος μὲν ἄρτι τοῦ νόμου τὸν Γράκχον εἰπεῖν ὅτι ἀθρόως τὴν βουλὴν καθῃρήκοι.

68. Since T. Mommsen, *Römische Forschungen*, 1 (Berlin, 1864), 120, it has often been assumed that he was born a patrician but transferred to the plebs; but, if so, it is odd that our sources do not so indicate. Nor, as D.R. Shackleton Bailey points out (*per litt.*), is it quite certain that he was descended from the patrician Sulpicii Rufi since the cognomen is attested only by V.Max. 6.5.7, who could have imported it from Servius; on the dubiousness of the cognomen see further Harold B. Mattingly, "The Consilium of Cn. Pompeius Strabo in 89 B.C.," *Athenaeum* 53 (1975), 262–66; for further possibilities cf. Tatum, 1999, 94–95.

totum genus dicendi penitus cognovimus). He used his control of the masses, however, to convert them into an armed force for achieving his will in the body politic. The violence was first directed against C. Caesar Strabo, who was seeking the consulate *extra ordinem,* then against the consuls, Sulla and Pompeius Rufus, the son of the latter of whom was killed. Driven out of Rome, Sulla marched his army on the city and outlawed his opponents; Sulpicius went into hiding at Laurentum but was betrayed by a slave and killed; his head was displayed on the rostra (Vell. 2.19.1), and his body was left unburied (*Rhet. Her.* 4.31; for the similar treatment of the remains of Ti. Gracchus and C. Marius cf. *ad* 2.56); his laws were annulled on grounds that they had been carried by force. Cf. Münzer, *RE* 4A1 (1931), 843.65 ff. (s.v. Sulpicius no. 92); Lintott, 1968, 134, 141, 155, 211; idem, "The Tribunate of P. Sulpicius Rufus," *CQ* 21 (1971), 442–53; Robin Seager, *CAH* 9, 167–69 and 171; Michael Lovano, *The Age of Cinna: Crucible of Late Republican Rome* (Stuttgart, 2002), 19 ff.—Quintus describes the use of armed force against Saturninus and Sulpicius as the *respublica* acting in self-defense (he uses the somewhat more neutral *ferrum* here as opposed to the sinister *sica* in the citation of Gracchus). The personification of *respublica* is characteristic of Ciceronian oratory at all periods; cf. material at Merguet, *Reden* s.v., 326–28; it appears with particular pathos just after the return from exile: . . . *cum me vestra auctoritas arcessierit, populus Romanus vocarit, respublica implorarit, Italia cuncta paene suis umeris reportarit . . . (Red. Sen.* 39).

21 Cur autem aut vetera aut aliena proferam potius quam et nostra et recentia?] Quintus has adduced *vetera* but not *aliena,* though he implies that he could do so; for the practice of balancing these two types of examples cf. *ad* 1.42 (*interrex noster*) and 2.33. Marcus cited the Spartan ephors as a *conferendum* for the tribunes at § 16.

quis umquam tam audax, tam nobis inimicus fuisset ut cogitaret umquam de statu nostro labefactando, nisi mucronem aliquem tribunicium exacuisset in nos?] Cicero often paints his opponents as *audaces* or characterized by *audacia;* cf. Achard, 198 and 247–48.—The discussion has now moved from the *reipublicae status* (§ 20) to *noster status,* i.e., that of the Tullii Cicerones. Clodius' action against Cicero is here implicitly attributed to personal animosity (*quis . . . tam nobis inimicus fuisset . . . ?*). H. Benner, 39, raises the possibility, however, that Clodius deliberately involved Cicero in his alibi in the Bona Dea affair because he saw him as a potentially popular target and wanted an excuse to destroy him; certainly the exile of Cicero was popular with the urban plebs (ibid., 55), something Cicero too readily overlooks or explains away (cf. the note after next and *ad* § 25).

Nevertheless one queries whether H. Benner's theory does not attribute to Clodius a preternatural ability to foresee the course of events: how could he be sure that Cicero would testify against him, that he could, in fact, succeed in transferring to the plebs, that attacks on Cicero would prove as popular as they did, etc.? More probably, Clodius was acting within the context of the traditional categories of *amicitia/inimicitia,* as argued by Jörg Spielvogel, "P. Clodius Pulcher—eine politische Ausnahme-Erscheinung der späten Republik?" *Hermes* 125 (1997), 56–74; sim. David F. Epstein, *Personal Enmity in Roman Politics 218–43 BC* (London, 1987), 94–95; Tatum, 1999, 151; for Cicero's motive for testifying against Clodius cf. W. Jeffrey Tatum, "Cicero and the *Bona Dea* Scandal," *CPh* 85 (1990), 202–8.— Emphatic repetition, like that of *umquam* here, though uncommon in good prose, is permissible; cf. Löfstedt, 2, 227 n. 1.—*Mucro,* like *sica* (§ 20), is used elsewhere as a vivid term for a weapon; cf. Achard, 450.

quem cum homines scelerati ac perditi non modo ulla in domo sed nulla in gente reperirent, gentes sibi in tenebris reipublicae perturbandas putaverunt; . . .] The "confounding of families" describes Clodius' transference from the patrician *gens Claudia* to the plebs, finally achieved by a *lex curiata de arrogatione Clodii* during Caesar's consulate (59); cf. H. Benner, 40–43; Tatum, 1999, 90–95 and 100–102.—The negation carries over from *non modo* to *ulla in domo* and need not be repeated; cf. *ad Off.* 1.77.—The metaphorical use of *tenebrae* to refer to a condition of the Roman state appears to have been pioneered by Cicero, first with reference to the civil war of the 80s (*Ver.* 3.177), then, as here, to Clodius' reign of terror in the 50s (*Dom.* 24; *Prov.* 43), and finally the civil war over Caesar's supersession (*Fam.* 4.3.2, to Varro: early September 47 or 46); cf. *OLD* s.v., 5.

quod nobis quidem egregium et ad immortalitatem memoriae gloriosum, neminem in nos mercede ulla tribunum potuisse reperiri, nisi cui ne esse quidem licuisset tribuno.] For Cicero's frequent assertion that his opponents are *mercennarii* or *conducti* cf. Achard, 137–40.—The invalidity of Caesar's legislation in view of the *spectio de caelo* of his consular colleague M. Bibulus was the chief argument against the validity of the laws of Clodius' tribunate (*cui ne esse quidem licuisset esse tribuno*); cf. the previous note; *Dom.* 34–42 together with Gelzer, *Caesar,* 70 = Engl. tr. 77–78; Taylor, 1949, 88; Tatum, 1999, 104–8.—This point actually runs counter to Quintus' case in that it suggests that the tribunate was not evil per se but was abused by an unscrupulous character contrary to law; cf. *ad* §§ 19b–22.

22 sed ille quas strages edidit! eas videlicet quas sine ratione ac sine ulla spe bona furor edere potuit impurae beluae, multorum inflammatus furoribus.] The rhetorical question of § 19 (*quid enim ille non edidit?*) is taken up in this exclamation.—This passage combines a number of the horrific images the optimates associated with their opponents: for *strages* cf. Achard, 340 and n. 819; for the attribution of *furor* or other forms of dementia ibid. 239–47; for the dehumanizing term *belua* ibid. 346–47; for the epithet *impurus* ibid. 139 n. 359; *inflammatus* suggests a fevered condition but perhaps also the incendiarism of which Cicero so often accuses the *improbi* (cf. Achard, 348–51). Quintus' invective does not draw nice distinctions, but some of the "destructions" wrought by Clodius were after his term as tribune was already over (at *Q.fr.* 1.4.3 Cicero expresses fear of Clodius even as a private citizen), including the incident of 23 January 57, when Quintus, supporting a motion of the tribune Q. Fabius for his brother's recall from exile, was attacked by a mob of Clodiani and left for dead (cf. *Sest.* 76; Plut. *Cic.* 33.4; Münzer, *RE* 7A2 [1943], 1293.46 ff.) or the burning of Quintus' house on the Palatine on 3 November 57 (*Att.* 4.3.2).

quamobrem in ista quidem re vehementer Sullam probo, qui tribunis plebis sua lege iniuriae faciendae potestatem ademerit, auxili ferendi reliquerit; . . .] The lex Cornelia Pompeia of 88 required prior approval by the senate for any measure brought before the *concilium plebis*. It remained without effect, however, because it was annulled the following year by Cinna. Sulla returned to the *tribunicia potestas* in the lex Cornelia of 82, probably among his first acts as dictator. It provided that only a senator could be a tribune and by accepting the post he renounced any further steps in the curule *cursus honorum;* it also effectively abolished the right to introduce legislation[69] and restricted the right to bring charges before the *concilium plebis;* cf. Rotondi, 343–44 and 350–51; Mommsen, *Staatsr.* 1, 486, and 553–54 n. 5; 2, 308, 312, and 326; Kunkel-Wittmann, 654 ff.; Thommen, 1989, 147 ff. (on the trials); Robin Seager, *CAH* 9, 172; T.P. Wiseman, ibid., 329–30 and n. 14. Whether, as Caesar twice asserts (*BC* 1.5.1 and 7.3), Sulla left the tribunician veto intact depends in part on one's interpretation of Cic. *Ver.* 1.155: under Verres' urban praetorship a fine is demanded from Q. Opimius *verbo, quod, cum esset tribunus plebis, intercessisset contra legem Corneliam;* this is often taken to show Sulla's restriction of intercession (cf., e.g., Duncan Cloud, *CAH* 9, 497 n. 23). A.W. Lintott, "The *quaestiones de sicariis et veneficis* and the Latin *lex Bantina*," *Hermes* 106 (1978), 127, followed by Seager, *loc. cit.,* 201, suggests, however, that seeking a fine through a private action, rather than a trial for *maiestas,* points rather to a contravention of the lex Cornelia that had established the *quaestio.* Another possibility is that Sulla allowed

69. Liv. *per.* 89; cf. Keaveney, 186–87 n. 3; Thommen, 1989, 251; Duncan Cloud, *CAH* 9, 497 n. 23 with literature.

intercession only to protect individuals; cf. Keaveney, 187 n. 5; Thommen, 1989, 228–29.—The tradition is divided between *auxilium* (BA^X) and *auxilii* (PɛL); either is possible; the gerundive construction is Cicero's overwhelming favorite, but this preference was reversed in later authors (cf. Kühner-Stegmann, 1, 735), the *uter in utrum?* test therefore clearly on the side of an original gerundive.

Pompeiumque nostrum ceteris rebus omnibus semper amplissimis summisque effero laudibus, de tribunicia potestate taceo; nec enim reprehendere libet, nec laudare possum.] For the chronological implications of the references to Pompey and Marcus' encomia on him cf. *ad* 1.8; *noster* emphasizes the shared personal tie, like *Magnus ille noster* at 2.6. The *tribunicia potestas* was much discussed in political circles at Rome in the 70s, with several stages of legislation: the rogatio (?) Sicinia of 76, the lex Aurelia of 75 (restoring the right to hold other offices after the tribunate [Asc. *Corn.* 59]), and finally the lex Pompeia Licinia of 70; cf. Rotondi, 364–65 and 369; Gruen, 1974, 28; Robin Seager, *CAH* 9, 210–11, 213, 224–25; T.P. Wiseman, ibid., 336; Thommen, 1988, 372–73 and n. 46. Pompey was able to reap some benefit in the 50s, when he and his allies Caesar and Crassus made adroit use of the tribunes to advance their political agenda; cf. Robin Seager, *loc. cit.*, 227, cited *ad* § 19b *supra;* similarly, Cicero worked closely in 58 with the tribune L. Ninnius Quadratus in attempts to thwart Clodius; cf. W. Jeffrey Tatum, "Cicero and the *Lex Clodia de collegiis,*" *CQ* 40 (1990), 190–92. The qualified criticism of Pompey fits the late 50s, when it was hoped he would champion the senate's cause (cf. Thommen, 1988, 367); there is a similar muting of criticism that might touch Pompey at *Off.* 2.60 (when he was already dead).

23–26a Here Marcus takes on the rôle of advocate for the defense. His speech amounts to 58 lines in the edition of Görler/Ziegler compared with 42 for Quintus or ca. 138 percent; for the generally greater length of the speeches of refutation in Cicero's dialogues (a mark of his skepticism) cf. Leonhardt, 25 ff. Marcus' case can be analyzed as follows:

(1) The tribunate provides the plebs with a leader who can also be held accountable (§ 23).
(2) The number of bad tribunes is small and subject to collegial veto (§ 24a).
(3) The plebs are kept content (§ 24b).
(4) His own exile was caused by slaves and the threat of military violence (§§ 25–26a).

(5) In reviving the tribunate, Pompey was guided by political exigencies
(§ 26b).

This defense is built on theoretical analysis of the power relations within the
state ([1], [3]), historical observations ([2], [4]), and pragmatic political
judgment ([5]). T.P. Wiseman, *CAH* 9, 330, suspects that this analysis may
have been influenced by Licinius Macer's history depicting Sulla's curtail-
ment of tribunician power as a throwback to the fifth-century patricians'
self-interested rule; but, given his negative view of Macer's style at 1.7, one
wonders how far Cicero was prepared to be influenced by his content. The
credit that Cicero gives to Pompey alone for restoring the tribunate (§ 26; cf.
§ 22) may be directed against the view attributed to Macer at Sal. *Hist.*
3.23–24 that all together should strive to restore the tribunate and not leave
the task to a single man; cf. Thommen, 1988, 373. There is some similarity
with the view at *Rep.* 2.57, where "the nature of things" is said to "force"
this increment in popular power (*sed id quod fieri natura rerum ipsa
cogebat, ut plusculum sibi iuris populus asciceret liberatus a regibus . . . :*
cf. [5]).[70] Apparently, he is guided by the idea that stability is promoted by a
balance of *potestas in magistratibus, auctoritas in principum consilio,* and
libertas in populo (ibid.; cf. *ad* § 17), though he deliberately frames the
argument in our passage so as to win over optimate sentiment, in particular
by holding out the prospect that the plebs can be induced to yield to the
authority of the *principes* (§ 25). Cf. *ad* § 26b; Thommen, 1988, 374.[71]

**23 Vitia quidem tribunatus praeclare, Quinte, perspicis; sed est iniqua in
omni re accusanda praetermissis bonis malorum enumeratio vitiorumque
selectio; . . .]** Here Marcus begins tactfully, praising Quintus' clear vision of
the *vitia tribunatus* but complaining of onesidedness.—Analysis of the main
idea into component parts (of which *enumeratio* is a form) can serve the end
of amplification (αὔξησις; *res augere*); cf. Lausberg § 838. The technique
will generally be of greater use to prosecution than defense (*Part.* 59: *enumeratio . . . laudatori numquam, suasori non saepe, accusatori saepius
quam reo necessaria*).

**nam isto quidem modo vel consulatus vituperari potest, si consulum (quos
enumerare nolo) peccata collegeris.]** This type of argument is criticized at

---

70. Cicero took this view in spite of the fact that in day-to-day politics he often found
himself attacking tribunician laws; cf. Lehmann, 30–31 n. 51.

71. Other discussions of our passage: G. Grosso, "Sul tribunato della plebe," *Labeo* 20
(1974), 7–11; L. Perelli, "Note sul tribunato della plebe nella riflessione ciceroniana," *Quaderni di storia* 10 (1979), 285–303; I. Pascucci, "Quid de tribunatu plebis Cicero senserit,"
Ciceroniana 7 (1990), 231–34.

Rhet. Her. 2.44: *item vitiosum est artem aut scientiam aut studium quodpiam vituperare propter eorum vitia, qui in eo studio sunt: veluti qui r⟨h⟩etoricam vituperant propter alicuius oratoris vituperandam vitam,* where magistracy/magistrate might also have been cited as an example. One wonders what consuls he had in mind. Obvious candidates include Cinna (87–84), Julius Caesar (59), and Piso and Gabinius (58). The refutation involves showing that some admitted good (here the consulate) would fall under the prosecution's strictures. Cicero similarly reins in the prosecution at *Cael.* 43: *multi . . . summi homines et clarissimi cives* (whom he declines to name) could be so criticized, for, like Caelius, they had sown youthful wild oats.— *Isto modo* = "according to that procedure of yours"; see the next note.— *Quidem solum* is emphatic here; cf. Solodow, 107.

ego enim fateor in ista ipsa potestate inesse quiddam mali, sed bonum quod est quaesitum in ea sine isto malo non haberemus.] Cicero combines a frank acknowledgement of the strong point in the opposing case with a palliative—the prospect of an entailed good; sim., e.g., § 24 (*et praeter eos quamvis enumeres multos licet—periculosas contentiones nullas facit*); *Sul.* 23: *'hoc dico', inquit, 'te esse ex municipio'. fateor et addo etiam: ex eo municipio unde iterum iam salus huic urbi imperioque missa est.* When it served his purpose he could, of course, argue against an "unholy alliance" of unlike entities; cf. *Off.* 3.119.—The second-person reference of *iste* is on display twice: "in that very power (that you excoriate)"; "without that evil (that you highlight)"; cf. *ad* 1.4 and 54.

nimia potestas est tribunorum plebis: quis negat?] Instead of constructing the dialogue as a series of shorter exchanges typical of Plato, Cicero prefers longer set speeches with an imaginary objector's interventions occasionally inserted in direct speech in diatribe style[72]—a form he also uses in his orations; cf. *ad* 2.47.

sed vis populi multo saevior multoque vehementior; quae ducem quod habet interdum lenior est quam si nullum haberet.] Here Marcus argues that the *vis populi* alone, unchanneled into the constitutional process by the tribunes, would be still worse. One thinks of Scipio's image of the mahout controlling an elephant as a metaphor for the statesman who is *prudens* as he tames the wild elements of the human character (*Rep.* 2.67). Marcus does not take the argument so far as M. Antonius in his defense of C. Norbanus, who apparently claimed that the just anger of the people was the motor

---

72. But Plato, too, sometimes invokes an imaginary questioner or objector to soften the directness of dialectical exchange or to add a point of view not otherwise represented (cf., e.g., *Gorg.* 452c–d; *Lg.* 885c with Szlezák, 73).

driving constitutional change at Rome; cf. *orat.* p. 231 = *de Orat.* 2.199 (see further *ad* § 11.3–5); Cicero used a similar argument at *Corn.* 1; cf. p. 475 n. 53 *supra.*—*Vis populi* takes up and varies Quintus' phrase *vis multitudinis* (§ 17); by using the more inclusive *populus,* rather than *plebs,* Marcus enlarges the perspective from Quintus' contextualization within the battle of the *plebs* and *patres;* indeed, in the Middle and Late Republic the upper class could and did make use of the *auxilii latio;* cf. Bleicken, 1955, 81 n. 4; Thommen, 1988, 360 n. 12.—*Quod* is causal.—Cf. Thommen, 1988, 369–70: "Cicero hat ... eine wesentliche Funktion des Volkstribunats richtig darin gesehen, als Artikulationspunkt einer nicht senatskonformen Politik und dadurch auch als 'Ventil' für oppositionelle Kräfte zu dienen." **dux enim suo ⟨se⟩ periculo progredi cogitat, populi impetus periculi rationem sui non habet.**] Similarly, the law *Ast quid turbassitur in agendo, fraus actoris esto* (§ 11.5) fixes responsibility for mob action with the presiding official; cf. the commentary *ad* § 42b. The psychology by which the individual member of a mob sloughs off responsibility for its actions is explored by Canetti, 17 = Eng. tr. 20 (cf. *ad* 2.65; sim. the last section of the chapter entitled "Der Befehl" = Eng. tr. 331–33).—The *recentiores* supplied *se.*

24 'At aliquando incenditur': et quidem saepe sedatur.] Sc. *a tribunis.* Adversative *quidem* in a partial concession; cf. Solodow, 83, who translates: "'But the populace is sometimes aroused by them.' And yet it is also calmed by them." For a similar remark about different types of music cf. *ad* 2.38.— The final rhythms of the two sentences—Cicero's two favorite clausulae— seem to mirror the sense: the more staccato ending of the prior (type *omni debebitur*) resolved in the majestic *omne debetur* type.—This is the critical point in Marcus' defense of the tribunate, reinforced with historical argument below, namely that it serves to pacify the populace and make them amenable to the *auctoritas senatus,* his policy being, as he candidly admits (§ 39), to give the people merely the *species libertatis;* cf. Nippel, 1980, 155. Examples of such activities by tribunes would include Cato in 63–62 and M. Caelius Rufus in 52; cf. *MRR* 2, 174–75 and 235. Fontanella, 1998, 206–7, reads the leading rôle of the senate (cf. § 28) in terms of an ideal senate embodying *lex* as *ratio summa insita in natura* (1.18b); certainly Cicero speaks at § 29 of his laws applying to an ideal future, but the premise seems to shift (see *ad loc.*); certainly, the laws given for senators (§ 10.3–5 with commentary §§ 40–41) look as though they were drafted with fallible individuals in mind, not embodiments of perfect *ratio.*

quod enim est tam desperatum collegium, in quo nemo e decem sana mente sit?] Sim. à propos the consuls Q. Catulus at *Red. Sen.* 9, quoted *ad* § 16 *supra.*—Marcus points to the possibility, opened up by the lex Hortensia (cf. *ad* § 9.6), of a collegial veto; hence the institution contains within itself a check against excesses; cf. Kunkel-Wittmann, 585. This was the traditional doctrine, but after Ti. Gracchus' deposition of his colleague it was very difficult for a single tribune to hold out in this way; see below. The tribune's veto could also be used against other magistrates, an aspect Cicero does not pursue here; cf. Thommen, 1988, 370–71.

quin ipsum Ti. Gracchum non solum neglectus sed etiam sublatus interces-
sor evertit; quid enim illum aliud perculit, nisi quod potestatem intercedenti
collegae abrogavit?] On intercession in general cf. *ad* § 42.—*Ipse* isolates Ti. Gracchus as the prime example of the phenomenon (cf. *OLD* s.v., 5) and thus implicitly concedes Quintus' characterization of his political activities (§ 20).—The *collega* was M. Octavius, whom Gracchus had removed from office for his veto of the grain bill; sim. *Brut.* 95: . . . *qui iniuria accepta fregit Ti. Gracchum patientia, civis in rebus optimis constantissimus, M. Octavius* with Linderski, 1995, 291–94. Plut. *TG* 15 shows the pressure on Tiberius in the aftermath; for *constantia* in such situations laying the ground-work for political reversal cf. Morstein-Marx, ch. 4. The constitutional consequences of Gracchus' act were considerable: no less than the transfor-mation of the popular assembly from a rubber stamp into an independent decision-making body; cf. Rilinger, 489. Stockton, 1979, 64–67, provides a narrative of the abrogation of Octavius' tribunate; for a similar judgment to Cicero's of the effect on Gracchus see ibid. 78–79. The removal of his colleague's sacrosanctity endangered Gracchus' own, as was implied by the *sponsio* to which the consular T. Annius Luscus challenged Gracchus;[73] cf. Kunkel-Wittmann, 586–87, esp. 587 n. 107.—Astin, 1964, 442, points to the revival of Gracchan tactics when in 67 Gabinius threatened to depose his fellow tribune L. Trebellius if he were to veto the *lex Gabinia*; in the event Trebellius backed down; hence in the controversies of 59 the optimates took refuge not in tribunician veto, but in *spectio de caelo*; see *ad* 2.14a and the detailed analysis of the weakness of the veto at Burckhardt, ch. 3.—*Evertit* is Vahlen's correction for *fuerat*; confusion of *e* and *f* is typical of transcripts from Beneventan.[74]

sed tu sapientiam maiorum in illo vide: concessa plebi a patribus ista
potestate, arma ceciderunt, restincta seditio est, inventum est temperamen-
tum quo tenuiores cum principibus aequari se putarent, in quo uno fuit
civitatis salus.] Quintus' approval of Sulla's reform (§ 22) implies a criticism

73. Plut. *TG* 14.5: Τίτος δ' Ἄννιος . . . εἰς ὁρκισμόν τινα προὐκαλεῖτο τὸν Τιβέριον, ἦ μὴν ἱερὸν καὶ ἄσυλον ἐκ τῶν νόμων ἠτιμωκέναι τὸν συνάρχοντα.

74. I owe this observation to J.G.F. Powell.

of the *sapientia maiorum,* which is here reaffirmed; cf. 2.62 and *Rep.* 2.30; Roloff, 68; Girardet, 1977, 189.—Since Quintus had dwelt upon the origin of the tribunate in armed force, not the sequel (*. . . quippe quae in seditione et ad seditionem nata sit,* etc.: § 19b), Marcus redresses the balance by providing full historical context.—*Plebi* is the reading of PF² for the otherwise transmitted *plebe. A patribus* is omitted by B, whereas AεL have *ista patribus* (before *ista potestate*).—*Ista potestas* refers to the tribunician power in its traditional form as enshrined in Cicero's law (§ 9.6); it has formed the topic since § 19a (*lex quae sancit eam tribunorum plebis potestatem quae ⟨est⟩ in republica nostra*); cf. also § 17: *ista potestate nata;* § 23: *fateor in ista ipsa potestate inesse quiddam mali.* Cicero is not speaking specifically of the power of veto, as Rudd *ad loc.* supposed, though that, of course, is included.—Our passage is the earliest attestation for *temperamentum* cited at *OLD* s.v., so the term may be Cicero's coinage; here it has the metaphorical sense of a "compromise between extremes of policy, conduct, character, etc." (ibid. 3); it is reminiscent of the *temperatio* Marcus attributes to his laws at § 12 (cf. also § 27) and the *temperatum genus* of constitution recommended for its durability by Scipio (*Rep.* 1.69; cf. *. . . in quo uno fuit civitatis salus*); sim. also the *sapiens temperatio* of § 17. This is, in fact, the one positive argument Marcus offers for the tribunate; the rest of his case consists in showing that, through the large number of tribunes and their equal possession of the right of intercession, the institution contains a self-checking mechanism; he fails to mention here other aspects of the institution, such as its function in checking consular abuses, the *ius relationis,* the right of prosecution before the *iudicium populi,* etc., though these points may have been touched on in the lacuna at § 17; cf. Thommen, 1988, 373.—The wording *quo tenuiores cum principibus aequari se putarent* makes it clear that Cicero's goal is perceived, rather than actual *aequalitas;* cf. *Rep.* 1.53; *ad* 2.25.—For Cicero's use of the term *tenues* and its comparative and superlative forms of a socioeconomic group cf. Achard, 376 and n. 162.

'At duo Gracchi fuerunt': . . .] The objection is premised upon a picture of the Gracchi similar to the one sketched by Quintus at § 20, according to which they endangered, rather than enhanced, the *salus civitatis.*

et praeter eos quamvis enumeres multos licet. cum deni creentur, ⟨non⟩nullos in omni memoria reperies perniciosos tribunos; leves etiam, non bonos, fortasse plures. invidia quidem summus ordo caret, plebes de suo iure periculosas contentiones nullas facit.] This response is based on the strategy of sinking the Gracchi into the mass of tribunes and thus diluting their significance (the numeral *duo* paling beside the *multi,* who are shown to be relatively harmless) then adding the palliative factors *invidia quidem summus* *ordo caret,* etc. Cf. *ad* § 23 (*ego enim fateor in ista ipsa potestate*—).—For *quamvis . . . multos* cf. *Caec.* 47: *vidi armatos quamvis paucos.*—*Cum deni—perniciosos tribunos:* translate: "Since ten are appointed at a time, in every age you will find some tribunes who are troublemakers." *Nonnullos* is the correction of Turnebus' 1538 edition. For *memoria* = "age, [historical] period" cf. *TLL* s.v., 680.57 ff. (our passage cited at 681.40); sim. 1.4: *in recenti memoria.*—As benefits of the tribunate Marcus cites the hindering of (1) *invidia* of the upper class (in the sequel he concedes merely *ex hypothesi* that *multitudinis furentis inflammata invidia* was the cause of his exile) and (2) *periculosae contentiones,* under which he no doubt has in mind a situation like the secession of the plebs in 494; cf. Girardet, 1977, 188 n. 40.

25 quamobrem aut exigendi reges non fuerunt, aut plebi re, non verbo, danda libertas; . . .] As the conclusion (*quamobrem*) drawn from the foregoing argument that the tribunate contained within itself not only the *malum* of *nimia potestas* excoriated by Quintus but also the *bonum* of checking the passions of the *populus,* Marcus poses these alternatives: either the kings ought not to have been expelled or the commons had to be granted true, not merely specious liberty, i.e., the latter was the logical outcome. The sequel, connected with *tamen,* offers a palliative for this "true liberty." Cf. Laser, 29. At § 39, however, he speaks of his voting law as giving the people merely the *libertatis species.*[75]

quae tamen sic data est ut multis praeclaris institutis adduceretur ut auctoritati principum cederet.] A statement of unusual clarity of the fundamental principle of the *respublica* that the *auctoritas principum* serves as a limit on the *libertas* of the plebs; cf. Bleicken, 1972, 27 and n. 32; sim. § 38: *. . . ita libertatem istam largior populo ut auctoritate et valeant et utantur boni;* cf. *Rep.* 1.43: *ipsa aequabilitas est iniqua cum habet nullos gradus dignitatis.* The point is not argued but taken for granted on the basis of Roman tradition; cf. Garnsey, 3.—*Praeclaris institutis* is Bake's correction for the transmitted *praeclarissimis* (cf. 3.44); for *instituta* in the sense "mores, ritus, usus" that have been established cf. *Leg.* 1.42 and in general *TLL* s.v. *instituo* 1994.19 ff.—At *Rep.* 1.69 Scipio describes the mixed constitution this way: *placet enim esse quiddam in republica praestans et regale, esse aliud auctoritati principum impertitum ac tributum, esse quasdam res servatas iudicio voluntatique multitudinis.* Our passage spells out a bit more clearly how this division is to function in practice: in exchange for *praeclara instituta,* the chief of which is the tribunate, the plebs are to be induced to yield to the *auctoritas principum.* Marcus thus aims to show that

---

75. This note has benefited from comments by Robert Morstein-Marx.

honor of the *patres* is, *pace* Quintus (§ 19b), not incompatible with the tribunate; indeed he sees the tribunate as "eine Einrichtung, die die Unterordnung befördert und erleichtert hat" (Thommen, 1988, 372). The consuls, although theoretically endowed with *regium imperium*, do not figure as a separate factor in the division of power; cf. *ad* § 8.2.

Nostra autem causa, quae, optime et dulcissime frater, incidit in tribuniciam potestatem, nihil habuit contentionis cum tribunatu; . . .] Since Quintus had invoked as his crown witness *et nostra et recentia* (§ 21), Marcus includes an interpretation of the family's recent difficulties that exculpates the tribunician power as such; for this interpretation of events cf. already *Red. Sen.* 17: *cum ego . . . non tribunicio sed consulari ictu concidissem . . .*—The Tullii Cicerones drew together as never before during the difficult time of Cicero's exile; cf. F. Münzer, *RE* 7A2 (1948), 1293.23 ff. Upon his return Marcus expressed his gratitude in public encomia, of which the address in our passage (*optime et dulcissime frater*) preserves some of the flavor; cf. *Red. Sen.* 1 (*qui mihi fratrem optissimum, me fratri amantissimo . . . reddidistis*) and 37 (*sed unus frater, qui in me pietate filius, consiliis parens, amore, ut erat, frater inventus est, squalore et lacrimis et cotidianis precibus desiderium mei nominis renovari et rerum gestarum memoriam usurpari coegit*); sim. *Red Pop.* 5 and 7 (*fratrisque miserrimi atque optimi cotidianae lacrimae sordesque lugubres a vobis deprecatae sunt*).—*Incido in* appears in the sense "come within the scope of (an authority, law, etc.)": *OLD* s.v. *incido* 7a.

non enim plebes incitata nostris rebus invidit, sed vincula soluta sunt et servitia incitata, adiuncto terrore etiam militari.] The first point is an application of the previously described general situation *invidia . . . summus ordo caret* (§ 24); even at *Dom.* 88 he grants the point merely *ex hypothesi: si me populus Romanus incitatus iracundia aut invidia e civitate eiecisset . . .* In general *invidiam concitare* was a major project of populist oratory at Rome; cf. J.-M. David, "'Eloquentia popularis' et conduites symboliques des orateurs de la fin de la République: problèmes d'efficacité," *Quaderni di storia* 12 (1980), 181 and 187.—Repetition of the same word within a short interval (as here *incitata*) is unusual for Cicero; cf. Hofmann-Szantyr, 820–22 with literature; cf. also *ad* § 21 (*umquam*); but Goerenz's *concitata* for the second *incitata*, though worth considering, is not absolutely necessary.—*Servitium* is abstract for concrete (= *servus*), and the plural is generic; cf. *Cat.* 4.4: *servitia excitantur* and *OLD* s.v., 3b. Cicero adopts L. Cotta's analysis (§ 45: *. . . armis gesta servilibus*); sim. *Fam.* 1.9.13 (to Lentulus, December 54): *. . . qui meos civis et a me conservatos et me servare cupientis spoliatos ducibus servis armatis obici noluerim . . .*—H. Benner, 71 ff., esp. 76 (sim.

Tatum, 1999, 211–12, with literature at 296 n. 152; cf. François Favory, "Clodius et le péril servile: Fonction du thème dans le discours polémique cicéronien," *Index* 8 [1978–79], 185–87; T. Loposzko, "Clodio e gli schiavi," *Acta Classica Univ. scient. Debrecen*. 21 [1985], 43–72), makes it likely that the majority of Clodius' followers belonged, in fact, to the urban plebs (*tabernarii*, members of *collegia*, etc.: cf. *Dom.* 13; Lintott [1968], 77–83), including freedmen but not slaves (in spite of App. *BC* 2.83 and 505); Cicero's description of them or some of them here and at *Dom.* 5 and 54[76] as slaves belongs to optimate defamation and is not repeated before the general public.[77] The shared optimate sentiments of his interlocutors[78] make such rhetoric possible here, as in *Luc*. It is also the case that Cicero and Cato, more than Caesar, Pompey, and Crassus, were Clodius' rivals in the struggle for influence with the urban plebs (cf. Lintott, 1968, 194), so Marcus' position here may reflect a wish to regain influence with that constituency now that Clodius is dead: the plebs can distance themselves from the work of Clodius' followers, constructed as mere slaves.—Though Clodius used street violence as a political weapon (cf. *ad* § 11.3–5), the phrase *adiuncto terrore etiam militari* points further: at the time of Cicero's withdrawal, Caesar was lingering near the capital with a considerable body of troops, and Clodius indulged in wild threats; cf. *Har.* 47: . . . *nisi exercitum C. Caesaris . . . signis infestis in curiam se inmissurum minitaretur . . .* ; cf. *Sest* 39–40; Gelzer, 137–38; Strasburger, 18.

neque ⟨solum⟩ nobis cum illa tum peste certamen fuit, sed cum gravissimo reipublicae tempore, cui ⟨nisi⟩ cessissem, non diuturnum beneficii mei patria fructum tulisset.] *Illa pestis* refers to P. Clodius, never mentioned by name in *Leg.* but often excoriated *tacito nomine*; cf. 2.37 and 42–43 and § 26; he is addressed as *funesta reipublicae pestis* at *Dom.* 5; on Cicero's avoidance of names cf. *ad* 2.42 (*nihil enim attinet quemquam nominari*). The insertion of *tum* between *illa* and *pestis* makes it clear that Clodius is dead (cf. 2.43); for the use of an adverb as a quasi-attribute, perhaps in origin a Grecism, cf. Kühner-Stegmann, 1, 218–20.—*Tempus* = "the circumstances existing at a particular time, the occasion, the moment": *OLD* s.v., 10a; *gravissimum tempus* can be rendered as "crisis." For the *iunctura* with *cedo* cf. *Fam.* 4.9.2 (to M. Marcellus ca. August–September 46): *primum tempori cedere,*

---

76. *Cum in tribunali Aurelio conscribebas palam non modo liberos sed etiam servos* . . . ; sim. *Sest.* 34; *Pis.* 64.

77. At *Red. Pop.* 13 the same people are described simply as *homines*: . . . *cum homines in tribunali Aurelio palam conscribi centuriarique vidissem* . . . Taking Cicero's words at face value, Lintott, 1968, 77–78 and 193, assumes that Clodius' ranks included both slave and free.

78. On Atticus cf. *ad* § 26: *nec mehercule ego sane a Quinto nostro dissentio.*

id est necessitati parere, semper sapientis est habitum.—Following *cui* the transmission is faulty: *si* goes back to A[b], *si non* at least to Manutianus (1498), improved by Halm to *nisi* (for the distinction cf. Kühner-Stegmann, 2, 411). If *si* is adopted, the reference is to the crisis precipitated by Catiline's conspiracy;[79] but Marcus is discussing the events that precipitated his exile from the point of view of the rôle played by the tribunate (for the use of *cedo* of his avoidance of confrontation through exile cf. *Sest.* 53: . . . *cum* . . . *furori hominis cessissem* . . .). Here he chooses to emphasize[80] the larger struggle; perhaps he means that Clodius himself, though a tribune, could not have exerted so much power; it was a concatenation of unfavorable circumstances: a pair of useless consuls, the unwillingness of Cicero's friends, notably Pompey, to stick out their necks for him, etc.; he describes the pressures he was then under in detail at *Sest.* 42. The argument is specious since it was essentially Clodius who orchestrated the situation (cf. Tatum, 1999, 151–56), but it does serve Cicero's purpose of exculpating the tribunate (besides saving him from having to admit that the tribune outsmarted him).[81]—Cicero's *beneficium* was, of course, the preservation of the *respublica* under threat from Catiline; cf., e.g., *Sul.* 26: . . . *tantis a me beneficiis in republica positis* . . . Cicero presumably means that if he had not yielded to Clodius, the result would have been a bloodbath perhaps followed by the establishment of a tyranny (cf. the scenario sketched at *Sest.* 47 ff.); in that case the enjoyment of the *fructus* of Cicero's *beneficium*, i.e., the free republic, would have been brief, lasting only from 62 to 58; as it was, however, Cicero's withdrawal prepared the way for the revival of the *respublica.*—The personified *patria* is hedged about by Cicero's deed and its consequences in terms both of sense and word order. This affective term (as opposed to *respublica* or *civitas*) is used sparingly in *Leg.* (only here in Book 3); other occurrences: 1.5 and 43, 2.3, 5–6, 42–43.—The interpretation that Cicero went into exile not to save his own life but to avoid a fundamental alteration of the Roman constitution is first mooted at *Dom.* 91–92 (*ad servos medius fidius respublica venisset*), then taken up at *Sest.* 43–44 (*erat enim altera eius modi contentio ut neque victi neque victores rempublicam tenere possemus*).

atque haec rerum exitus indicavit. quis enim non modo liber, ⟨sed etiam⟩

---

79. It is so taken by Michael Grant, tr., Cicero, *On Government* (London, 1993), 206 n. 2.

80. ⟨*Solum*⟩ is Powell's supplement; there was no need for Cicero to deny altogether that he was engaged in a struggle with Clodius.

81. My interpretation of this passage in general has benefited from discussion with J.G.F. Powell.

servus libertate dignus fuit, cui nostra salus cara non esset?] Marcus points to *rerum exitus* as a confirmation for his diagnosis of the recent troubles of the Tullii, namely the universal desire for his own *salus* (cf. 2.42); this would tend to show that not *plebes incitata* or *invidia* but darker forces were at work.—This is a variation of the theme sounded at *Sul.* 29: . . . *omnes boni omnium generum atque ordinum suam salutem cum mea coniungunt* . . .—By establishing the subjective category *servus libertate dignus* Cicero can construct the sentiments of the type as he will.—*Sed etiam* is P's (necessary) insertion.

26a Here Marcus goes on to consider an alternative scenario under which there *was* real disagreement in the citizen body about the policies of his consulate (not merely *servitia incitata* and threats of military force), with the consequence that his exile is permanent and he has to resort to the consolation afforded by previous cases of *clarissimi viri* who suffered a similar fate. He then turns to Quintus' final point (§ 22 *fin.*), Pompey's restoration of the tribunate, and comes to a different conclusion, approving Pompey's recognition of *quid necessarium*.

quodsi is casus fuisset rerum quas pro salute reipublicae gessimus ut non omnibus gratus esset, et si nos multitudinis furentis inflammata invidia pepulisset, . . .] *Casus* appears here in the sense "issue, outcome, fortune" (cf. *OLD* s.v., 6, where our passage is cited).—*Invidia* is personified for emphasis. In § 24 Marcus listed as a benefit of the tribunate that it freed the upper class (*summus ordo*) of *invidia;* in line with that, in § 25 he had denied that the envy of the plebs had precipitated his exile (*non enim plebes incitata nostris rebus invidit*). But now he accepts at least *ex hypothesi* that the *inflammata invidia multitudinis furentis* may have done (albeit he claims that the *multitudo* consisted mostly of slaves; see above); for Clodius' tactic of playing upon the *invidia Ciceronis* cf. Tatum, 1999, 79–80 and 151–55. The plundering of his house on the Palatine by the Clodiani (on which cf. *Sest.* 54; Gelzer, 139; H. Benner, 116–17) certainly suggests *invidia* as a factor. If in our passage *invidia* is exclusively or potentially directed by the lower at the upper classes, Cicero sometimes described his exile as due to the *invidia* of *nobiles;* cf. Achard, 87 and 416; A.J. Christopherson, "*Invidia Ciceronis:* Some Political Circumstances Involving Cicero's Exile and Return," in *Studia Pompeiana et Classica in Honor of Wilhelmina F. Jashemski*, 2 (New Rochelle, N.Y., 1989), 33–57, esp. 39 and 41.

. . . tribuniciaque vis in me populum, sicut Gracchus in Laenatem, Saturninus in Metellum incitasset, . . .] Cicero's refusal to mention Clodius by name is conspicuous here, where a proper name would be expected in parallel with Gracchus and Saturninus; cf. *ad ad* 2.42 (*nihil enim attinet quemquam nominari*); instead he paraphrases as *tribunicia vis;*[82] for Clodius' use of violence cf. *ad* § 11.3–5.—Though as consul in 132 P. Popillius Laenas may have helped with the settlement of the *ager publicus* in accord with the Gracchan law,[83] he also set up special courts to try and convict Ti. Gracchus' followers without any possibility of an appeal to the people. Hence in 123 C. Gracchus delivered speeches denouncing Popillius (*orat.* pp. 184–85) and carried a new law, the lex Sempronia *de capite civis Romani,* which included a clause making it retroactive to the events of 132. Popillius chose to forestall a judicial verdict through voluntary exile but returned in 121 after the death of C. Gracchus. Cf. Volkmann, *RE* 22.1 (1953), 63.9 ff. (= Popillius 28); Rotondi, 309–10; *MRR* 1, 497–98 and 513–14; Lintott, 1968, 163–64; Stockton, 1979, 90–91 and 118–21.—On the exile in 100 and recall in 99 of Q. Caecilius Metellus Numidicus (cos. 109) cf. *ad Off.* 3.79.—Cicero sets the exiles of Popillius and of Metellus in parallel with his own at *Red. Sen.* 37 and *Red. Pop.* 6.

. . . **ferremus, o Quinte frater; consolarenturque nos non tam philosophi qui Athenis fuerunt, qui hoc facere debe⟨ba⟩nt, quam clarissimi viri qui illa urbe pulsi carere ingrata civitate quam manere ⟨in⟩ improba maluerunt.**] This is the only instance of *Quinte frater* in *Leg.;* Quintus refers to Marcus simply as *frater;* cf. Pease *ad Div.* 2.150; Adams, 1978, 161–62; Shackleton Bailey, 1992, 95, and 1996, 61–62; Dickey, 2002, 123–24.—Athens provides two potential sources of consolation, its philosophers (cf., e.g., Cratippus' consolation of Pompey after Pharsalia [*ad Off.* 1.1]) and its exiled statesmen, of whom Cicero prefers the latter; Aristides, Themistocles, and Demosthenes were famous examples.—*Debebant* is Goerenz's correction for the transmitted *debent.* The sense is evidently not that philosophers ought to have done so but failed to but, rather, that they were under an obligation to; at *Fam.* 4.13.4 Cicero describes the task of consolation as deriving in part *ab exquisita quadam ratione et doctrina;*[84] *sunt . . . haec propria philosophorum* (*Div.* 2.10) would have been another way of expressing the same idea; on the *officia consolantium* see further *Tusc.* 3.75 ff. Underlying is Cicero's preference for acts of those engaged in the *vita activa* over the

---

82. Goerenz's certain correction of *tribunicia quis* (BAε).

83. If he was the one who set up an inscription claiming to be the first to make herdsmen yield to farmers of the public land and if it refers to his consulship, not his praetorship; for the alternative identification of T. Annius (pr. ca. 132) as author cf. Lintott, *CAH* 9, 73–74 and n. 48.

84. Cf. also the letter of consolation (presumably identical with the essay de *Virtute*) that Brutus addressed to Cicero from Asia (*Brut.* 11–12).

pronouncements of philosophers; cf. *Sen.* 12: *est in manibus laudatio* [sc. of Q. Fabius Maximus for the son who predeceased him], *quam cum legimus, quem philosophum non contemnimus?*—Sim. the words put in Milo's mouth at *Mil.* 93: *si mihi bona republica frui non licuerit, at carebo mala* . . . Our passage suggests that Cicero first thought of such consolation in connection with his own exile.

Pompeium vero quod una ista in re non ita valde probas, vix satis mihi illud videris attendere: non solum ei quid esset optimum videndum fuisse, sed etiam quid necessarium.] This refers back to Quintus' remarks in § 22 on Pompey's restoration of full powers to the tribunate in 70; see *ad loc.*— *Pompeium* is promoted ahead of the relative clause so as to announce clearly the next major topic; cf. *ad* § 9.6.—Here for the first time the *necessarium* becomes a factor in discussing legislation (cf. §§ 33 and 46); this is expected in discussing historical acts like the lex Pompeia Licinia on tribunician power,[85] but Marcus' own legislation on the tribunate is similar. So the justification of Pompey's procedure is in effect a justification of his own. The argument thus develops on two different planes: on the one side political "necessity," on the other side an ideal state not necessarily intended for those now alive (cf. *ad* § 29); cf. Lehmann, 10–11. The historical "necessity" presumably refers to the political compact underlying the *respublica* as delineated at § 25 *init.*

sensit enim deberi non posse huic civitati illam potestatem. quippe, quam tantopere populus noster ignotam expetisset, qui posset carere cognita?] Pompey evidently saw that the tribunate was needed as a means for ventilating public opinion; cf. Thommen, 1988, 369–70 (cited *ad* § 23); Kunkel-Wittmann, 651.—*Tantopere* refers discreetly to the *secessio plebis* (on which cf. *ad* § 19b).—The *a fortiori* argument features a chiastic arrangement of participles and verbs and a good clausula (type *omne debuit*).—For the instrumental *quī*, seen also in *nequīquam, quī fit?* etc., cf. Leumann, 472; Meiser § 75.5 and 113.6.

sapientis autem civis fuit causam nec perniciosam et ita popularem ut non posset obsisti, perniciose populari civi non relinquere.] Pompey is thus seen as a more recent counterpart of the statesmen praised at *Rep.* 2.54 (cited *ad* § 17). As these two passages illustrate, *popularis* is a neutral term, its particular coloring in Cicero depending on the context and the modifier; cf.

---

85. At *Clu.* 130 Cicero speaks of *ventus quidam popularis* in connection with censorial actions of 70, but the same applies to the legislation on the tribunate and the changed composition of the jury-courts; cf. Gelzer, *Pompeius*, 62–63. In our passage Cicero chooses to ignore the part that Pompey's own political ambitions played in his policy on the tribunate; cf. Yakobson, 1999, 233 n. 12.

Hellegouarc'h, 534–41; Robin Seager, "Cicero and the Word *popularis*," *CQ* 22 (1972), 328–38. Quintus, however, is hardly prepared to concede that the cause is not *perniciosa* (cf. § 19b); hence his dissent in the sequel. **26b** The debate on the tribunate of the plebs yields no consensus, Quintus and Atticus remaining unconvinced. The discussion of *N.D.* ends in a similar ἀπορία (3.94–95). This is Cicero's approach when the issues are difficult and contentious and several different positions plausible. The thesis of "Marcus" is tempered to this degree; cf. Heuss, 214; *aliter* Thommen, 1988, 375, who does not distinguish between "Marcus," the dialogue character, and Cicero, the author.

Scis solere, frater, in huiusmodi sermone, ut transiri alio possit, dici 'Admodum', aut 'Prorsus ita est'.] We are probably meant to imagine a pregnant pause, the silence finally filled by this remark. Marcus thus signals that, from his point of view, the topic is now exhausted. "This is without question the wittiest moment of the dialogue, and almost modern in its meta quality" (W. Jeffrey Tatum, *per litt.*).—These are typical formulas of assent, the Greek equivalents of which are often found in Plato's dialogues; cf. *OLD* s.v. *admodum* 6 and *prorsus* 2c.

Q. Haud equidem adsentior; tu tamen ad reliqua pergas velim.] Quintus remains obdurate, though he will not block the further course of the conversation; cf. Atticus' acceptance, for the sake of argument, of Marcus' postulate at 1.21, with note.

A. Nec mehercule ego sane a Quinto nostro dissentio; sed ea quae restant audiamus.] Atticus thus places himself, along with his brother-in-law, firmly in the optimate camp; this picture of Atticus' political views accords with the evidence of the letters, where Cicero "writes throughout as one *bonus* to another, and at times finds it necessary to apologize for certain aberrations of his own" (Shackleton Bailey, *Att.* 1, p. 14). Cf. also § 37; Nep. *Att.* 6.1 (cited p. 23 n. 82 *supra*).

27 M. Deinceps igitur omnibus magistratibus auspicia et iudicia dantur: iudicia ut ⟨ea⟩ esset populi potestas ad quam provocaretur, . . .] In spite of the unresolved disagreement Marcus continues, with his interlocutors' assent, the commentary on his laws, the next in order being *omnes magistratus auspicium iudiciumque habento* (§ 10.1).—For *deinceps* marking the transition to the next law to be treated in the commentary cf. 2.40.—On the magistrates' possession of *auspicia* cf. *ad* § 10.1.—Prior to *esset* B (?A¹) has *aut* (AˣPF²εL have *ut*), changed by Ziegler to ⟨it⟩a ut, but this destroys the parallelism to the following purpose clause (cf. du Mesnil *ad loc.*; Cancelli, 241; Lintott, 1972, 258, and 1999, 227 n. 53; Kunkel, 20 n. 43). Lintott, 1972, 258–59, interprets the transmitted text as follows: "The magistrates cannot be given *iudicia, in order that* another body may have power. The *potestas* must be the magistrates' and *populi* will be an objective, rather than subjective, genitive. Thus *populi potestas* should mean power over (opportunity to use) the people, i.e. power to summon a (judicial) assembly." *Potestas* is used, however, with the objective genitive of things, not of persons (cf. *TLL* s.v., 303.82 ff., citing *inter alia Rep.* 3.17: *... qui in populum vitae necisque potestatem habent ...*). Surely du Mesnil was right in supposing that the thought should be "damit seine *potestas* [sc. die des Volkes] von der Art wäre, dass sie erst auf Appellation einträte ...," which can be restored by his addition of *ea* before *esset.*—Evidently, Cicero has the will of the lawgiver in mind when he has imperfect subjunctives follow *dantur;* cf. Kühner-Stegmann, 2, 186.—Lintott, 1999, 227, suggests that our text is a Ciceronian innovation "whereby any magistrate can refer appeals to the assembly for decision, if he so wishes. He might have argued that this was a useful short-cut, but it also had the effect of making an inroad into the traditional competence of the tribune."

... auspicia ut multos inutiles comitiatus probabiles impedirent morae; saepe enim populi impetum iniustum auspiciis di immortales represserunt.] This sentence sets *inutiles comitiatus,* with five short syllables out of nine, in opposition to *probabiles morae,* whereby the stately double cretic clausula seems to mirror the slowing down. If § 29 suggests that Cicero is legislating for citizens of ideal character, this passage and §§ 42–43 show him envisioning the same problems of demagoguery and rashness that beset the legislative process of his day. Linderski, 1995, 477, remarks on the oddity that "one would expect that the magistrates are given the auspices in order to be able to perform their actions *auspicato,* with the approval of the gods. But in Cicero's state the magistrates have the auspices primarily in order to impede *inutiles comitiatus*"; surely Cicero had in mind the former purpose even though in justifying his measure to his optimate interlocutors he speaks only of the latter.—*Inutiles* from the point of view of the citizen body as a whole or merely the *principes?* Cicero fails to distinguish, as often.—Here *probabilis* means "worthy of approval, commendable, acceptable" (cf. *OLD* s.v., 1a), *impetus* "a violent mental impulse, urge" (ibid., s.v., 5a).—With the "pious" explanation of our passage (*di immortales represserunt*) contrast the utilitarian one offered by "Marcus" at *Div.* 2.70: *retinetur autem et ad opinionem vulgi et ad magnas utilitates reipublicae mos, religio, disciplina, ius augurium, collegii auctoritas;* cf. also (of *auspicium*) ibid. 2.74: *quod quidem institutum reipublicae causa est, ut comitiorum vel in iudiciis populi vel in iure legum vel in creandis magistratibus principes civitatis essent interpretes;* cf. Linderski, 1986, 2205 and n. 218; de Libero, 56–64 (including, at

56–57 n. 21, a list of the attested instances of *servatio de caelo* and *obnuntiatio* between 100 and 44); 3.10.1. In general, Cicero's religiosity has proved difficult to categorize because he speaks with different voices in different contexts; cf. Latte, 1960, 285–86; Goar, 108–11.

Ex eis autem qui magistratum ceperunt quod senatus efficitur, populare ⟨est⟩ sane neminem in summum locum nisi per populum venire, sublata co-optatione censoria.] *Quod* = "in regard to the fact that." Cicero now passes to the next clause *exque eis senatus esto* (§ 10.2). As in his defense of the tribunate at §§ 23–26a, he finds himself defending before two optimates a measure that could be called *populare;* hence the apologetic *sane* and the following admission that this is a *vitium.*—*Populare ⟨est⟩* is Turnebus' correction for the transmitted *popularem,* concessive *sane* (= "I admit": Reid) often adhering to a form of *sum* (cf. *ad* 1.1).—Marcus speaks of doing away with censorial adlection to the senate (not to be confused with the *lectio senatus,* which continued) as if this were a change in current practice (*sublata cooptatione censoria*). The traditional view is that this feature was eliminated by Sulla (in making the quaestorship prerequisite to a senate seat) and not revived until Augustus; cf. Mommsen, *Staatsr.* 1, 561; 2, 423 and 939–40; 3, 466. But the text cited in support, Tac. *An.* 11.22, does not say that censorial adlection was eliminated by Sulla, only that he added ex-quaestors to the senate (§ 6: *post lege Sullae viginti creati* [sc. *quaestores*] *supplendo senatui . . .*), and Cicero's language in our passage suggests that the power to do so still remained; cf. Kunkel-Wittmann, 442–43. The absence of reference to post-Sullan censorial adlection in our sources may be due to the fact that the problem was now excessive numbers (cf. Tatum, 1999, 134); hence in practice disputes were about expulsions.—Lintott, 1999, 230, explains this "popular" feature as "a form of balancing against the primacy in policy-making which Cicero assigns to the senate"; cf. *ad* § 10.3 and the note after next.

27–28a sed praesto est huius viti temperatio, quod senatus lege nostra confirmatur auctoritas; sequitur enim 'eius decreta rata sunto'.] For *temperatio* as the balance sought in the ideal state cf. *ad* § 12 (*quam maxime probat temperationem reipublicae*). As in the case of the tribunate, a concession to the plebs is argued to be justified as strengthening the *auctoritas principum* (cf. § 25).—*Senatus* is emphasized by its separation from the limited word *auctoritas.*—*Eius decreta rata sunto* = § 10.3.

28a nam ita se res habet ut si senatus dominus sit publici consili, quodque is creverit defendant omnes, et si ordines reliqui principis ordinis consilio rempublicam gubernari velint, . . .] Cf. *ad* § 10.3.—For *cerno* = "decerno" cf. *ad* 2.21.10.—*Princeps ordo* is a *variatio* for *summus ordo* (§ 24).—

Guberno is so often used at this period of the government of the state that the nautical metaphor seems hardly to be felt (hence the absence of *quasi*); cf. *TLL* s.v., 2351.73 ff. For the thought cf. *Dom.* 130, contrasting the time of C. Cassius' censorship (154) with Clodius' tribunate: *tempus illud erat tranquillum et in libertate populi et gubernatione positum senatus, tuum porro tempus libertate populi Romani oppressa, senatus auctoritate deleta.*

... *possit ex temperatione iuris, cum potestas in populo, auctoritas in senatu sit, teneri ille moderatus et concors civitatis status,* ...] For *temperatio* as an ideal cf. *ad* § 17; the content of *temperatio iuris* is defined by the following *cum*-clause.—So far Cicero has taken measures to insure the *auctoritas* of the senate, including the granting of *praeclara instituta,* above all the tribunate, to insure that the people will yield to that *auctoritas* (§ 25), as well as the law *eius* [sc. of the senate] *decreta rata sunto.* But nevertheless the people have the *potestas;* cf. *Har.* 11: *populus Romanus, cuius est summa potestas omnium rerum* ... , with other texts cited by Laser, ch. 2.2. Keyes, 1921, 321, à propos the law on voting, explains the power relations this way: "Absolute power is given to the People, but as many opportunities as possible are provided for the play of senatorial influence upon this all-powerful democracy ... Only aristocracy can govern the state wisely, but it cannot govern the state at all, except with the full approval of the People. This approval is in general to be gained by persuasion; but when this is found impossible, by trickery based on popular superstition. But no attempt is made to *force* the will of the governing class upon the people"; cf. the first note *ad* § 24.—*Moderatus* is expected as a synonym for *temperatus;* nor, in light of Cicero's catchphrase *concordia ordinum* (cf. p. 18 n. 74 *supra*), is it surprising to see *concors* as an epithet for the type of constitution he seeks; cf. *Rep.* 1.49: *concordi populo* ... *nihil est immutabilius;* for *concordia* as an optimate slogan cf. in general Burckhardt, 70 ff.

... *praesertim si proximae legi parebitur; nam proximum est 'Is ordo vitio careto, ceteris specimen esto'.*] The stability of the proposed state thus hinges on the moral probity of the senatorial class—a deep conviction of Cicero throughout his career.

28b–29 Quintus' wish for a censor to interpret what constitutes a *vitium* (*Praeclara—censorem quaerit interpretem*) has already been catered for (§ 7.3). Atticus escalates the criticism in claiming that no censors or judges could be adequate to the task. This critique of the senators, politely phrased so as not to offend Marcus and Quintus, goes to the heart of the problem. Marcus deflects the point by claiming that his legislation is not *de hominibus qui nunc sunt, sed de futuris.* But this argument seems to be invoked ad hoc; elsewhere Cicero does not make any assumptions about the character of the citizens living under his laws; indeed, their often hortatory nature (*Iusta imperia sunto* [§ 6.1] and the like) seems to take existing human character as its premise.

29 A. Ille vero, etsi tuus est totus ordo gratissimamque memoriam retinet consulatus tui . . .] Cf. *Att.* 1.19.4 (15 March 60): *is enim est noster exercitus, hominum, ut tute scis, locupletium.* The cultivation of the memory of his exploits by the senate was the cause of his recall from exile, as depicted at *Red. Pop.* 10: *nec rerum gestarum memoria in reditu C. Mari sed exercitus atque arma valuerunt; at de me ut valeret semper senatus flagitavit, ut aliquando proficeret, cum primum licuit, frequentia atque auctoritate perfecit;* for the *memoria* of Cicero as a factor during his exile cf. also *Har.* 48: *idem* [sc. Clodius] *postea quam . . . reviviscere memoriam ac desiderium mei vidit . . .* At § 37 Atticus makes clear why the memory of Cicero's consulate was so pleasing to that group (. . . *rempublicam . . . , quam hic consul constituerat, quae sit in potestate optimorum*). Besides the foiling of Catiline's conspiracy, he will have in mind the blocking of Servilius Rullus' *rogatio agraria,* the frustration of the prosecution of C. Rabirius, and the clearing of the way for Lucullus' triumph; cf. Gelzer, ch. 7; Mitchell, 1979, ch. 4.

. . . pace tua dixerim, non modo censores sed etiam iudices omnes potest defatigare.] A politely phrased but accurate and damning judgment, which Marcus cannot evade except by taking refuge in the hypothesis of presumably better "future" men as the addressees of his legislation; see Haury, 163, and the next note.

M. Omitte ista, Attice: non enim de hoc senatu nec his de hominibus qui nunc sunt, sed de futuris, si qui forte his legibus parere voluerint, haec habetur oratio.] A rather sharp rejoinder such as Marcus elsewhere reserves for Quintus (cf. *ad* §§ 17 and 33). He implicitly admits, however, that the present-day senate does not measure up to the moral standards he has in view; similar the criticism of current senators, but not of the senate as an institution, in Sallustian *contiones;* cf. Morstein-Marx, ch. 5 *sub fin.*—A similar point about the general application of the laws was already made at 1.57 and 2.35, and Quintus repeats it at § 37; nevertheless, Cicero does not stick consistently to this approach; cf. *ad* § 26 (*Pompeium vero quod una ista in re . . .*) and the provision of auspices at § 27, which is clearly predicated upon an imperfect citizen body (see *ad loc.*). For *si qui forte his legibus parere voluerint* cf. § 19: *si parebunt his legibus.* The Platonic Socrates similarly asserted the possibility of the implementation of his laws in some remote place or in the future (*Rp.* 499c–d). Keyes, 1921, 323, apparently has our passage in mind when he remarks that Cicero "goes so far as to recognize frankly that his ideal constitution would have no chance for practical success in his own day." Similarly, Heuss, 203 (cf. 259), and Lehmann, 10, speak of irony here. Girardet, 1983, 167 and n. 18, remarks à propos this passage that it presupposes the implementation ("Inkraftesetzung") of the laws and expresses doubt only on the score of future obedience to them; but "to be willing to obey (*parere velle*) the laws" is another way of saying "to be willing to put them into effect."

nam cum omni vitio carere lex iubeat,—id autem difficile factu est nisi educatione quadam et disciplina, de qua dicemus aliquid fortasse, si quid fuerit loci aut temporis.] The discussion of *disciplina*, with Atticus' encouragement, follows immediately under the heading *ceteris specimen esto;* there is some discussion of the knowledge needed by senators under *causas populi teneto* (§ 41). Marcus speaks here, however, as if education will form part of the present discussion (and in the sequel Atticus clears away the one supposed obstacle); and indeed the topic is expected per se, since, given the conservatism of Cicero's constitution, the major possibility for improvement lies in education; cf. Sprute, 170. It is thus commonly assumed that Cicero planned a more extensive discussion of the topic in *Leg.*[86] Given that Cicero was evidently composing *Rep.* and *Leg.* in tandem, P.L. Schmidt now suspects (in oral communication) that this reference may have become redundant after education was treated in *Rep.* 4; if so, Cicero would have deleted the reference to education here in final revision.

30a A. Locus certe non deerit, quoniam tenes ordinem legum; tempus vero largitur longitudo diei.] Atticus responds in turn to each of the factors raised by Marcus as possible impediments to such a discussion (*locus, tempus*): the *ordo legum*, to which Cicero is adhering in this commentary, will provide scope for such a discussion (see the previous note); for the setting in summer (*longitudo diei*) cf. *ad* 2.3 and the fragment from Book 5.

30b–32 *Cupiditas*, the underlying verb *cupio*, and *libido* form the theme of this homily, as they have of Cicero's criticisms of the upper class since his early speeches defending Roscius of Ameria and prosecuting C. Verres: not only are such tendencies bad per se, but they infect the whole citizen body; cf. *Rep.* 2.47 and 59, where the *vitium* or *libido* of a single man is made responsible for changes in the state or its institutions; *Off.* 1.140. This material continues and gives specific point to the attack on egotistical self-aggrandizement at 1.40 ff.

30b M. Tu vero et istum, Attice, et si quem alium prae⟨teriero. . . . 'ce⟩teris specimen esto': quod si tenemus, omnia ⟨tenemus⟩.] *Praeteriero. ceteris* is

---

86. Cf. Schmidt, 1959, 31, who thinks that Cicero may have devoted a part of a lost book to the subject; Lehmann, 6–7 n. 20.

Lambinus' correction for *praeteris* BAεL, *ceteris* F, *preterii* P. In addition, Powell posits a lacuna; indeed, elsewhere Cicero tends to preface some introductory matter to the quotation of the text of the given law (see, e.g, § 40; *ad* 2.23–45). The rhythm of ⟨*tenemus*⟩ *omnia* (Bake) is poor;[87] hence Powell's *omnia tenemus*, effecting a clausula of the *debuerat omne* type.

ut enim cupiditatibus principum et vitiis infici solet tota civitas, sic emendari et corrigi continentia.] For *continentia* cf. *Inv.* 2.164: *temperantia est rationis in libidinem atque in alios non rectos impetus animi firma et moderata dominatio. eius partes continentia, clementia, modestia.*—In this chiastically organized sentence the two nouns and one infinitive of the prior clause balance the two infinitives and one noun of the latter, with a fine clausula of the *omne debebitur* type.

vir magnus et nobis omnibus amicus L. Lucullus—non vides, Luculle, a te id ipsum natum, ut illi cuperent quibus id, si tu non faceres, non liceret?] L. Licinius Lucullus (cos. 74) was dead by 56 (*Prov.* 22) and hence available to be used as an example and even apostrophized in diatribe-style without offense being taken; cf. the diatribe against the dead Crassus at *Parad.* 42 ff. On Lucullus, this anecdote, and the underlying point about luxury cf. *ad Off.* 1.140.

. . . concedi sibi oportere quod eis qui inferioris ordinis essent liceret.] A cool response displaying the class-consciousness of the born noble. With *inferior ordo* cf. the terms *summus ordo* (§ 24) and *princeps ordo* (§ 27).

31 quis non frangeret eorum libidines, nisi illi ipsi qui eas frangere deberent, cupiditatibus eisdem tenerentur?] A rhetorical question in the form of an unreal condition: such *cupiditates* would be a prime target per se (*quis non frangeret . . . ?*), but they remain untouched because they have infected the entire political class. As counter-examples one thinks of Cicero's own prosecution of Verres or his (mostly private) complaints about the *piscinarii* (*Att.* 1.18.6; 1.19.6; 1.20.3; 2.1.7; 2.9.1; *Parad.* 38).

nam licet videre, si velis replicare memoriam temporum: qualescumque summi civitatis viri fuerint, talem civitatem fuisse; . . .] *Replico* is a metaphor from the unrolling of a book; cf. *OLD* s.v., 2a (where our passage is cited); *memoria temporum* can be rendered simply as "history": cf. *OLD* s.v. *memoria* 7 and s.v. *tempus* 12.—A similar premise underlies the somber meditation on the decline of the *respublica* at *Rep.* 5.1, which takes its starting point in the Ennian verse: *moribus antiquis res stat Romana virisque* (*Ann.* 156 Sk.) and includes the point: *itaque ante nostram memoriam et mos ipse patrius praestantes viros adhibebat, et veterem morem ac*

---

87. Sim. *quod si* ⟨*est*⟩, *tenemus omnia* R. Stephanus.

maiorum instituta retinebant excellentes viri. The idea is attributed to Plato at *Fam.* 1.9.12 (to Lentulus, December 54): *erant praeterea haec animadvertenda in civitate quae sunt apud Platonem nostrum scripta divinitus: quales in republica principes essent, tales reliquos solere esse cives.* Boyancé, 1970, 250–51 (followed by Rawson, 1991, 144), supposed the reference to be to *Lg.* 711b; but *Rp.* 421a is closer to the thought: ἀλλὰ τῶν μὲν ἄλλων ἐλάττων λόγος· νευρορράφοι γὰρ φαῦλοι γενόμενοι καὶ διαφθαρέντες καὶ προσποιησάμενοι εἶναι μὴ ὄντες πόλει οὐδὲν δεινόν· φύλακες δὲ νόμων τε καὶ πόλεως μὴ ὄντες ἀλλὰ δοκοῦντες ὁρᾷς δὴ ὅτι πᾶσιν ἄρδην πόλιν ἀπολλύασιν, καὶ αὖ τοῦ εὖ οἰκεῖν καὶ εὐδαιμονεῖν μόνοι τὸν καιρὸν ἔχουσιν. In our passage, however, the following criticism of Plato is surprising if this point comes from him; the pithy formulation suggests that the source is rather Xen. *Cyr.* 8.8.5: ὁποῖοί τινες γὰρ ἂν οἱ προστάται ὦσι, τοιοῦτοι καὶ οἱ ὑπ' αὐτοὺς ὡς ἐπὶ τὸ πολὺ γίγνονται; cf. Mehl, 53.

32 idque haud paulo est verius quam quod Platoni nostro placet, qui musicorum cantibus ait mutatis mutari civitatum status; . . .] Cf. *ad* 2.38 (*negat enim mutari posse musicas leges—*).

ego autem nobilium vita victuque mutato mores mutari civitatum puto; . . .] The *iunctura vita victusque* is fairly common in the sense "way of life," either word alone being ambiguous; cf. Lucr. 5.804 and 1080; *Fam.* 7.23.4 and 9.24.3; Nep. *Alc.* 1.3.

atque haec lex, dilatata in ordinem cunctum, coangustari etiam potest.] This is the earliest attestation of *coangusto;* here it has the sense "to narrow the scope or application of" (*OLD* s.v., 3; cf. *TLL* s.v.).

pauci enim atque admodum pauci, honore et gloria amplificati, vel corrumpere mores civitatis vel corrigere possunt.] The ponderously emphatic *atque admodum* is attested elsewhere in classical Latin only in Stratippocles' pompous speech at Pl. *Epid.* 104–5: *rem tibi sum elocutus omnem, Chaeribule, atque admodum / meorum maerorum atque amorum summam edictavi tibi.*[88] For corrective repetition cf. Wills, 68 ff.; E. Wölfflin, *Die Gemination im Lateinischen*, SBAW, philos.-philol. Cl., 1882, no. 3 (Munich, 1882), 476–77. For the thought cf. *ad* §§ 30b–32.

sed haec et nunc satis, et in illis libris tractata sunt diligentius; . . .] The theme of leadership was variously broached in *Rep.*; cf. 2.69 and 5.1, as well as the fragments of Books 5 and 6 pertaining to the *rector reipublicae.* For *nunc* = "for present purposes" cf. *ad* 1.2.

33–39 On the method of voting, as previously on the tribunate, Marcus must defend his proposal against strenuous criticism voiced from an opti-

---

88. Based on a search of PHI 5.3.

mate angle by Quintus. Voting had traditionally been oral and thus open to observation. In the second century a new style of politics developed based upon the personal appeal of the candidates and their ability to sway emotions in a speech. This trend threatened to sever the traditional links between the plebs and their upper-class patrons that had determined electoral outcomes. To counter this tendency, candidates increased the scale of bribery, and this in turn sparked legal curbs enacted in 181 and 159; cf. A.E. Astin, *CAH* 8, 178 and 193; Rotondi, 277 and 288. The pressure for ballot laws arose when the laws against *ambitus* were perceived to have been ineffective (cf. *ad* § 39). Change was effected by a series of ballot laws beginning ca. 139, which made balloting secret and in writing; cf. *ad* §§ 35–36a. The paradoxical result, however, was not to reduce but to increase the amount of bribery in play.

In fact, gift-giving was firmly rooted in the sociopolitical culture of Republican Rome, and the line separating gift-giving from electoral bribery (*ambitus*) often obscure; cf. Andrew Lintott, "Electoral Bribery in the Roman Republic," *JRS* 80 (1990), 1–16, esp. 10–11 (on Cicero's evidence); Gruen, 1991, 255–57; Luciano Perelli, *La corruzione politica nell'antica Roma* (Milan, 1994); Riggsby, 21–49. Cicero recognizes that elections are characteristic of a free people (cf. *Planc.* 11 and 14), but he wants to allow maximum influence of the wealthy upon the electoral process (cf. Keyes, cited *ad* § 28a). Hence his desire in our passage to turn back the clock to a degree; for the underlying principle cf. 2.30: *consilio et auctoritate optimatium semper populum indigere,* with note. But Marcus' proposed compromise, whereby the ballots should be written but not secret, is a "curious suggestion," as Taylor, 1966, 35, remarks, and one likely to please neither the optimates, who wanted to go back to the old system of oral voting, nor the plebs, who regarded the voting tablets as a guarantee of liberty (*quasi vindex libertatis:* § 39). The evidence consists of coins of descendants honoring the sponsors of various voting laws (cf. *ad* §§ 35–36), that seek to exploit their popularity. These include *RRC* 226/1, possibly 386, 428/2, and 437 and are dated between 126 and 51. One depicts Libertas (labeled: 428/2), another a female figure, usually interpreted as Libertas, on a quadriga carrying a *pilleus* and on the obverse a voting urn behind a head of Roma (266/1); cf. Taylor, 1966, 35–37. In spite of the rhetoric in which they were cloaked, "reforms of procedure, including the introduction of the *tabella,* probably did nothing to widen 'democratic' participation in public life, and were of limited effect in securing political change or increasing the 'libertas' of those who did participate" (Hall, 1998, 30); the appeal may have been the enhancement in dignity of the ordinary voter, though Marcus does not make that point. Quintus' objection seems to be based on the assumption that voting on a matter of public concern ought to be available to public scrutiny. As Robert Morstein-Marx points out (*per litt.*), "this view is not so silly as it often strikes us today—at least historically it has to be taken seriously. In effect, you should have to take responsibility for your vote, stand up and be counted among your peers; if you are afraid to do that, you must be up to something disreputable." The assumption that underlies our passage is that the laws were effective in concealing the contents of votes, but even this has been doubted; cf. Robert Morstein-Marx, review of Yakobson, 1999, *SCI* 19 (2000), 231.

What is odd is the amount of space devoted to what turns out to be, in fact, a pseudodebate with no serious disagreement (cf. Keyes, 1921, 322; *ad* § 34), especially in light of the brief discussion of the innovations in the censorship (§§ 46–47); however, even more space was given to the debate on the tribunate (§§ 16–17, 19b–26), where Marcus was essentially defending the status quo. These facts suggest that Cicero's primary goal is to make the views of the extreme optimates explicit and present his own positions in contrast to them; that no agreement is reached serves, as in the case of the tribunate, to emphasize the difficulty and contentiousness of the issue.

C. Nicolet, "Cicéron, Platon et le vote secret," *Historia* 19 (1970), 53 ff. and (on Plato) 58 ff., has argued that Cicero is influenced by Greek parallels here, esp. the complicated voting procedures for the νομοφύλακες at Pl. *Lg.* 753c–d; but Cicero is likely rather to be thinking of Roman conditions and trying to find a middle ground between the optimates and plebs on this issue; cf. Rawson, 1991, 143–44; Heuss, 256 n. 91a; Lehmann, 47. On voting procedures in general cf. Mommsen, *Staatsr.* 3, 403–5; Ursula Hall, "Voting Procedure in Roman Assemblies," *Historia* 13 (1964), 267–306, as well as Hall, 1990 and 1998; Taylor, *loc. cit.*, 34 ff.; Nicolet, 1980, 267 ff.; Yakobson, 1995 and 1999, 126–33.

33 Proximum autem est de{in} suffragiis, quae iubeo nota esse optimatibus, populo libera.] An allusion to the law formulated in full at § 10.6: *Creatio magistratuum, iudicia populi, iussa vetita cum suffragio consciscentur, optimatibus nota, plebi libera sunto.*—Transmitted *dein,* sometimes written as two words, has surely resulted from a double reading in the archetype *de* and *in,* of which the latter perhaps arose under the influence of *in illis libris* just above (the correction was effected by P and F²). For other possible examples see the Index of Topics s.v. "Archetype."

A. Ita mehercule attendi, nec satis intellexi quid sibi lex aut quid verba ista vellent.] Atticus' puzzlement is understandable. At 1.63 he plays a similar rôle in seeking elucidation of Marcus' meaning.

M. Dicam, Tite, et versabor in re difficili ac multum et saepe quaesita: . . .] Was the matter really so often investigated? As in the case of 1.4 (*multa quaeruntur in Mario fictane an vera sint*), doubts are possible. The common view is that the voting laws of the late second century "gained approbation and acceptance" or generated "little excitement."[89] The other evidence is slight, but Cicero's discussions suggest that the issue was still contentious and a subject of debate, or at least optimate grumbling, in the 50s; cf. *Sest.* 103: *tabellaria lex ab L. Cassio ferebatur: populus libertatem agi putabat suam; dissentiebant principes et in salute optimatium temeritatem multitudinis et tabellae licentiam pertimescebant*; *Planc.* 16: . . . *si populo grata est tabella, quae frontis aperit hominum, mentis tegit datque eam libertatem ut quod velint faciant, promittant autem quod rogentur* . . . ; Yakobson, 1995, 427–28.

suffragia in magistratu mandando ac de reo iudicando ⟨at⟩que in legum rogatione clam an palam ferri melius esset.] As often, *mando* appears in the sense "publice . . . munus, officium deferre"; cf. *TLL* s.v., 263.8 ff.—We adopt Madvig's ⟨*at*⟩*que in legum rogatione* for *qui in lege aut rogatione;* this provides a minimally invasive restoration of the three types of voting.

Q. An etiam id dubium est? vereor ne a te rursus dissentiam.] *Etiam id =* "this also," i.e., in addition to the desirability of severely limiting the powers of the tribunate, the subject of the brothers' disagreement at §§ 16–17 and 19b–26.

M. Non facies, Quinte; nam ego in ista sum sententia qua te fuisse semper scio, nihil ut fuerit in suffragiis voce melius. sed obtineri an possit, videndum est.] As in 1.21, Marcus is already familiar with his brother's views. The vocative *Quinte,* especially in conjunction with *non facies,* seems curt, far from the ingratiating *optime et dulcissime frater* of § 25 and more distant than the plain *frater* of § 26. In fact, Marcus' optimism is unwarranted, and agreement on this issue proves to be as elusive as on the tribunate.—For the appeal to feasibility see *ad* § 26 (*necessarium*).

34 Q. Atqui frater, bona tua venia dixerim, ista sententia maxime et fallit imperitos et obest saepissime reipublicae, cum aliquid verum et rectum esse dicitur, sed obtineri, id est obsisti posse populo, negatur.] The opening sentence of Quintus' reply has suffered a good deal in transmission. Feldhügel's *atqui* is surely needed for *quia* of the archetype; and prior to *obest* P's *et* is generally substituted for the otherwise transmitted *sed,* as well as Minutianus' *obtineri* for *-ere* (for the confusion of active and passive infini-

---

89. Gruen, 1991, 259; and W.V. Harris, *Ancient Literacy* (Cambridge, Mass., 1989), 169 n. 102, respectively.

tive endings cf. *ad* 2.27a).—For *imperitus* cf. *ad* 1.4.—*Posse* is doing double duty here, construed both with *obtineri* and *obsisti;* supply *dicitur* out of *negatur* as a complement to *id est obsisti posse.*—Quintus could have added that Marcus himself has just insisted that his laws are not necessarily for human beings as they now exist (§ 29), so there is a problem of consistency of premise; cf. the introduction to this Book. He thus acknowledges that his proposal to turn back the clock to oral voting is unrealistic; for the people had come to regard the right to vote as an essential component of their *libertas,* and Cicero himself, in opposing Rullus' agrarian law, played upon their fear of its being abridged (*Agr.* 2.16b–19; cf. Laser, 155–56).

primum enim obsistitur cum agitur severe; deinde vi opprimi in bona causa est melius quam malae cedere.] Marcus seems to have been striving for a "painless" reform of the state; Quintus' prior clause rebukes the idea that such a thing is possible: there will always be resistance to severe measures. His second clause reflects perhaps the redoubtable spirit of the historical Quintus, which very nearly cost him his life in one encounter with the Clodiani (cf. *ad* § 17). The contrast between the two brothers could not have been more sharply drawn; cf., however, *Sex. Rosc.* 10: *opprimi me onere officii malo quam id quod mihi cum fide semel impositum est . . . deponere.* Sallust prefers to frame the problem of victory or defeat differently: defeat is preferable if it occurs *bono more: sed bono vinci satius est quam malo more iniuriam vincere* (*Jug.* 42.3); in context this is an argument against the murder of the Gracchi, which Quintus' formulation could be used to support.

qui⟨s⟩ autem non sentit omnem auctoritatem optimatium tabellariam legem abstulisse?] As on the question of tribunician power, Quintus' concern is to maintain the position of the optimates; cf. § 17: *nam ista potestate* [sc. *tribunicia*] *nata gravitas optimatium cecidit, convaluitque vis multitudinis.* Lintott, 1968, 71, explains concretely how the oral ballot could be manipulated by the optimates: "Eminent senators used to act as *rogatores* and receive the votes at the elections of their relatives and others, no doubt, whose candidature they approved. There would thus have been ample opportunity for forcing a vote on an elector." But, in spite of Quintus' assertion, no sharp break is apparent in the consular *fasti* after 139; cf. Gruen, 1991, 259.—On the fluctuation of *qui* and *quis*[90] as the nominative singular interrogative pronoun in both adjectival and substantival usages in Cicero cf. Laughton, 73.

quam populus liber numquam desideravit, idem oppressus dominatu ac potentia principum flagitavit.] A curious statement, which would imply that

90. In our passage Lambinus' restoration.

prior to the first *lex tabellaria* (139) the Romans were "free," then around that time "oppressed." In fact, the oppression of the lower classes tended to decrease in the course of the Republic, but this view fits with a policy of tracing reform efforts to excesses of the upper class; similarly, Sallust excoriates the dominance of the "few" after the destruction of Carthage (*Cat.* 10–11; *Jug.* 41).—For *flagito* cf. *ad* 1.5.

itaque graviora iudicia de potentissimis hominibus exstant vocis quam tabellae.] *Itaque:* sc. because the people were freer in those days. This is an interesting observation that Marcus does not challenge (cf. § 39). Our evidence is insufficient to provide a control, but ten convictions of men of praetorian rank or higher are known from the period 149 to 107 (the year of the introduction of the secret ballot in trials for *perduellio*), *viz.* nos. 2, 12, 30, 45, 46, 52, 53, 55, 56, and 58 Alexander; the case of C. Papirius Carbo (no. 30), who committed suicide in the aftermath, was celebrated. If Quintus' claim is true, those "more severe judgments" may have resulted from a greater general severity of mores rather than the oral method of voting per se.

quamobrem suffragandi nimia libido in non bonis causis eripienda fuit potentibus, non latebra danda populo in qua, bonis ignorantibus quid quisque sentiret, tabella vitiosum occultaret suffragium.] Quintus thus voices what doubtless was the optimate position on voting laws in general, though it would not, of course, bear on Marcus' law, which explicitly allows the votes to be *nota optimatibus*. Cf. *ad* §§ 33–39. So the disagreement between the two brothers is really a pseudodebate; one misses a representative of the *popularis* position.—*Suffragandi nimia libido,* etc., can be taken in either of two ways: (1) "means should have been found to deprive powerful leaders of the people's undue eagerness to support them with their votes even in the case of bad measures": Keyes; cf. *OLD* s.v. *suffragor* 2; or (2) "the leaders should have been deprived of their excessive license in putting bad measures to the vote": Rudd; sim. Ziegler, Zetzel; *OLD* s.v., 1. Surely, however, Quintus sees the behavior of the powerful as the root of the problem (see above); theirs is the *libido* that should be curbed; this interpretation (2) also effects the better contrast to the following *non latebra danda populo . . .* For Quintus' general position on open voting cf. *ad* §§ 33–39.—For *latebra* cf. *Fam.* 3.12.1 (to App. Claudius Pulcher after his acquittal; cf. *ad* 2.32): *mirandum est . . . nullam ne in tabellae quidem latebra fuisse absconditam malevolentiam quae te impugnare auderet; Planc.* 16, quoted *ad* § 33.—Our lemma raises the question of what constitutes a *vitiosum suffragium*: is it a ballot cast contrary to a received bribe or one cast contrary to conscience and, in case of a trial, the juror's oath? In favoring open voting Quintus seems to assume the former.

itaque isti rationi neque lator quisquam est inventus nec auctor umquam bonus.] Lambinus' *rogationi* is often substituted for *rationi;* but the transmitted text is well defended by Vahlen with reference to *Att.* 1.19.4: *unam rationem non reiciebam, ut ager hac adventicia pecunia emeretur quae ex novis vectigalibus per quinquennium reciperetur,* a passage that suggests that *ratio* can mean something like "item of legislation, measure" ("proposal," tr. Shackleton Bailey); sim. the reference here to legislation on balloting.—*Bonus* is the operative term, emphatically placed; the following survey of legislation on the subject aims to demonstrate this point (note the connection with *enim*); in contrast to the usage at 1.41 ff., *bonus* is clearly being used here with reference to social class; cf. *ad* § 20 (. . . *quid iuris bonis viris Tiberi Gracchi tribunatus reliquit?*).

35–36a This is Quintus' potted history of ballot reform, in four stages, *viz.,* the laws of (1) A. Gabinius (139), (2) L. Cassius Longinus Ravilla (137), (3) C. Papirius Carbo (130), and (4) C. Coelius Caldus (107), successively providing secret ballot for election of officials, the people's courts (except *perduellio*), legislative assemblies, and *perduellio*; cf. Gruen, 1991, 258–59. Quintus does not carry his history down as far as the election of priests by seventeen tribes chosen by lot instituted in 104 by Cn. Domitius Ahenobarbus (cf. *MRR* 1, 559).

35 Sunt enim quattuor leges tabellariae, quarum prima de magistratibus mandandis. ea est Gabinia, lata ab homine ignoto et sordido.] It is interesting that the secret ballot was first introduced in elections, where it would have posed greater technical problems of administration than in legislative assemblies, where the vote takes the form of a simple yes or no; cf. Hall, 1998, 16. Though intended above all for the *comitia centuriata,* the law probably applied to the *comitia tributa* as well (ibid., 23; Yakobson, 1999, 132). Simultaneous voting did not, however, come into use until later (between 132 and 124); cf. Hall, *loc. cit.*—*Ea est Gabinia, lata ab homine ignoto et sordido:* the lex Gabinia is assigned to 139 because it is said to be two years earlier than that of L. Cassius, dated to 137 (*Brut.* 106; on the interval see the next note). To seek to discredit the sponsor (and hence the legislation itself) on the basis of family origin is vintage optimate rhetoric. But Gabinius may have been merely a cat's paw; substantial upper-class support was probably required in order for his legislation to have been passed at all. Cf. Lintott, *CAH* 9, 60: "We know nothing about the circumstances in which this bill was enacted. No doubt it was presented as a blow struck for the *libertas* of the people—which indeed it was—but it may also have been argued to be a blow against corruption, since those who bribed could no longer check who voted for them, and thus it would have been

acceptable to those who were afraid of demagogic canvassing, such as practiced by Q. Pompeius." Hall, *loc. cit.*, and, in more detail, 1990, also sees the
law as "largely supported by men of substance" but "aiming to challenge
aristocratic control of office"; *aliter* Yakobson, 1999, 132. One effect was
an increased use of coinage for self-advertisement by potential candidates;
cf. *RRC*, 728. Cf. also *ad* § 39 (*si n⟨on⟩ valuerint tamen leges*—); Münzer,
RE 7.1 (1910), 423.39 ff.; Rotondi, 297; *MRR* 1, 482.

**secuta biennio post Cassia est de populi iudiciis, a nobili homine lata Lucio
Cassio, sed (pace familiae dixerim) dissidente a bonis atque omnes rumusculos populari ratione aucupante.**] The relative dating is also given at *Amic.* 41:
*videtis in tabella iam ante quanta sit facta labes, primo Gabinia lege, biennio
autem post Cassia.*—In the case of L. Cassius Longinus Ravilla (cos. 127;
censor 125), Quintus cannot deny noble lineage, so he must criticize instead
the man's failure to hew to the optimate line. Our passage is a typical example
of a *color;* Cassius could have been more sympathetically presented, as at *Sex.
Rosc.* 84 (introducing Cassius' famous *cui bono?* test): *L. Cassius ille quem
populus Romanus verissimum et sapientissimum iudicem putabat . . .* At
Brut. 97 Cicero characterizes the speaking style and character of this atypical
*popularis: tum L. Cassius multum potuit non eloquentia, sed dicendo tamen;
homo non liberalitate, ut alii, sed ipsa tristitia et severitate popularis . . .* He
goes on to criticize Scipio Africanus for using his influence to remove a
tribunician obstacle to the passage of Cassius' voting bill, which applied to all
popular trials except *perduellio* (see the note after next). Cf. in general
Münzer, *RE* 3 (1899), 1742.11 ff. (Cassius no. 72); Rotondi, 297; *MRR* 1,
485; all the coins except one cited *ad* §§ 33–39 (*viz., RRC* 437/1a) commemo-
rate Cassius' voting bill.—Cicero is the only author the *OLD* cites for *ru-
musculus,* the diminutive of *rumor;* here as elsewhere the word implies the
speaker's contempt; for the *iunctura* cf. *Clu.* 105: . . . *illi quinque qui
imperitorum hominum rumusculos aucupati tum illum absolverunt . . . ; Pis.*
57: . . . *levitatis est inanem aucupari rumorem et omnes umbras etiam falsae
gloriae consectari . . . ;* cf. Hanssen, 113.—*Populari ratione* = "by means of
a popular policy" or the like; cf. *OLD* s.v. *ratio* 11c.—The use of the two
participles (*dissidente . . . aucupante*) to characterize Cassius, the latter governing an object, adumbrates the freer use of the present participle, including
its verbal properties, in the orator's late style, on which cf. Laughton, 45; the
description ibid., 156, of the function of participles in the speeches also fits
our passage: ". . . where there is a concentration of fact or thought which
requires brief or forceful expression."

**Carbonis est tertia de iubendis legibus ac vetandis, seditiosi atque improbi
civis, cui ne reditus quidem ad bonos salutem a bonis potuit adferre.**] Once

the secret ballot had been adopted for the general elections and the courts, its introduction into the legislative comitia was the next logical step. This was taken in a plebiscite sponsored by C. Papirius Carbo (cos. 120), one of the tribunes of 130; cf. Rotondi, 302; for the date *MRR* 3, 154. Since most legislation was by this date passed in the tribal comitia, the probable effect of the law may, with Hall, 1998, 23, be described thus: "The *comitia* are held in the forum, there is the possibility of the proceedings being halted by a veto of a fellow-tribune . . . [as the vote is taken] accumulating results are known after each tribe's vote, and a law is passed once the eighteenth tribe of the 35 has voted in its favour. This very public process worked to the advantage of the presiding tribune and the proposers of a law. As long as there was no veto then there was strong pressure for tribe after tribe to vote in favour, and for individual voters to be swept along with the majority view."—At *de Orat.* 3.74 Cicero refers to C. Papirius Carbo as *nobilissimus homo,* while at *Fam.* 9.21.3 he claims that the Carbones were plebeian; possibly they were originally patrician (cf. Shackleton Bailey, 1997, 309–10); in any case his birth is not criticized here. Few followed a consistently *popularis* line over a significant period of time (cf. Tatum, 1999, 3–7), so Carbo's "return" to the *boni* is unsurprising; it is also insufficient to save him from Quintus' vituperation in light of his *lex tabellaria.* This was evidently a bone that Scipio threw to popular sentiment after the defeat of Carbo's bill allowing the iteration of the tribunate, the point that had been the undoing of Ti. Gracchus. Carbo also served on the Gracchan land commission. Many suspected him of culpability in the sudden death of Scipio in 129. At some time before his consulate, he changed sides and successfully defended L. Opimius under accusation before the people for C. Gracchus' murder (at *Brut.* 103 Cicero approves his oratory but not his politics). The following year he committed suicide in the face of prosecution by the young L. Crassus; Cicero preserves a sample of the prosecution speech (*orat.* p. 241 = *de Orat.* 2.170): *non si Opimium defendisti, Carbo, idcirco te isti bonum civem putabunt. simulasse te et aliquid quaesisse perspicuum est, . . . quod eam legem in tribunatu tulisti, quod semper a bonis dissedisti.* Cf. *ad Off.* 2.47; Münzer, *RE* 18.3 (1949), 1015.31 ff. (= Papirius no. 33).—In our treatise *iubeo* and *veto* often form together a description of what the law does (cf. 1.19 and 33; 2.10); but here the two are used for "enacting" and "rejecting" the laws themselves; cf. *OLD* s.vv., 5a and 3, respectively; *de Orat.* 1.60 (Crassus): *num apud populum de legibus iubendis aut vetandis . . . dici sine summa rerum civilium cognitione et prudentia.*

36a uno in genere relinqui videbatur vocis suffragium, . . . perduellionis;

dedit huic quoque iudicio C. Coelius tabellam, doluitque quoad vixit se ut opprimeret Gaium Popillium nocuisse reipublicae.] Though a mediocre orator (*de Orat.* 1.117; *Brut.* 165), C. Coelius Caldus rose to consul for 94— the penultimate in a remarkable run of eight non-noble consuls in thirteen years (cf. Wiseman, 1971, 6 and n. 3; 203; Shackleton Bailey, 1997, 312); the tribunate of 107 was his first office. During that year he prosecuted for *perduellio* the legate C. Popillius Laenas, who, after the defeat of his commander L. Cassius Longinus (cos. 107) by the Tigurini in Aquitania, saved the lives of the men under his command by concluding a treaty with the enemy. Prior to the trial Coelius carried his *lex tabellaria*. With this in place, Popillius was convicted and went into exile, though he was later recalled by the optimates. Coelius' "regret" over his law is attested only here; it thus remains obscure whether it had some specific cause; certainly the law was still commemorated by a descendant of the sponsor in 51 (*RRC* 437/1a). In the aftermath of his own exile Cicero saw Popillius' case as parallel in the manner of expulsion and restitution; cf. *Dom.* 87: *fortis et constans in optima ratione civis P. Popilius semper fuit; tamen eius in omni vita nihil est ad laudem inlustrius quam calamitas ipsa; quis enim iam meminisset eum bene de republica meritum, nisi et ab improbis expulsus esset et per bonos restitutus?* Cf. Lintott, *CAH* 9, 92–93; Münzer, *RE* 4 (1901), 195.50 ff. (Coelius no. 12) with Wiseman, 1971, 225, no. 127; Volkmann, *RE* 22.1 (1953), 58.52 ff. (Popillius no. 19); *MRR* 1, 551; Brecht, 291–92; Rosenstein, 137–38 and 159–60.

36b Et avus quidem noster singulari virtute in hoc municipio quoad vixit restitit Marco Gratidio, cuius in matrimonio sororem, aviam nostram, habebat, ferenti legem tabellariam.] For "extending *quidem*" cf. Solodow, 112 ff.—The sister of M. Gratidius of Arpinum married M. Tullius Cicero, the grandfather of Marcus and Quintus and builder of the original (small) family house mentioned at 2.3. The dispute of the brothers-in-law over balloting procedures in the elections of Arpinum (*hoc municipium*) began during or shortly before 115, the year of M. Aemilius Scaurus' consulate (cf. the following words *M. Scaurus consul*; Nicolet, 1967, 279–80) and continued until the death of M. Tullius (*quoad vixit*); Quintus' stand in our passage is thus in line with their grandfather's opposition to the secret ballot. Presumably Gratidius' law was carried after his brother-in-law's death (ibid., 287). Gratidius later prosecuted C. Flavius Fimbria (cos. 104);[91] he died in Cilicia as a member of the staff of the proconsul M. Antonius (102– 100 [for his office cf. Kallet-Marx, 229–30 n. 27]); cf. *Brut.* 168; *MRR* 1,

---

91. On him cf. Wiseman, 1971, 231, no. 180.

568; Münzer, *RE* 7.2 (1912), 1840.38 ff. and 65–67 (Gratidius nos. 2 and 5); ibid. 7A1 (1939), 824.4 ff. (Tullius no. 27). In view of Gratidius' familial relation with the Marii (see next note), Nicolet, *loc. cit.*, 290–93, sees Gratidius as taking up the cudgels for the early policies of C. Marius, notably unsuccessful in Arpinum (cf. V.Max. 6.9.14: *Arpinatibus honoribus iudicatus inferior quaesturam Romae petere ausus est*; on Marius' balloting law cf. *ad* § 39).

excitabat enim fluctus in simpuio, ut dicitur, Gratidius, quos post filius eius Marius in Aegaeo excitavit mari.] The proverbial phrase *fluctus in simpuio*, equivalent to "a tempest in a teapot," is not attested elsewhere; cf. Otto, 323 § 1652; Häussler, 320 (*simpuio* was restored by Powell as the preferable spelling for the transmitted *sim/symp(u)lo*). The phrase *in Aegaeo excitavit mari* can be explained by assuming, with Nicolet, 1967, 277 n. 1, that the M. Marius who went as a legate from Sertorius to Mithradates in 74 (Plut. *Sert.* 24.3) and served until his death in 72 as a general with the Pontic king was, like M. Marius Gratidianus (pr. I 85?), a son of Gratidius; for the career of this M. Marius see in general Münzer, *RE* 14.2 (1930) 1818.38 ff. (Marius no. 23).

ac nostro quidem ⟨avo . . . M. Scaurus consul⟩ qui cum res esset ad se delata, 'Utinam{que}', inquit, 'M. Cicero, isto animo atque virtute in summa republica nobiscum versari quam in municipali maluisses.'] The text incorporates Powell's transposition of *M. Scaurus consul,* transmitted after *delata.* Puteanus and Lambinus had simply substituted *avo* for *qui;* but it is hard to see how one could have given rise to the other. The alternative is to assume, with Vahlen, a deeper corruption; he suggested *exempli gratia: ac nostro quidem ⟨avo magnam ea res attulit laudem⟩. cui cum res esset ad se delata . . .*—The senate did on occasion handle certain affairs of municipalities affecting the public order; nevertheless Madvig's *ad se⟨natum⟩* is unnecessary, indeed improbable, given the kinds of municipal matters the senate is known to have dealt with (cf. Nicolet, 1967, 286 and n. 3).—On M. Aemilius Scaurus (cos. 115; cens. 109), one of the most influential politicians of the immediate post-Gracchan period, cf. literature cited *ad Off.* 1.108, to which add Richard L. Bates, "*Rex in Senatu*: A Political Biography of M. Aemilius Scaurus," *PAPhS* 130 (1986), 251–88; Karl-Ludwig Elwers, *NP* 1, 182–83. Given this kind of encouragement, Cicero's grandfather might have been tempted, if not to embark on a political career himself, at least to prepare his son for the *vita activa*, but the latter's health did not allow it; cf. *ad* 2.3.—*In municipali*: sc. *re.*

37 Quamobrem, quoniam non recognoscimus nunc leges populi Romani sed aut repetimus ereptas aut novas scribimus, non quid hoc populo obtineri

possit sed quid optimum sit tibi dicendum puto.] Quintus returns to his starting point, *viz.*, that feasibility should be excluded from the discussion; cf. *ad* § 34.—*Recognosco* = "review, inspect" (*OLD* s.v., 1).—*Repetere ereptas* would apply to the restoration of a previous status quo, as some of these laws would do. Marcus has so far not been keen to acknowledge innovations in his laws[92] but, rather, in accord with optimate rhetoric, has emphasized their conservatism; cf. 2.62, 3.12, and esp. 2.23: *quae non sint in nostra republica nec fuerint, tamen erunt fere ⟨quae olim fuerunt⟩ in more maiorum, qui tum ut lex valebat.* Cf. the Introduction § 3.—*Hoc populo* is an ablative absolute; cf. *Tusc.* 1.60 (*hoc nebuloso et caliginoso caelo*) and other examples cited at Kühner-Stegmann, 1, 779–80; Nisbet *ad Dom.* 13.

nam Cassiae legis culpam Scipio tuus sustinet, quo auctore lata esse dicitur; . . .] Cf. *Brut.* 97 (immediately after the quotation at § 35: *secuta biennio post Cassia*—): . . . *cuius* [sc. *L. Cassii*] *quidem legi tabellariae M. Antius Briso tribunus plebis diu restitit, M. Lepido consule adiuvante; eaque res P. Africano vituperationi fuit, quod eius auctoritate de sententia deductus Briso putabatur.*—Scipio is *tuus* in light of *Rep.*; cf. *supra* p. 55 n. 22.

tu si tabellariam tuleris, ipse praestabis.] For *praesto* = "be responsible for making good (loss, damage, etc.), answer for" cf. *OLD* s.v. *praesto*[2] 15. Quintus implies that his brother will be assailed by the kind of regret felt by C. Coelius (cf. *ad* § 36a), but he ignores that Marcus' law is actually designed to restore some measure of control to the optimates (*optimatibus nota:* § 10.6; cf. § 33).

nec enim mihi placet, nec Attico nostro, quantum e vultu eius intellego.] For the reading of the *vultus* cf. *ad* 1.27; for an indication of assent by the *vultus* cf. Tac. *Dial.* 33.3. It is noticeable that Cicero avoids making Quintus' knowledge of Atticus' views depend upon previous discussion between the brothers-in-law; see the Index of Topics s.v. "Interlocutor(s), prior conversations among."

A. Mihi vero nihil umquam populare placuit, eamque optimam rempublicam esse dico quam hic consul constituerat, quae sit in potestate optimorum.] For Atticus' political views cf. *ad* § 26 (*Nec mehercule ego sane a Quinto nostro dissento.*). For Cicero's "optimate" policy cf. *ad* § 29 (*Ille vero, etsi tuus est totus ordo*—).

38 Vos ⟨qui⟩dem ut video legem antiquastis sine tabella.] Picking up the metaphor of Quintus' and Atticus' "voting" on his laws (cf. *ad* 2.24 and § 11.13), Marcus puns wittily on voting *sine tabella*, i.e., orally, the proce-

---

92. He is more candid at § 46.

dure they have just followed and the one that, as good optimates, they generally favor. For *antiquo* = "reject" cf. *TLL* s.v., 176.60 ff. (where our passage is cited).—⟨*Qui*⟩*dem* is Turnebus' necessary correction.

sed ego, etsi satis dixit pro se in illis libris Scipio, tamen ita libertatem istam largior populo ut auctoritate et valeant et utantur boni.] Scipio's policy on *libertas* is implicit in his praise of the *genus temperatum* (cf. *ad* § 17: *quo posteaquam modica et sapiens temperatio accessit . . .*); if Cicero has in mind a more specific discussion, it has been lost.—This essentially restates policy formulated at § 25 (cf. *ad loc.: quae tamen sic data est*—). For Cicero's common distinction between the *populus* and the *boni* cf. Achard, 47 and n. 69.—*Ita* is H.A. Koch's correction for (another) *istam* ε or *in istam* P or *ista* BL (there is an erasure of three or four letters in A, and the word was simply omitted by the earlier editors).—*Boni* is postponed for emphasis, like *bonus* at § 34 *fin.*

quae lex hanc sententiam continet ut omnes leges tollat quae postea latae sunt, quae tegunt omni ratione suffragium: 'ne quis inspiciat tabellam', 'ne roget', 'ne appellet'; . . .] Had Marcus offered this clarification earlier—and had Quintus sought clarification—considerable discussion could have been saved. It may seem odd that Cicero sent the interlocutors so far down a cul-de-sac, but he evidently sought a way to present the optimate position in detail without making any of the interlocutors into a *popularis.*—*Ne roget:* sc. *de tabella* (Reid).

38–39 pontes etiam lex Maria fecit angustos. quae si opposita sunt ambitiosis, ut sunt fere, non reprehendo.] The *pontes* of the Comitia were gangways leading to the voting compartments; cf. *OLD* s.v. *pons* 2c. The reference is to a law which C. Marius (cos. I 107) carried as tribune in 119; cf. Rotondi, 318; *MRR* 1, 526. "In both centuries and tribes the votes were gathered and counted by men known first as *rogatores* and later, when ballots were written, as *custodes,* chosen in general from upper-class voters, eventually from the jury lists" (Taylor, 1966, 8; cf. Mommsen, *Staatsr.* 3, 406–7); they positioned themselves on the *pontes.* In narrowing the *pontes,* Marius "must have sought to prevent jostling and physical interference during the vote. It would also have stopped men lining the *pontes* and threatening a voter as he passed": Lintott, 1968, 71; sim. Nicolet, 1967, 292–93. Against the supposition that Marius' bill was designed to further the political interests of the Caecilii Metelli cf. Gruen, 1991, 261 n. 54.—Per se the *ambitiosus* is a man canvassing for office or in behalf of a candidate; cf. Q. Cic. (?) *Comm. pet.* 18 (*homines ambitiosi*) with Robert Morstein-Marx, "Publicity, Popularity and Patronage in the *Commentariolum Petitionis,*" *CA* 17 (1998), 276–80; but in our context the *ambitiosus* is one who engages in *ambitus*, i.e., corrupt electioneering; cf. *TLL* s.v., 1855.32 ff. (our passage cited at 39).

39 si n⟨on⟩ valuerint tamen leges ut ne sit ambitus, habeat sane populus tabellam quasi vindicem libertatis, dummodo haec optimo cuique et gravissimo civi ostendatur ultroque offeratur, . . .] Here it is made explicit that the proponents of the secret ballot praised it as a defense against *ambitus;* cf. *ad* §§ 33–39 and 35 (*Sunt enim quattuor leges—*).—*Si n⟨on⟩* is Ziegler's correction; Vahlen had suggested *sin ⟨non⟩*.—The association of *libertas* with the *leges tabellariae* (cf. *ad* §§ 33–39) is a theme of *popularis* rhetoric that Cicero appropriated; cf. *Agr.* 2.4: *tabellam vindicem tacitae libertatis; Sest.* 103, cited *ad* § 33 (*Dicam, Tite, et versabor in re difficili . . .*); *Planc.* 16: *tabella . . . dat . . . eam libertatem ut quod velint faciant;* Bleicken, 1972, 34 ff., esp. 37–38.—A "*popularis*" would no doubt retort to Marcus' proposal that a written ballot so used is a far cry from a guarantee of liberty; cf. *ad* §§ 33–39.—For *dummodo . . . ultro . . . offeratur* cf. *ad* § 10.6.

. . . ut in eo sit ipso libertas in quo populo potestas honeste bonis gratificandi datur.] Cf. *Mur.* 70–71, where the *tenues* are said to join the candidate's entourage for this reason. Cicero's view on this has rightly been called "a naive compromise" (C. Wirszubski, *Libertas as a Political Idea at Rome during the Late Republic and Early Principate* [Cambridge, 1950], 50); see also the next two notes.

eoque nunc fit illud quod a te modo, Quinte, dictum est, ut minus multos tabella condemnet quam solebat vox, quia populo licere satis est. hoc retento, reliqua voluntas auctoritati aut gratiae traditur.] This refers back to Quintus' point at § 34 (*graviora iudicia de potentissimis hominibus exstant vocis quam tabellae*). Again, a naive conception of what satisfies (*satis est*) the people combined with a euphemistic description of the consequence of his proposal (that *auctoritas* or *gratia* would prevail, with no mention made of bribery).—*Minus multi* substitutes for *pauciores* as at *Off.* 1.73: . . . *quo minus multa patent in eorum vita quae fortuna feriat . . .*—*Hoc* refers back to *licere, viz.,* the freedom to condemn: if this element is kept, for the rest they deliver their support to those who enjoy respect or popularity.

itaque, ut omittam largitione corrupta suffragia, non vides, si quando ambitus sileat, quaeri in suffragiis quid optimi viri sentiant?] A naively optimistic assessment, like the supposition that Clodius' following consisted primarily of slaves and not of the urban plebs (§ 25). Cicero seems unable to conceive that there could be a substantial element in the citizen body with views opposed to the optimate position. This is, of course, in line with the broad definition of "optimate" at *Sest.* 97 (*omnes optimates sunt qui neque nocentes sunt nec natura improbi nec furiosi nec malis domesticis impediti*).

quamobrem lege nostra libertatis species datur, auctoritas bonorum retine-tur, contentionis causa tollitur.] The maintenance of the *auctoritas opti-matium* was the cause of Quintus' concern about the *lex tabellaria* (§ 34); sim. of the tribunate (§ 17). The last member of the tricolon highlights Marcus' concern, the preservation of the *concordia ordinum* (*contentionis causa tollitur:* note the clausula of cretic plus iamb); cf. *ad* § 28a.

40–47a These sections offer commentary on the final laws, pertaining to meetings, senatorial and popular, individuals, and the censors (this in addition to the duties described at § 7.3):

   I. Duties of the senator (40–41)
  II. Conduct in popular assemblies
     A. Violence (42)
       1. Outlawed
       2. Presiding magistrate to be held accountable
     B. Those who intercede against evils to be honored
     C. Auspices to be observed (43)
     D. Miscellaneous provisions
  III. Treatment of individuals (44–46a)
     A. Prohibition of *privilegia*
     B. Comitia centuriata to decide capital cases
     C. Prohibition of bribes
     D. Punishment to be fitted to the crime
  IV. New duties for the censors (46b–47a)
     A. Guarding of the laws
     B. Review of retiring magistrates

40 A difficult section, in which the train of thought is by no means clearly delineated. The transmitted matter is so elliptical and the transitions so abrupt that Powell suggests that the text comprises a series of excerpts and compares (*per litt.*) the *Collectaneum* of Hadoard. Possibly it is a rough draft, the form in which Cicero read Crassus' speech in favor of the Servilian law (*Brut.* 164).

Deinde sequitur, quibus ius sit cum populo agendi aut cum senatu.] The point is passed over as uncontroversial; cf. *ad* § 10.8.

gravis et, ut arbitror, praeclara lex: 'quaeque in patribus agentur, modica sunto', id est modesta atque sedata.] The lack of a connection was felt already by Turnebus, who supplied *deinde*, Vahlen, for greater variety, wrote *tum* instead, which, with the nasal written as a supralinear stroke, could easily have fallen out after *senatu*. One wonders whether some verb has also been lost, e.g, ⟨*tum excipitur*⟩ would be conceivable; but the problems of this chapter lie deeper and should perhaps not be smoothed over; see the headnote to this section. Comparison with § 10.8 led the *recentiores* to supply *quae cum populo* prior to *quaeque in patribus;* this is a possibility, but Cicero may not have been so pedantic; the *cum populo actiones* are dealt with separately in § 42.—*Modicum* has been an epithet for something approved of at several points already: ... *ex natura vivere* ... , *id est vita modica et apta* ⟨*e*⟩ *virtute perfrui* (1.56); ... *modica et sapiens temperatio* (§ 17); its opposite is *nimius* (Tac. *Ann.* 2.33.3); cf. *TLL* s.v. *modicus* 1229.18 ff. It is stipulated that private sacrifice be made *modo* at 2.20.4; and *modus* in social relations is repeatedly recommended in *Off.* (cf. *ad* 1.93). But what is viewed as *modicum* may vary from observer to observer; hence this is one of those provisions that is more like an exhortation than an enforceable law (cf. *ad* § 6.1: *Iusta imperia sunto*).

actor enim moderatur et fingit non modo mentes ac voluntates, sed paene vultus eorum apud quos agit.] Another hard transition; Powell indicates *per litt.* that he would expect a train of thought such as this: "And in the popular assembly too. Now this is an excellent law because it keeps unruly demagogues under control. The preservation of moderate proceedings depends on the *actor.*"—*Actor*[93] is here the orator, as often; cf. *TLL* s.v., 446.42 ff. ("qui orationem pronuntiat"), where our passage is cited (49–50); the word has a different sense at § 11.5; see *ad loc.* Crassus describes this power as the orator's outstanding asset at *de Orat.* 1.30: *neque vero mihi quicquam praestabilius videtur quam posse dicendo tenere hominum mentes, adlicere voluntates, impellere quo velit, unde autem velit deducere,* a passage Ziegler cited in support of writing *mentes* for the transmitted *mentem,* and indeed a search of PHI 5.3 for the two words in juxtaposition shows them always agreeing in number in Cicero's corpus. On the *vultus* cf. *ad* 1.27.

quod si in senatu, non difficile; est enim ipse senator is cuius non ab actore efferatur animus, sed qui per se ipse spectari velit.] What is "not difficult" in the senate is presumably the preservation of orderly proceedings, though once again the transition is abrupt.—The transmitted text is *is cuius non ab auctorem referatur animus.* Turnebus' *ad actorem* for *ab auctorem* was accepted by Ziegler but yields, as Görler points out *ad loc.,* no satisfactory sense. He proposes instead *ab actore* and a change of *referatur* to *reflectatur, regatur,* or *refingatur;* a more plausible verb is Powell's *efferatur* (cf. *OLD* s.v. *effero*[1] 13a: "to be carried away"). The sense will be that the senator in

---

93. Ascensius' correction of the transmitted *auctor.*

the audience is not prey to the speaker's *psychagogia;* he "rather would expect to have others looking at him to see what line he would take" (this latter the sense of *qui per se ipse spectari velit*): Powell *per litt.*

Huic iussa tria sunt: ut adsit, nam gravitatem res habet cum frequens ordo est; . . .] Hence Cicero's many references to measures taken by the *frequens senatus* (cf. § 18 *supra: approbante senatu frequentissimo*), especially regarding his own recall from exile, e.g., *Red. Pop.* 15: . . . *frequentissimus senatus, uno dissentiente, nullo intercedente, dignitatem meam quibus potuit verbis amplissimis ornavit, salutem vobis municipiis coloniis omnibus commendavit;* Merguet, *Reden,* s.v. *frequens;* Ryan, 36–41 and 46.

ut loco dicat, id est rogatus; . . .] On the rules for the order in which senators were asked for their opinion cf. Mommsen, *Staatsr.* 3, 965 ff.

ut modo, ne sit infinitus. nam brevitas non modo senatoris sed etiam oratoris magna laus est in ⟨dicenda⟩ sententia, . . .] On *brevitas* cf. *ad* 2.23; Tac. *Dial.* 41.4 (Maternus) gives this explanation: *quid enim opus est longis in senatu sententiis cum optimi cito consentiant?* Capito fr. 4.14 Strzelecki = Gel. 4.10.8 states, however: *erat enim ius senatori ut sententiam rogatus diceret ante quicquid vellet aliae rei et quod vellet.*—Prior to *sententia* one would expect *dicenda* to complete the thought (cf. *de Orat.* 3.163: . . . *summa laus est in verbis transferendis . . .*); the clausula (type *omni debebitur*) would not be altered by the insertion. This solution is rhythmically preferable both to Halm's deletion of *in sententia* and Moser's *in sententia ⟨dicenda⟩.*

. . . nec est umquam longa oratione utendum (quod fit ambitione saepissime) nisi aut ⟨cum⟩ peccante senatu, nullo magistratu adiuvante, tolli diem utile est, . . .] Bake's transposition of the clause *quod fit ambitione saepissime,* which is transmitted after *senatu,* is needed; otherwise *quod fit ambitione saepissime* would refer to the senate's making mistakes (*peccante senatu*), but this would hardly be attributable to *ambitio.* Here *ambitio* surely means emulousness, competition, i.e., each successive speaker vying to outdo the previous one (cf. *OLD* s.v., 2b). I have added the *cum* since the exception (*nisi*) should be expressed in two parallel *cum*-clauses (*nisi aut ⟨cum⟩ . . . aut cum . . .*); cf. *Orat.* 135 (7x), *de Orat.* 3.115 (4x), *Inv.* 1.30, *Har.* 19, *Cael.* 64 (these are only the instances after *aut*).—Among the synonymous expressions for *tollere diem* listed by de Libero, 15 n. 1, add under *diem dicendo eximere* reference to *Tull.* 6; Tac. *Dial.* 19.2.

. . . . aut cum tanta causa est ut opus sit oratoris copia vel ad hortandum vel ad docendum; . . .] *Brevitas* could be praiseworthy in certain contexts (see above), but what generally established an orator's reputation was *copia dicendi;* cf. *ad* 2.69.

quorum generum in utroque magnus noster Cato est.] The mention of Cato as still living is decisive against a dramatic date of *Leg.* after Thapsus/Utica; see the Introduction § 5.—Cato's art of filibuster was deployed most notably in efforts to block the career and policies of Julius Caesar, in particular against (1) Caesar's request to present himself as a consular candidate in absentia in 60 so as not to relinquish his triumph by entering the *pomerium* to announce his candidacy; (2) Caesar's land bill in behalf of Pompey's veterans (59); (3) Caesar's request to be permitted to seek the consulship in absentia in 52; cf. Taylor, 1949, 131, 133, and 150; on no. (2) in particular de Libero, 18–20. On the tactic in general cf. ibid. 15 ff.; P. Groebe, "Die Obstruktion im römischen Senat," *Klio* 5 (1905), 229–35.

41 quodque addit 'causas populi teneto', est senatori necessarium nosse rempublicam, . . .] Cf. in general *de Orat.* 3.76 (Crassus): *illa vis autem eloquentiae tanta est, ut . . . rempublicam regat . . .* ; ibid. 2.337 (Antonius on deliberative oratory): *ad consilium autem de republica dandum caput est nosse rempublicam . . .* It is only in our passage that Cicero spells out some of the implications.—For the unpreparedness of many entering public life cf. *de Orat.* 3.136; [Sal.] *Rep.* 2.10.9.

. . . idque late patet: quid habeat militum, quid valeat aerario, quos socios respublica habeat, quos amicos, quos stipendiarios, qua quisque sit lege condicione foedere; . . .] Cf. Arist. *Rh.* 1359b33; such an inventory for Attica at X. *Vect.* (cf. also *Mem.* 3.6.4–13); sim. for the Byzantine Empire Constantine Porphyrogenitus, *de Administrando Imperio.* The factors indicated would clearly figure in the evaluation of a crisis such as might lead to war (in which case, of course, corresponding knowledge would be needed of the enemy).—The term *socii* was used of autonomous allies of the Roman people, especially, prior to the Social War, the Italians; see Mommsen, *Staatsr.* 3, 659 ff.; Wegner, 72 ff.; the title *amicus populi Romani* was bestowed by the senate on request from a magistrate; cf. *OLD* s.v. *amicus* 2b; Mommsen, *loc. cit.*, 1026; A.J. Marshall, "Friends of the Roman People," *AJPh* 89 (1968), 39–55. The use of such terms seems not necessarily to imply treaty relations; cf. Mommsen, *loc. cit.*, 660; Kallet-Marx, 108 n. 50; 185; and 195 n. 51.—*Respublica* was deleted by Manutius; but cf. Madvig *ad Fin.* 1.3.—The study of usage conducted by Brunt, 1990, 349, leads him to conclude that "until the early Principate *stipendium* was the normal term for direct taxation imposed by Rome on her subjects in all provinces alike."—Any designated Roman citizen could conclude a treaty (*foedus*) with a foreign power in the form of an oral question and answer (*stipulatio* or *sponsio*); for details see Mommsen, *Staatsr.* 1, 246–57.

tenere consuetudinem decernendi, nosse exempla maiorum.] For the method of voting by change of place in the senate of the Republic cf. Mommsen, *Staatsr.* 3, 991–92.—For historical examples cf. *de Orat.* 1.18 (Crassus on the requisite knowledge for an orator): *tenenda praeterea est omnis antiquitas exemplorumque vis* . . . ; at Tac. *Dial.* 30.1 Messala complains that such matters are neglected in current education. There are various more detailed recommendations for their deployment in deliberative speeches: *Rhet. Her.* 3.9 recommends use of as many historical examples as possible in the *conclusio;* at *de Orat.* 2.335 Antonius remarks that *maiorum exempla* will tend to be invoked by the speaker *qui ad dignitatem impellit* (as opposed to *ad utilitatem*).

videtis iam genus hoc omne scientiae diligentiae memoriae, sine quo paratus esse senator nullo pacto potest.] These three elements (*scientia, diligentia,* and *memoria*) are requisites for the orator in general; cf. *de Orat.* 2.147–49 (Antonius), with emphasis on *diligentia,* whereas Crassus had emphasized *scientia* in Book 1; they likewise find a place in the art of divination (*Div.* 1.127 [Quintus]).—For the ancient art of memorization cf. *Rhet. Her.* 3.28–40 and *de Orat.* 2.350–60 (Antonius).

42 Deinceps sunt cum populo actiones, in quibus primum et maximum 'vis abesto'.] The introductory words clearly mark the transition to *cum populo actiones,* reserved for this place (cf. *ad* § 40 *init.*).—For the ellipsis of a form of *sum* in the relative clause cf. the following *quo nihil praest⟨abil⟩ius;* Alfred Klotz, "Sprachliche Bemerkungen zu einigen Stellen in Ciceros Reden," *Glotta* 6 (1915), 221–22.

nihil est enim exitiosius civitatibus, nihil tam contrarium iuri ac legibus, nihil minus civile et immanius, quam composita et constituta republica quicquam agi per vim.] A fine tricolon beginning with the general effect on the *civitas,* then within the *civitas* the relation to legal order, and finally the general negation of civil and humane behavior; the whole is capped with a fine clausula of the cretic plus trochee type.—*Immanius* is Powell's conjecture; *inhumanius* of some *recentiores* is usually adopted; transmitted is *human(i)us.*—The *constituta respublica* is the premise; for comparison with *Sest.* 92 cf. *ad* § 11.3–5.—Lintott, 1968, 132, notes that Cicero evidently cannot point to any preexisting law either in the Twelve Tables or elsewhere against *vis in populo;* cf. *ad* § 11.3–5.

parere iubet intercessori, quo nihil praest⟨ant⟩ius; impediri enim bonam rem melius quam concedi malae.] Intercession is the right of a magistrate of equal or greater *potestas* to annul an act of another magistrate. It developed as a consequence of the collegial system of magistracies, and the tribunate of the plebs was created on the basis of this principle. Cf. Mommsen, *Staatsr.* 1, 266–88. Between 70 and 49 de Libero, 33–36, counts twenty-four certain cases of intercession affecting legislation in the senate and seven in the *concilium plebis;* cf. in general ibid. 29 ff.; Rilinger. Cf. also § 24: *quin ipsum Ti. Gracchum non solum neglectus sed etiam sublatus intercessor evertit.*—The *recentiores* already correct to *praestantius.*—The conservative tendency of Cicero's provision is plain (*impediri enim bonam rem melius quam concedi malae*[94]), though he does not make ignoring an *intercessor* a capital crime as he does ignoring an augur (2.21.6).

quod vero actoris iubeo esse fraudem, id totum dixi ex Crassi sapientissimi hominis sententia, . . .] This is, as Rawson, 1991, 31, observes, "the one certain example of Cicero picking up a political idea of L. Crassus'"; she also notes (ibid.) that Cicero refers to Crassus in all seven times as *sapientissimus,* an unparalleled total.—The *actor* will be the man who has convened a legislative or judicial assembly and, in the former case, is hoping to win approval for his proposals; see *ad* § 11.3–5. An assembly leader (ordinarily a tribune of the plebs; cf. Kaj Sandberg, *Magistrates and Assemblies: A Study of Legislative Practice in Republican Rome* [Rome, 2001], esp. 147) will tend to be cautious as a result of this law since he will be held accountable for any violence (cf. § 23: *dux enim suo ⟨se⟩ periculo progredi cogitat*); hence this provision, together with the encouragement of the veto given in the previous sentence, will powerfully inhibit any move toward reform; cf. Lintott, 1999, 231.

. . . . quem est senatus secutus cum decrevisset, C. Claudio consule de Cn. Carbonis seditione referente, invito eo qui cum populo ageret seditionem non posse fieri, quippe cui liceat concilium . . . dimittere.] As consul of 92 C. Claudius Pulcher referred to the senate an unruly public meeting presided over by the tribunus plebis Cn. Carbo, the later follower of C. Marius. Our passage is the sole source for the incident. Cf. Münzer, *RE* 3 (1899), 2856.10 ff. (Claudius no. 302); idem, ibid., 18.3 (1949), 1024.17 ff. (Papirius no. 38), esp. 41 ff.; N. Häpke, ibid. 13.1 (1926), 261.61 ff. (though Crassus' words can hardly, as she suggests, come from the prosecution of C. Papirius Carbo); cf. *MRR* 2, 17–18 and on the date 19 n. 5; M. Krueger, *M. Antonii et L. Licinii Crassi oratorum Romanorum fragmenta* (diss., Bratislava, 1909), 55–56.

quod ⟨si⟩ qui permanet cum agi nihil potest, vim quaerit, cuius impunitatem amittit hac lege.] A difficult passage. The most plausible solution so far proposed is that of J.G.F. Powell, who inserts *si* before *qui* and adopts *permanet* of the *recentiores* for *permonet* P(?A¹)ε or *permovet* Aˣ and renders (*per litt.*) "but if anyone stands his ground when no business can be

---

94. Cf. § 34 (Quintus): *. . . vi opprimi in bona causa est melius quam malae cedere.*

done, he invites violence," i.e., the presiding magistrate ought to dissolve the assembly at the announcement of adverse omens (implied in *cum agi nihil potest*).—*Impunitas* is used, as often, with the genitive of the offense (*cuius* will refer back to *vim*); cf. *OLD* s.v.—For the magistrates endowed with the *ius agendi cum populo* cf. § 10.8. In practice those leading assemblies resulting in violence were likely to be tribunes endowed with *sacrosancta potestas* (cf. Mommsen, *Staatsr.* 2, 286 ff.), which apparently was to be modified to this degree.

42–43 (se)quitur illud: 'intercessor rei malae salutaris civis esto'. quis non studiose reipublicae subvenerit, hac tam praeclara legis voce laudatus?] For the *salutaris civis* cf. *ad* § 11.6.—Here Cicero acknowledges that he has provided not so much an enforceable law as a commendation for the statesman—a reward on a different level from that of *Rep.* 6.17.—I prefer *praeclarae* for the transmitted *praeclara* for the sake of Ciceronian chiasmus and balance; in addition, to say that the law has "this outstanding voice" suggests that it may have others (less outstanding?) as well; for *praeclara* as epithet of *lex* cf. §§ 28, 40, 44; *Rep.* 2.61; such common locutions as *hic tam praeclarus vir* might account for the change of ending from genitive to ablative.—For the *iunctura legis vox* cf. 2.18 (*legum vox*).

43 est autem boni auguris meminisse, (se) maximis reipublicae temporibus praesto esse debere, Iovique Optimo Maximo se consiliarium atque administrum datum, ut sibi eos quos in auspicio esse iusserit; . . .] These precepts reflect the ethos of the board of augurs, to which Cicero was elected in 53/52 (cf. *ad* 2.31).—*Meminisse (se)* (Lambinus) posits an easy haplographic error.—*Maxima tempora*, like *gravissima tempora* (§ 25), will be the "crises" of the state; cf. *ad* § 25.—The relation to Jupiter Optimus Maximus was emphasized already at 2.20.6: *Interpretes autem Iovis Optimi Maximi, publici augures . . .*—*Consiliarius* as a substantive has the sense "adviser, counsellor" (cf. *OLD* s.v. *consiliarius*[2] a).—The last clause is to be interpreted *ut sibi eos* [sc. *administros esse*] *quos in auspicio esse iusserit,* i.e., the augur is the assistant to Jupiter as his own assistants are to him. **caelique partes sibi definitas esse traditas, e quibus saepe opem reipublicae ferre possit.]** The cult acts of the augurs (*auguria*) were connected with observation of the sky; cf. Wissowa, *RE* 2.2 (1896), 2341.18 ff. For the *partes caeli* cf. *Div.* 2.42: *caelum in sedecim partes diviserunt Etrusci,* with Pease's note.—*Divinitus* is sometimes substituted for *definitas* (Bake, de Plinval), wrongly, for the augural discipline is not based on divine revelation but on *observatio;* cf. Linderski, 1986, 2214–15 n. 257.—The augur, like the *intercessor rei malae*, aids the state by hindering or impeding wrong action (cf. § 27).

Deinde de promulgatione, de singulis rebus agendis, de privatis magistratibusve audiendis.] These points are passed over as too obvious to require comment; cf. *ad* § 11.8.

44 tum leges praeclarissimae de XII tabulis tralatae duae, quarum altera privilegia tollit, altera de capite civis rogari nisi maximo comitiatu vetat.] *Praeclarissimae* is the correction of AˣPε for *praeclarissimas* B, *p(rae)clarisma* A¹(?), or *praeclaris mea* L.—The claim that the first of these provisions is taken over from the Twelve Tables (and the *sacratae leges* according to *Sest.* 65) has recently provoked skepticism; cf. A. Guarino, "I 'privilegia' dai romanisti a Cicerone," *Labeo* 37 (1991), 339–42, and Crawford on *Lex XII* 9.1–2, 4, 6 (with useful collection of parallel material [698–99]),[95] who, however, admits (698) that the skeptical case is "incapable of formal proof." To understand Cicero's position it is helpful to use as a point of departure his fullest statement of it, *Dom.* 43: *quo iure, quo more, quo exemplo legem nominatim de capite civis indemnati tulisti? vetant leges sacratae, vetant XII Tabulae leges privatis hominibus irrogari. id est enim privilegium. nemo umquam tulit; . . . proscriptionis miserrimum nomen illud et omnis acerbitas Sullani temporis quid habet quod maxime sit insigne ad memoriam crudelitatis?* Cicero is not using terms with the precision of a jurist; what he evidently means is *nominatim de capite civis indemnati legem ferre;* he calls this a *privilegium,* though *privilegium* is the broader category of which this is a type; cf. also below: *ferri de singulis nisi centuriatis comitiis noluerunt;* Mommsen, *Strafr.* 169 n. 3 and 1014 n. 2. *Nemo umquam tulit* is a rhetorical exaggeration, as the sequel shows, for precedent could be found in the Sullan proscriptions and thus in their legal basis, the lex Valeria (on which cf. *ad* 1.42). But, in spite of his terminological imprecision and rhetorical exaggeration, it seems unlikely that Cicero's explicit, repeated claim about the Twelve Tables, the text of which he knew so well (cf. 2.59), is wrong. We probably ought to accept that they contained such a provision as *Privilegia ne inroganto;* it should be seen as a reaction against the punitive use of *plebiscita;* cf. G. Wesenberg, *RE* 23.1 (1957), 19.1 ff. (s.v. Privilegium).—On the other hand, Crawford accepts the latter law for the Twelve Tables, in this form: *de capite civis, ⟨ni⟩ maximus comitiatus ⟨est⟩, ne ferunto (Lex XII* 9.2); cf. also Humbert, 466–67 n. 101. For the sense there of *maximus comitiatus* cf. *ad* § 11.10; Cicero, however, gives the phrase a different interpretation (see below).

et nondum in⟨ven⟩tis seditiosis tribunis plebis, ne cogitatis quidem, admiran-

---

95. Cf. also Delz, 82, who sees Cicero's law as an innovation inspired by the Athenian statute reported at Andoc. 1.87 and Dem. 23.86: μηδὲ ἐπ' ἀνδρὶ νόμον ἐξεῖναι θεῖναι, ἐὰν μὴ τὸν αὐτὸν ἐπὶ πᾶσιν Ἀθηναίοις.

dum tantum maiores in posterum providisse.] While not necessarily accepting Quintus' notion that the tribunate was *ad seditionem natus,* Marcus acknowledges the existence of latter-day *seditiosi tribuni plebis* (cf. *ad* § 19b).—*Inventis* is Turnebus' necessary correction.—*Ne cogitatis* is the correction of Puteanus and Lambinus for *negotia his* B (with slight variants elsewhere);[96] *cogito* is first attested in Cicero in the sense "imagine, conceive, picture": cf. *TLL* s.v., 1467.33 ff.; *OLD* s.v., 9.—For the praise of the *maiores* in such matters cf. Roloff, 94–95.

in privatos homines leges ferri noluerunt: id est enim privilegium, quo quid est iniustius, cum legis haec vis sit, ⟨ut sit⟩ scitum et iussum in omnes?] For Cicero's attribution of a provision against *privilegia* to the Twelve Tables cf. the note before last.—Here Cicero adds to the argument from tradition an argument drawn from the definition of *lex* itself. The universality is not usually emphasized this way (cf. in general the definitions at *TLL* s.v., 1238.80 ff., including *Leg.* 1.18b and 19), but see Festus p. 266M: *quod in omnis homines resve populus scivit lex appellatur;* Calc. *comm.* 179: *lex generaliter iubet omnibus quae facienda sint prohibetque omnes ab inconvenientibus.*—*Ut sit* is Scheffer's supplement.

ferri de singulis nisi centuriatis comitiis noluerunt . . .] This is Cicero's interpretation of the *maximus comitiatus* of *Lex XII;* sim. *OLD* s.v. *comitiatus* and L. Cotta's opinion quoted at *Sest.* 73: *de capite non modo ferri, sed ne iudicari quidem posse nisi comitiis centuriatis.*[97] This interpretation is open to doubt: there were, in fact, cases of legislation in the popular assembly against citizens who went into voluntary exile during judicial proceedings (Liv. 25.4.9 and 26.3.12.); cf. also *ad* § 11.10. But if Cicero is correct, the provision would "seem designed to curb tribunician attempts to force through plebiscites inflicting penalties on those who defied their intervention. Thus the restriction of measures imposing a capital penalty to the centuriate assembly (to which the tribunes can have had no access in the fifth century) clearly refers only to the passage of comitial proposals, not to the infliction of legally sanctioned penalties, and is evidently intended to prevent their presentation to the plebeian assembly": A. Drummond, *CAH* 7², 201–2.

discriptus enim populus censu ordinibus aetatibus, plus adhibet ad suffragium ⟨con⟩sili quam fuse in tribus convocatus.] *Discriptus* (Ziegler) is to be

---

96. An evident error in transcription from capitals, as in *N.D.* 2.18 (*negotiari* for *ne cogitari*), compared by Vahlen.

97. Cf. already Pl. *Pseud.* 1232 (Ballio is the speaker): *Pseudolus mihi centuriata habuit capitis comitia; Dom.* 33: *nego potuisse iure publico, legibus iis quibus haec civitas utitur, quemquam civem ulla eiusmodi calamitate affici sine iudicio;* sim. *Sest.* 65; *Rep.* 2.61.

read here for the transmitted *descriptus,* in accord with the modern doctrine on the semantic distinction of the two verbs; cf. *ad* 1.23.—P already corrected to *consili(i).* Robert Morstein-Marx remarks *(per litt.):* "The contrast of *discriptus populus censu* and *fuse in tribus convocatus* is interesting: sorting into rational units is necessary in order for reason to prevail."—For the origins and original principle of selection of the centuriate assembly cf. *ad* § 7.3 *(exin pecunias aevitatis ordines partiunto).* The centuriate organization facilitated control by the top social strata; this would apply whether Cicero is thinking in strict historical terms (the time of the Twelve Tables), as *enim* implies, or of his own time. For the early Republic Cornell, *CAH* 7², 402–3 summarizes the position thus: ". . . the distribution of the centuries among the classes went in inverse proportion to the actual numbers of citizens, so that the wealthiest class, which was numerically relatively small, contained by far the largest number of centuries; together with eighteen centuries of aristocratic knights, the eighty centuries of the first class could command an absolute majority of the total"; for Cicero's time cf. Yakobson, 1999, ch. 2. A further element of noble control was the disproportionate influence, under successive voting, of the first century called upon for its vote *(praerogativa centuria),* on the assumption that, as most scholars hold, it was always a century of the first class; cf. Christian Meier, *RE* Suppl. 8 (1956), 567.44 ff., esp. 572.37 ff. (s.v. *Praerogativa centuria).* The system of a *centuria praerogativa* seems to have been challenged by Ser. Sulpicius Rufus' bill, opposed successfully by Cicero as consul (cf. *Mur.* 47, where the text is corrupt at the critical point; [Sal.] *Rep.* 2.7 contains a reference to centuries being called by lot, possibly a revival of the earlier proposal). The organization of each class into *seniores* and *iuniores,* each group allotted an equal number of centuries, though the seniors amounted to less than 30 percent of the electorate, likewise helped insure a balance of conservative opinion; cf. Cornell, *loc. cit.* Hence the only known uses of the centuriate assembly for legislation between 70 and 49 were the lex curiata *de arrogatione Clodi* (59) and Lentulus Spinther's law recalling Cicero from exile (57); cf. Taylor, 1966, 103.—The *comitia tributa,* with which Cicero compares the *comitia centuriata* as if they were the available alternative, did not yet exist in 450; cf. Crawford on *Lex XII* 9.2 (p. 699); Laser, 45 n. 5.

45 quo verius in causa nostra vir magni ingeni summaque prudentia Lucius Cotta dicebat, nihil omnino actum esse de nobis; praeter enim quam quod irrita illa essent, ⟨cum essent⟩ armis gesta servilibus, praeterea neque tributa capitis comitia rata esse posse{nt} neque ulla privilegi. quocirca nihil nobis opus esse lege, de quibus omnino nihil actum esset legibus.] L. Aurelius Cotta (cos. 65; cens. 64) belonged to a family of some political influence in

the late Republic, his elder brothers Gaius and Marcus having preceded him
in the consulate (75 and 74 respectively). It was he who moved a *supplicatio*
for Cicero upon suppression of the Catilinarian conspiracy (*Phil.* 2.13). His
opinion of 1 January 57 is also reported at *Dom.* 68 and *Sest.* 73. He
likewise formulated this corollary: *me . . . in senatu iuratus dixit se, si censor tum esset cum ego aberam, meo loco senatorem recitaturum fuisse*
(*Dom.* 84). It was rumored that, in behalf of the *quindecimviri*, he was
planning to propose for Caesar the title *rex* at the time of the assassination
(Suet. *Jul.* 79.3; cf. *Div.* 2.110). Cf. Klebs, *RE* 2 (1896), 2485.59 ff.
(Aurelius no. 102).—Cotta adduced three grounds for supposing that no
valid law had been passed touching Cicero: (1) the proceedings were dominated by *arma servilia*, an analysis Cicero adopted at § 25 (see *ad loc.*); (2)
the *comitia tributa* were not competent to legislate *de capite civis* (cf. *ad* § 44
ferri de singulis nisi centuriatis comitiis noluerunt); (3) no *comitia* were
competent to pass a *privilegium de capite civis* (cf. *ad* § 44 init.). For *nihil
omnino actum esse de nobis* cf. *ad* 1.3 (*ita factum de Mario*).—*Irrita* is
Powell's correction for *amicitia* (BA^X; deleted by Madvig), *amicta* ES(?A¹),
amitta R, or *amicla* PL; Manutius' *comitia* is usually adopted, but there is no
parallel for the *iunctura comitia gerere* prior to Auson. 364.278–80 Peiper
= 419.42 (cf. *TLL* s.v. *comitium* 1809.1).—*Cum essent*, omitted by
saltation but supplied by Powell, clarifies that the following is a causal
clause.—Turnebus corrected *possent* to *posse*.

**sed visum est et vobis et clarissimis viris melius, de quo servi et latrones
scivisse ⟨se⟩ aliquid dicerent, de hoc eodem cunctam Italiam quid sentiret
ostendere.]** Turnebus inserted *se*, an easy saltation error; sim. § 43: *meminisse ⟨se⟩*.—In fact, it was Pompey, asked his opinion next after Cotta, who,
while praising the latter's view, offered this political solution (cf. *Sest.* 74).
Cicero expressly accepts Cotta's juristic appraisal in the fuller description at
Dom. 69: *neque hoc Cn. Pompeius . . . vosque, pontifices, . . . non vidistis,
⟨legem⟩ illam esse nullam, atque esse potius flammam temporis, interdictum
sceleris, vocem furoris; sed prospexistis ne quae popularis in nos aliquando
invidia redundaret, si sine populi iudicio restituti videremur.* The further
steps leading to Cicero's restoration are narrated by Gelzer, 145–49 (more
briefly, id., *Pompeius*, 125–26) and Tatum, 1999, 176–85; they included
the bill passed in the centuriate assembly (see the note before last), which
was greeted *mirifico studio omnium aetatum atque ordinum, incredibili
concursu Italiae* (*Att.* 4.1.4).—For the attribution of the laws against him to
servi cf. *ad* § 25; for *latro* as a term of abuse for Cicero's enemies cf. *ad* 2.13.
46 Sequuntur de captis pecuniis et de ambitu leges; . . .] Cf. § 11.11: *donum
ne capiunto neve danto neve petenda neve gerenda neve gesta potestate,*

with note.—*Sequuntur* is Cratander's correction for *sequitur* (BA).—*Pecunias capere* is the technical expression for an official's acceptance of money contrary to the Lex Cincia (cf. *ad Off.* 2.66); cf. Mommsen, *Strafr.* 714 and n. 1.

quae cum magis iudiciis quam verbis sanciendae sint, adiungitur 'noxiae poena par esto', ut in suo vitio quisque plectatur: vis capite, avaritia multa, honoris cupiditas ignominia sanciatur.] *Quae* is read (for *-que*) in A alone.— Cicero presents a rational system of punishment matched to crime; similar is Plato's question ζημία δή . . . τίς ἄρα γίγνοιτ' ἂν πρόσφορος (*Lg.* 944d3– 5). The implication is that the purpose of punishment is to persuade the criminal (and others) of the futility of criminal acts and thus cure the propensity to crime; on Plato's similar "curative" punishments in the *Laws* cf. Saunders, 351–52; Mary Margaret MacKenzie, *Plato on Punishment* (Berkeley–Los Angeles, 1981), 195 ff., esp. 199, emphasizes that, while he still speaks of reform as possible, Plato's attitude toward criminals has hardened since *Gorg.* The general improvement of society will be the consideration underlying the handling of *vis*. Cicero presumably means for those found guilty of capital crimes to be able to elect exile instead of execution, as was the practice in his day; cf. Mommsen, *Strafr.* 941–44; J.L. Strachan-Davidson, *Problems of the Roman Criminal Law,* 2 (Oxford, 1912), 23–24; Ernst Levy, *Die römische Kapitalstrafe,* SHAW, phil.-hist. Kl. 1930/31, no. 5 (Heidelberg, 1931), 18 ff.; Brecht, 177 and n. 3. Plato, on the other hand, like Greek penal codes of his day, did not hesitate to impose the death penalty for the worst offenses; cf. Winfried Knoch, *Die Strafbestimmungen in Platons Nomoi* (Wiesbaden, 1960), 149–51; Saunders, 355–56; Mac-Kenzie, *loc. cit.* Besides the question of type of crime, there is also that of its severity, a matter that Plato addresses sporadically while leaving considerable discretion to members of the jury; cf. Saunders, 355. Though Cicero makes no mention of compensation of the party injured by the *vis* or *avaritia* of others, Plato offers such, but not as part of his penal system; ibid., 351. The three types of punishment listed here were all meted out under Roman law but were not matched to the offense; Cicero, however, evidently does not mean to imply that these punishments are *only* to be used for these crimes; cf. § 6.2: *noxium civem multa vinculis verberibusve coerceto.*—For Augustin. *civ.* 21.11 and its possible relation to *Leg.* cf. *supra* p. 33 and n. 114.—On *plecto* = "punish" cf. *ad Off.* 1.89.

Extremae leges sunt nobis non usitatae, reipublicae necessariae.] This is a rare hint that Marcus' laws include some innovations (*nobis non usitatae*); cf. his statement at 2.23: *. . . quae non sint in nostra republica nec fuerint, tamen erunt fere ⟨quae olim fuerunt⟩ in more maiorum . . .* Quintus was more candid at § 37: . . . *quoniam non recognoscimus nunc leges populi Romani sed aut repetimus ereptas aut novas scribimus* . . . Cicero's censor is an original creation, combining aspects of Greek and Roman officials; cf. Mehl, 271, who, however, sees too much influence from philosophy here; see the note after next.—Presumably "necessary" in the sense of needed to keep the state strong and free of abuses. The term functions a bit differently at § 26, where Pompey is said to have calculated *quid necessarium* in restoring the full tribunician power (as opposed to *quid esset optimum*); similarly, at § 33 the "better" course is rejected on grounds of feasibility (*optineri an possit, videndum est*).

legum custodiam nullam habemus, itaque eae leges sunt quas apparitores nostri volunt. a librariis petimus, publicis litteris consignatam memoriam publicam nullam habemus; . . .] There was provision for storage of laws in the *aerarium* (cf. *ad* § 11.8), but apparently the system was unreliable for lack of official oversight. Badian, 1996, 211, describes the problem thus: "Modern scholars, depending on sources that never mention routine legislation and . . . not even important and controversial laws, have not usually realized how much of it there was, and how few magistrates to look after it"; see also Lintott, 1992, 8. In this situation, few aediles were prepared to exert themselves to verify drafts and root out mistakes as strenuously as Cato did (cf. Plut. *Cat. min.* 16.4 and 17.3–4). Cicero himself was accused of falsifying the decree with instructions to the embassy sent early in 43 to Mutina to treat with Marc Antony; cf. App. *BC* 3.250–52; Emilio Gabba, "Cicerone e la falsificazione dei senatoconsulti," *SCO* 10 (1961), 89–96. Dio 54.36 reports that ca. 11 B.C. Augustus removed custody of the archives from the tribunes and aediles, who had delegated it to their *apparitores* (ὑπηρέται) with resulting errors and confusion, and gave it to the quaestors; cf. Mommsen, *Staatsr.* 2, 490 n. 2.—An *apparitor* is a magistrate's attendant or clerk (cf. *OLD* s.v.); the *scriba librarius* ("a scribe, copyist, secretary": ibid. s.v. *librarius*) was the most prominent type of *apparitor*. Such persons were *mercennarii* and thus debarred from membership of the senate (cf. *ad Off.* 1.150 and 2.29a, as well as the contemptuous reference at *Ver.* 3.183–84); hence the irony of the Roman legislative record depending upon their claims (*quas apparitores nostri volunt;* for the sense of *volo* cf. *ad* 1.63). Cf. Mommsen, *Staatsr.* 1, 332–46 (*apparitores*) and 346–55 (*scribae librarii*); on their influence cf. E. Badian, "The *scribae* of the Roman Republic," *Klio* 71 (1989), 582–603, esp. 598 ff.; on the post as a means of social advancement cf. Nicholas Purcell, "The *Apparitores*: A Study in Social Mobility," *PBSR* 51 (1983), 125–73.—*Memoria* = "written record"; cf. *ad* 1.8; *publicis litteris consignatam* will mean "supported or attested by the public archives"; cf. Rawson, 1991, 146, who suggests that Cicero's concern in our passage is with unauthorized copies "circulating among the staffs of magistrates"; this would accord with the emphasis here on the need for a public record: *publicis litteris consignatam memoriam publicam nullam habemus;* cf. Fontanella, 1998, 186–87.

Graeci hoc diligentius, apud quos nomophylaces creantur. ⟨hi olim⟩ non solum litteras (nam id quidem etiam apud maiores nostros erat), sed etiam facta hominum observabant ad legesque revocabant; . . .] *Nomophylaces* is a rare instance of a Greek word deployed in *Leg.;* see *supra* p. 39 and n. 141. Here clarity dictates identifying the office by its Greek name. They existed in various Greek states and continued to be appointed (*creari:* cf. *OLD* s.v. *creo* 5) in Cicero's day (cf. Gehrke, 159–60 n. 53; Busolt-Swoboda, 1, 490–91 n. 3), albeit they were eliminated at Athens after Demetrius of Phalerum (ibid., 2, 931; on his νομοφύλακες cf. Gagarin, 2000, 352–53). Bake's *crea-⟨ba⟩ntur* is often adopted to parallel *observabant . . . revocabant* and on the assumption that Cicero means to cite the precedent of respected Greeks of the past, not his own day (cf. Rawson, 1991, 145 and n. 61); but, as Powell notes (*per litt.*), *creantur* follows nicely on *habemus*. Immediately following *creantur* the mss. present the nonsensical *nei,* for which *nec ei* is usually read; *hi olim non* is Powell's emendation to account for the shift of tense in describing the *nomophylaces*. They presided both over public archives and the constitutionality of legislation (Busolt-Swoboda, 1, 490). Did Cicero mean for the censors to have the power to reject laws, as did Demetrius' νομοφύλακες (cf. Gehrke, 152)? If so, this might have provided a means for blocking legislation such as that of Clodius (cf. L. Cotta's statement at *Sest.* 73 cited *ad* § 46) and, given the overwhelmingly aristocratic origin of the censors,[98] have strengthened optimate control generally. Gehrke, 151–62, esp. 157–58, shows that the νομοφύλακες of Plato's *Laws* and Aristotle's *Politics* are quite different from those of Demetrius of Phalerum and, implicitly, Cicero:[99] for the νομοφύλακες of Cicero and Demetrius are firmly rooted in the institutions of their respective states, whereas Plato and Aristotle give them much broader competence. Cicero provides, however, too few details to clarify whether he was influenced by Greek practice in general

---

98. Cf. Suolahti, 80–137, with summary of results at 599–600.

99. *Pace* Heuss, 260–61; cf. James Williams, "Ideology and the Constitution of Demetrius of Phalerum," in *Polis and Polemos: Essays in Politics, War, and History in Ancient Greece in Honor of Donald Kagan,* ed. C.D. Hamilton and P. Krentz (Claremont, Calif., 1997), 333–35, who wants to allow some background influence on Demetrius' use of the νομοφύλακες from his studies in the Peripatos; for the possibility of philosophical influence on his funerary legislation cf. *ad* 2.66.

or Demetrius in particular (see above; the latter is the supposition of Keyes, 1921, 317; Lehmann, 34 n. 56, is more reserved).—*Observo* here cannot mean "preserve," a poetic usage. Rather translate ⟨*hi olim*⟩ *non solum litteras . . . sed etiam facta hominum observabant ad legesque revocabant* "they once kept an eye not only on texts but also on the behavior of individuals and measured them against the laws"; cf. Rawson, 1991, 146; *OLD* s.v. *observo* 1a (contrast 2c) and s.v. *revoco* 20.—The text is puzzling because Cicero has just said that Rome had no *legum custodia,* yet here he claims that the ancestors provided oversight over *litterae.* But, in fact, the Roman censors traditionally had oversight over the *facta hominum* but not over *litterae* in the sense of an archive of legislation. Have the two spheres been reversed? Should we read: ⟨*hi olim*⟩ *non solum facta hominum (nam id quidem etiam apud maiores nostros erat), sed etiam litteras observabant, ad legesque revocabant?*—*Graeci hoc diligentius* implies criticism of the *maiores,* but this is muted; when they are mentioned, it is in order to emphasize what they *did* provide; cf. Roloff, 98–99 and 125.

47a haec ⟨igitur⟩ detur cura censoribus, quandoquidem eos in republica semper volumus esse.] Especially the last function of the *nomophylaces (facta hominum observare ad legesque revocare)* was bound to suggest the censors as the Roman equivalent. For the perpetual exercise of the office cf. *ad* § 7.3 (*magistratum quinquennium habento*).—*Igitur* is Powell's supplement.

Apud eosdem, qui magistratu abierint, edant et exponant quid in magistratu gesserint, deque eis censores praeiudicent.] At Rome retiring magistrates swore an oath on the rostra that they had administered their office according to the laws; cf. Mommsen, *Staatsr.* 1, 625. According to this proposal, they are to lay their official journals (*commentarii*) before the censors (*edere*) and explain (*exponere*) their conduct of office (cf. Kunkel-Wittmann, 106 n. 7); these will then render a preliminary judgment (*OLD* s.v. *praeiudico* 1a); see the note after next.—Keyes, 1921, 317, suggests that Cicero meant for the *praeiudicium* of the censors to carry considerable weight and help protect a magistrate, such as himself, "who had clearly acted for the best interests of the state, but who, by a technical violation of the law, had laid himself open to malicious prosecution."

hoc in Graecia fit publice constitutis accusatoribus, qui quidem graves esse non possunt nisi sunt voluntarii; . . .] Classical Athens had two sets of accounting officials, the ten λογισταί chosen by lot to handle financial accounting, and the ten εὔθυνοι also chosen by lot, one per tribe, who handled public or private wrongs. If wrongdoing were found, one of the συνήγοροι of the λογισταί would conduct the prosecution, whereas the εὔθυνοι would forward the case to the deme-judges or to the θεσμόθεται depending on whether it was a private or public wrong. Cf. A.R.W. Harrison, *The Law of Athens: Procedure* (Oxford, 1971), 28–31. Plato set great store by the εὐθυνταί, who were to perform this function in his Cretan colony (cf. *Lg.* 945d), and provided correspondingly elaborate regulations (ibid. 945e ff.).—Interesting the preference for a private prosecutor on grounds of *gravitas;* the rôle tended to be shunned, however, by established pleaders with political ambitions; cf. J.A. Crook, *Legal Advocacy in the Ancient World* (London, 1995), 138–39.

quocirca melius rationes referri causamque exponi censoribus, integram tamen legi accusatori iudicioque servari.] As he already hinted by the use of *praeiudicare* (see the note before last), Cicero does not intend to replace existing legal procedure, merely to add a systematic check. The lack of a regular auditing process for magistrates was highlighted, e.g., when in 60 Pompey asked for blanket approval of his acts in Asia, but Lucullus insisted on a point-by-point review of cases in which his own arrangements had been altered; cf. Gelzer, *Pompeius,* 113. In the meantime the lex Iulia (59) required the retiring governor to deposit copies of his accounts in two cities of his province and with the quaestor at the aerarium; cf. Andrew Lintott, "The leges de repetundis and Associate Measures under the Republic," *ZSS* 98 (1981), 203 and n. 156.—For the organization of three items as x, y, z*que* cf. Harm Pinkster, "A, B and C Coordination in Latin," *Mnemosyne* ser. 4, 22 (1969), 258–67, esp. 266–67.

sed satis {et}iam disputatum est de magistratibus, nisi forte quid desideratis.] *Iam* is Minutianus' correction of *etiam,* which, if correct, would have been expected before *de magistratibus*—"also" about magistrates, as about *religiones* (Book 2; cf. 2.69).

47b–49 Atticus raises the topic of *potestatum ius* by analogy with the handling of *ius Romanum,* in particular the relation of rites in honor of the dead to inheritances, appended to the commentary on the sacral laws at 2.46–53. Marcus, deferring to the extensive treatment of the topic in a work dedicated to Atticus' father by M. Junius Congus Gracchanus, undertakes to comply briefly before the text breaks off.

47b A. Quid si nos tacemus, locus ipse te non admonet quid tibi sit deinde dicendum?] Presumably, Atticus means that the topic (*locus*) Marcus has just touched upon, namely the regular judicial process (. . . *legi accusatori iudicioque servari*), should put him in mind of the *ius populi Romani* in relation to magistrates, though it could equally prompt a discussion *de iudiciis,* as Marcus suggests.

M. Mihine? de iudiciis arbitror, Pomponi; id est enim iunctum magistratibus.] For *mihine* and the following *egone?* cf. *ad* 1.14 (*egone?*).—This is our one indication of the topic of Book 4. Possibly it began with general reflections on human *pravitas* (see *ad* fr. 1 incertae sedis) and the classification of eight types of punishment which Augustin. *civ.* 21.11 (cited *supra* p. 33 n. 114) attributes to Cicero. Some reflections on corrupt verdicts in Roman courts such as are adumbrated at *In Clod. et Cur.* fr. or. T 1.16.9 = *Att.* 1.16.9, *Har.* 36 *alibi* (the perjured jury in the Bona Dea trial), and *Pis.* 95 might also have been expected to precede the formulation of Cicero's own laws on the subject, perhaps including reforms to make juries less susceptible to bribery (he throws out some hints on the subject at *Pis.* 94).

48 A. . . . quod [sc. ius p.R.] ignorari ab eis qui in republica versantur turpissimum puto; nam ut modo a te dictum est, leges a librariis peti, sic animadverto ⟨ple⟩rosque in magistratibus, ignoratione iuris sui, tantum sapere quantum apparitores velint.] *Plerosque* is R. Stephanus' correction.—"What the magistrates are ignorant of . . . is one particular department of Roman law—the one that concerns them, i.e., in broad terms, civil or praetorian law, and in particular the *ius potestatum* . . . , i.e., the law determining the powers of magistrates": J.G.F. Powell, *per litt.*—For *leges a librariis peti* and the *apparitores* cf. *ad* § 46.

quamobrem si de sacrorum alienatione dicendum putasti cum de religione leges proposueras, . . .] This special problem for *ius* in relation to *religio* was handled at 2.46–53.

. . . faciendum tibi est ut magistratibus lege {ob} constitutis, de potestatum iure disputes.] The *recentiores* already removed *ob*.—For the sense of *ius potestatum* see the note before last; in view of the connector *quamobrem*, *ius* in this sentence can hardly have the different, very broad sense ("condicio, status") claimed for our passage at *TLL* s.v., 687.56.

49 M. Faciam breviter si consequi potuero; nam pluribus verbis scripsit ad patrem tuum M. Iunius eo de iure, perite meo quidem iudicio et diligenter.] = *iur.* 13, 7, our sole testimony for the dedicatee of the *de Potestatibus* of the jurist and antiquarian M. Junius Congus Gracchanus, a friend not only of the elder T. Pomponius but also of the orator M. Antonius (cf. *de Orat.* 1.256); his second cognomen, never cited by Cicero, derived from his youthful friendship with C. Gracchus (cf. Shackleton Bailey, 1991, 54). The work comprised at least seven books (Ulp. *dig.* 1.13.1 pr.; hence *pluribus verbis*); the one explicitly attributed fragment (*iur.* p. 13, 12 = Lydus *Mag.* 1.24) maintains that the quaestorship existed as a popularly elected office prior to Tullus Hostilius (!). Cf. Wissowa, *RE* 10.1 (1917), 1031.34 ff. (Iunius no. 68).—*Eo de iure* is Powell's correction of the transmitted *sodalie*, for which Minutianus' *sodalis* is usually substituted, implausibly.

†nos ac de iure nate cogitari per nos et que dicere debemus†, de iure populi

Romani quae relicta sunt et tradita.] It is most unfortunate that this sentence is transmitted in so corrupt a form, for it indicates Cicero's method for the remainder of this Book. Evidently the project of Marcus and his interlocutors is being contrasted with that of M. Junius just described (*nos* . . .). Bake's *autem* for *ac*, P's *natur(a)e* for *nate* (AEL) or *nata* (SR), and Turnebus' *cogitare* and *atque* (for *et que*) are usually adopted. But *ac* may be correct and matter may have fallen out between *nos* and *ac*: what, one wonders, is the point of *per nos* with *nos* already placed emphatically at the beginning of the sentence? One thus suspects there may have been some extensive loss. Moreover, one doubts that Cicero and his interlocutors would be content merely to "state what has come down to us from earlier generations" (Rudd's paraphrase); and it is hard to see how *atque* could have been corrupted to *et que*. More plausible to suppose that *etqu(a)erere* was the original and, when this was found unintelligible, *dicere* extrapolated from *quod dicis* of the following sentence. If that is so, then the following clause may also be corrupt, at least to the point of requiring *sint* instead of *sunt*. Another possibility would be that some other verb, perhaps *explicare* or the like, has fallen out after *Romani*. It is also unclear that *de iure naturae* is correct (as Girardet, 1983, 88–89, assumes with further hypothesis built on this premise): it would be odd for *naturae* to be corrupted in the transmission of this work! Something like *nos autem de iure nationum ⟨omnium⟩* . . . would be just as plausible here in point of sense (as affording a contrast both to M. Junius, *de Magistratibus,* and the *ius populi Romani*); cf. 2.35: *non enim populo Romano sed omnibus bonis firmisque populis leges damus.* Görler-Ziegler smooth out the text through emendation, but their product fails to yield a satisfactory sense (see above); better to acknowledge the accumulated difficulties and possibilities by obelizing the text.—*Per nos,* if sound (see above), means "by our own efforts, independently," or the like; cf. *OLD* s.v. *per* 15b.

A. Sic prorsum censeo, et id ipsum quod dicis ⟨ex⟩specto.] For *prorsum* used with a demonstrative adverb to emphasize identity or correspondence cf. *OLD* s.v., 2b; for the similar use of *prorsus* cf. *ad* 2.12.—Eberhard Heck, "Zum Buchschluss von Cicero, De Legibus III," *Hermes* 107 (1979), 496–99, followed by Schmidt, 2001, 15, has argued that these words did, in fact, form the conclusion of *Leg.* 3. He points to Atticus' similar words at the very end of Book 2: *tu vero dic, et istam rationem quam coepisti tene;* and he calculates that the lacunae in Marcus' commentary on the laws, if proportionately filled out with what remains, would bring this Book up to about the requisite length. *Leg.* formed, however, the last element of the Leiden corpus (see the Introduction § 10); additional books are demonstrably lost (see on the fragment from Book 5); the truncation was probably due to mechanical causes and is unlikely to have coincided with a division between books. Likewise comparable to our passage are Atticus' words at 2.46 introducing the remarks on *pontificium ius* and *ius civile* that he has just cited (§ 48) as analogous to his current request: *sed tamen hoc magis eas res et memini et ⟨ex⟩specto, quod ad pontificium ius et ad civile pertinent*. And Marcus has just said that he plans to carry out Atticus' request *breviter*, so no very lengthy discussion is implied. Hence there need not have been any great disproportion of this Book as against the others; and, of course, the premise of even coverage in the commentary on the laws is itself by no means secure: some points are discussed at great length, others hardly or not at all (cf. *ad* 2.22.7, 26, 30–31, 34, 38–39, and 41; 3.19b–26, 33–39, 40, 43). So unless Cicero has been very misleading in raising the *iudicia* as the next topic (i.e., presumably the topic of the next Book) and in setting Atticus' request for a discussion *de iure magistratum* in parallel with his request for the discussion *de sacrorum alienatione* appended to Book 2 (with the implication that the former would be handled in a similar appendix to Book 3), we must assume that the handling of the *ius magistratuum* has been lost in a lacuna covering the final materials of Book 3.

Commentary on the Fragments

Fragment from Book 3:
Qui poterit socios tueri, si dilectum rerum utilium et inutilium non habebit?]
This sentence is cited at auct. inc. *de verbo* 37.4 and (through *tueri*) as from
Leg. 3 at Macr. *diff.* 17.6. Vahlen rightly placed it in the lacuna after § 17 as a
comment on *sociis parcunto* (§ 9.4).—The problem of the mistreatment of
Rome's allies weighed upon Cicero; cf. *ad Off.* 2.27–29; C.E.W. Steel, *Cicero, Rhetoric, and Empire* (Oxford, 2001), 192–202. Atticus' unclarified
statement in § 18 *eis qui in provinciis sunt minime placet* may allude to misrule by Roman provincial governors exemplified and excoriated in the missing matter; see *ad loc.* Perhaps Cicero went on to argue that fair treatment of
the allies was in the long-term interest of Rome, even if Rome might achieve
some short-term benefits by cheating them; cf. the example at *Off.* 1.33. In
that sense the defense of the allies will rest upon a (careful) choice between
utilia and *inutilia*.

Fragment from Book 5:
**Visne igitur, quoniam sol paululum a meridie iam devexus videtur, nequedum
satis ab his novellis arboribus omnis hic locus opacatur, descendamus ad
Lirem, eaque quae restant in illis alnorum umbraculis persequamur?**] In the
course of refuting the notion that Vergil coined the word *umbraculum*, Macr.
sat. 6.4.8 cites *inter alia* this passage with explicit attribution to *Leg.* 5 (. . . *et
Cicero in quinto de legibus* . . .). Luckily, he did not think to cite 3.14 instead,
where *umbraculum* also occurs (see *ad loc.*). Schmidt, 1965, 321, plausibly
assigned our fragment to the very beginning of its book, where it would be
likely to catch the eye. For the *visne* formula at the opening of a book cf. 2.1
(Atticus): *Sed visne . . . locum mutemus, et in insula quae est in Fibreno . . .
sermoni reliquo demus operam sedentes?* There is no difficulty in the placement of *igitur* at the beginning of a Book when a conversation is being
continued; cf. 3.1: *Sequar igitur, ut institui, divinum illum virum . . .* ; for
visne igitur cf. also 1.15. Perhaps Atticus was the speaker of our text, as he
generally takes charge of the stage-management of the dialogue (cf. the Introduction § 6; 1.14 and 2.1). For the different scenes of the conversation cf. *ad*
1.14; for the setting in summer cf. 2.3 and 69 and, implicitly, 3.30a. The

situation of seeking the shade of lofty trees is borrowed from Pl. *Lg.* 625b: πάντως δ' ἤ γε ἐκ Κνωσοῦ ὁδὸς εἰς τὸ τοῦ Διὸς ἄντρον καὶ ἱερόν . . . ἱκανή, καὶ ἀνάπαυλαι κατὰ τὴν ὁδόν, ὡς εἰκός, πνίγους ὄντος τὰ νῦν, ἐν τοῖς <u>ὑψηλοῖς δένδρεσίν</u> εἰσι σκιαραί . . .—*Novellus* is used only here and at *Fin.* 5.39 by Cicero,[1] both times with reference to trees; cf. *OLD* s.v., 1b.—*Opaco* is first attested at Pac. *trag.* 362: *nunc primum opacat flora lanugo genas* (possibly, as Ribbeck suggests *ad loc.*, an allusion to Parthenopaeus in the *Atalanta*); Cicero is the sole prose writer to use it prior to Columella and the elder Pliny (also of a tree's shade at *de Orat.* 1.28; cf. also *N.D.* 2.49 and 95); cf. *TLL* s.v.—*Descendamus,* Halm's correction for the transmitted *descendatur* (surely influenced by *opacatur*), seems natural in light of the parallel *persequamur* (2.1, cited above).—*Lirem* or *Lirim* were both possible spellings, but *Lirem* is to be restored here (for *Lirim* of the Macrobius mss.) in light of 1.14 and 2.6; cf. on the former passage and Schmidt, 1965, 331 n. 67.

Fragmenta ex incertis libris:

1. Sicut una eademque natura mundus omnibus partibus inter se congruentibus cohaeret ac nititur, sic omnes homines inter se natura coniuncti pravitate dissentiunt, neque se intellegunt esse consanguineos et subiectos omnes sub unam eandemque tutelam; quod si teneretur, deorum profecto vitam homines viverent.] This passage is quoted at Lact. *inst.* 5.8.10 with explicit attribution to *Leg.* Ziegler inserted it in the lacuna between 1.33 and 34 and corrected the transmitted *confusi* to *coniuncti.* It should be emphasized that the extent of this lacuna is quite uncertain. Cicero has established at some length the *hominum inter ipsos societas coniunctioque* (§ 28); if Ziegler is right, this explanation of the origin of diverging human views and interests, in spite of the common *tutela* (cf. § 23), contrasts with the godlike life (*deorum vita*) enjoyed by human beings at an earlier stage (and still possessed by the sages of § 34). It is perhaps not a decisive objection that *pravitas* at 1.31 is adduced in favor of human similarity; from another point of view it can also be a cause of difference. On the other hand, Schmidt, 1965, 319–20, sees the treatment of *pravitas* in this fragment as a prelude to the entire topic of crime and punishment in *Leg.* 4, *de iudiciis.* He seeks support for his case in Lactantius' reference nearby to such phenomena as *dissensiones, bella, fraudes, rapinae, adulteria, stupra, mulierum prostitutiones* (5.8.6), which he sees as a paraphrase of a Ciceronian polemic against Clodius' activities; however, *bella* fits less well than the other items. It is easier to picture this passage as part of Book 1 because of the several points

---

1. Based on a search of PHI 5.3.

it has in common with the argument there, but so little is known of Book 4 and its argumentation that Schmidt's theory cannot be excluded.

2. Gratulemurque nobis, quoniam mors aut meliorem quam qui est in vita aut certe non deteriorem adlatura est statum. nam sine corpore animo vigente divina vita est, sensu carente nihil profecto est mali.] Lact. *inst.* 3.19.2 cites this passage explicitly from *Leg.* (*quam sententiam Cicero de legibus sic explicavit: . . .*). The attribution has been doubted by Bake, XXXV, and Feldhügel, 1, 142, possibly rightly. The aim is to show that death is not a *malum*, a typical topic of consolation. It could form a basis, e.g., for *Cons.* F 9, cited by Lactantius a bit further on (3.19.14): *Cicero in Consolatione non nasci inquit longe optimum nec in hos scopulos incidere vitae, proximum autem, si natus sis, quam primum tamquam ex incendio effugere fortunae.* Those who want to claim the fragment for *Leg.* (Vahlen *ad* 2.68; Schmidt, 1965, 318–19) locate it in the lacuna between 2.53 and 54 and think that *eadem illa* at 2.68 points to a preceding discussion of the immortality of the soul including a citation of Pl. *Lg.* 959b. In particular it is claimed that the lacuna provided the premise for the consecration of the *boni* according to the conjecture ⟨*bo*⟩*nos leto datos divos habento* at 2.22.15. But in that passage ⟨*bo*⟩*nos* is unlikely; see *ad loc.*; and our fragment does not in any case differentiate the fate of the *boni*. It seems doubtful that Cicero can have referred back to a discussion of the immortality of the soul fourteen chapters earlier with the vague words *eadem illa* and have expected his readers to understand. Perhaps we ought rather to read *eodem loco*; see *ad* 2.68. Cicero's powers of incorporating seemingly irrelevant matter should not be underestimated, but nothing favors the theory that our fragment was lost in the lacuna between 2.53 and 54. In view of the fragmentary state of preservation of *Leg.*, certainty is unobtainable; but it is a distinct possibility that, by a slip of the pen, Lactantius may have cited *de Legibus* when he meant to write *de Consolatione*.

Fragmentum dubium:

Magnum Cicero audaxque consilium suscepisse Graeciam dicit, quod Cupidinum et Amorum simulacra in gymnasiis consecrasset.] = Lact. *inst.* 1.20.14. In view of Lactantius' immediately following comment, *adulatus est videlicet Attico et inrisit hominem familiarem*, this fragment was assigned by Turnebus to *Leg.* 2.28 (which Lactantius goes on to cite at 1.20.16: *. . . adiecit: virtutes enim oportere, non vitia consecrari*) without its having been convincingly integrated with the transmitted text of that passage; Vahlen *ad loc.* rejected Turnebus' thesis. Schmidt, 1965, 316–17, argued that the passage refers rather to *N.D.* 2.61 (*Cupidinis et Voluptatis et*

Lubentinae Veneris vocabula consecrata sunt). But the specific point of our text, namely the establishment of statues of Cupids in gymnasia, is not paralleled there. Moreover, Lactantius goes on to deplore the gymnasia of Greece as a breeding ground for vice before turning back again to the question of the divinization of vices (1.20.16), so this point is not likely to have been missing from the original Ciceronian context. We should probably, with Ziegler, posit a lacuna in 2.28 just prior to *virtutes enim non vitia consecrari decet* in order to accommodate this point. The immorality of Greek education was likewise excoriated by Scipio at *Rep.* 4.3 ff.

Addenda et Corrigenda

P. 11, l. 11: after "connected argument" delete period and add: "; cf. also p. 245 *infra* on the latter part of the 2.28."

P. 31, l. 22: after "the absence of reference to the work by Quintilian" add: "(possibly, however, *avium concentus* at *Inst.* 5.9.16 is a quotation of 1.21)."

P. 60, l. 1 (1.1): after "Hand, 2, 401 ff." add: "; cf. also W.S. Watt, "*enim* Tullianum," *CQ* 74 [1980], 120–21".

P. 66, l. 8 (1.4): after "308–12" delete period and add: "; see further Margalit Finkelberg, *The Birth of Literary Fiction in Ancient Greece* (Oxford, 1998)."

P. 76, l. 10 (1.6): after "(Paris, 1986);" add: "*Die frühen römischen Historiker,* ed. Hans Beck and Uwe Walter, vol. 1, *Von Fabius Pictor bis Cn. Gellius* (Darmstadt, 2001), 148–224;"

P. 80, n. 43 (1.7): after "slant of his work" delete period and add: "; cf. Wiseman, 1979, 45 and n. 25 with literature."

P. 81, fourth from last line of text (1.7): after "published later" delete period and add: "; cf. Ronald Syme, *Sallust* (Berkeley–Los Angeles, 1964), 47."

P. 112, l. 2 (1.19): after "Frier" delete period and add: "; G. Ciulei, *L'équité chez Cicéron* (Amsterdam, 1972)."

P. 150, second from last line of text (1.31): after "Powell *ad Sen.* 26" delete period and add: "; Beate Hintzen, *Das Partizip Präsens in Ciceros Reden* (Münster–New York, 1993), 38."

P. 193, l. 28 (1.45): after "the contained term" delete period and add: "; cf. Quint. *Inst.* 5.10.90."

P. 199, l. 22 (1.48): after "*optinere*" delete period and add: "; Quint. 4.5.22."

P. 207, l. 6 (1.52a): after "in the speeches" delete period and add: "; cf. also Berry *ad Sul.* 35.5."

P. 226, l. 19 (1.58): after "entire phrase;" add: "cf. Sal. *Cat.* 48.5: *tanta vis hominis;*"

P. 255, l. 13 (2.4): after *sepulcrum* delete period and add: "with Mary Jaeger, 'Cicero and Archimedes' Tomb,' *JRS* 92 (2002), 49–61."

P. 262, l. 31 (2.6b): after "Gasser, 40." add: "It may be relevant that, apparently at his Palatine home, Cicero had a *palaestra* that he was keen to equip *ad similitudinem gymnasiorum;* cf. *Fam.* 7.23.2 with Shackleton Bailey's note."

P. 282, l. 7 (2.14b): after "Lg. 722b4 ff.)." add: "On the implications of Plato's use of persuasion in the proems to his laws cf. Christopher Bobonich, 'Persuasion, Compulsion, and Freedom in Plato's Laws,' *CQ* 41 (1991), 365–88."

P. 293, l. 14 (2.19.3): after "24–54" delete period and add: " = *Collected Papers,* vol. 2, *The Greeks and Their Legacy* (Oxford, 1988), 135–57 with 'additional note,' 157–58."

P. 326, 5th from last line (2.25): after "esp. 113–14" delete period and add:

"; D.H. Berry, '*Equester ordo tuus est:* Did Cicero Win His Cases because of His Support for the *equites?*' *CQ* 53 (2003), 222–34."

P. 338, next to last line (2.29a): after lemma add: "For the *iunctura hostiae maiores* cf. *Agr.* 2.93.—"

P. 352, l. 30 (2.36): after "*ad* 1.3" add: "; Cicero had already imitated this passage at *Flac.* 62".

P. 360, last line of text (2.40): after lemma add: "= no. 135 in H.W. Parke and D.E.W. Wormell, *The Delphic Oracle,* 2: *The Oracular Responses* (Oxford, 1956).—"

P. 365, l. 3 (2.42): after "n. 60" delete period and add: "; the chronology is controversial, however, and the departure sometimes dated as late as the end of March; cf. Marinone, 104 with literature."

P. 370, l. 12 (2.43): after "Clodius" add: "(the latter point also to Catiline; cf. *Cat.* 1.18, cited on 1.42)".

P. 384, l. 18 (2.49): after "440.36–41." add: "E. Badian, *JRS* 57 (1967), 228–29, argues that Cicero's explicit statement at *Amic.* 1 (*ita eram deductus ad Scaevolam . . . ut quoad possem et liceret a senis latere numquam discederem*) is false; but it is more likely that the reading at *Brut.* 306 rests upon a confusion of *P.f.* and *Q.f.* Badian adduces Cicero's omission of reference to his military service in the *Brutus* as a parallel for Cicero's 'touching up' of his autobiography. But the omission is unremarkable: Cicero is discussing great oratory at Rome and the formation of the orator, not his autobiography *per se.*"

P. 432, 4th from last line (3.2): after "F. Sommer, 124–26" delete period and add: "; Michèle Ducos, 'Les magistrats et le pouvoir dans les traités politiques de Cicéron,' *Ciceroniana* n.s. 7 (1990), 83–96 at 91."

P. 500, l. 13 (3.20): after "442–53;" add: "Christine M. Chapman, 'Cicero and P. Sulpicius Rufus (tr. pl. 88 B.C.),' *Acta Classica* 22 (1979), 61–72;"

Ibid., l. 32 (3.21): after "cf." add: "C. Wirszubski, '*Audaces:* A Study in Political Phraseology,' *JRS* 51 (1961), 12–22;"

P. 530, l. 23 (3.36a): after "see the note after next)." add: "Cassius' law was for a time superseded by a Cornelian law of 82 that gave the defendant the choice whether the jurors' votes were to be secret or disclosed; cf. *Clu.* 55 and 75; Rotondi, p. 351; by the date of Cluentius' trial (66: Alexander no. 198) the *status quo ante* had been restored."

P. 541, l. 17 (3.41): after "(Antonius)" delete period and add: "; Harry Caplan, 'Memoria: Treasure-House of Eloquence,' in *Of Eloquence: Studies in Ancient and Mediaeval Rhetoric,* ed. Anne King and Helen North (Ithaca–London, 1970), 196–246."

P. 546, l. 24 (3.44): after "critical point;" add: "cf., however, Francis X. Ryan, 'Cicero, *Mur.* 47: Text and Meaning,' *Gymnasium* 101 (1994), 481–82, who proposes to emend *praerogationum* to *promulgationem;*"

P. 548, l. 3 (3.46): after "*ad Off.* 2.66" add: "; Berry *ad Sul.,* pp. 40–41".

P. 554, l. 7 (3.49): after "are usually adopted" delete period and add: "; Powell now moots (*per litt.*) *nos autem de iure naturae cogitata per nos et quae⟨sita⟩ dicere debemus, de iure populi Romani quae relicta sunt et tradita,* which gives a better balance."

Addenda et Corrigenda to A.R. Dyck, *A Commentary on Cicero, de Officiis*

P. 28, l. 3 "Cicero's Use of His Model": here and *passim* readers will want to consider the arguments of Eckard Lefèvre, *Panaitios' und Ciceros Pflichtenlehre*, Historia Einzelschriften 150 (Stuttgart, 2001).

P. 52, l. 19 "The Text": see now Paolo Fedeli, "Noterelli al *De officiis* di Cicerone," *Paideia* 55 (2000), 217–24.

P. 164. ll. 12–22 (1.49): "Hence Pohlenz, *AF,* 36, n. 3, comparing for the thought § 44 and 2.54–55, proposed *sine iudicio vel modo ⟨effusi⟩ vel⟨ut⟩ morbo in omnes* (*modo* appears as a weakly attested variant for *morbo*); for *effusi* Pohlenz compares *Parad.* 21: . . . *an virum . . . dices . . . temperantem qui se in aliqua libidine continuerit, in aliqua effuderit?* (his reference to *Att.* 5.9.3 is in error, however); for the participle *effusus* used for an adjective in the sense *largus, prodigiosus* cf. Leumann, *TLL* 5, 219.71 ff. However, *vel modo . . . vel⟨ut⟩ morbo* seems an unnecessary expansion. Surely either after Pohlenz *vel⟨ut⟩ morbo in omnes ⟨effusi⟩* or after Holford-Strevens (*apud* Winterbottom) *vel⟨ut⟩ morbo in omnes ⟨prodigi⟩* would restore the probable sense."

P. 186, l. 32 ff. (1.61): The solution to Ennius' *Salmaci da spolia* has now been provided (with telling parallel: Phld. *AP* 7.222 = 26 GP = 33 Sider, 1–2) by Hugh Lloyd-Jones, "The Pride of Halicarnassus: Corrigenda and Addenda," *ZPE* 127 (1999), 64.

P. 274, l. 16 (1.108): after "§ 76" add: "; *ad Leg.* 3.36b;"

P. 316, l. 16 (1.138–40): after "4 ff." add: "; Anne Leen, 'Cicero and the Rhetoric of Art,' *AJPh* 112 (1991), 237–38."

P. 320. ll. 18–19 (1.142): εὐταξία.

P. 335, l. 27 (1.150): after lemma add: "This view of merchants can be paralleled in Greek sources; cf. Pl. *Lg.* 918d with Glenn R. Morrow, *Plato's Cretan City* (Princeton, 1960), 144; Arist. *Pol.* 1328b39–41; D.L. 1.105."

P. 336, l. 16 (ibid.): after "§ 104" delete period and add: "; for an alternative interpretation cf. Russell on Quintilian 11.3.58."

P. 372, l. 33 (2.10): after lemma delete "A much disputed text." and add: "For the transference of *auctoritas* to the sphere of philosophy (*summa auctoritate philosophi*) and its implications cf. Richard Heinze, 'Auctoritas,' *Hermes* 60 (1925), 362 = *Vom Geist des Römertums*[3] (Darmstadt, 1960), 55.—The text is much disputed."

P. 378, fourth from last line (2.11): read "2, 154" (not "1, 154").

P. 400, l. 26 (2.26b–29a): add at end: "Cf. now C.E.W. Steel, *Cicero, Rhetoric, and Empire* (Oxford, 2001), 193–94."

P. 406, ll. 36 ff. (2.29a: the scribe Cornelius): cf. Ernst Badian, "The *scribae* of the Roman Republic," *Klio* 71 (1989), 582–603, esp. 586–87.

P. 407, l. 19 (ibid.): after "κεναί;" add: "the Pompeian view quoted at *Att.* 7.11.3: *non est . . . in parietibus respublica;*"

P. 419, l. 15 (2.40): after "*ad loc.*)." add: "Cicero could also have cited the example of Spartacus; cf. App. *BC* 1.541."

P. 446, l. 8 (2.58): after "cognomina" delete period and add: "; the same perhaps applies to Servius, as is suggested by the letters to Cicero of Servius Sulpicius Rufus; cf. T.A. Dorey, 'The Use of *praenomina* in Cicero's Letters,' *Humanitas* 9–10 (1957–58), 35."

P. 458, ll. 5–9 (2.69): delete "*E silentio* support . . . cites it only from *Planc.*": Antonius Julianus' critique is formulated on the basis of the specific wording of *Planc.* 68; therefore it cannot lend *e silentio* support to the omission of the enthymeme at *Red. Pop.* 23 or our passage (I owe this point to Miriam T. Griffin).

P. 563, l. 10 (3.54): after "with Wankel's note" delete period and add: "; Walter Burkert, *Savage Energies: Lessons of Myth and Ritual in Ancient Greece*, tr. Peter Bing (Chicago, 2001), 92 and 96 n. 37."

P. 565, 15–16 (3.58): after "Cicero will surely have heard the anecdote, as Frier suggests, during his Sicilian quaestorship." add: "Some have suggested, however, that Cicero owes the anecdote to Lucilius; cf. Jens S.T. Hanssen, *Latin Diminutives* (Bergen, 1952), 148–49."

P. 599, l. 6 (3.80–81): after "1–4" delete period and add: "; K. Verboven, 'The Monetary Enactments of M. Marius Gratidianus,' in C. Deroux, ed., *Studies in Latin Literature and Roman History*, 7 (Brussels, 1994), 117–31."

P. 656, l. 42 (addendum to p. 277, last line): substitute "⟨*potest*⟩" for "Κpotest1".

P. 657, ll. 2–3 (addendum to p. 325, l. 22): substitute "⟨*valent, id*⟩" for "kvalent, id1".

P. 658, addendum to p. 459, third line from bottom: read "Attica" not "Atticia."

P. 674 s.v. *Venustas:* read "1.95," not "1.94."

P. 713, left column: after 1.7 add: "Marius, M. (22), 3.80–81."

Indices

References below are to the section or sections of Cicero's text on which the relevant comment appears or, following "p." or "pp.," to the page number(s) of the introduction to this volume or to the individual Books. A repetition of section number may occur if there is a reference both in a comment on a group of sections and on an individual section within that group.

The Index of Authors includes references to pre–nineteenth-century authors and to passages in their works actually quoted verbatim or discussed, whether by way of interpretation or paraphrase, not to passages simply cited. The authors' names appear in the form most familiar to English readers, e.g., "Lucan," not "Annaeus Lucanus, M." Works are listed alphabetically with fragments unassigned to works at the end of the series, followed by spuria.

The Index of Proper Names is, for Romans, arranged alphabetically by *gentes,* next *familiae,* then *praenomina,* and then chronologically within this framework. Identification in parentheses is by year of first consulate or dictatorship or, in default of these, the highest office held, otherwise by article number in the *RE* (* indicates that there is only one article under the *gentilicium,* # indicates the absence of an *RE* article) or for well-known persons some more obvious identifier, e.g., "Tullius Cicero, M. (the orator)." In the case of Cicero, data bearing on his biography (i.e., other than his opinions and literary methods) are included in the Index of Proper Names, philosophical/literary data in the Index of Authors. To avoid a confusion of *Dichtung und Wahrheit,* names of characters in Cicero's dialogues are excluded.

Index of Topics

God(s) (*continued*)
  fear of, 1.43a
  foreign, expelled from Athens in Aris-
    tophanes' ‌Ὧραι, 2.37
    Roman acceptance of, 2.19.7
  human origin of some, 2.19.7
  proof for existence of, intro. to 2,
    2.15b–16, 15b, 16, p. 304 n. 56
  theriomorphic, 1.24
Gloss, supposed origin of a reading as,
  1.4, 25, 34b, 61, 2.28, 41
Golden age, Cicero's conception of,
  1.40
Good (as predicate of law), 2.11, 12
Goods, classification of, 1.37, 52a, 55
  hierarchy of, 1.48–52a, 54, 56. *See*
    Index of Latin Words s.v.
    Summus, Summum bonum, In-
    dex of Greek Words s.v. Τέλος.
Grave goods, restrictions on, 2.59
Greek institutions/practices
  as models, 2.22.2 and 5, 26, 47, 59,
    intro. to 3, 3.46
  criticism of, 2.36
"Greek rite." *See* s.v. *Worship, Graeco
  sacro*

Haplography, 1.14, 3.43. *See* s.v.
  Saltation error.
Haruspices, 2.14a, 21.2 and 4 and 8–
  10, 25, 29a, 34
Hedonism, Hedonist, 1.34a, 37
Hierarchy, reversal of, 1.28a. *See* s.v.
  Goods, hierarchy of.
Historicity, problems of, 1.1–4, 2.15a
Historiography, Intro. § 4, 1.1, 5a, 5b–
  12, 5b, 9, 13–15, 62
Honors, *ad hominem* vs. heritable, 2.58
Human being(s), definition of, 1.29
  false choices made by, 1.31
  nature of, 1.21
  possession of reason by, 1.30
  qualities of, 1.22, 23, 26b–27, 29
  similarity of to one another, 1.29, 31,
    34a
Humor, examples of, Intro. § 6, 1.8,
  28a, 54, 2.11 *fin.,* 3.18, 26b, 38

Ideal state or persons, Cicero's laws in-
  tended for, 3.11.3–5, 26a, 28b–
  29, 34
Illegal action, 1.42
Impiety, 2.42
  trials for, 2.19.2
Incompleteness or lack of final polish,
  possible signs of, Intro. §§ 9–10,
  1.32, 40–52, 56, p. 245, 2.14b–
  18, 17, 68, 3.6–11, 13a, 29
"Indifferents" (in Stoic philosophy),
  1.38, 55
Ingratitude, 1.32
Injustice, 1.28b–34a
Innovations in Ciceronian laws, 1.42,
  3.11.13–14, 12, 27, 46
  downplayed, 3.12
Institution(s), disappearance of, 2.33
  Greek, criticized, 2.36
Intent, as criterion for judging an act,
  2.22.1, 37
Intercalation, 2.23, 29a
Intercession, 3.6.2, 9, 24, 42
Interest of the state, p. 238 n. 3
Interlocutor(s)
  assignment of major speaking rôle
    among, 1.13. *See also* Index of
    Authors s.v. *Cicero, M. Tullius,
    "Heraclidean" vs. "Aristotelian"
    dialogues written by.*
  authority of buttressed, 1.58–62,
    3.13b–14
  choice of topics by, 1.13–15
  clarification sought by, 1.4, 63, 3.33
  contrast of characters among, 3.34
  expressions of satisfaction by, 1.63,
    2.69
  indications of parts of in ms., 1.1, 57
  modesty of, 1.14, 57, 63
  prior conversations among, 1.21, 56,
    2.2, 3.27
  rôle of keeping discussion on track or
    propelling it forward, Intro. § 6,
    1.4, 5a, 2.7a, 24, 45, 58, 62, 69,
    3.12
  rôle of stage-managing the dialogue,
    Intro. § 6, fr. Bk. 5

Index of Latin Words

Favor, 2.11
Faxo, 2.19.2
-fer, 1.2
Feriae, 2.19.9, 29a, 45, 55. See also s.v.
    Denicalis.
Ferrum, 3.20
Fetura, 2.20.1
Fetus, 1.25, 2.20.1
Fingo, 1.47
Finio, 2.20.1
Finis, 1.55, 2.55
    bonorum, intro. to 1, 1.37, 38, 46,
        47, 52b–57, 52b–56, 52b, 56.
        See Index of Greek Words s.v.
        Τέλος.
Fio de, 1.3
Flagito, 1.5b, 3.34
Flamen, 2.20.3
Focus, 2.29b
Foedus, 3.41
Fons, 1.16
Formula, 1.14
Fortitudo, 1.51
Forum, 2.61
Frango, 1.38
Fraus, 1.40, 3.11.3–5
Frequens, 3.40
Fructus, 1.25, 41
Fugo, 1.31
Fulgur, 2.21.4
Fulmen, 2.21.4
Fulvus, 1.2
Fundo, p. 164 n. 148
Funus, 2.55
    indictivum, 2.61
Furca, 2.22.7
Furiae, 1.40, 2.25
Furor, 3.22
Furtum, 2.22.5
Fuse. See s.v. Fundo.

Gaudium, 1.31
Gentilis, 1.23
Genus, 1.22, 24, 29, 30
    orationis, intro. to 2, 2.7b–18
Gigno, 2.28
Glandifer, 1.2

Gleba, 2.57, p. 398 n. 130
Gloria, 1.32
Gradus, 3.7.2
Graecia, 2.39
Graius, 2.26
Grammaticus, 2.59
Gratus deo, 2.41
Gravis, 2.41
Gravitas, 3.1, 17, 19b, 47a
Guberno, 3.28a

Habeo, 1.16, 24, 2.25, 45, 52
    Habessit, 2.19.3
Habilitas, 1.27
Habito, 3.14
Habitus, 1.45
Hercle, 1.8, 2.8, 3.1
Hermae, 2.65
Herous, 2.68
Hic, 1.1, 8, 33, 39, 58, 2.18, p. 289 n.
    45, 48a
Hic . . . ille, 1.1, 24
Honestas, 1.32
Honestus, 1.1, 37, 38–39, 42, 44b–46,
    45, 46, 48–52a, 55, 3.6.5
Honor amplior, 3.6–11
Horridus, 1.6
Hortulus, 1.39, 54
Hostis, 1.1, 2.57
Humanitas, 3.1
Humo, Intro. § 9, 2.57, 58

Iam, 1.50, 2.34
Iam nunc, 1.56
Iam vero, 1.25
Igitur, 1.18b, 25, 2.8, 14a, 3.5, 15, fr.
    Bk. 5
Igniculus, 1.33
Ignorantia, 1.18a
Ignoratio, 1.18a, 2.47
Ignoro, 1.42
Ignotus, 2.58
Ille, Intro. § 9, 1.1, 2.14b, 3.17. See s.v.
    Hic.
Illecebra, 1.31
Imitatio, 1.5a
Immanis, 1.49, 51, 3.42

civitatis, intro. to 1, 1.14–15, 14, 34
gentium, p. 103 n. 69
ipsum, intro. to 1, 1.18b–19, 20
naturae, 1.40
parietum, 1.14, 2.47
pontificale, 2.55, 56
pontificium, 2.46–53, 46, 58, intro. to 3
praetorium, 1 17
publicum, 2.17, 46
religionum, 2.42
religiosum, 2.55, 57
sacrum, 2.17
universum, 1.14–15, 14, 17, 20
unum, 1.42
Iussum, 1.17
Iustitia, 1.41, 42, 43a, 48, 49, 51
Iustus, 1.41, 2.13, 57
-ix, 1.47

Labellum, 2.66
Labes, 1.60, 2.24
  animi, 2.24
Lac, 2.20.1
Lar, 2.42
Latro, 2.13, 3.45
Laudabilis, 1.32, 46, 2.11
Laudes, 2.19.7
Lautus, p. 407 n. 134
Legatio, libera, 1.10a, 10b–11, 3.6–11, 18
Legatus, 1.10a
Lego, 1.1, 1.18b–19, 19
Levis, 3.18
Lessus, Intro. § 9, 2.59
Letum
  Leto datus, 2.22.15–16, 3.19b
Levis, 1.31
Lex, p. 109 n. 76, 1.16, 18b–19, 18b, 19, 20, 22, 23, 27, 33, 57, 58, intro to 2, 2.2, 7b–18, 8–9a, 8, 11, 12, 13, 16, 23, 3.2, 8.2, 44. *See* Index of Topics s.v. *Law*.
  leges, 1.5a, 20, 63, 2.8–9a, 11, 13, 16, 18, 69
  aeterna, Intro. § 8

naturalis, Intro. § 8
sacrata, 3.44
scripta, 1.19, 42
summa, 1.19, 20–21
suprema, 3.3
  legis actiones, 1.14
Libamen, p. 338 n. 79
Libamentum, 2.29a
Liber, 1.8, p. 164 n. 148. *See* s.v. *Legatio*.
Liberalitas, 1.43a, 48–52a, 48, 51
Libere. See s.v. *Liber*.
Libero, 2.21.4
Libertas, 2.42, 3.20, 25, 38, 39
Libido, 1.51, 3.30b–32
Libra, 2.51
Librariolus, 1.7
Librarius, 1.7
Libripens, 2.51
Licentia, 2.42
Liris, -em/-im, 1.14, 2.6b, fr. Bk. 5
Locus, 2.46, 3.19b
  religiosus, 2.54–68, 57, 58, 61
Loedus. See s.v. *Ludus*.
Loquor, 1.2, 55
Lorica, 3.6.4
Ludus, Intro. § 9, 2.22.2, 3.7.1

Magister, 1.54
  equitum, 3.6–11
  populi, 3.9.2, p. 461 n. 36
Magistratus, 2.69, 3.2–5, 2, 15
  maior, 3.6.5
  minor, 3.6.5
Magno opere, 1.53
Magnus (cognomen), 2.6a
Maiores, 2.55, 62, 3.7.1, 9.1, 12, 44, 46. *See* s.v. *Mos*.
Maleficus, 1.32
Malitia, 1.49, p. 201 n. 195
Malus, 1.44b–46, 46, 55, 3.11.6, fr. ex inc. lib. 2
  malum do/habeo, 1.41
Mando, 3.33
Maneo, 1.1
Manus, 1.36
Maturitas, 1.24

Index of Greek Words

Ἀγαθόν, 1.55
Ἄγαλμα, 1.59
Ἀγύρται, 2.22.4
Ἀγών, 2.37
Ἀδιαφορία, 1.38
Ἀδιάφορα, 1.38
Ἄδικον, 1.44b–46
Αἰδώς, 1.33
Αἰσχρόν, 1.2, 44b–46, 45
Ἀκριβέστερον, 2.22.9
Ἀλλότρια, Intro. § 5
Ἀναφέρομαι, 1.20
Ἀναφέρω, 1.20
Ἀναφορά, 1.20
Ἀνείλιξις, 1.24
Ἀνόητος, p. 190 n. 184
Ἀνομία, 1.42
Ἀποπροηγμένον, 1.55
Ἀπορία, 3.26b
Ἀρετή, 1.25, 45
Ἀρχή, 1.18a
Αὔξησις, 3.23
Ἀφορμή, 1.28b–34a, 33
Ἄφρων, 1.44a

Βαλανηφόρος, 1.2
Βραχυλογία, 2.23

Γέ, 2.23
Γνώμη, σύμπασα, 2.18
Γυναικονόμος, 2.66

Δαίμων, 2.28
Δεῖγμα, 2.18
Διαλεκτική, 1.62
Διάνοια, 1.22
Δίκαιον, τό, 1.23, 28b, 3.5
Δικαιοσύνη, 1.23
Δίκη, 1.23, 33

Διοίκησις, 1.23
Δύναμις, 1.19

Εἶδος, 1.22
*Εἴδω, 2.33
Εἶεν . . . δέ, 1.2
Εἰκών, 1.59
Ἐκπύρωσις, 1.61
Ἐκφορά, 2.66
Ἔννοια, Intro. § 9, 1.24, 26b, 59
    κοινή, 1.24, 26b
Ἐξηγητής, 2.67
Ἐπαχθής, 2.41
Ἐπιθυμία, 1.51, 60
Ἐπίστημα, 2.68
Ἐποχή, 1.52b, 2.33
Ἐργάσιμος, 2.67
Ἔργον, 1.51
    ἔργα γυναικῶν, 2.45
Ἕρματα, 2.65
Ἑστία, 2.29b
Ἔσχατος, p. 318 n. 67
Εὐαγής, 2.19.1, 45
Εὐδαιμονία, 1.52a
Εὔθυνος, 3.47a
Εὐθυντής, 3.47a
Ἐῶ χαίρειν, 1.39

Ζήτημα, 1.4

Ἡδονή, 1.20, 60
Ἡνωμένον, 1.24

Θεσμοθέτης, 3.47a
Θήκη, 2.67
Θριγκός, 1.62

Ἴαχος, 2.35
Ἰσοτιμία, 1.49

Index of Grammatical and Stylistic Features

Index of Authors

Accius
  praet. 39: 3.8.2
  trag.
    143: 1.22
    pp. 328–31: 2.54
Acilius, L.
  iur. anteh. 18: 2.59
Aelian
  Varia Historia
    2.39: 2.59
Aelius Paetus, Sextus
  Tripertita
    iur. 1 = *iur. anteh.* 15–16: p. 4
      n. 21
    iur. 1, 3 = *iur. anteh.* 16, 4: 2.59
Aelius Stilo Praeconinus, L., Intro. § 3,
    2.54–68, 58–62a, 60, 61
  gram. p. 61, fr. 13: 2.59
  gram. p. 64, fr. 24: 2.21.10
Aeschines
  3.203: 1.18b
  3.249: 1.18b
Aeschylus
  Choephori 519–21: 2.24
  Eumenides 261 ff.: 2.24
    804 ff.: 2.28
Alcidamas
  no. 3 Avezzù: 1.42
Alcinous
  Introductio in Platonem 7: 1.62
Andocides
  1.87: p. 544 n. 95
Annius Luscus, T.
  orat. p. 106, no. 5: 3.11.8
Anonymous
  auctor *hypotheseos in Platonis Leges,*
    1.15
  auctor *Prolegomenon in Platonis*
    philosophiam 26.57–58: 1.15

de verbo 37.4: fr. Book 3
de Viribus illustribus urbis Romae
    81. 2.3
Rhetorica ad Herennium
    2.44: 3.23
    3.9: 3.41
    3.23: 1.11
    3.28–40: 3.41
    4.31: 3.20
    trag. inc. 43: 2.36
    167: p. 164 n. 151
Antiochus of Ascalon: Intro. § 2a, in-
    tro. to 1, p. 47 n. 2, p. 51 n. 10, p.
    130 n. 101, 1.24, 26b, 27, 39, 54,
    56, p. 222 n. 223, 1.58–62, 61,
    intro. to 2
Antipater of Tarsus
    SVF 3, 252.31–32: intro. to 1
    SVF 3, 252.39–253.2: 1.56
Antonius, M.
  orat. pp. 229 ff.: 3.11.3–5
  orat. p. 231: 3.23
Appian
  Bellum Civile
    1.92: p. 499 n. 67
    1.459: 1.42
    2.83: 3.25
    2.505: 3.25
    3.250–52: 3.46
  Numidica 3: 3.6.4
Apuleius
  Metamorphoses 1.8: 3.14
Aratus
    1: 2.7b
    5: 1.22
Arcesilas, 1.39
Archias, A. Licinius, Intro. § 4
Aristides Quintilianus
    2.6: 2.38–39

2.25: 1.50
3.10 ff.: 1.40, 2.43
3.13: 1.27
3.25: 1.5b
4.4: 3.25
4.7: p. 318 n. 67
4.9: 3.8.2
4.11: p. 318 n. 67
4.18: 2.20.3
in Pisonem
1: 1.27
6: 1.53
9: 2.14a, 3.7.3
17: 3.7.2
21: 2.42
23: 3.8.2
28: p. 346 n. 91
33: 1.52a
35: 2.42
37: p. 217 n. 214
41: 2.42
46: 1.40
57: 3.35
68: 1.41
85–86: 2.47
94: 3.47b
95: 3.47b
frr. 9, 13, 14, 15, 16: p. 256 n. 32
in Vatinium
14: 2.26
16: 2.42
in Verrem
43: p. 177 n. 172
1.6: 1.40
1.13: 2.43
1.98: 2.14a
1.103: 1.12
1.111: 2.16
1.155: 3.22
2.37: 2.36
2.128–30: p. 337 n. 78
3.15: 3.3
3.45: 1.3
3.81: 1.42
3.132: p. 177 n. 172
3.177: 3.21
3.183–84: 3.46

3.195: 1.40
4.30: 3.18
4.107: 2.4
5.28: 3.11.7
5.133: 3.6.4
5.163: 3.6.2
Lucullus
4: 1.54
5: 1.2, 12
13: 3.20
17: 1.30
18: 1.30
21: 1.27
30: 1.59
31: 1.56, 59
54: p. 145 n. 120
62: 1.36
66: 1.39, 63
69: 1.17, 54
77: 1.55
78: 1.39
79–90: 1.47
80: 2.6b, 39, 43
92: 1.16
101: 1.21
104: 2.15a
112: p. 164 n. 152
113: 1.54
114: 1.58–62
118: 2.26
119: 1.36
120: 1.25
126: 1.22
131: 1.37
132: intro. to 1, 1.54, 55
144: 3.19b
Marius, Intro. §§ 4, 5, 6, 1.1–5a, 1, 4, 2.2
orationes post reditum habitae, Intro. §§ 4, 6
Orator, 2.9b
5: 1.36
10: 2.14b
12: 1.36, 63
14: 1.18a
30: 1.6, 62
40: 1.36

Index of Proper Names

Pompeius Rufus, Q. (40, son of the above), 3.20

Pomponius, T. (father of the following#), 3.49

Pomponius Atticus, T., Intro. §§ 2b, 5, 1.1, 2, 3, 13, 21, 3.1
avid reader of Cicero's speeches, 2.2
corrector of Cicero's Greek, 2.64
estate of at Buthrotum, 2.1–7a, 7a
political views of, 3.26b

Popillii (Laeni), 2.55

Popilius Laenas, C. (19), 3.36a

Popilius Laenas, P. (cos. 132), 3.26a

Porcius Cato, C. (tr. pl. 56), 2.30

Porcius Cato Censorius, M., 2.3, 5, 22, 3.6.2

Porcius Cato Uticensis, M., 3.40, 46

Porcius Laeca, P. (21), 3.6.4

Porta Capena, 2.28, 57

Porta Mugonia, 2.28

Poseidon, 1.2

Postumius, A. (dict. 499), 2.19.7

Postumius Albinus, M. (cens. 403), 3.7.3

Postumius Tubertus, A. (63), 2.58

Postumius Tubertus, P. (cos. 505), 2.58

Proculus Julius, 1.3

Praeneste, 2.28

Praetextatus, Vettius Agorius (cos. des. A.D. 385), 2.36

Prodicus of Ceus, 2.38

Ptolemaeum, 1.54, 56

Ptolemy XII Auletes, king of Egypt, 2.30

Punic War
First, 2.19.7, 28
Second, 2.28, 3.7.3, 9.1

Pupius Piso, M. (cos. 61), 1.54

Pyramus (river), 2.33

Pyrrhus of Epirus, 2.58

Pythagoras, Pythagorean(s), 1.33, 34a, 40, intro. to 2, 2.14b, 15a, 26, 29a, 3.2. *See* Index of Authors s.v. *Pythagorean Texts.*

Pythia, 2.1–7a

Quinctius, P. (16), 1.11

Quirinal (hill), 1.1, 2.28

Quirinus, 1.3, 2.19.7

Rabirius, C. (5), 3.29

Regillus, battle of Lake, 2.19.7

Remus, p. 84 n. 48

Rhodes, war with, 3.11.8

Roma, 3.39

Romulus, 1.3, 4, 2.28, 33, p. 348 n. 94, 2.40

Rosalia, 2.45

Roscius Gallus, Q. (16), 1.11

Rutilius Rufus, P. (cos. 105), 3.47b

Salus, 1.3, 2.28

Samian War, 2.65

Samnite(s), 1.1, 2.28

Samnite War, Third, 2.19.7, 28

Samos, 2.41

Sarapis, 2.19.3

Saturn, temple of, 2.22.5

Saturnalia, 2.29a

Scribonius Curio, C. (cos. 76), 1.53

Sempronius Atratinus, L. (cos. 444), 3.7.3

Sempronius Gracchus, C. (tr. pl. I 123), 3.11.11, 20, 22, 26a, 35, 49. *See* Index of Authors s.v. *Gracchus, C. Sempronius.*

Sempronius Gracchus, Ti. (cos. I 177), 2.31

Sempronius Gracchus, Ti. (tr. pl. 133), 2.56, 3.11.6, 20, 24, 26a, 35

Sempronius Tuditanus, P. (cos. 204), 2.28

Senones, 3.20

Septimius Severus, L. (emperor A.D. 193–211), 2.22.4

Sergius, L. (15), 2.42

Sergius Catilina, L. (pr. 68), Intro. § 4, 1.12, 2.13, 3.47b
his conspiracy, 2.62b, 3.29

Servilius Caepio, Q. (cos. 106), 3.11.3–5

Servilius Glaucia, C. (pr. 100), 3.11.11

Servilius Rullus, P. (tr. pl. 63), 3.29

Se(r)vius (*RE* s.v. Servius 5), 2.42

Servius Tullius (sixth king of Rome), 3.7.3